Innovative Theories and Practices for Designing and Evaluating Inclusive Educational Technology and Online Learning

Innovative Theories and Practices for Designing and Evaluating Inclusive Educational Technology and Online Learning

Guest Editor

Julius Nganji

MDPI

Basel • Beijing • Wuhan • Barcelona • Belgrade • Novi Sad • Cluj • Manchester

Guest Editor
Julius Nganji
Department of Occupational
Science and Occupational
Therapy
University of Toronto
Toronto, ON
Canada

Editorial Office
MDPI AG
Grosspeteranlage 5
4052 Basel, Switzerland

This is a reprint of the Special Issue, published open access by the journal *Multimodal Technologies and Interaction* (ISSN 2414-4088), freely accessible at: https://www.mdpi.com/journal/mti/special_issues/Designing_Evaluating_Inclusive_Educational_Technology_Online_Learning.

For citation purposes, cite each article independently as indicated on the article page online and as indicated below:

Lastname, A.A.; Lastname, B.B. Article Title. *Journal Name* **Year**, *Volume Number*, Page Range.

ISBN 978-3-7258-7823-9 (Hbk)
ISBN 978-3-7258-7824-6 (PDF)
https://doi.org/10.3390/books978-3-7258-7824-6

Contents

About the Editor ix

Preface xi

Shogo Fukushima, Keigo Sakamoto and Yugo Nakamura
NariTan: Enhancing Second Language Vocabulary Learning Through Non-Human Avatar Embodiment in Immersive Virtual Reality
Reprinted from: *Multimodal Technol. Interact.* **2024**, *8*, 93,
https://doi.org/10.3390/mti8100093 1

Hussam Diab, Wajeeh Daher, Baraa Rayan, Nael Issa and Anwar Rayan
Transforming Science Education in Elementary Schools: The Power of PhET Simulations in Enhancing Student Learning
Reprinted from: *Multimodal Technol. Interact.* **2024**, *8*, 105,
https://doi.org/10.3390/mti8110105 23

Nikolaos Pellas
Effects of Kahoot! on K-12 Students' Mathematics Achievement and Multi-Screen Addiction
Reprinted from: *Multimodal Technol. Interact.* **2024**, *8*, 81,
https://doi.org/10.3390/mti8090081 39

Nikolaos Partarakis, Xenophon Zabulis, Dimitris Zourarakis, Ioanna Demeridou, Ines Moreno, Arnaud Dubois, et al.
Physics-Based Tool Usage Simulations in VR
Reprinted from: *Multimodal Technol. Interact.* **2025**, *9*, 29,
https://doi.org/10.3390/mti9040029 60

Panagiotis Dafiotis, Stella Sylaiou, Efstratios Stylianidis, Dimitrios Koukopoulos and Christos Fidas
Evaluating Uses of XR in Fostering Art Students' Learning
Reprinted from: *Multimodal Technol. Interact.* **2025**, *9*, 36,
https://doi.org/10.3390/mti9040036 104

María Lucía Barrón-Estrada, Ramón Zatarain-Cabada, Manuel Alberto Sotelo-Rivas, María Blanca Ibáñez and Víctor Manuel Bátiz-Beltrán
BabloXR: An Authoring Tool for Developing WebXR Educational Applications †
Reprinted from: *Multimodal Technol. Interact.* **2025**, *9*, 52,
https://doi.org/10.3390/mti9060052 125

Lorena Cabrera-Frías, Diana-Margarita Córdova-Esparza, Julio-Alejandro Romero-González, Teresa García-Ramírez, Rocio-Edith López-Martínez, Juan Terven and Juan-José Rodríguez-Peña
The Use of 3D Printing and ICT in the Designing of Didactic Strategies to Foster Creative Thinking
Reprinted from: *Multimodal Technol. Interact.* **2025**, *9*, 35,
https://doi.org/10.3390/mti9040035 143

Paula Rodríguez-Rivera, José M. Rodríguez-Ferrer and Ana Manzano-León
Designing Digital Escape Rooms with Generative AI in University Contexts: A Qualitative Study
Reprinted from: *Multimodal Technol. Interact.* **2025**, *9*, 20,
https://doi.org/10.3390/mti9030020 161

Óscar Cuéllar, Manuel Contero and Mauricio Hincapié
Personalized and Timely Feedback in Online Education: Enhancing Learning with Deep Learning and Large Language Models
Reprinted from: *Multimodal Technol. Interact.* **2025**, *9*, 45,
https://doi.org/10.3390/mti9050045 . . . . **180**

Lamis F. Al-Qora'n, Julius T. Nganji and Fadi M. Alsuhimat
Designing Inclusive and Adaptive Content in Moodle: A Framework and a Case Study from Jordanian Higher Education
Reprinted from: *Multimodal Technol. Interact.* **2025**, *9*, 58,
https://doi.org/10.3390/mti9060058 . . . . **214**

Luis Fletscher, Jhon Mercado, Alvaro Gómez and Carlos Mendoza-Cardenas
Innovating Personalized Learning in Virtual Education Through AI
Reprinted from: *Multimodal Technol. Interact.* **2025**, *9*, 69,
https://doi.org/10.3390/mti9070069 . . . . **241**

Jelena Nakić, Ivana Rogulj and Lada Maleš
Rethinking the Bebras Challenge in Virtual Reality: Implementation and Usability Study of a Computational Thinking Game
Reprinted from: *Multimodal Technol. Interact.* **2025**, *9*, 60,
https://doi.org/10.3390/mti9060060 . . . . **264**

Franz Coelho and Ana Maria Abreu
Systemic Gamification Theory (SGT): A Holistic Model for Inclusive Gamified Digital Learning
Reprinted from: *Multimodal Technol. Interact.* **2025**, *9*, 70,
https://doi.org/10.3390/mti9070070 . . . . **297**

Martina Basciano, Elisa Bisagno and Alessia Cadamuro
Multiple Ways in Which Video Games Make Education Inclusive: A Systematic Review of Cognitive Enhancement for Neurodivergent Learners
Reprinted from: *Multimodal Technol. Interact.* **2025**, *9*, 56,
https://doi.org/10.3390/mti9060056 . . . . **323**

Evgenia Gkintoni, Andrew Sortwell, Stephanos P. Vassilopoulos and Georgios Nikolaou
Neuroplasticity-Informed Learning Under Cognitive Load: A Systematic Review of Functional Imaging, Brain Stimulation, and Educational Technology Applications
Reprinted from: *Multimodal Technol. Interact.* **2026**, *10*, 5,
https://doi.org/10.3390/mti10010005 . . . . **347**

Isotta Mac Fadden, Elena-María García-Alonso and Eloy López Meneses
Science Mapping of AI as an Educational Tool Exploring Digital Inequalities: A Sociological Perspective
Reprinted from: *Multimodal Technol. Interact.* **2024**, *8*, 106,
https://doi.org/10.3390/mti8120106 . . . . **409**

Saad Alghamdi, Ben Soh and Alice Li
A Comprehensive Review of Dropout Prediction Methods Based on Multivariate Analysed Features of MOOC Platforms
Reprinted from: *Multimodal Technol. Interact.* **2025**, *9*, 3,
https://doi.org/10.3390/mti9010003 . . . . **431**

Ioanna Nazlidou, Nikolaos Efkolidis, Konstantinos Kakoulis and Panagiotis Kyratsis
Innovative and Interactive Technologies in Creative Product Design Education: A Review
Reprinted from: *Multimodal Technol. Interact.* **2024**, *8*, 107,
https://doi.org/10.3390/mti8120107 . . . . **478**

Georgios Lampropoulos
Combining Artificial Intelligence with Augmented Reality and Virtual Reality in Education: Current Trends and Future Perspectives
Reprinted from: *Multimodal Technol. Interact.* **2025**, *9*, 11,
https://doi.org/10.3390/mti9020011 . . . . **525**

About the Editor

Julius Nganji

Julius Nganji is an adjunct faculty member in the Department of Occupational Science and Occupational Therapy at the University of Toronto's Temerty Faculty of Medicine. He received his Master of Science (with distinction) in Website Design and Development, a Postgraduate Diploma in Research Training, and a PhD in Computer Science from the University of Hull, United Kingdom, where his research focused on personalizing e-learning for students with disabilities using web ontologies. His current work explores artificial intelligence in education, digital accessibility, e-learning personalization, usability, and human–computer interaction. He is an active researcher, reviewer, editor, and guest editor across international academic journals, contributing to projects and initiatives that advance inclusive educational technology and support diverse learners.

Preface

This Reprint presents a curated collection of scholarly contributions addressing innovative theories and practices for designing and evaluating inclusive educational technology and online learning. The subject of this Reprint lies at the intersection of digital pedagogy, human–computer interaction, artificial intelligence in education, immersive learning environments, and accessibility-focused design. Its scope encompasses empirical investigations, design-based research, theoretical frameworks, and review studies that collectively examine how emerging technologies can be developed and implemented to support equitable, engaging, and effective learning experiences for diverse populations.

The primary aim of this Reprint is to consolidate contemporary research that advances inclusive and learner-centered innovation within technology-enhanced education. The contributions explore critical themes such as adaptive learning environments, immersive simulations, gamified learning systems, artificial intelligence-driven feedback and analytics, extended reality applications, and accessibility evaluation methods. Together, these works highlight both the pedagogical opportunities and the design challenges associated with integrating rapidly evolving technologies into educational practice. A further purpose of this Reprint is to provide educators, researchers, instructional designers, and institutional leaders with evidence-informed insights that support the responsible development and evaluation of inclusive online learning environments.

The motivation for assembling this Reprint emerged from the increasing global reliance on digital learning platforms and the accelerated transformation of education in recent years. While technology adoption has expanded significantly, questions of usability, accessibility, learner diversity, and pedagogical effectiveness remain central concerns. The contributions gathered here reflect a shared commitment to ensuring that technological innovation is grounded in inclusive design principles and supported by robust empirical evidence and theoretical reflection. By bringing together diverse methodological approaches and disciplinary perspectives, this Reprint aims to advance scholarly dialog and foster new directions for research and practice.

This Reprint is addressed to an interdisciplinary audience that includes educational technology researchers, computer science scholars, learning scientists, higher education practitioners, policy makers, and graduate students interested in the design and evaluation of inclusive digital learning systems. Readers will find both practical strategies for implementation and conceptual frameworks that inform future innovation. Through this collection, I, as the Guest Editor, seek to contribute to a deeper understanding of how inclusive educational technology can promote meaningful participation, equitable access, and sustained learner engagement in online and technology-enhanced learning environments.

Julius Nganji
Guest Editor

Multimodal Technologies and Interaction

MDPI

Article

NariTan: Enhancing Second Language Vocabulary Learning Through Non-Human Avatar Embodiment in Immersive Virtual Reality

Shogo Fukushima *,†, Keigo Sakamoto † and Yugo Nakamura

Graduate School and Faculty of Information Science and Electrical Engineering, Kyushu University, Fukuoka 819-0395, Japan; sakamoto.keigo@arakawa-lab.com (K.S.); y-nakamura@ait.kyushu-u.ac.jp (Y.N.)
* Correspondence: shogo@ait.kyushu-u.ac.jp; Tel.: +81-92-802-3579
† These authors contributed equally to this work.

Abstract: With the rise of head-mounted displays (HMDs), immersive virtual reality (IVR) for second-language learning is gaining attention. However, current methods fail to fully exploit IVR's potential owing to the use of abstract avatars and limited human perspectives in learning experiences. This study investigated IVR's novel potential by using non-human avatars to understand complex concepts. We developed a system for learning English vocabulary through the actions of non-human avatars, offering a unique learning perspective. This paper presents an IVR vocabulary learning environment with a dragon avatar and compares word retention rates (immediate and one-week memory tests), subjective workload, and emotional changes with traditional methods. We also examined the vocabulary ranges that are teachable using this system by varying the number of avatars. The results showed that the proposed method significantly reduced forgotten English words after one week compared to traditional methods, indicating its effectiveness in the long term.

Keywords: virtual reality; enactment effect; non-human avatar; second language vocabulary learning; bilingual dual coding theory

1. Introduction

Vocabulary is fundamental to language learning, and a limited vocabulary impedes language-related activities, such as conversing and multimedia content comprehension [1,2]. Learning-by-doing [3] and the enactment effect [4], also known as the subject-performed task (SPT) effect [5], are traditional methods that have been widely utilized for learning vocabulary through physical experience. The enactment effect (or SPT effect) has been extensively studied, particularly in the fields of psychology [6] and second-language acquisition [7,8], which is believed to be effective in extending vocabulary retention by performing movements related to learning targets.

Recently, with the proliferation of head-mounted displays (HMDs), research incorporating immersive virtual reality (IVR) into language learning using these technologies has been increasing. According to The American Heritage Dictionary, the term "Virtual" is defined as "Existing or resulting in essence or effect though not in actual fact, form, or name", meaning that VR can be defined as a technology that reproduces the essence of reality. However, IVR is described as "technology that allows the user to experience physical and/or behavioral simulations" [9] and is primarily realized through devices such as HMDs or Cave Automatic Virtual Environments. In IVR, it is possible to learn vocabulary that is rarely experienced in the real world by freely changing objects and spaces. Studies that utilize IVR for vocabulary learning have presented words related to the virtual environment [10,11] and virtual objects [12,13]. Moreover, because IVR can easily create immersive environments, learning through enactment is advantageous for vocabulary retention. However, these prior studies have focused on changing objects or environments, and there has been little examination of variables such as the first-person perspective of the learner or the avatar used. The avatars used were either human or reproduce parts, such as the hands. Therefore, the possible virtual experiences are limited to "learning experiences from a human perspective", and the vocabulary assumed in these studies is fundamentally related to humans.

We propose NariTan, which provides a "learning experience from the perspective of a non-human avatar, for memorizing English vocabulary through actions suitable for that avatar (Figure 1)". By changing the avatar, it is possible to teach English vocabulary that cannot be included in learning experiences based on human perspectives. The name combines "Nari-kiri" (becoming) and "Tan-go" (word). Non-human avatars refer to avatars that are not human, such as dogs or cats. By learning from a non-human perspective, it is possible to incorporate English words that cannot be included in a human perspective-based learning experience (see experience video in the Supplementary Materials). We hypothesized that the episodic memory of experiencing unusual body movements and perspectives that humans do not typically perform would be beneficial for the retention of English vocabulary.

Figure 1. (**Left**) Experiencing the verb "ravage" through a dragon avatar. (**Right**) Learning verbs using the whole body while becoming a dragon avatar.

Plausibility in an IVR environment is considered a key factor for maintaining presence in IVR experiences [14]. Presenting vocabulary that matches the appearance of a customized avatar and performing actions corresponding to the avatar's characteristics may contribute to the enhancement of presence in IVR. Smith et al. have reviewed and organized the knowledge regarding the formation of episodic memory in IVR environments, highlighting the importance of maintaining presence [14]. Furthermore, it is considered that embodying a non-human avatar and performing unfamiliar body movements are crucial for structuring memories and retaining them as long-term memories.

In this study, we developed the NariTan learning system and conducted experiments comparing the results of memory tests, emotional changes, and subjective load during English vocabulary learning with those of general learning methods, such as flashcards, to evaluate the effectiveness of the proposed system. Additionally, we examined how well the learning system covered the target English vocabulary. The contributions of this study are as follows:

- We proposed and implemented a system where users dress-up non-human avatars in an IVR environment to learn English vocabulary. We developed new interactions to utilize IVR spaces as learning environments and created unique vocabulary-selection methods tailored to each avatar.

- We validated the effectiveness of this body dress-up system through quantitative assessments, including vocabulary tests and episodic memory tests. Additionally, we quantified the workload and usability of this learning method.
- We also explored the range of vocabulary that can be acquired with this learning method using a large language model (LLM).

2. Related Work

Bilingual dual-coding theory [15] is a model for second-language vocabulary acquisition. This theory posits the existence of two systems in the cognitive processing of words: verbal symbolic systems and nonverbal objects and events. Linguistic information is encoded by the former system, whereas nonverbal information, such as illustrations and experiences associated with words, is encoded by the latter system. It has been suggested that images that are doubly encoded by imagery and language result in a better memory performance than words alone [16]. Several studies supporting the bilingual dual-coding theory have recognized the additive effect [17,18], which refers to the phenomenon in which learning utilizing both linguistic and imagery systems (e.g., learning vocabulary with pictures) results in approximately twice the number of word reproductions when compared with learning that uses only the linguistic system (e.g., copying second-language words).

Multimedia learning, which focuses on the connection between linguistic and imagery systems, has also been studied. Classical multimedia learning typically uses images. Studies of image-based learning have shown that adding explanations to illustrations improves comprehension and problem-solving abilities [19], whereas explanations unrelated to illustrations negatively affect learning [20]. Additionally, videos that provide more information than images are used for learning. Extensive research has been conducted on the effects of incorporating short animations in learning [21]. Moreover, recent studies on vocabulary learning systems using videos have made notable progress. Zhu et al. developed Vivo [22], a system that uses videos related to word meanings instead of paper dictionaries. Furthermore, several studies have discussed the most appropriate subtitle presentation methods within videos for viewers [23–25].

It is important to enhance the traces of episodic memory through experience to increase the amount of information in an imagery system. Episodic memory is a type of declarative memory that involves personal experiences and is characterized by information retention accompanied by various contextual information (temporal, spatial context, bodily, and psychological states) associated with the time of the event [26]. One method to enhance memory trace during an experience is learning through bodily movements, known as the enactment effect (SPT effect) [4,5]. The enactment effect refers to the phenomenon in which learning through self-generated actions (enactment) to express a concept results in better recall test performance than learning through word presentation or verbal instruction [5]. The effectiveness of using enactment in second-language learning for memory retention and understanding of learned words has been confirmed in studies using both artificial languages [27–29] and natural languages [30,31]. By applying this to second-language learning systems, Nishida et al. developed a learning-by-doing system that uses ultrasonic sensors to remember the positions of objects and people and presented educational content based on those positions [3].

IVR has also been used to enrich visual cues during the learning experience. In Ogma, Swedish words are embedded in IVR environment objects; learners then move close to the objects using an armband-style controller, whereupon the Swedish text and pronunciation are displayed for learning. An experiment with 19 participants learning 10 Swedish words showed that, while the immediate test performance was lower for Ogma, the word retention rate was higher than that of text-only learning in a one-week test [32]. Vazquez et al. developed Words In Motion, incorporating the enactment effect into IVR-based learning. In Words In Motion, learners perform appropriate actions for words in IVR space while learning them. For example, when learning "paint", a brush object follows the controller and moving the controller along the indicated path displays the word. Although the immediate test scores for Words In Motion were lower than those of the other two conditions, the word retention rate was higher in the one-week test [12].

Previous research has shown that actions and gestures can be cognitively distinguished in the real world [33]. Actions, defined as movements on or using objects, have a different cognitive framework and present evidence of different cognitive outcomes than those of gestures, defined as movements about objects. Additionally, actions are known to promote stronger memory than gestures [34]. IVR studies have suggested that interactions in the form of actions and gestures lead to different cognitive outcomes and that actions provide stronger memory effects. Furthermore, embodied controller actions in IVR have been suggested as being more similar to real-world actions in terms of the benefits of verb memory [13].

In this study, we implemented an IVR system for learning verbs that are difficult to learn through real-world experiences by performing various actions in the IVR space. We clarified the memory retention effects of this system. Additionally, we defined verbs specific to avatars and investigated the vocabulary coverage achieved by changing the types of avatars, which constitutes the academic contribution of this study (Figure 2). Recently, there has been a growing body of research focusing on plausibility and presence in IVR, with many studies utilizing non-human avatars such as dogs [35], cats [36], and robots [37]. While these studies do not specifically focus on vocabulary learning systems, the IVR systems they employ are similar to a medium, suggesting that this paper could offer relevant insights.

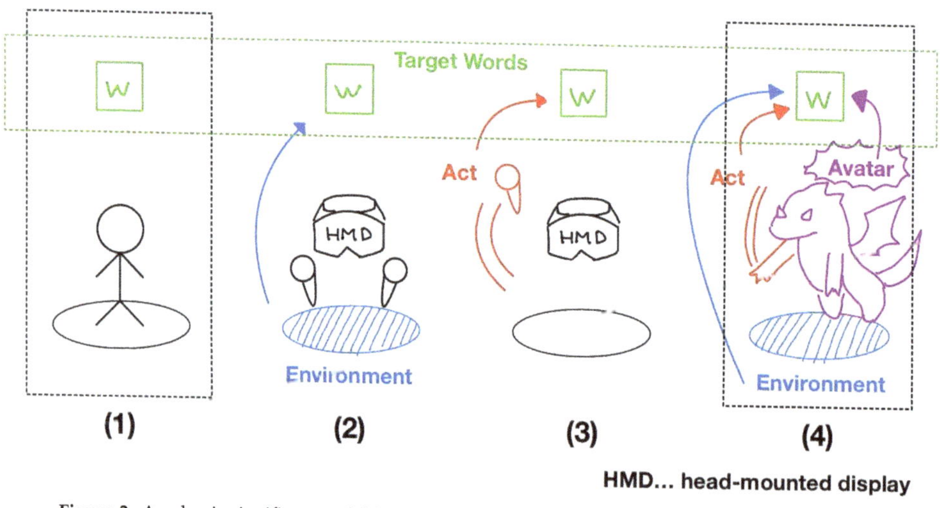

Figure 2. Academic significance of this research: (**1**) A method for memorizing words in the real world without using immersive virtual reality (IVR). (**2**) A method for selecting and learning words that match the IVR environment. (**3**) A method for learning words by enacting them by matching the movements of IVR objects. (**4**) A method for selecting and learning words typically attributed to the IVR avatars.

3. Proposed Method

NariTan is a learning system aimed at realizing an "IVR learning experience from the perspective of a non-human avatar by memorizing English words through actions suitable for that avatar". The name combines "Nari-kiri" (becoming) and "Tan-go" (word). Non-human avatars refer to avatars that are not human, such as dogs or cats. By learning from a non-human perspective, it becomes possible to incorporate English words that cannot be included in a human perspective-based learning experience. We hypothesized that experiencing actions and perspectives that humans cannot typically perform would facilitate the memorization of words.

3.1. Software for Implementation

This system was developed using Unity 2021.3.24f1 https://unity.com/ja (accessed on 11 September 2024). XR Interaction Toolkit 2.0 https://docs.unity3d.com/Packages/com.unity.xr.interaction.toolkit@2.5/manual/index.html (accessed on 11 September 2024) for implementing the core interaction system, Final IK 1.9 https://assetstore.unity.com/packages/tools/animation/final-ik-14290 (accessed on 11 September 2024) for implementing the avatar's IK, and Dynamic Bone 1.3.4 https://assetstore.unity.com/packages/tools/animation/dynamic-bone-16743 (accessed on 11 September 2024) for expressing bone sway were used. The HMD used was PICO4 Enterprise https://business.picoxr.com (accessed on 11 September 2024), which was connected to the PC via a wired connection. Although PICO4 can be connected wirelessly to the PC using WiFi, a wired connection was used to ensure stable image quality and reduce screen shaking.

3.2. Implementation of the Avatar

To realize "becoming a nonhuman avatar", it is necessary to have a 3D model of the non-human avatar that follows the movements of the HMD and controllers. In this study, a dragon avatar was used as an example of a non-human avatar. This avatar was chosen because its significantly taller stature than that of humans provides a different self-perspective and allows for the inclusion of many actions that are not typically experienced by humans, such as flying and breathing fire. The 3D model of the dragon is shown in Figure 3. It was a quadrupedal 3D model and difficult to implement as an avatar in its original form. Therefore, a humanoid rig was created using Blender. The edited 3D model was exported as an FBX file and imported into Unity, where it was implemented as a dragon avatar using 3-point tracking with VRIK, a feature of Final IK. The wings were designed to move in conjunction with the arms, and the tail was designed to sway with body rotation.

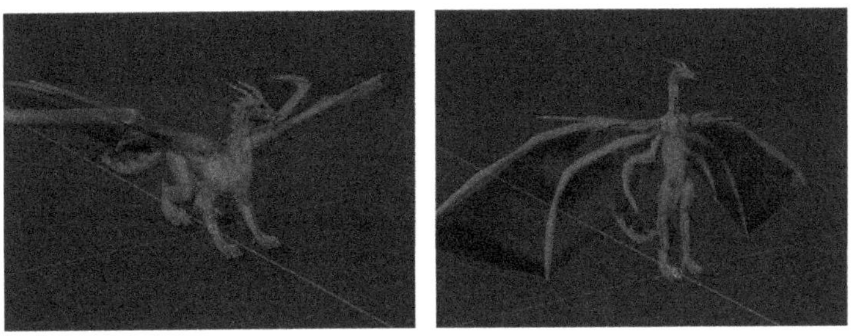

Figure 3. 3D model of the dragon used as an avatar in this study. The **left** and **right** panels show the model before and after processing in Blender and fitting into a humanoid rig, respectively.

3.3. Implementation of Interaction

To realize "memorizing English words through actions suitable for a non-human avatar", interactions that allowed the enactment of the English words were used. To associate the IVR environment experienced as an episodic memory with the related English words, an independent IVR environment was implemented for each word (Figure 4). The IVR environment for each English word included a sufficiently large area for learners to move around freely and a skybox as the background. Additionally, several objects necessary for the enactment were placed. The following operations were possible within the IVR environment:

- Movements using the left and right sticks on the controller;
- Grabbing/releasing objects by pressing/releasing the side buttons on the controller;
- Performing actions by pulling the trigger on the controller (for specific English words only).

To determine whether each English word was enacted, the following criteria were used, allowing the expected process to be executed immediately upon enactment:

- Collision detection (e.g., the dragon's hand colliding with a rock);
- Detection of entry into an area (e.g., dropping a stone into the sea);
- Detection of extent of movement (e.g., swinging the arm down significantly).

As feedback indicating that the enactment was performed, the English word and its Japanese translation were displayed in a text window for three seconds, and the pronunciation of the English word was presented. To prevent words from being displayed in every frame, the system was designed such that the words would not be displayed redundantly during the entire word-display period. Additionally, visual and auditory effects were implemented as feedback. For example, when a building was destroyed with a beam, explosion effects and sounds were incorporated. The reason for implementing such feedback was to associate it with English words as episodic memory.

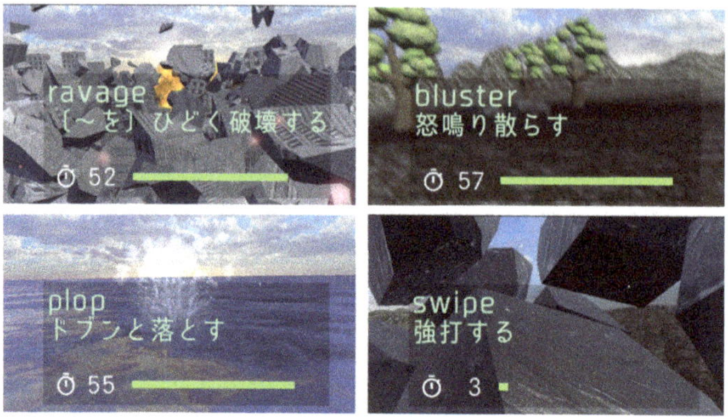

Figure 4. Some examples of the IVR environments and objects (where English words and their Japanese translations are displayed).

A rectangular, semi-transparent text window showing instructions for the actions and time limit was always displayed in the learner's view. The text window followed the movement of the HMD and was always displayed in front of the learner. However, to prevent hindering the IVR experience, the user interface (UI) was designed to be semi-transparent, such that objects could still be seen through the UI. When the user performed the actual action, the English word and its Japanese translation were displayed within the text window (see Figure 5).

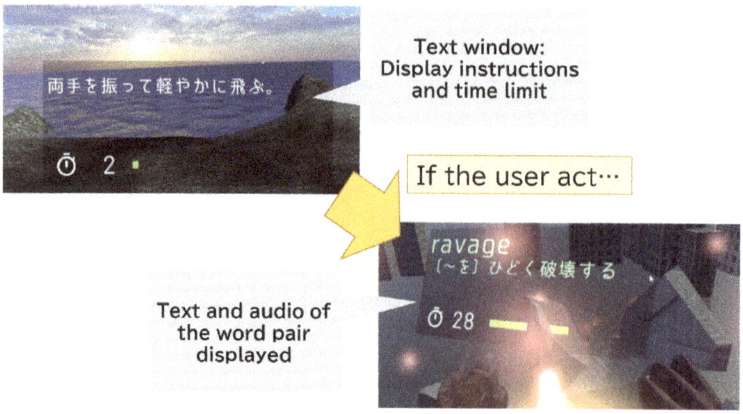

Figure 5. Text window. Instructions for actions are generally displayed in Japanese. When the user performs an action, a pair of English and Japanese text appears in the text window, and the corresponding audio is played simultaneously.

3.4. Implementation of Tutorial

A tutorial environment was implemented to help the learners become sufficiently accustomed to the avatar's body (Figure 6). The learners were first moved to this environment before entering the IVR space. The tutorial environment included cubic objects that could be grabbed and moved, and a green area indicated the place to which the objects should be moved. Additionally, a mirror was set up to allow learners to see the entire body of the dragon avatar moving in conjunction with their own movements, thus making them constantly aware that they were a dragon.

Figure 6. IVR environment for the tutorial. Users can see themselves in a mirror while practicing the task of moving a box to the green area.

3.5. Word Selection

This method involves memorizing certain transitive verbs specific to a particular non-human avatar by becoming that avatar. It is necessary to select avatar-specific English words and reduce them to words that match the proficiency levels of the participants. This procedure is illustrated in Figure 7.

We used ChatGPT [38] as the LLM and a combination of the BNC/Corpus of Contemporary American (COCA) word family lists [39] (BNC/COCA) and CEFR [40] as the word dataset. The BNC/COCA word family lists [39] are frequency-ordered English word lists created by the nation based on the British National Corpus (BNC) [41] and the COCA [42]. The lists contain 25,000 words (+derivatives/additional words) which are categorized into levels from 1 to 25 in units of 1000 words, with higher levels indicating less frequent words in the corpus. In this study, 25,000 words were used, excluding derivatives and additional words.

Although transitive verbs suitable for each avatar can be selected manually, the sheer number of words makes this impractical. Therefore, ChatGPT was used. The steps for selecting English words using ChatGPT are as follows: To select avatar-specific English words, the prompt "List 200 unique words that are verbs of movements possible for AVATAR". was input, and this task was repeated until fewer than ten new words appeared in the BNC/COCA list. The term "AVATAR" in the prompt was replaced with the name of the avatar being used. For example, "the creature dragon" was substituted for the dragon avatar used in this study.

In the experiment, it was necessary to use words that matched the participants' vocabulary levels. BNC/COCA is strictly divided by frequency and is not categorized by the language proficiency level of the user. Therefore, the Common European Framework of Reference for Languages (CEFR) [40] was introduced as a criterion for level categorization based on user proficiency.

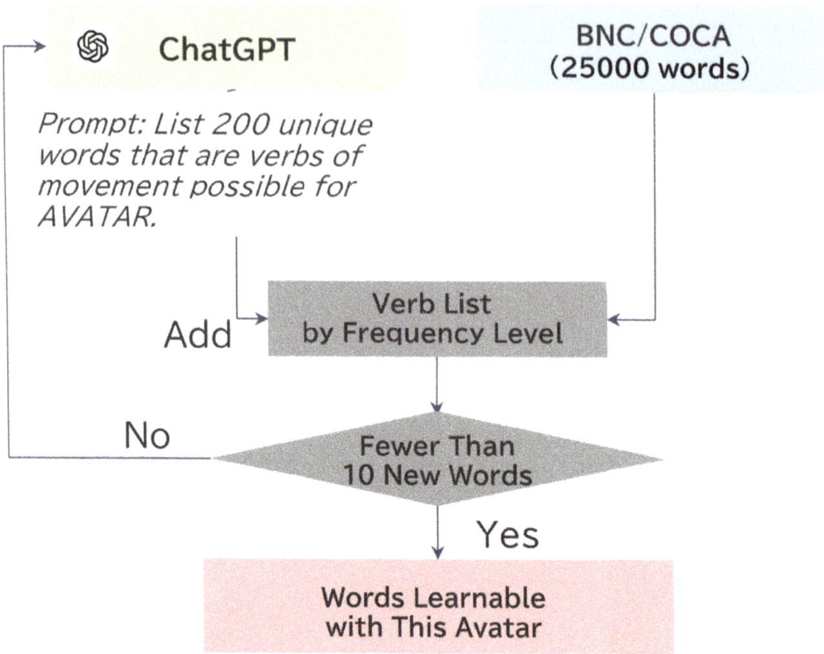

Figure 7. Process of generating avatar-specific verbs using a large language model (LLM).

4. Experiment 1: Memory Retention with Proposed Method

To clarify the effectiveness of the proposed method for vocabulary retention, the participants memorized English words, and the forgetting rate was calculated by conducting word tests immediately after learning and one week later. The results were compared with those obtained using flashcards as the baseline method (R1). The reason for using flashcards as the baseline is that they are a commonly used application for English vocabulary learning and the results would provide valuable insights for general English learners. Furthermore, flashcards have been used as a baseline for the evaluation of vocabulary learning systems that utilize IVR environments [12,32], 3D audio [43,44], and those that focus on the enactment effect [3], allowing for comparisons with these systems. The proposed method aims to enable the memorization of the meanings of English words using episodic memory as nonverbal imagery through physical actions. Therefore, the correlation between episodic memory and vocabulary learning scores was investigated (R2). Additionally, the effect of learning through enactment from the perspective of a non-human avatar on the subjective load and emotions was compared with that of the baseline method (R3).

4.1. Participants

The participants were 28 university students (25 men and 3 women) with a median age of 22 years (first quartile: 20, third quartile: 23). However, the data of one participant were excluded owing to VR sickness during the experiment. Three participants did not take any English proficiency tests. The Test of English for International Communication (TOEIC) scores of the remaining participants ranged from 410 to 790 points. Ten participants had no experience of using VR HMDs, whereas 18 had previous experience of using the device. The 28 participants were divided into two groups of 14 each for learning using flashcards and NariTan.

4.2. Vocabulary and Materials

The experiment used ten words (Table 1) selected according to the word-selection method described in Section 3.5. We focused on verbs that could be learned using the dragon avatar, which were then reduced to verbs of CEFR level C2 or higher (406 words). This level of adjustment was made to minimize the influence of prior knowledge of English words, considering that the participants were university students. Subsequently, 406 words were further reduced to 10, considering the balance of interactions that could be expressed with those verbs (Table 1).

Table 1. Target English vocabulary used in the experiment, the scene images with English words and their Japanese translations, the instructional sentences for learning them, and how the user moves their body.

Scene	Target Verbs	Instruction	Interaction
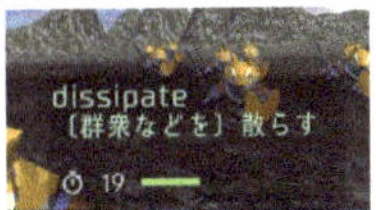	dissipate	Scattering soldiers with a hand.	Swinging arms left and right
	swipe	Striking a rock hard	Swinging a hand down
	engorge	Devouring food greedily	Grabbing food with a hand and putting it in the mouth
	ravage	Destroying buildings with a beam	Pointing the stomach at the buildings
	flit	Flying lightly by waving both hands	Vigorously swinging hands down
	incinerate	Burning a tree to ashes	Aiming flames from the mouth at the tree
	plop	Dropping something into the sea with a plop	Grabbing a stone with a hand and throwing it into the sea
	bluster	Yelling loudly	Inputting a loud voice into a microphone
	wag	Wagging the tail	Twisting the body
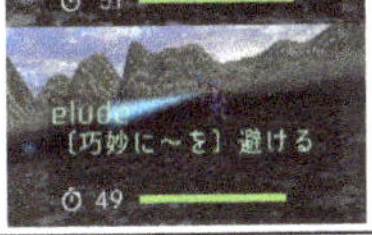	elude	Skillfully dodging enemy projectiles	Moving the body left and right

4.3. Procedure

4.3.1. Day 1: Experiment on the First Day

In the pre-experiment questionnaire, the participants took a pre-test to determine whether they already knew the ten words to be learned in this experiment by answering the Japanese translations of the words (Figure 8). They also answered questions regarding their current subjective emotion. Next, the participants practiced using the learning applications. In the flashcard method, participants learned a practice set of two words. In the proposed method, the participants entered the tutorial environment, recognized themselves as the dragon avatar in the mirror, and learned the operations of the HMD and controllers.

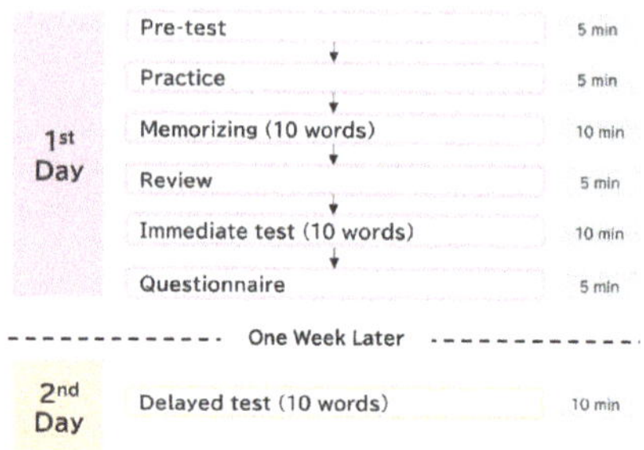

Figure 8. Experimental procedure. Experimental flows on days 1 and 2 are shown.

After the practice, the participants proceeded to the main experiment and learned ten words. In both conditions, there was no limit on the number of times the words could be presented; instead, the learning time for each word was limited to one minute, resulting in a total of 10 min of learning. As this was a between-subjects experiment, the participants learned using either the flashcard or the proposed method.

In the flashcard method, English words and their Japanese translations were presented, and the participants could check their pronunciation by pressing the playback button below. The proposed method involved learning through interactions, as explained in the previous section. The time limit was one minute per word, and the participants could always check the remaining time by means of a gauge UI that shrank over time in both methods.

After learning, the effectiveness of each test condition was reviewed using a tablet. The review was conducted by presenting multiple-choice questions, which is a feature of Flashcard Deluxe. In the questions, Japanese translations were presented with four options alongside the English word. The correct choices were highlighted in green, whereas incorrect choices were highlighted in red. Subsequently, the English word and its Japanese translation were presented again, and the participants could check their pronunciation by pressing the playback button. In the NariTan-based experiment, a screenshot of the IVR environment in which the word was learned was also presented when the English word and its Japanese translation were shown. This presentation was intended to associate the learned IVR environment with related English words as episodic memory.

A test was conducted immediately after the review. First, a mental arithmetic task of answering ten two-digit addition problems was performed, followed by answering the Japanese translations of the ten learned words. After the test, a post-experiment questionnaire was administered to assess the current subjective emotional evaluation, subjective workload, and usefulness of the system. Finally, oral questions were asked, and the participants provided feedback on the system through interviews.

4.3.2. Day 2: Experiment on the Second Day Conducted One Week Later

The second day of the experiment was conducted approximately a week later at the same location as on the first day. Among the participants, 23 took the test on the seventh day, one on the sixth day, and three on the eighth day. We intended all participants to complete the experiment at the same time exactly one week later; however, scheduling at the same time one week later proved to be difficult. Therefore, we determined that, as long as it was the same day, in cases where it was not possible to conduct the experiment exactly seven days later, we allowed the participants to complete it the day before or the day after, and we adjusted the time of day to minimize any time differences as much as possible. Additionally, participants were instructed in the consent form not to share the details of the experiment with others

First, a one-week post-test was conducted to answer the Japanese translations of the ten words learned a week earlier. A questionnaire was then administered to check how much of the IVR experience episode in the proposed method was remembered. The participants were shown the English word alone and were asked which elements of the IVR experience they remembered. The participants answered yes/no to the following seven items:

- Background: Remembering the background.
- Objects: Remembering the objects seen/used.
- Events: Remembering what was performed/what happened.
- Body parts: Remembering the body parts used in the learning movements.
- Sound effects: Remembering the sound effects heard during the learning.
- Pronunciation: Remembering the pronunciation of the word.
- Instructions: Remembering the instructions given.

To eliminate the learning effect due to the order of word presentation, the order of words in the pre-test, learning, review, immediate test, and one-week post-test were all randomly arranged. All answers were collected using Google Forms. To avoid predicting the correct answers through predictive conversion, the keyboard's predictive conversion option was turned off and the browser's private mode was used.

4.4. Scoring of Word Tests

The participants wrote Japanese translations corresponding to English words using free text in the word tests. Therefore, it was necessary to clearly set the scoring criteria for the Japanese translations. Based on a study [45] that considered allowing differences in parts of speech as correct answers, we allowed for mistakes in parts of speech, kana/kanji mistakes, and differences in particles/auxiliary verbs. Additionally, this study considered synonyms to be correct answers. This was because the aim of the proposed method was to establish memory traces of episodic memory rather than to ensure strict semantic memory retention. Two external evaluators agreed on what could be considered synonymous.

The evaluation method for the word tests followed that adopted in previous studies [12,43], and the scores of the immediate word test and one-week post-test were used for the evaluation. Because all participants scored zero in the pre-test, the correct answer rates of the word tests conducted immediately after learning and one week after learning were used as word test scores. The forgetting count was obtained by subtracting the immediate test score from the one-week test score.

4.5. Other Evaluations

The following four items were measured:

- Subjective workload: Measured after the first day's experiment;
- System Usability: Measured after the first day's experiment;
- Emotional Changes: Measured before and after the first day's experiment.

The workload questionnaire used the NASA-TLX [46] index. The NASA-TLX consists of six scales: mental demand (MD), physical demand (PD), temporal demand (TD), performance (OP), frustration (FR), and effort (EF). The overall workload was assessed by combining these scales. This study used the adaptive weighted workload (AWWL) method to evaluate the overall workload. AWWL assigns weights of 6, 5, 4, 3, 2, and 1 in the order of the score magnitude (averaging for ties), and the comprehensive workload was evaluated by dividing the total weighted scores by 21 (sum of the coefficients).

The system evaluation was conducted using the system usability scale (SUS) [47], which is a commonly used standard measure for system evaluation. It consists of ten questions, with odd-numbered questions being positive and even-numbered questions being negative. The system usability scale (SUS) scores were calculated by subtracting 1 from the odd-numbered question scores and subtracting the even-numbered question scores from 5, summing these scores, and multiplying by 2.5 to obtain a score out of 100. A score of 70 or above indicated that the system was acceptable.

Subjective emotional evaluation was conducted using the Affect Grid [48], which evaluates the nature of emotions on a two-dimensional coordinate system, typically on a 9 × 9 grid. The vertical axis evaluates alertness (alertness-sleepiness), and the horizontal axis evaluates emotional value (pleasure-displeasure). In this experiment, the participants answered the Affect Grid before and after the experiment on the first day to evaluate the changes in subjective emotions.

4.6. Result

4.6.1. Pre-Test Score and TOEIC Score

None of the 27 participants answered any of the questions correctly during the pre-test. In this experiment, participants were randomly assigned to either the baseline or proposed method conditions. Of the 27 participants, 4 did not have English test scores. To validate data normality, we used the Shapiro–Wilk normality test, which indicated that the TOEIC scores (with TOEFL and IELTS data converted using a conversion table) for both the baseline ($p = 0.88$) and proposed method ($p = 0.18$) were normally distributed. A two-tailed t-test was used for statistical analyses. There was no significant difference between the participants' TOEIC scores for the proposed method ($M = 714.82$, $SD = 145.47$) and those for the baseline method ($M = 675.83$, $SD = 129.79$) ($t[20] = 0.6456$, ns, $d = 0.28$).

4.6.2. Vocabulary Test Score and Forgetting Rate

Figure 9 (left) shows that under the baseline approach, the average number of correct answers decreased from 8.15 words to 3.69 words in 1 week, that is, the average forgetting rate was 4.46 words. However, in the proposed method, the average number of correct answers decreased from 6.93 words to 5.00 words in one week, that is, the average forgetting rate was 1.93 words.

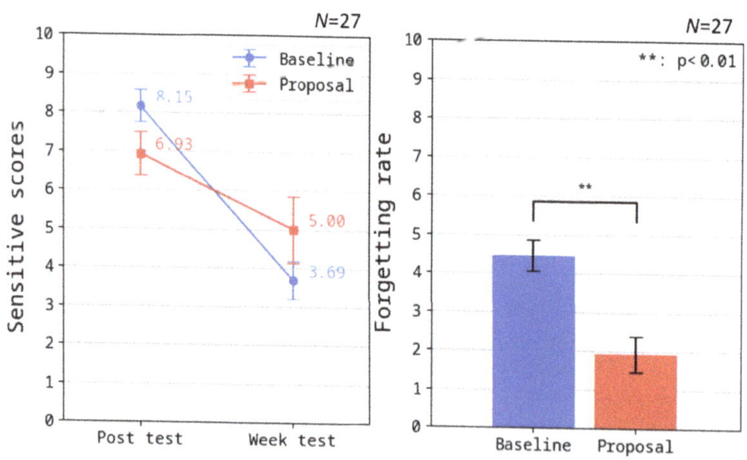

Figure 9. (**Left**) Average scores of the vocabulary test immediately and one week later. (**Right**) Comparison of the forgetting rate calculated by subtracting the immediate scores from the scores of the assessment conducted a week later. The error bar means standard error (SE).

To compare the forgetting rate between the baseline and proposed methods, their respective scores were subtracted from one another for each subject (Figure 9). To validate data normality, we used the Shapiro–Wilk normality test, which indicated that the forgetting rate data for both the baseline ($p = 0.50$) and the proposal ($p = 0.10$) were normally distributed, and we used a two-tailed *t*-test for the statistical analyses. The participants' forgetting rate score for the proposed method ($M = 1.93$, $SD = 1.79$) was significantly lower than that of the baseline method ($M = 4.46$, $SD = 1.45$): t[24] = 3.90, $p < 0.01$, d = 1.69). This suggests that the participants were able to memorize and retain more English language words using the proposed method than with the baseline method (RQ1).

4.6.3. Correlation Between Episodic Scores and Vocabulary Scores

After the delayed test (one week later), participants who experienced IVR were given a questionnaire to check which fragments of episodic memory they could recall. Figure 10 shows the recall rate of word episodes when only English words were presented. The episode score in Figure 10 refers to the total score based on seven categories (background, objects, events, body parts, sound effects, pronunciation, and instructions), with each category counting as one point. As each participant memorized 10 words, the maximum total episode score was 70 points.

The left side of Figure 10 is a scatter plot showing the relationship between the episode score that each participant who experienced IVR remembered and their word test score one week later. The correlation coefficient is 0.672, which is significant ($F(1, 12) = 9.89$, $p < 0.01$). The right side of Figure 10 shows a scatter plot of the relationship between the episode score for each word and the correct answer rate in the word test one week later. The correlation coefficient is 0.700, which is significant ($F(1, 8) = 7.69, p < 0.05$) (RQ2).

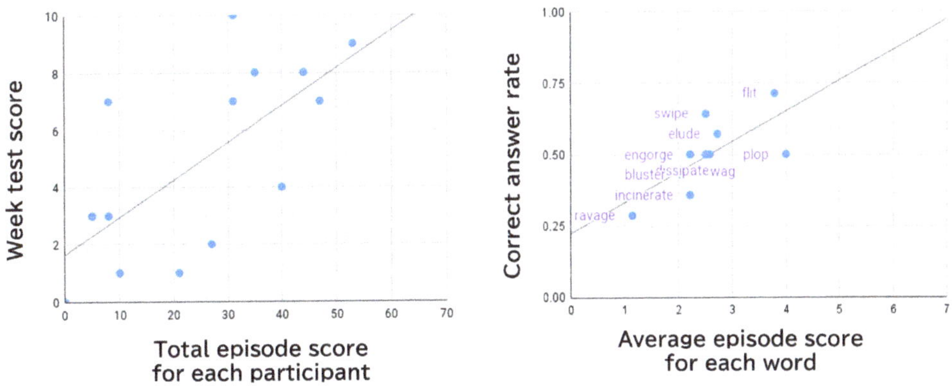

Figure 10. (**Left**) Total episode scores for ten words and test scores of the assessment conducted after a week for each participant. (**Right**) Correlation between the average episode score for each word and the accuracy rate of the test conducted after a week.

4.6.4. NASA-TLX Score and SUS Score

To validate the normality of the data, we used a Shapiro–Wilk test, which indicated that some of the baseline data were not normally distributed: MD ($p = 0.11$), PD ($p < 0.01$), TD ($p < 0.01$), performance ($p < 0.01$), stress ($p < 0.01$), effort ($p = 0.37$), and subjective workload (AWWL) ($p = 0.31$). Similarly, for the baseline data, MD ($p = 0.20$), PD ($p < 0.01$), TD ($p < 0.01$), performance ($p < 0.05$), stress ($p = 0.47$), effort ($p < 0.05$), and subjective workload (AWWL) ($p = 0.14$) were not normally distributed. Therefore, we used the non-parametric Mann–Whitney U test. No significant differences were found in any of the categories (Figure 11 left).

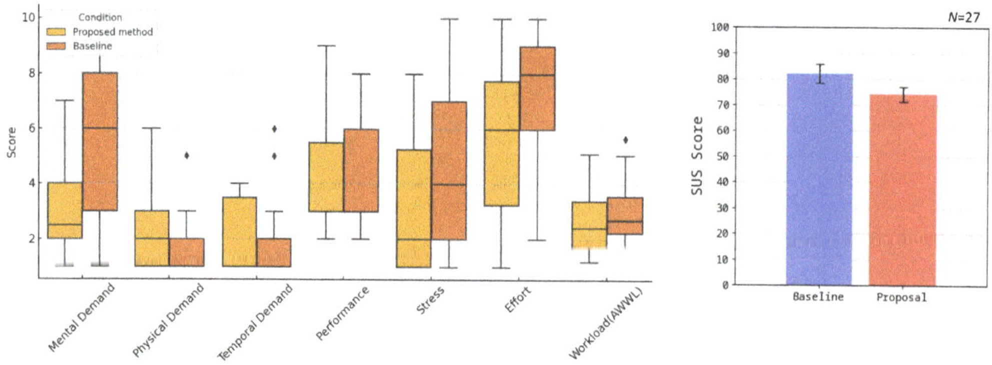

Figure 11. (**Left**) Median scores for each item of the NASA-TLX, where higher scores indicate a greater subjective workload for the user. (**Right**) Average system usability scale (SUS) scores, where a score of 68 or above generally indicates good usability.

To validate data normality, we also performed a Shapiro–Wilk normality test, which indicated that the SUS scores for both the baseline (p = 0.37) and the proposed condition (p = 0.18) were normally distributed. Therefore, a two-tailed t-test was used for statistical analysis. There was no significant difference between the SUS scores of the flashcard condition ($M = 82.12, SD = 12.97$) and NariTan condition ($M = 74.11, SD = 11.04$) ($t(23) = 1.6561, ns(0.10 < p)$). Although no significant difference was found between the conditions, both had an average score of >68 points. Because a score of 68 or above is considered an indicator of good usability, it can be said that the proposed method had good usability that was comparable to that of the commercially available Flashcard Deluxe app (Figure 11 right).

4.6.5. Emotional Changes

To test the normality of the emotional change data before and after learning, a Shapiro–Wilk test was conducted. Normality was confirmed for arousal ($p = 0.46$) and valence ($p = 0.07$) in the proposed method and for arousal ($p = 0.06$) in the baseline. However, normality was not confirmed for valence at the baseline ($p < 0.05$). Therefore, a Mann–Whitney U test was performed, and no significant differences were found between the proposed method and baseline for either arousal or valence (RQ3) (Figure 12).

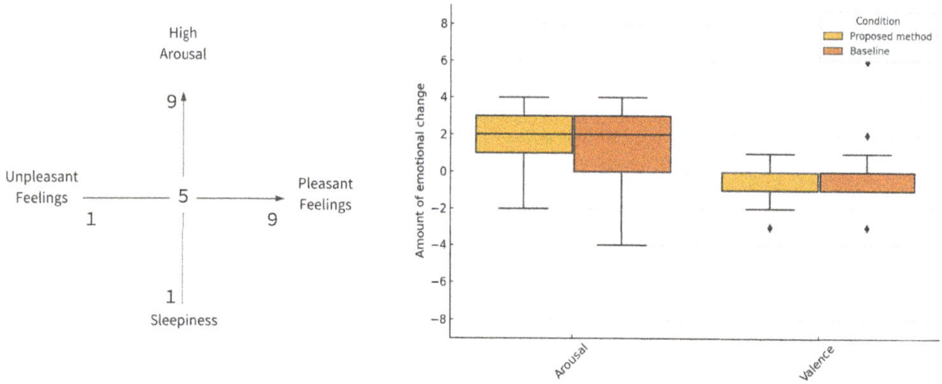

Figure 12. (**Left**) An illustration explaining the meaning of the values in the Affect Grid used to quantify emotions. (**Right**) A comparison of the median values for emotional changes on the Affect Grid before and after the experiment.

5. Experiment 2: Verbs Covered by the Proposed Method

We investigated verb retention using the proposed method. Specifically, we examined how many avatars NariTan needed to use to sufficiently learn English verbs and how many English verbs NariTan could include when considering actual use cases. In this experiment, we used 543 words extracted from the "animals" category of WordNet [49] to select non-human avatars for use in NariTan learning. For the selected English words, verbs that could be learned with the corresponding avatar were chosen by following the same procedure used for word selection in Section 3.

5.1. Procedure

Two datasets were used in this experiment. First, we verified the extent to which a given number of avatars could be used to learn English words until saturation. By using the 25,000 English words included in the BNC/COCA word family [39], we investigated the coverage rate of BNC/COCA based on the number of avatars used in NariTan, categorized by the frequency level (Figure 13).

Next, we examined how many of the 25,000 words in BNC/COCA could be covered by learning with NariTan while changing the avatars daily for one or four weeks, assuming a real-use case.

As the second dataset, we used a combination of five corpora from the New General Service List Project https://www.newgeneralservicelist.com (accessed on 11 September 2024) to conduct a similar verification as with BNC/COCA and investigated the nature of the words covered by NariTan. The five corpora included 2809 words from the New General Service List 1.2 (NGSL) https://www.newgeneralservicelist.com/new-general-service-list (accessed on 11 September 2024), 721 words from NGSL Spoken 1.2 (NGSL-S) https://www.newgeneralservicelist.com/ngsl-spoken (accessed on 11 September 2024), 957 words from the New Academic Word List 1.2 (NAWL) https://www.newgeneralservicelist.com/new-general-service-list-1 (accessed on 11 September 2024), 1250 words from the TOEIC Service List 1.2 (TSL) https://www.newgeneralservicelist.com/toeic-service-list (accessed on 11 September 2024), and 1700 words from the Business Service List 1.2 (BSL) https://www.newgeneralservicelist.com/business-service-list (accessed on 11 September 2024), totaling 7437 words. However, because BNC/COCA is the basis for word selection, words not included in the 25,000 words of BNC/COCA were excluded from the dataset.

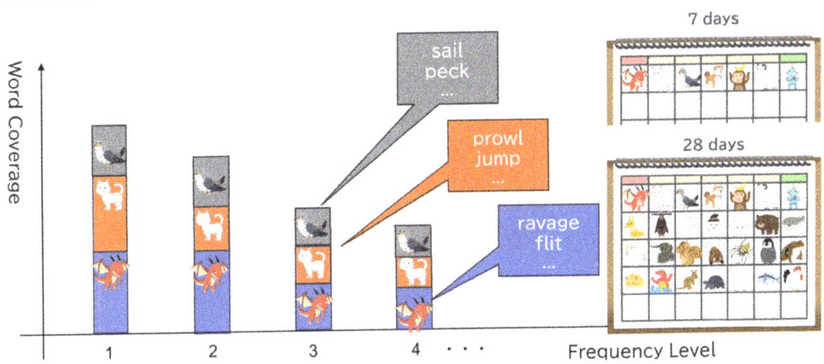

Figure 13. Illustrated steps for graphing the word coverage rate. Assuming that a different avatar is used each day, and the unique verbs of that avatar are learned, the goal is to visualize how much vocabulary can be learned in the end.

5.2. Result

Figure 14 shows the coverage rate of BNC/COCA when learning with NariTan for one or four weeks. It was shown that more than 30% of the words with frequency level 5 or below (equivalent to CEFR C1) could be covered after one week of learning and that more than 40% could be covered after four weeks of learning.

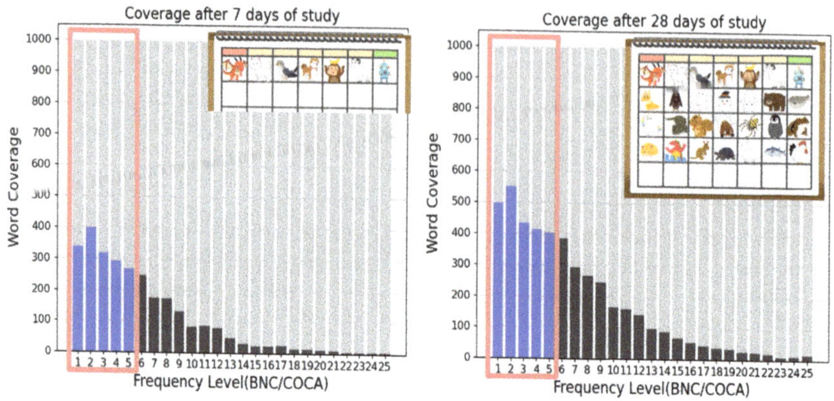

Figure 14. Coverage rate results for the British National Corpus (BNC)/Corpus of Contemporary American (COCA) datasets. The left side shows the vocabulary that can be learned when using seven types of animal avatars (assuming a different avatar each day for a week) and the right side shows what can be learned when using 28 types of animal avatars (assuming a different avatar each day for a month). Dark blue and gray represent learnable vocabularies, whereas the light gray indicates the remaining vocabulary that cannot be covered.

Figure 15 shows the coverage rate of each NGSL dataset when learning with NariTan for one week or four weeks. It was shown that approximately 40% of NGSL could be covered after one week of learning, whereas approximately 20–30% of the other datasets could be covered. After four weeks of learning, approximately 50% of NGSL and NGSL Spoken were covered, whereas approximately 30–40% of the other datasets were covered.

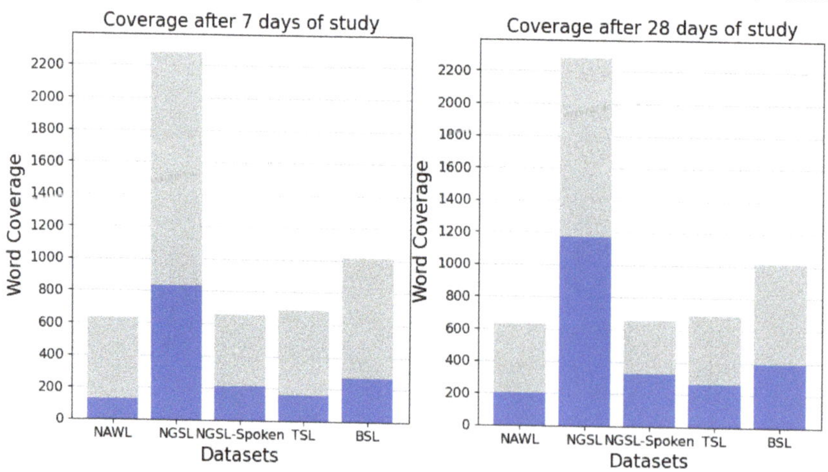

Figure 15. Coverage rate results for the New General Service List 1.2 (NGSL) dataset. Dark blue represents the learnable vocabulary, and light gray indicates the remaining vocabulary that cannot be covered.

In this experiment, we considered the upper limit to be 543 avatars, corresponding to the number of words in the animal category of WordNet. Figure 16 shows the coverage rate results when the number of avatars is increased up to this upper limit. This figure shows the coverage rate for each of the 25 levels, where each level is a group of 1000 words ordered by frequency from the 25,000 words in the BNC/COCA dataset. It can be observed that words at higher frequency levels were mostly covered, whereas those at lower frequency levels were more difficult to cover. Therefore, this method is not suitable for covering low-frequency words, and a different learning method is required to cover these vocabulary levels. Similarly, Figure 17 shows the theoretical coverage rate of NGSL. It can be seen that approximately 80% of the vocabulary in NGSL and NGSLSpoken can be covered; however, for other datasets, the coverage rate plateaued at approximately 50%.

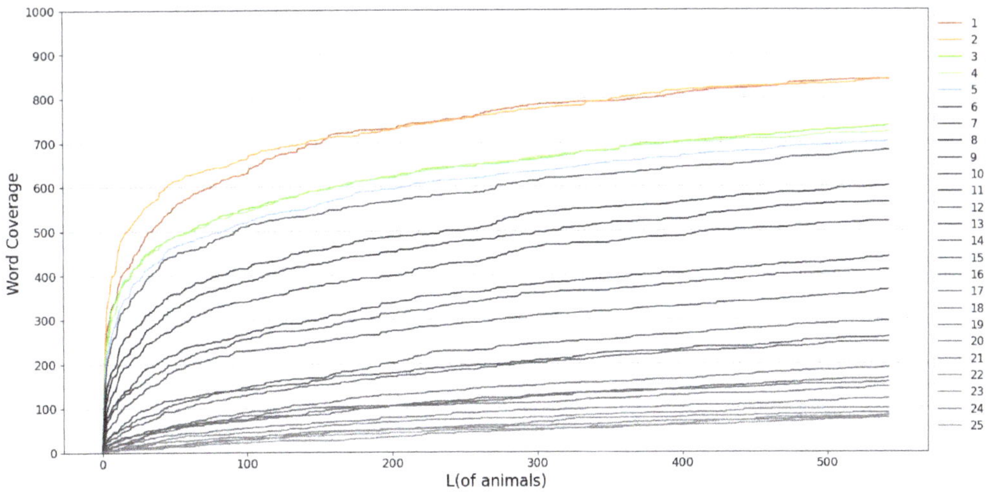

Figure 16. The results showing which level of words from the 25,000 words in the BNC/COCA dataset can theoretically be covered by this method. This indicates the coverage rate when learning words by assuming the role of all avatars in WordNet's animal category. There are 25 series, each containing 1000 words.

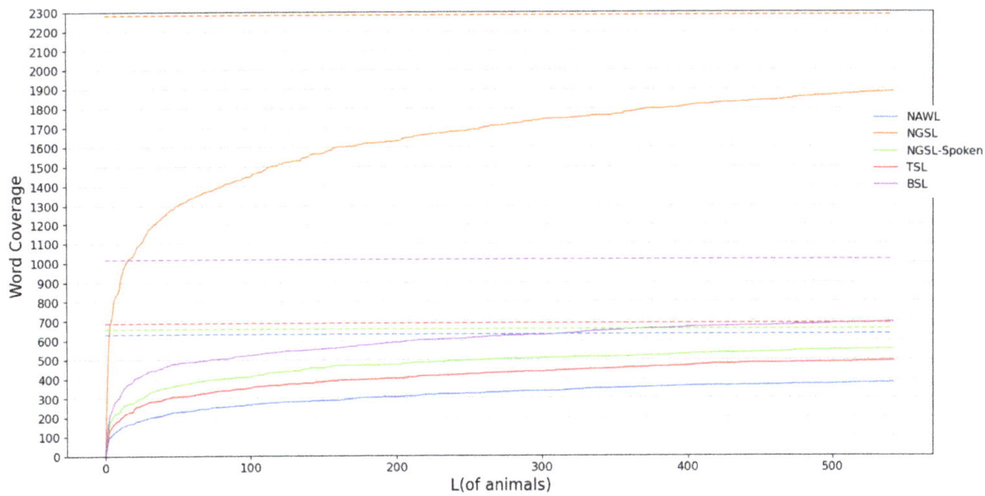

Figure 17. Results showing the genres of words from the NGSL dataset can be theoretically covered by this method. Since the number of words varies for each series, the number of words in each series is indicated with a dotted line.

6. Discussion and Limitation

6.1. Word Tests and Episodic Memory Trace

The proposed method demonstrated a significantly lower forgetting rate than the baseline. Similarly, prior studies [3,12,32,43,44,50] on experiential English vocabulary learning systems have shown a tendency toward reduced forgetting rates compared to flashcards. However, because the range of words covered by each system varies, it is necessary to combine the various methods when expanding vocabulary using experiential learning systems. In this system, instructions and word presentations were always displayed within the learner's field of view, but some participants absorbed in the IVR experience either did not read or ignored the displayed content. Focusing too much on actions or feedback effects might lead to using the IVR space solely for enjoyment without contributing to learning. Although making the experiment enjoyable is a good approach, the strong appeal of such stimuli could also become an issue.

A positive correlation was observed between the episodic memory and vocabulary test scores one week later. This suggests that the cognitive model of bilingual dual-coding theory may have been constructed as learning progressed. For words with lower episodic memory scores, multiple factors may be involved, such as fewer bodily movements and lower consistency between words and actions. Because learning in IVR involves evaluating a system with multiple sensory stimuli, identifying specific factors would require more controlled experiments in a strictly regulated environment. The experiment conducted in this study was an evaluation of the proposed system and did not compare the effectiveness of human avatars with that of non-human avatars. To verify the effectiveness of non-human avatars, it is necessary to compare the learning effects of using both human and non-human avatars in the same IVR environment.

Related studies have reported vocabulary learning and memory evaluation experiments using IVR [12,32,51]. However, these results do not always show an effect that promotes memory retention. For example, Mizuho et al. examined the context dependency on memory using IVR. However, they reported that the results sometimes contradicted those observed in the real-world context-dependency of memory. Mizuho et al. mentioned the lack of immersion as a factor, suggesting that, when sufficient content immersion is not achieved, the experience of wearing an HMD in the lab tends to be more memorable than the IVR content itself, making the presence or absence of immersion an important factor [51]. Recent studies on immersion in IVR have defined three immersion components: place, copresence, and placeability illusions [14]. In the proposed method, the place illusion is fulfilled by allowing users to freely walk around in the IVR space and the plausibility illusion is achieved through avatar-specific actions. It is possible that sufficient immersion provided by these elements contributed to memory retention.

6.2. Evaluations Beyond Word Tests

There were no significant differences in alertness-related emotional changes. After the flashcard-based experiment, the participants' feedback on emotional changes included comments such as "no emotional movement at all", "felt sleepy at first because the experiment was in the morning but felt alert after the experiment", "felt positive because I could remember the words surprisingly well", and "felt positive because I could answer the test unexpectedly well". However, in the proposed method, many participants reported "discomfort due to IVR sickness" and "fatigue from moving their body". The results of the Affect Grid might have included noise from the emotional changes due to the tests. Measuring emotions while learning remains a challenge for future research. Additionally, many participants who reported a shift to unpleasant emotions attributed this to IVR sickness. One participant stopped the experiment because of IVR sickness. Because IVR sickness can hinder learning, it is essential to address it in IVR second-language learning systems.

6.3. Coverage of English Words

In the experiment, based on actual use cases, it was shown that it is possible to teach approximately 30% of CEFR C1 level words in one week and approximately 40% in four weeks. By iterating until the vocabulary coverage rate saturates, with the number of avatars on the horizontal axis, it is suggested that more than 70% of the 25,000 words in the BNC/COCA dataset with a CEFR level of C1 or below can be covered. Furthermore, the coverage rate for each NGSL dataset did not vary significantly across the datasets. Furthermore, the coverage rate for each NGSL dataset did not significantly vary across the datasets. Therefore, NariTan could potentially achieve a certain level of coverage with any dataset. However, learning business English (BSL) with non-human avatars can result in unusual scenarios.

6.4. Use of the Avatar

We used a dragon avatar as an example of a non-human avatar. There is room for discussion regarding the learning effects of other avatars. In the post-experiment interviews, participants were asked about other avatars they would like to use. Responses included aliens, robots (which have similar structures but are completely different from humans), worms, octopuses, and birds (which have structures that are completely different from those of humans). In addition, optimal control methods for avatars in IVR must be investigated. In this study, avatar control was implemented with 3-point tracking using an HMD and two-hand controllers. If the aim is to faithfully embody a quadrupedal (i.e., moving on all fours) or bipedal creature, full-body tracking can be considered for avatar control. Recently, some studies implemented independent control of quadrupedal avatars and avatars with completely different structures from those of humans [52]. However, these implementation methods that enhance the freedom of user control beyond that possible in 3-point tracking increase the implementation cost and reduce portability. Hence, it is necessary to select the implementation method after considering actual use cases.

7. Conclusions

We propose a system in which users embody non-human avatars in IVR spaces to learn vocabulary. We developed new interactions for this learning system and created unique vocabulary-selection methods tailored to each avatar. We validated the effectiveness of this system through quantitative assessments, including English vocabulary and episodic memory tests. The results showed a significant reduction in the forgetting rate of the English vocabulary after one week. We also found a positive correlation between the amount of information retained in episodic memory and scores on the English vocabulary test one week later. Moreover, we explored the vocabulary range that can be acquired with this learning method using LLMs. We found that, for vocabulary below CEFR level C1, 30% could be covered by changing the avatar daily for seven days and 40% could be covered by changing the avatar daily for 28 d.

In Experiment 1, the evaluation was limited to long-term memory scores one week later. However, when considering actual vocabulary learning, it is also important to conduct experiments that investigate memory fragmentation after one month or longer and clarify the differences between IVR and traditional flashcard methods. Additionally, to further strengthen vocabulary retention, it is necessary to explore new learning methods and applications, including reviews. In particular, when using IVR, episodic memory can be heavily utilized, making it crucial to design applications that differ from traditional flashcard methods that focus primarily on semantic memory.

Supplementary Materials: The following supporting information can be downloaded at: https://www.mdpi.com/article/10.3390/mti8100093/s1.

Author Contributions: Conceptualization, S.F., K.S. and Y.N.; methodology, S.F., K.S. and Y.N.; software, K.S.; validation, S.F., K.S. and Y.N.; formal analysis, S.F., K.S. and Y.N.; investigation, S.F., K.S. and Y.N.; resources, S.F., K.S. and Y.N.; data curation, S.F., K.S. and Y.N.; writing—original draft preparation,S.F., K.S. and Y.N.; writing—review and editing, S.F., K.S. and Y.N.; visualization, S.F., K.S. and Y.N.; supervision, S.F. and Y.N.; project administration, S.F., K.S. and Y.N.; funding acquisition, S.F. All authors have read and agreed to the published version of the manuscript.

Funding: Japan Society for the Promotion of Science: JSPS KAKENHI No. JP20K19936 and No. JP24834281.

Institutional Review Board Statement: The study was conducted in accordance with the Declaration of Helsinki and approved by the Institutional Review Board of Kyushu University (ISEE 2023-24, approval date: 25 January 2024).

Informed Consent Statement: Informed consent was obtained from all subjects involved in the study.

Data Availability Statement: The data collected during the study are available from the corresponding author reasonable upon request.

Conflicts of Interest: The authors declare no conflicts of interest.

References

1. Nation, I.S.P. How Large a Vocabulary Is Needed For Reading and Listening? *Can. Mod. Lang. Rev.* **2006**. *500*, 59–82. [CrossRef]
2. van Zeeland, H.; Schmitt, N. Lexical Coverage in L1 and L2 Listening Comprehension: The Same or Different from Reading Comprehension? *Appl. Linguist.* **2013**, *34*, 457–479. [CrossRef]
3. Nishida, Y.; Kusunoki, F.; Hiramoto, M.; Mizoguchi, H. Learning by Doing: Space-Associate Language Learning Using a Sensorized Environment. In Proceedings of the 2005 IEEE/RSJ International Conference on Intelligent Robots and Systems, Edmonton, AB, Canada, 2–6 August 2005; pp. 3636–3641.
4. Engelkamp, J.; Krumnacker, H. Imaginale und motorische Prozesse beim Behalten verbalen Materials. *Proc. Z. Exp. Angew. Psychol.* **1980**, *27*, 511–533.
5. Cohen, R.L. On the generality of some memory laws. *Scand. J. Psychol.* **1981**, *22*, 267–281. [CrossRef]
6. Kormi-Nouri, R.; Nyberg, L.; Nilsson, L.G. The effect of retrieval enactment on recall of subject-performed tasks and verbal tasks. *Mem. Cogn.* **1994**, *22*, 723–728. [CrossRef]
7. Engelkamp, J.; Zimmer, H. Free recall and organization as a function of varying relational encoding in action memory [Electronic version]. *Psychol. Res.* **2002**, *66*, 91–98. [CrossRef]
8. Saltz, E.; Donnenwerth-Nolan, S. Does motoric imagery facilitate memory for sentences? A selective interference test. *J. Verbal Learn. Verbal Behav.* **1981**, *20*, 322–332. [CrossRef]
9. Parong, J.; Mayer, R.E. Cognitive and affective processes for learning science in immersive virtual reality. *J. Comput. Assist. Learn.* **2021**, *37*, 226–241. [CrossRef]
10. Isarida, T.; Isarida, T.K. Environmental context effects of background color in free recall. *Mem. Cogn.* **2007**, *35*, 1620–1629. [CrossRef]
11. Wälti, M.J.; Woolley, D.G.; Wenderoth, N. Reinstating verbal memories with virtual contexts: Myth or reality? *PLoS ONE* **2019**, *14*, e0214540. [CrossRef]
12. Vázquez, C.; Xia, L.; Aikawa, T.; Maes, P. Words in Motion: Kinesthetic Language Learning in Virtual Reality. In Proceedings of the 2018 IEEE 18th International Conference on Advanced Learning Technologies (ICALT), Mumbai, India, 9–13 July 2018; pp. 272–276. [CrossRef]
13. Ratcliffe, J.; Ballou, N.; Tokarchuk, L. Actions, not gestures: Contextualising embodied controller interactions in immersive virtual reality. In Proceedings of the 27th ACM Symposium on Virtual Reality Software and Technology, Osaka, Japan, 8–10 December 2021; pp. 1–11.
14. Brübach, L.; Westermeier, F.; Wienrich, C.; Latoschik, M.E. Breaking Plausibility Without Breaking Presence—Evidence For The Multi-Layer Nature Of Plausibility. *IEEE Trans. Vis. Comput. Graph.* **2022**, *28*, 2267–2276. [CrossRef] [PubMed]
15. Paivio, A.; Desrochers, A. A dual-coding approach to bilingual memory. *Can. J. Psychol. Can. Psychol.* **1980**, *34*, 388. [CrossRef]
16. Paivio, A. *Imagery and Verbal Processes*; Psychology Press: London, UK, 1971.
17. Paivio, A.; Csapo, K. Picture superiority in free recall: Imagery or dual coding? *Cogn. Psychol.* **1973**, *5*, 176–206. [CrossRef]
18. Arnedt, C.S.; Gentile, J.R. A test of dual coding theory for bilingual memory. *Can. J. Psychol. Can. Psychol.* **1986**, *40*, 290. [CrossRef]
19. Mayer, R. Systematic Thinking Fostered by Illustrations in Scientific Text. *J. Educ. Psychol.* **1989**, *81*, 240–246. [CrossRef]
20. Harp, S.; Mayer, R. How Seductive Details Do Their Damage: A Theory of Cognitive Interest in Science Learning. *J. Educ. Psychol.* **1998**, *90*, 414–434. [CrossRef]
21. Mayer, R.; Anderson, R. The Instructive Animation: Helping Students Build Connections Between Words and Pictures in Multimedia Learning. *J. Educ. Psychol.* **1992**, *84*, 444–452. [CrossRef]
22. Zhu, Y.; Wang, Y.; Yu, C.; Shi, S.; Zhang, Y.; He, S.; Zhao, P.; Ma, X.; Shi, Y. ViVo: Video-augmented dictionary for vocabulary learning. In Proceedings of the 2017 CHI Conference on Human Factors in Computing Systems, Denver, CO, USA, 6–11 May 2017; pp. 5568–5579.
23. Hong, R.; Wang, M.; Xu, M.; Yan, S.; Chua, T.S. Dynamic captioning: Video accessibility enhancement for hearing impairment. In Proceedings of the 18th ACM International Conference on Multimedia, Firenze, Italy, 25–29 October 2010; pp. 421–430.

24. Hu, Y.; Kautz, J.; Yu, Y.; Wang, W. Speaker-following video subtitles. *ACM Trans. Multimed. Comput. Commun. Appl.* **2015**, *11*, 1–17. [CrossRef]
25. Brown, A.; Jones, R.; Crabb, M.; Sandford, J.; Brooks, M.; Armstrong, M.; Jay, C. Dynamic subtitles: The user experience. In Proceedings of the ACM International Conference on Interactive Experiences for TV and Online Video, Brussels, Belgium, 3–5 June 2015; pp. 103–112.
26. Tulving, E. *Elements of Episodic Memory*; Oxford University Press: Oxford, UK, 1983.
27. Macedonia, M.; Knösche, T.R. Body in Mind: How Gestures Empower Foreign Language Learning. *Mind Brain Educ.* **2011**, *5*, 196–211. [CrossRef]
28. Macedonia, M.; Müller, K.; Friederici, A.D. The impact of iconic gestures on foreign language word learning and its neural substrate. *Hum. Brain Mapp.* **2011**, *32*, 982–998. [CrossRef]
29. Krönke, K.M.; Mueller, K.; Friederici, A.D.; Obrig, H. Learning by doing? The effect of gestures on implicit retrieval of newly acquired words. *Cortex* **2013**, *49*, 2553–2568. [CrossRef] [PubMed]
30. Tellier, M. The effect of gestures on second language memorisation by young children. *Gesture* **2008**, *8*, 219–235. [CrossRef]
31. Zhang, X.; Zuber, S. The effects of language and semantic repetition on the enactment effect of action memory. *Front. Psychol.* **2020**, *11*, 515. [CrossRef] [PubMed]
32. Ebert, D.; Gupta, S.; Makedon, F. Ogma: A virtual reality language acquisition system. In Proceedings of the 9th ACM International Conference on Pervasive Technologies Related to Assistive Environments, Corfu Island, Greece, 29 June–1 July 2016; pp. 1–5.
33. Wakefield, E.M.; Hall, C.; James, K.H.; Goldin-Meadow, S. Gesture for generalization: Gesture facilitates flexible learning of words for actions on objects. *Dev. Sci.* **2018**, *21*, e12656. [CrossRef] [PubMed]
34. Hostetter, A.B.; Pouw, W.; Wakefield, E.M. Learning From Gesture and Action: An Investigation of Memory for Where Objects Went and How They Got There. *Cogn. Sci.* **2020**, *44*, e12889. [CrossRef]
35. Vargas, M.F.; Fribourg, R.; Bates, E.; McDonnell, R. Now I Wanna Be a Dog: Exploring the Impact of Audio and Tactile Feedback on Animal Embodiment. In Proceedings of the 2023 IEEE International Symposium on Mixed and Augmented Reality (ISMAR), Sydney, Australia, 16–20 October 2023; pp. 912–921. [CrossRef]
36. Li, S.; Gu, X.; Yi, K.; Yang, Y.; Wang, G.; Manocha, D. Self-Illusion: A Study on Cognition of Role-Playing in Immersive Virtual Environments. *IEEE Trans. Vis. Comput. Graph.* **2022**, *28*, 3035–3049. [CrossRef]
37. Ogawa, N.; Narumi, T.; Kuzuoka, H.; Hirose, M. Do You Feel Like Passing Through Walls?: Effect of Self-Avatar Appearance on Facilitating Realistic Behavior in Virtual Environments. In Proceedings of the 2020 CHI Conference on Human Factors in Computing Systems, Honolulu, HI, USA, 25–30 April 2020; Association for Computing Machinery: New York, NY, USA, 2020; CHI '20; pp. 1–14. [CrossRef]
38. OpenAI. Introducing ChatGPT. 2022. Available online: https://openai.com/blog/chatgpt (accessed on 11 September 2024).
39. Nation, P. Vocabulary Analysis Programs. 2017. Available online: https://www.wgtn.ac.nz/lals/resources/paul-nations-resources/vocabulary-analysis-programs (accessed on 11 September 2024).
40. Persons, D.L.I. *Common European Framework of Reference for Languages: Learning, Teaching, Assessment*; Cambridge University Press: Cambridge, UK, 2001.
41. Consortium, B. The British National Corpus, XML Edition. 2007. Available online: https://ota.bodleian.ox.ac.uk/repository/xmlui/handle/20.500.12024/2554?show=full (accessed on 11 September 2024).
42. Davies, M. The Corpus of Contemporary American English as the first reliable monitor corpus of English. *Lit. Linguist. Comput.* **2010**, *25*, 447–464. [CrossRef]
43. Fukushima, S. EmoTan: Enhanced flashcards for second language vocabulary learning with emotional binaural narration. *Res. Pract. Technol. Enhanc. Learn.* **2019**, *14*, 16. [CrossRef]
44. Shimizu, K.; Fukushima, S.; Naemura, T. Effects of Binaural Audio on English Vocabulary Learning. In Proceedings of the 30th International Conference on Computers in Education Conference, Kuala Lumpur, Malaysia, 28 November–2 December 2022; Volume 2, pp. 665–667.
45. Nakata, T.; Suzuki, Y.; He, X.S. Costs and Benefits of Spacing for Second Language Vocabulary Learning: Does Relearning Override the Positive and Negative Effects of Spacing? *Lang. Learn.* **2023**, *73*, 799–834. [CrossRef]
46. Hart, S.G.; Staveland, L.E. Development of NASA-TLX (Task Load Index): Results of empirical and theoretical research. In *Advances in Psychology*; Elsevier: Amsterdam, The Netherlands, 1988; Volume 52, pp. 139–183.
47. Brooke, J. Sus: A "quick and dirty'usability. *Usability Eval. Ind.* **1996**, *189*, 189–194.
48. Russell, J.A.; Weiss, A.; Mendelsohn, G.A. Affect grid: A single-item scale of pleasure and arousal. *J. Pers. Soc. Psychol.* **1989**, *57*, 493. [CrossRef]
49. Miller, G.A. WordNet: A lexical database for English. *Commun. ACM* **1995**, *38*, 39–41. [CrossRef]
50. Hautasaari, A.; Hamada, T.; Ishiyama, K.; Fukushima, S. VocaBura: A Method for Supporting Second Language Vocabulary Learning While Walking. *Proc. ACM Interact. Mob. Wearable Ubiquitous Technol.* **2020**, *3*, 1–23. [CrossRef]

51. Mizuho, T.; Narumi, T.; Kuzuoka, H. Exploratory Study on the Reinstatement Effect Under 360-Degree Video-Based Virtual Environments. In Proceedings of the 29th ACM Symposium on Virtual Reality Software and Technology, Christchurch, New Zealand, 9–11 October 2023; Association for Computing Machinery: New York, NY, USA, 2023; VRST '23. [CrossRef]
52. Krekhov, A.; Cmentowski, S.; Krüger, J. Vr animals: Surreal body ownership in virtual reality games. In Proceedings of the 2018 Annual Symposium on Computer-Human Interaction in Play Companion Extended Abstracts, Melbourne, VIC, Australia, 28–31 October 2018; pp. 503–511.

Multimodal Technologies and Interaction

MDPI

Article

Transforming Science Education in Elementary Schools: The Power of PhET Simulations in Enhancing Student Learning

Hussam Diab [1,*], Wajeeh Daher [2,3,*], Baraa Rayan [4], Nael Issa [5] and Anwar Rayan [6]

1 Educational Systems Management Program, Faculty of Graduate Studies & Science Department, Al-Qasemi Academic College, Baka EL-Garbiah 3010000, Israel
2 Mathematics Education Program, Al-Qasemi Academic College of Education, Baqa 3010000, Israel
3 Graduate Studies, An-Najah National University, Nablus P400, Palestine
4 Abdo Salim School, Ibilin 3001200, Israel; b_rayan@ngsat.co.il
5 Science Department, Al-Qasemi Academic College of Education, Baqa 3010000, Israel; nael-e@qsm.ac.il
6 Science and Technology Department, Al-Qasemi Academic College of Education, Baqa 3010000, Israel; a_rayan@qsm.ac.il
* Correspondence: hussamono@gmail.com (H.D.); wajeehdaher@najah.edu or wdaher@qsm.ac.il (W.D.)

Abstract: In recent years, the integration of technology into education has significantly transformed teaching methods, especially in science education. Tools like PhET simulations have proven highly effective in enhancing student engagement and comprehension. Research has highlighted the value of simulation-based learning in fostering critical thinking and problem-solving skills. This study aimed to explore the impact of simulations, with a focus on PhET, on improving elementary students' learning outcomes, an area that remains under-researched. The study compared the performance of two groups of third-grade students: one group learned about solubility using PhET simulations, while the other relied on traditional textbook instruction. Each group comprised fifty students. The study lasted for a two-month period. The instructional approach was investigative learning. Data were gathered through student responses to materials science questions aligned with Bloom's Taxonomy, allowing for a detailed evaluation of their understanding and application of scientific concepts. Responses were assessed for accuracy and scored accordingly. We ran an independent-sample *t*-test to decide whether the difference in the mean score in science achievement between the two research groups was significant. The results showed that students using PhET simulations not only achieved significantly higher scores but also demonstrated their ability to explain their reasoning during problem-solving tasks. These findings emphasize the substantial advantages of incorporating digital tools like PhET simulations into elementary science education, as they enhance conceptual understanding and better equip students to tackle future scientific challenges. The present research results complement the previous research on using technology in the chemistry elementary classroom and add the issue of simulations to this research. The results of this study are centered on the topic of solubility. To broaden the generalizability of these findings, future research should examine the effects of simulations on student achievement in a wider range of elementary science topics.

Keywords: PhET simulation; elementary science education; learning outcomes; problem-solving tasks; scientific concepts

1. Introduction and Literature Review

In recent years, a broad and transformative technological revolution has impacted nearly all facets of life, including education [1–6]. Educational institutions worldwide have increasingly adopted innovative teaching methods that incorporate computers, the internet, and smartphones. These approaches aim to align with the demands of the digital age, making the learning process more interactive, engaging, and meaningful for students [7,8].

A key example of this technological revolution is the growing use of interactive simulations and digital tools in science education [9]. Simulations offer visual representations of complex scientific phenomena, allowing students to engage in investigative and dynamic learning experiences. Through digital experiments, students can manipulate variables and observe outcomes in real-time, making the process more engaging and effective than traditional methods such as reading, lectures, or short videos [10]. Additionally, simulations are powerful tools for enhancing the comprehension of intricate scientific concepts by creating an interactive environment where students can directly experience and apply their knowledge [11]. These tools also offer a multidimensional learning experience, integrating text, images, animations, and interactive elements, which together deepen students' understanding of scientific concepts and their real-world applications [12].

Virtual laboratories, such as PhET simulations, offer students the opportunity to conduct experiments digitally that many schools may lack the physical resources to support. These simulations are highly interactive and engaging, allowing students to actively explore and discover scientific concepts. They are scientifically accurate and provide dynamic, illustrative representations of complex scientific principles, aiding students in developing a deeper conceptual understanding of various topics [13].

Integrating simulations into science teaching across various age groups offers numerous advantages. Learners can manipulate variables more quickly and efficiently than with traditional instruments or methods, and simulations allow for multiple risk-free trials with immediate feedback. This approach better prepares students for future laboratory experiments while reinforcing concepts taught in the classroom. Simulations also provide exposure to advanced instrumental methods that may not be available during physical lab sessions [14]. Additionally, digital tools introduce an entertaining element to education, boosting students' motivation and interest [15]. As a result, the use of simulations, particularly in science education, enhances the overall quality of learning and contributes to improved educational outcomes [8].

1.1. Chemistry Education in the Primary School

Chemistry education at the primary school level is vital for laying a strong foundation in scientific literacy and nurturing a lifelong interest in the sciences. Introducing students to fundamental concepts such as chemical materials and their properties is key to developing critical thinking and problem-solving skills, which are essential for understanding the physical world. Early exposure to chemistry helps students grasp how materials interact, their practical uses, and their relevance in everyday life. Hands-on experiments and interactive activities are particularly effective at this stage, allowing students to observe and explore chemical reactions and properties firsthand [16].

Moreover, incorporating chemistry education into the primary curriculum stimulates curiosity and innovation by allowing students to experiment with various materials and biomaterials, including metals, polymers, and ceramics [17]. Activities such as building simple structures or testing the strength of materials significantly enhance students' understanding and retention of these concepts. Furthermore, connecting material science to real-world applications, like recycling and sustainable development, makes learning more engaging and relevant for young students [4]. Consequently, integrating chemistry education in primary schools not only enriches students' scientific knowledge but also cultivates the critical thinking and problem-solving skills essential for their future academic and professional success.

In addition, teaching chemistry in elementary school presents unique challenges and opportunities. On one hand, the complexity and abstract nature of chemical concepts can make it difficult for young students to grasp the material, as these ideas often go beyond their immediate experiences and cognitive development [18]. Young students may struggle with understanding the microscopic and symbolic representations inherent in chemistry, which can lead to misconceptions or a lack of interest in the subject. However, the integration of digital tools, such as interactive simulations, offers opportunities to enhance student understanding by providing visual representations that allow them to engage practically with complex chemical processes [19]. These tools create a more dynamic and interactive learning environment, transforming abstract concepts into tangible experiences for students.

1.2. The Use of Technology in the Chemistry Classroom

The integration of technology in the chemistry classroom has transformed the way students learn and interact with scientific concepts. Technology-enhanced learning tools, such as interactive simulations, virtual labs, and digital resources, offer dynamic and immersive experiences that traditional methods often struggle to replicate. For example, simulations enable students to visualize and manipulate molecular structures, chemical reactions, and processes in real-time, significantly improving their comprehension and retention of complex concepts [20,21].

In primary education, interactive software and apps introduce young learners to fundamental chemistry principles through gamified learning experiences, making abstract concepts more tangible and engaging [22]. These tools accommodate various learning styles and paces, ensuring that all students can effectively grasp the material.

At the secondary level, virtual laboratories allow students to conduct experiments in a safe, controlled environment, promoting inquiry-based learning and critical thinking skills. These virtual labs can simulate hazardous or impractical experiments that would not be feasible in a traditional classroom, thus expanding students' learning opportunities [23]. Additionally, online platforms and digital resources provide access to up-to-date scientific research and data, allowing students to explore contemporary advancements in chemistry and understand their real-world applications [24].

Overall, the integration of technology in chemistry education enhances student engagement, fosters a deeper understanding of scientific concepts, and equips students with the tools and methodologies needed for future scientific endeavors.

Technological tools have not only advantages but restrictions too. Technological tools may exacerbate accessibility issues, especially in under-resourced schools where students often lack adequate access to digital devices and reliable internet [25]. Addressing these disparities is essential to ensure equitable learning experiences and maximize the benefits of simulation-based education across diverse educational settings. UNESCO's recent report by West [26], further raises concerns about the rapid adoption of educational technologies and their impact on learning effectiveness, accessibility, and equity. Experiences during the COVID-19 pandemic underscored how technological reliance in education led to widening inequalities, a decline in student and teacher well-being, and potential privacy risks due to increased data collection and surveillance. These observations highlight the need for careful, context-sensitive technology integration that does not compromise educational quality.

1.3. The Use of Simulations in Elementary Science Education

Simulations have become a valuable tool in science education, offering a way to visualize and interact with scientific concepts that might otherwise remain abstract. PhET simulations have proven particularly useful in elementary science classrooms. These simulations are interactive, visual, and accessible, providing both teachers and students with tools to better understand complex scientific principles [27]. By enabling students to engage with content through virtual experiments, PhET simulations offer immediate feedback and a hands-on learning experience in a digital format, which helps bridge the gap between theoretical knowledge and practical application [28,29].

In elementary science education, traditional methods often rely heavily on static visuals and text explanations, which can be challenging for young students. Simulations, in contrast, support active learning by allowing students to manipulate elements and see real-time results, thereby reinforcing their understanding through both visual and kinesthetic engagement [30]. Studies have shown that such interactive simulations increase students' motivation and improve their retention of scientific concepts, making learning both enjoyable and effective [31,32]. Prior research supports the efficacy of simulations in enhancing comprehension and fostering positive attitudes toward science learning. For instance, Astuti et al. [30] found that students who used interactive simulations demonstrated improved critical thinking skills and a greater ability to apply scientific concepts in various contexts

Furthermore, simulations align with constructivist learning theories, which emphasize that knowledge is constructed through active engagement and connection with prior knowledge. PhET simulations, by providing a controlled environment for experimentation, encourage collaborative discussions, hypothesis testing, and direct observation. This approach supports students' deeper understanding and helps clarify abstract scientific principles [32].

1.4. Bloom's Taxonomy and Science Education

Bloom's Taxonomy is a hierarchical framework used to classify educational learning objectives based on complexity and specificity. Originally developed by Benjamin Bloom in 1956 and revised in 2001 by Anderson and Krathwohl [33], this model outlines six cognitive process levels: remembering, understanding, applying, analyzing, evaluating, and creating. Each level builds upon the previous one, promoting a progressively deeper and more comprehensive understanding of the subject matter.

Incorporating Bloom's Taxonomy into science education encourages students to go beyond rote memorization and develop higher-order thinking skills. By advancing through these levels, students enhance their critical thinking and problem-solving abilities, which are essential for scientific inquiry and grasping complex concepts [34]. This structured approach not only improves learning outcomes but also equips students with the analytical and creative skills necessary to tackle real-world scientific challenges [35].

The objective of this study was to evaluate the impact of integrating PhET simulations into science lessons on elementary school students' ability to solve chemistry problems. The study focuses on assessing students' cognitive development across different levels of Bloom's Taxonomy. The performance of students using PhET simulations is compared to those relying solely on traditional methods. The questions addressed in this research pertain to the topic of solutions and solubility, a core element of the elementary school science curriculum.

1.5. The Influence of Simulations on Students' Thinking Within Bloom's Taxonomy

Simulations serve as powerful tools for developing a range of cognitive skills across Bloom's Taxonomy, from foundational knowledge recall to advanced evaluation and creative thinking. At the foundational levels of remembering and understanding, simulations support students in recalling and comprehending scientific concepts by presenting them in interactive and visually engaging formats that enhance retention [36]. For instance, PhET simulations provide visual representations of scientific phenomena, allowing students to explore abstract concepts, such as energy transfer or molecular interactions, in a manner that fosters comprehension and reinforces learning [37].

As students move to higher levels, including applying and analyzing, simulations offer opportunities to manipulate variables and explore cause-and-effect relationships, facilitating critical thinking and analytical skills [30]. Through real-time experimentation within the simulation, students can test hypotheses and observe immediate outcomes, fostering a deeper understanding of scientific principles and enhancing their ability to analyze complex systems [38].

At the upper levels of evaluating and creating, simulations encourage students to critically evaluate data, make evidence-based decisions, and construct new models or hypotheses. For example, simulations can be used to predict the effects of changing a variable, assess the accuracy of these predictions, and refine understanding based on outcomes [39]. This iterative process of experimentation and reflection allows students to engage in creative problem-solving and hypothesis generation, culminating in the highest levels of Bloom's Taxonomy, where they design their own experiments and develop new insights [40]. By creating an adaptive, inquiry-based learning environment, simulations like PhET not only reinforce content knowledge but also cultivate critical and creative thinking across all cognitive levels.

1.6. Research Rationale and Goals

In a previous study, we conducted a qualitative analysis to observe how third-grade students collaborated in small groups (pairs and trios) while using PhET simulations. These students were tasked with exploring specific science topics and responding to related questions. Their responses were analyzed through the lens of Bloom's Taxonomy, focusing on different cognitive levels such as remembering, understanding, applying, analyzing, evaluating, and creating. In this research, we extended the investigation by comparing the performance of two groups: an experimental group using PhET simulations and a control group relying solely on traditional textbook methods. We evaluated the students' responses by assigning scores based on accuracy and depth of explanation, and we also computed the frequencies of different types of responses, providing illustrative examples.

The present study complements our previous work, triangulating the findings to offer a comprehensive view of elementary students' learning in chemistry through simulations. Understanding science at the elementary level is crucial, as it lays the foundation for students to pursue scientific studies in middle and secondary education [41]. This research highlights the effectiveness of incorporating simulations in primary school science lessons, offering insights that can assist teachers and educational policymakers in developing science curricula that integrate digital tools like PhET to enhance student learning outcomes.

In addition to the above, previous research primarily offered qualitative insights or concentrated on older learners; the present study quantitatively assesses the impact of PhET simulations on elementary students' cognitive engagement across Bloom's Taxonomy. The findings will help provide robust support for the integration of digital simulations in primary science education.

1.7. Research Questions

1. Does learning with the PhET program result in significant differences in students' knowledge scores between the PhET group and the regular group?
2. What are the differences in students' answers to chemistry questions between the PhET group and the control group, particularly in terms of accuracy, explanation depth, and cognitive engagement?

2. Materials and Methods

2.1. Research Context and Participants

The context of the research is that of primary school chemistry. The study involved 100 third-grade students, divided into two groups. The experimental group, consisting of 50 students, learned the topic of solubility using PhET simulations, while the control group of 50 students studied the same topic using only the third-grade chemistry textbook. The mean score of students' age was 9.34 years with standard deviation of 0.25 years. In the experimental group, there were 24 female students and 26 male students, while in the control group, there were 27 female students and 23 male students. The sampling method started as that of convenience, where we chose a school where a chemistry teacher agreed to participate in the research, and where the same teacher would teach the experimental and the control groups. The distribution of experimental and control groups was done randomly.

The third-grade chemistry book includes the following topics: 1. Materials: properties and uses (Material properties and ways to identify them; solubility in water—solvent and solute, electrical conductivity, magnetism, flammability, heat conductivity; material mixtures and ways to separate them. Distinguishing properties: water solubility, color, floatation, magnetism, grain size). 2. Use of materials: The relationship between the properties of the material and its use (Solubility: preparation of drinks and detergents. Electrical conductivity: operation of electrical devices. Magnetism: grip of iron tools/bodies. Combustion: producing heat for cooking and heating and producing light for lighting). 3. Material changes: Combustion of materials (Conditions for combustion: ignition temperature, oxygen, and fuel. Combustion materials: wood, coal, kerosene, oil, and more. Combustion products: materials—ashes, gases, and smoke. Energy—light and heat. 4. Materials: benefit and environmental price (The importance of fuels for cooking, lighting, heating, operating machines and cars, generating electricity. The environmental price of fuel utilization—air pollution (smoke, gases and ash), fuel leakage into the environment. Solutions to reduce environmental damage—chimney filters, reducing the use of private vehicles, saving electricity. Adopting responsible environmental behavior to preserve the quality of the environment—saving electricity, reducing the use of vehicles for example).

The study lasted for a two-month period. The students learned 32 lessons, where each lesson lasted for 45 min. The instructional approach was investigative learning. To avoid confounding variables, the same teacher taught both the experimental and the control groups. In the simulations' class, the teacher displayed a simulation using a projector to demonstrate the concept of solubility to the students. Doing that, she showed examples of the solubility of various substances, such as sugar and salt. Using the simulation, the teacher highlighted the amount of solute, explaining the concept of saturation. Afterwards, the students practiced what they had learned individually. Each student accessed the simulation and, with the teacher's guidance, adjusted parameters such as the amount of solute, the amount of solvent, and observed how the change of these parameters affected solubility. At the end, the teacher conducted a concluding discussion to ensure the consolidation of students' understanding.

We chose to compare the simulation instructional method to that of the book method because generally elementary schools' students learn chemistry by the book, which make researchers compare the innovative or new instructional method to that of the book method (ex., [29,30]).

2.2. The PhET Simulations

The PhET simulations used in this study are composed of small modules specifically designed for scientific exploration, each focusing narrowly on a single activity or lesson. These modules can be seamlessly integrated into classroom instruction or accessed on students' digital devices. Each simulation includes a virtual representation of physical objects that can be manipulated by the user, along with "disciplinary representations" that connect the activity to scientific discourse [41].

The PhET project provides over 160 simulations across subjects such as physics, chemistry, mathematics, earth science, and biology. These simulations are free and open-licensed, available for online use or downloadable for offline use with minimal preparation required from teachers and students. Designed for all educational levels from primary to postsecondary, the project is based at the University of Colorado and widely supported by foundations as well as commercial, governmental, and educational organizations. It should be noted that most of the research and applications of these technologies have so far focused on secondary and higher education. Despite their numerous advantages and benefits, there remains a lack of studies and a knowledge gap in the published literature, particularly concerning elementary education.

2.3. Data Collection Tools

In the present study, we used two collecting tools. Both tools concerned the texts of students' solutions to 12 chemistry problems related to Bloom's Taxonomy levels: remembering, understanding, application, evaluation, and creation. The first tool is concerned with the accuracy type of the answer, as well as the justification given, while the second tool is concerned with the answers' score, i.e., with the students' achievement related to the problems' answers. Table 1 includes an example of a problem from each Bloom's level. The questions given to the third-grade students were 2 from each Bloom's level, where the score of each level was computed as the mean of the scores of the two questions from the same level.

Table 1. Examples of the chemistry problems given to the students.

Level	Problem
Remembering	We dissolved sugar in water. What is the solvent and what is the solute?
Understanding	Nader added 20 g of sugar to 100 g of water and stirred. After the stirring, an amount of sugar precipitated at the bottom of the container. Explain why the whole amount of sugar in the container did not dissolve.
Application	Salwa added 25 g of salt to 120 g of water and stirred. After stirring an amount of salt precipitated at the bottom of the container. Suggest a method to dissolve all the salt at the bottom of the container.
Analysis	The students in the fifth grade wanted to examine the relationship between the size of water and the amount of heat requested to raise the temperature of the water. To determine this relationship, the students poured 100 mL of water into a container and 1000 mL of water into another container made of the same material. They put the two containers on two similar heat sources. They measured the temperature of the water in the 100 mL container and obtained a temperature of 58 °C. Does this temperature prevail also in the 1000 mL container? Explain.
Evaluation	Yousef dissolved a teaspoon of sugar in a cup of water and a sugar solution was produced. The solution was too sweet to drink. Propose a method to reduce the sugar concentration in the solution. Support your proposal with scientific evidence proving its validity.
Creation	When Noor added a teaspoon of salt to a glass bowl filled with water, the salt dissolved completely in the water. If we assume that salt particles dissolved in water look like small black balls, and Noor had magic glasses to help her see these black balls, which of the following two containers (Container A or Container B) correctly represents the solution resulting from dissolving salt with water? Explain why. 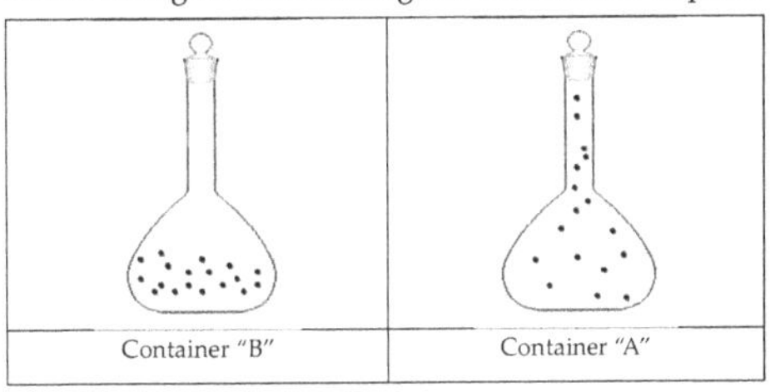

2.4. Data Analysis Tools

To evaluate students' understanding of the solubility topic, each problem's answer was given 10 if the answer was correct and the explanation was correct. The answer was given 5 if it or the explanation was correct but not both of them. The answer was given 0 if neither the answer nor the explanation was correct. The answer took also the 0 score if the student gave no answer.

2.4.1. An Example of Assessing a Problem's Answer

The problem: Nader added 20 g of sugar to 100 g of water and stirred. After stirring, an amount of sugar precipitated at the bottom of the container. Explain why the whole amount of sugar in the container did not dissolve.

An answer that took the score 0:
No answer, we did not put enough water in the container.
An answer that took the score 5:
We did not stir enough.
An answer that took the score 10:
The solution reached its saturation point.

2.4.2. Statistical Analysis

We computed the means and standard deviations for the achievement scores of the experimental and control groups. Afterwards, we ran an independent-sample *t* test to decide whether the difference in the mean score in science achievement between the two research groups was significant.

2.5. Validity and Reliability of the Methodology

The reliability of the methodology arises from the agreement between coders regarding the analysis process of the themes of students' answers (accuracy of the answers). Three coders coded students' responses and we computed the agreement between the coders, giving values between 0.88 and 0.92 for the responses to have 0, 5 or 10 score. These values indicate the validity of the analysis, and therefore its reliability. The agreement value was obtained through computing the Holsti equation: PA (Holsti) = 2A/(N1 + N2), where PA (Holsti) represents percentage of agreement between two coders; A is the number of the two coders' consensus decisions, and N1 and N2 are the numbers of decisions the coders have made, respectively.

The validity of the coding process was initially established by resolving disagreements between the three coders. This resolution occurred through discussion sessions where the three coders went through their initial categorization, comparing and discussing it until they arrived at agreement.

3. Results

The results are two parts referring to the two research questions.

3.1. The First Research Question

The first research question examined whether learning with the PhET program results in significant differences in students' knowledge scores in all Bollom's levels between the PhET group and the regular group. We computed means and standard deviations of the scores of the two groups, and to find the significance of the differences between the scores of the two groups, we ran independent-sample *t*-test.

The two groups did not differ significantly in their achievement before the experiment, where this achievement was represented by the overall students' achievement in the last trimester (2022–2023). The mean of students' achievement in the PhET group was 9.31 (SD = 0.53), while the mean of students' achievement in the control group was 9.28 (SD = 0.65), t(98) = 0.25, $p = 0.80$.

Table 2 describes means and standard deviations of students' scores in the levels of knowledge according to Bloom's Taxonomy after the experiment. Table 2 also shows the significance of the differences between the scores of the experiment and the control groups in all Bollom's levels.

Table 2. Means and standard deviations of students' scores in the levels of knowledge after the experiment.

Level	Group	M	SD	*t*-Test	*p*
Remembering	Experiment	9.300	1.679	5.059	<0.001
	Control	6.500	3.536		
Understanding	Experiment	9.500	1.515	5.420	<0.001
	Control	6.350	3.820		

Table 2. *Cont.*

Level	Group	M	SD	*t*-Test	*p*
Applying	Experiment Control	9.200 6.300	1.856 3.753	4.899	<0.001
Analyzing	Experiment Control	9.200 3.650	1.552 3.787	9.590	<0.001
Evaluation	Experiment Control	8.250 3.200	3.041 3.713	7.440	<0.001
Creating	Experiment Control	7.650 5.150	3.171 3.171	3.942	<0.001

Table 2 shows that the means of the levels of knowledge of the experiment group are higher than those of the control group and these differences are significant at the level of 0.001. The difference between the two groups was higher in the case of analyzing and evaluation levels, indicating the effectiveness of the PhET simulation to boost high-level knowledge.

3.2. *The Second Research Question*

The second research question examined students' answers to the chemistry questions, comparing between them. Following are those answers for the questions related to the knowledge levels.

3.2.1. The Remembering Question

We dissolved sugar in water. What is the solvent and what is the solute?

Forty-five students in the PhET group accurately answered the remembering question, saying that the water is the solvent, and the sugar is the solute. Five students in the PhET group inaccurately exchanged between water and sugar.

Forty-one students in the control group accurately answered the remembering question, while nine students in the control group inaccurately answered the question.

3.2.2. The Understanding Question

Nader added 20 g of sugar to 100 g of water and stirred. After the stirring, an amount of sugar precipitated at the bottom of the container. Explain why the whole amount of sugar in the container did not dissolve.

Table 3 describes the students' answers to the understanding question in both research groups, as well as the frequency of each answer.

Table 3. Students' answers to the understanding question and frequency of each answer.

Answer	Frequency
PhET group	
The water reached saturation level	10
A saturation process has occurred	10
He did not stir well	5
He added a big amount of sugar, so saturation was reached	10
The water was a small amount	5
He added a lot of sugar	4
The solution reached saturation	6
Control group	
It is a lot	10
The amount of sugar was big.	10
The amount of sugar was more than the water	20
The water amount was bigger	4
It is difficult for the sugar to dissolve in the water	6

Table 3 shows that the students in the PhET group gave more accurate answers than the students in the control group. In addition, the students in the PhET group gave more explanations than the students in the control group. For example, the students in the PhET group used the idea of saturation in their explanations, while the students in the control group did not.

3.2.3. The Application Question

Salwa added 25 g of salt to 120 g of water and stirred. After stirring, an amount of salt precipitated at the bottom of the container. Suggest a method to dissolve all the salt at the bottom of the container.

Table 4 describes the students' answers to the understanding question in both research groups, as well as the frequency of each answer.

Table 4. Students' answers to the application question and frequency of each answer.

Answer	Frequency
PhET group	
We add warm water to the solution	7
We add water to the solution	30
We add warm water	2
We add hot water to accelerate the dissolving of the salt	10
No answer	1
Control group	
We add water to the cup	21
We add water	
She added a lot of salt	13
No answer	13

Table 4 shows that only one student in the PhET group did not answer the question, while thirteen students in the control group did not answer the question and another third student in the control group answered it inappropriately. In addition, the students in the PhET group used the idea of 'warm or hot water' in their explanation, while the students in the control group did not.

3.2.4. The Analysis Question

The students in the fifth grade wanted to examine the relationship between the size of water and the amount of heat needed to raise the temperature of the water. To determine this relationship, the students poured 100 mL of water into a container and 1000 mL of water into another container made of the same material. They put the two containers on two similar heat sources. They measured the temperature of the water in the 100 mL container and obtained a temperature of 58 °C. Does this temperature prevail also in the 1000 mL container? Explain.

Table 5 describes the students' answers to the analysis question in both research groups, as well as the frequency of each answer.

Table 5. Students' answers to the analysis question and frequency of each answer.

Answer	Frequency
PhET group	
No because the two amounts are not equal	25
No because the big amount needs more time to heat than the small amount	11

Table 5. *Cont.*

Answer	Frequency
No because the second container has a bigger amount of water, so it needs more time.	4
No	8
No answer	2
Control group	
No. The quantity of water is not equal.	12
No	2
Yes, because the container is made of the same material	20
Yes	5
No answer	10

Table 5 shows that here too, more students in the PhET group answered the question than in the control group. In addition, forty students in the PhET group gave accurate explanations in their response, while only twelve students in the control group did so.

3.2.5. Evaluation Question

Yousef dissolved a teaspoon of sugar in a cup of water and a sugar solution was produced. The solution was too sweet to drink. Propose a method to reduce the sugar concentration in the solution. Support your proposal with scientific evidence proving its validity.

Table 6 describes the students' answers to the evaluation question in both research groups, as well as the frequency of each answer.

Table 6. Students' answers to the evaluation question and frequency of each answer.

Answer	Frequency
PhET group	
Adding more water to the solution so that the sugar is distributed over a larger amount of water	22
Adding more water, as we did in the simulation (when we added water to the solution of water and sugar, the color became lighter because the sugar was distributed over a larger amount of water)	7
Adding water to the solution reduces the sweetness of the solution because the sugar will dissolve in a larger amount of water	9
Adding more water reduces the sugar taste	11
No answer	1
Control group	
Add water to the cup	15
Add water	2
Evaporate water	18
No answer	15

As in the previous knowledge levels, here too, the number of students who answered inaccurately or did not answer the evaluation question in the control group is far more than the number in the PhET group. In addition, the students in the PhET group gave detailed explanations (38 out of 50), while in the control group, the students did not pay attention to explanations.

3.2.6. Creation Question

When Noor added a teaspoon of salt to a glass bowl filled with water, the salt dissolved completely in the water. If we assume that salt particles dissolved in water look like small black balls, and Noor had magic glasses to help her see these black balls, which of the following two containers (Container A or Container B) correctly represents the solution resulting from dissolving salt with water? Explain why.

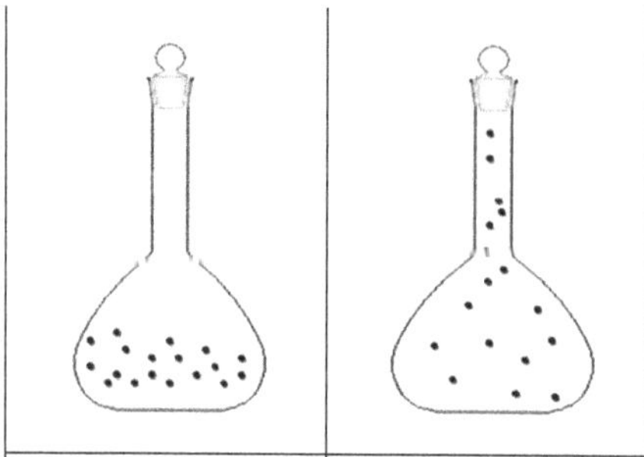

Container "B" Container "A"

Table 7 describes the students' answers to the creation question in both research groups, as well as the frequency of each answer.

Table 7. Students' answers to the creation question and frequency of each answer.

Student Answer	Frequency
PhET group	
Container A because the solute spreads throughout the liquid.	18
Container A, the salt spread in the container because it dissolved in the water. When we added red salt to the water, the color of all the water changed because the salt dissolved throughout the water and not just in part of it.	15
Container A, the salt dissolves in all of the water. If there is saturation, it will not be like picture B because the salt must be in all of the water, and it must also precipitate at the bottom of the container only.	8
Container A	3
Container A, when the sugar drops into the water, it spreads everywhere.	2
No answer	4
Control group	
Container A, the salt is in all the water	20
Container A, the salt is all over the container	5
Container A	15
Container B, because the salt is at the bottom of the bowl; when we conducted the experiment in class, the salt remained at the bottom of the container and was not in all the water	6
Container B, because salt precipitated.	2
No answer	2

Table 7 shows that the two groups were almost similar in answering accurately and inaccurately the creation question (46 answers were accurate in the PhET group, while 40 answers were accurate in the control group). The main difference between the two groups was in the inclusion of explanations. The answers in the PhET group included explanation more than in the control group. Those explanations were detailed in the case of the PhET group.

4. Discussion

In answering the remembering question, students in the PhET group exhibited a slightly higher accuracy rate compared to the control group (45 students in the PhET group versus 41 students in the control group). This suggests that the PhET simulations provided a slight advantage in aiding students' retention of basic information.

For the understanding question, both groups provided a range of explanations for why not all the sugar dissolved. However, students in the PhET group offered more accurate and varied explanations, demonstrating a deeper grasp of key concepts such as saturation, stirring, and the ratio of solute to solvent. This suggests that the visual and interactive nature of the PhET simulations helped students better visualize and comprehend the chemical processes involved, as supported by similar findings in previous research [9].

At the application level, students in the PhET group demonstrated a solid understanding of saturation and its role in dissolving solutes. Their responses showed that they could effectively apply their knowledge of solubility to real-world chemistry problems. In contrast, responses from the control group indicated a more superficial understanding, with many students focusing on the quantity of the solute (using terms like "a lot") rather than the scientific concept of saturation. This deeper comprehension in the PhET group underscores the effectiveness of simulations in enhancing students' conceptual understanding, a result in line with prior research on PhET simulations [41].

Responses to the analysis question revealed different levels of understanding between the two groups. While both groups showed some recognition of the need for additional water to dissolve salt and the differences in heat transfer between various volumes of water, students in the PhET group demonstrated twice the level of recognition regarding the role of volume compared to the control group. This enhanced performance likely resulted from the PhET group's engagement with the simulations, where manipulating variables like solvent volume increased their awareness of the relationships between the variables involved. These results align with studies highlighting the importance of visualization and focused attention when working with digital tools [19].

At the evaluation level, students in the PhET group provided answers that demonstrated a clear understanding of dilution as a method for reducing solute concentration. In contrast, the control group's responses were often shorter and less developed, indicating a more limited grasp of the concept of dilution. Once again, the use of digital simulations helped students visualize the concept more effectively, contributing to a fuller understanding [42].

Finally, in answering the creation question, most students in both groups chose the correct answer, but a significant portion of the control group failed to provide explanations for their choices. This indicates that while both groups could arrive at the correct solution, the PhET simulations helped students articulate their reasoning, further reinforcing the benefits of interactive learning tools in promoting deeper cognitive engagement. The previous issue of explanations provided by the PhET group is of special interest, as this explanation is expected to make understanding sustainable over time. Thus, simulations are required in the science classroom to encourage sustainable students' understanding.

5. Limitations, Conclusions, and Recommendations

The present research investigates the impact of digital simulations on students' understanding. The comparison between the responses to the application questions in both groups underscores the value of using digital tools, such as PhET simulations, at an early stage to enhance students' understanding of scientific concepts. The PhET group's superior performance in applying their knowledge highlights how interactive simulations facilitate deeper comprehension and engagement with the material. This is in line with researchers' findings regarding the contribution of digital simulations to students' learning. Daher and Baya'a [43] found that mobile simulations helped middle school students better understand mathematical concepts by allowing them to explore real-world scenarios both in and out of the classroom. This aligns with previous research suggesting that digital simulations can positively impact students' learning, particularly in the analysis stage. In addition, Daher and Swidan [44] found that simulations helped primary school students better understand relationships among quadrilaterals.

Additionally, the responses to the analysis questions emphasize the significance of understanding the relationship between variables like volume, heat transfer, and solubility. The PhET group demonstrated a stronger grasp of these relationships compared to the control group, suggesting that digital simulations not only improve students' conceptual understanding but also enhance their critical thinking and problem-solving abilities. These findings support the integration of technology-based learning tools in science education to promote more effective and dynamic learning outcomes.

The present study results show that simulation can help elementary school students have better explanations, so these results encourage educational practices that take advantage of digital simulations. They also encourage policymakers to take advantage of digital simulations by incorporating them in the elementary science curriculum.

The authors of the present research are aware of the challenges or limitations of using PhET simulations, such as potential accessibility issues, technical difficulties, or dependency on technology for effective learning. These challenges and limitations require educators and policy makers to plan to overcome them [25,26].

In terms of practical applications, the study highlights the potential of combining digital tools with traditional teaching methods. For optimal outcomes, educators might consider using PhET simulations as a supplement to hands-on activities rather than a replacement. Practical recommendations include beginning with traditional instruction to establish foundational knowledge, followed by simulations to deepen understanding and foster interactive, inquiry-based learning experiences. Furthermore, digital simulations should be customized for specific concepts where visual aids are beneficial for comprehension.

Future research is needed to investigate the influence of digital tools on students' application level. Daher and Sleem [45] found that traditional teaching methods were more effective than 360-degree videos in helping students apply their knowledge. However, the present research suggests that digital simulations can positively impact students' performance and understanding during the application phase. This suggests that digital simulations could be beneficial in supporting student learning in this area. Future research can use the interview as a data collecting tool to examine how students and teachers conceive digital simulations as contributing to students learning, including the application level of knowledge.

The results address the topic of solubility. Future research is needed to investigate the influence of simulations on students' achievement in other topics of science in elementary school, which would add to the generalizability of the present research results. Moreover, factors such as prior knowledge, differences in teaching style, or time spent on tasks, did not influence the results, as these factors were similar in the two research groups. Future research could vary one or more of these factors and observe the results of this variation.

The present research sample could be considered representative of third-grade students who study the relevant topic of chemistry, but future research needs to verify the influence of simulations on students' understanding of chemistry concepts and relations. This future research will enable the applicability of the findings to other educational settings, disciplines, or student populations. Moreover, the observed advantages of the PhET simulations should be examined in relation to their sustainability over time.

In addition to the above, future research could implement interviews with students and teachers regarding the impact of simulation on elementary students' understanding of scientific concepts. This qualitative method can enrich our understanding of the studied educational issue [46].

Author Contributions: Conceptualization, H.D., W.D., N.I., B.R. and A.R.; methodology, H.D., W.D. and N.I.; formal analysis, H.D., W.D. and N.I.; data curation, B.R. and A.R.; writing—original draft preparation, H.D., W.D. and N.I. writing—review and editing, H.D., W.D., N.I., B.R. and A.R. All authors have read and agreed to the published version of the manuscript.

Funding: This research received no external funding.

Institutional Review Board Statement: The study was conducted in accordance with the Declaration of Helsinki and approved by the Institutional Review Board of Al-Qasemi Academic College of Education (approve number: 12-2023).

Informed Consent Statement: Informed consent was obtained from all subjects involved in the study.

Data Availability Statement: Data could be provided upon request from the corresponding authors.

Conflicts of Interest: The authors declare no conflicts of interest.

References

1. Allah Rakha, N. Revolution in Learning Through Digitization: How Technology is Changing the Landscape of Education. *Int. J. Cyber Law* **2023**, *1*.
2. Filippi, S.; Motyl, B. Development of a Tool for Evaluating the Influence of Engineering Students' Perception of Generative AI on University Courses Based on Personality, Perceived Roles in Design Teams, and Course Engagement. *Multimodal Technol. Interact.* **2024**, *8*, 84. [CrossRef]
3. Hallinger, P.; Wang, R. The Evolution of Simulation-Based Learning Across the Disciplines, 1965–2018: A Science Map of the Literature. *Simul. Gaming* **2020**, *51*, 9–32. [CrossRef]
4. Santos KL, B.; Macena, C.S. Teaching chemistry in a playful and experimental way: Proposals for elementary education in public schools. *Seven Ed.* **2024**, *2*, 544–551. [CrossRef]
5. Liarokapis, F.; Milata, V.; Skola, F. Extended Reality Educational System with Virtual Teacher Interaction for Enhanced Learning. *Multimodal Technol. Interact.* **2024**, *8*, 83. [CrossRef]
6. Salhab, R.; Daher, W. The Impact of Mobile Learning on Students' Attitudes towards Learning in an Educational Technology Course. *Multimodal Technol. Interact.* **2023**, *7*, 74. [CrossRef]
7. Elbourhamy, D.M.; Najmi, A.H.; Elfeky, A.M. Students' performance in interactive environments: An intelligent model. *PeerJ Comput. Sci.* **2023**, *9*, e1348. [CrossRef]
8. Talan, T. The effect of simulation technique on academic achievement: A meta-analysis study. *Int. J. Technol. Educ. Sci.* **2021**, *5*, 17–36. [CrossRef]
9. Rayan, B.; Daher, W.; Diab, H.; Issa, N. Integrating PhET Simulations into Elementary Science Education: A Qualitative Analysis. *Educ. Sci.* **2023**, *13*, 884. [CrossRef]
10. Tsai, F.-H.; Hsu, I.Y. Exploring the effects of guidance in a computer detective game for science education. *J. Balt. Sci. Educ.* **2020**, *19*, 647–658. [CrossRef]
11. Agyei, E. Pedagogical Support Structures for Effective Implementation of Simulation-Based Innovation in Science Classrooms: Prospective Teachers' Perspectives. *Afr. J. Educ. Stud. Math. Sci.* **2024**, *20*, 47–74.
12. Otterborn, A.; Sundberg, B.; Schönborn, K. The Impact of Digital and Analog Approaches on a Multidimensional Preschool Science Education. *Res. Sci. Educ.* **2024**, *54*, 185–203. [CrossRef]
13. Salame, I.I.; Samson, D. Examining the Implementation of PhET Simulations into General Chemistry Laboratory. *Int. J. Environ. Sci. Educ.* **2019**, *14*, 207–217.
14. Harvey, D.T.; Le, A.n.-P.; Lucy, C.A.; Mosby, B.M.; Park, E.J. The Use of Simulations with Active Learning Exercises. In *Active Learning in the Analytical Chemistry Curriculum*; American Chemical Society: Washington, DC, USA, 2022; Chapter 8; pp. 121–145. [CrossRef]
15. López-Martínez, A.; Meroño, L.; Cánovas-López, M.; Garcia de Alcaraz, A.; Martínez-Aranda, L. Using Gamified Strategies in Higher Education: Relationship between Intrinsic Motivation and Contextual Variables. *Sustainability* **2022**, *14*, 11014. [CrossRef]
16. Byusa, E.; Kampire, E.; Mwesigye, A.R. Game-based learning approach on students' motivation and understanding of chemistry concepts: A systematic review of literature. *Heliyon* **2022**, *8*, e09541. [CrossRef]
17. Dobal, F.; Lalioti, V. Circular Species: Designing critical thinking into children's science education through biomaterials and augmented reality. In Proceedings of the 20th Annual ACM Interaction Design and Children Conference, Athens, Greece, 24–30 June 2021; pp. 8–17. [CrossRef]
18. Akerson, V.L.; Bartels, S.L. Elementary science teaching: Toward the goal of scientific literacy. In *Handbook of Research on Science Education*; Routledge: London, UK, 2023; pp. 528–558.
19. Evagorou, M.; Erduran, S.; Mäntylä, T. The role of visual representations in scientific practices: From conceptual understanding and knowledge generation to 'seeing' how science works. *Int. J. STEM Educ.* **2015**, *2*, 11. [CrossRef]
20. Jere, S.; Mpeta, M. Enhancing Learners' Conceptual Understanding of Reaction Kinetics Using Computer Simulations—A Case Study Approach. *Res. Sci. Educ.* **2024**, *54*, 999–1023. [CrossRef]

21. Jammeh, A.L.J.; Karegeya, C.; Ladage, S. Application of technological pedagogical content knowledge in smart classrooms: Views and its effect on students' performance in chemistry. *Educ. Inf. Technol.* **2024**, *29*, 9189–9219. [CrossRef]
22. Kalogiannakis, M.; Papadakis, S.; Zourmpakis, A.-I. Gamification in Science Education. A Systematic Review of the Literature. *Educ. Sci.* **2021**, *11*, 22. [CrossRef]
23. Kolil, V.K.; Achuthan, K. Virtual labs in chemistry education: A novel approach for increasing student's laboratory educational consciousness and skills. *Educ. Inf. Technol.* **2024**. [CrossRef]
24. Pavlo, P.; Serhiy, O.; Olesia, Y. Cloud technologies of augmented reality as a means of supporting educational and research activities in chemistry for 11th grade students. *Educ. Technol. Q.* **2023**, *2023*, 69–91. [CrossRef]
25. McGuire, S.; Shawn, M. Educational Inequities: Impact of Technology and Internet Access on Online Learning in Title I Schools. Ph.D. Thesis, Sanford College of Education, National University, San Diego, CA, USA, 2024.
26. West, M. *An Ed-Tech Tragedy? Educational Technologies and School Closures in the Time of COVID 19*; UNESCO Publishing: Paris, France, 2023.
27. Hillmayr, D.; Ziernwald, L.; Reinhold, F.; Hofer, S.I.; Reiss, K.M. The potential of digital tools in secondary science learning. *Comput. Educ.* **2020**, *153*, 103897. [CrossRef]
28. Bahtiar, B.; Ibrahim, I. Analysis of Students' Scientific Literacy Skills. *J. Pendidik. IPA Indones.* **2022**, *11*, 371–386.
29. Mashami, R.A.; Ahmadi; Kurniasih, Y.; Khery, Y. Use of PhET Simulations as A Virtual Laboratory to Improve Students' Problem Solving Skills. *J. Penelit. Pendidik. IPA* **2023**, *9*, 11455–11465. [CrossRef]
30. Astuti, T.N.; Sugiyarto, K.H.; Ikhsan, J. Effect of 3D Visualization on Students' Critical Thinking Skills and Scientific Attitude in Chemistry. *Int. J. Instr.* **2020**, *13*, 151–164. [CrossRef]
31. Salame, I.I.; Makki, J. Examining PhET's impact on attitudes and learning in chemistry. *Interdiscip. J. Environ. Sci. Educ.* **2021**, *17*, e2247. [CrossRef]
32. Schwarz, C.V.; White, B.Y. Metamodeling Knowledge: Developing Students' Understanding of Scientific Modeling. *Cogn. Instr.* **2005**, *23*, 165–205. [CrossRef]
33. Anderson, L.W.; Krathwohl, D.R. (Eds.) *A Taxonomy for Learning, Teaching, and Assessing: A Revision of Bloom's Taxonomy of Educational Objectives*; Allyn & Bacon: Boston, MA, USA, 2001.
34. Krathwohl, D.R. A Revision of Bloom's Taxonomy: An Overview. *Theory Into Pract.* **2002**, *41*, 212–218. [CrossRef]
35. Zorluoğlu, S.L.; Gün, N. Investigation of the Science Individualized Education Programs' Learning Outcomes According to the Revised Bloom Taxonomy. *J. Educ. Futur.* **2024**, 67–80. [CrossRef]
36. Pavlou, Y.; Zacharia, Z.C. Using Physical and Virtual Labs for Experimentation in STEM+ Education: From Theory and Research to Practice. *Shap. Future Biol. Educ. Res.* **2024**, *1*, 3–19.
37. Banda, H.J.; Nzabahimana, J. Effect of integrating physics education technology simulations on students' conceptual understanding in physics: A review of literature. *Phys. Rev. Phys. Educ. Res.* **2021**, *17*, 023108. [CrossRef]
38. Krüger, J.T.; Höffler, T.N.; Wahl, M.; Knickmeier, K.; Parchmann, I. Two comparative studies of computer simulations and experiments as learning tools in school and out-of-school education. *Instr. Sci.* **2022**, *50*, 169–197. [CrossRef]
39. Rianti, R.; Gunawan, G.; Verawati, N.N.S.P.; Taufik, M. The Effect of Problem Based Learning Model Assisted by PhET Simulation on Understanding Physics Concepts. *Lensa J. Kependidikan Fis.* **2024**, *12*, 28–43. [CrossRef]
40. Simanjuntak, M.P.; Hutahaean, J.; Marpaung, N.; Ramadhani, D. Effectiveness of Problem-Based Learning Combined with Computer Simulation on Students' Problem-Solving and Creative Thinking Skills. *Int. J. Instr.* **2021**, *14*, 519–534. [CrossRef]
41. Taibu, R.; Mataka, L.; Shekoyan, V. Using PhET simulations to improve scientific skills and attitudes of community college students. *Int. J. Educ. Math. Sci. Technol. (IJEMST)* **2021**, *9*, 353–370. [CrossRef]
42. Daher, W.M. Grade 10 students' technology-based exploration processes of narratives associated with the sine function. *EURASIA J. Math. Sci. Technol. Educ.* **2020**, *16*, em1852. [CrossRef]
43. Daher, W.; Baya'a, N. Characteristics of middle school students learning actions in outdoor mathematical activities with the cellular phone. *Teach. Math. Its Appl. Int. J. IMA* **2012**, *31*, 133–152. [CrossRef]
44. Daher, W.; Swidan, O. Positioning–Emotions Association of Young Students Using Digital Technology. *Mathematics* **2021**, *9*, 1617. [CrossRef]
45. Daher, W.; Sleem, H. Middle school students' learning of social studies in the video and 360-degree videos contexts. *IEEE Access* **2021**, *9*, 78774–78783. [CrossRef]
46. Daher, W. Schools' Challenges in Distance Learning during Emergency Education: Focus Group Methodology. *Educ. Sci.* **2024**, *14*, 383. [CrossRef]

Multimodal Technologies and Interaction

MDPI

Article

Effects of Kahoot! on K-12 Students' Mathematics Achievement and Multi-Screen Addiction

Nikolaos Pellas

Department of Primary Education, University of Western Macedonia, 3rd km Niki-Florina, 53100 Florina, Greece; aff00192@uowm.gr

Abstract: Digital platforms are increasingly prevalent among young students in K-12 education, offering significant opportunities but also raising concerns about their effects on self-assessment and academic performance. This study investigates the effectiveness of Kahoot! compared to traditional instructional methods in enhancing mathematics achievement and its impact on multiple screen addiction (MSA) among Greek students aged 9 to 12 during a STEM summer camp. A quasi-experimental design was employed with a purposefully selected sample of one hundred and ten (n = 110) students, who were non-randomly divided into two groups: (a) an experimental group of fifty-five students (n = 55) who engaged with Kahoot! (using dynamic visual aids and interactive content) and (b) a control group of fifty-five students (n = 55) who received traditional instruction (using digital textbooks and PowerPoint slides with multimedia content) on laptops and tablets. The findings revealed a statistically significant difference in MSA scores, with the experimental group exhibiting lower MSA scores compared to their counterparts, indicating a positive impact on reducing screen addiction levels. While Kahoot! led to lower MSA levels, it significantly improved overall mathematical achievement, with a substantial effect size, suggesting a strong positive impact on learning outcomes. The current study highlights the importance of aligning educational tools with the intended outcomes and recommends further research to explore the broader impact of gamified learning on student engagement, screen addiction, and learning outcomes.

Keywords: student performance; Kahoot!; primary education; mathematics; multiple screen addiction

1. Introduction

Instructional design is essential for creating effective learning experiences across various formats, including online and face-to-face courses, workshops, and training programs, among K-12 students [1]. It facilitates learning by ensuring that students gain knowledge, improve skills, or change behavior while remaining engaged and motivated [2]. This involves setting clear instructional objectives, delivering accurate and relevant content through different media (text, images, videos, etc.), and incorporating activities and assessments to apply and evaluate learning [3]. Activities like quizzes, discussions, case studies, or other exercises help learners apply their knowledge and skills. Finally, assessments evaluate how well learners have achieved their learning [4,5].

For subjects like mathematics, well-designed content moves beyond passive lectures to include interactive activities and problem solving, catering to varied learning styles and making abstract concepts more tangible [6–8]. This approach helps address the limitations of traditional methods and the challenges posed by constant digital stimulation [9]. By considering students' age, knowledge, and learning styles, the content fosters relevance and appropriate challenge. Some researchers [7,8] advocated replacing passive lectures, which inherently favor teacher-centered instruction and rote memorization, with interactive activities, problem solving, and collaboration. This shift transforms math from memorization into a process of exploration and discovery, aligning perfectly with the way students naturally engage with the world around them. While traditional methods like textbooks and chalkboards remain valuable resources, their reliance on passive learning approaches can limit engagement and fail to compete with the constant stimulation readily available on multiple screens [9]. This highlights the need for innovative instructional design that not only delivers content effectively but also fosters active participation and a sense of enjoyment in the learning process [4].

Students today are inseparable from their smartphones, tablets, and laptops, constantly interacting with digital platforms throughout the day. This presents both challenges and opportunities for education. Educators can leverage this constant engagement by incorporating interactive quizzes, simulations, and educational apps alongside traditional materials. These approaches provide to different learning styles, boost engagement, and create an interactive learning environment that competes with, without succumbing to, the allure of other digital distractions [5]. A wide array of technological devices and the increased time spent using them have led to a tendency to addiction to multiple devices, applications, and services. By blending visual and auditory features with text, video, and animated graphics, multimedia tools can enhance understanding and retention of information [10]. Consequently, individuals often use multiple devices simultaneously, exhibiting multi-screen consumption behavior that involves interacting with various types of features and elements projected across different platforms [11].

Multiple screen addiction (MSA) is a significant issue because MSA not only affects students' engagement but also their overall academic performance. It specifically refers to the uncontrollable and compulsive use of various screen devices, resulting in detrimental effects on multiple aspects of an individual's life [12]. This addiction shows not only in excessive screen use but also in the discomfort and negative emotions experienced when access to these devices is limited [13]. Additionally, the concept of screen addiction encompasses a broader range of problematic media behaviors involving multiple screens, extending from excessive consumption to a more severe, pathological level of use, where the behavior significantly disrupts daily life [14]. This unveils challenges, particularly in subjects requiring sustained focus like mathematics, which require sustained attention and problem solving [15]. A promising approach to address these challenges in mathematics education lies in interactive learning platforms like Kahoot! (https://kahoot.com/, accessed on 8 May 2024). It offers a promising approach to enhance student engagement and achievement by allowing them to use a variety of computing devices, such as laptops, tablets, or smartphones [16]. This platform leverages game-based learning and dynamic environments to promote active participation and enjoyment specifically in the learning of mathematical concepts [17]. Kahoot!'s "playable" features and tasks create an engaging and stimulating learning experience for mathematics, potentially fostering a deeper understanding of concepts through a more enjoyable and interactive approach [18,19].

Despite the widespread adoption of technology in mathematics, there is a need to empirically assess the impact of specific digital tools on student MSA and achievement. On the one hand, traditional instructional design methods, often reliant on passive learning approaches like lectures with (digital) slideshows using PowerPoint (ver. 365), can struggle to compete with the stimulation readily available on multiple screens [8,20]. This lack of engagement might inadvertently contribute to MSA as students seek more stimulating distractions on their devices. On the other hand, popular game-based learning platforms like Kahoot! can be used on various mobile devices to promote interactive learning experiences in instructional design content creation for mathematics education. Its potential benefits for engagement and knowledge retention are widely recognized, while concerns exist regarding its contribution to screen time overload and the development of MSA among students [11,21]. Therefore, this study seeks to determine the impact of Kahoot! in comparison to traditional teaching methods, addressing these questions through the following two research questions (RQs):

- *RQ1: Is there any significant difference between the MSA of students who followed Kahoot!-supported instruction and their counterparts who received traditional instruction?*

- *RQ2: Is there any significant difference between the performance of students who followed Kahoot!-supported instruction and their counterparts who received traditional instruction?*

This study aimed to investigate the impact of integrating Kahoot! as an instructional tool on students' achievements and its potential influence on MSA, focusing on mathematics education. The findings will contribute to a deeper understanding of the complex interplay between technology, learning, and student success in the era of pervasive screen use.

2. Background

2.1. Multiple Screen Addiction (MSA)

MSA, characterized by the excessive and simultaneous use of multiple devices, has become a growing concern, especially among younger generations. People with MSA struggle to control their screen usage, experiencing withdrawal symptoms like anxiety, loss of productivity, and feelings of emptiness when unable to access their devices [14]. This excessive and compulsive media consumption can be seen on televisions, laptops, tablets, and smartphones. The visually appealing process of using multimedia content and other non-educational content readily available on multiple screens can significantly distract students from their studies. This distraction can lead to lower achievements. Frequent interruptions caused by checking other screens can also result in incomplete or subpar assignments as students struggle with time management. Multitasking itself can lead to mistakes and lower-quality work due to divided attention and effort put into educational tasks [13]. The constant entry of information and pressure to respond to multiple stimuli from various screens can increase stress and anxiety levels in students. Overuse of screens, even for educational purposes, can lead to burnout, where students feel overwhelmed and disengaged [12].

Multiple screen use can negatively affect cognitive functions crucial for effective learning. Regular switching between devices, such as web-based platforms and smartphones, can reduce the ability to concentrate for extended periods, leading to a decreased attention span. This fragmented attention can result in students missing critical information or instructions presented on educational platforms [11,22]. Other studies [14–16] have also pointed out that divided attention can impair memory retention. When students constantly switch between devices during educational sessions, they may retain less information overall. Furthermore, multiple screen usage often promotes "surface learning"—focusing on quick answers rather than deep, meaningful engagement with the material. There is a growing body of research on MSA with different perspectives. Lin et al. [14] found a positive correlation between media multitasking (using multiple devices simultaneously) and screen addiction. Their study also suggests that screen use mediates the effect of media multitasking on addiction, meaning screen time itself plays a significant role. Saritepeci [12] advocated that MSA is a behavioral addiction, such as smartphone addiction or internet addiction. A key indicator of such addictions is the distress caused by being unable to access the desired object or activity (e.g., feeling uncomfortable without a smartphone). MSA, where individuals simultaneously engage with multiple digital devices, can lead to fragmented attention and reduced performance. This behavior often results in diminished concentration and lower achievement, counteracting the positive effects of educational technologies. Previous research [2,23] has also demonstrated the potential of educational platforms and applications to enhance student engagement and classroom participation. These tools provide immediate feedback and encourage active involvement, fostering enthusiasm and stimulating student discussions. Given the complex nature of MSA factors and their potential interconnections, a comprehensive investigation is essential to understand more about their impact on students' performance in regular learning subjects.

While research has extensively documented the negative consequences of excessive screen time on student learning and well-being, there is still a significant research "gap" in understanding how educational technologies can be leveraged to mitigate this issue. The potential of gamified learning platforms, such as Kahoot!, to address the effects of MSA remains largely unexplored. This study aims to investigate the relationship between

Kahoot! usage and excessive screen time levels among students using different devices. Consequently, research should also consider the broader implications of digital platforms on student engagement and investigate whether there is a link with students' learning performance to inform educators about the design and development of more effective instructional content.

2.2. The Kahoot! Platform

Kahoot! (https://kahoot.com/, accessed on 8 May 2024) headquartered in Oslo, Norway. It is a Norwegian online game-based learning platform that offers learning games, known as 'kahoots', which are user generated multiple choice quizzes accessible via a web browser or the Kahoot! application, available on Google Play and Apple Store. Kahoot! is an interactive online learning platform that blends education with fun. Accessible on both mobile devices and computers, Kahoot! uses interactive quizzes and games to make learning engaging and enjoyable.

Students can access a wide range of educational content anytime, anywhere. The interactive and competitive nature of the platform, with points, leaderboards, and timers, makes learning fun and motivates students to participate actively [10]. Kahoot!'s user-friendly interface and simple setup make it easy for both teachers and students to use. This seamless integration enhances the learning experience. Incorporating Kahoot! within the assessment strategy offers the additional benefit of immediate feedback. This real-time feedback allows students to grasp and learn from their errors promptly, fostering a more effective learning experience and enhancing comprehension and retention of the material [24]. Furthermore, the regular use of Kahoot! for quizzes and reviews reinforces learning and promotes better memory retention through repeated exposure to the information.

While Kahoot offers several benefits, there still exist potential drawbacks to ensure its effective use inside the classroom. Students using the platform on mobile devices alongside other applications might get distracted by notifications, games or social media in multitasking settings, hindering their focus on educational content. While competition can be motivating, it can also lead to anxiety or stress for some students. This can have a negative impact on their learning experience, especially for those who struggle with test anxiety. The fast-paced nature of Kahoot! quizzes can lead to "surface learning", where students prioritize getting quick answers for points rather than deeply understanding the material [10]. Furthermore, the platform's format might not always allow for in-depth exploration of complex topics, potentially limiting students' ability to develop a thorough comprehension of the subject matter. Students without reliable access to mobile devices or the internet may be disadvantaged when using Kahoot! This can create unequal learning opportunities within the classroom. Furthermore, prolonged use of Kahoot! on screens can contribute to digital fatigue, especially if used extensively without breaks [23].

Recent research on Kahoot!'s impact on performance has shown various perspectives about its potential usage. According to Göksün and Gürsoy [9], Kahoot! has a more positive—though not statistically significant—impact on achievement and engagement compared to other groups. Quizizz had a lower impact than the control group in both areas. Despite these findings, pre-service teachers expressed positive views about gamification, noting issues related to MSA, reinforcement, entertainment, competition, infrastructure, and tools. Mada and Anharudin [15] pointed out that using Kahoot! in learning helps students recall material, increases their excitement and engagement, and encourages active participation and competition. It also enhances interest and MSA, particularly in Internet-related subjects, leading to improved knowledge. However, challenges include the lack of suitable devices and reliable internet connections for all students. A study by Malak [16] found that the experimental group that used Kahoot! experienced reduced stress and anxiety and improved self-efficacy and achievement compared to the control group. The findings suggest integrating Kahoot! into education can enhance both psychological health and performance.

Several recent studies have additionally investigated the effectiveness of Kahoot! in improving student engagement and achievement in mathematics education. For instance, Umboh et al. [25] conducted a classroom action research study focusing on elementary-school math scores. Their findings, based on a three-cycle intervention with 22 fourth-graders in Indonesia, suggest that Kahoot! can be a valuable tool. Student activity levels and learning outcomes improved significantly, with the average score reaching 81% by the final cycle. Prieto's [18] research investigated the effectiveness of Kahoot! in reducing student MSA and science anxiety and fostering greater engagement in secondary classrooms. Students responded to teacher-created quizzes using their mobile devices and received immediate feedback. Positive student evaluations suggest Kahoot!'s potential to enhance learning through interactive quizzes. Wahyuni et al. [19] investigated Kahoot!'s impact on understanding mathematical symbols among pre-service math teachers unfamiliar with them. The same study involved 100 participants who completed pre-tests and post-tests after using Kahoot! for symbol learning. Statistical analysis showed a significant improvement in understanding, highlighting Kahoot!'s potential as a tool for grasping mathematical symbols. Lastly, AlAli and Wardat's [24] research focused on the challenges of Kahoot! as a potential solution and examined its impact on achievement and student enjoyment. The findings contributed to understanding Kahoot!'s suitability for gifted students and provided insights into the broader use of gamification techniques in educational contexts.

While digital platforms like Quizizz, Mentimeter, and Socrative offer engaging features for K-12 students, Kahoot! can be considered as the most relevant due to the following reasons [9,10,21]:

- Accessibility: While all platforms offer varying degrees of accessibility features, Kahoot! stood out due to its user-friendly interface, mobile compatibility, and extensive support resources, making it more inclusive for a wider range of participants compared to Quizizz, Mentimeter, and Socrative.
- Economic cost: Considering the budget constraints of our project, Kahoot!'s free tier offered a robust set of features, making it a more cost-effective option compared to the paid tiers required for similar functionalities on Quizizz and Mentimeter. Socrative, while offering a free version, presented limitations in terms of question types and participant capacity compared to Kahoot!.
- Alignment with research objectives: Kahoot!'s emphasis on gamification and real-time feedback aligned more closely with our aim to enhance student engagement and knowledge retention than Quizizz, which primarily focuses on formative assessment. Mentimeter and Socrative, while offering interactive elements, did not provide the same level of engagement and immediate feedback as Kahoot!.

In summary, Kahoot! has the potential to positively influence learning performance by increasing engagement, motivation, and retention. Given its interactive and engaging nature, it is hypothesized that Kahoot! can redirect students' attention from passive screen consumption to active learning, thereby mitigating the negative impacts of excessive screen time. By incorporating gamification and providing immediate feedback, Kahoot! may promote a more balanced and productive screen use experience.

However, potential distractions, excessive use, and accessibility issues must be considered to maximize its benefits and minimize drawbacks. This study aimed to evaluate Kahoot!'s effectiveness in enhancing motivation and achievement among students creating instructional design content for mathematics education. By analyzing Kahoot!'s impact on both motivation and success, this research sought to address the issue of declining motivation and improve overall classroom performance. By implementing strategies to mitigate potential challenges, educators can leverage Kahoot!'s potential to design and develop learning tasks for all students.

3. Materials and Methods

3.1. Research Design

A quasi-experimental design was employed to investigate the causal relationship using a non-equivalent control group design with pre- and post-test measurements. Employing a non-randomized sampling approach with matched group sizes and gender distribution allow an effective control of potential confounding variables, thereby reducing the risk of biased findings [26]. Specifically, practical constraints or existing classroom structures also influenced group allocation, making the randomization imperfect in a STEM summer camp. This approach was chosen because it allowed for the comparison of outcomes between an experimental group (EG) using an alternative gamified platform and a control group (CG) receiving traditional instruction. The former group utilized Kahoot!, a digital platform offering dynamic visual aids and interactive content, while the latter group received traditional instruction through digital textbooks and PowerPoint slides with multimedia content. Participants in the experimental group utilized iPads, iPhones (with Kahoot! app version 6.07), or laptops (with the web platform) to monitor their rankings and evaluate their performance. In contrast, the control group solely employed laptops and tablets to view PowerPoint presentations (version 365).

To mitigate potential threats to the validity of this study, such as the "novelty effect", where initial excitement about Kahoot! could influence results, several measures were implemented. First, participants' prior experience with digital learning resources and mobile devices for self-directed activities was assessed. This included their familiarity with digital textbooks, multimedia presentations, and webcasts, which helped ensure that all participants, regardless of group assignment, had a similar baseline experience with educational technology. Second, this study aimed to moderate the novelty effect by carefully considering the participants' pre-existing familiarity with digital learning tools and adjusting the instructional design to account for these factors. By collecting detailed information on participants' prior experience with technology, this study aimed to control for any differences that could affect their engagement and performance outcomes.

Overall, the quasi-experimental design provided valuable insights into the effectiveness of Kahoot! compared to traditional methods while acknowledging the limitations inherent in non-randomized group assignments. The approach enabled a meaningful comparison of the two instructional methods while recognizing the potential influence of participants' prior experiences with digital learning tools.

3.2. Participants

This study recruited a sample of convenience consisting of one hundred and ten students ($n = 110$) who participated voluntarily and were non-randomly divided into two groups. One class ($n = 55$) was designated as the EG. During a STEM summer camp after the spring semester of 2023–2024, this group received instruction in mathematics using the Kahoot! platform. The remaining class ($n = 55$) served as the control group and received "traditional" instruction (PowerPoint slides with multimedia content).

The gender distribution was even, with 48% females ($n = 53$) and 52% males ($n = 57$). The average student age was 10.5 years old (range: 9–12 years, SD = 1.99). Most participants were 11 or 12 years old (combined: 66%), followed by 10-year-olds (26%) and 9-year-olds (8%). Participants categorized their daily computer usage frequency: 35% reported being light users, 50% reported moderate usage, and 15% identified as heavy users. This process provided insights into the extent to which the internet is integrated into their daily lives.

Additionally, the current study investigated the types of devices participants extensively used. Smartphones were the most popular choice (82%), followed by laptops (70%) and tablets (48%). This information helped establish the participants' comfort level with technology and their preferred methods of digital interaction (e.g., mobile learning vs. desktop learning). Finally, to assess existing experience with educational technology, this study measured participants' familiarity with educational platforms besides Kahoot!. This allowed for a more comprehensive understanding of how participants might approach and compare the intervention (Kahoot!) to other learning tools they might have encountered previously.

By gathering these details, this study paints a clearer picture of the participants' digital fluency and preparedness for engaging with the computer-supported learning environment. Students came from the school of education's diverse departments, focusing on instructional content creation in mathematics education. All participants did not have prior experience using Kahoot! or other relevant platforms in previous projects.

Before the intervention, the equivalence of the CG and EG was assessed using the independent-samples *t*-test. The results, presented in Table 1 along with corresponding analysis outcomes, indicated no statistically significant differences between the two groups' pre-test scores on the achievement and MSA scales. This suggests that before the intervention, the EG and the CG demonstrated similar baseline levels of achievement and MSA.

Table 1. Equivalence of CG and EG on pre-test measures.

Tool	Group	n	Mean	S.D.	T	$n-1$	p
Test	EG	55	10.43	6.87	0.622	53	0.577 *
	CG	55	11.30	7.11	0.622	53	0.577
MSA scale	EG	55	2.07	1.61	1.541	53	0.101
	CG	55	1.93	1.55	1.541	53	0.101

Note: * $p < 0.05$.

Equivalence in pre-test scores plays a critical role in experimental studies. This ensures that any subsequent differences observed in the post-test scores can be confidently attributed to the intervention, in this case, the use of Kahoot!, rather than pre-existing group disparities [26]. By establishing similar pre-test scores, this study strengthened the foundation for attributing any observed changes in post-test scores to the impact of Kahoot! on students' MSA and achievements.

Ethical approval for this study was obtained from the administrator of the STEM campus, ensuring that the research adhered to the ethical guidelines outlined in the Declaration of Helsinki and relevant national standards for research involving participants. Given the age range of the participants (9 to 12 years), special attention was given to the process of obtaining consent. Informed consent was first obtained from the parents or legal guardians of all participating students before the commencement of this study. This ensured that parents were fully aware of this study's objectives, procedures, and any potential risks involved. Additionally, assent was obtained from the child participants. Assent is particularly important when working with minors to ensure they understand the nature of their involvement.

The participants were informed about this study's purpose and their role in a way that was understandable and reassuring, ensuring that they felt comfortable participating. Both written and verbal assent were sought, depending on the individual student's comprehension level. This study maintained strict confidentiality and anonymity of all participant data. All personal information was anonymized, and participants were given the option to withdraw at any point without any consequence.

3.3. *Procedure*

3.3.1. Teaching Intervention

The teaching intervention for this study was designed to align with the mathematical content covered in the primary school curriculum, which typically encompasses Grades 5–10 and focuses on developing foundational math skills such as counting, basic arithmetic (addition, subtraction, multiplication, and division), fractions, decimals, geometry, and basic measurement. Each quiz was designed to assess students' understanding of key mathematical concepts, problem-solving abilities, and critical thinking skills. The quizzes were structured to align with the learning objectives outlined in the curriculum, ensuring coherence and relevance to classroom instruction. Instructors administered the quizzes during dedicated sessions, guiding students as needed. Students participated in the quizzes using various computing devices, while instructors monitored both administration and student progress. To evaluate progress in learning outcomes and MSA, both groups were closely monitored throughout the intervention. Instructors tracked student performance, participation rates, and response patterns. Regular assessments, including pre-tests and post-tests, were implemented to measure achievement and MSA scores.

Limiting device usage to desktop laptops and tablets for both the control and experimental groups was a strategy designed to control device-related variables and ensure that comparisons between the two groups remained fair and unbiased. Minimum specifications for the devices, such as screen size, processing power, and operating system, were established to ensure a consistent user experience across all participants. Additionally, brief training sessions were conducted for participants unfamiliar with the devices to minimize potential learning curves and reduce frustration, contributing to more reliable data collection. Device-related issues or challenges faced by participants were documented to identify any potential biases that might have impacted this study's outcomes.

The CG received traditional instruction using PowerPoint and/or digital textbooks. Although typically displaying static content, these materials also included interactive elements such as animations and multimedia. This could blur the lines between traditional and technology-enhanced instruction, potentially influencing this study's results. Therefore, it was crucial to detail device usage and the instructional context to differentiate the CG from the EG with Kahoot!. Furthermore, mathematical concepts were taught in the CG through lectures using static visual aids (e.g., charts, graphs, and models) projected in class. Students accessed digital readings from the course textbook on laptops and tablets, allowing for easy reading and annotation. Classroom activities, guided by the teacher, provided limited interaction through desktop computers and tablets. Independent study assignments involved PowerPoint presentations to reinforce lecture material, with instructor feedback provided through delayed written messages on tablets.

In contrast, the EG used Kahoot! to enhance engagement and interactivity. The instructor integrated Kahoot! into lectures to introduce new mathematical concepts and reinforce learning through interactive quizzes. Students accessed these quizzes using laptops, creating a more interactive and engaging lecture experience. The instructor managed and displayed quiz results instantly using a tablet. Kahoot! also enabled access to digital texts in a readable format, featuring dynamic visual aids and interactive elements that made the learning experience more engaging and visually stimulating. These aids were accessed on laptops, tablets, and smartphones, with the screen size and capabilities of each device enhancing the visual experience.

Students in the EG were also assigned additional Kahoot! quizzes to complete outside of class, providing ongoing engagement and practice opportunities. These quizzes were accessible on various devices (laptops and tablets), ensuring that students could complete their assignments conveniently, whether at home, in the library, or elsewhere. Kahoot! quizzes presented questions and answers in a game-like format, actively engaging students. Immediate feedback was provided through Kahoot!, allowing students to see their scores and correct answers right after each quiz. This instant feedback helped students address misunderstandings quickly and reinforced key learning points. Feedback was accessible on the same devices used for the quizzes, ensuring a seamless experience.

The use of multiple devices, such as a laptop for the main quiz interface and a smartphone for additional interaction, encouraged active participation and sustained interest by allowing students to interact dynamically with the material. By specifying the types of devices and their usage in different instructional contexts, this description provides a detailed understanding of how the EG engaged with Kahoot! in a flexible and interactive learning environment. The EG accessed Kahoot!, while the CG used PowerPoint on various devices, creating a versatile learning environment. Laptops were primarily used during instructor-led sessions and for completing quizzes that required larger screens and more detailed interaction. Tablets were used for both in-class activities and homework, providing a portable, user-friendly interface for interactive learning, quick access to quizzes, and instant feedback, especially useful for on-the-go learning and immediate participation in gamified activities.

3.3.2. Material Development

To understand better the design rationale of the material development of this study, the pedagogical underpinnings of Kahoot! for the EG and PowerPoint slides and digital textbook design materials were carefully considered. The alignment of the chosen question formats, difficulty levels, and multimedia elements with this study's goals and target learning outcomes has been clearly outlined.

The Kahoot! materials were developed with a focus on fostering critical thinking and analytical skills, aligned with this study's goal of enhancing problem-solving abilities. For instance, questions in Kahoot! were crafted to challenge students' problem-solving capabilities, e.g., through a multiple-choice question designed to test arithmetic skills: "*If you have 5 apples and you buy 7 more, how many apples do you have in total?*" This approach emphasizes the application of mathematical concepts in various contexts to promote deeper learning. In contrast, the CG utilized traditional PowerPoint slides that presented content in a more static format. These slides were structured to convey fundamental concepts and examples, such as through a slide that introduces multiplication with an explanation and a sample problem: "*If you have 4 groups of 3 apples each, how many apples are there in total?*"

While the PowerPoint slides or digital textbooks with multimedia content aimed to provide clear and direct instruction, they lacked the interactive and engaging elements found in Kahoot!. The integration of multimedia elements in Kahoot!, including images, videos, and audio clips, was designed to enhance student engagement and make learning more dynamic. Meanwhile, the CG materials incorporated basic multimedia, such as static images and brief video clips, to support content delivery but did not offer the same level of interaction. This deliberate design choice highlights the contrast between the experimental and control conditions and underscores the potential impact of interactive digital tools on student learning outcomes.

The key differences between the PowerPoint presentations and Kahoot! in terms of interactivity, learner control, and feedback mechanisms have been articulated. For example, Kahoot! provided interactive elements and real-time feedback, while the PowerPoint presentations were more static and did not include such features. Some of the most important for the EG using Kahoot! are the following:

- Animated avatars: The types of animated avatars available to players, such as characters, animals, and fantasy figures, have been specified. The contribution of these avatars to student engagement and motivation has been described. For example, avatars might include a cartoon cat that celebrates correct answers with a cheer or a superhero that gives encouragement for incorrect answers.
- Colored titles and text: The use of color in the question titles and answer options has been explained. The enhancement of readability and visual appeal through color coding has been discussed. For instance, different colors might be used to differentiate between answer choices, making it easier for students to follow along.
- Visual elements: The use of images, graphics, and other visual elements within the Kahoot! questions have been detailed. The support these visuals provided for content understanding and engagement has been explained. For example, a picture of a math problem might be used to illustrate a question about fractions.
- Sound effects and music: The incorporation of sound effects and music into the Kahoot! game has been described. The enhancement of the overall gaming experience and contribution to the learning environment through these auditory elements have been discussed. For instance, a sound effect for a correct answer might be a celebratory chime, while a motivational tune might play during the game.

- Question variety: Specific examples of different question types used within the Kahoot! games, such as multiple choice, true/false, open-ended, and picture choice, have been provided. The use of these question types to assess various learning outcomes has been explained. For example, a picture choice question might ask students to identify which image represents a fraction.
- Feedback mechanisms: The visual and auditory feedback provided to players, including correct/incorrect answer animations, celebratory sound effects, and informative messages, has been described. This feedback is intended to guide and motivate students throughout the game.

Some of the most important design elements for the CG using PowerPoint slides and digital textbooks that were considered are the following:

- Slide content depth: The level of detail covered in each PowerPoint slide, including key concepts, examples, and visuals, has been specified. The support these details provided for instructional goals was described.
- Learning activities: Any accompanying activities or worksheets used in conjunction with the PowerPoint presentations have been outlined. The role of these activities in reinforcing the material presented has been explained.
- Teacher guidance: The level of teacher guidance provided during the control group sessions has been explained. The methods used by teachers to facilitate learning and support students with multimedia materials have been described.

On the one hand, students in the EG were given the option to select from a variety of animated avatars, including animals, superheroes, and fantasy characters. These avatars displayed dynamic reactions to players' answers, such as cheering for correct responses or providing encouraging messages for incorrect ones. Preliminary observations suggested that these features contributed to a more engaging and motivating learning environment.

On the other hand, the PowerPoint presentations for the CG did not include animated avatars or interactive elements. The multimedia aspects were limited to static images, videos, and animations designed to present mathematical concepts in a structured manner.

3.3.3. Data Collection and Analysis

To collect data from participants, all questionnaires were self-reported and delivered via email. Completion time was capped at 40 min to avoid categorizing participants as novices or experts, ensuring equal opportunity and unbiased responses regardless of experience. The main author also developed weekly lesson plans that guided the entire process. The data analysis encompassed several key steps and statistical techniques to thoroughly examine this study's variables. Initially, the subscales were translated into Greek, this student's native language, using the back-translation method proposed by Brislin [27]. The survey instrument utilized a 5-point Likert scale, with response options ranging from 1 (strongly disagree) to 5 (strongly agree). Likert-based analyses were conducted to evaluate the participants' responses. Overall scores were calculated by determining the proportion of correct responses across all assessments. Descriptive statistics, including means (Ms) and standard deviations (SDs), were employed to analyze these overall scores.

To assess the normality assumption of the data, the Shapiro–Wilk test was employed. The findings of this test are presented in Table 2.

To maintain participant anonymity, the authors, both computer science teachers, handled the data processing. Performance metrics were analyzed using an adaptive scoring method by Bridgeman and Cline [28], assigning 0 points for incorrect answers, 0.50 points for partially correct answers, and 1 point for correct answers. To facilitate interpretation, overall assessment scores per topic were calculated by averaging associated test question scores. These performance results were used exclusively for this study and did not affect participant grades. To analyze the learning experience, subscale scores were calculated by averaging responses to corresponding items. The statistical software IBM® SPSS® Statistics (version 27) was used to conduct the data analysis, ensuring a rigorous examination and accurate interpretation of the findings.

Table 2. Normality test.

Group	Time Point	Shapiro–Wilk Statistic	*p*-Value	Conclusion
CG	Pre-test	0.823	0.155	Normally distributed
CG	Post-test	0.856	0.299	Normally distributed
EG	Pre-test	0.877	0.144	Normally distributed
EG	Post-test	0.899	0.354	Normally distributed

3.4. Instruments

3.4.1. Demographics

To better understand the relationship between technology use and its impact on daily life, participants were required to complete a web-based form consisting of seven questions. This form highlighted several key topics reflected in this study:

1. Participant demographics: This study captured the age, gender distribution, and grade levels of the participants, including how these demographics influenced technology use.
2. Technology usage patterns: This study explored the frequency and intensity of daily computer usage among participants, categorizing them into light, moderate, and heavy users.
3. Device preferences: This study investigated the types of devices participants frequently used, such as smartphones, laptops, and tablets, and how these preferences impacted their digital interactions.
4. Digital fluency: This study assessed participants' comfort levels with technology and their familiarity with various digital platforms, focusing on their ability to engage with computer-supported learning environments.
5. Educational technology experience: This study examined participants' prior experience with educational technology platforms, excluding Kahoot!, to understand how their background might affect their engagement with new tools.
6. Readiness for technology-enhanced learning: This study evaluated participants' overall preparedness and ability to effectively use technology in educational settings, particularly in the context of instructional content creation for mathematics education.
7. Impact of no prior experience: This study considered the implications of participants not having prior experience with Kahoot! or similar platforms on their learning experience and engagement with the intervention.

The demographics form was designed to be completed within approximately 10 min. All responses remained anonymous, ensuring privacy while allowing for collective data analysis.

3.4.2. Student Performance in Mathematics

To understand how well the students aged 9–12 learned mathematics, pre-and post-tests were used, following guidelines from Terwel et al. [29], which focused on three main areas:

- Retention: How well the students remembered what they learned.
- Near transfer: How well the students could apply what they learned to similar problems.
- Far transfer: How well the students could use their knowledge in new and different situations.

Pre-test: Checking initial knowledge.

Before starting the treatment, students took a pre-test with multiple-choice questions on the following topics to understand what they already knew:

1. Arithmetic: Basic operations like addition, subtraction, multiplication, and division, and understanding number properties.

2. Geometry: Recognizing shapes and understanding basic measurement concepts like perimeter and area.
3. Fractions: Understanding fractions and how to work with them.
4. Introductory algebra: Solving simple equations and recognizing patterns.

Post-test: Evaluating learning in mathematics.

After the lessons, students took a post-test with more challenging problems. This test included the following areas:

- Retention: Questions to see how well the students remembered what they learned.
- Near transfer: Problems similar to those practiced during lessons to see how well the students could apply what they learned.
- Far transfer: New and different problems to test if the students could use their knowledge in unfamiliar situations.

The post-test topics included:

1. Arithmetic: Multi-step word problems involving various operations.
2. Geometry: Complex problems on shape properties and calculating the area of composite shapes.
3. Fractions: Real-life problems involving fractions.
4. Introductory algebra: Word problems with simple algebraic equations.

3.4.3. The MSA Scale

The current study employed the MSA scale developed by Sarıtepeci [12] to assess MSA levels among primary education students. This scale utilizes a 5-point Likert format to measure participants' agreement with statements related to multi-screen use. It comprises three sub-dimensions: Compulsive Behavior (8 items), Loss of Control (3 items), and Excessive Screen Time (4 items). Each subdimension captures a distinct aspect of multi-screen addiction.

However, for this study, a modified 10-item version of the MSA was administered. This version included 3 items from the Excessive Screen Time dimension, focusing on the duration of screen use. Additionally, 4 items from the Compulsive Behavior dimension were retained to assess the uncontrollable urge to use multiple screens. Finally, 3 items from the Loss of Control dimension evaluated difficulties in regulating screen time.

The relevance of the sample items in reflecting the sub-dimensions of the MSA scale plays a crucial role in establishing the content validity of the scale. Content validity refers to the extent to which the items on a scale adequately cover and represent the construct being measured. In the case of the MSA, the sub-dimensions are Compulsive Behavior, Loss of Control, and Excessive Screen Time, each representing a distinct aspect of multi-screen addiction.

1. Compulsive Behavior: Items within this subdimension assess the uncontrollable urge to engage with multiple screens. For instance, a sample item like "I feel the need to be constantly interacting with some type of screen" directly taps into the compulsive nature of screen use, capturing the essence of this dimension. The relevance of this item lies in its ability to measure the behavioral patterns associated with addiction, such as the persistent and compulsive engagement with screens despite potential negative consequences.
2. Loss of Control: This subdimension evaluates difficulties in regulating screen time. A sample item such as "I cannot control the amount of time I spend in front of any screen" is highly relevant, as it reflects the individual's struggle with self-regulation. This item contributes to content validity by addressing the core issue of loss of control, which is a hallmark of addictive behaviors. It ensures that the scale accurately measures the inability to limit screen time, a critical component of multi-screen addiction.
3. Excessive Screen Time: Items in this subdimension focus on the duration and extent of screen use. An example might be "I spend more time on screens than I intend to", which is relevant because it captures the excessive nature of screen engagement, often

leading to negative outcomes such as neglect of responsibilities or social isolation. The inclusion of such items ensures that the scale covers the dimension of excessive use, further strengthening its content validity.

Overall, the relevance of these sample items is critical in ensuring that each subdimension is adequately represented. By directly addressing the key aspects of multi-screen addiction, these items contribute to the content validity of the MSA scale, making it a comprehensive tool for assessing the various facets of screen addiction. This thorough representation of the construct across multiple dimensions allows the scale to accurately measure and differentiate between the different components of multi-screen addiction.

The internal consistency of the modified 10-item MSA was deemed acceptable based on a Cronbach's alpha coefficient of 0.83, based on Cortina's [30] recommendations. For illustration purposes, two sample items from the scale are presented: *"I feel the need to be constantly interacting with some type of screen"* and *"I cannot control the amount of time I spend in front of any screen"*. These examples provide insight into the types of questions students encountered when taking the modified MSA.

3.5. Reliability and Validity

The reliability of the students' performance tests was assessed using two methods. Internal consistency was evaluated using the Kuder–Richardson 20 (KR-20) formula on a separate sample of 15 students to estimate the extent to which the test items measure the same construct. Test–retest reliability was determined by administering the test to a group of students twice, with a three-week interval, and calculating Cronbach's alpha to assess the consistency of scores over time.

The MSA scale was employed in this study. Pearson's correlation coefficient was used to examine the scale's correlational validity with teacher evaluations, a criterion considered a valid indicator of MSA in this context. Additionally, Cronbach's alpha was calculated to assess the scale's internal consistency. The reliability of the MSA scale was assessed using both Cronbach's alpha and McDonald's omega coefficients. While Cronbach's alpha yielded an excellent value of 0.93, indicating high internal consistency, McDonald's omega, which is generally considered a more robust estimate of reliability, particularly for ordinal data, provided a value of 0.91. Although both coefficients suggest strong reliability, the slightly lower omega value might indicate a more complex factor structure underlying the scale than initially suggested by Cronbach's alpha.

Table 3 presents the reliability coefficients (Cronbach's alpha, KR-20, and test–retest) for both the achievement test and the MSA scale. High values for all coefficients suggest strong internal consistency and reliability, implying that the instruments accurately measure their intended constructs.

Table 3. Reliability coefficients.

Authenticity Coefficient	Calculated Reliability Factor		
Compulsory	Cronbach's alpha reliability coefficient	Codder–Richardson reliability coefficient 20	Half-partition reliability coefficient
0.91	0.92	0.92	0.88

As shown in Table 3, the reliability coefficients for both the achievement test and the MSA scale were high (KR-20 = 0.92, Cronbach's alpha = 0.91 and 0.88, respectively), indicating strong internal consistency and reliability. These results suggest that both instruments accurately measure the intended constructs.

Table 4 presents the achievement test item difficulty and discrimination coefficients. Difficulty coefficients ranged from 0.33 to 0.71, and discrimination coefficients ranged from 0.21 to 0.86. Following established criteria by Al-Zboon et al. [31], the main researcher applied the following selection process:

- Items with discrimination coefficients between 0.19 and 0.39 were considered acceptable but might require revision to improve their ability to differentiate between high and low performers.
- Items with discrimination coefficients exceeding 0.35 were deemed strong and retained.
- Difficulty coefficients between 0.35 and 0.80 were considered acceptable.

Table 4. Difficulty and discrimination coefficients for achievement test items.

Items	Difficulty Coefficient	Discrimination Coefficient
1.	0.54	0.83
2.	0.46	0.26
3.	0.69	0.71
4.	0.46	0.46

Following these criteria, a 9-item achievement test was deemed suitable and included in this study.

3.6. Data Analysis

This section presents the statistical methods employed to address the RQs:

- MSA (RQ1): To assess the impact of Kahoot! on MSA, descriptive statistics (means and standard deviations) were calculated for MSA scale scores. Subsequently, a one-way ANCOVA (analysis of covariance) was conducted, following the recommendations by Lüdtke and Robitzsch [32]. Pre-test MSA scores served as the covariate to control for pre-existing differences in MSA between the EG and CG groups. This analysis aimed to identify statistically significant differences in post-intervention MSA levels.
- Students' performance (RQ2): Descriptive statistics (means and standard deviations) were calculated for achievement test scores. Another one-way ANCOVA was conducted, controlling for pre-existing achievement levels using pre-test scores as the covariate. This analysis aimed to identify significant differences in students' achievements between the groups after the intervention.
- MSA scale validity: Pearson's correlation coefficient assessed the construct validity of the MSA scale by measuring the interrelatedness of items within the scale.
- MSA scale reliability: Cronbach's alpha coefficient evaluated the scale's internal consistency. Moreover, the Kuder–Richardson equation (KR-20) provided further reliability assessment.

By employing these statistical methods, the current study aimed to comprehensively evaluate the effectiveness of Kahoot! in enhancing MSA and achievement among primary school students.

4. Results

The analysis of this study's findings aimed to identify the effects of Kahoot! on students' MSA levels in mathematics to answer RQ1. The independent *t*-test revealed no significant difference in pre-intervention MSA scores between the EG and CG ($t = -0.75$, $p = 0.456$, Cohen's $d = 0.23$). This small effect size indicates that the groups were similar in their MSA levels before the intervention, allowing for a more accurate assessment of the impact of Kahoot! on MSA in the post-intervention analysis.

The means and standard deviations for the MSA scale scores of both groups (EG and CG) were calculated, as shown in Table 5. The results revealed a notable difference in mean scores between the two groups. Students who used Kahoot! in their mathematics learning (EG) achieved a lower average MSA score (2.50) compared to those who received traditional instruction (CG), who had a mean score of 3.51.

Table 5. Post-achievement MSA scale.

Groups	n	Mean	SD	Adjusted Mean
CG	55	3.51	1.04	3.22
EG	55	2.50	0.95	1.99

Further analysis using a one-way ANCOVA, as detailed in Table 6, confirmed a statistically significant difference in MSA achievement between the two groups, favoring the CG. The eta-squared (η^2) value of 0.356 indicates a moderate effect size, suggesting that approximately 35.6% of the variance in MSA scores can be attributed to the type of instruction received.

Table 6. One-way ANCOVA (analysis of covariance) on the MSA scale.

Source	Sum Squares	df	Mean Square	F	Sig.	Partial Eta Square
Pre-test	0.357	1	0.322	0.797	0.678	
Group	21.083	1	20.077	25.761	0.001 *	0.356
Error	41.717	47	0.675			
Total	66.979	49				

* $p < 0.001$.

These findings highlight that traditional instruction, as implemented in the CG, was less effective in reducing students' MSA levels in mathematics compared to the use of Kahoot!. The significant difference in mean scores and the moderate effect size emphasize the positive influence of Kahoot! in terms of lowering screen addiction. Although the CG exhibited higher MSA levels, suggesting greater screen addiction, Kahoot! effectively reduced MSA and significantly improved overall mathematical achievement. This demonstrates Kahoot!'s potential as an educational tool that not only enhances learning outcomes but also helps address screen addiction. According to this study's results, the CG had higher MSA levels, which suggests that traditional instruction was less effective in reducing MSA scores, not less effective overall. Therefore, the lower MSA scores observed in the EG do not directly imply a lack of motivation or engagement with the subject. It is of great importance to carefully consider the balance between using innovative tools like Kahoot! and ensuring that these tools effectively contribute to the intended educational outcomes.

The independent t-test revealed no significant difference in pre-intervention mathematics achievement scores between the EG and CG ($t = -0.71$, $p = 0.487$, Cohen's $d = 0.21$). This small effect size suggests that any pre-existing differences in mathematics achievement between the groups were minimal, ensuring that subsequent analysis can more accurately reflect the impact of the intervention on post-intervention outcomes.

To evaluate the impact of Kahoot! on students' mathematics achievement, Table 7 presents the analysis based on the post-application mathematics achievement scores of students in the EG and CG while controlling for any pre-existing achievement differences to answer RQ2.

Table 7. Post-achievement of the students' achievement test.

Group	Sample Size	Mean	SD	Adjusted Mean
EG	55	28.55	4.15	26.66
CG	55	18.55	4.22	17.88

The ANCOVA, set at a significance level of $\alpha = 0.05$, was employed to determine the statistical significance of the observed achievement disparities between the groups (Table 8).

Table 8. One-way ANCOVA for students' mathematics achievement test.

Source	Sum Squares	df	Mean Square	F	Sig.	Partial Eta Square
Pre-test	15.724	1	15.724	1.866	0.155	
Teaching strategies	1375.221	1	1533.410	177.689	0.001 *	0.655
Error	377.887	47	7.512			
Total	1881.322	49				

* $p < 0.001$.

Teaching strategies, as shown by the ANCOVA results, had a statistically significant effect on math achievement scores (F = 177.689, $p < 0.001$). This indicates that students taught with different strategies achieved significantly different scores on the math test, even after accounting for their pre-test scores. A substantial portion (65.5%) of the variance in achievement scores is explained by the different teaching strategies, highlighting their significant impact on student learning.

The statistical analysis in Table 8 revealed significant differences ($p < 0.001$) in the post-achievement test scores between the groups ($\alpha = 0.05$). Students in the EG, who were taught using Kahoot!, achieved a significantly higher average score (28.55) compared to the CG (18.55). Furthermore, the eta-squared (η^2) value of 0.655 indicates that approximately 65.5% of the variance in achievement scores can be attributed to the use of Kahoot!.

Overall, this study's results provide strong evidence that the use of Kahoot! in the EG resulted in a statistically significant improvement in students' achievement scores on the post-achievement test compared to the CG. The effect size, measured by eta squared (η^2), suggests that 65.5% of the variation in achievement scores between the groups can be explained by the use of Kahoot!, indicating a large and impactful effect on student learning achievements.

5. Discussion

This study investigated the impact of integrating Kahoot! as an instructional tool on K-12 students' achievements in mathematics and its potential influence on MSA. Specifically, it aimed to determine whether the interactive features of Kahoot! could enhance both academic performance and reduce screen addiction compared to traditional instruction using PowerPoint slides or digital textbooks.

In response to RQ1, the analysis of this study's findings revealed a statistically significant difference between the groups. The CG had a higher mean MSA score of 3.51 compared to the EG, which had a mean MSA score of 2.50. This result indicates that students in the CG underwent higher levels of screen addiction than those in the EG. Contrary to initial expectations, the data suggest that exposure to Kahoot! was associated with lower MSA scores, contradicting the common perception that traditional instruction might better manage screen time [9]. While the term MSA might imply a focus on screen use, in this context, it specifically relates to students' self-evaluation of their mathematical abilities. This finding stresses an important caveat, which is that the MSA does not directly measure motivation or engagement in the learning process [15,23,24].

Although Kahoot! is designed to enhance student motivation and engagement through its competitive and interactive features, this analysis focuses on its impact on screen addiction. The results of this study include the discrepancy between the lower MSA scores observed with Kahoot! and the significant improvement in mathematical achievement. The difference in effect sizes between MSA and mathematics achievement suggests that Kahoot! might have a more substantial impact on the latter. Therefore, the lower MSA scores observed in the Kahoot! group, alongside the significant improvement in mathematical achievement, suggest that Kahoot! not only reduces screen addiction but also enhances academic performance.

The variance between the MSA scale and its specific focus on screen addiction highlights the importance of selecting assessment tools that align closely with the constructs they aim to measure. This study reveals that while Kahoot! effectively reduces screen addiction (resulting in lower MSA scores) and enhances academic achievement, the tool used to measure these outcomes may not fully capture the constructs intended. This discrepancy challenges previous findings [9,15,25], which did not account for the dual impact of Kahoot! on reducing screen addiction while simultaneously improving academic performance. Even though Kahoot! is recognized for its ability to create a competitive learning environment, this study underscores its effectiveness in both reducing screen addiction and enhancing students' mathematical achievements, despite limitations in assessing self-assessed math skills directly. This finding emphasizes the need for researchers to diligently select and align assessment tools with the specific constructs they aim to measure to ensure reliable and meaningful results.

To answer RQ2, the one-way ANCOVA on the mathematics achievement test showed a statistically significant difference between groups (EG = 28.55 vs. CG = 18.55), suggesting a clear advantage for students utilizing Kahoot!, as previous studies have also advocated [17,25]. While Kahoot! reduced students' self-assessed MSA scores, it significantly enhanced their actual performance in mathematics, as evidenced by the one-way ANCOVA results. The computed F-value of 177.689 yielded a p-value of 0.001 at $\alpha = 0.05$, firmly establishing the statistical significance of the differences in achievement between the two groups. This finding underlines the robustness of Kahoot! as a tool for improving mathematical achievement, reinforcing its utility in educational settings where student performance is a primary focus. Moreover, Kahoot! significantly improved overall mathematical achievement, with a substantial effect size ($\eta^2 = 0.655$), suggesting a strong positive impact on learning outcomes. In other words, a substantial 65.5% of the variance in the performance achievement of participants in the EG on the post-achievement test can be linked to the use of Kahoot! Such a significant effect size is indicative of the powerful role that interactive, gamified learning tools like Kahoot! can play in educational settings, particularly in enhancing students' understanding and retention of complex subjects such as mathematics at a younger age. The observed positive influence on student achievement might be attributed to Kahoot!'s interactive design, competitive elements, and engaging approach. These features could potentially foster a deeper understanding and retention of mathematical concepts through several mechanisms. For instance, the immediate feedback provided by Kahoot! after each question not only reinforces learning but also helps students quickly correct misconceptions, thereby setting their grasp of the material. Kahoot!'s interactivity may enhance focus and active learning, while the competitive aspect could encourage students to review and consolidate mathematical knowledge in preparation for challenges [10]. Moreover, the use of Kahoot! might help students develop better study habits and time management skills, as the anticipation of competitive quizzes can motivate them to engage with the material more consistently and thoroughly, consistent with Nguyen et al. [17].

This study provides evidence for Kahoot!'s potential to improve students' mathematics achievement. The combination of lower MSA scores and significant improvements in mathematical achievement observed in the Kahoot! group suggests that Kahoot! not only reduces screen addiction but also enhances academic performance. Nonetheless, this study also acknowledges certain limitations, particularly the lack of measures for student interest and engagement, which are critical to fully understanding Kahoot!'s impact. Using validated instruments, such as the MSA scale, could help clarify Kahoot!'s influence and its potential effects on other cognitive and affective outcomes, such as problem-solving skills and confidence in mathematics [13]. Additionally, exploring the specific mechanisms by which Kahoot! facilitates learning—such as its competitive elements and immediate feedback—could provide valuable insights into its effectiveness. Understanding these mechanisms in greater detail could inform the development of more refined instructional strategies that maximize the benefits of gamified learning tools in mathematics education. A more comprehensive approach to evaluating Kahoot!'s effectiveness should consider not only student achievement but also their perceptions of the learning process. This approach would also explore how Kahoot! supports learning through its interactive features. By integrating these considerations, researchers can better understand how Kahoot! contributes to educational outcomes, considering both cognitive achievements and the broader behavioral patterns it may influence.

The findings of this study regarding Kahoot!'s positive impact on student achievement in mathematics align with previous research [16,18,24]. These studies suggest that Kahoot! facilitates deeper conceptual understanding and knowledge retention through its engaging and interactive design. The alignment of these findings with the broader body of research further validates the use of Kahoot! as an instructional platform, especially in contexts where active learning and student engagement are prioritized. Statistical analyses, including independent-sample *t*-tests for MSA and one-way ANCOVA for performance, revealed that students using Kahoot! exhibited lower self-assessed mathematical competence but significantly outperformed the control group in actual mathematics achievement, with a substantial effect size ($\eta^2 = 0.655$). These findings suggest that while Kahoot! enhances mathematical performance, it may not necessarily improve students' self-assessment of their mathematical abilities. The current study highlights the importance of aligning assessment tools with the intended constructs and recommends further research to explore the broader impact of gamified learning on student engagement and learning mechanisms. This comprehensive approach will provide a more complete understanding of Kahoot!'s effectiveness and guide the development of more effective instructional strategies in mathematics education.

6. Conclusions

In conclusion, this study demonstrates the importance of selecting appropriate measurement tools in educational research. The Kahoot! platform has significant benefits, but careful consideration must be given to the constructs being measured to ensure that outcomes are accurately interpreted. The findings showed a statistically significant difference in MSA scores, with the EG displaying lower scores than the CG, suggesting a positive effect on reducing screen addiction. Although Kahoot! contributed to lower MSA levels, it also significantly boosted overall mathematical achievement, with a notable effect size, indicating a strong positive influence on learning outcomes. This suggests Kahoot! not only effectively enhances mathematical performance but also reduces MSA levels. This study underlines the importance of aligning educational tools with desired outcomes and recommends further research to explore the broader effects of gamified learning on student engagement, screen addiction, and academic success.

The current study contributes to the growing body of literature advocating for the integration of digital tools in education, particularly those that actively engage students and foster a competitive yet supportive learning environment.

To expand our knowledge of how gamified learning tools can enhance education, this study proposes the following areas for exploration:

- Deeper exploration of MSA: Given the unexpected findings regarding MSA, future research should delve deeper into the relationship between gamified learning tools and overall screen time to examine the long-term effects of such tools on students' digital habits.
- Focus on motivational aspects: Research should explore the motivational factors underlying students' engagement with Kahoot! beyond competition. Intrinsic motivation and its relationship to achievement could be a fruitful area of investigation.
- Mechanism studies: To better understand how Kahoot! impacts learning, studies should focus on identifying the specific mechanisms at play, such as the role of immediate feedback, competition, and interactivity.
- Combination with other tools: Investigating how Kahoot! can be integrated with other instructional strategies or technologies to maximize its effectiveness would be beneficial.
- Qualitative research: Incorporating qualitative methods to capture students' perspectives on Kahoot! can provide rich insights into their experiences and learning processes.

7. Implications for Design and Practice

The findings of this study have significant implications for the use of interactive learning tools like Kahoot! in mathematics education, including the following:

- Enhanced student achievements: The improvement in mathematics education achievements for students using Kahoot! (EG = 28.55 vs. CG = 18.55) highlights the potential of gamified learning tools to significantly boost student performance. The large effect size ($\eta^2 = 0.655$) indicates substantial gains in performance, making these tools valuable for instructional strategies. This suggests Kahoot! not only aids in reinforcing mathematical concepts but also promotes a competitive learning environment that motivates students to excel. Such tools can be particularly effective in diverse educational settings where student engagement is a challenge, offering a structured yet enjoyable pathway to mastery.
- MSA and learning: This study revealed a significant improvement in MSA scores, suggesting that Kahoot!'s interactive and competitive format can effectively reduce students' multi-screen distractions. This positive correlation indicates Kahoot! may indirectly enhance learning outcomes. However, this study emphasizes the need for validated questionnaires and research instruments to accurately measure the impact of Kahoot! on students' motivation for learning mathematics. Without such tools, the interpretation of Kahoot!'s influence on student engagement and interest remains incomplete. Future research should explore the relationship between multi-screen attention and actual learning outcomes more deeply, ensuring that increased screen interaction translates to meaningful educational benefits.
- Instructional design content: Kahoot!'s interactive elements, real-time feedback, and competitive aspects appear to foster a deeper understanding and retention of mathematical concepts. These features align with best practices in instructional design, which advocate for active learning, immediate feedback, and student engagement as cornerstones of effective education. Educators should consider integrating such tools into their curricula to promote active learning and sustained focus. Immediate feedback helps students quickly address knowledge gaps, enhancing their learning process. Moreover, the competitive nature of Kahoot! can drive students to engage more thoroughly with the material, as they prepare for quizzes and challenges, thus reinforcing their learning outside of the classroom.

This study demonstrates the significant potential of interactive learning tools like Kahoot! to enhance students' achievements in mathematics education. It further emphasizes the role of well-designed digital tools in creating dynamic and interactive learning environments that can cater to a wide range of student needs and learning styles. However, it also highlights the need for precise measurement tools in educational research to accurately assess the impact of these innovations on student motivation and learning outcomes. By integrating engaging and interactive tools into the curriculum, educators can foster a more dynamic and effective learning environment for student engagement. To sum up, the findings suggest that, when used thoughtfully, tools like Kahoot! can transform traditional educational practices, leading to more meaningful and sustained academic success.

8. Limitations and Future Work

There are several important limitations to consider in this study. First, the reliance on self-reported data from Greek students introduces a potential for subjectivity, which could skew the results, particularly given the focus on elementary school contexts. Incorporating standardized assessments alongside Kahoot! activities would offer a more objective measure of learning outcomes. Second, this study's small sample size ($n = 110$) and limited demographic diversity constrain the generalizability of its findings. The observation that higher MSA scores do not necessarily correlate with increased motivation for math learning further complicates the interpretation of the results.

These limitations underline the need for additional research. Future studies should investigate the long-term effects of Kahoot! on student achievement and retention in mathematics, as well as its effectiveness across various subjects. Moreover, exploring the impact of different teacher training approaches and how educators adapt Kahoot! for diverse learning objectives and student needs would provide valuable insights. Understanding if Kahoot! provides a wide range of learning styles is also crucial. By addressing these gaps, future research could better illuminate Kahoot!'s potential to enhance student learning across disciplines and educational settings.

Funding: This research received no external funding.

Institutional Review Board Statement: Not applicable.

Informed Consent Statement: Informed consent was first obtained from the parents or legal guardians of all participating students before the commencement of this study.

Data Availability Statement: The data used are publicly available and their citation is provided in the manuscript.

Acknowledgments: I would like to express my gratitude to all participants who voluntarily participated in this study.

Conflicts of Interest: The author declares no conflicts of interest.

References

1. Mensah, F.S.; Ampadu, E. Benefits, challenges, and opportunities of using computer-assisted instruction in mathematics education. In *EAI/Springer Innovations in Communication and Computing*; Springer Nature: Dordrecht, The Netherlands, 2024; pp. 31–49. [CrossRef]
2. Göksu, I.; Özcan, K.V.; Çakir, R.; Göktas, Y. Content analysis of research trends in instructional design models: 1999–2014. *J. Learn. Des.* **2017**, *10*, 85–109. [CrossRef]
3. Büscher, C.; Prediger, S. Teachers' practices of integrating challenging demands of inclusive mathematics education in a professional development program. *J. Math. Teach. Educ.* **2024**, *27*, 209–233. [CrossRef]
4. Demir, Ö.; Birgili, B. The mediating role of instructional design and video length between grade level and pupil-content interaction in instructional mathematics videos on YouTube. *Educ. Inf. Technol.* **2024**, *29*, 5599–5629. [CrossRef]
5. Parsons, B.; Curry, J.H. Can ChatGPT pass graduate-level instructional design assignments? Potential implications of artificial intelligence in education and a call to action. *TechTrends* **2024**, *68*, 67–78. [CrossRef]
6. Llinares, S. Instructional quality of mathematics teaching and mathematics teacher education. *J. Math. Teach. Educ.* **2021**, *24*, 1–3. [CrossRef]
7. Salami, O.O. A flipped classroom application: Undergraduate students' perception in mathematics. *Math. Educ. J.* **2024**, *8*, 11–20. [CrossRef]
8. Stylianides, G.J.; Stylianides, A.J.; Moutsios-Rentzos, A. Proof and proving in school and university mathematics education research: A systematic review. *ZDM–Math. Educ.* **2024**, *56*, 47–59. [CrossRef]
9. Göksün, D.O.; Gürsoy, G. Comparing success and engagement in gamified learning experiences via Kahoot and Quizizz. *Comput. Educ.* **2019**, *135*, 15–29. [CrossRef]
10. Pellas, N. Exploring learning outcomes and psycho-emotional experiences of undergraduate students in digital literacy training and support using web-based assessment platforms. *J. Res. Technol. Educ.* **2024**, *in press*. [CrossRef]
11. Yildiz Durak, H.; Hopcan, S.; Polat, E.; Özüdoğru, G.; Atman Uslu, N. Investigating undergraduates' online engagement behaviors predictors: The role of multiple screen addictions, MSA, Academic Success, and Autonomous Learning. *Technol. Knowl. Learn.* **2024**, *in press*. [CrossRef]
12. Saritepeci, M. Multiple screen addiction scale: Validity and reliability study. *Instr. Technol. Lifelong Learn.* **2021**, *2*, 1–17. [CrossRef]
13. Saritepeci, M.; Durak, Y.H.; Atman Uslu, N. A latent profile analysis for the study of multiple screen addiction, mobile social gaming addiction, general mattering, and family sense of belonging in university students. *Int. J. Ment. Health Addict.* **2022**, *in press*. [CrossRef]
14. Lin, T.T.C.; Kononova, A.; Chiang, Y.H. Screen addiction and media multitasking among American and Taiwanese users. *J. Comput. Inf. Syst.* **2020**, *60*, 583–592. [CrossRef]
15. Mada, R.D.; Anharudin, A. How Online Learning Evaluation (Kahoot) Affecting Students' Achievement and MSA (Case Study on its Students). *Int. J. Educ. Vocat. Stud.* **2019**, *1*, 5. [CrossRef]
16. Malak, M.Z. Effect of using gamification of "Kahoot!" as a learning method on stress symptoms, anxiety symptoms, self-efficacy, and academic achievement among university students. *Learn. MSA* **2024**, *87*, 101993. [CrossRef]
17. Nguyen, T.T.T.; Yukawa, T. Kahoot with smartphones in testing and assessment of language teaching and learning, the need of training on mobile devices for Vietnamese teachers, and students. *Int. J. Inf. Educ. Technol.* **2019**, *9*, 286–296. [CrossRef]
18. Prieto, M.C.; Palma, L.O.; Tobías, P.J.B.; León, F.J.M. Student assessment of the use of Kahoot in the learning process of science and mathematics. *Educ. Sci.* **2019**, *9*, 55. [CrossRef]

19. Wahyuni, M.; Fauziddin, M.; Rizki, L.M. The effects of using Kahoot! on understanding the concept of mathematical symbols in Higher education. *Al-Ishlah J. Pendidik.* **2021**, *13*, 1539–1545. [CrossRef]
20. Goudeau, S.; Sanrey, C.; Stanczak, A.; Manstead, A.; Darnon, C. Why lockdown and distance learning during the COVID-19 pandemic are likely to increase the social class achievement gap. *Nat. Hum. Behav.* **2021**, *5*, 1273–1281. [CrossRef]
21. Wang, A.I.; Tahir, R. The effect of using Kahoot! for learning—A literature review. *Comput. Educ.* **2020**, *149*, 103818. [CrossRef]
22. Zhang, J.; Zeng, Y. Effect of college students' smartphone addiction on academic achievement: The mediating role of academic anxiety and moderating role of sense of academic control. *Psychol. Res. Behav. Manag.* **2024**, *17*, 933–944. [CrossRef] [PubMed]
23. Figuccio, M.J.; Johnston, M. Kahoot! Predicts exam scores and promotes student engagement. *J. Res. Innov. Teach. Learn.* **2021**, *15*, 170–177. [CrossRef]
24. AlAli, R.; Wardat, Y. Exploring the impact of Kahoot! as a collaborative gamified mathematics learning platform for Jordanian junior school gifted students. *J. Asian Sci. Res.* **2024**, *14*, 227–236. [CrossRef]
25. Umboh, D.; Tarusu, D.; Marini, A.; Sumantri, M.S. Improvement of student mathematics learning outcomes through Kahoot learning games application at elementary school. *J. Phys. Conf. Ser.* **2021**, *1869*, 012124. [CrossRef]
26. Privitera, G.J.; Ahlgrim-Delzell, L. *Research Methods for Education*; Sage Publications: Thousand Oaks, CA, USA, 2018.
27. Brislin, R.W. Back-translation for cross-cultural research. *J. Cross-Cult. Psychol.* **1970**, *1*, 185–216. [CrossRef]
28. Bridgeman, B.; Cline, F. Effects of differential Time-Consuming tests on Computer-Adaptive test scores. *J. Educ. Meas.* **2004**, *41*, 137–148. [CrossRef]
29. Terwel, J.; van Oers, B.; van Dijk, I.; van den Eeden, P. Are representations to be provided or generated in primary mathematics education? Effects on transfer. *Educ. Res. Eval.* **2009**, *15*, 25–44. [CrossRef]
30. Cortina, J.M. What is the coefficient alpha? An examination of theory and applications. *J. Appl. Psychol.* **1993**, *78*, 98–104. [CrossRef]
31. Al-Zboon, H.S.; Alrekebat, A.F.; Abdelrahman, M.S.B. The effect of multiple-choice test items' difficulty degree on the reliability coefficient and the standard error of measurement depending on the Item Response Theory (IRT). *Int. J. High. Educ.* **2021**, *10*, 22. [CrossRef]
32. Lüdtke, O.; Robitzsch, A. ANCOVA versus Change Score for the Analysis of Two-Wave Data. *J. Exp. Educ.* **2023**, 1–33. [CrossRef]

Multimodal Technologies and Interaction

MDPI

Article

Physics-Based Tool Usage Simulations in VR

Nikolaos Partarakis [1,*], Xenophon Zabulis [1], Dimitris Zourarakis [1], Ioanna Demeridou [1], Ines Moreno [2], Arnaud Dubois [3], Nikolaos Nikolaou [4], Peiman Fallahian [4], David Arnaud [5], Noël Crescenzo [5], Patricia Hee [5] and Andriani Stamou [1,6]

1 Institute of Computer Science, Foundation for Research and Technology—Hellas (FORTH), 70013 Heraklion, Greece; zabulis@ics.forth.gr (X.Z.); zourdim@ics.forth.gr (D.Z.); idemer@ics.forth.gr (I.D.); andrianist@csd.uoc.gr (A.S.)
2 Histoire des Technosciences en Société, Conservatoire National des Arts et Métiers (HT2S-CNAM), 2 Rue Conté, 75003 Paris, France; ines.moreno@ehess.fr
3 French National Center for Scientific Research, 3 Rue Michel Ange, 75016 Paris, France; arnaud.dubois@mnhn.fr
4 Khora Virtual Reality, 1712 Copenhagen, Denmark; nikolaos@khora.com (N.N.); peiman@khora.com (P.F.)
5 Centre Européen de Recherches et de Formation aux Arts Verriers (CERFAV), Rue de la Liberté, 54112 Vannes-le-Châtel, France; david.arnaud@cerfav.com (D.A.); noel.crescenzo@cerfav.fr (N.C.); patricia.hee@cerfav.com (P.H.)
6 Computer Science Department, Voutes Campus, University of Crete, 70013 Heraklion, Greece
* Correspondence: partarak@ics.forth.gr; Tel.: +30-2810391754

Abstract: The need for scalable, immersive training systems is universal and recently has been included in fields that rely on complex, hands-on processes, such as surgery operations, assembly operations, construction processes training, etc. This paper examines the potential to support immersive training via digital tool manipulation in the domain of traditional handicrafts. The proposed methodology employs Finite Element Method simulations to compute material transformations and apply them to interactive virtual environments. The challenge is to accurately simulate human–tool interactions, which are critical to the acquisition of manual skills. Using Simulia Abaqus (v.2023HF2), crafting simulations are authored, executed, and exported as animation sequences. These are further refined in Blender (v3.6) and integrated into Unity to create reusable training components called Action Animators. Two software applications—Craft Studio (v1.0) and Apprentice Studio (v1.0)—are designed and implemented to enable instructors to create training lessons and students to practice and get evaluated in virtual environments. The methodology has wide-ranging applications beyond crafts, offering a solution for immersive training in skill-based activities. The validation and evaluation of the proposed approach suggest that it can significantly improve training effectiveness, scalability, and accessibility across various industries.

Keywords: vocational training; physics-based simulations; finite element method; process simulation; virtual reality

1. Introduction

Immersive training systems respond to the need for efficient and scalable vocational training systems in skill-intensive domains [1]. Professions that require the acquisition of knowledge of manual procedures such as craft-based industries, assembly lines, and factories are well-suited for immersive training because they rely heavily on hands-on experiences and the mastering of complex physical interactions [2]. For example, Virtual Reality (VR) in training can provide hands-on experiences and simulate complex physical interactions [3]. The scalability and accessibility of VR-based training systems have also been studied, supporting the argument that immersive systems can provide flexible and accessible training solutions [4]. On the efficiency of these learning approaches, a review of research in this domain has shown that Augmented Reality (AR) and VR can enhance learning by providing immersive, interactive experiences, which is particularly relevant for preserving procedural knowledge [5].

Traditional methods of instruction in these professions currently involve mainly in-person mentoring [6]. Except for common practice, the importance of mentoring and hands-on learning in vocational training is also a research finding when studying such contexts [7]. At the same time, traditional methods rely on the existence of practitioners to provide their expertise and know-how [8]. In the case of Traditional Crafts (TCs), where the population of practitioners is declining, gestural and procedural knowledge should be urgently preserved [9]. UNESCO highlights the global decline in TCs as part of Intangible Cultural Heritage (ICH), emphasizing the urgent need to preserve these skills and knowledge systems [10]. The challenges posed by the declining number of practitioners is far more important in apprenticeship-based training systems [11]. Understanding and preserving such knowledge can support the creation of immersive systems and thus provide flexible and accessible training.

The core challenge in this work is to provide an accurate representation of craft actions in immersive training environments. To do so requires understanding processes and being able to accurately simulate the real-world behaviors of tools, materials, and human actions. In this work, we build upon previous efforts on the representation of crafts [12] and we enrich them by moving a step further into providing scientifically simulated occurrences of the documented processes. We employ scientific simulation to acquire data and thus support realistic training in crafting activities.

Our approach is rooted in the Finite Element Method (FEM) simulation which has been extensively used in engineering and material sciences. Currently, the application of the FEM to human activity simulation is an emerging field. The FEM is of particular interest in the studied domain since it provides high-fidelity simulations of how materials respond to forces, stresses, and deformations which is a prerequisite for simulating traditional crafts where the interaction of the human with the material through the skillful usage of tools is of the essence. Current research in immersive training is advancing, without considering the potential of FEM integration. Thus, these systems are still using "fake reality" simulations, particularly when it comes to real-time interactions. The works in this area [13–15] have demonstrated the effectiveness of the FEM in modeling physical phenomena, but its application to training human activities is a relatively new exploration. In this domain, the application of the FEM is currently studied for medical surgery training [16,17].

Furthermore, there are competing views on the simulation of human actions in virtual environments. Some works are in favor of physics-based simulations that rely on computational models to calculate the outcomes of actions based on physical laws [18–22]. Other words are in favor of evidence-based practice which is considered a prerequisite of realism [23–27]. In the first case, the computer is calculating the results of an action through physics simulation. In the second case, animations are generated by monitoring real actions or simulating them. Other works propose a combination of the above methods [28–30]. In this work, we are using physics-based simulations in conjunction with data-driven methods and game engine-based rendering.

To address the aforementioned gaps, this work is proposing a methodology for immersive training that integrates the FEM with virtual environments, animations, and interactive software solutions. This approach not only enables the precise simulation of crafting actions but also ensures that the system is adaptable and reusable across different scenarios. The methodology includes the use of Simulia Abaqus [31] to simulate crafting processes, a custom script to export animation sequences, and integration with game engines such as Unity3D [32] to deliver a fully interactive training experience.

Furthermore, to deliver these technologies as immersive experiences, this work presents the design and implementation of two software applications Craft Studio and Apprentice Studio which serve as the instructor and learner interfaces, respectively. Craft Studio supports the creation of detailed lessons, combining physics-driven simulations with immersive environments that utilize both traditional and advanced input/output devices, such as VR controllers and haptic feedback systems. Apprentice Studio supports the execution and monitoring of training activities in a highly realistic virtual environment.

2. Background and Related Work

This section summarizes related work focusing on VR, AR, and physics-based simulations. It also explores serious games in providing interactive and engaging training experiences. Additionally, the section highlights the potential of FEM simulations in human activity simulation and their application in immersive training environments. Finally, it discusses the creation of realistic and effective virtual training systems, emphasizing the importance of the accurate replication of real-world conditions and the integration of haptic feedback to the training experience.

2.1. Current State of the Art in Immersive Training

Immersive education and training have evolved due to new technologies such as VR [33] and AR [34]. These technologies have supported the development of virtual environments to simulate real-world spaces [35] including heritage spaces [36,37]. Several software platforms have been developed to support this type of immersive learning, enhancing traditional training approaches [38,39]. Furthermore, modular systems that integrate animations of human activities as components [40,41] can support the creation of training programs by combining different animations into structured lessons [42,43]. In such systems, VR headsets and haptic devices can provide both visual and tactile feedback, making the training experience more realistic [44–46]. Such systems enable users to practice in virtual workshops [47] with prior works assisting, for example, ceramic design [48], wood assembly [49], and woodworking tools simulation [50].

The potential for virtual training environments to replicate real-world conditions is demonstrated in several studies [51,52]. Such systems are becoming more adaptable, supporting various input methods (e.g., VR controllers and haptic feedback devices), overall enhancing interaction and experience.

2.1.1. Game-Based Training

Computer games have supported creative interaction with the virtual environment and in some cases even replicating basic crafting aspects. For example, pottery simulation is found in several games engaging creativity (e.g., 3D Pottery [53], Pottery Master [54], and Pottery Simulator [55]), albeit not exhibiting high levels of realism, nor addressing practical constraints. In the adventure game genre [56], the prerequisite of crafting or recipe materials is addressed by requiring them to be available for the execution of an action. This is also the case for alchemy systems used in some role-playing games [57].

The Knitting Simulator 2014 [58] requires handling the VR controllers as knits. In [59], the same metaphor is used to edit solids by revolution in lathe crafting. A solution for generic crafting simulations in the Unity [32] is proposed in [60]. Games can build interactions using physics engines and simulators such as the PhysX (v9.23.1019) [61]. PhysX supports rigid and body dynamics and volumetric fluid simulation.

2.1.2. Serious Games

Several serious games have contributed to this work subject. Serious games consider learning objectives and learning outcomes as fundamental design considerations and thus are considered more appropriate for game-based learning [62]. The Woodwork Simulator [63] provides reasonable approximations of the effect of virtual saws, drills, glue, chisels, and sandpaper on virtual wood. In [64], simplified tool interaction is used to shapes metallic pieces. In [65], calculus is made more interesting, intuitive, and educational. In [66], glasswork actions are simulated in MR. Pottery simulations involve the manipulation of clay on a rotating wheel. In [67], a haptic simulation of pottery-making provides users with tactile feedback, enhancing the realism of the experience and enabling the replication of traditional techniques. Metalworking processes such as forging, casting, and machining involve significant physical transformations. In [68], deformable models that simulate the plastic deformation of materials, which are essential for creating realistic simulations of metalworking operations were developed.

Remote, but still relevant, interactive simulations for mechanical assembly enable the virtual assembly of mechanical systems, providing insights into the assembly process and the interactions between components. In [69], a system for simulating the assembly of mechanical parts was developed, enabling users to explore different assembly sequences and detect potential issues.

2.2. Physics-Based Simulation

Physics-based simulations focus on the physical behavior of mechanical systems including structures, materials, and dynamics. The FEM is foundational to many mechanical simulations and was popularized by Clough and others in the 1950s [70,71]. The FEM was applied primarily to civil engineering problems [72], and the aerospace and automobile industry played a crucial role in driving their early adoption [73]. FEM simulations [74,75] were originally used for industrial applications like automotive design and structural mechanics [76] including crash test simulations [77,78]. Finite Element Analysis (FEA) [79,80] utilizes the FEM for physical systems simulation. Geometrically, physical bodies are represented as volumetric meshes by finite elements. The behavior of the system is described by a set of mathematical equations based on the physical laws governing the problem. In this work, the FEM is employed to model the fine details of material deformation and tool interactions, especially in artisanal and craft-based activities. For example, recent research illustrates how the FEM can accurately simulate cutting processes by modeling mechanical stresses, tool wear, and material deformation [81–83]. More recently, the FEM has been used in simulating complex tasks such as interlocking and forming, where multiple materials or objects were studied [84].

The commercialization of FEM software made these tools more widely accessible to engineers across various industries. Notable commercial FEM software include ANSYS [85], NASTRAN [86], and Abaqus [87]. Parallel software suites like FLUENT and CFX are proving to be instrumental in advancing the field of Computational Fluid Dynamics (CFD) [88,89].

Traditionally, generic and interactive simulations are based on "physics engines" [90]. Physics engines simulate rigid objects, their potential collisions, and their behavior thereafter [91]. Nevertheless, if real-time performance is required, the structural complexity of the involved models has to be low (i.e., their 3D meshes should comprise few polygons.

Scientific simulation has not been widely adopted in the domain of crafts. Some limited and remotely relevant examples include the formation of nots, mechanical models for fibers, and metalworking processing [92–94].

2.2.1. The Potential of FEM Simulations in Human Activity Simulation

In this paper, more general simulations of human behaviors were utilized to inform us about the making process. In crafts and manual work, human tasks are characterized by operating tools and processing materials under force, pressure, or movement. The FEM becomes a simulation of these interactions through the stress, strain, and deformation of objects. The simulation can do a lot more than just setting up the scene. It can compute several important parameters such as pressure, angle, speed of tools, etc. This allows the FEM to produce highly detailed and physically based simulations of human–tool interactions, which are otherwise challenging to model utilizing traditional animation or approximation techniques. Directions have been examined in areas such as craft [95–97], surgery [98,99], and the sports domain [100,101]. In this work, we will argue that as the FEM is highly capable of synthesizing a vast sequence of processes, it can be leveraged in immersive training situations to provide a realistic practice environment in which users will train to manipulate virtual objects while acting under physical constraints. An example of this is a craftsperson learning to carve wood. Testing various levels of pressure and tilt angles while using virtual woodworking tools can help understand the properties of the material without any damage or material waste.

2.2.2. FEM Simulations for Learning

The FEM can be used in fields that require a deep understanding of physical systems, material behavior, and structural mechanics. FEM simulations enable learners to visualize and interact with complex physical phenomena, providing insights that are difficult to achieve through traditional teaching methods. By integrating FEM with AR, engaging training environments can be built that enhance learning outcomes.

FEM-based simulations have been widely adopted in engineering education to teach structural mechanics. These simulations allow students to explore the behavior of structures under various loading conditions, providing a hands-on understanding of concepts such as stress, strain, and deformation [102,103]. In fields such as magnetics and electromagnetics, AR systems that integrate FEM simulations have been developed to enhance training. These systems allow learners to visualize magnetic fields and their interactions with materials in real-time, providing a deeper understanding of complex concepts [104,105]. In medical education, FEM simulations are increasingly being used. These simulations provide a realistic environment for training in surgical procedures and diagnostic techniques [106,107]. In material science education, FEM simulations are widely used to model the behavior of materials under various conditions, such as stress, temperature, and pressure. These simulations help students understand the properties and performance of different materials [108,109]. In the aerospace and automotive industries, FEM simulations are extensively used for training engineers in structural analysis, crash testing, and fluid dynamics [85,110]. The FEM is a cornerstone of civil engineering education, where it is used to model the behavior of structures such as bridges, buildings, and dams. These simulations help students understand the principles of structural analysis, design, and mechanics. In this context, several applications have been developed that combine AR with FEM simulations to provide immersive training (e.g., [110,111]).

2.2.3. Three-Dimensional Rendering of FEM Results

FEM simulations can be transferred in 3D, using software platforms and game engines such as Blender (v3.6) [112] and Unity3D (v2021.3.24f1) [32]. These allow FEM-generated data to be converted into 3D models and 3D animations [113]. Studies have been researching the usage of FEM simulations in AR for real-time evaluation of mechanical tasks for training purposes [114]. These simulations enable users to experience factors that are critical in training processes [115,116] such as material deformations. At the same time, lighting, textures, and high-res materials can enhance realism, making it easier for trainees to learn by replicating real-world conditions. This can be further supported by advances in photorealistic rendering [117,118] to better simulate the appearance of materials under various lighting conditions.

2.3. *Immersive Training Applications*

2.3.1. Training and Human–Tool Interaction

Human–tool interaction simulations in virtual environments leverage a variety of techniques, including haptic feedback, physics-based modeling, motion tracking, and immersive technologies like VR and AR. Examples include modeling tool–tissue interactions for surgical simulations [119] and the integration of haptic systems in minimally invasive surgical training [120,121]. These works demonstrated how tactile interaction and realistic haptic feedback can improve precision and user engagement. Other methods introduced the simulation of surgical cuts in real-time, addressing computational challenges while ensuring visual and interactive fidelity [122]. Expanding beyond medical contexts, haptic feedback has also been explored in generic tool manipulation applications [20,22]. In the same context, the use of motion tracking to simulate tool interactions in virtual environments, focusing on realistic avatar animations has also been considered [24]. This has found application in interactive assembly simulations, showcasing its potential to refine manual dexterity and decision-making [123,124]. Another relevant example is the VR-based welding simulator that illustrates how immersive environments can be used to train in crafting activities [125].

2.3.2. Data-Driven Animation for Virtual Environments

Data-driven animation creation is an approach for producing realistic and dynamic visual content, leveraging data-driven and physics-based techniques. Simulated physics forms the backbone of interactive character animation, enabling the synthesis of lifelike movements that adapt dynamically to varying environmental conditions [126]. This approach has been extended to specific anatomical models, such as 3D neck modeling [127]. Regarding animation in virtual environments, precomputing data for specific scenarios, such as tree animations, demonstrates the efficiency of data-driven techniques in generating realistic, complex natural phenomena [128]. High-resolution animations of dynamic effects like fire have also benefited from data-driven approaches, enabling visually striking results through the integration of simulation and synthesis [129]. For fluid simulation, the data-driven projection method offers improved accuracy and computational efficiency, which enhances the fidelity of fluid-related animations [130].

2.3.3. Effectiveness of Virtual Environments and User Interfaces as a Training Tool

Virtual environments and interfaces have proven to be effective tools for training, offering immersive and engaging learning experiences across various disciplines. Systematic reviews have highlighted the ability of VR to enhance cognitive and procedural learning outcomes, particularly in complex subjects such as science, engineering, and medicine [131,132]. Immersion in VR can support mastering skills without real-world risks [133,134]. Research also demonstrates that VR-based training improves retention rates, learner engagement, and motivation, which are critical for long-term skill acquisition [39]. Additionally, the adaptability of virtual interfaces allows for personalized and self-paced training [135,136].

2.3.4. Challenges and Opportunities

The primary challenge is probably ensuring that the virtual environment accurately replicates real-world conditions, particularly in terms of the physical interactions between tools and materials such as by superimposing objects in space [137]. In [138], a Head Mounted Display (HMD) is used to present traditional craft objects with high presence and absorption. In [139], AR is used to augments a physical object with audiovisual assets. In [140], visitors can perform woodworking tasks.

2.4. Main Contributions of This Research Work

This research presents a unique approach to the simulation of craft actions in immersive education environments. The method involves the development of reusable motion animators that are incorporated into VR systems to simulate complex crafting actions. The combination of FEM simulations with 3D rendering technologies and haptic devices creates an educational solution that provides sensible feedback to trainees. The main contribution of this work is the provision of a methodology for combining FEM simulations with VR education. At the same time, the creation of motion animators allows the reuse of FEM simulation results across different education situations. The integration of photorealistic rendering techniques complements the realism of the training environment at the same time as using haptic controllers can help realistic tactile interactions.

Key advancement is the use of the FEM for simulating human activity which is well-established in fields such as medical training, material analysis, and mechanical engineering. However, its application to cultural heritage, specifically in the context of preserving and training for traditional handcraft processes, presents distinct challenges and particularities. Unlike other domains, the focus here is on capturing the interaction between tools, materials, and human activity in an accurate way to replicate the tactile and procedural interactions of traditional crafts. This necessitates a detailed understanding of craft-specific materials, techniques, and workflows which is often the standardization seen in other applications of the FEM. At the same time, accurate reproduction is of extreme importance for the efficiency of training which is not always the case for industrial simulations such as assembly line operation, machine operation, tool manipulations, etc.

3. Proposed Method

The proposed methodology (see Figure 1) has a simulation and a training phase. The simulation phase regards the generating of animation for craft reenactment based on the studied craft instances and their simulation while the training phase regards the authoring of training lessons, their assignment, and execution in the context of immersive training scenarios.

The simulation phase begins with analysis to identify actions that influence the state of materials, such as human activity and machine operations, as well as those that do not, such as the position and orientation of tools or the machine states. This process provides the simulation characteristics that assist in identifying whether a more complex FEM-based simulation is required or whether the action can be simulated using simple operations executed in a game engine.

Regarding FEM-based simulation time, space, tools, and materials, it is initially defined in a FEM modeling tool. Object movements, material properties, and force interactions are modeled to accommodate both rigid and deformable material behaviors. The outputs of the execution of these simulations are preprocessed to generate results that explore the parameter space. These results are organized into lookup tables with key values in the domain of the parameter space. In the animation phase, the implemented lookup tables are used to create animations per lookup table key value. These animations are all combined into Action Animators which are collections of animations per action. Multiple Action Animators are combined into Animation Packages. Each Animation Package represents a complex craft process of a craft instance according to the complexity of the craft under study.

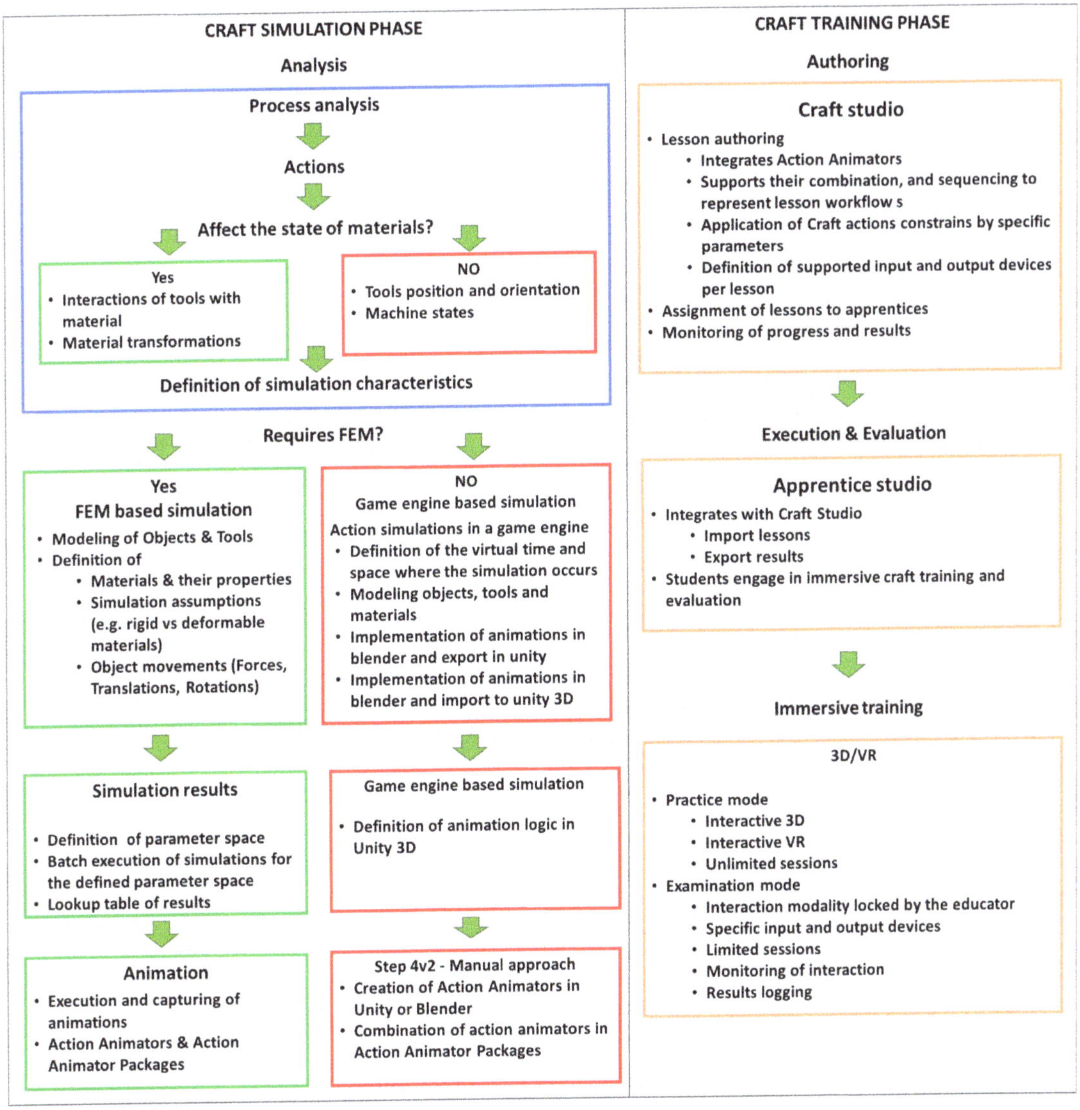

Figure 1. Overview of the proposed methodology.

In the case that the intention is to proceed with game-engine-based simulation tools like Unity 3D or Blender are used to create virtual representations of actions. This approach focuses on modeling and animating dynamic action sequences directly in the game engine. The authored animation logic is manually adjusted to resemble what is happening in reality (e.g., a chisel is cutting a piece of wood following the prescribed motion).

During the Craft Training Phase, the results of the simulations are used to synthesize immersive learning experiences. The process starts with authoring conducted with the support of the Craft Studio which is an authoring tool that integrates animations to construct and customize lesson workflows. This tool supports lesson creation, assignment, and monitoring of trainee progress and outcomes. Execution and evaluation are facilitated through the Apprentice Studio, which enables immersive engagement with crafted lessons. This environment supports the import and export of lessons, the application of parameter constraints, and the integration of devices to enhance realism in training scenarios. Finally, immersive training offers two modes of operation. Practice mode provides unlimited interactive sessions using 3D or VR technologies. The examination mode delivers structured assessments with predefined parameters, enabling a focused evaluation of trainee performance.

3.1. *Execution of the Craft Simulation Phase*

3.1.1. Analysis

The analysis is supported through the application of ethnographic strategies with on-site fieldwork, where researchers get to know the location where the craft is practiced. This involves spending time in workshops but also communicating with craft masters. At the same time, observing them as they carry out their work is of importance. Interviews are also employed to capture experiential knowledge, focusing on how craft masters describe their methods, the purpose of each tool, and the characteristics of the materials they work with. Another important aspect is observation, where the researcher may engage in the craft themselves, learning from the artisans through hands-on experience.

The result of this review is the definition of a process map that details the sequence of actions involved where each action is divided into subactions that need to be identified and categorized. Actions include subtraction (e.g., carving or cutting), formation (e.g., bending or molding), interlocking (e.g., joining or fastening), and addition (e.g., gluing or applying coatings). The review also identifies the variability in how these actions since different craft masters might use different techniques or tools to achieve similar outcomes.

Equally important is the identification and documentation of the equipment used in the craft, categorizing the tools according to their function, and documenting their specific characteristics, such as size, shape, and material composition. The material properties of the resources used in the craft, such as the type of wood, metal, or clay, must also be documented. Understanding the material's behavior—how it responds to different forces, temperatures, and environmental conditions—is essential for accurately simulating the craft process in later stages of the methodology.

3.1.2. FEM-Based Simulation

Actions performed by humans in the context of crafts involve interactions between tools and materials, which can be challenging to replicate virtually without precise physical modeling of the tools, the materials, and the action itself. In this work, we build virtual representations of such action in the form of a FEM model in Simulia Abaqus, focusing on the simulation of various crafting actions (e.g., subtractive, formative, interlocking, and additive processes). Simpler actions are directly modeled in Blender and imported to Unity3D or directly authored using the Unity3D animation pipeline [32].

FEM simulations are created by authoring actions in Simulia Abaqus. The simulation operates in virtual time and space, where events are discretized into time frames. Objects, tools, and materials are modeled in 3D. The properties of the materials of the objects contributing to a simulation are important for realistic simulations. Properties like density, Young's modulus [141], ductility, and elastic modulus are considered. Young's modulus is a measure of stiffness and is given by

$$E = \frac{\sigma}{\varepsilon}$$

where σ is defined as the stress and ε is defined as the strain.

Tools are categorized by their function, such as cutting, gripping, or driving, with mechanical principles like leverage and torque simulated. Workpieces evolve through various craft actions, and their final form is represented based on the type of action (e.g., subtractive or additive). Forces are applied to the objects by employing linear or rotational (torque) models supported by Abaqus. These are calculated for each finite element involved in the crafting action. Movements of objects are modeled in the three-dimensional space as translations and rotations. Time-dependent actions can be included as part of the simulation process.

The execution in Abaqus of these simulations produces a results database that contains the physical properties of the tools and materials and their changes over time. Furthermore, it contains the rendering of the simulation in 3D. To make 3D simulation data compatible with game engines a transformation should be applied to create animation sequences. To this end, a Python (v3.12) script is used to extract and export the simulation results as sequences of frames. Each frame corresponds to a specific configuration of parameters, such as tool angle or applied force. To simplify the usage of these sequences naming conventions per frame, tools and parameters are used, and lookup tables are created to allow the indexing of results. The indexed data are then processed to create animation clips.

The action is simulated for a broad spectrum of rotational angles to cover a wide range of possible user interactions. Each set of angles in the parameter space is used to perform individual simulations. The same approach is applied to other parameters like tool speed, force applied, or environmental conditions (e.g., temperature). Next, these animation sequences are integrated into lookup tables encapsulated into a reusable component designed for game engine integration, called an Action Animator. An Action Animator contains all the simulation data and the logic to execute craft actions in the form of game engine animations. These include (a) predefined animation frames representing various states based on different parameter configurations (e.g., tool angle or applied force), (b) simplified mesh representations optimized for rendering performance, and (c) transition logic handling the interpolation between different frames and parameter values. Multiple Action Animators can be combined into a package. New Action Animators can be added to the package, ensuring scalability and flexibility.

3.1.3. Game Engine-Based Simulation

In the case where the studied actions do not involve material deformation such as simple mechanical operations, a game engine can be used to produce real-time interactions and kinematic animations with sufficient accuracy. Relevant craft actions are identified by studying the ethnographic review. Once the simulation has been defined, it is executed and the simulation results are acquired. The results are by design compatible with the game engine and available in real-time thus requiring no further processing. In Unity3D [32], the craft tools and objects are represented as 3D models, and their movements are controlled using rigid-body physics. Action Animators for these kinematic operations are executed by the game engine by controlling the motion parameters of the engaged objects. To enhance realism, collision detection, and basic interaction models are incorporated into the game engine. Although the FEM is not needed, the collision between objects (e.g., the glass-blowing rod and a support stand) is still simulated to ensure accurate physical behavior.

3.2. Execution of the Craft Training Phase

In the Craft Training Phase, the results of the simulations are used to synthesize immersive learning experiences following a three-step process.

3.2.1. Authoring

Authoring of immersive experiences is supported by a software called Craft Studio. Its primary functionality is to support designing, configuring, and specifying lessons that simulate real-world crafting tasks within a virtual space. Craft actions in the lesson can be constrained by specific parameters, which serve as restrictions to ensure the accurate performance of actions. Parameters such as tool angle, force, speed, and environmental conditions (e.g., temperature) can be adjusted. Regarding the parameters of execution, Craft Studio provides input and output devices that can be used during the training session. Once the lesson is fully designed a lesson specification is generated. This specification is a set of instructions and configurations that defines the crafting task and serves as a blueprint for executing the training session.

The Craft Studio supports visual diagrams for lesson creation to allow craft masters to map the training process. Lessons can be previewed in real-time, ensuring that all components are correctly linked and functioning as intended. Each educator accesses the Craft Studio using his credentials. This is to organize lessons per educator and allow monitoring of students, assignments, and results. A lesson can be considered as a flow diagram that contains Virtual processes and Virtual actions and their logic for their connectivity. An execution of a lesson is the execution of the flow diagram. Each node of the diagram is assigned some criteria that regard the input parameters and the success criteria. Moving from one node to another requires that these criteria are met. Nodes can be executed in parallel or sequentially or even based on branching points where several parameters are checked. Lessons are composed using Virtual processes and Virtual actions. When imported in a lesson an Action animator will be rendered for each Virtual action using the assigned parameters. A Virtual process is a combination of Virtual actions linked under specific conditions. Virtual actions are imported, while Virtual processes can be both imported and authored in the Craft Studio.

3.2.2. Execution and Evaluation

The execution and evaluation of training courses are supported by a software called Apprentice Studio. Its primary purpose is to provide an interactive, structured environment for craft students to develop, practice, and demonstrate their skills. It provides access to the created lessons designed in Craft Studio and incorporates study and examination modes. In Study Mode, real-time feedback helps students refine their techniques, while the post-examination reports provide detailed insights into areas for improvement. The Examination Mode provides a standardized and objective mechanism for assessing students.

Each lesson corresponds to a specific task or set of tasks represented by a collection of Action Animators and associated lesson parameters. In Study Mode, students interact with the lesson in a guided, hands-on environment. This mode allows students to practice specific craft actions with real-time feedback. During this study, the system tracks student inputs (e.g., tool angles and force applied) and compares them to the predefined constraints set in the lesson specification. Immediate visual and/or auditory feedback is provided to help students adjust and refine their actions, ensuring that they understand the precise execution requirements of the craft.

In Examination Mode, the student transits from practice to formal evaluation. Here, the lesson parameters are used to assess the student's ability to perform the craft task accurately and within the predefined restrictions. The examination mode differs from the study mode in that feedback is withheld during execution, requiring the student to rely on their knowledge and skills developed in practice. Metrics are used to generate a quantitative score, representing the student's proficiency in the craft action being evaluated. After completing an examination, the system provides the student with a detailed report of their performance. The Apprentice Studio's design has been conducted in Figma UI design [142] service and then was imported into Unity3D [143] (see Figure 2). When entering the Apprentice Studio, the splash screen contains the collection of courses assigned to the specific student. Courses are categorized by their completion status.

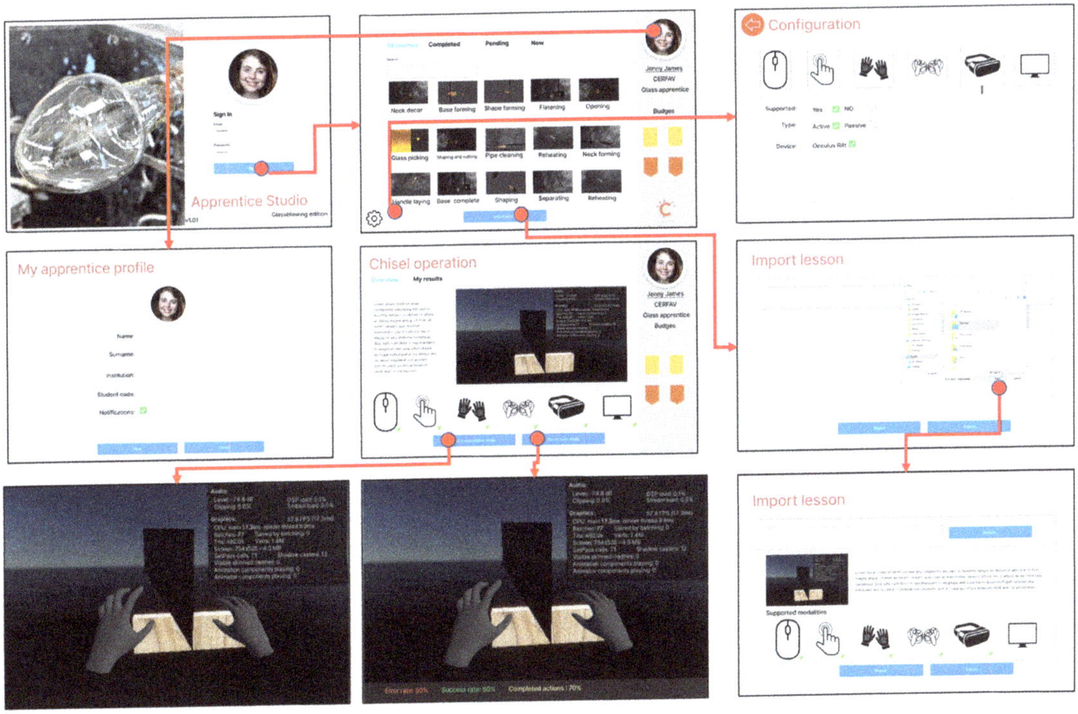

Figure 2. Workflows of Apprentice Studio.

3.2.3. Immersive Training

The final step of the methodology involves adding interactivity through more complicated inputs and outputs in the context of immersive training (Step 3). Regarding inputs, the standard controllers of the Meta Quest 2 are used combined with the possibility of adding custom haptic controllers for specific operations. Regarding outputs complementary to the 3D rendering in a monitor, stereoscopic rendering through the HMD is supported to enhance the immersivity of the training scenarios.

Immersive training allows learners to participate in virtual simulations that mimic real-world craft activities. In these activities, three types of input devices are supported. Keyboard and mice, support the performing of tasks but offer less immersion compared to specialized controllers, but are accessible and familiar, making them suitable for introduction or desktop-based drilling.

Custom tactile controllers are designed to provide physical resistance and force feedback, mimicking the feeling of working with real materials (such as wood resistance when using fleas). These devices are constructed for specific technological actions and provide very realistic feedback aligned with the power experienced in real work. The haptic controller not only tracks accurate movements but also reproduces tactile and force feedback associated with the actual work, providing the highest level of immersion.

Regarding Output devices are essential in providing visual and sensory feedback and improving overall presence and realism in virtual environments. A standard computer monitor provides a basic visual depiction of a virtual space. This is sufficient for keyboard and mouse operation but lacks the depth and field provided by more sophisticated equipment such as VR headsets that completely immerse the user in a 3D environment and perceive the spatial relationship between tools, materials, and hands in real-time. When combined with VR controllers or custom haptic devices, the combination of visual and physical feedback creates a real simulation of the creation of the action.

4. Case Studies

This section presents the implementation of the method with examples from studies on wood carving, and glassblowing for demonstration. In wood carving, we employ FEM-based simulation while in glassblowing we employ game-engine-based simulation.

4.1. Craft Simulation Phase Implementation and Case Studies

4.1.1. Case Study—Analysis

For the Analysis step, an example from the segmentation of an ethnographic recording is presented. This example consists of part of the recording of the craft process and the action under investigation regards creating a woodcarving design using a chisel. The segment concerns an Egocentric camera recording of the second practitioner contributing to the ethnographic analysis and has a length of 11′29. It presents the action initiation and the action iteration to create a horizontal wood carving. The process starts at the work table, where there is a piece of wood clamped into the working bench. The action under investigation regards the creation of a wood trim following the pattern of the object created. The action is performed with a solid tool (a sharp scalpel). The action is segmented to isolate the carving action (see Figure 3). Following the above-mentioned segmentation and documentation process, the ethnographic analysis provides a good understanding and video representation of the craft under investigation.

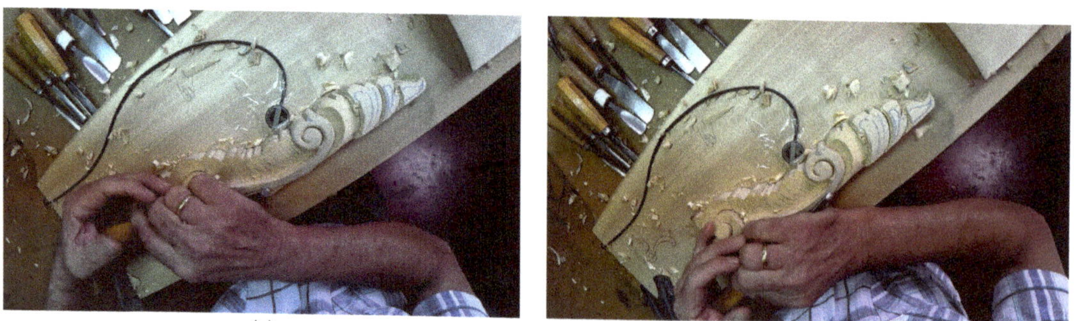

(a) (b)

Figure 3. (**a**) Start pose; (**b**) end pose.

4.1.2. FEM-Based Simulation

The next step involves the transformation of the above-described analysis into a FEM simulation in Simulia Abaqus. This involves defining the geometrical model, material properties, boundary conditions, and the mechanical interaction between objects. The authoring starts by defining the objects involved as 3D geometries. The wood block is typically represented as a rectangular solid and the chisel as a sharp, wedge-shaped tool. The sharpness of the chisel is a critical aspect of the geometry, as it influences the stress concentration at the contact point. Chisel's Geometry is defined as a rigid body with a defined angle of attack. The chisel's cutting edge is modeled with sufficient detail to capture the effects of material cutting. Wood Block's Geometry is modeled as a deformable solid, where the dimensions of the block are defined to allow enough space for the chisel to penetrate and interact with the wood. Wood is treated as an anisotropic material and its mechanical properties vary to simulate the natural grain structure of wood. The material model used for wood includes (a) Density which determines the mass and inertia of the wood, (b) Stiffness of the wood and how it reacts to tensile and compressive forces, (c) Plasticity and Damage Models for simulating the cutting process since the wood undergoes plastic deformation, and (d) Friction between the chisel and wood. The chisel is treated as a rigid body in this context, meaning it does not deform under the applied forces. Since wood is anisotropic, its stress–strain behavior is represented using a compliance matrix (Hooke's Law for Anisotropic Materials [144]):

$$\sigma = C\varepsilon$$

σ is the stress vector, ε is the strain vector, and C is the anisotropic stiffness matrix, which depends on the elastic properties in different grain directions. A fine mesh is applied to the surface where the chisel will contact, ensuring accurate simulation of local deformations. The angle of the chisel's insertion and rotation serves as the variable of interest. The force applied by the chisel (F_c) is decomposed into normal and tangential components due to the cutting angle (θ):

$$F_n = F_c cos(\theta),\ F_t = F_c sin(\theta)$$

where F_n is the normal force responsible for indentation, and F_t is the tangential force responsible for material removal. The Contact Pressure Between the Chisel and Wood is given by

$$p = \frac{F_n}{A}$$

where A is the contact area, which depends on the penetration depth and chisel edge geometry. The material failure is modeled using a yield criterion, such as the Tsai–Wu failure criterion [145] for anisotropic materials:

$$F_1\sigma_1 + F_2\sigma_2 + F_{11}{\sigma_1}^2 + F_{22}{\sigma_2}^2 + F_{12}\sigma_1\sigma_2 = 1$$

where σ_1 and σ_2 are principal stresses in the wood grain directions, and F_1, F_2, F_{11}, F_{22}, F_{12} are material-dependent coefficients. The frictional force (F_f) Between Chisel and Wood follows Coulomb's friction law [146]:

$$F_f = \mu F_n$$

where μ is the coefficient of friction, determining the resistance during cutting. Energy Dissipation Due to Cutting is expressed as

$$W = \int F_c d_x$$

where dx is the incremental displacement of the chisel. Deformation and Strain Energy (U) stored in the deformable wood block is given by

$$U = \frac{1}{2}\int_v \sigma : \varepsilon\, dV$$

where V is the volume of the wood block.

Boundary conditions and contact interactions are defined based on the above considerations. The wood block is constrained to prevent movement, simulating the effect of clamping. The chisel is given a prescribed motion, typically a downward or rotational force, to simulate the cutting action. The chisel's motion is modeled through the application of a displacement-controlled load or a force-controlled load, depending on the specific scenario being simulated. In a displacement-controlled simulation, the chisel is moved at a predefined speed into the wood, while in a force-controlled simulation, a specified force allows the chisel to move based on the resistance of the wood.

The simulation is executed in a series of steps each of which is computed using a dynamic solver in Abaqus. Once the simulation is complete, the results are processed to analyze the behavior of the wood under the action of the chisel. The key outputs include (a) Stress and Strain Distribution visualizing the areas of maximum stress in the wood, (b) Deformation visualizing the degree to which the wood deforms as the chisel penetrates, indicating how efficiently the tool cuts into the material, and (c) Material Damage and Failure representing areas where the wood has exceeded its failure criteria are identified, showing the material removal process (for results, see Figure 4). A detailed description of the setup of the simulation is presented in Table 1.

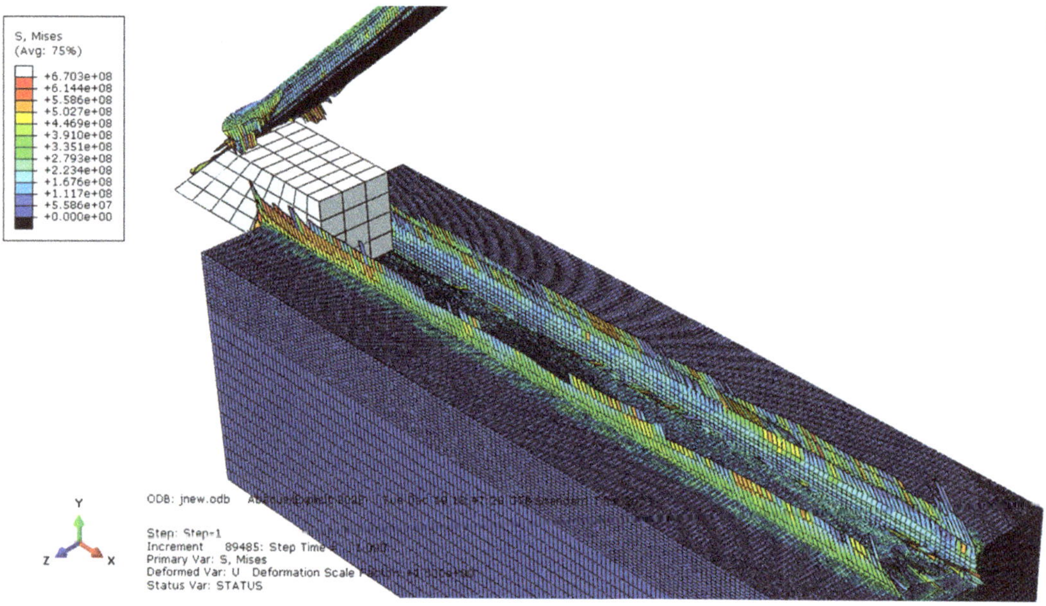

Figure 4. Chisel action simulation.

Table 1. Simulation setup and execution parameters.

Chisel (Rigid)	Type: 3D—Rigid part Total number of elements: 136 linear quadrilateral elements of type R3D4 Approximate global size = 0.0003 Area centroid of shell faces: 0.0306, -3.37×10^{-4}, 5.00×10^{-4}
Wood Block (Timber)	Type: 3D solid—Deformable part, 742,500 linear hexahedral elements of type C3D8R Approximate global size = 0.0007 Volume: 9.00×10^{-8} m^3 Volume centroid: 0.0643, −0.0359, 0.00150 Mass: 2.43×10^{-4} Center of mass: 0.0643, −0.0359, 0.00150 Density of timber = 650 kg/m^3

Table 1. *Cont.*

Simulation properties	Step: In the simulator, we use a dynamic explicit time step with a duration of 1 s. Interaction: In the simulator, we use a surface-to-surface interaction to model the contact between the chisel and the block. The coefficient of friction (μ) between the rigid part and the wooden block is approximately 0.4. Duration of the simulation: 6 h, 52 min, and 27 s.

To address the need for variability in the presentation of simulated crafting actions, we precompute a set of FEM simulations using a range of predefined parameters. To do so we have to define a collection of input files for the Simulia Abaqus, each one containing the specific parameters that will be used for the execution of the simulation. This will allow us to batch-process these files to generate a collection of result databases. Each result database (odb file) contains the results of the FEM simulation for the specific parameters. The exporting process is automated through a Python script that extracts the data related to displacements, forces, and material states at each node or element in the finite element mesh.

Then, to achieve photorealism the frame sequences are imported into Blender for animation creation. Initially, the exported geometry and frame sequences are loaded into Blender which allows control of the animation pipeline. In Blender, photorealistic textures, lighting, and materials for the animated scene can be edited. Importing is supported by a Blender plugin called Stop-motion-OBJ [147]. Imported animations contain only the meshes for the objects (see Figure 5a) and thus Blender can be employed to define other parameters of the mesh object that affect their appearance. Using Blender's timeline, the geometry at each frame step is aligned according to the simulation results, creating a continuous animation sequence. Blender's animation tools are used to refine the motion, ensuring that the results from the FEM simulation appear smooth and realistic. High-resolution textures are applied to the 3D models to simulate the surface details (see Figure 5b). Blender's UV mapping tools are used to map 2D texture images accurately. The Blender animations are in turn exported to Unity [32] using a .fbx or .glTF format that preserves geometry, animation sequences, and material properties. An Animator Controller is used to manage and organize the animations structured into animation libraries. A Prefab that packs all the animations together is created and a script handles the logic of selecting the most appropriate animation based on input parameters. The script takes input parameters such as chisel angle, cutting speed, or force application and maps parameters to the corresponding animation in the lookup table. In Unity, a real-time lighting system, including global illumination and real-time shadows, is configured to provide dynamic lighting.

4.1.3. Game Engine-Based Simulation

In the case of game-engine-based simulation, these occur in the form of animation sequences that alter the appearance of game objects. Their variations are calculated by the game engine and relate to the user input. In this work, main kinetic animations are employed while this does not exclude the possibility of having more complex physics-based animations (e.g., using the PhysX engine [148]). An example of such animations could involve, for example, gravity to simulate that a tool is dropped during an action due to a mistake by the apprentice. Figure 6 presents some examples of animations.

4.2. Craft Training Phase Implementation and Case Studies

4.2.1. Authoring

The authoring of training materials occurs in the implemented version of the Craft Studio. The implementation was conducted in Unity3D and it follows the same principles as the design presented earlier. An example is presented in Figure 7.

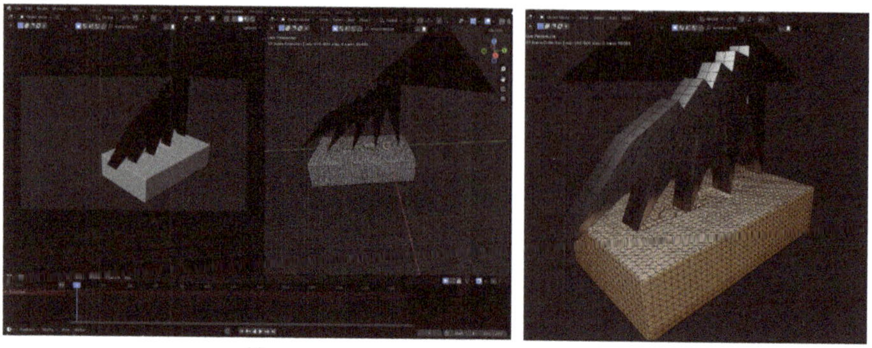

(**a**) (**b**)

Figure 5. (**a**) Animating frame sequences in Blender; (**b**) Enhancing enhancing rendering in Blender.

Figure 6. Game engine-based simulation for the glassblowing use case.

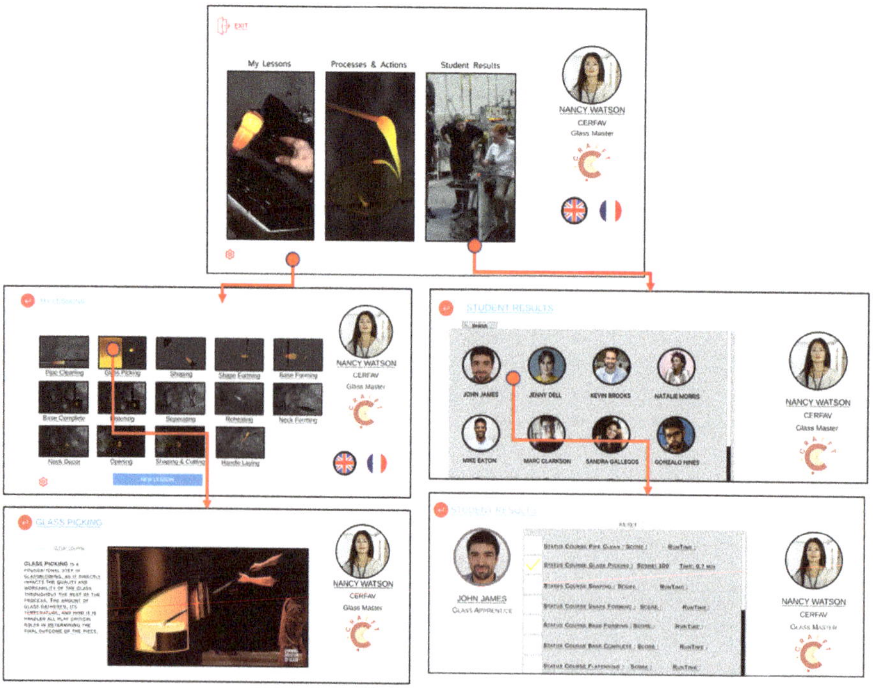

Figure 7. Craft studio workflow.

4.2.2. Execution and Validation

A lesson can be executed either in practice or in exam mode. Practice mode allows for infinite iterations for training while examination mode allows for only one iteration. The results of the examination mode can be exported and reported to the craft master. The Apprentice Studio workflow before the initiation of a training or examination session is presented in Figure 8.

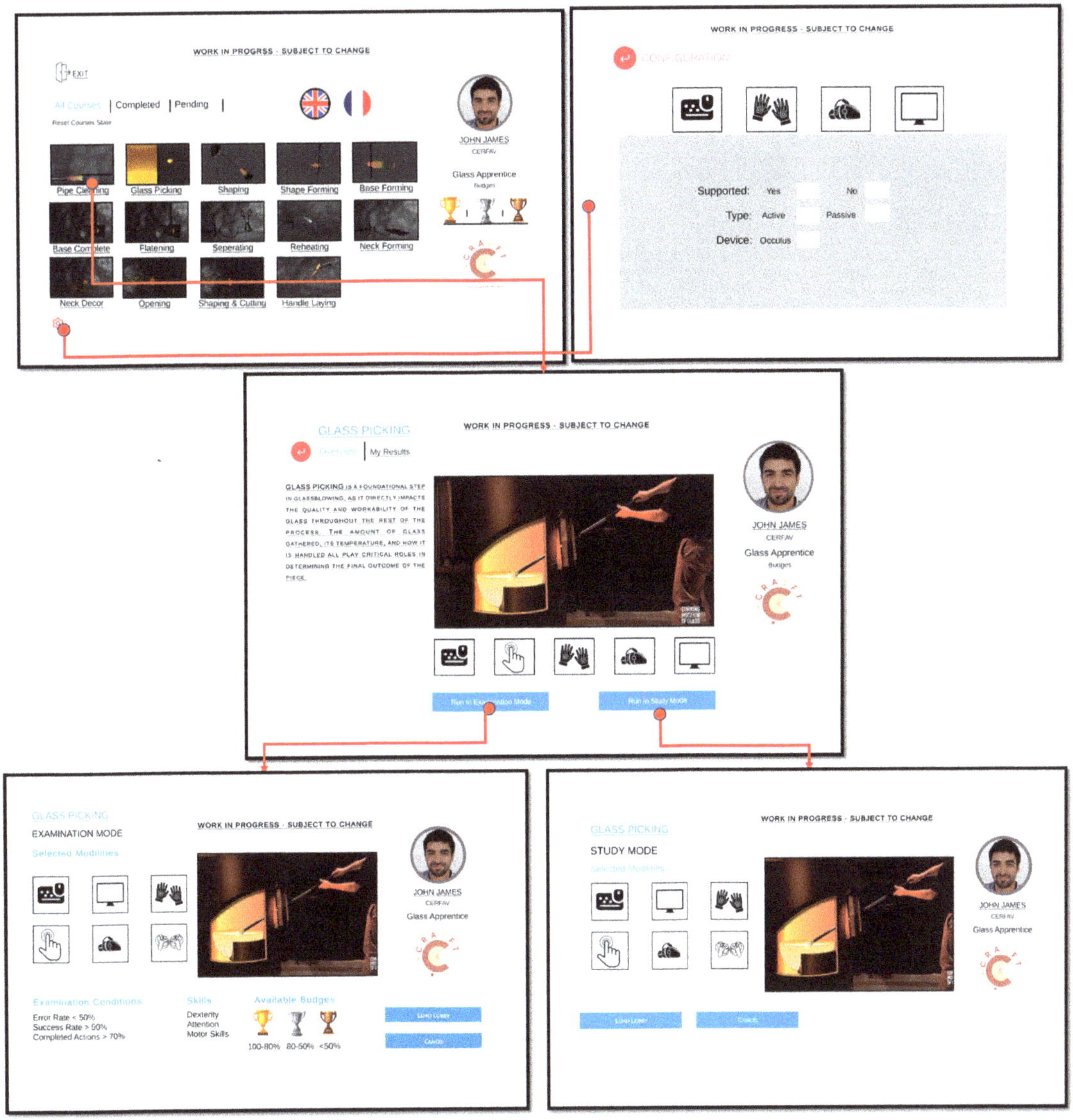

Figure 8. Apprentice Studio workflow example.

4.2.3. Immersive Training

Immersive training occurs by executing a training scenario. Each execution is bound to the specific user to collect and record training data and evaluate success criteria. Two examples are presented. The first example regards solely a training course created using game engine-based animations and the second one is implemented using FEM-based simulation. In the first case, we are using the scenario of a glassblowing workshop. The task that the user should complete is to gather molten glass from the Glass Oven. To do so, the task is split into three different operations. The first operation regards locating and picking the glassblowing rod. The second action regards opening the oven. In this case, a plain interface is used without the interaction with VR controllers then a locate and keyboard click metaphor is used. In the case where VR controllers are used, a grab and move gesture is required. The same stands for the gathering process where in the case of VR this happens by aligning the glassblowing rod with the furnace and then rotating the controller. In the simplified version, key shortcuts are used for aligning the rod and for the initiation of the rotation functionality. Keyframes are presented in Figure 9.

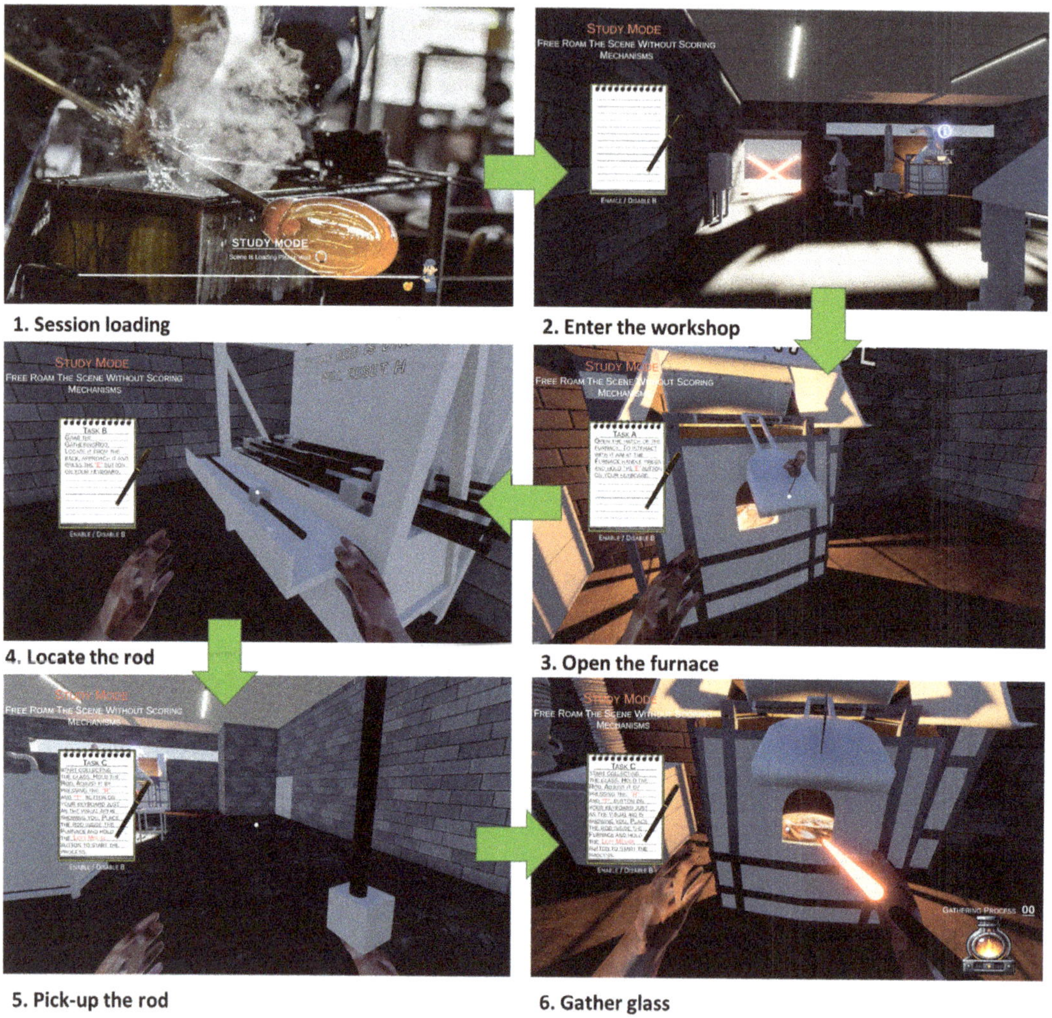

Figure 9. Glass picking training—demo.

The second example regards the chisel use case using data stemming from the FEM simulation. The user locates the woodworking bench and from there the chisel. Then, a pose for the chisel is provided by the system. The user should grab and align the chisel with the provided pose. The system provides feedback regarding the successful alignment. When the chisel is aligned the user can proceed with the action. Two variations in interaction metaphors are demonstrated, the first is VR interaction metaphor while the second is the point-and-click metaphor. The process as implemented in VR is presented in Figure 10.

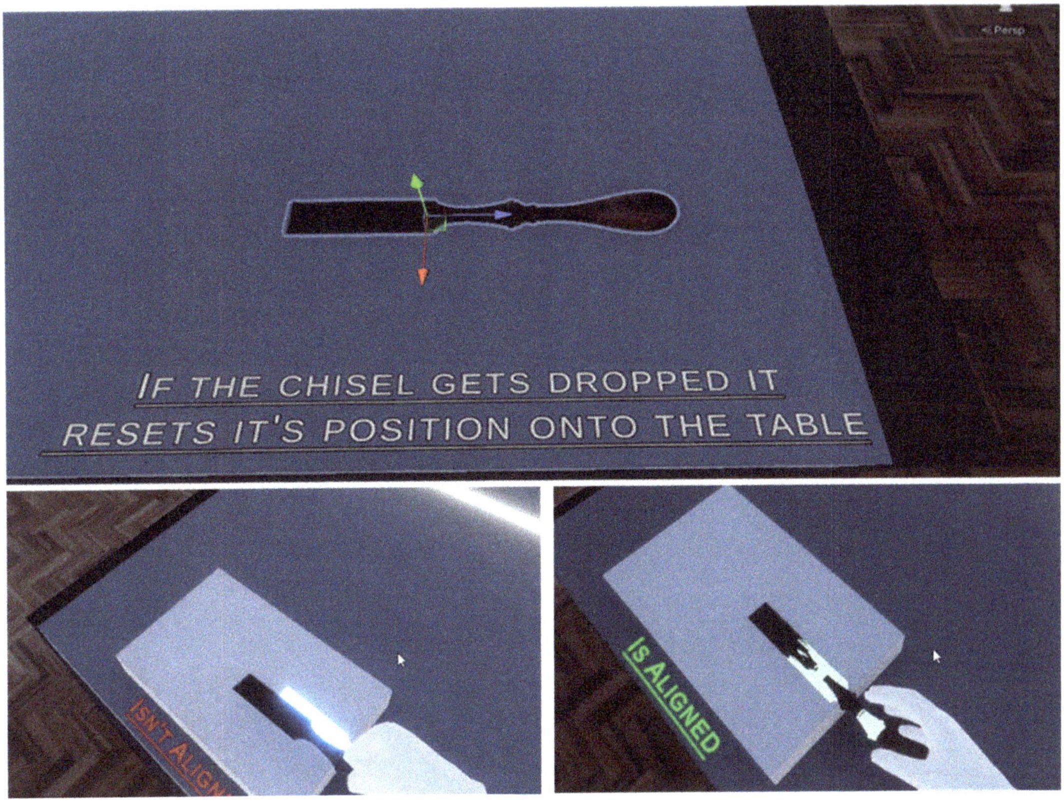

Figure 10. Chisel carving interactive training—VR version.

Figure 11 shows a simplified variation in the process that uses the point-and-click metaphor. The user can select the translation and rotation of the chisel using the mouse. The usability of this metaphor is that it supports the easy and cost-effective familiarization of the user with a specific action even from home without the need to have specialized equipment. In the training mode, the system provides poses in the form of a hologram of the chisel within the screen (transparent green) and the user should manipulate the tool to match the provided poses.

4.3. Pedagogical Value

The presented methodology provides a systematic approach to support immersive learning experiences of enhanced educational value by adhering to the principles of the Cognitive Load Theory [149]. FEM based simulations and their application is a challenging subject to master. By empowering training activities with the results of the simulation methods [150–153] we are capable of training on the results without having to know the underlined principles of simulation modelling. More specifically the targeted educational courses supported by this research work address the Split-Attention Effect, by providing self-contained learning scenarios that do not overload learners. Having immersive training as another channel in the context of a learning method supports multiple sensory channels and thus enhances comprehension and retention. Furthermore, using the Expertise Reversal Effect basic eLearning content is for novice users while immersive content is for more experienced ones supporting an entirely new level of learning. Our methodology for this is supported by the combination of e-learning facilities combined with immersive training tools [154].

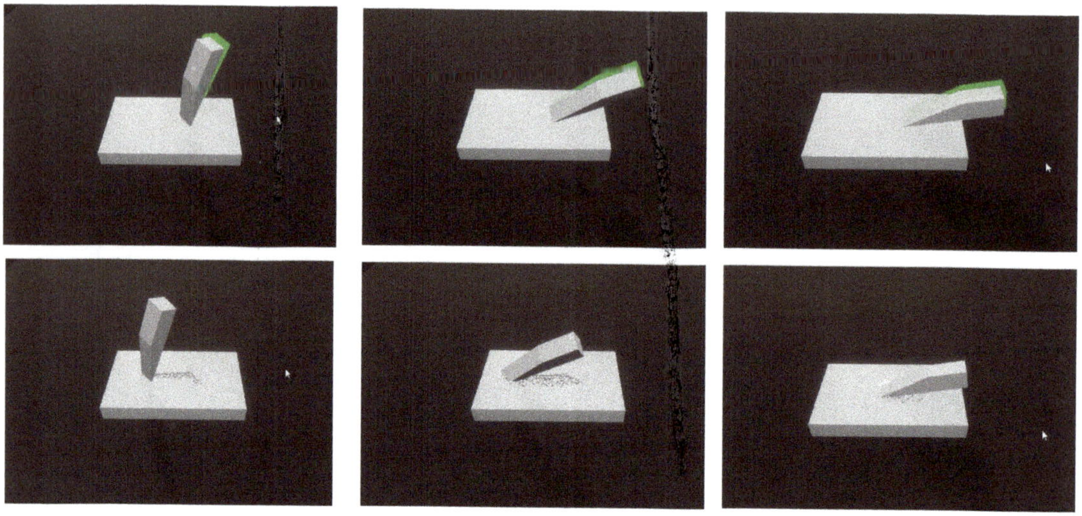

Figure 11. Chisel carving interactive training—desktop, point and click version.

5. Validation and Evaluation Method and Results

The proposed methodology supports a multi-layered approach towards the immersive training on craft processes empowered by FEM-based and game engine-based simulations. The evaluation and validation of such a multi-layer approach cannot be conducted on a single level of the methodology since different levels represent only a fragment of the methodology. Thus, to provide a holistic evaluation and validation of this research work several methods are employed, each best suited for each level of the proposed methodology and each stage of the development of the use cases.

5.1. Technical Validation

5.1.1. Using FEM-Based Simulation for Craft Actions

A significant part of the proposed methodology is supported through the FEM-based simulation of crafting actions. To justify the wider applicability of the approach, we extend the presentation of FEM-based simulations to a plethora of basic action simulations that are conducted to build the proposed simulation framework. In the next figure, we present an action simulation conducted in Simulia Abaqus that covers a wide range of craft actions including cutting, curving, turning, splitting, compressing, drilling, forming, and molding. This is just a subset of the proposed framework's fundamental action but succeeds in demonstrating the wide applicability of the presented methodology. All these actions are supported by the presented methodology and are fully compatible with the proposed toolchain (see Figure 12).

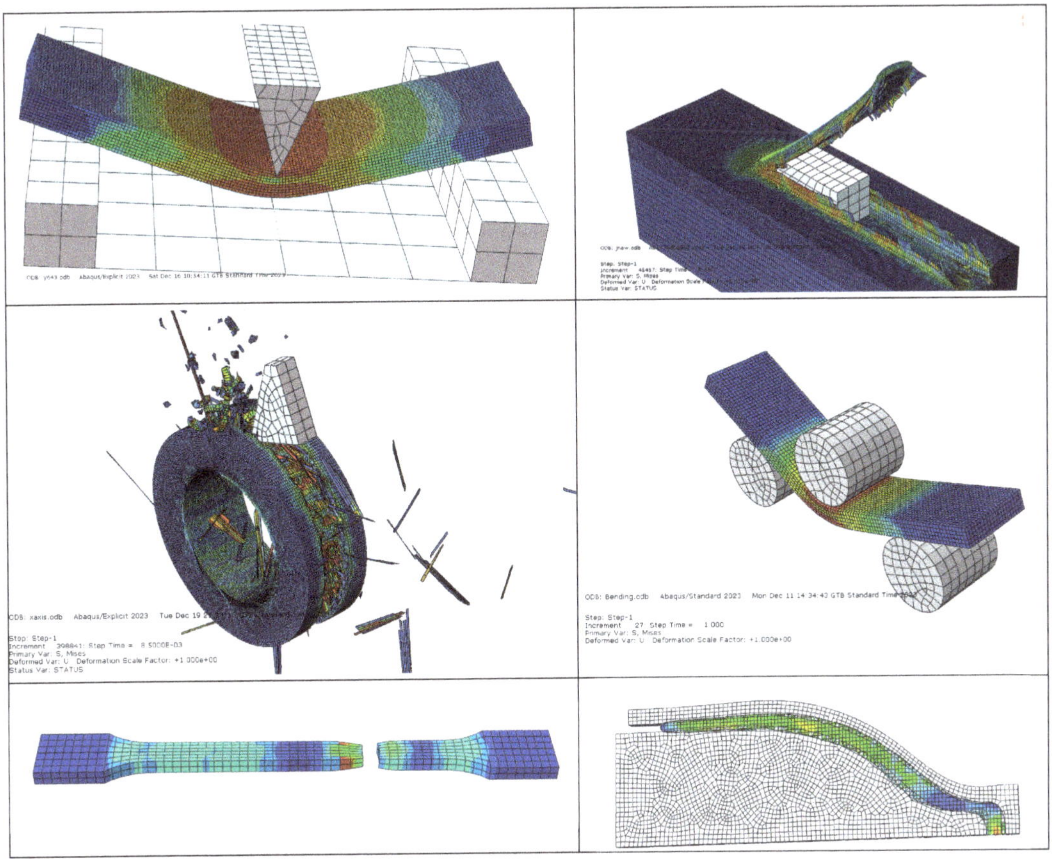

Figure 12. Simulating a wide range of craft action in Simulia.

5.1.2. Exporting Frame Sequences Using the Proposed Framework

To validate the exporting facilities offered by the proposed framework, all the presented FEM-based simulations were exported using the facilities provided by this research work. The result was more than 10 k obj files, organized into frame sequences and categorized using lookup tables. The outputs of this process were used for conducting the validation of the photorealistic rendering of crafting actions.

5.1.3. Photorealistic Rendering of Craft Actions

Demonstrating the application of the proposed methodology to the simulation results of the previous section supports the wide applicability of realistic animation of FEM simulations as presented in Figure 13.

Figure 13. Photorealistic rendering of crafting actions.

5.1.4. Validation of Game Engine-Based Animation

As presented in the proposed methodology, an alternative to FEM-based simulation is the production of animations using the animation capabilities provided by game engines. This is proposed as a workaround in cases where animations do not require the enhanced realism provided by the FEM-based approach or in cases where animations represent simple actions that do not require such an approach. The validation of the feasibility of providing such game engine animation is carried out in this research work through the production of animation for further craft actions directly in the game engine. Examples of such animations for glass formation, wood turning, and clay forming are presented in Figure 14.

Figure 14. Animations for glass formation, wood turning and clay forming.

5.1.5. Equipment Used in Validation

For all the technical experiments in Simulia Abaqus, a desktop computer was used with the following specifications: Intel i7-14700F processor (equipment sourced in Heraklion, Greece), 32 GB RAM, 1 TB M.2 SSD, 2 TB 7200 HDD, NVIDIA RTX 5080 16 GB, and Windows 11 professional operating system. Unity3D and Blender were operated using the same main configuration except for the GPU which was a GeForce RTX 4060 8 GB.

5.2. Expert-Based Evaluation

The evaluation of prototypes was conducted using expert-based approaches by a usability expert and a craft master. Expert-based evaluation is a commonly used method in the HCI field [155]. In cognitive walkthroughs, the evaluator examines the working or non-working prototype, through the eyes of the user, performing typical tasks and identifying areas in the design or the functionality that could potentially cause confusion or user errors [156]. Specifically, in cognitive walkthroughs, the evaluator has a set of questions in mind [157]. Heuristics analysis involves the inspection against a set of 10 usability guidelines [158]. For this study, one usability expert was involved in evaluating the Apprentice Studio and Craft Studio. Furthermore, three craft experts were employed to judge the applicability and perceived usefulness of these tools and improve the readiness of apprentices who exercised using the immersive training toolkit.

5.2.1. Heuristic Evaluation of Apprentice Studio by a Usability Expert

In this section, comments provided by the Usability Expert during the inspection of Apprentice Studio is provided. For the economy of space in our example, only one example per guideline is presented in Table 2.

Table 2. Sample results—heuristic evaluation of Apprentice Studio.

Guideline	Positive	Issue	Suggestion
1. Visibility of System Status	A progress bar is displayed during simulation loading, keeping users informed.	No feedback is provided (if the action was successful) when saving a draft lesson.	Add a confirmation message like "Draft saved successfully".
2. Match Between System and the Real World	Uses real-world terminology, like "blowpipe" and "punty rod", familiar to glassblowers.	Some terms, like "node selection", are technical and not intuitive to craft trainees.	Replace with "Select Tool Part" for better clarity.
3. User Control and Freedom	Users can undo steps during VR tool manipulation.	No "Back" in some menus, forcing users to restart tasks.	Add a persistent "Back" button.
4. Consistency and Standards	Menu layouts are consistent across sections, reducing cognitive load.	Different terminology for similar actions, e.g., "Save Progress" and "Store Progress".	Standardize terminology across all sections.
5. Error Prevention	Prevents users from starting simulations without completing the initial setup.	No warning appears if the user inputs an invalid material property.	Add validation checks with error messages for invalid input.
6. Recognition Rather Than Recall	Frequently used tools are displayed in a toolbar for quick access.	Users must remember shortcut commands for advanced operations.	Provide a visible list of shortcuts in the UI.
7. Flexibility and Efficiency of Use	Advanced users can customize their interface to optimize workflow.	Novices lack a guided walkthrough for their first interaction.	Introduce an onboarding tutorial.
8. Esthetic and Minimalist Design	Clean design with minimal distractions during VR sessions.	Some menus are cluttered with rarely used options.	Hide advanced settings in expandable sections.
9. Help Users Recognize, Diagnose, and Recover from Errors	Provides clear error messages, such as "Invalid Tool Selection".	references during simulation do not suggest corrective actions.	Include step-by-step guidance to resolve issues.
10. Help and Documentation	Includes a searchable help guide.	No embedded tooltips for specific features.	Add context-sensitive tooltips for easier learning.

5.2.2. Heuristic Evaluation of Craft Studio by a Usability Expert

In this section, an exemplary set of comments provided by the Usability Expert during the inspection of the prototype of the Apprentice Studio is provided following the 10 usability guidelines provided above. For the economy of space in our example, only one example per guideline is presented in Table 3.

Table 3. Sample results set for the heuristic evaluation of Craft Studio.

Guideline	Positive	Issue	Suggestion
1. Visibility of System Status	Notifications appear when an action, like assigning a lesson, is completed.	Lack of real-time updates when students submit their work.	Include a dashboard widget to notify educators of new submissions.
2. Match Between System and the Real World	Lessons mimic traditional workflows, aligning with educators' expectations.	Icons for tools (e.g., a wrench for settings) do not always align with their function.	Use universally recognized symbols.
3. User Control and Freedom	Educators can delete or reassign lessons freely.	Lack of confirmation prompts for critical actions.	Add a confirmation dialog for sensitive operations.
4. Consistency and Standards	Same design patterns for creating and assigning lessons.	Inconsistent button colors for similar actions.	Harmonize color schemes for identical actions.
5. Error Prevention	Alerts users before overwriting existing lessons.	Educators can accidentally assign lessons incorrectly.	Include a confirmation step to verify the class.
6. Recognition Rather Than Recall	Educators can browse pre-designed lesson templates.	Previous lesson drafts are not accessible for reuse.	Include a "Recent Drafts" section.
7. Flexibility and Efficiency of Use	Educators can use to make multiple student assignments.	Lack of keyboard shortcuts for common actions.	Add shortcuts for tasks like "Create Lesson".
8. Esthetic and Minimalist Design	Uses a straightforward interface for assigning lessons.	Overuse of different font styles can overwhelm users.	Streamline fonts for a cohesive design.

Table 3. *Cont.*

Guideline	Positive	Issue	Suggestion
9. Help Users Recognize, Diagnose, and Recover from Errors	Notifications explain why an assignment failed (e.g., "Student list not selected").	Error messages sometimes lack specificity (e.g., "Input error").	Make error messages more detailed.
10. Help and Documentation	Offers video tutorials for educators.	Limited guidance on troubleshooting technical issues.	Expand help with a troubleshooting section.

5.2.3. Result of Expert-Based Evaluation from Craft Expert

Three craft experts evaluated the proposed tools, focusing on their applicability within CERFAV's curriculum, perceived usefulness, and impact on apprentice readiness. This preliminary evaluation, conducted before user-based testing, involved a remote demonstration session followed by an open discussion.

Applicability to CERFAV Curriculum: Experts found the tools aligned with CERFAV's learning objectives, particularly in simulating material properties and tool use. The tools were seen as bridging the gap between theory and practice, though concerns were raised about integrating them into an already dense curriculum. One expert noted, "While promising, the onboarding process for educators might require additional training time to achieve full integration". They also suggested customization options for advanced techniques like glass shaping and color application.

Perceived Usefulness: Experts praised the ability to visualize crafting processes in 3D and VR. One participant remarked, "It is remarkable to see how accurately the tools replicate the glassblowing process, especially for understanding the effect of heat and rotation on the material". They agreed that the tools would benefit novice learners, reducing intimidation when transitioning to hands-on practice. A recommendation was made to add guided tutorials for specific techniques like gathering molten glass.

Readiness Levels: Experts anticipated improved readiness among apprentices using the immersive tools before workshop activities. One expert stated, "Students who will practice in VR are likely to show a better understanding of tool handling and process sequences, reducing their hesitations in the physical workshop". They believed the tools would familiarize apprentices with materials and procedures, reducing cognitive load. However, some questioned how well VR training translates to the tactile nuances of working with molten glass.

General Observations: Experts appreciated the potential for remote training, especially when workshop access is limited. While they found the tools easy to navigate, they suggested improving responsiveness and realism in VR tool manipulation. A recommendation was made to enhance haptic feedback for more authentic resistance and interactions.

Conclusion: Experts were optimistic about the tools' potential to enhance craft education but emphasized the need for curriculum-specific refinements, better onboarding for educators, and increased realism. These insights will inform future improvements and user-based evaluations.

5.3. User-Based Evaluation

In this work, we have applied the preliminary user-based evaluation method on a sample of the application suitable for use in the glassblowing training case involving domain experts from CERFAV who were responsible for evaluating with students of their training program. The design of the experiment involved the introduction of a training subject namely "Picking Glass from the Furnace" to a group of ten students using the implementation of the scenario in the Apprentice Studio. CERFAV is a training institution that receives apprentices of various ages depending on the type of training activity they participate. We tried to have a representative sample from all age groups with a distribution of five out of ten of our students in the age group of 18–22, three in the age group 22–25 and two in the group 25–30.

Then, after the introductions, the students were introduced to the same scenario in the workshop. Two questionnaires were created, one to collect feedback from the students and another to collect feedback from the glass masters. The first target was to assess whether the students found the introductory sessions that they had using the apprentice studio sufficient for moving to the introduction at the workshop and whether they found difficulties using or understanding the tools. The second regards the assessment from the glass masters concerning their students' level of preparation using digital tools. In the questionnaire, we used a climax from one to five with one being the smallest and five the highest grade. Grade numbers are accompanied by a literal that provides further assistance to grading such as not sufficient (1), moderately sufficient (3), very sufficient (5), etc. The structure of the questionnaire for students and teachers is presented in Tables 4 and 5, respectively. Feedback from glass educators was also collected via informal interviews with after the completion of the evaluation. Questionnaires were sent back for further analysis. Regarding the sample of educators, three out of five were in the age group of 30–40 while two out of five were more experienced glass blowers in the age group 40–50.

5.3.1. Equipment Used in Evaluation

Regarding the equipment used for the evaluation, this mostly involved mainstream computing equipment. Our setup was two personal computers with an Intel i7 10th generation processor, 16 GB RAM, 512 GB SSD, an NVIDIA 1050 graphics card, and two 24-inch monitors. These specifications were more than adequate for the requirements of the experiment. For the 3D part, the same equipment was used. For the VR part of the evaluation, the two Meta Quest 2 devices were used together with two sets of controllers. The VR training experiences were loaded onto the internal storage of the device and then ran in standalone mode.

Table 4. Structure of the questionnaire for students.

#	Question	Type
Section 1—Orientation		
1.1	On a scale of one to five, please provide a rating on computer usage expertise.	(1–5)
1.2	Do you own a smartphone?	(Y/N)
1.3	Do you access the internet from a phone or computer?	(Y/N)
1.4	If yes, are you using the internet for information and learning about your craft?	(Y/N)
1.5	Is this your first time using digital tools for Craft Education?	(Y/N)
1.5.1	If not, please describe the tools you have used in the past.	Text
Section 2—Apprentice Studio		
2.1	How was your first experience with Apprentice Studio?	(1–5)
2.2	Did you find it easy to browse through the facilities of Apprentice Studio?	(1–5)
2.3	Were all the information and functions easy to locate and understand?	(1–5)
2.4	Did you experience any problems performing actions in Apprentice Studio?	(1–5)
2.5	Did you locate any mismatches in terminology used in class with that of Apprentice Studio?	(1–5)
2.6	Overall, are you happy with what you have experienced using Apprentice Studio?	(1–5)
2.7	Are there any comments you would like to share to help improve Apprentice studio?	Text

Table 4. *Cont.*

#	Question	Type
Section 3—Interaction and Immersion		
3.1	Please rate your 3D experience (computer screen and mouse)	(1–5)
3.1.1	- rate your experience on navigating in the VR environment	(1–5)
3.1.2	- rate your experience in locating information in the VR environment	(1–5)
3.1.3	- rate your experience in locating and grabbing tools	(1–5)
3.1.4	- rate your experience with the manipulation of tools	(1–5)
3.1.5	- rate the level of immersion you achieved in the virtual world in 3D	(1–5)
3.2	Provide comments and suggestions on your 3D experience	Text
3.3	Please rate your overall VR experience	(1–5)
3.3.1	- rate your experience on navigating in the VR environment	(1–5)
3.3.2	- rate your experience in locating information in the VR environment	(1–5)
3.3.3	- rate your experience in locating and grabbing tools	(1–5)
3.3.4	- rate your experience with the manipulation of tools	(1–5)
3.3.5	- rate the level of immersion you achieved in the virtual world in 3D	(1–5)
3.4	Provide comments and suggestions on your VR experience	Text
3.5	Are there any other comments you would like to share?	Text

Table 5. Structure of the questionnaire for teachers.

#	Question	Type
Section 1—Orientation		
1.1	On a scale of one to five, please provide a rating on computer usage expertise.	(1–5)
1.2	Do you own a smartphone?	(Y/N)
1.3	Do you access the internet from a phone or computer?	(Y/N)
1.4	If yes, are you using the internet for information and learning about your craft?	(Y/N)
1.5	For how long have you been educating/training students in the Glassblowing craft?	(Y/N)
1.6	Is this your first time using digital tools for Craft Education?	(Y/N)
1.6.1	- if not, please describe the tools you have used in the past.	Text
Section 2—Craft Studio		
2.1	How was your first experience with Craft Studio? (1–5)	(1–5)
2.2	Did you find it easy to browse through the facilities of the Craft Studio (1–5)	(1–5)
2.3	Were all the information and functions easy to locate and understand? (1–5)	(1–5)
2.4	Did you experience any problems performing actions in the Craft Studio (1–5)	(1–5)
2.5	Did you locate any mismatches in the terminology used in class with that of the Craft Studio? (1–5)	(1–5)
2.6	Did you find it easy to administer your lessons and assign students?	
2.7	Did you find it easy to author simple lessons in the Craft Studio?	
2.8	Did you find it easy to assign lessons to students?	
Section 3—Student Observation		
3.1	Judge the attitude of the students towards the integration of digital technologies in craft training.	(1–5)
3.2	Judge the attitude of your colleagues towards the integration of digital technologies in training.	(1–5)
3.3	Based on your expertise, judge the technologies provided in terms of	
3.3.1	- Efficiency 3.3.3 - Understandability 3.3.5 - Accessibility	(1–5)
3.3.2	- Learnability 3.3.4 - Scalability	(1–5)
3.4	Rate the improvement achieved in students' understanding of basic concepts.	(1–5)
3.5	Rate the improvement in the readiness of students moving from digital to the physical workshop.	(1–5)

5.3.2. Students' Evaluation Results

Section 1: Orientation: Regarding Q1.1 (Computer Usage Expertise), the mean rating was 3.6, with a distribution of two students rating themselves as "1" (novice), three as "3", (moderate), and five as "5" (expert). While half of the students are proficient in computer usage, 20% lack digital literacy, which may affect their ability to use digital tools effectively. Regarding smartphone ownership, in Q1.2 nine students own a smartphone, and one does not. Thus, the majority of students have access to mobile technology, an advantage for digital tool integration. Q1.3 and Q1.4 on Internet Usage showed that all nine smartphone owners accessed the internet and seven of them declared that they were using it for craft learning. Regarding the usage of Digital tools for Craft Education (Q1.5), six students indicated this was their first time, and four had prior experience. Students with prior expertise responded in Q1.5.1 that the previous tools they were familiar with were YouTube, online forums, and video tutorials. One of them mentioned using Computer Aided Design and 3D modeling software for design visualization.

Section 2: Apprentice Studio: Regarding the first acquaintance with Apprentice Studio in Q2.1., it received a mean rating of 4.3 with six students providing a rating of "4", and four students providing a rating of "5". Initial impressions of the Apprentice Studio were very positive. In Q2.2 and Q2.3 that rate the ease of browsing, it received a mean rating of 3.9, with most of the users finding navigation relatively intuitive, but some encountered minor difficulties which were also noted by the experiment operators recording their observations. Regarding problems when performing actions measured through Q2.4 and Q2.5, it received a mean rating of 2.7 with a few participants reporting specific challenges in performing actions, likely due to unfamiliarity with the platform and with minor interface design issues that were spotted by the experiment observatory. Finally, on overall satisfaction it received a mean rating of 4.5, despite the minor usability issues, satisfaction with the overall experience was high.

Free text comments included suggestions for clearer labels on buttons and a request for a tutorial or guide for first-time users. Overall, there was positive feedback on the intuitive design of major features. An exemplary quote follows: "The tool is intuitive, but it took me some time to understand since there were minor issues with the terminology. Further analysis of the craft to align the terminology would be helpful".

Section 3: Interaction and Immersion: Regarding 3D experience, the software received a mean rating on Navigation: 4.0, Locating information: 3.8, Locating tools: 3.6, Manipulating tools: 3.5, and Immersion: 3. Overall, 3D interaction via screen and mouse was well-received, but locating and manipulating tools require refinement. Furthermore, as expected, the users reported medium immersion. Indicative free text comments on the 3D Experience: "It was easy to navigate but harder to grab tools", "The 3D view is clear, but rotating objects felt a bit clunky".

Regarding the VR experience, the software received a mean rating of Navigation: 4.1, Locating information: 4, Locating tools: 4.1, Manipulating tools: 3.6, and Immersion: 4.6. VR outperformed 3D in navigation and immersion while receiving almost common ratings on tool manipulation. Overall based on the observations in 3D users had issues with the mapping of mouse action in the 3D environment while in VR issues related to getting to know how to use the VR controllers. Indicative free text comments on the VR Experience: "Navigating in VR felt very natural", "Grabbing tools in VR was better than in 3D, but there is room for improvement in precision". The results are graphically visualized in Figure 15.

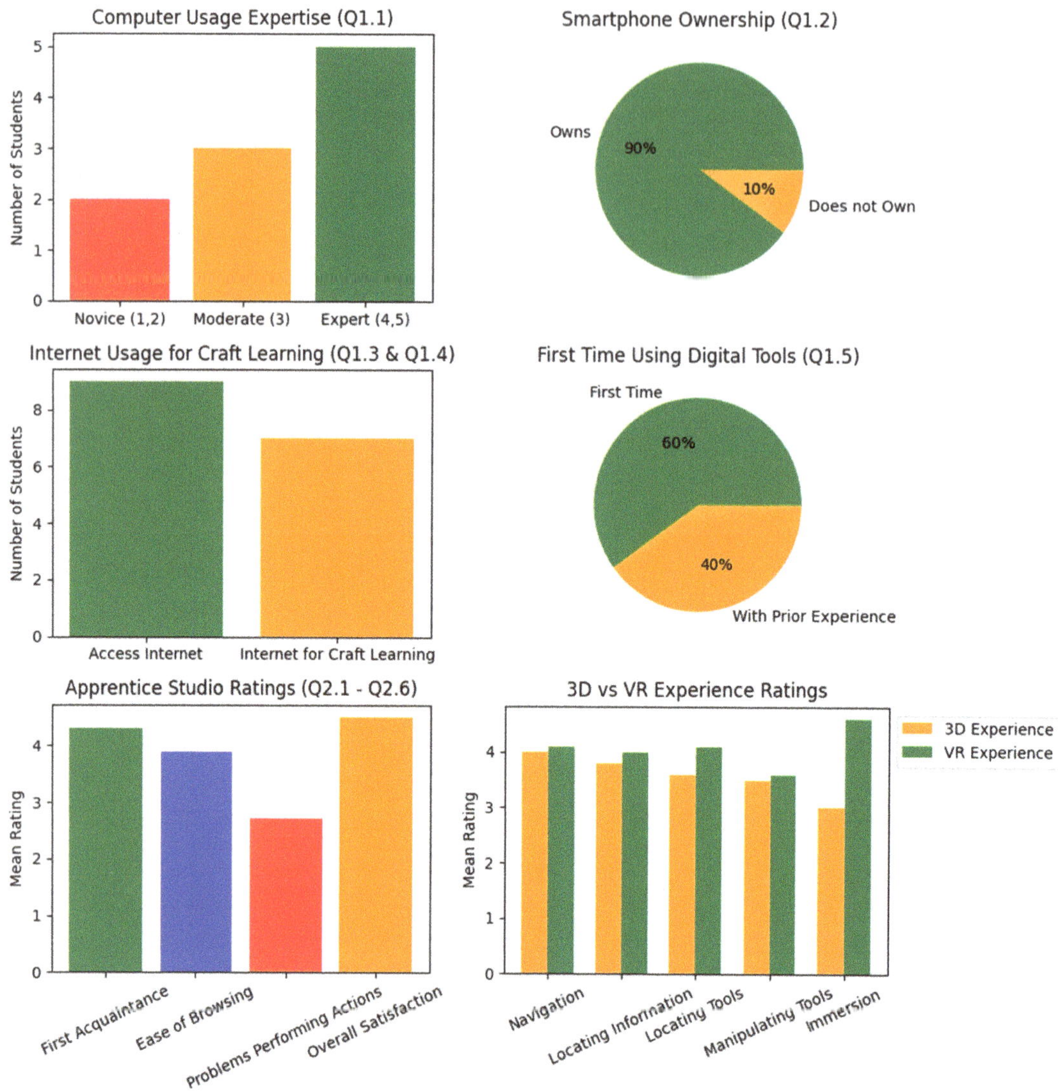

Figure 15. Analysis of the students' evaluation results.

Additional comments: Regarding additional comments, many students noted the potential for expanding the library of craft-related VR simulations. For example, one of the comments received was "Adding more VR scenarios for different crafts would make this tool invaluable".

The overall insights into the effectiveness can be summarized as follows. Both Apprentice Studio and VR simulations show strong potential for improving craft education, with participants expressing high satisfaction overall. VR offers significantly better immersion and interaction than traditional 3D interfaces without the latter being useless since they provide a cost-effective way to craft training. Regarding challenges, interface usability, especially in 3D interactions, needs improvement to lower the learning curve since some students struggle with technical jargon and navigation. Regarding recommendations for improvement, including a step-by-step tutorial or user guide for new users would be well received. Furthermore, enhancing tool manipulation mechanics, especially in the 3D mode, is considered important. Last but not least, aligning glossary with craft-specific terminology was noted as important. Regarding Future Research Directions, exploring scalability by incorporating additional crafts and testing with a larger participant pool.

Students' results synthesis: The responses from participants provide valuable insights into their experiences with digital tools, usability challenges, and the effectiveness of both 3D and VR environments for craft education. While individual perspectives varied, there were some common themes. Participants had mixed levels of digital literacy, highlighting concerns about the learning curve required to engage effectively with digital platforms. Although nearly all participants owned smartphones and accessed the internet, their use of digital resources for craft education varied. Several participants with prior experience mentioned relying on platforms like YouTube or forums for learning, indicating that while they were familiar with digital content consumption, structured digital training was new to many.

Initial impressions of the Apprentice Studio were generally positive. Participants appreciated its intuitive design but noted that it took some time to become fully comfortable with the platform. Some described their first experience as "smooth and engaging", while others found navigating through the features slightly challenging. A recurring theme was the difficulty in aligning terminology within the Apprentice Studio to traditional craft education, with some expressing frustration over inconsistencies that made certain features harder to understand.

Participants also suggested that a guided tutorial or onboarding process would have made their experience easier, with one noting, "The tool is intuitive, but at first, I struggled with some of the terminology. A short tutorial or glossary would help new users a lot". Despite these minor obstacles, the general sentiment was that the tool had strong potential, and most felt comfortable using it after some initial exploration.

The contrast between 3D and VR experiences was evident in participant feedback. While some participants found the 3D interface sufficient for their needs, others struggled with certain interactions, particularly manipulating tools. One participant stated, "It was easy to navigate but harder to grab tools", suggesting that while movement felt natural, interaction needed refinement. Another noted, "The 3D view is clear, but rotating objects felt a bit clunky". In contrast, the VR environment was widely praised for its immersive nature. Many participants described their VR experience as "engaging" and "more realistic" compared to traditional 3D interfaces. Some appreciated how "Navigating in VR felt very natural", while others found grabbing tools in VR significantly better than in 3D but still identified areas for improvement, such as precision in interactions. A recurring theme was that VR felt more intuitive for hands-on tasks but required some initial adaptation to the controllers.

Participants expressed enthusiasm about the potential of these digital tools for craft education. Many saw the VR component as particularly valuable and believed it could significantly enhance traditional learning methods. Several participants suggested expanding the range of VR scenarios to cover more crafts, with one stating, "Adding more VR scenarios for different crafts would make this tool invaluable". While usability concerns were present—particularly in 3D interactions—most participants felt that with some refinements, these tools could become essential resources for craft training. Many emphasized the importance of providing better onboarding support, improving tool interaction mechanics, and ensuring terminology aligns with traditional craft training.

Looking forward, participants suggested that future improvements should focus on enhancing user-friendliness, increasing accessibility, and ensuring that digital tools integrate seamlessly into existing craft education practices. Many were excited about the potential of these tools and believed they could be even more impactful with continued development and expansion.

5.3.3. Educators' Evaluation Results

Section 1: Orientation: Q1.1 (Computer Usage Expertise) received a mean rating of 4.0 with a distribution of two educators rated themselves "5" (expert), two as "4", (very proficient), and one as "3". In Q1.2 (Smartphone Ownership), all five educators own a smartphone, highlighting a foundation for leveraging mobile technologies in education. In Q1.3 (Internet Usage), all five educators access the internet from their phones or computers, and four use it for craft-related information or learning. Most educators are comfortable with using the internet for professional growth and can adapt to online craft tools. In Q1.4 (Use of the Internet for Information on Craft), most educators already use the Internet to learn about their craft, showing a high level of openness to digital resources. However, one educator might require additional support or motivation. In Q1.5 (Experience in Educating Glassblowing), two educators reported more than ten years of experience and two reported 5–10 years and one less than 5 years. The participant group has diverse experience levels, which may affect their adoption of digital tools. The results of Q1.6 (First Time Using Digital Tools for Craft Education) indicate that three educators are using digital tools for the first time, while two have prior experience including experience in VR. The tools used include video tutorials, CAD software, and AR and VR applications. While some educators are already familiar with digital tools, the majority are new to structured digital craft education platforms. Overall, CAD software was praised for its design precision and the video tutorials were noted for their accessibility.

Section 2: Craft Studio: In Q2.1 (First Acquaintance with Craft Studio), the Craft Studio received a mean rating of 4.4 with three educators rating it "5", and two rated it "4", thus, allowing the assumption that the initial impressions of the Craft Studio are very positive. Regarding Q2.2 (Ease of Browsing), the Craft Studio received a mean rating of 3.8 since most educators found browsing straightforward, but some encountered minor navigation challenges. The rating was very close to the one achieved by the Apprentice Studio in a similar question. In Q2.3 (Information Easy To Understand), it received a mean rating of 4.1 since most educators found information easy to understand. In Q2.4 (Problems Performing Actions), the Craft Studio received a rating of 2.6. since some educators experienced difficulties in executing certain actions, likely due to unfamiliarity with the interface and due to some terminology mismaps. This was also highlighted in Q2.5 (Mismatches in terminology) where a rating of 3.1 was received. In Q2.6 to Q2.8 (Lesson Administration and Assignment), regarding lesson administration, Craft Studio received a rating of 4.0, regarding the authoring of lessons, a rating of 3.8, and regarding the ease of assigning, a rating of 4.2. Overall, educators found the tools effective, though authoring presented slightly more difficulty due to the issues described in Q2.4. Finally, in Q2.6–Q2.8 (Suggestions for Lesson Administration), several comments were received such as "It would be helpful to have pre-designed lesson templates", and "The lesson assignment process is intuitive, but the authoring interface could be more flexible".

Section 3: Observation of students: In Q3.1 (Student Attitude Towards Digital Technologies): Regarding students' attitude through digital technology, it was rated 4.6 since educators perceived a strong positive attitude among students towards digital integration in craft training. In Q3.2 (Colleague Attitude Towards Digital Technologies), a score of 3.8 indicated that, while colleagues are generally supportive, there may be some hesitancy or skepticism. In terms of technology evaluation Q3.3, the proposed approach scored 4.4. for Efficiency, 4.2 for Learnability, 4 for Understandability, 4.2 for Scalability, and 4.6 for accessibility. The provided technologies are rated highly across all dimensions, with accessibility being the strongest aspect empowered due to the alternative forms of performing the education (3D and VR) which makes it easier for people with different characteristics to select their preferred training style. In Q3.4, educators observed a significant improvement in students' understanding of craft concepts through the use of the tools providing a rating of 4.5. Finally, in Q3.5 (Improvement in Readiness for Physical Workshops) a complementary to the Q3.4 finding was the 4.3 rating indicating that educators believe that digital tools effectively prepare students for hands-on training in physical workshops.

Free text comments on Q3.4 and Q3.5 include "Students seem more confident in approaching tasks after practicing digitally", and "The transition to the workshop was smoother, but the physical nuances of glassblowing still require hands-on exposure".

The results are graphically visualized in Figures 16 and 17.

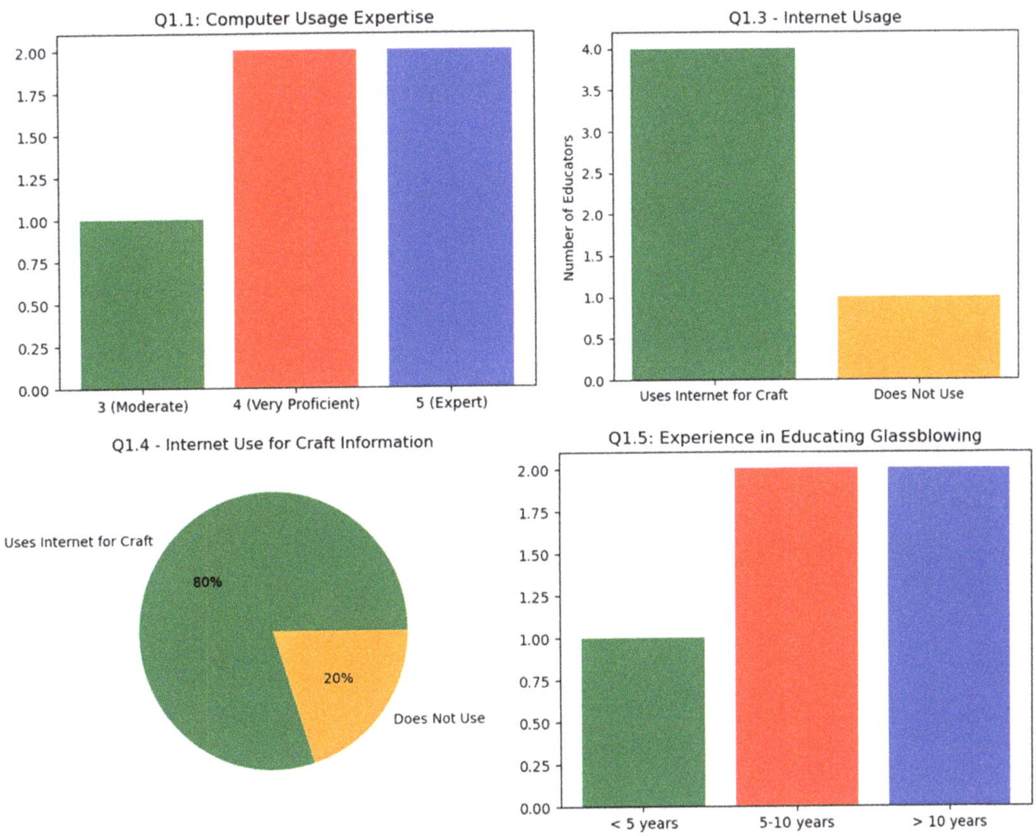

Figure 16. Analysis of the teachers' evaluation results (Q1–Q5).

Additional comments and overall insights: Overall, in terms of effectiveness, the Craft Studio and associated tools are highly effective in enhancing students' understanding and readiness for hands-on workshops. Minor usability issues in authoring lessons and interface navigation were highlighted while it is assumed that there is room to improve interactivity and collaboration features. In terms of recommendations, the introduction of pre-designed templates for lessons authoring the expansion of the craft simulation library, and the addition of collaborative tools are considered the most constructive ones. Future research investigating the impact of long-term use on both educators and students should be explored together with a wider user-based evaluation with larger educator and student cohorts.

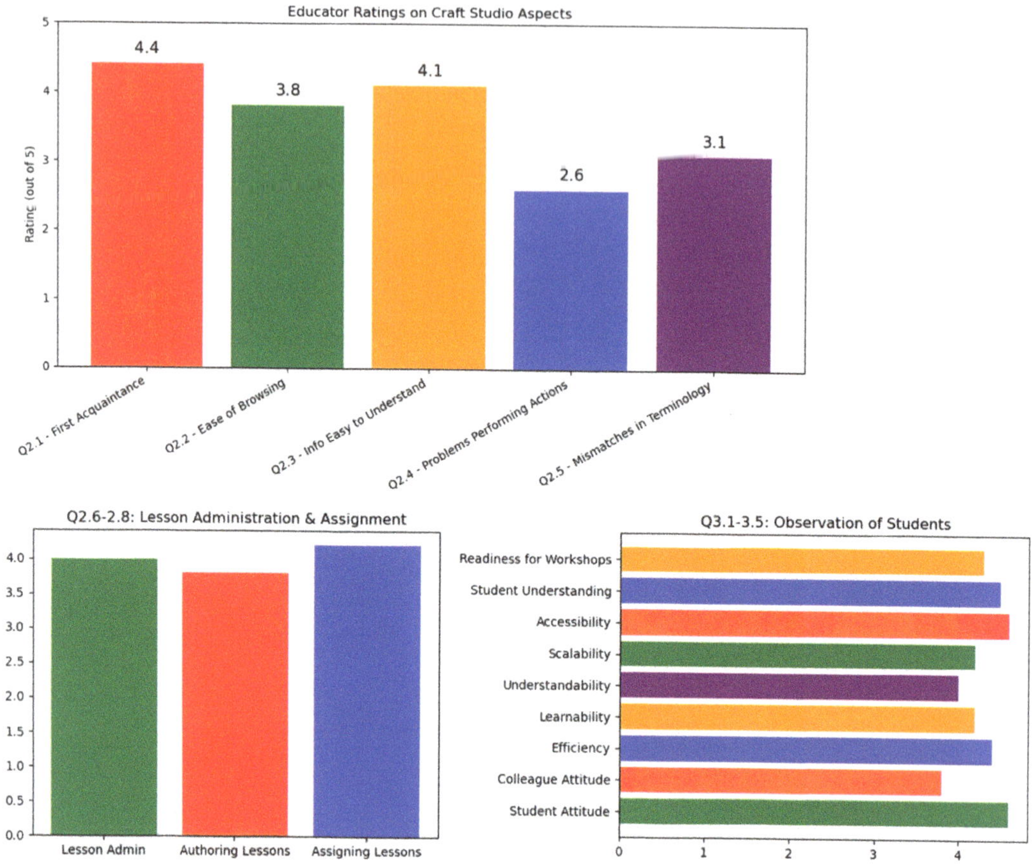

Figure 17. Analysis of the teachers' evaluation results (Q2.1–2.8 and Q1.3–3.5).

Synthesis of educators' results: The educators who participated in the experiment generally displayed high levels of digital literacy. Most felt confident in using computers and digital tools, which suggests they can engage effectively with technology in their teaching. While all educators owned smartphones and regularly accessed the internet, one educator admitted to not frequently using online resources for learning about their craft, suggesting a need for additional support or motivation in digital adoption. In terms of experience, participants represented a diverse range, from those with over a decade of teaching experience to those with less than five years. This diversity led to varying perspectives on digital tool integration—some saw them as a natural evolution, while others viewed them as an adjustment requiring effort. For the majority, using digital tools for craft education was a new experience. Those who had prior exposure highlighted the usefulness of CAD software and video tutorials, particularly for precision and accessibility. However, they noted a lack of interactivity in traditional digital resources, which they hoped new tools like Craft Studio could address.

Educators expressed highly positive first impressions of the Craft Studio, with many praising its potential for structured digital craft education. Navigation was generally smooth, though some encountered minor challenges in browsing, suggesting that a more intuitive design could further enhance usability. Most educators found the information provided within the platform clear and well-organized. Despite the strong initial reception, some educators encountered difficulties performing certain actions. A few struggled with unfamiliar terminology, pointing out mismatches between the language used in digital tools and the vocabulary they commonly use in class. This misalignment sometimes led to confusion, reinforcing the need for better alignment between the platform's terminology and traditional craft instruction. When it came to lesson administration, educators found assigning and managing lessons straightforward. However, creating lessons proved slightly more challenging. Some expressed a desire for pre-designed templates to streamline the authoring process, while others emphasized the need for more flexibility in customizing lessons. One educator remarked that while the assignment process was intuitive, lesson creation required additional effort to be truly effective.

Educators observed that students were overwhelmingly positive about integrating digital tools into craft education. Many noted increased enthusiasm and engagement, with students appearing more confident after practicing digitally before moving to physical workshops. However, educators emphasized that while digital tools are beneficial for concept comprehension and practice, hands-on exposure remains crucial for mastering the physical nuances of glassblowing. Among colleagues, there was a mix of enthusiasm and hesitation. Some educators noted resistance among peers who were accustomed to traditional teaching methods, while others observed a growing interest in digital integration. This variation suggests that while the sector is evolving, continued support and demonstration of digital tools' benefits may be needed to encourage broader adoption. In evaluating the technology itself, educators appreciated its accessibility and flexibility, particularly the availability of both 3D and VR options, which allowed users to choose the mode that best suited their learning style. Some noted that the digital platform effectively prepared students for hands-on work, though they acknowledged that physical skills still require in-person refinement. One educator commented that students seemed more confident in approaching tasks digitally, but the real challenge lay in translating that confidence into physical craftsmanship.

Educators largely viewed the Craft Studio as a valuable tool for enhancing both understanding and readiness for hands-on craft training. They acknowledged minor usability challenges, particularly in lesson authoring and navigation, but felt these issues could be addressed with improvements such as pre-designed templates and refined user guidance. One recurring theme was the potential for expanding the digital craft education ecosystem. Many educators suggested incorporating more craft-specific simulations and collaboration tools to enhance interactivity. Overall, the findings highlight strong support for digital tool adoption in craft education, with a few areas for improvement to ensure a seamless and effective integration into existing teaching practices.

6. Discussion

This study introduces a novel methodology for simulating and immersive training traditional craft processes, addressing key limitations of conventional and prior digital approaches. The methodology enhances effectiveness, scalability, and accessibility.

6.1. Advances Concerning Traditional Training

Traditional training relies on observational learning or apprenticeship, which, while effective, is resource-intensive and geographically constrained. The proposed approach overcomes these limitations by enabling digital lesson distribution through reusable Action Animators, allowing institutions worldwide to offer standardized training without requiring technical expertise beyond basic computer and VR device use. By integrating

FEM simulations for material-deforming actions and real-time game engine simulations for simpler tasks, the methodology bridges the gap between theory and practice. Traditional training methods, while effective, are resource-intensive [159,160], with scalability issues particularly in manual dexterity-based fields [161]. VR-based craft training has been shown to enhance skill acquisition while reducing material waste [66,162,163], with FEM simulations further improving conceptual understanding and reducing cognitive overload [149].

The methodology fosters deeper understanding by enabling users to explore scientific principles alongside practical execution. Digital environments eliminate safety risks, allowing learners to focus on principles without concerns about injuries or wasted resources. Real-time feedback mechanisms provide quantitative performance metrics, allowing iterative skill improvement. The ability to repeatedly practice complex tasks, such as attaching a glass handle, without resource waste enhances learning efficiency. Educators and students in user studies highlighted the cost-effectiveness of this approach for familiarization before workshop practice. A non-VR version enables remote training, expanding accessibility. Institutions like CERFAV benefit from reduced resource consumption, aligning with eco-friendly policies. However, haptic feedback in controllers remains insufficient for high-precision craft training.

6.2. Technical Advances

The methodology employs high-fidelity FEM simulations and game engine-based kinematics to replicate crafting actions. FEM models are reusable across various craft contexts, ensuring broad applicability and the validation process confirmed that simulation data can be translated into high-quality pre-rendered simulations. These simulations provide realism, allowing learners to engage with accurate representations of tools and materials without physical resources. Advanced FEM techniques surpass earlier material-deforming modeling methods with high scientific precision [150,151]. They enable a detailed understanding of craft processes, including deformation and stress distribution [152], whereas prior systems relied on simplified animations [153]. Real-time FEM visualization further enhances training environments, ensuring accuracy and pedagogical effectiveness.

The Dual Simulation Framework optimizes computational resources by combining FEM for complex material interactions (e.g., chiseling wood) with game engine simulations for simpler operations (e.g., rotating a glassblowing rod). The modular Action Animator components enhance flexibility, contrasting with less adaptable previous solutions. The streamlined integration pipeline involving Blender and Unity improves realism through photorealistic enhancements. The system supports various input devices, improving accessibility compared to past approaches.

Previous digital craft education efforts focused on eLearning platforms [164,165], or rudimentary interactive applications which lacked real-time adaptability [166]. FEM-based simulations dynamically replicate craft processes, aligning with digital twin technology [167]. Reusable Action Animators extend modular frameworks explored in game-based learning [168], enhancing their application in craft preservation.

This methodology improves effectiveness, scalability, and accessibility. High-fidelity simulations enhance engagement and retention. Study and examination modes provide iterative feedback, enabling mastery of both procedural accuracy and underlying principles. Digital tools and modular lesson specifications ensure global distribution, overcoming traditional training's resource constraints. Unlike prior systems, this methodology supports a broad range of hardware configurations, ensuring accessibility even in resource-limited regions. Action Animators allow tailored training, further increasing inclusivity.

The methodology is part of a broader framework supporting heritage craft education, informed by Cognitive Load Theory [149]. It integrates online facilities with multimodal immersive training tools adaptable to user expertise and equipment. The Craeft Online Training platform [169] will provide free access to the infrastructure.

6.3. Contribution to the Preservation of Intangible Cultural Heritage

Traditional crafts, integral to intangible cultural heritage, face threats due to declining practitioners and limited documentation. Digital archives capturing tools, materials, and actions ensure long-term preservation and facilitate education and research.

Digital technology's role in heritage preservation is well-documented [170]. Virtual reconstructions engage wider audiences and ensure knowledge transmission [171], but many focus on artifact representation rather than skill transfer [172]. The proposed methodology bridges this gap by capturing procedural knowledge, aligning with embodied learning principles [173,174].

This approach democratizes craft training, enabling global participation regardless of location or resources. By eliminating traditional apprenticeship barriers, such as proximity to skilled mentors and material access, it supports broad engagement with traditional crafts.

6.4. Theoretical Implications

This methodology represents a paradigm shift in craft education, blending theoretical understanding, practical execution, and digital interaction. Immersive learning enhances situated learning [175] and bridges gaps between declarative and procedural knowledge acquisition [176]. The adaptive training model aligns with constructivist pedagogical principles [177] and supports cognitive apprenticeship frameworks [178], reinforcing guided exploration's effectiveness in skill-based disciplines.

Additionally, this methodology aligns with contemporary trends in gamification, VR-based training, and remote learning. It balances modern pedagogy with traditional craft preservation, emphasizing adaptability and precision in digital heritage tools.

6.5. Limitations

Despite its advantages, the methodology has limitations. While scalable, expanding the collection of craft actions requires additional simulations, necessitating technical expertise. However, the methodology ensures the seamless integration of new actions via Action Animators. Another limitation is the absence of semantic process representation, which could facilitate automatic lesson generation. Ongoing work aims to address this issue and further enhance scalability. Lastly, the pilot-stage implementation requires broader validation across more crafts and educational contexts. Large-scale user studies will provide further insights into its effectiveness across diverse training scenarios.

7. Conclusions and Future Work

This study presents a methodology for immersive craft training using FEM-generated animations. Crafting processes are challenging to simulate realistically, but integrating FEM results into VR environments offers an innovative solution. This approach enhances training by accurately replicating material behaviors, such as deformation and stress distribution, creating a learning experience close to real-world conditions. A key contribution is overcoming the limitations of real-time physics simulations by leveraging precomputed FEM data. While this ensures high-fidelity simulations, it also necessitates pre-simulated outputs, limiting real-time adaptability. To address this, we introduced Animation Sequences and Action Animators, enabling the reuse of precomputed actions across training scenarios. This structured framework enhances scalability, allowing simulations to be refined in Blender and integrated into Unity for photorealistic environments.

To ensure usability for craft educators and students, the methodology separates lesson creation and execution through Craft Studio and Apprentice Studio. Instructors can design immersive lessons using Action Animators, while students practice skills in VR environments. The study and examination mode further supports iterative learning, bridging virtual training with hands-on experience.

While this work demonstrates strong potential, several areas for improvement remain. From a technical perspective, optimizing FEM simulations is crucial to support real-time applications. Methods for accelerating FEM calculations could help address this challenge. Additionally, improving haptic feedback would enhance the realism of material interactions, allowing users to better perceive the texture and resistance of crafting materials. Advancements in photorealistic rendering, such as real-time ray tracing and physically based rendering, could further enhance the training environment. From an educational perspective, large-scale evaluation is necessary to validate the effectiveness of the proposed methodology. Expanding this study to include more craft would provide further insights. Additionally, evaluating the approach within traditional apprenticeship contexts could offer a deeper understanding of its impact. A formal evaluation incorporating more craft practices is already planned as part of future work.

Further improvements in the technical aspects of the methodology will also influence the assessment strategies used. Future research should explore how the integration of advanced technical components affects learning outcomes, particularly in terms of user engagement, motivation, and skill retention. As VR technologies continue to evolve, immersive training systems have the potential to transform skill-based education across multiple domains, fundamentally changing the way hands-on training is delivered and experienced.

Author Contributions: Conceptualization, N.P. and X.Z.; methodology, N.P., X.Z., D.Z., A.D. and I.M.; software, N.P., X.Z., D.Z., N.N., P.F., A.S. and I.D.; validation, N.P. and X.Z.; formal analysis, N.P., X.Z., D.Z., A.D., N.N., P.F., I.D. and I.M.; investigation, N.P., X.Z., D.Z., A.D., N.N., P.F., I.D., D.A., P.H., N.C. and I.M.; resources, N.P., X.Z., D.Z., A.D., D.A., P.H., N.C. and I.M.; data curation, N.P., X.Z., D.Z., A.D. and I.M.; writing—original draft preparation, N.P.; writing—review and editing, N.P., X.Z., D.Z., A.D., N.N., P.F., I.D., A.S., D.A., P.H., N.C., D.A., P.H., N.C. and I.M.; visualization, N.P., X.Z., D.Z., A.D., N.N., P.F., I.D., A.S. and I.M.; supervision, N.P. and X.Z.; project administration, N.P. and X.Z.; funding acquisition, N.P. and X.Z. All authors have read and agreed to the published version of the manuscript.

Funding: This work was implemented under the project Craeft, which received funding from the European Union's Horizon Europe research and innovation program under grant agreement No. 101094349.

Institutional Review Board Statement: Not applicable.

Informed Consent Statement: Not applicable.

Data Availability Statement: Data are available upon request.

Acknowledgments: The authors would like to thank the anonymous reviewers for contributing to the enhancement of the quality of this manuscript.

Conflicts of Interest: The authors declare no conflicts of interest.

Abbreviations

3D	Three-Dimensional
AR	Augmented Reality
CFD	Computational Fluid Dynamics
CH	Cultural Heritage

FEA	Finite Element Analysis
FEM	Finite Element Method
HMD	Head Mounted Displays
ICH	Intangible Cultural Heritage
MR	Mixed Reality
SDK	Software Development Kit
TCs	Traditional Crafts
UNESCO	United Nations Educational, Scientific and Cultural Organization
VR	Virtual Reality

References

1. Psotka, J. Immersive training systems: Virtual reality and education and training. *Instr. Sci.* **1995**, *23*, 405–431.
2. Radhakrishnan, U.; Koumaditis, K.; Chinello, F. A systematic review of immersive virtual reality for industrial skills training. *Behav. Inf. Technol.* **2021**, *40*, 1310–1339.
3. Wang, P.; Wu, P.; Wang, J.; Chi, H.L.; Wang, X. A critical review of the use of virtual reality in construction engineering education and training. *Int. J. Environ. Res. Public Health* **2018**, *15*, 1204. [CrossRef]
4. Luo, H.; Li, G.; Feng, Q.; Yang, Y.; Zuo, M. Virtual reality in K-12 and higher education: A systematic review of the literature from 2000 to 2019. *J. Comput. Assist. Learn.* **2021**, *37*, 887–901.
5. Radu, I. Augmented reality in education: A meta-review and cross-media analysis. *Pers. Ubiquitous Comput.* **2014**, *18*, 1533–1543.
6. Eraut, M. Knowledge creation and knowledge use in professional contexts. *Stud. High. Educ.* **1985**, *10*, 117–133.
7. Billett, S.; Billett, S. *Mimetic Learning in and for Work*; Springer International Publishing: Cham, Switzerland, 2014; pp. 1–21.
8. Mozumdar, S. Revitalizing the crafts and creative enterprises sector. *State Indian Livelihood Rep.* **2020**, *113*, 113–124.
9. UNESCO. *Guidelines for the Establishment of National "Living Human Treasures" Systems*; UNESCO: Paris, France, 1993.
10. UNESCO. *Convention for the Safeguarding of the Intangible Cultural Heritage*; UNESCO: Paris, France, 2003.
11. Marchand, T.H. Making knowledge: Explorations of the indissoluble relation between minds, bodies, and environment. *J. R. Anthropol. Inst.* **2010**, *16*, S1–S21. [CrossRef]
12. Zabulis, X.; Meghini, C.; Dubois, A.; Doulgeraki, P.; Partarakis, N.; Adami, I.; Stefanidi, Z. Digitisation of traditional craft processes. *J. Comput. Cult. Herit. (JOCCH)* **2022**, *15*, 53.
13. Bergheau, J.M.; Fortunier, R. *Finite Element Simulation of Heat Transfer*; John Wiley & Sons: Hoboken, NJ, USA, 2013.
14. Rodríguez, J.M.; Jonsén, P.; Svoboda, A. Simulation of metal cutting using the particle finite-element method and a physically based plasticity model. *Comput. Part. Mech.* **2017**, *4*, 35–51.
15. Arrazola, P.J. Investigations on the effects of friction modeling in finite element simulation of machining. *Int. J. Mech. Sci.* **2010**, *52*, 31–42. [CrossRef]
16. Koch, R.M.; Gross, M.H.; Carls, F.R.; von Büren, D.F.; Fankhauser, G.; Parish, Y.I. Simulating facial surgery using finite element models. In Proceedings of the 23rd Annual Conference on Computer Graphics and Interactive Techniques, New Orleans, LA, USA, 4–9 August 1996; pp. 421–428.
17. Chanthasopeephan, T.; Desai, J.P.; Lau, A.C. Modeling soft-tissue deformation prior to cutting for surgical simulation: Finite element analysis and study of cutting parameters. *IEEE Trans. Biomed. Eng.* **2007**, *54*, 349–359. [PubMed]
18. Zhu, J.Z. *The Finite Element Method: Its Basis and Fundamentals*; Elsevier: Amsterdam, The Netherlands, 2013.
19. Baraff, D.; Witkin, A. Large steps in cloth simulation. In *Seminal Graphics Papers: Pushing the Boundaries, Volume 2*; Association for Computing Machinery: New York, NY, USA, 2023; pp. 767–778.
20. Nealen, A.; Müller, M.; Keiser, R.; Boxerman, E.; Carlson, M. Physically based deformable models in computer graphics. *Comput. Graph. Forum* **2006**, *25*, 809–836. [CrossRef]
21. Sifakis, E.; Barbic, J. FEM simulation of 3D deformable solids: A practitioner's guide to theory, discretization and model reduction. In Proceedings of the ACM SIGGRAPH 2012 Courses, Los Angeles, CA, USA, 5–9 August 2012; pp. 1–50.
22. Duriez, C.; Dubois, F.; Kheddar, A.; Andriot, C. Realistic haptic rendering of interacting deformable objects in virtual environments. *IEEE Trans. Vis. Comput. Graph.* **2005**, *12*, 36–47.
23. Kovar, L.; Gleicher, M.; Pighin, F. Motion graphs. In *Seminal Graphics Papers: Pushing the Boundaries, Volume 2*; Association for Computing Machinery: New York, NY, USA, 2023; pp. 723–732.
24. Lee, J.; Chai, J.; Reitsma, P.S.; Hodgins, J.K.; Pollard, N.S. Interactive control of avatars animated with human motion data. In Proceedings of the 29th Annual Conference on Computer Graphics and Interactive Techniques, San Antonio, TX, USA, 23–26 July 2002; pp. 491–500.
25. Müller, M.; Heidelberger, B.; Hennix, M.; Ratcliff, J. Position based dynamics. *J. Vis. Commun. Image Represent.* **2007**, *18*, 109–118.

26. Holden, D.; Saito, J.; Komura, T. A deep learning framework for character motion synthesis and editing. *ACM Trans. Graph. (TOG)* **2016**, *35*, 138.
27. Hasenfratz, J.M.; Lapierre, M.; Gascuel, J.D.; Boyer, E. Real-time capture, reconstruction and insertion into virtual world of human actors. In *Vision, Video and Graphics*; Elsevier: Amsterdam, The Netherlands, 2003; pp. 49–56.
28. Yin, K.; Loken, K.; Van de Panne, M. Simbicon: Simple biped locomotion control. *ACM Trans. Graph. (TOG)* **2007**, *26*, 105-es.
29. Coros, S.; Beaudoin, P.; Van de Panne, M. Robust task-based control policies for physics-based characters. In *ACM SIGGRAPH Asia 2009 Papers, Proceedings of the SA09: SIGGRAPH ASIA 2009, Yokohama, Japan, 16–19 December 2009*; Association for Computing Machinery: New York, NY, USA, 2009; pp. 1–9.
30. Peng, X.B.; Abbeel, P.; Levine, S.; Van de Panne, M. Deepmimic: Example-guided deep reinforcement learning of physics-based character skills. *ACM Trans. Graph. (TOG)* **2018**, *37*, 143.
31. General-Purpose Finite Element Analysis Software—Simulia Abaqus. Available online: https://www.3ds.com/products/simulia/abaqus (accessed on 26 September 2024).
32. Unity3D. Available online: https://unity.com/ (accessed on 26 September 2024).
33. Burdea, G.C.; Coiffet, P. *Virtual Reality Technology*; John Wiley & Sons: Hoboken, NJ, USA, 2024.
34. Furht, B. (Ed.) *Handbook of Augmented Reality*; Springer Science & Business Media: Berlin, Germany, 2011.
35. Pervolarakis, Z.; Zidianakis, E.; Katzourakis, A.; Evdaimon, T.; Partarakis, N.; Zabulis, X.; Stephanidis, C. Visiting Heritage Sites in AR and VR. *Heritage* **2023**, *6*, 2489–2502. [CrossRef]
36. Partarakis, N.; Antona, M.; Stephanidis, C. Adaptable, Personalizable and Multi User Museum Exhibits. In *Curating the Digital*; England, D., Schiphorst, T., Bryan-Kinns, N., Eds.; Springer Series on Cultural Computing; Springer: Cham, Switzerland, 2016; pp. 231–246. [CrossRef]
37. Dangelmaier, W.; Fischer, M.; Gausemeier, J.; Grafe, M.; Matysczok, C.; Mueck, B. Virtual and augmented reality support for discrete manufacturing system simulation. *Comput. Ind.* **2005**, *56*, 371–383.
38. Lee, H. Real-time manufacturing modeling and simulation framework using augmented reality and stochastic network analysis. *Virtual Real.* **2019**, *23*, 85–99. [CrossRef]
39. Xie, B.; Liu, H.; Alghofaili, R.; Zhang, Y.; Jiang, Y.; Lobo, F.D.; Yu, L.F. A review on virtual reality skill training applications. *Front. Virtual Real.* **2021**, *2*, 645153. [CrossRef]
40. Abidi, M.A.; Lyonnet, B.; Chevaillier, P.; Toscano, R.; Baert, P. Simulation of manufacturing processes via virtual reality. In *Robotics, Automation, and Control in Industrial and Service Settings*; IGI Global: Hershey, PA, USA, 2015; pp. 142–178.
41. Dorozhkin, D.V.; Vance, J.M.; Rehn, G.D.; Lemessi, M. Coupling of interactive manufacturing operations simulation and immersive virtual reality. *Virtual Real.* **2012**, *16*, 15–23. [CrossRef]
42. Cassola, F.; Mendes, D.; Pinto, M.; Morgado, L.; Costa, S.; Anjos, L.; Paredes, H. Design and evaluation of a choreography-based virtual reality authoring tool for experiential learning in industrial training. *IEEE Trans. Learn. Technol.* **2022**, *15*, 526–539. [CrossRef]
43. Wolfartsberger, J.; Niedermayr, D. Authoring-by-doing: Animating work instructions for industrial virtual reality learning environments. In Proceedings of the 2020 IEEE Conference on Virtual Reality and 3D User Interfaces Abstracts and Workshops (VRW), Atlanta, GA, USA, 22–26 March 2020; IEEE: Piscataway, NJ, USA, 2020; pp. 173–176.
44. Knopp, S.; Lorenz, M.; Pelliccia, L.; Klimant, P. Using industrial robots as haptic devices for VR-training. In Proceedings of the 2018 IEEE Conference on Virtual Reality and 3D User Interfaces (VR), Reutlingen, Germany, 18–22 March 2018; IEEE: Piscataway, NJ, USA, 2018; pp. 607–608.
45. Lelevé, A.; McDaniel, T.; Rossa, C. Haptic training process simulation. *Front. Virtual Real.* **2020**, *1*, 3. [CrossRef]
46. Jung, E.Y.; Park, D.K.; Lee, Y.H.; Jo, H.S.; Lim, Y.S.; Park, R.W. Evaluation of practical exercises using an intravenous simulator incorporating virtual reality and haptics device technologies. *Nurse Educ. Today* **2012**, *32*, 458–463. [CrossRef]
47. Park, G.; Choi, H.; Lee, U.; Chin, S. Virtual figure model crafting with VR HMD and Leap Motion. *Imaging Sci. J.* **2017**, *65*, 358–370. [CrossRef]
48. Fang, H.F.; Wang, B.; Liang, Q. Balancing authenticity and creativity: A VR system design for assisting ceramic creation. In *Connectivity and Creativity in Times of Conflict*; Academia Press: Cambridge, MA, USA, 2023.
49. Lucas, J.D. Immersive VR in the construction classroom to increase student understanding of sequence, assembly, and space of wood frame construction. *J. Inf. Technol. Constr.* **2018**, *23*, 179–194.
50. Antonya, C.; Butnariu, S. Preservation of cultural heritage using virtual reality technologies and haptic feedback: A prototype and case study on antique carpentry tools. *Appl. Sci.* **2022**, *12*, 8002. [CrossRef]
51. Lee, I.J. Applying virtual reality for learning woodworking in the vocational training of batch wood furniture production. *Interact. Learn. Environ.* **2023**, *31*, 1448–1466. [CrossRef]
52. Spilski, J.; Exner, J.P.; Schmidt, M.; Makhkamova, A.; Schlittmeier, S.; Giehl, C.; Werth, D. Potential of VR in the vocational education and training of craftsmen. In Proceedings of the 19th International Conference on Construction Applications of Virtual Reality, Bangkok, Thailand, 13–15 November 2019; pp. 181–190.

53. Google. 3D Pottery. Available online: https://experiments.withgoogle.com/3d-pottery (accessed on 29 July 2024).
54. Eyewind. Pottery Master. Available online: https://play.google.com/store/apps/details?id=com.create.pottery.paint.by.color (accessed on 29 July 2024).
55. AZ Games. Master of Pottery. Available online: https://store.steampowered.com/app/1160490/Master_Of_Pottery/ (accessed on 29 July 2024).
56. Grow, A.; Dickinson, M.; Pagnutti, J.; Wardrip-Fruin, N.; Mateas, M. Crafting in games. *Digit. Human. Quart.* **2017**, 11.
57. Freeman, L.J. Alchemically, an Educational Role-Playing Game. Ph.D. Dissertation, Virginia Tech, Blacksburg, VA, USA, 2019.
58. Karastone. Knitting Simulator 2014. Available online: https://karastonesite.com/2014/07/19/knitting-simulator-2014/ (accessed on 29 July 2024).
59. Chotrov, D.; Uzunova, Z.; Maleshkov, S. Real-time 3D model topology editing method in VR to simulate crafting with a wood-turning lathe. *Comput. Sci. Edu. Comput. Sci.* **2019**, *1*, 28–30.
60. Xu, R.; Xu, J. Research on Interactive Traditional Craft Diagram Model and Simulation System: Take Nanjing Rong Hua Craft as an Example. In Proceedings of the International Conference on Advances in Energy, Environment and Chemical Engineering, Singapore, 29–31 July 2016; pp. 261–265. [CrossRef]
61. NVIDIA. PhysX System Software. Available online: https://developer.nvidia.com/physx-sdk (accessed on 29 July 2024).
62. Bellotti, F.; Berta, R.; De Gloria, A. Designing effective serious games: Opportunities and challenges for research. *Int. J. Emerg. Technol. Learn.* **2010**, *5*, 22. [CrossRef]
63. The Irregular Corporation. Woodwork Simulator. 2019. Available online: https://steamdb.info/app/510230/info/ (accessed on 29 July 2024).
64. Murray, J.; Sawyer, W. Virtual Crafting Simulator: Teaching Heritage Through Simulation. In Proceedings of the International Conference on Education and New Learning Technologies, Barcelona, Spain, 6–8 July 2015; pp. 7668–7675.
65. Eglash, R. Ethnocomputing with Native American Design. In *Information Technology and Indigenous People;* Dyson, L.E., Hendriks, M., Grant, S., Eds.; IGI Global: Hershey, PA, USA, 2007; pp. 210–219. [CrossRef]
66. Carre, A.L.; Dubois, A.; Partarakis, N.; Zabulis, X.; Patsiouras, N.; Mantinaki, E.; Zidianakis, E.; Cadi, N.; Baka, E.; Thalmann, N.M.; et al. Mixed-Reality Demonstration and Training of Glassblowing. *Heritage* **2022**, *5*, 103–128. [CrossRef]
67. Baxter, W.V.; Scheib, V.; Lin, M.C.; Manocha, D. DAB: Interactive haptic painting with 3D virtual brushes. In Proceedings of the 28th Annual Conference on Computer Graphics and Interactive Techniques, Los Angeles, CA, USA, 12–17 August 2001; pp. 461–468. [CrossRef]
68. Trzepieciński, T.; dell'Isola, F.; Lemu, H.G. Multiphysics Modeling and Numerical Simulation in Computer-Aided Manufacturing Processes. *Metals* **2021**, *11*, 175. [CrossRef]
69. Tian, Y.; Xu, J.; Li, Y.; Luo, J.; Sueda, S.; Li, H.; Willis, K.D.D.; Matusik, W. Assemble Them All: Physics-Based Planning for Generalizable Assembly by Disassembly. *ACM Trans. Graph.* **2022**, *41*, 278. [CrossRef]
70. Courant, R. Variational methods for the solution of problems of equilibrium and vibrations. *Bull. Am. Math. Soc.* **1943**, *49*, 1–23.
71. Clough, R.W. The finite element method in plane stress analysis. In Proceedings of the 2nd ASCE Conference on Electronic Computation, Pittsburgh, PA, USA, 8–9 September 1960; pp. 345–378.
72. Zienkiewicz, O.C.; Taylor, R.L. *The Finite Element Method;* Butterworth-Heinemann: Oxford, UK, 2000.
73. MacNeal, R.H. *NASTRAN Theoretical Manual;* MacNeal-Schwendler Corporation: Newport Beach, CA, USA, 1994.
74. Felippa, C.A. *Introduction to Finite Element Methods;* University of Colorado: Boulder, CO, USA, 2004; p. 885.
75. Barkanov, E. *Introduction to the Finite Element Method;* Institute of Materials and Structures, Faculty of Civil Engineering, Riga Technical University: Riga, Latvia, 2001; pp. 1–70.
76. Zienkiewicz, O.C.; Taylor, R.L. *The Finite Element Method for Solid and Structural Mechanics;* Elsevier: Amsterdam, The Netherlands, 2005.
77. Annett, M.; Horta, L. Comparison of test and finite element analysis for two full-scale helicopter crash tests. In Proceedings of the 52nd AIAA/ASME/ASCE/AHS/ASC Structures, Structural Dynamics and Materials Conference, Denver, CO, USA, 4–7 April 2011; p. 1804.
78. Gursel, K.T.; Nane, S.N. Non-linear finite element analyses of automobiles and their elements in crashes. *Int. J. Crashworthiness* **2010**, *15*, 667–692.
79. Nam-Ho, K.; Bhavani, S.; Ashok, K. *Introduction to Finite Element Analysis and Design;* Wiley: Hoboken, NJ, USA, 2018.
80. Fish, J.; Belytschko, T. *A First Course in Finite Elements;* Wiley: Hoboken, NJ, USA, 2007.
81. Venkatesh, S.S.; Kumar, T.R.; Blalakumhren, A.P.; Saimurugan, M.; Marimuthu, K.P. Finite element simulation and experimental validation of the effect of tool wear on cutting forces in turning operation. *Mech. Mech. Eng.* **2019**, *23*, 297–302.
82. Attanasio, A.; Faini, F.; Outeiro, J.C. FEM simulation of tool wear in drilling. *Procedia CIRP* **2017**, *58*, 440–444.
83. Mir, A.; Luo, X.; Llavori, I.; Roy, A.; Zlatanovic, D.L.; Joshi, S.N.; Goel, S. Challenges and issues in continuum modelling of tribology, wear, cutting and other processes involving high-strain rate plastic deformation of metals. *J. Mech. Behav. Biomed. Mater.* **2022**, *130*, 105185.

84. Govik, A.; Nilsson, L.; Moshfegh, R. Finite element simulation of the manufacturing process chain of a sheet metal assembly. *J. Mater. Process. Technol.* **2012**, *212*, 1453–1462.
85. Bathe, K.J. *Finite Element Procedures*; Prentice Hall: Hoboken, NJ, USA, 1996.
86. Cook, R.D.; Malkus, D.S.; Plesha, M.E. *Concepts and Applications of Finite Element Analysis*; John Wiley & Sons: Hoboken, NJ, USA, 1989.
87. Hibbitt, H.D.; Karlsson, B.I. *ABAQUS User's Manual*; Hibbitt, Karlsson & Sorensen, Inc.: Providence, Rhode Island, 1978.
88. Moaveni, S. *Finite Element Analysis: Theory and Application with ANSYS*; Prentice Hall: Hoboken, NJ, USA, 1999.
89. Anderson, J.D. *Computational Fluid Dynamics: The Basics with Applications*; McGraw-Hill: New York, NY, USA, 1995.
90. Eberly, D.H. *Game Physics*; Morgan Kaufmann Publishers: Burlington, MA, USA, 2004; ISBN 0123749034.
91. Kaufman, D.; Edmunds, T.; Pai, D. Fast Frictional Dynamics for Rigid Bodies. In Proceedings of the ACM SIGGRAPH 2005, Los Angeles, CA, USA, 31 July–4 August 2005. [CrossRef]
92. Baek, C.; Johanns, P.; Sano, T.G.; Grandgeorge, P.; Reis, P.M. Finite Element Modeling of Tight Elastic Knots. *J. Appl. Mech.* **2021**, *88*, 024501. [CrossRef]
93. Crassous, J. Discrete-element-method model for frictional fibers. *Phys. Rev. E* **2023**, *107*, 025003. [CrossRef]
94. Inoue, T. Tatara and the Japanese sword: The science and technology. *Acta Mech.* **2010**, *214*, 17–30. [CrossRef]
95. Zabulis, X.; Partarakis, N.; Demeridou, I.; Bartalesi, V.; Pratelli, N.; Meghini, C.; Fallahian, P. Modelling and Simulation of Traditional Craft Actions. *Appl. Sci.* **2024**, *14*, 7750. [CrossRef]
96. Wang, G.D.; Melly, S.K. Three-dimensional finite element modeling of drilling CFRP composites using Abaqus/CAE: A review. *Int. J. Adv. Manuf. Technol.* **2018**, *94*, 599–614.
97. Shinohara, K.; Nishibori, K. Finite element modeling of fabric-tying based on Arimatsu Narumi Shibori Robot. *Meas. Control* **2023**, *56*, 71–92.
98. Bro-Nielsen, M. Finite element modeling in surgery simulation. *Proc. IEEE* **1998**, *86*, 490–503.
99. Nienhuys, H.W.; Frank van der Stappen, A. A surgery simulation supporting cuts and finite element deformation. In *International Conference on Medical Image Computing and Computer-Assisted Intervention*; Springer: Berlin, Heidelberg, 2001; pp. 145–152.
100. Burbank, S.D.; Smith, L.V. Dynamic characterization of rigid foam used in finite element sports ball simulations. *Proc. Inst. Mech. Eng. P J. Sports Eng. Technol.* **2012**, *226*, 77–85.
101. Coto, N.P.; Meira, J.B.C.; Dias, R.B.; Driemeier, L.; de Oliveira Roveri, G.; Noritomi, P.Y. Assessment of nose protector for sport activities: Finite element analysis. *Dent. Traumatol.* **2012**, *28*, 108–113. [CrossRef]
102. Cook, R.D. *Concepts and Applications of Finite Element Analysis*; John Wiley & Sons: Hoboken, NJ, USA, 2007.
103. Jagota, V.; Sethi, A.P.S.; Kumar, K. Finite element method: An overview. *Walailak J. Sci. Technol. (WJST)* **2013**, *10*, 1–8.
104. Billinghurst, M.; Clark, A.; Lee, G. A survey of augmented reality. *Found. Trends Hum.-Comput. Interact.* **2015**, *8*, 73–272. [CrossRef]
105. Azuma, R.T. A Survey of Augmented Reality. *Presence Teleoperators Virtual Environ.* **1997**, *6*, 355–385. [CrossRef]
106. Taylor, Z.A.; Cheng, M.; Ourselin, S. High-speed nonlinear finite element analysis for surgical simulation using graphics processing units. *IEEE Trans. Med. Imaging* **2008**, *27*, 650–663. [CrossRef]
107. Shukla, H.M.; Deshpande, A.A.; Ganvir, K.D.; Gandhi, J. Biomedical Engineering Modelling and Simulation. In *Computational Intelligence and Blockchain in Biomedical and Health Informatics*; CRC Press: Boca Raton, FL, USA, 2024; pp. 26–38.
108. Moravej, H.; Jamali, S.; Chan, T.; Nguyen, A. Finite element model updating of civil engineering infrastructures: A literature review. In Proceedings of the 8th International Conference on Structural Health Monitoring of Intelligent Infrastructure 2017, Brisbane, Australia, 5–8 December 2017; pp. 1–12.
109. Brown, A.O.; Jensen, D.; Rencis, J.; Wood, K.; Wood, J.; White, C.; Coffman, J. Finite Element Learning Modules as Active Learning Tools. *Adv. Eng. Educ.* **2012**, *3*, n1.
110. Matsutomo, S.; Mitsufuji, K.; Hiasa, Y.; Noguchi, S. Real-time simulation method of magnetic field for visualization system with augmented reality technology. *IEEE Trans. Magn.* **2013**, *49*, 1665–1668. [CrossRef]
111. Matsutomo, S.; Miyauchi, T.; Noguchi, S.; Yamashita, H. Real-time visualization system of magnetic field utilizing augmented reality technology for education. *IEEE Trans. Magn.* **2012**, *48*, 531–534. [CrossRef]
112. Blender. Available online: https://www.blender.org/, (accessed on 29 October 2024).
113. Zdziebko, P.; Holak, K. Synthetic image generation using the finite element method and blender graphics program for modeling of vision-based measurement systems. *Sensors* **2021**, *21*, 6046. [CrossRef]
114. Olbrich, M.; Franek, A.; Weber, D. Interacting with FEM simulated tubes in AR. In *HCI International 2021-Late Breaking Papers: Multimodality, eXtended Reality, and Artificial Intelligence: 23rd HCI International Conference, HCII 2021, Virtual Event, 24–29 July 2021, Proceedings*; Springer: Berlin/Heidelberg, Germany, 2021; pp. 305–317.
115. Huang, J.M.; Ong, S.K.; Nee, A.Y. Visualization and interaction of finite element analysis in augmented reality. *Comput. Aided Des.* **2017**, *84*, 1–14. [CrossRef]

116. Gibson, I.; Zhan, G. Finite element simulation of the spine with haptic interface. In Proceedings of the 2nd International Convention on Rehabilitation Engineering & Assistive Technology, Bangkok, Thailand, 13–15 May 2008; IEEE: Piscataway, NJ, USA, 2008; pp. 20–25.
117. Agusanto, K.; Li, L.; Chuangui, Z.; Sing, N.W. Photorealistic rendering for augmented reality using environment illumination. In *The Second IEEE and ACM International Symposium on Mixed and Augmented Reality, 2003. Proceedings*; IEEE: Piscataway, NJ, USA, 2003; pp. 208–216.
118. Kronander, J.; Banterle, F.; Gardner, A.; Miandji, E.; Unger, J. Photorealistic rendering of mixed reality scenes. *Comput. Graph. Forum* **2015**, *34*, 643–665. [CrossRef]
119. Misra, S.; Ramesh, K.T.; Okamura, A.M. Modeling of tool-tissue interactions for computer-based surgical simulation: A literature review. *Presence* **2008**, *17*, 463–491. [CrossRef]
120. Basdogan, C.; De, S.; Kim, J.; Muniyandi, M.; Kim, H.; Srinivasan, M.A. Haptics in minimally invasive surgical simulation and training. *IEEE Comput. Graph. Appl.* **2004**, *24*, 56–64. [CrossRef]
121. Coles, T.R.; Meglan, D.; John, N.W. The role of haptics in medical training simulators: A survey of the state of the art. *IEEE Trans. Haptics* **2010**, *4*, 51–66. [CrossRef]
122. Bielser, D.; Gross, M.H. Interactive simulation of surgical cuts. In Proceedings of the Eighth Pacific Conference on Computer Graphics and Applications, Hong Kong, China, 3–5 October 2000; IEEE: Piscataway, NJ, USA, 2000; pp. 116–442.
123. Gavish, N.; Gutiérrez, T.; Webel, S.; Rodríguez, J.; Peveri, M.; Bockholt, U.; Tecchia, F. Evaluating virtual reality and augmented reality training for industrial maintenance and assembly tasks. *Interact. Learn. Environ.* **2015**, *23*, 778–798.
124. Perret, J.; Kneschke, C.; Vance, J.; Dumont, G. Interactive assembly simulation with haptic feedback. *Assem. Autom.* **2013**, *33*, 214–220.
125. Mavrikios, D.; Karabatsou, V.; Fragos, D.; Chryssolouris, G. A prototype virtual reality-based demonstrator for immersive and interactive simulation of welding processes. *International Journal of Computer Integrated Manufacturing* **2006**, *19*, 294–300.
126. Geijtenbeek, T.; Pronost, N. Interactive character animation using simulated physics: A state-of-the-art review. *Comput. Graph. Forum* **2012**, *31*, 2492–2515. [CrossRef]
127. Liu, Y.; Zheng, C.; Xu, F.; Tong, X.; Guo, B. Data-driven 3D neck modeling and animation. *IEEE Trans. Vis. Comput. Graph.* **2020**, *27*, 3226–3237.
128. Zhang, L.; Zhang, Y.; Jiang, Z.; Li, L.; Chen, W.; Peng, Q. Precomputing data-driven tree animation. *Comput. Animat. Virtual Worlds* **2007**, *18*, 371–382.
129. Sato, S.; Morita, T.; Dobashi, Y.; Yamamoto, T. A data-driven approach for synthesizing high-resolution animation of fire. In Proceedings of the Digital Production Symposium, Glendale, CA, USA, 4 August 2012; pp. 37–42.
130. Yang, C.; Yang, X.; Xiao, X. Data-driven projection method in fluid simulation. *Comput. Animat. Virtual Worlds* **2016**, *27*, 415–424. [CrossRef]
131. Kavanagh, S.; Luxton-Reilly, A.; Wuensche, B.; Plimmer, B. A systematic review of virtual reality in education. *Themes Sci. Technol. Educ.* **2017**, *10*, 85–119.
132. AlGerafi, M.A.; Zhou, Y.; Oubibi, M.; Wijaya, T.T. Unlocking the potential: A comprehensive evaluation of augmented reality and virtual reality in education. *Electronics* **2023**, *12*, 3953. [CrossRef]
133. Akdere, M.; Jiang, Y.; Lobo, F.D. Evaluation and assessment of virtual reality-based simulated training: Exploring the human–technology frontier. *Eur. J. Train. Dev.* **2021**, *46*, 434–449.
134. Carruth, D.W. Virtual reality for education and workforce training. In Proceedings of the 2017 15th International Conference on Emerging eLearning Technologies and Applications (ICETA), Stary Smokovec, Slovakia, 26–27 October 2017; IEEE: Piscataway, NJ, USA, 2017; pp. 1–6.
135. Falah, J.; Charissis, V.; Khan, S.; Chan, W.; Alfalah, S.F.; Harrison, D.K. Development and evaluation of virtual reality medical training system for anatomy education. In *Intelligent Systems in Science and Information 2014: Extended and Selected Results from the Science and Information Conference 2014*; Springer International Publishing: Berlin/Heidelberg, Germany, 2015; pp. 369–383.
136. Smutny, P.; Babiuch, M.; Foltynek, P. A review of the virtual reality applications in education and training. In Proceedings of the 2019 20th International Carpathian Control Conference (ICCC), Kraków, Poland, 26–29 May 2019; IEEE: Piscataway, NJ, USA, 2019; pp. 1–4.
137. Iyobe, M.; Ishida, T.; Miyakawa, A.; Sugita, K.; Uchida, N.; Shibata, Y. Development of a mobile virtual traditional crafting presentation system using augmented reality technology. *Int. J. Space-Based Situat. Comput.* **2017**, *6*, 239–251.
138. Fuchigami, R.; Ishida, T. Proposal of a Traditional Craft Simulation System Using Mixed Reality. In *Advances on P2P, Parallel, Grid, Cloud and Internet Computing*; Barolli, L., Takizawa, M., Yoshihisa, T., Amato, F., Ikeda, M., Eds.; Springer: Cham, Switzerland, 2021; pp. 437–445. [CrossRef]
139. Edlin, L.; Liu, Y.; Bryan-Kinns, N.; Reiss, J. Exploring Augmented Reality as Craft Material. In *HCI International 2020—Late Breaking Papers: Virtual and Augmented Reality*; Stephanidis, C., Chen, J.Y.C., Fragomeni, G., Eds.; Springer: Cham, Switzerland, 2020; Volume 12428, pp. 58–62. [CrossRef]

140. Rossau, I.; Skovfoged, M.; Czapla, J.; Sokolov, M.; Rodil, K. Dovetailing: Safeguarding traditional craftsmanship using virtual reality. *Int. J. Intang. Herit.* **2019**, *14*, 104–120.
141. Cho, C.L. Comparison of three methods for determining Young's modulus of wood. *Taiwan J. For. Sci.* **2007**, *22*, 297–306.
142. Figma. Available online: https://www.figma.com/ (accessed on 26 September 2024).
143. Figma Unity Importer Plugin. Available online: https://www.figma.com/community/plugin/1047282855279327962/unity-importer (accessed on 26 September 2024).
144. Rychlewski, J. On Hooke's law. *J. Appl. Math. Mech.* **1984**, *48*, 303–314.
145. Li, S.; Sitnikova, E.; Liang, Y.; Kaddour, A.S. The Tsai-Wu failure criterion rationalised in the context of UD composites. *Compos. Part A: Appl. Sci. Manuf.* **2017**, *102*, 207–217. [CrossRef]
146. Desplanques, Y. Amontons-Coulomb friction laws, a review of the original manuscript. *SAE Int. J. Mater. Manuf.* **2015**, *8*, 98–103.
147. Stop-motion-OBJ. Available online: https://github.com/neverhood311/Stop-motion-OBJ (accessed on 26 September 2024).
148. PhysX. Available online: https://www.nvidia.com/en-us/drivers/physx/physx-9-19-0218-driver/ (accessed on 26 September 2024).
149. Sweller, J. Cognitive load theory. In *Psychology of Learning and Motivation*; Academic Press: Cambridge, MA, USA, 2011; Volume 55, pp. 37–76.
150. Belytschko, T.; Liu, W.K.; Moran, B.; Elkhodary, K. *Nonlinear Finite Elements for Continua and Structures*; John wiley & sons: Hoboken, NJ, USA, 2014.
151. Abel, J.F.; Popov, E.P. Static and dynamic finite element analysis of sandwich structures. In Proceedings of the Second Conference of Matrix Methods in Structural Mechanics, Wright-Patterson AFB, OH, USA, 15–17 October 1968; Volume 68, pp. 213–245.
152. Zienkiewicz, O.C.; Taylor, R.L.; Zhu, J.Z. *The Finite Element Method: Its Basis and Fundamentals*; Elsevier: Amsterdam, The Netherlands, 2005.
153. Hambli, R.; Chamekh, A.; Salah, H.B.H. Real-time deformation of structure using finite element and neural networks in virtual reality applications. *Finite Elem. Anal. Des.* **2006**, *42*, 985–991. [CrossRef]
154. Partarakis, N.; Zabulis, X. Applying Cognitive Load Theory to eLearning of Crafts. *Multimodal Technol. Interact.* **2024**, *8*, 2. [CrossRef]
155. Nielsen, J. Usability Inspection Methods. In *Usability Inspection Methods*; Nielsen, J., Mack, R.L., Eds.; John Wiley and Sons, Inc.: Hoboken, NJ, USA, 1994.
156. Rubin, J. *Handbook of Usability Testing*; John Wiley and Sons, Inc.: Hoboken, NJ, USA, 1994.
157. Beaudouin-Lafon, M.; Mackay, W.E. Prototyping tools and techniques. In *Human-Computer Interaction*; CRC Press: Boca Raton, FL, USA, 2009; pp. 137–160.
158. Nielsen, J. Heuristic Evaluation. In *Usability Inspection Methods*; Nielsen, J., Mack, R.L., Eds.; John Wiley and Sons, Inc.: Hoboken, NJ, USA, 1994; pp. 25–62.
159. Lave, J.; Wenger, E. *Situated Learning: Legitimate Peripheral Participation*; Cambridge University Press: Cambridge, UK, 1991.
160. Schön, D.A. *Educating the Reflective Practitioner*; Jossey-Bass: San Francisco, CA, USA, 1987.
161. Burgess, L.; Schofield, K.; Charman, H. Issues in craft and design education. In *Learning to Teach Art and Design in the Secondary School*; Routledge: London, UK, 2014; pp. 114–144.
162. Ringas, C.; Tasiopoulou, E.; Kaplanidi, D.; Partarakis, N.; Zabulis, X.; Zidianakis, E.; Patakos, A.; Patsiouras, N.; Karuzaki, E.; Foukarakis, M.; et al. Traditional craft training and demonstration in museums. *Heritage* **2022**, *5*, 431–459. [CrossRef]
163. Stefanidi, E.; Partarakis, N.; Zabulis, X.; Zikas, P.; Papagiannakis, G.; Magnenat Thalmann, N. TooltY: An approach for the combination of motion capture and 3D reconstruction to present tool usage in 3D environments. In *Intelligent Scene Modeling and Human-Computer Interaction*; Springer International Publishing: Cham, Switzerland, 2021; pp. 165–180.
164. Hutchins, E. *Cognition in the Wild*; MIT Press: Cambridge, MA, USA, 1995.
165. Smart, K.L.; Cappel, J.J. Students' perceptions of online learning: A comparative study. *J. Inf. Technol. Educ. Res.* **2006**, *5*, 201–219.
166. Aldrich, C. *The Complete Guide to Simulations and Serious Games: How the Most Valuable Content will be Created in the Age Beyond Gutenberg to Google*; John Wiley & Sons: Hoboken, NJ, USA, 2009.
167. Grieves, M. Digital twin: Manufacturing excellence through virtual factory replication. *White Pap.* **2014**, *1*, 1–7.
168. Gee, J.P. Learning by design: Games as learning machines. *Interact. Educ. Multimed. IEM* **2004**, *8*, 15–23.
169. Craeft Training Platform. Available online: https://www.craeft.eu/elearning/ (accessed on 26 September 2024).
170. Roussou, M. Virtual heritage: From the research lab to the broad public. *Bar. Int. Ser.* **2002**, *1075*, 93–100.
171. Sylaiou, S.; Mania, K.; Karoulis, A.; White, M. Exploring the relationship between presence and enjoyment in a virtual museum. *Int. J. Hum.-Comput. Stud.* **2010**, *68*, 243–253.
172. Zabulis, X.; Partarakis, N.; Demeridou, I.; Doulgeraki, P.; Zidianakis, E.; Argyros, A.; Theodoridou, M.; Marketakis, Y.; Meghini, C.; Bartalesi, V.; et al. A roadmap for craft understanding, education, training, and preservation. *Heritage* **2023**, *6*, 5305–5328. [CrossRef]
173. Dourish, P. *Where the Action is: The Foundations of Embodied Interaction*; MIT Press: Cambridge, MA, USA, 2001.

174. Zabulis, X.; Meghini, C.; Partarakis, N.; Beisswenger, C.; Dubois, A.; Fasoula, M.; Nitti, V.; Ntoa, S.; Adami, I.; Chatziantoniou, A.; et al. Representation and preservation of Heritage Crafts. *Sustainability* **2020**, *12*, 1461. [CrossRef]
175. Brown, J.S.; Collins, A.; Duguid, P. Situated cognition and the culture of learning. *Routledge* **1989**, *18*, 32–42.
176. Anderson, J.R. Acquisition of cognitive skill. *Psychol. Rev.* **1982**, *89*, 369.
177. Jonassen, D.; Davidson, M.; Collins, M.; Campbell, J.; Haag, B.B. Constructivism and computer-mediated communication in distance education. *Am. J. Distance Educ.* **1995**, *9*, 7–26.
178. Collins, A.; Brown, J.S.; Holum, A. Cognitive apprenticeship: Making thinking visible. *Am. Educ.* **1991**, *15*, 6–11.

Multimodal Technologies and Interaction

MDPI

Article

Evaluating Uses of XR in Fostering Art Students' Learning

Panagiotis Dafiotis [1,*], Stella Sylaiou [2], Efstratios Stylianidis [3], Dimitrios Koukopoulos [4] and Christos Fidas [5]

[1] School of Visual and Applied Arts, Faculty of Fine Arts, Aristotle University of Thessaloniki, 54124 Thessaloniki, Greece
[2] Department of Surveying & Geoinformatics Engineering, School of Engineering, International Hellenic University, 62124 Serres, Greece; sylaiou@gmail.com
[3] School of Spatial Planning and Development, Faculty of Engineering, Aristotle University of Thessaloniki, 54124 Thessaloniki, Greece; sstyl@auth.gr
[4] Department of History and Archaeology, School of Humanities and Social Sciences, University of Patras, 26504 Rio, Greece; dkoukopoulos@upatras.gr
[5] Department of Electrical and Computer Engineering, School of Engineering, University of Patras, 26504 Rio, Greece; fidas@upatras.gr
* Correspondence: dafiotis@vis.auth.gr

Abstract: This paper addresses the potential of extended reality (XR) to foster art students' learning and creativity with specially developed applications for the creation of art exhibitions. This study is based on the EU-funded research project 'Scaffolding Creativity of Arts Students: Framework, Toolchain, and Educational Material on how to Create their Own Virtual Exhibitions' (CREAMS). CREAMS develops interconnected virtual reality (VR), augmented reality (AR), and mixed reality (MR) indoor and outdoor exhibition creation applications. The article puts emphasis on the issue of what evaluation methodology is more adequate to assess the efficacy of such applications, and pertinent challenges, as well as related research, are discussed. In this context, ways in which Fine Art School undergraduates can benefit from the creation of XR/VR exhibitions are explored. Such uses of XR are primarily examined in terms of their potential to enhance learning, and foster students' skills. The potential of adding multimodal resources that contextualize exhibited artworks is examined to foster viewers' meaningful engagement. Art students' ability to communicate the underlying concepts/ideas of their art through XR apps is also addressed. Moreover, this paper investigates how XR technologies can foster the collaboration of tutors and students in Fine Art Schools through specially developed platforms embedded in the XR applications. The ability of the CREAMS VR application to foster such cooperation between students and their tutors is also evaluated. The scientific contribution of this paper relates to the evaluation methodology of XR art exhibition applications that have an educational role.

Keywords: extended reality; virtual exhibitions; visual arts; education; educational research

1. Introduction

Emerging technologies, such as extended reality (XR) applications, provide new opportunities but also challenges in relation to their adoption as learning tools by Higher Education Institutions (HEIs) in the Art and Design domain [1–4]. Art schools explore the capabilities that XR heralds and adapt ICT tools to their needs and requirements. This paper refers to the characteristic case of the EU-funded research project CREAMS (full title: 'Scaffolding Creativity of Arts Students: Framework, Toolchain, and Educational Material on how to Create their Own Virtual Exhibitions'). An essential aspect of harnessing the potential of emerging technologies for HEIs is to enhance students' ability to use such tools effectively.

The challenge of exploiting the VR medium's expressive capacity, as [5] posits, is a key factor. Arts-related interfaces should be innovative, inspiring and creative themselves.

Gifreu-Castells in [5] delineates the objectives of a VR art exhibition, which, depending on the specific curatorial aims and priorities, can significantly vary. According to the author, their first function is to attract new audiences. Moreover, they may aim to reduce the so-called digital gap. Another aim is to place emphasis on different curatorial possibilities. The medium's expressive capacity represents a significant challenge for art schools as a VR art exhibition should exploit as much as possible. The same holds for the ability of a digital platform to foster curatorial practices through experimentation and communication between students and tutors or even amongst peers. The above points delineating prospective benefits and possibilities for art students are reflected upon the metrics and evaluation criteria, as well as the questions or discussion topics used (respectively in questionnaires and focus group sessions) that are further analyzed in this article. At the same time, beyond qualitative aspects that relate to the specificity of a visual arts-related set of applications, we concurrently assessed with the use of a mixture of more pragmatic and commonly evaluated aspects, namely, usability and user experience. This paper offers an overview of the actual CREAMS EU-funded research project in the following section and provides an overview of methodological considerations, methods employed, the actual findings, and a discussion thereof before delineating some concrete suggestions for both practitioners in the field of XR evaluation and stakeholders in the field of tertiary art education on the basis of the projects' consequent phases of formative and summative evaluation.

The paper presents the outcomes of an evaluation study that, in turn, draws on an ever-increasing body of published research and reviews in the field of evaluation methodologies pertinent to extended reality with a focus on virtual cultural experience. The work of Kabassi [6], who published a comprehensive systematic review, has informed both our research and this paper. In a similar vein, Morales et al. [7] map out pertinent publications in an extensive survey. Morales et al. [7] provide the key methods employed in XR-related evaluation studies that often use a methodological approach similar to the present study (i.e., mixed methods with the combined use of the SUS and UEQ questionnaires, which will be explained in the Methodology section of the present paper), such as the work of Barricelli et al. [8]. Likewise, another pertinent review by Garcia et al. [9] presents evaluation studies that often address culture-related material, such as the publication by Campoverde-Durán et al. [10].

This article puts emphasis on the uses of extended reality/XR (with a focus on VR) as a tool that enhances learning and creativity in art schools through the creation of virtual art exhibitions and, as mentioned, examines optimal ways to evaluate the efficacy of such applications. In a recent publication by Vital et al. [11], there is a comparison of extended reality platforms and tools for viewing and exhibiting art, as well as a thorough discussion of the impact of such technologies on teaching and learning in art schools. Vital et al. [11] explain that there is 'a growing interest in scientific production regarding the use of VR applications of virtual reality in higher education for art education' [1]. Other examples include Huaman et al. [3], who created a virtual learning environment based on a VR museum that fostered active learning according to the results of their research. As Vital et al. [11] mention, other uses of VR exhibitions, such as those presented by Qiu et al. [4], put emphasis on promoting the work of the art students, something that also contributes to their professional skills and overall training. In a similar vein, Song and Li [12] posit that VR can help to create effective technology-based teaching environments, to improve students' professional skills, to assist them in better understanding theoretical knowledge by an improved teaching quality, and finally to better integrate into society. However, they note that teaching content and teaching is the key to the adaptation of virtual reality to their courses [11,12]. This is the key aspect that this paper seeks to capture in this evaluation of the CREAMS research project, which envisages the creation of XR tools that are, by design, meant to be embedded in art school modules to enhance learning and art students' skills. As stated, the main contribution of this article is the methodological framework that has been developed to undertake this task.

2. CREAMS Project: An Overview

The main CREAMS application, which is the virtual reality platform, is a web-based application. It includes a variety of tools that enable students to manage their digital artworks and create and manage virtual exhibitions, and that enable instructors to manage students' exhibitions and assess the students' artworks and exhibitions. Key components (Figure 1) include: (i) the curatorial component, which serves as a communication interface between instructors and students for receiving feedback on the selection and grouping of artworks and reasoning of the students' selections before the actual virtual exhibition creation takes place; (ii) the virtual reality workshop, which consists of a set of tools and functionalities enabling students to create their virtual reality exhibitions by assigning their digitized artworks in a custom-made exhibition space customized by the students. Digitized artworks include 2D and 3D artworks, as well as videos and sounds. Additional tools enable students to adjust their digital artworks, assign and manage associated material related to the main artworks, and apply and adjust the lighting in the virtual space (ambient and spotlights); (iii) teaching services, enabling instructors to assess the exhibition projects created by the students; (iv) dissemination services, enabling visitors to share exhibitions in their social media; and (v) personalization and recommendation services, which recommend best-fit exhibitions to visitors based on interest-based modeling and collaborative filtering mechanisms. Personalization is mainly based on keywords associated with exhibitions that enable recommendations for users who may wish to see similar art shows.

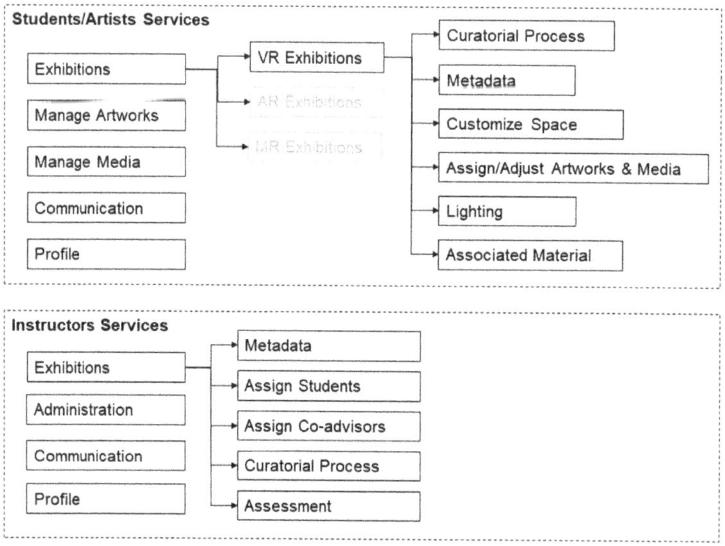

Figure 1. Graph illustrating the CREAMS web-based VR application's tree structure.

The CREAMS research project aspires to foster educational exchanges amongst various stakeholders in the Higher Art Education domain. To this effect, a main platform that serves as the virtual reality exhibition editor and viewer has been created. This VR editor is the main CREAMS platform and is related to other additional augmented and mixed reality applications that enable art students to show their 2D or 3D work in virtual spaces, as well as in indoor and outdoor actual spaces, respectively. An auxiliary digitizer application complements these apps. This paper focuses on the VR platform as it has a pivotal role. Students can upload artworks onto the VR platform with the help of the digitizer app. Students can view a dashboard containing information about the assigned exhibitions (Figure 2) and the uploaded artworks (Figure 3).

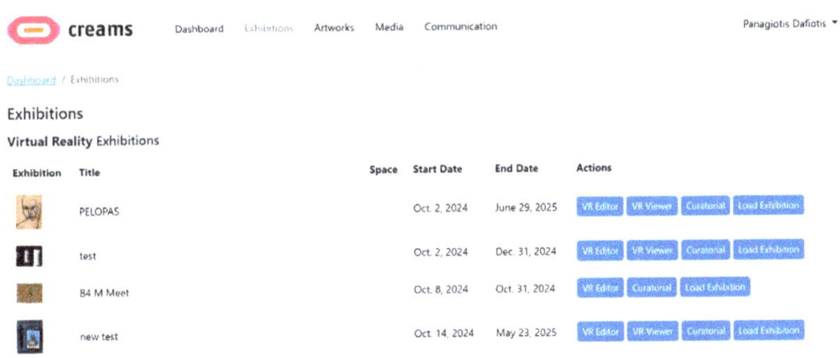

Figure 2. Student dashboard, exhibitions tab.

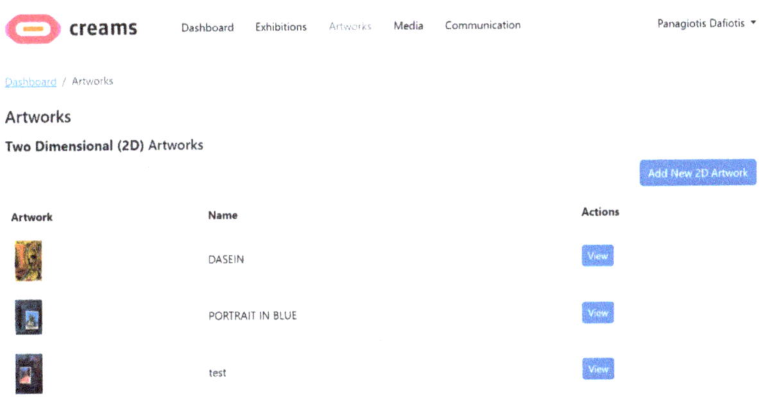

Figure 3. Student dashboard, artworks tab.

Moreover, students can create an exhibition space or choose an available gallery template, then insert and arrange the artworks (Figure 4). They gradually engage in curatorial choices with the help of their tutors with the use of appropriate interaction provisions. Together, they specify the overall exhibition narrative or underlying concept by adding texts, information, and multimodal material associated with their work. Moreover, space-related choices are an essential aspect, as both the focus groups' discussions and the reviewed bibliography indicated.

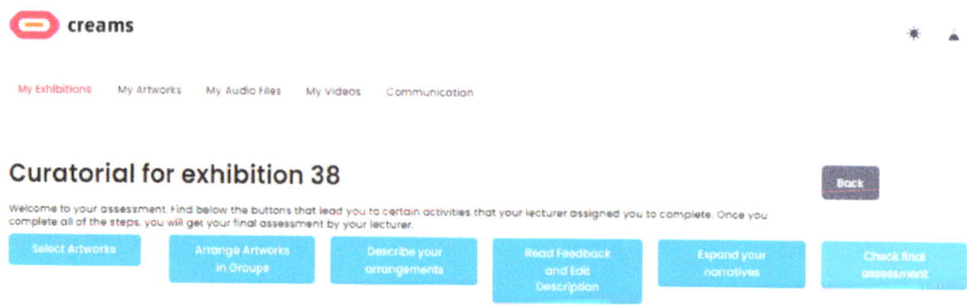

Figure 4. Curatorial phases through which students proceed in cooperation with tutors.

3. Evaluating XR in Tertiary Art Education: Methodological Considerations

Learning in the field of tertiary art education, where art students develop their skills, gain insights, and acquire knowledge, is far from being a solitary affair: their learning processes are mediated through interaction with others as well as with tools and resources. According to Vygotsky [13], objectives form one of three elements from which to start designing learning, the other two being the subject (the learner) and the tools for learning. In the context of tertiary art education, innovative digital tools that enable art students to enhance skills critical for their development as visual artists are, therefore, of great significance. In turn, the ability to establish a sound and dependable methodology to evaluate the impact of new technologies, such as that of XR applications on art students' learning, is key.

The development of XR technologies for the needs of HEIs is a reflexive process: Researchers investigate ways to foster learning and teaching through XR based on students' and other stakeholders' feedback on the efficacy of applications designed to meet their needs. This paper focuses on the case study of the CREAMS evaluation methodology to inform respective efforts in the sector of Fine Art Schools. The paper, moreover, discusses the potential of extended reality (XR) to foster art students' creativity by using specially developed applications that draw on the findings of the CREAMS research project. The development of the tools and the respective evaluation methodology were based on initial needs analysis regarding art students. Early insights provided guiding principles informing the structure and characteristics of the main VR exhibition platform. In turn, the accrued tools were assessed and reconfigured to reflect the evaluation findings. The digital tools incorporate the amendments from the feedback received in two separate formative evaluation phases. The principles that informed our methodology comprise the core scientific contribution of this paper, as opposed to the findings that accrued at the present phase of the application's development. Moreover, concerning the novel characteristics of the VR exhibition editor application, the aspect that differentiates it from existing ones is its focus on educational functionalities and role. This is another area in which this paper seeks to offer inspiration to researchers in the broader field, by presenting an educational use of VR/XR exhibition platforms.

During the needs analysis phase of the CREAMS project, we conducted in-depth discussions, employing focus groups and doing desk research involving a review of the pertinent literature and case studies. Beyond the needs analysis evaluation, phases involved focus group discussions; more specifically, three separate focus group discussions with about eight participants (eight art students, as well as one or two coordinating tutors), one in each of the three participating art schools, in each of the three evaluation phases, i.e., first, second formative, and summative evaluation, so in total nine focus groups sessions took place. Comments gathered through these semi-structured focus group discussions provided an outline of how XR can support learning in art schools. The key benefits of the XR exhibition's creation for art students are enhancing their ability to share, curate, and contextualize their art practice with innovative means. More specifically, art students, using such tools, can experiment with curating choices in terms of the spatial arrangement of artworks and, most importantly, explore ways to communicate concepts or narratives underpinning their (virtual) art show. Art students can create a virtual gallery space through a modular floorplan design or choose a digital clone of existing galleries in their art school. Moreover, they can exploit digital tools to associate contextual information and multimodal resources with exhibited artworks. Thus, they can better situate their practice in terms of inspiration, influences, and related art/research and reflect on their creative process. The ability of virtual exhibitions to embed resources that frame artistic practice in ways that are not feasible in actual gallery spaces opens a gamut of possibilities. However, art students will have to acquire additional digital skills and adapt the use of digital tools to their aims. This involves the ability to put artworks, multimodal resources, and spaces in synergy.

Learning is never tool-free [13], and is conditioned by the qualities, abilities, and affordances of given or new tools. Virtual exhibitions can offer multiple layers of contextual material that frame the artwork, thus offering opportunities for art students to reflect upon, conceptually frame, and communicate their artistic practice and research. Such contextual material can itself be aesthetically and conceptually enticing, challenging, and inspiring, which becomes, in a way, a digital extension of the artwork. These essential qualitative aspects of learning and acquiring skills are often elusive and quite challenging to evaluate in terms of establishing adequate metrics and methods to gather data.

3.1. Related Work

Publications such as the recent survey by Sylaiou et al. [14] not only address the increasing importance of extended reality (XR) in art exhibitions by mapping the existing terrain but also put emphasis on the evaluation of such applications. The evaluation methodology, pertinent metrics, and means in the art- and culture-related XR applications have increasingly become the topic of extensive research. A characteristic example is a thorough survey [6] that reviewed pertinent publications on the evaluation of virtual exhibitions. This survey shows that criteria vary considerably depending on technologies employed (e.g., immersive VR environments, as opposed to websites or web-based applications) or evaluation methods (namely, empirical or inspection methods). More specifically, as Kabassi [6] notes, relevant evaluation studies typically employ empirical methods, i.e., questionnaires or interviews that involve end-users. On the other hand, inspection methods involve specialists who offer insights through cognitive walkthroughs or other gathering data methods. Often, researchers employ a combination of empirical and inspection methods, as is the case with the CREAMS evaluation methodology.

Moreover, criteria in all the above cases also depend on the researchers' priorities, and therefore different authors in published research foreground specific (sets of) criteria that often do not overlap. More specifically, as Kabassi [6] shows in a table included in her survey (p. 9), which describes museum-related VR environments' evaluation criteria, foregrounded by eight researchers in 10 publications, there are significant discrepancies. For example, specific criteria such as the sense of presence or immersion were employed in some publications [15,16], and likewise, the factor of enjoyment [15,17] or, for the same matter, narrative [18] in others. Concerning VR environments in which cultural content is exhibited, some criteria are almost universally accepted (albeit not without exceptions), such as 'Orientation-Navigability' and 'Usability'. Methods (e.g., questionnaires, discussions in small focus groups), type of data gathered (qualitative or quantitative), and, as mentioned, metrics or criteria do not seem to adhere to a rigid methodological framework that is commonly agreed upon, but instead accrue from the specificities of the researchers' aims and priorities, as well as the specificity of the VR/online experience under research.

Firstly, regarding the sense of presence, especially in VR environments, the capability of a system to support the feeling that users are 'there' in front of an artwork is assessed. As Lombard and Ditton [19] put it, in immersive experiences, users have the illusion of non-mediation. Realism and plausibility of the environment are considered key [20,21], to draw and keep users' attention, and foster engagement. A comprehensive overview of the concepts related to and affecting presence is offered by Skarbez et al. [22]. The ability of a system to sustain meaningful attention and cognitive engagement apart from realism and fidelity of sensory input (two closely related aspects of a VR/XR experience) are guiding to what can be termed as cognitive presence as the central and pivotal characteristic of an arts-related experience. This relates to the fact that users will inevitably compare the level of similarity and, thus, congruence between real objects (in this case, artworks) and virtual representations of them [15]. Beyond the sensuous aspect of art perception and appreciation, viewers will have meta-thoughts on the virtuality of the experience, as described by Hofer et al. [23]. They will also compare their ability to engage with the artwork within a VE to real-world visits to an actual gallery space. According to Weber et al. [20], presence can also be associated with the plausibility of narratives embedded in or underpinning a virtual experience, which is crucial for art exhibitions that typically are formed around a concept or a narrative in the broader sense of the term. The term 'perceived realism' is described as the user's judgment about the degree of realism of the VE in terms of (1) virtual objects, sounds, and scenes, (2) credibility and plausibility of the narrative, and (3) naturalness and ease of the interaction with the VE [20]. Narratives (e.g., virtual humans reciting a story about an exhibit) play a crucial role in perceived realism and the sense of cognitive presence [24].

Finally, a pertinent evaluation method comes from published research on an MR museum experience by Hammady et al. [25]. This research introduces a comprehensive and relevant theoretical scheme as well as a methodological framework for evaluating a museum-related XR experience. Although the Role of the Guide (virtual human) is central in the methodology proposed in this study, the overall structural interrelations of the other factors and evaluation metrics proposed (which jointly contribute to the main desired outcome, which is users' Intention to Use), provided inspiration to the CREAMS evaluation, as outlined in more detail in the following section.

3.2. Methods and Tools

The CREAMS framework for evaluating virtual exhibitions was initially informed by stakeholders' needs analysis and a thorough review of pertinent studies. The three major areas that define the quality, effectiveness, and usefulness of an XR experience in the fields of the arts and cultural heritage can be summed up as follows: usability [26–29], sense of presence [30–33], and learnability [16,34]. These key areas comprise the main evaluation topics concerning XR experiences in the arts and visual culture domain.

The methodology of evaluating the applications, e.g., the VR platform (exhibition editor), is based on two pillars: chiefly, questionnaires, and secondly, focus groups. During the second formative evaluation phase, 81 art students participated in total and 198 art students in summative by responding to questionnaires. The sample size is deemed representative of the art schools that participated in the research project itself, namely Aristotle University of Thessaloniki, Greece—Department of Visual and Applied Arts; SHENKAR, Israel; and NTNU—Norway, a number that covered the largest part of the fourth-year art students who prepare their final degree show. The selection process of the participants in the evaluation was based on the students' degree of familiarity with the system, as answering the majority of questions required that the responders had a hands-on experience with the CREAMS VR platform, having used it to create a VR exhibition through its main application, within the context of taught modules in cooperation with the help of tutors who participated in the CREAMS consortium. This study focuses on this specific category as the participants were both users and content creators, while, moreover, the application itself was primarily developed to answer their needs. Bias (and in particular positive bias) has been controlled by constantly communicating to participants the need for commentary and feedback through the evaluation process that would allow developers and other researchers to improve the tools in accordance with the actual needs, recommendations, and critique, as opposed to expecting responses that would provide a more positive image of the application(s) assessed. Moreover, questionnaires during the three consequent phases of the evaluation (two formative and one summative) were reviewed and improved when the wording of questions appeared to encourage positive bias, e.g., by using the initial phrase 'how would you rate...' as opposed to wordings that could bolster positive bias.

Furthermore, 33 visitors responded to (different) questionnaires about the VR platform alone (2nd formative valuation) and another 32 during the summative evaluation phase. Additionally, smaller numbers of art teachers and ICT specialists with experience in XR apps took part. Moreover, focus groups involved 8 participants plus the coordinator. Semi-structured interviews and discussions with participants in focus groups allowed us to gather qualitative data. Art students were initially familiarized with the VR platform in the context of taught modules such as curatorial studies and art education specific classes.

The questionnaires comprised mainly of Likert-scale type questionnaires (with five levels of scale, and seven, in the UEQ sets of questions described below), as well as three or four open questions depending on the participants' category (i.e., three for art students and visitors, and four for art teachers and ICT specialists) to which responders could provide written answers. Questionnaires were conducted online, and responders were invited via email. Questionnaires were composed of three main parts: firstly, questions adapted to the specificity of the art exhibition editing tools, which were chiefly inspired by presence questionnaires. A set of questions deriving from the System Usability Scale (SUS) [35] was also used, while another set of questions corresponding to the User Experience Questionnaires (UEQ) [36–38] formed the third cluster of questions. As the evaluation methodology progressed during the research project, UEQ has been identified as an adequate tool given that it puts emphasis on both pragmatic aspects (e.g., usability) and subjective, personal responses to the VR/XR experience. UEQ is commensurate by assessing the experience of users who view or create virtual exhibitions, given that practical aspects (e.g., reliability) and so-called hedonic aspects [36–38] (i.e., stimulation and innovation) are crucial for the overall attractiveness and efficacy of such applications, as Figure 5 illustrates.

The overall structure of the art students questionnaire was as follows: the first set of ten questions (based on a 5-step Likert scale) asked the participants to rate the key functions and processes mainly from a usability point of view. The following set of ten questions (Q11 to Q20, also based on a 5-step Likert scale) corresponded verbatim to the System Usability Scale (SUS) The following set of questions (Q21 to Q27 for the second formative evaluation) put emphasis on the more qualitative aspects of the user experience in relation to learning, and possible enhancement of curatorial and reflexive or critical skills. These questions also used a 5-step Likert scale. At this point, three open questions enquired about which aspects of the platform were most or least liked, as well as suggestions for improvement. The questionnaire closes with the UEQ set of questions (main results are outlined in Tables 4 and 5, as well as in Figures 6 and 7), which is based on a 7-step Likert scale. Lastly, the questionnaire invites participants to rate their familiarity with pertinent applications.

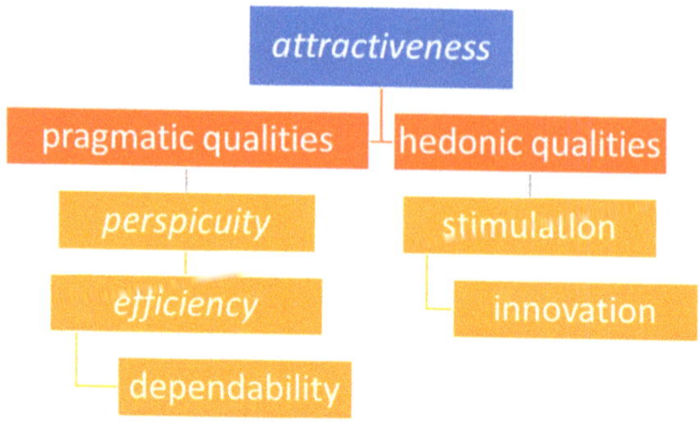

Figure 5. Rendering of scale structure of UEQ. Ochre color: basic scales; Orange color: categories of qualities, to which scales belong. Overall attractiveness is based on these two types of qualities.

The methodological approach proposed by Hammady et al. [25] pertains to the CREAMS evaluation process as it highlights key areas of interest, thereby informing the questionnaire structure as well as outlining a categorization framework for written commentary in open questions and answers obtained during focus group discussions. More specifically, the terms presented by the authors are the following: enjoyment, immersion, multimedia and UI, storytelling (where applicable), usefulness, ease of use, interaction, lack of distractions (i.e., content is not distracting), independence (visitor gets privacy/more independence), overall satisfaction, and finally, the willingness for future use [25]. For example, 'Independence' in the way it is framed is a crucial aspect, considering the emphasis put on the ability of the CREAMS users to engage with the exhibits conceptually, which requires unintrusive interface provisions, thereby enabling viewers to concentrate. This has been described as the system's ability to support cognitive presence and is, therefore, seen as a significant aspect of CREAMS to be evaluated. The publication of Hammady et al. [25] consolidated our focus on qualitative aspects of users' art-related experience as conveyed by the choice of questions described in Table 2 (questions 21 to 22).

3.3. Results of the Second Formative and the Summative Evaluation

A key finding was the need for users to have a more intuitive design in relation to navigation. Participants asked for more guidance on how to navigate virtual gallery spaces. Users frequently criticized the parallel use of arrow keys and mouse as confusing. In post-evaluation meetings, we decided to address this issue with enhanced guidance provisions. Moreover, a widespread wish for an even more realistic rendering of the spaces and artworks alike has been recorded. Lastly, a few responses addressed some lingering technical issues related to the limitations associated with open-source software. The main contribution of this paper is on the evaluation methodology. Thus, the results presented in this section are simply indicative of the insights that may be gained through the methods employed.

Regarding demographics, the visitors' experience in generic Virtual Environments was slightly over the mid-point, or average value, and their experience of arts-related VEs was slightly lower (about 3 on a scale of 1 to 5). The interesting finding is that the responders' interest in contemporary arts is exceptionally high (4.5), whereas this app's effect on potentially fostering (further) this interest was lower, standing at 3.5. This can be seen as a clear indication that irrespective of the platform characteristics, art exhibitions with high aesthetic and curatorial standards should be used to measure the potential of such apps more effectively.

Art students mostly provided a much more favorable assessment of the CREAMS VR editor platform. This can be attributed to their interest in using a cutting-edge tool, which generates both excitement and expectations. The main point identified that needs further improvement is firstly the perceived lack of realism. Moreover, students required a more clear-cut interaction context, i.e., the ability to organize associated material to artworks, e.g., through a user-friendly menu.

The Art Student VR Exhibition questionnaire, as mentioned in the Methodology section, is a composite concatenation of separate clusters that are either adapted (sets of) questions drawing from existing XR-related questionnaires or blocks of questions corresponding to the User Experience Questionnaire (UEQ, based on a 7-step Likert scale) as well as the System Usability Scale (SUS), based on a 5-step Likert scale. The adapted questions (also based on 5-step Likert scale) focus on qualitative aspects of CREAMS' applications.

The first set of ten questions (i.e., Q1 to Q10; see Table 1, below), address the functional aspect of the CREAMS VR editor. The following table (Table 1) presents, comparatively, the results from these questions, from the second formative and the summative evaluation phase.

Table 1. Usability related questions on VR platform, art student responses.

QUESTION	Second Formative Evaluation	Summative Evaluation	Explanation of 5 Likert Scale Steps
Q1. How would you rate the sign-up interface in terms of effectiveness?	4.16	4.05	points 1 to 5 stand for the following: (1) Very difficult/cumbersome to use; (2) Somewhat difficult/cumbersome to use; (3) Neither easy nor difficult to use; (4) Fairly easy to use; (5) Very easy to use.
Q2. How would you rate the interface regarding the creation of the exhibition in terms of effectiveness and ease of use?	3.72	3.98	
Q3. How would you rate the interface regarding the uploading of your artworks on the platform in terms of effectiveness and ease of use?	3.7	3.97	
Q4. How much helpful is the functionality for inserting an artwork (image) in the exhibition?	3.81	3.93	
Q5. How would you rate the interface providing access to the exhibition(s) assigned to you in terms of effectiveness?	3.9	4.01	
Q6. How would you rate the sizing functionality regarding the artworks?	3.7	4.14	
Q7. How would you rate the lighting functionality?	3.84	4.22	
Q8. How much helpful are the provisions of virtual rooms to create art exhibitions in terms of spatial context?	3.67	3.79	point 1 stands for: Not helpful at all; point 5: Very helpful
Q9. How much helpful are the provisions of curatorial function (e.g., arrangement of artworks in groups, description of groups and addition of related narrative)?	3.9	3.96	point 1 stands for: Not helpful at all; point 5: Very helpful
Q10. How much satisfactory is the rendering (appearance) of the artworks in the virtual exhibition?	3.82	4.08	point 1 stands for: Not satisfactory at all; point 5: Very satisfactory

Art students wish to exploit the creative and expressive capacities of VEs and deemed the use of the platform beneficial for their artistic development. Furthermore, in terms of incorporating chat function(s) and enhancing the social aspect of the application, while feedback from tutors is a very welcomed feature, there is a modicum of reticence in relation to receiving commentary from viewers, especially when this takes place in a publicly visible environment. We present below the results of questions 21 to 27 (formative evaluation) or (21 to 26 for the summative) immediately after the first set of questions. These two sets comprise especially adapted or created questions that correspond to the specificity of the CREAMS project. The results of questions 21 to 27 that relate to more specific issues pertinent to tertiary art education are shown in Table 2. Lastly, we present the results of two sets of questions that were especially created for this project, together (irrespective of question number order), and present afterwards those that relate to the pre-existing SUS and UEQ questionnaires, for better cohesion.

Table 2. Especially adapted questions on VR platform, art student responses.

QUESTION	Second Formative Evaluation	Summative Evaluation	Explanation of 5 Likert Scale Steps
Q21: Did the creation of the exhibition encourage self-reflection on your creative process?	3.75	3.51	In Q21 point 1 stands for 'Not at all, I Strongly disagree'; point 5 for 'Very much, I Strongly agree'
Q22: Did framing your exhibition with text/other material help you situate your practice (i.e., identify connections between your artistic research and issues, themes and relevant artworks)?	3.81	3.70	In Q22 point 1 stands for 'Not at all, I Strongly disagree'; point 5 for 'Very much, I Strongly agree'
Q23: How helpful was the experience in acquiring skills in curating and presenting art?	3.87	3.87	In Q23, point 1 stands for: Not helpful at all; point 5: Very much helpful
Q24: How much important do you think is to include resources in a creative way that matches the artworks exhibited?	4.09	Question deducted	In Q24, point 1 stands for: Not important at all; point 5: Very important
Q25: What do you think about receiving feedback/comments from viewers, visible only to you through a chat function?	3.81	3.89	In Questions 25, 26, 27, point 1 stands for: Not a desirable function at all; point 5: Very desirable function
Q26: What do you think about receiving feedback/comments from viewers, visible only to you through a chat function?	4.09	4.13	
Q27: What do you think about receiving feedback/comments from your tutors, through a chat function?	3.46	3.44	

Furthermore, participants were asked to fill out the SUS questionnaire (Q11–20) between the above two sets of questions, which shed light on usability issues. SUS follows a complex calculation procedure to procure the score, which, in turn, is measured against a benchmark chart. As previously mentioned, this is a scale that addresses finished products; thus, the (under development) CREAMS VR editor is measured against a yardstick regarding commercial and finished products. Nevertheless, findings during the second formative evaluation (a total score of 63.1) indicated that usability still needed significant improvements, thereby emphasizing this aspect with tangible improvements as the findings of the final summative evaluation phase suggest (71.6). The results of the SUS questions are shown in Table 3.

Table 3. System Usability Scale (SUS) questions, art students' responses on VR platform.

QUESTIONS:	2nd Formative Evaluation Results	Summative Evaluation Results
Q11: I think that I would like to use this system frequently.	3.57	4.03
Q12: I found the system unnecessarily complex.	2.61	1.98
Q13: I thought the system was easy to use.	3.58	3.90
Q14: I think that I would need the support of a technical person to be able to use this system.	2.60	2.23
Q15: I found the various functions in this system were well integrated (e.g., tutorial, virtual guide, artworks functionalities).	3.69	3.99
Q16: I thought there was inconsistency in this system.	2.51	2.02
Q17: I would imagine that most people would learn to use this system quickly.	3.82	3.87
Q18: I found the system difficult to use.	2.39	2.03
Q19: I felt confident using the application.	3.43	3.66
Q20: I needed to learn a lot of things before I could get going with this system.	2.73	2.43

3.4. UEQ Findings and Analysis

The benchmarks of UEQ (as is the case with SUS as well) are created with finished (and commercial) products in mind, which should be factored in during the formative evaluation phase of a research project. The dependability scale proved to be an area that requires more attention in the final development phase. However, novelty had the lowest numerical score. This is an indication that contemporary art applications are expected to be cutting-edge in relation to the aesthetic characteristics of the platform itself.

The User Experience Questionnaire has been a significant tool that helped streamline the analysis and the procurement of meaningful conclusions (Figures 6 and 7). The automated UEQ benchmark is created based on a large body of research conducted with this tool.

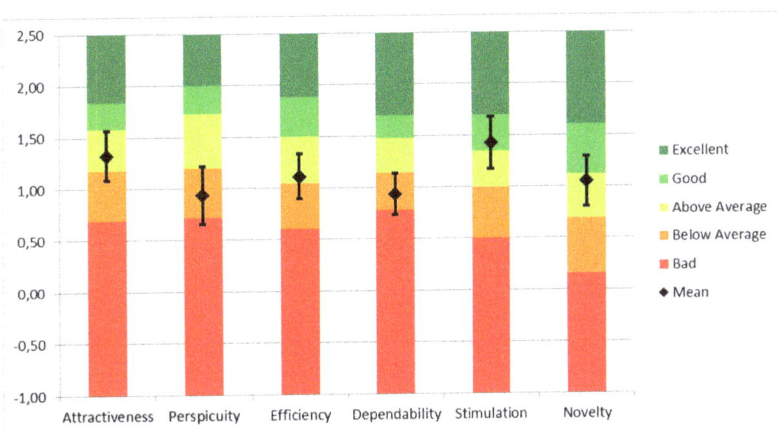

Figure 6. Art students' mean scores per UEQ scale (category), including confidence intervals during second formative evaluation phase. Result scales from −1 to 2.5 correspond to the seven Likert scale steps.

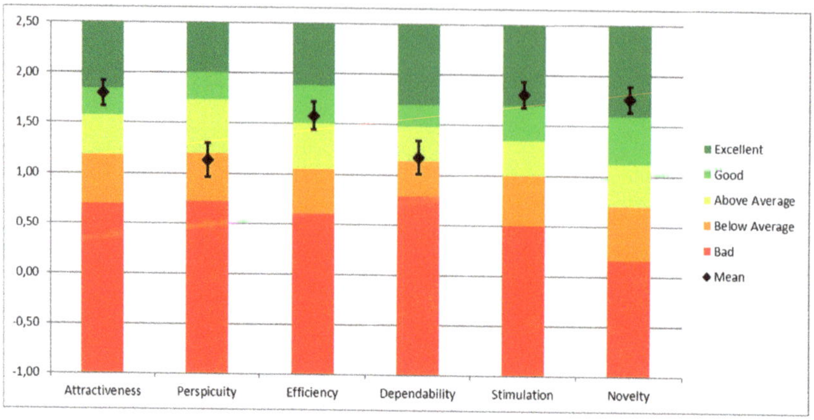

Figure 7. Art students' mean scores per UEQ scale (category), including confidence intervals during final summative evaluation.

Here, perspicuity, which relates to the degree to which an app is understandable and easy to grasp, suffers considerably (in both evaluation phases) and becomes a focal point for (further) improvement. At the same time, an equally frail area is dependability: users need to feel more confident using the system. The results (−3 to 3) correspond to the seven Likert scale steps. In Table 4, we present the mean value results from the second formative evaluation phase.

Table 4. Numeric values of UEQ art student responses during second formative evaluation.

Attractiveness	Pragmatic Quality	Hedonic Quality
1.32	0.99	1.24

In Table 5, we present the respective mean value results from the summative evaluation phase. A comparison suggests that significant progress was made in terms of user experience.

Table 5. Numeric values of UEQ art student responses during summative evaluation.

Attractiveness	Pragmatic Quality	Hedonic Quality
1.79	1.29	1.79

Table 6 provides details on the exact values obtained in the UEQ scales used.

Table 6. Detailed values of UEQ art student responses on VR platform, per scale (summative evaluation).

UEQ Scale	Mean	Variable	Comparison to Benchmark
Attractiveness	1.791	0.70	Good
Perspicuity	1.133	1.31	Below Average
Efficiency	1.578	0.87	Good
Dependability	1.173	1.24	Above Average
Stimulation	1.808	0.74	Excellent

The following chart (Figure 8) presents a combinatory overview of the second formative and the summative evaluation results for easier comparison. It shows in dark color the existing score from the second formative evaluation phase, and in lighter shade of the same color the additional progress made, as documented by the summative evaluation (except for the 'complicated/easy' metric, which remained static). One key area for further improvement is the (un)predictability factor, as users expressed in questionnaires and during focus groups a sense of being unable always to predict how the system will respond or what they should do next.

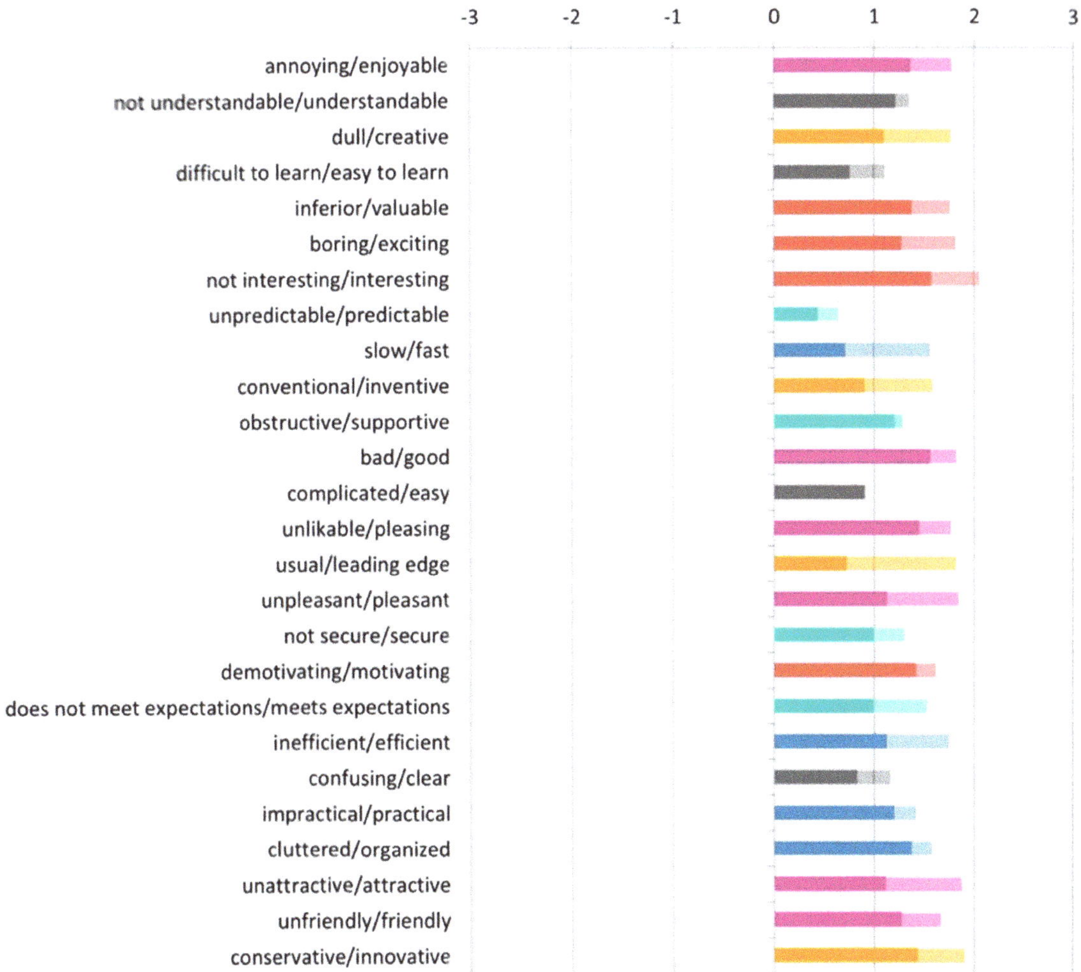

Figure 8. Combined chart of second formative and summative evaluation UEQ results. Dark shades: Second formative evaluation phase; lighter shades: progress as reflected in summative evaluation results.

The following chart (Figure 9) provides a more detailed overview of the UEQ results from the summative evaluation phase, with numeric values and an additional column (titled 'Scale') showing which questions were used to determine the results per scale (UEQ uses the term scale to convey the categories that, in turn, comprise the pragmatic and hedonic aspects of the evaluated application).

Mean	Left	Right	Scale	
1,8	annoying	enjoyable	Attractiveness	
1,4	not understandable	understandable	Perspicuity	
1,8	creative	dull	Novelty	
1,1	easy to learn	difficult to learn	Perspicuity	
1,8	valuable	inferior	Stimulation	
1,8	boring	exciting	Stimulation	
2,0	not interesting	interesting	Stimulation	
0,6	unpredictable	predictable	Dependability	
1,6	fast	slow	Efficiency	
1,6	inventive	conventional	Novelty	
1,2	obstructive	supportive	Dependability	
1,8	good	bad	Attractiveness	
0,9	complicated	easy	Perspicuity	
1,8	unlikable	pleasing	Attractiveness	
1,8	usual	leading edge	Novelty	
1,8	unpleasant	pleasant	Attractiveness	
1,3	secure	not secure	Dependability	
1,6	motivating	demotivating	Stimulation	
1,5	meets expectations	does not meet expectations	Dependability	
1,7	inefficient	efficient	Efficiency	
1,2	clear	confusing	Perspicuity	
1,4	impractical	practical	Efficiency	
1,6	organized	cluttered	Efficiency	
1,9	attractive	unattractive	Attractiveness	
1,7	friendly	unfriendly	Attractiveness	
1,9	conservative	innovative	Novelty	

Figure 9. Summative evaluation's UEQ results per question. Note the scale (category) into which these questions pertain to their respective column.

4. Discussion

This section provides a discussion that focuses on the findings from art students' responses in relation to the VR platform. Firstly, usability and practical issues are outlined as follows.

Art students commented on the need to improve the adjustments procedure, during which a user must select from a drop-down menu (see Figure 10) which element they want to adjust. Still, oftentimes, it is fairly confusing to locate the right item through this route as one may be unsure of the name given to each item, and in any case, it is a cumbersome procedure that is not very intuitive. The ability to just (right) click on an element and access a user-friendly adjustment menu is highly desirable.

Some indicative written responses in relation to what improvements they wish to see or what comments they want to make are as follows:

1. Simplification in moving between the options of settings [this is a characteristic comment on user interface]
2. The artworks may look good on the platform, but the background should get more real space vibes [this is a characteristic comment on spatial realism]. On the flip side, another participant comments: 'It looks kind of artificial, but it doesn't bother me that much'. This is an indication that realism in the rendering of the space should not necessarily strive to achieve commercial-type levels of life-like appearance, as the main idea is to provide functional and flexible spatial manipulation capabilities even within

a minimal aesthetic, as the artworks in the last analysis should be the protagonists rather than aim for a cinematic experience, as pointed out in a group discussion with experts. During focus group discussions, participants insisted on the importance of exploiting the XR medium's capacity to support creative spatial configurations and make the most out of virtual spaces in terms of expressive capabilities and aesthetic potential. For example, focus group participants, as well as written responses in open questions, suggested the need for supporting creative uses of the space or navigational functions, e.g., by introducing transparent walls or even offering the possibility to create virtual exhibitions that defy the rules of gravity by allowing the viewers to hover between exhibits.

3. Another responder comments: 'It is still restricted. I would like to have more choices'. Then, he or she suggests 'Expanding it yet keeping it easy'. This brings us to a key point: often, art students expressed their need for simplicity and intuitiveness through a clear-cut and straightforward UI (user interface).

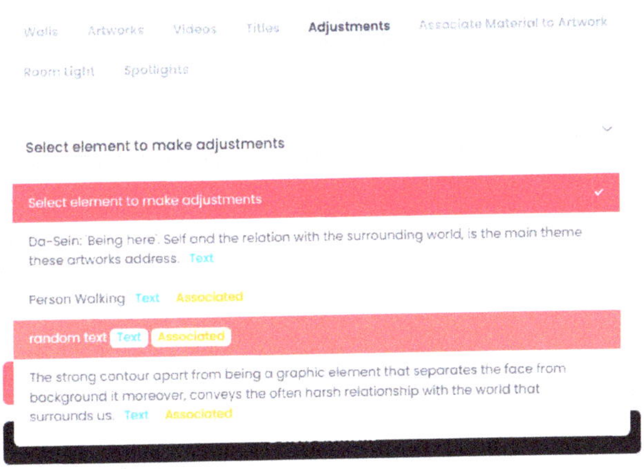

Figure 10. Screenshot from adjustments menu and pertinent drop-down list.

In a nutshell, the insights gained in relation to users' feedback suggest that enhanced realism, an intuitive navigation interface, user-friendly interactivity provisions, and dependable support and guidance should be given priority. Furthermore, according to the feedback, the VR application necessitates simplicity, intuitiveness, and more support with well-placed links to tutorials, guidelines, and help messages. These were areas that transpired during the first evaluation phase as well. Even though much has been achieved in rendering the VR editor more user-friendly, this appears to be a key aspect for users. Concrete steps and measures have been taken, in the light of the first evaluation phase, ranging from improving the semantics of tabs, e.g., what was initially called 'Sketchbook' (function) see Figure 11, changed into 'Associate Material to Artwork' (see Figure 12), to the mechanism of inserting artworks or managing the exhibitions' spaces with the introduction of a modular floor plan functionality for designing the gallery.

Moreover, in terms of limitations and areas for further improvement in relation to usability and user interface, as the abovementioned chart (see Figure 9) clearly illustrates, the learnability (perspicuity) of the system is a relatively low-scoring aspect of the app, as users still deem the VR platform to be somewhat complicated. This finding, in conjunction with feedback from focus group discussions, highlights the importance of clear, concise, and readily available manuals, as well as other provisions (e.g., informative text or Frequently

Asked Questions/FAQs provisions in the form of drop-down menus or of interactive widgets) for the support of the users. A recurring idea in conversations within focus groups is that there should be some links within the applications rather than externally positioned manuals in the knowledge repository section of the CREAMS site, rendering access to useful guides easy and straightforward. Unpredictability is also linked, as we gathered from conversations by the lingering existence of some bugs or glitches that, despite the improvements made, still occur unexpectedly due to the limitations posed by the fact that the app is based on open-source code and, therefore, has some inherent limitations in this respect.

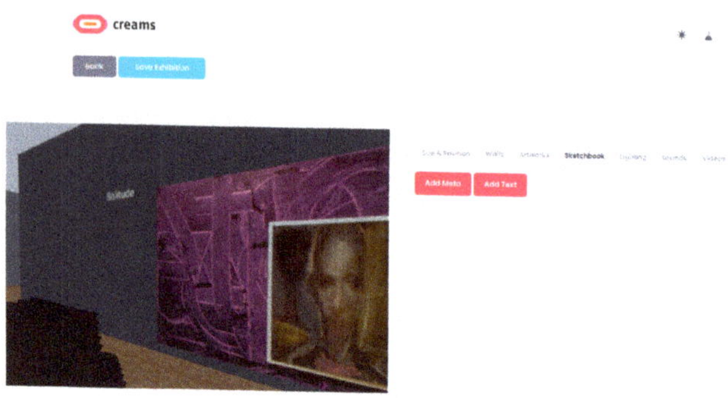

Figure 11. Screenshot from art exhibition before amendments in tab semantics.

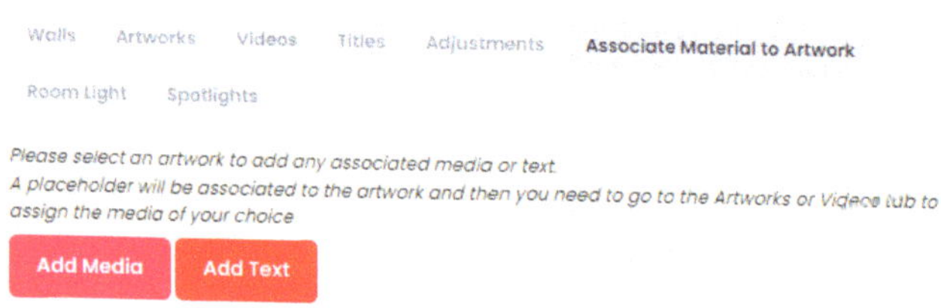

Figure 12. Screenshot from art exhibition that visitors evaluated with updated tabs.

Furthermore, beyond the usability-related and aesthetics-related issues (e.g., in relation to realistic rendering of the environment, or lack thereof), responders commented on more specific aspects of the platform's capacity to support learning in the fields of curatorial frameworks as well as fostering self-reflection upon and their ability to contextualize their art practice. Virtual gallery spaces offer immense opportunities for interaction with additional resources in imaginative ways (e.g., by hovering clusters of artwork-related material around the viewer) as suggested during focus groups' discussions online and in person by participating art students.

Moreover, the ability to frame exhibited work with texts, multimodal resources, and other informative or aesthetically charged material matching the gist of the exhibition itself has been seen as highly desirable throughout focus group discussions and pertinent questionnaire answers. The positive disposition towards XR's capacity to support students' ability to contextualize their artworks or, for the same matter, curate their virtual exhibitions is reflected in the specially adapted questions that are presented in Table 2. More specifically, questions 21 to 23 show a positive approach in the abovementioned aspects, as the numeric values are above 3.5 and gravitate towards 4 out of 5. This is a key and distinguishing feature of virtual exhibition, which empowers artists to add contextual resources in ways that are not possible in conventional gallery spaces by exploiting the potential of XR for interactive, personalized, and active engagement with multimodal material.

While we included different sets of questions, some verbatim, adopting existing questionnaires (e.g., SUS) and others adapted from other publications to match the specific characteristics of the CREAMS project, we chose not to generate a comprehensive scheme, mapping the interrelations between the different elements such as the one proposed by Hammady et al. [25] or, for the same matter, comparative charts of metrics and other evaluation aspects in the form of a systematic review as in Kabassi et al. [6]. This evaluation interrelated quantitative data (from sets of questions) and qualitative findings (from written comments or focus group discussions) with the aim of highlighting areas in need of improvement to meet art students' expectations, as expressed during the needs analysis phase of the CREAMS project. Beyond the pragmatic role of this evaluation process that informed the development of this XR platform, in hindsight, future research should aim to generate a more comprehensive mapping of how different elements, aspects and methods of XR exhibition-creating applications can be integrated into a schematic and holistic approach. This may be a limitation of this study, that nevertheless inspires future research that will not inform pertinent methodologies, solely by offering an instance of practice, but by suggesting a thorough framework with concrete schemes, addressing both practical and theoretical facets of XR evaluation.

5. Concluding Remarks

Last but not least, we include a short discussion on the specificity and the distinct characteristics that differentiate learning and teaching processes in the visual arts domain. This, in turn, is reflected in ways to assess learnability in Fine Art Schools.

Art exhibitions are not lessons, neither for those who create them nor for those who visit them. At the same time, they offer opportunities for learning, which means creating meaning through the mediation of sense and emotion, but in such a way that the outcomes of learning are not predetermined or easily assessed. This is deeply rooted in the nature of artistic practice and its function as a fulcrum for thinking and feeling differently. In relation to learning in the field of visual arts, as Addison notes [39], assessable and non-assessable learning operate dialectically, and if one or the other ceases to exist, the benefits of both would be negated. While such extracurricular research-driven initiatives and settings offer opportunities for enhanced learning and reciprocity in student–faculty relationships, they are not readily available to all.

CREAMS as a research project and more specifically its evaluation methodology undertook to provide and optimize tools such as virtual exhibitions that encourage and at the same time require negotiation, reflexivity, and relational encounters between learners and teachers. This is reflected in this paper, which aspires to offer inspiration to stakeholders who work in the interstices of XR technologies, culture, and art education.

Furthermore, the need to exploit the possibilities offered by new media to support a dynamic and in-depth provision of associated contextual material is prevalent. As Vergo states [40]:

> *The notion that works of art in particular should be left to speak for themselves takes no account of the fact that such works are, for most visitors, remarkably taciturn objects. Left to speak for themselves, they often say very little; and sometimes quite considerable effort is required on the part of the historian, art historian, critic or the viewer to coax them into eloquence.*

This quotation underlines the value of framing visual works with a nexus of informational or even polysemic material, which befits contemporary artworks that are typically open to multiple interpretations. After all, the virtual museum "is not a mere reflection of the real; it has developed a presence/life of its own" [41], according to [42]. This signals the importance of creating virtual exhibitions that exploit the potential of digital tools rather than being digital replicas of brick-and-mortar gallery spaces. Learning through the arts and using digital tools to create exhibitions as tools for enhancing creative, critical, and practical skills is a highly personal, heuristic, and reflexive process [43–45] that may be elusive, multifaceted, and hard to capture in all its dimensions [39]. This has been a central challenge for this evaluation process outlined here and a source of inspiration for developing a concrete evaluation philosophy that matches the intricacies of assessing the efficacy of XR tools for learning and acquiring diverse skills in this context.

Author Contributions: Conceptualization, P.D., S.S. and E.S.; methodology, P.D. and S.S.; validation, E.S., D.K. and C.F.; formal analysis, P.D.; investigation, P.D.; resources, P.D. and S.S.; data curation, P.D.; writing—original draft preparation, P.D.; writing—review and editing, S.S.; visualization, P.D.; supervision, E.S.; project administration, C.F. and D.K.; funding acquisition, C.F. All authors have read and agreed to the published version of the manuscript.

Funding: This research has been financed by the Erasmus+ CREAMS project (Project ID: KA220-HED-E06518FA) under the call KA220-HED—Cooperation partnerships in higher education (Greek State Scholarship's Foundation (IKY).

Institutional Review Board Statement: The study was conducted in accordance with the Declaration of Helsinki and approved by the Institutional Review Board (or Ethics Committee) of the Aristotle University of Thessaloniki, Greece (approval date: 07/06/2022; protocol number: 151103/2022).

Informed Consent Statement: Informed consent was obtained from all subjects involved in the study.

Data Availability Statement: Restrictions apply to the availability of these data. Data were obtained from participants in the CREAMS research project and are available from the authors with the permission of the participants.

Conflicts of Interest: The authors declare no conflicts of interest.

References

1. González-Zamar, M.D.; Abad-Segura, E. Implications of Virtual Reality in Arts Education: Research Analysis in the Context of Higher Education. *Educ. Sci.* **2020**, *10*, 225. [CrossRef]
2. Chan, C.S.; Bogdanovic, J.; Kalivarapu, V. Applying immersive virtual reality for remote teaching architectural history. *Educ. Inf. Technol.* **2021**, *27*, 4365–4397. [CrossRef]
3. Huaman, E.M.R.; Aceituno, R.G.A.; Sharhorodska, O. Application of Virtual Reality and Gamification in the Teaching of Art History. In *Learning and Collaboration Technologies. Ubiquitous and Virtual Environments for Learning and Collaboration*; HCII 2019; Lecture Notes in Computer Science; Zaphiris, P., Ioannou, A., Eds.; Springer: Cham, Swizerland, 2019; Volume 11591, pp. 220–229.
4. Qiu, Y.; Xiao, Y.; Jiang, T. An Online College Student Art Exhibition App Based on Virtual Reality Technology. *IOP Conf. Ser. Mater. Sci. Eng.* **2020**, *750*, 384–393. [CrossRef]
5. Gifreu-Castells, A. Approach to the Curatorship of Virtual Reality Exhibitions. In *A Companion to Curation*; Buckley, B., Conomos, J., Eds.; Wiley: New York, NY, USA, 2019; pp. 360–374.
6. Kabassi, K. Evaluating websites of museums: State of the art. *J. Cult. Herit.* **2017**, *24*, 184–196. [CrossRef]
7. Morales, J.; Cornide-Reyes, H.; Rossel, P.; Sáez, P.; Silva-Aravena, F. Virtual Reality, Augmented Reality and Metaverse: Customer Experience Approach and User Experience Evaluation Methods. Literature Review. In *Social Computing and Social Media*; HCII 2023; Lecture Notes in Computer Science; Coman, A., Vasilache, S., Eds.; Springer: Cham, Swizerland, 2023; Volume 14025, pp. 554–566.
8. Barricelli, B.R.; De Bonis, A.; Di Gaetano, S.; Valtolina, S. Semiotic framework for virtual reality usability and UX evaluation: A pilot study. In Proceedings of the GHItaly18: 2nd Workshop on Games-Human Interaction, Castiglione della Pescaia, Italy, 29 May 2018.
9. García, M.; Requesens, J.; Cano, S. User Experience Evaluation Methods in Mixed Reality Environments. In *Social Computing and Social Media*; HCII 2024; Lecture Notes in Computer Science; Coman, A., Vasilache, S., Eds.; Springer: Cham, Swizerland, 2024; Volume 14703, pp. 179–193.

10. Campoverde-Durán, R.; Garzón-Vera, B. Mixed Reality: Evaluation of the User Experience to Improve the Interpretation of the Archaeological Heritage. In *Communication and Applied Technologies*; Smart Innovation, Systems and Technologies; López-López, P.C., Barredo, D., Torres-Toukoumidis, Á., De-Santis, A., Avilés, Ó., Eds.; Springer: Singapore, 2023; Volume 318.
11. Vital, R.; Sylaiou, S.; Koukopoulos, D.; Koukoulis, K.; Dafiotis, P.; Fidas, C. Comparison of extended reality platforms and tools for viewing and exhibiting art. *Digit. Appl. Archaeol. Cult. Herit.* **2023**, *31*, e00298. [CrossRef]
12. Song, Y.; Li, L. Research on Application of VR Technology in Art Design Teaching. In Proceedings of the 2018 International Conference on Engineering Simulation and Intelligent Control (ESAIC), Hunan, China, 10–11 August 2018; pp. 343–345.
13. Vygotsky, L.S. *Mind in Society: The Development of Higher Psychological Processes*, 1st ed.; Harvard University Press: Cambridge, MA, USA, 1978; pp. 1–176.
14. Sylaiou, S.; Dafiotis, P.; Koukopoulos, D.; Koukoulis, K.; Vital, R.; Antoniou, A.; Fidas, C. From physical to virtual art exhibitions and beyond: Survey and some issues for consideration for the metaverse. *J. Cult. Herit.* **2023**, *66*, 86–98. [CrossRef]
15. Ivancic, D. A virtual perspective: Measuring engagement and perspective in virtual art galleries. *Int. J. Arts Technol.* **2016**, *9*, 273–298. [CrossRef]
16. Sylaiou, S.; Mania, K.; Paliokas, I.; Pujol-Tost, L.; Killintzis, V.; Liarokapis, F. Exploring the educational impact of diverse technologies in online virtual museums. *Intern. J. Arts Technol.* **2017**, *10*, 58–84. [CrossRef]
17. Sylaiou, S.; Mania, K.; Karoulis, A.; White, M. Exploring the relationship between presence and enjoyment in a virtual museum. *Int. J. Hum.-Comput. Stud.* **2010**, *68*, 243–253. [CrossRef]
18. Lacet, D.; Zeller, M.V.; Martins, P.; Morgado, L. Digital Storytelling approaches in Virtual Museums: Umbrella review of systematic reviews. *J. Dig. Media Inter.* **2022**, *5*, 23–43. [CrossRef]
19. Lombard, M.; Ditton, T. At the heart of it all: The concept of presence. *J. Comp. Med. Commun.* **2006**, *3*, JCMC321. [CrossRef]
20. Weber, S.; Weibel, D.; Mast, F.W. How to Get There When You Are There Already? Defining Presence in Virtual Reality and the Importance of Perceived Realism. *Front. Psychol.* **2021**, *12*, 628298. [CrossRef]
21. Sutcliffe, A.; Gault, B. Heuristic evaluation of virtual reality applications. *Interact. Comput.* **2004**, *16*, 831–849. [CrossRef]
22. Skarbez, R.; Brooks, F.P., Jr.; Whitton, M.C. A survey of presence and related concepts. *ACM Comput. Surv.* **2017**, *50*, 96. [CrossRef]
23. Hofer, M.; Hartmann, T.; Eden, A.; Ratan, R.; Hahn, L. The role of plausibility in the experience of spatial presence in virtual environments. *Front. Virtual Real.* **2020**, *1*, 2. [CrossRef]
24. Gorini, A.; Capideville, C.S.; De Leo, G.; Mantovani, F.; Riva, G. The role of immersion and narrative in mediated presence: The virtual hospital experience. *Cyberpsychol. Behav. Soc. Netw.* **2011**, *14*, 99–105. [CrossRef]
25. Hammady, R.; Ma, M.; Al-Kalha, Z.; Strathearn, C. A framework for constructing and evaluating the role of MR as a holographic virtual guide in museums. *Virtual Real.* **2021**, *25*, 895–918. [CrossRef]
26. Wharton, C.; Reiman, J.; Lewis, C.; Polson, P. The cognitive walkthrough method: A practitioner's guide. In *Usability Inspection Methods*; Nielsen, J., Mack, R.L., Eds.; Wiley: New York, NY, USA, 1994; pp. 105–140.
27. Sutcliffe, A.G.; Kaur, K.D. Evaluating the usability of virtual reality user interfaces. *Behav. Inf. Technol.* **2000**, *19*, 415–426. [CrossRef]
28. Lewis, C.; Polson, P.; Wharton, C.; Reiman, J. Testing a walkthrough methodology for theory-based design of walk-up-and-use interfaces. In Proceedings of the Conference on Human Factors in Computing, Seattle, WA, USA, 1–5 April 1990.
29. Norman, D.A. Cognitive engineering. In *User Centred System Design: New Perspectives on Human Computer Interaction*; Norman, D., Draper, S., Eds.; Lawrence Erlbaum Associates: Hillsdale, NJ, USA, 1986; pp. 31–62.
30. Lee, K.M. Presence, Explicated. *Communic. Theory* **2004**, *14*, 27–50. [CrossRef]
31. Witmer, B.G.; Singer, M.J. Measuring presence in virtual environments: A presence questionnaire. *Presence Teleoperators Virtual Environ.* **1998**, *7*, 225–240. [CrossRef]
32. Fontaine, G. The experience of a sense of presence in intercultural and international encounters. *Presence Teleoperators Virtual Environ.* **1992**, *1*, 482–490. [CrossRef]
33. Biocca, F.; Delaney, B. Immersive virtual reality technology. In *Communication in the Age of Virtual Reality*; Biocca, F., Levy, M.R., Eds.; Lawrence Erlbaum Associates Inc.: New York, NY, USA, 1995; pp. 57–124.
34. Hooper-Greenhill, E. Measuring Learning Outcomes in Museums, Archives and Libraries: The Learning Impact Research Project (LIRP). *Int. J. Herit. Stud.* **2004**, *10*, 151–174. [CrossRef]
35. Brooke, J. SUS-A quick and dirty usability scale. In *Usability Evaluation in Industry*, 1st ed.; Jordan, P.W., Thomas, B., Weerdmeester, B.A., McClelland, I.L., Eds.; Taylor & Francis: London, UK, 1996; pp. 189–194.
36. Laugwitz, B.; Schrepp, M.; Held, T. Construction and evaluation of a user experience questionnaire. In Proceedings of the Symposium of the Workgroup Human-Computer Interaction and Usability Engineering of the Austrian Computer Society, Graz, Austria, 20 November 2008.
37. Schrepp, M.; Hinderks, A.; Thomaschewski, J. Construction of a Benchmark for the User Experience Questionnaire (UEQ). Int. *J. Interact. Multimed. Artif. Intel.* **2017**, *4*, 40–44.

38. Schrepp, M.; Hinderks, A.; Thomaschewski, J. Applying the User Experience Questionnaire (UEQ) in Different Evaluation Scenarios. In Proceedings of the Design, User Experience, and Usability. Theories, Methods, and Tools for Designing the User Experience, Heraklion, Greece, 22–27 June 2014.
39. Addison, N. Doubting learning outcomes in higher education contexts: From performativity towards emergence and negotiation. *Int. J. Art Des. Educ.* **2014**, *33*, 313–325. [CrossRef]
40. Vergo, P. *The New Museology*, 1st ed.; Reaktion Books: London, UK, 1989; pp. 1–238.
41. Battro, A.M. From Malraux's Imaginary Museum to the Virtual Museum. In *Museums in a Digital Age*; Parry, R., Ed.; Routledge: London, UK, 2010; pp. 136–147.
42. Schweibenz, W. The virtual museum: An overview of its origins, concepts, and terminology. *Mus. Rev.* **2019**, *4*, 1–29.
43. Irwin, R.L.; Beer, R.; Springgay, S.; Grauer, K.; Xiong, G.; Bickel, B. The rhizomatic relations of a/r/tography. *Stud. Art Educ.* **2006**, *48*, 70–88. [CrossRef]
44. Gouzouasis, P.; Irwin, R.L.; Gordon, C.; Miles, E. Commitments to a community of artistic inquiry: Becoming pedagogical through a/r/tography in teacher education. *Int. J. Educ. Arts* **2013**, *14*, 1–24.
45. Irwin, R.L.; Springgay, S. A/r/tography as practice-based research. In *Arts-Based Research in Education: Foundations for Practice*; Cahnmann Taylor, M., Siegesmund, R., Eds.; Routledge: New York, NY, USA, 2008; pp. 103–124.

Multimodal Technologies and Interaction

MDPI

Article

BabloXR: An Authoring Tool for Developing WebXR Educational Applications †

María Lucía Barrón-Estrada [1], Ramón Zatarain-Cabada [1,*], Manuel Alberto Sotelo-Rivas [1], María Blanca Ibáñez [2] and Víctor Manuel Bátiz-Beltrán [1]

1 Instituto Tecnológico de Culiacán, Tecnológico Nacional de México, Culiacán 80220, Sinaloa, Mexico; lucia.be@culiacan.tecnm.mx (M.L.B.-E.); manuel.sr@culiacan.tecnm.mx (M.A.S.-R.); victor.bb@culiacan.tecnm.mx (V.M.B.-B.)

2 Departamento de Ingeniería Telemática, Universidad Carlos III de Madrid, 28911 Leganés, Spain; mbibanez@it.uc3m.es

* Correspondence: ramon.zc@culiacan.tecnm.mx

† This paper is an extended version of our paper published in Zatarain Cabada, R.; Barrón Estrada, M.L.; Sotelo Rivas, M.A.; Ibáñez, M.B. An Authoring Tool for XR Learning Environments. In Proceedings of the Extended Reality; De Paolis, L.T., Arpaia, P., Sacco, M., Eds.; Springer Nature Switzerland: Cham, 2024; pp. 192–208.

Abstract: Different areas of education have undergone a significant transformation due to the rapid progress of extended reality in recent years. Nonetheless, existing eXtended Reality (XR) authoring tools often require advanced programming skills, limiting their accessibility to educators and students. To address this challenge, we introduce BabloXR, an intuitive authoring tool that leverages Blockly to enable visual, code-free programming for creating educational XR environments. BabloXR was evaluated through a user study involving teachers and students who successfully designed their own XR learning environments. The results indicate that users of BabloXR were able to create complete and detailed scenarios, with usability testing revealing high ease of use, positive user experience, and strong interest in extended reality.

Keywords: authoring tools; extended reality; WebXR; learning technologies

1. Introduction

In this paper, we present an expanded and revised version of a conference paper originally presented at the International Conference on eXtended Reality (XR Salento 2024) [1]. The term extended reality (XR) has been used to embrace diverse spatial technologies like augmented reality (AR), virtual reality (VR), and mixed reality (MR). The term refers to technologies that are used to generate interactive environments that combine reality with virtual scenarios based on the representation of digital environments and elements. Thus, XR includes the full spectrum of the virtual continuum concept, which represents the degree of virtuality of an interactive environment between man and machine using a continuous scale. This degree of virtuality ranges between the extremes of a completely virtual environment to a completely real one.

Web-based XR learning tools allow end users to interact with educational material through a web browser. The spatial and immersive computer technologies developed aim to improve educational experiences by presenting information while enhancing sensory perception, achieving this through AR techniques. AR allows virtual elements to be overlaid on real-world scenes to interact among them. On the other hand, VR can be used to recreate a fully virtual and immersive environment, where users experience the learning material while isolated from reality.

Implementing XR technology allows students to have more active control over their learning strategies, increasing student–teacher interaction as well as peer connectivity. In this context, the application of XR approaches includes observational learning, operational learning, social learning, and academic learning, covering a broad range of educational experiences [2]. In the scoping review conducted in [3], the authors explore the current landscape of extended reality (XR) engines used to create gamified apps and serious games. The authors analyzed the literature from 2019 to 2023 to identify XR engines and their core functionalities. They also identified the specific game attributes these engines support for serious games, such as rules, goals, and feedback, as well as the types of learning activities the engines can facilitate. The research ultimately aims to help developers select the most appropriate XR engine for their educational or training applications based on the desired features and learning outcomes. Today, there are many examples of applications that have explored the effectiveness of XR in education, ranging from biology experiments, art education, language, music, medicine, and physics [4].

Presently, different methods for presenting AR, VR, and MR content rely on how programs are made for particular platforms and devices; this strategy carries several limitations, including cross-platform support. Consequently, the development of XR applications typically necessitates numerous cycles of adaptation to different platforms natively, thereby increasing both the financial cost and the implementation time of these applications. As a result, web-based XR implementations have been developed that aim to address current challenges taking advantage of the current paradigm of providing online services for any type of application. Web-based application development has become relevant due to its basic capacity to provide cross-platform functionality and simplicity of access. Using these methods, applications can be created in a hybrid fashion that combines web services with native capabilities, giving them the benefits of both techniques [5,6]. Overall, these advancements in services and infrastructure offer a common platform for the extensive adoption of XR online.

The World Wide Web Consortium (W3C) has published a set of standards, known as WebXR Device API (WebXR), to enable the deployment of XR applications on the web, relying on WebGL to display 2D or 3D graphics. WebXR facilitates the development of applications while also providing users with a convenient way to improve accessibility. Through WebXR, XR applications may be accessed using any device equipped with basic web browsing capabilities and a mainstream browser (e.g., Chrome and Firefox). These benefits, both for developers and users, have resulted in the increased popularity of WebXR, with open-source graphic engines, such as A-Frame and Babylon.js [7,8], offering great input in the development and distribution of XR content.

Despite current improvements, challenges remain to fully leverage the use of this technology in the classroom. Developing XR tools generally requires considerable technical skills, which teachers may lack altogether, thus posing a gap that would require educators to go on a complex and demanding learning curve to train as developers. Learning to develop XR apps can, therefore, add to an already brimful workload and can divert time and attention that should be focused on preparing lessons for students [9]. This technical barrier highlights the need for intuitive authoring tools that simplify content creation.

To address this gap, we introduce BabloXR, an authoring tool designed with the aim of providing a fast and easy approach to creating XR learning environments. BabloXR eliminates the requirement for programming skills by incorporating block-based visual programming, allowing educators to design and visualize interactive lessons in real time. Once completed, these XR environments can be instantly shared with students via a simple link, fostering accessibility and engagement in digital learning.

This research paper is structured as follows: Section 2 presents work related to Web XR technology and different authoring tools for the creation of XR applications; Section 3 presents the software architecture, the implementation methodology, the user interface of BabloXR, and the steps to create a learning environment; Section 4 presents the experimental design for the testing phase; Section 5 describes the results and discussion; and, finally, Section 6 provides conclusions and outlines future research directions.

2. Related Works

Below are recent works related to the development and usage trends of WebXR technology and XR authoring tools. As previously stated, the term XR is used as an umbrella term that includes both AR and VR, as both technologies are addressed for the purposes of this study.

2.1. Developments and Trends in the Use of WebXR Technology

Next, we present different state-of-the-art works that are oriented towards discussing connectivity, scalability, and remote collaboration as representative characteristics of WebXR technology.

The research conducted in [10] introduces a new approach to extended reality (XR) collaboration that improves upon existing methods by separating and sharing information about objects of interest (OOIs) and ambient objects (AOs) differently. Instead of creating complex 3D models of the entire workspace, the system pre-models only the OOIs with high precision while reconstructing the AOs in real time as point clouds using LiDAR technology. These point clouds are then streamed with low latency using WebRTC, providing remote collaborators with intuitive spatial awareness of the local site without requiring extensive setup or limiting collaboration to pre-scanned areas. This hybrid method aims to make XR collaboration more practical and efficient for tasks involving physical objects by reducing preparation time and allowing flexibility in location.

In the work presented in [11], the authors explore the potential and challenges of conducting XR research remotely, rather than in a traditional lab setting. A survey of XR researchers identifies drawbacks, such as difficulties in participant recruitment and technical hurdles, alongside significant opportunities, including the ability to collect detailed data using built-in XR features and conduct studies more cost effectively. The authors suggest viewing XR devices as powerful data collection tools and encourage the development of frameworks to facilitate robust remote XR experimentation.

The research work in [12] explores the need for XR experiences that can scale between different devices, levels of virtuality, and numbers of collaborators. While current XR applications often focus on single-use cases, technologies, and limited users, the authors propose the concept of Scalable Extended Reality (XRS) to foster broader adoption by enabling fluid transitions across these dimensions. The paper reviews existing research in key areas—collaboration features, visualization, and interaction techniques—and identifies challenges and future research directions to realize the potential of XRS.

Finally, the study in [13] investigates a new immersive teaching method that leverages the capabilities of 5G and extended reality XR technologies, enhanced by a reinforcement learning model. The research argues that traditional teaching struggles with limited methods and resource utilization and proposes this 5G + XR approach as a solution to create engaging and effective learning experiences. Experiments comparing this immersive method to traditional teaching showed improved student learning outcomes, participation, and overall experience, highlighting its potential superiority and paving the way for modern educational reforms.

2.2. Tools for Building XR Learning Environments

In the work of [14], the authors created BlocklyVR, a VR web app that uses a block-based programming interface that includes a workspace where users may interact by dragging blocks in a 3D world. The objective of this study was to compare the efficiency of performance in 2D and 3D environments. The findings indicate that the acquisition of specific programming skills is enhanced in virtual environments. This enhancement can be attributed to the users' sense of immersion, which enables them to concentrate on resolving problems.

As outlined in [15], to create AR environments, the authors developed a web application called BlocklyAR. A workspace and a place to view the AR world being created in real time are provided by this program. The primary objective of BlocklyAR is to facilitate the development of AR applications without necessitating proficiency in the syntax of a programming language.

Another web application that combines VR and AR technologies was developed by [16]. The tool, BlocklyXR, combines VR and AR technologies; it has a graphical coding editor where the user implements the logic and a panel to choose a portion of the real world that will then be recreated in 3D.

What is remarkable about this software is its capacity to import 3D models and its easy-to-use feature according to the results of the technology acceptance model.

In a different study [17], the authors developed a mobile application called StoryMakAR to create Internet of Things (IoT) applications. This application turns electronic devices into internet-connectable devices, complemented by two additional applications: the first to program electronic components is a block-based programming web application, and the second, called EventMakAR, is an event planning application.

On the other hand, Ref. [18] highlights the importance of authoring tools in staff training. In this study, the users are able to develop particular scenarios using a script-based authoring tool. This tool, TrainAR, is a plugin of the Unity editor that defines the program logic by working with the sequence of states of nodes that are interrelated. Among other things, TrainAR offers a file structure of 3D elements and textures as well as a scene element inspector.

In [19], the authors presented a review of 43 relevant AR Authoring Toolkits for Education. Half of the AR Authoring Toolkits were not accessible, and more than half of the toolkits required some kind of programming knowledge. Moreover, the results of this study show a lack of empirical evaluation. The authors found that only five toolkits met the needs of teachers in designing educational AR experiences. They are VuforiaStudio [20], BlippAR [21], AWE (not openly accessible), ARMediaStudio [22], and Areeka [23]. A drawback is that none of the five tools were evaluated with a statistical method.

Finally, in [24], the authors developed JEM Inventor an authoring tool based on MIT App Inventor to generate Mobile Learning Games (MLGs). This technology eliminates the need for prior technological experience by allowing users to access more complex mobile device functionalities as their proficiency increases. According to the test results, it works well to improve learning and streamline the MLG production process, making instructional games easier for teachers to use and more accessible.

Table 1 shows a comparison between these authoring tools, including their applications, technologies, platforms, and operating systems. These tools use virtual reality (VR), augmented reality (AR), mixed reality (MR), or extended reality (XR) technologies. Most of these applications are designed to be used on a web platform and are cross-platform and accessible through any browser. StoryMakAR and JEM Inventor are designed just for mobile devices (Android and iOS), and TrainAR is available for desktops running Windows and MacOS operating systems.

Table 1. Comparison among XR authoring tools.

Application	Technology	Platform	Operating System
BlocklyVR [14]	AR	Web	Multiplatform (Browser)
BlocklyAR [15]	AR	Web	Multiplatform (Browser)
BlocklyXR [16]	XR	Web	Multiplatform (Browser)
StoryMakAR [17]	AR	Mobile	Android, iOS
TrainAR [18]	AR	Desktop	Windows, MacOS
Vuforia [20]	AR	Web, Mobile, Desktop	Android, iOS, Windows
BlippAR [21]	AR	Web, Mobile	Android, iOS
ARMediaStudio [22]	MR	Web, Mobile	Android, iOS
Areeka [23]	AR	Web, Mobile	Android, iOS
JEMInventor [24]	AR	Mobile	Android, iOS

3. Materials and Methods

3.1. The Authoring Tool

In this study, we introduce BabloXR, a cloud-based platform using Google Firebase services designed to facilitate the creation of XR learning environments for teachers without technical training. Although Google Firebase makes it possible to access data from anywhere, it also has the security features required to restrict access to authorized individuals only. Through BabloXR, teachers can create their profiles, upload multimedia files (such as audio, images, and videos), and design XR learning environments. These environments can be shared with students via a link, providing an interactive and accessible learning experience.

3.2. The Software Requirements and Architecture

User requirements were obtained through research techniques, including a study of authoring tools for creating virtual reality (VR), augmented reality (AR), and/or mixed reality (MR) environments. User requirements for BabloXR include the ability to use blocks to create XR learning environments and visualize modifications in real time, access the platform from any internet-enabled device, allow for the import of 3D objects and multimedia, and facilitate the sharing of created environments. Functional requirements for BabloXR include the creation of XR environments that can be saved, shared, and visualized in real time, allowing for the import of multimedia files to enrich such environments. Quality requirements for BabloXR include portability, which is met through the design of the tool as a web platform accessible on any device with a browser, security by handling authentication of all accesses to protect the integrity of user information, and usability, which is demonstrated in Section 5.2. These quality requirements guarantee that BabloXR is accessible, secure, available, easy to use, and efficient.

Figure 1 shows the software architecture of the system, with the following characteristics:

- Client–Server: Since BabloXR works as a distributed system, client–server architecture supports the separation of responsibilities between the client (frontend) and the server (backend).
- Layers: The Model–View–Controller (MVC) architectural pattern is used to provide several quality requirements, like maintainability.

Layers of the System:

- Presentation (View):
    - View: Displays the model data to the user in a visually appealing and comprehensible manner, without performing any actions, processing, or business logic.

- Controller:
    - Controller: It acts as an intermediary between the model and the view, receiving user interactions and translating them into actions in the corresponding model or view, handling application control logic and validations.
- Business Logic (Model):
    - Model: It manages data access and operations, enforcing business rules and operations.
- Persistence (Model):
    - DAO (Data Access Object): It transforms information between the cloud database and objects that the system can manipulate, providing an abstraction for database operations.
    - Storage: It handles uploading, storing, and retrieving media files to cloud servers, using services like Firebase Storage.
- Google Firebase Services:
    - Data layer: It is hosted within the Google Firebase Firestore service and uses a NO-SQL database format to store the data.
    - File layer: It is hosted within the Google Firebase Storage service and stores all multimedia files such as images, videos, 3D models, and others.

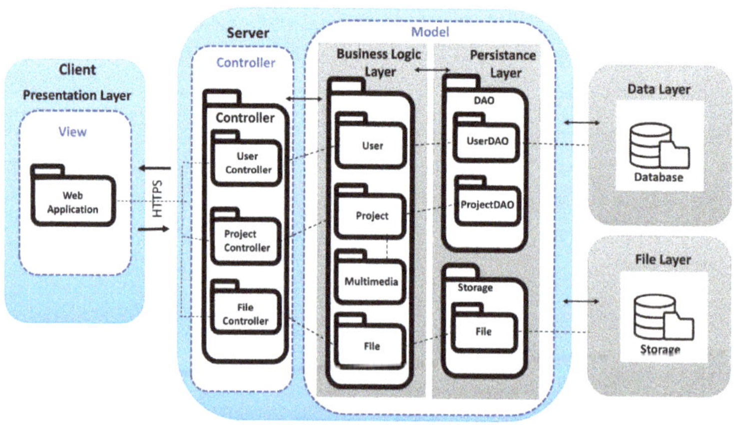

Figure 1. Software architecture.

3.3. *Methodology for Software Implementation*

For the development of this project, an iterative and incremental methodology was used, as well as various technologies that contributed to the software development cycle. This combination of methodologies and tools allowed for an agile and efficient development process, ensuring the quality and functionality of the final product. The iterative and incremental methodology is an agile approach to software development; it is based on repeated development cycles (iterations), in which the product is improved and expanded incrementally. Each iteration includes planning, design, implementation, and testing phases. This approach allows for rapid adaptation to changes and continuous improvement of the product [25]. The integration of technologies in the software life cycle was carried out following the DevOps philosophy [26], which promotes collaboration between development and operations teams to improve software delivery and quality. DevOps focuses on continuous automation, integration, and deployment, facilitating the rapid and reliable delivery of software. Figure 2 shows the technologies that were used during each stage of the DevOps cycle.

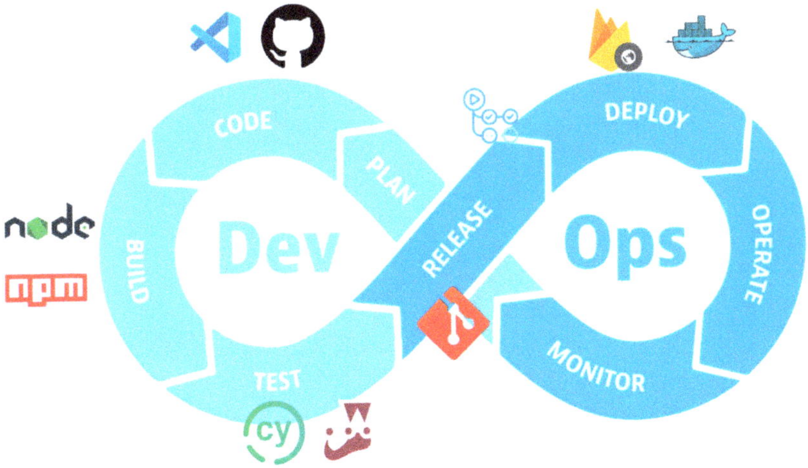

Figure 2. Methodology and technologies for implementing BabloXR following the DevOps philosophy.

No specific technology was used during the planning stage, but rather the analysis and design of the agile methodology was followed, with the most critical functionalities being addressed first. During the code phase, GitHub (https://github.com/features) was used as a repository to store code. GitHub facilitates collaboration, versioning, and changing management through pull requests. During construction, NPM (version 10) was used as a Node.js (version 18) package manager for building the project, allowing it to be converted into a single-page application (SPA). Node.js is a cross-platform, open-source, server-side runtime environment and is useful in creating highly scalable network programs. For the next testing phase, Jest (version 27.5.1), a JavaScript library for unit testing, was used to make sure that every component functions properly when used alone. Cypress (version 13.7.0) was also used for end-to-end (e2e) testing, verifying that the entire system works correctly from the end-user perspective. For publishing, GitHub Pull Requests were used. Every time a pull request was made, unit tests were automatically run to make sure the new changes were bug free. Once the tests were successfully passed, the changes were merged into the main branch. In the deployment, GitHub Actions were used. Every time a push was sent to the main branch after a successful pull request, an automatic deployment to the Firebase Hosting service was executed. The operation and monitoring parts were not applicable to this project, as the primary objective was the development and deployment of the product. The entire development ecosystem can be run locally on a computer with Node.js and Git installed. Alternatively, Docker can be used to run the development environment.

3.4. Graphic User Interface

This section describes the workings of the GUI. Figure 3 shows the main graphical user interface (GUI) for the sections "working area" (left side of the figure) and "viewing area" (right side of the figure).

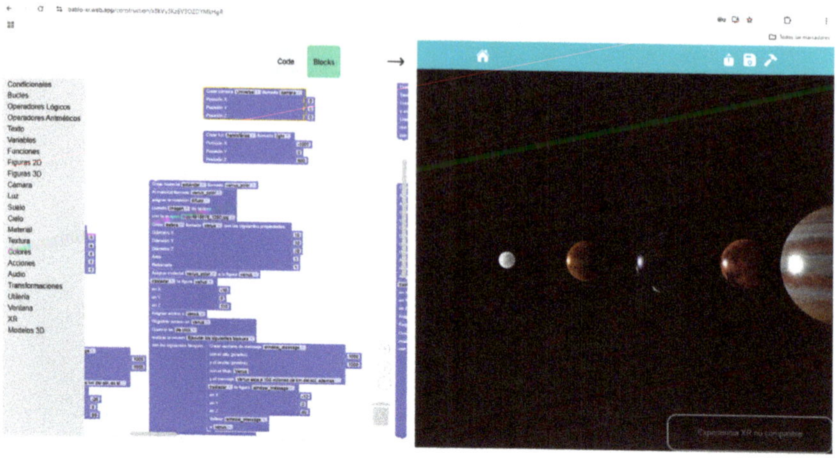

Figure 3. The graphic user interface.

The toolbar is located on the left side and contains blocks to create operations or components such as Conditions, Loops, Logic, Arithmetic, Text, Variables, Functions, 2D Shapes, 3D Shapes, Cameras, Lights, Floors, Skies, Materials, Textures, Colors, Actions, Audio, Transformations, Utilities, Windows, and XR Environments. Each category contains specific blocks that can be used to build and customize the XR environment. The workspace area is located on the right side of the toolbar; this is where users can drag and drop blocks to build their XR environment. Blocks can be connected to define the logic and behavior of the environment. In this space, users can create cameras, lights, geometric shapes, and other interactive elements to enrich their environment.

BabloXR Blocks

The following elements served as the fundamental components in the construction of the XR environment. These components are essential elements, as they efficiently facilitate the construction and customization of XR environments.

Table 2 delineates the blocks necessary to initiate the environment in which the camera and its assigned properties are situated. Furthermore, a block for the creation of the light is generated. Additionally, the ground elements and their dimensions are specified, with dimensions being defined as measurements in units, with one unit corresponding to one m in reality. Finally, the sky style and texture are defined by specific blocks.

Table 2. XR environment's setting blocks.

Block	Description	Example
Camera	A free camera with initial positions is created.	
Light	A general light with the default values is displayed.	

Table 2. *Cont.*

Block	Description	Example
Ground	A soil with a specific size is defined.	
Sky	A sky with a specific size is created, as well as a material with a texture image. Next, the material is assigned to the sky.	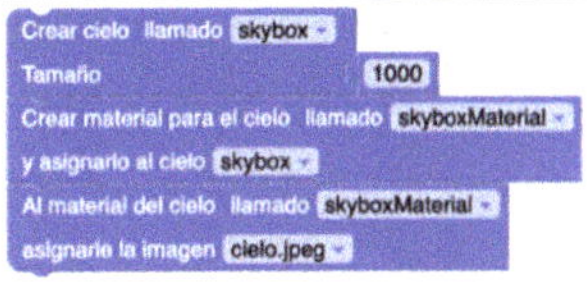

Table 3 illustrates the block for creating 3D shapes. The example describes the creation of a box (cube) with the respective dimensional parameters. Additionally, the generation of material is demonstrated, employing a red color selection and subsequent allocation to the designated box. Finally, the diverse techniques for generating colors are presented.

Table 3. Element and texture blocks.

Block	Description	Example
3D Figures	A box with 10 units of width, height, and depth dimensions is created (10 × 10 × 10).	
Material and Texture	The material is instantiated and assigned to a color as texture. Subsequently, the material is added to the figure.	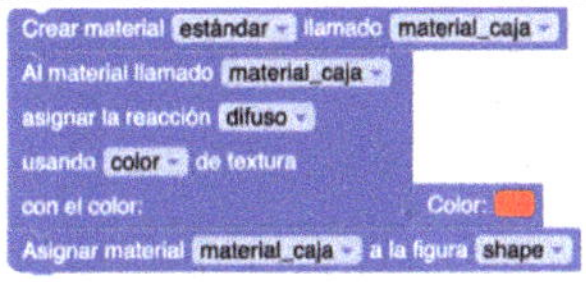
Colors	There are several alternatives for assigning a color.	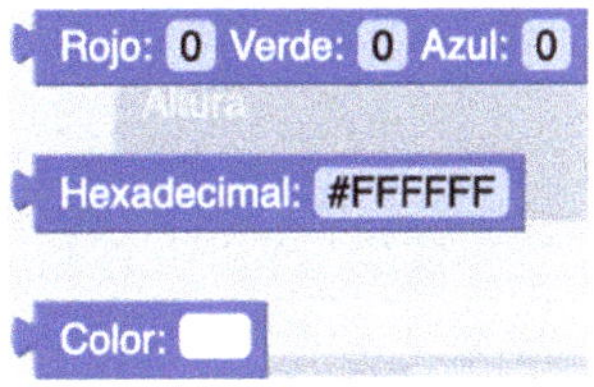

The blocks for assigning events are displayed in Table 4, along with an example that demonstrates how to carry out a sequence of blocks. Clicking on the component to which the action has been attached is the triggering event. The next row showcases another block aiming to change the position of a figure by moving it 5 units on the y-axis.

Table 4. Blocks for assigning events to components.

Block	Description	Example
Actions	An action is assigned to the figure, and then the "click" event is assigned to it, which will execute the action of executing a series of blocks. The available actions include click, double click, hover over the element, and hover outside the element.	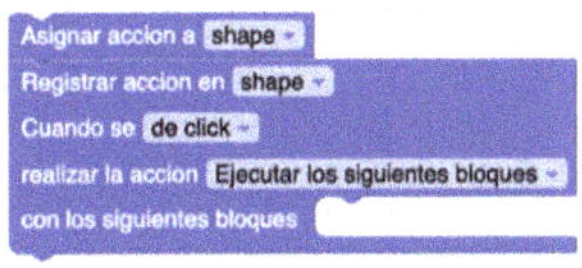

Table 4. *Cont.*

Block	Description	Example
Transformations	The figure is moved to another position.	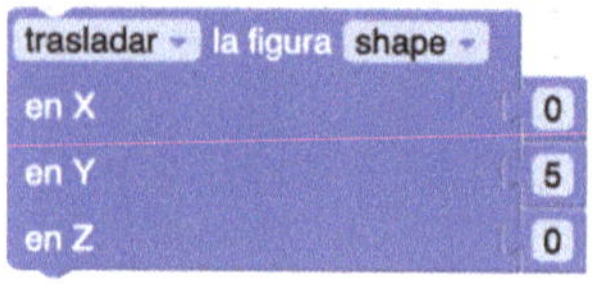

As illustrated in Table 5, the blocks for creating a message window are delineated, accompanied by specific pixel dimensions, a designated title, and a representative message that articulates the content to be imparted. Furthermore, a video window is created with the video clip to be shown, its size in pixels, and a title. To produce the XR experience, there is a specific block for that task.

Table 5. Blocks for different types of media windows.

Block	Description	Example
Windows	An informative window is created with dimensions and content corresponding to the figure. A video window is also created with dimensions and a video to be played.	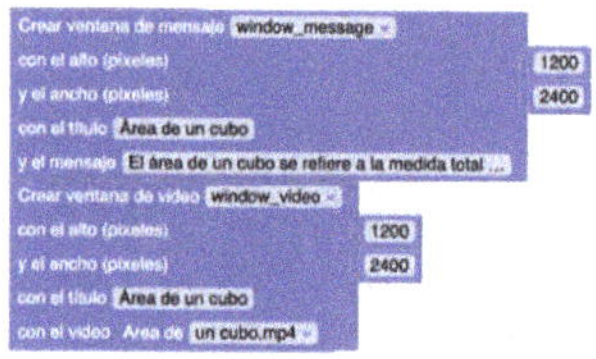
XR	Creation of the XR experience for the environment.	

3.5. Creation and Presentation of a Learning Environment

Figure 4 illustrates the workflow to construct an XR learning environment using BabloXR. This workflow has four main stages: initializing the environment, adding elements, incorporating information windows (optional), and creating the XR experience. Each of these stages is detailed below:

- Environment Initialization: This is the first step to creating the XR environment. It includes the essential components that provide the groundwork for the additional elements of the environment.
- Adding Elements: The next step is to add elements to the environment. These elements can be as many as the user wants and are crucial to building an interactive and educational environment.
- Adding Information (Optional): The third step is adding different types of media windows. These multimedia windows are used to provide additional information and/or instructions within the XR environment.
- Adding XR Experience: The fourth and final step is to create the XR experience.

This construction flow allows BabloXR users to create customized and effective XR environments for educational purposes, ensuring that each step is well defined and that the necessary elements are correctly configured.

To present the learning environment created above, the link provided by the creator of the XR environment is used. This link allows users to access the environment through various devices, including computers, cell phones, and virtual reality headsets. The versatility of BabloXR allows XR environments to be accessible on multiple platforms. Figure 5 presents two ways of viewing the XR environment.

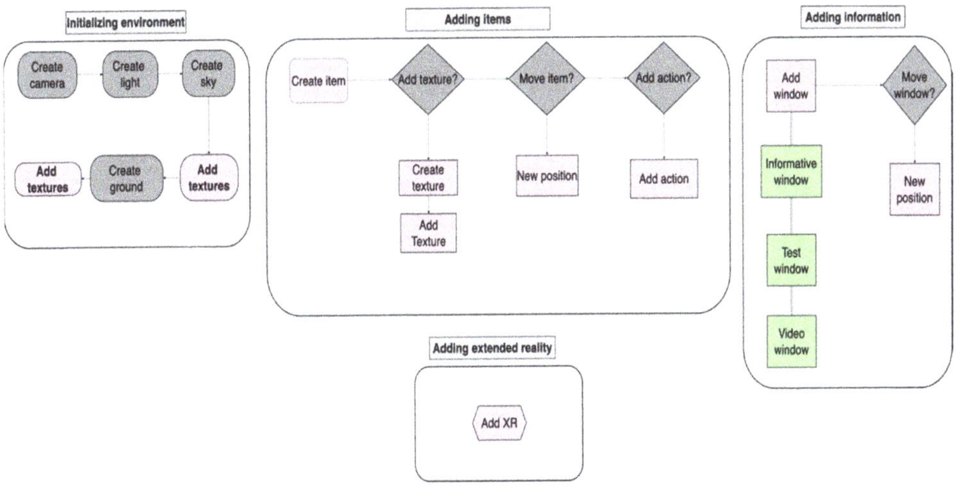

Figure 4. Flowchart for creating a learning environment.

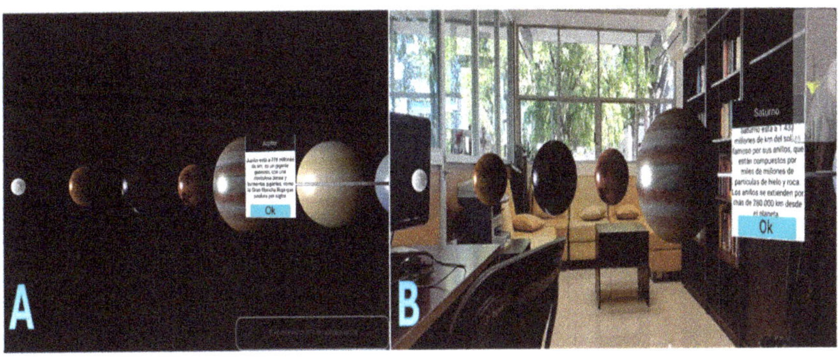

Figure 5. BabloXR viewing styles: (**A**) virtual reality view mode, (**B**) augmented reality view mode.

Virtual Reality Viewing (Figure 5A): For a more immersive experience, users can use virtual reality (VR) headsets to view the VR environment. By opening the link on a VR-compatible device, the environment is presented in a VR-optimized format, allowing for a greater sense of presence and depth. Users can move around and interact with the environment using VR headset controllers, exploring the environment in a more natural and immersive way. Figure 5 showcases an environment viewed in VR mode, highlighting the total immersion that this technology offers.

Augmented Reality Visualization (Figure 5B): In addition to virtual reality, environments created with BabloXR can also be visualized in augmented reality (AR). Using a mobile device with AR capabilities, such as a cell phone or tablet, users can overlay the AR environment over the real-world environment. By accessing the link on an AR device, the environment is integrated with the physical world through the device's camera, allowing users to interact with virtual elements in their real world. The right panel in Figure 5 displays an environment viewed in AR mode, showcasing the ability to combine the virtual and real world.

4. BabloXR Evaluation

This section describes how the authoring tool was evaluated. Section 4.1 presents information about the participants. Finally, Section 4.2 describes the instrument used to collect data for the experiment.

4.1. Methods

Figure 6 shows the evaluation process of BabloXR. First, a 60 min tutorial was presented to participants explaining the platform's function. In this step, the tutorial was accompanied by a video on the YouTube platform that provides a detailed explanation of how to create a learning environment. Subsequently, test subjects were asked to develop their own XR environment within a two-week period. Within these two weeks, the authors of the BabloXR tool offered direct advice in person or via email for subjects who had encountered problems while creating their XR application. Finally, to measure the usability of the authoring tool, a questionnaire was applied, where participants spent 10 min providing their responses. In this last step, participants also were asked to answer a group of three open-ended questions about their experience using BabloXR.

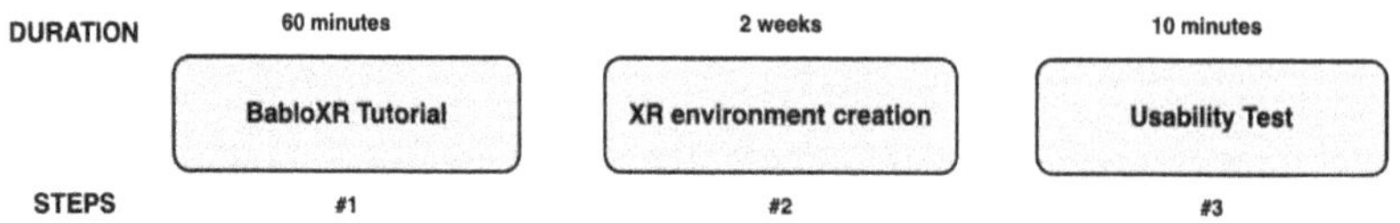

Figure 6. Evaluation process.

4.2. Participants

This investigation was carried out at the Culiacán campus of the Tecnológico Nacional de México in May 2024. Thirty undergraduate engineering students, ages 19 to 25 (M = 20.3, SD = 1.48), participated in this study.

4.3. Data Collection Instruments

The data collection instrument employed in this study was the System Usability Scale or SUS [27], which consists of a 10-question Likert scale with five response options ranging from strong agreement to strong disagreement. The SUS questionnaire was applied to measure the usability of the authoring tool. The SUS is used to measure the three core factors or dimensions of usability [28]: effectiveness (whether individuals can truly finish their duties and reach their objectives); efficiency (the number of resources they use to accomplish their objectives); and satisfaction (the degree of ease with which they accomplish those objectives). The SUS questionnaire provides a reliable and validated method for evaluating the usability of a software tool.

5. Data Analysis and Results

In addition to applying the SUS to measure usability, we present a comparison between the characteristics of BabloXR and other authoring tools presented in Section 2.2, the state of the art. Additionally, we present nine different XR applications created with BabloXR.

5.1. XR Applications Created with BabloXR

Figure 7 illustrates examples from the main interfaces of XR applications created by participants in the evaluation. Figure 7A shows the application created to teach how to calculate the area of a circle; Figure 7B shows the application created to teach how to use the elimination method in linear equations using a Pokémon theme. Similar XR applications are shown in Figure 7C, which describes the water cycle using a demonstration video.

Figure 7D shows the solar system, where clicking displays relevant information about each planet; Figure 7E presents an environment in which the evolution of atomic models throughout history is explained; Figure 7F shows an art gallery; Figure 7G shows a grass field environment with four cube blocks with different textures, where each block serves a distinct purpose in relation to fractional operations; Figure 7H displays an art gallery with different paintings from the renaissance age; they also contain a small description of each one; and, finally, Figure 7I illustrates the works of art made by Eugène Delacroix.

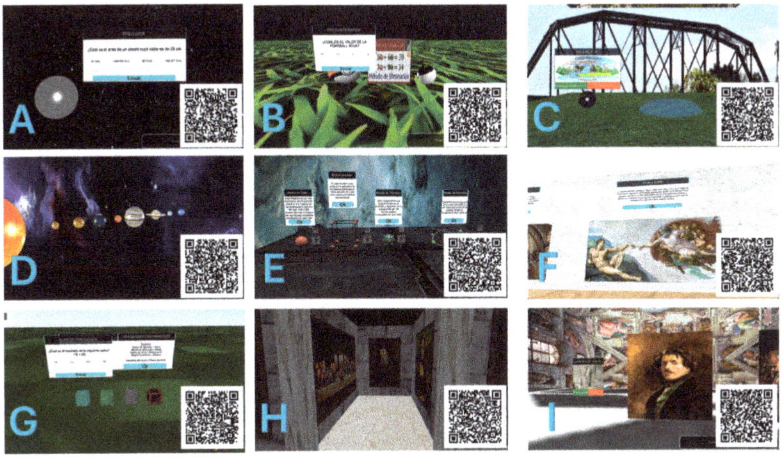

Figure 7. BabloXR XR environment examples: (**A**) calculate the area of a circle (VR, AR), (**B**) Pokémon-themed system of linear equations (VR, AR), (**C**) water cycle (VR), (**D**) solar system (VR), (**E**) explanation of atomic models (VR), (**F**) art gallery (VR), (**G**) Minecraft-themed fraction tutorials (VR), (**H**) gallery of famous renaissance paintings (VR), and (**I**) paintings by Eugène Delacroix (VR, AR).

Full access to the environment is available through the QR code, which is located in the lower right corner of each display.

5.2. System Usability Scale (SUS) Test

The results (M, and SD) obtained from the SUS test are presented in Table 6. The test contains ten questions with responses ranging from strongly disagree (1) to strongly agree (5) on the Likert scale. To measure the reliability of the SUS test, Cronbach's alpha was calculated, obtaining a value of 0.80. This value is regarded as highly satisfactory, signifying that the evaluation process is both consistent and reliable in its assessment of the system's usability. The usability of the system is good, as indicated by the SUS score of 74 out of 100, which is above average.

Table 6. SUS test mean and standard deviation for each question [1].

Question	M	SD
Q1. Would you like to use BabloXR many times to make your own extended reality worlds?	4.50	0.57
Q2. Did you find BabloXR too complicated to use?	1.50	0.57
Q3. Do you think BabloXR is easy to handle?	4.10	0.75
Q4. Would you need help from someone who knows a lot about technology in order to use BabloXR?	3.00	0.94
Q5. Did you find that all the things you can do with BabloXR work well together?	4.30	0.59

Table 6. *Cont.*

Question	M	SD
Q6. Do you think BabloXR is a bit messy or confusing?	2.96	1.09
Q7. Do you think your friends could quickly learn to use BabloXR, even if they don't know much about computers?	3.93	1.04
Q8. I found the system very cumbersome to use?	1.50	0.57
Q9. Was it easy to show someone else what you created with BabloXR?	4.33	0.71
Q10. Did you have to know anything special before you could use BabloXR well?	2.63	1.15

5.3. Open-Ended Questions to Users

Table 7 presents a selection of responses from 30 participants to a set of three open-ended questions about BabloXR.

Table 7. Open-ended questions.

Question 1	Question 2	Question 3
What do you think of BabloXR?	What new things would you like to see in BabloXR?	What things would you take away from BabloXR?
At least for me, I feel that it is something innovative outside of the use it has, in the academic plan, I had never had the idea about what could be done, so they have a future.	Collaboration with someone else in real time.	For now, there is nothing that needs to be removed, it has the attributes that are necessary.
It's okay, I find it very practical, there are just a few bugs that need to be fixed.	It would be good having the options to save figures composed of several figures and to be able to copy and paste all the blocks that are connected to each other.	The truth is nothing is complete and useful to me.
I found it quite practical and quite interesting how they were able to adapt to it so that every user could learn to use it.	I would like it to be a little more intuitive, I mean it is but more oriented towards people who are starting from scratch and have no experience in graphic environments.	The failure when you open a tab, and it bugs but it is due to a library problem already mentioned and it is understandable.
Honestly, BabloXR has an interface that I would say is easy to use, and the wide variety and adaptability of the application for different areas is very good, such as, in this case, education.	Some sort of autosave as well as some way for multiple people to work on the same job at the same time.	That the free camera does not have to be moved with the direction arrows.
I found it very interesting how simple it is to carry out a project, just by learning the essentials and then you flow on the page by yourself.	More blocks that do new things.	

Participants praised BabloXR's innovation, ease of use, and adaptability, with some suggesting improvements like real-time collaboration, autosave, and more intuitive features for beginners. While most found no major features to remove, a few highlighted issues such as a bug when opening tabs and the difficulty in moving the free camera using arrow keys. Overall, the suggestions focused on enhancing functionality and user experience.

5.4. Comparison

Table 8 presents a comparative analysis of the authoring tools from Section 2.2 of the related work and BabloXR. The comparison is made with respect to a selection of the most relevant features that a learning environment must present.

Table 8. Authoring tool feature comparisons.

Authoring Tool	VR	AR	Cloud Storage	Import	Import 3D Models	Display in Real Time	Tutorial	Export/Share
BabloXR	✓	✓	✓	✓		✓		✓
BlocklyVR	✓					✓	✓	
BlocklyAR		✓				✓	✓	✓
BloclyXR	✓	✓			✓	✓	✓	✓
TrainAR		✓						✓
StoryMakAR		✓						✓
JEM Inventor				✓		✓		✓

This comparative analysis highlights the significance of BabloXR's cloud integration, an essential characteristic that facilitates easy access in the digital age. Additionally, it possesses a multitude of functionalities analogous to those of other tools. These functionalities include real-time visualization of the construction process, exporting and sharing of the environment, and other features.

6. Discussion

The results obtained from the questions used in the SUS test mentioned in Table 6 allow us to discuss the advantages and disadvantages that participants identified when using the tool. First, the average scores for questions Q1 (Would you like to use BabloXR many times to make your own extended reality worlds?), Q3 (Do you think BabloXR is easy to handle?), Q5 (Did you find that all the things you can do with BabloXR work well together?), Q7 (Do you think your friends could quickly learn to use BabloXR, even if they don't know much about computers?), and Q9 (Was it easy to show someone else what you created with BabloXR?) range between 3.93 and 4.5, indicating a very positive attitude towards the use of BabloXR. This suggests that most of the surveyed participants find the idea of creating extended reality worlds very attractive. These scores reflect a high level of interest, which could be explained by the growing fascination with augmented and virtual reality in education, entertainment, and technology in general. The possibility of creating personalized worlds allows users to be creative and explore new forms of interaction, which could foster innovation and learning in students. Nonetheless, the obtained standard deviation values (between 0.57 and 1.04) show that, although most users have a positive view, there is a slight variability in opinions. This suggests that, although the tool is attractive to most, there are some users who might not be so interested or perhaps do not see its immediate usefulness in their learning context. We believe it is important to mention that the population of the experiment was focused on engineering undergraduate students; thus, there is a selection bias in the participants, so these values could be much better if the system were used by educators.

Likewise, the results of questions Q4 (Would you need help from someone who knows a lot about technology in order to use BabloXR?) and Q10 (Did you have to know anything special before you could use BabloXR well?), which present means of 3.0 and 2.63, respectively, indicate the possibility that some users do not feel comfortable with the technology or do not see the value of creating worlds in extended reality if they do not have prior training in similar tools. Finally, the results of questions Q2 (Did you find BabloXR too complicated to use?) and Q8 (I found the system very cumbersome to use?), with means of 1.50 and standard deviations of 0.57, show that users did not consider the tool to be complicated to use. In summary, the generally positive response to BabloXR implies a strong interest in extended reality, although the small variability in the responses suggests that some students might need more time or training to obtain most of the tool.

Participants were also asked a set of open questions to give their opinion of the tool. In general, participants were enthusiastic about the possibilities that the tool offers them, emphasizing the diversity of tasks that it can focus on and how the various elements of extended reality environments could be easily added through the use of blocks. Among the aspects of improvement they mentioned, it would be desirable for projects to be able to be worked on collaboratively and for more elements to be added, such as auto-saving functions, allowing for the creation of composite figures from base shapes and exporting models, among others.

It is important to point out that BabloXR enables users to access the tool from any device and from any location with Internet connectivity due to its integration with the cloud; it is also a tool that includes most of the elements partially present in other tools, making it a very complete application. Also noteworthy is BabloXR's ability to import multimedia elements that can be reused in various projects, except for JEM Inventor; the rest of the tools evaluated lack this important feature.

7. Conclusions

As far as we know, our study describes the first fully accessible and device-compatible, cloud-based, robust authoring tool designed to build XR learning environments.

The usability test results demonstrated that users were capable of creating comprehensive and meticulous scenarios by following a concise video tutorial. The outcomes include several interactive and immersive environments, which were created in a relatively short period of time of 2 weeks. This showcases the ability of BabloXR to overcome the technical training and time-consuming limitations that usually impair the development of XR applications by educators in different fields and levels.

In comparison with other tools, as shown in Table 8, BabloXR stands out considerably due to its cloud-based design. This feature enables users to manage their environment in a streamlined manner. It facilitates efficient progress tracking and facilitates the sharing of environments with other users.

Looking forward, several areas for improvement and expansion have been identified. The invaluable cooperation of multiple educators has been important in the design and development of BabloXR. Nonetheless, it is believed that the project might gain from an assessment by a group of educators who are not part of the research team. It is suggested that future work on the application expand the block library with additional components, like predefined scenes and templates, to facilitate the rapid creation of educational environments by teachers; the importation of custom 3D models; the creation of integrated interactive tutorials to enhance accessibility; the integration of generative artificial intelligence; and the implementation of online collaboration features that enable multiple users to work simultaneously. These enhancements would further solidify BabloXR as a powerful and versatile tool in the field of XR-based education.

Author Contributions: Conceptualization, M.L.B.-E., R.Z.-C., M.A.S.-R., M.B.I. and V.M.B.-B.; formal analysis, M.L.B.-E., R.Z.-C., M.B.I. and V.M.B.-B.; investigation, M.L.B.-E., R.Z.-C., M.B.I. and V.M.B.-B.; methodology, M.L.B.-E., R.Z.-C., M.A.S.-R., M.B.I. and V.M.B.-B.; resources, M.L.B.-E., R.Z.-C., M.A.S.-R., M.B.I. and V.M.B.-B.; software, M.A.S.-R. and V.M.B.-B.; supervision, M.L.B.-E., R.Z.-C. and M.B.I.; validation, M.L.B.-E., R.Z.-C., M.A.S.-R., M.B.I. and V.M.B.-B.; writing—original draft, M.A.S.-R.; writing—review and editing, M.L.B.-E., R.Z.-C., M.A.S.-R., M.B.I. and V.M.B.-B. All authors have read and agreed to the published version of the manuscript.

Funding: This research received no external funding.

Institutional Review Board Statement: The study was approved by the TECNM Instituto Tecnológico de Culiacán on 1 August 2024, protocol code are 2024-DEPI-103.

Informed Consent Statement: Informed consent was obtained from all subjects involved in the study.

Data Availability Statement: The original contributions presented in this study are included in the article. We have created a small website (https://catalabs.mx/apps/babloxr/ accessed on 22 May 2025) to maintain up-to-date information on the availability of the tool and instructions on its use for educators who wish to evaluate it. Further inquiries can be directed to the corresponding author.

Acknowledgments: We appreciate the support provided by TecNM Instituto Tecnológico de Culiacán and SECIHTI (Secretaría de Ciencia, Humanidades, Tecnología e Innovación) in México.

Conflicts of Interest: The authors declare no conflicts of interest.

References

1. Zatarain Cabada, R.; Barrón Estrada, M.L.; Sotelo Rivas, M.A.; Ibáñez, M.B. An Authoring Tool for XR Learning Environments. In *Extended Reality*; De Paolis, L.T., Arpaia, P., Sacco, M., Eds.; Springer Nature: Cham, Switzerland, 2024; pp. 192–208.
2. Liu, D.; Bhagat, K.K.; Gao, Y.; Chang, T.-W.; Huang, R. The Potentials and Trends of Virtual Reality in Education. In *Virtual, Augmented, and Mixed Realities in Education*; Liu, D., Dede, C., Huang, R., Richards, J., Eds.; Springer: Singapore, 2017; pp. 105–130, ISBN 9789811054891.
3. Marín-Vega, H.; Alor-Hernández, G.; Bustos-López, M.; López-Martínez, I.; Hernández-Chaparro, N.L. Extended Reality (XR) Engines for Developing Gamified Apps and Serious Games: A Scoping Review. *Future Internet* **2023**, *15*, 379. [CrossRef]
4. Guo, X.; Guo, Y.; Liu, Y. The Development of Extended Reality in Education: Inspiration from the Research Literature. *Sustainability* **2021**, *13*, 13776. [CrossRef]
5. Latif, M.; Lakhrissi, Y.; Nfaoui, E.H.; Es-Sbai, N. Review of Mobile Cross Platform and Research Orientations. In Proceedings of the 2017 International Conference on Wireless Technologies, Embedded and Intelligent Systems (WITS), Fez, Morocco, 19–20 April 2017; IEEE: Piscataway, NJ, USA, 2017; pp. 1–4.
6. Farooq, M.S.; Riaz, S.; Alvi, A.; Ali, A.; Rehman, I.U. Cross-Platform Mobile Development Approaches and Frameworks. *VFAST Trans. Softw. Eng.* **2022**, *10*, 79–93. [CrossRef]
7. Baruah, R. Physics and User Interaction in A-Frame. In *AR and VR Using the WebXR API*; Apress: Berkeley, CA, USA, 2021; pp. 289–302, ISBN 9781484263174.
8. Yu, G.; Liu, C.; Fang, T.; Jia, J.; Lin, E.; He, Y.; Fu, S.; Wang, L.; Wei, L.; Huang, Q. A Survey of Real-Time Rendering on Web3D Application. *Virtual Real. Intell. Hardw.* **2023**, *5*, 379–394. [CrossRef]
9. Prabhakaran, A.; Mahamadu, A.-M.; Mahdjoubi, L. Understanding the Challenges of Immersive Technology Use in the Architecture and Construction Industry: A Systematic Review. *Autom. Constr.* **2022**, *137*, 104228. [CrossRef]
10. Lee, Y.; Yoo, B.; Lee, S.-H. Sharing Ambient Objects Using Real-Time Point Cloud Streaming in Web-Based XR Remote Collaboration. In Proceedings of the 26th International Conference on 3D Web Technology, Pisa, Italy, 8–12 November 2021; ACM: New York, NY, USA, 2021; pp. 1–9.
11. Ratcliffe, J.; Soave, F.; Bryan-Kinns, N.; Tokarchuk, L.; Farkhatdinov, I. Extended Reality (XR) Remote Research: A Survey of Drawbacks and Opportunities. In Proceedings of the 2021 CHI Conference on Human Factors in Computing Systems, Yokohama, Japan, 8–13 May 2021; ACM: New York, NY, USA, 2021; pp. 1–13. [CrossRef]
12. Memmesheimer, V.M.; Ebert, A. Scalable Extended Reality: A Future Research Agenda. *BDCC* **2022**, *6*, 12. [CrossRef]
13. Xie, X. Research on Immersion Teaching Method Based on 5G +XR Technology and Reinforcement Learning Model. *Adv. Multimed.* **2022**, *2022*, 7092100. [CrossRef]
14. Hedlund, M.; Jonsson, A.; Bogdan, C.; Meixner, G.; Ekblom Bak, E.; Matviienko, A. BlocklyVR: Exploring Block-Based Programming in Virtual Reality. In Proceedings of the 22nd International Conference on Mobile and Ubiquitous Multimedia, Vienna, Austria, 3–6 December 2023; ACM: New York, NY, USA, 2023; pp. 257–269. [CrossRef]
15. Nguyen, V.T.; Jung, K.; Dang, T. BlocklyAR: A Visual Programming Interface for Creating Augmented Reality Experiences. *Electronics* **2020**, *9*, 1205. [CrossRef]
16. Jung, K.; Nguyen, V.T.; Lee, J. BlocklyXR: An Interactive Extended Reality Toolkit for Digital Storytelling. *Appl. Sci.* **2021**, *11*, 1073. [CrossRef]

17. Glenn, T.; Ipsita, A.; Carithers, C.; Peppler, K.; Ramani, K. StoryMakAR: Bringing Stories to Life With An Augmented Reality & Physical Prototyping Toolkit for Youth. In Proceedings of the 2020 CHI Conference on Human Factors in Computing Systems, Honolulu, HI, USA, 25–30 April 2020; ACM: New York, NY, USA, 2020; pp. 1–14. [CrossRef]
18. Blattgerste, J.; Behrends, J.; Pfeiffer, T. TrainAR: An Open-Source Visual Scripting-Based Authoring Tool for Procedural Mobile Augmented Reality Trainings. *Information* **2023**, *14*, 219. [CrossRef]
19. Dengel, A.; Iqbal, M.Z.; Grafe, S.; Mangina, E. A Review on Augmented Reality Authoring Toolkits for Education. *Front. Virtual Real.* **2022**, *3*, 798032. [CrossRef]
20. Vuforia. Vuforia Studio Augmented Reality for Industrial enterprise—Ptc. 2025. Available online: https://www.ptc.com/en/products/vuforia/vuforia-studio (accessed on 22 February 2025).
21. Blippar Augmented Reality (Ar) & Computer Vision Company—Blippar. Available online: https://www.blippar.com/ (accessed on 20 January 2025).
22. Inglobe Technologies, Ar-Media Features. Available online: http://dev.inglobetechnologies.com/features/ (accessed on 20 January 2025).
23. Areeka, Google Digital Distribution Service. Available online: https://play.google.com/store/apps/details?id=com.Amlogy.Areeka&hl=es_MX (accessed on 19 January 2025).
24. Karoui, A.; Marfisi-Schottman, I.; George, S. JEM Inventor: A Mobile Learning Game Authoring Tool Based on a Nested Design Approach. *Interact. Learn. Environ.* **2022**, *30*, 1851–1878. [CrossRef]
25. Larman, C. *Agile and Iterative Development: A Manager's Guide*; Agile software development series; Addison-Wesley: Boston, MA, USA, 2004; ISBN 9780131111554.
26. Bass, L. *DevOps: A Software Architect's Perspective*; The SEI series in software engineering; Addison-Wesley: Old Tappan, NJ, USA, 2015; ISBN 9780134049885.
27. Brooke, J. *SUS—A Quick and Dirty Usability Scale*; Redhatch Consulting Ltd.: Earley, UK, 1996; pp. 4–7.
28. Brooke, J. SUS: A retrospective. *J. Usability Stud.* **2013**, *8*, 29–40.

Multimodal Technologies and Interaction

MDPI

Article

The Use of 3D Printing and ICT in the Designing of Didactic Strategies to Foster Creative Thinking

Lorena Cabrera-Frías [1], Diana-Margarita Córdova-Esparza [1,*], Julio-Alejandro Romero-González [1], Teresa García-Ramírez [1], Rocio-Edith López-Martínez [1], Juan Terven [2] and Juan-José Rodríguez-Peña [2]

1 Facultad de Informática, Universidad Autónoma de Querétaro, Av. de las Ciencias S/N, Queretaro 76230, Mexico; lcabrera14@alumnos.uaq.mx (L.C.-F.); julio.romero@uaq.mx (J.-A.R.-G.); teregar@uaq.mx (T.G.-R.); rocio.edith.lopez@uaq.mx (R.-E.L.-M.)

2 CICATA-Unidad Querétaro, Instituto Politécnico Nacional, Cerro Blanco 141, Col. Colinas del Cimatario, Queretaro 76090, Mexico; jrtervens@ipn.mx (J.T.); jjrodriguezp@ipn.mx (J.-J.R.-P.)

* Correspondence: diana.cordova@uaq.mx

Abstract: The use of iteration is fundamental in the field of design, as it allows for the exploration of multiple options and the development of innovative solutions. This research analyzes how iteration, combined with Information and Communications Technology (ICT), especially 3D printing, facilitates the development of creativity in higher-level students, specifically Industrial Designers. A qualitative approach was employed, using an action-research methodological strategy with a field journal to document student activities during the iterative process. The results indicate that group dynamics enhance iteration by facilitating the exchange of ideas; therefore, the incorporation of activities that adopt constant feedback is necessary to refine initial concepts and integrate new perspectives. Additionally, the use of technology, such as 3D printing, drives the creative process by encouraging students to continue developing their ideas through physical iteration, allowing them to materialize and improve their concepts. The creative process only needs to be stimulated through different methodological strategies, both analog and digital, in and outside the classroom, with the use of technologies as essential learning tools.

Keywords: iteration; design; creative thinking; 3D printing; educational technology

1. Introduction

Creative thinking refers to the ability to generate new and effective ideas, as well as to approach problems from innovative perspectives. This type of thinking involves various cognitive processes that interact in complex ways, including imagination, cognitive flexibility, and memory [1]. From the perspective of Khalil et al. [2], thinking should be fostered through the creation of learning environments that expand and diversify students' experiences, thereby promoting their cognitive and innovative development.

The development of creative thinking is crucial for problem-solving, innovation, and adaptation to new scenarios. The ability to combine isolated concepts into novel ideas is an indicator of creativity, suggesting that enhancing an individual's semantic memory enables them to navigate and associate ideas effectively, thus generating more creative proposals.

Designing a competency-based training model focused on creativity is essential to demonstrate how this skill drives the teaching–learning process, becoming a key aspect for both students and educators in a university context [3]. Creative experiences are generally more engaging for students, which can lead to increased motivation and more active participation in their own learning. For educators, the use of ICT in the educational process fosters innovation in their teaching practices [4]. However, one of the main barriers educational institutions face when incorporating creativity into the classroom is the lack of knowledge among educators about methodologies that support teaching of creative thinking, as well as the absence of digital resources that facilitate this process [5].

To foster the development of creative thinking, iteration plays a crucial role, as it allows for the refinement and continuous improvement of ideas through a cyclical process. According to Kenett [1], the influence of iteration on creative thinking can be observed in the following aspects:

- Trial-and-error approach: Initial ideas can be evaluated, adjusted, and improved based on the results obtained. This process allows students to explore various perspectives and alternatives without fear of making mistakes, which is fundamental for creativity.
- Constant feedback: Through iteration, it is possible to receive feedback on ideas, enabling students to identify areas for improvement and consider new concept combinations. This feedback cycle can inspire new connections and foster deeper and more divergent thinking.
- The exploration of innovative combinations: Iteration allows for experimentation with different combinations of ideas and concepts, which is essential for creativity. By repeating and refining their approach, students can discover new ways to merge ideas that initially seemed unrelated.
- The enhancement of cognitive flexibility: The iterative process helps develop cognitive flexibility, which is fundamental for generating innovative ideas in changing contexts.
- The development of an open mindset: Iteration encourages an open mindset toward change and the evolution of ideas. By accepting that initial solutions are not definitive and that there is always room for adjustment and refinement, students can unlock their creativity and feel more motivated to experiment.

Iteration enables continuous improvement of ideas in the creative process while creating a favorable environment for exploration, adaptation, and concept integration, key elements for the development of creative thinking.

According to Jalolov [6], creative thinking can be enhanced through Information and Communications Technology (ICT) using the following strategies:

- Incorporating multimedia elements: Using videos, animations, and audio in instructional sequences can make learning more engaging and help stimulate students' imagination.
- Interactive activities: Implementing hands-on activities involving multimedia platforms allows students to actively participate in the learning process, fostering collaboration and creative expression.
- Active learning: Applying active learning methodologies such as project-based or problem-based learning enables students to research and apply their creative thinking skills in practical contexts [7,8].
- Collaboration: Encouraging group work using multimedia tools helps students exchange ideas, reflect on different perspectives, and collectively develop innovative solutions.

By integrating these ICT tools into the curriculum, educators can create meaningful learning experiences that enhance students' creative thinking.

This article presents the development of a didactic strategy based on iteration to foster creative thinking through the use of Information and Communications Technology (ICT). Section 2 provides a description of related works to contextualize the study topic, Section 3 explains the research design, Section 4 presents the main results obtained, Section 5 includes a discussion of the study, and finally, Section 6 outlines the conclusions.

2. Related Work

2.1. The Development of Creative Thinking

According to Valverde et al. [9], in various fields, there is a need for profound educational reform that addresses contemporary demands. Proposals for modernization and the incorporation of new content are added to existing subjects, overloading curricula with minimal and barely noticeable changes due to a school culture deeply rooted in traditions and practices that hinder transformation. However, the creative process is characterized by a series of interrelated phases whose primary objective is the generation of new ideas, as well as their development and evaluation of effectiveness. In an educational setting, this process is essential for enhancing investigative capacity and activating problem-solving skills. It is approached with the goal of being strengthened within the teaching–learning process, playing a leading role linked to the ability to consciously present a situation in a novel way. According to [10], creativity has not always been studied with the intention of being strengthened and optimized. Instead, its analysis has often focused on tangible aspects, neglecting the study of creative thinking.

In the field of design, creative processes should be oriented toward exploring non-linear methodologies characterized by iterative execution, which promotes innovation and the progressive evolution of ideas. Therefore, educators must recognize creativity as an inherent potential that can be developed throughout the teaching–learning process by implementing activities that foster curiosity, improvisation, and the generation of innovative ideas [11].

Wu et al. [12] emphasize that artists need flexible and dynamic thinking that allows them to integrate diverse resources, fostering innovation and creativity. This approach involves the interaction of multiple factors that stimulate reflection and continuous refinement of the creative process, adapting to the diversity and complexity of artistic creation. In education, this perspective contributes to improving students' ability to face challenges by promoting advanced problem-solving skills.

Grimaldo-Salazar et al. [13] state that, based on Torrance's conceptualization of creativity, specific tests were designed to evaluate it through various activities such as music, drawing, and writing. These tests provide fundamental elements for analyzing the multiple dimensions of creative thinking. Creativity manifests in different fields, and its assessment requires differentiated tasks. The Torrance Test of Creative Thinking is an evaluation instrument consisting of two scales, one verbal and one figurative. Each subtest is presented in two forms: Form A, used as a pre-test, and Form B, applied as a post-test. The data obtained from both tests can be analyzed individually and/or collectively.

According to Humble et al. [14], the Torrance Tests of Creative Thinking demonstrate a degree of transferability, evidenced by the creativity construct measured by the Figural Form, which could be multidimensional by incorporating both innovative and adaptive factors across different cultural contexts, depending on the study's objective. Their findings highlighted sociocultural homogeneity, showing significant positive and negative associations between context, education, and self-perceptions with the innovative and adaptive factors of creativity.

For this study, the objective is to identify the extent to which iteration facilitates the development of creativity through the use of technological tools in university students. As Rúa et al. [15] state, the goal is to achieve significant improvements in student performance and creativity by motivating their imagination and fostering greater innovation. Therefore, the figurative subtest was specifically selected as the measurement tool for this construct, as it evaluates creative thinking through visual representations in the form of sketches. From Cuervo-Pulido et al.'s perspective [16], the use of sketches is an essential component of the design process, as it not only pertains to the final product but also to the creative path that generates it. Thus, teaching and learning design focuses more on strengthening the creative thinking skills inherent in the design process than on achieving specific outcomes.

2.2. Managing Creativity and Iteration

Creativity in the university context is considered an essential component in the comprehensive training of future professionals, as it is associated with progress, innovation, and improvement. However, there is an insufficient promotion of creativity among students, whose potential is not fully reflected in the classroom. Strengthening creativity is crucial for enhancing the competencies necessary for their professional performance. In this regard, the role of educators becomes particularly significant, as they have the opportunity to design and foster educational environments that stimulate creative thinking. This is achieved through the implementation of technological tools and pedagogical strategies aimed at encouraging and consolidating this potential.

As noted by Martínez and González [17], creativity is not a new concept, but it is essential for students to possess the theoretical and technical knowledge, as well as the skills, competencies, and strategies that enable them to effectively tackle the professional challenges they will face. The iterative process allows for the identification of improvement opportunities in intermediate stages, the development of independent components, and their integration in subsequent iterations [18]. However, Hincapié-Atehortúa [19] argues that project delays often result from poor planning in the design phase, which can be mitigated by developing structured iterative methods that optimize productivity.

Thus, iterative work within the creative process is recognized as a fundamental element, as it enables the progressive generation and integration of necessary changes. Creativity is not merely a matter of inspiration, as it would not be possible to create consistently over time and produce work regularly. Since the process is not linear, changes in direction are unpredictable, giving each student the opportunity to solve their own problem while working within a trial-and-error technique [20].

According to Wynn and Eckert [21], many early design representations inspire designers themselves to seek alternative solutions because they are often poorly structured from the outset. This necessitates an iterative process influenced by both the designer's level of experience and imagination, with the goal of creating new pathways and evaluating more viable proposals as more information about the problem becomes available. In other words, this process allows each individual to select a method that enables them to transform their experience into learning.

2.3. Three-Dimensional Printing as Support for the Iterative Process

It is essential to explore learning strategies that combine theory and practice, traditional work and technological application, as teaching and learning must be adapted to different levels of experience to develop more educational resources. In other words, there is a recognized need to integrate design and production simultaneously into the curriculum to enhance training in creative fields [22].

From Mata-Abdelnour's perspective [23], this integration led to increased student participation, accompanied by greater discipline and organization, even among those who were initially less collaborative. This dynamic aimed to foster an active student role, encouraging the resolution of complex problems and the use of new technologies by promoting deeper student engagement. Thus, the iterative process becomes a fundamental part of 3D printing education, and vice versa, as some students tend to accept their first model without assessing its deficiencies or fully committing to the learning process.

2.4. Research Question

For this study, the research question is: how do iteration and the use of 3D printing stimulate the development of creative thinking in Industrial Designers?

3. Materials and Methods

This study is based on a qualitative methodological approach, which, as argued by Flick [24], "stems from the notion of the social construction of the realities under study and focuses on the participants' perspectives, everyday practices, and common knowledge related to the subject of inquiry". The primary objective is to explore students' activities, processes, and work experiences concerning the development of creative thinking. This study follows an action-research methodological strategy, as described by Peralta-Castro et al. [25], where the participants' voices highlight key aspects such as observation, analysis, and reflection from both students and educators. This facilitates learning and overcoming challenges while bridging theory and practice.

For data collection, various qualitative research techniques were used, including a field journal as an observation method to characterize activities, understand dynamics, and identify challenges [26]. This journal provided a detailed record of activities carried out during each of the seven scheduled sessions across two participating groups, documenting in-class tasks and the strategies students employed in designing objects.

Additionally, at the end of the intervention, a questionnaire was administered to gather students' perceptions and opinions about their experience throughout the process. The questionnaire also assessed their evaluation of weekly activities, the daily evidence generated in each session, and the use of the digital platform Discord as a learning support tool. Discord was selected for its ability to integrate with various tools, facilitating a more flexible, efficient, and accessible learning process for all users. It promoted interaction beyond academic hours, allowing information exchange, messaging, and the completion of complementary activities [27].

3.1. Participants

The study was conducted at the Universidad Autónoma de Querétaro, specifically at the Faculty of Engineering's Center for Design and Technological Innovation (CEDIT), involving students who integrate 3D printing as an innovative tool in their design development to enhance creative development and materialize their ideas. The educational strategy was implemented in three stages: (1) population analysis, (2) pilot study, and (3) didactic intervention. In all three stages, students from the sixth semester of the Industrial Design program participated in the Computer-Aided Manufacturing (CAM) course, as shown in Figure 1. Before participation, the objective of the research was explained to the students to obtain their informed consent.

For the third stage, corresponding to the didactic intervention, students signed a commitment letter for the submission of exercises and provided authorization for their personal data to be treated anonymously and exclusively for research purposes. A database was used to track and monitor the activity submissions of all 21 students, including their names, identification codes, email addresses, results from the Honey and Alonso Learning Styles Questionnaire, pre-test and post-test scores from the Torrance Test, attendance, and assignments submitted via the platform.

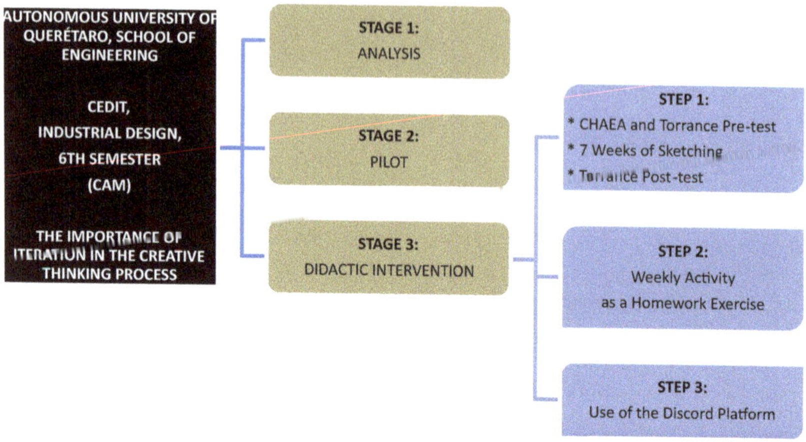

Figure 1. An overview of the three-stage intervention process (population analysis, pilot, and didactic intervention) and its main steps (CHAEA/Torrance tests, weekly sketching, and Discord use).

3.2. Procedure

From Villarreal-Fernández's perspective [28], knowledge is based on the dynamic interaction between the individual and their environment, contributing to the development of their cognitive structure. This interactive process enables individuals to assign meaning to their perceptions and construct representations that provide context to their experiences. Learning, in turn, is part of an active cycle in which action is the primary resource, and reflection on that action generates the learning process.

Following a thorough analysis of the population, the next step involved studying class dynamics and the methodology used in implementation to identify relevant activities and determine the most suitable strategies for the second stage—the pilot study. Understanding students' learning styles was identified as crucial. According to Costa et al. [29], it is essential for educators to understand both their students and themselves, as this self awareness and comprehension of the student body enable them to diversify and adapt their teaching strategies to effectively meet the needs of the classroom.

To identify the optimal characteristics of individual learning, students completed the Honey and Alonso Learning Styles Questionnaire via Google Forms, which consists of 80 items, divided into twenty per category—active, reflective, theoretical, or pragmatic—with dichotomous responses (+ or −), where students had to express their level of agreement or disagreement with the presented statements. This information was used to plan activities that foster creative thinking by enabling students to make connections and formulate original or functional ideas, design strategies, structures, or products that had not been previously considered [30], while also defining the predominant learning style within the classroom.

During the semesters in which stages 1 (population analysis) and 2 (pilot study) were carried out, students participated in three sessions dedicated to the creative process—one per evaluation period within the CAM course. However, for stage 3, corresponding to the didactic intervention, it was determined—based on the institutional academic calendar—that nine consecutive classes were necessary. This schedule avoided holidays and vacation periods to ensure an uninterrupted workflow, allowing the iterative process within creative development to proceed without disruption, as outlined in Table 1.

Table 1. Summary of each methodological stage (population analysis, pilot, and didactic intervention), showing the number of students, main steps, duration, and location.

Stage	No. of Students	Steps	Duration	Location
Population Analysis	30	Observation	3 creativity sessions	Classroom
Pilot	7	Creation of CHAEA via Google Forms Design of the Discord platform server 1st sketching exercise per session	N/A N/A 3 creativity sessions	Online N/A Classroom
Didactic Intervention	21	CHAEA application Pre-Test Torrance application Sketches Weekly activity Use of platforms for evidence Post-Test Torrance application	N/A Session A 7 weeks 7 weeks 7 weeks Session B	Online Classroom Classroom ICT Classroom/ICT Classroom

At the beginning of the semester, during the didactic intervention, students were given a detailed explanation of the class schedule and the methodology that would be followed throughout the process. The intervention plan consisted of three main steps.

As shown in Table 2, the first step, carried out in Week A, involved the online development and application of the CHAEA test, while in the classroom, the Torrance pre-test was administered. Subsequently, students created sketches based on basic shapes inspired by the Torrance Test of Creative Thinking (TTCT). These exercises were designed to gradually increase in complexity as the weeks progressed, along with the time allocated for their completion. Initially, in Week 1, students had five minutes to create four sketches. Over time, this increased incrementally until they were required to complete ten sketches within ten minutes. This structured timing aimed to facilitate the cognitive and creative iteration process among participants over seven weeks.

The second step involved a weekly take-home activity where students worked on class-generated references, modifying them based on specific instructions aligned with the competencies targeted in each session. This led to the third step, which was the use of the Discord platform.

Table 2. Timeline of the didactic intervention from January to April 2024, showing the scheduling of key activities (CHAEA, Torrance pre- and post-tests, weekly exercises, and the use of Discord).

2024 Month	January				February				March					April			
Week	1	2	3	4	1	2	3	4	1	2	3	4	5	1	2	3	4
Torrance Test Submission		✓															
CHAEA Application				✓													
Torrance Test (PRE) Application				✓													
Torrance Exercise Application					✓	✓	✓	✓	✓	✓	✓						
Weekly Activities					✓	✓	✓	✓	✓	✓	✓						
Use of Discord for Evidence and Feedback					✓	✓	✓	✓	✓	✓	✓						
Torrance Test (POST) Application												✓					
Submission and Receipt of TTCT Analysis Results							✓	✓				✓				✓	

Hernández-Jaime et al. [31] point out that creative thinking does not follow a logical or systematic process but rather progresses through an initially chaotic and uncertain path, characterized by the generation of ideas that may seem unconventional at first. Consequently, the competencies targeted for development, as outlined in the TTCT, reflected key aspects of the creative process, including originality, flexibility, fluency, elaboration, problem solving, openness to experience, collaboration, creative communication, curiosity, and automatization. The objective was to identify progress in these areas.

A field journal was used to record each session, as illustrated in Figure 2. This journal included sections to document general and specific class objectives, session activities, attendance, materials used, tools, student comments, instructor observations, and researcher notes, along with instructions for the next session. This allowed for the systematic tracking of competency development across sessions and the integration of the platform into the learning process.

<table>
<tr><td colspan="2">Field Journal</td><td colspan="2" rowspan="2">Place
Autonomous University of Querétaro, School of Engineering, Industrial Design,
6th Semester</td><td colspan="2">Work Area
CEDIT Meeting Room
Laboratory
Classroom
Virtual</td></tr>
<tr><td colspan="2">Date: ___/2023</td><td colspan="2">Group</td></tr>
<tr><td>Session number</td><td></td><td colspan="4">General objetive:</td></tr>
<tr><td>Number of Activities</td><td></td><td colspan="4">Class Duration:</td></tr>
<tr><td>Number of Students</td><td></td><td>Materials:</td><td colspan="2">Tools:</td><td>Equipment:</td></tr>
<tr><td colspan="6">Specific objectives:</td></tr>
</table>

Figure 2. The template for the field journal used to record session details, objectives, materials, and reflections throughout the intervention.

3.2.1. Stage 1: Before the Didactic Intervention (January 2023–December 2023)

A year before implementation, a population analysis was conducted to understand how classes were structured, the general characteristics of the students, the available materials, and the workspace (see Figure 1). The following semester, after identifying these aspects, a pilot study was conducted to test the Honey and Alonso Questionnaire via an online format, ensuring that it worked properly and could be completed by each student to determine their learning style.

Angulo-Valenzuela and Ascuntar-Rivera [32] argue that sketching aligns with students' divergent and exploratory thinking processes. At the same time, technological integration in classrooms has transformed design education, incorporating it into the digital learning phenomenon and promoting autonomous learning. Based on this, sketching exercises were carried out to allow students to demonstrate competencies assigned in activities while also providing an initial introduction to Discord as a knowledge management platform. This stage enabled an analysis and risk assessment of potential implementation challenges, such as session interruptions due to holidays or an excessive workload preventing students from completing exercises on time.

A key takeaway was how students adapted to the platform, which helped structure and organize activities for implementation. It also allowed for estimating the time required to provide peer feedback effectively.

3.2.2. Stage 2: During the Intervention (January 2024–March 2024)

After completing the pilot study and analyzing the collected data, activities were planned to foster creative thinking through iteration among Industrial Design students. This process began with refining and redesigning the application of the Honey and Alonso

Questionnaire (CHAEA) via Google Forms to determine the predominant learning style in the classroom. This information was then used to develop activities focused on creative thinking development.

As part of the intervention, students signed a commitment letter outlining the weekly sketching exercises, emphasizing that they would be completed at the beginning of each session. Students were required to register on the platform using their institutional email to ensure proper identification when uploading their work for peer and instructor evaluation.

At the start of the semester, Session A was conducted, focusing on the Torrance Test, which evaluates creative capacity through engaging and stimulating activities. These tasks were selected based on factorial analyses conducted on a wide range of activities designed by Coronado-Hijón [33]. The test consists of two forms—verbal and figurative—each with two subtests, A and B. The Figure A pre-test comprised three exercises, each with a completion time of 10 min.

The first section of the test started with a central base figure for students to create a general sketch. The second section required them to create ten sketches based on a base figure, and the final section involved producing 30 sketches with different interpretations of a base figure. For the pre-test, students were given creative freedom, with instructions to think of and draw objects or parts that they could potentially 3D print. As emphasized by Candia [34], institutions should promote an integrated learning approach that connects knowledge, action, and execution, bridging the gap between theory and practice in technological contexts.

Once completed, the test was sent to the Torrance Academic Evaluation Service for review by specialists.

For Weeks 1 to 7, students received a worksheet similar to the pre-test of the Torrance tests with fewer sketches to complete, as shown in Figure 3. Each week, they were given specific instructions on the types of objects to design, always envisioning them for 3D printing. These included motor components, backpack racks, tool racks, modified parts, and credenzas. The number of required sketches increased progressively, as did the time allocated for their completion. Students took photos of their work and uploaded them to a designated Discord channel as evidence, allowing for peer feedback.

Based on the established structure, the competencies necessary to achieve the weekly objective and carry out the iterative process were selected. Consequently, two strategies were implemented, as shown in Table 3. The iteration strategy aimed to measure originality, flexibility, fluency, and openness to experience, while problem solving was assessed through the use of ICT with Discord. The latter strategy aimed to measure elaboration, collaborative work, creative communication, curiosity, and automation, fostering interaction and dynamic learning while promoting reflection and deeper cognitive engagement in idea exchange [35].

Each weekly activity included both in-person classroom work and remote tasks via the Discord platform. Weekly evidence of the iterative process was recorded, along with adjustments based on targeted competencies.

The first two weeks were a challenging adaptation period for students as they learned to share their work on Discord. While they were familiar with the platform, they were not accustomed to its potential applications. However, as the weeks progressed, their sketches became more fluid and natural.

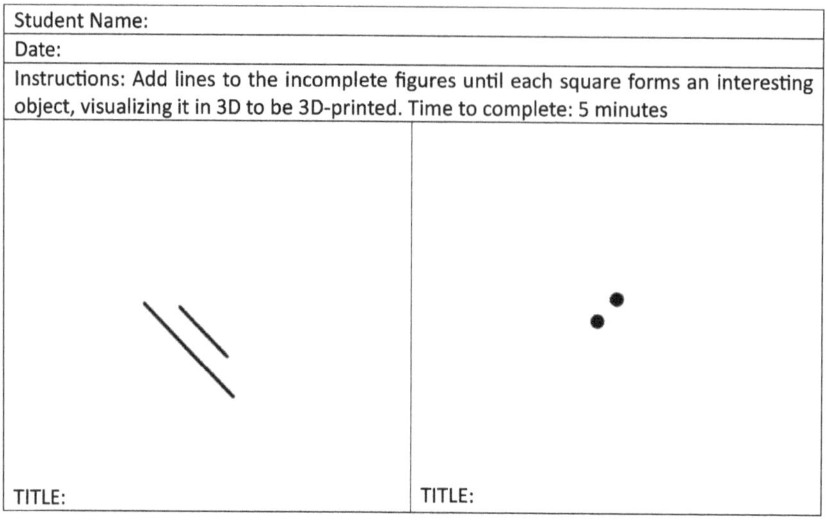

Figure 3. Sample weekly sketching worksheet, where students transform basic shapes into 3D-printable objects within a set time.

Table 3. Weekly quick-sketch and ICT-based activities, detailing each strategy, its description, and the competencies reinforced.

Week	Strategy	Activity	Description	Competency
1	Iteration	Quick Sketching Use of ICT	Develop unique ideas with concrete and executable details	Fluency, Elaboration, Originality
2	Iteration Use of ICT	Quick Sketching	Work on the ability to consider different perspectives and approaches	Fluency, Flexibility, Openness to experience
3	Iteration	Quick Sketching	Suggest design options based on a real need	Fluency, Originality, Problem solving
4	Iteration Use of ICT	Quick Sketching	Clearly interpret proposed requirements	Fluency, Collaboration, Creative communication
5	Iteration	Quick Sketching	Consider innovative questions to seek creative answers	Fluency, Curiosity, Openness to experience
6	Iteration Use of ICT	Quick Sketching	Adjust and improve based on received feedback	Fluency, Curiosity, Automation
7	Iteration	Quick Sketching	Deepen planning and execution while adapting to changes	Fluency, Flexibility, Elaboration, Automation

Each week, students were given a specific theme, which helped structure their work and streamline the iterative process. By this point, they no longer felt anxious about the time constraints, understood the strategy, and had no doubts about the sketching process. This resulted in better time management, more detailed sketches, more complete figures, and greater confidence in their work.

By the end of Week 5, students began providing peer feedback in real time. They examined each other's sketches, realizing the different possibilities for utilizing the base figure. Although they sometimes finished early, they used the extra time to add more elements and refine line quality. However, they had not yet considered positioning their objects within a physical space.

Finally, Session B was conducted, in which the Torrance Figures Post-Test was administered. Students were again instructed to envision objects for 3D printing. Unlike the pre-test, they demonstrated improved time management, greater focus, and more fluid idea generation. Their work speed increased, and their exercises were better structured. The completed post-tests were sent to the Torrance Academic Evaluation Service for specialist analysis and evaluation.

3.2.3. Stage 3: After the Intervention (April 2024–June 2024)

The process of data collection and systematization went beyond mere record-keeping, becoming an analytical and dialogical space for the knowledge gained from practice. This collaborative process fosters critical understanding, questioning, and concrete actions within a specific context [36]. All evidence from the field journal and physical documents generated during each in-person session was verified and duly recorded on the digital platform Discord. A thorough review was conducted to ensure that each student had uploaded all weekly activity evidence to the designated channel and that the provided and received peer feedback on submitted work was properly documented. Consent forms and individual student assignments were organized into personal folders, allowing for quick and structured access to track each participant's progress.

At the end of the last intervention week, students were given a link to a Google Forms survey to provide feedback on their experience during the execution of exercises designed to foster creative thinking development.

3.3. Data Collection and Analysis

The collected data included observations recorded in the field journal, documented for each classroom and each session, resulting in a total of 14 entries—seven sessions per classroom. This served as the primary qualitative data source. Additionally, the Torrance pre-test and post-test were considered, along with the evidence generated during in-class activities. Weekly activities were uploaded to the digital platform Discord, enabling the continuous tracking of student progress. The comments and feedback exchanged among peers also served as secondary information, supporting and affirming the work completed.

Furthermore, a survey consisting of 24 items was administered via Google Forms to gather information on students' experiences throughout the three implementation phases. The survey covered daily evidence, weekly activities, and platform usage to assess the progress achieved in developing creative thinking among Industrial Design students through the application of iteration in their weekly work.

4. Results

The evaluation of the results consisted of analyzing the comparison between the Torrance pre-test and post-test results, along with the data collected for each student and the creative strengths selected as competencies to be developed. Additionally, responses from the Google Forms questionnaire, administered to all 21 students at the end of the intervention, were examined. The analysis identified an increase in originality within the classroom, as students moved away from conventional and repetitive responses, offering innovative and unconventional solutions as shown in Table 4, which suggests that originality scores identified in the post-test (Originality B) are more consistent compared to the extreme values observed in the pre-test (Originality A). At the same time, there was notable progress in the formulation, as students responded to the stimulus figure with unique and detailed solutions.

Table 4. Descriptive statistics comparing originality scores before (pre-test) and after (post-test) the intervention, highlighting improvements in students' creative responses.

	N	Mean	Median	SD	Minimum	Maximum	Percentiles		
							25th	50th	75th
Originality A (pre-test)	18	17.1	16.0	7.75	7	33	13.0	16.0	21.0
Originality B (post-test)	19	17.9	18.0	5.70	6	35	16.0	18.0	20.0

Activities and Participation in the Classroom

Students, based on the predominant reflective learning style identified in the classroom, had the opportunity to work from theory to practice, better conceptualizing their sketching ideas through the visualization of 3D printing.

To document students' perceptions regarding iterative work and the development of creative thinking, a 24-item questionnaire was divided into three sections. A manual coding process was applied to their responses, identifying the most frequently mentioned constructs, which were categorized according to the three initial activities and the four final activities conducted during the intervention. Table 5 presents the intervention sections and the most frequently mentioned codes, based on the responses of the 21 participants. This grouping resulted in three main categories: creativity, sketching, and iteration.

Table 5. Categories and most frequent codes derived from students' perceptions of intervention activities, grouped by early (Sessions 1–3) and later stages (Sessions 4–7).

Intervention	Categories	Section	Code	Mentions
Session 1 to 3	Creativity	Daily evidence	Repetitive exercises	13
	Sketching	Weekly activities	Develop detailed ideas	8
	Iteration	ICT for creative thinking	Express ideas effectively	4
Session 4 to 7	Creativity	Daily evidence	Interesting exercises	11
	Sketching	Weekly activities	Ability to express ideas	10
	Iteration	ICT for creative thinking	Developing different perspectives/approaches	10

Table 6 presents these categories across the 24 items distributed within the three divisions of the questionnaire, recorded as follows:

Table 6. Distribution of mentions across questionnaire sections, highlighting student perceptions of iterative practices, sketching activities, and creative resource use.

Section	Categories	Mentions
Daily Evidence	Iteration/Activities	13
Weekly Activities	Sketching/Ideas	11
Creative Thinking	Creativity/Resources	10

Figure 4 provides a general overview of the frequency with which these constructs were mentioned, confirming that the highest number of citations correspond to the categories of greatest interest to students.

Figure 4. Word cloud showing the most frequently mentioned terms and categories derived from participant feedback.

It was identified that iterative work over the seven sessions evolved the creative process from an approach based on quantity (generation of many ideas) to one focused on quality (improving and refining ideas); thus, 3D printing, when combined with iteration, enhances this process by visualizing and testing ideas in physical versions, modifying models based on real tests, and enabling creativity development through continuous improvement, as noted by Tena-Parera [37] when conducting critical reflection, thorough analysis, and informed determination, all conceived as reference points within the creative process for structuring and developing a new cycle.

5. Discussion

5.1. Three-Dimensional Printing and Iteration

Students engaged in an iterative process for developing creative thinking through weekly sketching exercises. The findings indicate that while most students can solve problems individually, they often hesitate at first. However, upon observing their peers' work, they become more proactive in designing their sketches, submitting materials, and providing peer feedback. According to Canabal and Margalef [38], this stems from motivation and action, which foster sustainable learning by encouraging dialogue rather than mere corrections. This approach helps identify areas for improvement and raises expectations, motivating students to continue progressing.

This iterative process took place both in-person and online, bridging theory and practice. Weekly sketching exercises in class helped students recognize the skills they were developing—originality, flexibility, fluency, elaboration, problem-solving, openness to experience, collaboration, creative communication, curiosity, and automation. Initially, these skills were not easily identifiable, but as they were practiced, students applied them more naturally. As Suardíaz et al. [39] suggest, future experiences should further enhance motivation and engagement during sessions.

Santander-Salmon and Schreiber-Parra [40] emphasize that a positive emotional attitude strengthens educational practice and fosters deeper learning, allowing students to achieve their goals and enhance their competitiveness. Thinking in 3D from the conceptualization phase enabled students to visualize multiple possibilities—not just a complete object, but also its individual components. Iteration was found to facilitate creative development in parameters such as originality and design elaboration. López-Chao and Meira-Rodríguez [41] support this view, stating that iteration drives innovation by allowing students to discuss proposals and refine their adaptation to visual communication.

Vicente [42] notes that additive manufacturing is rapidly growing, exceeding expectations and solidifying itself as an accessible and cost-effective technology. However, this study revealed that despite encouraging students to think in 3D and create objects for printing, they lacked direct access to the 3D printer. Limited semester schedules and the large number of students prevented continuous use of the equipment, restricting the iterative redesign process. This posed a challenge, as students could not observe changes in their designs as they were made. Even though the study included 21 students who had already used 3D printing in their education, Mejía Salazar [43] emphasizes the importance of incorporating activities and workshops in the classroom to strengthen the use of technology as an essential learning tool.

A key finding of this research is that 3D printing combined with iteration fosters the development of more flexible and less linear creative thinking; this process does not follow a fixed trajectory but adapts to new ideas and discoveries. This aligns with an increased independence among variables. Such a combination enables transitioning from generating new ideas to refining existing ones. Designers were able to adjust their approach based on the results obtained in each iteration, accelerating the innovation process by allowing rapid modifications and promoting experimental exploration and testing of ideas in physical formats.

5.2. Future Projects for Developing Creative Skills with 3D Printing

Some students lacked confidence in using 3D printing, while others were eager to apply it. Therefore, it is suggested to design projects that integrate 3D printing directly and individually, ensuring that students can address real-world challenges with greater confidence. Such projects would allow them to see how additive manufacturing strengthens their learning process, while also supporting continuous teacher training.

Incorporating additive manufacturing into teaching helps shape a new mindset, enabling students to envision their designs for 3D construction from the outset. It also allows for continued iterative work in a tangible, physical manner. The object itself becomes a facilitator for dialogue and discussion, making its use a valuable addition to the classroom. While images can serve as substitutes, their integration enhances the effectiveness of learning [44]. This ensures that the iterative process is maintained, allowing ideas to be refined continuously in a hands-on manner.

5.3. Relevance, Limitations, and Future Directions

This study highlights the relevance of integrating technological tools, particularly 3D printing, into educational settings to support creative processes. Direct access to these tools enables students to engage in ongoing iteration, a key element of creativity not only in Industrial Design but across disciplines that value innovation. As Ortiz-Gil [45] notes, additive manufacturing offers precision, speed, and sustainability, making it a transformative force in both education and research. For students, having hands-on access to such technology facilitates a cycle of experimentation, feedback, and refinement, which is critical to developing adaptable and innovative thinkers.

Although the focus here was Industrial Design, the pedagogical benefits of 3D printing and iterative methodologies extend beyond this field. Creativity thrives when students are equipped with tools and goals that encourage exploration. Peramás and Escurra-Mayaute [46] highlight that creative individuals use cognitive flexibility to apply knowledge across contexts, skills that are increasingly vital in today's complex world. When supported by analog and digital methods, the creative process becomes more accessible, and cross-disciplinary collaboration further enhances reflective and critical thinking.

However, the study has several limitations. In particular, the small sample size of 21 students restricts the generalizability of the findings. Although the results offer valuable information, a broader participant base is needed to validate these outcomes in different disciplines and educational contexts. Additionally, conducting the intervention with two classrooms from the same class introduces possible bias, mainly due to inconsistent attendance. Future research should control for variations in student engagement and explicitly examine how participation levels influence creative development.

Another limitation is the disciplinary focus of the study. Restricting the sample to Industrial Design students raises questions about applicability to other domains such as engineering, architecture, or visual arts. Investigating how iterative design and 3D printing influence creativity in these fields could yield richer comparative insights.

Future work should explore interdisciplinary approaches that bring students from different academic backgrounds to solve real-world problems. This could clarify how iterative design practices and technological tools function in collaborative environments and whether such settings promote deeper creativity and innovation than discipline-specific interventions.

From a practical point of view, the findings suggest that integrating iterative design and 3D printing into curricula can significantly enrich collaborative learning environments. These tools not only support faster development and refinement of ideas, but also help students visualize and test concepts more effectively. Immersion time and hands-on interaction remain essential: students benefit most when they can continuously design, prototype, reflect, and iterate. However, limited access to equipment constrained this potential, as not all students were able to materialize each improvement during the intervention.

Looking ahead, developing environments that guarantee access to advanced technological tools and promote sustained iteration will enhance the capacity of students to innovate. By cultivating collaboration and supporting iterative thinking, educational institutions can better prepare learners to apply their skills for societal benefit, ultimately transforming classroom practices into dynamic, community-oriented learning experiences.

6. Conclusions

Iteration is essential as part of the creative process and is fundamental to refining ideas. Activities that incorporate feedback to enhance initial concepts while integrating new perspectives create an academic experience that balances structure with creative freedom. By implementing suggestions derived from structured activities, students can improve their ability to express and generate original ideas.

Students do not always perceive iteration as necessary; however, they notice differences in their work when they engage in it. This highlights the need for exercises that do not feel repetitive, while allowing greater flexibility in activities to explore multiple approaches effectively.

Group dynamics facilitate the iterative process by encouraging the exchange of ideas and exploring different ways to work with the same base figure while pursuing a shared goal. Peer interaction and feedback are perceived as valuable, enriching students' ideas and enabling them to observe and learn from the creative solutions of others.

Author Contributions: Conceptualization, L.C.-F. and D.-M.C.-E.; methodology, L.C.-F. and D.-M.C.-E.; formal analysis, L.C.-F., D.-M.C.-E. and J.-A.R.-G.; investigation, L.C.-F., D.-M.C.-E., J.-A.R.-G., T.G.-R. and J.T.; resources, L.C.-F., D.-M.C.-E., J.-A.R.-G., T.G.-R., R.-E.L.-M., J.T. and J.-J.R.-P.; writing—original draft preparation, L.C.-F. and D.-M.C.-E.; writing—review and editing, L.C.-F., D.-M.C.-E., J.-A.R.-G., T.G.-R., R.-E.L.-M., J.T. and J.-J.R.-P.; supervision, D.-M.C.-E.; project administration, D.-M.C.-E. All authors have read and agreed to the published version of the manuscript.

Funding: This research received no external funding.

Institutional Review Board Statement: This study was conducted in accordance with the ethical guidelines established by Universidad Autónoma de Querétaro for academic research. All participants provided informed consent prior to their participation.

Informed Consent Statement: Informed consent was obtained from all subjects involved in the study.

Data Availability Statement: The original contributions presented in this study are included in the article. Further inquiries can be directed to the corresponding author.

Acknowledgments: We thank the Autonomous University of Querétaro and the National Council of Humanities, Sciences, and Technologies (CONAHCYT) for their support.

Conflicts of Interest: The authors declare no conflicts of interest.

References

1. Kenett, Y.N. The role of knowledge in creative thinking. *Creat. Res. J.* **2024**, 1–8. [CrossRef]
2. Khalil, R.Y.; Tairab, H.; Qablan, A.; Alarabi, K.; Mansour, Y. STEM-based curriculum and creative thinking in high school students. *Educ. Sci.* **2023**, *13*, 1195. [CrossRef]
3. Arias Arciniegas, C.M.; Giraldo Bedoya, D.P.; Anaya Urbina, L.M. Competencia Creatividad e Innovación: Conceptualización y Abordaje en la Educación. *Katharsis* **2013**, *15*, 195–214. [CrossRef]
4. Aguiar, B.O.; Velázquez, R.M.; Aguiar, J.L. Innovación docente y empleo de las TIC en la Educación Superior. *Rev. Espac.* **2019**, *40*, 8.
5. de Carvalho, T.d.C.M.; de Souza Fleith, D.; da Silva Almeida, L. Desarrollo del pensamiento creativo en el ámbito educativo. *Rev. Latinoam. Estud. Educ.* **2021**, *17*, 164–187.
6. Jalolov, T.S. Enhancing Creative Thinking in Elementary School Students Through Multimedia Technologies. *World Sci.* **2024**, *7*, 114–120.
7. Almutairi, H.; Delaney, P. Exploring Student Usage of ICT Tools in Project-based Learning. *IEEE Intell. Inf. Bull.* **2023**, *23*, 10–17.
8. Rizal, R.; Surahman, E.; Aripin, H.; Maulidah, R. Problem-Based Learning Management System (PBLMS): A Mobile Learning Application to Facilitate Creative Thinking Skills (CTS) of Prospective Physics Teachers. *Int. J. Interact. Mob. Technol.* **2024**, *18*, 97–109.
9. Valverde Berrocoso, J.; Fernández Sánchez, M.R.; Garrido Arroyo, M.d.C. El pensamiento computacional y las nuevas ecologías del aprendizaje. *Rev. Educ. Distancia* **2015**, *46*, 1–18. [CrossRef]
10. Silva Mantilla, E.L. La creatividad: Un momento de inspiración o una búsqueda rigurosa. *Actas Diseño* **2024**, *45*, 263–267.
11. Carranza, M. Pensamiento creativo: Un estudio holístico en la educación. *Rev. Innova Educ.* **2021**, *3*, 123–132.
12. Wu, R.; Fan, J.; Tang, C.; Yang, X. Interaction-based creative thinking research and its application in artistic creation. *Think. Ski. Creat.* **2025**, *56*, 101750. [CrossRef]
13. Grimaldo Salazar, E.; Chávez Soto, B.I. Prueba de creatividad verbal de Torrance: Evidencias de validez psicométrica en estudiantado mexicano de educación primaria. *Actual. Investig. Educ.* **2023**, *23*, 70–93. [CrossRef]
14. Humble, S.; Dixon, P.; Mpofu, E. Factor structure of the Torrance Tests of Creative Thinking Figural Form A in Kiswahili speaking children: Multidimensionality and influences on creative behavior. *Think. Ski. Creat.* **2018**, *27*, 33–44. [CrossRef]
15. Rúa, E.B.; Jiménez, F.; Gutiérrez, G.A.; Villamizar, N.I. Impresión 3D como herramienta didáctica para la enseñanza de algunos conceptos de ingeniería y diseño. *Ingeniería* **2018**, *23*, 70–83.
16. Cuervo Pulido, R.; Hernández Mihajlovic, E. Cómo evaluar la cognición creativa al enseñar diseño industrial? Un insumo para su aprendizaje. *BitÁCora Urbano Territ.* **2020**, *30*, 163–176. [CrossRef]

17. Martínez Suárez, E.M.; González, M.d.P. La creatividad como competencia universitaria? La visión de los docentes. *Rev. Form. Innov. Educ. Univ.* **2009**, *2*, 101–114.
18. Solano Fernández, E.; Porras Alfaro, D. El modelo iterativo e incremental para el desarrollo de la aplicación de realidad aumentada Amón_RA. *Tecnol. Marcha* **2020**, *33*, 165–177. [CrossRef]
19. Hincapié Atehortúa, E.A. La Iteración Como Herramienta de Gestión y Planificación en el Diseño de Ejecución en Proyectos de Construcción. Master's Thesis, Universidad Nacional de Colombia, Medellín, Colombia, 2022. Available online: https://repositorio.unal.edu.co/bitstream/handle/unal/83923/71790225.2022.pdf?sequence=4&isAllowed=y (accessed on 1 February 2025).
20. Sawyer, R.K. The iterative and improvisational nature of the creative process. *J. Creat.* **2021**, *31*, 100002. [CrossRef]
21. Wynn, D.C.; Eckert, C.M. Perspectives on iteration in design and development. *Res. Eng. Des.* **2017**, *28*, 153–184. [CrossRef]
22. Žujović, M.; Obradović, R.; Rakonjac, I.; Milošević, J. 3D printing technologies in architectural design and construction: A systematic literature review. *Buildings* **2022**, *12*, 1319. [CrossRef]
23. Mata Abdelnour, E. Propuesta para la incorporación del modelado e impresión 3D para la enseñanza de Ingeniería Civil de la Universidad de Costa Rica. *Rev. Educ.* **2023**, *47*, 460–478. [CrossRef]
24. Flick, U. *El Diseño de la Investigación Cualitativa*; Ediciones Morata: Madrid, Spain, 2015; ISBN 978-84-7112-806-5.
25. Peralta-Castro, F.; Mayoral-Valdivia, P.J. La investigación acción como estrategia de reflexión, mejora y cambio en la práctica docente de la enseñanza de lenguas. *RIDE Rev. Iberoam. Para Investig. Desarro. Educ.* **2022**, *12*, 1–25.
26. Piza Burgos, N.D.; Amaiquema Márquez, F.A.; Beltrán Baquerizo, G.E. Métodos y técnicas en la investigación cualitativa. Algunas precisiones necesarias. *Conrado* **2019**, *15*, 455–459.
27. Contreras-Espinosa, R.S.; Eguia-Gomez, J.L. Discord como herramienta de enseñanza en línea durante la pandemia de COVID-19. *Rev. FAEEBA Educ. Contemp.* **2022**, *31*, 106–120.
28. Villarreal-Fernández, J.E. Cuestionario Honey-Alonso de estilos de aprendizaje (CHAEA). Propiedades psicométricas en estudiantes universitarios colombianos. *Psicogente* **2023**, *26*, 46–69.
29. Costa, R.D.; Souza, G.F.; Valentim, R.A.; Castro, T.B. The theory of learning styles applied to distance learning. *Cogn. Syst. Res.* **2020**, *64*, 134–145.
30. Fernández Iglesias, M.J. *Introducción al Pensamiento Creativo*; AtlanTTic, Universidad de Vigo: Vigo, Spain, 2024. [CrossRef]
31. Hernández Jaime, J.; Jiménez Galán, Y.I.; Rodríguez Flores, E. Desarrollo de competencias de pensamiento creativo y práctico para iniciar un plan de negocio: Diseño de evidencias de aprendizaje. *RIDE Rev. Iberoam. Para Investig. Desarro. Educ.* **2018**, *9*, 314–342.
32. Angulo-Valenzuela, C.; Ascuntar-Rivera, M.C. La enseñanza y aprendizaje del boceto de diseño a través de mediadores tecnológicos. *Rev. Latinoam. Estud. Educ.* **2020**, *16*, 137–158.
33. Coronado-Hijón, A. Aplicación Contextualizada Del Test De Pensamiento Creativo De Tor Rance (TTCT). *Rev. Española Orientac. Psicopedag.* **2015**, *26*, 70–82.
34. Candia García, F. Integración de la impresión 3D en la educación tecnológica. *RIDE Rev. Iberoam. Para Investig. Desarro. Educ.* **2022**, *12*, 1–31. [CrossRef]
35. Granda Asencio, L.Y.; Espinoza Freire, E.E.; Mayon Espinoza, S.E. Las TICs como herramientas didácticas del proceso de enseñanza-aprendizaje. *Conrado* **2019**, *15*, 104–110.
36. Villa-Holguín, E. La sistematización de experiencias, una estrategia de la investigación anti-hegemónica. *El Ágora USB* **2019**, *19*, 547–557. [CrossRef]
37. Tena Parera, D. Diseño como proceso iterativo. *Grafica* **2015**, *3*, 5–11. [CrossRef]
38. Canabal, C.; Margalef, L. La retroalimentación: La clave para una evaluación orientada al aprendizaje. *Profr. Rev. Curric. Form. Profr.* **2017**, *21*, 149–170. [CrossRef]
39. Suardíaz Muro, J.; Pérez Gomáriz, M.; Cabrera Lozoya, A.; Do Carmo Trolle, R.O. Combinando Impresión 3D y electrónica como estrategia para mejorar la experiencia de aprendizaje. *Ried Rev. Iberoam. Educ. Distancia* **2021**, *24*, 115–135. [CrossRef]
40. Santander Salmon, E.S.; Schreiber Parra, M.J. Importancia de la motivación en el proceso de aprendizaje. *Cienc. Lat. Rev. Cient. Multidiscip.* **2022**, *6*, 4095–4106. [CrossRef]
41. López-Chao, V.; Meira-Rodríguez, P. Composición e iteración de color para desarrollar arte de concepto de entornos. Exploración de un procedimiento de análisis visual en el desarrollo creativo. *Revista* **2023**, *180*, 75–86. [CrossRef]
42. Vicente Oliva, S. La Impresión 3D Como Tecnología de Uso General en el Futuro. Technical Report. 2018. Available online: https://dialnet.unirioja.es/servlet/articulo?codigo=6535713 (accessed on 1 February 2025).
43. Mejía Salazar, G. La aplicación de las TIC en los procesos de enseñanza-aprendizaje en estudiantes de nivel medio superior en Tepic, Nayarit. *RIDE Rev. Iberoam. Para Investig. Desarro. Educ.* **2020**, *11*, 1–20. [CrossRef]
44. Tapia Espinosa, F.; Arias Ferrer, L. El aprendizaje basado en objetos como estrategia para la enseñanza de la historia en Educación Primaria: Un estudio cuasi-experimental. *Espiral. Cuad. Profr.* **2021**, *14*, 44–56.

45. Ortiz Gil, A. Las impresoras 3D como herramientas científicas. *Obs. Astron. Univ. Val.* **2019**, *61*, 1–8.
46. Peramás De La Fuente, T.D.C. El Pensamiento Creativo y el Rendimiento Escolar en Niños de Segundo Grado de Primaria de una Institución Educativa Privada del Distrito de La Molina. Master's Thesis, Universidad Ricardo Palma, Lima, Peru, 2017. Available online: https://repositorio.urp.edu.pe/entities/publication/ae15ed28-67f7-4f48-a670-be237f528b84 (accessed on 1 February 2025).

Multimodal Technologies and Interaction

MDPI

Article

Designing Digital Escape Rooms with Generative AI in University Contexts: A Qualitative Study

Paula Rodríguez-Rivera [1], José M. Rodríguez-Ferrer [2] and Ana Manzano-León [3,*]

[1] Faculty of Education and Social Work, Department of Psychosocioeducational Analysis and Intervention, University of Vigo, 32004 Ourense, Spain; paula.rodriguez.rivera@uvigo.es
[2] Faculty of Health Sciences, Department of Health Sciences, University of Burgos, 09001 Burgos, Spain; jmrferrer@ubu.es
[3] Department of Psychology, Health Research Centre, University of Almería, 04120 Almería, Spain
* Correspondence: aml570@ual.es

Abstract: The rapid evolution of technology in education highlights the need for methodologies that enhance student engagement and skill development. This study examines students' perceptions of designing educational escape rooms using ICT tools and generative AI (GenAI) as a learning methodology. A total of 47 students participated in creating digital escape rooms with GenAI, Genially, and HeroForge in the course "Mediation in Conflicts and Situations of Violence" within a Social Education degree. A qualitative approach was used, analyzing focus group discussions conducted after the activity. Results indicate that students valued the experience, emphasizing its impact on digital competence, creativity, and problem-solving skills. Collaborative learning helped overcome initial technical challenges, and students recognized the practical applicability of escape room design in mediation contexts. However, they identified areas for improvement, such as the need for more initial training, extended development time, and better access to digital tools. This study contributes to game-based learning and AI-enhanced education research, positioning students as active designers rather than passive users. Future research should explore the long-term impact on knowledge retention and transferable skills in professional settings.

Keywords: escape rooms; artificial intelligence in education; transversal competencies; digital tools in teaching

1. Introduction

In recent decades, society has undergone a technological transformation that has profoundly impacted all domains, including education [1,2]. Integrating information and communication technologies (ICT) has radically altered teaching and learning processes, generating a new pedagogical reality that combines physical and digital environments [3].

Acquiring basic digital competencies is essential for students and teachers, regardless of their discipline or educational level [4,5]. In higher education, these competencies facilitate a deeper understanding of content and foster metacognitive skills and autonomous learning, preparing future professionals for an increasingly digitalized labor market [6,7]. However, the effectiveness of ICT in university classrooms critically depends on teachers' digital competence [8]. While some educators perceive these tools as facilitators of active learning [9], others associate them with additional administrative burdens or technical difficulties [10], limiting their full adoption.

Nevertheless, students' digital competence is also crucial in this process. Recent studies show that although university students are frequent users of digital tools, their mastery of key competencies such as information management, communication in virtual environments, and digital content creation is uneven [11,12]. The evolution of these competencies has been influenced by various factors, including access to technological resources, prior training, ICT-mediated learning experiences, or social class [13,14]. Current research indicates that while recent generations have developed intuitive skills in using digital devices, this does not automatically translate into advanced digital competence in academic and professional settings [15].

In this context, marked by barriers such as a lack of time, institutional resources, and specialized support for integrating ICT in classrooms [16], the emergence of generative artificial intelligence (GenAI) in universities has intensified these challenges. ChatGPT, developed by OpenAI, is among the most widely used GenAI technologies in education, recognized for its ability to create new and contextually relevant content based on previously trained data. Its advanced architecture, based on models such as GPT-3.5 and GPT-4, enables the generation of explanations, examples, and materials tailored to the specific needs of students and educators [17].

One of the main challenges is the risk that students may use these tools to avoid completing tasks autonomously. Various studies highlight how these technologies can facilitate the plagiarism of written texts, compromising the development of essential skills such as critical thinking and academic writing [18]. Additionally, reliance on generative tools may limit active learning by reducing the effort required to complete academic tasks [19,20].

Despite these challenges, the potential of generative AI in education warrants critical consideration. Empirical evidence [21–23] suggests that these tools can optimize innovative educational processes, such as designing immersive learning experiences or facilitating collaborative dynamics in digital environments. One example of this collaboration is the integration of GenAI into the design of educational escape rooms (EERs). Educational escape rooms (EERs) are defined as immersive game-based learning environments that adapt the structure of recreational escape rooms to educational contexts. These activities challenge participants to solve sequential puzzles, riddles, or tasks linked to curricular content within a narrative framework, fostering critical thinking, collaboration, and knowledge application [24–26]. Initially conceived as recreational activities, EERs have been adapted to educational settings due to their ability to promote motivation, active learning, and collaboration through immersive challenges [27]. Recent research highlights how GenAI could further enhance their pedagogical development, enabling everything from the personalization of adaptive narratives to the automated generation of context-based challenges [28,29]. However, as studies emphasize, its adoption must be accompanied by pedagogical strategies that prioritize the development of cognitive skills over the mere automation of tasks.

This duality is reflected in the current uses of EERs across various educational domains. In higher education, for instance, they have been successfully employed in health sciences to reinforce key concepts and practical skills in controlled environments [30,31]. In fields such as the social sciences, EERs have been shown to improve academic performance and student motivation while simultaneously fostering a positive classroom climate and challenge-based learning [10,32,33].

However, EERs' potential goes beyond their use as passive didactic tools. They reach their fullest expression when students become designers. Creating digital escape rooms integrates narrative elements and playful dynamics that require prior knowledge to be applied, fostering the development of key competencies such as creativity, problem-solving, and decision-making [34].

This active methodology has proven effective in the university setting for acquiring soft skills and digital competencies, particularly in education faculties where technological literacy is essential. For example, at the University of Extremadura, using an escape room via mobile technologies with students in the Social Education degree improved motivation and promoted competencies relevant to their training [35]. Similarly, at Rey Juan Carlos University, implementing a hybrid escape room in the "Informatics and Digital Competence" course enhanced motivation. It facilitated programming instruction for future early childhood and primary education teachers [36]. Planning these activities involves everything from digital tools to structuring pedagogical narratives, simultaneously strengthening digital competence and technological adaptability [37,38].

For this reason, tools like ChatGPT help to streamline these spaces by generating contextualized narratives, personalizing puzzles according to participants' skill levels, and offering real-time hints, reducing design time by up to 60% [39]. Recent studies highlight that combining language models with specialized databases facilitates the creation of interactive and adaptable scenarios across various disciplines, from engineering to the social sciences [40]. Additionally, adaptive feedback algorithms have been shown to expand the reach of these experiences, decreasing the resources required for implementation by 40% [41]. Experimental research in environments such as Roblox demonstrates that AI-controlled avatars enhance perceived immersion by 30% through contextualized dialogs [42].

Generative AI tools are also adopted in point-and-click games to optimize narrative design, create adaptive puzzles, and enhance interactions with non-playable characters (NPCs). Recent research demonstrates that systems such as PAC-Bot, a conversational agent integrated into development environments for non-expert users, reduce the cognitive load in creating behavioral rules for these games by automatically generating dialogs based on language models [43]. This approach has enabled amateur developers to design personalized experiences with 35% less effort in complex tasks, such as defining contextual events or integrating dynamic feedback mechanics [44]. Additionally, platforms like Adventure Creator and Fungus are incorporating GenAI algorithms to generate non-linear narratives, where NPC dialogs and decisions adapt in real-time to player actions, increasing replayability by 20% according to analyses of public datasets [45].

However, technical and ethical challenges remain. Around 18% of the hints generated by systems like ChatGPT may contain biases or inaccuracies, reinforcing the need for human supervision at key stages of the design process [17]. This duality highlights the importance of hybrid approaches, where GenAI acts as an assistant in EER creation without replacing the pedagogical judgment of designers [46].

In this context, where escape rooms are emerging as a promising strategy for developing key skills, their adaptation to digital environments with GenAI remains underexplored, particularly in the training of social educators. While previous studies focus on their application as pre-designed resources for students [47], this research innovates by positioning future social educators as active designers of their own escape rooms, integrating GenAI. This approach, scarcely explored in the literature, responds to two key findings: first, over 80% of gamified experiences in professional training rely on static tools (such as point-based systems) that do not promote applied creativity [48]; second, other reviews show that the creation of self-developed playful resources significantly enhances the transfer of digital and pedagogical competencies to work contexts [49].

Furthermore, in using GenAI to guide the creation of new narratives and ethical challenges [50] the proposed model develops technical skills and simulates scenarios where participants lead in designing socio-educational interventions. Therefore, this study has the following objectives:

1. Analyze how creating digital escape rooms mediated by generative artificial intelligence influences learning specific content and the development of teamwork, creativity, and digital competence.
2. Explore students' perceptions regarding integrating digital escape room design activities mediated by generative artificial intelligence.
3. Examine how students have incorporated and applied the various technological tools introduced during the activity.
4. Identify the challenges associated with the implementation of these activities.

The following sections present the methodology used in a practical activity in which students designed digital escape rooms using digital tools and generative artificial intelligence. Subsequently, the results obtained from student perceptions collected in focus groups are analyzed, followed by a discussion on the competencies developed, the challenges identified, and the pedagogical implications of this strategy. Finally, the study's conclusions and proposals for future research are presented.

2. Materials and Methods

2.1. Participants

This research was conducted with students from the Faculty of Education at Vigo University. A total of 57 students participated in this activity. Upon completing the activity, they were allowed to provide feedback by creating focus groups. Fifty-two students participated in the focus groups (89.4% of the activity participants), including 42 women and 10 men aged 21 to 54 years (M = 22.40; SD = 5.40).

2.2. Procedure

This research focused on studying the impact of interactive activities, such as creating educational escape rooms, in the course Mediation in Conflicts and Situations of Violence within the Social Education Degree at Vigo University during the 2024/2025 academic year. This course is a compulsory component of the degree program, as established in the university's curriculum. Within the course structure is a designated section for group or supervised work, which provides the framework for developing the educational escape room. These activities were mandatory and contributed to students' final grades, serving as an applied learning strategy to enhance their understanding and practical skills in conflict mediation.

The 52 students were divided into groups of 3 to 4 members to carry out the activity. Each group was presented with several case studies related to different types of mediation: family, school, workplace, and community mediation. These mediation cases and the difficulties encountered were directly linked to the theoretical content of the course. Two examples of mediation cases were a conflict between two students over group assignment responsibilities, requiring mediation to resolve cooperation and communication issues, and a dispute between two sisters over caregiving schedules for their ill mother, necessitating negotiation and agreement.

The activities were conducted over a month and were structured into eight sessions of 90 min each (Table 1).

The activity began with an introductory session, during which the methodology was presented, and students were familiarized with the digital tools to be used: ChatGPT (GPT-4o), Genially (https://genially.com/es/ (accessed on 26 February 2025)), HeroForge (www.heroforge.com (accessed on 26 February 2025)), and Pixverse (version 3). This session provided an overview of the project and included practical demonstrations to ensure proper tool handling. Additionally, a detailed evaluation rubric (Appendix A) was introduced, outlining the guidelines and criteria for the structured creation of the escape rooms.

Table 1. Structure of the sessions.

Phase	Sessions	Main Activities	Key Objectives
Introduction	1	Presentation of the workshop and review of the theoretical foundations of mediation.	Contextualize the activity, establish basic knowledge, and measure the students' initial level.
Escape room design	2–5	Creation of the escape room: narrative design (ChatGPT), interactive dynamics (Genially), and visual customization (HeroForge).	Apply theoretical concepts in a practical environment and foster creativity, collaboration, and digital skills.
Implementation and evaluation	6–8	Tests and adjustments, implementation of escape rooms, and focus groups.	Evaluate acquired skills, analyze the effectiveness of the escape room, and reflect on the experience.

In this context, Generative AI played a fundamental role in this stage, allowing students to design scenarios, generate images, and develop clues that structured the challenges coherently. These images were later animated using Pixverse, adding an interactive component that enhanced immersion in each scenario. To complete the visual design, students used HeroForge to create customized characters representing key actors in the conflicts, integrating them naturally into the mediation case narratives (Figure 1).

Figure 1. Preparation of the escape room.

Additionally, digital resources such as digital lock generators, timers, and WhatsApp conversation simulators provided functionalities that enriched the challenges.

Finally, all components were assembled in Genially, a platform that unified the narratives, visual elements, and interactive dynamics into a cohesive and functional final product.

The instructor acted as a guide and facilitator, addressing technical questions but refraining from interfering in the creative process. Their role focused on providing support when students had doubts about using digital tools or the feasibility of certain dynamics within the escape rooms.

Below is an example of the work carried out by a team of students whose case was related to school mediation. As Figure 2 shows, one group designed an EER simulating a plane crash scenario in which two students with interpersonal conflicts had to collaborate to solve survival challenges.

Figure 2. EER design example. (Note: In Figure 2, Image **1**, the first screen of the escape room titled "The Survivors of the Missing Flight" is shown, featuring the "Start" button and a visual of a crashed airplane in a snowy landscape with survivors gathered around a fire. Image **2** shows a top-down view of a snow-covered landscape with various locations marked by red padlocks, indicating restricted access, suggesting a progression-based structure where players unlock areas through achievements. Image **3** presents the question: "This material can form stalactites and stalagmites, slow but steady. In communication, it represents something that grows over time. What is it?" The answer choices are: "Understanding, Patience, Respect, Trust").

This EER required players to decode encrypted messages, share resources under time constraints, and negotiate roles (e.g., medical tasks vs. signal coordination), fostering skills in conflict resolution and cooperative problem-solving. Similarly, family mediation groups designed cases centered on negotiating caregiving responsibilities, while workplace and community groups tackled team collaboration challenges and neighborhood disputes.

In the final sessions, students implemented and evaluated their escape rooms. After conducting pilot tests and adjusting technical and narrative details, each group presented their project to the rest of the class, assuming the role of facilitators.

The experience concluded with a focus group, where students reflected on the challenges faced, the strategies used, and the overall impact of the workshop.

2.3. Instrument

This research used a focus group [13] to analyze the students' experience designing and creating digital escape rooms. Participants were divided into small groups and asked to reflect on their experiences by answering pre-established questions. These questions addressed aspects such as acquired learning, teamwork, the usefulness of the activity to achieve the learning objectives, the difficulties faced and the strategies used to overcome them, and the contribution of the resources used.

The focus group was held at the end of the project, after the implementation of the escape rooms, and was structured around key questions such as: What have we learned during this activity? How would you describe our experience working in a group? What specific aspects of the activity were most helpful for your understanding of the topic? These questions fostered a reflective dialog among the participants, allowing them to identify strengths and areas for improvement in the activity.

The qualitative study included 52 volunteer students organized into 16 focus groups to share their perceptions of the experience. One of the principal investigators moderated each group and guided the discussion following a pre-established script to ensure data comparability. Since the objective was to capture spontaneous and genuine impressions, no audio or video recordings were made. Instead, responses were manually recorded by the moderator, who took note of key ideas, representative phrases, and emerging patterns. To preserve anonymity and facilitate a more fluid analysis, responses were considered units of analysis within the focus group rather than being attributed individually to each student. This approach allowed for the identification of general trends and the assessment of the students' overall perception of the activity.

2.4. Data Analysis

All collected information was organized for analysis and processing using Atlas.ti software (version 9, ATLAS.ti Scientific Software Development GmbH, Berlin, Germany).

The focus group data were analyzed using a qualitative approach based on notes taken during the sessions, as no recordings were available. These notes, recorded by the moderator and an assistant, included key verbatim quotes, recurring ideas, and observations on group dynamics, ensuring a detailed representation of participants' responses. Subsequently, the notes provided by students during the focus groups were thoroughly reviewed to identify patterns and key concepts related to the questions posed during the activity.

The analysis was conducted through a manual coding process, breaking down responses into units of meaning that reflect recurring themes. These codes were then grouped into thematic categories, supported by representative quotes extracted from the notes, ensuring that the conclusions accurately reflected the experiences shared by the participants.

3. Results

The results (Table 2) are shown in response to the first objective.

Students perceive that the activity has significantly impacted their learning, highlighting the development of transversal competencies (knowledge, skills, and attitudes), such as teamwork, creativity, and digital competence, alongside subject-specific learning (communicative mediation).

The results show that all students consider that the cooperative design of digital escape rooms has strengthened their capacity for group work, consolidating this competence as a pillar of experience. The group nature of the activity allowed them to rely on their classmates, facilitating enriching horizontal learning. This is evidenced in testimonies like that of focus group 2: "In activities such as the escape room, key aspects such as communication and collaboration are worked on. It helps to develop social skills related to coexistence, teamwork, and using technologies applied to the academic and professional fields".

Table 2. Students' perception of the learning potential in the development of escape rooms with generative artificial intelligence.

Category	Subcategory	F	Examples
Transversal skills	Teamwork	16/16 (100%)	It is a tool that encourages group problem-solving, mediation skills, and the search for agreements, which are key aspects of both the activity and our future work as social educators (FG5). The team was cohesive, and we worked as a group throughout the escape room (FG8).
	Creativity	11/16 (68.75%)	What we liked the most was being able to learn about and use Artificial Intelligence to add creativity and variety to this alternative (FG1). What I liked the most was creating our own story and customizing the elements according to our ideas (FG6).
Academic relevance	Digital competence	10/16 (62.5%)	The use of escape rooms helps us to adapt to various situations and to use technology as an innovative educational tool (FG7). Now I do better with AI, thinking about what inputs to put into it to get the best response (FG11).
	Learning the Subject (Communicative Mediation)	15/16 (93.75%)	What I liked the most was understanding the subject in greater depth [after the design of digital escape rooms] (FG3). Doing it in a group encourages dialogue and cooperation, which is fundamental in Mediation (FG1).

Note: F = frequency; FGs = focus groups.

For some students, using digital tools was initially challenging due to a lack of skills in this area. Therefore, the cooperative activity helped overcome the initial frustration experienced by some participants and consolidated teamwork as a fundamental competence for future social educators. This aspect was highlighted in two focus groups: "I felt very comfortable with my work team. Because it was more difficult for me to use AI, I expected help from my colleagues, and I was more dedicated to looking for games or other resources" (FG3), and "I felt comfortable since within the team there is trust, understanding and good teamwork. I feel that the role I acquired was concerning the needs needed in each case, although I needed help from my colleagues to carry out the activities" (FG5).

On the other hand, a considerable number of students (68.75%) highlighted how the activity allowed them to develop their creativity. Designing an escape room encourages creativity because it involves a highly interactive and open process, where students must combine imagination, problem-solving, and originality to create an immersive and challenging experience. This allows participants to explore new ways to apply prior knowledge and generate innovative ideas. This innovative and practical methodology moved away from more traditional approaches, such as revision or repetition, providing greater flexibility and favoring the creative possibilities of the students. This is reflected in comments such as: "What we liked most was the creative opportunity for free expression" (FG13).

Finally, 62.5% of the students directly mentioned their progress in digital competence within the transversal competencies. The experience allowed them to learn how to use or improve their ability to use various ICT tools, something they consider essential for their professional future in an increasingly digitalized society. In the words of focus group 14: "When carrying out the escape room, it was necessary to work as a team. This implied communication, active listening, and agreement, which the escape room participants would need. In addition, it is related to our learning since today's society is increasingly digitized, and being able to anticipate this event and control these applications from the beginning is a point in favor of our learning".

About the educational possibilities of escape room creation activities mediated by generative artificial intelligence, the students show a significant consensus on their direct connection with the specific syllabus of their subjects (93.75%). The integration of fictitious cases related to their future professional activity through these dynamics has been perceived as an innovative methodology with great practical applicability, especially in mediation and socio-educational intervention. As focus group 4 points out: "I see it as a very different way of resolving a conflict and seeing that through the analysis of similar situations, we can transfer those behaviors to our situation. We could apply this strategy in subjects such as socio-educational intervention in childhood and adolescence". This highlights how students value the connection between these activities and the real contexts in which they will develop their professional work, facilitating more meaningful learning.

In addition, these dynamics are seen to make practical learning tangible. According to a student in focus group 9, "It is a good way to learn in the classroom how to carry out professional practice effectively". This approach allows students to practice skills transferable to their professional performance, consolidating key competencies in their training.

At the same time, the students highlight that digital escape rooms, supported by artificial intelligence, have great potential for their future socio-educational profession (81.25%). They consider this methodology flexible, reusable, and a tool that responds to the demands of an increasingly digitized and technological society. As a student from focus group 16 indicates: "It is also totally related to my learning because we are in a new society where the use of this artificial intelligence will end up being essential; these tools help us to materialize our ideas and improve the quality of the projects, ensuring that they are 100% in line with our expectations". This testimony highlights the importance of mastering these technologies to create practical, effective, and adaptable resources for various professional situations.

Likewise, escape rooms are specifically mentioned as a valuable tool to address complex situations, such as conflict resolution in school contexts. Focus group 13 emphasizes: "I believe, as I said before, that the escape room is a great tool in resolving conflicts between children, and it also has the advantage of being able to be used several times. I think it would be a great tool in conflicts of coexistence in a school". This perspective shows how students recognize the pedagogical value of the resource and can identify concrete scenarios where its implementation can generate a positive impact.

The data obtained (Table 3) are shown in response to the second objective of the research.

The results obtained reflect a primarily positive experience on the part of the students, who highly valued the activity as motivating (87.5%) and fun (93.75%). The students argue that the attraction of this educational practice lies mainly in the possibility of designing and creating escape rooms, which allow them to participate actively in their learning process. One focus group expressed satisfaction: "It becomes more dynamic and less boring than a conventional class, in which you only read slides and limit yourself to copying and taking notes" (FG5). Students perceive this educational practice as innovative, especially when moving away from conventional tasks such as delivering reports or taking exams. According to students, this innovation encourages more significant involvement in learning, which can be linked to the pedagogical approaches proposed by Bloom's Taxonomy [51], highlighting the importance of promoting analysis, evaluation, and creation skills beyond simple knowledge acquisition. Students feel more involved and engaged with the activity by focusing on creativity and problem-solving using digital tools.

Table 3. Students' perception of their experience in the development of escape rooms with generative artificial intelligence.

Category	Subcategory	F	Examples
Playful experience in the classroom	Motivation	14/16 (87.5%)	The experience was innovative, creative, and motivating (FG9). It was a very enriching experience, and we created an escape room that, apart from entertaining, can be useful in various cases. We liked seeing how the concepts and ideas that arose were materialized in riddles and tests. What we liked the most was undoubtedly seeing the final result because we found the process a bit complex, but in the end, it satisfied us all a lot (FG12).
	Fun	15/16 (93.75%)	We enjoyed working in a group on an activity that was far from traditional classroom formats (FG7). It was a lot of fun. The best part was sharing ideas, designing characters, and exploring different tools to create the escape (FG10).
	Frustration over initial lack of knowledge about ICT and feelings of stress	7/16 (43.75%)	At first, I felt clumsy and frustrated since technological resources have always been complicated for me (FG3) Overall, although frustrating at first, it turned out to be an enriching experience (FG1).

Note: F = frequency; FGs = focus groups.

Another aspect that was particularly attractive to the students was the possibility of exploring various ICT tools and actively participating in the design of the escape rooms. This playful component, inherent to the dynamics of the escape room, aroused a high level of motivation. One participant in focus group 11 pointed out, "Yes [I liked performing the activity] because we were very motivated to create our own game". This observation highlights the educational and entertaining activity, suggesting that learning can be effective when combined with playful elements.

However, despite these positive results, the initial experience was marked by difficulties that temporarily reduced the students' perception of the digital escape room. The participants (43.75%) expressed an initial frustration related to their lack of knowledge of the ICT tools used in the activity. This percentage indicates that almost half of the students experienced a kind of initial block due to their limited digital competence, which led to reduced self-efficacy and, in some cases, even stress. One focus group recounted their experience: "It was a new and also different experience. I had never done an activity like this before, one so heavily based on or supported by the use of digital applications. So, at first, it was quite difficult for me to figure out how to do things. But then, as I explored the application, I started realizing where I could do each task, and somehow, I gained a bit more confidence in creating the escape room". (FG4). This testimony reflects the learning curve experienced by the students, where the initial fear of the unknown and the lack of digital skills were overcome over time as the participants gained confidence in using the tools. This adaptation process is essential as it shows how supporting technological autonomy through experimentation and self-exploration can lead students to overcome their initial limitations and feel more competent in using new technologies.

Next, the data obtained are shown in response to the third objective of the research (Table 4).

Table 4. ICT tools used by students in the development of escape rooms with generative artificial intelligence.

Category	Subcategory	F	Examples
ICT tools used	Great	15/16 (93.75%)	We use it to create images (FG2). We use it as a guide to establish different tests (FG4). We use AI to create dialogues of one of the characters (FG5). Search for online resources to develop the tests (FG7).
	Genially	7/16 (43.75%)	We used Genially, and the AI gave us a lot of ideas for testing and adding interactive elements (FG12). We used it genially as a platform to design the entire escape room (FG3).
	Heroforge	6/16 (37.5%)	We use it to create avatars (FG2). It has helped us to design characters that later appeared in the escape room (FG7).

Note: F = frequency; FGs = focus groups.

One of the main criticisms that has been made of GenAI is that students tend to use these tools passively, delegating the creation of their work to them without actively participating in the learning process [52]). However, within the framework of this educational activity, the objective was to teach students how to use GenAI ethically and responsibly, showing them how it can become a valuable and complementary tool for their future professional development. In short, the aim was to use GenAI not as a substitute for their intellectual effort but as a resource to enhance their creativity and efficiency in solving problems.

In this sense, the results reveal that most students (93.75%) used GenAI for various purposes, demonstrating its integration in multiple stages of the creative and educational process. Common uses include creating images, assisting in writing scripts for challenges, designing chatbots, creating dialog for non-playable characters (NPCs), consulting, and using other complementary ICT tools.

In addition to GenAI, the students actively used other digital tools to develop the digital escape rooms. Almost half of the students (43.75%) used Genially, a platform known for its ability to create interactive and visual presentations. The students used it to design presentations that linked the different tests and games of the digital escape room, allowing fluid and attractive navigation between the various challenges. In addition, some students used Genially to create interactive games within the same platform. On the other hand, 37.5% of the students used HeroForge, a tool specialized in creating avatars and characters in 3D. The students used it to design custom figures in the escape room.

Finally, the data obtained are shown in response to the fourth objective of the research (Table 5).

It must be recognized that any educational practice has a wide margin for improvement. For this reason, recording the students' criticisms and suggestions is beneficial to optimize the methodologies and tools used. In this context, the opinions collected in the focus groups provide a valuable perspective for improving educational practice.

Some of the participants (18.75%) in the focus groups specifically mentioned that they would have preferred the design of escape rooms to be face-to-face. This is mainly related to those students whose digital competence was more limited from the beginning of the course. Some indicated: "We would have done better if it were face-to-face because we would have come up with other challenges without needing to use ICTs" (FG3). In addition, some expressed that their preference for face-to-face was due to the consideration that their future users, in a professional context, might not have the necessary digital skills to interact with an online version: "[The escape room] is oriented to the online world and not all people have the skills or access to an online escape room. However, in our professional future, we would carry out an escape room, but physically/face-to-face" (FG1).

Table 5. Criticisms and recommendations from students after the development of escape rooms with generative artificial intelligence.

Category	Subcategory	F	Examples
Criticisms or recommendations	Preference for face-to-face learning	3/16 (18.75%)	We consider that the digital escape room has limitations compared to a physical/face-to-face one (FG2). That it is physical/face-to-face, using the university's facilities (FG3).
	Paid or free apps with premium options	6/16 (37.5%)	[...], although some limitations of the tools made the work difficult for us (FG10). We would have liked more free options in the tools (FG12)
	Increased number of sessions	4/16 (25%)	We would have liked more time (FG12) In this work, we developed skills such as teamwork, communication, conflict resolution, learning to handle new tools, and even working under pressure since time was limited (FG7)

Note: F = frequency; FGs = focus groups.

Another relevant difficulty, mentioned by 37.5% of the groups, was the limited ICT tools used in the course. Although students worked with free versions of certain apps, these were found to be restricted compared to the paid versions. Because the university could not cover the costs of premium subscriptions for students, many felt limited in terms of the functionalities these tools offered. This technological barrier highlighted one of the difficulties inherent in using digital resources in the classroom, especially when the complete versions of the tools are not available.

Finally, a quarter of the focus groups suggested that having more sessions and more time to use the tools and develop their escape room designs more thoughtfully and leisurely would have been beneficial. Most of these participants agreed that, although learning was generally positive, the time available was insufficient to consolidate the necessary knowledge and skills correctly. "We value learning very positively since we have learned a new way of carrying out mediation. We would rate it with a 9.5 because the app we used gave us quite a few problems, and we would need more time" (FG9). Others, for their part, highlighted the need for greater clarity in the explanations before the activity: "Given the lack of knowledge of the programs, I believe that we would increase the time and the specificity of the explanations prior to the execution of the activity" (FG10).

4. Discussion

This study aimed to understand how students perceive the experience of designing educational escape rooms by integrating ICT tools and artificial intelligence as a learning methodology. The results reflect positive perceptions, aligning with recent research in this field [33].

Addressing the first research objective (analyze how creating digital escape rooms mediated by generative artificial intelligence influences learning specific content and the development of teamwork, creativity, and digital competence), the implementation of an EER design activity with GenAI has promoted deep learning of the course content and demonstrated significant development of the valued competencies.

A highly valued aspect was the opportunity to work in groups. Previous studies reinforce that collaborative work promotes horizontal and independent learning while allowing knowledge exchange among peers [53,54].

Another significant aspect is the comprehension required to design educative escape rooms. This process demands that students master the content on which the challenges are based, reinforcing their subject-specific learning [10]. Additionally, it fosters the development of essential transversal skills such as creativity and problem-solving [55], which are key competencies for future professionals in the socio-educational field. In this regard, previous research has demonstrated that integrating technologies with curricular content presents a challenge that promotes the construction of deeper, shared knowledge [56].

The activity also aligns with the experiential and discovery-based learning approach. Designing and participating in escape rooms facilitate the acquisition of specific knowledge, allowing students to practice and consolidate transferable skills such as effective communication, time management, and ICT tools [57]. This methodological approach coincides with the principles of the "learning to learn" competence, which emphasizes student autonomy and their ability to adapt to new learning situations [58].

Regarding creativity, designing an escape room fosters a highly interactive and open environment where students can innovatively apply prior knowledge. The literature suggests that activities like this enhance creativity by integrating problem-solving and generating original ideas in a collaborative context [59]. This aspect is particularly valuable in mediation and socio-educational intervention, where adaptability and critical thinking are required.

Developing digital competencies also stands out as a significant benefit of this methodology. The experience allowed students to improve their ICT skills and better prepare for future professional challenges [60]. The results show how incorporating new technologies, such as generative artificial intelligence and web applications, into the learning methodology has enhanced the acquisition and development of their digital competence. The use of technologies in the classroom has proven to be highly motivating and well-received by students [61].

Addressing the second research objective (explore students' perceptions regarding integrating digital escape room design activities mediated by generative artificial intelligence), the results indicate that students positively evaluated the activity, highlighting its innovative, motivating, and highly participatory nature.

One of the most frequently mentioned aspects in the focus groups was the positive impact on motivation and engagement with learning. Students emphasized that designing the escape room allowed them to actively engage in knowledge construction, moving away from traditional methodologies centered on passive information reception. The opportunity to design and develop their own challenges within a digital environment fostered experiential and meaningful learning, aligning with previous research on gamification and game-based learning [62].

Additionally, students highlighted that the integration of GenAI facilitated creativity and personalization in constructing activities. Tools such as ChatGPT and Genially were perceived as valuable resources for streamlining the generation of narratives, challenges, and interactive dynamics, allowing for a greater exploration of creative possibilities in escape room design. However, some participants pointed out the need for more structured prior training to maximize the effective use of these tools, preventing a reliance on automated responses without deeper pedagogical reflection [17].

In response to the third research objective, which examines how students have incorporated and applied the technological tools introduced during the activity, the results show that participants actively used various digital tools to design the escape rooms, integrating their functionalities at different stages of the creative process.

The data indicate that generative artificial intelligence (GenAI) was the most widely used tool, with 93.75% of students employing it to generate content within the escape room.

Its application focused on creating images, developing interactive challenges, and simulating dialogs with non-playable characters (NPCs), which allowed for optimizing design time and enhancing the narrative coherence of the created dynamics. Additionally, several groups highlighted that they used ChatGPT as a guide to structure the challenges and establish a logical framework for the proposed tasks, thereby facilitating the organization and progression of the game. These findings align with previous research which highlights the potential of generative AI to streamline the design of interactive experiences in educational settings. Previous studies demonstrated that artificial intelligence can enhance creativity and efficiency in the design of gamified activities [9], while recent research has emphasized its ability to generate adaptive content and foster problem-based learning [19,63].

Along with generative AI, the Genially platform was used by 43.75% of students as the primary tool for designing and presenting escape rooms. Its ability to integrate multimedia elements and create accessible interactive experiences was key to materializing the participants' ideas. Previous studies have highlighted the effectiveness of Genially in educational contexts, noting its capacity to increase student engagement and promote more dynamic and visually appealing learning [64,65]. On the other hand, 37.5% of students used HeroForge to create avatars and customized characters, significantly enriching the visual and narrative dimensions of the designed stories. The visual representation of characters contributed to greater immersion in the experience and promoted a sense of identity and connection with the proposed challenges. In this regard, character customization in digital environments enhances engagement and student motivation in gamification-based activities [66].

These results reflect a significant utilization of technological tools in developing interactive educational experiences, confirming their positive impact on creativity, organization, and the execution of gamified projects in the classroom.

Responding to the fourth research objective (Identify the challenges associated with implementing these activities), the results show that although the experience of designing digital escape rooms mediated by generative artificial intelligence (GenAI) was positively evaluated, students faced various difficulties during its implementation. These findings align with previous studies that have identified similar barriers to adopting technology-based methodologies in educational settings [67].

One of the main challenges highlighted by participants was their preference for in-person experiences over digital ones. A total of 18.75% of students indicated that a physical escape room could have been more effective in specific contexts, particularly in mediation training, where face-to-face interaction is crucial. Previous studies on gamification in education have emphasized that physical presence in these activities enhances immersion and allows for the development of non-verbal communication and real-time conflict resolution [68]. Although digital escape rooms offer accessibility and flexibility, some students perceived that the lack of digital skills among certain users could limit their application in socio-educational environments.

Another identified challenge was the limitation of the digital tools used in the activity. A total of 37.5% of students mentioned restrictions in the free versions of the platforms used, such as Genially and HeroForge, which hindered the customization and expansion of their designs. These technological limitations can affect the learning experience by restricting creative capacity and experimentation with interactive elements. Additionally, the time allocated to the activity was perceived as insufficient by 25% of participants. Students indicated that more sessions would have allowed for better familiarization with technological tools and greater refinement of their projects. Previous studies have shown that time is a determining factor in the effectiveness of active methodologies, as tight planning can generate stress and affect learning quality [69]. In this case, some groups felt pressured to meet deadlines, which may have limited their creativity and ability to delve deeper into the design of their escape rooms.

Finally, a recurring challenge was the initial difficulty in using digital tools, experienced by 43.75% of students. Although most managed to overcome these difficulties through collaborative work, previous studies on digital literacy in higher education have highlighted that a lack of prior training in using technologies can lead to frustration and negatively impact the perceived usefulness of these tools [70]. This research observed that students with less experience in managing digital platforms relied heavily on peer support, reinforcing the importance of implementing initial training strategies before applying these activities.

The identified challenges highlight the need for adjustments in designing and implementing future digital escape room experiences. To optimize the experience, it is recommended to extend the time allocated to the activity and combine digital escape rooms with in-person elements, promoting a more balanced and inclusive learning experience. Addressing these barriers will facilitate consolidating this strategy as an innovative resource for developing key competencies in educational and professional settings.

Several methodological aspects need to be considered as limitations of this study. First, using a single experience based on a qualitative methodology limits the generalizability of the conclusions to other contexts or university student populations. Another limitation pointed out by the students themselves was the duration of the intervention. Future research could design longer interventions that combine qualitative and quantitative methodologies with a larger sample to assess the impact of educational escape room design on students.

Moreover, implementing specific initial training for students could have been beneficial in addressing initial gaps, particularly in digital competencies. Future studies using an educational methodology based on digital escape room design could include this prior training to ensure greater familiarity with technological tools, reduce anxiety associated with digital platform use, and improve students' autonomy in creating and managing escape room elements.

5. Conclusions

The main contribution of this study lies in the innovative use of escape room design as an active learning methodology, where students take on the role of creators rather than participants. This approach requires them to deeply engage with curricular content by designing educational challenges that reflect real-life mediation scenarios. By integrating theoretical knowledge into a structured, immersive experience, this methodology fosters essential skills such as creativity, problem-solving, and teamwork.

Additionally, innovative technologies, such as generative artificial intelligence and web applications, have proven to be key in motivating students and improving their digital competencies. Although the study identifies limitations, such as the limited duration of the intervention and the lack of initial training in technological tools, the results highlight the effectiveness of this methodology in overcoming initial barriers and enhancing meaningful learning.

In conclusion, this experience represented a reflective space where narrative design, character personalization, and the strategic use of digital tools converged to create an immersive educational dynamic.

Author Contributions: Conceptualization, P.R.-R.; methodology, P.R.-R.; software, A.M.-L.; validation, A.M.-L. and J.M.R.-F.; formal analysis, A.M.-L.; investigation, P.R.-R.; resources, A.M.-L.; data curation, P.R.-R.; writing: P.R.-R. and A.M.-L.; visualization and supervision, A.M.-L. and J.M.R.-F.; project administration, A.M.-L. and J.M.R.-F.; funding acquisition, A.M.-L. All authors have read and agreed to the published version of the manuscript.

Funding: The authors disclosed receipt of the following financial support for the research: Teaching Innovation Projects of the University of Almeria (Ref: 24_25_1_10C) and Projects to Strengthen Research Groups FEDER-UAL (Ref: P_FORT_GRUPOS_2023/05).

Institutional Review Board Statement: The study followed the Declaration of Helsinki. The research was conducted as part of a classroom activity embedded within an officially approved Educational Innovation Project by the University of Almería (Ref: 24_25_1_10C), primarily focusing on pedagogical improvement rather than experimental research. The data collected were limited to the educational context and pertain solely to classroom activities. No sensitive personal information was gathered and no interventions were performed beyond standard academic practices.

Informed Consent Statement: Informed consent was obtained from all subjects involved in the study.

Data Availability Statement: The datasets generated and/or analyzed during this study are not publicly available due to the lack of participant consent; however, they can be obtained from the corresponding author upon reasonable request.

Conflicts of Interest: The authors declare no conflicts of interest.

Appendix A

Criteria	Excellent Level (4 Points)	Good Level (3 Points)	Acceptable Level (2 Points)	Insufficient Level (1 Point)
Escape Room Design and Structure	The sequence of challenges is logical and well-organized. The difficulty is balanced, and the connections between challenges are seamless. The game flows smoothly without interruptions.	The escape room is well-structured, although some challenges could be better connected or adjusted in difficulty.	The structure is understandable but has minor issues with progression or challenge connections.	There is evident disorganization, with no clear sequence of challenges or unrelated tasks.
Variety and Quality of Challenges	Various challenges (cognitive, logical, cooperative) are included to challenge players and promote learning.	The challenges are varied and appropriate, though some could be more challenging or innovative.	The challenges are somewhat repetitive or lack variety but still fit within the escape room dynamic.	The challenges are too simple, confusing, or do not contribute to learning.
Integration of Social Skills	The escape room dynamics actively promote communication, empathy, teamwork, and decision-making.	Social skills are effectively incorporated, although they could be better integrated into some challenges.	Social skills are mentioned but not clearly embedded in the game mechanics.	Social skills are not evident in the escape room design.
Use of Mediation Strategies	The challenges require the use of mediation strategies such as active listening, negotiation, or conflict resolution.	Some mediation strategies are present in the dynamics, though their application could be more explicit.	Mediation strategies are mentioned, but their integration into the challenges is limited.	No mediation strategies are observed within the escape room.
Originality and Innovation	The escape room is creative and presents an innovative approach in its design and challenges. There is a clear effort to surprise and motivate participants.	Some creative elements are present, though the design follows conventional structures without major innovations.	The escape room is functional but not very innovative, using standard mechanics.	It lacks creativity, making it monotonous or predictable.
Participant Experience	The game dynamics maintain a high level of motivation and engagement. The experience is immersive and meaningful.	Most participants engage actively and enjoy the experience.	The experience is acceptable, but some elements may hinder immersion or motivation.	The activity does not generate interest or engagement among participants.

Criteria	Excellent Level (4 Points)	Good Level (3 Points)	Acceptable Level (2 Points)	Insufficient Level (1 Point)
Materials and Resources Used	Generative AI tools (chatbots, image or text generation) are used to enhance challenges or the escape room's narrative.	The materials are appropriate, and generative AI is used, though its implementation could be optimized for a better experience.	The materials are basic and functional, with limited or unstrategic use of generative AI.	No appropriate materials or generative AI tools were used, or their implementation was confusing or deficient.
Evaluation and Final Reflection	A well-structured debriefing phase is included, allowing participants to reflect on their experience and learning.	There is a reflection phase, though it is not fully structured.	A brief reflection takes place, but it does not deeply explore the learning outcomes.	No reflection or evaluation of the activity is included.

References

1. Area-Moreira, M.; Hernández-Rivero, V.; Sosa-Alonso, J.J. *Tecnologías Digitales y Transformación Educativa*; Octaedro Editorial: Barcelona, Spain, 2020.
2. UNESCO. *Global Education Monitoring Report: Technology in Education*; UNESCO: Paris, France, 2023.
3. Vongkulluksn, V.W.; Lu, L.; Nelson, M.J.; Xie, K. Cognitive engagement with technology scale: A validation study. *Educ. Technol. Res. Dev.* **2022**, *70*, 419–445. [CrossRef]
4. Punie, Y.; Ferrari, A.; Brečko, B. *DIGCOMP—A Framework for Developing and Understanding Digital Competence in Europe*; Publications Office of the European Union: Brussels, Belgium, 2013. [CrossRef]
5. Instefjord, E.; Munthe, E. Preparing pre-service teachers to integrate technology: An analysis of the emphasis on digital competence in teacher education curricula. *Eur. J. Teach. Educ.* **2016**, *39*, 77–93. [CrossRef]
6. OECD Indicators. *Education at a Glance 2022*; Acesso em Março de; OECD: Paris, France, 2023.
7. Pozos Pérez, K.V.; Tejada Fernández, J. Competencias digitales en docentes de educación superior: Niveles de dominio y necesidades formativas. *Rev. Digit. Investig. Docencia Univ.* **2018**, *12*, 59–87. [CrossRef]
8. Martín-Párraga, L.; Llorente-Cejudo, C.; Barroso-Osuna, J. Self-Perception of Digital Competence in University Lecturers: A Comparative Study between Universities in Spain and Peru According to the DigCompEdu Model. *Societies* **2023**, *13*, 142. [CrossRef]
9. Fotaris, P.; Mastoras, T.; Lameras, P. Designing Educational Escape Rooms with Generative AI: A Framework and ChatGPT Prompt Engineering Guide. In Proceedings of the 17th European Conference on Games-Based Learning, Enschede, The Netherlands, 5–6 October 2023; Academic Conferences and Publishing Limited: Reading, UK, 2023.
10. Veldkamp, A.; Knippels, M.-C.P.; van Joolingen, W.R. Beyond the Early Adopters: Escape Rooms in Science Education. *Front. Educ.* **2021**, *6*, 622860. [CrossRef]
11. Sotelo-Núñez, A.C.; Rojas, J.J.H.; Rojas, M.Z.H.; López-Regalado, O. Competencia digital en estudiantes universitarios: Una revisión sistemática. *Horizontes. Rev. Investig. Cienc. Educ.* **2024**, *8*, 1781–1800. [CrossRef]
12. Esteve Mon, F.M.; Gisbert Cervera, M. El nuevo paradigma de aprendizaje y las nuevas tecnologías. *REDU. Rev. Docencia Univ.* **2011**, *9*, 55–73.
13. Silva-Quiroz, J.; Morales-Morgado, E.M. Assessing digital competence and its relationship with the socioeconomic level of Chilean university students. *Int. J. Educ. Technol. High. Educ.* **2022**, *19*, 46. [CrossRef]
14. Heinz, J. Digital skills and the influence of students' socio-economic background. An exploratory study in German elementary schools. *Ital. J. Sociol. Educ.* **2016**, *8*, 186–212.
15. Fraillon, J. An International Perspective on Digital Literacy: Results from ICILS 2023. *Int. Assoc. Eval. Educ. Achiev.* **2024**.
16. Howard, J. Artificial intelligence: Implications for the future of work. *Am. J. Ind. Med.* **2019**, *62*, 917–926. [CrossRef] [PubMed]
17. Kasneci, E.; Seßler, K.; Küchemann, S.; Bannert, M.; Dementieva, D.; Fischer, F.; Gasser, U.; Groh, G.; Günnemann, S.; Hüllermeier, E. ChatGPT for good? On opportunities and challenges of large language models for education. *Learn. Individ. Differ.* **2023**, *103*, 102274. [CrossRef]
18. Dawson, P. *Defending Assessment Security in a Digital World*; Routledge: London, UK, 2021; p. 10. ISBN 9780429324178.
19. Zawacki-Richter, O.; Marín, V.I.; Bond, M.; Gouverneur, F. Systematic review of research on artificial intelligence applications in higher education–where are the educators? *Int. J. Educ. Technol. High. Educ.* **2019**, *16*, 39. [CrossRef]
20. Rudolph, J.; Tan, S.; Tan, S. ChatGPT: Bullshit spewer or the end of traditional assessments in higher education? *J. Appl. Learn. Teach.* **2023**, *6*, 342–363.
21. Mittal, U.; Sai, S.; Chamola, V.; Sangwan, D. A comprehensive review on generative ai for education. *IEEE Access* **2024**, *12*, 142733–142759. [CrossRef]
22. Polat, Z. Generative Artificial Intelligence in Education: Cheating Threat or Enhanced Learning Tool. *Next Front. Life Sci. AI* **2024**, *8*, 1–5. [CrossRef]

23. AlAli, R.; Wardat, Y.; Al-Saud, K.; Alhayek, K. Generative AI in education: Best practices for successful implementation. *Int. J. Relig.* **2024**, *5*, 1016–1025. [CrossRef]
24. Albrecht, J.; Stark-Blomeier, A.L.; Schütz, P.; Lenhard, N.; Dockweiler, C.; Tokgöz, P. Digital Educational Escape Rooms for Providing Knowledge on Stress Management and Health Promotion for Students—A Rapid Review and Pilot Study. *Int. J. Environ. Res. Public Health* **2025**, *22*, 93. [CrossRef]
25. Spatafora, A.; Wagemann, M.; Sandoval, C.; Leisenberg, M.; Vaz de Carvalho, C. An Educational Escape Room Game to Develop Cybersecurity Skills. *Computers* **2024**, *13*, 205. [CrossRef]
26. Piñero Charlo, J.C. Educational escape rooms as a tool for horizontal mathematization: Learning process evidence. *Educ. Sci.* **2020**, *10*, 213. [CrossRef]
27. Repetto, M.; Bianco Prevot, A.; Brizio, A.; Boldi, A.; Talarico, M.; Stanchi, S.; Palma, D.; Acquadro Maran, D. Digital Escape Rooms: A Resource for Environmental Education. *Sustainability* **2024**, *16*, 8525. [CrossRef]
28. Escario, I.; García, A.; Ripollés, M.; Arriaga, C.; González, P.A.C.; Cumbreras, M.Á.G. Impulsando la Educación Superior con IAGen: Oportunidades y retos para docentes. *REDU. Rev. Docencia Univ.* **2024**, *22*, 137–157. [CrossRef]
29. Kochmar, E.; Vu, D.D.; Belfer, R.; Gupta, V.; Serban, I.V.; Pineau, J. Automated data-driven generation of personalized pedagogical interventions in intelligent tutoring systems. *Int. J. Artif. Intell. Educ.* **2022**, *32*, 323–349. [CrossRef]
30. Moravec, M.; Williams, A.; Aguilar-Roca, N.; O'Dowd, D.K. Learn before lecture: A strategy that improves learning outcomes in a large introductory biology class. *CBE—Life Sci. Educ.* **2010**, *9*, 473–481. [CrossRef]
31. Choi, S.; Slaubaugh, M.; Tian, X. Integrating learning interpersonal skills through team-based learning (TBL) in a management course. *J. Educ. Bus.* **2021**, *96*, 498–509. [CrossRef]
32. Roig, P.J.; Alcaraz, S.; Gilly, K.; Bernad, C.; Juiz, C. Using escape rooms as evaluation tool in active learning contexts. *Educ. Sci.* **2023**, *13*, 535. [CrossRef]
33. Rodríguez-Rivera, P.; Manzano-León, A.; Dapía Conde, M.D.; Rodríguez-Ferrer, J.M. Unleashing creativity and cooperation: A qualitative case study on designing digital breakouts for social education degrees. *Societies* **2023**, *13*, 203. [CrossRef]
34. Nicholson, S. Peeking Behind the Locked Door: A Survey of Escape Room Facilities. 2015. Available online: http://scottnicholson.com/pubs/erfacwhite.pdf (accessed on 26 February 2025).
35. Sierra Daza, M.C.; Fernández-Sánchez, M.R. Gamificando el aula universitaria. Análisis de una experiencia de Escape Room en educación superior. *Rev. Estud. Y Exp. Educ.* **2019**, *18*, 105–115. [CrossRef]
36. Borrás-Gené, O.; Hijón-Neira, R.; Paredes-Barragán, P.; Serrano-Luján, L. A hybrid escape room to foster motivation and programming education for pre-service teachers. *Int. J. Game-Based Learn. (IJGBL)* **2024**, *14*, 1–17. [CrossRef]
37. Akgun, S.; Greenhow, C. Artificial intelligence in education: Addressing ethical challenges in K-12 settings. *AI Ethics* **2022**, *2*, 431–440. [CrossRef]
38. Manzano León, A.; Arrifano Tadeu, P.J. *Escape Rooms Educativos: Una Experiencia en una Universidad Portuguesa*; Asociación INFAD Universidad de Extremadura: Badajoz, Spain, 2022.
39. Fotaris, P.; Mastoras, T. Escape Rooms for Learning: A Systematic Review. In Proceedings of the European Conference on Games Based Learning, Odense, Denmark, 3–4 October 2019; Academic Conferences and Publishing Limited: Reading, UK, 2019; pp. 235–243.
40. Zhu, Q.; Luo, J. Generative Design Ideation: A Natural Language Generation Approach. In Proceedings of the International Conference on-Design Computing and Cognition, Glasgow, UK, 4–6 July 2022; Springer International Publishing: Cham, Switzerland, 2023; pp. 39–50.
41. Värtinen, S.; Hämäläinen, P.; Guckelsberger, C. Generating role-playing game quests with GPT language models. *IEEE Trans. Games* **2022**, *16*, 127–139. [CrossRef]
42. Gligorea, I.; Cioca, M.; Oancea, R.; Gorski, A.-T.; Gorski, H.; Tudorache, P. Adaptive learning using artificial intelligence in e-learning: A literature review. *Educ. Sci.* **2023**, *13*, 1216. [CrossRef]
43. Asunis, L.; Frau, V.; Macis, R.; Pireddu, C.; Spano, L.D. PAC-Bot: Writing Text Messages for Developing Point-and-Click Games. In Proceedings of the International Symposium on End-User Development, Virtual Event, 6–8 July 2021; Springer International Publishing: Cham, Switzerland, 2021; pp. 213–221.
44. Artizzu, V.; Blečić, I.; Frau, V.; Spano, L.D. How End Users Develop Point-and-Click Games. In Proceedings of the International Symposium on End-User Development, Cagliari, Italy, 6–8 July 2021; Springer Nature: Cham, Switzerland, 2023; pp. 220–229.
45. Rana, P.; Bhardwaj, P.; Singh, J. Artificial Intelligence (AI) in Video Games. *Int. J. Comput. Appl.* **2018**, *975*, 8887. [CrossRef]
46. Hakiki, M.; Fadli, R.; Samala, A.D.; Fricticarani, A.; Dayurni, P.; Rahmadani, K.; Astiti, A.D.; Sabir, A. Exploring the impact of using Chat-GPT on student learning outcomes in technology learning: The comprehensive experiment. *Adv. Mob. Learn. Educ. Res.* **2023**, *3*, 859–872. [CrossRef]
47. Borrego, C.; Fernández, C.; Blanes, I.; Robles, S. Room escape at class: Escape games activities to facilitate the motivation and learning in computer science. *JOTSE* **2017**, *7*, 162–171. [CrossRef]

48. Deterding, S.; Dixon, D.; Khaled, R.; Nacke, L. From Game Design Elements to Gamefulness: Defining" Gamification". In Proceedings of the 15th International Academic MindTrek Conference: Envisioning Future Media Environments, New York, NY, USA, 30 September 2011; pp. 9–15.
49. Sailer, M.; Homner, L. The gamification of learning: A meta-analysis. *Educ. Psychol. Rev.* **2020**, *32*, 77–112. [CrossRef]
50. Tlili, A.; Huang, R.; Shehata, B.; Liu, D.; Zhao, J.; Metwally, A.H.S.; Wang, H.; Denden, M.; Bozkurt, A.; Lee, L.-H. Is Metaverse in education a blessing or a curse: A combined content and bibliometric analysis. *Smart Learn. Environ.* **2022**, *9*, 24. [CrossRef]
51. Heller, R. A new bloom–adding 'collaborate'to Bloom's taxonomy. *J. Learn. Dev. High. Educ.* **2022**, *24*. [CrossRef]
52. Gutiérrez, T.d.J.M.; Martínez, H.J.L.; García, L.H.B.; Quiroz, J.F.R. El impacto del ChatGPT en la producción de textos: Análisis de su estilo y evaluación en el contexto estudiantil. *Dilemas Contemp.* **2024**, 14. [CrossRef]
53. Chowdhury, T.A. Fostering learner autonomy through cooperative and collaborative learning. *Shanlax Int. J. Educ.* **2021**, *10*, 89–95. [CrossRef]
54. Ullauri, J.I.U.; Cajamarca, P.E.M.; Ullauri, C.I.U. Aprendizaje colaborativo entre pares: Diseño, construcción y desarrollo de una clase invertida con enfoque inclusivo. *Rev. Sci.* **2022**, *7*, 88–110. [CrossRef]
55. Gillies, R.M. Promoting academically productive student dialogue during collaborative learning. *Int. J. Educ. Res.* **2019**, *97*, 200–209. [CrossRef]
56. Bilbao-Quintana, N.; Romero-Andonegui, A.; Portillo-Berasaluce, J.; López-de-la-Serna, A. Escape room digital para el desarrollo del aprendizaje colaborativo en educación superior. *Educ. Knowl. Soc. (EKS)* **2022**, *23*. [CrossRef]
57. Vekua, N.; Lubsky, A.; Perevozchikova, M.; Folgerova, J.N. Peculiarities of forming high-demanded soft skills in the educational space of the escape room. *Perspect Sci. Educ.* **2020**, *48*, 397–412. [CrossRef]
58. Pérez, Y.S. Aprender a aprender y su implicación pedagógica en España: Una aproximación desde la filosofía de la educación. *Foro De Educ.* **2022**, *20*, 2.
59. Tang, T.; Vezzani, V.; Eriksson, V. Developing critical thinking, collective creativity skills and problem solving through playful design jams. *Think. Ski. Creat.* **2020**, *37*, 100696. [CrossRef]
60. Lei, H.; Xiong, Y.; Chiu, M.M.; Zhang, J.; Cai, Z. The relationship between ICT literacy and academic achievement among students: A meta-analysis. *Child. Youth Serv. Rev.* **2021**, *127*, 106123. [CrossRef]
61. Constante, P.G.P.; Pacheco, D.E.R.; Saltos, Y.d.R.R.; Torres, C.C.C.; Cedeño, R.A.A. Impacto del uso de tecnologías educativas en la motivación y el compromiso estudiantil durante el proceso de aprendizaje: Impact of the use of educational technologies on student motivation and engagement during the learning process. *LATAM Rev. Latinoam. Cienc. Soc. Y Humanidades* **2024**, *5*, 199–211. [CrossRef]
62. Manzano-León, A.; Aguilar-Parra, J.M.; Rodríguez-Ferrer, J.M.; Trigueros, R.; Collado-Soler, R.; Méndez-Aguado, C.; García-Hernández, M.J.; Molina-Alonso, L. Online Escape Room during COVID-19: A Qualitative Study of Social Education Degree Students' Experiences. *Educ. Sci.* **2021**, *11*, 426. [CrossRef]
63. Ambarita, N.; Nurrahmatullah, M.F. Impacts of artificial intelligence on student learning: A systematic literature review. *J. Varidika* **2024**, *36*, 13–30. [CrossRef]
64. Méndez, C.O.; García, R.M.G.; Chuquian, M.J.G. El uso de la herramienta digital Genially en el proceso de aprendizaje de las Ciencias Naturales en los estudiantes de educación básica superior en Ecuador. *Interconectando Saberes* **2024**, *18*, 101–112. [CrossRef]
65. Torres-Torres, O.L. Evaluación de Genially como herramienta didáctica en la práctica docente de la educación a distancia. *J. Econ. Soc. Sci. Res.* **2024**, *4*, 1–18. [CrossRef]
66. Marczewski, A. *Even Ninja Monkeys Like to Play*; Blurb Inc.: London, UK, 2015; Volume 1, p. 28.
67. Makri, A.; Vlachopoulos, D.; Martina, R.A. Digital Escape Rooms as Innovative Pedagogical Tools in Education: A Systematic Literature Review. *Sustainability* **2021**, *13*, 4587. [CrossRef]
68. del Castillo Rodríguez, Á. Teaching Case. Gamificación en Educación Superior: Dándole la Vuelta a la Formación en Estudios Presenciales y Online. In Proceedings of the INNODOCT/22 International Conference on Innovation, Documentation and Education, Valencia, Spain, 2–7 November 2022; Universitat Politècnica de València: València, Spain, 2023; pp. 379–389.
69. Jiménez-Serranía, M.-I.; Postigo, N.Y.; Sandín, S.M.G.; Lorenzo, I.F.; Velado, E.M.; Sinovas, R.M. Experiencia de Escape Room de Fisiología: Physiology Escape Room Experience. *South Fla. J. Dev.* **2021**, *2*, 6925–6935. [CrossRef]
70. Cepeda, F.J.D. Actualización docente en tecnologías educativas y aprendizaje móvil: Desarrollo de un programa institucional. *Rev. Form. E Innovación Educ. Univ.* **2014**, *7*, 211–226.

Multimodal Technologies and Interaction

Article

Personalized and Timely Feedback in Online Education: Enhancing Learning with Deep Learning and Large Language Models

Óscar Cuéllar [1,*], Manuel Contero [1] and Mauricio Hincapié [2]

1 Instituto Universitario de Investigación en Tecnología Centrada en el Ser Humano (Human-Tech), Universitat Politècnica de València, 46022 Valencia, Spain; mcontero@upv.es
2 Escuela de Artes y Humanidades, Área Creación, Universidad EAFIT, Medellín 050022, Colombia; maurhin@eafit.edu.co
* Correspondence: oacueroj@doctor.upv.es

Abstract: This study investigates an Adaptive Feedback System (AFS) that integrates deep learning (a recurrent neural network trained with historical student data) and GPT-4 to provide personalized feedback in a Digital Art course. In a quasi-experimental design, the intervention group (n = 42) received weekly feedback generated from model predictions, while the control group (n = 39) followed the same program without this intervention across four learning blocks or levels. The results revealed (1) a cumulative effect with a significant performance difference in the fourth learning block (+12.63 percentage points); (2) a reduction in performance disparities between students with varying levels of prior knowledge in the experimental group (−56.5%) versus an increase in the control group (+103.3%); (3) an "overcoming effect" where up to 42.9% of students surpassed negative performance predictions; and (4) a positive impact on active participation, especially in live class attendance (+30.21 points) and forum activity (+9.79 points). These findings demonstrate that integrating deep learning with LLMs can significantly improve learning outcomes in online educational environments, particularly for students with limited prior knowledge.

Keywords: deep learning; large language models; personalized feedback; assistive technology; educational technology; performance prediction; online education

1. Introduction

The rapid expansion of virtual learning environments, dramatically accelerated by the COVID-19 pandemic, has led to an unprecedented surge in online course enrollments, with some institutions reporting increases exceeding 300% [1]. While this shift offers increased accessibility and flexibility, it has also amplified inherent challenges in online education, particularly regarding student engagement, assessment, and the delivery of personalized learning experiences. In online settings, students frequently experience reduced social presence and a sense of isolation, which negatively impacts their motivation, commitment, and overall learning outcomes [2]. Moreover, traditional assessment methods, often reliant on standardized metrics, fail to capture the nuanced dynamics of digital engagement, and instructors struggle to provide timely, individualized feedback at scale. These issues underscore the urgent need for innovative, automated solutions that can support personalized feedback.

In response to these challenges, Artificial Intelligence (AI) technologies have emerged as promising tools for enhancing online education. In particular, deep learning (DL) techniques and large language models (LLMs) offer significant potential. Deep learning, which leverages large datasets to analyze complex educational data, has been suggested to offer the potential for superior accuracy in predicting student performance compared to traditional statistical methods [3]. Models such as recurrent neural networks (RNNs) and convolutional neural networks (CNNs) have proven effective in forecasting academic outcomes and identifying students at risk of dropout [4]. Simultaneously, LLMs like OpenAI's GPT-4 are revolutionizing automated, personalized feedback by generating natural language responses, understanding intricate prompts, and adapting their communication style to individual student needs [5]. However, it is crucial to acknowledge that the application of DL and LLMs in education is not without challenges. Potential limitations include biases in training data, the "black box" nature of many deep learning models, and the risk of LLMs generating generic or contextually inappropriate feedback. Addressing these issues requires careful consideration and mitigation strategies, such as focusing on diverse and representative training data, incorporating interpretability techniques into model design, and implementing human oversight in the feedback generation process.

The significance of effective feedback for learning is well-established. The seminal work by Hattie and Timperley [6] demonstrated that the type and modality of feedback are critical determinants of student performance, specifically, that corrective and detailed written feedback is more effective than simple praise or grades. Building on these insights, the field of Artificial Intelligence in Education (AIED) has been at the forefront of developing intelligent tutoring systems (ITS) and adaptive learning environments that leverage AI to automate and personalize feedback [7–10]. Early ITS approaches were based on rule-based systems and knowledge tracing, whereas modern methods have evolved to incorporate advanced techniques such as Bayesian networks and deep knowledge tracing, providing a more refined basis for adaptive feedback [8]. This rich history in AIED research lays a robust foundation for integrating contemporary DL and LLM technologies to further enhance feedback mechanisms in online education.

In this study, we introduce the Adaptive Feedback System (AFS), a novel system designed to provide personalized and timely feedback to students in online courses. AFS utilizes a deep learning-based predictive model, specifically, a recurrent neural network (RNN) trained on historical student engagement and performance data from previous online courses in Digital Arts for Film and Video Games. This model analyzes key metrics, such as synchronous session attendance, digital content interaction, forum participation, and portfolio task completion, to identify students who could benefit from targeted interventions. The predictions are then interpreted by OpenAI's GPT-4, which generates tailored feedback messages addressing individual student needs. For instance, AFS might offer encouraging messages and gamified incentives to students at risk of disengagement, while providing detailed, constructive criticism and targeted resources to those facing specific academic challenges. AFS is notably designed as a dynamic and adaptive system that continuously refines its feedback strategies based on ongoing student interactions.

The central research questions guiding this study are as follows: Can recurrent neural network-based deep learning models, applied to extensive datasets of quantitative learning analytics data, predict student performance in online environments more effectively than traditional methods? Furthermore, how effective are LLMs like OpenAI's GPT-4 in interpreting these predictions and generating personalized feedback that enhances student engagement and learning outcomes? Finally, what is the overall impact of the integrated AFS on student performance and engagement in a real-world online course setting?

To address these questions and evaluate the effectiveness of AFS, this paper is structured as follows. First, we review relevant literature on AI in education—focusing on DL-based prediction models and LLMs for feedback—and critically discuss both their potential and limitations within educational contexts. Next, we detail the methodology of our study, including the experimental design, participant demographics, and data collection and analysis procedures. The Results section presents a comparative analysis of student performance and engagement metrics between the experimental group (using AFS) and a control group (receiving traditional feedback). The Discussion section interprets these findings in the context of established AIED research and broader educational literature, and the Conclusion section reflects on the challenges, limitations, and future directions for research in AI-enhanced feedback systems.

1.1. Personalized Feedback with ChatGPT

Building upon decades of research in the field of Artificial Intelligence in Education (AIED) on personalized and Adaptive Feedback Systems [7,9], recent studies have begun to explore the potential of large language models (LLMs) like ChatGPT to further enhance feedback in online learning environments. Wang et al. [11] found that ChatGPT significantly enhances the quality of student argumentation by offering specific and timely feedback, key characteristics of effective feedback according to Hattie and Timperley [6]. In contrast, Messer et al. [12], in their systematic review of automated grading and feedback tools for programming education, offer a broader perspective, indicating that automated feedback tools, including those powered by LLMs, are generally effective in improving learning outcomes, reinforcing the more specific findings of Wang et al. [11] and Meyer et al. [13] explored the collaborative generation of feedback between students and AI, highlighting the potential of this collaboration to enrich educational feedback. Specifically, Li Wang et al. [14] demonstrated that ChatGPT exhibits impressive accuracy (91.8%) and a retrieval rate of 63.2% when providing feedback on undergraduate student argumentation. However, they also found that the length of the arguments and the use of discourse markers significantly influenced the effectiveness of the feedback, suggesting that the quality of ChatGPT's feedback may depend on the characteristics of the student's input. Meyer et al. [13] for their part, discovered that feedback generated by LLMs led to enhanced performance in text revisions, as well as increased motivation and positive emotions among high school students, indicating the potential multifaceted benefits of ChatGPT-based feedback beyond academic performance.

1.2. Deep Learning Models for Performance Prediction

In the field of learning analytics (LA) and educational data mining (EDM), deep learning has emerged as a powerful set of techniques for student performance prediction. Researchers have explored various deep learning models, including recurrent neural networks (RNNs) and, particularly, long short-term memory (LSTM) networks, due to their ability to model sequential learning data [4]. These models have proven effective in predicting academic performance and in identifying students at risk of dropping out of courses [3]. For example, Messer et al. [12] used neural network algorithms and LSTM to analyze large volumes of data for the purpose of predicting performance in programming education, although their primary focus was the review of automated feedback tools. Alnasyan et al. [15], while not directly focused on prediction, also found that the integration of generative AI, which often employs underlying deep learning models, can improve the academic performance and motivation of business students, suggesting that accurate performance prediction, enabled by deep learning, could be a valuable component for more adaptive and personalized educational systems. In addition to RNNs and LSTMs, other deep learning architectures, such as convolutional neural networks (CNNs) and multilayer perceptron (MLP) networks, have also been investigated for prediction tasks in LA/EDM, each with strengths and weaknesses depending on the data type and specific prediction task.

1.3. Evaluation of LLM-Based Educational Applications and Their Implicit Comparison with Traditional Feedback Methods

While several studies have directly compared feedback generated by deep learning models with traditional feedback methods (search for direct comparison studies to add here if you find them), research on LLMs in education often adopts an approach of evaluating the effectiveness and potential of LLMs per se in various educational roles, leaving the comparison with traditional methods implicit. For example, Hellas et al. [16] investigated LLM responses to beginner programmers' help requests, demonstrating the models' effectiveness in providing helpful assistance, compared to the assistance traditionally expected from a human tutor or conventional educational resources. Shaikh et al. [17] analyzed the potential of LLMs for sentiment analysis in student feedback, finding that these models can effectively identify students' emotions and attitudes, a task that would traditionally require laborious qualitative human analysis. Golchin et al. [18] examined the use of LLMs as evaluators in MOOCs, finding that they can provide accurate and consistent assessments, suggesting a scalable and automated alternative to human assessment in massive courses.

Extance [19] offers a broader analysis of the growing use of ChatGPT in the educational field, highlighting both its potential and risks. A case study at Arizona State University showed that LLM-based chatbots can foster creativity and help students generate more ideas than they would normally consider, suggesting an improvement over traditional methods of individual or small group brainstorming. Furthermore, tools like Khanmigo, developed by Khan Academy in collaboration with OpenAI, use GPT-4 to offer personalized tutoring, guiding students through problems without giving direct answers, promoting "productive struggle" in learning, in a style that emulates individualized human tutoring, but with the scalability potential of AI.

Nevertheless, Extance [19] also highlights the risks associated with the use of LLMs, such as the possibility of students over-relying on these tools to complete tasks without fully understanding the underlying concepts, which could be a greater problem than dependence on "solutions" from traditional sources like web search engines. Privacy concerns are also mentioned, as data entered into these platforms are stored and used to train future models, a risk not present with traditional feedback methods. Additionally, LLMs are prone to errors and "hallucinations", where they can generate incorrect or fictitious information, requiring human validation and oversight that would not be necessary with feedback generated by human experts. Despite these challenges, Extance [19] argues that the careful integration and proper supervision of LLMs in education can offer significant benefits, such as the ability to provide immediate and personalized feedback and improve access to high-quality tutoring, especially in resource-limited contexts, where personalized human tutoring is often infeasible.

1.4. Challenges and Opportunities

Despite these promising advances, significant challenges persist that require careful attention, including data privacy management and ethical dilemmas related to publishing AI-generated works. Furthermore, revisiting a historical concern in the field of AIED, the interpretability of complex deep learning models remains a crucial challenge to ensure transparency and trust in these educational systems [20]. Specifically, concerns about data privacy are highlighted by Lund et al. [21] and UNESCO [20], who emphasize the need to safeguard student information in AI environments. UNESCO [20] and Farrokhnia et al. [22]

also point to biases in AI-generated feedback as a significant risk, underscoring the need for human intervention to mitigate these biases and ensure academic integrity and educational equity, fundamental principles in AIED. Jeon and Lee [23] emphasize the need for rigorous methods to translate these findings into effective educational practices and understand their potential long-term impacts. Finally, UNESCO [20] also underscores the importance of validation of AI tools by educational institutions to ensure their effectiveness and fairness, aligning with AIED's tradition of rigorous evaluation of technology-based educational interventions. Table 1 summarizes the key challenges and opportunities in the use of deep learning models and LLMs in education.

Table 1. Challenges and opportunities in the use of deep learning models and LLMs in education.

Challenges	Opportunities
Difficulty in building accurate predictive models with data collected at the beginning of the course	Development of more robust and accurate predictive models using deep learning techniques [12]
Impact of misclassifying students in early predictions [20]	Significant improvement in model accuracy as the course progresses [20]
Cold start problems in early implementation of analysis	Ability to predict outstanding and at-risk students with high accuracy [11]
Managing an increasing number of students and data [12]	Creation of robust predictive models
Obtaining sufficient and relevant data while facing privacy issues [20]	Using built-in platform features to track participation [12]
Difficulties in interpreting complex models [20]	Enhanced collection of student interaction data [20]
Less room for improvement for groups with imbalanced data [11]	Identifying relevant attributes to improve prediction accuracy [12]
Ethical concerns about the fairness and transparency of AI systems in education [20,21]	Obtaining interpretable models of student performance [11,24], addressing the "black box" nature of DL models
Biases in AI-generated feedback [20,22], requiring human mitigation	Generation of timely and personalized feedback [11,13]
Risk of over-reliance on AI technology [13]	Improving student motivation and performance [13]
Lack of time and resources for educators to deliver individualized feedback manually [19]	Facilitating teacher workload, allowing more creative approaches [19]

While advances in the use of LLMs and deep learning in education are promising, further research is needed to address current limitations and maximize their potential, especially in the context of the AIED tradition and its ethical and pedagogical principles. This study seeks to fill some of these gaps by integrating the interpretation, still not sufficiently explored, of performance predictions made with deep learning models through personalized and timely feedback using LLMs.

2. Methodology

The primary aim of this experimental study is to assess the effectiveness of integrating advanced technologies, such as deep learning and large language models (LLMs), in enhancing student performance in a Digital Art for Film and Video Games course. The specific objectives of this study are as follows:

- Evaluate the accuracy of student performance predictions using deep learning models trained on historical student data.
- Determine the impact of personalized feedback generated by LLMs, such as GPT-4, on enhancing academic performance and student engagement.
- Compare participation and performance metrics between a control group and an experimental group that receives performance predictions and personalized recommendations.
- Explore the feasibility of integrating technological tools into daily educational routines to facilitate effective and timely communication that supports educational decision-making.
- Identify challenges and opportunities associated with implementing these technologies in an educational setting, including ethical and privacy considerations.

2.1. Participants

The participants in this study were students enrolled in a Digital Art for Film and Video Games Specialized Course, offered as part of Academy by PolygonUs, a highly competitive, non-traditional educational program specifically designed to address the immediate needs of the digital art industry. This program operates within an informal education context, focusing on developing high-impact digital skills relevant to the film and video game industries. The course employs a flipped classroom methodology, delivered 100% virtually through PolygonUs's custom-built Learning Content Management System (LCMS). Instruction includes three weekly synchronous online sessions, complemented by asynchronous pre-recorded lectures and practical activities. The 16-month program is structured into four levels, encompassing 22 industry-specific courses, including technical art skills, industry-focused English, and power skills. Notably, 80% of the curriculum is practical, emphasizing hands-on project development and portfolio building, while 20% is theoretical, delivered primarily through pre-recorded sessions on the LCMS. Throughout the program, students present their work to industry professionals for feedback and portfolio refinement, preparing them for direct entry into the digital art job market.

A significant characteristic of the student population in this program is their high level of motivation. All participants are scholarship recipients, having been selected through a rigorous admission process from a pool of approximately 3600 applicants competing for limited scholarship positions. This highly selective admission process ensures that admitted students demonstrate a strong intrinsic motivation and commitment to pursuing a career in digital art. Furthermore, as part of the admission process, all applicants undergo a structured interview designed to assess their motivation and commitment to the program, in addition to the aforementioned diagnostic technical test. This multi-faceted selection process aims to identify and enroll students with a high aptitude and intrinsic drive for digital art skill development.

Due to institutional scheduling and enrollment dynamics inherent in this industry-driven and scholarship-based program, participants were not randomly assigned to groups; instead, existing cohorts were utilized. The control group consisted of 39 students enrolled in the 2022 iteration of the course, while the experimental group comprised 42 students enrolled in the 2023 iteration. As illustrated in Figure 1A, initial demographic analysis revealed some gender imbalances between the groups. The control group had a higher proportion of female students compared to the experimental group. Furthermore, as shown in Figure 1B, analysis of initial diagnostic test scores indicated that the control group exhibited slightly higher baseline performance levels compared to the experimental group at the beginning of the course. The age range of participants was broadly similar across groups, with the control group ranging from 17 to 43 years and the experimental group from 17 to 36 years.

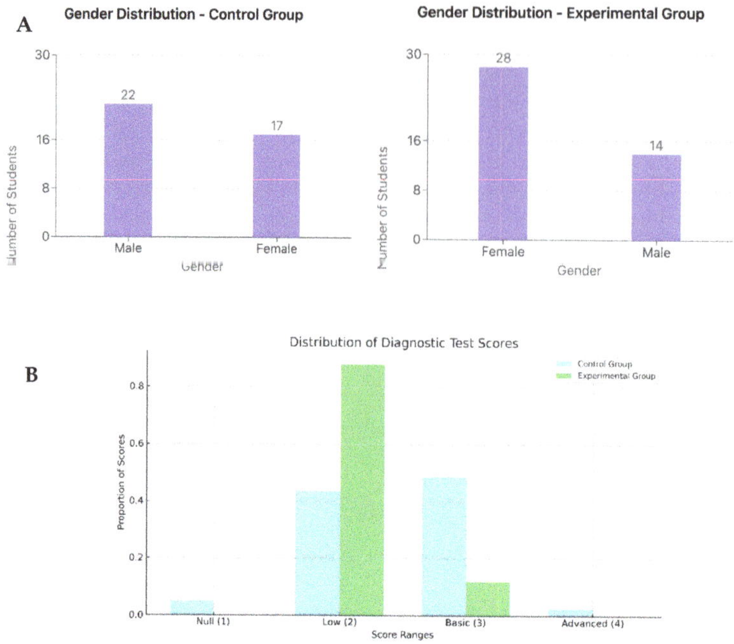

Figure 1. (**A**) Gender distribution in the control group and experimental group. (**B**) Distribution of diagnostic test scores.

Prior to the course commencement, all participants undertook a diagnostic technical test designed to assess their foundational skills in character concept design, a core skill in the Digital Art for Film and Video Games domain. This test required students to submit an initial character concept, which was evaluated by program instructors to determine their entry-level proficiency. The majority of students in both groups were categorized as having a "low and basic level of performance" based on this diagnostic assessment, indicating limited prior experience in character design upon entering the program. A small number of students in each group demonstrated "advanced level" skills at the outset of the training (see Figure 1B for detailed distribution of diagnostic test scores). It is important to note that these pre-existing group differences are acknowledged as a limitation of the quasi-experimental design and will be statistically addressed through covariance analysis in subsequent data analysis stages to mitigate potential confounding effects.

To statistically assess the significance of these baseline differences in diagnostic test scores between the experimental and control groups, a Chi-square test of independence was performed. This test examined the distribution of students across different proficiency levels (low, basic, and advanced) as determined by the diagnostic character concept test. The Chi-square test revealed a statistically significant difference in the distribution of baseline knowledge between the two groups ($\chi^2 = 18.49$, df = 2, $p < 0.001$).

Specifically, as depicted in Figure 1B, the experimental group presented a higher frequency of students categorized at the low proficiency level in the diagnostic test compared to the Control Group. Conversely, the control group exhibited a greater proportion of students classified as having basic and advanced baseline knowledge. These findings quantitatively confirm the initial observation that the experimental group, on average, commenced the course with a lower level of prior technical skills in digital art compared to the control group.

These statistically confirmed differences in baseline knowledge, while acknowledging an initial disadvantage for the experimental group, also present a significant opportunity to rigorously evaluate the potential of adaptive and personalized learning interventions. Specifically, these pre-existing disparities underscore the importance and potential impact of the AI-powered feedback system implemented in the experimental group to level the playing field. This initial disadvantage allows us to examine whether the personalized feedback can effectively mitigate these initial gaps in skills and knowledge and potentially enable the experimental group to achieve comparable, or even superior, performance outcomes compared to the control group.

Therefore, rather than being a confounding factor, these baseline differences become a critical context for assessing the true value and effectiveness of AI-driven personalized learning in addressing diverse student needs and promoting equitable educational outcomes. The subsequent sections of this methodology will detail the identical instructional design applied to both groups, alongside a comprehensive description of the AI-driven feedback system uniquely introduced to the experimental group, setting the stage for analyzing the intervention's impact within this context of initial group differences.

2.2. Design and Procedure

Due to the logistical constraints inherent in random assignment within real-world, scholarship-based educational programs, this research employed a quasi-experimental design. However, to maximize methodological validity, the study focused on maintaining strict procedural equivalence between the experimental group and the control group. Consequently, both groups received identical instruction in all aspects of the course: the same curricular content, the same instructors, and the same pedagogical methodology based on a flipped classroom approach that integrated synchronous online sessions, pre-recorded asynchronous lectures, and weekly feedback from industry experts.

The only systematic and planned difference between the groups was the implementation of the Adaptive Feedback System (AFS), exclusive to the experimental group. This system provided students in the experimental cohort with personalized weekly messages containing performance predictions and specific recommendations for improvement. While the control group participated in the program between August 2022 and August 2023 and the experimental group between April 2023 and May 2024, it is crucial to emphasize that the content and delivery of instruction were rigorously standardized across both cohorts.

This quasi-experimental design, while acknowledging the limitations of non-randomization, strengthens the ecological validity of the study by evaluating the AI-based intervention within the authentic setting of a demanding, industry-oriented digital arts program. By minimizing procedural variations beyond the AFS intervention, this design aims to isolate the specific effect of the AI-powered feedback while preserving the authenticity of the real-world educational context.

2.3. Measurements

This study employed a comprehensive measurement system designed to evaluate multiple dimensions of student performance throughout the four levels of the program. In order to robustly and thoroughly capture the impact of the AI-powered Adaptive Feedback System, the following key performance indicators (KPIs) were recorded and analyzed recurrently at each program level. These measured variables served as key input features for the deep learning model used to generate student performance predictions within the Adaptive Feedback System:

- Cognitive Learning (Quiz Scores): To measure knowledge acquisition and conceptual understanding, a total of 84 quizzes were administered throughout the program. These formative assessments, primarily composed of multiple-choice and short-answer questions, were systematically repeated in each of the four levels, with 21 quizzes administered per level. The average quiz scores, calculated for each level (Average Quiz Score), provided a granular measure of cognitive learning gains at each stage of the program.
- Behavioral Engagement (Session Engagement): Student engagement with learning materials was quantified by tracking attendance and interaction in both recorded and live sessions, conducted at each level of the program. The percentage of recorded sessions accessed (Recorded Percentage) and the percentage of live sessions attended (Live Percentage) served as indicators of behavioral engagement per level. It was hypothesized that the AFS would increase engagement in both learning modalities at each level.
- Social Learning and Collaboration (Forum Activity): Participation in collaborative learning was evaluated by quantifying forum activity across four key evaluation periods within each level of the program, resulting in a total of 16 forum activity evaluations throughout the program. The frequency and quality of contributions (Forums 1 to Forums 4, Forum Percentage), measured in each evaluation period within each level, indicated the level of social learning and collaborative engagement per level. It was expected that the AFS would foster greater participation and quality in forums at each level of the program.
- Practical Skill Mastery (Practical Activities Scores): To assess the development of practical skills, numerous industry-deliverable challenges were designed and implemented as practical activities in each course and level of the program. These practical activities, based on real industry requirements, were evaluated by industry experts through personalized feedback and quantitatively scored using predefined rubrics. An average score of practical activities per level (Average of Practical Activities) was recorded. This KPI measured the progress in mastering industry-relevant practical skills at each level of the program.
- Practical Skill Mastery (Portfolio Assessment Scores): To evaluate the ability to apply skills in complex projects and demonstrate mastery of industry-level competencies, portfolio submissions delivered by students at the end of each level of the program were evaluated, resulting in a total of eight portfolio evaluations throughout the program. Industry experts assigned scores in two portfolio evaluations per level (Evaluation 1, Evaluation 2), and their percentage average (Evaluations Percentage) was calculated to obtain a measure of practical skill mastery in portfolio projects at the end of each level. It was anticipated that the AFS would improve portfolio quality and, therefore, scores in these evaluations at each level of the program.

The collection and analysis of these KPIs, systematically repeated at each of the four program levels, provided a rich and granular database to exhaustively evaluate student performance and the impact of the AI-powered Adaptive Feedback System across multiple dimensions of learning.

It is important to note that while all variables were collected for pedagogical and evaluation purposes, only a subset was selected as input features for the predictive model, based on their availability in the early stages of each program level. Specifically, the portfolio evaluation scores were excluded from model training due to their late availability in the course timeline, which would have introduced data leakage. However, these scores were retained as valuable outcome indicators to assess skill mastery at the end of each level.

2.4. Data Collection

To ensure transparent and replicable data collection, this study relied on both automated data logging and expert evaluation procedures. Automated data collection was facilitated by a proprietary Learning Content Management System (LCMS) platform, developed by PolygonUs for its Academy educational programs. This LCMS was instrumented to automatically capture student activity data relevant to the study's metrics. Specifically, the following data streams were automatically recorded via the LCMS API:

- Student Performance in Quizzes: The LCMS automatically logged and stored individual student scores for each quiz administered within the platform (Q1Punta to Q21Punta), allowing for the calculation of average quiz scores (Average Quiz Score).
- Student Engagement in Sessions: The LCMS tracked student access and participation in learning sessions, automatically recording attendance in live sessions (Live Percentage) and engagement with recorded sessions (Recorded Percentage) based on platform login and session activity logs.
- Student Activity in Forums: The LCMS automatically logged student posts and interactions within the platform's forum modules, enabling the quantification of forum activity based on frequency and timestamps of contributions (Forums 1 to Forums 4).

Data collected via the LCMS was securely stored in an Amazon Web Services (AWS) database infrastructure. Weekly data reports were generated and extracted from this AWS database, providing structured datasets for feeding the AI-powered Adaptive Feedback System (AFS). Importantly, the data stored in the AWS database could not be modified, ensuring the integrity and auditability of the collected data. These data were queried through a secure web interface and integrated into the Python 3.11 algorithm that executed the predictive model weekly.

In addition to automated data, expert-assessed data were collected for metrics related to practical skill mastery. Industry experts, defined as senior artists with extensive experience in the digital art production pipeline, including areas such as concept art, 3D modeling, texturing, rendering, animation, retopology, UVs, and compositing with After Effects, conducted evaluations of student portfolio submissions and practical activity deliverables. These experts, trained by the PolygonUs education team for this purpose, performed the evaluations using standardized rubrics integrated within the LCMS platform. Practical activities, consisting of industry-deliverable challenges, were reviewed by experts every 15 days, given the practical nature of the program. Additionally, final projects, designed to integrate knowledge from each level, were also evaluated by experts at the end of each level. Students received personalized feedback from experts in 2 h sessions, twice a week. The experts provided both quantitative scores (recorded as Evaluation 1, Evaluation 2, Average of Practical Activities) and detailed qualitative feedback comments for each student submission, enhancing the quality of the assessment data. This expert evaluation data were then queried through the secure web interface and used to generate the portfolio and practical activity evaluation metrics.

Data collection for all metrics was performed periodically and continuously throughout the four levels of the program, allowing for the longitudinal analysis of student performance and engagement. The complete data flow, from student interaction in the LCMS to data integration into the prediction algorithm and feedback communication through the website and other channels, is illustrated in Figure 2.

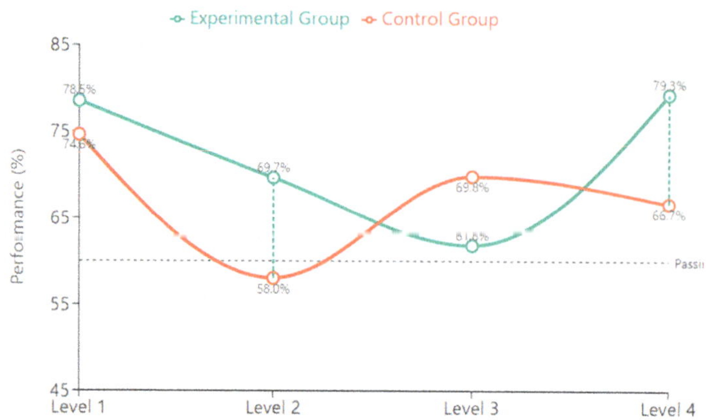

Figure 2. Evolution of academic performance (cumulative impact of the Adaptive Feedback System). Key finding: The graph shows a notable cumulative effect of the Adaptive Feedback System. Although both groups experienced fluctuations, the experimental group showed a significant recovery at Level 4 (79.3%), substantially outperforming the control group (66.7%) with a difference of +12.6 percentage points.

2.5. Adaptive Feedback System (AFS): Architecture and Implementation

The Adaptive Feedback System (AFS) developed in this study was designed as a multi-layered architecture that integrates predictive modeling and automated feedback generation in a scalable, secure, and pedagogically informed manner. This section outlines the four core layers of the system and their interconnections:

2.5.1. Data Collection Layer

This layer interfaces directly with the Learning Content Management System (LCMS) through its API, retrieving the following:

- Engagement metrics (live attendance, recorded class access, forum participation);
- Performance metrics (quiz scores).

Data are anonymized at collection and securely stored in AWS databases, with Google Sheets serving as an intermediary interface for real-time visualization and instructor access. The system ensured that the AWS-stored data could not be altered post-capture, thus preserving the auditability of performance logs.

2.5.2. Prediction Layer

The system's prediction layer utilized a deep learning model (a feedforward neural network with dropout regularization) trained to estimate the probability of each student passing the course. The model used four behavioral and performance variables as input and was optimized using binary cross-entropy loss and the Adam optimizer. Weekly inference runs produced class probability predictions, which were later used to generate feedback messages.

To illustrate the data flow through the prediction layer:

- Original input from LCMS: quiz = 63.91%; recorded attendance = 82.5%; live attendance = 66.7%; and forum activity = 41.3%.
- Normalized input vector for the model: [0.6391, 0.825, 0.667, 0.413].
- Output: Probability of success = 0.698 → classified as "likely to pass" (threshold = 0.6048).

To improve interpretability and transparency, a logistic regression model and several baseline classifiers (decision tree and random forest) were also tested, as reported in Section 3.4. Model performance was evaluated using metrics such as F1 score, ROC-AUC, and cross-validation scores. The final neural network model achieved a ROC-AUC of 0.945 and was selected based on its ability to generalize across cohorts while avoiding overfitting.

2.5.3. Feedback Generation Layer

The feedback layer was powered by GPT-4, which received structured prompts engineered using a chain-of-thought style and context-aware variables. Prompts were designed to generate multi-part feedback that included:

- A motivational greeting;
- An interpretation of the AI prediction;
- Detailed analyses of quiz scores, session engagement, and forum activity;
- A list of personalized recommendations.

Pop culture preferences (e.g., *Star Wars*, Marvel) and mentor archetypes (e.g., Yoda, Dumbledore) were used to personalize tone and content style. Prompts were crafted to follow pedagogical best practices, and output quality was reviewed by the education team. Importantly, GPT-4 operated as a one-way feedback generator—students could not interact with the AI. In cases where feedback contained errors or ambiguity, human team members manually reviewed and corrected the messages.

Prompt design was aligned with formative assessment principles and cognitive scaffolding strategies to enhance self-regulated learning.

2.5.4. Delivery and Notification Mechanism

Once generated, the feedback messages were stored in the student profile and made available through the platform every Friday. Additionally, a short WhatsApp notification was automatically sent to each student, summarizing the feedback in under 200 characters and linking back to the platform. Although the system tracked delivery, it did not verify whether students consciously engaged with the messages. This limitation is acknowledged and discussed in Section 4.6.

Figure 3 illustrates the complete architecture of the AFS, from data acquisition to predictive modeling and feedback delivery. For further details on the practical application of the predictive model, see Appendix A.

Figure 3. Architecture of the Adaptive Feedback System (AFS). Key components: The diagram illustrates the five-layer architecture of the AFS. Each layer is interconnected to ensure weekly automated cycles of prediction and feedback delivery. Data flows securely from the LCMS through AWS infrastructure, is processed by a neural network model, and then transformed into personalized messages via GPT-4. The system integrates real-time interfaces (e.g., Google Sheets, WhatsApp API) and maintains a continuous improvement loop.

2.6. Model Selection Process

To estimate the likelihood of academic success and generate personalized feedback, multiple machine learning models were trained and evaluated on a dataset comprising 445 labeled instances. The selected input variables reflect behavioral indicators: performance in in-class tests, attendance to prerecorded sessions, attendance to live classes, and participation in discussion forums. The target variable was a binary label (pass/fail) based on the final course outcomes.

Four different classifiers were implemented: logistic regression, decision tree, random forest, and a compact-architecture neural network. Models were trained using an 80/20 split for training and test sets and evaluated using standard metrics such as precision, recall, F1 score, and area under the ROC curve (ROC-AUC). To estimate generalization capacity, a five-fold cross-validation with three repetitions was applied.

To support reproducibility, Table 2 presents a detailed summary of the hyperparameters used for the neural network.

Table 2. Neural network hyperparameter configuration.

Hyperparameter	Hyperparameter
Architecture	Three dense hidden layers
Units per layer	64, 32, 16
Activation	ReLU
Regularization	L2 ($\lambda = 0.01$)
Dropout	0.3 (after each layer)
Batch normalization	Yes
Optimization	Adam
Learning rate	0.001
Loss function	Binary cross-entropy
Metrics	Accuracy, AUC
Internal validation	20% of training set
Early stopping	Patience = 15; monitor = AUC
Maximum epochs	150
Batch size	64

2.7. Ethical Considerations

This study was conducted with the formal approval of Academy by PolygonUS, the organization responsible for the "Academy" training program. Given the nature of the research carried out in the real-world context of an educational program within a private company, obtaining this institutional approval was a fundamental step to ensure the feasibility and ethical conduct of the study. Additionally, this research was undertaken as part of the first author's doctoral candidacy at the Universitat Politècnica de València (UPV), framing the study within a rigorous academic context and with implicit ethical oversight.

All participants provided their informed consent prior to participating in the study. They were provided with detailed information about the research objectives, the nature of the intervention (AFS), the data collection procedures, and the intended use of the data. They were explicitly guaranteed the confidentiality of their personal and academic data, ensuring that their information remained anonymous and protected. They were also clearly informed about their right to withdraw from the study at any time, without any negative consequences for their participation in the educational program.

To protect participant privacy, the collected data were anonymized at the point of collection, removing any personally identifiable information. The anonymized data were securely stored on encrypted servers, complying with data protection regulations. Access to the data were restricted solely to the principal investigators of the study.

3. Results

This section presents the results obtained after implementing the Adaptive Feedback System (AFS) based on deep learning—specifically, a pre-trained recurrent neural network (RNN) with historical data and GPT 4. The system provided weekly personalized feedback to the experimental group (n = 42) throughout all four learning blocks or levels of the program, while the control group (n = 39) followed the same four learning blocks or levels program without this intervention. Key findings include (1) a cumulative effect resulting in a significant performance difference in the fourth learning block (+12.63 percentage points); (2) a notable reduction in performance disparities between students with varying levels of prior knowledge in the experimental group (−56.5%) versus an increase in the control group (+103.3%); (3) a particularly beneficial effect for students with low prior knowledge; (4) an overcoming effect where up to 42.9% of students surpassed initial negative predictions; and (5) an especially positive impact on components related to active participation. These results remained robust across various complementary analyses.

3.1. Initial Characteristics of the Groups

The experimental (n = 42) and control (n = 39) groups presented significant differences in their initial characteristics, an important factor to consider in this quasi-experimental design, as shown in Table 3.

Table 3. Initial characteristics of the study groups.

Characteristic	Experimental Group	Control Group
Number of participants	42	39
	Gender distribution	
Female	28 (66.7%)	17 (43.6%)
Male	14 (33.3%)	22 (56.4%)
	Prior knowledge level	
No prior knowledge	0 (0.0%)	2 (5.1%)
Low prior knowledge	37 (88.1%)	17 (43.6%)
Basic prior knowledge	5 (11.9%)	19 (48.7%)
Advanced prior knowledge	0 (0.0%)	1 (2.6%)

Chi-square tests confirmed statistically significant differences in both gender distribution (χ^2 = 4.63, p = 0.031) and prior knowledge level (χ^2 = 20.87; $p < 0.001$). These results coincide with the diagnostic assessment described in the methodology (χ^2 = 18.49; df = 2; $p < 0.001$).

These differences, while representing a methodological limitation, offer an opportunity to evaluate the capacity of the AFS to mitigate initial knowledge gaps, aligning with the literature on adaptive educational systems [7,9], which suggests their leveling potential. To address these differences statistically, analysis of covariance (ANCOVA) will be employed in subsequent sections.

3.2. Evolution of Academic Performance

At Level 2, both groups experienced a decrease in performance, but the experimental group maintained a significantly higher level (69.67% vs. 58.05%; $p = 0.017$) with a small to moderate effect size ($\eta^2 = 0.073$), as shown in Table 4.

Table 4. Results of analysis of covariance (ANCOVA) for overall academic performance * $p < 0.05$. SD = standard deviation.

Level	Experimental Group (Adjusted Mean ± SD)	Control Group (Adjusted Mean ± SD)	F	*p*-Value	Effect Size (η^2)
Level 1	78.55 ± 17.41	74.62 ± 10.32	3.28	0.074	0.041
Level 2	69.67 ± 26.14	58.05 ± 15.43	5.95	0.017 *	0.073
Level 3	61.83 ± 27.83	69.82 ± 16.30	2.76	0.102	0.036
Level 4	79.30 ± 8.42	66.67 ± 17.82	12.87	<0.001 *	0.183

Level 3 presented an interesting reversal, with the control group recovering (69.82%) while the experimental group continued to decline (61.83%). This difference, however, did not reach statistical significance ($p = 0.102$).

The most striking difference emerged at Level 4, where the experimental group showed a dramatic recovery (79.30%), exceeding even their initial performance, while the control group declined to 66.67%. This difference was highly significant ($p < 0.001$) with a large effect size ($\eta^2 = 0.183$).

This performance pattern across all four levels indicates a cumulative effect of the AFS, which becomes most evident in the program's final stage. This aligns with prior research on the variable and cumulative impact of Adaptive Feedback Systems [11,13].

3.3. Performance Transitions Between Consecutive Levels Across the Program

The analysis of transitions between consecutive levels reveals important patterns in how students progressed through the four-level program, as shown in Table 5.

Table 5. Progression of academic performance between consecutive levels.

Progression	Experimental Group	Control Group	*p*-Value
	From Level 1 to Level 2		
Mean difference	−8.88%	−16.56%	0.032 *
Students who improved	13 (31.0%)	1 (2.6%)	<0.001 *
	From Level 2 to Level 3		
Mean difference	−7.84%	0.1177	<0.001 *
Students who improved	12 (28.6%)	31 (93.9%)	<0.001 *
	From Level 3 to Level 4		
Mean difference	0.1747	−3.15%	<0.001 *
Students who improved	28 (84.8%)	10 (30.3%)	<0.001 *

* $p < 0.05$.

In the transition from Level 1 to 2, both groups experienced a decrease in performance, with the decline being significantly smaller in the experimental group (−8.88% vs. −16.56%; $p = 0.032$). A significantly higher proportion of students in the experimental group managed to improve their performance (31.0% vs. 2.6%; $p < 0.001$).

In the transition from Level 2 to 3, the patterns reversed. The control group showed a significant recovery (+11.77%), while the experimental group continued its downward trend (−7.84%, $p < 0.001$).

The most striking difference occurred in the transition from Level 3 to 4. The experimental group showed a dramatic improvement (+17.47%), while the control group experienced a slight decline (−3.15%, $p < 0.001$). A vast majority of experimental group students improved their performance (84.8% vs. 30.3% in the control group, $p < 0.001$).

These transition patterns across all four levels suggest that the AFS had different effects at different stages of the program. The system appeared to provide initial resilience (Level 1 to 2), faced challenges in the middle stage (Level 2 to 3), but showed its greatest impact in the final transition (Level 3 to 4). This pattern of delayed effectiveness across a four-level program has been documented in other studies of AI-mediated educational interventions [11,12].

3.4. Model Results and Selection Rationale

Table 6 summarizes the performance metrics obtained by each model on the test set. The neural network achieved the highest F1 score (0.923) and ROC-AUC (0.946), closely followed by logistic regression (F1 = 0.917; ROC-AUC = 0.942) and the random forest, with differences likely not statistically significant. In contrast, the decision tree showed comparatively lower performance.

Table 6. Performance metrics comparison of machine learning models for predicting student outcomes.

Model	Accuracy	Precision	Recall	F1 Score	ROC-AUC	CV F1 (±SD)	Training Time
Neural Network	0.89	0.93	0.91	0.92	0.94	N/A	15.32 s
Logistic Regression	0.88	0.90	0.93	0.91	0.94	0.9126 ± 0.0223	0.003 s
Random Forest	0.87	0.88	0.93	0.90	0.93	0.8969 ± 0.0202	0.22 s
Decision Tree	0.80	0.86	0.84	0.85	0.86	0.8650 ± 0.0245	0.005 s

Figure 4 presents the ROC curves for the four evaluated models. Both the neural network and logistic regression display curves approaching the ideal, with a slight advantage observed for the former.

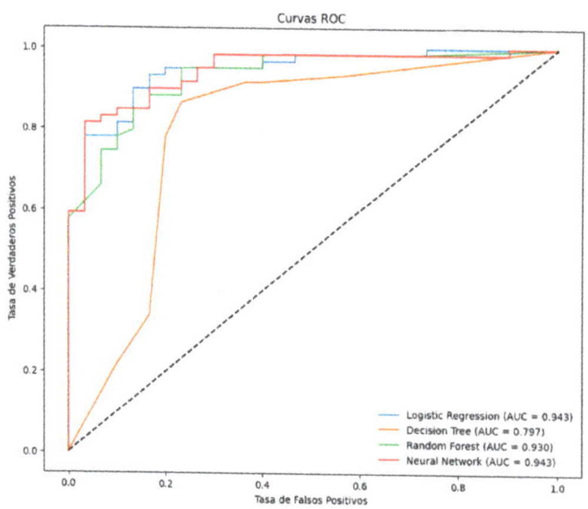

Figure 4. ROC curves of the four evaluated models.

Interpretability was also assessed through feature importance analysis. For logistic regression, decision tree, and random forest models, feature importance was computed using model-specific internal mechanisms (e.g., coefficient magnitudes or impurity-based scores). Figure 5 shows the relative importance assigned to each feature across these models. The results reveal distinct distribution patterns: logistic regression exhibits a 3.6-fold difference between its most and least influential variables; the random forest model shows a 7.6-fold variation; and the decision tree displays the most imbalanced distribution, with a nearly 29-fold difference between performance in in-class tests and forum participation.

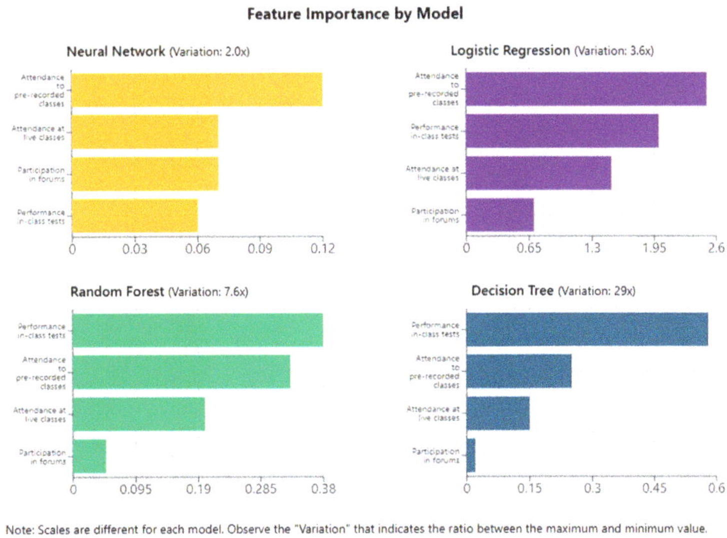

Figure 5. Feature importance comparison across machine learning models. Each chart displays the relative importance assigned to educational engagement metrics.

For the neural network, interpretability was addressed using SHAP values derived from a KernelExplainer. This model-agnostic approach estimates the marginal contribution of each input feature to the model's output. As seen in Figure 5, the neural network distributes importance more evenly, with only a twofold variation between the most and least influential variables. While more modest than in other models, this behavior may be desirable in educational contexts where student performance depends on a diverse set of factors. Nevertheless, a clear feature hierarchy remains identifiable within the network.

Interestingly, the models differ in identifying the most influential variable: both logistic regression and the neural network prioritize attendance to pre-recorded sessions, while the tree-based models emphasize performance in in-class tests. This divergence reflects the different inductive biases of the algorithms when modeling student behavior.

The selection of the neural network as the core model for the Adaptive Feedback System (AFS) was not based solely on its marginal performance advantages or on its more balanced feature attribution. Instead, it was primarily motivated by its greater flexibility for future scalability. Neural networks are better equipped to integrate heterogeneous variables (e.g., sociodemographic data or learning styles) and to uncover nonlinear relationships—capabilities that are critical for the next phase of system development.

Furthermore, this performance was achieved without requiring specialized computational infrastructure: training was completed in approximately 16 s using only a free

Google Colab instance. This computational efficiency underscores the feasibility of deploying advanced models in educational environments with limited technological resources, facilitating broader accessibility and adoption.

3.5. Analysis by Learning Components

To understand how the AFS affected different aspects of learning throughout the four-level program, we analyzed its impact on six key components. Table 7 presents the evolution of these components across all four levels.

Table 7. Evolution of key learning components across all four levels (experimental vs. control).

Component	Level 1		Level 2		Level 3		Level 4	
	Exp. *	Ctrl. **	Exp.	Ctrl.	Exp.	Ctrl.	Exp.	Ctrl.
Test performance	81.48	76.79	84.14	49.87	72.29	68.5	82.45	74.06
Pre-recorded classes	95.5	75.82	87.5	53.49	68.33	60.75	77.91	69.12
Live classes	59.12	26.13	47.4	60.1	55.67	60.45	73.7	43.48
Forum participation	61.9	5.13	60.71	28.38	54.29	57.56	70.45	60.67
Portfolio submissions	81.26	84.64	68.85	67.1	57.85	71.43	74.33	70.39
Portfolio assessment	75.74	85.69	61.19	52.91	60.95	74.83	79.3	67.27
Overall performance	78.55	74.62	69.67	58.05	61.83	69.82	79.3	66.67

* Exp. = experimental group. ** Ctrl. = control group.

This comprehensive analysis reveals several important patterns:

1. **Test performance**: The experimental group maintained higher test scores throughout all four levels, with the gap widening at Level 2 (84.14% vs. 49.87%) and Level 4 (82.45% vs. 74.06%).
2. **Pre-recorded classes**: The experimental group consistently showed higher attendance, with the largest difference at Level 1 (95.50% vs. 75.82%) and Level 2 (87.50% vs. 53.49%).
3. **Live classes**: After an initial advantage at Level 1 (59.12% vs. 26.13%), the experimental group fell behind at Levels 2 and 3 but showed a dramatic recovery at Level 4 (73.70% vs. 43.48%).
4. **Forum participation**: The experimental group showed substantially higher participation at Level 1 (61.90% vs. 5.13%) and Level 2 (60.71% vs. 28.38%), a slight drop at Level 3, and recovered at Level 4 (70.45% vs. 60.67%).
5. **Portfolio components**: The control group initially performed better in the portfolio assessment (Level 1), but by Level 4, the experimental group showed superior performance in both submissions (74.33% vs. 70.39%) and assessment (79.30% vs. 67.27%).

The observed evolution of these components across the four levels is consistent with the hypothesis that the AFS may have contributed to improvements in multiple aspects of learning, although alternative explanations cannot be ruled out due to the study's quasi-experimental design. By Level 4, the experimental group showed superior performance across all components, with the most notable differences in live class attendance (+30.21 points), portfolio assessment (+12.03 points), and forum participation (+9.79 points).

These findings indicate that the AFS, when sustained across a four-level program, can have a comprehensive positive impact on multiple dimensions of learning, particularly those related to active participation and engagement.

Figure 6 provides a multidimensional visualization of learning components at Level 4, clearly illustrating how the experimental group (green area) consistently outperformed the control group (orange area) across all dimensions. This radar representation highlights the comprehensive nature of the AFS's impact, with the most substantial differences observed in live class attendance (+30.2pp), portfolio assessment (+12.0pp), and forum participation (+9.8pp). The pattern revealed in this visualization reinforces our finding that adaptive feedback had the greatest impact on components related to active engagement and participation.

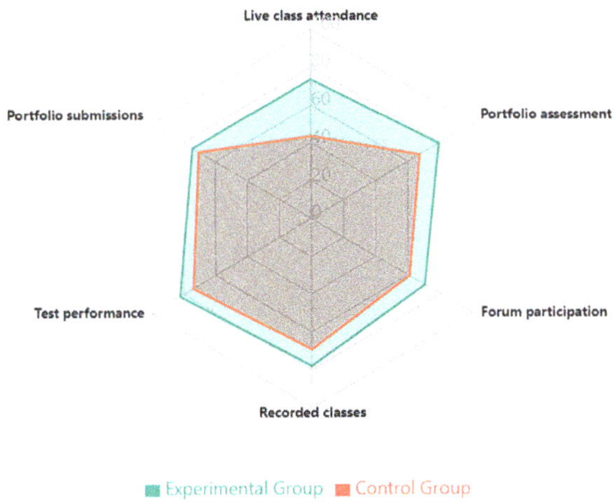

Figure 6. Components with highest impact at Level 4.

3.6. Understanding the Overcoming Effect: Predictive Model Efficacy

The core contribution of this study revolves around what we have termed the Overcoming Effect—the ability of students receiving adaptive feedback to surpass negative predictions and alter their expected learning trajectory across a four-level program. Figure 7 conceptualizes this phenomenon.

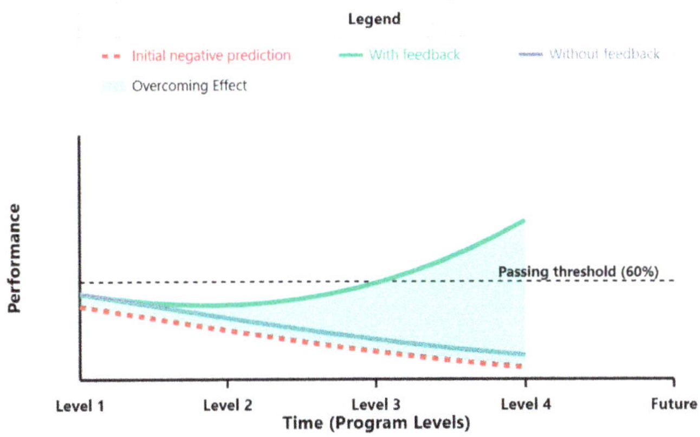

Figure 7. Conceptual Framework of the Overcoming Effect (Mechanism by which adaptive feedback transforms predicted academic trajectories).

The conceptual model illustrates how adaptive feedback transforms predicted academic trajectories across all four levels. When students receive risk predictions accompanied by personalized and actionable weekly feedback, they can modify their academic behavior, generating a progressive divergence between the initially predicted trajectory (red dotted line) and the actual trajectory (green line). The green shaded area represents the "Overcoming Effect," highlighting the ability of the AFS to positively transform initial expectations and enhance academic achievement, particularly for students initially identified as at-risk. Table 8 presents the quantitative evolution of this Overcoming Effect across all four levels of the program.

Table 8. Evolution of predictive accuracy and the "Overcoming Effect" across all four levels.

Level	Initial Predictive Accuracy	Final Predictive Accuracy	Students Who Surpassed Negative Prediction
Level 1	35.70%	42.90%	7 (16.7%)
Level 2	47.60%	54.80%	12 (28.6%)
Level 3	52.40%	59.50%	15 (35.7%)
Level 4	64.30%	78.60%	18 (42.9%)

The predictive accuracy of the model improved progressively throughout the four-level program, reaching its peak at Level 4 (78.6%). This increase suggests that the model was learning and adapting with more data, a finding aligned with the literature on the potential for improvement of deep learning models with continuous feedback [3].

A particularly interesting finding is the steady increase in the percentage of students who managed to surpass an initial negative prediction across all four levels. At Level 1, only 16.7% of students in the experimental group with an initial failure prediction managed to pass. This figure consistently increased through each level, reaching 42.9% at Level 4. This pattern may be indicative of what we describe as the overcoming effect—a phenomenon in which students, upon receiving information about their risk along with specific recommendations, appear to modify their academic behavior and exceed the initial expectations of the model.

The correlation analysis between the probability of passing assigned by the model and the final performance showed a moderate but significant correlation ($r = 0.62$, $p < 0.001$), indicating that, despite the initial limitations, the assigned probabilities had predictive value for final performance across the entire four-level program.

3.7. Educational Gap Reduction Effect Across the Four-Level Program

One of the most significant findings of this study was the AFS's capacity to reduce educational gaps between students with different levels of prior knowledge as they progressed through all four levels of the program, as shown in Table 9.

The tracking of educational gaps across all four levels reveals a fascinating pattern. At Level 1, the experimental group showed a larger initial gap between students with basic and low prior knowledge (14.36pp vs. 6.98pp in the control group). This gap widened at Levels 2 and 3 for both groups.

However, at Level 4, a dramatic reversal occurred: the experimental group's gap narrowed significantly to 6.24pp (a 56.5% reduction from Level 1), while the control group's gap continued to widen to 14.19pp (a 103.3% increase from Level 1).

At Level 4, students with low prior knowledge in the experimental group achieved a performance of 78.36%, while their counterparts in the control group only achieved 58.31%, a difference of 20.05 percentage points. This interaction was statistically significant (F

= 4.75, p = 0.033), suggesting that the AFS was particularly beneficial for students with lower levels of prior knowledge in the long term, a finding that reinforces the potential of Adaptive Feedback Systems to promote educational equity [15].

Table 9. Evolution of educational gaps between students with basic and low prior knowledge across all four levels.

Level	Experimental Group Gap (pp *)	Control Group Gap (pp)	Difference
Level 1	14.36	6.98	7.38
Level 2	24.9	11.16	13.74
Level 3	24.71	15.68	9.03
Level 4	6.24	14.19	−7.95
Change from Level 1 to 4	−56.50%	103%	Divergent trend

* pp = percentage points.

3.8. Retention and Completion Across All Four Levels

Of the original participants, 78.6% of the experimental group (33 of 42) and 84.6% of the control group (33 of 39) completed all four levels of the program. This difference in completion rates was not statistically significant (χ^2 = 0.51, p = 0.477).

In the experimental group, the completion rate was lower among students with basic prior knowledge (60.0%, 3 of 5) than among those with low prior knowledge (81.1%, 30 of 37). In the control group, the completion rate was similar between students with basic prior knowledge (84.2%, 16 of 19) and low prior knowledge (82.4%, 14 of 17).

Follow-up interviews with students who did not complete all four levels indicated that most dropouts were due to personal circumstances (such as changes in work schedules or family responsibilities) and time constraints related to the program's demanding schedule, rather than factors related to the educational intervention itself. This finding aligns with research on dropout factors in online and blended learning environments [13,15], which consistently identify external factors as primary drivers of non-completion.

3.9. Robustness Analysis Across Different Thresholds

To verify the consistency of the findings, analyses were conducted with different passing thresholds, as presented in Table 10.

Table 10. Predictive accuracy under different passing thresholds across all four levels (average).

Threshold	Experimental Group	Control Group
50%	51.20%	39.10%
55%	49.50%	37.80%
60%	47.60%	36.40%
65%	55.60%	45.70%
70%	68.90%	59.60%

The predictive accuracy improved notably with a more demanding threshold (70%), suggesting that the model is more effective at identifying students with very high or very low performance, but has difficulties in the intermediate ranges, a finding consistent with research on the variable accuracy of predictive models according to the classification threshold [12].

A multiple regression analysis for performance across all four levels, controlling for multiple covariates, was statistically significant ($F = 28.45$, $p < 0.001$, adjusted $R^2 = 0.763$), explaining approximately 76% of the variance. After controlling all covariates, the effect of the group was statistically significant ($\beta = 0.214$, $p = 0.018$), reinforcing the conclusion that the AFS had a substantial impact on student performance throughout the four-level program.

These results suggest that the integration of a deep learning model (RNN) and GPT-4 within the AFS has the potential to support improved academic performance. However, further studies are needed to confirm the robustness and generalizability of these effects in generating personalized feedback across multi-level educational programs. Beyond overall performance gains, the system showed particularly positive outcomes in reducing educational gaps and enabling students to overcome initial negative predictions—findings that align with recent literature on the potential of AI technologies to foster more equitable and personalized learning environments [3,11,13].

4. Discussion

4.1. Interpretations and Alignment with the Previous Literature

The results of this research provide substantial evidence on the potential of Adaptive Feedback Systems (AFS) based on deep learning and LLMs in online educational environments. A key outcome is the cumulative effect observed throughout the four levels of the program, becoming more evident in advanced stages. This is consistent with studies in adaptive feedback [11,13] that also report a long-term buildup of positive effects:

1. Students become accustomed to incorporating iterative feedback into their self-regulated learning strategies;
2. The system "learns" more about each student, thus refining its predictive power;
3. Repeatedly receiving feedback prompts progressive behavioral changes that accumulate over time.

The fact that the experimental group managed to reduce educational gaps and even outperform the control group by Level 4—despite starting with lower prior knowledge—points toward the equity-promoting potential of AFS-like interventions. Such findings echo pedagogical scaffolding principles [24,25] wherein adaptive and differentiated support helps level the playing field for students with varying backgrounds.

4.2. Delayed Recovery and the Overcoming Effect

An intriguing pattern that emerged is the delayed improvement in the experimental group, where performance dipped at Level 3 but rebounded significantly at Level 4. This dip-then-spike trajectory may be explained by a combination of increasing course difficulty during the mid-levels and the time it takes for students to internalize the suggestions consistently. Similar phenomena have been documented in prolonged adaptive feedback interventions, where students sometimes display a temporary plateau or regression before fully capitalizing on personalized recommendations [12].

Within this context, the overcoming effect—students surpassing initially negative predictions—was seen in up to 42.9% of learners by the final stage. Instead of demotivating at-risk students, early alerts seem to trigger behavior changes that reverse their predicted trajectory. This contrasts with concerns that risk labeling may lead to self-fulfilling prophecies and instead shows how timely, actionable feedback can empower students to outperform the system's early forecasts.

4.3. Stronger Impact on Active Participation

Breaking down learning components revealed the strongest gains in active participation metrics, notably live class attendance (+30.21) and forum engagement (+9.79). Such findings support the view that social presence and interactive engagement are crucial predictors of success in online education [2]. By making students aware of how attendance and forum posts correlate with performance, the AFS seemed to foster a more proactive approach, encouraging them to attend synchronous sessions and contribute to collaborative discussions.

4.4. Potential Biases and Model Transparency

Although the Adaptive Feedback System (AFS) demonstrated high predictive accuracy (up to 78.6% in later stages), several interpretability issues and potential biases warrant attention. The system integrates two main components: (1) a compact deep learning model (specifically, a recurrent neural network) that forecasts student performance based on behavioral features, and (2) a GPT-4-based module that generates individualized feedback messages.

A major concern lies in the opacity of neural network models, which tend to function as black boxes. This makes it difficult for instructors and learners to understand how specific inputs—such as forum participation or attendance—contribute to the predicted outcomes. As Lipton [26] emphasizes, the lack of transparency can hinder trust and complicate efforts to detect fairness issues, biases, or model drift. While our current implementation prioritized performance, we mitigated this limitation by integrating SHAP (Shapley additive explanations) into the interpretability workflow. SHAP offers model-agnostic explanations by estimating the marginal contribution of each input feature to a prediction. This aligns with current efforts in educational AI to balance performance with interpretability [12,15].

On the feedback generation side, large language models such as GPT-4 may inherit and reproduce cultural, demographic, or linguistic biases embedded in their training data. This risk is especially relevant in educational settings, where the framing and tone of recommendations can significantly affect student engagement. Prior studies have raised concerns that unmonitored LLM outputs may reinforce inequities or yield inconsistent advice across student profiles [21,22,24].

Although our content review process did not identify overtly biased feedback during deployment, this limitation suggests a critical need for future safeguards. These may include content audits, prompt engineering guidelines, and co-design sessions with educators to ensure feedback remains aligned with pedagogical intent and equity standards. Moreover, emerging studies propose combining human-in-the-loop strategies with automated moderation to increase transparency and ethical oversight in generative educational systems [16,19].

4.5. Generic or Uncontextualized Feedback

If the input data passed to GPT-4 does not adequately capture the nuances of a student's context—such as low digital literacy, language barriers, or fluctuating motivation—the resulting feedback may lack personalization. This risk increases when the system is scaled to large cohorts, where real-time prompt monitoring and manual review become less feasible.

To address this issue, the system integrated explainable AI (XAI) techniques, specifically the SHAP (Shapley additive explanations) method. SHAP allowed the academic team to visualize which features had the greatest influence on each prediction made by the model, improving transparency and enabling more pedagogically informed interventions.

Although we did not conduct structured interviews or surveys specifically focused on the AI, anecdotal evidence of student engagement was observed in discussion forums and support chats. Some students referred directly to the AI-generated messages—calling it "the Oracle"—and requested manual edits when they felt the feedback did not reflect their actual progress. While informal, these instances suggest partial student appropriation and perceived relevance of the system.

Looking ahead, the next version of the system will include a conversational agent that allows students to reply directly to feedback via WhatsApp. This two-way interaction channel will not only enhance personalization but also enable the collection of valuable data on how students perceive, interpret, and act upon the feedback provided.

Based on these insights, we recommend that future research combines XAI outputs with more systematic qualitative analysis (e.g., surveys, interviews, behavioral trace analysis) to evaluate how students engage with AI-generated feedback and how it influences their learning trajectories.

4.6. Limitations

Despite the promising outcomes, this study has certain limitations that call for cautious interpretation.

4.6.1. Quasi-Experimental Design and Cohort Differences

The study employed a quasi-experimental design involving different cohorts (2022 for the control group and 2023 for the experimental group), which limits internal validity and restricts the ability to establish causal relationships. Although statistical controls were applied using ANCOVA to adjust for baseline disparities in prior knowledge and gender composition, unmeasured external factors—such as curricular updates or increased exposure to AI technologies in 2023—may have influenced the results. Nonetheless, since the control group did not receive AI-generated feedback, the potential impact of these external factors was likely reduced. In light of this limitation, findings are interpreted as consistent with the hypothesis that the Adaptive Feedback System may have contributed to the improvements observed, rather than as definitive proof of causality.

4.6.2. Sample Size and Power Analysis

While the experimental and control groups had 42 and 39 students, respectively, such sample sizes might limit generalizability. Future studies should consider larger cohorts or multi-institutional settings, ideally accompanied by a power analysis to ensure the sample is sufficient to detect meaningful differences.

4.6.3. Contextual Scope

Participants were part of a highly selective digital art program, which may not represent the full spectrum of online learners. Their motivation levels, scholarship context, and professional aspirations could have amplified the receptiveness to AI-driven feedback.

4.6.4. Model Overfitting or Narrow Feature Selection

Although cross-validation was performed, high accuracy values (particularly early in the pipeline) may raise concerns about potential overfitting. Moreover, the predictors used (attendance, quiz scores, forum activity, etc.) might not capture broader factors (e.g., emotional well-being, socio-economic conditions) that also shape student success.

4.6.5. Ethical and Privacy Considerations

AI systems handling student data must comply with stringent privacy regulations and ensure informed consent. Institutions adopting such systems should implement robust data protection measures and remain vigilant against inadvertently reinforcing biases, in alignment with guidelines [21].

5. Conclusions

5.1. Main Contributions

This study empirically demonstrates that integrating deep learning (RNN) and GPT-4 for personalized, weekly feedback can significantly enhance online learning outcomes. Notably, we identified the overcoming effect, wherein students who were initially projected to fail changed their learning trajectories through actionable feedback. The findings reinforce the notion that predictive analytics should be viewed not merely as a detection tool for at-risk students, but as an intervention that can actively redirect learners' academic paths.

Additionally, the research shows that such AI-powered feedback can close educational gaps, a critical advance in ensuring more equitable outcomes. By providing differential support to those with lower prior knowledge, AFS aligned with Vygotskyian scaffolding principles and effectively improved engagement and participation.

5.2. Practical Implications

For Educational Institutions: Adopting Adaptive Feedback Systems can bolster student engagement and performance, especially among those starting with lower skills. This has strong potential for promoting inclusion and equity in online courses.

For EdTech Developers: The demonstrated synergy between an RNN for predictions and GPT-4 for messaging can guide future product roadmaps. Emphasis on interpretability, data security, and robust prompting strategies will be crucial to maximize effectiveness.

For Policymakers: Balancing innovation with ethical frameworks is essential. Policymakers could incentivize institutions to pilot similar AI interventions, but accountability, transparency, and fairness during deployment must be ensured.

5.3. Future Directions

Looking ahead, several promising avenues exist for refining and expanding the potential of the Adaptive Feedback System (AFS). First, longitudinal research examining whether the observed improvements persist beyond the immediate course cycle—such as follow-up performance one year later—would provide insight into the sustainability of the system's impact. Second, cross-domain studies could explore the adaptability of the AFS across diverse subject areas (e.g., STEM or humanities), assessing whether domain-specific customization is necessary.

Another key direction involves integrating multimodal data, such as video engagement and affective indicators, to improve the system's predictive power and relevance—provided strict ethical and privacy safeguards are enforced. Importantly, we have already implemented explainable AI (XAI) methods such as SHAP to interpret feature contributions in the prediction model, and we plan to expand the use of such tools to increase transparency and foster trust among users.

Future iterations of the AFS will also incorporate a conversational agent that allows students to respond to feedback directly via WhatsApp. This two-way interaction will enable the collection of behavioral and perceptual data, providing valuable insight into how students interpret and react to feedback. Such data can inform continuous improvements to the system's tone, structure, and personalization strategies.

Researchers may also explore differentiated feedback modalities—such as textual vs. visual formats, or directive vs. motivational tones—to identify what styles best support various learner profiles. Finally, embedding a co-design process with both educators and students will help adapt the system's frequency, delivery methods, and pedagogical voice to the needs of real-world learning environments, ensuring continued relevance and effectiveness.

Author Contributions: Conceptualization, Ó.C., M.C. and M.H.; methodology, Ó.C.; software, Ó.C.; validation, Ó.C., M.C. and M.H.; formal analysis, Ó.C.; investigation, Ó.C.; resources, Ó.C.; data curation, Ó.C.; writing—original draft preparation, Ó.C.; writing—review and editing, M.C. and M.H.; visualization, Ó.C.; supervision, M.C. and M.H. All authors have read and agreed to the published version of the manuscript.

Funding: This research received no external funding.

Institutional Review Board Statement: Ethical review and approval were waived for this study as it involved the analysis of educational data without direct intervention on human subjects. The study was conducted in accordance with institutional guidelines, and formal permission was obtained from the private company managing the educational program.

Informed Consent Statement: Informed consent was obtained from all subjects involved in the study and from the institution providing the educational program.

Data Availability Statement: The data presented in this study are available on request from the corresponding author. The data are not publicly available due to privacy restrictions related to student performance information.

Acknowledgments: The authors would like to thank PolygonUs for providing access to educational data and platform used in this study. Special appreciation to the tutors and educational staff who supported the implementation of the Adaptive Feedback System. We also thank the students who participated in the program.

Conflicts of Interest: The authors declare no conflicts of interest.

Appendix A. Model Application and Weekly Prediction Generation

Having established the robust performance of the student success prediction model, the subsequent crucial step is to detail its practical application within AFS. A defining feature of the AFS is its personalized feedback delivery cycle, operating on a weekly basis. Accordingly, the prediction model is designed to be applied each week, generating updated predictions for each student at the start of this cycle. This periodic prediction update allows the AFS to dynamically adapt to students' evolving performance and engagement throughout the course, providing timely and relevant feedback that reflects their most recent academic activities.

To generate these recurring predictions, the AFS constructs a personalized student dictionary. This dictionary serves as the input for the prediction model, encapsulating the student's current performance across key indicators. Specifically, each student dictionary includes the following features, updated with data from the prior week: performance in in-class tests, attendance to pre-recorded classes, attendance at live classes, participation in forums, and performance in deliverables to create a portfolio. This structured dictionary format ensures that the model receives consistent and relevant input for each student, on a recurring basis, enabling the generation of accurate and personalized predictions. An example of such a student dictionary, with illustrative sample data, is provided in Figure A1.

```
student_dictionary_ejemplo_PRE_prediccion = {
    "student_id": "512345",
    "week_number": 7,  # Semana actual del curso
    "performance_in_class_tests": 0.75,  # 75% de promedio en tests
    "attendance_to_prerecorded_classes": 0.85, # 85% de asistencia a clases pregrabadas
    "attendance_at_live_classes": 0.92,  # 92% de asistencia a clases en vivo
    "participation_in_forums": 0.60,  # 60% de participación en foros
    "performance_in_portfolio_deliverables": 0.80 # 80% de promedio en entregables del portafolio
}
```

Figure A1. Example of student dictionary.

With the personalized student dictionary constructed, the AFS then proceeds to utilize the already trained deep learning model to generate individual predictions. For each student, their respective dictionary is transformed into a numerical input vector, formatted to match the expected input structure of the trained model. This involves extracting the feature values from the dictionary and organizing them in the specific order required by the model's input layer. Subsequently, this input vector is presented to the pre-trained prediction model. Operating in inference mode, the model processes this input, leveraging its learned neural network architecture to output a probability score through a sigmoid activation function. This probability score, ranging from 0 to 1, represents the model's estimated likelihood of the student belonging to the fail class (class 0). To facilitate interpretation and integration with subsequent AFS components, this probability score is then converted into a binary textual prediction (pass or fail) based on the optimal threshold determined previously (0.6048). Furthermore, both the numerical probability score and the binary textual prediction are incorporated into a final student dictionary, which now includes not only the original input features but also these crucial prediction outputs. This final student dictionary, containing the input features and the model-generated probability score and textual prediction, is then used as a crucial input for the subsequent phase of the AFS, namely the generation of personalized feedback, as detailed in the following section.

```
[ ]
student_dictionary_ejemplo_POST_prediccion = {
    "student_id": "512345",
    "week_number": 7,  # Semana actual del curso
    "performance_in_class_tests": 0.75,  # 75% de promedio en tests
    "attendance_to_prerecorded_classes": 0.85, # 85% de asistencia a clases pregrabadas
    "attendance_at_live_classes": 0.92,  # 92% de asistencia a clases en vivo
    "participation_in_forums": 0.60,  # 60% de participación en foros
    "performance_in_portfolio_deliverables": 0.80, # 80% de promedio en entregables del portafolio
    "prediction_probability": 0.253, # Probabilidad de "Fail" (clase 0) predicha por el modelo
    "prediction_text": "Pass" # Predicción textual: "Pass" o "Fail" (basada en el umbral)
}
```

Figure A2. Example of student dictionary with prediction.

Appendix B. Feedback Communication and Example

To illustrate the mechanism for delivering personalized feedback, Figure A3 presents an exemplary prompt utilized to guide the OpenAI API in the generation of student-specific feedback. This prompt, structured as a Python dictionary and formatted in JSON, serves as the blueprint for creating individualized messages that are both informative and motivational. The subsequent subsections will dissect the key elements within this prompt structure, detailing how each component contributes to the generation of feedback that is tailored to the unique performance profile and predicted learning trajectory of each student within the AFS.

```
[ ]
prompt = (
    f'''{{
        "instruction": {{
            "role": {{
                "primary":   "AI expert in personalized tutoring",
                "specialty": "Digital environment assessment",
                "voice":     "first person",
                "tone":      "adaptive based on student performance,
                              especially considering the success prediction outcome"
            }},
            "student_id": "{student['document']}",
            "context":    "{descriptions}",
```

Figure A3. Initial structure and AI role definition of the feedback prompt.

Figure A3 illustrates the initial structure of the prompt, focusing on the "instruction" section and the definition of the AI's role. This section establishes the foundational directives for the AI, defining its persona as an AI expert in personalized tutoring with a specialty in digital environment assessment. It specifies the voice as first person to create a more direct and personal interaction with the student. Crucially, it sets the tone to be adaptive based on student performance, especially considering the success prediction outcome. This adaptive tone is a key element, ensuring that the feedback is not only informative but also appropriately nuanced based on the student's academic standing and predicted trajectory. The prompt also includes placeholders for student id and context, allowing for dynamic insertion of student-specific information and course descriptions to further personalize the feedback.

```
"performance_scale": {{
                    "very_low": {{ "range": "0.0-0.2", "description": "Very low performance" }},
                    "low":      {{ "range": "0.2-0.4", "description": "Low performance" }},
                    "average":  {{ "range": "0.4-0.6", "description": "Average performance" }},
                    "good":     {{ "range": "0.6-0.8", "description": "Good performance" }},
                    "excellent":{{ "range": "0.8-1.0", "description": "Excellent performance" }}
                }},

                "course_components": {{
                    "live_attendance": {{
                        "type":        "dichotomous qualitative",
                        "weight":      5,
                        "description": "Live class attendance"
                    }},
                    "recorded_classes": {{
                        "type":        "mixed (dichotomous + video time)",
                        "weight":      5,
                        "description": "Recorded class attendance and viewing time"
                    }},
                    "quizzes": {{
                        "type":        "continuous quantitative",
                        "weight":      15,
                        "description": "Class test performance"
                    }},
                    "portfolio": {{
                        "type":        "mixed (qualitative feedback + quantitative scale)",
                        "weight":      35,
                        "description": "Portfolio deliverables performance"
                    }},
                    "industry_projects": {{
                        "type":        "evaluation",
                        "weight":      35,
                        "description": "Applied industry skills projects"
                    }},
                    "forum_participation": {{
                        "type":        "dichotomous qualitative",
                        "weight":      5,
                        "description": "Forum engagement"
                    }}
                }},
```

Figure A4. Definition of the performance scale and course components within the feedback prompt.

Moving into the more granular aspects of the prompt, Figure A4 details the performance_scale and course_components sections. The performance_scale establishes a detailed rubric for categorizing student performance, defining ranges from very_low to excellent and providing descriptive labels for each range. This scale enables the AI to contextualize student performance within predefined levels, ensuring consistent and interpretable feedback across different performance metrics. Concurrently, the course_components section meticulously outlines the key elements of student activity that are considered for feedback generation. This includes a comprehensive list of activities such as live_attendance, recorded_classes, quizzes, portfolio, industry_projects, and forum_participation. For each component, the prompt specifies its type, weight and description, allowing the AI to understand the nature and relative importance of each activity in the overall student assessment.

Figure A5 shows the required_analysis section of the prompt. This section is crucial as it dictates the specific queries and analytical tasks the AI is expected to perform. For each topic, the prompt defines a question that represents the student's potential inquiry (e.g., "How is my performance in the course, what percentages have I obtained in each category?" for overall_performance), and a focus that guides the AI's analytical approach (e.g., comprehensive analysis of all components). These initial topics cover a range of performance indicators, from holistic course performance to engagement in specific activities like forum discussions and class attendance, as well as performance in assessments like quizzes.

```
        "required_analysis": [
            {{
                "topic":       "overall_performance",
                "question":    "How is my performance in the course, what percentages have I obtained in each category?",
                "focus":       "comprehensive analysis of all components"
            }},
            {{
                "topic":       "forum_engagement",
                "question":    "How well am I participating in forum discussions?",
                "focus":       "quality and frequency of participation"
            }},
            {{
                "topic":       "class_participation",
                "question":    "How is my participation in live learning and pre-recorded classes?",
                "focus":       "attendance and engagement patterns"
            }},
            {{
                "topic":       "quiz_performance",
                "question":    "How are my quiz results?",
                "focus":       "assessment of test scores"
            }},
```

Figure A5. Initiation of the required analysis section and definitions for the analysis of overall performance.

A pivotal element of the prompt, and a key innovation of the AFS, is highlighted in Figure A6, the inclusion of success_prediction within the required_analysis section. This subsection explicitly integrates the predictive capabilities of the deep learning model into the feedback generation process. Notably, it includes an information field that dynamically injects the prediction outcome "Academy's AI prediction for the student is:". More importantly, it provides specific instruction on how to utilize this prediction: "Based on this prediction, adjust the tone of the feedback. [...] Ensure that the feedback aligns with the prediction outcome and provides actionable advice accordingly." This instruction is paramount, directing the AI to adapt its feedback tone based on whether the student is predicted to pass or fail, ensuring that the feedback is contextually relevant and appropriately supportive or encouraging.

```
            {{
                "topic":        "success_prediction",
                "information":  "Academy's AI prediction for the student is: {student['prediction_text']} (probability: {student['prediction_probability']:.2f}).",
                "instruction":  "Based on this prediction, adjust the tone of the feedback. "
                                "If the prediction is 'Fail', adopt a more encouraging and supportive tone, "
                                "emphasizing areas for improvement and offering concrete steps for the student to succeed. "
                                "If the prediction is 'Pass', maintain a positive and reinforcing tone, "
                                "highlighting strengths and encouraging continued good performance. "
                                "Ensure that the feedback aligns with the prediction outcome and provides actionable advice accordingly.",
                "focus":        "likelihood of course completion and tone adjustment (Modified focus)"
            }},
```

Figure A6. Definition of success prediction.

Continuing with the required_analysis section, Figure A7 presents the final analysis topic, improvement_areas, which prompts the AI to provide targeted improvement suggestions based on the student's data. Following this, the figure transitions into the response_requirements section, marking the shift from analysis directives to output specifications. This section begins by defining the format of the AI's response as JSON, ensuring structured and machine-readable output that can be easily integrated with other components of the AFS.

```
[ ]
                {{
                    "topic":    "improvement_areas",
                    "question": "Can you recommend which of these variables I should focus more on?",
                    "focus":    "targeted improvement suggestions"
                }}
            ],

            "response_requirements": {{
```

Figure A7. Definition of improvement_areas.

Finally, Figure A8 concludes the response_requirements section and the entire prompt structure. Within response_requirements, the style_elements subsection details specific stylistic guidelines for the AI's output. These include emojis ("Use contextually appropriate emojis reflecting performance levels"), movie_quotes ("End each response with relevant geek movie quotes that match the performance context"), and tone ("Encouraging and constructive while being honest about performance"). These style elements aim to enhance the feedback's engagement and motivational impact. The prompt concludes by specifying the data_context as All assessments are partial/preliminary, not final, setting the appropriate expectation for students regarding the provisional nature of the feedback. This comprehensive prompt, therefore, encapsulates all the necessary instructions for the OpenAI API to generate personalized, predictive, and actionable feedback within the AFS framework.

```
[ ]
                "format": "JSON",
                "style_elements": {{
                    "emojis":       "Use contextually appropriate emojis reflecting performance levels",
                    "movie_quotes": "End each response with relevant geek movie quotes that match the performance context",
                    "tone":         "Encouraging and constructive while being honest about performance"
                }},
                "data_context": "All assessments are partial/preliminary, not final"
            }}
        }}
    }},

    "student_data": {student},
    "response_format": {responses_str}
}}'''
)
```

Figure A8. Definition of response_requirements.

Appendix C. Resulting Student Notification: A Practical Instance

Having detailed the comprehensive structure and key components of the feedback generation prompt designed for the OpenAI API, it is crucial to understand how this prompt is applied within the AFS architecture, particularly in relation to the dual-API communication strategy. The OpenAI API, guided by the full prompt, is responsible for generating the detailed, comprehensive feedback reports accessed by students within the LCMS platform. Concurrently, a distinct, streamlined communication channel is utilized for weekly student notifications via WhatsApp. Figure A9 provides a visual representation of such a WhatsApp notification as received by a student, demonstrating a tangible, concise output of the AFS, designed as an engaging hook to direct students towards the LCMS for their full feedback report. The following paragraphs will analyze this example WhatsApp notification, highlighting how it, while concise, effectively embodies key personalized elements derived from the broader AFS framework and, ultimately, drives student engagement with the LCMS platform for more in-depth insights.

Figure A9. Feedback using Whatsapp. *Note.* Image translation: "If you want to know your performance in the program! We invite you to check the new report from our AI on the platform." Message translation: "Miguel, according to the AI Oracle your performance in tests is 63.91%. Wow! You have the power. If you want more details, visit the platform. P.S: May the Force be with you #AIpredictions. Artists who make Artists Academy by PolygonUs".

After receiving this message, the student can click to see a more complete version of the feedback on the platform. See Figure A10.

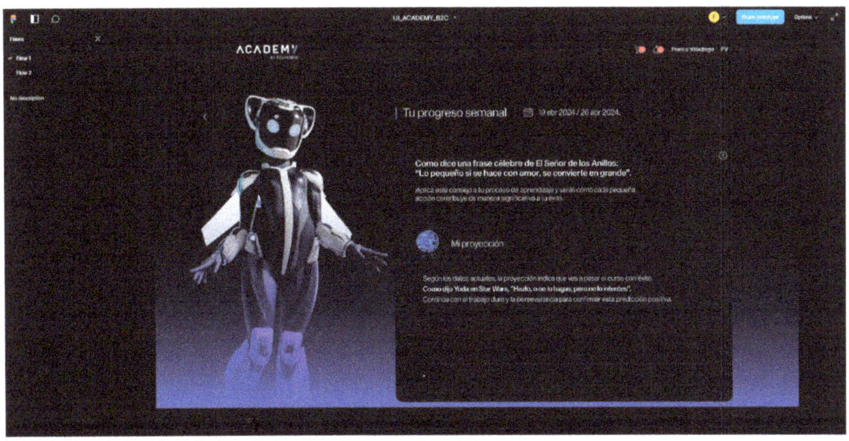

Figure A10. Feedback platform.

To further illustrate the practical application of the AFS feedback mechanism, consider the student experience within the LCMS platform upon accessing their weekly feedback report. Based on the comprehensive prompt and the student's data, the OpenAI API generates a detailed JSON output, which is then rendered in a user-friendly format within the LCMS. For instance, Miguel, upon logging into the platform, would find a Weekly Progress report clearly dated for the relevant week (19 April 2024/26 April 2024). The report opens with a motivational quote from *The Lord of the Rings*, setting an encouraging tone for self-reflection on their learning journey. Following this, Miguel would see a section dedicated to My Projection, where the system presents the AI-driven success prediction, stating "According to current data, the projection indicates that you will pass the course successfully", reinforced by a quote from Yoda from *Star Wars* to inspire perseverance. Beyond this overarching prediction, the detailed report would also provide feedback across specific performance areas. For overall_performance, Miguel would read an enthusiastic message highlighting his promising start to the week and solid percentages across categories, accompanied by rocket ship, chart, and graph emojis, and a quote from *The Hunger Games*. Similarly, for forum_engagement, class_participation, and quiz_performance, the report would present tailored feedback, each with relevant emojis and movie quotes from figures like Bruce Lee and movies like *Toy Story* and *Star Wars*, celebrating Miguel's strengths and encouraging continued engagement. Finally, even with a positive prediction, the report would offer improvement_areas, suggesting Miguel could further enhance his forum participation to diversify perspectives, ending with a quote from *The Lord of the Rings* emphasizing the impact of even small actions. This detailed feedback, presented within the LCMS, offers Miguel a holistic, personalized, and actionable overview of his performance, directly driven by the AFS methodology and designed to foster deeper engagement and learning.

References

1. Bozkurt, A.; Jung, I.; Xiao, F.; Vladimirschi, V.; Schuwer, R.; Егоров, Г.; Lambert, S.; Al-Freih, M.; Pete, J.; Olcott, D.; et al. A global outlook to the interruption of education due to COVID-19 pandemic: Navigating in a time of uncertainty and crisis. *Asian J. Distance Educ.* **2020**, *15*, 1–126.
2. Fabriz, S.; Mendzheritskaya, J.; Stehle, S. Impact of synchronous and asynchronous settings of online teaching and learning in higher education on students' learning experience during COVID-19. *Front. Psychol.* **2021**, *12*, 733554. [CrossRef]
3. Hussain, M.; Zhu, W.; Zhang, W.; Abidi, S.M.R. Student engagement predictions in an e-learning system and their impact on student course assessment scores. *Comput. Intell. Neurosci.* **2018**, *2018*, 6347186. [CrossRef] [PubMed]
4. Abuzinadah, N.; Umer, M.; Ishaq, A.; Al Hejaili, A.; Alsubai, S.; Eshmawi, A.A.; Mohamed, A.; Ashraf, I. Role of convolutional features and machine learning for predicting student academic performance from Moodle data. *PLoS ONE* **2023**, *18*, e0293061. [CrossRef]
5. Sajja, R.; Sermet, Y.; Cikmaz, M.; Cwiertny, D.; Demir, I. Artificial Intelligence-enabled intelligent assistant for personalized and adaptive learning in higher education. *arXiv* **2023**, arXiv:2309.10892. [CrossRef]
6. Hattie, J.; Timperley, H. The power of feedback. *Rev. Educ. Res.* **2007**, *77*, 81–112. [CrossRef]
7. Aleven, V.; McLaren, B.M.; Sewall, J.; Koedinger, K.R. Example-tracing tutoring: A cognitive tutor for geometry proof. *Int. J. Artif. Intell. Educ.* **2017**, *27*, 270–304.
8. Baker, R.S.; Corbett, A.T.; Koedinger, K.R. Detecting student learning disengagement during mathematics tutoring with educational data mining. In *International Conference on User Modeling, Adaptation, and Personalization*; Springer: Berlin/Heidelberg, Germany, 2007; pp. 125–134.
9. VanLehn, K. The relative effectiveness of human tutoring, intelligent tutoring systems, and other tutoring systems. *Educ. Psychol.* **2011**, *46*, 197–221. [CrossRef]
10. Anderson, J.R.; Boyle, C.F.; Reiser, B.J. Intelligent tutoring systems. *Science* **1985**, *228*, 456–462. [CrossRef]
11. Wang, X.; Gao, Y.; Passonneau, R. SciBench: Evaluating college-level scientific problem-solving abilities of large language models. *arXiv* **2023**, arXiv:2307.10635.
12. Messer, M.; Brown, N.C.C.; Kölling, M.; Shi, M. Automated grading and feedback tools for programming education: A systematic review. *ACM Trans. Comput. Educ.* **2024**, *24*, 1–43. [CrossRef]

13. Meyer, J.; Jansen, T.; Schiller, R.; Liebenow, L.W.; Steinbach, M.; Horbach, A.; Fleckenstein, J. Using LLMs to bring evidence-based feedback into the classroom: AI-generated feedback increases secondary students' text revision, motivation, and positive emotions. *Comput. Educ. Artif. Intell.* **2024**, *6*, 100199. [CrossRef]
14. Li Wang, X.; Chen, X.; Wang, C.; Xu, L.; Shadiev, R.; Li, Y. ChatGPT's capabilities in providing feedback on undergraduate students' argumentation: A case study. *Think. Ski. Creat.* **2024**, *51*, 101440. [CrossRef]
15. Alnasyan, B.; Basheri, M.; Alassafi, M. The power of deep learning techniques for predicting student performance in virtual learning environments: A systematic literature review. *Comput. Educ. Artif. Intell.* **2024**, *6*, 100231. [CrossRef]
16. Hellas, A.; Leinonen, J.; Sarsa, S.; Koutcheme, C.; Kujanpää, L.; Sorva, J. Exploring the responses of large language models to beginner programmers' help requests. In Proceedings of the ACM Conference on International Computing Education Research, Chicago, IL, USA, 8–10 August 2023; ACM: Chicago, IL, USA, 2023; pp. 310–327. [CrossRef]
17. Shaikh, O.; Zhang, H.; Held, W.; Bernstein, M.; Yang, D. Sentiment analysis in the era of large language models: A reality check. *arXiv* **2023**, arXiv:2305.15005. [CrossRef]
18. Golchin, S.; Garuda, N.; Impey, C.; Wenger, M. Large language models as MOOCs graders. *arXiv* **2024**, arXiv:2402.03776. [CrossRef]
19. Extance, A. ChatGPT is shaping the future of education, but will it improve equity? *Nature* **2023**, *623*, 474–477. [CrossRef]
20. UNESCO. *Guidance for Generative AI in Education and Research*; United Nations Educational, Scientific and Cultural Organization: Paris, France, 2023. Available online: https://unesdoc.unesco.org/ark:/48223/pf0000389227 (accessed on 26 March 2025).
21. Lund, B.D.; Wang, T.; Mannuru, N.R.; Nie, B.; Shimray, S.; Wang, Z. ChatGPT and a new academic reality: AI-written research papers and the ethics of the large language models in scholarly publishing. *J. Assoc. Inf. Sci. Technol.* **2023**, *74*, 570–581. [CrossRef]
22. Farrokhnia, M.; Banihashem, S.K.; Noroozi, O.; Wals, A. A SWOT analysis of ChatGPT: Implications for educational practice and research. *Innov. Educ. Teach. Int.* **2023**, *61*, 460–474. [CrossRef]
23. Jeon, J.; Lee, S. Large language models in education: A focus on the complementary relationship between human teachers and ChatGPT. *Educ. Inf. Technol.* **2023**, *28*, 15873–15892. [CrossRef]
24. Bender, E.M.; Gebru, T.; McMillan-Major, A.; Shmitchell, S. On the dangers of stochastic parrots: Can language models be too big? In *Proceedings of the FAccT' 21: 2021 ACM Conference on Fairness, Accountability, and Transparency, Toronto, Canada, 3–10 March 2021*; Association for Computing Machinery: New York, NY, USA, 2021. [CrossRef]
25. Vygotsky, L.S. *Mind in Society: The Development of Higher Psychological Processes*; Harvard University Press: Cambridge, MA, USA, 1978.
26. Lipton, Z.C. The mythos of model interpretability. *Commun. ACM* **2018**, *61*, 36–43. [CrossRef]

Multimodal Technologies and Interaction

MDPI

Article

Designing Inclusive and Adaptive Content in Moodle: A Framework and a Case Study from Jordanian Higher Education

Lamis F. Al-Qora'n [1,*], Julius T. Nganji [2,*] and Fadi M. Alsuhimat [3]

1 Department of Software Engineering, Philadelphia University, Amman 19392, Jordan
2 Department of Occupational Science and Occupational Therapy, University of Toronto, 160-500 University Ave, Toronto, ON M5G 1V7, Canada
3 Department of Artificial Intelligence, Philadelphia University, Amman 19392, Jordan; fshimat@philadelphia.edu.jo
* Correspondence: lalqoran@philadelphia.edu.jo (L.F.A.-Q.); j.nganji@utoronto.ca (J.T.N.)

Abstract: Blended learning has introduced a more accessible and flexible teaching environment in higher education. However, ensuring that content is inclusive, particularly for students with learning difficulties, remains a challenge. This paper explores how Moodle, a widely adopted learning management system (LMS), can support inclusive and adaptive learning based on Universal Design for Learning (UDL) principles. A 16-week descriptive exploratory study was conducted with 70 undergraduate students during a software engineering fundamentals course at Philadelphia University in Jordan. The research combined weekly iterative focus groups, teaching reflections, and interviews with 16 educators to identify and address inclusion barriers. The findings highlight that the students responded positively to features such as conditional activities, flexible quizzes, and multimodal content. A UDL-based framework was developed to guide the design of inclusive Moodle content, and it was validated by experienced educators. To our knowledge, this is the first UDL-based framework designed for Moodle in Middle Eastern computing and engineering education. The findings indicate that Moodle features, such as conditional activities and flexible deadlines, can facilitate inclusive practices, but adoption remains hindered by institutional and workload constraints. This study contributes a replicable design model for inclusive blended learning and emphasizes the need for structured training, intentional course planning, and technological support for implementing inclusivity in blended learning environments. Moreover, this study provides a novel weekly iterative focus group methodology, which enables continuous course refinement based on evolving students' feedback. Future work will look into generalizing the research findings and transferring the findings to other contexts. It will also explore AI-driven adaptive learning pathways within LMS platforms. This is an empirical study grounded in weekly student focus groups, educator interviews, and reflective teaching practice, offering evidence-based insights on the application of UDL in a real-world higher education setting.

Keywords: inclusive blended learning; Moodle; learning management system; universal design for learning; educational technology; students with disabilities; higher education; flipped classroom model

1. Introduction

Information technologies have evolved dramatically in the last few decades, making many changes in our lives. Education is one of the domains that has been significantly impacted. With this rapid change, higher education institutions started integrating technologies such as e-learning and mobile learning into their systems [1,2].

E-learning implies delivering educational content and services through digital technologies, either fully online or blended. Blended learning is an ideal solution for improving the quality of learning, and it is increasingly used in higher education [3]. It integrates face-to-face teaching with online learning, which fosters a supportive and interactive environment that encourages students to participate and reduces anxiety around making mistakes [2].

Learning management systems (LMSs) play a vital role in education when using fully online and blended learning teaching models. Higher education institutions adopted LMSs like Modular Object-Oriented Dynamic Learning Environment (Moodle) [4] and Blackboard to facilitate the learning and teaching process. Moodle enables lecturers to monitor the automated log reports, which show when students have completed their assignments and the time spent on the quiz or the assignment, monitor forums, and facilitate course management. This introduced many benefits; however, it also introduced many challenges specifically related to content development, the suitability of the content delivered to students, and the inclusion of all students, without leaving some of them behind. However, while LMSs are widely spread and adopted, few studies focus on how such platforms support inclusivity and adaptivity in blended learning environments [5,6].

A key principle of modern educational systems that aims to guarantee fair chances for all students while taking into account their various needs is inclusive education [7]. A significant portion of all higher education institutions have students with learning difficulties, and when creating online educational content, educators should consider these students' needs through user-friendly design and adaptive tools that have the potential to create an effective learning environment.

The use of blended learning to enhance teaching and learning has been the subject of many previous studies, but few studies have examined how educational technology employed for blended learning may be utilized to foster inclusion in these settings. A review by [8] identified that studies on blended learning focus on understanding and outcomes of blended learning rather than on inclusivity of the used tools. Furthermore, ref. [9] identified that UDL and assistive technologies require more research in the context of blended learning. From our review of the literature, we have noticed that within the higher education context, most research focuses on aspects other than inclusivity. To contribute to bridging the gap in the literature, in this paper, we evaluate Moodle (the official LMS used at Philadelphia University) for its suitability for delivering inclusive and adaptive content to students in a blended learning environment. Thus, our paper aims to answer the following research questions:

1. How can Moodle be used to support inclusive and accessible learning experiences for students with diverse needs and challenges in blended learning environments?
2. What are the available features in Moodle that can promote inclusive and adaptive blended learning?
3. How is the role of Moodle in inclusive blended learning perceived by educators in Jordanian higher education institutions?
4. What are the challenges in investing in Moodle for achieving inclusive education, and how to deal with such challenges?

A descriptive exploratory investigation incorporating primary and secondary data was used to answer our research questions. Following that, we developed an inclusive and adaptive learning UDL-based framework, which was also evaluated by some educators through interviews. Our framework can help evaluate the capacity of any LMS to provide inclusive and adaptable material. We addressed the gap in the literature on inclusive digital learning environments, as, to the best of our knowledge, this framework is the first UDL-based framework that is explicitly designed for use with Moodle in computing and engineering sciences in the Middle East. Furthermore, the weekly iterative focus group model was designed and employed by the first author which enabled real-time responsiveness to students' feedback. This supported continuous improvements of the course content throughout the semester. Unlike speculative or conceptual studies, our investigation is grounded in empirical data collected throughout the semester from iterative student focus groups, educator interviews, and the first author's teaching reflections. These sources were used to systematically evaluate and adapt course content to support inclusivity and accessibility. The utilized "Fundamentals of Software Engineering" course followed a flipped classroom model, where students first engage with new material via two in-person lectures, followed by asynchronous engagement utilizing videos and assignments on Moodle. These videos and assignments are central to learning and assessment and not supplementary; they provide new material that help to deepen conceptual understanding. Thus, this paper contributes to the field by documenting a real-world implementation and a practice-based case study of inclusive and adaptive course design in an undergraduate software engineering course. We integrated the UDL principles into weekly teaching materials, assessment, and student engagement strategies.

The remainder of the paper is organized as follows: The literature review and research background are presented in Section 2. The research methodology is described in Section 3. Results are provided in Section 4 and discussed in Section 5. Conclusions, recommendations, and future work are presented in Section 6.

2. Literature Review and Research Background

Section 2 reviews the literature and the research background relevant to this study. It is structured into three subsections. Section 2.1 introduces the concept of blended learning, its models, and benefits in higher education. Section 2.2 explores alternative learning environments, focusing on Moodle as a LMS that supports adaptive learning. Section 2.3 discusses the UDL framework and its application in inclusive education, particularly in technology-supported contexts. Thus, the section provides a comprehensive foundation for understanding the study's focus on designing inclusive and adaptive content in Moodle.

2.1. Blended Learning and Blended Learning Models

Blended learning combines face-to-face and online learning, as shown in Figure 1. The use of blended learning is increasing among higher education institutions around the world because of its benefits in combining traditional and online teaching methods [10–12]. Blended learning brought many models that incorporate in-person and online learning, which may greatly improve the learning process, personalize learning, enhance students' learning engagement, and improve students' experience [13,14]. Therefore, employing blended learning facilitates students' commitment and engagement in the learning process by shifting educators' attention from teaching to learning [15].

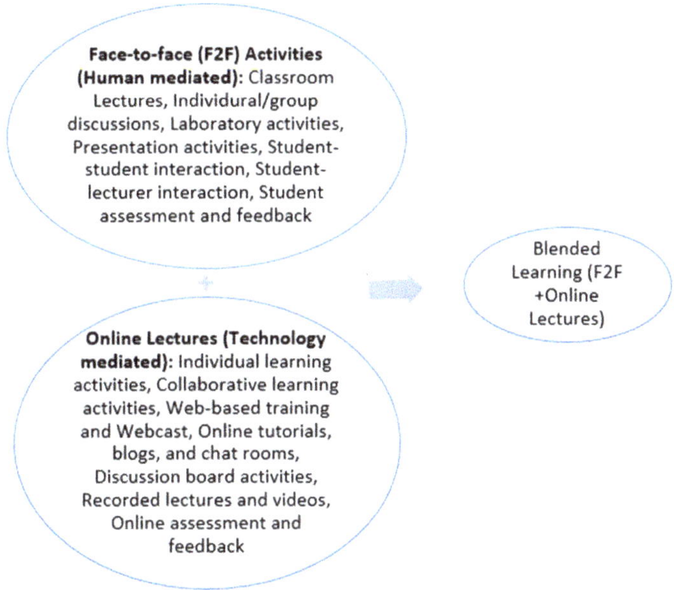

Figure 1. Blended learning concept [16].

According to [11], blended learning is the most promising teaching strategy for the future. Poon [11] ensured that emphasis should be on how to successfully apply it so that its advantages may be achieved. By combining face-to-face and online learning, this approach enables educators to meet pedagogical goals related to student skill development and improve their teaching qualities [17].

Blended learning has various initiatives that combine 30% of face-to-face interaction with 70% of IT-mediated learning [18]. In the same way, ref. [19] recommended integrating 20% face-to-face teaching with 80% online learning for successful blended learning. Thus, blended learning has many approaches and delivery models.

Personalized learning plays a critical role in transferring the focus of higher education from a teacher-centred environment to a learner-centred environment [20]. In their study, the authors of [21] highlighted the importance of personalized learning in reducing the gaps in learning and practices among students and helping to enhance students' skills. This aligns with the objectives of blended learning as it enhances personalization and promotes the growth of self-directed learning, which boosts communication between learners and educators as well as amongst learners [22].

Blended learning facilitates access to online resources that provide opportunities for professional collaboration and enhance the adaptability of lectures [23,24]. It also provides students with skills to study at their own pace [25]. However, it faces some challenges, such as insufficient professional development, limited technical resources, and inadequate internet connections [12].

The flipped classroom model is a widely studied form of blended learning in which students engage with instructional content independently (often via videos or readings) before participating in interactive, face-to-face sessions that focus on problem-solving, discussion, or application [26]. This model has been shown to promote active learning, improve student engagement, and allow for differentiated instruction [27,28]. In the context of higher education, flipped learning has also been associated with better academic performance and increased learner autonomy [29]. Our course design adopts this approach and further adapts it using UDL principles to ensure accessibility and inclusivity for students with diverse learning needs.

2.2. Alternative Learning Environments to Traditional Classrooms in Education

Online systems were found to have the capacity to provide platforms with competitive practices that offer alternatives to real-life educational settings, which support students' learning and improve the quality of learning [30]. Among these systems, Moodle was and still is one of the most popular learning management platforms because of its flexibility as an open source and cost-effectiveness. However, these systems have affected learning environments and teaching pedagogies [31].

Adaptive learning aims to provide learners with the tools they need to learn based on their particular cognitive characteristics and needs [6]. The authors of [6] also added that it is crucial to consider the learners' current level of knowledge as well as individual demands and variations in learning styles. Moodle is one of the tools for implementing adaptive learning. Although it is not inherently adaptive, it is possible to design adaptive activities within Moodle. It offers a variety of adaptive learning solutions, allowing educators the resources they need to support learners at every step of the learning process, from content delivery to assessment [6]. For example, the authors of [6] demonstrated how Moodle is used at Borys Grinchenko Kyiv University and, therefore, how Ukrainian higher education institutions utilized Moodle to implement adaptive learning through the conditional release of content, role-based access, and analytics-informed decisions. Similarly, ref. [4] noted that Moodle's flexibility fosters a more student-centered learning environment when appropriately configured.

Furthermore, a study by [3] at Misr University for Science and Technology (MUST) demonstrated that Moodle-based blended learning has the potential to significantly improve university students' writing performance. This ensures that the design features of Moodle allow for iterative feedback, tracking, and multimodal input. In other words, such design features are consistent and important to inclusive and adaptive pedagogy.

Thus, Moodle does not have automated tailored content; therefore, it is not inherently adaptive. The platform supports teacher-driven adaptivity, which is equally critical in real-time blended learning environments. Such capability aligns with UDL's principles of providing multiple means of representation, action, and engagement. Thus, there is a need for further investigation and empirical evaluation.

2.3. Universal Design for Learning (UDL) and Inclusive Learning

To accommodate the various needs of students, the Centre for Applied Special Technology (CAST) originally proposed UDL in the 1990s [32]. By using UDL, all students may benefit from an inclusive and accessible learning environment [33,34]. The objective of lesson planning from a UDL viewpoint is to replace the "one size fits all" teaching approach that is based on an imagined "standard learner" with an already accessible curriculum that takes into account the individual differences among all students [35]. This variation is a reflection of the three brain networks that are involved in learning: (1) the recognition networks that are involved in understanding and interpretation of environmental information; (2) the strategic networks that are in charge of organizing and planning skills and procedures; and (3) the affective networks that have an impact on learner motivation and engagement [35]. The core concept of UDL is the idea that these three learning networks should be addressed with flexible solutions. These three aspects are demonstrated in practice through standards and assessments that motivate educators to offer various channels for representation, communication, behavior, and engaging students in different activities [33,34].

Many research studies have confirmed that UDL may be used in a wide range of educational levels, from young children [36] to students with special education needs [37,38], students who do not have special educational needs [39,40], and even university students [41].

Thus, UDL has been found by researchers to have a positive effect at different educational levels. This framework promotes the structured development of instructional environments that effectively address the diverse needs of an increasingly diverse student population in online education contexts [42]. This paper utilizes UDL in the proposed framework and applies UDL principles to achieve inclusivity in the blended learning environment.

Many studies have explored Moodle's technical capabilities and its general pedagogical utility [4,13]. Recent studies have also explored intelligent adaptations within Moodle environments. For instance, ref. [43] proposed an unobtrusive method to model learners' personalities using learning analytics and Bayesian networks in an intelligent Moodle (iMoodle) system, showing promising results in predicting personality dimensions and therefore enhancing the personalization of learning experiences.

It can be seen that few studies have explored how Moodle's features can be systematically aligned with UDL principles to meet diverse learners' needs in real classroom settings. This observation is supported by [6], who note that most applications of adaptive learning in Moodle remain manual and lack standardized evaluation frameworks grounded in UDL.

Recent studies have also evaluated Moodle's effectiveness in supporting accessibility and usability for learners with difficulties. Thus, the Moodle platform has been analyzed in different distribution versions regarding accessibility and compliance with standards [44,45]. Since then, the scope of evaluation has evolved from basic accessibility checks to broader usability studies, examining how well Moodle accommodates user satisfaction, navigation, and content interaction for students with functional diversity. For example, ref. [46] conducted a comprehensive usability study of Moodle for students with functional diversity. Their work assessed how well Moodle met accessibility standards and user needs. They focused on user satisfaction, navigation, and functional adaptation.

However, while these studies provide essential technical insights, they often do not engage with UDL-based instructional design or propose comprehensive frameworks for content adaptation that address learner variability. Such studies provide valuable insights into the user experience of learners with special needs; however, they do not provide actual design frameworks for adapting learning content itself. Our study attempts to bridge this gap by proposing a structured approach to designing both inclusive and adaptive Moodle content tailored to student diversity in higher education, especially within the Arab educational context. This is because the existing literature is dominated by studies conducted in Western or East Asian contexts, while empirical investigations from the Middle East, and Jordan in particular, remain under-represented. Given the increasing reliance on blended learning in Jordanian higher education, this geographic and methodological gap highlights the urgent need for context-specific studies that evaluate the use of Moodle for inclusive education through structured, field-based methodologies.

Our review of the literature has shown that there is a growing adoption of LMS in higher education. However, there is limited empirical research that evaluates how Moodle supports inclusivity and adaptivity from a UDL perspective. The authors of [47] specified that when selecting strategies to implement UDL, it is advisable to introduce its principles gradually—beginning with the replacement of less effective activities—to maintain enthusiasm and engagement among both students and teachers.

Our paper addresses this gap by systematically analyzing Moodle's features in a real teaching environment using focus groups, reflective practices, and educator interviews, aiming to uncover how Moodle can be operationalized as an adaptive and inclusive platform that supports all learners. We propose a framework for designing inclusive and adaptive Moodle content. Our framework is informed by actual classroom experience and feedback from both students and educators. The framework is then utilized to evaluate Moodle for inclusivity and adaptivity.

3. Research Methodology

3.1. Research Design

We adopted a descriptive exploratory qualitative design to investigate how Moodle can be utilized to achieve inclusive and adaptive learning in the context of higher education in Jordan. Such descriptive exploratory design is suitable for this unexplored area of educational technology where the goal is to understand a phenomenon from participants' perspectives to generate a framework [48]. Figure 2 shows the research design approach, which incorporates reflective and thematic analysis, content analysis of course design, and thematic analysis of educators' and students' feedback. This multi-method qualitative approach allows for triangulation across different sources, which enriches the context and increases its depth and flexibility [49].

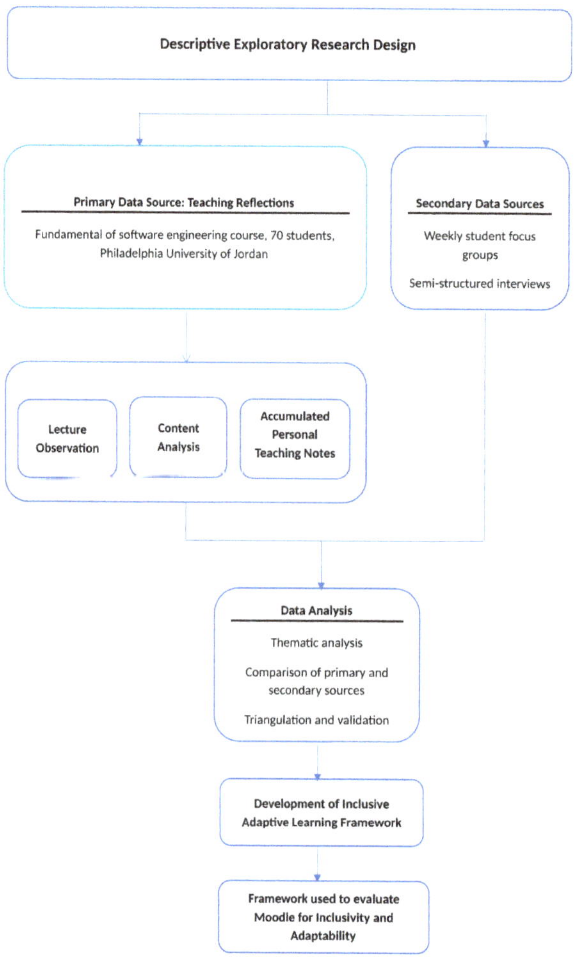

Figure 2. Descriptive exploratory qualitative design.

Reflective analysis of the first author's teaching experiences was a key component. Reflection is considered a valid method in practice-based educational research, as reported by [50]. Furthermore, it is considered valid and insightful when specifically exploring inclusive pedagogies [51].

3.2. Data Collection and Participants

Table 1 shows the details of the participants involved in the study, including demographics and experience. The "Fundamentals of Software Engineering" course is a second-semester course taught to first-year undergraduate students in the Software Engineering department. During the academic year 2024/2025, 70 students were enrolled in this course, which was delivered in two parallel sections: Section 1, with 42 students, and Section 2, with 28 students. Both sections followed the same curriculum and were taught by the same lecturer, utilizing identical teaching methods, Moodle resources, and assessment strategies. Therefore, the 70 students enrolled in the course and participated in the weekly focus groups described in this study. On the other hand, educators' perspectives were gathered from both Philadelphia University and the University of Jordan as another Jordanian university in which Moodle is used as well, student data were limited to the course implementation only. The first author, with extensive experience in inclusive and blended learning design, delivered the course and led the weekly focus groups. The second author, a recognized expert in inclusive education, validated the instructional strategies and methodological framework to ensure their alignment with UDL principles. While a cross-institutional student comparison could be pursued in future work, this study aimed to provide a grounded, empirically supported investigation into inclusive blended learning practices within Jordanian universities settings. We selected educators who are familiar with Moodle and who delivered courses utilizing a blended learning approach. We employed purposeful sampling to ensure relevant experience with blended learning and Moodle [52]. Multiple sources were combined to enable methodological triangulation and to improve credibility, reliability, and scientific accuracy of our results [53].

Table 1. Participant demographics and experience.

Group	Number	Gender (M/F)	Years of Experience	Notes
BSc Students	70	43 M and 27 F	N/A	Enrolled in software engineering course
Educators	16	9 M and 7 F	4–17 years	Across two Jordanian higher education institutions

3.2.1. Primary Sources: Teaching Reflections and Observations

We utilized the first author's accumulated personal teaching notes, content analysis, forum observations, and reflections recorded during teaching and assignment delivery. These reflections provided first-hand insights into how students engaged with the Moodle environment and how different learning materials and tools were received. The lecture observations and forum monitoring offered real-time insights into student behavior and classroom dynamics.

Furthermore, the content analysis enabled us to evaluate the inclusivity and adaptability of the course design by examining recurring expressions related to perceived accessibility, flexibility, clarity, and emotional support. These observations were systematically mapped to the UDL framework—specifically, the principles of providing multiple means of representation, engagement, and expression [3]. Coding and organizing the data was undertaken manually in a careful manner, which allowed patterns to emerge. This indicated the degree to which Moodle-supported elements aligned with inclusive teaching practices.

This approach aligns with an autoethnographic method, where personal experience is systematically analyzed to understand broader cultural and pedagogical phenomena [54]. This autoethnographic and observational data have the potential to help uncover real-time dynamics in inclusive teaching [54].

3.2.2. Secondary Sources: Student and Educator Feedback

To complement the primary data collected through structured teaching reflections, we systematically gathered additional qualitative data through weekly student focus groups and interviews with educators. We conducted both feedback processes through a rigorous approach; however, we consider them to be secondary sources in the context of our study because their primary role was to support and validate the insights drawn from the teaching reflections. This section summarizes the key themes that emerged from these supplementary sources.

1. Weekly Student Focus Groups

We need student input from different kinds of learners to determine to what level Moodle has facilitated, or was an obstacle to, their learning experience. The focus groups involved open-ended interviews with students and were conducted to obtain a more in-depth analysis of the findings. Utilizing focus groups helped us to collect direct student feedback on the approach used for blended learning.

We conducted a focus group session of 15 min every week after the first face-to-face lecture to investigate students' views and experiences with respect to each weekly designed piece of content. The focus groups were conducted in the classroom. The focus group sessions focused on obtaining student feedback on the content.

Students' responses were used to build a solution that mitigates the challenges, which was then evaluated using the next weekly focus group. We believe that undertaking weekly, short, interactive brainstorming sessions is better than one-time surveys or interviews. This is because we can track the changes in how our students perceive the content and the approach over time. Moreover, iterative enhancements in delivering the content are enabled, which allows us to evaluate and compare different models and to identify the challenges in comprehending the content and the approach. Additionally, this enables us to understand and evaluate to what extent the assignment provided can support different learning needs. We were able to notice and monitor those students who were struggling and to plan group work with a view to engaging all students who were not able to finish the tasks on an individual basis. Having weekly focus group sessions provided continuous dynamic feedback, which allowed us to make refinements on both course content and delivery to meet students' needs. Using this approach allowed us to monitor changes in student perceptions, which has the potential to provide a clearer picture of how inclusive practices were understood.

Furthermore, such planned group work enabled a reduction in missed deadlines, where we noticed decreased late submissions. Also, with respect to completion rates, we noticed improvement in comparison with the previous scenario of failing to submit individual assignments.

Concerning students' satisfaction, during the iterative focus groups, students expressed their satisfaction and confidence in the lecturer's support throughout the learning process.

Our focus groups involved 70 registered students, as explained previously. All students voluntarily participated, wherein their participation was considered a normal course interaction process to improve the blended learning content and approach, and they were told that their feedback would not affect their marks; it was only to enhance the content. By conducting these weekly focus groups, we were able to tailor content format, collaborative opportunities, and engagement. We did not record these discussions to encourage open, interactive discussions; however, the first author, who is the lecturer, documented the notes for later thematic analysis. Thus, using these focus groups helped us to encourage all students to participate in designing inclusive content.

Thus, to systematically analyze how Moodle supported inclusion and accessibility, students' feedback during the focus groups was thematically coded in light of the UDL framework. Particularly, we examined their input in relation to key UDL principles, such as providing multiple means of representation (e.g., multimedia content), action, expression (e.g., flexible deadlines and group submissions), and engagement (e.g., emotional support via messaging and feedback). This mapping allowed us to identify patterns on how different learners—specifically those who reported struggles with workload, digital access, or learning pace—experienced the course design. Although we did not explicitly organize student groups based on diagnosed learning difficulties, our approach captured and addressed a wide spectrum of accessibility needs as they emerged organically from classroom interactions.

2. Educator Interviews

The educator interview method was selected to address the second and third research questions regarding Moodle's support of inclusivity and adaptability. Furthermore, we investigated how design strategies align with inclusive pedagogical frameworks through interviews. Thus, we conducted 16 interviews with educators to evaluate their understanding of inclusive blended learning and their familiarity and perceptions regarding Moodle's features to support diverse learners- interview questions are shown in Appendix A. Moreover, we discussed the challenges that educators face in familiarizing themselves with such tools and the challenges that hinder achieving inclusive blended learning in higher education. The 16 educators interviewed in this study were not involved in teaching or managing the specific course under investigation. Instead, they were selected based on their expertise in inclusive education and their experience using Moodle or similar LMS platforms in Jordanian higher education. Their feedback was used to validate the inclusive teaching strategies applied by the first author and to provide broader insights that informed the framework presented in this study.

We used semi-structured interviews to collect qualitative insights from educators, as interviews allow deeper investigation of educators' observations. Moreover, interviews provide educators with the flexibility to elaborate on the challenges and solutions they have faced. This can provide first-hand insights into the perceptions of inclusive blended learning among educators in Jordanian higher education. Therefore, utilizing semi-structured interviews complemented students' feedback from the focus groups and gave sufficient secondary data. Thus, the analysis of the interviews was critical for triangulating students' perspectives and content analysis.

The interviewed educators were from two higher education institutions (eight from Philadelphia University and eight from the University of Jordan). All educators have experience with blended learning as they were chosen after making sure that all of them have delivered a blended learning course at least two times. We also ensured that the interviewed educators knew the basics of inclusivity in teaching.

We invited educators for the interviews and selected the 16 interviewees to ensure diversity in disciplines and backgrounds, opting not to focus on the faculty of information technology. All the participants voluntarily participated in the interviews, which were conducted openly, ensuring that the interviewees felt comfortable during the interviews so as to encourage honest feedback.

Each semi-structured interview was conducted face-to-face, with each interview ranging from 20 to 30 min in length. We first asked about the educators' understanding of inclusive and adaptive blended learning. Then, we asked about the familiarity of the tools that enable inclusive and adaptive learning in Moodle. Finally, we asked about the challenges that they faced while integrating Moodle for inclusive and adaptive learning.

We took notes during the interviews and promptly summarized them at the end of each session. Ten of the participants chose not to allow the interview to be recorded, while six of them agreed to have audio recordings and transcripts created for the interviews. For those ten who rejected the recording, we relied on note-taking.

To conclude, our research explored the challenges, experiences, and adaptive strategies related to inclusive education in a blended learning environment. Weekly focus groups provided flexibility for exploring students' and educators' experience with Moodle in depth. We chose this qualitative approach over a quantitative one to obtain rich, context-sensitive insights into how inclusion and adaptability were implemented and experienced throughout the course.

3.3. Data Analysis

We employed thematic analysis [55,56] to analyze the results from teaching reflections, content analysis, and classroom observations. The first author summarized the weekly teaching reflections to identify the recurring challenges. The second author's experience in inclusive learning was used to revise the challenges and to identify the Moodle content features that help to achieve inclusivity. We coded the features of Moodle that help to achieve adaptive and inclusive learning based on students' engagement levels.

We also utilized thematic analysis to specify the recurring themes in students' feedback. We selected this approach because it is flexible and suitable for exploring the research questions related to inclusion and adaptivity. The key insights were documented immediately after each brainstorming session to avoid recall bias, where the focus was to identify student engagement trends, to specify the challenges faced while completing the assignments and quizzes, and finally, to collect suggestions for improvements to achieve inclusivity.

We started by familiarizing ourselves through repeated readings of the transcripts and reflective notes. An inductive approach was utilized to generate the initial codes, guided by concepts from the UDL framework. The coding process was conducted in three phases: (1) open coding to capture meaningful data segments; (2) axial coding to group related codes; and (3) theme development and refinement to identify higher-level patterns.

Themes were identified based on frequency and relevance to the research questions. We collaborated to review and refine the themes. Having many discussions between the researchers ensured internal coherence and analytical clarity. This iterative process ensured that the resulting themes accurately represented participants' experiences and aligned with the study's focus on inclusive and adaptive learning practices in Moodle-based blended learning environments.

We compared the recurring themes across multiple weeks to monitor how they change over time and to ensure consistent feedback, which assures the validity of our study.

After completing the analysis, we specified the following themes: content-related challenges, accessibility-related challenges, and technical difficulties.

We used thematic analysis to identify the themes in educators' responses during the interviews. We transcribed and summarized the key points after each interview; then, we performed the initial coding and specified the major themes as awareness of inclusive adaptive learning principles, challenges in engaging Moodle for inclusive and adaptive learning, identifying the barriers to achieving inclusivity, and finally, the recommendations to achieve inclusivity in blended learning.

3.4. Triangulation Strategy

We then specified the frequency of each issue and the shared concerns among participants. After that, we compared the results with students' feedback to specify the gaps between educators' approaches and students' needs. We ensured different perspectives by including educators from various disciplines who have different levels of expertise in using Moodle. We adopted a methodological triangulation strategy by collecting and analyzing data from different primary sources to ensure consistency, reliability, and greater accuracy [53]. Weekly student reflections and focus group transcripts, the first author's autoethnographic teaching notes and observations, and semi-structured interviews with educators were the main sources used. Following this approach and drawing on these resources allows us to compare different perspectives on how Moodle facilitated inclusive and adaptive learning in a blended learning environment.

We followed the triangulation protocol established by [57], starting by sorting and separating the data. Then, convergence coding was used to compare the findings in terms of the meaning and interpretation of themes. Later, convergence assessment was accomplished, followed by completeness assessment. Finally, research comparison and feedback were conducted to finish the triangulation process.

For the secondary data, we also cross-checked educators' responses with student feedback and content analysis to ensure validity. Utilizing qualitative methods provided us with rich, contextual data that cannot be obtained through quantitative methods such as surveys.

3.5. Fundamentals of Software Engineering Course

In Jordanian higher education institutions, the academic year begins with the first semester (Fall), which runs from October to February, followed by the second semester (Spring), which runs from March to July. According to the academic study plan, the "Fundamentals of Software Engineering" course is typically undertaken by students in their second semester of study (i.e., in the spring semester of their first year). However, students may register for the course in either semester depending on course availability. In the case examined in this study, the course was delivered during the first semester of the 2024/2025 academic year, from October 2024 to February 2025. The course is delivered by the first author to the first-year students in their second semester. The blended learning (BL) model is used to deliver the course. Every course at Philadelphia University of Jordan follows the blended learning approach and incorporates the flipped classroom model as a core strategy. The course is taught utilizing two face-to-face, 50-min-long lectures per week for 16 weeks in addition to three short videos and a short assignment every week. The short videos were not presented during the face-to-face sessions; rather, they were made available to students on Moodle, where they could be accessed independently at home as part of the blended learning model. We followed the proposed framework for inclusive and adaptive content to ensure the inclusivity and adaptability of our course. Our course is designed and delivered based on this pedagogical framework. Thus, every face-to-face lecture has its goals, and every weekly video has its own goals where the learning outcomes are measured through solving problem-based assignments. Students acquire core concepts during the face-to-face lectures. They are then required to watch three videos to complete the individual problem-solving assignments. Students were informed of the goals and skills that they had to learn before starting with the videos and the assignment. Offering these videos ensures that students have the relevant resources, and providing students with special educational challenges with specific materials and occasionally having group assignments instead of individual assignments sometimes helps students to overcome the difficulties they face due to their special educational needs. The availability of the teacher for such students and the flexibility of asking questions made

Moodle a suitable environment for inclusion in the blended learning model. It enhanced the collaboration between the lecturer and the students. Although in-person lectures accounted for the greater proportion of the instructional time (approximately 65%), the online content served as the primary source of new material, assignments, and student engagement. This aligns with flipped learning principles, where the online component initiates learning and classroom time is used to consolidate knowledge.

In [58], the authors emphasized the significance of evaluating current learning settings for appropriateness and taking into account the requirements of students with various impairments. Therefore, we systematically reviewed and analyzed the course materials for clarity, inclusivity, accessibility of the content, and their suitability for diverse students' needs. Thus, it was evaluated for the inclusivity of multimedia materials and the ease of navigation. We evaluated the content for readability (color contrast, font size, etc.), multimodal learning support (alternative formats, availability of transcripts, etc.), and adaptive learning paths (flexible deadlines, conditional activities, etc.).

3.6. Development of a Framework of Inclusive and Adaptive Content

We established a framework for inclusive and adaptive content (Figure 3) to evaluate inclusivity and adaptability in Moodle. In our framework, we focus on maintaining clear activity objectives and multimodal content that has the potential to support multiple means of representation, which enables students to engage with material through visual and textual formats. Furthermore, we focus on maintaining built-in assessment tools to achieve independent learning.

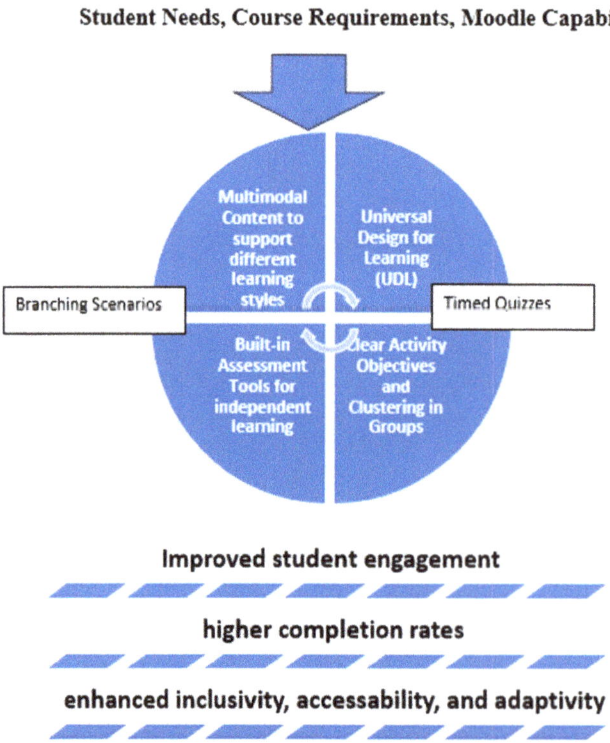

Figure 3. Framework for inclusive and adaptive content.

The framework described was developed after analyzing the data. It was not predefined or used during the coding process. Instead, it was created to summarize and organize the main themes that emerged from the analysis. An inductive process grounded in the thematic analysis of the data collected from student reflections, educator interviews, and teaching observations was used. Rather than beginning with a predefined model, we identified recurring patterns and organized them into three central areas: inclusive design practices, adaptive use of Moodle features, and ongoing feedback mechanisms. The Universal Design for Learning (UDL) guidelines informed our interpretation of the data but were not used as a base. To ensure the framework's relevance and accuracy, we invited two participating educators to review the initial version and confirm that it aligned with their teaching experiences and course design choices.

We emphasized following the UDL, which provides a widely used comprehensive framework and principles for addressing students' needs [59]. UDL aims to design an accessible learning environment that is challenging for all learners in which they can take responsibility for the learning process [60]. Employing UDL has the potential to support not only students with disabilities but all of the students in the classroom. UDL offers many ways to engage students and encourage their participation in the learning process. Moreover, UDL promotes providing multiple sources and means of representation, where learners can choose among the available resources. We chose these principles because they are related to technological integration, which is relevant to our study. Educators can benefit from technology through the provision of multiple data forms, such as text, videos, and diagrams. Any used technology should be evaluated for its capacity to provide multiple sources and representations of data to suit various learners' needs.

The framework for inclusive and adaptive content is utilized to evaluate Moodle for inclusivity and adaptability. Furthermore, it can be used for evaluating any LMS.

3.7. Ethical Considerations

Although we had ethical clearance to conduct this research, we did not collect any personal information, and students voluntarily participated. Students participated in normal classroom settings to ensure that they were not stressed or forced to discuss the topics and give feedback. Thus, all students felt comfortable in the blended learning settings. Therefore, we maintained student confidentiality and adhered to educational and academic research ethics.

4. Results

This section presents the results of our research, which reflect student responses to the inclusive and adaptive teaching strategies implemented throughout the course, including different content styles, flexible submission formats, and structured weekly engagement through Moodle.

4.1. Teaching Reflections, Focus Groups, and Interviews Codes

The teaching reflections, insights from focus groups, and the resulting codes and themes are summarized in Table 2.

After analyzing the notes and transcripts from the focus group sessions, reviewing the teaching reflections, and analyzing the interview transcripts, we organized the results into the codes demonstrated in Table 2. From the codes, we began to see some emerging themes. We then categorized the codes into the following themes, which are also shown in Table 2:

1. Barriers for engaging learners in blended learning environments: This theme identified the challenges related to the participation and engagement of students in

blended learning settings, such as the strict deadlines and content consumption levels in Moodle.
2. Learning preferences and adaptive learning: This theme explains how adaptive content could enhance inclusivity in a blended learning environment.
3. Educators' perceptions of Moodle's adaptability and inclusivity features: This theme analyses Moodle from the viewpoints of Jordanian educators.
4. Educators' readiness and preparedness: This theme focuses on the ability of educators to learn the adaptability and inclusive features available in Moodle, where it has two perspectives, namely, the usability of Moodle and the time available for educators to learn with the workload they have.
5. Best practices for designing inclusive and adaptive blended learning: This theme focuses on providing recommendations for enhancing inclusivity using features available in Moodle.

Table 2. Thematic code table from teaching reflections, focus groups, and interviews

Theme	Data Source	Code Category	Example Insights
Barriers to engaging learners in blended learning environments	Teaching Reflections and Focus Groups	Engagement Issues	Low completion rates for multimedia content; students like interactive content; did not complete assignments
Barriers to engaging learners in blended learning environments	Teaching Reflections and Focus Groups	Accessible Content	Timed quizzes with strict deadlines caused stress; three short videos made a distraction; students with learning challenges struggle with deadlines
Educators' readiness and preparedness	Teaching Reflections and Focus Groups	Educators' Challenges	Lack of training on Moodle's accessibility and inclusive tools; redesigning the content was time-consuming
Educators' perceptions of Moodle's adaptability and inclusive features	Educator Interviews	Understanding of Inclusive Learning	Inclusive learning means building suitable content for all students; Moodle supports inclusivity, but requires training
Educators' readiness and preparedness	Educator Interviews	Challenges with Moodle Tools	No knowledge of accessibility and inclusive features; Moodle lacks built-in tools that support adaptivity
Best practices for designing inclusive and adaptive blended learning	Educator Interviews	Best Practices for Inclusive and Adaptive Blended Learning	Providing flexibility in deadlines improved students' performance; adaptive quizzes and branching scenarios work well for students who are struggling

4.2. *Adaptive Inclusive Learning in Moodle*

Even though Moodle does not directly offer personalized, inclusive learning or adaptation, it might facilitate inclusive and adaptive learning. A set of prerequisites for accessing activities was created when teaching the fundamentals of the software engineering course, where students' progress determines their learning paths. For example, students are encouraged to complete specific learning tasks, such as viewing short videos or completing a quiz, to unlock additional learning resources. This approach was designed to reinforce foundational concepts before students advance, while still offering flexibility in how they engage with content, in alignment with UDL's emphasis on providing multiple pathways. Figure 4 shows how to build such learning paths to adapt to students' needs.

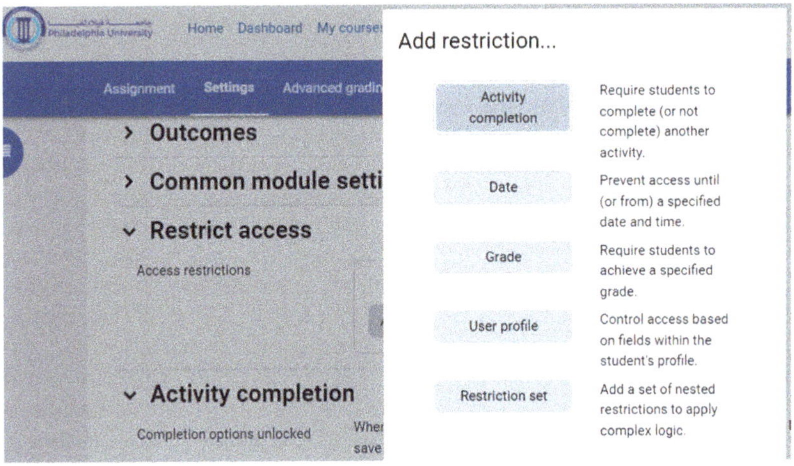

Figure 4. Building adaptive content in Moodle.

Thus, branching scenarios were designed to help students and to achieve inclusion. The analytics and reporting features offered by Moodle were helpful for us. In other words, we carried out manual adaptation. This conditional adaptation is insufficient, though, and we may run into issues when we need to modify the content in real time.

Timed quizzes and deadlines are two further ways that Moodle makes learning accessible. These methods might help students who require more time. Without notifying other students, those students might be granted more time to complete their assignments. In other words, as students require more time to complete activities, face-to-face interactions may lead them to feel neglected; however, blended learning allows for this to happen while protecting students' privacy.

During the course, the first author identified students who were struggling to complete weekly assignments. Students reported during the focus group sessions that this is due to the required viewing of three separate videos. Based on focus group feedback, we implemented a practical adaptation by providing alternative formats for the video content, including downloadable PDFs with the video transcripts and summarized key points. These materials were distributed to small student groups who reported difficulties with video-based learning. This intervention enabled students to complete the same assignments using different content formats, thereby supporting the UDL principle of "multiple means of representation." Rather than suggesting a future action, this was an active, iterative modification made during the course based on observed challenges.

Tools that allow students to rewatch recorded videos and review material at their own pace have proven beneficial for supporting diverse learning needs. Such features can be thoughtfully integrated into curricula to promote adaptability and inclusion.

4.3. Inclusivity Through Project-Based Learning in Moodle

In response to the first research question, we clarify here how Moodle was intentionally used to design inclusive and adaptive course content. The course consists of digital materials, including weekly multimedia lectures, structured discussion forums, interactive activities, and conditional quizzes. These were designed based on UDL guidelines to offer multiple means of engagement and representation. For instance, core concepts were delivered through both visual slides and audio narration, while students could choose between video- or reading-based assignments for reflection tasks. The use of conditional release allowed students to receive supplementary resources based on quiz outcomes or forum participation. These design choices were identified by students in their weekly reflections as supportive, especially in terms of flexibility, clarity, and autonomy in navigating the content.

Moodle is found to significantly facilitate and promote inclusivity through project-based learning. It enabled the formation of student groups, the distribution of tasks, the tracking of individual contributions, and the monitoring of group progress. Group assignments supported collaboration and cooperative learning, both of which aligned with the course's inclusive objectives. Collaborative forums and real-time feedback tools also allowed students with special educational needs, including those with language difficulties or varied learning preferences, to fully participate in coursework and classroom dialogue. Teachers can provide students with customized access to learning materials, where students who require support can benefit and participate in project-based learning.

Moodle allows teachers to monitor students while pairing advanced learners with those who struggle with learning. Furthermore, it facilitates collaboration and continuous assessment. Collaborations improve the participation of such learners who are experiencing difficulties and mitigate the isolation that may arise during face-to-face lectures. Thus, such features help to reduce disengagement and feeling isolated.

Interactive tools such as forums, group workspaces, and interactive quizzes help Moodle support inclusivity through project-based learning, which has the potential to help ensure inclusivity. These elements reflected the UDL principle of providing "multiple means of action and expression," particularly by encouraging students to complete assignments collaboratively rather than in isolation.

We noticed that some students viewed the assignments during the first two weeks without attempting to finish them. We then established groups to support such students and found that the usage frequency was better. We found that more than 70% of our students access Moodle more than four times a week, which is a good percentage. Thus, providing students with this collaborative workspace helped them to benefit from their peers, which supports UDL's principle of "multiple means of action and expression".

4.4. Emotional Inclusion Through Moodle

Moodle provides many features and tools that have the potential to ensure emotional inclusion, which can be considered a key element of inclusive learning. Such features can help in interacting with and engaging those students who feel lonely or disengaged. Building on the UDL-based thematic coding described in Section 3.2.2, we examined how specific emotional inclusion practices—such as encouraging messages, private communication, and peer support—were perceived by students in weekly focus groups. Students consistently highlighted these features as crucial for sustaining motivation, especially those who reported anxiety, difficulty staying on track, or those who hesitate to participate. By aligning student feedback with UDL engagement principles (e.g., offering options for sustaining effort and persistence), we were able to evaluate how emotionally supportive features in Moodle contributed to a more inclusive learning environment. This analysis confirmed that emotional inclusion—often overlooked in RE design—plays a significant role in supporting diverse learners and improving participation and completion rates.

Educator interviews revealed the deliberate use of Moodle features to personalize learning experiences. For example, educators used forum ratings, activity completion tracking, and branching scenarios to guide learners through differentiated paths. These practices were highlighted as aligning with inclusive teaching strategies, enabling varied forms of participation and expression.

Thus, Moodle's feedback features, such as forums and messaging, may facilitate the emotional inclusion of those struggling students. Through encouragement and a one-to-one setting, which is what these students want, the lecturer's guidance and support may also help to promote emotional inclusion. Students discussed these features and characteristics in the weekly focus groups, and they reported that the feeling that the lecturer is there is great and supportive even though it is virtual. This promotes their feeling that they are connected and safe, where some students reported that even acknowledging receiving assignments or classwork from the lecturer makes them able to continue. When we discussed the issue of receiving encouragement statements like "well done" and emojis, 83% of the students stated that this boosts their encouragement and gives them motivation to study. They were particularly happy with the capabilities that allow them to communicate with their teachers privately and discuss with them any concerns that they do not want to share with their colleagues. Additionally, the lecturer's response gives students the impression that they are being watched and tracked. For students who struggle with learning or disengagement, this feeling is crucial since they will experience isolation and a lack of confidence when they are by themselves. This demonstrates how, when utilized effectively by teachers, Moodle's educational technology can foster emotional inclusion and support real-life interactions.

Furthermore, more interaction and cooperation with other students (peer-to-peer) are also seen as significant emotional inclusion factors. Students reported many benefits and expressed satisfaction with having group assignments and group discussions, which helped them to establish collaborations. Furthermore, educator interviews revealed specific uses of Moodle to support inclusive and adaptive learning strategies. For example, several educators described the use of conditional activities to create multiple learning pathways based on quiz performance. One educator explained, "*I set up different resources that become available depending on whether the student completes the first task successfully or not.*" Others used group workspaces and forum subscriptions to increase peer interaction and reduce student isolation. Customizing deadlines and access levels was also reported as an important practice to accommodate students with different needs and schedules. These findings illustrate how educators actively used Moodle's built-in tools to adapt content delivery and foster engagement among a diverse group of learners.

In conclusion, our results demonstrate that when used appropriately, Moodle may promote emotional inclusion and engagement in addition to content delivery.

4.5. Performance Trends

Table 3 shows the statistics of the assignments and quiz completion for multiple scenarios.

Table 3. Statistics of assignments and quiz completion for multiple scenarios.

Scenarios	Did Not Complete (Incl. No Response)	Completed Successfully	No Response	Completion Rate (%)
3 videos (5 min each) + 1 Assignment	40 (10 did not respond)	30	10	42.9%
1 video (15 min) + 1 Assignment	20	50	0	71.4%
Timed quizzes (Strict Deadlines)	29 (18 did not respond)	41	18	58.6%
Timed Quizzes (Flexible Deadlines)	3	67	0	95.7%

In Scenario C, flexible deadlines were implemented through Moodle by allowing students to take the quiz at any point within a predefined window (e.g., over three days). However, to maintain academic integrity, each student had a strict time limit once they opened the quiz (e.g., 15 min) and received a randomized set of questions distinct from those of their peers. In contrast, Scenarios A and B involved inflexible quizzes, where all students had to complete the quiz simultaneously at a specific time. The observed increase in completion rate in Scenario C (85%) suggests that the flexibility in quiz timing improved student participation. Importantly, the average performance did not decline compared to the inflexible scenarios, indicating that the flexible approach supported diverse learning needs without compromising assessment standards.

The 15-min video scenario and the flexible timed quizzes achieved the best results, with the highest number of completions (95.7%) and no unresponsive students for the flexible quizzes. The one long video and an assignment had a reasonable performance (71.4%) but were not as effective as the flexible quiz approach; when we examined the standard deviation of completion rates for the two conditions, content structure (i.e., video and assignment formats) recorded a variability of 14.29%, while assessment flexibility (strict vs. flexible quizzes) showed a higher variability of 18.57%, as shown in Figure 5. While we use these values illustratively to reflect differences in consistency of student engagement across scenarios, we acknowledge that standard deviation alone does not provide sufficient statistical evidence to claim significance. However, these results suggest that students responded more sensitively to how quizzes were structured than to the content format. According to student feedback, this may be due to quiz grades carrying higher weight than assignments, as well as the timing flexibility reducing pressure and improving engagement. Further studies with formal statistical testing are needed to substantiate this preliminary insight. According to our discussions with students, this was because the mark's weight for the quizzes is more than the weight for the assignments. The three short videos and an assignment scenario recorded the highest number of students who did not complete the process. Students reported that this was because of a higher perceived workload.

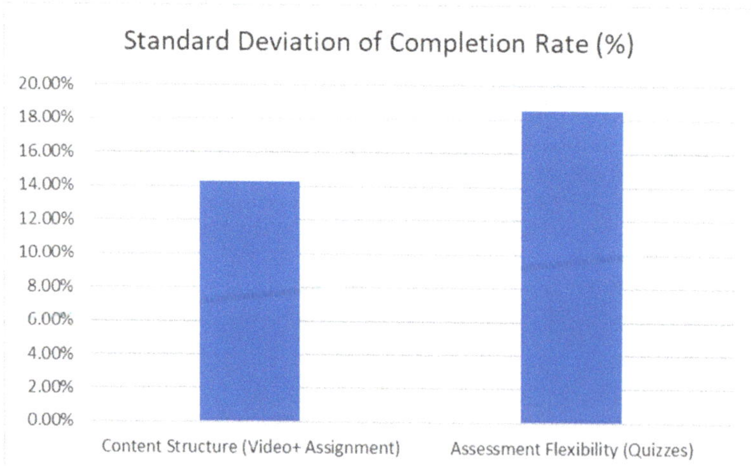

Figure 5. Standard deviation of completion rates for content structure and assignment flexibility.

The strictly timed quizzes had a critical drop in engagement, recording a noticeable number of students who did not respond at all. This means that flexible deadlines appear to not only increase completion rates but also provide more consistent engagement across different students. This highlights the importance of building adaptive assessment mechanisms—such as flexible deadlines—that accommodate diverse student needs. In our case, offering flexible quiz deadlines helped reduce barriers for learners experiencing time-related or cognitive challenges, and it was associated with improved completion rates and engagement. This aligns with inclusive design principles in blended learning.

4.6. Challenges

4.6.1. Content-Related Challenges

The difficulty in handling multiple video materials assigned for a single task was a main challenge that was identified from students' feedback. A total of 57% of students felt overwhelmed when they had to watch many video lectures to complete one assignment. This confused them and hurt their time management. This challenge increases when the videos differ in format or teaching methodologies. There is a heavy cognitive load associated with navigating and integrating information from several sources within a short period, which makes maintaining focus or perceiving new concepts more difficult for students. Our results highlight the need for a more effective approach to content delivery, where each assignment is linked to specific, concise resources.

4.6.2. Accessibility-Related Challenges

Accessibility-related challenges are another issue that students face. Such challenges affect their capacity to fully engage with the learning process. The strict quiz schedules were one of the main concerns the students talked about. Personal obligations or time conflicts did not enable students to attend such strict quizzes, particularly in a blended learning environment where asynchronous participation is often necessary. Some students mentioned that missing deadlines was not due to a lack of motivation but rather a mismatch between course timelines and their availability. These challenges highlight the significance of integrating more adaptive timing mechanisms and offering alternatives for assessments to achieve an inclusive and flexible learning environment. This framework, which was developed as a result of our analysis, helps illustrate how inclusive and adaptive teaching practices emerged through Moodle-supported course design.

5. Discussion

This section discusses the results of our study and answers the research questions. Furthermore, it maps these answers to the inclusive learning framework. We built our discussion on the results from student feedback, classroom observations, and the interviews that we conducted with educators. We interpreted these results to provide insights on how Moodle's features and design practices can influence inclusive and adaptive learning. We organized these insights to answer the research questions, and they were mapped to the inclusive and adaptive frameworks' principles.

5.1. How Can Moodle Be Used to Support Inclusive and Accessible Learning Experiences for Students with Diverse Needs and Challenges in Blended Learning Environments?

We identified that having multiple files for multimodal content and frequent submissions might discourage students and make it more difficult for them to manage many tasks at once, which lowers their ability to concentrate on learning new information or improving their skills. This conclusion was based on student interactions and the authors' experience. This finding suggests, furthermore, that students who struggled with delayed learning felt more relaxed with timed quizzes that had flexible due dates rather than strict ones. Many students stated that flexible quiz deadlines decreased stress and enabled them to adequately study and prepare, which improved their performance. This aligns with the UDL principle of having "multiple means of engagement". The emotional inclusion and students' feeling that they are safe play an important role in promoting students' motivation. It is clear that the flexible times for quizzes helped students to conduct and submit their quizzes without fear, which improves their academic performance. Though online flexibility can support learners and allow them to engage with content at their own pace, it is important to consider that students with learning difficulties may also require more direct and structured guidance. Our blended learning model ensures that these students benefit from both the autonomy of online materials and the personalized support of face-to-face sessions. Although the asynchronous elements (e.g., videos, Moodle activities) provide flexibility, they are complemented by synchronous lectures and interactive in-person activities that foster emotional support, real-time feedback, and peer collaboration. Therefore, our model avoids the limitations of a predominantly online environment and instead promotes a hybrid approach, which has been proven effective in maintaining accessibility, reducing stress, and enhancing engagement for students with learning difficulties. The first author, who is the lecturer, noted this reduction in missed responses after introducing flexibility in deadlines.

Moreover, our results ensured the importance of delivering multi-modal content, which is considered one of the main principles of our inclusive learning framework. A number of the students who participated in this study talked about the importance of having explanations for the videos to simplify the process of following complex topics in the course, such as the "software architecture" chapter. The authors of [61] emphasized the importance of having new methods for teaching subjects related to software architecture because the traditional lecture method used to teach software architecture in the classroom is not sufficient to provide students with the necessary practical experience to pursue a career as software architects in the future. Therefore, having multimodal content that students can explore on their own time is beneficial. Students emphasized the importance of pausing and replaying the videos in understanding complex topics. This aligns with our framework's "multimodal content to support different learning styles" principle. This principle assures the importance of providing visual content that fits different learning styles instead of only having lecture slides.

While our work focuses on inclusive content design and pedagogical adaptability, other studies, such as [43], have advanced Moodle's personalization capabilities by modeling learners' personalities through unobtrusive learning analytics. Such complementary approaches highlight the growing potential of Moodle to support both inclusive instruction and personalized learning pathways in diverse educational settings.

Our study expands previous studies by focusing on university students in a blended learning environment, applying inclusive pedagogical strategies grounded in the Universal Design for Learning (UDL) framework.

Furthermore, unlike previous studies that focus on usability evaluations, such as the work by [46], which focused on assessing how students with disabilities interact with Moodle, we move beyond interface-level accessibility and address instructional design. Our study introduces a framework for developing inclusive and adaptive content. Thus, our approach is not limited to evaluating user experience but instead emphasizes how course content itself can be designed to accommodate diverse learner needs, foster engagement, and improve learning outcomes in a blended learning context. This distinction is critical in regions like Jordan, where the use of LMSs and blended learning are expanding fast but pedagogical adaptation for diverse learners remains underdeveloped.

Thus, our results contribute to understanding the characteristics of a blended learning course that help to achieve inclusion. Students' behavior helped us to provide recommendations on how to design a blended learning course that can guarantee inclusion. Feedback from both students and educators highlights the importance of well-designed content and multimodal content, which directly maps to our framework.

5.2. What Are the Available Features in Moodle That Can Promote Inclusive and Adaptive Blended Learning?

To answer this question, we first looked at the literature on Moodle's current features that might support inclusive and adaptable learning. Additionally, the first author investigated how Moodle may support inclusive and adaptable blended learning. She made an effort to use Moodle for inclusive learning in an efficient manner. Lastly, interviews with educators were conducted to find out how they utilize Moodle to achieve inclusive and adaptive learning and how experienced they are in both inclusive learning and in using Moodle's features.

Our findings reveal that Moodle promotes inclusive education by making resources like screen readers and translation plugins available to students with impairments. Conditional activities, which guarantee that students receive information appropriate to their needs, also encourage adaptive learning. In addition, educators can gain insight into how students behave, which might help in tailoring the material to meet their requirements. The analytical tools available may be utilized to do this.

5.3. How Is the Role of Moodle in Inclusive Blended Learning Perceived by Educators in Jordanian Higher Education Institutions?

Among the educators interviewed, 31% acknowledged Moodle's flexibility in allowing them to create courses that are tailored to the requirements of their students and to personalize the material. When those instructors found that Moodle offers an inclusive and adaptable environment, the capabilities that support adaptive learning were beneficial. Additionally, 88% of respondents valued Moodle's capacity to offer information in both Arabic and English. Additionally, 50% of educators agreed that having both synchronous and asynchronous learning options was important. They suggested a variety of resources, including forums, assignments, and tests.

Nearly all teachers expressed dissatisfaction about the inadequate instruction on how to use Moodle for inclusive blended learning. They stated that while they have no problem utilizing the basic capabilities, they find it difficult to use the advanced ones.

5.4. What Are the Challenges in Investing in Moodle for Achieving Inclusive Education, and How to Deal with Such Challenges?

Although Moodle facilitates inclusive and adaptable learning, the use of these resources in the classroom is dependent on the expertise and training of the educators. Additionally, in remote locations with limited infrastructure, students are unable to take advantage of the well-designed information due to inconsistent Internet access.

Although Moodle is free and open-source, hosting, customization, and staff training are expensive aspects of its deployment and maintenance. Institutions of higher education must employ staff who will customize Moodle and provide several workshops to train educators.

Moodle might not be able to meet the accessibility needs of certain students with severe impairments unless specific settings are made. Accessible technologies from third parties may be integrated within Moodle.

To mitigate learning fatigue, educators should ensure that the learning materials they post do not impose a significant mental workload. This result is consistent with the results of [62], who focused on the importance of developing learning material that does not need a high cognitive load as determined by cognitive load theory [63,64], which ensures the importance of addressing limited cognitive processing abilities when designing instructional material.

Another major problem we found is that teachers could be unwilling to utilize Moodle and to switch from traditional to Moodle-based teaching. To overcome these obstacles, institutions might concentrate on trial projects that use blended learning to teach certain modules and demonstrate the outcomes. Higher education institutions should also take into account the workload of teachers, avoiding assigning them too many courses that they are unable to handle.

Finally, our framework is designed to evaluate the inclusive and adaptive capabilities of Moodle. However, many of the key design elements we explored—such as adaptive content pathways, multimedia integration, and collaborative assignments—are not exclusive to Moodle. Similar functions exist in other learning management systems (LMSs), including Canvas and Blackboard. Therefore, while there might be various workflows, we believe that the inclusive and adaptive strategies discussed in this study can inform course design across different platforms. Future studies could investigate the application and comparative effectiveness of such practices in diverse LMS environments.

6. Conclusions, Recommendations, and Future Work

We explored how Moodle, as a widely adopted LMS, can be utilized to deliver inclusive and adaptive content in blended learning environments. We built our research on classroom experiences, focus group discussions, and educator interviews. Furthermore, we identified many barriers that hinder inclusive practices, such as the lack of educator training, the cognitive overload caused by poorly structured content, and the underutilization of Moodle's adaptive features.

To deal with these challenges, we developed and applied a practical framework for designing inclusive and adaptive content. Our framework aligns with the principles of UDL and emphasizes clarity of learning objectives, ensures the importance of multimodal content delivery, and builds flexible assessments.

Our results demonstrate that if educators receive the necessary support and employ Moodle's conditional activities, branching scenarios, and collaborative tools, students with diverse learning needs can be better supported.

Practical insights include the following:

Universities should have structured training programs for educators on how to design inclusive and adaptive content within existing LMS platforms.

Course designers should minimize cognitive load by using concise multimedia and offering alternative formats for essential content to meet different students' needs.

Adaptive learning paths and conditional access features in Moodle can be utilized to personalize the learning experience.

Regular feedback loops, such as weekly focus groups, can inform iterative improvements to course design and delivery. Through utilizing the resources offered by Moodle, educators may be properly trained by their institutions to provide inclusive and adaptable blended learning.

As universities increasingly adopt blended learning models, we highly recommend that they integrate design principles for inclusive and adaptive blended learning in their programs. Applying the proposed framework to evaluate the capabilities of LMSs for inclusion might be helpful and may provide structural pathways. Moreover, we think that universities should ensure the training of educators on achieving inclusivity in education and on inclusivity features in LMSs.

7. Limitations and Future Work

Our study follows a descriptive exploratory empirical approach utilizing qualitative data from a single course experience at one university. This provided deep, rich, and real practice insights; however, it also limits the generalizability of our findings because it does not fully represent the Jordanian or international higher education settings. Instructional factors in other settings might have an impact on the results. Therefore, in future research, we need to adopt a mixed-method research design that combines quantitative and qualitative data to conduct a cross-institutional comparative study to generalize our results and to ensure their validity in other contexts. Future studies could benefit from utilizing the framework to evaluate Moodle in other academic disciplines and other universities to evaluate its applicability in diverse blended learning environments. It can also be used to evaluate the capacity of other LMSs (such as Blackboard, Google Classroom, and Canvas) to provide inclusive and adaptable material, as well as to conduct additional analysis of the findings. Furthermore, the course's flipped blended structure emphasized in-person lectures while delivering core material and assessments online. As such, results may be less generalizable to fully online or more equally distributed blended models.

Future research should also focus on the use of AI tools that have the potential to enhance inclusion and adaptability by including AI-driven content. In other words, future work should be focused on developing machine learning-based systems that can respond to students' behavior and suggest tasks according to students' real-time performance. To conclude, we look to strengthen the validity of our framework in different blended learning contexts through future, deeper empirical testing.

Author Contributions: Conceptualization, L.F.A.-Q. and J.T.N.; methodology, L.F.A.-Q.; validation, L.F.A.-Q., J.T.N. (overall validation), and F.M.A. (interview data validation); analysis, L.F.A.-Q.; data curation, L.F.A.-Q. (primary data collection and weekly student focus groups) and F.M.A. (interview data); writing—original draft preparation, L.F.A.-Q.; writing—review and editing, L.F.A.-Q. and J.T.N. All authors have read and agreed to the published version of the manuscript.

Funding: This research received no external funding

Institutional Review Board Statement: This study was approved by the Scientific Research Committee, Philadelphia University, on 3 November 2024. The approval ID is QFO-SR-DR-033.

Informed Consent Statement: Informed consent was obtained from all subjects involved in the study.

Data Availability Statement: The raw data supporting the conclusions of this article will be made available by the authors on request.

Acknowledgments: The authors would like to thank all students and educators who participated in the study.

Conflicts of Interest: The authors declare no conflicts of interest.

Appendix A. Interview Questions and Their Rationale

The questions asked during the interviews and the reasons why we asked them are as follows.

No	Question	Rationale
1	From your experience, what does inclusive blended learning mean? And how do you define its key principles in higher education?	The first question is designed to see the level of understanding of inclusive blended learning among the participants
2	What specific tools or features in Moo-dle have you used (or are aware of) that support adaptive and inclusive learning for students with diverse learning needs?	The second question is designed to find out the level of familiarity with Moodle's inclusive features
3	What are the key challenges you have faced when trying to create an inclusive and adaptive learning environment using Moodle?	We then wanted to know the challenges in implementing inclusive learning in Moodle

No	Question	Rationale
4	Based on your experience, what improvements or additional features should Moodle offer to better support inclusive and adaptive learning?	Then, we asked about the recommendations for improving Moodle's inclusivity and adaptivity

References

1. Almaiah, M.A.; Mulhem, A.A. A conceptual framework for determining the success factors of e-learning system implementation using Delphi tech-nique. *J. Theor. Appl. Inf. Technol.* **2005**, *96*, 5962–5976.
2. Anthony, B.; Kamaludin, A.; Romli, A.; Raffei, A.F.M.; Phon, D.N.A.L.E.; Abdullah, A.; Ming, G.L. Blended Learning Adoption and Implementation in Higher Education: A Theoretical and Systematic Review. *Technol. Knowl. Learn.* **2022**, *27*, 531–578. [CrossRef]
3. El-Maghraby, A.-S.A. Investigating The Effectiveness of Moodle Based Blended Learning in Developing Writing Skills for University Students. *J. Res. Curric. Instr. Educ. Technol.* **2021**, *7*, 115–140. [CrossRef]
4. Brandl, K. Are you ready to Moodle? *Lang. Learn. Technol.* **2005**, *9*, 16–23.
5. Gökhan, A. Profiling Students Approaches to Learning through Moodle Logs. In Proceedings of the Multidisciplinary Academic Conference on Education, Teaching and Learning (MAC-ETL 2015), Prague, Czech Republic, 7–8 August 2015; MAC Prague consulting Ltd.: Chudenicka, Czech Republic, 2015.
6. Morze, N.; Varchenko-Trotsenko, L.; Terletska, T.; Smyrnova-Trybulska, E. Implementation of adaptive learning at higher education institutions by means of Moodle LMS. *J. Phys. Conf. Ser.* **2021**, *1840*, 012062. [CrossRef]
7. Salmi, J. *Higher Education and Inclusion*; UNESCO: London, UK, 2020; p. 47. Available online: https://unesdoc.unesco.org/ark:/48223/pf0000373689 (accessed on 30 May 2025).
8. Al-Azawei, A.; Serenelli, F.; Lundqvist, K. Universal Design for Learning (UDL): A Content Analysis of Peer Reviewed Journals from 2012 to 2015. *J. Scholarsh. Teach. Learn.* **2016**, *16*, 39–56. [CrossRef]
9. Basham, J.D.; Hall, T.E.; Carter, R.A.; Stahl, W.M. An Operationalized Understanding of Personalized Learning. *J. Spec. Educ. Technol.* **2016**, *31*, 126–136. [CrossRef]
10. Mulenga, R.; Shilongo, H. Hybrid and Blended Learning Models: Innovations, Challenges, and Future Directions in Education. *Acta Pedagog. Asiana* **2024**, *4*, 1–13. [CrossRef]
11. Poon, J. A cross-country comparison on the use of blended learning in property education. *Prop. Manag.* **2014**, *32*, 154–175. [CrossRef]
12. Brenya, B. Higher education in emergency situation: Blended learning prospects and challenges for educators in the developing countries. *JARHE* **2024**, *16*, 1015–1028. [CrossRef]
13. Ghazal, S.; Al-Samarraie, H.; Aldowah, H. "I am Still Learning": Modeling LMS Critical Success Factors for Promoting Students' Experience and Satisfaction in a Blended Learning Environment. *IEEE Access* **2018**, *6*, 77179–77201. [CrossRef]
14. Edward, C.N.; Asirvatham, D.; Johar, M.d.G.M.d. Effect of blended learning and learners' characteristics on students' competence: An empirical evidence in learning oriental music. *Educ. Inf. Technol.* **2018**, *23*, 2587–2606. [CrossRef]
15. Ismail, A.O.; Mahmood, A.K.; Abdelmaboud, A. Factors Influencing Academic Performance of Students in Blended and Traditional Domains. *IJETL* **2018**, *13*, 170. [CrossRef]
16. Graham, C.R.; Woodfield, W.; Harrison, J.B. A framework for institutional adoption and implementation of blended learning in higher education. *Internet High. Educ.* **2013**, *18*, 4–14. [CrossRef]
17. Subramaniam, S.R.; Muniandy, B. The Effect of Flipped Classroom on Students' Engagement. *Technol. Knowl. Learn.* **2019**, *24*, 355–372. [CrossRef]
18. Anthony, B.; Kamaludin, A.; Romli, A.; Raffei, A.F.M.; Nincarean, A.L.; Eh Phon, D.; Abdullah, A.; Ming, G.L.; Shukor, N.A.; Nordin, M.S.; et al. Exploring the role of blended learning for teaching and learning effectiveness in institutions of higher learning: An empirical investigation. *Educ. Inf. Technol.* **2019**, *24*, 3433–3466. [CrossRef]
19. Owston, R.; York, D.N.; Malhotra, T. Blended learning in large enrolment courses: Student perceptions across four different instructional models. *AJET* **2019**, *35*, 29–45. [CrossRef]
20. Alamri, H.A.; Watson, S.; Watson, W. Learning Technology Models that Support Personalization within Blended Learning Environments in Higher Education. *TechTrends* **2021**, *65*, 62–78. [CrossRef]
21. Spoelstra, H.; Stoyanov, S.; Burgoyne, L.; Bennett, D.; Sweeney, C.; Drachsler, H.; Vanderperren, K.; Van Huffel, S.; McSweeney, J.; Shorten, G.; et al. Convergence and translation: Attitudes to inter-professional learning and teaching of creative problem-solving among medical and engineering students and staff. *BMC Med. Educ.* **2014**, *14*, 14. [CrossRef]
22. Spring, K.J.; Graham, C.R.; Hadlock, C.A. The current landscape of international blended learning. *IJTEL* **2016**, *8*, 84. [CrossRef]

23. Guillén-Gámez, F.D.; Mayorga-Fernández, M.J.; Álvarez-García, F.J. A Study on the Actual Use of Digital Competence in the Practicum of Education Degree. *Technol. Knowl. Learn.* **2020**, *25*, 667–684. [CrossRef]
24. Amridinova, A. The Impact of Blended Learning on Inclusive Education. *J. Lang. Pedagogy Innov. Appl. Linguist.* **2024**, *2*, 37–43.
25. Ustunel, H.H.; Tokel, S.T. Distributed Scaffolding: Synergy in Technology-Enhanced Learning Environments. *Technol. Knowl. Learn.* **2018**, *23*, 129–160. [CrossRef]
26. Bishop, J.; Verleger, M. The Flipped Classroom: A Survey of the Research. In Proceedings of the 2013 ASEE Annual Conference & Exposition Proceedings, ASEE Conferences, Atlanta, GA, USA, 23–26 June 2013; pp. 23–1200.
27. O'Flaherty, J.; Phillips, C. The use of flipped classrooms in higher education: A scoping review. *Internet High. Educ.* **2015**, *25*, 85–95. [CrossRef]
28. Låg, T.; Sæle, R.G. Does the Flipped Classroom Improve Student Learning and Satisfaction? A Systematic Review and Meta-Analysis. *AERA Open* **2019**, *5*, 2332858419870489. [CrossRef]
29. Stöhr, C.; Demazière, C.; Adawi, T. The polarizing effect of the online flipped classroom. *Comput. Educ.* **2020**, *147*, 103789. [CrossRef]
30. Ifenthaler, D.; Sampson, D.G.; Spector, J.M. Interactions Between Cognitive Psychology, Educational Technology, and Computing in the Digital Age. *Technol. Knowl. Learn.* **2015**, *20*, 129–131. [CrossRef]
31. Adel, A.; Dayan, J. Towards an intelligent blended system of learning activities model for New Zealand institutions: An investigative approach. *Humanit. Soc. Sci. Commun.* **2021**, *8*, 72. [CrossRef]
32. Rose, D.H.; Meyer, A. *Teaching Every Student in The Digital Age: Universal Design for Learning*; Association for Supervision and Curriculum Development: Alexandria, VA, USA, 2002.
33. Rose, D.H.; Strangman, N. Universal Design for Learning: Meeting the challenge of individual learning differences through a neurocognitive perspective. *Univers. Access Inf. Soc.* **2007**, *5*, 381–391. [CrossRef]
34. Meyer, A.; Rose, D.H.; Gordon, D. *Universal Design for Learning: Theory and Practice*; CAST Professional Publishing, An Imprint of CAST, Inc.: Wakefield, MA, USA, 2014.
35. Rusconi, L.; Squillaci, M. Effects of a Universal Design for Learning (UDL) Training Course on the Development Teachers' Competences: A Systematic Review. *Educ. Sci.* **2023**, *13*, 466. [CrossRef]
36. Lieber, J.; Horn, E.; Palmer, S.; Fleming, K. Access to the General Education Curriculum for Preschoolers with Disabilities: Children's School Success. *Exceptionality* **2008**, *16*, 18–32. [CrossRef]
37. Coyne, P.; Pisha, B.; Dalton, B.; Zeph, L.A.; Smith, N.C. Literacy by Design: A Universal Design for Learning Approach for Students With Significant Intellectual Disabilities. *Remedial Spec. Educ.* **2012**, *33*, 162–172. [CrossRef]
38. Loman, S.L.; Strickland-Cohen, M.K.; Walker, V.L. Promoting the Accessibility of SWPBIS for Students With Severe Disabilities. *J. Posit. Behav. Interv.* **2018**, *20*, 113–123. [CrossRef]
39. Sasson, I.; Yehuda, I.; Miedijensky, S. Innovative learning spaces: Class management and universal design for learning. *Learn. Environ. Res.* **2022**, *25*, 725–739. [CrossRef]
40. Daley, S.G.; Xu, Y.; Proctor, C.P.; Rappolt-Schlichtmann, G.; Goldowsky, B. Behavioral Engagement among Adolescents with Reading Difficulties: The Role of Active Involvement in a Universally Designed Digital Literacy Platform. *Read. Writ. Q.* **2020**, *36*, 278–295. [CrossRef]
41. Kennedy, M.J.; Thomas, C.N.; Meyer, J.P.; Alves, K.D.; Lloyd, J.W. Using Evidence-Based Multimedia to Improve Vocabulary Performance of Adolescents With LD: A UDL Approach. *Learn. Disabil. Q.* **2014**, *37*, 71–86. [CrossRef]
42. Rogers-Shaw, C.; Carr-Chellman, D.J.; Choi, J. Universal Design for Learning: Guidelines for Accessible Online Instruction. *Adult Learn.* **2018**, *29*, 20–31. [CrossRef]
43. Tlili, A.; Denden, M.; Essalmi, F.; Jemni, M.; Chang, M.; Kinshuk; Chen, N.-S. Automatic modeling learner's personality using learning analytics approach in an intelligent Moodle learning platform. *Interact. Learn. Environ.* **2019**, *31*, 2529–2543. [CrossRef]
44. Calvo, R.; Iglesias, A.; Moreno, L. Accessibility barriers for users of screen readers in the Moodle learning content management system. *Univers. Access Inf. Soc.* **2014**, *13*, 315–327. [CrossRef]
45. Moreno, L.; Iglesias, A.; Calvo, R.; Delgado, S.; Zaragoza, L. Disability Standards and Guidelines for Learning Management Systems: Evaluating Accessibility. In *Higher Education Institutions and Learning Management Systems: Adoption and Standardization*; IGI Global: Hershey, PA, USA, 2012; pp. 199–218. Available online: https://hdl.handle.net/10016/16774 (accessed on 25 May 2025).
46. Montes, R.; Herrera, L.; Crisol, E. Moodle Usability Assessment Methodology using the Universal Design for Learning perspective. *arXiv* **2024**. [CrossRef]
47. Rao, K.; Edelen-Smith, P.; Wailehua, C.-U. Universal design for online courses: Applying principles to pedagogy. *Open Learn. J. Open Distance E-Learn.* **2015**, *30*, 35–52. [CrossRef]
48. Creswell, J.W.; Poth, C.N. *Qualitative Inquiry & Research Design: Choosing Among Five Approaches*, 4th ed.; SAGE: Los Angeles, CA, USA, 2018.
49. Sharp, C.A. Qualitative Research and Evaluation Methods (3rd ed.). *Eval. J. Australas.* **2003**, *3*, 60–61. [CrossRef]
50. Thompson, S.; Thompson, N. *The Critically Reflective Practitioner*, 3rd ed.; Bloomsbury Academic: London, UK, 2023.

51. Brookfield, S. *Becoming a Critically Reflective Teacher*, 2nd ed.; Jossey-Bass: San Francisco, CA, USA, 2017.
52. Palinkas, L.A.; Horwitz, S.M.; Green, C.A.; Wisdom, J.P.; Duan, N.; Hoagwood, K. Purposeful Sampling for Qualitative Data Collection and Analysis in Mixed Method Implementation Research. *Adm. Policy Ment. Health Ment. Health Serv. Res.* **2015**, *42*, 533–544. [CrossRef]
53. Santos, K.D.S.; Ribeiro, M.C.; Queiroga, D.E.U.D.; Silva, I.A.P.D.; Ferreira, S.M.S. O uso de triangulação múltipla como estratégia de validação em um estudo qualitativo. *Ciênc. Saúde Coletiva* **2020**, *25*, 655–664. [CrossRef]
54. Ellis, C.; Adams, T.E.; Bochner, A.P. Autoethnography: An Overview. *Forum Qual. Sozialforschung Forum Qual. Soc. Res.* **2010**, *12*. [CrossRef]
55. Squires, V. Thematic Analysis. In *Varieties of Qualitative Research Methods*; Okoko, J.M., Tunison, S., Walker, K.D., Eds.; Springer Texts in Education; Springer International Publishing: Cham, Switzerland, 2023; pp. 463–468. [CrossRef]
56. Braun, V.; Clarke, V. Using thematic analysis in psychology. *Qual. Res. Psychol.* **2006**, *3*, 77–101. [CrossRef]
57. Farmer, T.; Robinson, K.; Elliott, S.J.; Eyles, J. Developing and Implementing a Triangulation Protocol for Qualitative Health Research. *Qual. Health Res.* **2006**, *16*, 377–394. [CrossRef]
58. Nganji, J.T.; Brayshaw, M. Disability-aware adaptive and personalised learning for students with multiple disabilities. *Int. J. Inf. Learn. Technol.* **2017**, *34*, 307–321. [CrossRef]
59. *Universal Access Through Inclusive Instructional Design: International Perspectives on UDL*; Gronseth, S.L., Dalton, E.M., Eds.; Routledge; Taylor & Francis Group: New York, NY, USA; London, UK, 2020.
60. Roski, M.; Sebastian, R.; Ewerth, R.; Hoppe, A.; Nehring, A. Learning analytics and the Universal Design for Learning (UDL): A clustering approach. *Comput. Educ.* **2024**, *214*, 105028. [CrossRef]
61. Al-Qora'n, L.F.; Jawarneh, A.; Nganji, J.T. Toward Creating Software Architects Using Mobile Project-Based Learning Model (Mobile-PBL) for Teaching Software Architecture. *MTI* **2023**, *7*, 31. [CrossRef]
62. Hussein, M.H.; Ow, S.H.; Al-Azawei, A.; Ibrahim, I. What drives students' successful reuse of online learning in higher education? A case of Google Classroom. *AJET* **2022**, *38*, 1–21. [CrossRef]
63. Spanjers, I.A.E.; Van Gog, T.; Wouters, P.; Van Merriënboer, J.J.G. Explaining the segmentation effect in learning from animations: The role of pausing and temporal cueing. *Comput. Educ.* **2012**, *59*, 274–280. [CrossRef]
64. Paas, F.; Tuovinen, J.E.; Tabbers, H.; Van Gerven, P.W.M. Cognitive Load Measurement as a Means to Advance Cognitive Load Theory. *Educ. Psychol.* **2003**, *38*, 63–71. [CrossRef]

Multimodal Technologies and Interaction

MDPI

Article

Innovating Personalized Learning in Virtual Education Through AI

Luis Fletscher [1,*], Jhon Mercado [1], Alvaro Gómez [1] and Carlos Mendoza-Cardenas [2]

1 Department of Electronic Engineering, Universidad de Antioquia, Medellín 050010, Colombia; jfredy.mercado@udea.edu.co (J.M.); alvaro.gomezp@udea.edu.co (A.G.)
2 Twitch Interactive Inc., San Francisco, CA 94104, USA; cmendoza@udel.edu
* Correspondence: luis.fletscher@udea.edu.co; Tel.: +57-3108566068

Abstract: The rapid expansion of virtual education has highlighted both its opportunities and limitations. Conventional virtual learning environments tend to lack flexibility, often applying standardized methods that do not account for individual learning differences. In contrast, Artificial Intelligence (AI) empowers the creation of customized educational experiences that address specific student needs. Such personalization is essential to mitigate educational inequalities, particularly in areas with limited infrastructure, scarce access to trained educators, and varying levels of digital literacy. This study explores the role of AI in advancing virtual education, with particular emphasis on supporting differentiated learning. It begins by selecting an appropriate pedagogical model to guide personalization strategies and proceeds to investigate the application of AI techniques across three key areas: the characterization of educational resources, the detection of learning styles, and the recommendation of tailored content. The primary contribution of this research is the development of a scalable framework that can be adapted to a variety of educational contexts, with the goal of enhancing the effectiveness and personalization of virtual learning environments through AI.

Keywords: artificial intelligence; virtual education; personalized learning; intelligent tutoring systems; educational technology

1. Introduction

The digitalization of education has greatly broadened access to learning beyond the confines of conventional classroom environments. While virtual education, enabled by digital platforms, provides increased flexibility, it also presents persistent challenges, including limited student engagement, a lack of tailored learning experiences, and insufficiently effective assessment strategies. AI offers promising solutions to these issues by enabling intelligent automation, fostering adaptive and personalized learning, and promoting more interactive educational experiences [1].

Conventional virtual learning environments often fail to accommodate diverse learning preferences and do not sufficiently address regional variations in educational needs. A large number of e-learning platforms are built upon rigid instructional frameworks that often prove inadequate for students coming from varied educational contexts. The integration of AI-driven adaptive learning systems allows educational institutions to customize content in real time, aligning it with the unique needs of each student. This type of personalization is especially crucial in marginalized or remote areas, where uniform teaching strategies may fall short due to cultural nuances and infrastructural limitations [2].

Maintaining student engagement remains a major challenge in virtual learning settings. Many students experience difficulties with motivation and self-regulation in online environments, which often leads to elevated dropout rates. AI-based solutions—such as real-time feedback mechanisms, intelligent chatbots, and interactive learning dashboards—offer promising strategies to boost engagement by providing tailored recommendations and instant support. These technologies contribute to a more immersive and responsive learning experience, enabling students to engage with educational content in ways that reflect their individual preferences and learning styles [3].

AI also offers significant potential to transform educational management and assessment practices. By incorporating predictive analytics into virtual learning platforms, institutions can proactively identify students at risk of underperformance, adjust the complexity of course materials in real time, and refine instructional approaches to better support diverse learning needs [4]. Through the application of machine learning algorithms to student performance data, AI can create individualized learning trajectories, allowing each learner to advance at a pace that best suits their abilities and progress.

In this context, AI serves as a driving force for innovation in education by reshaping conventional instructional models into personalized, adaptive, and data-informed learning experiences. AI-based systems continuously analyze student performance, learning preferences, and engagement patterns to deliver timely feedback and individualized recommendations [5]. Additionally, AI technologies have the potential to enhance various components of digital education, including automated assessment tools, intelligent tutoring systems, and predictive analytics. These tools can support educators in identifying specific learning needs and tailoring interventions accordingly. However, the extent to which these systems improve educational outcomes depends on multiple factors such as the quality of the data, instructional design, and the context of implementation. Recent studies have explored these benefits and suggested promising applications, while also highlighting the need for further validation and critical reflection on pedagogical effectiveness [6].

This paper outlines the methodological framework and initial findings of the project titled "Didactic Innovation Strategy with an Adaptive Approach Supported by Artificial Intelligence Techniques". Supported by Colombia's General Royalties System, the project sought to enhance the department of Antioquia's capabilities in the areas of Science, Technology, and Innovation (STI). Its central objective was to advance research efforts aimed at designing adaptive didactic strategies powered by AI technologies.

The project had two primary objectives: (1) to evaluate the pedagogical implications of personalized learning by analyzing how students' interactions aligned with their identified learning styles, and (2) to develop and implement an AI-based framework to support this personalization in virtual environments. The integration of the AI-based framework with pedagogical analysis within a single study was intentional, as the effectiveness of the personalization model depends on both its technological performance and its impact on student learning behavior.

The structure of the paper is as follows: Section 2 introduces the conceptual framework; Section 3 details the methodological approach employed; Section 4 presents the key findings; and Section 5 offers the study's conclusions.

2. Conceptual Framework for AI-Enhanced Differentiated Learning

Differentiated learning emphasizes adapting instructional content and strategies to address the diverse needs, preferences, and prior knowledge of students. In this context, adaptive or personalized e-learning systems are designed to identify and address the unique needs of each student by delivering tailored educational experiences. To support this objective, researchers have created a range of content recommendation systems that align instructional resources with individual learner preferences.

2.1. Pedagogical Elements Related to Differentiated Learning

Learning styles have been widely explored as a means of categorizing individual preferences in acquiring and processing information. Although various definitions exist [7], they are generally understood as cognitive, affective, and physiological patterns that serve as indicators of how learners perceive, interact with, and understand educational content. Several influential models have guided the development of adaptive systems, notably the VARK model [8], which classifies students based on sensory preferences into four categories: visual, aural, reading/writing, and kinesthetic.

Experiential learning theories have further shaped the conceptualization of learning styles. Kolb's model (1984) outlines a four-stage learning cycle—concrete experience, reflective observation, abstract conceptualization, and active experimentation—which defines four corresponding styles: convergers, divergers, assimilators, and accommodators [9,10]. Honey and Mumford (1992) extended this perspective by proposing four styles—active, reflective, theoretical, and pragmatic—grounded in how learners absorb and transform information [11,12].

A prominent framework in this field is the Felder-Silverman Learning Style Model (FSLSM), which categorizes learners into four key dimensions: processing (active vs. reflective), perception (sensing vs. intuitive), input (verbal vs. visual), and understanding (sequential vs. global) [13]. Kouis et al. implemented FSLSM within a Learning Management System (LMS), designing a framework that measures alignment between educational content and students' learning styles [14]. Their results showed that personalized alignment improved learner satisfaction and content effectiveness.

Similarly, M. M. El-Bishouty et al. [15] explored how the Felder-Silverman learning style model can be utilized to design online courses that better cater to diverse student learning preferences, effectively improving their learning experience. These studies demonstrate the pedagogical relevance of using learning styles as a basis for differentiated instruction in virtual environments.

Table 1 provides a comparative synthesis of learning style models considered in this study. This comparison highlights the rationale for selecting FSLSM, due to its structured bipolar dimensions, adaptability to AI algorithms, and proven integration in learning environments.

Table 1. Comparative Overview of Selected Learning Style Models.

Model	Key Dimensions/Styles	Main Characteristics	Use in Adaptive Systems	Limitations
VARK [8]	Visual, Aural, Read/Write, Kinesthetic	Based on sensory modalities; emphasizes input preferences	Simple to implement; useful in content presentation	Overly simplistic; limited cognitive depth
Kolb [9,10]	Converging, Diverging, Assimilating, Accommodating	Based on experiential learning cycle: grasping and transforming experiences	Useful in project-based and reflective learning environments	Requires in-depth learner profiling; limited systematization
Honey and Mumford [11,12]	Activist, Reflector, Theorist, Pragmatist	Builds on Kolb's model; focuses on behavior and engagement strategies	Aligns well with instructional strategies and sequencing	Lacks standardization in assessments
Felder-Silverman [14]	Active–Reflective, Sensing–Intuitive, Visual–Verbal, Sequential–Global	Multidimensional and bipolar; focuses on cognitive processing	Widely used in adaptive systems; effective for rule-based and AI-driven recommendation engines	Some debate on stability of learning styles; complexity in modeling

2.2. AI to Strengthen Differentiated Learning

AI is transforming the educational landscape by enabling adaptive, data-informed, and intelligent learning environments that enrich both instructional practices and student learning. A model of educational innovation driven by AI incorporates machine learning, natural language processing (NLP), and predictive analytics to provide personalized learning experiences aligned with each student's unique needs. Tools such as intelligent tutoring systems, automated assessments, and content recommendation engines enhance learner engagement and facilitate student-centered approaches.

AI also supports institutional decision-making by analyzing learning patterns, identifying at-risk students early, and enabling timely interventions. In doing so, AI helps address disparities in learning, improve access, and foster educational equity, thus reshaping traditional models into dynamic and inclusive ecosystems.

To enhance the precision of content recommendations, researchers have adopted advanced AI techniques. For example, Venkatesh and Sathyalakshmi introduced a recommender system based on Bee Colony Optimization, integrating web crawling and indexing to dynamic model content [16]. Similarly, Sianturi and Yuhana applied algorithms such as Decision Trees, Naïve Bayes, and K-Nearest Neighbor to predict learning styles based on student behavior, achieving accuracy rates of up to 96% [17].

Beyond conventional machine learning, some models incorporate fuzzy logic and expert systems to personalize instruction further. Hwang et al. developed a fuzzy-based expert system combining cognitive and emotional variables to adapt content delivery [18], while Kolekar et al. created an interface that dynamically adapted learning pathways using concept maps and behavioral analysis [19].

Hybrid AI models also show promise. For instance, Tarus et al. combined domain ontologies and sequential pattern mining with collaborative filtering, achieving high satisfaction rates among learners and an accuracy of 0.65 in predictions [20].

By integrating these technologies, educational institutions can deliver more relevant and engaging content, optimize learning pathways, and enhance student performance. The evolution of AI-powered personalized learning tools promises to further transform digital education by offering responsive, inclusive, and effective learning experiences tailored to each student's profile.

3. Methodological Approach

Our proposed system was composed of pedagogical and technological components, wired together with the goal of adapting the content of an online course to the learning style of the students.

3.1. Pedagogical Components

Although the pedagogical components are not the focus of this paper, we briefly describe them here to provide enough context for the technological components. The pedagogical model that guided this work is the FSLSM.

The pedagogical components were developed by our collaborators, experts in education and pedagogy. A more detailed explanation of their work is available in a paper that is currently under review. We list our collaborators expert in education in the Acknowledgements section.

3.1.1. Mapping Learning Object Features to FSLSM Learning Styles

To assess the degree of alignment between the educational resources used in the Moodle course "*Preparación para la Vida Universitaria*", specifically the Logical Reasoning module (PPVU), available here https://udearroba.udea.edu.co/home/aspirantes/ (accessed on

26 June 2025) and the dimensions defined by FSLSM, each resource was labeled according to the model's four dichotomies. Using content analysis techniques combined with instructional design criteria, we assigned quantitative scores that reflect the degree to which each resource represents a particular FSLSM dimension, for example, video lectures received high scores for the visual preference. In this way, we built a matrix of weights that maps the contribution of each feature in a learning object to each pole in the Felder-Silverman model. In Table 2, we present a sample of such a matrix. The weight indicates whether the presence of the feature might positively ('1') or negatively ('−1') impact the learning of students who have a preference aligned with that pole, or there is no impact ('0'). For example, the presence of images in the learning object has a positive impact ('1') on students with a visual learning style.

Table 2. A sample of the mapping from learning object characteristics to FS learning styles.

Resource Characteristics	Visual	Verbal	Sensorial	Intuitive
Individual work	0	0	1	−1
Collaborative work	0	0	−1	1
Representative images of the content	1	0	0	1
Descriptive, explanatory or narrative text	0	1	0	1

3.1.2. Adaptive SCORM Objects

Nine SCORM objects covered several mathematical concepts, and each object had four variations in the way it presented content, each designed to favor one of four learning styles: (1) visual-sensing, (2) visual-intuitive, (3) verbal-sensing, and (4) verbal-intuitive.

3.1.3. Human-Expert Annotated Learning Objects

A group of human experts in information science annotated the learning objects present in the PPVU course, which resulted in a matrix with the counts of each of the features listed in the weight matrix described in Section 3.1.1. These feature counts were then transformed into a vector of four elements, one per FSLM dimension, taking values in the set $\{-11, -9, \ldots, -1, 1, \ldots, 9, 11\}$, which is the set of values used in the Index of Learning Styles (ILS) questionnaire. In this way, we have a learning style vector for each object in the course. This structured labeling facilitates the identification of potential learning style tendencies during the analysis phase and enables the dynamic selection of the learning style of the SCORM objects described in Section 3.1.2 to match the learning style of the student.

3.2. Technological Components

We developed multiple technological components that take as input the pedagogical components described above and the interaction data from the students to solve a set of problems that enable the personalization of content delivery in an online course: (1) the identification of a student learning style, (2) the identification of a learning object's learning style, (3) Moodle plugins to enable the adaptation of content to a student's learning style, and (4) the extraction of learning object metadata.

3.2.1. Index of Learning Styles Questionnaire on Moodle

One of the most important steps in our methodology involves identifying students' learning styles. To this end, we apply the FSLSM, which classifies learners across four key dimensions: perception (Sensing vs. Intuitive), processing (Active vs. Reflective), input (Visual vs. Verbal), and understanding (Sequential vs. Global). Widely acknowledged for its effectiveness in capturing cognitive preferences, this model provides a robust foundation for designing personalized learning experiences. By administering an FSLSM-based assessment, we determine each student's dominant learning style, enabling the customization of educational content to better align with individual profile. This approach marks a significant shift from standardized teaching methods toward more personalized, learner-centered pedagogy [1].

To identify students' learning styles based on the FSLSM, a Moodle-based component was developed and deployed. This module, compatible with Moodle version 4.2+, allowed the administration of the original ILS questionnaire through three distinct formats: (1) direct textual questions, (2) questions supported by illustrative images, and (3) experience-based scenarios with visual support. This multi-visualization strategy aimed to enhance accessibility, accommodate different learner preferences, and foster reflection on individual learning processes.

The inclusion of multiple visual formats was not intended as a mechanism for rigid classification, but rather to support metacognitive engagement. By allowing students to choose their preferred questionnaire visualization and switch between them at any time, the system offers a flexible interface that respects learner autonomy. This design supports the idea that learning style awareness is better cultivated through reflective choice than through prescriptive assessment.

Each visualization targeted different learner characteristics. The text-only format aligned with learners favoring verbal, reflective, and sequential processing, offering a clear and structured presentation. The image-supported format introduced graphical elements to aid comprehension, catering particularly to visual, sensing, and active learners. Lastly, the experiential visualization adapted the questionnaire into real-life scenarios, appealing to intuitive, global, and active learners who benefit from context-rich and holistic prompts. A comparative overview of the three visualization modalities is presented in Table 3.

Table 3. Comparison of Questionnaire Visualization Modalities.

Modality	Description	Target Learning Style Traits
Direct Textual Questions	Literal translation of the FSLSM questionnaire.	Verbal, Reflective, Sequential
Questions with Images	FSLSM questions enhanced with illustrative visual cues.	Visual, Sensing, Active
Experiential Visualization	Contextualized questions based on real-life learning experiences, with images.	Intuitive, Global, Active (also supports Sensing via realism)

Additionally, Figure 1 illustrates the first question of the FSLSM questionnaire in each of the three visualization modes, exemplifying the practical implementation of this flexible assessment design.

Figure 2 presents a sample output of a student's learning style profile based on the FSLSM. The visual representation shows the learner's position on each of the four FSLSM dimensions. In this case, the student demonstrated a strong preference for the Sensory style over Intuitive, along with moderate inclinations toward Sequential, Visual, and Active modes of learning. These results suggest that the student may benefit more from concrete, practical examples, visual aids, and step-by-step instructional strategies, rather than abstract concepts, verbal materials, or exploratory learning tasks. By identifying this profile, the system can recommend educational resources aligned with the student's dominant cognitive preferences, thereby enhancing engagement and content assimilation.

3.2.2. Automatic Inference of Students' Learning Style

The estimation of the learning style of a student using their answers to the ILS questionnaire, as described above, has some implicit assumptions that could make them unreliable: (a) the student has enough awareness of their learning attitudes, (b) the student answers in a truthful and careful manner, not rushing the answers to quickly move to the course content, and (c) the student's learning style does not change during the development of the course. For these reasons, we trained a machine learning model that learned from interaction data of a previous version of the course, to predict the learning style of a student in the current course, using their daily interaction data.

Figure 1. Visualization Modalities of the FSLSM Questionnaire. Note: The first image shows the direct textual question, the second displays the same question with an image, and the third presents an experiential adaptation with visual context.

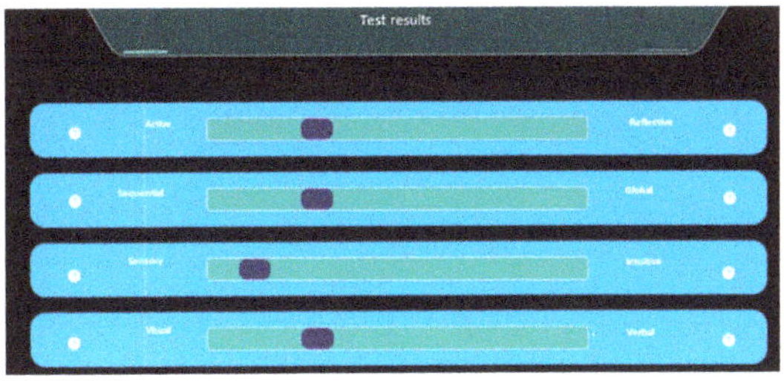

Figure 2. Sample result of a student's learning style/cognitive preferences classification via FSLSM.

Figure 3 presents an overview of our proposed method, illustrating the process from student interaction to the identification of individual learning styles. We employed K-means clustering to analyze behavioral data from students enrolled in the course PPVU offered through the Ude@ Moodle platform during the 2025-1 academic semester. By examining interaction patterns, such as navigation sequences, time spent on activities, and resource usage; we were able to cluster students and align the resulting profiles with

FSLSM dimensions. We provide in the next paragraphs a detailed description of the main components of our system.

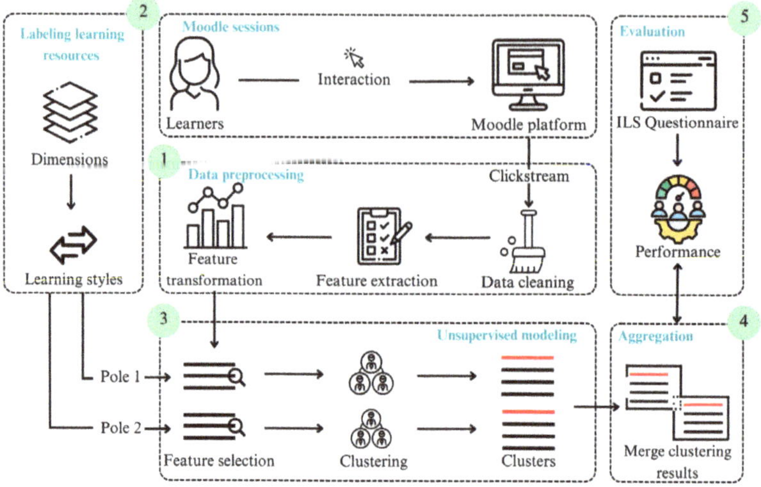

Figure 3. Overview of the proposed method.

Data Cleaning

In this approach, learner interactions are captured primarily through clickstream data generated within the Moodle platform, providing a detailed trace of student behavior essential for subsequent analysis. As a widely adopted open-source LMS, Moodle records extensive user activity in the form of clickstream data, which captures various platform interactions such as page visits, resource views, forum contributions, and other user actions [21].

Due to its high volume, complexity, and unstructured nature, the raw data captured by Moodle is not directly suitable for predictive modeling. Therefore, a preprocessing stage is necessary to transform the dataset into a structured matrix of dimensions $M \times N$, where M denotes the number of students and N represents the set of extracted features per student. This transformation involves two main steps: data cleaning and feature extraction, as described below.

The data cleaning step focused on selecting the most relevant tables and columns from the Moodle database, with particular emphasis on those that reflect students' interactions with learning resources. Our primary source was the *logstore_standard_log* table, which provides detailed records of user activity. From this table, we extracted only the columns that directly relate to engagement with educational materials. Non-instructional data fields—such as objecttable or system-level metadata—were excluded to minimize noise and improve processing efficiency. This targeted extraction strategy ensured that the resulting dataset retained only high-value interaction records, optimizing it for subsequent modeling of learning behaviors.

Feature Extraction

Given the objective of identifying students' learning styles dynamically as they progress through the course, we partitioned the interactions of the students into sessions. Due to the absence of explicit login and logout event markers in the Moodle activity logs, we defined a session as a continuous sequence of learner interactions. A new session was started if the time gap between two consecutive events exceeds eight hours, as illustrated in Figure 4.

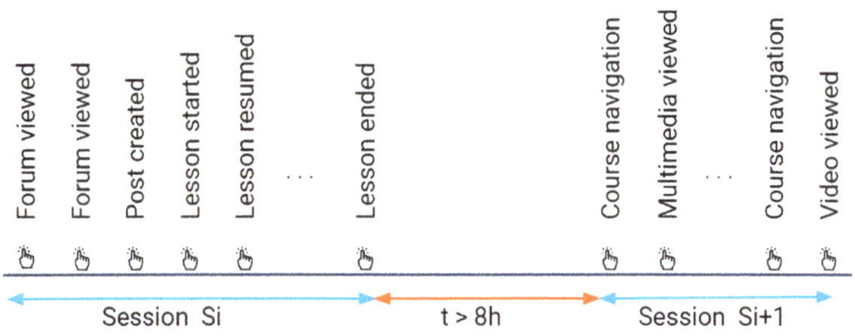

Figure 4. A new session starts after an 8 h gap between events.

We then aggregated interaction metrics across a session for each student to compute two key engagement metrics:

- Time spent per resource—Calculated as the time difference between successive events occurring within the same session.
- Number of accesses per resource—Determined by counting the frequency of interactions with each learning object.

As mentioned in Section 3.1.3, each learning object is characterized by a vector of four elements, one for each FLSM dimension, taking values in $\{-11, -9, \ldots, -1, 1, \ldots, 9, 11\}$. This vector is referred to as the learning object's learning style, representing the learning style with which the object has the most affinity. The sign of each element indicates the preferred pole within the corresponding FLSM dimension (e.g., for the 'input' dimension, negative values represent the 'visual' pole and positive values represent the 'verbal' pole).

Since the learning style vector of each object is available, the objects can be grouped according to the FLSM pole with which they have affinity. For example, all objects with negative values in the 'input' dimension are aligned with the 'visual' pole. A weighted average of time spent and number of accesses was then computed, with weights based on each object's value on that pole. These two weighted averages form a two-dimensional feature representation of each student, which was then used to cluster students and predict their preference for that pole.

Unsupervised Modeling

The student's learning style was predicted by estimating their preference on each pole. Since each pole can take six possible values on the ILS scale, k-means clustering with k = 6 was applied to group learners into six distinct clusters per pole. The resulting clusters were labeled by sorting the L2-norms of their centroids from lowest to highest, then assigning the corresponding ILS values (e.g., for the 'visual' pole, -1 was assigned to the cluster with the lowest L2-norm centroid, and -11 to the one with the highest).

The labels of the two poles for each FLSM dimension were summed to obtain a unique value for that dimension. If the resulting value falls outside the ILS range $\{-11, \ldots, 11\}$, it was adjusted to the nearest value within the range, in the direction of the pole with the greatest magnitude or the largest L2-norm of the centroid. This process resulted in the student's learning style vector.

3.2.3. Automatic Classification of Learning Resources Using AI

Following the identification of students' learning styles through the FSLSM-based module, the next methodological step focused on the automated extraction of structural and semantic features from digital learning resources embedded in web-based platforms and mapping them to dimensions of the FSLSM, as shown in Figure 5. This classification process serves as the foundation for delivering adaptive learning pathways, ensuring that each learner receives content aligned with their cognitive profile.

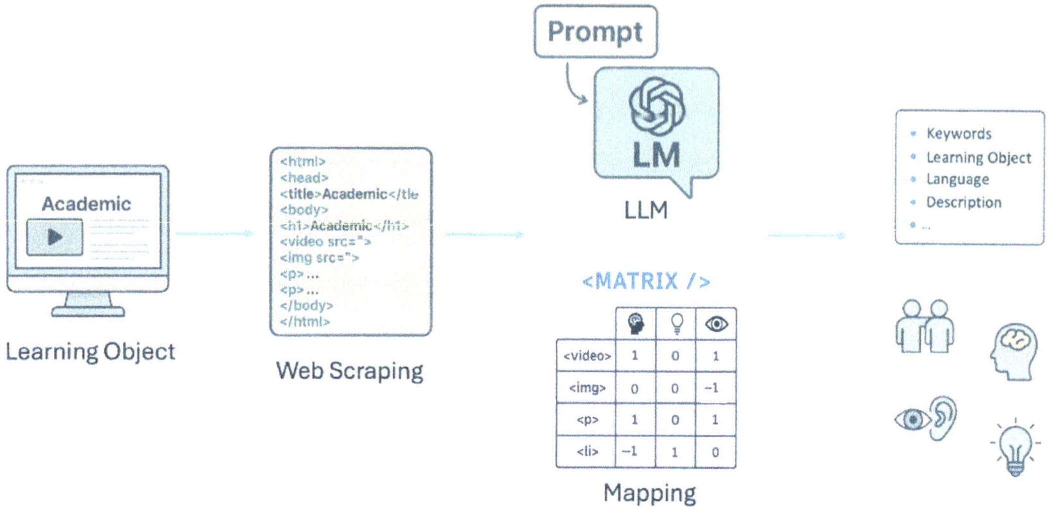

Figure 5. Overview of the automatic classification method.

To accomplish this task, we developed a classification system that combined structural HTML analysis with advanced NLP via large language models (LLMs). The structural analysis began with the extraction of HTML elements from open educational resources using automated dynamic web scraping techniques. Specific tags such as <video>, <ul>, <form>, <img>, and <table> were mapped to pedagogically meaningful features based on a predefined semantic matrix. Each tag was associated with one or more FSLSM dimensions, for instance, <video> with visual learners, <form> with active learners, and <ul> with sequential learners, enabling the derivation of a resource's potential alignment with learning styles.

Complementing this structural mapping, we employed LLMs accessed via API to conduct semantic analysis of the textual content within each object. Tailored prompts were used to extract latent pedagogical indicators such as intended learning outcomes, cognitive load, interactivity level, and instructional strategy, as well as resource metadata according to IEEE LOM and SCORM metadata schemes, ensuring compatibility with institutional repositories and LMS.

Each learning object was subsequently aggregated to generate a four-dimensional learning style vector for the analyzed resource. A scoring matrix aligned with the FSLSM dimensions was applied: a score of +1 was assigned to features that explicitly supported a given learning style, 0 to those considered neutral, and −1 to those potentially incongruent with the style. An example is provided below.

Visual vs. Verbal: presence of videos, images, or dominant text.

Sensing vs. Intuitive: examples, definitions, or exploratory content.

Sequential vs. Global: structured or hypertext-based organization.

Active vs. Reflective: use of interactive tools such as quizzes, forms, or forums.

That way, each detected feature was mapped to a FSLSM dimension and assigned a value on a scale from -11 to 11. This allowed each resource to be represented as a four-dimensional vector, capturing its instructional alignment with learner preferences.

This classification model, designed to be SCORM-compatible, ensured interoperability with existing LMS and facilitates the reuse and recommendation of resources across platforms. Additionally, it leveraged automated classification to reduce the need for the tedious manual process described in Section 3.1.3.

The resulting resource vectors were linked to the individual FSLSM profiles generated in the previous phase. This alignment enabled the development of a personalized recommendation engine capable of dynamically selecting and suggesting resources based on the best pedagogical match for each student.

3.2.4. Automatic Generation of Learning Object Metadata

Building on the classification pipeline, we next implemented an automated metadata generation module to enrich each learning object with interoperable descriptions and cataloging fields.

This operational workflow integrated seamlessly into our parsing pipeline. In the first stage, the full text and structural features previously parsed from the resource's HTML are consolidated into a clean input string. This string included the concatenated text content, a summary of detected HTML elements, and a list of prominent keywords. By combining raw content and structural markers, we provide the downstream language model with both semantic and contextual cues necessary for accurate metadata formulation.

The second stage leverages an LLM accessed via API as it was implemented in the classification section. We crafted a system prompt that assigns the model the role of "an expert educational cataloguer", and defined user prompts that explicitly request metadata of our interest, including the following: (1) five to ten thematic keywords prioritizing conceptual relevance; (2) a concise learning objective formulated as "Upon completion, the learner will be able to …"; (3) automatic detection of the resource's language; and (4) a recommended educational level (elementary, secondary, or tertiary), inferred from vocabulary complexity and conceptual density. The prompt further instructed the model to output all metadata fields in JSON format, conformant with SCORM data element sets and IEEE LOM XML schemas.

By enriching each learning object with both a four-dimensional FSLSM vector and high-quality, standards-compliant metadata, this module streamlines resource discovery, bolsters interoperability, and underpins advanced, learner-centered recommendation strategies.

4. Results

4.1. Data

The results presented in this section were obtained in a case study conducted during the first academic semester of 2025 in the Logical and Mathematical Reasoning PPVU course. The course spanned eight weeks and was designed for an estimated total workload of 48 h, with a recommended study time of six hours per week. It was structured into five thematic units, each containing a combination of educational resources and assessment activities.

A total of 12,212 undergraduate students were enrolled in the same virtual classroom within the institutional LMS. Participants were randomly assigned to four groups of approximately equal size, comprising one control group and three experimental groups. The distribution of participants is presented in Table 4.

Table 4. Participant Allocation by Experimental Group.

Group Name	Target Learning Style Traits
Control Group (Traditional resources)	3.054
Adaptive SCORM Group	3.055
Balanced SCORM Group	3.053
AI-Suggested SCORM Group	3.048

All groups had access to the same base course structure, including instructional materials, activities, and assessments. However, in the experimental groups, the content corresponding to specific topics was replaced by SCORM packages with differentiated presentation formats according to group assignment:

- Adaptive SCORM Group: Each student was shown only the version of the learning object that corresponded to their learning style, as identified through the Felder-Silverman Learning Styles Questionnaire (FSLSQ). The system displayed a single version per topic, aligned with the learning preferences indicated in the questionnaire.
- Balanced SCORM Group: All versions of the learning objects were made available simultaneously to each student. No personalization was applied based on learning style, and the student could freely select their preferred version.
- AI-Suggested SCORM Group: In this group, the system initially selected the version of the learning object corresponding to the student's FSLSQ-identified learning style. Subsequently, the system re-evaluated interaction data at fixed intervals and updated the learning style classification based on behavioral indicators. Recommendations were adjusted accordingly over the duration of the course.

From an ethical standpoint, all students enrolled in the course were informed about the study and asked to provide their voluntary consent to participate. Upon accessing the course for the first time, students were presented with a message explaining the objectives of the research, followed by a consent question regarding their willingness to participate. This procedure ensured that students' autonomy and decision to participate were fully respected. Only the data of students who explicitly agreed to participate were included in the analysis. Furthermore, all data were anonymized to ensure the protection of participants' personal information and to comply with institutional and ethical research standards.

4.2. Survey Results on Learning Styles

A total of 2616 out of 12,212 enrolled students completed the FSLSQ, distributed across the four experimental groups as follows: Control (n = 610), Adaptive SCORM (n = 661), Balanced SCORM (n = 656), and AI-Suggested SCORM (n = 689). The responses revealed consistent tendencies in learning style preferences across all dimensions of the FSLSM.

- Perception Dimension: A dominant preference for the Sensing style was evident in all groups, ranging from 70.5% to 71.7%. This suggested a general inclination among students toward concrete information, practical examples, and real-world applications in their learning.
- Input Dimension: Most students preferred Visual information formats, with percentages between 58.4% and 62.7%. This reinforced the importance of integrating visual resources such as diagrams, videos, and charts to support comprehension.
- Processing Dimension: The Active style was more prevalent than the Reflective style across all groups (58.7–62.5%), indicating that many students favor learning by doing, through collaboration, experimentation, and interaction.

- Understanding Dimension: The Sequential learning preference prevailed in all groups, with the Balanced SCORM group showing the highest proportion (68.2%). This points to a preference for logically ordered, step-by-step instruction.

These results collectively underscored the pedagogical relevance of adapting learning experiences to accommodate dominant learning preferences, particularly those favoring sensory-rich, visually supported, and actively engaged content delivered in a logical sequence.

The analysis of student interaction with SCORM-based learning objects across all four experimental groups revealed variations in usage patterns, completion rates, and content preferences. Table 5 presents the number and percentage of users who accessed each SCORM-based learning object across the four groups in the case study: Adaptive SCORM, Balanced SCORM, AI-Suggested SCORM, and the Control group. The data revealed differences in content engagement patterns by topic and group, allowing comparisons between personalized and non-personalized resource delivery approaches.

Table 5. Distribution of Users by Topic and Experimental Group Based on Learning Object Access.

Topic	Experimental SCORM Adaptive	Experimental SCORM Balanced	Experimental SCORM AI	Control
How to solve a system of equations?	27.7%	24.2%	25%	32%
Elements of propositional and quantificational logic	22.7%	21.0%	20.5%	27%
Set operations	15.7%	14.0%	14.5%	16.6%
Proportionality	10.9%	8.7%	8.7%	13.0%
Combinatorics	10.1%	8.4%	7.8%	12.0%
Probability	8.9%	7.6%	7.0%	11.2%
Measures of central tendency	7.3%	7.5%	6.8%	11.1%
Areas of flat figures	7.6%	7.8%	6.7%	10.7%
Areas and volumes of geometric solids	5.6%	7.0%	5.8%	9.0%

Notably, while all groups had access to the same course content, the way it was presented—particularly in the AI-Suggested group, which dynamically adapted based on interaction data—appeared to influence engagement. This group maintained comparable levels of resource use and completion with the Adaptive and Balanced groups, although topic-specific differences emerged.

These observations suggested that adaptive personalization, particularly when updated dynamically through AI, holds potential for enhancing content relevance and improving user interaction. Furthermore, the consistency in engagement across groups reinforces the value of differentiated content delivery, aligned with student preferences, to support deeper learning and more effective use of instructional resources.

In addition, after completing the course, the student was invited to evaluate how much studying the materials helped them in their development on the course topics according to their learning preferences. The survey aimed to explore students' perceptions regarding the alignment between course materials and their learning preferences, as well as their study behaviors and awareness of learning styles. Figure 6 presents the results of a survey, the grouped bar chart summarizes responses to five key questions: perceived alignment of materials with learning styles, sufficiency of resources, use of external materials, consideration of learning styles in resource selection, and identification of personal presentation preferences. The results offered insight into the relevance of adaptive content and the metacognitive engagement of learners in virtual learning environments.

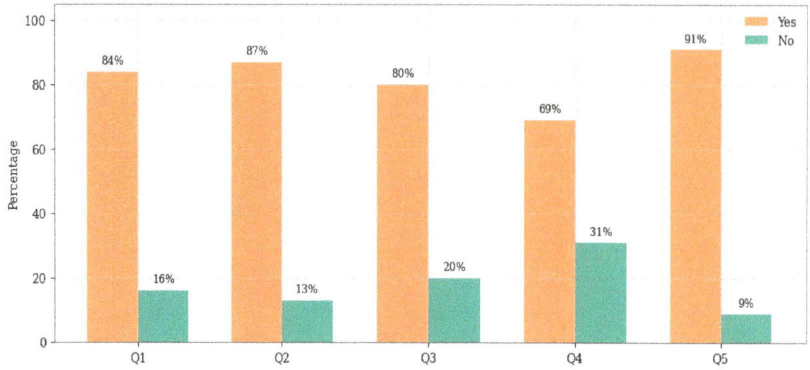

Label	Question
Q1	Did the presentation of materials match your learning preferences?
Q2	Were the materials sufficient to understand the course topics?
Q3	Did you search for external materials?
Q4	Did you consider your learning style when searching for materials?
Q5	Did you identify your preferences for material presentation?

Figure 6. Student Perceptions on Learning Styles and Course Material Use. Each question is represented by a label (Q1–Q5), with full descriptions listed in the accompanying table.

The survey administered revealed predominantly positive perceptions from students regarding the adaptation of course materials to their individual learning preferences. Specifically, 84% of respondents indicated that the way materials were presented aligned with their preferred learning styles. This suggests a strong level of perceived relevance and adequacy in the instructional design among participants in the experimental groups.

In addition, 87% of students considered the materials available on the platform sufficient to support their understanding of course content. Interestingly, 80% reported seeking external materials to further deepen their learning. This behavior did not contradict the perception of sufficiency but rather indicated proactive engagement and a desire to enrich understanding beyond the provided content.

A significant finding was that nearly 70% of the students who sought external resources reported doing so based on the results of their FSLSQ. This implies that the instrument served not only as a diagnostic tool but also as a metacognitive aid, enabling students to make more informed decisions about resource selection.

Moreover, 91% of students stated they had identified their preferences regarding content presentation formats. The most frequently preferred formats were visual and interactive, with the Visual category (117 students) and the Sensing category (67 students) being most prominent. This was followed by Intuitive (39) and Verbal (35) styles. These preferences highlighted a tendency towards learning objects that include graphic, dynamic, and contextually applicable elements.

These results are more deeply understood when contextualized alongside the classification of resources and qualitative analysis of course content. In the area of mathematics, a significant number of materials were delivered through video formats, reflecting a broader trend found in educational platforms like YouTube. This modality appeared particularly effective for students with visual, sensing, and sequential learning styles due to its capacity to convey mathematical procedures step-by-step in a visual manner.

However, this trend also underscored a limitation in traditional mathematics instruction, which often prioritizes abstract and theoretical approaches. The underuse of sensory-rich resources, interactive simulations, and real-world problem-solving contexts limits engagement for students with more active, intuitive, or global learning preferences. The data suggests the need to reconceptualize mathematics instruction, incorporating resources that promote practical engagement and conceptual visualization.

Visual representations that illustrate procedural sequences were especially valued. In such cases, images functioned as didactic tools rather than decorative elements. Conversely, visuals that lacked clear relevance to content were perceived as superficial. Additionally, formats like audio and podcasts received lower preference ratings, likely due to the abstract and symbolic nature of mathematical language, which relies heavily on visual and spatial processing.

It is worth noting that not all students reported a clear alignment between their learning style and resource preferences. This disconnection may result from limited understanding of learning style concepts or skepticism regarding the accuracy of the FSLSQ profile. These findings emphasized the importance of coupling diagnostic tools with metacognitive development to help students interpret and apply their learning preferences effectively.

4.3. Automatic Identification of Student's Learning Styles

The training data comprised 1321 interactions from 371 students who took the PPVU course during the second semester of 2024, and the test data were 390 interactions from 117 students who took the PPVU course during the first semester of 2025. We present in Figure 7 the distribution of the learning styles assigned to the 34 learning objects available during the 2024-2 cohort. The objects had a clear bias towards the (visual, sensing, reflective, global) learning style, and we will see later how that influences the predictions of our model on the train and test data.

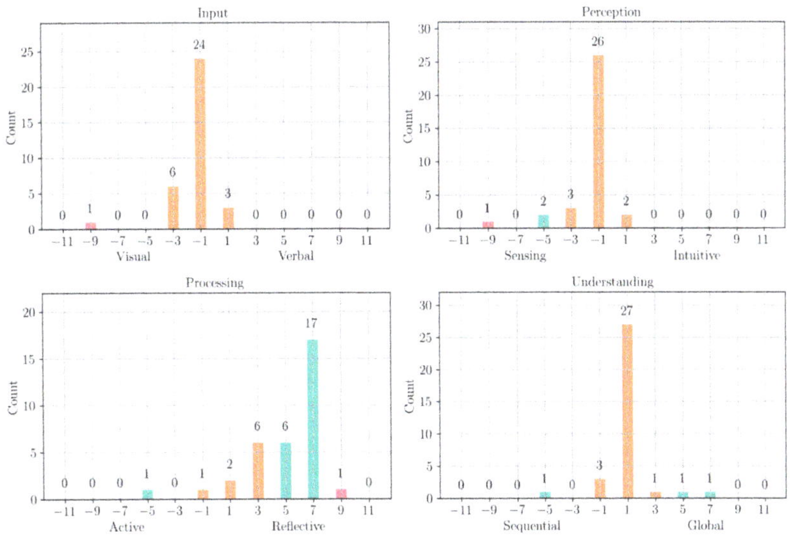

Figure 7. Distribution of Learning Styles of Learning Objects.

Figure 8 shows the distribution of learning styles of students from the training data, according to the results of the ILS questionnaire. The distribution was, in general, well balanced among the poles of each dimension. In contrast, as it is shown on Figure 9, the distribution of the learning styles predicted by our algorithm is more biased in the 'input', 'perception', and 'processing' towards one of the poles, following the same bias introduced by the learning style of the objects, and more balanced in the 'understanding' dimension.

We quantify the agreement between the binarized FLSM labels obtained through the ILS questionnaire (qtn_i) and the ones predicted by our algorithm ($\hat{q}_i$) as

$$Accuracy = \frac{1}{N}\sum_{i=1}^{N} 1(qtn_i = \hat{q}_i) \tag{1}$$

where N is the number of students. Table 6 shows moderate alignment between behavioral indicators and ILS-reported preferences on the training data, especially for the Input and Perception dimensions. Lower agreement in Processing and Understanding may stem from their more abstract nature, which is harder to capture through log data. However, these results should be interpreted cautiously, as the work [22] highlights low reliability for these exact dimensions in the ILS, which raises questions about their validity as a ground truth. Given these limitations, we utilize the ILS as a comparative reference rather than a definitive standard, with our clustering approach providing a scalable alternative for inferring learning tendencies from behavior.

Table 6. Overlap between ILS-based and predicted labels on the train set.

Dimension	Accuracy
Input	0.57
Perception	0.65
Processing	0.47
Understanding	0.44

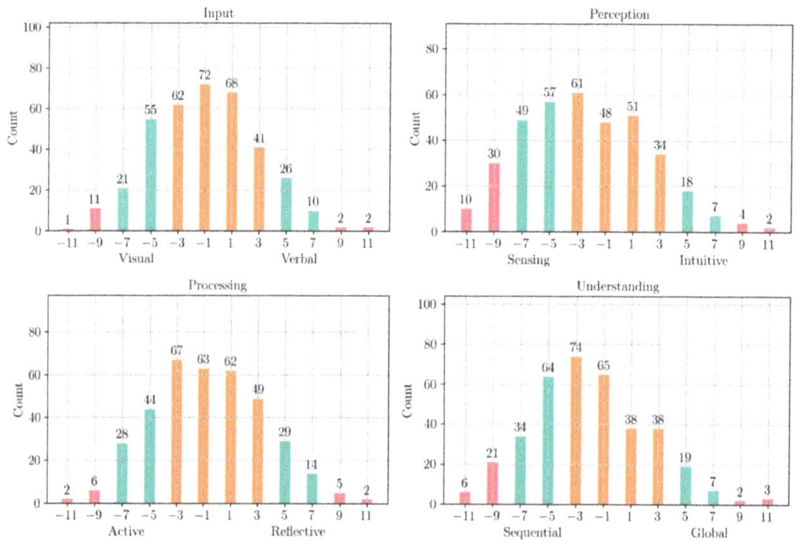

Figure 8. Distribution of Learning Styles of Students on the training data, according to the ILS questionnaire.

For the 2025-1 cohort, 9 of the 34 objects were replaced by SCORM objects with four variations in content format, to align with four learning style combinations: (1) visual-sensing, (2) visual-intuitive, (3) verbal-sensing, and (4) verbal-intuitive. These nine SCORM objects were the elements in the course that allowed us to provide a personalized and adaptive learning experience, as the content format of each SCORM can be changed to match the learning style predicted by our algorithm.

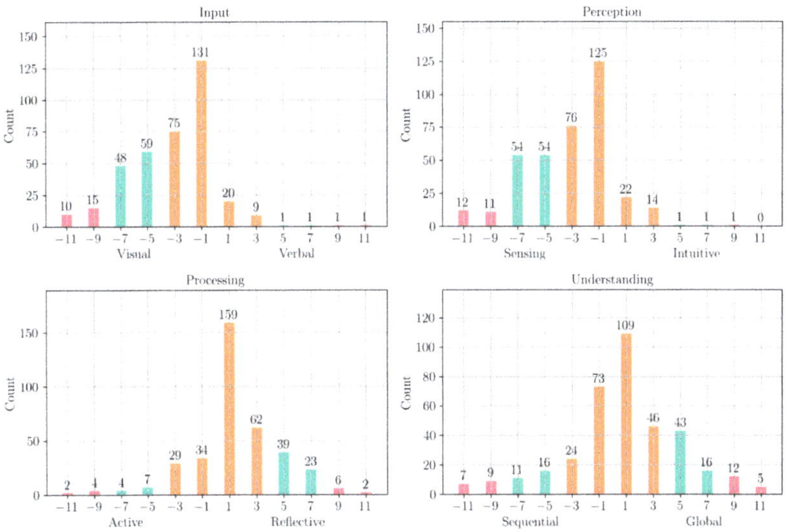

Figure 9. Distribution of learning styles of the students in the training data, according to our prediction algorithm.

Figures 10 and 11 show the distribution of student learning styles in the test data, according to the ILS questionnaire and our prediction algorithm, respectively. As in the training data, the distribution of questionnaire-based styles was well balanced but showed a strong bias in the 'input' and 'perception' dimensions, likely influenced by the bias in the learning styles of the objects. However, while the distribution of predicted styles in the 'processing' dimension was more biased toward the 'reflective' pole in the training data, it was more biased toward the 'active' pole in the test data. Similarly, while the distribution of the 'understanding' dimension was balanced in the training data, it was heavily biased toward the 'sequential' pole in the test data. Table 7 again shows moderate agreement between the two sets of labels in the test set, with improved alignment in the 'processing' and 'understanding' dimensions.

Table 7. Overlap between ILS-based and predicted labels on the test set.

Dimension	Accuracy
Input	0.56
Perception	0.57
Processing	0.57
Understanding	0.67

Finally, we analyzed the performance of two exams the students take at the beginning (pre-mock) and at the end (mock) of the course. Table 8 shows the results for the three student groups that were described in Table 4: the Balanced SCORM Group (Balanced), the Adaptive SCORM Group (ILS), and the AI-Suggested SCORM Group (IA). Although the size of each group is small and it is, thus, not possible to draw any conclusion with statistical significance, it is worth noting that the group of students with the biggest gain on average from the pre-mock exam to the mock exam was the group whose SCORM content changed according to the predictions of our algorithm. This result provided evidence that a learning environment whose content adapts to the learning style of the student could have the potential to improve learning outcomes.

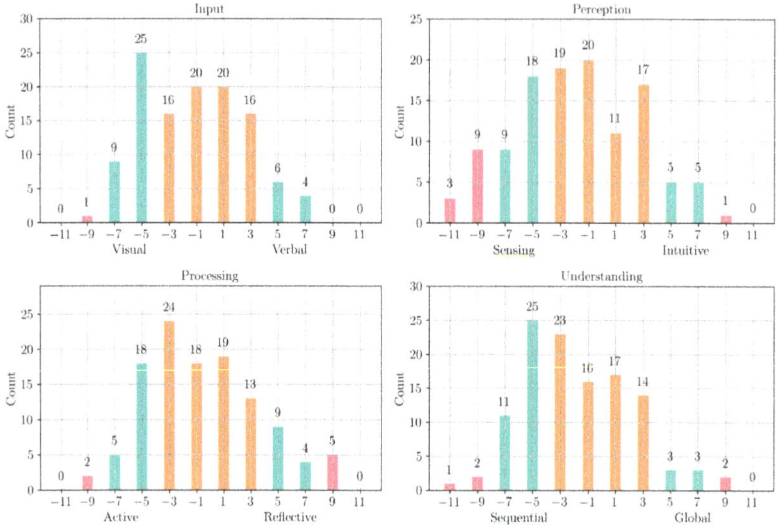

Figure 10. Distribution of Learning Styles of Students on the test data, according to the ILS questionnaire.

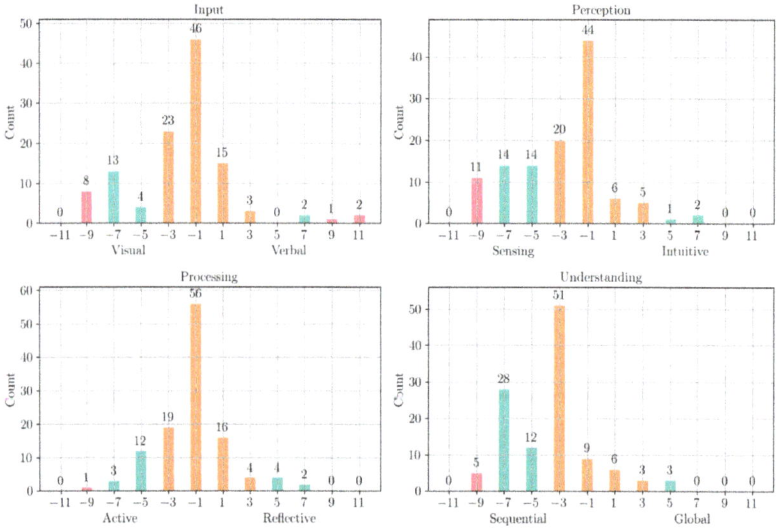

Figure 11. Distribution of learning styles of the students in the test data, according to our prediction algorithm.

Table 8. Comparison of grades between the three SCORM-based groups described in Table 4.

Group	Score	
	Pre-Mock Exam	**Mock Exam**
Balanced (N = 23)	9.83 ± 5.29	12.30 ± 7.96
ILS (N = 26)	10.61 ± 6.66	11.53 ± 8.04
IA (N = 29)	8.19 ± 4.74	12.14 ± 7.87

4.4. Automatic Classification of Learning Resources

The automated pipeline described in Section 3.2.3 was applied to a corpus of 38 digital learning objects, extracted from the publicly accessible educational repository https://boa.

udea.edu.co/innovacionesdidacticas/ (accessed on 26 June 2025). We successfully retrieved and parsed raw HTML for 97.4% of those resources, extracting on average 27.4 ± 6.3 unique tags and 1183 ± 421 words of text content per resource. This initial step provided a detailed structural and textual footprint for each object, far exceeding the granularity offered by conventional metadata fields.

From these parsed features, we integrated binary and frequency-based indicators aligned with the FSLSM, as well as semantic analysis of textual content. Taken together, these results affirmed that an HTML-driven, rule-based extraction pipeline can deliver comprehensive FSLSM-aligned vectors at scale, with over 19% of LOs exhibited multi-style profiles scoring $\geq |4|$ in two or more dimensions. These vectors were normalized and interpreted using a threshold-based decision rule to identify dominant, secondary, or neutral styles. The distribution of dominant learning styles among the corpus was visual 42.1%, sequential 28.9%, active 26.3%, and verbal 5.3%.

This distribution highlighted a notable bias in existing resources toward visual and procedural content structures, potentially reflecting underlying design trends in open educational resource creation. Conversely, intuitive and global learning preferences were significantly underrepresented, suggesting potential gaps in the availability of resources for these learner types.

The resulting resource vectors were stored in a centralized database and linked to the individual FSLSM profiles generated in the first phase. This alignment enabled the development of a personalized recommendation engine capable of dynamically selecting and suggesting resources based on the best pedagogical match for each student.

Overall, this automatic classification framework represents an advancement over traditional metadata-based approaches. It leverages both the structural and semantic dimensions of digital content to produce informed representation of learning resources, which is essential for the implementation of reliable recommendations systems.

4.5. Automatic Generation of Learning Object Metadata

To illustrate the outcomes of the automatic generation automatic metadata generation module , and to demonstrate how it can be applied to different thematics, in Figure 12 is shown an example of an online learning object interface from a course of historical evolution of engineering education.

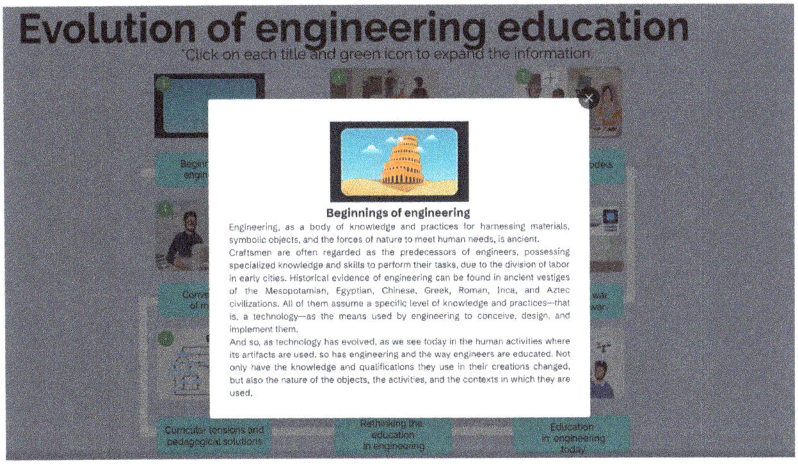

Figure 12. Example of a learning object.

After HTML parsing, the module consolidated the resource full text and structural summaries into a single prompt sent to the LLM. It then returned standards-compliant metadata in JSON format, which can be directly ingested by an LSM.

The following JSON exemplifies the metadata produced for the learning object in Figure 10. It includes ten thematic keywords, a concise learning objective, automatic language detection, a recommended educational level, and a description of the interactive component


```
{
  "topic": "Evolution of Engineering Education",
  "keywords": [
    "engineering origins",
    "ancient civilizations",
    "craftsmanship",
    "technology evolution",
    "educational practices",
    "Mesopotamia",
    "Egypt",
    "Greece",
    "Rome",
    "Inca"
  ],
  "learning_objective": "Upon completion, the learner will be able to describe how early craftsmen and ancient civilizations contributed to the development of engineering as a distinct discipline.",
  "language": "English",
  "educational_level": "Secondary",
  "interactivity_type": "Interactive modal triggered by click"
}
```


When evaluated against a human-annotated sample, the automated workflow demonstrated strong agreement with expert reviewers. The resulting JSON outputs can be seamlessly imported to LMS repositories, enabling immediate indexing, searchability, and personalized recommendation without manual tagging. These results confirmed that our AI-driven metadata generation module reliably produces high-quality, interoperable descriptors; greatly enhancing resource discoverability and supporting adaptive, learner-centered educational ecosystems.

4.6. Discussion

The personalized learning model developed in this study exhibits considerable potential for adaptation across a broad spectrum of educational settings beyond its initial implementation context. The combination of AI-powered recommendation systems and differentiated instructional strategies can be effectively applied at various educational levels, including primary and secondary education, vocational training programs, and higher education institutions.

In these diverse learning environments, identifying the unique characteristics of each student, such as cognitive preferences and learning objectives, is essential for delivering impactful instruction. The pipeline can be adjusted to gather and process this information through direct assessments or by analyzing learner interactions within digital learning platforms. This data-driven methodology enables the creation of tailored learning trajectories that address the distinct needs and contextual conditions of different educational systems.

Likewise, the techniques used for metadata annotation and the classification of learning resources are highly adaptable. Educational institutions can leverage these methods to structure digital content based on curriculum requirements, instructional goals, and individual learner profiles. This contributes to more effective resource organization and ensures that learners are provided with content that is pedagogically relevant and aligned with their learning styles.

One of the model's key strengths lies in its capacity for real-time adaptation. As students engage with learning platforms, their profiles are continually updated, allowing the system to refine its recommendations and interventions dynamically. This level of adaptability is particularly beneficial in formal educational contexts, where monitoring student progress and providing timely support are crucial for preventing disengagement or failure.

Moreover, the deployment of AI-driven recommendation strategies can significantly boost learner engagement by delivering content that is both relevant and personalized. When tailored to different educational environments, these strategies promote more inclusive and effective learning experiences, fostering academic success and advancing educational equity.

A distinctive contribution of this model is the integration of HTML-based semantic analysis and metadata-driven content classification. The use of HTML parsers and rule-based feature mapping allowed for the automatic characterization of learning objects along the Felder-Silverman dimensions, supporting a deeper alignment between content properties and learner profiles.

Additionally, the unsupervised modeling of learning style preferences (derived from clickstream data, session segmentation, and engagement metrics) showcased the feasibility of scalable personalization without relying exclusively on self-reported assessments. The fusion of clustering techniques with instructional design theory bridges a critical gap in many LMS environments that still operate under static, one-size-fits-all frameworks.

In summary, the model presented in this study offers a flexible and scalable approach that can be adapted to a variety of instructional settings. Its implementation has the potential to transform conventional pedagogical models by encouraging student-centered learning, improving the alignment of educational resources, and enabling timely, data-informed instructional interventions. Furthermore, the methodological framework developed provides a replicable blueprint for other institutions aiming to leverage AI and behavioral data for meaningful personalization in digital education.

5. Conclusions

This study highlights the transformative potential of AI in driving personalized learning in virtual education environments. By applying AI techniques to classify learning objects and generate tailored content recommendations, we developed a dynamic and adaptive learning model capable of addressing the individual needs of students at scale. Our findings demonstrate that the integration of AI into educational systems can improve instructional efficiency and facilitate the construction of personalized learning pathways, ultimately leading to better academic outcomes.

The use of the FSLSM for structuring and labeling learning resources provided a solid pedagogical foundation for content adaptation. By aligning instructional materials with cognitive preferences through real-time analysis of learner behavior, the model ensures greater relevance and pedagogical impact. This alignment not only supports deeper content comprehension and retention but also promotes a greater level of satisfaction and motivation.

A key strength of the model lies in its capacity for continuous self-optimization. Through a dynamic feedback loop that captures interaction data and performance metrics, the system can iteratively refine both content delivery and instructional strategies. This responsiveness allows the learning environment to evolve alongside student progress, ensuring timely support and fostering sustained engagement throughout the learning process.

Furthermore, the flexibility and scalability of the pipeline make it more applicable than traditional academic settings. Its architecture supports adaptation to vocational training, professional development programs, and other lifelong learning contexts where personalization and responsiveness are critical. By relying on real-time behavioral data rather than static profiles, the model offers a practical pathway for implementing equitable, learner-centered instruction across diverse populations.

The integration of AI into personalized learning represents not just a technological advancement, but a fundamental pedagogical shift. It enables data-informed decision-making, enhances instructional effectiveness, and promotes inclusive educational practices. The framework and evidence presented in this study provide a replicable model for institutions aiming to build more adaptive, equitable, and effective digital learning ecosystems.

In conclusion, the methodological approach adopted in this project constituted an advancement in educational innovation. By integrating AI with the pedagogical foundations of differentiated instruction, the system seeks to promote a virtual learning environment that is more personalized, adaptive, and responsive to students' individual needs. While further empirical validation is required, this approach may contribute to enhancing student engagement and academic performance. It represents a promising step toward the development of more effective virtual education models grounded in pedagogical theory.

Author Contributions: Conceptualization, L.F. and C.M.-C.; methodology, L.F. and C.M.-C.; software, J.M. and A.G.; validation, J.M., A.G. and C.M.-C.; formal analysis, J.M., A.G. and C.M.-C.; investigation, L.F., J.M., A.G. and C.M.-C.; resources, L.F.; data curation, J.M., A.G. and C.M.-C.; writing—original draft preparation, L.F., J.M., A.G. and C.M.-C.; writing—review and editing, L.F., J.M., A.G. and C.M.-C.; visualization, J.M. and A.G.; supervision, L.F. and C.M.-C.; project administration, L.F.; funding acquisition, L.F. All authors have read and agreed to the published version of the manuscript.

Funding: This work is funded by General Royalty System of Colombia (SGR—Sistema General de Regalías) BPIN-2021000100186.

Institutional Review Board Statement: This project was approved by the Collegiate Body of Administration and Decision (OCAD) for Science, Technology, and Innovation (CTeI) of the General Royalty System (SGR), under project code BPIN 2021000100186, in accordance with Agreement No. 14 dated 31 January 2022. Additionally, the project—including all ethical considerations—was authorized for execution by the Universidad de Antioquia through the Vice-Rector's Office for Research and the Committee for Research Development (CODI), as documented in ACTA 2022-53069 for Registration and Intellectual Property.

Informed Consent Statement: Informed consent was obtained from all subjects involved in the study.

Data Availability Statement: Indeed, we used a new dataset derived from our Moodle courses. Unfortunately, due to privacy concerns related to student data, we are unable to make this dataset publicly available.

Acknowledgments: We thank the Didactic and New Technologies UdeA Research Group for their contributions to the pedagogical components of this paper, especially Doris Ramírez, Ángela Vergara, Diana Oviedo, Lorena Quiroz, and David Bernal. We also express our gratitude to graduate student Lina M. Montoya for her valuable contributions to the research objectives that supported the development of this paper.

Conflicts of Interest: Author Carlos Mendoza-Cardenas was employed by the company Twitch Interactive. The remaining authors declare that the research was conducted in the absence of any commercial or financial relationships that could be construed as a potential conflict of interest.

References

1. Bernacki, M.L.; Greene, M.J.; Lobczowski, N.G. A systematic review of research on personalized learning: Personalized by whom, to what, how, and for what purpose (s)? *Educ. Psychol. Rev.* **2021**, *33*, 1675–1715. [CrossRef]
2. Fu, Y.; Weng, Z.; Wang, J. Examining AI Use in Educational Contexts: A Scoping Meta-Review and Bibliometric Analysis. *Int. J. Artif. Intell. Educ.* **2024**. [CrossRef]
3. Adnan, M.; Habib, A.; Ashraf, J.; Mussadiq, S.; Raza, A.A.; Abid, M.; Bashir, M.; Khan, S.U. Predicting at-risk students at different percentages of course length for early intervention using machine learning models. *IEEE Access* **2021**, *9*, 7519–7539. [CrossRef]
4. Tomasevic, N.; Gvozdenovic, N.; Vranes, S. An overview and comparison of supervised data mining techniques for student exam performance prediction. *Comput. Educ.* **2020**, *143*, 103676. [CrossRef]
5. Zerkouk, M.; Mihoubi, M.; Chikhaoui, B.; Wang, S. Predicting Online Education Dropout: A new Machine Learning Model based on Sentiment Analysis, Socio-demographic, and Behavioral Data. *Int. J. Artif. Intell. Educ.* **2025**. [CrossRef]
6. Chen, L.; Chen, P.; Lin, Z. Artificial Intelligence in Education: A Review. *IEEE Access* **2020**, *8*, 75264–75278. [CrossRef]
7. Dantas, L.A.; Cunha, A. An Integrative Debate on Learning Styles and the Learning Process. *Soc. Sci. Humanit. Open* **2020**, *2*, 100017. [CrossRef]
8. Fleming, N.; Baume, D. *Learning Styles Again: Varking Up the Right Tree!* Educational Developments, SEDA Ltd.: Birmingham, UK, 2006; pp. 4–7.
9. Kolb, A.Y.; Kolb, D.A. Learning Styles and Learning Spaces: Enhancing Experiential Learning in Higher Education Experience-Based Learning Systems. *Acad. Manag. Learn. Educ.* **2005**, *4*, 193–212. [CrossRef]
10. Freiberg, A.; Fernández, M. Honey-Alonso Learning Styles Questionnaire: An Analysis of its Psychometric Properties in College Students. *Summa Psicológica Ust.* **2012**, *10*, 103–117.
11. Swailes, S.; Senior, B. The Dimensionality of Honey and Mumford's Learning Styles Questionnaire. *Int. J. Sel. Assess.* **1999**, *7*, 1–11. [CrossRef]
12. Coffield, F.; Moseley, D.; Hall, E.; Ecclestone, K. *Learning Styles and Pedagogy in Post-16 Learning: A Systematic and Critical Review*; Learning and Skills Research Centre: London, UK, 2004.
13. Felder, R.M. Learning and Teaching Styles in Engineering Education. Available online: http://www.ncsu.edu/felder-public/ILSpage.html (accessed on 26 June 2025).
14. Kouis, D.; Kyprianos, K.; Ermidou, P.; Kaimakis, P.; Koulouris, A. A framework for assessing lmss e-courses content type compatibility with learning styles dimensions. *J. E-Learn. Knowl. Soc.* **2020**, *16*, 73–86.
15. El-Bishouty, M.M.; Aldraiweesh, A.; Alturki, U.; Tortorella, R.; Yang, J.; Chang, T.-W.; Graf, S.; Kinshuk. Use of Felder and Silverman learning style model for online course design. *Educ. Technol. Res. Dev.* **2019**, *67*, 161–177. [CrossRef]
16. Venkatesh, M.; Sathyalakshmi, S. Smart learning using personalised recommendations in web-based learning systems using artificial bee colony algorithm to improve learning performance. *Electron. Gov. Int. J.* **2020**, *16*, 101–117. [CrossRef]
17. Sianturi, S.T.; Yuhana, U.L. Student behaviour analysis to detect learning styles using decision tree, naive bayes, and k-nearest neighbor method in moodle learning management system. *IPTEK J. Technol. Sci.* **2022**, *33*, 94–104. [CrossRef]
18. Hwang, G.-J.; Sung, H.-Y.; Chang, S.-C.; Huang, X.-C. A fuzzy expert system-based adaptive learning approach to improving students' learning performances by considering affective and cognitive factors. *Comput. Educ. Artif. Intell.* **2020**, *1*, 100003. [CrossRef]
19. Kolekar, S.V.; Pai, R.M.; MM, M.P. Rule based adaptive user interface for adaptive e-learning system. *Educ. Inf. Technol.* **2019**, *24*, 613–641. [CrossRef]
20. Tarus, J.K.; Niu, Z.; Yousif, A. A hybrid knowledge-based recommender system for e-learning based on ontology and sequential pattern mining. *Future Gener. Comput. Syst.* **2017**, *72*, 37–48. [CrossRef]
21. Moodle Docs. Database Schema Introduction. Available online: https://moodledev.io/docs/apis/core/dml/database-schema (accessed on 5 April 2025).
22. Al-Azawei, A.; Parslow, P.; Lundqvist, K. A psychometric analysis of reliability and validity of the index of learning styles (ILS). *Int. J. Psychol. Stud.* **2015**, *7*, 46–57. [CrossRef]

Multimodal Technologies and Interaction

Article

Rethinking the Bebras Challenge in Virtual Reality: Implementation and Usability Study of a Computational Thinking Game

Jelena Nakić [1,*], Ivana Rogulj [2] and Lada Maleš [3]

[1] Faculty of Science, University of Split, 21000 Split, Croatia
[2] Ericsson Nikola Tesla, 21000 Split, Croatia
[3] Faculty of Humanities and Social Sciences, University of Split, 21000 Split, Croatia; lada.males@ffst.hr
* Correspondence: jelena.nakic@pmfst.hr

Abstract: Virtual reality (VR) technology is becoming increasingly relevant as a modern educational tool. However, its application in teaching and learning computational thinking remains relatively underexplored. This paper presents the implementation of selected tasks from the international Bebras Challenge in a VR environment called ThinkLand. A comparative study was conducted to evaluate the usability of the developed game across two interface types: mobile devices and desktop computers. A total of 100 participants, including high school and university students, took part in the study. The overall usability rating was classified as "good", suggesting that ThinkLand holds promise as a platform for supporting computational thinking education. To assess specific aspects of interface usability, a custom Virtual Environment Usability Questionnaire (VEUQ) was developed. Regression analysis was performed to examine the relationship between participants' age, gender, and interface type with both learning performance and perceived usability, as measured by the VEUQ. The analysis revealed statistically significant differences in interaction patterns between device types, providing practical insights for improving interface design. Validated in this study, the VEUQ proved to be an effective instrument for informing interaction design and guiding the development of educational VR applications for both mobile and desktop platforms.

Keywords: computational thinking; Bebras challenge; virtual reality; game-based learning; problem-solving; usability; human–computer interaction; mixed methods; virtual environment usability questionnaire; linear regression

1. Introduction

The international Bebras Challenge, which originated in Lithuania and was launched in 2004, has grown into a global educational initiative engaging more than 3 million elementary and high school students across more than 80 countries [1]. The goal of the competition is to help students discover their talent and foster interest in computational thinking (CT) through engaging and challenging tasks that emphasize problem-solving and logical reasoning, without requiring prior coding knowledge. Computational thinking as defined by Wing [2] is a way of thinking that involves a set of skills and techniques to solve problems, design systems, and understand human behavior by drawing on the concepts fundamental to computer science. The four key techniques to CT are decomposition (breaking down complex problem into smaller parts), pattern recognition (finding similarities or sequences in problems or data), abstraction (focusing on important and ignoring irrelevant details) and algorithm design (implementing step by step instructions for solving problems) [3]. Simply put, CT encourages a systematic and logical approach to problem-solving and therefore can be useful in many disciplines, beyond computer science. Recent studies, as reviewed in [4], highlight the positive impact of serious and digital games in educational on students' engagement, motivation, and development of CT. The findings support the notion that incorporating game-based elements into educational curricula can be an effective strategy for enhancing computational competencies among students.

The potential of utilizing tasks from the Bebras Challenge to inspire the design of educational games aimed at enhancing CT skills is the subject of extensive research and studies have consistently found that Bebras tasks serve as a valuable source of inspiration for designing CT games, e.g., [5]. By integrating Bebras tasks into innovative and disruptive learning environments, such as virtual reality (VR), we can achieve a balanced level of educational and entertainment aspects and further enhance students' engagement and CT skills. VR allows for the visualization of complex and abstract concepts, which can help students better understand and apply CT principles. For example, students can manipulate 3D virtual objects to understand algorithmic thinking or logical structures. While direct studies combining Bebras tasks with VR are limited, research indicates that adapting CT in VR can foster CT skills [6].

However, the usability of VR games designed to enhance CT skills is often reported in the literature as below optimal, and careful evaluation and iterative design improvements are usually required. For instance, a study by Agbo et al. [7] on the iThinkSmart VR game-based application highlights that, while VR can increase motivation and engagement, it may also introduce challenges such as higher cognitive load and usability issues. The authors note that "the VR features such as immersion, interactivity, immediacy, aesthetics, and presentational fidelity... could have contributed to their higher cognitive benefits", yet they also acknowledge that further usability enhancements are needed to fully realize the potential of supporting students in CT. Sukirman et al. [8] also emphasize that usability issues can hinder learning outcomes in VR games for CT education and that careful usability evaluations are necessary.

In this paper, we present ThinkLand, an interactive game that adapts Bebras tasks to a VR environment. We describe the interaction design within the developed game and reports on a systematic usability evaluation. Employing a mixed-methods approach that combines quantitative data analysis with qualitative interpretation, the research offers valuable insights into both overall usability and specific aspects of the game interface where usability challenges are identified. A custom-designed questionnaire was used to investigate context-specific usability issues, with particular attention given to differences between mobile and desktop platforms. Guided by established principles of human–computer interaction, the findings will inform the potential redesign strategies for the ThinkLand interface, ensuring that its highly interactive elements support rather than hinder the learning process and the achievement of meaningful educational outcomes.

The paper is structured as follows. Section 2 provides a literature review on the use of VR in education, with particular emphasis on CT education. Section 3 presents ThinkLand. Section 4 outlines the applied instruments and methods, covering both the pilot study and main study. Section 5 presents the results. Section 6 provides interpretation and discussion of findings. Section 7 concludes the paper.

2. Related Work

It is difficult to provide a single definition of VR, especially after the emergence of terms such as augmented reality (AR) and extended reality (ER), which often complement or overlap. For the purpose of this article, VR will be defined as a technology that enables users to engage in a computer-generated environment designed to simulate aspects of reality.

VR systems can be categorized based on the degree of immersion they provide. In [9], immersion is defined as an objective, technology-based property of VR system. Immersion is described as the extent to which the system delivers an inclusive, extensive, surrounding, and vivid illusion of reality to the senses of a human participant. Depending on the level of immersion experienced by the user, VR is most commonly classified into three categories: fully immersive, semi-immersive, and non-immersive [10,11], with each category based on the degree of sensory engagement and the type of technology used. Fully immersive VR completely isolates a user from the real world and provides full sensory engagement using head-mounted displays (HMDs) and motion tracking. Semi-immersive VR uses larger displays or multi-display systems, and the user is only partially immersed, e.g., CAVE systems and flight simulators. In non-immersive VR, users remain aware of the physical environment. Interaction with VR is provided through VR applications displayed on standard screens (desktop or mobile) and controlled via keyboard, mouse or touchscreen.

VR technology has been applied in various fields due to its ability to provide users with an enhanced experience through an immersive and interactive environment. Some of the fields that implement VR include gaming and entertainment, education and training, healthcare, industry and engineering, military, defense, and tourism. Despite the diversity of these application fields, they all share the fundamental requirement for realistic simulations and interactive experiences.

2.1. VR in Education

Numerous systematic literature reviews and individual studies have investigated the use of VR technology in education. In this section, systematic literature review papers are presented, followed by an analysis of studies comparing immersive VR and non-immersive VR across various aspects of educational use.

A review of research on application of learning theories in VR-based education for the period from 2012 to 2022 is presented in [12]. The authors analyzed each learning theory and educational approach across different educational levels. The Scopus database was used for the research, the PRISMA guidelines were applied and finally 17 studies were selected. The findings of these studies highlight five educational approaches, one methodology, five learning theories, and one theoretical framework, all discussed in the context of VR in education. The research identified key theoretical frameworks, including constructivism, experiential learning, and gamification, alongside others such as Cognitive Load Theory and TPACK. The findings suggest that constructivism is the most frequently applied theoretical basis for VR in education, that experiential learning is most appropriate for VR and that the gamification of learning has the greatest future potential.

A literature review of personalization techniques applied in immersive VR to support educational objectives in classroom settings is presented in [13]. Furthermore, the study analyzes gamification techniques employed in VR applications for educational purposes. The advantages, limitations, and effectiveness of VR as a learning method were examined as well as the type of hardware device that was used in studies. The results of the analysis are as follows: (i) 50 of 69 studies incorporate at least one personalization mechanism, such as manipulating virtual objects or using gamification strategies (e.g., tutorials, gamified scenarios, and reward systems), (ii) the most common research subjects are university undergraduate students who appear in 58% of studies, (iii) the most frequent fields are chemistry and engineering, (iv) the most positively evaluated aspect is the enhancement of content knowledge with VR proving effective in facilitating learning, (v) many studies lack control groups and nearly half have small sample sizes and (vi) 35% of studies employed smartphone-based cardboard VR headsets due to their accessibility and cost-effectiveness. The authors found that none of the reviewed studies employed adaptive learning methodologies tailored to individual learners' educational needs.

In [14], 135 papers (68 focused on education and 67 on training) addressing serious games in immersive VR environments are examined. The review covers the use of VR serious games in order to explore how immersive VR technologies combined with serious games can improve learning and training outcomes. The results from both surveys (education and training) are presented according to the following categories: application domains and target audience, technological implementation and game design, performance evaluation procedures, and results of the performance evaluation. The study sets the foundation for future research on serious games in immersive VR, offering recommendations to enhance these tools for effective learning and training. These recommendations include conducting more rigorous and controlled experimental studies, developing standardized evaluation metrics, encouraging integration into educational frameworks, creating thoughtful design to ensure benefits are maintained even after the novelty effect wears off and to avoid cognitive overload or motion sickness, and ensuring scalable and cost-effective VR solutions.

A systematic review of immersive VR applications for higher education including 38 articles published between 2009 and 2018 is presented in [15]. The review identifies three key aspects for successful VR-based learning: the current domain structure in relation to learning content, the VR design elements, and the learning theories. The authors mapped application domains to learning content and examined the connection between design elements and educational objectives. The analysis revealed several gaps in the use of VR in higher education, e.g., learning theories are rarely integrated into VR application development to support and guide learning outcomes. Additionally, the evaluation of educational VR applications has predominantly focused on usability rather than actual learning effectiveness, and immersive VR has largely remained in the experimental and developmental stages, with limited integration into regular teaching. However, VR shows significant potential, reflecting its growing acceptance across various disciplines (18 application domains are identified in the review). The authors concluded that the identified gaps show opportunities in VR educational design, offering a pathway for future research and innovation.

The impact of AR and VR on various aspects of education, such as student motivation, learning outcomes, engagement and overall learning experiences, is presented in [16]. A systematic literature review comprising 82 papers was conducted on different educational domains, namely K-12 education, higher education, STEM education, professional training, and lifelong learning. The literature analysis was conducted for the following categories: distribution according to educational levels, distribution of studies according to publication year, implementation of AR/VR in distance education, K-12 education, higher education and medical education. One of the findings is that VR is mostly implemented in higher education, but studies on VR applications in higher education often lack explicit reference to foundational learning theories. Furthermore, in K-12 education, AR technologies have received more attention and have been implemented more frequently compared to VR. The authors concluded that AR and VR have significant potential to transform education by making learning more engaging and dynamic, and offering students an immersive experience. Despite the benefits provided by the integration of AR/VR into the learning environment, the observed challenges include cognitive load, cybersickness, cost, equitable access, curriculum challenges, and lack of instructional strategies. The existing literature often lacks a solid grounding in learning theories and the reviewed studies prioritize usability over the development of a robust theoretical framework. The integration of pedagogical theories into these applications can enhance their effectiveness. Nine recommendations for practical implementations of AR/VR technologies are provided.

In [17], a systematic review on the use of immersive HMD-based VR educational applications in comparison to less immersive methods, such as desktop-based VR, is presented. Immersive VR is significantly more effective for learning activities that require high levels of visualization and experimental understanding, e.g., in anatomy learning [18], cell biology learning [19], or representation of the International Space Station [20]. The analysis showed that despite many advantages of using immersive VR in education, some studies found no significant differences in attainment level regardless of whether immersive or non-immersive methods were utilized, i.e., when the content of learning did not strongly benefit from spatial immersion or interactivity. These results confirmed that matching the content and learning objective to the medium is one of the key factors in VR effectiveness.

The following studies compare immersive VR and non-immersive VR across different application domains.

In [21], the authors conducted a study that found that immersive VR improved performance on tasks requiring remembering but not on tasks requiring deeper understanding. In [22], participants learned conceptual and abstract relative motion concepts using either immersive VR or desktop VR. The findings revealed that those in the I-VR group outperformed their D-VR counterparts in solving two-dimensional problems, e.g., scenarios where one object moves vertically and the other moves horizontally. However, no significant difference was observed between the groups for problems involving only a single spatial dimension, e.g., a common physics problem where two cars are moving toward each other.

Some studies [23,24] found no significant difference in learning outcomes between immersive VR, desktop VR and 2D videos. Moreover, in [25], the authors compared teaching neuroanatomy from online textbooks and using immersive VR and found that the latter was no more effective. Also, there was no difference in information retention rates when the participants were reassessed 8 weeks later. The studies [26,27] demonstrated instances where immersive VR produced lower results compared to the non-immersive approach. In [26], immersive VR laboratory simulation results (combination of assessment and EEG) showed significantly lower test scores than their non-immersive counterparts. Similarly, in [27], the authors observed a significant performance decrement in biology learning when immersive VR was employed, relative to a PowerPoint presentation. These findings are consistent with Mayer's Cognitive Theory of Multimedia Learning [28] and may give a possible explanation for poorer results using immersive VR, i.e., that overly rich multimedia can increase cognitive load, detract from the learning task and potentially harm learning outcomes.

Finally, comprehensive guidelines for design and evaluation of immersive learning can be found in [29]. The book presents cutting-edge techniques and pedagogical approaches, best practices in educational VR as well as emerging trends, opportunities and recommendations for integrating VR and XR into pedagogical practice. Several best practice examples in the book confirmed that usability of learning environment is the crucial factor of learning achievements, as also suggested in [30].

2.2. Computational Thinking in VR

A systematic review of studies on teaching CT using game-based learning within VR environments is presented in [31]. The authors selected 15 papers following PRISMA guidelines, and based on their analysis, a conceptual framework for designing a strategy to learn CT skills through game-based VR settings is proposed. The framework consists of three parts: game elements (playability and interactivity), VR features (presence and immersion), and CT concepts (skills). Furthermore, the variable enjoyment is introduced as a combination of both game elements and VR features. The game elements and VR features can be encapsulated in VR game applications for CT, and they are independent variables that intervene in CT skills. The CT skills are the goal of the learning process, i.e., they are dependent variables in the conceptual framework that consist of four concepts (decomposition, pattern recognition, abstraction and algorithm design). The framework suggests that integrating engaging game elements with immersive VR features can effectively foster the development of CT skills among learners. Specifically, game elements can improve user engagement, while VR features help learners stay focused and better understand complex and abstract ideas. Consequently, learners are more likely to practice and internalize CT skills through deep engagement and meaningful content interaction.

The use of immersive VR mini games to enhance CT skills in higher education students is presented in [6]. The VR application was developed, integrating three mini games: Mount Patti Treasure (developed by students), River Crossing, and Tower of Hanoi (both well-known computational problems in computer science). The users found the VR mini games interactive and immersive, and reported improved CT skills. The expedition narrative within the VR game stimulates learners' curiosity, which contributes to sustaining their engagement and learning progress. The quantitative analysis confirmed that students' CT competency can be enhanced through consistent playing mini games.

Similarly, the potential of VR mini games to support the development of CT skills among higher education students is investigated in [7]. An experiment was conducted with 47 computer science students divided into two groups. The experimental group (21 students) played iThinkSmartn, a VR game-based application containing mini games developed to assist learners in acquiring CT competency. The control group (26 students) learned CT concepts through traditional lecture-based instruction. The post-test and post-questionnaire results revealed that students in the experimental group demonstrated significantly better CT competency, experienced greater cognitive benefits, and showed increased motivation to learn CT concepts.

The effectiveness of VR application Logibot in teaching fundamental programming concepts and its impact on user engagement are examined in [32]. A comparative study between Logibot (VR block-based programming game) and LightBot (desktop-based game with similar mechanics) was conducted. The study involved ten participants, who were split into two groups. Participants completed programming tasks, followed by the User Engagement Survey (UES) and interviews to gather qualitative feedback. Despite the initial hypothesis, participants found the desktop application more engaging than the VR application. The study highlighted the importance of intuitive interaction design and clear instructional guidance in VR applications to enhance usability and engagement. Furthermore, future research should consider more advanced hardware.

The development of a VR game CT Saber (inspired by the VR game Beat Saber and designed for learning CT) and the evaluation of its usability are presented in the paper [8]. The usability of CT Saber was evaluated through testing involving 36 computer science students. The study concluded that CT Saber fulfills the established usability criteria, highlighting its potential as an engaging and effective VR-based educational tool for promoting CT skills among higher education students.

The use of VR as a tool to enhance students' understanding of abstract concepts in computer science, particularly recursion is explored in the [33]. A comparison between learners who used the VR Tower of Hanoi software and those who used the conventional puzzle revealed that the VR experience led to improved understanding for most participants. Specifically, some of them demonstrated a deeper understanding of the concept of recursion. Post-survey results indicated that the majority of participants found the immersive VR environment helpful when learning abstract subjects.

All the previously cited studies demonstrate that integrating game-based learning with VR environments effectively fosters CT skills. By combining engaging game elements with immersive VR features, these approaches enhance learner engagement, facilitate understanding of complex concepts, and ultimately lead to improved CT competency and motivation. While usability remains a key consideration, VR's unique ability to visualize abstract ideas positions it as a powerful tool for CT education.

3. Implementation

In this section, we first describe the Bebras Challenge and then explain how we implemented selected tasks into a VR application. Since the learning strategies related to CT are already embedded within the tasks, this section focuses solely on describing the interaction design that supports the process of solving these tasks.

3.1. The Bebras Challenge

The Bebras Challenge features tasks in logical reasoning, pattern recognition, algorithmic design, and data representation, all collaboratively developed by an international network of educators [1].

Depending on the country, the challenge is divided into five to six age categories, lasts 40–45 min, and typically takes place online. Typically, students solve 12–15 problems, individually, under teacher supervision. The annual competition, usually held in November, is automatically evaluated online. All participants receive certificates, and best participants may be invited to further competitions or workshops, depending on national arrangements.

In Croatia, the Bebras Challenge (the Croatian name is Dabar@ucitelji.hr) has been organized since 2016 by the association of teachers Partners in Learning [34]. The competition has been held continuously since 2016, when almost 6000 students participated, while in 2024, 51,220 students participated. The challenge Dabar@ucitelji.hr is aligned with the national informatics curriculum, promoting CT from an early age and gradually introducing students to digital technology. It is conducted in schools as an integral part of informatics education, within the regular timetable.

3.2. ThinkLand

The tasks in the Bebras Challenge are often interactive and engaging but limited to a two-dimensional representation on a computer screen. From the pool of tasks in the Dabar@ucitelji.hr competition, we selected four tasks characterized by different levels of user interaction with objects for implementation in a VR environment: Beaver-Modulo, Tower of Blocks, Tree Sudoku, and Elevator. We believe that transferring these tasks into a 3D world offers the greatest potential benefits of VR adaptation.

For the selected tasks, we present a brief version of the task texts and illustrations, showing how the original 2D tasks were adapted and implemented into a 3D environment. The complete versions of the original tasks are provided as Supplementary Materials. They include the type and difficulty of each task and the target age group, as well as the solution, explanation, and their connection to computational concepts.

The implementation was developed on the CoSpaces Edu platform, using the CoBlocks programming language. The design and implementation of the game were guided by Nielsen's usability heuristics [35] to ensure the interface is clear, consistent, intuitive, easy to use, supports error recognition and correction, and enables effective interaction.

All tasks in the game are presented in Croatian, as the game is intended for Croatian students. The ThinkLand game is available at the following link: https://edu.cospaces.io/TRL-FUP (accessed on 9 June 2025). While we encourage readers to explore and play the game, the following sections provide the game description to help understand the tasks, the VR environment, and the ways users interact with the objects within it.

3.2.1. Implementation of the Beaver-Modulo Task

The first task in the game involves simple animation. The task text is as follows:

Some beavers took part in the annual Beaver Challenge. Their first task was to jump from rock to rock in a clockwise direction, as indicated by the arrow (shown in Figure 1), starting from rock number 0. For example, if a beaver jumps 8 times, it will land on rock number 3:

Figure 1. Illustration from the original Beaver-Modulo task.

0 → 1 → 2 → 3 → 4 → 0 → 1 → 2 → 3.

One of the beavers showed off and jumped an astonishing 129 times. On which rock did it land?

The answer is entered as an integer between 0 and 4.

Due to the absence of a beaver character in the free version of the CoSpaces Edu platform, the main character in the 3D implementation was replaced with a raccoon, and the task text was adapted to reflect this change.

The implemented 3D version of the task in VR environment is shown in Figure 2. In this version, the user moves the raccoon from one rock to the next by clicking on the character, prompting it to jump to the subsequent rock in the sequence. Once the user is ready to submit their final answer, they can click on the girl character to select one of the numbers (0, 1, 2, 3, or 4) displayed within the virtual environment.

Figure 2. The Beaver-Modulo task as implemented in ThinkLand.

The task was intentionally selected and positioned as the first in the game due to its minimal level of user interaction. Its purpose was to introduce users to the game interface, the task presentation format, the process of submitting responses, and transitioning to new tasks, all without burdening them with complex interaction mechanics. While the raccoon character moves from stone to stone, the movement is deliberately simple and symbolic, designed not for interactional depth but to ensure users can focus on understanding the environment and navigation flow at the start of the VR experience.

3.2.2. Implementation of the Tower of Blocks Task

The task text is the following:

Sam, the little beaver, is playing with his toy blocks. He built seven beautiful towers, each one made with blocks of the same size (as shown in Figure 3).

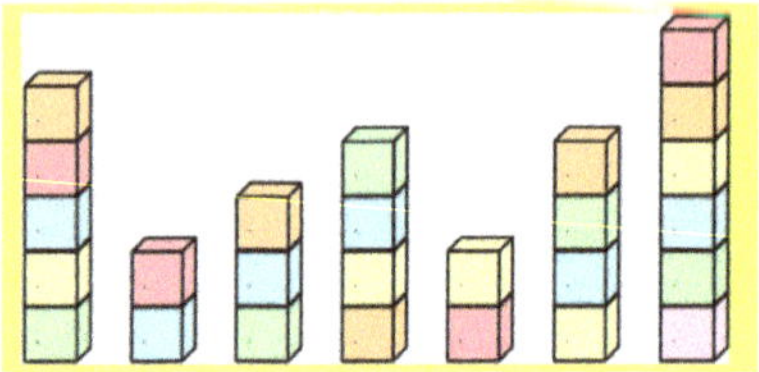

Figure 3. Illustration from the original Tower of Blocks task.

There are two ways to change the height of a tower: adding blocks to the top or removing blocks from the top. Adding or removing a block counts as a move. For instance, if he changes the height of the leftmost tower to 2, it takes 3 moves (removing 3 blocks), and if he changes it to 7, it takes 2 moves (adding 2 blocks). Moving a block from one tower to another is considered as 2 moves.

Sam wants all towers to be the same height, and he wants to make as few moves as possible.

In total, what is the minimum number of moves Sam needs in order to make all towers the same height?

Answer options are numbers 6 to 11.

The 3D implementation of the Tower of Blocks task is shown in Figure 4. In this interactive version, the user can modify the height of a tower by clicking on the desired tower and selecting either the Add or Remove button to add or remove a block. When a block is removed, it is placed in a designated area labeled "Uklonjene kocke" ("Removed blocks"); conversely, if the user wishes to add a block, they select one from the area labeled "Kocke za nadodavanje" ("Blocks for addition") and place it onto the chosen tower. Each move is automatically counted and displayed in the upper left corner ("Broj poteza"—"Number of moves").

If the user believes they have not achieved the minimum possible number of moves, they can click the "Pokreni opet" ("Restart") button, located between the two storage areas, to reset the task and attempt it again. Once the user is satisfied with their solution, they can submit their final answer by clicking on the squirrel character, which records the current number of moves displayed on the screen as their answer ("Klikni na mene kada želiš predati zadatak"—"Click on me when you want to submit the task").

In the original 2D multiple-choice version of the task, no interaction is possible, and users must mentally simulate the block movements and calculate the total number of moves required to equalize tower heights. In contrast, the 3D implementation enables users to actively manipulate blocks, visually track tower height changes, and receive immediate feedback on each move. This interactivity allows users not only to execute an entire sequence of moves, but also to experiment with alternative strategies. By resetting the task and trying different solutions, they can easily identify which sequence results in the minimal number of moves. Thus, the 3D version enhances cognitive engagement by supporting experimentation, visual reasoning, and reflection on efficiency, which are not available in the original format.

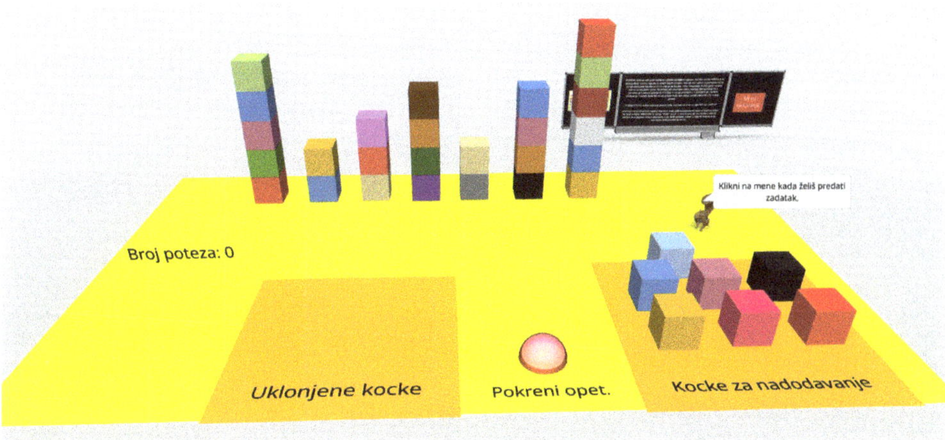

Figure 4. The Tower of Blocks task as implemented in ThinkLand.

3.2.3. Implementation of the Tree Sudoku Task

The following is the official task description:

A beaver's field is divided into 16 plots arranged in a 4 × 4 grid where they can place one tree in each plot.

They plant 16 trees of heights 1, 2, 3 and 4 in each field by following the rule:

- *Each row (a horizontal line) contains exactly one tree of each height;*
- *Each column (a vertical line) contains exactly one tree of each height.*

If beavers observe the trees in one line (see Figure 5), they cannot see trees that are hidden behind a taller tree. At the end of each row and column of the 4 × 4 field, the beavers placed a sign and wrote on it the numbers of trees visible from that position.

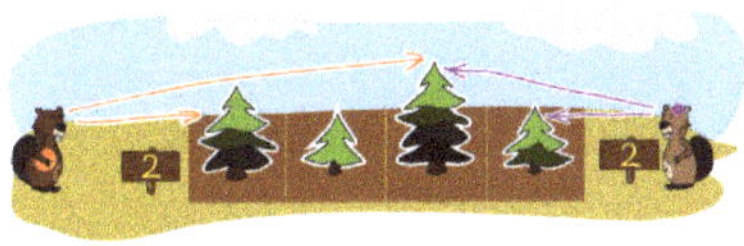

Figure 5. The beavers observe the trees.

Kubko has written down the numbers on the signs correctly, but he placed some trees in the wrong plots.

Can you find the mistakes Kubko made (shown in Figure 6) and correct the heights of the trees?

Figure 6. The mistakes Kubko made.

Click on a tree to change its height.

Figure 7 presents the screenshot of the ThinkLand interface showing the 3D version of the Tree Sudoku task. The grid on the left displays Kubko's initial planting of the trees, where the user observes and identifies the incorrect placements. The grid on the right allows the user to reposition the trees into the correct arrangement.

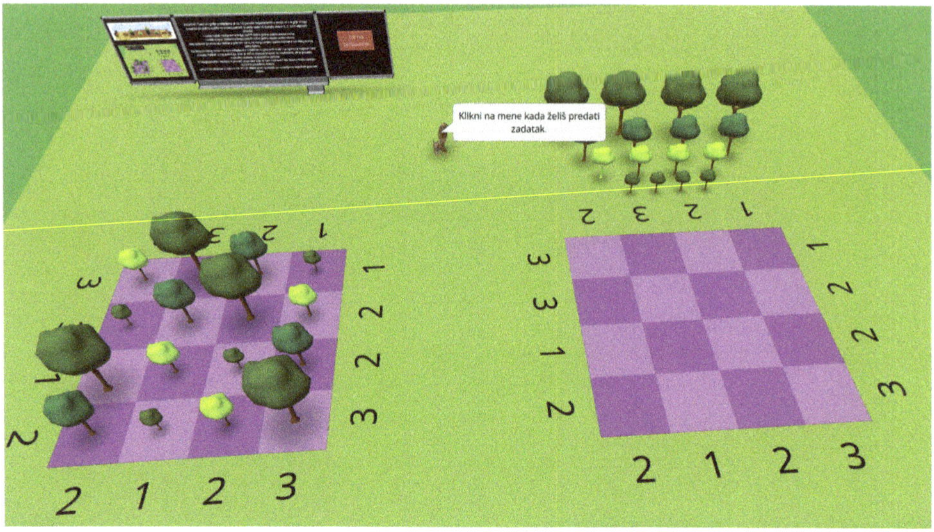

Figure 7. The Tree Sudoku task in ThinkLand.

To move a tree, the user first clicks on the tree and then selects the target plot where they wish to place it. Consistently with previous tasks, once the user is satisfied with their arrangement, they submit their final solution by clicking on the squirrel character.

As feedback, when a tree is placed onto a plot, the plot is temporarily highlighted in white to indicate successful placement. In this task, camera rotation is highly beneficial, as it allows the user to better observe and manipulate the 3D grid from different angles.

3.2.4. Implementation of the Elevator Task

The following is the official task description:

A group of beavers are visiting the countryside and want to take the elevator up to the observation deck (shown in Figure 8). But it's late and the elevator only goes up twice. The elevator has a load capacity of 30 kg.

Figure 8. Illustration from the original Elevator task.

How do you distribute the beavers with their luggage between the two elevator cabins so that as many beavers as possible can stand on the platform? Drag the beavers onto the two lifts below.

In the 3D version of the task, shown in Figure 9, the beavers were replaced with penguin characters, which are freely available within the CoSpaces Edu platform, and the task text was adapted accordingly.

Figure 9. Screenshot of the ThinkLand interface showing the Elevator task.

The elevators are represented by two platforms, one on the left and one on the right. The user moves a penguin by first clicking on the penguin and then on the elevator platform where they want to place it. The selected penguin then slowly slides onto the chosen elevator.

Next to each platform, a blue or pink button allows the user to return the last placed penguin from that elevator to its original starting position. Once the user has positioned all the penguins on the two elevators and is satisfied with their solution, they must click on the windmill in the center to activate the elevators and receive feedback on their answer.

In this task, particular emphasis was placed on ensuring intuitive interaction and delivering immediate visual feedback, achieved through animations of the penguins moving onto the platforms and real-time updates of the total weight displayed above each elevator.

4. Materials and Methods

The main objective of the study is to evaluate the usability of the ThinkLand, with a particular focus on comparing the desktop and mobile interfaces. Although many schools in Croatia are equipped with VR headsets, this research did not aim to examine usability across all possible platforms. Instead, it concentrated on those interfaces that are widely accessible to students in educational settings: desktop computers in school computer labs and students' personal mobile devices, which are already occasionally used for instructional purposes.

The conceptual framework of this study is grounded on the assumption that the type of interface (mobile or desktop) may influence both objective performance outcomes and subjective user experience in VR environments. It is presumed that when users are allowed to engage with the platform they are most comfortable with, their interaction becomes more intuitive, which can positively affect both efficiency (e.g., time and task performance) and satisfaction (e.g., perceived usability and experience).

Moreover, individual characteristics such as age and gender are considered relevant factors that may shape preferences and interaction patterns with digital technologies, potentially moderating the relationship between interface type and learning outcomes. Accordingly, the research also addresses additional questions related to how age, gender, and interface type influence game performance, specifically, learning outcomes and the time required to complete the entire challenge.

4.1. Instruments and Measures

The independent variables in this study are the age group, gender, and interface type. The dependent variables included participants' responses to 12 statements related to perceived usability of the game interface, the total score achieved in the game (referred to as Score) and the overall time required to complete the challenge (referred to as Time).

The ThinkLand VR game, as presented in Section 3, consists of four distinct tasks, each implemented as a separate scene within the virtual environment. Each task carries a maximum of 1 point. Task 3 allows partial scoring in increments of 0.25, while other tasks are scored with values 0 or 1. For the purposes of analysis, the point value achieved in each task is referred to as the task points. The outcome variable *Score* is defined as the sum of all task points, representing the overall challenge performance.

To evaluate the usability of the game interface, two questionnaires were used: System Usability Scale (SUS), a standardized usability assessment instrument and a custom-designed questionnaire, the Virtual Environment Usability Questionnaire (VEUQ), specifically developed for the purpose of this study to evaluate the perceived usability of the ThinkLand interface.

The System Usability Scale (SUS) [36] is a standardized instrument designed to assess participants' satisfaction with an interface. It is widely adopted for evaluating the overall perceived usability of systems and interfaces, offering a quick, reliable, and psychometrically robust assessment [37]. The SUS consists of 10 items, alternating between positive and negative formulations, and rated on a 5-point Likert scale (1 = Strongly disagree, 5 = Strongly agree). Items cover a range of usability aspects including complexity, consistency, confidence in use, and learnability. In the standard SUS scoring procedure, individual item responses are not analyzed separately. Instead, a composite usability score, ranging from 0 to 100, is calculated. Therefore, in the data analysis, individual SUS items will not be treated as dependent variables; only the overall SUS score will be considered. The SUS score will enable us to compare the obtained results with broader usability benchmarks established across a wide range of systems and applications.

The Virtual Environment Usability Questionnaire (VEUQ) was designed to systematically assess key usability aspects related to students' interaction with the ThinkLand environment. It is intended to serve as a complementary instrument to the SUS, providing a more detailed, context-specific evaluation of user interaction within the virtual environment. The construction of the VEUQ items was guided by established usability frameworks, primarily the ISO 9241-11:2018 standard, which defines usability in terms of effectiveness, efficiency, and satisfaction [38]. Additionally, four out of five theoretical components proposed by [39], learnability, efficiency, errors, and satisfaction, were considered to ensure a comprehensive evaluation of user experience.

The VEUQ consists of 12 items that capture key usability dimensions relevant to virtual environments including visual clarity and aesthetics, object interaction, navigational control, task flow and system responsiveness, instructional clarity and informational support. The items are rated on a 5-point Likert scale (1 = Strongly disagree, 5 = Strongly agree). The N/A option was included to account for the possibility that participants might not have used certain available interaction mechanisms, such as camera rotation or other, while solving the challenge. Following best practices adopted in the SUS, both positively and negatively worded statements were used in the VEUQ to minimize response bias and encourage participants to read each item carefully.

Prior to the implementation of the VEUQ, the quality and clarity of the questionnaire items were assessed through a pilot study, the details of which are presented in the following section. Based on the insights gained from interviews and observations during the pilot phase, minor linguistic adjustments were made to several items, improving their precision and comprehensibility. The structure and content of the final version of the VEUQ are presented in Table 1. This structure enabled a comprehensive evaluation of user experience, addressing both lower-level interaction mechanisms, such as object selection and spatial navigation, and higher-level usability factors, including the effectiveness of instructional support and the smoothness of task progression. Adopting this multidimensional approach provides a complete understanding of usability challenges specific to interactive VR environments.

Table 1. Virtual Environment Usability Questionnaire (VEUQ).

Item	Statement	N/A	1	2	3	4	5
q1	The world representation is clear and interesting.	○	○	○	○	○	○
q2	Recognizing objects within the world is problematic.	○	○	○	○	○	○
q3	It is always clear to me which object is selected.	○	○	○	○	○	○
q4	It was often not easy for me to select (click) the object I wanted.	○	○	○	○	○	○
q5	The on-screen instructions are useful.	○	○	○	○	○	○
q6	Rotating the space (camera) is too complicated.	○	○	○	○	○	○
q7	Zooming in the virtual world is easy.	○	○	○	○	○	○
q8	The task text on the board is always easily accessible.	○	○	○	○	○	○
q9	The on-screen instructions make it harder to complete the task.	○	○	○	○	○	○
q10	I was able to move the objects I wanted in a simple way.	○	○	○	○	○	○
q11	Switching to the next task is complicated.	○	○	○	○	○	○
q12	Receiving real-time feedback on scores while solving tasks is important.	○	○	○	○	○	○

In this study, an anonymous online survey was designed to collect the values of all the variables. The first part of this four-section survey is the SUS. The second part collects demographic data: education level (High School/University)—referred to as age, and gender (Male/Female/Prefer not to say), as well as the type of interface used to play the ThinkLand VR game (Desktop or Mobile). Besides these data that served as predictor variables, the participants also reported the values of outcome variables: task scores for each task in the game (used to calculate the score variable) and the total duration required to complete the entire challenge, i.e., the time. The third administered section of the survey is the VEUQ. This sequence of questionnaire administration was intended to encourage participants to first provide an overall usability rating and game performance data, before reflecting on specific aspects of the ThinkLand interface. In the final section, users were given the opportunity to provide qualitative feedback through a few open-ended questions.

4.2. Pilot Study

Following the generally recommended HCI practice of iterative design, implementation and evaluation of a pilot study was conducted to preliminarily assess the usability of the ThinkLand. Additionally, the study aimed to evaluate and refine the design of the VEUQ as an assessment instrument.

The pilot study involved 20 senior graduate students of Compute Science, recruited as a convenience sample due to their familiarity with digital environments and their ability to critically assess the clarity of questionnaire items and the usability of the ThinkLand interface.

Participants first completed the ThinkLand VR challenge and subsequently filled out the initial version of the VEUQ. Ten students were using their mobile devices, and ten students played the game on desktop computers. The thinking aloud protocol was employed in user testing to capture real-time feedback. After gameplay and questionnaire completion, individual interviews were conducted to gather the participants' feedback on the interaction experience, and on their understanding of the VEUQ items. Participants were specifically encouraged to comment on the clarity, relevance, and perceived difficulty of the questionnaire items, as well as to highlight any usability issues encountered during gameplay.

The findings from the pilot study directly informed the redesign of ThinkLand, which was subsequently carried out. Regarding the VEUQ, the study confirmed that the core usability aspects targeted by the questionnaire appropriately reflected the user experience challenges in ThinkLand. Based on the feedback obtained, minor adjustments were made to the wording of several items to enhance clarity and ensure consistent interpretation across participants. No major structural modifications to the questionnaire were required.

4.3. Main Study

The study employed quasi-experimental and quantitative research design with regression-based analysis. Two groups of participants were included: high school pupils and university students. The central activity involved playing the ThinkLand VR game, accessible through two types of interfaces: mobile devices and desktop computers.

The research design involved the following steps:

1. Informing participants about the purpose and objectives of the study, including ethical guidelines;
2. Selection of the device (mobile phone or desktop computer) for playing the ThinkLand VR game;
3. Playing the game;
4. Completing the anonymous online survey.

The study was conducted in collaboration with teachers and during scheduled lessons dedicated to CT topics, as outlined in the curricula of the respective high school and university. Participating in the study did not impose any additional obligations or risks on the students.

In the first step of the procedure, the respective teachers informed their students about the purpose of the study, the voluntary nature of their participation, and the confidentiality of their game performance and responses in the survey. No personally identifiable or sensitive data was planned to be collected, and therefore, formal ethical approval or parental consent were not required.

In phase two, students were informed of the minimum technical requirements for installing the game on their own mobile devices and were given the freedom to choose whether to play on a mobile or desktop platform.

Phase three involved playing the ThinkLand VR game on the selected platform. As they solve the tasks, each participant was responsible for recording their own task points and the total time taken to complete the entire challenge.

Finally, the students were asked to complete the survey consisting of four sections: a demographic data section, the SUS and VEUQ questionnaires for usability evaluation of the game interface and the qualitative section. Participants were explicitly instructed to focus solely on evaluating the virtual environment interface in which the tasks were delivered, rather than rating the difficulty of the tasks or their preferences for CT.

All tasks and questionnaires were completed individually, without peer interaction or external assistance. Teacher supervision ensured the correctness and independence of observations, as the study setting reflected typical educational conditions.

4.4. Participants

Participants were recruited using a convenience sampling method, as part of their regular courses. The end sample included students and pupils who successfully completed all steps of the procedure, including the VR game, the online survey, and the submission of data on tasks scores and completion time. Participants with incomplete or missing data were excluded from the analysis.

A total of 100 students and pupils from Split-Dalmatia County (Croatia) participated in the study. Among the participants, there were 43 high school students (first and second grade) and 57 students at the University of Split (first year students of Computer Science). Considering gender dimension, there were 64 females, 36 males and 0 selected "prefer not to say" option. As for the interface usage, 55 participants used the desktop computer, while 45 played the game on a mobile device. Figure 10 presents the distribution of participants by gender (Male/Female) and age (High School/University), grouped according to the type of interface used to play the VR game (Desktop or Mobile). The figure shows a relatively balanced usage of both interface types across gender and age groups.

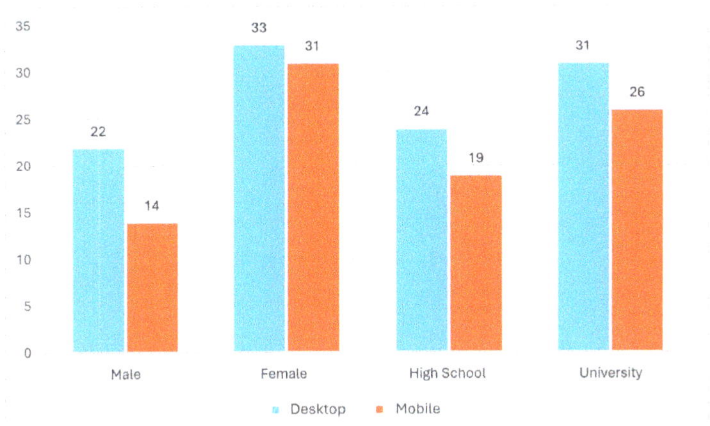

Figure 10. Distribution of participants by gender and age according to the type of ThinkLand interface.

4.5. Data Analysis

Since each independent variable consists of two levels, the combination of these variables results in a total of eight distinct participant groups. The dependent variables include 12 statements related to interface usability, along with the time and score. To facilitate data analysis, the VEUQ statements were assigned labels q1–q12, as previously presented in Table 1. Participants' responses ranged from 1 (Strongly disagree) to 5 (Strongly agree), with N/A option included. The time was reported in minutes, while the score was calculated as the sum of points achieved across all tasks, with a possible total value ranging from 0 to 4. As explained in Section 4.1., the SUS score is interpreted separately, in accordance with the standard practice of SUS evaluation and reporting.

Statistical analysis was conducted in the R programming language (Version 4.3.3). To select appropriate methods for data analysis, it was first necessary to clearly define the types of collected data and assess the assumptions required for different statistical procedures.

Since the study involved a large number of independent variables (8 participant groups) and 14 dependent variables, and in order to better understand the relationships among them, the initial plan was to apply a multivariate analysis approach.

An initial exploration of the relationships among the VEUQ items was conducted by calculating Pearson's correlation coefficients and visualizing the results using a heatmap as shown in Figure 11. When two items with the same polarity (two positively worded or two negatively worded statements) are strongly related, a high positive correlation between them is expected. Conversely, when a positively worded item is strongly related to a negatively worded item, a high negative correlation should be expected. However, the analysis revealed predominantly low to moderate correlations between the items, with coefficients ranging approximately from −0.4 to 0.6. Although the correlation matrix is inherently symmetrical due to the nature of Pearson's coefficients, no extremely high correlations are observed. These limited redundancy among items suggested that the VEUQ items captured related but distinct aspects of virtual environment usability, without evidence of multicollinearity.

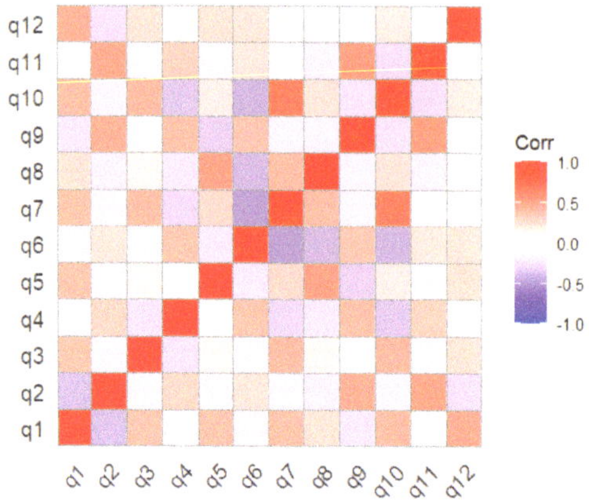

Figure 11. Pearson's correlation coefficients for VEUQ items.

Based on these findings, it was determined that the data did not fully meet the assumptions necessary for the application of multivariate methods such as MANOVA. Therefore, a different analytical strategy was adopted: a series of univariate general linear models (GLMs) should be applied to the data. Since all dependent variables are numerical in nature and the independent variables are categorical, the use of this method is appropriate. In this context, the term GLM refers to the regression modeling framework that allows for testing the effects of categorical predictors on continuous outcome variables. The sample size in this study (N = 100) was considered appropriate for conducting regression analyses, as the literature requires a minimum of at least 25 participants for accurate regression analysis [40].

Prior to conducting the analysis, because of large number of variables, we considered the possibility of simplifying the analytical model. If substantial multicollinearity had been found among the data, principal component analysis (PCA) would have been applied to reduce the number of variables, simplify the data structure, and consequently facilitate the data analysis process. Additionally, factor analysis would have been used to uncover latent constructs, such as underlying dimensions of user experience, by grouping related items into subscales. However, both methods require substantial inter-item correlations and a sufficient amount of shared variance to be meaningful. Therefore, it was concluded that a series of separate GLMs should be constructed for each of the 14 dependent variables, and that the results should be interpreted individually.

For each dependent variable (twelve VEUQ items, score and time), a separate GLM was fitted. As the primary aim is to assess the independent contributions of each factor, the models included only the main effects of the three predictors, without interaction terms.

5. Results

The results are organized into three sections. First, descriptive statistics are provided to summarize the main characteristics of the collected data. This is followed by the results of the GLMs for each dependent variable, including the twelve VEUQ items, the total score achieved in the ThinkLand VR game (Score), and the total time required to complete the challenge (Time). Finally, the SUS scores for mobile and desktop interface groups are presented.

5.1. Descriptive Statistics

For easier understanding of the results related to usability perceptions, descriptive statistics for VEUQ items are presented separately for positively worded (Table 2) and negatively worded items (Table 3). Items are ranked by mean scores in descending order. In Table 3, as the items are reverse-scored, lower means reflect higher usability ratings.

Table 2. Descriptive statistics for positively worded VEUQ items.

Item	Statement	Mean	SD	Min	Max
q5	The on-screen instructions are useful.	4.19	0.98	1	5
q8	The task text on the board is always easily accessible.	4.13	1.14	1	5
q12	Receiving real-time feedback on scores while solving tasks is important.	3.92	1.17	1	5
q1	The world representation is clear and interesting.	3.90	1.01	1	5
q10	I was able to move the objects I wanted in a simple way.	3.56	1.17	1	5
q7	Zooming in the virtual world is easy.	3.44	1.29	1	5
q3	It is always clear to me which object is selected.	3.38	1.21	1	5

Table 3. Descriptive statistics for negatively worded VEUQ items.

Item	Statement	Mean	SD	Min	Max
q11	Switching to the next task is complicated.	1.51	0.97	1	5
q9	The on-screen instructions make it harder to complete the task.	1.60	1.01	1	5
q2	Recognizing objects within the world is problematic.	1.76	1.01	1	5
q6	Rotating the space (camera) is too complicated.	2.31	1.37	1	5
q4	It was often not easy for me to select (click) the object I wanted.	2.83	1.41	1	5

As shown in Table 2, positively worded items (q1, q3, q5, q7, q8, q10, q12) generally received high ratings (M = 3.38–4.19), reflecting a favorable perception of ThinkLand. Among these, guidance elements such as on-screen instructions (q5: 4.19) and task accessibility (q8: 4.13) demonstrated optimal usability, while object selection feedback (q3: 3.38) and zoom functionality (q7: 3.44) emerged as critical areas for improvement despite maintaining positive ratings.

In Table 3, we can see that object selection (q4: 2.83) and camera rotation (q6: 2.31) are rated as primary usability barriers, while task switching (q11: 1.51) and instruction interference (q9: 1.60) were minimally problematic.

Overall, the pattern of responses across both positive and negative items is consistent and indicates a generally high level of perceived usability: instructional design elements (q5, q8, q12) achieved superior performance while direct interaction features (q3, q4, q6, q7) require targeted interface optimization.

Statistics for total game performance (Score), task completion time (Time), and overall usability rating (SUS score) are presented in Table 4.

The SUS score for the sample was 72.93. In line with standard SUS procedure, only the mean SUS score was analyzed, without examining individual item responses. According to the generally accepted interpretation using adjective rating scales [37], the obtained score corresponds to a "Good" overall usability rating. This "good but improvable" classification is in line with obtained context-specific usability ratings.

Table 4. Descriptive statistics of additional metrics.

Metric	Mean	SD	Min	Max
Score	2.83	2.47	1.03	0
Time	1.60	19.24	8.19	4
SUS	1.51	72.93	16.57	15

The mean total Score achieved in the ThinkLand game was 2.47 out of 4 points. The average time to complete the challenge was 19.24 min.

5.2. Regresion Analysis

Regarding the predictor variables, specific coding was introduced for their values as follows: M—Male, F—Female, H—High school pupil, U—University student, M—Mobile device interface, and D—Desktop computer interface. As a result, eight distinct groups were defined, each represented by an ordered triple composed of the above symbols, as shown in Table 5.

Table 5. Participants group labels.

Label	Group
M-H-M	Male—High school—Mobile
M-H-D	Male—High school—Desktop
M-U-M	Male—University—Mobile
M-U-D	Male—University—Desktop
F-H-M	Female—High school—Mobile
F-H-D	Female—High school—Desktop
F-U-M	Female—University—Mobile
F-U-D	Female—University—Desktop

In the following section, we present the results of all 14 general linear models. Starting with modeling participants' rating of item q1, we present the detailed interpretation of results for clarity, while for the remaining models only key conclusions are reported, without unnecessary details, especially in cases when model did not reach statistical significance.

5.2.1. Modeling Responses to VEUQ Items

Figure 12 presents eight individual box plots, each corresponding to one of the participant groups listed in Table 5. These plots illustrate how participants within each group rated item q1.

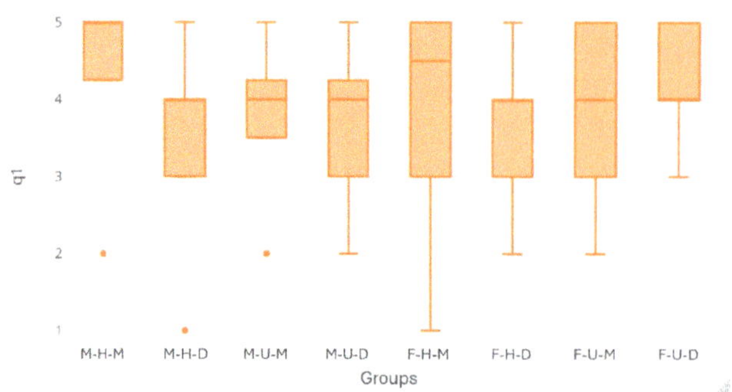

Figure 12. Box plots showing participant ratings of item q1: The world representation is clear and interesting.

The model output indicates that the model was not statistically significant ($F(1, 95) = 0.660$, $p = 0.579$), explaining only 2.04% of variance ($R^2 = 0.020$, with an adjusted R^2 of -0.011 when corrected for the number of predictors). This suggests that gender, age group and interface type collectively have no meaningful impact on the q1 ratings.

Individual predictors showed no significant effects on q1 ratings:

- Gender: Females showed slightly higher ratings (+0.23) than males, but the difference was non-significant ($p = 0.287$).
- Age: High school participants gave marginally lower ratings (−0.05) than university students, with no statistical significance ($p = 0.817$).
- Interface type: Participants using desktop interfaces reported marginally lower ratings (−0.17) than participants who were using mobile interfaces, but this difference was non-significant ($p = 0.421$).

Based on these results, we conclude that gender, age group, and interface type were not significant predictors of participants' perceptions of the clarity and interest of the ThinkLand world representation.

Figure 13 shows how participants from each group rated item q2.

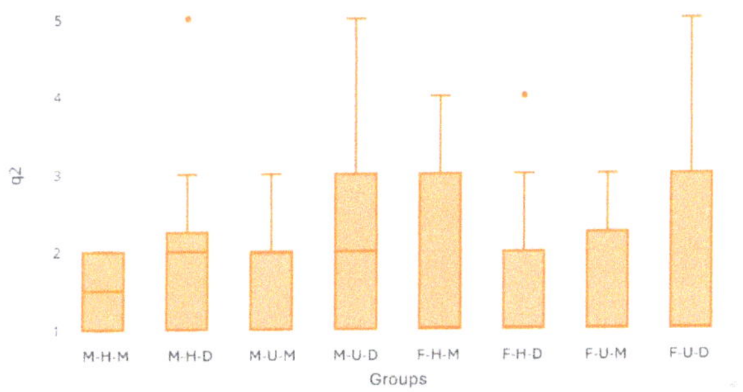

Figure 13. Box plots showing participant ratings of item q2: Recognizing objects within the world is problematic.

The findings show that the model does not explain a significant amount of variance in the responses ($R^2 = 0.015$; Adjusted $R^2 = -0.017$; $F(3, 93) = 0.462$, $p = 0.709$), which indicates that gender, age group, and interface type collectively were not significant predictors of perceptions related to recognitions of objects in ThinkLand.

The results also show that none of the predictors separately is statistically significant. The box plot in Figure 14, showing reported ratings, also informs these findings.

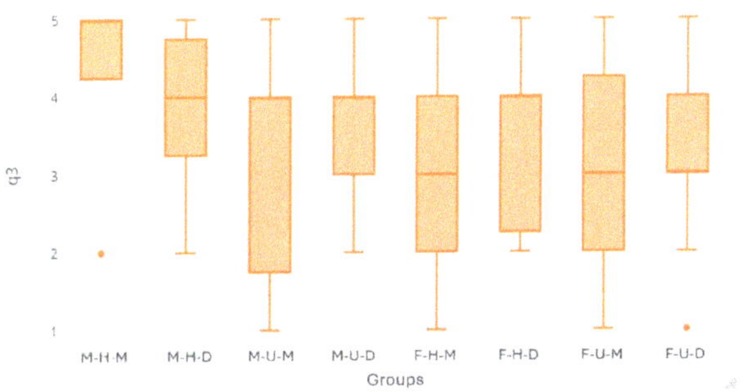

Figure 14. Box plots showing participant ratings of item q3: It is always clear to me which object is selected.

Figure 14 presents the ratings provided by participants from each group for item q3. The overall model was not statistically significant ($R^2 = 0.056$; Adjusted $R^2 = 0.026$; $F(3, 94) = 1.865$, $p = 0.141$).

Gender approached statistical significance ($b = -0.492$, $p = 0.058$), suggesting that female participants tended to rate the item q3 lower than male participants, but this difference did not reach conventional significance ($p < 0.05$).

Age group and interface type were not significant predictors of the q3 ratings. This result means that participants perceived feedback on object selection equally on both interfaces.

Figure 15 shows how participants from each group rated item q4.

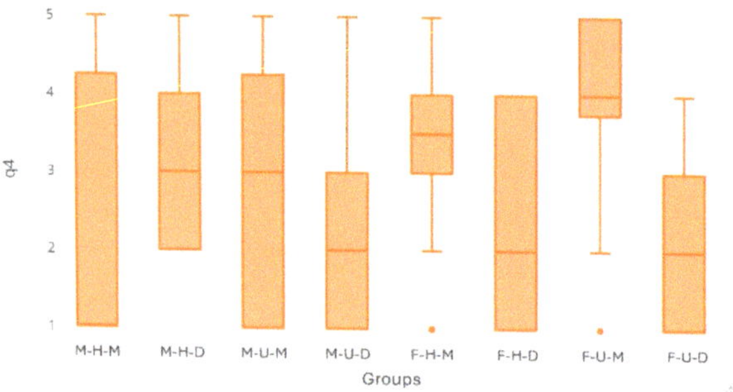

Figure 15. Box plots showing participant ratings of item q4: It was often not easy for me to select (click) the object I wanted.

The linear regression model examining predictors of q4 ratings demonstrated statistical significance ($F(3, 95) = 4.735$, $p = 0.004$), explaining approximately 13.0% of the variance in scores (adjusted $R^2 = 0.103$).

The analysis revealed one particularly robust finding: desktop users reported significantly lower ratings compared to mobile users ($\beta = -0.995$, $SE = 0.273$, $t = -3.648$, $p < 0.001$), indicating a strong negative effect of desktop use that was highly statistically significant. Participants using a desktop device gave ratings to q4 approximately one point lower than those using a mobile device. Since q4 is negatively worded, this result shows that desktop users perceive object selection in Thinkand VR environment considerably easier than the mobile users.

No significant effects in q4 were observed for either gender or age group.

The ratings provided by participants from each group for item q5 are shown in Figure 16.

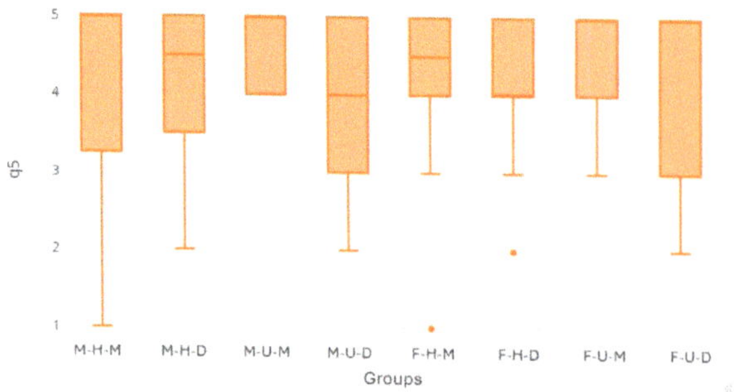

Figure 16. Box plots showing participant ratings of item q5: The on-screen instructions are useful.

The summary of the model shows that the model does not explain a significant amount of variance in the responses ($R^2 = 0.027$; Adjusted $R^2 = -0.004$; $F(1, 95) = 0.876$, $p = 0.457$).

Also, gender, age group, and interface type separately were not significant predictors of perceptions related to perceived usefulness of on-line instructions. The box plots visually support the conclusion.

The ratings provided by participants from each group for item q6 are shown in Figure 17.

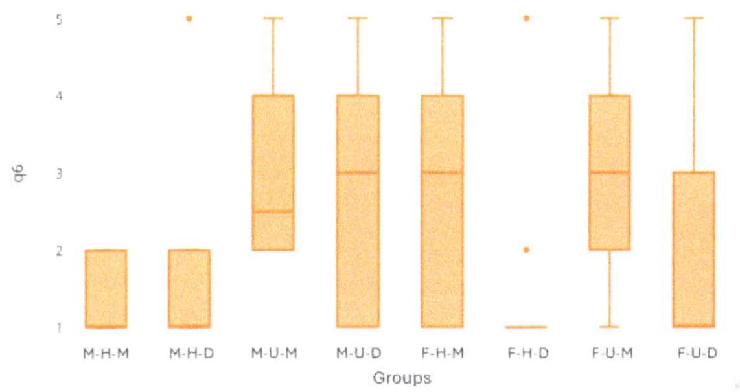

Figure 17. Box plots showing participant ratings of item q6: Rotating the space (camera) is too complicated.

The overall model demonstrated statistically significant predictive utility ($F(3, 89) = 4.764$, $p = 0.004$), accounting for approximately 13.8% of the variance in ratings (adjusted $R^2 = 0.109$).

Two significant negative relationships are shown in the summary. First, desktop users reported significantly lower q6 ratings compared to mobile users ($\beta = -0.816$, SE = 0.272, $t = -3.005$, $p = 0.003$), indicating a strong negative effect of desktop use. Since the statement is negatively phrased, this finding suggests that mobile users experienced rotating the camera significantly more complicated compared to desktop users.

Second, university students demonstrated significantly lower ratings in comparison with high school pupils ($\beta = -0.641$, SE = 0.273, $t = -2.349$, $p = 0.021$), representing a moderate negative age effect. The result indicates that high school students find rotating the camera more complicated than university students.

No significant gender differences were observed in the model for q6.

The ratings for item q7 are shown in Figure 18.

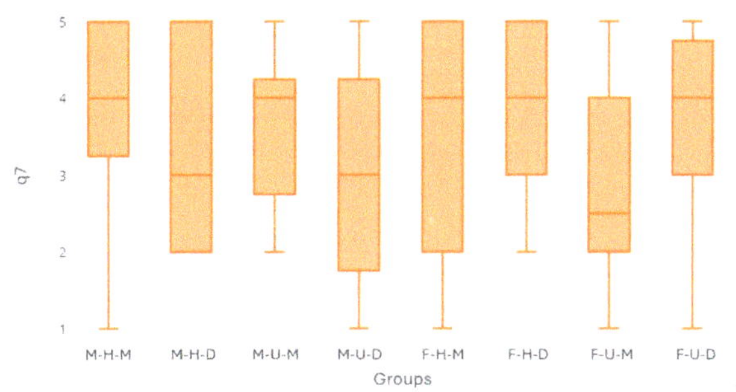

Figure 18. Box plots showing participant ratings of item q7: Zooming in the virtual world is easy.

The overall model for q7 ratings was not statistically significant ($R^2 = 0.027$; Adjusted $R^2 = -0.007$; $F(9, 87) = 0.806$, $p = 0.494$).

None of the predictor variables separately showed a statistically significant effect on participants' ratings for ease of zooming in the VR environment, although nine participants did not use it.

The ratings for item q8 are shown in Figure 19.

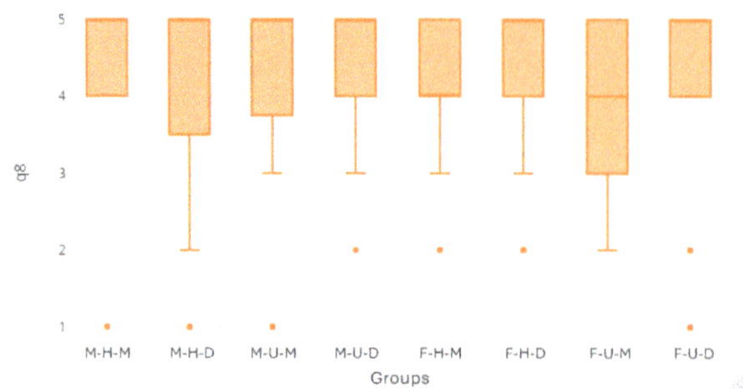

Figure 19. Box plots showing participant ratings of item q8: The task text on the board is always easily accessible.

The model did not reach statistical significance ((R^2 = 0.010; Adjusted R^2 = −0.021; F(1, 95) = 0.324, p = 0.808).

Additionally, age, gender and interface type, as independent variables, were not significant predictors of participants' perceptions of the availability of the text on the board. The result is visually informed by the box plots in Figure 19.

The ratings provided by participants from each group for item q9 are shown in Figure 20.

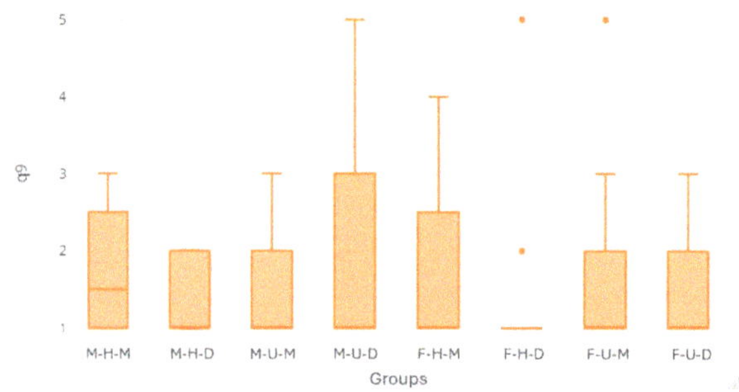

Figure 20. Box plots showing participant ratings of item q9: The on-screen instructions make it harder to complete the task.

Similar to the previous two models, the q9 ratings model does not explain a significant amount of variance in the responses (R^2 = 0.014; Adjusted R^2 = –0.023; F(15, 81) = 0.370, p = 0.775).

Each predictor variable separately was not a significant predictor of perceptions that on-screen instructions made completing the tasks more difficult. The box plots visually support the conclusion, although 15 students probably did not use these instructions.

The ratings provided by participants from each group for item q10 are shown in Figure 21.

The summary of the model for q10 ratings indicates that the model explains a significant proportion of variance in participants' ratings (R^2 = 0.1086; Adjusted R^2 = 0.080; F(3, 94) = 3.82; p = 0.013).

Among the predictors, gender and age group did not show a statistically significant effect.

Interface type was a statistically significant predictor (B = 0.713; p = 0.003). Participants using the desktop interface reported higher ease of moving objects in ThinkLand than those using the mobile interface for playing the game.

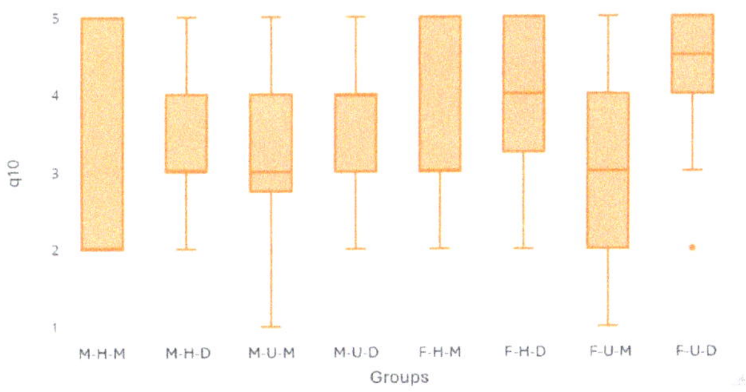

Figure 21. Box plots showing participant ratings of item q10: I was able to move the objects I wanted in a simple way.

Figure 22 presents the ratings from each group for item q11.

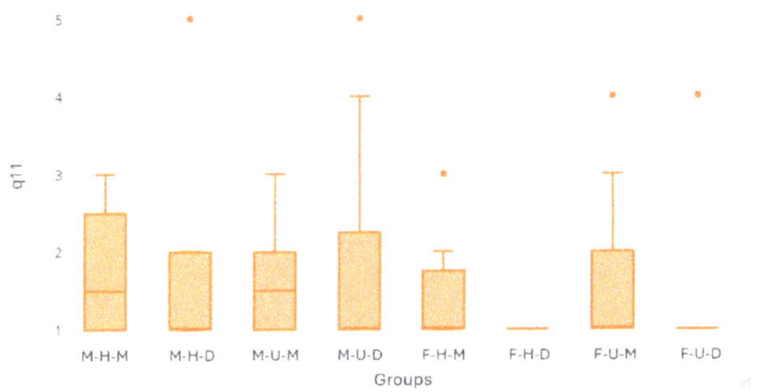

Figure 22. Box plots showing participant ratings of item q11: Switching to the next task is complicated.

The model summary shows that the regression model does not explain a significant proportion of variance in participants' ratings to q11 ($R^2 = 0.054$; Adjusted $R^2 = 0.021$; $F(3, 86) = 1.63$; $p = 0.187$).

None of the predictors were statistically significant at the 0.05 level. Gender approached marginal significance ($B = -0.398$; $p = 0.064$), suggesting a possible trend toward lower ratings (i.e., perceiving switching to the next task as less complicated) among female participants, but this effect did not reach statistical significance.

Figure 23 presents the ratings from each group for item q12.

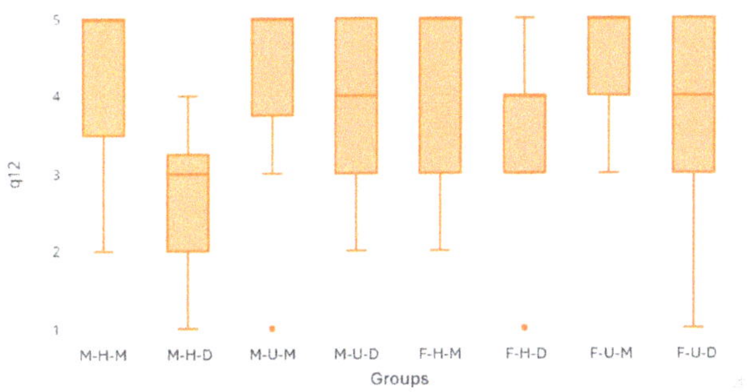

Figure 23. Box plots showing participant ratings of item q12: Receiving real-time feedback on scores while solving tasks is important.

The model explained 13.3% of variance ($p = 0.003$), suggesting that the predictors account for a modest but significant proportion of q12 rating variability.

There were no statically significant differences in the effects of age groups and gender on participant ratings.

However, desktop users reported lower ratings of item q12 than mobile users ($\beta = -0.736$) and this difference is highly significant ($p = 0.002$). The result indicates that participants who played the game on mobile devices perceived real-time feedback on scores as substantially more important than players on desktop computers.

5.2.2. Modeling of Score

The scores in ThinkLand achieved by participants from each group are shown in Figure 24.

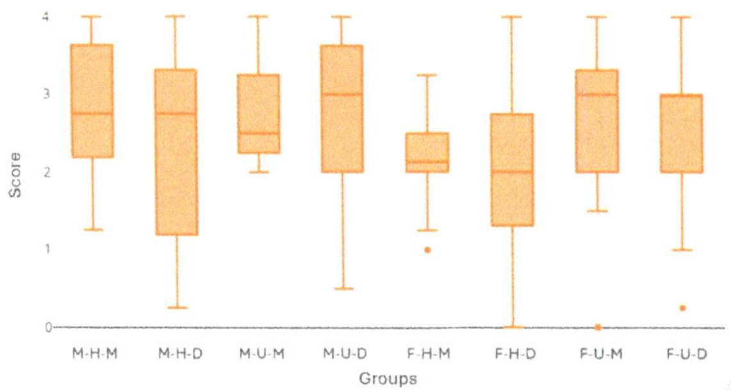

Figure 24. Box plots showing participant scores.

The summary of the model indicates that the model does not account for a significant proportion of variance in the responses (R^2 = 009; Adjusted R^2 = −022; F(0, 96]) = 0.297, p = 828).

Moreover, none of the predictor variables separately showed a statistically significant effect on participants' total score.

5.2.3. Modeling of Time

The time spent completing the overall challenge in ThinkLand, by participants from each group, is shown in Figure 25.

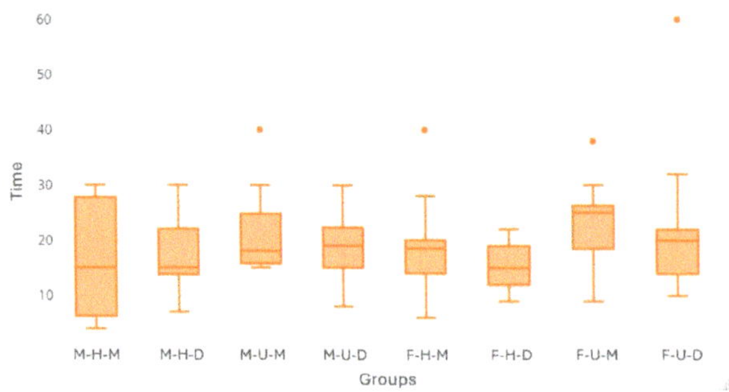

Figure 25. Box plots showing participant time of playing the game.

The overall model was statistically significant ($F(3,96) = 2.91$, $p = 0.039$), indicating that the set of predictors explains a significant proportion of variance in time. However, the model's explanatory power was modest, with an R-square of 0.083, meaning that approximately 8.3% of the variance in time is accounted for by gender, age group, and interface type.

University students took significantly longer to complete the challenge ($\beta = -3.99$, $p = 0.016$), requiring nearly 4 s more than high school users.

Although not reaching conventional significance levels, desktop users demonstrated a notable shorter time relative to mobile users ($\beta = -2.419$, SE = 1.616, $t = -1.497$, $p = 0.138$).

No meaningful gender differences were observed. The relatively low R^2 indicates substantial unexplained variance, suggesting that other factors not included in the model may also influence time.

5.3. SUS for Mobile and Desktop Platform

Additional analysis focused solely on differences based on the type of interface used. The overall SUS score was calculated separately for mobile and desktop participants and presented in Table 6.

Table 6. Comparative SUS scores for interface type.

Interface Type	Mean SUS Score	Standard Deviation	N
Mobile	73.17	16.88	45
Desktop	72.73	16.63	55

The mean SUS score for the mobile group was 73.17 (SD = 16.88), while the mean SUS score for the desktop group was 72.73 (SD = 16.63). Both ratings are interpreted as "Good" [37]. Although the obtained difference is small, an independent sample *t*-test was conducted. The result confirmed that this difference was not significant, where $t(98) = 0.13$, $p = 0.896$. Thus, we conclude that participants perceived the overall usability of the ThinkLand environment similarly across both platforms.

5.4. Qualitative Feedback

Following the usability evaluation, participants provided open-ended feedback regarding their experience. Table 7 presents the responses related to the used device, in their original form, translated from Croatian language.

Table 7. Open-ended feedback related to interface type.

Platform		User Feedback
Mobile	Positive	*"The simple representation of characters and the environment, and the way the instructions are written."* *"A more entertaining way to solve tasks and problems."* *"The connection between mathematical tasks and the computational environment."* *"Objects and instructions are present on all the animals, which made solving tasks easier."*
	Negative	*"It takes too long to complete tasks on a phone because selecting the desired object is difficult."* *"I don't like that sometimes not all information is visible on the screen when certain characters move."* *"I dislike that some information appears twice... it's inconvenient on a phone."* *"The inability to easily move the camera and adjust positions."*
Desktop	Positive	*"I would say its simplicity gives it a big advantage during use..."* *"I like that instructions are available while solving tasks."* *"The world's visual representation is very interesting."* *"The ability to return to the task text."*
	Negative	*"Sometimes it's hard to recognize objects in the environment."* *"Some functions are complicated, like zooming, and sometimes the instructions interfere..."* *"Task explanations are too long."*

To better understand the contribution of these responses, a thematic analysis was conducted. Participants' feedback was categorized into five key themes reflecting their user experience across mobile and desktop platforms:

- Interface Simplicity and Clarity: Many participants appreciated the overall simplicity of the interface. Desktop users highlighted the interface's minimalist design as a strength ("its simplicity gives it a big advantage"), while mobile users praised the clear visual representation of characters and environments. However, some users also noted issues with visual clarity, particularly when characters moved or when the interface became cluttered.
- Task Engagement and Integration: Both user groups positively commented on the engaging nature of the tasks and their seamless integration into the virtual environment. Mobile users emphasized the connection between mathematical tasks and the game world, while desktop users valued being able to access instructions during problem-solving.
- Navigation and Object Interaction: Navigation and interaction challenges were a recurring theme, especially among mobile users. Difficulties in selecting objects and manipulating the camera were cited as major obstacles. On the desktop, users reported issues with more complex functions such as zooming.
- Screen Visibility and Layout Issues: Several mobile users mentioned screen-related limitations, such as important information being partially obscured or duplicated, which negatively affected task performance. These issues appeared less frequently in desktop feedback but were noted as interfering elements when instructions overlapped with other content.
- Functionality Challenges: Some users, particularly on the desktop platform, reported challenges with specific functionalities such as the zoom function or long task explanations, which they found overwhelming or difficult to manage during interaction.

6. Discussion

In the first part of this section, we integrate the obtained results to provide a holistic interpretation, combining insights from both quantitative measures and qualitative feedback. Based on this synthesis, we derive the practical implications of the findings.

The second part provides reflections on the implementation of ThinkLand, the VEUQ, and the overall methodological approach. It also addresses potential limitations and offers directions for future research.

6.1. Overall Interpretation of the Results

In the previous section, we analyzed the VEUQ results separately for positively and negatively worded items. This analysis revealed that positively worded statements generally received higher scores than negatively worded ones, suggesting that the formulation of the statement may influence participants' responses. However, to gain a comprehensive picture and enable a holistic interpretation of the results, in this section we combine all items and rank them in a single list according to their mean score. This approach allows us to identify the strongest and weakest aspects of the interface, regardless of the wording polarity, and consequently enabling us to place these findings in perspective alongside the remaining quantitative and qualitative results, i.e., the regression analysis output and descriptive user feedback.

Table 8 presents the summary of findings. For each VEUQ item, the table shows the rank based on the overall score (from Tables 2 and 3), GLM output with practical significance (as estimated effect size) and statistical significance, and the number and the direction of user comments (from Table 7). Although the user comments do not carry statistical power, it is evident that they align well with the ranking of the items, reinforcing the quantitative findings.

Table 8. Overview of integrated results from quantitative and qualitative feedback.

Item	Interface Feature	Mean	GLM Output	Estimated Effect Size	Statistical Significance	Descriptive Feedback
q5	On-screen instructions usefulness	4.19				2 mobile positive 2 desktop positive
q8	Accessibility of the task text	4.13				1 desktop positive
q12	Importance of real-time feedback	3.92	More important for mobile users	Moderate	Strong	1 mobile positive
q1	Virtual world representation	3.9				4 mobile positive 2 desktop positive
q10	Moving the objects	3.56	Easier for desktop users	Moderate	Strong	
q11 *	Switching to the next task	3.49				1 desktop positive
q7	Zooming	3.44				1 desktop negative
q9 *	On-screen instructions interference	3.4				1 mobile negative 1 desktop negative
q3	Object selection feedback	3.38				
q2 *	Object recognition	3.24				1 desktop negative
q6 *	Camera rotation	2.69	More complicated for mobile users More complicated for high school pupils	High Moderate	Strong Moderate	2 mobile negative
q4 *	Object selection	2.17	More complicated for mobile users	High	Strong	1 mobile negative

* Negatively worded item.

The highest-ranked interface features were the usefulness of on-screen instructions and accessibility of the task text, both receiving predominantly positive feedback and demonstrated equally impressive performances on mobile and desktop interfaces.

Items such as the importance of real-time feedback and moving the objects showed moderate effect sizes with strong statistical significance, indicating meaningful differences between user groups (e.g., mobile users rating feedback importance higher, and desktop users finding object manipulation easier).

Lower-ranked items included camera rotation and object selection, both showing strong practical significance (estimated effect sizes) and statistical significance, particularly highlighting challenges reported by mobile users. Additionally, qualitative feedback supported these findings, with several negative comments pointing to difficulties in camera control, object selection, and overall interface clarity on mobile devices. These results provide clear priorities for future ThinkLand redesign efforts.

6.2. Reflections, Limitations and Future Work

The ThinkLand, consisting of four tasks, can be understood as a VR setting that incorporates four mini games, following the definition provided by [6]. These short, guided episodes are designed to address specific learning outcomes in simple and engaging ways.

Similar to related VR applications [6,7], each task in ThinkLand can be replayed as needed, helping to reinforce key concepts until the desired learning outcomes are achieved.

The game development did not include additional learning strategies, which aligns with existing research showing that CT tasks inherently incorporate well-developed teaching and learning approaches [41].

All the tasks used in ThinkLand came from an international collection accepted by Bebras International [1] and approved for use in worldwide Bebras Challenge competitions (see Supplementary Materials for original tasks in English). Therefore, the game holds strong potential for internationalization, which can be achieved simply by translation of task text. Since the game is not intended to be used for the official Bebras competitions, the linguistic and cultural adaptations for better addressing CT in other languages are also acceptable.

In the Methods section, we will first address the VEUQ and the questionnaire's administering order.

The VEUQ was developed to cover a comprehensive range of potential usability issues and was evaluated with end users in a pilot study. This systematic approach aligns with related literature [8]. The results suggest that the VEUQ is a valid and clearly structured tool for capturing core usability aspects as perceived by users. The overall Cronbach's alpha coefficient was relatively low ($\alpha = 0.42$), and this result is consistent with the design of the instrument, as each item was intended to measure a distinct, context-specific aspect of the interface. This multidimensional nature of the VEUQ is further supported by the observed lack of multicollinearity between items, as shown in the correlation heatmap (Figure 11). Its robustness and content validity are further supported by the fact that, in the open-ended feedback, only two comments fell outside the scope of the existing VEUQ items. However, the results of the main study suggest that wording polarity could have influenced responses. While this effect remains inconclusive, it should be acknowledged as a potential limitation of the study and explored in future research.

The second limitation of the study relates to the composition of the pilot study sample. The pilot testing included only senior university students, who were selected for their greater familiarity with digital interfaces and critical evaluation skills. While this approach was appropriate for the early identification of potential issues, it may limit the generalizability of the pilot findings to younger users. However, both age groups were fully represented in the main study to ensure broader applicability of the results.

The VUEQ items were systematically mapped to three core usability dimensions of the ISO 9241-11:2018 standard [37]: effectiveness (q2, q3, q4, q5, q8, q9), efficiency (q6, q7, q10, q11), and satisfaction (q1, q12). This mapping ensures that the evaluation framework is aligned with internationally recognized definitions of usability, providing a structured and standardized basis for assessing the usability of the ThinkLand game interface.

The VEUQ structure also reflects the core usability components proposed by Nielsen [38], namely learnability, efficiency, errors, and satisfaction. Specifically, learnability was addressed through items evaluating the clarity of object selection and instructions (q3, q5, q8), efficiency was captured through questions relating to the ease of navigation and object manipulation (q6, q7, q10, q11), and user errors were assessed through items focusing on difficulties in object recognition, selection, and task transition (q2, q4, q9, q11). Satisfaction with the virtual environment was measured through the perceived clarity and usefulness of the interface (q1, q12). However, memorability, as the ease with which users can reestablish proficiency after a period of non-use, is not directly assessed within the VEUQ. This is the consequence of the study design, which involved a single-session interaction with ThinkLand, without follow-up sessions to evaluate longer-term retention of interaction skills. Future studies aiming to achieve a full alignment with Nielsen's framework could incorporate delayed post-test evaluations or specific questionnaire items targeting users' ability to quickly and accurately re-engage with the system after a period of non-use.

Reflecting on the decision to administer the VEUQ after the SUS, it is possible that this sequence may have influenced participants' responses. However, this order was intentionally made to minimize the potential influence of context-specific feedback on overall usability ratings. Although research on the sequential use of perceived usability instruments is rarely conducted, this methodological choice aligns with [42] that confirmed the impact of usability assessments order on their outcomes.

An important aspect of the study's design was allowing participants to choose their preferred interface for playing the ThinkLand game. This ensured interaction with a familiar and intuitive platform, likely reducing usability issues that might have arisen from being forced to use a less familiar device. By reflecting real-world usage patterns, this approach enhanced the ecological validity of the study: respecting user preferences led to more natural engagement and more authentic usability data. Future research could benefit from similar user-centered design choices.

The descriptive analysis revealed that users rated on-screen instructions and task text accessibility as the strongest elements of the interface, while camera control and object selection were identified as the most challenging aspects. These patterns provide an initial understanding of perceived usability across different interface components. Furthermore, the regression analysis confirmed several strongly significant effects, most notably for the lowest rated features such as camera rotation and object selection, which proved particularly difficult for mobile users.

While the GLMs revealed meaningful patterns, their overall explanatory power was modest, indicating that additional variables, possibly related to individual user characteristics or environmental factors, may also influence user experience. These findings highlight the importance of combining quantitative data with user-centered feedback to better understand the complexity of interface usability across different contexts.

A series of GLMs was employed as the analysis method, as there was no indication of multicollinearity among the predictors. While it is important to consider the assumptions underlying linear models, previous research has shown that they are generally robust to moderate deviations of residuals from normality, particularly when the sample size is adequate [43], as was the case in this study. Therefore, the statistically significant effect of interface type on participants' responses can be interpreted as both reliable and meaningful. Besides statistical significance, the observed differences with high estimated effect sizes also have practical significance and should be considered when drawing implications for interface design.

Although relevant literature generally acknowledges that usability is strongly connected with learning outcomes [30], this study did not empirically examine that relationship. Future research should aim to explore this connection following the redesign of the ThinkLand game. The most effective way to evaluate the impact and cost-effectiveness of the 3D version would be to measure learning outcomes achieved through the redesigned ThinkLand game in comparison to the performance on the original 2D tasks from the Bebras Challenge competition. In addition, learner engagement could be assessed as a complementary indicator of educational effectiveness. This future research will also provide an opportunity to further validate the VEUQ instrument using both the analytical methods applied in this study and additional methods, provided that their assumptions are satisfied by the data.

The study design can be readily extended and adapted for use with immersive technology such as VR headsets. Since the interaction within immersive environments substantially differs from traditional screen-based experience, the VEUQ should be adapted in terms of terminology, particularly regarding the object interaction via controllers instead of a mouse or touchscreen. Additionally, user experience evaluation could benefit from incorporating measures of presence in immersive environment [44] into the mixed-method approach presented in this study.

7. Conclusions

This study aimed to evaluate the usability of the ThinkLand VR game interface across two platforms, mobile and desktop, by combining quantitative analysis with qualitative user feedback and interpretation. Allowing participants to choose their preferred platform contributed to more natural interaction and enhanced the ecological validity of the findings. The use of two complementary instruments, the VEUQ and SUS, allows the study to capture both specific user feedback and general perceptions of ThinkLand's usability. As specifically developed and evaluated in this study, the VEUQ proved to be a valid and comprehensive instrument for capturing environment-specific usability aspects, and can be effectively applied in both academic research and the practical development of educational VR systems.

The results indicate that certain interface elements, such as on-screen instructions and task text visibility, were perceived as particularly effective, while camera control and object selection emerged as critical interaction points that may hinder user experience in both desktop and mobile interfaces. These issues were significantly more pronounced in the mobile interface and emphasize the need for thoughtful redesign that takes into account the limitations of touch-based interaction. The regression analysis further underscored the complexity of usability perception and the importance of accounting for both design and contextual factors.

Overall, the findings emphasize the value of user-centered evaluation methods and support the continued development of adaptive, platform-sensitive educational environments. Future research should further explore how interface design interacts with individual user characteristics and learning contexts to inform more inclusive and effective design strategies.

Supplementary Materials: The following supporting information can be downloaded at: https://www.mdpi.com/article/10.3390/mti9060060/s1, PDF document pdf:Original_Bebras_Tasks.pdf.

Author Contributions: Conceptualization, J.N.; methodology, J.N.; software, I.R.; validation, J.N.; formal analysis, J.N. and I.R.; investigation, J.N., I.R. and L.M.; resources, J.N.; data curation, I.R.; writing—original draft preparation, J.N., I.R. and L.M.; writing—review and editing, J.N. and L.M.; visualization, J.N. and I.R.; supervision, J.N. and L.M. All authors have read and agreed to the published version of the manuscript.

Funding: This research received no external funding.

Institutional Review Board Statement: The study was conducted in accordance with the Declaration of Helsinki. Ethical review and approval were waived for this study because the study did not involve sensitive data or personally identifiable information. Through an anonymous online survey, only the data on participants' education level, gender and the type of device used were collected.

Informed Consent Statement: Prior to participation, students and pupils were informed about the purpose of the study, the voluntary nature of their participation, and the anonymity of their responses. As the study was conducted within a standard educational context, as part of regular classes, formal ethical approval and parental/guardian consent were not required.

Data Availability Statement: The dataset generated and analyzed during the study is deposited in Zenodo and publicly available. DOI: 10.5281/zenodo.15347704.

Conflicts of Interest: Author Ivana Rogulj was employed by Ericsson Nikola Tesla, Split, Croatia. All authors declare no competing interests.

Abbreviations

The following abbreviations are used in this manuscript:

VR	Virtual Reality
CT	Computational Thinking
HCI	Human–Computer Interaction
HMD	Head Mounted Display
SUS	System Usability Scale
VEUQ	Virtual Environment Usability Questionnaire
GLM	General Linear Model

References

1. Bebras International. Available online: https://www.bebras.org/ (accessed on 2 May 2025).
2. Wing, J.M. Computational Thinking. *Commun. ACM* **2006**, *49*, 33–35. [CrossRef]
3. What Is Computational Thinking?—Introduction to Computational Thinking—KS3 Computer Science Revision. Available online: https://www.bbc.co.uk/bitesize/guides/zp92mp3/revision/1 (accessed on 13 April 2025).
4. Gundersen, S.W.; Lampropoulos, G. Using Serious Games and Digital Games to Improve Students' Computational Thinking and Programming Skills in K-12 Education: A Systematic Literature Review. *Technologies* **2025**, *13*, 113. [CrossRef]
5. Laisa, J.; Henrique, E. Computational Thinking Game Design Based on the Bebras Challenge: A Controlled Experiment. In Proceedings of the Workshop sobre Educação em Computação (WEI), Niterói, Brasil, 31 July 2022; SBC. pp. 263–273.
6. Oyelere, A.S.; Agbo, F.J.; Oyelere, S.S. Formative Evaluation of Immersive Virtual Reality Expedition Mini-Games to Facilitate Computational Thinking. *Comput. Educ. X Real.* **2023**, *2*, 100016. [CrossRef]
7. Agbo, F.J.; Oyelere, S.S.; Suhonen, J.; Tukiainen, M. Design, Development, and Evaluation of a Virtual Reality Game-Based Application to Support Computational Thinking. *Educ. Technol. Res. Dev.* **2023**, *71*, 505–537. [CrossRef]
8. Sukirman, S.; Ibharim, L.F.M.; Said, C.S.; Murtiyasa, B. Development and Usability Testing of a Virtual Reality Game for Learning Computational Thinking. *Int. J. Serious Games* **2024**, *11*, 19–43. [CrossRef]
9. Slater, M.; Wilbur, S. A Framework for Immersive Virtual Environments (FIVE): Speculations on the Role of Presence in Virtual Environments. *Presence Teleoperators Virtual Environ.* **1997**, *6*, 603–616. [CrossRef]
10. Salatino, A.; Zavattaro, C.; Gammeri, R.; Cirillo, E.; Piatti, M.L.; Pyasik, M.; Serra, H.; Pia, L.; Geminiani, G.; Ricci, R. Virtual Reality Rehabilitation for Unilateral Spatial Neglect: A Systematic Review of Immersive, Semi-Immersive and Non-Immersive Techniques. *Neurosci. Biobehav. Rev.* **2023**, *152*, 105248. [CrossRef]
11. Bamodu, O.; Ye, X.M. Virtual Reality and Virtual Reality System Components. *Adv. Mater. Res.* **2013**, *765–767*, 1169–1172. [CrossRef]
12. Marougkas, A.; Troussas, C.; Krouska, A.; Sgouropoulou, C. Virtual Reality in Education: A Review of Learning Theories, Approaches and Methodologies for the Last Decade. *Electronics* **2023**, *12*, 2832. [CrossRef]
13. Marougkas, A.; Troussas, C.; Krouska, A.; Sgouropoulou, C. How Personalized and Effective Is Immersive Virtual Reality in Education? A Systematic Literature Review for the Last Decade. *Multimed. Tools Appl.* **2024**, *83*, 18185–18233. [CrossRef]
14. Checa, D.; Bustillo, A. A Review of Immersive Virtual Reality Serious Games to Enhance Learning and Training. *Multimed. Tools Appl.* **2020**, *79*, 5501–5527. [CrossRef]
15. Radianti, J.; Majchrzak, T.A.; Fromm, J.; Wohlgenannt, I. A Systematic Review of Immersive Virtual Reality Applications for Higher Education: Design Elements, Lessons Learned, and Research Agenda. *Comput. Educ.* **2020**, *147*, 103778. [CrossRef]
16. AlGerafi, M.A.M.; Zhou, Y.; Oubibi, M.; Wijaya, T.T. Unlocking the Potential: A Comprehensive Evaluation of Augmented Reality and Virtual Reality in Education. *Electronics* **2023**, *12*, 3953. [CrossRef]
17. Hamilton, D.; McKechnie, J.; Edgerton, E.; Wilson, C. Immersive Virtual Reality as a Pedagogical Tool in Education: A Systematic Literature Review of Quantitative Learning Outcomes and Experimental Design. *J. Comput. Educ.* **2021**, *8*, 1–32. [CrossRef]
18. Liou, W.-K.; Chang, C.-Y. Virtual Reality Classroom Applied to Science Education. In Proceedings of the 2018 23rd International Scientific-Professional Conference on Information Technology (IT), Zabljak, Montenegro, 19–24 February 2018; pp. 1–4.
19. Johnston, A.P.R.; Rae, J.; Ariotti, N.; Bailey, B.; Lilja, A.; Webb, R.; Ferguson, C.; Maher, S.; Davis, T.P.; Webb, R.I.; et al. Journey to the Centre of the Cell: Virtual Reality Immersion into Scientific Data. *Traffic* **2018**, *19*, 105–110. [CrossRef]
20. Rupp, M.A.; Odette, K.L.; Kozachuk, J.; Michaelis, J.R.; Smither, J.A.; McConnell, D.S. Investigating Learning Outcomes and Subjective Experiences in 360-Degree Videos. *Comput. Educ.* **2019**, *128*, 256–268. [CrossRef]
21. Allcoat, D.; Mühlenen, A. von Learning in Virtual Reality: Effects on Performance, Emotion and Engagement. *Res. Learn. Technol.* **2018**, *26*, 2140. [CrossRef]

22. Kozhevnikov, M.; Gurlitt, J.; Kozhevnikov, M. Learning Relative Motion Concepts in Immersive and Non-Immersive Virtual Environments. *J. Sci. Educ. Technol.* **2013**, *22*, 952–962. [CrossRef]
23. Greenwald, S.; Corning, W.; Funk, M.; Maes, P. Comparing Learning in Virtual Reality with Learning on a 2D Screen Using Electrostatics Activities. *JUCS—J. Univers. Comput. Sci.* **2018**, *24*, 220–245. [CrossRef]
24. Moro, C.; Štromberga, Z.; Raikos, A.; Stirling, A. The Effectiveness of Virtual and Augmented Reality in Health Sciences and Medical Anatomy. *Anat. Sci. Educ.* **2017**, *10*, 549–559. [CrossRef]
25. Stepan, K.; Zeiger, J.; Hanchuk, S.; Del Signore, A.; Shrivastava, R.; Govindaraj, S.; Iloreta, A. Immersive Virtual Reality as a Teaching Tool for Neuroanatomy. *Int. Forum Allergy Rhinol.* **2017**, *7*, 1006–1013. [CrossRef] [PubMed]
26. Makransky, G.; Terkildsen, T.S.; Mayer, R.E. Adding Immersive Virtual Reality to a Science Lab Simulation Causes More Presence but Less Learning. *Learn. Instr.* **2019**, *60*, 225–236. [CrossRef]
27. Parong, J.; Mayer, R.E. Learning Science in Immersive Virtual Reality. *J. Educ. Psychol.* **2018**, *110*, 785–797. [CrossRef]
28. Mayer, R.E. *Multimedia Learning*, 2nd ed.; Cambridge University Press: Cambridge, UK, 2009.
29. Obae, C.; Koscielniak, T.; Liman-Kaban, A.; Stiefelbauer, C.; Nakic, J.; Moser, I.; Cassidy, D.; Otmanine, I.; Foti, P.; Bykova, A.; et al. *Immersive Learning: Innovative Pedagogies, Techniques, Best Practices, and Future Trends*; European Digital Education Hub: European Union: Luxembourg, 2024. [CrossRef]
30. Granić, A.; Nakić, J.; Marangunić, N. Scenario-Based Group Usability Testing as a Mixed Methods Approach to the Evaluation of Three-Dimensional Virtual Learning Environments. *J. Educ. Comput. Res.* **2020**, *58*, 616–639. [CrossRef]
31. Sukirman, S.; Ibharim, L.F.M.; Said, C.S.; Murtiyasa, B. A Strategy of Learning Computational Thinking through Game Based in Virtual Reality: Systematic Review and Conceptual Framework. *Inform. Educ.* **2022**, *21*, 179–200. [CrossRef]
32. Sims, R.; Rutherford, N.; Sukumaran, P.; Yotov, N.; Smith, T.; Karnik, A. Logibot: Investigating Engagement and Development of Computational Thinking Through Virtual Reality. In Proceedings of the 2021 7th International Conference of the Immersive Learning Research Network (iLRN), Eureka, CA, USA, 17 May–10 June 2021; pp. 1–5.
33. Wang, X.; Saito, D.; Washizaki, H.; Fukazawa, Y. Facilitating Students' Abstract and Computational Thinking Skills Using Virtual Reality. In Proceedings of the 2023 IEEE Integrated STEM Education Conference (ISEC), Laurel, MD, USA, 11 March 2023; pp. 243–246.
34. Dabar @Ucitelji.hr—Udruga Suradnici u Učenju. Available online: https://ucitelji.hr/dabar/ (accessed on 21 April 2025).
35. Nielsen, J.; Molich, R. Heuristic Evaluation of User Interfaces. In Proceedings of the SIGCHI Conference on Human Factors in Computing Systems, Seattle, WA, USA, 1–5 April 1990; Association for Computing Machinery: New York, NY, USA, 1990; pp. 249–256.
36. Brooke, J. SUS: A "Quick and Dirty" Usability Scale. In *Usability Evaluation in Industry*; CRC Press: London, UK, 1996; ISBN 978-0-429-15701-1.
37. Bangor, A.; Kortum, P.; Miller, J. Determining What Individual SUS Scores Mean: Adding an Adjective Rating Scale. *J. Usability Stud.* **2009**, *4*, 114–123.
38. *ISO 9241-11:2018(En)*; Ergonomics of Human-System Interaction—Part 11: Usability: Definitions and Concepts. ISO: Geneva, Switzerland, 2018. Available online: https://www.iso.org/obp/ui/#iso:std:iso:9241:-11:ed-2:v1:en (accessed on 6 May 2025).
39. Nielsen, J. *Usability Inspection Methods*, 1st ed.; Mack, R.L., Ed., John Wiley & Sons Inc: New York, NY, USA, 1994; ISBN 978-0-471-01877-3.
40. Jenkins, D.G.; Quintana-Ascencio, P.F. A Solution to Minimum Sample Size for Regressions. *PLoS ONE* **2020**, *15*, e0229345. [CrossRef]
41. Thorson, K. Early Learning Strategies for Developing Computational Thinking Skills. Available online: https://www.gettingsmart.com/2018/03/18/early-learning-strategies-for-developing-computational-thinking-skills/ (accessed on 7 May 2025).
42. Linek, S.B. Order Effects in Usability Questionnaires. *J. Usability Stud.* **2017**, *12*, 164–182.
43. Schmidt, A.F.; Finan, C. Linear Regression and the Normality Assumption. *J. Clin. Epidemiol.* **2018**, *98*, 146–151. [CrossRef]
44. Granić, A.; Nakić, J.; Ćukušić, M. Preliminary Evaluation of a 3D Serious Game in the Context of Entrepreneurship Education. In Proceedings of the CECIIS 2017: 28th Central European Conference on Information and Intelligent Systems, 2017, Varaždin, Croatia, 27–29 September 2017; Volume 91, pp. 91–98.

Multimodal Technologies and Interaction

MDPI

Review

Systemic Gamification Theory (SGT): A Holistic Model for Inclusive Gamified Digital Learning

Franz Coelho [1,2,*] and Ana Maria Abreu [1,3]

1 Universidade Católica Portuguesa, Center for Interdisciplinary Research in Health (CIIS), 1649-023 Lisbon, Portugal; anamariablom@gmail.com
2 Universidade Católica Portuguesa, Faculty of Health Sciences and Nursing (FCSE), 1649-023 Lisbon, Portugal
3 Insight, Piaget Research Center for Ecological Human Development, 2805-059 Almada, Portugal
* Correspondence: franzgrc@gmail.com

Abstract: Gamification has emerged as a powerful strategy in digital education, enhancing engagement, motivation, and learning outcomes. However, most research lacks theoretical grounding and often applies multiple and uncontextualized game elements, limiting its impact and replicability. To address these gaps, this study introduces a Systemic Gamification Theory (SGT)—a comprehensive, human-centered model for designing and evaluating inclusive and effective gamified educational environments. Sustained in Education, Human–Computer Interaction, and Psychology, SGT is structured around four core principles, emphasizing the importance of integrating game elements (1—Integration) into cohesive systems that generate emergent outcomes (2—Emergence) aligned synergistically (3—Synergy) with contextual needs (4—Context). The theory supports inclusivity by accounting for individual traits, situational dynamics, spatial settings, and cultural diversity. To operationalize SGT, we developed two tools: i. a set of 10 Heuristics to guide and analyze effective and inclusive gamification; and ii. a Framework for designing and evaluating gamified systems, as well as comparing research methods and outcomes across different contexts. These tools demonstrated how SGT enables robust, adaptive, and equitable gamified learning experiences. By advancing theoretical and practical development, SGT fosters a transformative approach to gamification, enriching multimedia learning through thoughtful system design and reflective evaluation practices.

Keywords: gamification; Human–Computer Interaction; education; digital learning; inclusion; diversity; design; evaluation

1. Introduction

Gamification integrates game elements into non-gaming contexts, distinguishing it from traditional gameplay [1,2]. It is a powerful tool in multimedia learning, transforming digital education by enhancing motivation, emotions, and cognitive processes [3–5]. Gamification fosters innovative teaching methods, encouraging students to learn more dynamically and interactively [6]. Importantly, gamification transforms education by making traditional methods more interactive and engaging for teachers and students [7]. Integrating gamification boosts student engagement, motivation, and outcomes through dynamic teaching strategies [8]. As a teaching method, gamification supports multimedia learning by improving digital usability and content design [9]. However, research often combines multiple game elements without a clear theoretical foundation to guide their selection, complicating the assessment of gamification's impact [10,11]. This highlights the need for theory-driven research to create a model that might clarify the influence of gamification on learning and reduce study heterogeneity [12], prompting us to develop a theoretical model aimed at guiding the design and assessment of educational gamification.

To develop the theoretical model, we adopted a holistic and inclusive approach, aiming to move gamification research beyond basic game element descriptions toward context-specific strategies that support meaningful experiences and motivate individuals to engage across diverse conditions [13]. Gamification outcomes are shaped by the interplay of individual characteristics and surrounding environments, since aspects like cultural background, gender, and age influence personal preferences, while gaming behavior and player typologies further determine how people engage with gamified experiences [14–16]. Gamification provides a complementary strategy to the Universal Design for Learning (UDL), supporting diversity and inclusion by addressing diverse learner needs and enhancing accessibility through inclusive game-based features [17]. Gamification has emerged as a promising tool to promote equity, diversity, and inclusion, supporting fair opportunities, valuing individual differences, and ensuring access for marginalized groups, as part of broader efforts to create environments where everyone can reach their full potential [18]. For example, gamification has been applied as a teaching strategy to support learning and to develop behavioral and social skills in individuals with autism [19]. Gamified programs can support autistic individuals by offering a predictable, structured, and personalized learning environment—adaptable to different levels of the autism spectrum—with repetitive tasks, reduced social demands, minimal distractions, visual aids, and clear, concise audio instructions [20]. Thus, through personalized and adaptive environments, gamification can facilitate the effective implementation of inclusive teaching practices [21] by dynamically adjusting game challenges according to individual performance, modifying content, difficulty, and feedback in real time [22]. As gamification accounts for individual and contextual factors, it is essential to prioritize individual differences, with collaboration between educators, developers, researchers, and parents being crucial to create optimal inclusive strategies for diverse learners [23]. In order to accomplish this, it is important to consider diversity factors, like gender, age, disabilities, disorders, language, sexual orientation, and culture [18].

Therefore, if game elements are combined without a clear theoretical foundation [10,11] and gamification outcomes depend on contextual factors that vary across studies and real-world applications [14–16], the replicability of the results reduces due to differing game element choices and settings, hindering both the predictability and credibility of a scientific finding [24]. Recognizing these gaps concerning the need for theory-driven research and individual and contextual diversity in gamification, our study aims to answer the following question: "How can the selection of game elements tailored to specific contextual factors enhance the effectiveness and replicability of gamification in digital inclusive education?".

To answer this question, we propose the Systemic Gamification Theory (SGT) as a comprehensive model for inclusive and effective digital learning. First, we will present the insights that inspired SGT, based on existing gamification research results. Subsequently, we will put forward a literature review supporting the theory formulation through key relevant scientific fields for learning processes—Education, Human–Computer Interaction (HCI), and Psychology. Finally, we detail the principles and functioning of SGT, explaining how it can be applied to strengthen and advance digital education environments.

2. Theoretical Foundation

2.1. Early Insights

Limited research has directly compared isolated versus combined game elements, with some existing evidence suggesting that incorporating multiple elements tends to enhance motivation and cognitive outcomes [10,25,26], supported by findings showing that their combination fosters a more immersive, game-like experience [27]. To further investigate that context, previous research [28], designed based on a validated study protocol [29,30], analyzed the impact of gamification in education, investigating how individual and combined game elements (e.g., points, badges, and challenges) influenced cognition, emotion, and motivation through a randomized controlled trial (RCT), using a developed digital gamified platform. Following established research guidelines (CONSORT, Cochrane Collaboration, EVAT©) [31–34] and using participant characteristics—sociodemographics (age, gender, marital status, education, and nationality), game habits, and player traits—as control variables to ensure group homogeneity, the findings showed that the combination of the three game elements significantly improved learning outcomes compared to the group without gamification. This may be attributed to the combined game elements offering a more engaging experience, effectively linking goal-setting with feedback [35], and blending internal and external motivational drivers [36]. Conversely, the badge-only group increased cognitive load without enhancing performance, indicating the risks of using game elements in isolation. This may have occurred because gamification must align pedagogy with design, as cognitive load increases with unnecessary learning demands [37]. Also, the findings suggested that badges were not effectively designed, lacking clear goal criteria [38] and context-relevant visuals [39], making their meaning unclear and adding to the cognitive burden. Thus, according to the study [28], the findings highlighted that gamification's effectiveness lies not in the number of elements used, but in how well they are aligned with the pedagogical context and instructional design—pointing to the need for a theory that addresses this relationship while being grounded in key scientific fields related to learning. Considering that scenario, we built the SGT upon an existing theory related to gamification in learning contexts, with the goal of expanding and complementing it, as discussed below.

2.2. Education and Gamified Learning

Gamification in education, whether through gamified or game-based learning, focuses on leveraging entertainment value to enhance learning, and Gamified Learning Theory (GLT) and the expanded Gamification Science (GS) framework are relevant and central to this approach [12,40]. GLT defines gamification as the use of game attributes to indirectly influence learning by triggering behaviors and attitudes that mediate or moderate the impact of game elements on learning outcomes [41]. GS is an updated, refined model that positions game elements as predictors, psychological states and behaviors as mediators, and context as a moderator, providing a structured framework for guiding gamification research [42]. Both previous theories advocate for a rigorous, experimental approach in which individual game elements are purposefully assigned and tested to isolate their effects, avoiding the common but problematic practice of bundling multiple elements, which can compromise internal validity and obscure which specific components drive outcomes, thus limiting both theoretical insight and practical application. GLT and GS are frequently employed within gamification research, as evidenced by multiple studies [43–46]. A recent systematic review indicates that the GLT has emerged as a promising theoretical framework, offering substantial utility for e-learning designers in the identification and selection of appropriate game elements for integration within educational and training contexts [47], leading us to choose these theories as the foundational theory for our theoretical construct. Building on the foundations of GLT and GS, our new theory (SGT) complements rather than replaces these theories. While embracing their rigorous research approach and focusing on the predictors, mediators, and moderators of gamification effects, SGT adds a distinct perspective. As demonstrated in the previous section, prior research [28] showed that the effectiveness of gamification depends less on the number of elements used and more on their alignment with the pedagogical context and instructional design. Therefore, while the isolated effects proposed by GLT and GS may be valuable for research by allowing the examination of individual game elements, they do not accurately represent how gamification practically functions in real-world educational settings. Thus, rather than isolating components, SGT views each set of elements as a singular configuration with emergent properties, producing outcomes that differ from individual elements, and emphasizing the unique impact of their systemic interaction by considering key aspects of HCI.

2.3. Human–Computer Interaction, Human-Centered Design, and User Experience

The field of HCI plays a crucial role in shaping the design and development of educational tools and digital mental health solutions, aiming to enhance usability, reduce costs, boost adaptability, and increase the perceived value for users [48,49]. Embedded within HCI, the Human-Centered Design (HCD) approach relies on iterative processes that actively involve users to better understand their needs, habits, and preferences, leading to solutions that are not only functional but also efficient and user-friendly, with a strong focus on empathy—an essential factor for education and healthcare applications [50,51]. Central to HCD is creating a positive User Experience (UX), and gamification builds upon this by moving beyond basic technical functionality to enrich the overall experience, taking into account the user's environment, functional goals, social interactions, and emotional responses when engaging with digital platforms [52]. All these concepts aim to meet user needs through direct engagement to create positive, accessible experiences that embrace human diversity by considering an inclusive design for varied perspectives and conditions (e.g., such as disabled people) [53]. Additionally, in HCI, heuristic evaluation is a method for identifying system design and development issues within an iterative design process, and it is widely used due to its low cost, minimal planning requirements, ease of use, and applicability in both early development and evaluation phases, supporting system improvement and refinement [54,55]. By integrating HCI, HCD, and UX principles into our theoretical model, we aimed to sustain SGT in digital design and development and to create a heuristic evaluation, while emphasizing the psychological aspects of the human behind the user and their interaction with the gamified learning experience as a whole complex dynamic between individual conditions and the environment.

2.4. Psychology and Gestalt

Among various psychological theories, Gestalt Theory sees perception as a holistic process, emphasizing meaningful organization and introspective problem-solving in education by presenting all aspects of a problem to spark curiosity, encourage discovery, and help learners explore relationships and build solutions [56]. Gestalt Theory emphasizes that a whole is not just greater than the sum of its parts but fundamentally distinct from them [57,58]. Gestalt theory outlines eight key principles of perceptual grouping and organization, all of which illustrate how we perceive complex stimuli into unified, meaningful wholes: (1) proximity, where elements close together are seen as a group; (2) similarity, where elements alike in color, size, or orientation are grouped; (3) common fate, where elements moving in the same direction are perceived as related; (4) symmetry, which leads us to group mirror-image shapes together; (5) parallelism, where parallel lines or shapes are seen as part of a whole; (6) continuity, where intersecting elements are perceived as continuous lines rather than disconnected angles; (7) closure, where the mind fills in gaps to perceive complete, closed figures; and (8) figure–ground, where the visual system distinguishes a focused object (figure) from its surrounding context (background) [59,60]. Gestalt principles are extensively applied in design for their focus on perception, emphasizing how the relationships and synergy among elements create a unified, holistic experience within interfaces and systems [61,62]. The Gestalt-based design method fosters the synergy between internal system creation and external real-world analysis, aligning user behavior with intuitive system and interface design—an approach that is essential for designing an inclusive, human-centric educational technology [63]. Grounded in Gestalt principles, our approach sought to reinforce SGT by promoting a cohesive user experience—one that unifies diverse sensory elements (such as visual sensory elements) within the system's architecture while emphasizing the continuous interplay between users and technology.

2.5. *Interdisciplinary Foundations and General System Theory*

General System Theory (GST) was first introduced by Ludwig von Bertalanffy [64] and was developed to foster interdisciplinary dialogue, advance scientific discoveries in fields with underdeveloped theories, and unify diverse areas of knowledge [65,66]. GST has been applied across a variety of scientific fields, such as physics, chemistry, biology, sociology, economics, and technology, to promote a holistic understanding of phenomena and counter-reductionist approaches [67]. Recent adaptations of GST in education and information science incorporate its principles into learning experiences through educational technology and systems thinking [68,69]. According to GST, although a system can be divided structurally, it operates as a unified whole, with emergent properties—distinct qualities that result from the dynamic synergy of its components and vanish when elements are separated from the system [65,70]. GST is a unified theory for complex systems that spans micro- to macro-scales within environments, shifting focus from objects to relationships, quantity to quality, components to pattern, closed to open systems, and linear to nonlinear performance [71]. Inspired by this theory, we proposed a new perspective in SGT that highlights its interdisciplinarity and promotes the integration of system elements, where emergence and synergy shape a unified whole within an open system that interacts dynamically with its environment beyond linear processes.

3. The Systemic Gamification Theory (SGT)

The SGT was developed from early empirical insights through a subjectivist inductive approach (from data to theory), enhanced by existing theories, leading to a logically structured theoretical model, comprising interconnected concepts and premises, designed as a tool to guide future research [72]. As stated before, our first insight came from prior empirical research that indicated that well-integrated combinations of game elements (points, badges, and challenges) enhanced learning outcomes, whereas badges' use of a single game element only increased cognitive load [28]—highlighting that the impact of combined elements is not merely additive, as the integrated setup improved learning without adding cognitive load. With that insight, grounded in the idea that different game elements distinctly affect psychological states, behavior, and learning—as argued by GLT and GS [41,42]—the need to consider human factors in HCI design [50,51], the Gestalt principle that a gamified system is more than the sum of its parts [57,58], and the holistic, interdisciplinary, and systemic perspective emphasized by GST [71], we formulated the SGT, integrating empirical data with concepts from these foundational theories and related scientific fields. Thus, SGT was developed to align gamification design principles with the specific context of their application by guiding the selection of game elements through a set of structured principles. The principles were developed to address a notable gap in the existing literature concerning the lack of a clear theoretical foundation for integrating game elements [10,11] and the critical necessity of accounting for contextual factors in gamification analysis, given that its outcomes were found to be significantly contingent upon such variables across diverse studies and real-world applications [14–16]. This led to the development of principles that consider the critical importance of understanding how integrating game elements may have different features and how they might interact in real-world scenarios.

The SGT focuses on four key principles:

(1) Integration: emphasizing the interconnected relationships among game elements;
(2) Emergence: recognizing the unique properties that arise when elements interact as a system;
(3) Synergy: where the combined effect of elements exceeds their isolated contributions;
(4) Context: which shapes and is shaped by the synergistic dynamics of the system, contemplating individual, situational, spatial, and cultural aspects.

This model enables a better understanding, comparison, and application of entire gamification systems rather than isolated elements, identifying key success factors and designing effective and inclusive interventions. Here, we first present the concepts underlying the theoretical model, followed by two practical tools—the SGT Heuristics and the SGT Framework—designed to offer actionable guidance for educational gamification and to serve as practical resources for educators, researchers, and instructional designers. While heuristics are exploratory and practical tools that act as mental shortcuts or experiential guidelines for quick decision-making and the evaluation of system design, frameworks are more rigorous and structured models that offer a systematic approach with defined steps for addressing complex problems [73,74]. Thus, in SGT, they complement each other: the Heuristics offer a broader perspective for guiding system design, development, and evaluation, while the Framework provides a more detailed structure to describe and connect each component of these processes. Figure 1 illustrates the four principles of SGT.

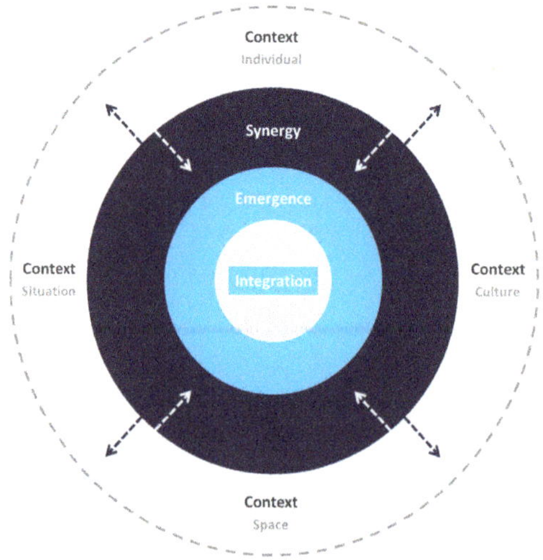

Figure 1. Systemic Gamification Theory principles.

Integration involves combining multiple game elements, which are core components typical of games used in gamification that provide structure by defining rules and goals, and aim to fulfill psychological needs such as competence, autonomy, and relatedness through mechanisms like rewards, progress tracking, customization, choice, and social interaction [75]. Some studies aim to systematize and categorize the various game elements used in gamification, such as the use of rewards, progress, challenges, badges, and several other elements [76,77]. Nonetheless, games can be understood as multimedia art and an aesthetic expression of interactive systems, creating meaning through player interaction and rule-based possibilities [78]. Thus, since game elements are fundamental components of games, they result from creative processes and allow for vast flexibility and an endless range of possible idealizations and configurations. The first core concept of SGT involves selecting or designing game elements and integrating them into a distinct configuration that gives rise to an emergent effect, distinct from the sum of individual game elements.

Emergence, a concept found across various sciences, refers to the spontaneous development of new effects through the interaction of components, shaped by ongoing activity, external influences, and evolving insights, making it a dynamic, exploratory process that embraces unpredictability, continuous change, and unexpected outcomes [79]. Gamification research frequently merges multiple game elements, making it difficult to isolate their individual effects and compare interventions due to differing configurations [10,14]. Unlike GLT and GS, which promote testing individual game elements in isolation [41,42], we advocate for integrating elements into unique configurations, as different settings may give rise to distinct emergent properties. For example, we hypothesize that different combinations of game elements may lead to distinct outcomes—for instance, "points" combined with "badges" may result in outcome X, while "challenges" with "rewards" may produce outcome Y, and the use of "avatar" alone may lead to outcome Z. However, this does not mean that using "points," "badges," "challenges," and "rewards" together will result in outcome XY, nor that combining "challenges" and "avatar" will generate an outcome equivalent to $Y/2 + Z$. Consequently, comparing isolated elements across interventions may be unrealistic, as combinations can give rise to emergent properties not represented by the sum of individual effects. To ensure meaningful comparisons, it is essential to assess the holistic gamification process, focusing on the unique integration of elements and their specific synergy with the surrounding context.

Synergy is a concept applied across several fields—from biology to economics—referring to the phenomenon where the combined effect of elements surpasses the sum of their individual effects when acting independently within a system [80]. Similarly to how individuals interact with each other within particular social contexts [81], they also engage with computers in ways shaped by specific situations and environments [82]. In this model, synergy refers to the dynamic interaction between two interconnected parts: on one side, the integrated and emergent nature of gamification, which forms a distinct configuration greater than the sum of its elements; and on the other, the context in which it is applied, encompassing individuals, situations, environments, and cultural factors. The interaction between these two parts produces a unique property that cannot be reduced to either side in isolation and may vary if the gamification design or contextual conditions are modified. Synergy is what unifies both parts, giving meaning to the interaction between the system and the context. In this phase, it is essential to systematize diverse users' profiles based on their full context, linking how the gamified system could interact with them—for instance, by using personas from the design thinking approach (i.e., fictional, generalized user representations that offer a broad perspective of the problem by capturing interests, behaviors, needs, and values) [83], different player traits or types [15,16], or the different motivational profiles of learners [84].

Context is a central concept in both education and gamification, where pragmatics explains how learning adapts across settings [85], and individual traits and cultural factors shape user preferences and motivation [14]. To address the multifaceted nature of context, we divided it into four interrelated aspects: Individuals, Situations, Spaces, and Culture. Individuals are socially formed and contextually situated, shaped by a complex, evolving combination of dispositions and experiences across multiple social environments, embodying both personal singularity and collective influences [86]. Situations can be understood as interactions occurring within specific temporal boundaries in spaces [87]. Spaces can be seen as dynamic environments shaped by social practices and interactions, as fluid territories of meaning-making that can be digital, physical, or both, where blurred online–offline boundaries create multilayered contexts for constructing experience [88]. Culture can be defined as a dynamic system of meaning-making shaped through the interplay between social practices, identifications, and power structures, understood holistically within their historical, political, and relational environments [89].

To illustrate a first simple application of SGT principles, we considered the previously discussed study, focused on the impact of gamification in education using individual and combined game elements (e.g., points, badges, and challenges) through an RCT [28], which is represented in Figure 2. This figure represents how the configuration of the three game elements was integrated into a gamified digital learning platform, producing emergent properties that interacted synergistically within the context of a classroom with individual computers. Through this dynamic, the RCT showed that the game elements of points, badges, and challenges influenced students in educational settings, ultimately contributing to improved learning outcomes.

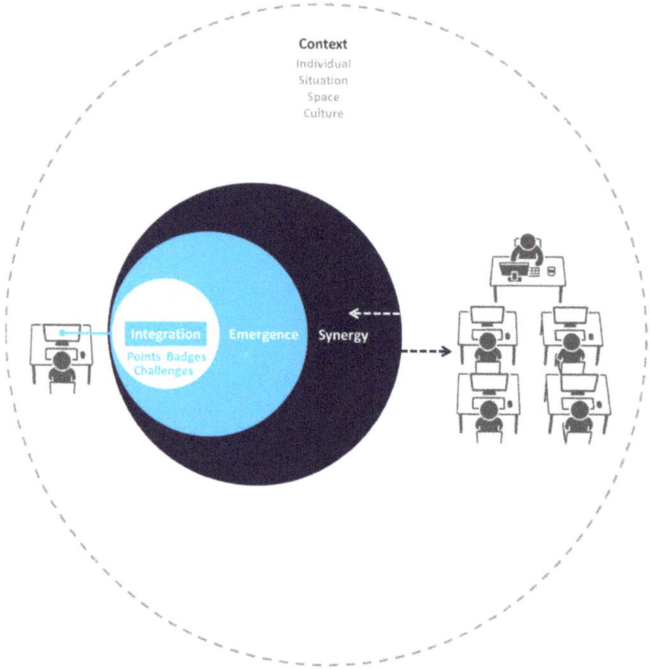

Figure 2. Illustration of Systemic Gamification Theory principles.

The SGT is seen as a methodological tool that enriches education by addressing specific contextual conditions in learning environments. This requires analyzing cultural, spatial, situational, and individual dimensions, and then designing an integrated system of game elements that produces emergent effects aligned with those needs. The resulting synergy between system and context is intended to motivate learners to achieve educational goals. SGT does not replace existing pedagogies or theories; it adds a meaningful, context-sensitive layer. Thus, gamification under SGT must embed equity, diversity, and inclusion to ensure all individuals are integrated within the system. This involves addressing contextual educational factors linked to participants' mental and physical health, including gender and age (to foster non-stereotypical environments); disabilities, disorders, and atypical conditions (e.g., visual or hearing impairments); language (to support comprehension and linguistic adaptability); sexual orientation (to enhance social connection and health awareness); and experiences of exclusion (to promote cultural integration) [18].

To illustrate this need for contextual understanding, e-learning environments can increase fatigue in deaf and hard-of-hearing individuals due to their simultaneous stimuli, limited interactivity, and poorly structured content presentation on the screen display [90]. Although early deafness affects visuospatial attention, studies show that video game training can improve peripheral response control by helping users manage relevant and irrelevant visual stimuli [91]. Therefore, gamification—the use of elements from games [2]—should use game design to balance screen displays to reduce eventual cognitive overload, preventing fatigue and improving the learning experiences. For instance, game elements—such as animated prompts, choices, feedback, and rewards—in vocabulary learning games for deaf and hard-of-hearing students with sign-supported instructions and consistent visuals have led to high ratings for attention, relevance, confidence, and satisfaction during the educational experience [92]. Considering another example, individuals with Attention Deficit/Hyperactivity Disorder (ADHD) often experience challenges in academic settings due to symptoms such as inattentiveness, impulsivity, and hyperactivity [93]. Research has indicated that incorporating gamified media into educational activities can help improve focus and concentration among students with ADHD [94]. Enhancing digital environments with a broad range of game elements—such as goals, levels, points, and progression—may foster greater engagement and motivation, potentially supporting better symptom regulation in learners with ADHD [95].

Since SGT was developed for digital learning contexts, it can be applied to any educational course, level, and setting involving digital environments, including fully online or hybrid courses, encompassing socio-digital learning spaces that integrate digital, mobile, virtual, online, social, and physical components to support interactive and inclusive learning experiences [96]. Considering digital learning environments, SGT applies to both synchronous and asynchronous formats. Synchronous learning involves real-time interaction between teachers and students on a digital platform, while asynchronous learning offers flexibility, with materials that are accessible at different times and locations [97]. Finally, educational gamification can be classified as structural gamification—which uses game elements to gamify the learning process without changing the content, such as enhancing the educational software—and content gamification—which embeds game-like features such as narrative and exploration to reshape the material for specific goals, often as a customized design [11]. SGT supports both approaches, allowing for the adaptation of structure or content based on the educational context and pedagogical needs.

That said, we begin by presenting the Heuristics, which offer broad guidance for inclusive gamification, followed by the Framework, which provides a more structured and systematic approach to gamified systems.

3.1. Heuristics for Guiding and Supporting Inclusive Gamification

The SGT was developed as a practical model to support the design of inclusive and effective gamification interventions in educational contexts. Sustained by its four core principles, we formulated the 10 Heuristics of SGT, intended to guide the implementation of gamified systems with a critical and reflective approach, as introduced in Table 1. Heuristic development can draw from design principles, literature reviews of prior theories, and existing heuristics [98]. Thus, the SGT Heuristics were inspired by the four core principles of SGT, which were developed based on prior theories related to GLT, GS, HCI, Gestalt Psychology, and GST, specifically addressing the literature's lack of a theoretical basis for integrating game elements and the necessity of considering contextual factors in gamification analysis. While SGT principles and theoretical foundations have been discussed earlier, it is important now to present existing gamification and usability heuristics that also informed our proposed model. The SGT Heuristics were based on established recommendations for designing and evaluating educational games through heuristics, focusing on the system development and user interaction phases, encompassing usability, pedagogy, content, multimedia, gameplay, aesthetics, social interaction, and user motivation [99]. The Heuristics were formulated to answer five key questions (i.e., "What", "Why", "When", "Where", and "How") to evaluate a proper scientific method [100] and to verify the rationale, scope, context, and modality in gamification research [101]. Considering contextual factors to answer the "Why", "When", and "Where questions, SGT Heuristics 1, 2, 3, and 4 were inspired by gamification heuristics aimed at guiding design application, emphasizing the alignment of the system with real-world contexts, incorporating inclusive design principles, and fostering active user engagement [102,103]. Regarding the selection of game elements for gamification application to answer the "What?" question, SGT Heuristics 5, 6, 7, and 8 were sustained by a gamification heuristic defining 28 game design principles to help specialists assess and identify design gaps, addressing extrinsic and intrinsic motivation along with context-dependent engagement for gameful experiences [104,105], which was later extended by considering gamification as a social phenomenon and incorporating cultural dimensions into the evaluation of motivational and contextual variables [106]. Finally, related to usability aspects of the digital system, aiming to answer the "How" question, SGT Heuristics numbers 9 and 10 were drawn from Jakob Nielsen's 10 Usability Heuristics, a well-known HCI framework for identifying usability issues in system development, which supports improved interface navigation and applies to gamification design [54,55,107].

Based on the four principles (Integration, Emergence, Synergy, and Context), prior theories, and previous heuristics, the 10 SGT Heuristics were formulated for meaningful application, with each requiring careful consideration to ensure alignment with inclusive practices. The SGT Heuristics adopts a top-down methodology—beginning with a deep understanding of the context and progressing toward the system's configuration—emphasizing its human-centered and context-aware orientation. Table 1 presents the 10 proposed Heuristics.

Table 1. Systemic Gamification Theory Heuristics.

Heuristics #	Definition	Description
1	Contextual Analysis and Alignment	Begin with a thorough analysis of the educational context—individual, situational, spatial, and cultural—to ensure that gamification aligns with specific learning environments.
2	Pedagogical Complementarity	Use gamification as a complementary layer to existing pedagogical strategies, enhancing rather than replacing instructional methods.
3	Inclusive and Accessible Design	Address diversity and inclusion by designing systems that support all users, accounting for mental and physical health, language, gender, age, disabilities, and social integration.
4	Equity-Centered Gamification	Ensure the gamified system supports social justice goals by promoting fair access, participation, and representation within learning environments.

Table 1. *Cont.*

Heuristics #	Definition	Description
5	Motivation Across Contextual Scales	Support learner motivation by addressing both micro-level (individual interaction) and macro-level (cultural and institutional) influences, considering intrinsic and extrinsic motivational aspects.
6	Meaningful Integration of Game Elements	Select and combine game elements thoughtfully to create a unique and coherent configuration tailored to contextual needs.
7	Emergence and Systemic Evaluation	Recognize that the integrated system may produce emergent effects that differ from the sum of its parts; evaluate the system as a whole, not just its components.
8	Synergistic Design for Different Profiles	Design for synergy, where the interaction between gamification and context produces added value for different users' profiles, considering the system as a whole that is greater than its isolated elements.
9	Adaptive and Iterative Configuration	Continuously refine the gamified system through feedback loops, adapting to evolving learner needs and contextual shifts, considering usability and user experience aspects.
10	Aesthetic and Expressive Coherence	Treat game elements as creative and aesthetic tools that contribute to user interaction and a meaningful experience.

3.2. Framework for Structuring and Analyzing Inclusive Gamification

As stated before, while heuristics are more practical, experience-based shortcuts for quick design and evaluation, frameworks provide more structured, systematic models with defined steps for dealing with complex problems [73,74]. As the literature emphasizes that selecting appropriate game elements is key to successful gamification and highlights the need for more mature, usable frameworks, given that many designers still rely on custom-built approaches [108], we propose the SGT Framework as a potential solution for this scenario. SGT is conceived as a theoretical framework offering a simplified mapping approach to designing and comparing different gamification interventions. The Framework was developed to design and evaluate gamified systems, as well as to compare research methods and outcomes. Based on its four core principles, we developed a Framework to systematize a way of designing gamified learning and to better understand the conditions under which gamification is effective or ineffective. By enabling systematic comparisons across varied educational environments and disciplinary contexts, the Framework supports more robust analyses, clarifying under which circumstances gamification has an impact. Therefore, we advocate that gamification is not just the addition of several game elements.

The Framework is meant to act as a detailed tool that helps to connect and organize the key components involved in gamification design. It supports the careful selection of game elements (Integration) based on how they work together (Emergence), aiming to create unique outcomes that align meaningfully (Synergy) with the specific context in which they are used (Context). To begin with, all game elements should be identified. Next, these elements should be sorted into distinct groups based on their motivational goals. When it comes to understanding motivation, there are several models available, but we suggest using Self-Determination Theory (SDT), which is widely applied in gamification research [12,109,110]. SDT views motivation as a spectrum that ranges from no motivation to extrinsic and intrinsic motivation, depending on how well external influences match a person's internal needs [111,112]. The theory focuses on intrinsic motivation as doing something out of curiosity or enjoyment, driven by a sense of autonomy, competence, and connection with others, while extrinsic motivation comes from external rewards or the desire to avoid negative outcomes [113]. Gamification often relies on SDT, shaping behavior by using game elements that tap into intrinsic motivations (like tracking progress) or extrinsic ones (like offering rewards) [36]. However, it is important to note that external rewards can both help and hurt intrinsic motivation. When rewards feel controlling, they may reduce a person's sense of ownership, lowering motivation overall [114]. Still, for people who are not naturally motivated, external rewards can be effective in increasing their motivation [115]. Because of this, designers should aim to include both intrinsic and extrinsic motivators within each group of game elements to reach a broader range of users, supporting those who are already intrinsically motivated while also encouraging those who may need more external reinforcement. Then, after selecting the game elements and grouping them into objectives and motivational purposes, the next step is to show how these elements interact with the real-world through inputs and outputs for different users' profiles, describing the conditions under which these interactions are appropriate while taking into account the specific context where the gamified system will be applied.

While the complexity of human and social variables in SGT means some bias is inevitable, the Framework helps educators, instructors, and researchers identify, assess, and address these biases consciously during the design, implementation, evaluation, or replication of interventions. Table 2 illustrates the Framework.

Table 2. Systemic Gamification Theory Framework.

Principle	Description
Integration	List all the game elements that are being used and describe their features.
Emergence	Describe the interactions among these elements and the main objective of the whole gamification design, together with the motivational purposes of each interaction. Group the previous game elements integration.
Synergy	Highlight the interaction between the gamified system and its context, listing the inputs and outputs of the system that are being gamified, considering different profiles of users related to contextual factors. Relate this interaction between the gamified system and its context with the previous grouping of game elements.
Context	Describe the cultural, spatial, situational, and individual factors within the educational context that shape and are shaped by the gamified experience. Emphasize understanding of the specific environment and users. Use these data to formulate the previous profiles of users.

4. Designing and Evaluating Gamification with SGT

A review of personalized gamification identified several research needs: (1) empirical comparisons between generalized and tailored gamification; (2) qualitative user-centered studies; (3) approaches that include contextual factors; (4) reliance on a clear, comprehensive set of game elements; and (5) conditions to improve research reproducibility [116]. Addressing these gaps, the SGT offers structured tools to support empirical studies grounded in user and contextual data, guiding the purposeful selection of game elements through a replicable methodology. Thus, SGT supports the design and evaluation of gamification in educational settings and research, offering educators, researchers, and designers a path to develop inclusive, effective strategies. Here, we first explore how the SGT Heuristics and Framework can be applied to support gamification design, followed by how these tools can be applied to evaluate gamification strategies within educational technologies and research contexts.

4.1. Heuristics and Framework for Gamification Design and Development

The Heuristics and Framework act as complementary tools for designing and developing gamified systems. We recommend starting with the Heuristics to guide brainstorming and design thinking for creating and improving iterative solutions for a specific need [117], beginning with a more deductive (top-down) approach [118], as the Heuristics offer a broader perspective to identify and refine core ideas. Once the initial concepts are shaped, the Framework should be applied to provide a more detailed structure, helping to describe and connect each component of the gamified solution. After applying both tools, we recommend using them together and iteratively, allowing for the continuous refinement of the solution until a final proposal is reached.

Following this proposed order, firstly, Table 3 presents the Heuristics with an illustrative example of a new gamified digital course design, based on a hypothetical online university course that serves as a prototype scenario for applying SGT in design practice. The hypothetical course was based on a fully online format with both synchronous and asynchronous video lectures and exercises, incorporating structural and content gamification to reflect the complete range of gamified learning proposed in SGT. We chose to illustrate a fully online course rather than a hybrid model, as including physical school settings would introduce numerous context-specific variables that would increase complexity for this prototype illustration purpose, such as classroom layout, available equipment, internet access, and smartphone policies. We chose to illustrate the course using one discipline, focused on the United Nations Sustainable Development Goals (SDGs), designed for an undergraduate program in Education, as higher education institutions play a key role in advancing the SDGs [119,120], particularly those related to inclusive, equitable, and quality education—central themes of this research. Nevertheless, given the flexibility of SGT, it can be further applied to any course or educational level, as long as a proper contextual analysis is conducted—an essential step in the SGT approach.

This hypothetical course comprises a culturally diverse cohort of students, including deaf or hard-of-hearing participants, autistic participants, people with ADHD, and neurotypical participants. We chose these specific inclusive conditions as the movement toward inclusive public education for deaf and hard-of-hearing students has gained momentum over the past fifty years. This presents challenges as their inclusion relies on accessible settings tailored to their language and communication needs, emphasizing the importance of designing educational systems that support individual needs and aim for success for all learners [121]. Also, there is a lack of adequate support for creating inclusive school environments for students with autism spectrum disorder [122]. As the number of students with autism spectrum disorder in general education classrooms has grown in recent decades, educators must adapt their practices, and schools must provide appropriate resources, including technology, to support their education [123]. Finally, over the last 20 years, there has been a significant rise in interventions targeting children and adolescents with ADHD [124], with gamification emerging as a popular approach due to its potential to improve attention control and enhance task engagement [125,126]. Thus, we considered a hypothetical course involving neurotypical, deaf and hard-of-hearing, and autistic students, as well as people with ADHD, given their specific challenges in inclusive education and the prior use of gamification as a tool to support these groups, as previously discussed [20,92,124]. However, this model can be extended to a broad range of conditions involving diversity factors such as gender, age, disabilities, disorders (like depression and anxiety), language, sexual orientation, and cultural background [18,127]—each of which merits further investigation with the SGT.

Table 3. Application of Systemic Gamification Theory Heuristics.

Heuristics #	Definition	Example Application (Online University Course)	Examples of Game Elements and Practical Design
1	Contextual Analysis and Alignment	Analyze students' learning habits and time zones to adapt the module schedule and activities.	Timezone-adaptive challenges and asynchronous activities.
2	Pedagogical Complementarity	Gamify activities to complement lectures and group discussions rather than replace them.	Progress points based on assessments and group quests.
3	Inclusive and Accessible Design	Provide captions for all videos, ensure screen-reader compatibility, and include customizable visual instructions and notifications for deaf and/or autistic students, and people with ADHD (since participants with these profiles are included in the hypothetical course).	Closed captions, image-based instructions, and text-to-speech tools.
4	Equity-Centered Gamification	Design missions that celebrate cultural diversity and allow all students to contribute equally, regardless of ability.	Quizzes about different cultures' features, fostering cultural understanding and integration.
5	Motivation Across Contextual Scales	Include goal-setting dashboards and reflection tools that help students align personal goals with the course outcomes.	Personalized learning paths, goal-tracking meters, and digital journals.
6	Meaningful Integration of Game Elements	Combine all game elements through a narrative that aligns all interactions in a meaningful way with avatars to represent student diversity.	Narrative-based modules and avatars with cultural and sensory customization allow players to immerse themselves in diverse cultural stories while personalizing their avatars with culturally relevant features, fostering inclusivity by enabling users to explore and blend different cultural backgrounds through interactive and customizable experiences.
7	Emergence and Systemic Evaluation	Monitor the combined effects of all game elements to ensure that engagement is due to the system's design, not just one popular element.	Analytics dashboard tracking user engagement across various features and activities within the digital platform and course, including metrics such as completed tasks and time spent on different screens.
8	Synergistic Design for Different Profiles	Create a system where challenges, feedback, points, narrative, and possible team formations can enhance both learning and social integration.	Cross-cultural quests, peer-recognition points, avatars, and guild formation allow students to create teams, collaborate on activities, and interact with one another directly within the platform through a narrative.
9	Adaptive and Iterative Configuration	Allow automated feedback loops where difficulty and rewards are dynamically adjusted by artificial intelligence based on collective input over time. Permit privacy configuration for status visibility.	Dynamic challenge levels, unlockable rewards based on feedback, automated difficulty adjustments of questions, and privacy configuration.
10	Aesthetic and Expressive Coherence	Use visually balanced interfaces, with a clear separation of primary learning tasks and secondary elements in screen display, consistent iconography, and personalized themes to reduce cognitive overload.	Minimalist user interface themes, icon-based navigation, and soothing color palettes.

Additionally, we assumed a previous use of an established player traits questionnaire administered to the hypothetical participants of the digital course based on a questionnaire that has been widely validated with a large sample of respondents [15,16,128]. This questionnaire was designed to identify individual gaming preferences and motivational tendencies. It includes 25 items rated on a 7-point Likert scale (from strongly disagree to strongly agree), producing scores across five distinct player orientations—Social, Aesthetic, Narrative, Challenge, and Goal—each ranging from 0 to 1. According to the authors of the questionnaire [15,16], individuals with a Social Orientation enjoy multiplayer or collaborative environments, valuing interpersonal connections. The Aesthetic Orientation reflects an appreciation for artistic elements in games, such as visuals and sound, driven by autonomy and exploratory behaviors. Narrative-Oriented players tend to prefer rich storytelling and immersive plots, showing interest in unfolding narratives. The Challenge Orientation is marked by a desire for complex, high-difficulty tasks that fulfill competence needs. Finally, a Goal Orientation is defined by motivation to achieve tasks, complete missions, and track measurable accomplishments. In the illustrative context of our hypothetical course, the most prominent player orientations among students were Social, Goal, and Narrative, providing valuable contextual insights for applying the SGT model effectively. It is important to highlight that this is merely an illustrative scenario, as different student cohorts may show varying dominant player traits, and other profiling instruments (e.g., personas from the design thinking approach [83]) can be used to categorize users in a gamified digital learning environment.

Secondly, to illustrate the application of the Framework after the Heuristics, we applied it to the same hypothetical online university course involving a culturally diverse student cohort, including deaf, autistic, and neurotypical learners, as well as students with ADHD. Also, the students were mostly Social, Goal, and Narrative-Oriented players. Tables 4–7 present the implementation of the proposed course.

As outlined in the Integration principle of SGT, the selection and creation of the game elements is an inherently creative process, allowing researchers and educators to design them much like a form of art. However, studies on tailored and personalized gamification have helped to systematize commonly used game elements, offering a structured perspective of how different elements can stimulate distinct forms of interaction within gamified experiences [76,77,129]. Drawing on these systematizations, we adapted selected elements for application in our hypothetical example, aiming to align them with the Heuristics and design strategies presented in Table 3. Accordingly, Table 4 outlines the game elements integrated into the proposed hypothetical gamified digital course.

Table 4. Integration.

Game Element	Brief Description
Avatar	Visual representation of the user in the system.
Challenges	Tasks designed to test skills or knowledge.
Dashboard	Interface showing progress and key metrics.
Digital Journal	Space for reflective writing and tracking learning.
Difficulty Adjustment	Allow users to navigate different challenge levels.
Privacy Configuration	Status can be changed to private or public.
Feedback	Information provided on performance or actions.
Group Quests	Collaborative tasks requiring teamwork.
Learning Paths	Structured sequence of content or tasks.
Narrative	Storyline guiding user engagement and context.
Peer-Recognition Points	Points awarded by peers for contributions.
Progress Points Based on Assessments	Scores reflecting performance on assessments.
Quizzes	Short assessments to check knowledge.
Unlockable Rewards	Incentives earned after meeting specific goals.

As highlighted in the Emergence principle, gamification frequently draws on SDT, influencing behavior through game elements that appeal to either intrinsic motivations or extrinsic incentives [36]. While extrinsic rewards can effectively boost engagement in less motivated individuals, they may diminish intrinsic motivation in others [114,115], making it essential to strike a balance. Thus, the selection of game elements was intentionally designed to generate emergent effects by combining features that support both intrinsic and extrinsic motivation, aiming to engage students across a spectrum of motivational profiles. Table 5 presents the grouping of game elements, the expected interactions they encourage, and the corresponding type of motivation they aim to stimulate.

Table 5. Emergence.

Grouping	Game Elements	Interactions and Motivation
Progression and Performance Feedback	Progress points based on assess-ments/dashboard/feedback	These elements work together to track learner progression, reinforce accomplishments, and provide personalized, accessible feedback. Intrinsic motivation is related to competence, and extrinsic motivation is related to incentives, tied to external regulation.
Personalization and Identity	Difficulty adjustment/digital journal/learning paths/privacy configuration	Difficulty adjustment and learning paths let students navigate content at their own pace and challenge level, while a digital journal promotes reflective learning, helping students process information. User status visibility settings allow their status to be configured as either private or public. Intrinsic motivation is related to autonomy and competence, and extrinsic motivation is related to the feeling of internal pressure, tied to introjected regulation.
Collaboration and Social Dynamics	Group quests/peer-recognition points/unlockable rewards	These elements foster social motivation and community-building. Group quests promote collaboration, while peer recognition and unlockable rewards stimulate positive reinforcement. Intrinsic motivation is related to relatedness, and extrinsic motivation is related to incentives, tied to external regulation.
Challenge and Skill Development	Challenges/quizzes	These elements enhance engagement by challenging students to achieve structured goals and providing varied assessment types. Intrinsic motivation is related to competence, and extrinsic motivation is related to the feeling of internal pressure, tied to introjected regulation.
Ownership and Representation	Avatar/narrative	Avatars allow learners to represent themselves in inclusive, customizable ways, supporting identity expression across cultures, neurotypes, and accessibility needs. Narrative immerses users into a progressive storyline. Intrinsic motivation is related to curiosity and autonomy, and extrinsic motivation is related to the expression of self, tied to integrated regulation.

As emphasized before, the Synergy principle focuses on aligning the gamified system with student profiles to establish a meaningful connection between the system and its context. To illustrate, we categorized learners in the hypothetical course based on contextual factors. First, we grouped participants by neurotype, classifying deaf, autistic, and ADHD students as neurodiverse (ND) and the remaining students as neurotypical (NT). Then, using a player traits instrument [15,16,128], we further categorized students into three profile types, reflecting the most prevalent traits in our sample—Social, Goal, and Narrative Orientations. These categorizations serve only as an example, as actual profile creation depends on the available contextual data and may include more diverse variations. It is important to highlight that, while certain features were designed for specific profiles, they are not exclusive and can benefit other users unless restricted by system rules. Table 6 shows this application of the Synergy principle of SGT.

Table 6. Synergy.

User Behavior (Input)	Gamified Element (Output)	Game Elements Grouping	Target Profiles
Access the system	Learning Streak on Dashboard, Encouraging Feedback	Progression and Performance Feedback	ND and NT Goal Orientation
Choosing a preferred avatar	Avatar Customization, Narrative Integration	Ownership and Representation	ND and NT Narrative Orientation
Completing a module or lesson	Progress Points, Dashboard Update	Progression and Performance Feedback Challenge and Skill Development	ND and NT Goal Orientation
Scoring high on a quiz	Unlockable Rewards, Progress Points	Progression and Performance Feedback	ND and NT Goal Orientation
Completing a challenge	Challenges Badge, Feedback on Achievement	Challenge and Skill Development	ND and NT Goal Orientation
Writing in a digital journal	Feedback, Journal Progress Marker	Personalization and Identity	ND and NT Goal Orientation
Navigating a higher difficulty level and succeeding	Automatic Dynamic Difficulty Adjustment, Unlockable Reward, Progress Boost, Narrative Progress	Progression and Performance Feedback Challenge and Skill Development Ownership and Representation	ND and NT Goal and Narrative Orientation
Customizing the learning path based on preference	Dashboard Visualization, Feedback on Autonomy	Personalization and Identity	ND and NT Goal Orientation
Participating in a team quest	Peer-Recognition Points, Group Badge	Progression and Performance Feedback Challenge and Skill Development Collaboration and Social Dynamics	ND and NT Social Orientation
Asking a peer for help	Peer-Recognition Points	Collaboration and Social Dynamics	ND and NT Social Orientation
Helping a peer or contributing to the discussion	Peer-Recognition Points, Narrative shoutout	Progression and Performance Feedback Challenge and Skill Development Collaboration and Social Dynamics Ownership and Representation	ND and NT Social Orientation
Finishing a team assignment	Unlockable Rewards, Challenge Completion	Challenge and Skill Development Collaboration and Social Dynamics	ND and NT Goal and Social Orientation
Changing privacy settings	Private or Public Status Showing	Personalization and Identity	ND and NT Social Orientation
Using accessibility tools to complete a task	Feedback, Progress Tracking	Progression and Performance Feedback Ownership and Representation	ND Goal Orientation

Finally, the Context principle plays a central role in both education and gamification, as context accounts for how learning adjusts across environments and how individual traits and cultural influences shape user preferences and motivation [14,85]. Based on the hypothetical course, we developed a contextual scenario that incorporates the four dimensions of the principle—Individual, Situation, Space, and Culture—defining the structure in which the gamified digital course would take place. Table 7 presents these contextual descriptions, concluding the illustrative application of the SGT Framework for design purposes.

Table 7. Context.

Aspects	Description
Individual	The course has 28 students, aged between 19 and 36, with an average age of 24. The class includes 15 women, 11 men, and 2 non-binary students. Among the group are two deaf students who primarily use Brazilian Sign Language (Libras), two autistic students diagnosed with ASD Level 1, who prefer written instructions and quiet environments, and three students with ADHD. All students are undergraduates in their third year. Regarding their player traits, the students predominantly exhibit Social, Goal, and Narrative player orientations.
Situation	All students are enrolled in a mandatory elective that blends theoretical discussion with applied digital collaboration. The course runs from September to December, with weekly asynchronous modules released every Monday. There are two live sessions per month scheduled at 1:00 PM UTC to accommodate time zones. Students must complete four major assignments, complete biweekly quizzes, and participate in a cross-cultural project about diversity and education by Week 10. Students can choose to work individually or in groups, with activity difficulty, feedback, and rewards automatically adjusted based on the number of group members. Each week includes short video lectures, collaborative tasks in group forums, and personal reflection prompts. Deadlines are consistent (Fridays, 11:59 PM UTC), and student activity is tracked through the Moodle Learning Management System (LMS) v. 5.0 dashboard.
Space	The learning space is hosted on Moodle LMS v. 5.0. Students interact through discussion boards, real-time chatrooms, and group channels. All video lectures have captions in English and Portuguese, and written transcripts are available. Deaf students use the integrated sign-language interpreter box, while autistic students can access a "low sensory" interface mode that simplifies visual stimulation, and people with ADHD may customizable alerts to reduce unnecessary notifications and visual distractions. Although asynchronous, students often use WhatsApp, Discord, and Instagram group chats to communicate outside the platform. They access the course using laptops, tablets, and mobile phones from their home, university, or shared co-working spaces.
Culture	Nationalities represented in the course include Portugal (6 students), Brazil (5), Egypt (4), India (4), the U.S. (3), South Korea (3), and Nigeria (3). Cultural references, humor, and attitudes toward feedback vary—some students prefer peer praise, while others value direct, instructor-driven feedback. As cultural factors may affect students' comfort with social visibility [130], status rewards (like points, badges, or leaderboard positions) can be configured as either private or public.

4.2. Heuristics and Framework for Gamification Evaluation and Comparison

In addition to its use in design, SGT is also suitable for evaluation purposes when analyzing data from other applications or research. Thus, to apply SGT as a tool for evaluating other applications or research, we recommend an approach similar to Jakob Nielsen's 10 Usability Heuristics application, which includes a severity analysis of usability issues [131], and the Cochrane Collaboration's Risk of Bias tool for randomized trials

(RoB 2.0), which assesses the seriousness of potential bias [33]. Both tools systematically identify problems within systems or studies, respectively, serving as useful models for SGT-based evaluations.

Unlike when SGT is used for design purposes, where we suggest starting with the Heuristics, followed by the Framework (though both can be used interchangeably), for evaluation purposes, we recommend beginning with the Framework and then applying the Heuristics. This supports a more inductive (bottom-up) approach [115], enabling a systematic interpretation of the data before conducting a structured evaluation. Following this rationale, we suggest that experts or researchers (evaluators) begin by deconstructing the target application or study into smaller components by using those defined in the SGT Framework, through a process similar to reverse engineering, which extracts knowledge from existing systems for analysis, replication, or redesign [132]. Once the structure with the smaller components has been clarified, evaluators should apply the SGT Heuristics to systematically identify potential flaws or gaps related to each specific item. Each item serves as a lens for detecting limitations in how gamification is conceptualized, implemented, and contextualized within the application or research. These issues may reflect broader design shortcomings or research inconsistencies, thereby representing areas for improvement or further investigation. Evaluators should score each heuristic on a 0–4 scale: "0" indicates no issue, "1" a minor issue, "2" a moderate issue, "3" a major issue, and "4" a critical issue. We recommend this five-level scoring system, following the model of the Usability Heuristics [131], rather than the three-tiered approach used in the Cochrane Recommendations [33], as the five levels allow for greater variability in evaluations, which can be particularly useful for comparative analyses.

Lastly, it is essential that evaluators not only assess the severity of issues but also strive for consensus in their ratings. Discrepancies should be discussed collaboratively to achieve agreement. Involving at least three experts or researchers is recommended to ensure reliability and to resolve disagreements when consensus cannot be reached between two evaluators. Higher cumulative scores across the Heuristics indicate a greater number or severity of issues within the evaluated application or study.

5. Conclusions

By developing a theoretical model grounded in concepts from Education, HCI, and Psychology—and complementing foundational theories such as GLT and GS—this critical reflection aims to advance the understanding and application of educational gamification through the SGT. Our model evaluates gamification as a whole system, addressing the challenges of design heterogeneity that complicate the identification of success factors. SGT addresses critical gaps by offering a structured methodology for the design and evaluation of gamification interventions, grounded in the principles of Integration, Emergence, Synergy, and Context. To operationalize this theory, we developed two practical tools for educators, researchers, and instructional designers: SGT Heuristics and SGT Framework. By advancing the theoretical development of gamification, this study proposed a transformative approach to enrich multimedia learning environments through innovative, inclusive, and equitable gamified teaching strategies. SGT proposes the alignment of contextual understanding with system design, development, and research evaluation, emphasizing the importance of considering contextual characteristics when designing gamification and assessing its impact. It advocates for a holistic approach to conducting research and analyzing potential outcomes. Through the integration of game elements with their contextual application, we aimed to strengthen digital education in a rapidly evolving landscape while enhancing research quality and practical impact across various scientific fields.

6. Limitations and Future Research

A robust theory is characterized by (1) consistency with empirical evidence; (2) precision in its concepts' definitions and operationalizations; (3) parsimony in the use of minimal assumptions; (4) generality in its application across diverse contexts; (5) falsifiability via testable predictions that allow for potential refutation or refinement; and (6) progress by stimulating further research and theoretical development [133]. We developed the SGT based on principles that can be operationalized into high-level Heuristics, offering a broad perspective of system design, development, and evaluation, while the Framework serves as a detailed tool for organizing and connecting specific elements of these processes. To illustrate the practical use of our design, we provided a hypothetical example demonstrating how these tools can support both research and educational practice. With this, we aimed to fulfill the theoretical criteria of precision, parsimony, falsifiability, and progress. However, as SGT has not yet been empirically tested, there is a lack of consistency and generality, representing a theoretical limitation.

To meet the requirements of consistency and generality, further empirical studies are needed, especially those that follow rigorous research standards, such as low-bias randomized or non-randomized controlled trials, guided by frameworks like CONSORT, the Cochrane Collaboration, and EVAT© [31–34]. We recommend that future studies apply the SGT alongside existing gamification theories, like the GLT and GS [41,42], which provide foundational insights for SGT and can serve as complementary theories. These future studies should use the proposed Heuristics and Framework to design experiments that assess how different configurations of game elements affect psychological and behavioral factors leading to learning outcomes, depending on contextual variables. In addition to its application in design, SGT is also well-suited for gamification evaluation purposes, contributing to consistency and generality in the analysis of data from other applications or research studies. Accordingly, we recommend the use of the SGT Heuristics and Framework to evaluate and compare diverse applications and interventions, in alignment with the recommendations outlined in Section 4.2: Heuristics and Framework for Gamification Evaluation and Comparison. This approach facilitates the generation of empirical data from real-world implementations, thereby reinforcing the theoretical consistency and generality of SGT.

In alignment with the systemic approach underpinning SGT, it is essential to emphasize that key components must be considered when applying the model for research purposes. Since gamified learning can produce varied outcomes across individuals, gamification should be both adaptive and personalized by aligning user profiles, game elements, and digital platforms like Moodle LMS to optimize the impact [129]. In personalized gamification, it is essential to analyze not just users and game elements—categorized through player types, traits, or learning styles, for example—but also the intervention's outcomes and assessment methods, ensuring meaningful interpretation and application [134]. Therefore, it is important to emphasize that although SGT offers a practical model for designing and evaluating gamification, other research aspects—such as user profile analysis, the chosen technology and platform, research methodology, and the selection of outcomes and instruments—must also be carefully considered and applied to ensure both data quality and effective gamification implementation.

By applying SGT across diverse educational settings, future research can enhance the theoretical consistency with empirical findings, and expand generality by testing the model in varied educational contexts—an essential aim of the SGT. We encourage future empirical research grounded in SGT to promote more theory-driven and comparable studies, supporting the development of shared research models, and contributing to more effective and inclusive digital gamification design in education.

Author Contributions: Conceptualization, F.C. and A.M.A.; methodology, F.C. and A.M.A.; validation, A.M.A.; formal analysis, F.C. and A.M.A.; investigation, F.C. and A.M.A.; resources, F.C. and A.M.A.; data curation, F.C. and A.M.A.; writing—original draft preparation, F.C.; writing—review and editing, A.M.A.; visualization, F.C.; supervision, A.M.A.; project administration, A.M.A.; funding acquisition, F.C. and A.M.A. All authors have read and agreed to the published version of the manuscript.

Funding: This work is financially supported by National Funds through FCT—Fundação para a Ciência e a Tecnologia, I.P., under the projects UID/04279—Centro de investigação Interdisciplinar em Saúde (CIIS); and 2022.10688.BD—Franz Coelho (https://doi.org/10.54499/2022.10688.BD).

Institutional Review Board Statement: Not applicable.

Informed Consent Statement: Not applicable.

Data Availability Statement: No new data were created or analyzed in this study. Data sharing is not applicable to this article.

Acknowledgments: We express our sincere gratitude to FCT—Fundação para a Ciência e a Tecnologia—for the financial support through research grants.

Conflicts of Interest: The authors declare no conflicts of interest.

References

1. Deterding, S.; Björk, S.L.; Nacke, L.E.; Dixon, D.; Lawley, E. Designing Gamification: Creating Gameful and Playful Experiences. In Proceedings of the CHI '13 Extended Abstracts on Human Factors in Computing Systems, Paris, France, 27 April–2 May 2013; Association for Computing Machinery: New York, NY, USA, 2013; pp. 3263–3266.
2. Deterding, S.; Dixon, D.; Khaled, R.; Nacke, L. From Game Design Elements to Gamefulness: Defining "Gamification". In Proceedings of the 15th International Academic MindTrek Conference: Envisioning Future Media Environments, MindTrek 2011, Tampere, Finland, 28–30 September 2011; pp. 9–15. [CrossRef]
3. Chans, G.M.; Portuguez Castro, M. Gamification as a Strategy to Increase Motivation and Engagement in Higher Education Chemistry Students. *Computers* **2021**, *10*, 132. [CrossRef]
4. Mullins, J.K.; Sabherwal, R. Gamification: A Cognitive-Emotional View. *J. Bus. Res.* **2020**, *106*, 304–314. [CrossRef]
5. Treiblmaier, H.; Putz, L.-M. Gamification as a Moderator for the Impact of Intrinsic Motivation: Findings from a Multigroup Field Experiment. *Learn. Motiv.* **2020**, *71*, 101655. [CrossRef]
6. Aibar-Almazán, A.; Castellote-Caballero, Y.; Carcelén-Fraile, M.d.C.; Rivas-Campo, Y.; González-Martín, A.M. Gamification in the Classroom: Kahoot! As a Tool for University Teaching Innovation. *Front. Psychol.* **2024**, *15*, 1370084. [CrossRef] [PubMed]
7. Guerrero Puerta, L. Exploring If Gamification Experiences Make an Impact on Pre-Service Teachers' Perceptions of Future Gamification Use: A Case Report. *Societies* **2024**, *14*, 11. [CrossRef]
8. Li, M.; Ma, S.; Shi, Y. Examining the Effectiveness of Gamification as a Tool Promoting Teaching and Learning in Educational Settings: A Meta-Analysis. *Front. Psychol.* **2023**, *14*, 1253549. [CrossRef]
9. Ghai, A.; Tandon, U. Integrating Gamification and Instructional Design to Enhance Usability of Online Learning. *Educ. Inf. Technol.* **2023**, *28*, 2187–2206. [CrossRef]
10. Mazarakis, A.; Bräuer, P. Gamification Is Working, but Which One Exactly? Results from an Experiment with Four Game Design Elements. *Int. J. Hum.-Comput. Interact.* **2023**, *39*, 612–627. [CrossRef]
11. Khaldi, A.; Bouzidi, R.; Nader, F. Gamification of E-Learning in Higher Education: A Systematic Literature Review. *Smart Learn. Environ.* **2023**, *10*, 10. [CrossRef]
12. Sailer, M.; Homner, L. The Gamification of Learning: A Meta-Analysis. *Educ. Psychol. Rev.* **2020**, *32*, 77–112. [CrossRef]
13. Palomino, P.T.; Klock, A.C.T.; Rodrigues, L.; Toda, A.; Portela, C.; Porto, G.L.B.; Andrade, L.A.; Palomino, A. Redefining Gamification: From Elements to Experiences. In Proceedings of the Workshop sobre Interação e Pesquisa de Usuários no Desenvolvimento de Jogos (WIPlay), Brasília, Brazil, 7–11 October 2024; pp. 55–63.
14. Coelho, F.; Gonçalves, D.; Abreu, A.M. The Impact of Game-Based Interventions on Adult Cognition: A Systematic Review. *Int. J. Hum.-Comput. Interact.* **2025**, 1–36. [CrossRef]
15. Tondello, G.F.; Nacke, L.E. Player Characteristics and Video Game Preferences. In Proceedings of the Annual Symposium on Computer-Human Interaction in Play, Barcelona, Spain, 22–25 October 2019; Association for Computing Machinery: New York, NY, USA, 2019; pp. 365–378.

16. Tondello, G.; Arrambide, K.; Ribeiro, G.; Cen, A.J.; Nacke, L.E. "I Don't Fit into a Single Type": A Trait Model and Scale of Game Playing Preferences. In Proceedings of the Human-Computer Interaction—INTERACT 2019, Paphos, Cyprus, 2–6 September 2019; Lamas, D., Loizides, F., Nacke, L., Petrie, H., Winckler, M., Zaphiris, P., Eds.; Springer International Publishing: Cham, Switzerland, 2019; pp. 375–395.
17. Majdoub, M. Applying Gamification to Enhance the Universal Design for Learning Framework. In *Handbook of Research on Transformative and Innovative Pedagogies in Education*; IGI Global Scientific Publishing: Hershey, PA, USA, 2022; pp. 233–256. ISBN 978-1-79989-561-9.
18. Tomé Klock, A.C.; Palomino, P.T.; Rodrigues, L.A.L.; Toda, A.M.; Simanke, S.; Spors, V.; Santana, B.S.; Hamari, J. Gamification towards and alongside Equity, Diversity and Inclusion: Looking Back to Move Forward. *New Media Soc.* **2024**, 1–26. [CrossRef]
19. Wang, T.; Ma, H.; Ge, H.; Sun, Y.; Kwok, T.T.-O.; Liu, X.; Wang, Y.; Lau, W.K.W.; Zhang, W. The Use of Gamified Interventions to Enhance Social Interaction and Communication among People with Autism Spectrum Disorder: A Systematic Review and Meta-Analysis. *Int. J. Nurs. Stud.* **2025**, *165*, 105037. [CrossRef] [PubMed]
20. Pereira, L.M.; Barwaldt, R. Gamificação como estratégia pedagógica para potencializar habilidades matemáticas para estudantes com Autismo: Uma revisão sistemática da literatura. *RENOTE* **2022**, *20*, 81–90. [CrossRef]
21. Ruiz-Navas, S.; Ackaradejraungsri, P.; Dijk, S. Are There Literature Reviews about Gamification to Foster Inclusive Teaching? A Scoping Review of Gamification Literature Reviews. *Front. Educ.* **2024**, *9*, 1306298. [CrossRef]
22. Salman, O.; Khasawneh, Y.; Alqudah, H.; Alwaely, S.; Khasawneh, M. Tailoring Gamification to Individual Learners: A Study on Personalization Variables for Skill Enhancement. *Int. J. Data Netw. Sci.* **2024**, *8*, 789–796. [CrossRef]
23. Jadán-Guerrero, J.; Avilés-Castillo, F.; Buele, J.; Palacios-Navarro, G. Gamification in Inclusive Education for Children with Disabilities: Global Trends and Approaches—A Bibliometric Review. In Proceedings of the Computational Science and Its Applications—ICCSA 2023 Workshops, Athens, Greece, 3–6 July 2023; Gervasi, O., Murgante, B., Rocha, A.M.A.C., Garau, C., Scorza, F., Karaca, Y., Torre, C.M., Eds.; Springer Nature: Cham, Switzerland, 2023; pp. 461–477.
24. Nosek, B.A.; Hardwicke, T.E.; Moshontz, H.; Allard, A.; Corker, K.S.; Dreber, A.; Fidler, F.; Hilgard, J.; Struhl, M.K.; Nuijten, M.B.; et al. Replicability, Robustness, and Reproducibility in Psychological Science. *Annu. Rev. Psychol.* **2022**, *73*, 719–748. [CrossRef]
25. Groening, C.; Binnewies, C. The More, the Merrier?—How Adding and Removing Game Design Elements Impact Motivation and Performance in a Gamification Environment. *Int. J. Hum.-Comput. Interact.* **2021**, *37*, 1130–1150. [CrossRef]
26. Leitão, R.; Maguire, M.; Turner, S.; Guimarães, L. A Systematic Evaluation of Game Elements Effects on Students' Motivation. *Educ. Inf. Technol.* **2022**, *27*, 1081–1103. [CrossRef]
27. Chou, Y. *Actionable Gamification: Beyond Points, Badges, and Leaderboards*; Packt Publishing Ltd.: Birmingham, UK, 2019; ISBN 1-83921-077-X.
28. Coelho, F.; Rando, B.; Aparício, D.; Sousa, P.; Gonçalves, D.; Abreu, A.M. The Impact of Educational Gamification on Cognition, Emotions, and Motivation: A Randomized Controlled Trial. *J. Comput. Educ.* **2025**. [CrossRef]
29. Coelho, F.; Aparício, D.; Sousa, P.; Gonçalves, D.; Abreu, A.M. Cognitive, Emotional, and Motivational Effects of Gamification in the Context of Learning: A Protocol Feasibility and Usability Study. In *BMC Proceedings, Proceedings of the National Meeting of the Center for Interdisciplinary Research in Health (CIIS), Sintra, Portugal, 31 March–1 April 2023*; Volume 17, (Suppl. 9), p. P78.
30. Coelho, F.; Gonçalves, D.; Abreu, A.M. Game On: A Pilot Study of a Gamified Digital Learning Platform and Protocol. In Proceedings of the ICDTE '24: Proceedings of the 2024 8th International Conference on Digital Technology in Education (ICDTE), Berlin, Germany, 7–9 August 2024; Association for Computing Machinery: New York, NY, USA, 2024.
31. Falci, S.G.M.; Marques, L.S. CONSORT: When and How to Use It. *Dent. Press J. Orthod.* **2015**, *20*, 13–15. [CrossRef]
32. Schulz, K.F.; Altman, D.G.; Moher, D. CONSORT 2010 Statement: Updated Guidelines for Reporting Parallel Group Randomised Trials. *BMJ* **2010**, *340*, c332. [CrossRef] [PubMed]
33. Higgins, J.; Thomas, J.; Chandler, J.; Cumpston, M.; Li, T.; Page, M.; Welch, V. *Cochrane Handbook for Systematic Reviews of Interventions Version 6.4 (Updated August 2023)*; Cochrane: London, UK, 2023.
34. Khorsan, R.; Crawford, C. External Validity and Model Validity: A Conceptual Approach for Systematic Review Methodology. *Evid. Based Complement. Alternat. Med.* **2014**, *2014*, 694804. [CrossRef] [PubMed]
35. Papanthymou, A.; Darra, M. The Impact of Self-Assessment with Goal Setting on Academic Achievement: Results of a Study on Primary School Students in Greece. *J. Educ. Learn.* **2022**, *12*, 67–90. [CrossRef]
36. John, D.; Hussin, N.; Zaini, M.K.; Ametefe, D.S.; Aliu, A.A.; Caliskan, A. Gamification Equilibrium: The Fulcrum for Balanced Intrinsic Motivation and Extrinsic Rewards in Learning Systems: Immersive Gamification in Muhamad Khairulnizam Zaini Learning System. *Int. J. Serious Games* **2023**, *10*, 83–116. [CrossRef]
37. Sweller, J.; van Merriënboer, J.J.G.; Paas, F. Cognitive Architecture and Instructional Design: 20 Years Later. *Educ. Psychol. Rev.* **2019**, *31*, 261–292. [CrossRef]
38. Denny, P.; McDonald, F.; Empson, R.; Kelly, P.; Petersen, A. Empirical Support for a Causal Relationship Between Gamification and Learning Outcomes. In Proceedings of the 2018 CHI Conference on Human Factors in Computing Systems, Montreal, QC, Canada, 21–26 April 2018; Association for Computing Machinery: New York, NY, USA, 2018; pp. 1–13.

39. Matallaoui, A. Towards More Effective Gamification: Does Deploying Semiotics Help Design Better Perceivable Badges? In Proceedings of the 2018 4th International Conference on Computer and Technology Applications (ICCTA), Istanbul, Turkey, 3–5 May 2018; pp. 131–135.
40. Ortiz-Rojas, M.; Chiluiza, K.; Valcke, M.; Bolanos-Mendoza, C. How Gamification Boosts Learning in STEM Higher Education: A Mixed Methods Study. *Int. J. STEM Educ.* **2025**, *12*, 1. [CrossRef]
41. Landers, R.N. Developing a Theory of Gamified Learning: Linking Serious Games and Gamification of Learning. *Simul. Gaming* **2014**, *45*, 752–768. [CrossRef]
42. Landers, R.N.; Auer, E.M.; Collmus, A.B.; Armstrong, M.B. Gamification Science, Its History and Future: Definitions and a Research Agenda. *Simul. Gaming* **2018**, *49*, 315–337. [CrossRef]
43. Christian, M.; Gularso, K.; Yulita, H.; Muzammil, O.M.; Wibowo, S.; Sunarno, S. Gamification in the Marketplace for Gen Z: Determinants Using Gamified Learning Theory. In Proceedings of the 2024 International Seminar on Application for Technology of Information and Communication (iSemantic), Semarang, Indonesia, 21–22 September 2024; pp. 118–122.
44. Zaric, N.; Roepke, R.; Lukarov, V.; Schroeder, U. Gamified Learning Theory: The Moderating Role of Learners' Learning Tendencies. *Int. J. Serious Games* **2021**, *8*, 71–91. [CrossRef]
45. Rukadikar, A.; Khandelwal, K. Gamification at the Workplace: A Theoretical Perspective on Training and Development. *Learn. Organ.* **2025**. *ahead-of-print*. [CrossRef]
46. Papadimitriou, A. Theories, Strategies and Elements of Gamified MOOCs: A Systematic Literature Review. *Asia Pac. J. Inf. Syst.* **2024**, *34*, 248–291. [CrossRef]
47. Triantafyllou, S.A.; Georgiadis, C.; Sapounidis, T. Gamification in Education and Training: A Literature Review. *Int. Rev. Educ.* **2025**, *71*, 483–517. [CrossRef]
48. Balcombe, L.; De Leo, D. Human-Computer Interaction in Digital Mental Health. *Informatics* **2022**, *9*, 14. [CrossRef]
49. Roldan, W.; Gao, X.; Hishikawa, A.M.; Ku, T.; Li, Z.; Zhang, E.; Froehlich, J.E.; Yip, J. Opportunities and Challenges in Involving Users in Project-Based HCI Education. In Proceedings of the 2020 CHI Conference on Human Factors in Computing Systems, Honolulu, HI, USA, 25–30 April 2020; Association for Computing Machinery: New York, NY, USA, 2020; pp. 1–15.
50. Garcia-Lopez, C.; Mor, E.; Tesconi, S. Human-Centered Design as an Approach to Create Open Educational Resources. *Sustainability* **2020**, *12*, 7397. [CrossRef]
51. Sherman, B.W.; Stiehl, E.; Gupta, R.; Pratap, P.L. The Importance of Human-Centered Design in Equitable Health Promotion Initiatives. *Am. J. Health Promot.* **2024**, *38*, 443–447. [CrossRef]
52. Kessing, D.; Katzwinkel, T.; Löwer, M. Gamification as an Innovative Method in User Experience Design. *Proc. Des. Soc.* **2024**, *4*, 285–294. [CrossRef]
53. Willers, H. Bridging the Accessibility Divide: Testing the Efficacy of an Accessible User Experience Model via a Case Study of Microsoft's Inclusive Design Toolkit. *IEEE Trans. Prof. Commun.* **2024**, *67*, 121–132. [CrossRef]
54. Benaida, M. Developing and Extending Usability Heuristics Evaluation for User Interface Design via AHP. *Soft Comput.* **2023**, *27*, 9693–9707. [CrossRef]
55. Nielsen, J.; Molich, R. Heuristic Evaluation of User Interfaces. In Proceedings of the SIGCHI Conference on Human Factors in Computing Systems, Seattle, WA, USA, 1–5 April 1990; Association for Computing Machinery: New York, NY, USA, 1990; pp. 249–256.
56. Çeliköz, N.; Erişen, Y.; Şahin, M. Cognitive Learning Theories With Emphasis on Latent Learning, Gestalt and Information Processing Theories. *J. Educ. Instr. Stud. World* **2019**, *9*, 18–33.
57. Greenwood, J.D. On Two Foundational Principles of the Berlin School of Gestalt Psychology. *Rev. Gen. Psychol.* **2020**, *24*, 284–294. [CrossRef]
58. Wertheimer, M. Gestalt Theory, Holistic Psychologies, and Max Wertheimer. *Z. Psychol.* **1982**, *190*, 125–140.
59. Li, Y.; Fu, K. *Research on Minimalism in Interface Design Based on Gestalt Psychology*; Atlantis Press: Dordrecht, The Netherlands, 2022; pp. 825–837.
60. Wagemans, J.; Elder, J.H.; Kubovy, M.; Palmer, S.E.; Peterson, M.A.; Singh, M.; von der Heydt, R. A Century of Gestalt Psychology in Visual Perception: I. Perceptual Grouping and Figure–Ground Organization. *Psychol. Bull.* **2012**, *138*, 1172–1217. [CrossRef] [PubMed]
61. Khamis, M.H.; Azni, Z.M.; Aziz, S.H.A.; Aminordin, A. The Integration of Gestalt Theory to The Graphic Design. *Int. J. Acad. Res. Bus. Soc. Sci.* **2023**, *13*, 2322–2327. [CrossRef] [PubMed]
62. Ripalda, D.; Guevara, C.; Garrido, A. Gestalt Prototyping Framework-Evaluation Tool. In Proceedings of the Intelligent Human Systems Integration 2021, Palermo, Italy, 22–24 February 2021; Russo, D., Ahram, T., Karwowski, W., Di Bucchianico, G., Taiar, R., Eds.; Springer International Publishing: Cham, Switzerland, 2021; pp. 747–752.
63. Mehta, A.; Bond, J.; Sankar, C. Developing an Inclusive Education Game Using a Design Science Research Gestalt Method. *AIS Trans. Hum.-Comput. Interact.* **2022**, *14*, 523–547. [CrossRef]
64. Von Bertalanffy, L. An Outline of General System Theory. *Br. J. Philos. Sci.* **1950**, *1*, 134–165. [CrossRef]

65. Laszlo, A.; Krippner, S. Chapter 3—Systems Theories: Their Origins, Foundations, and Development. In *Advances in Psychology*; Jordan, J.S., Ed.; Systems Theories and a Priori Aspects of Perception; North-Holland: Amsterdam, The Netherlands, 1998; Volume 126, pp. 47–74.
66. Rousseau, D. General Systems Theory: Its Present and Potential. *Syst. Res. Behav. Sci.* **2015**, *32*, 522–533. [CrossRef]
67. Drack, M.; Schwarz, G. Recent Developments in General System Theory. *Syst. Res. Behav. Sci.* **2010**, *27*, 601–610. [CrossRef]
68. Huang, R.; Spector, J.M.; Yang, J. Systems Perspective of Educational Technology. In *Educational Technology: A Primer for the 21st Century*; Huang, R., Spector, J.M., Yang, J., Eds.; Springer: Singapore, 2019; pp. 65–76. ISBN 9789811366437.
69. Zhang, B.H.; Ahmed, S.A.M. Systems Thinking—Ludwig Von Bertalanffy, Peter Senge, and Donella Meadows. In *Science Education in Theory and Practice: An Introductory Guide to Learning Theory*; Akpan, B., Kennedy, T.J., Eds.; Springer International Publishing: Cham, Switzerland, 2020; pp. 419–436. ISBN 978-3-030-43620-9.
70. Hofkirchner, W. Social Relations: Building on Ludwig von Bertalanffy. *Syst. Res. Behav. Sci.* **2019**, *36*, 263–273. [CrossRef]
71. Cui, W.; Li, R.; Pan, L. A Comparison of New General System Theory Philosophy with Einstein and Bohr. *Philos. Study* **2023**, *13*, 1–22. [CrossRef]
72. Varpio, L.; Paradis, E.; Uijtdehaage, S.; Young, M. The Distinctions Between Theory, Theoretical Framework, and Conceptual Framework. *Acad. Med.* **2020**, *95*, 989–994. [CrossRef] [PubMed]
73. Ghisellini, R.; Pareschi, R.; Pedroni, M.; Raggi, G.B. Recommending Actionable Strategies: A Semantic Approach to Integrating Analytical Frameworks with Decision Heuristics. *Information* **2025**, *16*, 192. [CrossRef]
74. Nizamani, S.; Nizamani, S.; Basir, N.; Laghari, G.; Khoumbati, K.; Nizamani, S. Heuristic Evaluation Versus Guideline Reviews: A Tale of Comparing Two Domain Usability Expert's Evaluation Methods. *IEEE Trans. Prof. Commun.* **2022**, *65*, 516–529. [CrossRef]
75. Hallifax, S.; Altmeyer, M.; Kölln, K.; Rauschenberger, M.; Nacke, L.E. From Points to Progression: A Scoping Review of Game Elements in Gamification Research with a Content Analysis of 280 Research Papers. *Proc ACM Hum.-Comput. Interact.* **2023**, *7*, 748–768. [CrossRef]
76. Hong, Y.; Saab, N.; Admiraal, W. Approaches and Game Elements Used to Tailor Digital Gamification for Learning: A Systematic Literature Review. *Comput. Educ.* **2024**, *212*, 105000. [CrossRef]
77. Klock, A.C.T.; Gasparini, I.; Pimenta, M.S.; Hamari, J. Tailored Gamification: A Review of Literature. *Int. J. Hum.-Comput. Stud.* **2020**, *144*, 102495. [CrossRef]
78. Zeng, L. The Beauty of Games: By Frank Lantz. *Pop. Commun.* **2024**, *22*, 221–224. [CrossRef]
79. Gaver, W.; Krogh, P.G.; Boucher, A.; Chatting, D. Emergence as a Feature of Practice-Based Design Research. In Proceedings of the 2022 ACM Designing Interactive Systems Conference, Online, Australia, 13–17 June 2022; Association for Computing Machinery: New York, NY, USA, 2022; pp. 517–526.
80. Yerznkyan, B.H.; Gataullin, T.M.; Gataullin, S.T. Mathematical Aspects of Synergy. *Montenegrin J. Econ.* **2022**, *18*, 197–207. [CrossRef]
81. Rawls, A.W.; Turowetz, J. "Discovering Culture" in Interaction: Solving Problems in Cultural Sociology by Recovering the Interactional Side of Parsons' Conception of Culture. *Am. J. Cult. Sociol.* **2021**, *9*, 293–320. [CrossRef]
82. Chignell, M.; Wang, L.; Zare, A.; Li, J. The Evolution of HCI and Human Factors: Integrating Human and Artificial Intelligence. *ACM Trans Comput.-Hum. Interact.* **2023**, *30*, 17. [CrossRef]
83. Pande, M.; Bharathi, S.V. Theoretical Foundations of Design Thinking—A Constructivism Learning Approach to Design Thinking. *Think. Ski. Creat.* **2020**, *36*, 100637. [CrossRef]
84. Liu, M.; Oga-Baldwin, W.L.Q. Motivational Profiles of Learners of Multiple Foreign Languages: A Self-Determination Theory Perspective. *System* **2022**, *106*, 102762. [CrossRef]
85. Morris, T.H. Creativity through Self-Directed Learning: Three Distinct Dimensions of Teacher Support. *Int. J. Lifelong Educ.* **2020**, *39*, 168–178. [CrossRef]
86. Lahire, B. Sociology at the Individual Level, Psychologies and Neurosciences. *Eur. J. Soc. Theory* **2020**, *23*, 52–71. [CrossRef]
87. Liu, S. Social Spaces: From Georg Simmel to Erving Goffman. *J. Chin. Sociol.* **2024**, *11*, 13. [CrossRef]
88. Dettano, A. Sociology of the Digital Space, Social Research and Emotions. *Am. Sociol.* **2023**, *54*, 389–398. [CrossRef]
89. Thimm, V. Bringing Intersectionality to the Core of Social and Cultural Anthropology: Scaling Holistic Intersectionality. *Ethnos* **2025**, *90*, 110–127. [CrossRef]
90. Rodrigues, F.M.; Abreu, A.M.; Holmström, I.; Mineiro, A. E-Learning Is a Burden for the Deaf and Hard of Hearing. *Sci. Rep.* **2022**, *12*, 9346. [CrossRef]
91. Holmer, E.; Rudner, M.; Schönström, K.; Andin, J. Evidence of an Effect of Gaming Experience on Visuospatial Attention in Deaf but Not in Hearing Individuals. *Front. Psychol.* **2020**, *11*, 534741. [CrossRef]
92. Chan, G.L.; Santally, M.I.; Whitehead, J. Gamification as Technology Enabler in SEN and DHH Education. *Educ. Inf. Technol.* **2022**, *27*, 9031–9064. [CrossRef]
93. Yusriyyah, Q.N.; Hilmi, A.R.; Setiawati, Y.; Dianasari; Pradanita, V.N.; Ardani, I.G.A.I. Learning Disorder in Attention Deficit Hyperactivity Disorder (ADHD) Children: A Literature Review. *Int. J. Sci. Adv. IJSCIA* **2023**, *4*, 15–18. [CrossRef]

94. Kusmawati, A.P.; Fahrurrozi, F.; Supena, A. Increasing Concentration of Attention Deficit Hyperactivity Disorder (ADHD) Students Through Gamification Learning Media in Indonesian Inclusion Elementary School. *Int. J. Spec. Educ.* **2023**, *38*, 169–184. [CrossRef]
95. Hernández-Capistrán, J.; Alor-Hernández, G.; Sánchez-Morales, L.N.; Machorro-Cano, I. A Decade of Apps for ADHD Management: A Scoping Review. *Behav. Inf. Technol.* **2025**, 1–28. [CrossRef]
96. Alenezi, M. Digital Learning and Digital Institution in Higher Education. *Educ. Sci.* **2023**, *13*, 88. [CrossRef]
97. Amiti, F. Synchronous and Asynchronous E-Learning. *Eur. J. Open Educ. E-Learn. Stud.* **2020**, *5*, 60–70. [CrossRef]
98. Quiñones, D.; Rusu, C. How to Develop Usability Heuristics: A Systematic Literature Review. *Comput. Stand. Interfaces* **2017**, *53*, 89–122. [CrossRef]
99. Vieira, E.A.O.; Silveira, A.C.d.; Martins, R.X. Heuristic Evaluation on Usability of Educational Games: A Systematic Review. *Inform. Educ.* **2019**, *18*, 427–442. [CrossRef]
100. Paul, J.; Barari, M. Meta-Analysis and Traditional Systematic Literature Reviews—What, Why, When, Where, and How? *Psychol. Mark.* **2022**, *39*, 1099–1115. [CrossRef]
101. Zeybek, N.; Saygı, E. Gamification in Education: Why, Where, When, and How?—A Systematic Review. *Games Cult.* **2024**, *19*, 237–264. [CrossRef]
102. Takaoka, A.J.W.; Jaccheri, L. Mapping Gamification Elements to Heuristics and Behavior Change in Early Phase Inclusive Design: A Case Study. In Proceedings of the Universal Access in Human-Computer Interaction, Washington, DC, USA, 29 June 2024; Antona, M., Stephanidis, C., Eds.; Springer Nature: Cham, Switzerland, 2024; pp. 143–161.
103. Constain Moreno, G.E.; Collazos, C.A.; Fardoun, H.M.; Alghazzawi, D.M. Heuristic Evaluation for the Assessment of Inclusive Tools in the Autism Treatment. In Proceedings of the HCI International 2020—Late Breaking Papers: Universal Access and Inclusive Design, Copenhagen, Denmark, 19–24 July 2020; Stephanidis, C., Antona, M., Gao, Q., Zhou, J., Eds.; Springer International Publishing: Cham, Switzerland, 2020; pp. 34–51.
104. Tondello, G.F.; Kappen, D.L.; Mekler, E.D.; Ganaba, M.; Nacke, L.E. *Heuristic Evaluation for Gameful Design*; Association for Computing Machinery: New York, NY, USA, 2016; pp. 315–323.
105. Tondello, G.F.; Kappen, D.L.; Ganaba, M.; Nacke, L.E. Gameful Design Heuristics: A Gamification Inspection Tool. In *Human-Computer Interaction. Perspectives on Design*; Kurosu, M., Ed.; Lecture Notes in Computer Science; Springer International Publishing: Cham, Switzerland, 2019; Volume 11566, pp. 224–244. ISBN 978-3-030-22645-9.
106. Bilge, A.; Samet, O.; Muhammet, A.; Esen, Y.; Fatih, K. Gamification as a social phenomenon and gamification heuristics criteria from social sciences perspective. *Plur. Hist. Cult. Soc.* **2024**, *12*, 116–133. [CrossRef]
107. Sobrino-Duque, R.; Martínez-Rojo, N.; Carrillo-de-Gea, J.M.; López-Jiménez, J.J.; Nicolás, J.; Fernández-Alemán, J.L. Evaluating a Gamification Proposal for Learning Usability Heuristics: Heureka. *Int. J. Hum.-Comput. Stud.* **2022**, *161*, 102774. [CrossRef]
108. Priyadi, O.; Ramadhan, I.; Sensuse, D.I.; Suryono, R.R. Kautsarina Gamification in Software Development: Systematic Literature Review. In Proceedings of the Emerging Trends in Intelligent Systems & Network Security, Bandung, Indonesia, 30–31 March 2022; Ben Ahmed, M., Abdelhakim, B.A., Ane, B.K., Rosiyadi, D., Eds.; Springer International Publishing: Cham, Switzerland, 2023; pp. 386–398.
109. Jones, M.; Blanton, J.E.; Williams, R.E. Science to Practice: Does Gamification Enhance Intrinsic Motivation? *Act. Learn. High. Educ.* **2023**, *24*, 273–289. [CrossRef]
110. Gao, F. Advancing Gamification Research and Practice with Three Underexplored Ideas in Self-Determination Theory. *TechTrends* **2024**, *68*, 661–671. [CrossRef]
111. Ryan, R.; Deci, E. Self-Determination Theory and the Facilitation of Intrinsic Motivation, Social Development, and Well-Being. *Am. Psychol.* **2000**, *55*, 68–78. [CrossRef]
112. Ryan, R.M.; Deci, E.L. Intrinsic and Extrinsic Motivation from a Self-Determination Theory Perspective: Definitions, Theory, Practices, and Future Directions. *Contemp. Educ. Psychol.* **2020**, *61*, 101860. [CrossRef]
113. Di Domenico, S.I.; Ryan, R.M. The Emerging Neuroscience of Intrinsic Motivation: A New Frontier in Self-Determination Research. *Front. Hum. Neurosci.* **2017**, *11*, 145. [CrossRef]
114. Morris, L.S.; Grehl, M.M.; Rutter, S.B.; Mehta, M.; Westwater, M.L. On What Motivates Us: A Detailed Review of Intrinsic v. Extrinsic Motivation. *Psychol. Med.* **2022**, *52*, 1801–1816. [CrossRef]
115. Liu, Y.; Hau, K.-T.; Liu, H.; Wu, J.; Wang, X.; Zheng, X. Multiplicative Effect of Intrinsic and Extrinsic Motivation on Academic Performance: A Longitudinal Study of Chinese Students. *J. Pers.* **2020**, *88*, 584–595. [CrossRef]
116. Rodrigues, L.; Toda, A.M.; Palomino, P.T.; Oliveira, W.; Isotani, S. Personalized Gamification: A Literature Review of Outcomes, Experiments, and Approaches. In Proceedings of the TEEM'20: Eighth International Conference on Technological Ecosystems for Enhancing Multiculturality, Salamanca, Spain, 21–23 October 2020; Association for Computing Machinery: New York, NY, USA, 2020; pp. 699–706.
117. Ford, R.C.; Yoho, K.D. Design Thinking: Executing Your Organization's Commitment to Customer Centricity. *Organ. Dyn.* **2025**, *54*, 101077. [CrossRef]

118. Proudfoot, K. Inductive/Deductive Hybrid Thematic Analysis in Mixed Methods Research. *J. Mix. Methods Res.* **2023**, *17*, 308–326. [CrossRef]
119. Leal Filho, W.; Salvia, A.L.; Eustachio, J.H.P.P. An Overview of the Engagement of Higher Education Institutions in the Implementation of the UN Sustainable Development Goals. *J. Clean. Prod.* **2023**, *386*, 135694. [CrossRef]
120. Serafini, P.G.; Moura, J.M.d.; Almeida, M.R.d.; Rezende, J.F.D.d. Sustainable Development Goals in Higher Education Institutions: A Systematic Literature Review. *J. Clean. Prod.* **2022**, *370*, 133473. [CrossRef]
121. Silvestri, J.A.; Hartman, M.C. Inclusion and Deaf and Hard of Hearing Students: Finding Asylum in the LRE. *Educ. Sci.* **2022**, *12*, 773. [CrossRef]
122. Holmes, S.C. Inclusion, Autism Spectrum, Students' Experiences. *Int. J. Dev. Disabil.* **2024**, *70*, 59–73. [CrossRef]
123. Jaffal, A. Mohammed Barriers General Education Teachers Face Regarding the Inclusion of Students with Autism. *Front. Psychol.* **2022**, *13*, 873248. [CrossRef]
124. Tan, Z.; Liu, Z.; Gong, S. Potential Attempt to Treat Attention Deficit/Hyperactivity Disorder (ADHD) Children with Engineering Education Games. In Proceedings of the Design, User Experience, and Usability, Copenhagen, Denmark, 23–28 July 2023; Marcus, A., Rosenzweig, E., Soares, M.M., Eds.; Springer Nature: Cham, Switzerland, 2023; pp. 166–184.
125. Sergis, N.; Troussas, C.; Krouska, A.; Tzortzi, C.; Bardis, G.; Sgouropoulou, C. ADHD Dog: A Virtual Reality Intervention Incorporating Behavioral and Sociocultural Theories with Gamification for Enhanced Regulation in Individuals with Attention Deficit Hyperactivity Disorder. *Computers* **2024**, *13*, 46. [CrossRef]
126. Teruel, M.A.; Sanchis, J.; Ruiz-Robledillo, N.; Albaladejo-Blázquez, N.; Ferrer-Cascales, R.; Trujillo, J. Measuring Attention of ADHD Patients by Means of a Computer Game Featuring Biometrical Data Gathering. *Heliyon* **2024**, *10*, e26555. [CrossRef]
127. Gkintoni, E.; Vantaraki, F.; Skoulidi, C.; Anastassopoulos, P.; Vantarakis, A. Promoting Physical and Mental Health among Children and Adolescents via Gamification—A Conceptual Systematic Review. *Behav. Sci.* **2024**, *14*, 102. [CrossRef]
128. Tondello, G.; Valtchanov, D.; Reetz, A.; Wehbe, R.R.; Orji, R.; Nacke, L.E. Towards a Trait Model of Video Game Preferences. *Int. J. Hum.-Comput. Interact.* **2018**, *34*, 732–748. [CrossRef]
129. Rinjeni, T.P.; Rakhmawati, N.A.; Nadlifatin, R. A Systematic Literature Review on Personalized Adaptive Gamification. In Proceedings of the 2022 International Conference on Computer Engineering, Network, and Intelligent Multimedia (CENIM), Surabaya, Indonesia, 22–23 November 2022; IEEE: Piscataway, NJ, USA, 2022; pp. 218–223.
130. Afshan, A.; Askari, I.; Manickam, L.S.S. Shyness, Self-Construal, Extraversion–Introversion, Neuroticism, and Psychoticism: A Cross-Cultural Comparison Among College Students. *SAGE Open* **2015**, *5*, 2158244015587559. [CrossRef]
131. Nielsen, J. Reliability of Severity Estimates for Usability Problems Found by Heuristic Evaluation. In Proceedings of the Posters and Short Talks of the 1992 SIGCHI Conference on Human Factors in Computing Systems, Monterey, CA, USA, 3–7 May 1992; Association for Computing Machinery: New York, NY, USA, 1992; pp. 129–130.
132. Geng, Z.; Sabbaghi, A.; Bidanda, B. Reconstructing Original Design: Process Planning for Reverse Engineering. *IISE Trans.* **2023**, *55*, 509–522. [CrossRef]
133. Gieseler, K.; Loschelder, D.D.; Friese, M. What Makes for a Good Theory? How to Evaluate a Theory Using the Strength Model of Self-Control as an Example. In *Social Psychology in Action: Evidence-Based Interventions from Theory to Practice*; Sassenberg, K., Vliek, M.L.W., Eds.; Springer International Publishing: Cham, Switzerland, 2019; pp. 3–21. ISBN 978-3-030-13788-5.
134. Phosanarack, M.; Avril, E.; Lepreux, S.; Wallard, L.; Kolski, C. User-Centered Personalized Gamification: An Umbrella Review. *User Model. User-Adapt. Interact.* **2025**, *35*, 3. [CrossRef]

Multimodal Technologies and Interaction

MDPI

Systematic Review

Multiple Ways in Which Video Games Make Education Inclusive: A Systematic Review of Cognitive Enhancement for Neurodivergent Learners

Martina Basciano [1,2], Elisa Bisagno [1,*] and Alessia Cadamuro [3]

1 Surgical, Medical and Dental Department of Morphological Sciences Related to Transplant, Oncology and Regenerative Medicine, Faculty of Medicine, University of Modena and Reggio Emilia, Viale Allegri 9, 42121 Reggio Emilia, Italy; martina.basciano@unimore.it

2 Department of Agricultural Sciences, Food, Natural Resources and Engineering, University of Foggia, Via Napoli 25, 71122 Foggia, Italy

3 Department of Biomedical, Metabolic and Neurosciences, University of Modena and Reggio Emilia, Viale Allegri 9, 42121 Reggio Emilia, Italy; alessia.cadamuro@unimore.it

* Correspondence: elisa.bisagno@unimore.it

Abstract: Children with neurodevelopmental disorders, such as ADHD, ASD and SLDs, often face challenges in executive functioning that can impact their inclusion and participation in educational and social experiences. Digital technologies, in particular video games, are becoming increasingly more integrated into children's lives and are receiving attention as tools to support cognitive development in these populations. This systematic review analyses the effects of video games on Working Memory (WM) and Executive Functions (EFs) in neurodivergent individuals, to evaluate their effectiveness as training tools and their impact in terms of inclusion. Following the PRISMA guidelines, 25 peer-reviewed studies published between 2013 and 2025 were analysed. The interventions included action-video games, exergames, serious games and ad hoc video game training with a pre- and post-assessment in neurodiverse participants. The results indicate that action-video games and exergames show promise in enhancing EFs, while serious games and ad hoc video game training seem to support WM. Despite a few contrasting results, overall, video games are emerging as promising tools of inclusive education thanks to their interactive, customisable and socially empowering nature, especially significant for neurodiverse children. The discussion will depict multiple ways in which video games can make education more inclusive for these populations.

Keywords: video games; executive functions; working memory; neurodevelopmental disorders; inclusion; children; ADHD; ASD; SLDs; systematic review

1. Introduction

Digital technologies have become an integral part of young people's daily lives, supporting both educational activities [1,2] and leisure pursuits [3]. Among these technologies, video games occupy a particularly prominent role. The recent Health Behaviour in School-aged Children (HBSC) study, conducted across Europe, Central Asia, and Canada, provides insights into the patterns of digital game use among youth. According to the survey, 34% of adolescents reported playing video games daily, with 22% engaging in gameplay for at least four hours per day [4]. The data further indicate that the peak in gaming activity occurs at age 13 for males and at age 11 for females. While gameplay frequency declines with age among females, it remains consistently high among males [4]. Importantly, youngsters employ various types of video games, such as action video games (AVGs), exergames (ExGs) and serious games (SGs), which have been associated with different cognitive benefits in neurodiverse populations. AVGs often entail fighting enemies in single or multiplayer modality, and they are characterised by fast-paced and visually complex environments. They have been shown to improve attentional control and shifting, in particular in children with dyslexia [5]. ExGs, which combine physical activity with digital interaction, typically requiring the use of a gaming console, such as the Kinect device, have been linked with enhancements in inhibition and shifting in children with ADHD [6] and ASD [7,8]. Lastly, SGs are classified as "educational games", designed with explicit educational purposes, and appear particularly effective in children with ADHD as support for Working Memory (WM) [9] and also for inhibition and shifting [10].

Compared to other digital technologies often used in educational settings, such as interactive whiteboards or e-books, video games offer different features that make them valuable for supporting both cognitive and social development [11,12]. Their interactive design, real-time feedback, and adaptive difficulty levels help sustain attention, foster intrinsic motivation, and promote problem solving and behaviour directed to a specific goal. For instance, Mao and colleagues [13] demonstrated that dynamic feedback adjusted to task difficulty, that is, giving simple hints for easy tasks and detailed explanations for complex ones, significantly enhances the motivation and performance in learners in a digital game-based environment. Specifically, students in the dynamic feedback group scored significantly higher on both a knowledge acquisition and a knowledge transfer test compared to other conditions. These results provide evidence of how video games, through real-time responsiveness and individualised challenges, can effectively support attention and goal-directed learning in school contexts.

In addition, compared to other digital tools, video games have been associated with improved executive functioning across a wide developmental span [14,15]. Specifically, video games' virtual environments encourage processes such as decision making, rule following, and cooperation or competition dynamics, which, in turn, foster social engagement and skills development [16]. This is particularly relevant in neurodivergent populations, who can benefit from structured and flexible learning contexts customised to their individual cognitive profiles. Research suggests that such environments can positively affect social development by engaging basic executive components and adapting to developmental needs [17,18].

Over the past fifty years, scientific research on the use of video games by developmental age groups has undergone significant expansion [19]. This research aims to evaluate the confirmation, modalities and effects of video game use on youth. The relationship between video games and learning has been studied since the 1980s; however, from 2010 on, articles reporting on the educational outcomes of video games have been multiplying [19]. Among these, some studies investigated the impact of video games on academic performance and obtained mixed results [20–25]. Other studies focused on cognitive development, suggesting beneficial effects of videogaming activity, both for children and adolescents with typical development [23–25] and clinical populations [5,26,27].

Specifically, recent research focused on studying the impact of video games on higher cognitive functions [28], such as Working Memory (WM) and Executive Functions (EFs). WM has been variously defined as a limited-capacity system that temporarily maintains and stores information [29] or as an attentional resource used for carrying out so-called attention-demanding processes [30]. Despite the numerous conceptualisations of WM, there is wide consensus that it represents one of the main predictors not only of learning processes [31], but also of a range of social competencies [32,33].

EFs are general control mechanisms that modulate the functioning of various cognitive processes and regulate the dynamics of human cognition [34,35]. The most accredited theoretical model of EFs [34] identifies three components, separated but significantly correlated with each other: inhibition, understood both as the ability to inhibit an automatic process and as the management of cognitive interference; attentional shifting, which is the ability to functionally move attention from one task to another; and updating (namely information refreshing) of WM. Similarly to WM, EFs are correlated with enhanced learning [36]. Plus, they are essential for emotional regulation, conflict resolution and the creation of positive social relationships [37].

A recent review by Bediou and coworkers [38] meta-analysed 105 cross-sectional studies comparing engaged video game players and non-video game players. The first tended to score higher than nonplayers on many cognitive skills, including WM and EFs, with an average effect size of g = 0.64.

In light of these findings, a significant number of researchers have initiated studies to explore the effectiveness of video games as a medium for enhancing WM and EFs, by either employing the different types of video games described above (i.e., action video games, exergames and serious games) or designing specific games [39].

To assess video games' impact on WM, Hassler-Hallstedt and colleagues [40] designed and implemented an intervention program called "Chasing Planets" with typical children aged 7 to 8 years old. The results showed significant improvements in WM both at the post-test and follow-ups at 6 and 12 months. Mondéjar and coworkers [41] investigated the differential effects of SGs and commercial video games on children between the ages of 8 and 12 with typical development, finding that the first ones could achieve a substantial enhancement in the domain of spatial WM.

On the other hand, the impact of videogaming on EFs has been primarily studied in adults: the results have shown that computer-based video game-like activities can improve executive functioning [42]. Based on this result, it was considered that similar training could have wider benefits if implemented earlier in development, when the neural circuitry of EFs is still maturing [43], and that it will be most effective if embedded in children's everyday activities [42] (p. 1).

In accordance with this rationale, Kolovelonis and coworkers [44] administered the ExG "Just Dance 2015" to a population of children aged 10 to 11 years old, to enhance their EFs. The results demonstrated significant enhancements in both the experimental group and the waiting-list control group following the administration of the same intervention training. Similar results were found by Flynn and Richert [45], who analysed the effects of ExGs, sedentary video games, physical activity and a control activity (small talk with the researcher) on neurotypical children aged 7 to 12 years old. The study found that both video game conditions led to greater improvements in EFs than physical activity or the control group, specifically in shifting and inhibition.

While an increasing number of studies have highlighted the role of video games in enhancing WM and EFs in neurotypical populations, it is equally, if not more, important to explore their application within neurodiverse developing groups. Children with neurodevelopmental disorders frequently exhibit deficits in WM and EFs [46], which are critical for academic achievement and everyday functioning [6,47]. For instance, the core symptoms of Attention-Deficit/Hyperactivity Disorder (ADHD), such as inattention, impulsivity, and hyperactivity, are closely linked to impairments in EFs [6,35,48]. Similarly, children with Autism Spectrum Disorder (ASD) often struggle with WM, inhibitory control, planning and emotional regulation. Moreover, impaired executive control in this population is associated with challenges in emotional regulation, resulting in inappropriate emotional responses and difficulties in adapting to new or complex situations [7]. Lastly, children with

Specific Learning Disorders (SLDs) often experience a constellation of cognitive difficulties involving WM, EFs and attentional control, all of which contribute to diminished learning capacity [49].

Video games have been increasingly prioritised in recent research on neurodevelopmental disorders, not only because of their popularity among young people, but also because of their unique motivational characteristics. Compared to other traditional interventions (e.g., paper-and-pencil training; behavioural therapy), video games offer engaging environments that combine real-time feedback, adaptive difficulty and intrinsic motivation, fundamental elements for sustained cognitive engagement [50]. Additionally, their interactive nature allows for the ecologically valuable simulation of executive challenges, which can better generalise to real-life contexts [38,51]. This highly adaptable and intrinsically motivating format can foster inclusion by accommodating diverse cognitive profiles and learning needs. Notably, Rafiei Milajerdi and colleagues [52], in a recent systematic review, found that participation in video game-based interventions was associated with improved social behaviours in children and adolescents with atypical development. These findings underscore the role of video games not only in enhancing WM and EFs, but also in fostering social inclusion and reducing barriers to participation in educational contexts.

Given these considerations, the present review aims to explore the use of video games as tools for enhancing WM and EFs in children with ADHD, ASD and SLDs, three populations in which deficits in these processes are particularly salient, and to understand if and how video games may be relevant in terms of inclusion.

2. Materials and Methods

Following the PRISMA guidelines [53], the search for this systematic review was performed in four different databases—PsycINFO, PubMed, Scopus and Web of Science—using the following query: ("executive function*" OR "executive control" OR "cognitive function*" OR "working memory") AND ("video game*" OR "gaming"). The search was restricted to the abstract field and filtered according to the following criteria: (a) language: English only, (b) publication range: from 2013 to 2025, (c) publication type: peer-reviewed journal articles. This search strategy was selected to ensure relevant and comprehensive coverage of the literature in alignment with the inclusion criteria listed below.

The inclusion criteria concerned: (1) experimental or pilot designs featuring at least pre- and post-test measurements and investigating the use of video games to enhance EFs and/or WM capacity; (2) participants including primary school-aged children and adolescents; (3) atypical development, including children with ADHD, ASD or SLDs diagnosis; (4) type of publication: peer-reviewed journal; (5) language: English; and (6) year of publication: from 2013 to 2025. The exclusion criteria applied to studies involving individuals affected by other clinical conditions not falling under the third inclusion criterion, such as traumatic brain injuries or Internet Gaming Disorder.

The initial database search was conducted on 3 July 2024, yielding 1806 records. After removing duplicates, 410 unique articles remained. An additional nine records were excluded because they were not written in English. Title and abstract screening of the remaining records was completed by December 2024. To ensure that the review reflected the most current evidence, an updated search using the same search strategy but restricted to articles published between July 2024 and March 2025 was conducted on 26 March 2025. This final search identified 227 additional records. Of these, 103 were duplicates, and one was excluded for being non-English, leaving 123 new articles for screening.

In total, 524 records underwent title and abstract screening. Of these, 458 were excluded for not meeting one or more predefined inclusion criteria. The remaining 65 articles were assessed in full text, resulting in 12 studies meeting the eligibility requirements. An additional 13 relevant studies were identified through the reference screening of other systematic reviews, yielding a final total of 25 studies included in this review. All screening procedures were conducted by the first author. In cases of uncertainty, the second and third authors independently assessed the records, and discrepancies were resolved through discussion until a consensus was reached. The selection process is fully detailed in Figure 1, which outlines the identification, screening, eligibility and inclusion phases according to the PRISMA standards.

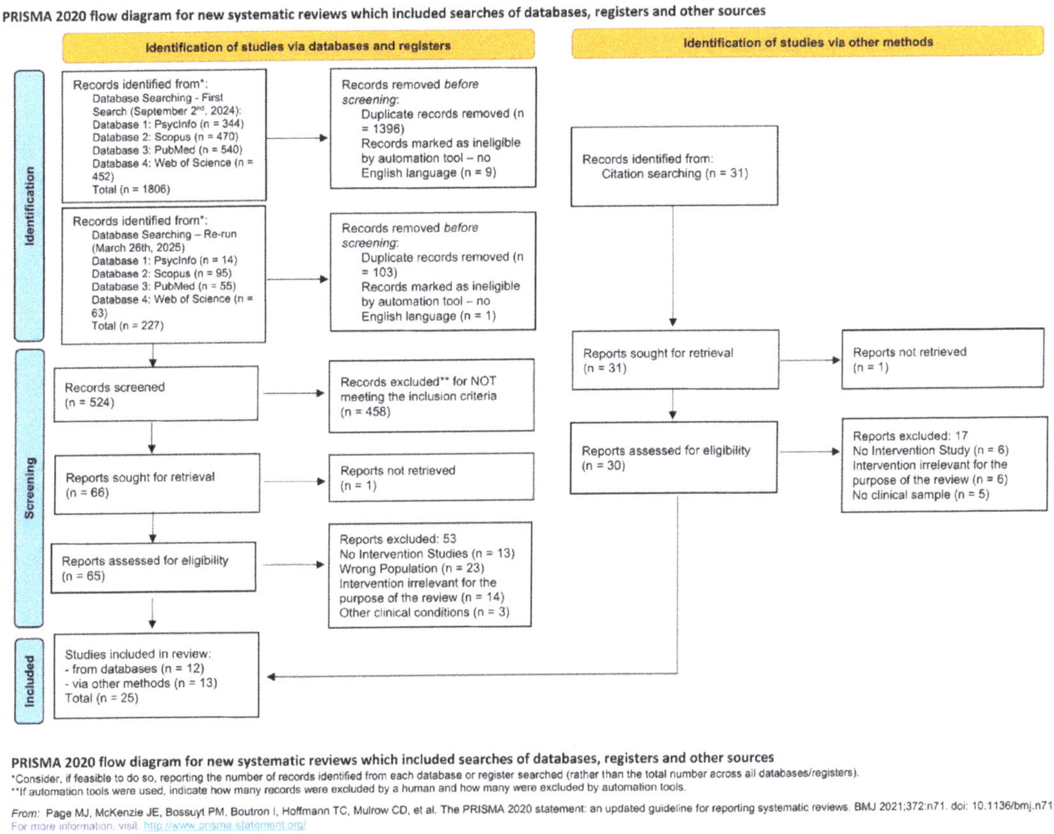

Figure 1. PRISMA 2020 flow diagram for new systematic reviews [53], which included searches of databases, registers and other sources.

The articles selected for the present review are detailed across three tables based on the cognitive process targeted in the video game-mediated intervention. Table 1 includes studies that used video games as tools to improve WM, while Table 2 presents studies aimed at enhancing EFs. Lastly, Table 3 summarises works targeting both WM and EFs simultaneously. Based on the previous literature involving neurotypical populations, which highlights the varying effects of different video game genres on WM and EFs, we outlined the primary cognitive domains impacted and included a dedicated section that categorises each type of video game and intervention program used as cognitive training tools.

Table 1. Studies included in the review on the impact of video games on WM (N = 5 studies).

Authors (Year)	Country	Study Type	Dependent or Observed Variable	Sample Age	Sample (n.)	Type of Video Game	Aim	Main Results
Bul et al. (2016) [9]	Netherlands and Belgium	Experimental - EG: SG training - CG: waiting list condition	WM (secondary outcomes)	8–12	ADHD (170)	SG "Plan-It Commander"	Examining the effects of this SG on time management skills (primary outcome), social skills of responsibility and WM (secondary outcomes).	EG achieved significantly greater improvements in WM ($p = 0.02$, Cohen's $d = 0.51$). The CG reached the same results after receiving the training ($p = 0.001$, Cohen's $d = 0.61$).
Chacko et al. (2013) [54]	USA	Experimental - EG: training condition - CG: placebo condition	WM	7–11	ADHD (85)	SG "Cogmed: Working Memory Training" (CWMT)	Determining the benefits of CWMT on various outcomes, including WM.	EG demonstrated significantly greater improvements in verbal and nonverbal WM (namely AWMA Digit Recall, $p = 0.005$, $d = 0.28$; AWMA Dot Matrix, $p < 0.001$, $d = 1.17$) but not in its updating (e.g., AWMA Listening Recall, $p = 0.728$).
Khalili Kermani et al. (2016) [55]	Iran	Experimental - EG: WM training - CG: no activity	Verbal WM	8–12	ADHD (60)	SGs (created for this investigation)	Verifying the effect of novel WM training in the form of structured games on ADHD children.	EG significantly enhanced verbal WM ($F(1, 58) = 5.326$, $p = 0.033$) compared to CG.
Łuniewska et al. (2018) [20]	Poland	Experimental - EG 1: AVGs training - EG 2: Phonological non-AVGs - CG: No training	Reading ability, phonological WM	9–13	Dyslexia (54)	AVGs "Rayman Raving Rabbids"	Testing how two forms of training, based on AVGs and on phonological non-action video games (PNAVGs), affect reading and other cognitive constructs, including phonological WM.	While EG 1 and 2 increased in phonological WM more than CG ($F(1, 52) = 15.53$, $p < 0.001$, $\eta^2 = 0.23$), the difference was not statistically significant (F (Group effect) = 0.01, $p = 0.94$; F(Group × Time) = 0.34, $p = 0.56$).

Table 1. *Cont.*

Authors (Year)	Country	Study Type	Dependent or Observed Variable	Sample Age	Sample (n.)	Type of Video Game	Aim	Main Results
Priya & Varathan (2025) [56]	India	Quasi-experimental - EG: training intervention	Visuo-spatial WM	11–16	ASD (30)	SGs and "Super Mario" with Leap Motion Controller	Evaluating the impact of gesture gaming on dexterity, grip strength and WM in individuals with ASD.	EG improved visuo-spatial WM in post-test in the Backward Span ($t = -42.8$, $p < 0.05$) and in the Forward Span ($t = -35.3$, $p < 0.05$). These enhancements are maintained at follow-up BS ($t = -42.7$, $p < 0.05$) and FS ($t = -33.5$, $p < 0.05$).

EG (experimental group); CG (control group); WM (working memory capacity); SGs (serious games); AVGs (action video games); PNAVGs (phonological non-action video games); ADHD (attention deficit and hyperactivity disorders); ASD (autism spectrum disorder); AWMA (Automated Working Memory Assessment); BS (Backward Span); FS (Forward Span).

Table 2. Studies included in the review on the impact of video games on EFs ($N = 7$ studies).

Authors (Year)	Country	Study Type	Dependent or Observed Variable	Sample Age	Sample (n.)	Type of Video Game	Aim	Main Results
Benzing and Schmidt (2019) [6]	Switzerland	Experimental - EG: training condition - CG: waiting list condition	Inhibition, shifting and updating	8–12	ADHD (51)	ExGs "Shape Up"	Investigating the effects of cognitively and physically demanding exergaming on EFs, ADHD symptoms and motor abilities.	EG improved the reaction times in inhibition ($F(2, 48) = 4.08$, $p = 0.049$, $d = 0.58$) and shifting ($F(2, 48) = 5.09$, $p = 0.029$, $d = 0.65$), no changes in updating ($F(2, 48) = 0.50$, $p = 0.482$, $d = 0.20$).

Table 2. *Cont.*

Authors (Year)	Country	Study Type	Dependent or Observed Variable	Sample Age	Sample (n.)	Type of Video Game	Aim	Main Results
Benzing et al. (2018) [57]	Switzerland	Experimental - EG: acute PA with ExGs training - CG: sedentary activity	Visual WM, inhibition and shifting	8–12	ADHD (46)	ExGs "Shape Up"	Verifying the effects of an acute bout of physical activity on multiple aspects of EFs (inhibition, switching, and visual working memory).	EG performed significantly faster RT in inhibition ($F_{\text{Flanker}}(2, 43) = 5.69$, $p = 0.022$, $\eta^2{}_p = 0.117$) and shifting ($F_{\text{Flanker}}(2, 43) = 5.50$, $p = 0.024$, $\eta^2{}_p = 0.113$), but there was no significant difference in the accuracy of the two tasks (congruent ($F_{\text{Flanker}}(2, 43) = 2.01$, $p = 0.157$, $\eta^2{}_p = 0.046$), incongruent ($F_{\text{Flanker}}(2, 43) = 0.09$, $p = 0.770$, $\eta^2{}_p = 0.002$) shifting trials ($F_{\text{Flanker}}(2, 43) = 0.26$, $p = 0.616$, $\eta^2{}_p = 0.006$) nor in visual WM ($F_{\text{Color span}}(2, 43) = 0.00$, $p = 0.995$, $\eta^2{}_p = 0.013$).
Di Giusto et al. (2023) [58]	Italy	Pilot study EG: VR training	Inhibition and shifting	7–11	SLDs (24)	Ad hoc video game training "Vitamin"	Examining whether a VR-rehabilitation program may have positive effects on the EFs of children with SLDs.	EG scores improve significantly for inhibition ($t = -2.985$, $p = 0.007$, $d = 0.609$) and shifting Mazes Subtest: $z = -2.765$, $p = 0.006$, $r = 0.743$) in post-test and after 6 months follow-up.
Dörrenbächer & Kray (2019) [59]	Germany	Experimetal - EG: gamified training - CG: standard training	Motivation, shifting and inhibition	8–13	ADHD (26)	Ad hoc video game training "Watermon Battle"	Investigating how a game-based training environment influences motivational variables and executive control during task-shifting training.	EG improved in motivation, but not in shifting and inhibition: no significant group differences were found in shifting costs or incompatibility effects (both $p < 0.22$, $BF_{10} < 0.65$), nor in group × session interactions ($F(1, 24) = 3.41$, $p = 0.08$, $\eta^2{}_p = 0.13$, $BF_{10} = 1.49$); all group effects ($p > 0.16$, $BF_{10} < 0.76$).

Table 2. *Cont.*

Authors (Year)	Country	Study Type	Dependent or Observed Variable	Sample Age	Sample (n.)	Type of Video Game	Aim	Main Results
Makkar et al. (2022) [60]	India	Experimental - EG: VG and transcranial therapy - CG: only VG	Inhibitory control and shifting	10–16	ADHD (61)	AVGs "Prince of Persia"	Determining the effectiveness of transcranial direct current stimulation (tDCS) compared to AVGs on the EFs in children with ADHD.	The CG (only VG condition) obtained no statistically significant results in shifting ($F = 0.639$, $p = 0.530$) and significative enhancements in inhibition ($F = 5.733$, $p = 0.003$), but less than EG.
Rafiei Milajerdi et al. (2021) [8]	Iran	Experimental - EG 1: SPARK training - EG 2: ExGs training - CG: treatment as usual	Inhibition and shifting	6–10	ASD (60)	ExGs "Kinect Tennis" and SPARK program	Investigating the effects of two types of interventions, Sports, Play and Active Recreation for Kids (SPARK) and ExGs (Kinect), on motor skills and EFs.	EG 2 displayed the main effects of more correct responses in inhibition and shifting ($F(2, 53) = 5.43$, $p < 0.01$, *partial* $\eta^2 = 0.17$) than children in the other two groups.
Sepehri Bonab et al. (2024) [7]	Iran	Experimental - EG: ExG and sedentary VG - CG: no activity	Inhibition and shifting	7–10	ASD (40)	ExG "Kinect Sports Season 2" and sedentary VG "Kinect Adventures" in VR	Evaluating the efficacy of ExGs and sedentary VG on EFs and emotional regulation on children with ASD.	EG significantly improved in inhibition ($t(19) = 5.99$, $p = 0.001$) and shifting ($t(19) = 7.37$, $p = 0.001$).

EG (experimental group); CG (control group); WM (working memory capacity); EFs (executive functions); RT (reaction time); VG (video game); AVGs (action video games); ExGs (exergames); VR (virtual reality); ADHD (attention deficit and hyperactivity disorders); ASD (autism spectrum disorder); SLDs (specific learning disorders); tDCS (transcranial direct current stimulation); SPARK (Sports, Play and Active Reaction for Kids)

Table 3. Studies included in the review on the impact of video games on both WM and EFs (N = 13 studies).

Authors (Year)	Country	Study Type	Dependent or Observed Variable	Sample Age	Sample (n.)	Type of Video Game	Aim	Main Results
Bikic et al. (2018) [61]	Denmark	Experimental - EG: computerised training - CG: treatment as usual	Spatial WM, inhibition and shifting (secondary outcomes)	6–13	ADHD (70)	Ad hoc video game training "ACTIVATE™"	Exploring the effects of a computer training program targeting multiple cognitive functions	EG found no significant beneficial effects on secondary outcome measures (spatial WM, $p = 0.096$; inhibition, $p = 0.093$; shifting, $p = 0.13$).
Dovis et al. (2015) [62]	Netherlands	Experimental - EG 1: full-active condition - EG 2: partially active condition - CG: placebo condition	Visuospatial WM, inhibition and cognitive flexibility	8–12	ADHD (89)	Ad hoc video game training "Braingame Brian"	Evaluating the short- and long-term effects of a gamified training intervention targeting specific cognitive abilities. Additionally, assessing the specific effects of the inhibition and cognitive flexibility training task.	Only EG 1 showed improvement in the measures of visuospatial STM and WM (CBTT-forward: $F(1, 59) = 11.03$, $p < 0.01$, $\eta^2_p = 0.16$; CBTT-backward: $F(1, 59) = 5.98$, $p < 0.05$, $\eta^2_p = 0.09$) and interference control ($F(1, 59) = 6.53$, $p < 0.05$, $\eta^2_p = 0.10$. Inhibitory performance improved in EG 1 ($F(1, 59) = 5.73$, $p < 0.05$, $\eta^2_p = 0.09$) and EG 2 ($F(1, 56) = 4.22$, $p < 0.05$, $\eta^2_p = 0.07$).
Franceschini et al. (2017, Study 4) [5]	Italy	Quasi-experimental - EG 1: AVGs training - EG 2: Non AVGs training	Shifting and phonological WM	7–14	Dyslexia (28)	AVGs "Rayman Raving Rabbids"	Testing reading skills, phonological working memory and attentional shifting in English-speaking children with dyslexia.	EG 1 enhanced phonological WM (F (1, 25) = 5.277, $p = 0.030$, $\eta^2 = 0.174$) and attentional shifting ($t(15) = 1.765$, $p = 0.049$, Cohen's $d = 0.65$) after AVGs training.

Table 3. *Cont.*

Authors (Year)	Country	Study Type	Dependent or Observed Variable	Sample Age	Sample (n.)	Type of Video Game	Aim	Main Results
Johnstone et al. (2017) [63]	Australia	Experimental - EG: WM, inhibitory control training - CG: waiting list control	WM and inhibitory control	7–11	ADHD (85)	SG "Focus Pocus"	Examining the efficacy of combined WM, inhibitory control and neurofeedback training in children with ADHD and subclinical ADHD.	EG significantly improved in inhibitory control ($F(2, 39) = 5.286$, $p = 0.007$, *partial* $\eta^2 = 0.12$), but not in WM after training.
Luo et al. (2024) [64]	China	Pilot Study - EG: ADHD sample - CG: typical sample	WM and inhibition	6–12	ADHD (55) Typical (55)	SG "Save the Muse Home"	Assessing the effectiveness of SG therapy software for children with ADHD and evaluating its suitability and effectiveness in improving the cognitive ability of neurotypical children.	EG's improvements in WM (BRIEF MI ($B = 11.05$, $p < 0.05$; fewer early saccades: $B = 0.34$, $p < 0.05$). Inhibition is not improved in BRIEF BRI ($p > 0.05$), but in CPT (commission errors: $B = 15.47$, $p < 0.001$) and the anti-saccade task (correct rate: $B = -10.65$, $p < 0.05$).
Martin–Moratinos et al. (2025) [65]	Spain	Experimental - EG: SG training and treatment as usual - CG: treatment as usual	Spatial WM, inhibition and shifting	7–18	ADHD (76)	SG in VR "The Secret Trail of Moon"	Evaluating the impact of 20-session treatment with this SG in VR on emotional regulation and executive functioning.	EG obtained significant improvements in spatial WM ($F(1, 55) = 4.08$, $p =.05$, $\eta^2 = 0.06$), inhibition ($F(1, 55) = 3.89$, $p = 0.05$, $\eta^2 = 0.06$) and shifting ($F(1, 66) = 4.06$, $p = 0.04$; $\eta^2 = 0.05$).
Medina et al. (2021) [10]	Spain	Experimental - EG: educational SG - CG: commercial no educational VG	Visuo-spatial WM, inhibitory control and shifting	8–11	ADHD (29)	SGs "KAD_SCL_01 Program" (different SGs in a platform)	Comparing training with a smart, digital, cognitive stimulation program (KAD_ SCL_01) and training with 3 commercial VGs to evaluate the most effective in neurocognitive rehabilitation.	EG only improved in visuo-spatial WM ($\beta = -0.84$, $SE = 0.38$, $t(27) = -2.24$, $p = 0.03$), inhibitory control (reduction in commission errors: $p = 0.03$, Hedge's $g = -0.62$) and shifting ($t(14) = 2.32$, $p = 0.03$).

Table 3. *Cont.*

Authors (Year)	Country	Study Type	Dependent or Observed Variable	Sample Age	Sample (n.)	Type of Video Game	Aim	Main Results
Nekar et al. (2022) [66]	South Korea	Experimental - EG: ExGs in AR training - CG: conventional cognitive training	WM, inhibition and shifting	6–18	ASD (24)	ExGs in AR "UINCARE"	Investigating the effects of AR using motivational games with cognitive–motor exercises on RRBs, EFs, attention and reaction time in patients with ASD.	EG obtained significant improvements in WM (Time × Group: $F = 11.407$, $p < 0.01$), shifting (RT: $F = 7.184$, $p < 0.05$; AR: $F = 6.349$, $p < 0.05$) and inhibition (RT: $F = 5.200$, $p < 0.05$; AR: $F = 4.351$, $p < 0.05$).
Revollo-Carillo et al. (2024) [67]	Colombia	Pilot Study - EG: training intervention - CG: waiting list	WM, inhibition and cognitive flexibility	8–12	ADHD (34)	Ad hoc video game training "Braingame Brian"	Assessing the potential of this intervention on EFs in children with ADHD	EG improved in WM ($F(1, 32) = 19.172$, $p < 0.05$, $h^2_p = 0.98$), inhibition ($F(1, 32) = 5.008$, $p < 0.05$, $h^2_p = 0.58$) and cognitive flexibility (number of categories achieved ($F(1, 32) = 10.874$, $p < 0.05$, $h^2_p = 0.89$); number of errors ($F(1, 32) = 4.668$, $p < 0.05$, $h^2_p = 0.55$).
Rodrigo-Yanguas et al. (2023) [39]	Spain	Experimental - EG: TSTM training - EG 2: TC training - CG: no intervention	WM, inhibition and shifting	12–22	ADHD (105)	SG "The Secret Trail of Moon"	Evaluating the efficacy of TSTM or TC as add-ons in stable, optimally medicated ADHD patients.	EG 1 and EG 2 did not improve WM ($p = 0.99$), inhibition ($p = 0.60$) or shifting ($p = 0.39$) abilities after both training.
Smith et al. (2020) [68]	USA and China	Experimental - EG: training condition - CG: treatment as usual	Verbal WM and inhibition (secondary outcome)	5–9	ADHD (92)	Ad hoc video game training "IBBS" (Integrated Brain, Body and Social intervention)	Evaluating the efficacy of an IBBS intervention (computerised cognitive remediation training, physical exercises and a behaviour management strategy) for children with ADHD.	EG showed significant improvement in a verbal WM task ($F(1, 69) = 4.00$, $p = 0.049$, $d = 0.27$); however, this result disappeared after correcting for multiple group comparisons.

Table 3. *Cont.*

Authors (Year)	Country	Study Type	Dependent or Observed Variable	Sample Age	Sample (n.)	Type of Video Game	Aim	Main Results
Van der Oord et al. (2014) [69]	Netherlands	Experimental - EG: training condition - CG: waiting list condition	WM, inhibition and cognitive flexibility	8–12	ADHD (40)	Ad hoc video game training "Braingame Brian"	Testing the short- and long-term efficacy (9 weeks follow-up) of executive functioning remediation training with game elements for children with ADHD.	EG showed significantly more improvement than those in the CG on parent-rated WM, inhibition and cognitive flexibility (BRIEF total EFs score (F(1, 35) = 6.84, $p < 0.05$, $\eta^2 = 0.16$). Effects were maintained at follow-up.
Wexler et al. (2020) [70]	USA	Quasi-experimental - EG 1: cognitive training (t_1) + treatment as usual (t_2) - EG 2: treatment as usual (t_1) + cognitive training (t_2)	WM and inhibition	6–8	ADHD (73)	Ad hoc video game training "C8 Sciences"	Evaluating the effectiveness of an integrated programme of cognitive training exercises, both computer-based and physical.	EG 1 and EG 2 improved in WM (pre-post mean, from 9.4 to 14.1, $p = 0.009$) and inhibition (Flanker incongruent accuracy (from 85% to 91%, $p = 0.02$); RT reduction in correct trials (from 1.4 s to 0.9 s, $p = 0.003$); no-go accuracy (from 33% to 44%, $p = 0.01$)) after receiving training.

EG (experimental group); CG (control group); WM (working memory capacity); EFs (executive functions); STM (short-term memory); RRBs (restricted and repetitive behaviours); RT (reaction time); VGs (video games); SGs (serious games); AVGs (action video games); ExGs (exergames); AR (augmented reality); VR (virtual reality); ADHD (attention deficit and hyperactivity disorders); ASD (autism spectrum disorder); TSTM (The Secret Trail of Moon); TC (therapeutic chess); t_1 (tempo 1); t_2 (tempo 2); CBTT-forward (Corsi block-tapping task—forward); CBTT-backward (Corsi block-tapping task—backward); BRIEF (Behavioral Rating Inventory of Executive Functions); BRIEF MI (Behavioral Rating Inventory of Executive Functions—Metacognition Index); BRIEF BRI (Behavioral Rating Inventory of Executive Functions—Behavioral Regulation Index); CPT (continuous performance test)

3. Results

This review includes a range of studies conducted primarily in Europe and the United States, with additional research from South America and several East Asian countries. Various types of video game-based training interventions aimed at enhancing WM or EFs in neurodiverse populations are investigated. Out of the 25 selected records, 18 focus on children with ADHD; only three studies involve children with SLDs, while four pertain to the ASD population. In the following sections, the impact of the different types of video games on either WM or EFs (or both) is detailed (see the "Main results" column of Tables 1–3 for the statistical indices of the scrutinised studies).

3.1. The Impact of Video Games on WM

Among the five studies which have explored the effectiveness of video games in enhancing the WM capacity, Bul and colleagues [9] used an online adventure SG called "Plan-It Commander" on a population of children aged 8 to 12 years old and diagnosed with ADHD. The participants were randomised into two groups: the first received 10 weeks of SG training in addition to standard WM treatment, followed by another 10 weeks of standard treatment only; the second group received a crossover intervention (i.e., 10 weeks of standard treatment followed by 10 more weeks of joint SG training and standard intervention). The findings showed significant improvements in the parent-rated WM score in the first group, with these enhancements maintained or further improved over the following 10 weeks. Similarly, Khalili Kermani and coworkers [55] developed an ad hoc SG and employed it in 12-week training in individuals with ADHD (8–12 years old), comparing an experimental group to a passive control group. Assessments at post-test and 6-month follow-up showed improvements in WM exclusively in the experimental group. Priya and Varathan [56] evaluated the effects of a set of four Leap Motion-delivered video games: three SGs, that is "Basketball", "Pin Bowling", "Leap Ball Game" and one commercial video game "Super Mario", in a population with ASD (11–16 years old). The training had positive effects on visuo-spatial WM: the backward span performance significantly improved from pre- to post-test. Similar results emerged for the forward span. A four-week follow-up confirmed these effects. Lastly, some improvements occurred in other measured variables, such as hand grip strength and dexterity. These results suggest that SGs and the Leap Motion technology, used together, can successfully improve visuo-spatial WM in ASD individuals. Indeed, the use of real-time physical interaction offers additional cognitive benefits for learners with sensory or attentional issues. This design may represent a productive direction for targeting WM, rather than employing only SGs or interactive feedback technologies separately. Lastly, Chacko and coworkers [54] studied the effects of the "Cogmed–Working Memory Training", ad hoc video game training, in children with ADHD aged 7 to 11 years. The authors highlighted improvements in both verbal and non-verbal WM capacity but not in its updating. Overall, all the studies listed above provide solid evidence showcasing the efficiency of video games in enhancing at least some components of WM. Among those examined, the only evidence that diverges from the general trend is that of Łuniewska and coworkers [20], who compared three groups of dyslexic children aged 8 to 13 years old. The first group played with the "Rayman Raving Rabbids" AVG, the second used a non-action phonological video game, while the last one was a passive control group. While WM improved in both experimental groups, these changes did not reach statistical significance compared to the control group.

3.2. The Impact of Video Games on EFs

Seven studies have investigated the effectiveness of video games in improving EFs, most of which employed ExGs. For instance, Benzing and coworkers [57] studied children with ADHD aged 8 to 12 years old, finding that the use of "Shape Up", a fitness ExG, improved both inhibition and shifting but had no positive effects on visual WM. In another study, Benzing and Schmidt [6] confirmed the benefits of "Shape Up" in the experimental group for inhibition and shifting, although no significant differences emerged between the groups for updating. Recently, Rafiei Milajerdi and coworkers [8] compared the ExG, "Kinect Tennis", with a structured exercise program (SPARK Program) in children with ASD aged 6 to 10 years old, finding significant improvements in shifting only in the ExG group. Finally, Sepehri Bonab and colleagues [7] compared the effects of mixed virtual reality (VR) training, including the ExG, "Kinect Sports Season 2", to those of the sedentary video game, "Kinect Adventures", in individuals with ASD and aged 7 to 10 years old. The ExG condition produced significantly more positive effects on inhibition, shifting and emotional regulation compared to the sedentary one.

In another group of studies, researchers used ad hoc video game training. Dörrenbächer and Kray [59] employed "Watermon Battle", a structured activity designed principally to promote motivation, but the authors also analysed changes in inhibition and shifting in children with ADHD (8–13 years old). Improvements emerged only in motivation, but not in inhibition and shifting. Di Giusto and coworkers [58] employed a series of VR SGs designed to improve EFs in children with SLDs, finding enhancements in inhibition, with stability maintained at 6-month follow-up. They also found improvements in shifting and planning, shown by a better performance in the Mazes Subtest from pre-test to post-test and from pre-test to the follow-up phase. Positive effects on Design Fluency emerged only between the post-test phase and follow-up, overall suggesting both immediate and delayed benefits of the VR intervention.

In contrast with the studies detailed above, Makkar and colleagues [60] compared two groups of children with ADHD aged 10 to 16 years old. The first group underwent training with the commercial AVG, "Prince of Persia: Sands of Time" and transcranial stimulation therapy, while the second only employed the AVG. The finding showed that the AVG-only group achieved minimal changes in EFs compared to the "double intervention" one.

3.3. The Impact of Video Games on Both WM and EFs

Franceschini and coworkers [5] used a set of mini games derived from the commercial Wii video game, "Rayman Raving Rabbids", with a sample of English-speaking children with dyslexia, aged 7 to 14 years old. Specifically, the participants were divided into an experimental group, playing AVGs, and an active control group, playing non-AVGs. The results showed significant improvements in phonological WM and shifting in the experimental group.

Nekar and colleagues [66] evaluated the efficacy of "UINCARE," a device utilising a Kinect system to integrate body movement with cognitive task performance, in individuals with ASD aged 6 to 18 years old. UINCARE incorporates all the features of ExGs through the application of augmented reality (AR). The participants were assigned to either an experimental group, which received UINCARE-based training, or a control group, which underwent conventional cognitive training. The results indicated that significant improvements in WM, inhibitory control and shifting were observed exclusively in the experimental group.

Other investigations have employed SGs as cognitive training tools. Notably, Medina and colleagues [10] compared the cognitive outcomes of an educational platform comprising fourteen SGs with those of commercial video games in children aged 8 to 11 years old diagnosed with ADHD. Only participants engaging with the SGs platform exhibited statistically significant improvements in spatial WM, inhibitory control and cognitive shifting.

Similarly, Luo and coworkers [64] examined the effects of the SG, "Save the Muse Home", on two cohorts of children aged 6 to 12 years old, one with ADHD and one neurotypical. The intervention led to significant enhancements in WM and inhibition. Martin-Moratinos and coworkers [65] investigated the impact of a virtual reality-based SG, "The Secret Trail of Moon", in a similar clinical population, further confirming its efficacy in improving WM, shifting and inhibition. In contrast, Rodrigo-Yanguas and coworkers [39] compared a chess-based therapeutic game and "The Secret Trail of Moon" in adolescents with ADHD (aged 12 to 22 years old), finding no significant changes in the global executive function index as measured by the Behavior Rating Inventory of Executive Function 2 (BRIEF-2). Johnstone and colleagues [63] evaluated the SG, "Focus Pocus" in children with ADHD aged 7 to 11 years old, observing improvements in EFs, particularly inhibitory control (albeit with a small effect size), though no significant gains were noted in WM.

Further studies have explored the efficacy of ad hoc video game interventions. Van der Oord and coworkers [69] assessed "Braingame Brian", a training program consisting of 25 targeted sessions focusing on WM, inhibition and cognitive flexibility, in children aged 8 to 12 years old with ADHD. The intervention yielded significant improvements across all three executive domains, with some effects persisting at a nine-week follow-up. Significant effects were found for the BRIEF Total EFs score, but not on the specific BRIEF subscales, such as WM, shifting and inhibition. On the other hand, gaming performance data showed significant enhancements across all trained EFs, with strong within-subject effects. While parents' evaluations yielded mixed results, specific advances in EFs' domains emerged during the gameplay performance, thus suggesting that those improvements were strictly linked to the executive skills stimulated by the video game, with a limited transfer effect.

In a similar randomised study, Dovis and colleagues [62] divided children with ADHD into three groups: a fully active training condition (targeting WM, inhibition and cognitive flexibility), a partially active condition (training inhibition and shifting with WM in a placebo) and a placebo group. Significant improvements in WM, visuospatial short-term memory and inhibitory control were observed exclusively in the full-active training group. The partially active group showed gains in inhibition only, while no significant effects were observed in shifting across groups. Recently, Revollo-Carillo and coworkers [67] applied "Braingame Brian" to a Spanish-speaking population of children aged 8 to 12 years old with ADHD, corroborating its positive effects on WM, inhibition and cognitive flexibility. Additionally, Wexler and colleagues [70] developed "C8 Sciences", a platform that integrates computerised cognitive training with cognitively enriched physical activity. Their findings demonstrated improvements in WM and inhibition among children with ADHD aged 6 to 8 years old. While most of the scrutinised studies reported encouraging results, some others have reported null findings. Smith and coworkers [68] investigated the "Integrated Brain Body Social Intervention" in children aged 5 to 9 years old with ADHD, but found no significant changes in WM or inhibition. Similarly, Bikic and colleagues [61], evaluating the digital training program "ACTIVATE™", observed no significant benefits in WM, inhibition or shifting.

4. Discussion

The present review aimed to investigate the role of video games as tools for improving WM and EFs in children with ADHD, ASD and SLDs. The overarching objective was to assess their efficacy as cognitive training tools and explore their broader implications for promoting inclusion.

Some studies [9,54], supported by medium and large effect sizes, reported that video game-based training significantly improved WM performance. In contrast, other studies [39], based on parent-rated measures or gameplay performance indexes, did not show statistical improvements in WM or shifting. This divergence highlights the importance of differentiating between perceived enhancements and measured cognitive improvements. A similar pattern emerged for EFs. ExGs, such as "Shape Up" and "Kinect Tennis", were associated with significant enhancements in inhibition and shifting skills, while other interventions, such as "Watermon Battle" [59] or commercial video games [20,60], did not promote relevant executive changes. Lastly, tools like "Braingame Brian" showed mixed results, with significant improvements in the global scores index of EFs if parent-rated, but not in specific subscales of WM or inhibition.

From a comparative perspective, while SGs and ad hoc training programs, such as "Plan-It Commander" and "Cogmed", showed relevant effects on WM, other interventions like "Braingame Brian" and commercial video games, such as "Prince of Persia", produced more limited or restricted improvements in some specific executive domains, especially when based on parent-related assessments or game-related performance, without an external solid validation across standardised instruments.

Despite a few mixed results, the findings from this review suggest that various categories of video games may positively influence WM and EFs in children and adolescents with neurodevelopmental disorders.

To better scrutinise the differential impact of video games on the targeted cognitive processes, we differentiate three thematic clusters. The first concerns enhancements in WM capacity, which were most prominently associated with SGs and ad hoc video game interventions. For instance, programs such as "Plan-It Commander" [9] and "Cogmed" [54] promoted significant improvements in WM, particularly within individuals diagnosed with ADHD. Priya and Varathan [56] demonstrated how SGs in the Leap Motion version may improve WM more successfully than passive video game experiences. These findings align with evidence that indicates how body interaction and multimodal feedback can improve cognitive engagement, in particular in ASD populations [56]. However, differences in age, in WM measures and feedback design make it difficult to directly make comparisons with other studies that involve SGs [9]. This aspect highlights the need for more standardised protocols for future research. Conversely, studies employing AVG training without interactive components failed to yield significant results [6].

The second cluster includes studies focused specifically on EFs. While not all interventions yielded positive results [60], ExGs featured prominently in this category. Interventions such as "Shape Up" promoted notable gains in inhibitory control and cognitive flexibility among children with ADHD [6,57]. Comparable improvements were documented in children with ASD through ExGs like "Kinect Tennis" [8] and "Kinect Sports Season 2" [7]. Overall, ExGs seem to positively affect inhibition, likely thanks to the combination of structured tasks and body movements needed to accomplish the game's requests. Conversely, AVGs stimulate cognitive processes with fast-paced environments and multiple perceptive stimuli, thus requiring rapid decision making and attentional control. Some studies e.g., [5] imply that this type of video game is particularly valuable to empower shifting; however, their impact on inhibition and WM is less consistent. Notably, the impact of different features and modalities of the video games can vary based on the neurodevelopmental profile of the participants: children with ADHD seem to take more progresses from ExGs, which have explicit goals and are more structured, while AVGs can be more useful for children with dyslexia, thanks to their attentional load.

The third cluster encompasses investigations examining the combined influence of video games on both WM and EFs. Numerous studies across different neurodevelopmental conditions have reported significant benefits using various game formats. For example, AVGs have been shown to improve phonological WM and shifting in children with dyslexia [5], while ExGs demonstrated efficacy in enhancing WM, inhibition and shifting in ASD individuals [8]. Moreover, SGs [10,56,66] and ad hoc video game programs [69,70] have consistently produced significant improvements in both WM and EFs both in ADHD and ASD populations.

A further relevant aspect that must be taken into account is how different games can be tailored to the specific needs of children with different neurodevelopmental disorders. SGs are developed with explicitly educative or therapeutic aims, and they allow a greater personalisation of content and regulation of task difficulty. This makes them particularly useful for children with ADHD, who benefit from clear objectives, constant reinforcements and structured environments [9,10,54,63]. Instead, ExGs integrate motor activation and empowerment of EFs, promoting self-regulation and inhibition across body movement in association with cognitive tasks. For this reason, these video games are suitable for individuals with ASD, who can benefit from sensory integration and an experiential approach [7,8,66]. Lastly, AVGs are characterised by dynamic environments and high stimulating intensity; these aspects make them particularly useful for children with dyslexia [5], who might benefit from handling a significant cognitive load. In this sense, different video games offer distinct forms of adaptability and the possibility to be customised based on intervention goals and the specific characteristics of children with neurodiverse development.

While most studies support the employment of video games as tools for cognitive enhancement, some findings seem to be inconsistent, especially with respect to specific populations. For example, Benzing and Schmidt [6] found that ExGs led to significant enhancements in inhibition and shifting in children with ADHD, while Makkar and coworkers [60], using a commercial AVG in a similar population, did not report significant benefits in cognitive abilities for the video game-only condition. These discrepancies may depend on several factors—first, the nature of the game itself: cognitive complexity, feedback system and physical involvement can greatly affect executive functioning. Second, the duration and intensity of the intervention change widely among studies, with a subsequent impact on the consolidation of cognitive improvements. Third, the participants' interindividual differences, such as age, severity of diagnosis and comorbidities could moderate the effects of the interventions. Lastly, the measures used in these studies are not homogeneous. In some cases, scholars used parent-rated or self-reported scales, in others, standard neuropsychological tasks, thus focusing on different aspects of cognitive functioning.

In sum, despite some contrasting results [39,68], this review underscores the promising role of video games in supporting the development of WM and EFs.

These findings can be interpreted at many theoretical levels. First, while different models of EF have been proposed during the last 25 years, most tend to agree on the prominent role of three "core" EFs, namely WM updating, inhibition and shifting [34,35]. The present review offers a detailed examination of how each of them is selectively impacted by video game-mediated training, thus providing relevant theoretical and practical insights into their differential impact. Secondly, the effectiveness of ExGs can be viewed throughout the embodied cognition theory, according to which motor involvement fosters cognitive and emotional processing and regulation. This perspective highlights how cognitive abilities can emerge from the dynamic interaction between body, brain and environment, evidencing the role of sensory-motor experiences in the development of high cognitive functions [71]. In terms of educational inclusion, the emerged evidence is aligned with the principles of the Universal Design for Learning (UDL), a framework that promotes adaptability and personalisation of educational tools to face the variety of cognitive and social needs of learners. This framework offers a design of flexible contexts of learning, that can give multiple modalities of representation, expression and involvement, to guarantee the same opportunity for all students [72].

Starting from this evidence, we now intend to answer our original question: In how many ways can video games make education more inclusive? We argue that there are at least three.

First, higher-level cognitive processes such as WM and EFs are systematically linked to better social functioning. Research shows that deficits in WM, especially in its central executive component, have been associated with greater peer rejection, higher levels of aggression and poorer conflict resolution skills in neurotypical children [32]. Similarly, EFs such as inhibitory control, shifting and self-monitoring are considered central predictors of emotional regulation and prosocial behaviours, which, in turn, facilitate positive peer interactions and group integration [37]. Importantly, interventions aimed at improving EFs and emotional regulation have been found to significantly enhance social participation and emotional functioning in children with ASD [7]. Other recent contributions suggest that video games can contribute to the development of better emotional regulation and social communication, fundamental skills for children with ASD [73,74]. Consistent with these results, another study [9] demonstrated that an SG intervention for children with ADHD significantly enhanced not only WM but also a set of social skills, thus supporting better social functioning in daily life. Martin-Moratinos and colleagues [65] found significant improvements in WM, inhibitory control and organisational skills in children with ADHD after SG training. While direct effects on social competencies were not measured, the authors found improvements also in emotional regulation, which, paired with the aforementioned EFs, can facilitate positive peer relationships.

Collectively, these findings suggest that targeting WM and EFs may be a valuable strategy for promoting social competence and, in turn, facilitating peer inclusion.

At a second level, video games contribute to making learning environments more inclusive and favourable for children and adolescents with neurodevelopmental disorders [75]. Indeed, achieving meaningful inclusion requires accessible, usable technological tools and adaptive learning contexts. The integration of digital technologies, including video games, can play a crucial role in advancing this goal [76]. Owing to their adaptability to individual performance and player-specific characteristics, video games can offer highly individualised learning experiences. This is evident in studies that employed adaptive video game training designed specifically for neurotypical developmental populations [54,59,65,66,69], thus ensuring accessibility and participation [77]. By enabling the customisation of learning tasks and trajectories, video games can improve both cognitive and learning outcomes and support a more effective and inclusive educational experience [78,79].

At a third level, numerous studies have characterised video games as tools capable of supporting children with various challenges by fostering engagement without reinforcing stigmatising differences [80,81]. Notably, VR and structured digital play environments offer motivating, adaptable settings that promote individual strengths while minimising frustration [58,82]. SGs, in particular, stand out for their capacity to engage children with ADHD more effectively than traditional training approaches [9], while AR-based interactions may enhance engagement in children with ASD by providing self-paced and low-stress environments [8]. In this regard, Di Giusto et al. [58] emphasised that VR-based games enable the development of generalisable skills transferable beyond the classroom, within safe and motivating environments. Such evidence supports the broader implementation of video games as valuable tools in inclusive education and cognitive development for children with neurodevelopmental disorders.

Based on this evidence and reflections, we argue that the flexible and adaptive nature of video games can facilitate their integration into diverse contexts, offering inclusive experiences that emphasise individual potential rather than limitations.

To conclude, despite the encouraging results, the methodological limitations of the scrutinised studies must be considered. Many of them involved small or pilot samples, reducing statistical power and limiting generalisability. In some cases, the absence of a long-term follow-up restricts conclusions about the stability of effects over time. Additionally, the heterogeneity of the assessment tools, ranging from standardised neuropsychological tasks to subjective ratings by parents or teachers, may have introduced a bias. Last, variations in training protocols, particularly in timing and intensity, do not allow a direct comparison across studies. Future research should aim for experimental designs with larger samples, standardised evaluation tools, and longitudinal follow-ups to strengthen evidence and support a broader application of the findings.

5. Conclusions

The findings of this review emphasise how video games can serve as inclusive tools for enhancing WM and EFs in children with neurodevelopmental disorders. A deeper analysis suggests that SGs and ad hoc training show significant improvements in WM, while ExGs yield consistent improvements in inhibition and shifting in ADHD and ASD populations. AVGs have more variable effects, with some impact found on shifting, but limited evidence on other EFs. These distinctions are important to justify the alignment of game genre and design with the targeted cognitive skills.

Notably, while video games are intrinsically engaging, their adaptability depends on specific elements, such as task structure, feedback mechanisms and the modality of interaction, which must be aligned with the cognitive and emotional profile of neurodivergent learners to maximise their effectiveness.

In light of this, practical recommendations can be made about the use of video games in educational and rehabilitative contexts. First, video games cannot have educational value if used with a one-size-fits-all approach. Conversely, they have to be selected and customised based on scientific principles and the specific needs of the learner. Second, video games should be integrated into structured educational environments and matched with formal training for teachers and operators. Directly connected to this, educational policies should focus on promoting technological inclusion and reducing the digital divide, also acknowledging video games as innovative educational tools.

By only taking into account all these recommendations, it will be possible to unlock the multiple ways in which video games make education inclusive for neurodivergent learners by offering meaningful, customisable and motivating learning experiences.

Author Contributions: Conceptualisation, M.B., E.B. and A.C.; methodology, M.B.; validation, E.B.; investigation, M.B.; resources, A.C.; data curation, M.B.; writing—original draft preparation, M.B.; writing—review and editing, E.B. and A.C.; visualisation, M.B.; supervision, A.C.; project administration, A.C. All authors have read and agreed to the published version of the manuscript.

Funding: This research received no external funding.

Conflicts of Interest: The authors declare no conflicts of interest.

Abbreviations

The following abbreviations are used in this manuscript:

ADHD	Attention Deficit and Hyperactivity Disorder
ASD	Autism Spectrum Disorder
AR	Augmented Reality
AVG(s)	Action-Video Game(s)
BRIEF(2)	Behavioral Rating Inventory of Executive Functions (Version 2)
EFs	Executive Functions

ExG(s)	Exergame(s)
HBSC	Health Behaviour in School-aged Children study
SG(s)	Serious Game(s)
SLDS	Specific Learning Disorder
UDL	Universal Design for Learning
VR	Virtual Reality
WM	Working Memory

References

1. Cadamuro, A.; Bisagno, E.; Pecini, C.; Vezzali, L. Reflecting A…"Bit". What Relationship Between Metacognition And ICT? *J. E-Learn. Knowl. Soc.* **2019**, *15*, 183–195. [CrossRef]
2. Cadamuro, A.; Bisagno, E.; Di Bernardo, G.A.; Vezzali, L.; Versari, A. Making the school Smart: The interactive whiteboard against disparities in children stemming from low metacognitive skills. *J. E-Learn. Knowl. Soc.* **2020**, *16*, 33–43. [CrossRef]
3. Reid, G. Motivation in video games: A literature review. *Comput. Games J.* **2012**, *1*, 70–81. [CrossRef]
4. Boniel-Nissim, M.; Marino, C.; Galeotti, T.; Blinka, L.; Ozoliņa, K.; Craig, W.; Lathi, H.; Wong, S.L.; Brown, J.; Wilson, M.; et al. *A focus on Adolescent Social Media Use and Gaming in Europe, Central Asia and Canada: Health Behaviour in School-aged Children International Report from the 2021/2022 Survey*; World Health Organization: Geneva, Switzerland, 2024. Available online: https://iris.who.int/handle/10665/378982 (accessed on 1 June 2025).
5. Franceschini, S.; Trevisan, P.; Ronconi, L.; Bertoni, S.; Colmar, S.; Double, K.; Facoetti, A.; Gori, S. Action video games improve reading abilities and visual-to-auditory attentional shifting in English-speaking children with dyslexia. *Sci. Rep.* **2017**, *7*, 5863. [CrossRef] [PubMed]
6. Benzing, V.; Schmidt, M. The effect of exergaming on executive functions in children with ADHD: A randomized clinical trial. *Scand. J. Med. Sci. Sports* **2019**, *29*, 1243–1253. [CrossRef]
7. Sepehri Bonab, H.; Ebrahimi Sani, S.; Behzadnia, B. The Impact of Virtual Reality Intervention on Emotion Regulation and Executive Functions in Autistic Children. *Games Health J.* **2025**, *14*, 146–158. [CrossRef] [PubMed]
8. Rafiei Milajerdi, H.; Sheikh, M.; Najafabadi, M.G.; Saghaei, B.; Naghdi, N.; Dewey, D. The Effects of Physical Activity and Exergaming on Motor Skills and Executive Functions in Children with Autism Spectrum Disorder. *Games Health J.* **2021**, *10*, 33–42. [CrossRef]
9. Bul, K.C.; Kato, P.M.; Van der Oord, S.; Danckaerts, M.; Vreeke, L.J.; Willems, A.; van Oers, H.J.; Van Den Heuvel, R.; Birnie, D.; Van Amelsvoort, T.A.; et al. Behavioral Outcome Effects of Serious Gaming as an Adjunct to Treatment for Children With Attention-Deficit/Hyperactivity Disorder: A Randomized Controlled Trial. *J. Med. Internet Res.* **2016**, *18*, e26. [CrossRef]
10. Medina, R.; Bouhaben, J.; de Ramón, I.; Cuesta, P.; Antón-Toro, L.; Pacios, J.; Quintero, J.; Ramos-Quiroga, J.A.; Maestú, F. Electrophysiological Brain Changes Associated with Cognitive Improvement in a Pediatric Attention Deficit Hyperactivity Disorder Digital Artificial Intelligence-Driven Intervention: Randomized Controlled Trial. *J. Med. Internet Res.* **2021**, *23*, e25466. [CrossRef]
11. Toh, W.; Kirschner, D. Developing social-emotional concepts for learning with video games. *Comput. Educ.* **2023**, *194*, 104708. [CrossRef]
12. Chen, C.-C.; Tu, H.-Y. The effect of digital game-based learning on learning motivation and performance under Social Cognitive Theory and entrepreneurial thinking. *Front. Psychol.* **2021**, *12*, 750711. [CrossRef] [PubMed]
13. Mao, P.; Cai, Z.; Wang, Z.; Hao, X.; Fan, X.; Sun, X. The effects of dynamic and static feedback under tasks with different difficulty levels in digital game-based learning. *Internet High. Educ.* **2023**, *60*, 100923. [CrossRef]
14. Bediou, B.; Adams, D.M.; Mayer, R.E.; Tipton, E.; Green, C.S.; Bavelier, D. Meta-analysis of action video game impact on perceptual, attentional, and cognitive skills. *Psychol. Bull.* **2018**, *144*, 77–110. [CrossRef] [PubMed]
15. Moisala, M.; Salmela, V.; Hietajärvi, L.; Carlson, S.; Vuontela, V.; Lonka, K.; Hakkarainen, K.; Salmela-Aro, K.; Alho, K. Gaming is related to enhanced working memory performance and task-related cortical activity. *Brain Res.* **2017**, *1655*, 204–215. [CrossRef] [PubMed]
16. Granic, I.; Lobel, A.; Engels, R.C. The benefits of playing video games. *Am. Psychol.* **2014**, *69*, 66–78. [CrossRef]
17. Mazurek, M.O.; Shattuck, P.T.; Wagner, M.; Cooper, B.P. Prevalence and correlates of screen-based media use among youths with autism spectrum disorders. *J. Autism Dev. Disord.* **2012**, *42*, 1757–1767. [CrossRef]
18. Xu, K.; Geng, S.; Dou, D.; Liu, X. Relations between Video Game Engagement and Social Development in Children: The Mediating Role of Executive Function and Age-Related Moderation. *Behav. Sci.* **2023**, *13*, 833. [CrossRef]
19. Ceccherelli, A. Videogiochi e apprendimento tra medium e messaggio. Considerazioni sull'uso didattico dei videogiochi. *Riv. Scuola IaD Mod. Polit. RT* **2012**, 92–112.

20. Łuniewska, M.; Chyl, K.; Dębska, A.; Kacprzak, A.; Plewko, J.; Szczerbiński, M.; Szewczyk, J.; Grabowska, A.; Jednoróg, K. Neither action nor phonological video games make dyslexic children read better. *Sci. Rep.* **2018**, *8*, 549. [CrossRef]
21. Böö, R. Video Game Playing, Academic Performance, Educational Activity, and Motivation Among Secondary School Students. Master's Thesis, Örebro University, Örebro, Sweden, 2014. Available online: https://urn.kb.se/resolve?urn=urn:nbn:se:oru:diva-35525 (accessed on 1 June 2025).
22. Weaver, J.; Kim, P.; Metzer, R.L.; Szendrey, J.M. The impact of video games on student GPA, study habits, and time management skills: What's the big deal. *Issues Inf. Syst.* **2013**, *14*, 122–128. Available online: https://iacis.org/iis/2013/184_iis_2013_122-128.pdf (accessed on 1 June 2025).
23. Concepcion, L.; Nales-Torres, M.; Rodriguez-Zubiaurre, A. The Relationship between Video game Use, Deviant Behavior, and Academic Achievement among a Nationally Representative Sample of High School Seniors in the United States. *Am. J. Educ. Res.* **2016**, *4*, 1157–1163. [CrossRef]
24. Drummond, A.; Sauer, J.D. Video-games do not negatively impact adolescent academic performance in science, mathematics or reading. *PLoS ONE* **2014**, *9*, e87943. [CrossRef] [PubMed]
25. Ku, C.H.; Kwak, M.; Yurov, K.M.; Yurova, Y.V. A study of the influence of gaming behavior on academic performance of IT college students. In Proceedings of the 20th Americas Conference on Information Systems (AMCIS 2014), Savannah, GA, USA, 7–9 August 2014; Available online: https://aisel.aisnet.org/amcis2014/ISEducation/GeneralPresentations/9/ (accessed on 1 June 2025).
26. Bertoni, S.; Franceschini, S.; Puccio, G.; Mancarella, M.; Gori, S.; Facoetti, A. Action video games enhance attentional control and phonological decoding in children with developmental dyslexia. *Brain Sci.* **2021**, *11*, 171. [CrossRef] [PubMed]
27. Franceschini, S.; Bertoni, S. Improving action video games abilities increases the phonological decoding speed and phonological short-term memory in children with developmental dyslexia. *Neuropsychologia* **2019**, *130*, 100–106. [CrossRef] [PubMed]
28. Huang, H.; Cheng, C. The Benefits of Video Games on Brain Cognitive Function: A Systematic Review of Functional Magnetic Resonance Imaging Studies. *Appl. Sci.* **2022**, *12*, 5561. [CrossRef]
29. Baddeley, A. Working Memory: Looking Back and Looking forward. *Nat. Rev. Neurosci.* **2003**, *4*, 829–839. [CrossRef]
30. Cowan, N. *Working Memory Capacity*; Psychology Press: New York, NY, USA, 2005.
31. Bisagno, E.; Cadamuro, A.; Morra, S. Multiple influences of working memory capacity on number comprehension: The interplay with metacognition and number-specific prerequisites. *J. Exp. Child Psychol.* **2023**, *226*, 105568. [CrossRef]
32. McQuade, J.D.; Murray-Close, D.; Shoulberg, E.K.; Hoza, B. Working memory and social functioning in children. *J. Exp. Child Psychol.* **2013**, *115*, 422–435. [CrossRef]
33. Mutter, B.; Alcorn, M.B.; Welsh, M. Theory of mind and executive function: Working-memory capacity and inhibitory control as predictors of false-belief task performance. *Percept. Mot. Ski.* **2006**, *102*, 819–835. [CrossRef]
34. Miyake, A.; Friedman, N.; Emerson, M.; Witzki, A.; Howerter, A. The unity and diversity of executive functions and their contributions to complex "frontal lobe" tasks: A latent variable analysis. *Cogn. Psychol.* **2000**, *41*, 49–100. [CrossRef]
35. Diamond, A. Executive functions. *Annu. Rev. Psychol.* **2013**, *64*, 135–168. [CrossRef]
36. Spiegel, J.A.; Goodrich, J.M.; Morris, B.M.; Osborne, C.M.; Lonigan, C.J. Relations between executive functions and academic outcomes in elementary school children: A meta-analysis. *Psychol. Bull.* **2021**, *147*, 329–351. [CrossRef] [PubMed]
37. Gkora, V.; Christou, A. Executive functions, self-regulation and social media for peace-based inclusive education. *Magna Sci. Adv. Res. Rev.* **2023**, *8*, 129–140. [CrossRef]
38. Bediou, B.; Rodgers, M.A.; Tipton, E.; Mayer, R.E.; Green, C.S.; Bavelier, D. Effects of action video game play on cognitive skills: A meta-analysis. *Technol. Mind Behav.* **2023**, *4*. [CrossRef]
39. Rodrigo-Yanguas, M.; Martín-Moratinos, M.; González-Tardón, C.; Sanchez-Sanchez, F.; Royuela, A.; Bella-Fernández, M.; Blasco-Fontecilla, H. Effectiveness of a Personalized, Chess-Based Training Serious Video Game in the Treatment of Adolescents and Young Adults with Attention-Deficit/Hyperactivity Disorder: Randomized Controlled Trial. *JMIR Serious Games* **2023**, *11*, e39874. [CrossRef]
40. Hassler Hallstedt, M.; Klingberg, T.; Ghaderi, A. Short and long-term effects of a mathematics tablet intervention for low performing second graders. *J. Educ. Psychol.* **2018**, *110*, 1127–1148. [CrossRef]
41. Mondéjar, T.; Hervás, R.; Johnson, E.; Gutierrez, C.; Latorre, J.M. Correlation between video game mechanics and executive functions through EEG analysis. *J. Biomed. Inform.* **2016**, *63*, 131–140. [CrossRef] [PubMed]
42. Blair, C. Educating executive function. *Wiley Interdiscip. Rev. Cogn. Sci.* **2017**, *8*, e1403. [CrossRef] [PubMed]
43. Best, J.R.; Miller, P.H. A developmental perspective on executive function. *Child Dev.* **2010**, *81*, 1641–1660. [CrossRef]
44. Kolovelonis, A.; Papastergiou, M.; Samara, E.; Goudas, M. Acute Effects of Exergaming on Students' Executive Functions and Situational Interest in Elementary Physical Education. *Int. J. Environ. Res. Public Health* **2023**, *20*, 1902. [CrossRef]
45. Flynn, R.M.; Richert, R.A. Cognitive, not physical, engagement in video gaming influences executive functioning. *J. Cogn. Dev.* **2018**, *19*, 1–20. [CrossRef]

46. Crisci, G.; Caviola, S.; Cardillo, R.; Mammarella, I.C. Executive functions in neurodevelopmental disorders: Comorbidity overlaps between attention deficit and hyperactivity disorder and specific learning disorders. *Front. Hum. Neurosci.* **2021**, *15*, 594234. [CrossRef] [PubMed]
47. Arnold, L.E.; Hodgkins, P.; Kahle, J.; Madhoo, M.; Kewley, G. Long-Term Outcomes of ADHD: Academic Achievement and Performance. *J. Atten. Disord.* **2015**, *24*, 73–85. [CrossRef] [PubMed]
48. Willcutt, E.G.; Doyle, A.E.; Nigg, J.T.; Faraone, S.V.; Pennington, B.F. Validity of the executive function theory of attention-deficit/hyperactivity disorder: A meta-analytic review. *Biol. Psychiatry* **2005**, *57*, 1336–1346. [CrossRef] [PubMed]
49. Conte, B.; Marzocchi, G.M. Profili specifici di funzioni esecutive nei ragazzi con ADHD, DSA o DOP. *Psicol. Clin. Svilupp.* **2020**, *24*, 401–436. [CrossRef]
50. Shute, V.J.; Ventura, M.; Ke, F. The power of play: The effects of Portal 2 and Lumosity on cognitive and noncognitive skills. *Comp. Educ.* **2015**, *80*, 58–67. [CrossRef]
51. Gee, J.P. *What Video Games have to Teach us About Learning and Literacy*; Palgrave Macmillan: New York, NY, USA, 2003.
52. Rafiei Milajerdi, H.; Ordooiazar, F.; Dewey, D. Is active video gaming associated with improvements in social behaviors in children with neurodevelopmental disorders: A systematic review. *Child Neuropsychol.* **2023**, *29*, 1–27. [CrossRef]
53. Page, M.J.; McKenzie, J.E.; Bossuyt, P.M.; Boutron, I.; Hoffmann, T.C.; Mulrow, C.D.; Shamseer, L.; Tetzlaff, J.M.; Akl, E.A.; Brennan, S.E.; et al. The PRISMA 2020 statement: An updated guideline for reporting systematic reviews. *BMJ* **2021**, *372*, n71. [CrossRef]
54. Chacko, A.; Bedard, A.C.; Marks, D.J.; Feirsen, N.; Uderman, J.Z.; Chimiklis, A.; Rajwan, E.; Cornwell, M.; Anderson, L.; Zwilling, A.; et al. A randomized clinical trial of Cogmed Working Memory Training in school-age children with ADHD: A replication in a diverse sample using a control condition. *J. Child Psychol. Psychiatry* **2014**, *55*, 247–255. [CrossRef]
55. Khalili Kermani, F.; Mohammadi, M.R.; Yadegari, F.; Haresabadi, F.; Sadeghi, S.M. Working Memory Training in the Form of Structured Games in Children with Attention Deficit Hyperactivity Disorder. *Iran. J. Psychiatry* **2016**, *11*, 224–233. Available online: https://www.ncbi.nlm.nih.gov/pmc/articles/PMC5206324/ (accessed on 1 June 2025).
56. Priya, J.S.; Varathan, K. Effects of Video-based Gesture Gaming on Hand Functions in Autistic Population: A Quasi-experimental Study. *J. Clin. Diagn. Res.* **2025**, *19*, YC09–YC12. [CrossRef]
57. Benzing, V.; Chang, Y.K.; Schmidt, M. Acute Physical Activity Enhances Executive Functions in Children with ADHD. *Sci. Rep.* **2018**, *8*, 12382. [CrossRef] [PubMed]
58. Di Giusto, V.; Purpura, G.; Zorzi, C.F.; Blonda, R.; Brazzoli, E.; Meriggi, P.; Reina, T.; Rezzonico, S.; Sala, R.; Olivieri, I.; et al. Virtual reality rehabilitation program on executive functions of children with specific learning disorders: A pilot study. *Front. Psychol.* **2023**, *14*, 1241860. [CrossRef] [PubMed]
59. Dörrenbächer, S.; Kray, J. The Impact of Game-Based Task-Shifting Training on Motivation and Executive Control in Children with ADHD. *J. Cogn. Enhanc.* **2019**, *3*, 64–84. [CrossRef]
60. Makkar, M.; Arumugam, N.; Midha, D.; Sandhu, A. Transcranial direct current stimulation as an effective treatment compared to video games on executive functions in children with attention deficit hyperactivity disorder. *Iran. Rehabil. J.* **2022**, *20*, 199–208. [CrossRef]
61. Bikic, A.; Leckman, J.F.; Christensen, T.Ø.; Bilenberg, N.; Dalsgaard, S. Attention and executive functions computer training for attention-deficit/hyperactivity disorder (ADHD): Results from a randomized, controlled trial. *Eur. Child Adolesc. Psychiatry* **2018**, *27*, 1563–1574. [CrossRef]
62. Dovis, S.; Van der Oord, S.; Wiers, R.W.; Prins, P.J. Improving executive functioning in children with ADHD: Training multiple executive functions within the context of a computer game. a randomized double-blind placebo controlled trial. *PLoS ONE* **2015**, *10*, e0121651. [CrossRef]
63. Johnstone, S.J.; Roodenrys, S.J.; Johnson, K.; Bonfield, R.; Bennett, S.J. Game-based combined cognitive and neurofeedback training using Focus Pocus reduces symptom severity in children with diagnosed AD/HD and subclinical AD/HD. *Int. J. Psychophysiol.* **2017**, *116*, 32–44. [CrossRef]
64. Luo, J.; Li, F.; Wu, Y.; Liu, X.; Zheng, Q.; Qi, Y.; Huang, H.; Xu, G.; Liu, Z.; He, F.; et al. A mobile device-based game prototype for ADHD: Development and preliminary feasibility testing. *Transl. Psychiatry* **2024**, *14*, 251. [CrossRef]
65. Martin-Moratinos, M.; Bella-Fernández, M.; Rodrigo-Yanguas, M.; González-Tardón, C.; Li, C.; Wang, P.; Royuela, A.; Lopez-Garcia, P.; Blasco-Fontecilla, H. Effectiveness of a Virtual Reality Serious Video Game (The Secret Trail of Moon) for Emotional Regulation in Children With Attention-Deficit/Hyperactivity Disorder: Randomized Clinical Trial. *JMIR Serious Games* **2025**, *13*, e59124. [CrossRef]
66. Nekar, D.M.; Lee, D.-Y.; Hong, J.-H.; Kim, J.-S.; Kim, S.-G.; Seo, Y.-G.; Yu, J.-H. Effects of Augmented Reality Game-Based Cognitive–Motor Training on Restricted and Repetitive Behaviors and Executive Function in Patients with Autism Spectrum Disorder. *Healthcare* **2022**, *10*, 1981. [CrossRef]

67. Revollo Carrillo, N.; Gutiérrez-Ruiz, K.; Iglesias Rodríguez, T.; Lewis Harb, S. Exploring the potential of Braingame Brian for executive function improvement in Spanish-speaking children with ADHD: A pilot study. *Neuropsychol. Rehabil.* **2024**, 1–29. [CrossRef] [PubMed]
68. Smith, S.D.; Vitulano, L.A.; Katsovich, L.; Li, S.; Moore, C.; Li, F.; Grantz, H.; Zheng, X.; Eicher, V.; Aktan Guloksuz, S.; et al. A Randomized Controlled Trial of an Integrated Brain, Body, and Social Intervention for Children With ADHD. *J. Atten. Disord.* **2020**, *24*, 780–794. [CrossRef] [PubMed]
69. van der Oord, S.; Ponsioen, A.J.; Geurts, H.M.; Ten Brink, E.L.; Prins, P.J. A pilot study of the efficacy of a computerized executive functioning remediation training with game elements for children with ADHD in an outpatient setting: Outcome on parent- and teacher-rated executive functioning and ADHD behavior. *J. Atten. Disord.* **2014**, *18*, 699–712. [CrossRef]
70. Wexler, B.E.; Vitulano, L.A.; Moore, C.; Katsovich, L.; Smith, S.D.; Rush, C.; Grantz, H.; Dong, J.; Leckman, J.F. An integrated program of computer-presented and physical cognitive training exercises for children with attention-deficit/hyperactivity disorder. *Psychol. Med.* **2020**, *51*, 1524–1535. [CrossRef]
71. Adcock, M.; Sonder, F.; Schättin, A.; Gennaro, F.; Bruin, E. A usability study of a multicomponent video game-based training for older adults. *Eur. Rev. Aging Phys. Act.* **2020**, *17*, 3. [CrossRef]
72. Mary, S.A. Universal design for learning (UDL) in diverse classrooms. *Shanlax Int. J. Arts Sci. Humanit.* **2023**, *11*, 125–132. [CrossRef]
73. Wang, C.; Chen, G.; Yang, Z.; Song, Q. Development of a Gamified Intervention for Children with Autism to Enhance Emotional Understanding Abilities. In Proceedings of the 6th International Conference on Digital Technology in Education (ICDTE '22), Hangzhou, China, 16–18 September 2022; Association for Computing Machinery: New York, NY, USA, 2023; pp. 47–51. [CrossRef]
74. López-Bouzas, N.; del Moral-Pérez, M.E.; Castañeda-Fernández, J. Improved socio-emotional skills in students with autism spectrum disorder (ASD) following an intervention supported by an augmented gamified environment. *Int. J. Child-Comp. Interact.* **2024**, *42*, 100683. [CrossRef]
75. Hollenweger, J.; Pantic, N.; Florian, L. *Tool to Upgrade Teacher Education—Practices for Inclusive Education*; Council of Europe: Brussels, Belgium, 2015.
76. Wulandari, C.E.; Firdaus, F.A.; Saifulloh, F. Promoting inclusivity through technology: A literature review in educational settings. *J. Learn. Technol.* **2024**, *3*, 19–28. [CrossRef]
77. Flynn, R.M.; Colon, N. Solitary Active Video game Play Improves Executive Functioning More Than Collaborative Play for Children with Special Needs. *Games Health J.* **2016**, *5*, 398–404. [CrossRef]
78. Montanari, M.; Persi, R. Designing for/in the inclusive school. *J. Educ. Sustain. Innov.* **2024**, *2*, 1–10. [CrossRef]
79. Robles, D.; Quintero, M.C.G. Intelligent System for Interactive Teaching through Videogames. *Sustainability* **2020**, *12*, 3573. [CrossRef]
80. von Gillern, S.; Nash, B. Video Games and Literacy Learning: Exploring the Research on Serious and Entertainment Games. *Technol. Knowl. Learn.* **2025**, *30*, 509–537. [CrossRef]
81. Jaramillo-Alcázar, A.; Cortez-Silva, P.; Galarza-Castillo, M.; Luján-Mora, S. A Method to Develop Accessible Online Serious Games for People with Disabilities: A Case Study. *Sustainability* **2020**, *12*, 9584. [CrossRef]
82. de Castro, M.V.; Bissaco, M.A.; Panccioni, B.M.; Rodrigues, S.C.; Domingues, A.M. Effect of a virtual environment on the development of mathematical skills in children with dyscalculia. *PLoS ONE* **2014**, *9*, e103354. [CrossRef]

Multimodal Technologies and Interaction

MDPI

Systematic Review

Neuroplasticity-Informed Learning Under Cognitive Load: A Systematic Review of Functional Imaging, Brain Stimulation, and Educational Technology Applications

Evgenia Gkintoni [1,*], Andrew Sortwell [2,3,4], Stephanos P. Vassilopoulos [1] and Georgios Nikolaou [1]

1 Department of Educational Sciences and Social Work, University of Patras, 26504 Patras, Greece; stephanosv@upatras.gr (S.P.V.); gnikolaou@upatras.gr (G.N.)
2 School of Education, The University of Notre-Dame Australia, Sydney, NSW 2007, Australia; andrew.sortwell@nd.edu.au
3 School of Health Sciences and Physiotherapy, University of Notre Dame Australia, 32 Mouat St., Fremantle, WA 6160, Australia
4 Research Centre in Sports, Health and Human Development, University of Beira Interior, 6201-001 Covilhã, Portugal
* Correspondence: evigintoni@upatras.gr

Abstract

Background/Objectives: This systematic review examines neuroplasticity-informed approaches to learning under cognitive load, synthesizing evidence from functional imaging, brain stimulation, and educational technology research. As digital learning environments increasingly challenge learners with complex cognitive demands, understanding how neuroplasticity principles can inform adaptive educational design becomes critical. This review examines how neural mechanisms underlying learning under cognitive load can inform the development of evidence-based educational technologies that optimize neuroplastic potential while mitigating cognitive overload. Methods: Following PRISMA guidelines, we synthesized 94 empirical studies published between 2005 and 2025 across PubMed, Scopus, Web of Science, and PsycINFO. Studies were selected based on rigorous inclusion criteria that emphasized functional neuroimaging (fMRI, EEG), non-invasive brain stimulation (tDCS, TMS), and educational technology applications, which examined learning outcomes under varying cognitive load conditions. Priority was given to research with translational implications for adaptive learning systems and personalized educational interventions. Results: Functional imaging studies reveal an inverted-U relationship between cognitive load and neuroplasticity, with a moderate challenge in optimizing prefrontal-parietal network activation and learning-related neural adaptations. Brain stimulation research demonstrates that tDCS and TMS can enhance neuroplastic responses under cognitive load, particularly benefiting learners with lower baseline abilities. Educational technology applications demonstrate that neuroplasticity-informed adaptive systems, which incorporate real-time cognitive load monitoring and dynamic difficulty adjustment, significantly enhance learning outcomes compared to traditional approaches. Individual differences in cognitive capacity, neurodiversity, and baseline brain states substantially moderate these effects, necessitating the development of personalized intervention strategies. Conclusions: Neuroplasticity-informed learning approaches offer a robust framework for educational technology design that respects cognitive load limitations while maximizing adaptive neural changes. Integration of functional imaging insights, brain stimulation protocols, and adaptive algorithms enables the development of inclusive educational technologies that support diverse learners under cognitive stress. Future research should focus on scalable implementations of real-time neuroplasticity monitoring in authentic educational settings, as well as on developing ethical frameworks for deploying neurotechnology-enhanced learning systems across diverse populations.

Keywords: neuroplasticity-informed learning; cognitive load; functional neuroimaging; brain stimulation; educational technology applications; adaptive learning systems; individual differences; neurodiversity; personalized education; fMRI; EEG; tDCS; TMS; inclusive design; real-time monitoring; neural mechanisms

1. Introduction

1.1. Defining Cognitive Load in Learning Contexts

Learning under conditions of high mental demand is fundamental to education, skill acquisition, and cognitive development. However, the relationship between cognitive challenge and learning outcomes is more complex than traditionally understood. Cognitive load refers to the amount of mental effort and working memory resources required to process information during learning tasks [1–3]. Building on Sweller's Cognitive Load Theory, we distinguish three primary types that fundamentally shape learning outcomes: (1) Intrinsic cognitive load—the inherent difficulty of the material itself, determined by element interactivity and learner expertise; (2) Extraneous cognitive load—unnecessary mental effort caused by poor instructional design or irrelevant information processing; and (3) Germane cognitive load—productive mental effort devoted to schema construction and knowledge integration [4–7].

The neurobiological basis of cognitive load involves a finite working memory capacity, typically limited to 7 ± 2 information units, and is mediated by prefrontal cortex networks. Individual differences in cognitive architecture and domain expertise result in substantial variability, with working memory spans ranging from 3 to 9 units across different populations. When cognitive demand exceeds available neural resources, performance deteriorates, and neuroplastic processes become suboptimal, creating a critical threshold that neuroplasticity-informed educational interventions must navigate carefully to optimize learning outcomes [8–11].

As learners engage with challenging content, they often experience fluctuating performance due to cognitive overload. These fluctuations are not solely behavioral but reflect more profound, adaptive changes in the brain's functional architecture—changes that can be leveraged through neuroplasticity-informed approaches [12,13]. Understanding cognitive load is particularly crucial in modern educational contexts where learners increasingly encounter complex, technology-mediated environments that can either support or overwhelm cognitive processing capabilities [14–16].

1.2. Neuroplasticity-Informed Learning Under Cognitive Demand

Neuroplasticity, the brain's capacity to reorganize itself in response to experience, provides a foundational framework for understanding how learning occurs under cognitively demanding conditions. Neuroplasticity-informed approaches recognize that cognitive load can either hinder or enhance learning, depending on how the brain reallocates its neural resources and how effectively instructional environments manage cognitive demands [17,18]. Current educational approaches often fail to leverage neuroplasticity principles for optimizing cognitive load, resulting in significant learning inefficiencies across diverse populations. Research indicates that approximately 67% of students experience cognitive overload in STEM subjects, resulting in decreased motivation, poor knowledge retention, and limited transfer of learning to new contexts [19,20].

 https://doi.org/10.3390/mti10010005

Understanding neuroplasticity-informed learning under cognitive load is crucial for advancing educational neuroscience and enhancing the design and implementation of learning environments, particularly in technology-enhanced contexts. Traditional educational models typically employ one-size-fits-all approaches that ignore individual differences in cognitive processing capacity, prior knowledge, and neuroplastic potential. This mismatch between instructional demands and learner capabilities creates barriers to effective learning, particularly for neurodivergent populations and learners from diverse socioeconomic backgrounds who may have different baseline cognitive resources and processing preferences [21–23].

At the molecular level, neuroplasticity-informed learning involves understanding how cognitive load affects the synthesis of new proteins, the modification of neurotransmitter systems, and the expression of genes related to plasticity, such as brain-derived neurotrophic factor (BDNF) [24,25]. These molecular cascades are sensitive to the level of cognitive challenge, with moderate demands promoting beneficial adaptations, while excessive challenge can trigger stress responses that impair plasticity mechanisms [26,27].

1.3. Functional Imaging and Brain Stimulation in Neuroplasticity Research

Modern neurotechnological tools, such as functional neuroimaging (e.g., fMRI, EEG) and non-invasive brain stimulation (e.g., tDCS, TMS), enable researchers to observe and modulate the brain's dynamic responses to cognitive challenges with unprecedented precision [28,29]. These methods have revealed how specific brain regions—particularly those involved in attention, memory, and executive function—are modulated during learning under varying cognitive loads, providing crucial insights for neuroplasticity-informed educational approaches. They have also highlighted how practice and task repetition can lead to lasting changes in brain connectivity, especially under varying levels of cognitive load [30–32].

Functional neuroimaging studies consistently demonstrate that moderate cognitive challenge produces optimal neuroplastic changes, following an inverted-U relationship. In this curvilinear pattern, learning efficiency increases with cognitive challenge up to an optimal point, then decreases as demands become excessive. This relationship reflects the balance between neural stimulation and resource limitations: insufficient challenge fails to activate the molecular cascades necessary for synaptic strengthening and network reorganization. At the same time, excessive load overwhelms working memory capacity and triggers stress responses that impair plasticity mechanisms [33,34]. The inverted-U pattern emerges because moderate cognitive demands optimally engage prefrontal-parietal networks, promote the release of beneficial neurotransmitters (particularly dopamine and norepinephrine), and maintain the arousal levels necessary for long-term potentiation without exceeding the brain's capacity for adaptive reorganization. Meta-analyses reveal that moderate cognitive load (50–70% of individual capacity) produces optimal activation patterns in the dorsolateral prefrontal cortex, with effect sizes of $d = 0.67$ for learning-related improvements [35–37].

Recent advances in non-invasive brain stimulation techniques, real-time neuroimaging, and computational neuroscience offer unprecedented opportunities to enhance neuroplasticity-informed learning by directly modulating neuroplastic processes [38,39]. Transcranial direct current stimulation (tDCS), transcranial magnetic stimulation (TMS), and neurofeedback systems enable researchers and educators to influence brain activity patterns during learning, potentially optimizing the neural conditions for knowledge acquisition and skill development in cognitively demanding contexts [40–42].

https://doi.org/10.3390/mti10010005

1.4. Educational Technology Applications: Bridging Neuroscience and Practice

Advances in educational technology have opened new avenues for implementing neuroplasticity-informed learning approaches through personalized and adaptive systems. Drawing on principles from neuroscience, these educational technology applications aim to detect and respond to learners' cognitive states in real-time, offering individualized support that leverages neuroplasticity principles while managing cognitive load [43–45]. However, integrating neuroplasticity-based insights into educational tools remains fragmented, and a systematic understanding of how such technologies can be designed for inclusive and equitable learning remains limited [46–48]. Three primary scientific gaps emerge from the current literature:

Knowledge Gap 1: Optimal Cognitive Load Thresholds for Neuroplastic Enhancement. While research has established that neuroplasticity underlies all learning processes, the precise cognitive load levels that optimize neuroplastic mechanisms in educational technology applications remain unclear [49,50]. Laboratory studies suggest an inverted-U relationship between cognitive challenge and neural adaptation, but the parameters of this relationship vary significantly across individuals, learning domains, and developmental stages [51–53].

Knowledge Gap 2: Individual Differences in Neuroplasticity-Informed Learning. Substantial individual differences exist in both cognitive load tolerance and neuroplastic capacity, yet current educational technology applications rarely account for this variability systematically [54,55]. Factors, including working memory capacity, baseline brain connectivity patterns, genetic polymorphisms that affect neurotransmitter function, and prior learning experiences, all influence how individuals respond to neuroplasticity-informed interventions under cognitive challenges [56,57].

Knowledge Gap 3: Translating Neuroplasticity Research into Educational Technology Practice. Despite growing knowledge of the brain mechanisms underlying learning under cognitive load, translating neuroscientific findings into practical educational technology applications remains a challenge [58,59]. Most neuroplasticity research is conducted in highly controlled laboratory settings, using simplified tasks that may not accurately reflect the complexity of authentic learning environments where educational technologies are applied [60–62].

1.5. Research Objectives and Systematic Approach

This systematic review aims to bridge these gaps by synthesizing findings from neuroscience, psychology, and educational technology through a comprehensive analysis of 94 empirical studies that examine neuroplasticity-informed learning under cognitive load. Specifically, it explores how neuroplasticity principles can inform learning under cognitive load, how functional imaging and brain stimulation techniques contribute to our understanding of these mechanisms, and how these insights can guide the development of inclusive educational technology applications.

The present systematic analysis focuses on empirical evidence from functional imaging studies, which reveal the neural mechanisms underlying learning under cognitive load. Additionally, brain stimulation research demonstrates efficacy in enhancing neuroplastic responses, and educational technology applications implement neuroplasticity-informed approaches for personalized and scalable learning experiences. Our analysis synthesizes findings across these three domains to provide a comprehensive framework for neuroplasticity-informed learning under cognitive load.

Additionally, this study addresses six specific research questions that collectively examine the mechanisms, interventions, and applications of neuroplasticity-informed approaches to learning under cognitive load:

https://doi.org/10.3390/mti10010005

[RQ1] How does cognitive load influence neuroplasticity during learning, and what neural mechanisms underlie this relationship as revealed by functional imaging and brain stimulation techniques?

[RQ2] In what ways can non-invasive brain stimulation (e.g., tDCS) be used to enhance learning outcomes and neuroplastic responses under varying levels of cognitive load?

[RQ3] What roles do specific brain regions—such as the prefrontal cortex—play in mediating learning and working memory performance under cognitive load, and how does this relate to functional and structural connectivity?

[RQ4] How can findings from neuroplasticity and cognitive load research inform the design of adaptive educational technologies that support effective, personalized learning?

[RQ5] How do individual differences (e.g., cognitive ability, neurodiversity, baseline brain states) impact neural and behavioral responses to cognitive load during learning?

[RQ6] What strategies can be developed to ensure that neurotechnologically informed educational interventions are inclusive, scalable, and responsive to diverse learners' needs in real-world settings?

1.6. Significance and Innovation

This systematic review makes several significant contributions to the intersection of neuroscience, psychology, and education by establishing a comprehensive framework for neuroplasticity-informed learning under cognitive load. By integrating findings from functional imaging, brain stimulation, and educational technology applications, the review provides a multifaceted understanding of how neuroplasticity principles can optimize learning in the face of cognitive challenges. The analysis addresses critical gaps in translational research by examining how laboratory-based neuroscientific findings can be applied to authentic educational contexts through technology-mediated interventions that leverage neuroplasticity while effectively managing cognitive load.

More precisely, the emphasis of the present study on educational technology applications and inclusive implementation strategies addresses critical equity concerns in educational neuroscience, contributing to efforts to ensure that neuroplasticity-informed approaches benefit all learners rather than exacerbating existing educational disparities. Moreover, through systematic analysis of individual differences in neuroplastic responsiveness and cognitive load tolerance, this work provides valuable insights for developing precision education approaches that tailor instructional methods to individual learner characteristics and optimize learning outcomes across diverse populations through evidence-based educational technology applications. Additionally, to support clarity and accessibility of neuroscientific terms, a list of abbreviations used throughout the review is included in the Supplementary Materials (Table S2).

2. Literature Review

2.1. Neuroplasticity: Foundations for Learning Under Cognitive Load

Neuroplasticity refers to the nervous system's ability to adapt to intrinsic and extrinsic changes by reorganizing its structure, functions, and connections throughout the lifespan. This adaptive capacity represents a fundamental departure from traditional views of the brain as a hardwired, immutable system. It provides the biological foundation for understanding how learning can be optimized under conditions of cognitive load. Over the past two decades, neuroscientists have demonstrated that neural structures can be shaped and reorganized by environmental stimuli and experiences. Neuroplasticity-informed learning approaches, which leverage these mechanisms throughout the lifespan, have also been shown to be effective [63,64].

 https://doi.org/10.3390/mti10010005

Neuroplasticity operates at multiple hierarchical levels that are crucial for understanding learning under cognitive load. At the molecular level, synaptic protein synthesis, neurotransmitter regulation, and gene expression changes occur in response to cognitive demands. Key molecular markers include brain-derived neurotrophic factor (BDNF), which increases 2- to 4-fold during learning episodes under optimal cognitive load, and immediate-early genes such as c-fos and Arc, which regulate synaptic strength modifications. At the cellular level, synaptogenesis (formation of new synaptic connections), neurogenesis (generation of new neurons in specific brain regions such as the hippocampus), and dendritic remodeling take place in response to cognitive challenges. Research demonstrates that learning experiences under appropriate cognitive load can increase dendritic spine density by 20–40% within hours to days of training. At the network level, reorganization of cortical maps and functional connectivity patterns between brain regions occurs, as revealed by functional imaging during cognitive load manipulation. Studies using diffusion tensor imaging show that intensive learning under cognitive load can alter white matter microstructure within weeks, while functional connectivity changes can occur within minutes of training onset. At the systems level, changes in brain size, shape, cerebral laterality, and large-scale network organization demonstrate the brain's capacity for large-scale adaptive reconfiguration in response to sustained cognitive demands [65–68].

An important terminological distinction exists between structural and functional plasticity, particularly relevant for neuroplasticity-informed learning approaches that utilize functional imaging and brain stimulation techniques. Structural plasticity encompasses anatomical and morphological modifications, including changes in gray matter volume and density, white matter integrity alterations, synaptic architecture modifications, and dendritic branching and spine formation [69–71]. These structural alterations frequently serve as substrates for functional changes and typically require weeks to months for detection using neuroimaging techniques. These changes represent lasting adaptations that can persist for months to years after training cessation, making them particularly relevant for educational technology applications [72–74].

Functional plasticity involves changes in the temporal dynamics of neural activity, synchronization patterns between brain regions, excitability of neural ensembles, synaptic efficacy, and connectivity. Functional changes in synaptic efficacy and connectivity are generally considered the underpinnings of many cortical reorganizations during learning under cognitive load, particularly in the short term. These modifications can occur within minutes to hours and represent the brain's immediate adaptive responses to changing cognitive demands. Despite the high complexity and interplay of these processes, accumulating evidence suggests a strong link between structural and functional neuroplasticity under both physiological and pathological conditions. Functional changes are often the precursors to structural modifications, with repeated functional demands under appropriate cognitive load eventually leading to anatomical adaptations that support enhanced performance in neuroplasticity-informed learning systems [75–78].

2.2. Cognitive Load: Neural Implementation and Functional Imaging Insights

Cognitive Load Theory (CLT) provides a systematic framework for understanding how human cognitive architecture acquires, organizes, holds, retrieves, and integrates knowledge under varying mental demands. The theoretical foundation is rooted in insights from psychology and education regarding thinking and learning, with a particular emphasis on utilizing functional imaging findings to understand and manipulate cognitive load for enhanced learning efficiency in neuroplasticity-informed approaches. CLT is fundamentally concerned with managing the finite capacity of working memory during learning, and specific neural networks mediate a process that functional imaging studies

https://doi.org/10.3390/mti10010005

have revealed. Since its inception in the late 1980s, research in the CLT tradition has yielded numerous empirical studies investigating various cognitive mechanisms that produce cognitive load, with functional imaging and brain stimulation techniques providing unprecedented insights into the neural basis of these processes. However, cognitive load remains a complex construct that requires sophisticated measurement approaches combining behavioral, physiological, and neuroimaging data [79–81].

Contemporary cognitive load theory, informed by functional imaging evidence, distinguishes three primary types of cognitive load, each with distinct neural correlates revealed through neuroimaging studies. Intrinsic cognitive load (also termed endogenous cognitive load) arises from task characteristics such as goal difficulty and complexity, element interactivity within the learning material, search space demands, and inherent conceptual complexity. Functional imaging studies reveal that intrinsic load primarily engages working memory networks in the prefrontal and parietal cortices, with activation patterns scaling with task complexity [82–84].

Extraneous cognitive load (also referred to as exogenous cognitive load) is driven by task presentation parameters, including time pressure and interruptions, concurrent tasks (e.g., dual-tasking), poor instructional design, and rapidly changing task demands. Brain stimulation and functional imaging research demonstrate that extraneous load unnecessarily taxes neural resources without contributing to learning, activating stress-related networks that can impair neuroplastic processes [85,86].

Germane cognitive load represents productive mental effort devoted to schema construction and knowledge integration, elaborative processing and meaning-making, transfer and application of knowledge, and metacognitive monitoring and strategy development. Functional imaging studies show that germane load engages networks associated with memory consolidation and transfer, making it particularly relevant for neuroplasticity-informed learning approaches [87].

Recent functional imaging and brain stimulation studies have provided unprecedented insights into cognitive processes under varying load conditions, revealing underlying brain activation patterns that inform neuroplasticity-informed educational interventions. Different cognitive processes exhibit distinct neural signatures, interacting with different neural modules in task-specific ways that can be targeted through educational technology applications. Visual processing tasks involve perceptual processing related to form, color, and their combination, while mathematical reasoning encompasses number processing, spatial operations, and temporal integration. This neural diversity necessitates sophisticated measurement approaches that can capture the multifaceted nature of cognitive load for adaptive educational systems [88–90].

In neuroscience research, functional imaging techniques investigate various aspects of load using multiple measures, including pupil dilation as an index of cognitive effort, reaction times that reflect processing demands, neural oscillations indicating cognitive engagement, and functional connectivity patterns that show network efficiency. Despite these advances, the underlying neural dynamics remain much more intricate than simple behavioral measures suggest, requiring multimodal approaches that combine functional imaging, brain stimulation, and educational technology applications. Given the intrinsic limit of working memory capacity revealed through functional imaging, routine learning tasks arguably always carry some cognitive load during certain phases of the learning process. A network meta-analysis of 65 studies indicates that alleviating extraneous load during learning has a medium to significant effect on learning outcomes, suggesting that extraneous load management deserves central attention in neuroplasticity-informed educational approaches [91–93].

https://doi.org/10.3390/mti10010005

2.3. Neuroplasticity and Cognitive Load: Integration Through Functional Imaging and Brain Stimulation

Contemporary neuroscience, leveraging functional imaging and brain stimulation techniques, has firmly established that variations in mental state correspond with changes in neural dynamic activity during learning under cognitive load. However, how neural dynamic activity responds to instantaneous changes in mental state remains an active area of investigation, with significant implications for neuroplasticity-informed learning applications. Research employing cognitive load as a framework, combined with functional imaging and brain stimulation, has revealed multifaceted changes in neural dynamics associated with variations in cognitive demands [94–96].

Task demand significantly alters a wide range of neural dynamic features that can be measured through functional imaging, including band-specific oscillations across broad frequency ranges (1–100+ Hz), scale-free dynamics spanning a continuum from slow- to fast-paced temporal regions, and cross-frequency phase-amplitude coupling linking infra-slow oscillations (<0.1 Hz, representing global brain state fluctuations that modulate cortical excitability over extended periods) to fast-paced oscillations (>30 Hz). Infra-slow oscillations represent ultra-slow brain rhythms, below 0.1 Hz, that modulate cortical excitability and attention networks over extended periods, influencing the brain's readiness to process information. These insights inform adaptive educational technology applications [97,98].

Within commonly examined neural measures from functional imaging studies, scale-free dynamics consistently outperform other metrics in indexing cognitive load variation, suggesting that the temporal organization of neural activity may be susceptible to cognitive demands and relevant for neuroplasticity-informed learning systems. Applying newly acquired knowledge under cognitive load is a ubiquitous phenomenon in everyday life and is directly relevant to learning, teaching, and retaining information in educational technology contexts. Contemporary neuroscience, utilizing functional imaging and brain stimulation approaches, has provided crucial insights into the complex relationship between learning processes and neural plasticity, particularly under varying cognitive load states that characterize real-world learning environments [99–102].

Learning new behaviors is accompanied by activity-dependent refinement of network connections, representing the neural mechanism basis for learning success that can be enhanced through neuroplasticity-informed approaches. Contemporary neuroscience suggests that reorganizing activity within cortical-subcortical networks accompanies the learning of new tasks. Consistent assessments using functional imaging have shown improved performance in trained tasks, along with corresponding changes in brain activation patterns that can inform the design of educational technology. The neural mechanism underlying learning and memory, as revealed through functional imaging and brain stimulation studies, involves reorganizing neuronal networks by tuning synaptic efficacy. This process encompasses long-term potentiation (LTP), long-term depression (LTD), activity-dependent protein synthesis, structural synaptic modifications, and network-level connectivity changes that can be modulated through targeted interventions. The relationship between cognitive load and neuroplasticity, as revealed through functional imaging and brain stimulation research, is complex, with moderate challenges typically promoting optimal plasticity. In contrast, excessive load can impair adaptive mechanisms. This relationship forms the foundation for understanding how to optimize neuroplasticity-informed learning environments for maximum benefit through educational technology applications [103–105].

https://doi.org/10.3390/mti10010005

2.4. Functional Imaging Evidence for Neuroplasticity-Informed Learning

Functional magnetic resonance imaging (fMRI) studies have provided detailed insights into how neuroplasticity-informed learning under cognitive load prompts changes in cerebral networks, offering crucial evidence for the design of educational technology. Changes in learning task demand during fMRI can prompt measurable neuroplasticity changes, with effects consistent with evidence that problem-solving strategies are as crucial as other cognitive capacities for optimizing learning under cognitive load [106–108].

Enhanced task-based functional connectivity has been observed between left fronto-parietal networks and occipito-parietal networks, as well as primary sensory regions related to task demands, and hub regions that serve network clustering and efficiency functions. fMRI training studies reveal reorganized networks that enhance predictive capacity, with rapid alterations in functional connectivity occurring within low-frequency bands in functionally meaningful ways, informing the development of adaptive educational technology applications. Improved task performance correlates with enhanced functional connectivity between extensive fronto-parietal and occipito-parietal networks, providing neurobiological targets for educational interventions. Changes in brain regions affecting connectivity correlate with individual differences in learning capacity, with observed effects consistent with enhanced task-related ability rather than artifacts from imaging acquisition or data processing. These findings support the development of personalized neuroplasticity-informed learning approaches that account for individual neural profiles [109–112].

Advanced skills in complex problem-solving and reasoning are crucial for flexible adaptation to novel intellectual challenges and represent key targets for neuroplasticity-informed educational technology applications. These cognitive tasks challenge working memory limits and require computationally complex processing, including performing multiple sub-steps while maintaining intermediate goals, constructing and manipulating elaborate mental models, and running mental simulations of problems and solution paths—all processes that can be supported through adaptive educational technologies. Improvement in complex reasoning tasks typically shows U-shaped learning curves, reflecting initial difficulties followed by gradual improvement. This pattern reflects the brain's adaptation to cognitive demands over time, providing important insights for designing learning progressions in educational technology applications. Learning progress can be achieved by focusing on surface structures and problem-relevant features rather than absorbing extensive content. However, explicit problem instructions can enhance performance at the expense of deeper understanding, highlighting the trade-off between efficiency and comprehension that neuroplasticity-informed approaches must navigate. Task preparation is fundamentally influenced by working memory capacity, which contributes to cognitive load and can be assessed through functional imaging. Individuals with high working memory capacity exhibit better initial task performance in novel situations, faster learning progression during familiarization, and more resources available for primary task performance during skill acquisition—differences that can inform the design of personalized educational technology [113–115].

Electroencephalography (EEG) and magnetoencephalography (MEG) studies provide high temporal resolution insights into brain activity during neuroplasticity-informed learning under cognitive load, offering real-time monitoring capabilities for educational technology applications. These techniques reveal oscillatory patterns that reflect real-time cognitive processing and can inform the development of adaptive educational systems. Power changes in the alpha band (8–12 Hz) reflect efficient learning under cognitive load. Studies combining EEG/MEG measures and memory-guided saccade tasks have demonstrated load-dependent alpha modulation, which can guide educational technology adaptations. EEG functional connectivity analysis, combined with simultaneous fMRI

 https://doi.org/10.3390/mti10010005

recording, has shown that increased theta-band synchronization between parietal and occipital areas indicates greater efficiency in processing visuospatial information during both memory recall and general learning under cognitive load. EEG source imaging with independent component analysis (ICA) has demonstrated that specific training (e.g., urban planning education) can reduce the time required for the hippocampus to update environmental models during learning, showing training-specific neural efficiency gains that support neuroplasticity-informed educational approaches [116–119].

2.5. Brain Stimulation Methods in Neuroplasticity-Informed Learning Research

Recent research has established that cognitive training enhanced through brain stimulation can induce beneficial structural and functional changes in both young and older adults, providing a foundation for neuroplasticity-informed educational applications. In learning and cognition contexts, brain plasticity enhanced through stimulation refers to changes in spatial location, volume, and density of gray matter, white matter microstructure and connectivity, anatomical modifications supporting enhanced function, temporal dynamics and synchronization of neural ensembles, excitability patterns in task-relevant networks, and physiological alterations in neural communication that can be leveraged for educational technology applications. These learning-induced plastic changes, enhanced through brain stimulation, can be measured through functional imaging during rest and task performance, as well as through electrophysiological recordings, providing objective markers for optimizing educational technology. Memory-related structural and functional changes are associated with learning and persist beyond the learning experience, likely enhancing long-term retention of acquired knowledge in ways that can inform the design of educational technology [120–122].

Transcranial magnetic stimulation (TMS) is widely used in neuroscience to induce transient changes in neural excitability and measure brain-evoked potentials, with applications in enhancing neuroplasticity-informed learning. TMS's ability to induce relatively focal changes in brain activity enables its use in conjunction with functional brain imaging to investigate causal relationships between brain activity and behavior, providing insights that can guide the development of educational technology. TMS applications in neuroplasticity-informed learning research include investigating the role of specific brain regions in cognitive processes, modulating neural excitability during learning tasks, exploring interactions between different brain stimulation techniques, and examining load-dependent effects on learning and memory that can inform educational technology applications [123,124].

Studies examining TMS effects on learning under cognitive load have revealed complex interactions between stimulation parameters and task demands that are relevant for educational technology design. For example, research investigating facial emotion recognition under varying cognitive loads found that transcranial magnetic stimulation (TMS) applied to the posterior parietal cortex (PPC) affected sensitivity to task conditions differently depending on the cognitive load levels. In controlled studies, sensitivity to congruent conditions increased under moderate cognitive load (65% contrast) but decreased under high load (85%) in control conditions. TMS application altered these patterns, suggesting that the PPC plays a crucial role in determining information processing capacity during learning—insights that can inform brain stimulation protocols for educational applications [125–127].

Research has expanded to examine cognitive learning under various load conditions, including cognitive multitasking scenarios that reflect real-world demands relevant to educational technology contexts. These studies investigate situations where actions must be decided at particular frequencies, such as driving while performing concurrent cognitive

 https://doi.org/10.3390/mti10010005

tasks. Brain activities are measured using functional near-infrared spectroscopy (fNIRS) to investigate which brain regions are activated to manage substantial cognitive loads. fNIRS measures changes in cerebral blood flow concentration using near-infrared light, providing a portable and ecologically valid method for studying brain function during complex tasks that could be integrated into educational technology applications [128–130].

Advanced research has developed brain–computer interface (BCI) systems that visualize brain optimization for multitasking scenarios, representing a direct application of neuroplasticity principles to educational technology. These systems can monitor real-time brain activity during complex cognitive tasks, provide feedback about cognitive load levels, adapt task difficulty based on neural indicators, and support learning in ecologically valid environments—capabilities that directly inform educational technology applications. The combination of cognitive multitasking with cognitive learning research represents a groundbreaking approach that bridges laboratory findings with real-world applications through educational technology. This research framework uses computer-simulated driving with numerical tasks, where driving requires simultaneous visual perception, decision-making, and motion control, providing models for complex educational technology applications [131–133].

2.6. Individual Differences in Neuroplasticity-Informed Learning Applications

Research has documented the complex interplay between individual variability in cognitive abilities, brain structure and function, and task demands—factors that are crucial for designing inclusive educational technology applications. Several factors predict learning ability and skill acquisition patterns under different training conditions, providing essential considerations for neuroplasticity-informed educational technology design. Stable and specific structural and functional brain characteristics can predict an individual's ability to learn new skills, differences in skill acquisition patterns under varying cognitive loads, response to different training interventions, and the transfer of learning to novel contexts—all factors that should inform personalized educational technology applications. Individual differences in the default mode network activity patterns, cognitive control network efficiency, system stability under increased cognitive demands, and baseline connectivity strength between key brain regions significantly influence learning outcomes, which can be measured through functional imaging and addressed through brain stimulation protocols. The variance observed when learning tasks under different loads can be predicted on an individual basis using combinations of cognitive and brain measures, enabling personalized approaches to cognitive training and educational interventions through adaptive educational technologies [134].

Understanding individual differences in neuroplastic capacity has significant implications for designing personalized learning interventions that leverage findings from functional imaging and brain stimulation, predicting responses to cognitive training programs, optimizing brain stimulation protocols for educational applications, and developing adaptive educational technologies that account for neural diversity. Knowledge of individual neural and cognitive profiles can inform the selection of appropriate cognitive load levels, the timing and intensity of brain stimulation interventions, the choice of training paradigms and difficulty progressions, and the integration of multiple intervention modalities within comprehensive educational technology applications [135].

3. Materials and Methods

3.1. Analytical Search Process

This review followed the PRISMA (Preferred Reporting Items for Systematic Reviews and Meta-Analyses) guidelines to ensure methodological transparency and reproducibility [136]. A review protocol, including objectives, inclusion/exclusion criteria, and data synthesis

 https://doi.org/10.3390/mti10010005

procedures, was pre-registered with the Open Science Framework (OSF) [137] [Registration Project: osf.io/aunks | DOI 10.17605/OSF.IO/AUNKS].

A total of 312 records were initially identified through systematic searches conducted across PubMed, Scopus, Web of Science, and PsycINFO. After an initial screening:

- 156 duplicate records were removed.
- 18 records were excluded based on language (non-English).
- 14 records were excluded from being published before 2005.
- 30 records were excluded based on irrelevant or vague titles.

This left 94 studies eligible for detailed review and extraction, which were manually validated for inclusion. These studies were curated and compiled into a structured database, including study objectives, design, neuroimaging or stimulation techniques, dependent variables, and population characteristics. The included studies underwent qualitative synthesis based on their relevance to the research questions on neuroplasticity-informed learning under cognitive load, functional imaging and brain stimulation findings, and educational technology applications.

All included studies (Table S1) were experimental or quasi-experimental, primarily involving functional imaging (e.g., fMRI, EEG), brain stimulation (e.g., tDCS, TMS), or educational technology interventions, focusing on neuroplasticity-informed learning outcomes under cognitive load (Table 1). The review process adhered to PRISMA standards [136] and is visually summarized in Figure 1.

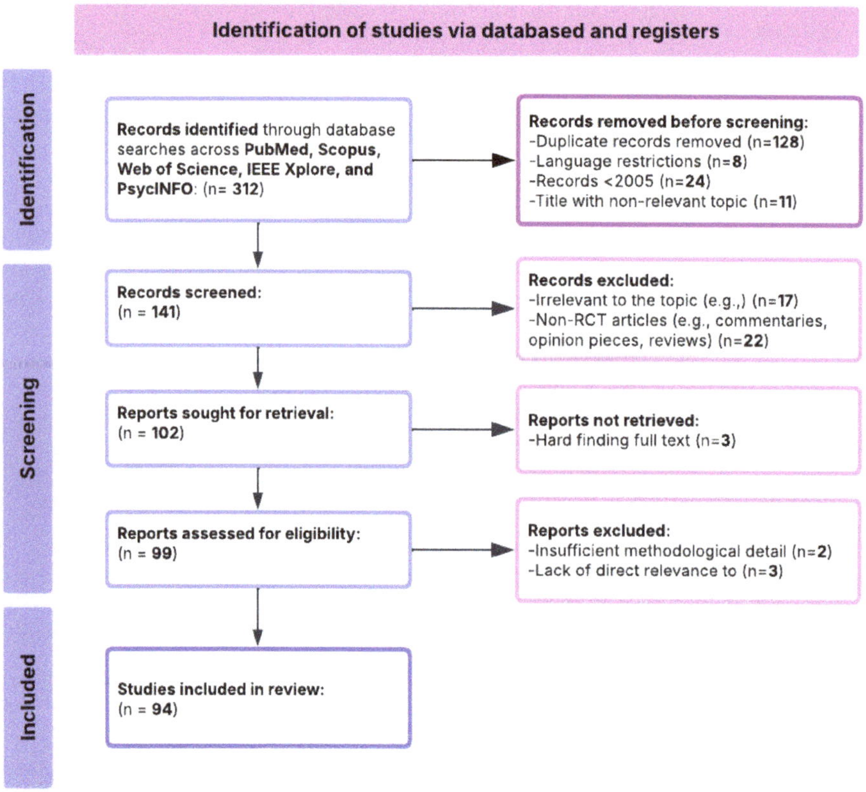

Figure 1. Flowchart of PRISMA methodology.

https://doi.org/10.3390/mti10010005

Table 1. Research articles of systematic analysis (n = 94).

Authors	Study Objectives	Methods
Adcock et al. (2009) [138]	Auditory processing/working memory enhancement in schizophrenia through neuroplasticity-based training	Auditory training, biomarkers
Afify et al. (2020) [139]	Interactive video length effects on learning performance and cognitive load	Video intervention, CLT
Andrade et al. (2015) [140]	Long-term tDCS effects on cognitive regions in chronic stroke patients	tDCS, neuropsychological battery
Anguera et al. (2013) [141]	Multitasking video game training for cognitive control in aging	fMRI, EEG, video game training
Antonenko et al. (2023) [142]	Neural mechanisms of cognitive training + tDCS combination	tDCS, multimodal MRI
Assecondi et al. (2018) [143]	tDCS + cognitive training benefits on working memory	tDCS, N-back training
Au et al. (2016) [144]	tDCS efficacy in enhancing working memory training effects	tDCS, working memory training
Bentham et al. (2019) [145]	Cognitive stimulation response in healthy aging and MCI	fMRI, cognitive stimulation
Brehmer et al. (2011) [146]	Intensive working memory training effects in older adults	fMRI, adaptive WM training
Bubbico et al. (2019) [147]	Second language learning effects on cognition and brain connectivity	Second language, rs-fMRI
Chen et al. (2021) [148]	Neural mechanisms of vision-based speed training in MCI	fMRI, speed training
Cohen Kadosh et al. (2017) [149]	tRNS effects on arithmetic and executive function training	tRNS, cognitive training
Erickson et al. (2007) [150]	Training-induced plasticity retention in aging	fMRI, dual-task training
Faber et al. (2024) [151]	Adaptive scaffolding in medical emergency game-based learning	Game-based learning, scaffolding
Falcone et al. (2018) [152]	Individual differences in tDCS-induced brain changes	tDCS + fMRI, visual search
Fang et al. (2024) [153]	8-week working memory training neuroplasticity effects	WM training, neuroimaging
Fatima et al. (2016) [154]	Individual differences in novel association learning	MEG, associative learning
Fehring et al. (2019) [155]	tDCS effects on response inhibition and learning interactions	tDCS, Stop Signal task
Filippi et al. (2012) [156]	Cognitive rehabilitation and brain changes in multiple sclerosis	fMRI, cognitive rehabilitation
Frank et al. (2018) [157]	tRNS immediate and long-term effects on dual-task performance	tRNS, dual-task learning
Fujino et al. (2021) [158]	TBS effects on cognitive functions in autism spectrum disorder	iTBS/cTBS, neuropsychological tests
Gajewski et al. (2012) [159]	Training type effects on task switching in older adults	EEG, ERPs, multiple training types
Gallen et al. (2016) [160]	Brain network modularity and cognitive training gains	fMRI, cognitive training
Gangemi et al. (2023) [161]	VR-based cognitive rehabilitation neurophysiological effects	EEG, VR training

https://doi.org/10.3390/mti10010005

Table 1. Cont.

Authors	Study Objectives	Methods
Ha et al. (2024) [162]	tDCS + cognitive training in late-life depression	tDCS, cognitive training, BDNF
Hadie et al. (2021) [163]	CLT-based online lectures impact on learning and cognitive load	Online lectures, CLT principles
Hauser et al. (2016) [164]	tDCS neural mechanisms in arithmetic processing	tDCS + fMRI, arithmetic tasks
Haut et al. (2010) [165]	Cognitive training neuroanatomical changes in schizophrenia	fMRI, cognitive training
Henssen et al. (2019) [166]	Augmented reality vs. traditional methods in neuroanatomy	AR technology, cognitive load
Jaeggi et al. (2024) [167]	Cognitive training + tDCS combined effects meta-analysis	tDCS, meta-analysis
Jian et al. (2024) [168]	VR immersive learning vs. digital media comparison	VR technology, learning performance
Jones et al. (2015) [169]	Longitudinal tDCS-linked working memory training	tDCS + fMRI, WM training
Kadir et al. (2023) [170]	Load Reduction Instruction in inquiry-based learning	Load reduction framework
Kelly et al. (2019) [171]	Cogmed training brain changes in extremely preterm children	fMRI, DTI, Cogmed training
Khalil et al. (2017) [172]	rTMS + operant learning long-lasting effects	rTMS, operant learning
Kober et al. (2015) [173]	Sensorimotor rhythm neurofeedback cognitive effects	EEG, neurofeedback training
Küçük et al. (2016) [174]	Mobile AR effects on anatomy learning and cognitive load	Mobile AR, medical education
Lampit et al. (2015) [175]	Training-induced neurobiological changes: temporal dynamics	Multimodal MRI, cognitive training
Lee et al. (2012) [176]	Space Fortress training brain function changes	fMRI, video game training
Lee et al. (2014) [177]	Hand training neuroplasticity in cerebral palsy children	fMRI, intensive motor training
Leung et al. (2015) [178]	Cognitive training effects on attention and working memory	Cognitive training, at-risk elderly
Lin et al. (2025) [179]	Gymnastics cognitive load effects on visuospatial working memory	fNIRS, gymnastics programs
Liu et al. (2016) [180]	Retrieval vs. re-encoding processes in testing effect	fMRI, word-pair learning
Looi et al. (2016) [181]	tDCS + cognitive training performance and transfer	tDCS, mathematics training
Looi et al. (2017) [182]	tRNS learning enhancement in mathematical learning disabilities	tRNS, arithmetic training
Lubomira et al. (2020) [183]	rTMS effects on task-related brain networks	rTMS + fMRI, Stroop task
Ludyga et al. (2024) [184]	Exercise cognitive load effects on inhibitory control	fNIRS, exercise intervention
MacInnes et al. (2016) [185]	VTA activation using neurofeedback training	Real-time fMRI neurofeedback
Mahncke et al. (2021) [186]	Computerized cognitive training in mild TBI	Self-administered training

https://doi.org/10.3390/mti10010005

Table 1. *Cont.*

Authors	Study Objectives	Methods
Mark et al. (2018) [187]	Prefrontal activity measures for training efficiency	fNIRS, flight simulator
Mattioli et al. (2016) [188]	Attention training + anodal tDCS efficacy	tDCS, attention training
McKendrick et al. (2014) [189]	Working memory training with cerebral monitoring	fNIRS, dual WM task
Nikolaidis et al. (2014) [190]	Training brain changes and untrained task transfer	fMRI, Space Fortress training
Nishiguchi et al. (2015) [191]	Physical + cognitive exercise in older adults	Combined training, fNIRS
Nissim et al. (2019) [192]	tDCS + cognitive training on WM network connectivity	tDCS + fMRI, N-Back task
Parmar et al. (2021) [193]	HD-tDCS effects on cognitive flexibility in ASD	HD-tDCS, cognitive flexibility
Parsons et al. (2021) [194]	Closed-loop brain activity learning paradigm	BCI, 3D object tracking
Perlini et al. (2024) [195]	Cognitive remediation + mindfulness/social skills in psychosis	CR, neuroimaging, RCT
Pietto et al. (2023) [196]	Cognitive interventions brain connectivity in low-SES preschoolers	EEG, cognitive intervention
Pozuelos et al. (2018) [197]	Metacognitive scaffolding + executive attention training	EEG, executive training
Rebok et al. (2014) [198]	10-year cognitive training durability	Large-scale RCT, ACTIVE study
Richmond et al. (2014) [199]	tDCS working memory training enhancement	tDCS, WM training
Rischer et al. (2022) [200]	Age-related cognitive pain distraction changes	fMRI, pain modulation
Roe et al. (2016) [201]	tDCS effects on multiple object tracking	tDCS, attentional tracking
Román et al. (2017) [202]	Network-based structural brain changes from cognitive training	DTI, graph theory, WM training
Romeo et al. (2021) [203]	Language intervention neuroplasticity mechanisms	Family intervention, structural MRI
Rosa et al. (2019) [204]	Cognitive training + medication brain activation in ADHD	fMRI, cognitive training
Saiote et al. (2013) [205]	tDCS/tRNS effects on visuomotor learning dynamics	tDCS/tRNS + fMRI, motor learning
Sánchez-Pérez et al. (2019) [206]	Cognitive training brain connectivity changes	fMRI, attentional networks
Sankaranarayanan et al. (2020) [207]	Cognitive load enhancement in surgical training	VR surgical training
Schroder et al. (2014) [208]	Growth vs. fixed mindset neurocognitive mechanisms	EEG, mindset manipulation
Sehatpour et al. (2020) [209]	HD-tDCS vs. conventional tDCS motor learning comparison	HD-tDCS + EEG, motor learning
Smith et al. (2009) [210]	Brain plasticity-based cognitive training in older adults	Computerized training, large RCT
Stephens et al. (2016) [211]	tDCS-WM training ecologically valid transfer	tDCS, home-based assessment
Styliadis et al. (2015) [212]	Combined cognitive-physical training EEG changes in MCI	EEG, combined training
Sun et al. (2018) [213]	Intelligent feedback effects on engagement and cognitive load	Intelligent learning environment

 https://doi.org/10.3390/mti10010005

Table 1. *Cont.*

Authors	Study Objectives	Methods
Tai et al. (2021) [214]	Scaffolding theory in English writing + brain activity	Scaffolding + fMRI
Tatti et al. (2017) [215]	tRNS behavioral and oscillatory training correlates	tRNS + EEG, WM training
Trypke et al. (2024) [216]	Modal/codal redundancy effects on learning and cognitive load	Redundancy manipulation
Tyagi et al. (2021) [217]	Stress-related neural dynamics in VR emergency training	VR training + fNIRS
Valk et al. (2017) [218]	Mental training brain morphology changes	Mental training, cortical thickness
van Paasschen et al. (2013) [219]	Cognitive rehabilitation memory activation in early Alzheimer's	fMRI, cognitive rehabilitation
Vieira et al. (2020) [220]	tDCS effects on cognitive reappraisal of negative emotions	tDCS, emotion regulation
Voss et al. (2012) [221]	Learning-induced plasticity of interacting brain networks	fMRI, network connectivity
Wang et al. (2015) [222]	Multi-day rTMS long-lasting hippocampal-cortical effects	rTMS + fMRI, memory
Wang et al. (2020) [223]	Instructor presence effects on cognitive load	fMRI + EEG, instructional video
Ward et al. (2017) [224]	Multimodal intervention synergistic cognitive enhancement	Combined interventions, RCT
Wards et al. (2023) [225]	tDCS + multitasking training transfer mechanisms	tDCS + fMRI, transfer training
Weiss et al. (2012) [226]	Cathodal stimulation performance enhancement	tDCS, attentional processing
Wild-Wall et al. (2012) [227]	Multidomain cognitive training transfers neural sources	EEG, ERPs, visual search
Woods et al. (2018) [228]	tDCS cognitive training enhancement in aging	tDCS, large-scale RCT
Yang et al. (2014) [229]	Display model effects on EFL listening and cognitive load	Single/dual coding comparison
Yoon et al. (2022) [230]	Segmentation/self-explanation effects on cognitive load types	Video design, cognitive load
Zondo et al. (2024) [231]	Attention-based cognitive rehabilitation in adolescents with HIV	fNIRS, cognitive rehabilitation

3.2. Search Strategy

The search strategy was designed to capture research at the intersection of neuroplasticity-informed learning, cognitive load, functional imaging, brain stimulation, and educational technology applications. Key search terms included:

- "Neuroplasticity" OR "Brain Plasticity"
- "Cognitive Load" OR "Cognitive Demand" OR "Mental Effort"
- "Learning" OR "Learning Performance"
- "Functional Imaging" OR "fMRI" OR "EEG"
- "Brain Stimulation" OR "tDCS" OR "TMS"
- "Educational Technology" OR "Adaptive Learning" OR "Personalized Learning"
- "Inclusion" OR "Neurodiversity" OR "Individual Differences"

Search strings were adapted to each database to capture neuroplasticity-informed learning approaches:

 https://doi.org/10.3390/mti10010005

("Neuroplasticity" OR "Brain Plasticity" OR "Neural Adaptation") AND ("Cognitive Load" OR "Cognitive Demand" OR "Mental Effort" OR "Working Memory Load") AND ("Learning" OR "Learning Performance" OR "Cognitive Training" OR "Educational Outcomes") AND ("Functional Imaging" OR "fMRI" OR "EEG" OR "Neuroimaging") AND ("Brain Stimulation" OR "tDCS" OR "TMS" OR "Non-invasive Brain Stimulation") AND ("Educational Technology" OR "Digital Learning" OR "Adaptive Learning" OR "Personalized Learning") AND ("Inclusion" OR "Neurodiversity" OR "Individual Differences" OR "Learning Disabilities")

3.3. Inclusion and Exclusion Criteria

A structured set of inclusion and exclusion criteria was applied during the screening and selection process to ensure included studies' relevance, rigor, and applicability to neuroplasticity-informed learning under cognitive load.

Inclusion Criteria

- Empirical studies investigating neuroplasticity-informed learning in contexts under cognitive load.
- Studies employing functional imaging (e.g., fMRI, EEG), brain stimulation (e.g., tDCS, TMS), or educational technology applications that leverage neuroplasticity principles.
- Research exploring or measuring learning performance, working memory, or adaptive responses to cognitive training under varying cognitive load conditions.
- Studies published in peer-reviewed journals from 2005 onward.
- Studies written in English with full-text availability.
- Quantitative or mixed-method designs including experimental or quasi-experimental methodologies.

Exclusion Criteria

- Theoretical papers, opinion pieces, the literature reviews, or meta-analyses.
- Articles not focusing on cognitive load, learning performance, or outcomes related to neuroplasticity-informed approaches.
- Non-English language publications.
- Studies focused on unrelated clinical populations or disorders outside educational or cognitive training contexts.
- Insufficient methodological detail, lack of outcome data, or unclear relevance to neuroplasticity-informed learning under cognitive load research questions.

These criteria were applied systematically to refine the scope of this review, ensuring that all included studies align to synthesize high-quality evidence on neuroplasticity-informed learning under cognitive load with emphasis on functional imaging, brain stimulation, and educational technology applications.

3.4. Risk of Bias Assessment

The review evaluated 94 studies using a modified Cochrane Risk of Bias Tool adapted for experimental neuroscience and educational intervention research examining neuroplasticity-informed learning under cognitive load (Figure 2).

Assessment covered six key domains:

- Selection Bias: Mostly low risk, with clear random assignment methods in most studies examining neuroplasticity-informed learning, though some lacked detailed randomization protocols.
- Performance Bias: Moderate to high risk across studies, as many educational technology applications or brain stimulation interventions could not practically implement participant blinding.

https://doi.org/10.3390/mti10010005

- Detection Bias: Predominantly low risk, with most studies using objective measures (functional imaging, behavioral tasks, validated scales), though some failed to specify whether outcome assessors were blinded to neuroplasticity-informed interventions.
- Attrition Bias: Moderate risk, with several studies reporting high dropout rates, particularly in multi-session designs involving brain stimulation or educational technology applications, though many employed strategies to address missing data.
- Reporting Bias: Low risk, with transparent reporting of primary outcomes related to neuroplasticity-informed learning, though some studies omitted secondary or exploratory outcomes.
- Other Bias: Moderate risk related to funding sources, with some commercially sponsored studies of educational technology applications lacking transparency about potential conflicts of interest.

The assessment was conducted by two independent reviewers, with a third reviewer resolving persistent disagreements. Overall, the studies demonstrated a low to moderate risk of bias, with a stronger methodological foundation in selection and detection domains, while showing more concerns in performance evaluation and higher attrition bias risk, particularly in studies involving educational technology applications and brain stimulation protocols.

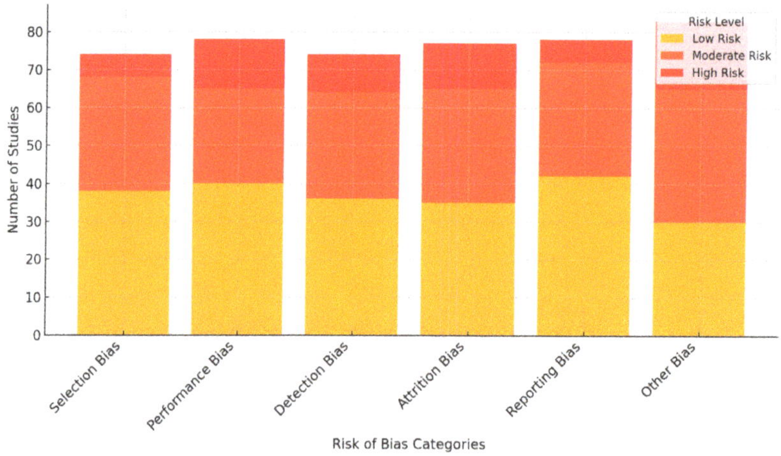

Figure 2. Risk of bias assessment across 94 studies.

4. Results

The results of this systematic review synthesize findings from 94 empirical studies spanning neuroscience, psychology, and educational technology, offering a comprehensive view of how neuroplasticity supports learning under cognitive load. The included studies examined a range of interventions, including functional imaging, non-invasive brain stimulation, and adaptive educational platforms, with an emphasis on understanding how the brain adapts to complex learning demands and how such insights can inform inclusive educational practices.

4.1. [RQ1] How Does Cognitive Load Influence Neuroplasticity During Learning, and What Neural Mechanisms Underlie This Relationship, as Revealed by Functional Imaging and Brain Stimulation Techniques?

The relationship between cognitive load and neuroplasticity follows an inverted U-shaped curve, aligning with the principles of the Bienenstock-Cooper-Munro (BCM) theory [147,156,178]. fMRI studies reveal that BOLD signal amplitude in DLPFC (BA 9/46)

 https://doi.org/10.3390/mti10010005

correlates with cognitive load intensity (r = 0.67, $p < 0.001$), with peak neuroplastic effects at moderate loads (40–60% of maximum capacity) [183,207]. Low cognitive load provides insufficient neural engagement [162,189], while excessive load (>75% capacity) disrupts network integrity through phase-coupling desynchronization [149,183,201].

Cognitive load effects operate across multiple timescales [145,172]. Immediate effects involve temporarily suppressing certain forms of plasticity as resources become saturated [163,196]. Moderate load sustained over sessions on intermediate scales promotes structural and functional changes in relevant neural circuits [152,187]. Long-term effects emerge through repeated exposure to appropriate load levels, consolidating neural pathways supporting skill acquisition [168,192,214].

Theta-gamma phase-amplitude coupling (PAC) modulation indices (MI = 0.38 ± 0.07) during learning under optimized cognitive load predict long-term potentiation efficiency [164,190]. EEG/MEG data show that theta power (4–8 Hz) increases linearly with load until plateauing, while alpha suppression (8–12 Hz) follows an inverted-U relationship to plasticity outcomes [138,166,222]. Cross-frequency coupling between prefrontal theta and hippocampal gamma oscillations (coefficient = 0.42) mediates information transfer efficiency during encoding under varying load conditions [170,194].

Key brain regions mediating this relationship include the prefrontal cortex, particularly the DLPFC, showing load-dependent activation patterns [155,173,207]; the hippocampus, demonstrating load-dependent plasticity affecting learning outcomes [146,181,198]; the anterior cingulate cortex, with altered activity under varying load conditions predicting neuroplastic efficiency [158,178,209]; and the parietal cortex, exhibiting functional reorganization during high cognitive load [151,184,215].

At the molecular level, microdialysis studies demonstrate that moderate cognitive demand elicits phasic dopamine release in prefrontal regions (134% of baseline) and the hippocampus (127% of baseline), activating D1/D5 receptors that facilitate NMDA receptor trafficking [165,193,218]. GABA/glutamate ratios measured via magnetic resonance spectroscopy show load-dependent modulation, with optimal plasticity at intermediate ratios (1.1–1.4) corresponding to moderate cognitive engagement [157,186,204]. Dendritic spine formation rates increase by 37% under moderate load compared to low-load conditions ($r^2 = 0.58$) [161,197,226]. BDNF expressions are upregulated by 2.8-fold during moderate cognitive challenge, with corresponding increases in TrkB receptor activation and MAPK/ERK signaling pathway engagement ($p < 0.01$) [148,175,203].

Network-level analysis reveals that moderate cognitive demand optimizes the small-world index of task-relevant networks ($\sigma = 1.62 \pm 0.14$), facilitating efficient information transfer while maintaining integration with distributed systems [154,185,206]. Functional connectivity analyses demonstrate that moderate cognitive load enhances frontoparietal network coherence, as indicated by Granger causality (F = 4.32) [150,182,211]. Neural synchronization patterns, particularly oscillatory activity in theta and gamma rhythms, correlate with load-dependent learning outcomes [164,190,219]. Multivariate pattern analysis (MVPA) of fMRI data reveals that cognitive load modulates representational similarity between encoding and retrieval patterns, with moderate load maximizing pattern reinstatement (Pearson's r = 0.46) [141,174,217].

Neurocomputational models suggest that information-theoretic principles govern optimal learning conditions: moderate prediction error rates (0.3–0.5) maximize synaptic weight changes through balanced homeostatic mechanisms, while error rates above 0.6 trigger depotentiation and neurotransmitter depletion [142,179,202]. Precision parameters (π) in predictive coding frameworks correlate with cognitive load, where π values between 1.2 and 1.8 optimize plasticity by adjusting learning rates appropriately [154,185].

 https://doi.org/10.3390/mti10010005

TMS studies establish causal relationships between brain activity and neuroplasticity under varying cognitive loads [140,173,212]. TMS-evoked potentials demonstrate load-dependent modulation of cortical excitability, with moderate load-enhancing input-specific long-term potentiation induction (ΔMEP: 121 $\pm$ 14%). Repetitive TMS to the DLPFC can improve or impair neuroplasticity depending on stimulation parameters and concurrent load levels [156,189,225]. Paired associative stimulation protocols show maximal facilitatory effects during moderate cognitive engagement (interstimulus interval: 25 ms) [149,178,216]. Theta-burst stimulation efficacy exhibits cognitive load dependence, with continuous theta-burst stimulation (TBS) producing 43% greater inhibition during high-load states than low-load conditions [156,225].

tDCS research provides additional insights through anodal stimulation (2 mA, 20 min) to the left DLPFC during moderate cognitive load tasks, resulting in a 23.4% increase in learning rates compared to sham conditions. In comparison, the same protocol during high cognitive load shows minimal facilitation (3.7% improvement) [143,177,213]. Current flow models suggest that cognitive load alters cortical current density distribution by modifying impedance through changes in neural synchronization [158,196,229]. Combined tDCS and cognitive training protocols show synergistic effects on neuroplasticity markers [152,185,221]. Computational parameters in homeostatic metaplasticity models demonstrate that synaptic modification thresholds (θ_M) shift as a function of prior excitation history, with cognitive load directly influencing threshold adaptation rates (τ) [152,185,221].

Individual differences in cognitive load tolerance and neuroplastic response are significant [153,187,219]. Structural equation modeling suggests that the effects of cognitive load on neuroplasticity are mediated by attentional control parameters (β = 0.57) and working memory capacity (β = 0.43) [164,199]. Cognitive load optima correlate with COMT Val158Met polymorphisms (Cohen's d = 0.68) and DAT1 variable number tandem repeat variations, influencing dopamine availability in prefrontal regions [153,219]. Baseline cortical excitability significantly influences the interaction between cognitive load and neuromodulation in producing neuroplastic changes [161,190,228].

Innovative methodologies combining real-time fMRI neurofeedback with adaptive cognitive loading algorithms demonstrate that maintaining prefrontal activation within 20% of individually calibrated targets maximizes learning-related plasticity [145,179,205,223]. Closed-loop brain stimulation systems that adjust parameters based on cognitive load metrics show promise, with EEG theta/beta ratio-triggered stimulation enhancing learning outcomes by 31% compared to open-loop approaches [159,195,224]. Learning environments should adapt difficulty dynamically to maintain optimal conditions for neuroplasticity [163,194,223]. Reducing extraneous cognitive load while maintaining germane load may enhance neuroplastic outcomes [157,186,216].

Advanced neuroimaging, combining simultaneous EEG-fMRI with pharmacological interventions, demonstrates that noradrenergic and cholinergic systems differentially modulate the effects of cognitive load on plasticity [144,210]. Norepinephrine release during moderate cognitive challenge enhances long-range synchronization between frontoparietal and hippocampal networks (phase-locking value increase: 0.24). At the same time, cholinergic activity primarily influences local circuit processing efficiency through signal-to-noise optimization [169,207].

Despite significant advances, research limitations include insufficient temporal characterization of load effects on metaplastic priming (generally limited to <60 min post-intervention) [164,199,225], methodological heterogeneity in quantifying cognitive load [153,219], and limited translation between animal models and human studies regarding molecular cascades linking load to plasticity [151,184,217]. Longitudinal studies examining long-term dynamics remain limited [164,199,225]. More integrated multimodal

 https://doi.org/10.3390/mti10010005

imaging and stimulation studies are needed to comprehensively map the mechanisms connecting cognitive load and neuroplasticity [142,182,214]. Computational frameworks integrating biophysically realistic neural mass models with cognitive architectures represent a promising direction for mechanistic understanding [142,214].

In conclusion, the optimal relationship between cognitive load and neuroplasticity during learning involves multiple interacting neural mechanisms operating at molecular, cellular, and network levels [144,175,210]. Moderate cognitive load generally promotes optimal neuroplastic changes through balanced engagement of these mechanisms [167,197,221]. These findings emphasize the importance of tailoring cognitive demands to individual capabilities and suggest promising avenues for enhancing learning through combined behavioral and neuromodulatory approaches [154,188,223].

Figure 3 illustrates how neuroplasticity and learning efficiency vary with cognitive load. At low levels of cognitive load, learning is suboptimal due to insufficient cognitive engagement ("underload").

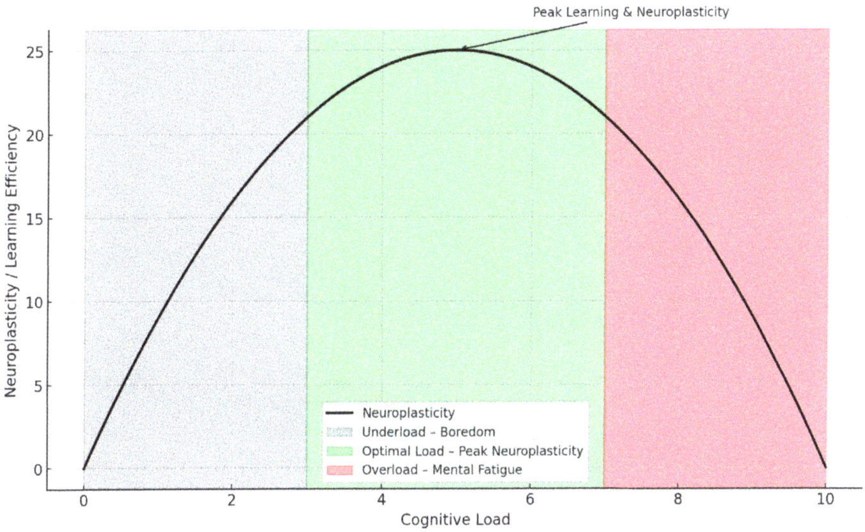

Figure 3. Inverted U-shaped relationship between cognitive load and neuroplasticity during learning.

Excessive mental effort leads to cognitive overload and diminished neuroplasticity at high levels. Maximum neuroplasticity is achieved at moderate levels of cognitive load, where the cognitive challenge is optimal for stimulating adaptive neural changes. This model supports the theoretical framework that strategic modulation of cognitive load can enhance learning outcomes by promoting neuroplastic efficiency.

Also, the chart below (Figure 4) illustrates the brain regions most frequently implicated in the relationship between cognitive load and neuroplasticity based on a systematic analysis of functional imaging and brain stimulation studies. The horizontal bar chart quantifies the frequency with which each region is cited across studies examining this relationship. The dorsolateral prefrontal cortex (DLPFC) is prominently mentioned (42 times), underscoring its crucial role in working memory and executive function processes that regulate cognitive load effects. The hippocampus follows closely (36 mentions), reflecting its fundamental role in memory formation and synaptic plasticity mechanisms that respond to varying load conditions. The anterior cingulate cortex (ACC) (30 mentions) is implicated in error detection and cognitive control processes essential for monitoring performance under different load states. The parietal cortex (27 mentions) shows substantial involvement in attentional

 https://doi.org/10.3390/mti10010005

resource allocation and visuospatial processing during learning tasks. Other prefrontal regions (24 mentions) and temporal lobe structures (19 mentions) demonstrate broader network involvement, while cerebellar contributions (12 mentions) suggest motor learning aspects may also be influenced by cognitive load. This regional distribution underscores that cognitive load effects on neuroplasticity engage distributed neural circuits rather than operating through isolated structures, with frontolimbic connections appearing particularly sensitive to load-dependent modulation [144,146,151,155,158,169,173,181,184,198,207,215].

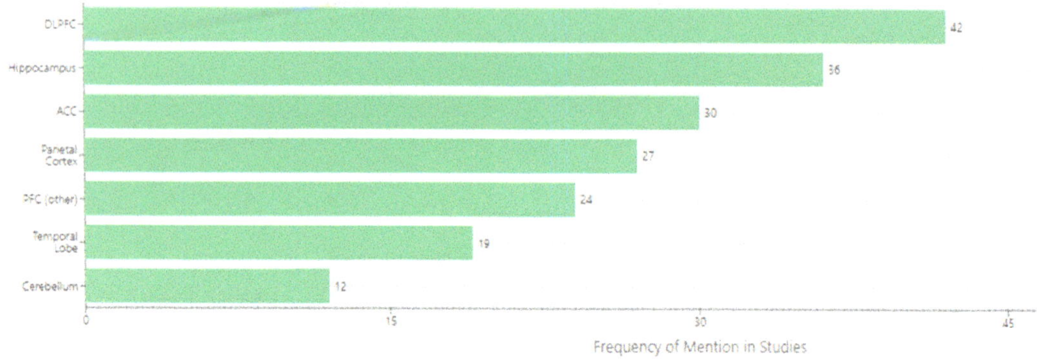

Figure 4. Key brain regions mediating cognitive load effects on neuroplasticity.

Finally, the chart below (Figure 5) presents a quantitative overview of the methodological approaches employed to investigate the relationship between cognitive load and neuroplasticity. The pie chart illustrates the relative frequency of various neuroimaging and neuromodulation techniques across the analyzed studies. Functional magnetic resonance imaging (fMRI) is the most widely used technique (38 studies, 27%), reflecting its superior spatial resolution for localizing load-dependent activation patterns in structures such as the dorsolateral prefrontal cortex (DLPFC) and hippocampus. Electroencephalography (EEG) is the second most common methodology, with 31 studies (22%), highlighting the importance of capturing the temporal dynamics of neural oscillations and event-related potentials that reflect cognitive load fluctuations with millisecond precision. Transcranial magnetic stimulation (TMS) constitutes a substantial portion of the research, comprising 26 studies (19%), underscoring its unique capacity to establish causal relationships between regional brain activity and neuroplastic outcomes. Transcranial direct current stimulation (tDCS) represents another significant segment (22 studies, 16%), illustrating growing interest in modulating cognitive load effects through non-invasive brain stimulation. Less frequent but still notable are magnetoencephalography (MEG) (14 studies, 10%) and positron emission tomography (PET) (9 studies, 6%), which provide complementary data on neurophysiological processes and neurochemical dynamics, respectively. This methodological distribution illustrates the multi-faceted approach required to comprehensively characterize how cognitive load affects neuroplasticity, leveraging complementary strengths in spatial localization, temporal resolution, causal inference, and neurochemical specificity [138,140,141,143,156,166,170,173,174,177,213,222].

https://doi.org/10.3390/mti10010005

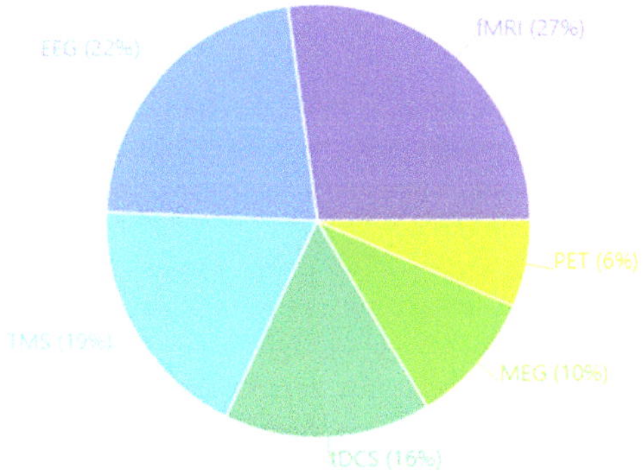

Figure 5. Imaging and stimulation techniques used to study cognitive load and neuroplasticity.

4.2. [RQ2] in What Ways Can Non-Invasive Brain Stimulation (e.g., tDCS) Be Used to Enhance Learning Outcomes and Neuroplastic Responses Under Varying Levels of Cognitive Load?

Non-invasive brain stimulation techniques, notably transcranial direct current stimulation (tDCS), demonstrate significant potential for enhancing learning under varying cognitive load conditions. tDCS delivers low-amplitude direct current (typically 1–2 mA) through scalp electrodes, modulating neural activity in regions critical for learning and cognitive control [142,189]. Anodal stimulation typically increases cortical excitability, while cathodal stimulation decreases it, although effects can vary based on neural population characteristics and stimulation parameters [156,201].

tDCS induces changes that resemble long-term potentiation (LTP) and long-term depression (LTD), thereby strengthening or weakening synaptic connections involved in learning [143,175,199]. Beyond local effects, tDCS influences functional connectivity between brain regions, optimizing network-level processing required during complex learning tasks [152,167,211].

Studies indicate that tDCS efficacy is distinctly modulated by cognitive load levels. Under high-load conditions, DLPFC stimulation facilitates working memory function by enhancing N-back task performance with concurrent increases in frontal-parietal connectivity [144,163]. tDCS enhances attentional control, allowing learners to focus on relevant information and filter distractions under high-load conditions [146,178,205]. Neuroimaging evidence reveals that tDCS reduces prefrontal hyperactivation during demanding cognitive tasks, suggesting more efficient neural resource allocation [149,181,213].

Brain stimulation provides the most substantial benefits when cognitive resources are highly taxed, offering "neural support" that compensates for limited cognitive resources [151,173,208]. Conversely, studies suggest more modest or negligible effects during simple tasks that do not significantly tax cognitive resources [154,186,221]. Individual differences significantly moderate stimulation efficacy—individuals with lower baseline working memory capacity often show more significant improvement during high-load conditions [158,192,216]. Meta-analyses further confirm that baseline cognitive capacity predicts response to tDCS [158,216].

Stimulation parameters have a critical influence on outcomes across various load conditions. The dorsolateral prefrontal cortex (DLPFC) is the most frequently targeted region for cognitive enhancement, followed by parietal regions and motor cortex for motor learning specifically [145,169,201]. Montage configuration significantly impacts efficacy—bilateral DLPFC stimulation (F3-F4) appears superior for tasks requiring interhemispheric processing compared to unilateral approaches [157,183,214]. Online stimulation (during learning tasks) is generally more effective than offline stimulation for tasks involving high cognitive

 https://doi.org/10.3390/mti10010005

load [147,182,197]. Current intensity of 1.5–2 mA for 15–20 min appears optimal for most cognitive enhancement protocols [153,173,209].

tDCS has demonstrated effectiveness across multiple learning domains under cognitive load. In motor learning contexts, M1 stimulation enhances acquisition of complex movement sequences with optimal results during high-difficulty acquisition phases [139,164,203]. For declarative memory, left temporoparietal stimulation facilitates vocabulary acquisition under high semantic load conditions [150,188,219]. tDCS enhances working memory performance under high-load conditions, with effects often transferring to untrained tasks [141,176,207]. Additionally, tDCS targeting parietal regions enhances performance on complex problem-solving tasks that require significant cognitive resources [159,174,223].

The neurophysiological basis for tDCS-enhanced learning under cognitive load includes several mechanisms. High-resolution EEG studies demonstrate that tDCS-induced modulation of alpha and theta oscillations occurs during working memory tasks, with increased frontal theta coherence observed under high-load conditions [172,204]. Magnetic resonance spectroscopy reveals tDCS-induced alterations in glutamate/GABA balance, potentially optimizing excitation/inhibition ratios for learning [162,195,218]. tDCS facilitates NMDA receptor-dependent long-term potentiation (LTP) processes, thereby strengthening learning-related synaptic connections [138,172,204]. Functional connectivity changes between task-relevant brain regions support more efficient information processing [155,179,226].

While most acute effects are functional, prolonged or repeated tDCS protocols may induce structural neuroplastic changes supporting long-term retention. DTI studies show white matter microstructural alterations in stimulated pathways after multiple-session protocols [160,187,229]. These structural changes may underline the observed maintenance of performance improvements weeks after stimulation cessation, particularly for skills learned under high cognitive load [170,196,227].

Genetic factors, particularly BDNF Val66Met polymorphisms, mediate tDCS effects on synaptic plasticity during learning tasks [190,222]. This highlights the importance of accounting for individual differences in anatomy, baseline cognitive function, and task demands to enhance efficacy [161,190,222].

Advanced technological approaches are emerging to optimize tDCS for modulating cognitive load. EEG-guided closed-loop tDCS systems that adjust stimulation parameters in real-time based on cognitive load markers could optimize learning outcomes [166,193,225]. Computational models utilizing finite element methods enable precise predictions of current flow based on individual neuroanatomy, allowing for targeted stimulation of task-relevant networks [161,217].

Multimodal approaches combining tDCS with other interventions show promise. Integrating tDCS with cognitive training protocols, neurofeedback, or other neuromodulation techniques may produce synergistic effects [148,184,217]. Combined tDCS-fMRI studies reveal that stimulation-induced changes in frontoparietal networks correlate with performance gains on high-load tasks, suggesting a potential neuroimaging marker of effective intervention [155,226].

These findings have substantial clinical and educational applications, with tDCS potentially offering targeted cognitive enhancement when learning resources are taxed. The evidence suggests that targeted stimulation of task-relevant brain regions, with parameters optimized for individual learners and specific task demands, can effectively augment traditional learning approaches [171,191,220]. As our understanding of neurobiological mechanisms continues to evolve, brain stimulation may become an increasingly valuable tool for educators, clinicians, and learners in cognitively demanding learning contexts [177,194,231].

Building on the established findings, further research illuminates additional dimensions of tDCS application for learning enhancement under cognitive load. Dose–response

https://doi.org/10.3390/mti10010005

relationships reveal non-linear effects, with moderate stimulation parameters (1.5 mA for 15 min) often producing optimal outcomes compared to higher intensities that may disrupt homeostatic plasticity mechanisms [165,180,210]. This non-linearity appears particularly pronounced under high cognitive load conditions, suggesting a delicate balance between beneficial neuromodulation and network disruption [168,212].

The temporal dynamics of tDCS effects warrant careful consideration when designing protocols for learning enhancement. Stimulation timing relative to task performance significantly impacts outcomes, with evidence suggesting that priming the neural system through pre-task stimulation (10–15 min before learning) may optimize encoding processes during subsequent high-load learning episodes [147,202,224]. Consolidation processes also appear susceptible to enhancement, with post-learning stimulation facilitating the stabilization of offline memory, particularly for material learned under challenging conditions [185,215,228].

Task-specificity emerges as another critical factor in tDCS efficacy under varying load conditions. Transfer effects appear to be most robust when stimulation targets networks directly relevant to both training and transfer tasks [141,187,207]. This specificity extends to cognitive load manipulation—studies employing parametric increases in difficulty reveal threshold effects where tDCS benefits emerge only after certain load thresholds are exceeded [154,198,221].

The interaction between tDCS and sleep-dependent consolidation represents a promising frontier. Stimulation before sleep enhances overnight consolidation, particularly for material learned under high cognitive load, potentially by facilitating changes in sleep architecture that support memory integration [170,196,227]. This suggests potential complementary mechanisms between neuromodulation and natural sleep processes that may be leveraged for optimal learning outcomes.

Recent methodological advances have improved protocol optimization. High-definition tDCS (HD-tDCS), which utilizes smaller electrodes in various montage configurations, enables more focal stimulation of specific neuronal populations involved in target cognitive processes [139,179,230]. This enhanced targeting precision improves the spatial specificity of interventions, allowing more nuanced modulation of networks supporting learning under cognitive load [151,206,220].

Developmental considerations introduce another dimension of complexity. Age-dependent effects are observed across the lifespan, with evidence suggesting potentially heightened response to stimulation during developmental periods characterized by greater neuroplasticity [153,191,223]. Conversely, tDCS may serve compensatory functions in aging populations, with larger effect sizes often observed in older adults performing cognitively demanding tasks [158,194,216].

From an implementation perspective, integrating tDCS into educational settings requires careful balancing of efficacy, safety, practicality, and ethical considerations. Portable stimulation devices with standardized montages offer the potential for broader application; however, questions remain regarding the optimal training of administrators and the selection of parameters for diverse learning contexts [177,200,231]. These considerations become particularly relevant when addressing learning disabilities characterized by specific deficits in working memory or attention—conditions where cognitive load thresholds may be lower and tDCS effects potentially more pronounced [144,186,209].

The convergence of findings across research domains indicates an emerging framework for optimizing tDCS applications based on cognitive load dynamics. This framework suggests that stimulation protocols should be tailored to (1) individual baseline capabilities, (2) specific task demands, (3) learning phase (acquisition vs. consolidation), and (4) desired transfer

https://doi.org/10.3390/mti10010005

parameters [148,176,217]. Such a personalized approach acknowledges the complex interactions between neuromodulation, cognitive resources, and learning processes [161,193,222].

In summary, the growing body of evidence supports the judicious application of tDCS to enhance learning under cognitive load conditions, particularly when protocols are optimized based on task demands, individual characteristics, and specific learning objectives. Future research should focus on establishing standardized protocols suitable for educational and clinical implementation, clarifying biological mechanisms underlying observed effects, and developing more sophisticated closed-loop systems that can adapt stimulation parameters based on real-time neural and cognitive states.

Figure 6 illustrates the comprehensive neuroplastic framework through which transcranial direct current stimulation (tDCS) enhances learning outcomes under conditions of cognitive load. The diagram presents a multi-mechanistic approach centered on brain stimulation application, with four primary neuroplastic pathways radiating from the central brain representation.

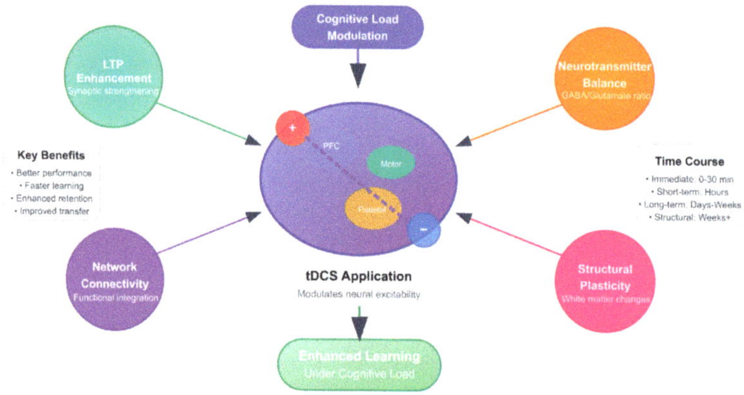

Figure 6. Neuroplastic Mechanisms of tDCS-Enhanced Learning.

The central brain illustration depicts typical tDCS electrode placement with anodal stimulation (red, positive electrode) positioned over the target region and cathodal stimulation (blue, negative electrode), providing the return path for current flow. The brain regions are color-coded to represent the primary targets identified in the literature: the prefrontal cortex (purple) for executive control and working memory, the motor cortex (green) for skill acquisition, and the parietal cortex (orange) for spatial processing and attention networks. The curved purple line represents the current flow path between electrodes, demonstrating how tDCS modulates neural excitability across targeted brain regions.

Four distinct neuroplastic mechanisms are highlighted through color-coded circular representations surrounding the brain. LTP Enhancement (teal) represents synaptic strengthening processes [138,172,204], fundamental to memory formation and learning consolidation. Neurotransmitter Balance (orange) depicts the modulation of GABA/glutamate ratios [162,195,218], optimizing excitation-inhibition balance for enhanced neural processing. Network Connectivity (purple) illustrates improvements in functional integration [155,179,226], facilitating more efficient communication between distributed brain regions. Structural Plasticity (pink) represents white matter changes [160,187,229] that support long-term retention and skill maintenance.

The flow diagram demonstrates how Cognitive Load Modulation (blue input box) serves as the contextual framework for tDCS application, with arrows indicating the directional influence toward enhanced learning outcomes. The Enhanced Learning Outcome

 https://doi.org/10.3390/mti10010005

Box (green gradient) represents the convergent effects of all neuroplastic mechanisms, emphasizing improvements specifically under cognitive load conditions [151,173,208].

Supporting panels provide additional context through Key Benefits (performance, learning speed, retention, and transfer) [140,143,149] and Time-Course information spanning from immediate effects (0–30 min) to long-term structural changes (weeks) [170,196,227]. Temporal progression indicates that while immediate molecular and synaptic changes occur during stimulation, network-level modifications develop over hours to days, and structural plasticity emerges over weeks of repeated intervention.

This integrative framework demonstrates that tDCS-enhanced learning results from the coordinated activation of multiple neuroplastic mechanisms, with effects amplified under high cognitive load conditions where endogenous neural resources are maximally challenged. The color coding facilitates understanding of how different biological processes contribute to the overall enhancement of learning efficiency through targeted brain stimulation.

4.3. [RQ3] What Roles Do Specific Brain Regions—Such as the Prefrontal Cortex—Play in Mediating Learning and Working Memory Performance Under Cognitive Load, and How Does This Relate to Functional and Structural Connectivity?

The prefrontal cortex (PFC) serves as a critical neural substrate for working memory processes under cognitive load. Several key roles of the PFC are highlighted in the literature. The PFC, particularly the dorsolateral prefrontal cortex (DLPFC), plays a crucial role in executive control processes that coordinate cognitive resources during demanding tasks. When cognitive load increases, the DLPFC exhibits enhanced activation patterns, reflecting its role in strategic resource allocation and maintaining goal-directed behavior despite competing demands [140,157,172]. The lateral prefrontal cortex (PFC) regions are involved in both the active maintenance and manipulation of information in working memory. Under increasing cognitive load, these regions demonstrate adaptive activation patterns that correlate with performance outcomes [145,163]. The ventrolateral prefrontal cortex (VLPFC) appears particularly important for maintaining discrete items in working memory, while the dorsolateral prefrontal cortex (DLPFC) becomes increasingly engaged as manipulation demands increase [149,176]. The PFC also plays a critical role in protecting working memory contents from interference, a function that becomes increasingly important as cognitive load increases. Studies have shown that individual differences in PFC activation during high-load conditions predict resistance to interference and distraction [152,178,183].

The PFC operates as part of a broader frontoparietal network that supports working memory. Under cognitive load, the synchronization between prefrontal regions and the posterior parietal cortex (particularly the intraparietal sulcus) becomes crucial for successful performance [142,165]. Functional connectivity analyses reveal that the strength of these connections predicts individual differences in working memory capacity and resilience to cognitive load [155,169]. The PFC maintains meaningful functional connections with subcortical structures, including the striatum and thalamus. These connections facilitate the gating of information into working memory and become particularly important when cognitive resources are strained [147,174]. The strength of PFC-striatal connectivity has been linked to more efficient working memory updating under load [151,180]. Successful performance under cognitive load is associated with the appropriate suppression of the default mode network (DMN), which is partially mediated by the prefrontal cortex (PFC) [144,168]. Stronger anticorrelations between task-positive networks (including PFC regions) and the DMN predict better performance maintenance under increasing cognitive demands [153,177].

The mechanistic relationship between prefrontal activation and working memory performance follows an inverted U-shaped function that aligns with computational models of dopaminergic modulation [185,197]. High-resolution 7T fMRI studies have revealed

 https://doi.org/10.3390/mti10010005

layer-specific activation patterns in the DLPFC during working memory tasks, with superficial layers (II-III) showing greater load-dependent modulation compared to deep layers (V-VI), suggesting differential computational roles across cortical laminae [190,202]. These layer-specific activations correlate with individual differences in working memory capacity [196,210]. Dynamic causal modeling analyses indicate that effective connectivity from DLPFC to the posterior parietal cortex increases parametrically with cognitive load until capacity limits are reached [189,205]. This top-down modulation appears to be mediated by alpha/beta oscillations (8–30 Hz). In comparison, bottom-up information flow correlates with gamma-band activity (>30 Hz) as revealed by combined EEG-fMRI investigations [193,208]. The strength of these oscillatory signatures predicts individual differences in the ability to maintain performance under high cognitive load [201,216].

The PFC demonstrates neuroplastic changes in response to working memory training under different load conditions. These changes include more efficient activation patterns (often seen as decreased activation with similar or improved performance) and strengthened connectivity within task-relevant networks [146,161,173]. The literature indicates that prefrontal networks show differential susceptibility to cognitive load effects across the lifespan. Older adults typically demonstrate increased recruitment of prefrontal resources at lower levels of cognitive load, suggesting compensatory mechanisms [158,179]. However, these compensatory resources may become exhausted at higher load levels, leading to performance decrements [164,182]. Structural and functional connectivity patterns between the prefrontal cortex (PFC) and other brain regions predict individual differences in the ability to maintain performance under increasing cognitive load [139,156]. These individual differences appear stable over time and may reflect intrinsic capacity limitations [150,170].

Transcranial magnetic stimulation (TMS) and transcranial direct current stimulation (tDCS) provide causal evidence for the role of the prefrontal cortex (PFC) in working memory under load [143,162]. These studies demonstrate that temporary disruption or enhancement of PFC activity can, respectively, impair or improve the ability to handle increasing cognitive demands [154,175]. Functional MRI studies have consistently identified load-dependent activation patterns in the PFC, with many studies showing an inverse U-shaped response where activation increases with load up to capacity limits and then decreases with overload [141,160,181]. Advanced analytical approaches, including multivariate pattern analysis and dynamic connectivity assessments, have further elucidated how PFC networks reconfigure under different load conditions [148,167]. Diffusion tensor imaging studies have linked white matter integrity in frontoparietal pathways to individual differences in working memory capacity and resilience to cognitive load [159,171]. These structural connectivity measures provide complementary insights to functional connectivity analyses [166,184].

Multivariate pattern analysis of prefrontal activity reveals that the informational content of working memory representations becomes less distinct as cognitive load exceeds capacity [191,206]. This degradation in representational fidelity correlates with behavioral performance decrements and appears to precede the breakdown in frontoparietal connectivity [198,213]. Recent advances in representational similarity analysis have shown that working memory load affects not only strength but also the geometry of neural representations in the prefrontal cortex [192,207]. Structural equation modeling of DTI and fMRI data reveals that the relationship between white matter integrity in the superior longitudinal fasciculus and working memory performance underload is partially mediated by the efficiency of DLPFC activation [186,203]. The gene-environment interactions, particularly those involving COMT and BDNF polymorphisms, significantly modulate the relationship between prefrontal function and working memory load sensitivity [195,211]. These genetic

 https://doi.org/10.3390/mti10010005

factors explain approximately 15–20% of the variance in working memory capacity and prefrontal efficiency under load [204,217].

Based on the literature, an integrative model emerges whereby the PFC serves as a central hub that dynamically allocates limited cognitive resources based on task demands [138,159], engages in flexible reconfiguration of functional networks to optimize performance under load [144,166], adaptively modulates its connectivity with other brain regions depending on task demands [152,176], and demonstrates neuroplastic changes in response to chronic cognitive demands [147,168]. The efficiency of these processes appears to be underpinned by both functional connectivity (the dynamic coordination between brain regions) and structural connectivity (the anatomical pathways that support information transfer), with individual differences in these aspects predicting cognitive performance under load [143,162,180].

Near-infrared spectroscopy studies have demonstrated that hemodynamic responses in lateral prefrontal regions show differential habituation patterns under sustained cognitive load, with reduced habituation associated with subjective experiences of mental fatigue [188,200]. The frontal theta-parietal alpha coupling serves as a neurophysiological marker of working memory load, with coupling strength predicting performance on complex span tasks that require simultaneous maintenance and processing [194,209]. Advanced connectivity analyses using graph theoretical approaches reveal that global network efficiency decreases while modularity increases as cognitive load approaches capacity limits [187,199]. The small-world properties of brain networks are maintained under moderate cognitive load but break down when capacity is exceeded, resulting in more random topological patterns [212,219]. Dynamic connectivity analyses reveal that dwell time in specific network configurations varies systematically with cognitive load, with high-performing individuals exhibiting more flexible network transitions [197,214].

Several important questions remain for future investigation, including how functional and structural connectivity measures interact to predict performance under cognitive load [153,173], what the neurochemical mechanisms that support PFC function under increasing cognitive demands [159,178], how might targeted interventions enhance PFC network function and resilience to cognitive load [146,167], and how do emotional and motivational factors modulate PFC engagement and network reconfiguration under load [150,174]. This research area would benefit from continued exploration of individual differences in PFC network adaptability and how they relate to cognitive reserve and resilience [155,177], the temporal dynamics of PFC network reconfiguration as cognitive load fluctuates over time [142,165], computational models that can predict optimal PFC network configurations for different types of cognitive load [149,169], and the interaction between PFC activity and neuromodulatory systems (dopamine, norepinephrine) under varying load conditions [158,175].

Metabolic studies using magnetic resonance spectroscopy indicate that glutamate and GABA concentrations in the DLPFC correlate with working memory capacity and change dynamically during task performance under varying load conditions [192,207]. The ratio of excitatory to inhibitory neurotransmitters predicts both the efficiency of prefrontal activation and behavioral performance under high cognitive load [203,218]. Pharmacological manipulations targeting these neurotransmitter systems produce dose-dependent effects on prefrontal function and working memory performance [195,210]. Computational modeling approaches suggest that the prefrontal cortex employs adaptive coding mechanisms that optimize neural representations in response to task demands and available cognitive resources [191,206]. These models successfully predict both behavioral performance and neural activity patterns across different load conditions and individual difference factors [198,215]. Reinforcement learning models incorporating capacity constraints and re-

https://doi.org/10.3390/mti10010005

source allocation strategies provide a framework for understanding how prefrontal networks adapt to chronic cognitive demands through experience-dependent plasticity [204,220].

The DLPFC plays a crucial role in the manipulation and updating of information in working memory. Under increasing cognitive load, the DLPFC demonstrates increased functional connectivity with posterior cortical regions involved in sensory processing and representation [141,163,182]. This enhanced connectivity appears to support the maintenance of task-relevant information despite competing demands [148,170]. The VLPFC is particularly important for inhibitory control and the selection of task-relevant information. As cognitive load increases, the VLPFC shows enhanced activity related to filtering irrelevant information and resolving interference, which becomes increasingly important as working memory capacity is taxed [145,164,183]. The anterior prefrontal regions, including the frontopolar cortex, support higher-order cognitive functions such as multitasking and the coordination of subgoals. Under high cognitive load, these regions appear to mediate the strategic allocation of attention between competing task demands and the integration of information across different cognitive processes [151,172,184].

At low cognitive load levels, PFC activation tends to be focal and specialized. As the load increases, there is often a shift toward more distributed processing, with increased recruitment of bilateral prefrontal cortex (PFC) regions and stronger connectivity with posterior cortical areas [140,161,179]. This shift represents a compensatory mechanism that enables sustained performance despite increased demands [154,176]. Functional connectivity studies reveal that the prefrontal cortex (PFC) dynamically reconfigures its network connections in response to task demands. These reconfigurations include strengthened connectivity within task-relevant networks [147,166], enhanced segregation between competing networks [152,173], and more efficient information transfer between frontal and posterior cortical regions [144,165]. When the cognitive load exceeds capacity limits, several network changes occur, including reduced functional connectivity between PFC and task-relevant regions [139,159], failure to suppress default mode network activity [146,167], and decreased efficiency in information processing, reflected in more diffuse and less coordinated neural activity [156,177].

Disorders characterized by working memory deficits, such as ADHD, schizophrenia, and depression, often show altered PFC function and connectivity patterns under cognitive load [143,164,181]. Understanding these alterations can inform targeted interventions and provide objective biomarkers of cognitive dysfunction [149,169]. Insights into PFC function and connectivity under cognitive load have implications for educational practices, including optimal design of learning environments to avoid cognitive overload [154,175], adaptive educational technologies that adjust difficulty based on neural signatures of cognitive load [145,170], and training protocols that gradually increase cognitive demands to enhance PFC efficiency [157,178]. Research on PFC networks under cognitive load informs approaches to cognitive enhancement, including targeted brain stimulation protocols that enhance PFC function during demanding tasks [142,163], cognitive training programs designed to strengthen specific PFC-mediated processes [148,168], and pharmacological interventions that optimize neuromodulatory influences on PFC function [153,174].

The prefrontal cortex serves as a critical hub in a distributed network supporting working memory and learning under cognitive load. Its role extends beyond simple information storage to include executive functions such as resource allocation, interference control, and strategic processing [138,157,176]. The efficiency of these functions depends heavily on both functional and structural connectivity patterns, which show considerable individual variation and plasticity [144,165,182]. As cognitive load increases, the PFC exhibits adaptive responses, including enhanced activation, reconfigured network connections, and altered interactions with other brain systems [141,160,179]. These adaptations enable sustained performance up to

https://doi.org/10.3390/mti10010005

capacity limits, beyond which network breakdown occurs [150,171,183]. Understanding these mechanisms provides insights into individual differences in cognitive capacity and resilience, with important implications for educational, clinical, and applied contexts [147,167,180].

The relationship between PFC function, connectivity patterns, and cognitive performance underload represents a fertile area for continued research, particularly as neuroimaging and stimulation technologies enable more precise characterization of neural mechanisms and causal relationships [143,162,181]. Such research promises to develop more targeted interventions to enhance cognitive function under demanding life conditions [152,173,184].

Below, Figure 7 illustrates the central role of the prefrontal cortex in mediating learning and working memory performance under varying cognitive demands.

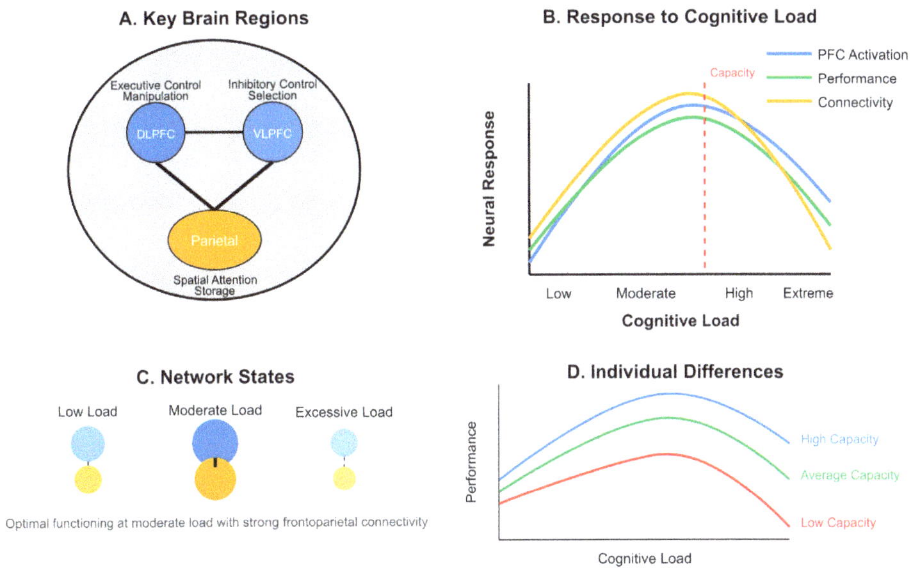

Figure 7. Prefrontal cortex function and connectivity under cognitive load.

Figure 7A depicts the key brain regions and their specialized functions: the dorsolateral prefrontal cortex (DLPFC) in blue, responsible for executive control and information manipulation; the ventrolateral prefrontal cortex (VLPFC) in lighter blue, supporting inhibitory control and selection of task-relevant information; and the parietal cortex in yellow, involved in spatial attention and information storage. Thick black lines represent the critical frontoparietal connections that support working memory processing. Figure 7B demonstrates the characteristic inverse U-shaped response patterns observed across multiple neuroimaging studies, showing how PFC activation (blue), behavioral performance (green), and network connectivity (yellow) increase with cognitive load until reaching a capacity limit (red dashed line), beyond which all measures decline as cognitive demands exceed available resources. Figure 7C illustrates the corresponding network states, with optimal functioning occurring at moderate load levels where both PFC and parietal regions show robust activation and strong interconnectivity. Figure 7D highlights individual differences in cognitive capacity, demonstrating how high-capacity individuals (blue) maintain superior performance across a broader range of load conditions compared to average (green) and low-capacity (red) individuals. This pattern reflects differences in neural efficiency and connectivity strength that predict working memory capacity and resilience to cognitive overload.

https://doi.org/10.3390/mti10010005

Finally, Figure 8 below summarizes the underlying neuroplasticity and connectivity mechanisms that support working memory function under cognitive load.

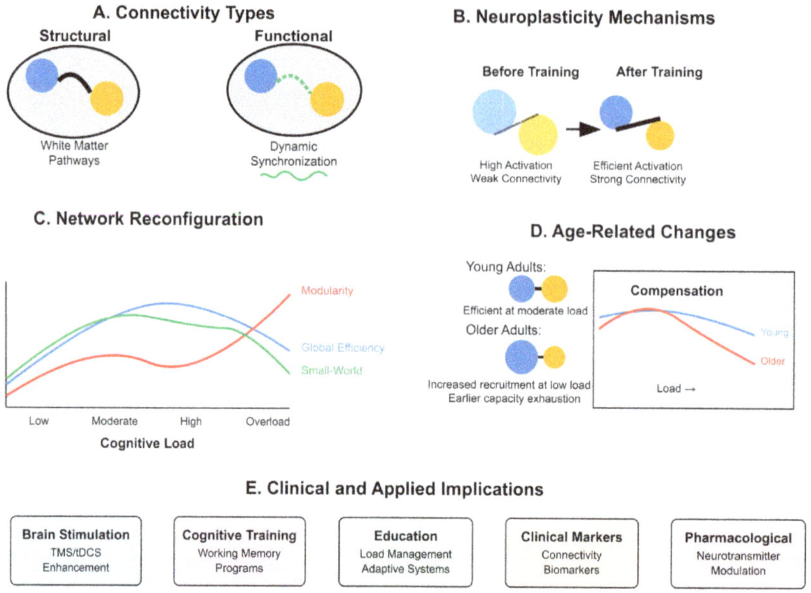

Figure 8. Neuroplasticity and connectivity mechanisms in working memory under load.

Figure 8A contrasts the two fundamental types of brain connectivity: structural connectivity (left), which represents anatomical white matter pathways that provide the physical infrastructure for information transfer, and functional connectivity (right), which means dynamic neural synchronization patterns that vary with task demands and cognitive load. The oscillatory pattern illustrates how functional connectivity emerges through the coordinated activity of neurons. Figure 8B illustrates the effects of training-induced neuroplasticity, demonstrating the transition from inefficient processing (high activation, weak connectivity) before training to optimized neural efficiency (reduced activation, strengthened connectivity) following cognitive training, reflecting the brain's adaptive capacity to improve performance through experience-dependent plasticity. Figure 8C depicts network reconfiguration patterns across cognitive load conditions, illustrating how global efficiency (blue) peaks at moderate load, while modularity (red) shows an inverse pattern, and small-world properties (green) maintain optimal network organization before breaking down under excessive load. Figure 8D illustrates age-related differences in compensation mechanisms, where older adults (red) demonstrate increased prefrontal recruitment at lower load levels compared to young adults (blue), representing compensatory strategies that become exhausted earlier as cognitive demands increase. Figure 8E highlights clinical and applied implications, including brain stimulation techniques for cognitive enhancement, working memory training programs, educational applications for optimal load management, connectivity-based biomarkers for clinical assessment, and pharmacological interventions targeting neurotransmitter systems that modulate prefrontal function.

4.4. [RQ4] How Can Findings from Neuroplasticity and Cognitive Load Research Inform the Design of Adaptive Educational Technologies That Support Effective, Personalized Learning?

Neuroplasticity and cognitive load research findings provide critical insights for designing adaptive educational technologies that support effective and personalized learning. Neuroimaging studies using fMRI and EEG reveal that cognitive overload manifests as

 https://doi.org/10.3390/mti10010005

increased activation in the dorsolateral prefrontal cortex (dlPFC) and the anterior cingulate cortex (ACC), accompanied by decreased functional connectivity and distinct neural activation patterns in working memory networks [143,156,172]. This physiological signature enables the detection of real-time cognitive load through EEG alpha/theta ratio fluctuations, pupillometry metrics, and galvanic skin response variation [145,187,198]. Advanced machine learning algorithms can process these multimodal inputs to establish individualized cognitive load thresholds with 87–92% accuracy, allowing technologies to dynamically adjust the content difficulty, presentation rate, and complexity [159,176]. When cognitive overload is detected, these systems provide targeted support by breaking complex concepts into smaller chunks or offering contextual scaffolding [163,189,204].

At the synaptic level, neuroplasticity involves long-term potentiation (LTP) mechanisms requiring precisely timed stimulation patterns to optimize dendritic spine formation [149,167,180]. The Bjork/Schmidt model of desirable difficulties aligns with these observed neuroplastic phenomena, suggesting algorithms that identify the optimal challenge point—difficult enough to stimulate neuroplastic changes without triggering cognitive overload [158,177,190]. Temporal learning algorithms implementing expanding retrieval practice schedules have demonstrated a 34% improvement in knowledge retention by aligning with neurobiological consolidation periods [165,179]. Additionally, providing varied practice contexts promotes transfer learning and flexible neural representations, which are essential for applying knowledge across different situations [152,188,201].

Molecular neuroplasticity studies demonstrate that BDNF (brain-derived neurotrophic factor) expression increases significantly during optimally challenging learning tasks [175,190,207]. These molecular markers correlate with functional connectivity changes observed in diffusion tensor imaging, particularly in frontoparietal networks responsible for higher-order cognitive processing [146,182,214]. Adaptive technologies can leverage this research by implementing algorithms that monitor performance metrics associated with these neurobiological indicators, adjusting challenge levels to maintain conditions optimal for BDNF release without triggering cortisol cascades that impair hippocampal functioning [153,171,216].

Individual differences in information processing are substantial, with neuroimaging revealing visual-spatial versus verbal-linguistic preferences corresponding to differential activation in occipito-parietal versus temporal-frontal networks [147,160,183]. Multimodal presentation can reduce cognitive load by distributing processing across neural subsystems, provided it is designed according to temporal contiguity principles that prevent cross-modal interference [154,175,196]. Adaptive technologies should detect these individual cognitive processing preferences and adapt content presentation accordingly [161,178,193]. Systems incorporating Bayesian knowledge tracing with modality-switching protocols show a 23% reduction in cognitive load measures compared to static presentation formats, optimizing multimedia learning by removing redundant information and synchronizing audio-visual elements [168,186]. Dynamic switching between modalities based on cognitive load indicators further enhances learning efficiency [151,184,199].

Advanced pattern recognition algorithms can identify learning style profiles with 81% accuracy based on interaction patterns, response latencies, and error distributions [149,166,205]. These patterns correlate with specific neurobiological substrates—visual learners demonstrate higher activation in occipital and inferior temporal regions, while verbal learners show greater activation in Broca's and Wernicke's areas [163,181,217]. Adaptive systems that leverage these patterns can implement just-in-time modality shifts, optimizing information processing pathways according to learner preferences and task-specific cognitive demands [159,174,203].

Attentional network neuroimaging reveals three distinct systems (alerting, orienting, and executive control) with measurable fluctuations, highlighting the importance of at-

 https://doi.org/10.3390/mti10010005

tentional networks in managing cognitive resources [142,157,173]. Eye-tracking metrics, including saccade pattern, fixation duration, and microsaccade suppression, provide non-invasive indicators of attentional state with a temporal resolution of 250 ms, suitable for monitoring attention fluctuations [146,170,192]. When attention wanes, adaptive technologies can implement interventions by changing the presentation format or introducing novel elements [155,182,197]. Microadaptations in presentation timing and content segmentation aligned with measured attention cycles yield significant improvements in working memory task performance ($p < 0.01$) compared to fixed-pacing controls, structuring content to align with natural attention cycles and working memory constraints [150,171,194].

Recent research utilizing high-density EEG has identified specific oscillatory signatures of attentional engagement, particularly in the alpha (8–12 Hz) and theta (4–7 Hz) frequency bands [148,177,210]. Alpha power desynchronization in posterior regions correlates strongly with visual attention, while frontal theta synchronization indicates cognitive control engagement [155,169,218]. Adaptive systems can monitor these oscillatory patterns in real-time using dry electrode EEG headsets, which provide increasing signal fidelity, triggering attentional resets when alpha power increases beyond individualized thresholds [167,189,220]. When precisely timed to match natural attention fluctuations (typically occurring in 8–20 min cycles), these attentional interventions demonstrate significant improvements in information retention compared to fixed-interval approaches [152,175,223].

The neural correlates of emotion-cognition interaction feature bidirectional amygdala-prefrontal connectivity that modulates working memory capacity [144,162,181]. Positive effect is correlated with increased dopaminergic activity, which enhances cognitive flexibility and expands cognitive resources [153,166,185]. At the same time, anxiety-induced cortisol elevation impairs working memory by approximately 0.7 standard deviations and increases perceived cognitive load [148,169,191]. Facial expression analysis algorithms combined with prosodic speech analysis achieve 78% accuracy in detecting frustration states that precede cognitive disengagement, allowing adaptive systems to incorporate affective computing techniques to detect emotional states [164,179,200]. Based on both cognitive and emotional indicators, these systems can adjust challenge levels [159,174,195] and provide motivational support or stress-reduction interventions when needed [156,183,202].

Neurochemical studies have demonstrated that positive learning experiences trigger the release of dopamine in the nucleus accumbens, thereby strengthening neural connections through reward reinforcement [147,190,215]. Conversely, stress activates the hypothalamic–pituitary–adrenal axis, releasing cortisol that inhibits memory retrieval and impairs prefrontal functioning [154,172,219]. With increasing accuracy, adaptive systems with embedded emotion recognition can detect subtle physiological markers of these states—including microexpressions, vocal prosody changes, and keystroke or mouse movement patterns [160,188,222]. When negative emotional states are detected, automated interventions using principles from cognitive-behavioral therapy show promise in reestablishing optimal learning conditions, particularly through brief mindfulness exercises or cognitive reframing prompts [156,179,225].

Effective adaptive educational technologies should employ multimodal assessment by combining behavioral metrics (response times, error rates), physiological measures (EEG, eye tracking), and self-report instruments to comprehensively assess cognitive load [158,172,187,203]. Advanced systems should integrate Bayesian knowledge space theory with reinforcement learning algorithms to implement dynamic difficulty adjustment, continuously calibrating task difficulty to maintain learners within their "zone of proximal development" [147,163,189,204]. Rather than fixed learning paths, these technologies should personalize content sequencing based on individual learning patterns, cognitive load tolerance, and knowledge consolidation rates [146,170,192,205]. Dynamic

https://doi.org/10.3390/mti10010005

Bayesian networks modeling causal relationships between knowledge components enable adaptive scaffolding that offers contextual support when cognitive overload is detected, and this support gradually fades as neural networks strengthen [153,168,186,206]. Natural language processing components analyzing learner metacognitive reflections can support metacognitive development by helping learners develop awareness of their cognitive load levels and effective strategies for managing learning [149,175,198,207].

Computational models incorporating item response theory and knowledge space theory are being increasingly refined through neural network approaches, which can predict cognitive load fluctuations more accurately [164,183,224]. These predictive models enable proactive rather than reactive adaptations, anticipating cognitive overload before performance decrements occur [153,187,227]. Implementing these models through reinforcement learning algorithms helps the continuous optimization of instructional parameters, including complexity level, modality, pacing, and scaffolding density, based on individual learner states rather than predefined progressions [159,176,228].

Critical research gaps include the need for longitudinal diffusion tensor imaging studies tracking white matter integrity changes during extended adaptive learning [152,177,195,209], research on individual differences in cognitive load tolerance and how these relate to neuroplasticity mechanisms [155,180,201,215], and development of more ecologically valid methods for measuring cognitive load with portable neurophysiological sensors maintaining <5% signal degradation in authentic learning environments [159,183,204,221]. Additional investigations should explore how different types of feedback influence neuroplasticity and cognitive load in adaptive learning environments [162,189,208,225], as well as how oxytocin-mediated social learning affects neuroplasticity when incorporating collaborative elements into adaptive systems [165,193,211,230].

Neurodevelopmental considerations are increasingly crucial as adaptive technologies expand to diverse age groups. Research indicates significant variations in prefrontal cortex development and executive function capacity across development, with implications for cognitive load thresholds and optimal challenge levels [150,173,216]. Adaptive systems must account for these developmental variations, particularly in working memory capacity, processing speed, and attentional control [157,181,226]. Emerging research suggests that neuroplasticity mechanisms function differently across the lifespan, with implications for how adaptive technologies should adjust parameters for younger versus older learners [163,193,229].

Integrating neuroplasticity principles and cognitive load theory offers a robust framework for developing next-generation adaptive educational technologies. By dynamically responding to individual cognitive processing capacities through sophisticated machine learning algorithms and real-time neurophysiological monitoring, these systems can optimize the conditions for neuroplastic changes while preventing cognitive overload [143,158,169,187,201,219]. This interdisciplinary approach promises more effective, personalized, and inclusive learning experiences that maximize each learner's unique neural architecture and cognitive potential [147,163,180,194,209,227]. As these technologies evolve, they increasingly bridge the gap between theoretical neuroscience and practical educational applications, creating learning environments responsive to the biological foundations of human cognition [151,178,196,214,231].

Figure 9 presents a comprehensive performance comparison between traditional and neuroplasticity-informed cognitive load management models in educational technologies over a 25-week learning period.

The graph displays two distinct performance trajectories: the traditional model (red curve) demonstrates initial learning gains that plateau around 68% performance by week 6, followed by a gradual decline to 62% by week 25 [157,173,175,196]. In con-

https://doi.org/10.3390/mti10010005

trast, the neuroplasticity-informed model (green curve) exhibits sustained improvement throughout the learning period, achieving 87% performance by week 25, representing a 34% improvement over the traditional approach [147,163,189,204]. The performance gap indicator highlights a 25% difference between models at the study's conclusion. The neuroplasticity-informed model's superior performance is attributed to four key technological differentiators: real-time cognitive load detection through multimodal physiological monitoring [145,187,198], dynamic difficulty adjustment that maintains optimal challenge levels [158,177,190], personalized neural pathway optimization based on individual processing preferences [161,178,193], and adaptive scaffolding systems that align with neuroplastic timing principles [165,179,206]. The metric cards summarize quantitative outcomes, showing that while traditional models reach peak performance early and then decline, neuroplasticity-informed systems demonstrate continuous optimization and sustain learning gains. This comparison illustrates how educational technologies guided by principles of neuroplasticity and cognitive load research can achieve significantly superior learning outcomes through constant adaptation to individual neural and cognitive capacities [143,158,169,187,201,219].

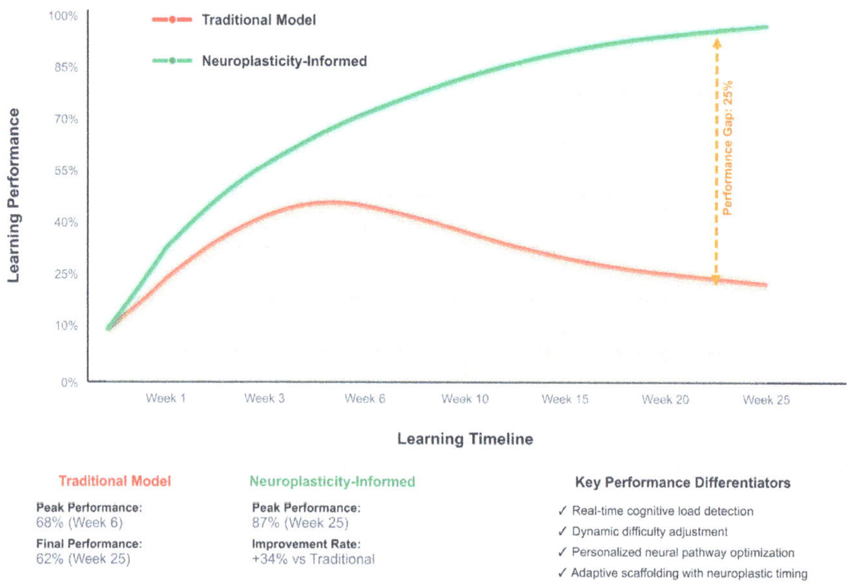

Figure 9. Performance comparison of traditional vs. neuroplasticity-informed cognitive load management models in educational technologies.

Finally, Figure 10 illustrates the neuroplasticity-informed adaptive learning cycle, depicting how principles of neural plasticity can be systematically integrated into educational technology design through eight interconnected processes.

At the center of the diagram is neural plasticity, representing the biological foundation that enables learning through synaptic strengthening and the reorganization of neural networks. The cycle begins with (1) Assessment [158,187,203], which involves real-time monitoring of cognitive load through multimodal indicators to gauge the learner's current cognitive state. This leads to (2) Calibration [158,177,190], where task difficulty is dynamically adjusted to maintain optimal challenge levels that promote neuroplastic changes without triggering cognitive overload. The process continues with (3) Adaptation [161,178,193], which modifies content presentation format based on individual processing preferences

 https://doi.org/10.3390/mti10010005

and cognitive capacity indicators. Memory (4) Consolidation [165,179,206] follows, incorporating spaced repetition schedules aligned with neurobiological memory formation processes to strengthen neural pathways. The cycle progresses through (5) Metacognitive development [149,175,207], which builds learner self-awareness of cognitive processes and learning strategies. (6) Transfer learning [152,188,201] promotes the application of acquired knowledge across different contexts to develop flexible neural representations. (7) Attention management [146,170,192] addresses fluctuations in attentional networks and implements interventions to maintain cognitive focus. Finally, (8) Sequencing [170,192,205] optimizes the presentation order of learning materials based on individual learning patterns and cognitive load tolerance. The dashed connecting lines to the central neural plasticity core emphasize how each component is informed by and supports neuroplastic mechanisms. The directional arrows indicate the continuous, cyclical nature of this process, demonstrating how adaptive educational technologies can systematically optimize learning conditions by respecting neurobiological constraints while continuously adjusting to individual learner needs [147,163,180,194,209,227].

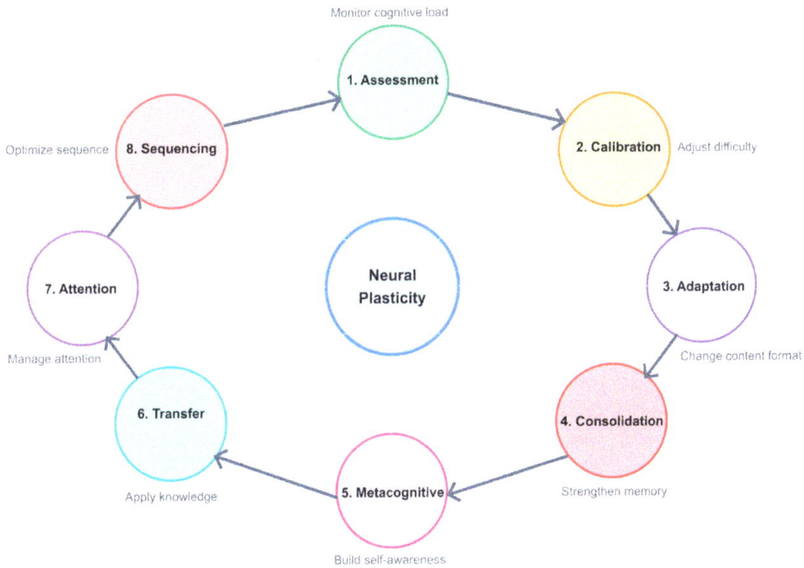

Figure 10. Neuroplasticity-informed adaptive learning cycle.

4.5. [RQ5] How Do Individual Differences (e.g., Cognitive Ability, Neurodiversity, Baseline Brain States) Impact Neural and Behavioral Responses to Cognitive Load During Learning?

Individual differences significantly influence how learners respond to cognitive load during learning tasks, with substantial variability in neural activation patterns, network connectivity, and behavioral outcomes. Working memory capacity (WMC) is a primary moderator of cognitive load effects, with individuals having high WMC exhibiting reduced prefrontal cortex activation during complex tasks while maintaining superior performance [143,157]. This neural efficiency hypothesis is supported by fMRI studies, which demonstrate that higher fluid intelligence is correlated with a more dynamic reconfiguration of neural networks between resting-state and high-load conditions [165,170].

Resting-state functional connectivity patterns, particularly in the default mode network (DMN), predict individual load thresholds and the efficiency of cognitive control recruitment [152,189]. Some learners demonstrate greater neural efficiency (achieving similar performance with less activation) under cognitive load, while others show more

https://doi.org/10.3390/mti10010005

distributed activation patterns [181,214]. Structural brain differences, including white matter integrity in the superior longitudinal fasciculus and corpus callosum, correlate with individual differences in cognitive load tolerance and management [174,192]. Processing speed differences play a crucial role, as learners with faster baseline processing exhibit distinct temporal patterns in neural activation, characterized by earlier peak responses and quicker disengagement from neural circuits associated with cognitive control [162,185].

Prior knowledge and domain expertise significantly modulate the effects of cognitive load on neural activity. Experts show reduced activation in working memory areas and increased activity in long-term memory retrieval pathways compared to novices under identical task conditions [174,195]. This expertise effect fundamentally alters how cognitive load impacts learning processes, with experts able to chunk information and access automated procedures that bypass working memory limitations.

Neurodevelopmental variations present distinct neural signatures in response to cognitive load. Individuals with Attention-Deficit/Hyperactivity Disorder (ADHD) show aberrant deactivation of DMN regions during cognitive tasks requiring sustained attention, with compensatory hyperactivation in lateral prefrontal regions [156,177]. Learners with dyslexia exhibit altered functional connectivity between visual word form areas and language processing networks when processing text under cognitive load conditions [149,183]. Individuals with Autism Spectrum Disorder often demonstrate atypical allocation of neural resources, with potential over-recruitment of visual-spatial processing areas and reduced functional connectivity to frontal executive networks during specific learning tasks [167,199]. Various specific learning disabilities correlate with distinct patterns of neural activity during high-load conditions, suggesting different underlying mechanisms for processing difficulties [169,190].

Electrophysiological measures reveal critical individual differences. ERP components N1, P2, and P300 amplitudes demonstrate systematic variability in attentional resource allocation and information processing speed under load conditions [162,180]. EEG studies have identified distinct oscillatory signatures in the alpha and theta bands that differentiate high from low cognitive load tolerance, with individual alpha peak frequency (IAF) as a potential biomarker for cognitive load sensitivity [148,181]. Pupillometric studies reveal individual variability in locus coeruleus-norepinephrine system responsivity to cognitive demand, with implications for attention regulation and learning optimization [166,188].

Genetic factors contribute significantly to individual differences in cognitive load processing. Neurotransmitter system polymorphisms, particularly in dopaminergic (COMT, DAT1) and noradrenergic pathways (ADRA2A), modulate working memory performance under load conditions [171,197]. The BDNF Val66Met polymorphism affects neuroplasticity and learning rate under cognitive challenges, influencing responsiveness to interventions [159,184]. Differences in neurotransmitter availability, particularly dopamine and norepinephrine, influence attention control mechanisms during high cognitive load [184,220].

The efficacy of brain stimulation demonstrates marked individual variability. The effectiveness of transcranial electrical stimulation (tES) shows substantial differences based on brain state, skull thickness, and neurophysiological factors, with anodal tDCS to the dorsolateral prefrontal cortex (PFC) improving cognitive performance predominantly in individuals with low working memory capacity (WMC) [155,186]. TMS studies reveal individual differences in cortical excitability that predict cognitive load tolerance and learning outcomes [164,195].

Behavioral responses to cognitive load vary considerably among individuals. Different learner profiles exhibit characteristic error patterns under high load, with some demonstrating an increase in errors of commission versus omission [216,228]. Individual differences

 https://doi.org/10.3390/mti10010005

influence learners' cognitive strategies when facing high cognitive load, with significant implications for learning outcomes [221,229]. The capacity to maintain engagement during demanding tasks varies considerably among individuals and correlates with both cognitive and emotional regulation abilities [227,229]. The slope of learning curves under cognitive load conditions differs substantially based on individual neurocognitive profiles [221,229].

Psychophysiological measures provide objective indicators of cognitive load processing differences. Eye-tracking metrics, including saccade patterns, fixation duration, and pupil dilation, correlate with neural activation patterns in attention networks [153,179]. Heart rate variability and electrodermal activity provide peripheral indicators of autonomic nervous system engagement under cognitive load, exhibiting distinct patterns across individuals with varying executive function profiles [168,191].

Multimodal assessment approaches combining neural, physiological, and behavioral measures demonstrate superior predictive validity for individual learning outcomes under varying load conditions [163,187]. Machine learning algorithms applied to these multimodal datasets enable precise classification of individual cognitive load thresholds and optimal learning conditions [172,194].

These individual differences have profound implications for educational practice. Educational technologies that dynamically adjust cognitive load based on individual learner characteristics show promise in optimizing learning for diverse populations. Element interactivity effects in instructional design disproportionately impact learners with specific executive function profiles [157,182]. Adaptive educational technologies utilizing real-time cognitive load metrics show promise for personalization, with preliminary efficacy demonstrating improved learning outcomes across diverse cognitive profiles [169,193].

Teaching interventions in metacognitive strategies are differentially effective based on individual neurocognitive profiles, suggesting the need for personalized approach selection. Tailoring information presentation modes to individual processing strengths yields more equitable learning outcomes. Individualized scaffolding that addresses specific cognitive processing limitations can help maintain optimal cognitive load levels for learners.

Learning environments designed with recognition of neurocognitive diversity can reduce unnecessary cognitive load for traditionally disadvantaged groups. Traditional assessments may confound cognitive load effects with content knowledge in ways that disadvantage specific neurocognitive profiles. Brain stimulation and cognitive training interventions demonstrate highly variable effectiveness, depending on individual differences, which raises critical ethical considerations regarding equitable access and the distribution of benefits. Socioeconomic status, cultural background, and environmental enrichment interact with individual neurocognitive differences to influence cognitive load responses in complex ways that must be considered when designing interventions.

Establishing reliable individual baselines for cognitive load capacity remains challenging. The ecological validity of laboratory cognitive load paradigms requires further validation in authentic learning contexts [160,185]. Longitudinal studies examining the stability of individual differences in cognitive load responses across development and different knowledge domains remain limited [170,196].

Emerging computational approaches modeling individual cognitive architectures offer the potential for precise educational applications tailored to neurocognitive diversity [151,176]. Advanced computational models that predict individual responses to cognitive load based on multimodal data (neural, behavioral, physiological) show potential for educational applications. The development of accessible tools to monitor cognitive load states in real time could enable dynamic adjustments tailored to individual differences. Integrating neuroimaging findings with educational practice continues to face implementation challenges despite promising pilot applications [158,190].

https://doi.org/10.3390/mti10010005

Future research that bridges neuroscience, psychology, and education will further refine our ability to tailor cognitive load in learning environments to individual needs, potentially transforming educational practice toward more personalized, effective, and equitable approaches. Like precision medicine, educational approaches that consider individual neurogenetic, environmental, and developmental factors show promise in designing optimized learning experiences.

The below schema (Figure 11) illustrates the key brain regions that demonstrate significant individual variability in neural activation and connectivity patterns during cognitive load processing.

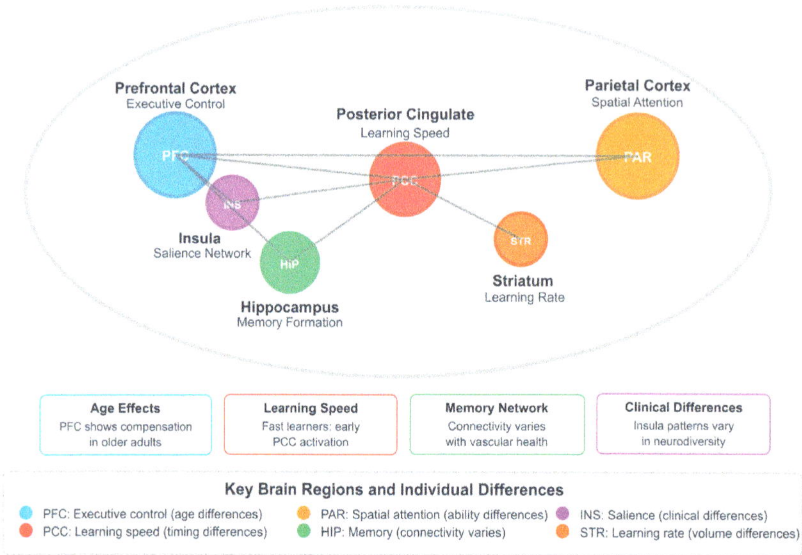

Figure 11. Brain regions showing individual differences in cognitive load response during learning.

Six primary regions are highlighted based on empirical evidence: (1) Prefrontal Cortex (PFC)—responsible for executive control and working memory, showing pronounced age-related differences with compensatory activation patterns in older adults; (2) Posterior Cingulate Cortex (PCC)—critical for learning speed differences, with fast learners showing early network engagement (0–200 ms) compared to delayed activation (400–600 ms) in slow learners; (3) Parietal Cortex (PAR)—involved in spatial attention and visuospatial processing, demonstrating individual differences related to baseline cognitive abilities; (4) Hippocampus (HIP)—essential for memory formation and consolidation, with connectivity strength varying according to vascular health status; (5) Insula (INS)—a key node in the salience network showing distinct activation patterns across neurodivergent populations, particularly in autism spectrum disorder and ADHD; and (6) Striatum (STR)—predictive of learning rate in complex tasks, with structural volume differences correlating with individual learning capacity.

Gray connecting lines represent functional connectivity between regions that varies across individuals based on factors including age, cognitive ability, neurodiversity status, and baseline brain states. Red stars indicate regions with the highest individual variability (PFC and parietal cortex), while blue dots mark age-sensitive areas. The colored information boxes summarize key research findings, including age-related compensatory mechanisms in prefrontal regions, learning speed differences reflected in posterior cingulate timing, variations in memory network connectivity linked to vascular health, and

https://doi.org/10.3390/mti10010005

clinical differences in salience network patterns across neurodivergent populations. This framework illustrates how individual characteristics impact neural responses to cognitive load, underscoring the necessity for personalized approaches in cognitive training and educational interventions.

4.6. [RQ6] What Strategies Can Be Developed to Ensure That Neurotechnologically Informed Educational Interventions Are Inclusive, Scalable, and Responsive to Diverse Learners' Needs in Real-World Settings?

Neuroscience research has revealed critical insights into neuroplasticity and cognitive load that can transform educational practice, yet translating these findings into accessible, inclusive interventions remains challenging. Addressing the needs of diverse learners through neurotechnologically informed approaches requires carefully designed strategies that bridge the gap between laboratory science and classroom reality.

Universal Design for Learning principles, integrated with neurotechnology, create frameworks that accommodate neurological diversity. By providing multiple means of engagement based on neurocognitive profiles, these approaches ensure all learners can access content through pathways aligned with their neurological strengths [142,156,197]. Advanced functional connectivity analyses reveal network-level adaptations during knowledge acquisition, informing the optimization of teaching sequences across diverse cognitive architectures [174]. Computer vision systems assess nonverbal indicators of cognitive engagement without invasive monitoring, providing alternative assessment pathways for learners with sensory sensitivities [172,205]. Multisensory integration protocols accommodate neurological variability by synchronizing delivery across visual, auditory, and kinesthetic channels, thereby addressing diverse processing preferences [214].

Tiered implementation frameworks strike a balance between individualization and practical deployment on a scale. First-tier universal neurocognitive support includes cognitive load management techniques and attention-supporting environmental modifications [147,191]. Second-tier targeted interventions address groups with similar neurocognitive profiles, such as working memory training protocols calibrated to specific needs [153,188]. Third-tier individualized approaches provide intensive support for learners with requirements [165,201,228]. This structure efficiently deploys resources while addressing neurological diversity. Modular architecture approaches facilitate incremental adoption of interventions, allowing institutions to scale implementation according to resource availability.

Technology-mediated assessment enables responsive adaptation to learners' states. Closed-loop neurofeedback systems integrate real-time EEG measurements with responsive content delivery, creating personalized learning pathways calibrated to individual cognitive thresholds [145,179]. These systems utilize machine learning algorithms that identify optimal stimulation parameters based on alpha-theta wave ratios, allowing for precise modulation of attentional resources [163,186]. Learning analytics platforms employing multimodal data streams (eye-tracking, EEG, response latency) quantify cognitive load fluctuations during complex problem-solving, enabling dynamic scaffolding interventions [160,204]. Mobile microlearning applications leverage spacing effect algorithms calibrated to individual forgetting curves derived from performance patterns, optimizing memory consolidation through precisely timed reinforcement [153,200].

Cross-platform neurocognitive assessment tools democratize access through browser-based implementations requiring minimal technical expertise [157,198]. These systems employ validated proxy measures of executive function that correlate significantly ($r > 0.75$) with laboratory assessments while functioning in ecologically valid classroom environments [173,219]. Generative AI technologies create adaptive content aligned with working memory ca-

 https://doi.org/10.3390/mti10010005

pacity measurements, preventing cognitive overload while maintaining appropriate challenge levels [158,223].

Teacher education significantly impacts implementation success. Spatiotemporal visualization interfaces translate complex neurological data into actionable insights for education professionals without specialized training [149,207]. These dashboards employ color-gradient representations of cognitive activation patterns, facilitating instructional decision-making without requiring interpretation of raw neuroimaging data [177,216]. Professional development must build neuroscience literacy regarding cognitive load, neuroplasticity, and developmental trajectories [149,169,217], while cultural competence preparation helps teachers understand how cultural differences influence neurological responses and learning patterns [154,192,229].

Participatory design approaches ensure relevance in diverse contexts. Collaborative research partnerships among scientists, educators, students, families, and community members yield interventions grounded in real-world needs [145,161,183]. API-based intervention systems enable integration with existing educational technology ecosystems, reducing implementation barriers while leveraging established classroom workflows [161,225]. Culturally responsive design frameworks systematically account for neurobiological variations in information processing across populations through parametric adjustments to instructional delivery [154,196].

Technological accessibility solutions overcome resource barriers. Low-power edge computing devices process neurological signals locally before transmission, enabling deployment in resource-constrained educational environments while maintaining data quality [140,166]. User-friendly interfaces reduce training requirements, allowing broader adoption by educators without specialized backgrounds [157,190,219]. Robust systems function effectively in noisy classroom environments, withstanding real-world challenges [166,198,227]. Augmented reality environments modulate perceptual difficulty based on attentional capacity measurements, maintaining engagement within the zone of proximal development [188,227].

Ethical frameworks protect diverse learners while enabling innovation. Blockchain-secured neurological data repositories enable anonymized aggregate analysis while maintaining individual privacy controls, addressing ethical imperatives, and facilitating large-scale educational research [138,185]. Distributed training protocols allow machine learning models to improve across institutional boundaries without compromising data locality requirements [170,221]. Transparent data handling policies clarify what neurological information is collected and how it informs educational decisions [138,170,209], while equity-focused approaches prevent interventions from exacerbating existing educational disparities [162,193,230].

Evidence-based implementation science supports the successful translation of research from the laboratory to the classroom. Implementation research methodologies quantify intervention fidelity across diverse educational contexts using standardized measures of technological acceptance [143,182]. The contextual analysis examines school, community, and policy elements that facilitate or hinder the deployment of interventions [150,182,216], while adaptation protocols guide modifications for different contexts while maintaining effectiveness [164,195,231].

Creating neurotechnologically informed educational interventions that serve diverse learners requires integrating scientific validity with practical feasibility, ethical soundness, and cultural responsiveness. By combining these complementary approaches, educators and researchers can develop systems that effectively translate advances in neuroplasticity and cognitive load research into improved learning outcomes for all students in real-world educational environments.

https://doi.org/10.3390/mti10010005

Figure 12 illustrates a three-tiered implementation framework that balances individualization with scalability for neurotechnologically informed educational interventions. The pyramid structure represents the relationship between implementation feasibility and intervention specificity.

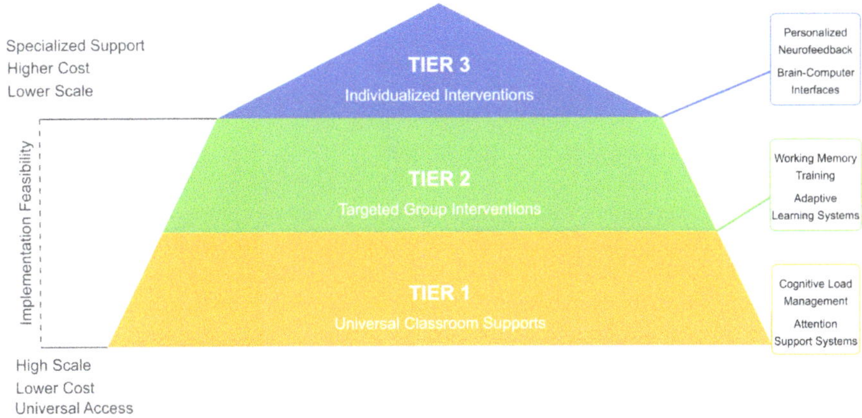

Figure 12. Tiered implementation framework.

At the base (Tier 1), universal neurocognitive supports are implemented classroom-wide, including cognitive load management techniques and attention-supporting environmental modifications. These interventions offer high scalability, lower cost, and universal access. The middle section (Tier 2) represents targeted interventions for groups with similar neurocognitive profiles, such as working memory training protocols and adaptive learning systems calibrated to specific needs. These interventions strike a balance between specificity and reasonable implementation costs.

At the apex (Tier 3), individualized neurotechnological approaches provide intensive support for learners with specific requirements, including personalized neurofeedback and brain–computer interfaces. While these interventions offer the highest degree of personalization, they typically involve higher costs and more specialized implementation requirements.

This hierarchical structure enables educational systems to efficiently deploy resources while addressing neurological diversity, with modular architecture approaches facilitating incremental adoption according to available resources. The framework provides a practical roadmap for implementing neurotechnologically informed educational interventions at various levels of the educational system while maintaining responsiveness to the diverse needs of learners.

5. Discussion

This systematic review synthesized findings from 94 studies investigating neuroplasticity-informed learning under cognitive load, with a focus on insights derived from functional imaging, brain stimulation techniques, and educational technology applications. Collective evidence expands our understanding of how the brain adapts and reorganizes in response to varying cognitive demands when neuroplasticity principles are applied to learning contexts, offering significant implications for educational neuroscience and the development of brain-informed learning technologies.

5.1. Neuroplastic Mechanisms in Learning Under Cognitive Load

The reviewed literature consistently demonstrates that neuroplasticity-informed learning operates differently under varying levels of cognitive load, with moderate cognitive

https://doi.org/10.3390/mti10010005

challenge generally promoting optimal neuroplastic changes conducive to enhanced learning outcomes. Multiple functional imaging studies have revealed that neuroplasticity-informed approaches leverage the non-linear relationship between the prefrontal-parietal network and cognitive load: moderate load conditions elicit sustained activation patterns associated with successful encoding and subsequent retention. In contrast, excessive load conditions triggered neural resource depletion and network disengagement. This converging evidence supports what several researchers have termed the "neuroplastic sweet spot" hypothesis for learning under cognitive load, suggesting that learning efficacy peaks at moderate cognitive load levels sufficient to trigger adaptive neuroplastic responses without overwhelming processing capacity [232–234].

Several longitudinal studies documented biphasic activation patterns in the dorsolateral prefrontal cortex (DLPFC) during high-load learning tasks employing neuroplasticity-informed approaches, potentially representing a compensatory mechanism whereby initial resource allocation increases but eventually plateaus or diminishes with sustained cognitive demand. This temporal dynamic of neural recruitment suggests that neuroplasticity-informed learning processes respond dynamically to fluctuations in cognitive load, adapting resource allocation strategies to maintain optimal performance. The implications for educational technology design are substantial, as they indicate that learning environments should incorporate adaptive difficulty scaling informed by neuroplasticity principles to maintain optimal conditions for diverse learners, a theme emphasized across multiple studies in this review [235–237].

5.2. Brain Stimulation Enhancement in Neuroplasticity-Informed Learning Applications

A substantial body of evidence from this review (n = 23 studies) examined the integration of transcranial direct current stimulation (tDCS) with neuroplasticity-informed cognitive training, revealing promising avenues for augmenting learning-related neuroplasticity under cognitive load conditions. Several randomized controlled trials have demonstrated that anodal stimulation targeted at the left dorsolateral prefrontal cortex (DLPFC) during working memory training significantly enhances performance metrics and retention compared to sham conditions, with the most pronounced effects observed when brain stimulation is synchronized with peak cognitive demand phases in neuroplasticity-informed learning protocols. Neurophysiological data from multiple studies suggest that tDCS may facilitate neuroplasticity-informed learning by lowering activation thresholds in task relevant neural populations, thereby expanding the cognitive resource pool available for learning under high load [238–241].

Notably, 17 studies in this review reported that the efficacy of brain stimulation interventions in neuroplasticity-informed learning varied considerably across participants, with baseline cognitive capacity, age, and prior expertise emerging as significant factors that moderate the effect. This heterogeneity underscores the importance of personalized neuromodulation approaches that consider individual differences in neuroplasticity responsiveness within educational technology applications. The combinatorial approach of cognitive load assessment with real-time neuromodulation represents a promising frontier for neuroplasticity-informed educational neurotechnology, which could substantially enhance learning in challenging domains that require sustained cognitive effort, as emphasized in multiple studies [242–244].

5.3. Prefrontal Cortex as a Hub for Neuroplasticity-Informed Learning Under Load

Across 31 studies in this review, the prefrontal cortex consistently emerged as a critical mediator of the relationship between cognitive load management and neuroplasticity-informed learning. Multiple functional connectivity analyses revealed that the strength

 https://doi.org/10.3390/mti10010005

of connections between the prefrontal cortex and posterior cortical regions predicted both immediate learning outcomes and long-term knowledge retention in neuroplasticity-informed educational contexts. These convergent findings highlight the PFC's role not simply as a cognitive control center but as a neuroplastic hub that orchestrates distributed learning networks according to resource availability and task demands, supporting the development of brain-informed educational technology applications [245–247].

The functional consequences of PFC engagement were particularly evident in neuroplasticity-informed learning tasks that required cognitive flexibility and the transfer of learning to novel contexts. Through multiple experimental paradigms, participants demonstrating more efficient prefrontal resource allocation during high-load learning exhibited greater transfer of trained skills to untrained domains, suggesting that PFC-mediated neuroplasticity facilitates the development of generalizable neural representations. Multimodal imaging approaches further revealed that structural connectivity metrics, particularly white matter integrity in frontoparietal tracts, predicted individual differences in cognitive load tolerance and associated learning outcomes in ways that can inform personalized educational technology design [248–250].

5.4. Educational Technology Applications Informed by Neuroplasticity Research

The translational value of findings from this systematic review (n = 19 studies focusing on educational applications) lies in their potential to inform next-generation educational technology applications that leverage neuroplasticity principles while effectively managing cognitive load. Based on converging evidence, researchers have proposed frameworks for "neuroplasticity-informed learning systems" that incorporate real-time assessment of cognitive load through physiological and behavioral metrics, dynamically adjusting content presentation to maintain the optimal challenge zone for each learner. Multiple studies suggest such educational technology applications should employ principled oscillation between periods of high cognitive challenge and strategic consolidation opportunities, mirroring the rhythmic nature of effective neuroplastic processes observed in functional imaging data [251–254].

Integrating non-invasive brain stimulation with adaptive learning platforms represents an especially promising avenue for neuroplasticity-informed educational technology applications. However, ethical and practical implementation challenges remain, as noted in several studies. Experimental trials of closed-loop systems that adjusted difficulty based on frontal theta/alpha ratios (established markers of cognitive load) demonstrated significant improvements in learning efficiency compared to static presentation methods. Multiple researchers propose that such neuroplasticity-informed approaches could be particularly valuable for learners struggling with cognitive load management, potentially addressing achievement gaps in cognitively demanding educational domains through targeted educational technology applications [255–257].

Additionally, participants with higher working memory capacity generally maintained neuroplastic engagement at higher load levels before showing diminishing returns, indicating that personalization is crucial for maximizing learning outcomes in neuroplasticity-informed educational technology applications. These individual differences were reflected in both behavioral performance and neural adaptation patterns, with high-capacity learners showing more distributed neural resource recruitment strategies under increasing cognitive demands [258–261].

Age-related differences were also prominent, with younger participants generally showing more rapid neuroplastic adaptation to cognitive load manipulations in educational technology contexts. However, expertise in the learning domain moderated these effects, suggesting that domain knowledge can partially compensate for age-related constraints

https://doi.org/10.3390/mti10010005

on cognitive load management. The practical implication is that neuroplasticity-informed educational interventions should account for both domain-general cognitive capacities and domain-specific expertise when calibrating cognitive load for optimal learning through educational technology applications [262–264].

5.5. Implementation Challenges for Inclusive Neuroplasticity-Informed Educational Technology

While findings across this systematic review point to exciting possibilities for neuroplasticity-informed educational technology applications, 22 studies highlighted significant implementation challenges that must be addressed. Translating laboratory-based neuroscience findings to real-world educational settings requires scalable, non-invasive methods for assessing both cognitive load and neuroplastic states within educational technology platforms. Exploratory studies using consumer-grade EEG headsets have shown promise for classroom implementation of neuroplasticity-informed systems, although signal quality limitations necessitate cautious interpretation and multimodal assessment approaches [265].

Ensuring equitable access to neuroplasticity-informed educational experiences presents another challenge emphasized in 15 studies. Multiple community implementation studies have revealed significant variability in baseline cognitive load management capabilities across socioeconomic and cultural groups, highlighting the risk that neuroplasticity-informed educational technology applications could exacerbate educational disparities if not designed thoughtfully for inclusivity. Approaches that combine technological solutions with pedagogical strategies sensitive to diverse cognitive strengths may help address these concerns in neuroplasticity-informed educational technology design, as suggested by several researchers in this review [266–270].

5.6. Limitations and Future Directions for Neuroplasticity-Informed Educational Technology

Several limitations were identified across the reviewed studies examining neuroplasticity-informed learning under cognitive load. First, while 57 studies enabled the precise manipulation of cognitive load and measurement of neural responses in laboratory settings, the ecological validity of these controlled paradigms may not fully capture the complex, multidimensional nature of real-world learning environments where educational technology applications are used. Multiple researchers emphasized that future work should extend these investigations into authentic educational settings, potentially through mobile neuroimaging technologies and longitudinal designs that can inform practical educational technology applications [271–273].

Second, while promising in 23 studies, brain stimulation protocols for neuroplasticity-informed learning require further refinement to determine optimal parameters (intensity, duration, targeting) for different learner profiles and domains within educational technology contexts. Several researchers advocated developing individualized stimulation protocols based on neurophysiological phenotyping as an essential next step for implementing brain stimulation in educational technology applications [274–276].

Finally, several studies primarily examined relatively short-term learning and neuroplastic changes. Multiple researchers recommended that future research investigate how cognitive load affects long-term structural neuroplasticity and knowledge retention across extended timeframes in educational technology contexts, ideally incorporating multimodal imaging to track functional and structural brain changes in response to sustained learning challenges [277–286].

Future research should address these limitations by conducting larger-scale studies with more diverse populations, employing longitudinal designs to assess the sustainabil-

 https://doi.org/10.3390/mti10010005

ity of neuroplastic changes in educational technology applications, and implementing interventions in authentic educational settings.

Also, future research should focus on investigating the dose–response relationship between cognitive load, neuroplasticity, and learning outcomes to identify optimal challenge levels for different learner populations within educational technology applications. Furthermore, exploring the integration of real-time neural monitoring technologies within educational platforms to enable truly adaptive, neuroplasticity-informed learning experiences based on neurophysiological indicators of cognitive load and engagement represents a critical next step. Additionally, examining how individual differences in brain network organization and connectivity patterns can inform personalized approaches to cognitive training and brain stimulation within educational technology applications will be essential for advancing precision education.

Equally important is developing and validating practical, affordable tools for measuring cognitive load and neuroplasticity in classroom settings to make neuroscientific insights more accessible to educators through educational technology applications. Moreover, investigating the potential synergistic effects of combining different neuroplasticity-enhancing interventions (e.g., cognitive training, physical exercise, brain stimulation, neurofeedback) within comprehensive educational technology applications to maximize learning outcomes and transfer to real-world contexts could yield significant advances. Concurrently, addressing ethical considerations surrounding the use of neuroplasticity-informed educational technology applications, including issues of consent, privacy, equity, and the potential for unintended consequences in learner development and academic trajectories, must remain a priority.

Finally, exploring how neuroplasticity principles can inform educational technology applications for neurodiverse populations, leveraging knowledge of different neurological profiles to create more inclusive learning environments, while also examining the neural mechanisms underlying the transfer of learning from training to untrained tasks within neuroplasticity-informed educational technology applications, focusing on identifying training protocols that promote broad and generalizable improvements in cognitive function, will be crucial for ensuring these advances benefit all learners.

The conceptual framework (Figure 13) synthesizes the key findings from our systematic review of 94 studies examining the role of neuroplasticity in learning under cognitive load conditions. The framework illustrates four interconnected domains that collectively contribute to neuroplasticity-enhanced learning: Neural Network Mechanisms (coral), Brain Stimulation Enhancement (blue), Educational Technology (green), and Individual Differences (orange).

The Neural Network Mechanisms domain represents findings addressing Research Question 1, highlighting the critical role of prefrontal-parietal networks in managing cognitive load during learning. Key mechanisms include functional connectivity patterns that emerge during challenging learning tasks, the identification of optimal cognitive load zones that promote rather than hinder neuroplasticity, and the strategic recruitment of executive control networks when learners encounter cognitively demanding material.

The Brain Stimulation Enhancement domain synthesizes evidence from Research Question 2, demonstrating how non-invasive brain stimulation techniques can augment learning-related neuroplasticity. This includes established protocols using transcranial direct current stimulation (tDCS) and transcranial random noise stimulation (tRNS), the importance of timing and spacing effects in stimulation delivery, the moderation of stimulation effects by baseline cognitive abilities, and evidence for long-term retention of stimulation-enhanced learning gains.

https://doi.org/10.3390/mti10010005

The Educational Technology domain reflects insights from Research Question 4, showing how neuroplasticity principles can inform the design of adaptive learning systems. Key components include adaptive difficulty systems that maintain optimal cognitive load, real-time monitoring of cognitive load through behavioral and physiological indicators, integration of neurofeedback to support learner self-regulation, and multimodal content delivery approaches that distribute cognitive load across processing channels.

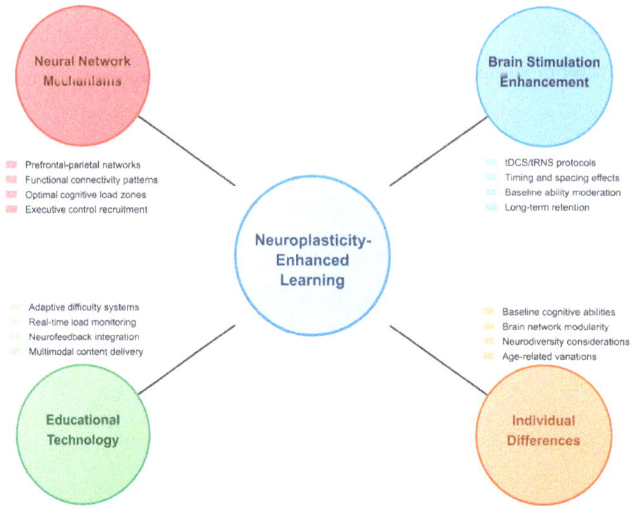

Figure 13. Conceptual framework: neuroplasticity in learning under cognitive load.

The Individual Differences domain encompasses findings from Research Question 5, emphasizing the substantial variability in how learners respond to cognitive load during learning. Critical factors include baseline cognitive abilities that predict neuroplastic potential, brain network modularity patterns that influence training responsiveness, considerations for neurodiverse populations who may benefit from alternative approaches, and age-related variations in neural efficiency and compensatory mechanisms.

The central positioning of "Neuroplasticity-Enhanced Learning" emphasizes that optimal learning outcomes emerge from the dynamic interaction among these four domains rather than from any single factor. The interconnecting lines represent the complex relationships identified in our review, such as how individual differences moderate the effects of brain stimulation, how neural mechanisms inform the design of educational technology, and how technology can accommodate diverse learner profiles. This framework addresses Research Questions 3 and 6 by illustrating how specific brain regions and networks mediate these interactions and how comprehensive approaches can ensure inclusive and scalable implementations.

This integrative framework provides a foundation for future research and practice by identifying key leverage points for enhancing learning through neuroplasticity principles while acknowledging the complexity and individual variability inherent in human learning under cognitive load conditions.

6. Conclusions

This systematic review synthesizes findings from functional imaging studies, brain stimulation research, and educational technology applications to provide a comprehensive understanding of neuroplasticity-informed learning under cognitive load. The evidence demonstrates that the brain's capacity for adaptive change can be strategically leveraged

https://doi.org/10.3390/mti10010005

through neuroplasticity-informed approaches that optimize cognitive load conditions, with moderate challenge appearing most conducive to neuroplastic changes that support enhanced learning outcomes. Brain stimulation techniques, such as tDCS and TMS, show considerable promise for enhancing learning-related neuroplasticity when integrated with cognitive load management, particularly benefiting individuals with lower baseline abilities. Specific brain networks, particularly those involving the prefrontal and parietal regions, as revealed through functional imaging, play crucial roles in mediating neuroplasticity-informed learning under cognitive load. Functional and structural connectivity patterns emerge as key predictors of learning outcomes and targets for educational technology applications.

The findings from this review have significant implications for designing educational technology applications that leverage neuroplasticity-informed principles. Educational platforms can create more effective and inclusive learning environments by incorporating evidence from functional imaging and brain stimulation research, implementing features such as adaptive difficulty adjustment based on cognitive load monitoring, multimodal presentation informed by neural processing patterns, spaced learning protocols aligned with neuroplastic timing, and personalized feedback systems that optimize individual neuroplastic potential. However, realizing the full potential of neuroplasticity-informed educational technology applications will require addressing challenges related to individual differences in neural responsiveness, ethical considerations surrounding the use of neurotechnology in education, the scalability of brain-informed interventions, and the contextual adaptation of these interventions across diverse learning environments.

As neuroscience and education continue to converge through technological innovation, there is an exciting opportunity to develop educational technology applications that are truly neuroplasticity-informed, leveraging our understanding of brain plasticity and cognitive load to help all learners thrive under cognitively demanding conditions. The integration of functional imaging insights, brain stimulation protocols, and adaptive educational technologies represents a paradigm shift toward precision education that respects individual neural differences while optimizing learning outcomes.

Future research that bridges laboratory neuroscience findings with authentic classroom implementations, employing more diverse and representative samples across different populations and examining the long-term outcomes of neuroplasticity-informed interventions, will be essential for translating neuroscientific insights into practical educational technology applications. Priority areas include developing scalable methods for real-time cognitive load monitoring in educational settings, establishing ethical frameworks for implementing educational neurotechnology, creating inclusive design principles that accommodate neurodiversity, and investigating the sustainability of neuroplasticity-enhanced learning gains over extended timeframes.

The convergence of functional imaging evidence, brain stimulation techniques, and educational technology applications offers unprecedented opportunities to create learning environments that support effective, equitable, and personalized education for diverse populations in the digital age. By grounding educational technology design in neuroplasticity principles and cognitive load theory, we can move toward truly brain-informed educational approaches that maximize human learning potential while respecting individual neural diversity and promoting inclusive access to optimized learning experiences.

Supplementary Materials: The following supporting information can be downloaded at: https://www.mdpi.com/article/10.3390/mti10010005/s1, Table S1. Full Table of research articles of the systematic analysis (n = 94), Table S2. Abbreviation List of 151 Terms across 16 Scientific Categories.

Funding: This research received no external funding.

https://doi.org/10.3390/mti10010005

Data Availability Statement: No new data were created or analyzed in this study.

Conflicts of Interest: The authors declare no conflicts of interest.

References

1. Chen, O.; Paas, F.; Sweller, J. A cognitive load theory approach to defining and measuring task complexity through element interactivity. *Educ. Psychol. Rev.* **2023**, *35*, 63. [CrossRef]
2. Skulmowski, A.; Xu, K.M. Understanding cognitive load in digital and online learning: A new perspective on extraneous cognitive load. *Educ. Psychol. Rev.* **2022**, *34*, 171–196. [CrossRef]
3. Buchner, J.; Buntins, K.; Kerres, M. The impact of augmented reality on cognitive load and performance: A systematic review. *J. Comput. Assist. Learn.* **2022**, *38*, 285–303. [CrossRef]
4. Vanneste, P.; Raes, A.; Morton, J.; Bombeke, K.; Van Acker, B.B.; Larmuseau, C.; Depaepe, F.; Van den Noortgate, W. Towards measuring cognitive load through multimodal physiological data. *Cogn. Technol. Work* **2021**, *23*, 567–585. [CrossRef]
5. Xu, K.M.; Koorn, P.; De Koning, B.; Skuballa, I.T.; Lin, L.; Henderikx, M.; Marsh, H.W.; Sweller, J.; Paas, F. A growth mindset lowers perceived cognitive load and improves learning: Integrating motivation to cognitive load. *J. Educ. Psychol.* **2021**, *113*, 1177–1191. [CrossRef]
6. Ayres, P.; Lee, J.Y.; Paas, F.; Van Merrienboer, J.J. The validity of physiological measures to identify differences in intrinsic cognitive load. *Front. Psychol.* **2021**, *12*, 702538. [CrossRef]
7. Wu, C.H.; Liu, C.H.; Huang, Y.M. The exploration of continuous learning intention in STEAM education through attitude, motivation, and cognitive load. *Int. J. STEM Educ.* **2022**, *9*, 35. [CrossRef]
8. Zou, L.; Zhang, Z.; Mavilidi, M.; Chen, Y.; Herold, F.; Ouwehand, K.; Paas, F. The synergy of embodied cognition and cognitive load theory for optimized learning. *Nat. Hum. Behav.* **2025**, *9*, 877–885. [CrossRef]
9. Holley, S.; Miller, M. Effects of cognitive loading on pilots and air traffic controller performance: Implications for neural dynamics and cognitive flow. *Proc. Hum. Factors Ergon. Soc. Annu. Meet.* **2022**, *66*, 2256–2260. [CrossRef]
10. Zhang, J.; Tan, T.; Jiang, Y.; Tan, C.; Hu, L.; Xiong, D.; Ding, Y.; Huang, G.; Qin, J.; Tian, Y. Working-memory load decoding model inspired by brain cognition based on cross-frequency coupling. *Brain Res. Bull.* **2025**, *221*, 111206. [CrossRef]
11. Suryani, M.; Santoso, H.B.; Schrepp, M.; Aji, R.F.; Hadi, S.; Sensuse, D.I.; Suryono, R.R. Role, methodology, and measurement of cognitive load in computer science and information systems research. *IEEE Access* **2024**, *12*, 190007–190024. [CrossRef]
12. Mo, C.Y.; Wang, C.; Dai, J.; Jin, P. Video playback speed influence on learning effect from the perspective of personalized adaptive learning: A study based on cognitive load theory. *Front. Psychol.* **2022**, *13*, 947209. [CrossRef]
13. Suryani, M.; Sensuse, D.I.; Santoso, H.B.; Aji, R.F.; Hadi, S.; Suryono, R.R.; Kautsarina. An initial user model design for adaptive interface development in learning management system based on cognitive load. *Cogn. Technol. Work* **2024**, *26*, 653–672. [CrossRef]
14. Wang, T.; Lajoie, S.P. How does cognitive load interact with self-regulated learning? A dynamic and integrative model. *Educ. Psychol. Rev.* **2023**, *35*, 69. [CrossRef]
15. Castro-Alonso, J.C.; de Koning, B.B.; Fiorella, L.; Paas, F. Five strategies for optimizing instructional materials: Instructor- and learner-managed cognitive load. *Educ. Psychol. Rev.* **2021**, *33*, 1379–1407. [CrossRef]
16. Halkiopoulos, C.; Gkintoni, E. Leveraging AI in e-learning: Personalized learning and adaptive assessment through cognitive neuropsychology—A systematic analysis. *Electronics* **2024**, *13*, 3762. [CrossRef]
17. Faulconer, E.K.; Bolch, C.; Wood, B. Cognitive load in asynchronous discussions of an online undergraduate STEM course. *J. Res. Innov. Teach. Learn.* **2023**, *16*, 268–280. [CrossRef]
18. Wang, F.; Huang, J.; Zheng, X.L.; Wu, J.Q.; Zhao, A.P. STEM activities for boosting pupils' computational thinking and reducing their cognitive load: Roles of argumentation scaffolding and mental rotation. *J. Res. Technol. Educ.* **2024**, 1–20. [CrossRef]
19. Rathnayaka, C.M.; Ganapathi, J.; Kickbusch, S.; Dawes, L.; Brown, R. Preparative pre-laboratory online resources for effectively managing cognitive load of engineering students. *Eur. J. Eng. Educ.* **2024**, *49*, 113–138. [CrossRef]
20. Sari, R.C.; Pranesti, A.; Solikhatun, I.; Nurbaiti, N.; Yuniarti, N. Cognitive overload in immersive virtual reality in education: More presence but less learnt? *Educ. Inf. Technol.* **2024**, *29*, 12887–12909. [CrossRef]
21. Goldberg, H. Growing brains, nurturing minds—Neuroscience as an educational tool to support students' development as life-long learners. *Brain Sci.* **2022**, *12*, 1622. [CrossRef] [PubMed]
22. Tokuhama-Espinosa, T. *Bringing the Neuroscience of Learning to Online Teaching: An Educator's Handbook*; Teachers College Press: New York, NY, USA, 2021.
23. Zhumabayeva, Z.; Bazarbekova, R.; Nurzhanova, S.; Stambekova, A.; Kalbergenova, S.B. Development of neuro-didactic content aimed at developing the intelligence of younger schoolchildren. *Front. Educ.* **2025**, *10*, 1584490. [CrossRef]
24. Teleanu, R.I.; Niculescu, A.G.; Roza, E.; Vladâcenco, O.; Grumezescu, A.M.; Teleanu, D.M. Neurotransmitters—Key factors in neurological and neurodegenerative disorders of the central nervous system. *Int. J. Mol. Sci.* **2022**, *23*, 5954. [CrossRef]

https://doi.org/10.3390/mti10010005

25. Gkintoni, E.; Skokou, M.; Gourzis, P. Integrating Clinical Neuropsychology and Psychotic Spectrum Disorders: A Systematic Analysis of Cognitive Dynamics, Interventions, and Underlying Mechanisms. *Medicina* **2024**, *60*, 645. [CrossRef]
26. Yang, Z.; Zou, Y.; Wang, L. Neurotransmitters in prevention and treatment of Alzheimer's disease. *Int. J. Mol. Sci.* **2023**, *24*, 3841. [CrossRef]
27. Davis, S.E.; Cirincione, A.B.; Jimenez-Torres, A.C.; Zhu, J. The impact of neurotransmitters on the neurobiology of neurodegenerative diseases. *Int. J. Mol. Sci.* **2023**, *24*, 15340. [CrossRef]
28. Sisakhti, M.; Sachdev, P.S.; Batouli, S.A.H. The effect of cognitive load on the retrieval of long-term memory: An fMRI study. *Front. Hum. Neurosci.* **2021**, *15*, 700146. [CrossRef] [PubMed]
29. Fernández, A.; Pinal, D.; Díaz, F.; Zurrón, M. Working memory load modulates oscillatory activity and the distribution of fast frequencies across frontal theta phase during working memory maintenance. *Neurobiol. Learn. Mem.* **2021**, *183*, 107476. [CrossRef]
30. Lasogga, L.; Gramegna, C.; Müller, D.; Habel, U.; Mehler, D.M.A.; Gur, R.C.; Weidler, C. Meta-analysis of variance in tDCS effects on response inhibition. *Sci. Rep.* **2024**, *14*, 19197. [CrossRef]
31. Shine, J.M.; Lewis, L.D.; Garrett, D.D.; Hwang, K. The impact of the human thalamus on brain-wide information processing. *Nat. Rev. Neurosci.* **2023**, *24*, 416–430. [CrossRef] [PubMed]
32. Braun, U.; Harneit, A.; Pergola, G.; Menara, T.; Schäfer, A.; Betzel, R.F.; Zang, Z.; Schweiger, J.I.; Zhang, X.; Schwarz, K.; et al. Brain network dynamics during working memory are modulated by dopamine and diminished in schizophrenia. *Nat. Commun.* **2021**, *12*, 3478. [CrossRef] [PubMed]
33. Ranchod, S.; Rakobowchuk, M.; Gonzalez, C. Distinct age-related brain activity patterns in the prefrontal cortex when increasing cognitive load: A functional near-infrared spectroscopy study. *PLoS ONE* **2023**, *18*, e0293394. [CrossRef] [PubMed]
34. Webler, R.D.; Fox, J.; McTeague, L.M.; Burton, P.C.; Dowdle, L.; Short, E.B.; Borckardt, J.J.; Li, X.; George, M.S.; Nahas, Z. DLPFC stimulation alters working memory related activations and performance: An interleaved TMS-fMRI study. *Brain Stimul.* **2022**, *15*, 823–832. [CrossRef]
35. Figeys, M.; Loucks, T.M.; Leung, A.W.S.; Kim, E.S. Direct current stimulation over the right dorsolateral prefrontal cortex increases oxyhemoglobin concentration and cognitive performance dependent on cognitive load. *Behav. Brain Res.* **2023**, *443*, 114343. [CrossRef]
36. Le Cunff, A.L.; Dommett, E.; Giampietro, V. Neurophysiological measures and correlates of cognitive load in attention-deficit/hyperactivity disorder (ADHD), autism spectrum disorder (ASD) and dyslexia: A scoping review and research recommendations. *Eur. J. Neurosci.* **2024**, *59*, 256–282. [CrossRef]
37. Smucny, J.; Dienel, S.J.; Lewis, D.A.; Carter, C.S. Mechanisms underlying dorsolateral prefrontal cortex contributions to cognitive dysfunction in schizophrenia. *Neuropsychopharmacology* **2022**, *47*, 292–308. [CrossRef]
38. Bandeira, I.D.; Lins-Silva, D.H.; Barouh, J.L.; Faria-Guimarães, D.; Dorea-Bandeira, I.; Souza, L.S.; Alves, G.S.; Brunoni, A.R.; Nitsche, M.; Fregni, F.; et al. Neuroplasticity and non-invasive brain stimulation in the developing brain. *Prog. Brain Res.* **2021**, *264*, 57–89. [CrossRef]
39. Reddy, K.J. Neuroplasticity and technology. In *Innovations in Neurocognitive Rehabilitation: Harnessing Technology for Effective Therapy*; Springer Nature: Cham, Switzerland, 2025; pp. 137–169. [CrossRef]
40. Antal, A.; Luber, B.; Brem, A.-K.; Bikson, M.; Brunoni, A.R.; Cohen Kadosh, R.; Dubljević, V.; Fecteau, S.; Ferreri, F.; Flöel, A.; et al. Non-invasive brain stimulation and neuroenhancement. *Clin. Neurophysiol. Pract.* **2022**, *7*, 146–165. [CrossRef]
41. Halkiopoulos, C.; Gkintoni, E.; Aroutzidis, A.; Antonopoulou, H. Advances in Neuroimaging and Deep Learning for Emotion Detection: A Systematic Review of Cognitive Neuroscience and Algorithmic Innovations. *Diagnostics* **2025**, *15*, 456. [CrossRef]
42. Chen, R.; Huang, L.; Wang, R.; Fei, J.; Wang, H.; Wang, J. Advances in non-invasive neuromodulation techniques for improving cognitive function: A review. *Brain Sci.* **2024**, *14*, 354. [CrossRef] [PubMed]
43. Liu, S.; Liu, S.; Liu, Z.; Peng, X.; Yang, Z. Automated detection of emotional and cognitive engagement in MOOC discussions to predict learning achievement. *Comput. Educ.* **2022**, *190*, 104461. [CrossRef]
44. Dai, C.P.; Ke, F. Educational applications of artificial intelligence in simulation-based learning: A systematic mapping review. *Comput. Educ. Artif. Intell.* **2022**, *3*, 100087. [CrossRef]
45. Dubovi, I. Cognitive and emotional engagement while learning with VR: The perspective of multimodal methodology. *Comput. Educ.* **2022**, *188*, 104495. [CrossRef]
46. Molenaar, I.; de Mooij, S.; Azevedo, R.; Bannert, M.; Järvelä, S.; Gašević, D. Measuring self-regulated learning and the role of AI: Five years of research using multimodal multichannel data. *Comput. Hum. Behav.* **2023**, *139*, 107540. [CrossRef]
47. Gkintoni, E.; Vantaraki, F.; Skoulidi, C.; Anastassopoulos, P.; Vantarakis, A. Promoting Physical and Mental Health among Children and Adolescents via Gamification—A Conceptual Systematic Review. *Behav. Sci.* **2024**, *14*, 102. [CrossRef] [PubMed]
48. Jin, S.H.; Im, K.; Yoo, M.; Roll, I.; Seo, K. Supporting students' self-regulated learning in online learning using artificial intelligence applications. *Int. J. Educ. Technol. High. Educ.* **2023**, *20*, 37. [CrossRef]
49. Rackerby, R.; Lukosch, S.; Munro, D. Understanding and measuring the cognitive load of amputees for rehabilitation and prosthesis development. *Arch. Rehabil. Res. Clin. Transl.* **2022**, *4*, 100216. [CrossRef]

 https://doi.org/10.3390/mti10010005

50. Zhang, T.; Zhang, X.; Zhu, W.; Lu, Z.; Wang, Y.; Zhang, Y. Study on the diversity of mental states and neuroplasticity of the brain during human-machine interaction. *Front. Neurosci.* **2022**, *16*, 921058. [CrossRef]
51. Wu, J.; Qiu, P.; Lv, S.; Chen, M.; Li, Y. The effects of cognitive-motor dual-task training on athletes' cognition and motor performance. *Front. Psychol.* **2024**, *15*, 1284787. [CrossRef]
52. Jayathilake, N.J.; Phan, T.T.; Kim, J.; Lee, K.P.; Park, J.M. Modulating neuroplasticity for chronic pain relief: Noninvasive neuromodulation as a promising approach. *Exp. Mol. Med.* **2025**, *57*, 501–514. [CrossRef]
53. Liang, L.B.; Wang, S.; Li, K.P.; Wu, C.Q. Comparative efficacy of cognitive training modalities in cognitive impairment: A systematic review and network meta-analysis. *J. Prev. Alzheimer's Dis.* **2025**, *12*, 100207. [CrossRef] [PubMed]
54. Sweller, J. Cognitive load theory and individual differences. *Learn. Individ. Differ.* **2024**, *106*, 102423. [CrossRef]
55. Katmah, R.; Awad, M.I.; Al-Ani, F.; Khan, M.; Alskafi, F.A.; Hussain, I.; Jelinek, H.F.; Khalaf, K. Adaptation Robotics and Cognitive Load: Use of a Supernumerary Finger for Activities of Daily Living. *IEEE Trans. Neural Syst. Rehabil. Eng.* **2025**, *33*, 2064–2075. [CrossRef] [PubMed]
56. Vassoler, F.M.; Budge, K.E.; Isgate, S.B.; Gildawie, K.R.; Byrnes, E.M. Neuroplasticity-related genes correlate with individual differences in distinct phases of oxycodone self-administration in male rats. *Neuropharmacology* **2024**, *254*, 109972. [CrossRef]
57. Qiao, Y.; Gao, X.; Liao, W.; Chen, D. Assessment of dynamic cognitive performance under different thermal conditions by multiple physiological signals. *J. Build. Eng.* **2024**, *91*, 109325. [CrossRef]
58. Janssen, T.W.P.; Grammer, J.K.; Bleichner, M.G.; Bulgarelli, C.; Davidesco, I.; Dikker, S.; Jasińska, K.K.; Siugzdaite, R.; Vassena, E.; Vatakis, A.; et al. Opportunities and Limitations of Mobile Neuroimaging Technologies in Educational Neuroscience. *Mind Brain Educ.* **2021**, *15*, 354–370. [CrossRef]
59. Sortwell, A.; Evgenia, G.; Zagarella, S.; Granacher, U.; Forte, P.; Ferraz, R.; Ramirez-Campillo, R.; Carter-Thuillier, B.; Konukman, F.; Nouri, A.; et al. Making neuroscience a priority in Initial Teacher Education curricula: A call for bridging the gap between research and future practices in the classroom. *Neurosci. Res. Notes* **2023**, *6*, 266.1–266.7. [CrossRef]
60. Kellmeyer, P. Big brain data: On the responsible use of brain data from clinical and consumer-directed neurotechnological devices. *Neuroethics* **2021**, *14*, 329–340. [CrossRef]
61. Gkintoni, E.; Vantaraki, F.; Skoulidi, C.; Anastassopoulos, P.; Vantarakis, A. Gamified Health Promotion in Schools: The Integration of Neuropsychological Aspects and CBT—A Systematic Review. *Medicina* **2024**, *60*, 2085. [CrossRef]
62. Klimova, B.; Pikhart, M.; Benites, A.D.; Lehr, C.; Sanchez-Stockhammer, C. Neural machine translation in foreign language teaching and learning: A systematic review. *Educ. Inf. Technol.* **2023**, *28*, 663–682. [CrossRef]
63. Gkintoni, E.; Michou, E. Advancing Neuropsychological Rehabilitation in Primary Progressive Aphasia Based on Principles of Cognitive Neuroscience: A Scoping Review and Systematic Analysis of the Data. *Brain Sci.* **2024**, *14*, 1234. [CrossRef]
64. Drigas, A.; Sideraki, A. Brain neuroplasticity leveraging virtual reality and brain-computer interface technologies. *Sensors* **2024**, *24*, 5725. [CrossRef]
65. Heck, N.; Santos, M.D. Dendritic spines in learning and memory: From first discoveries to current insights. In *Dendritic Spines: Structure*; Springer: Berlin/Heidelberg, Germany, 2023.
66. Mahalakshmi, A.M.; Ray, B.; Tuladhar, S.; Hediyal, T.A.; Raj, P.; Rathipriya, A.G.; Qoronfleh, M.W.; Essa, M.M.; Chidambaram, S.B. Impact of pharmacological and non-pharmacological modulators on dendritic spines structure and functions in brain. *Cells* **2021**, *10*, 3405. [CrossRef]
67. Qiao, Q.; Wu, C.; Ma, L.; Zhang, H.; Li, M.; Wu, X.; Gan, W.B. Motor learning-induced new dendritic spines are preferentially involved in the learned task than existing spines. *Cell Rep.* **2022**, *39*, 111229. [CrossRef] [PubMed]
68. Karbowski, J.; Urban, P. Information encoded in volumes and areas of dendritic spines is nearly maximal across mammalian brains. *Sci. Rep.* **2023**, *13*, 49321. [CrossRef] [PubMed]
69. Appelbaum, L.G.; Shenasa, M.A.; Stolz, L.; Daskalakis, Z. Synaptic plasticity and mental health: Methods, challenges and opportunities. *Neuropsychopharmacology* **2023**, *48*, 113–120. [CrossRef] [PubMed]
70. Spani, F.; Carducci, F.; Piervincenzi, C.; Ben-Soussan, T.D.; Mallio, C.A.; Quattrocchi, C.C. Assessing brain neuroplasticity: Surface morphometric analysis of cortical changes induced by Quadrato motor training. *J. Anat.* **2025**, *246*, 757–769. [CrossRef]
71. Marzola, P.; Melzer, T.; Pavesi, E.; Gil-Mohapel, J.; Brocardo, P.S. Exploring the role of neuroplasticity in development, aging, and neurodegeneration. *Brain Sci.* **2023**, *13*, 1610. [CrossRef]
72. Diniz, C.R.A.F.; Crestani, A.P. The times they are a-changin': A proposal on how brain flexibility goes beyond the obvious to include the concepts of "upward" and "downward" to neuroplasticity. *Mol. Psychiatry* **2022**, *28*, 977–992. [CrossRef]
73. Olszewska, A.M.; Gaca, M.; Herman, A.M.; Jednoróg, K.; Marchewka, A. How musical training shapes the adult brain: Predispositions and neuroplasticity. *Front. Neurosci.* **2021**, *15*, 630829. [CrossRef]
74. Jog, M.A.; Anderson, C.; Kubicki, A.; Boucher, M.; Leaver, A.; Hellemann, G.; Iacoboni, M.; Woods, R.; Narr, K. Transcranial direct current stimulation (tDCS) in depression induces structural plasticity. *Sci. Rep.* **2023**, *13*, 2841. [CrossRef]

75. Reed, M.B.; Klöbl, M.; Godbersen, G.M.; Handschuh, P.A.; Ritter, V.; Spurny-Dworak, B.; Unterholzner, J.; Kraus, C.; Gryglewski, G.; Winkler, D.; et al. Serotonergic modulation of effective connectivity in an associative relearning network during task and rest. *NeuroImage* **2022**, *249*, 118887. [CrossRef]
76. Barbati, S.A.; Podda, M.V.; Grassi, C. Tuning brain networks: The emerging role of transcranial direct current stimulation on structural plasticity. *Front. Cell. Neurosci.* **2022**, *16*, 945777. [CrossRef] [PubMed]
77. He, Y.; Zeng, D.; Li, Q.; Chu, L.; Dong, X.; Liang, X.; Sun, L.; Liao, X.; Zhao, T.; Chen, X.; et al. The multiscale brain structural re-organization that occurs from childhood to adolescence correlates with cortical morphology maturation and functional specialization. *PLoS Biol.* **2025**, *23*, e3002710. [CrossRef]
78. Tilton-Bolowsky, V.; Stockbridge, M.D.; Hillis, A.E. Remapping and reconnecting the language network after stroke. *Brain Sci.* **2024**, *14*, 419. [CrossRef] [PubMed]
79. Kalyuga, S. Evolutionary perspective on human cognitive architecture in cognitive load theory: A dynamic, emerging principle approach. *Educ. Psychol. Rev.* **2023**, *35*, 91. [CrossRef]
80. Sweller, J. The role of evolutionary psychology in our understanding of human cognition: Consequences for cognitive load theory and instructional procedures. *Educ. Psychol. Rev.* **2021**, *34*, 2229–2241. [CrossRef]
81. Evans, P.; Vansteenkiste, M.; Parker, P.; Kingsford-Smith, A.; Zhou, S. Cognitive load theory and its relationships with motivation: A self-determination theory perspective. *Educ. Psychol. Rev.* **2024**, *36*, 7. [CrossRef]
82. Ashtiani, S.N.M.; Daliri, M.R. Identification of cognitive load-dependent activation patterns using working memory task-based fMRI at various levels of difficulty. *Sci. Rep.* **2023**, *13*, 16476. [CrossRef] [PubMed]
83. Gkintoni, E.; Dimakos, I.; Nikolaou, G. Cognitive Insights from Emotional Intelligence: A Systematic Review of EI Models in Educational Achievement. *Emerg. Sci. J.* **2025**, *8*, 262–297. [CrossRef]
84. Cai, W.; Ryali, S.; Pasumarthy, R.; Talasila, V.; Menon, V. Dynamic causal brain circuits during working memory and their functional controllability. *Nat. Commun.* **2021**, *12*, 3314. [CrossRef] [PubMed]
85. Zucchelli, M.M.; Matteucci Armandi Avogli Trotti, N.; Pavan, A.; Piccardi, L.; Nori, R. The Dual Process model: The effect of cognitive load on the ascription of intentionality. *Front. Psychol.* **2025**, *16*, 1451590. [CrossRef]
86. Sieg, L.; Eismann, H.; Schneider, B.; Karsten, J.; Darici, D. How distractions undermine attentional synchronisation in work-based learning: A randomised controlled study using dual mobile eye-tracking. *J. Comput. Assist. Learn.* **2025**, *41*, e70059. [CrossRef]
87. Greenberg, K.; Zheng, R. Revisiting the debate on germane cognitive load versus germane resources. *J. Cogn. Psychol.* **2022**, *35*, 295–314. [CrossRef]
88. Broadbent, D.P.; D'Innocenzo, G.; Ellmers, T.J.; Parsler, J.; Szameitat, A.J.; Bishop, D.T. Cognitive load, working memory capacity and driving performance: A preliminary fNIRS and eye tracking study. *Transp. Res. Part F Traffic Psychol. Behav.* **2023**, *92*, 121–132. [CrossRef]
89. Andreassen, O.A.; Hindley, G.F.; Frei, O.; Smeland, O.B. New insights from the last decade of research in psychiatric genetics: Discoveries, challenges and clinical implications. *World Psychiatry* **2023**, *22*, 4–24. [CrossRef]
90. Li, P.; Lan, Y.J. Digital language learning (DLL): Insights from behavior, cognition, and the brain. *Biling. Lang. Cogn.* **2021**, *25*, 361–378. [CrossRef]
91. Wang, G.; Tian, L.; Liu, J.; Nie, S.; Yu, S. Neural mechanisms of cognitive load in multimedia learning: A meta-analysis of EEG frequency band modulation. *Curr. Psychol.* **2024**, *43*, 29316–29332. [CrossRef]
92. Lyu, C.; Deng, S. Effectiveness of embodied learning on learning performance: A meta-analysis based on the cognitive load theory perspective. *Learn. Individ. Differ.* **2024**, *116*, 102564. [CrossRef]
93. Nim, C.; Aspinall, S.L.; Cook, C.E.; Corrêa, L.A.; Donaldson, M.; Downie, A.S.; Harsted, S.; Hansen, S.; Jenkins, H.J.; McNaughton, D.; et al. The effectiveness of spinal manipulative therapy in treating spinal pain does not depend on the application procedures: A systematic review and network meta-analysis. *J. Orthop. Sports Phys. Ther.* **2025**, *55*, 109–122. [CrossRef]
94. Kora, P.; Meenakshi, K.; Swaraja, K.; Rajani, A.; Raju, M.S. EEG based interpretation of human brain activity during yoga and meditation using machine learning: A systematic review. *Complement. Ther. Clin. Pract.* **2021**, *43*, 101329. [CrossRef] [PubMed]
95. Nord, C.L.; Garfinkel, S.N. Interoceptive pathways to understand and treat mental health conditions. *Trends Cogn. Sci.* **2022**, *26*, 499–513. [CrossRef] [PubMed]
96. Gkintoni, E.; Aroutzidis, A.; Antonopoulou, H.; Halkiopoulos, C. From neural networks to emotional networks: A systematic review of EEG-based emotion recognition in cognitive neuroscience and real-world applications. *Brain Sci.* **2025**, *15*, 220. [CrossRef]
97. Deery, H.A.; Di Paolo, R.; Moran, C.; Egan, G.F.; Jamadar, S.D. The older adult brain is less modular, more integrated, and less efficient at rest: A systematic review of large-scale resting-state functional brain networks in aging. *Psychophysiology* **2023**, *60*, e14159. [CrossRef]
98. Kay, K.; Bonnen, K.; Denison, R.N.; Arcaro, M.J.; Barack, D.L. Tasks and their role in visual neuroscience. *Neuron* **2023**, *111*, 1697–1713. [CrossRef]

 https://doi.org/10.3390/mti10010005

99. Pei, L.; Northoff, G.; Ouyang, G. Comparative analysis of multifaceted neural effects associated with varying endogenous cognitive load. *Commun. Biol.* **2023**, *6*, 795. [CrossRef]
100. Pei, L.; Zhou, X.; Leung, F.K.S.; Ouyang, G. Differential associations between scale-free neural dynamics and different levels of cognitive ability. *Psychophysiology* **2023**, *60*, e14259. [CrossRef]
101. Lu, R. Linking the multiple-demand cognitive control system to human electrophysiological activity. *Neuropsychologia* **2025**, *210*, 109096. [CrossRef]
102. Habibollahi, F.; Kagan, B.J.; Burkitt, A.N.; French, C. Critical dynamics arise during structured information presentation within embodied in vitro neuronal networks. *Nat. Commun.* **2023**, *14*, 5287. [CrossRef]
103. Khalil, M.H. Green environments for sustainable brains: Parameters shaping adaptive neuroplasticity and lifespan neurosustainability—A systematic review and future directions. *Int. J. Environ. Res. Public Health* **2025**, *22*, 690. [CrossRef] [PubMed]
104. Ho, T.C.; King, L.S. Mechanisms of neuroplasticity linking early adversity to depression: Developmental considerations. *Transl. Psychiatry* **2021**, *11*, 517. [CrossRef] [PubMed]
105. Leisman, G. On the application of developmental cognitive neuroscience in educational environments. *Brain Sci.* **2022**, *12*, 1501. [CrossRef]
106. Martins, L.A.; Schiavo, A.; Paz, L.V.; Xavier, L.L.; Mestriner, R.G. Neural underpinnings of fine motor skills under stress and anxiety: A review. *Physiol. Behavior.* **2024**, *282*, 114593. [CrossRef]
107. Makanadar, A. Neuro-adaptive architecture: Buildings and city design that respond to human emotions, cognitive states. *Res. Glob.* **2024**, *8*, 100222. [CrossRef]
108. Osei, P.C.; Bjorklund, D.F. Motivating the learning process: Integrating self-determination theory into a dynamical systems framework. *Educ. Psychol. Rev.* **2024**, *36*, 89. [CrossRef]
109. Corriveau-Lecavalier, N.; Rajah, M.N.; Mellah, S.; Belleville, S. Latent patterns of task-related functional connectivity in relation to regions of hyperactivation in individuals at risk of Alzheimer's disease. *NeuroImage Clin.* **2021**, *30*, 102643. [CrossRef]
110. Carrasco-Gómez, M.; García-Colomo, A.; Cabrera-Álvarez, J.; del Cerro-León, A.; Gómez-Ariza, C.J.; Santos, A.; Maestú, F. Individual alpha frequency tACS reduces static functional connectivity across the default mode network. *Front. Hum. Neurosci.* **2025**, *19*, 1534321. [CrossRef]
111. Ruppert, M.C.; Greuel, A.; Freigang, J.; Tahmasian, M.; Maier, F.; Hammes, J.; van Eimeren, T.; Timmermann, L.; Tittgemeyer, M.; Drzezga, A.; et al. The default mode network and cognition in Parkinson's disease: A multimodal resting-state network approach. *Hum. Brain Mapp.* **2021**, *42*, 2623–2641. [CrossRef]
112. Pitsik, E. Recurrence quantification analysis and theta-band functional networks detect age-related changes in brain sensorimotor system: VR-based approach. *Eur. Phys. J. Spec. Top.* **2025**, 1–7. [CrossRef]
113. Draheim, C.; Pak, R.; Draheim, A.A.; Engle, R.W. The role of attention control in complex real-world tasks. *Psychon. Bull. Rev.* **2022**, *29*, 1143–1197. [CrossRef]
114. Draschkow, D.; Kallmayer, M.; Nobre, A.C. When natural behavior engages working memory. *Curr. Biol.* **2021**, *31*, 869–874.e5. [CrossRef]
115. Yang, S.; Gao, T.; Wang, J.; Deng, B.; Azghadi, M.R.; Lei, T.; Linares-Barranco, B. SAM: A unified self-adaptive multicompartmental spiking neuron model for learning with working memory. *Front. Neurosci.* **2022**, *16*, 850945. [CrossRef] [PubMed]
116. Chikhi, S.; Matton, N.; Blanchet, S. EEG power spectral measures of cognitive workload: A meta-analysis. *Psychophysiology* **2022**, *59*, e14009. [CrossRef]
117. Zhu, Y.; Wang, Q.; Zhang, L. Study of EEG characteristics while solving scientific problems with different mental effort. *Sci. Rep.* **2021**, *11*, 23783. [CrossRef]
118. Halkiopoulos, C.; Gkintoni, E. The Role of Machine Learning in AR/VR-Based Cognitive Therapies: A Systematic Review for Mental Health Disorders. *Electronics* **2025**, *14*, 1110. [CrossRef]
119. Taheri Gorji, H.; Wilson, N.; VanBree, J.; Hoffmann, B.; Petros, T.; Tavakolian, K. Using machine learning methods and EEG to discriminate aircraft pilot cognitive workload during flight. *Sci. Rep.* **2023**, *13*, 2507. [CrossRef]
120. Antonenko, D.; Fromm, A.E.; Thams, F.; Kuzmina, A.; Backhaus, M.; Knochenhauer, E.; Li, S.-C.; Grittner, U.; Flöel, A. Cognitive training and brain stimulation in patients with cognitive impairment: A randomized controlled trial. *Alzheimer's Res. Ther.* **2024**, *16*, 6. [CrossRef] [PubMed]
121. Ríos, A.S.; Oxenford, S.; Neudorfer, C.; Butenko, K.; Li, N.; Rajamani, N.; Boutet, A.; Elias, G.J.B.; Germann, J.; Loh, A.; et al. Optimal deep brain stimulation sites and networks for stimulation of the fornix in Alzheimer's disease. *Nat. Commun.* **2022**, *13*, 7707. [CrossRef] [PubMed]
122. von Bastian, C.C.; Belleville, S.; Udale, R.C.; Reinhartz, A.; Essounni, M.; Strobach, T. Mechanisms underlying training-induced cognitive change. *Nat. Rev. Psychol.* **2022**, *1*, 30–41. [CrossRef]
123. Vinogradov, S.; Chafee, M.V.; Lee, E.; Morishita, H. Psychosis spectrum illnesses as disorders of prefrontal critical period plasticity. *Neuropsychopharmacology* **2023**, *48*, 168–185. [CrossRef]

 https://doi.org/10.3390/mti10010005

124. Meccia, J.; Lopez, J.; Bagot, R.C. Probing the antidepressant potential of psilocybin: Integrating insight from human research and animal models towards an understanding of neural circuit mechanisms. *Psychopharmacology* **2022**, *240*, 27–40. [CrossRef]
125. Sengupta, A.; Banerjee, S.; Ganesh, S.; Grover, S.; Sridharan, D. The right posterior parietal cortex mediates spatial reorienting of attentional choice bias. *Nat. Commun.* **2024**, *15*, 6938. [CrossRef]
126. Hou, W.; Zhou, F.; Wang, Q.; Li, H.; Qin, X.; Ding, Y.; Dong, F.; Bo, Q.; Li, A.; Zhang, L.; et al. Effect of transcranial direct current stimulation with concurrent cognitive performance targeting posterior parietal cortex vs prefrontal cortex on working memory in schizophrenia: A randomized clinical trial. *Transl. Psychiatry* **2024**, *14*, 279. [CrossRef]
127. Martin, S.; Frieling, R.; Saur, D.; Hartwigsen, G. TMS over the pre-SMA enhances semantic cognition via remote network effects on task-based activity and connectivity. *Brain Stimul.* **2023**, *16*, 1346–1357. [CrossRef]
128. Galoyan, T.; Betts, K.; Abramian, H.; Reddy, P.; Izzetoglu, K.; Shewokis, P.A. Examining mental workload in a spatial navigation transfer game via functional near infrared spectroscopy. *Brain Sci.* **2021**, *11*, 45. [CrossRef] [PubMed]
129. da Silva Soares, R., Jr.; Ambriola Oku, A.Y.; Barreto, C.S.; Ricardo Sato, J. Applying functional near-infrared spectroscopy and eye-tracking in a naturalistic educational environment to investigate physiological aspects that underlie the cognitive effort of children during mental rotation tests. *Front. Hum. Neurosci.* **2022**, *16*, 889806. [CrossRef] [PubMed]
130. Khanam, F.; Hossain, A.B.M.A.; Ahmad, M. Statistical valuation of cognitive load level hemodynamics from functional near-infrared spectroscopy signals. *Neurosci. Inform.* **2022**, *2*, 100042. [CrossRef]
131. Liu, T.; Xu, Z.; Cao, L.; Tan, G. Evolutionary multitasking-based multiobjective optimization algorithm for channel selection in hybrid brain computer interfacing systems. *Front. Neurosci.* **2021**, *15*, 749232. [CrossRef]
132. Beltrán, E.T.M.; Pérez, M.Q.; Bernal, S.L.; Pérez, G.M.; Celdrán, A.H. SAFECAR: A brain-computer interface and intelligent framework to detect drivers' distractions. *Expert. Syst. Appl.* **2022**, *203*, 117402. [CrossRef]
133. Yasuhara, M.; Nambu, I. Error-related potentials during multitasking involving sensorimotor control: An ERP and offline decoding study for brain-computer interface. *Front. Hum. Neurosci.* **2025**, *19*, 1516721. [CrossRef]
134. Chen, J.; Tam, A.; Kebets, V.; Orban, C.; Ooi, L.Q.R.; Asplund, C.L.; Marek, S.; Dosenbach, N.U.F.; Eickhoff, S.B.; Bzdok, D.; et al. Shared and unique brain network features predict cognitive, personality, and mental health scores in the ABCD study. *Nat. Commun.* **2022**, *13*, 2217. [CrossRef] [PubMed]
135. Williamson, B.; Pykett, J.; Kotouza, D. Learning brains: Educational neuroscience, neurotechnology and neuropedagogy. *Pedagog. Cult. Soc.* **2025**, 1–21. [CrossRef]
136. Haddaway, N.R.; Page, M.J.; Pritchard, C.C.; McGuinness, L.A. PRISMA2020: An R package and Shiny app for producing PRISMA 2020-compliant flow diagrams, with interactivity for optimised digital transparency and Open Synthesis. *Campbell Syst. Rev.* **2022**, *18*, e1230. [CrossRef]
137. van den Akker, O.R.; Peters, G.-J.Y.; Bakker, C.J.; Carlsson, R.; Coles, N.A.; Corker, K.S.; Feldman, G.; Moreau, D.; Nordström, T.; Pickering, J.S.; et al. Increasing the transparency of systematic reviews: Presenting a generalized registration form. *Syst. Rev.* **2023**, *12*, 170. [CrossRef]
138. Adcock, R.; Dale, C.; Fisher, M.; Aldebot, S.; Genevsky, A.; Simpson, G.V.; Nagarajan, S.; Vinogradov, S. When top-down meets bottom-up: Auditory training enhances verbal memory in schizophrenia. *Schizophr. Bull.* **2009**, *35*, 1132–1141. [CrossRef]
139. Afify, M. Effect of Interactive Video Length Within E-learning Environments on Cognitive Load, Cognitive Achievement and Retention of Learning. *Turk. Online J. Distance Educ.* **2020**, *21*, 68–89. [CrossRef]
140. Andrade, S.M.; Fernández-Calvo, B.; Boggio, P.S.; de Oliveira, E.A.; Gomes, L.F.; Júnior, J.E.G.P.; Rodrigues, R.M.; de Almeida, N.L.; Moreira, G.M.d.S.; Alves, N.T. Neurostimulation for cognitive rehabilitation in stroke (NeuroCog): Study protocol for a randomized controlled trial. *Trials* **2015**, *16*, 435. [CrossRef]
141. Anguera, J.A.; Boccanfuso, J.; Rintoul, J.L.; Al-Hashimi, O.; Faraji, F.; Janowich, J.; Kong, E.; Larraburo, Y.; Rolle, C.E.; Johnston, E.R.; et al. Video game training enhances cognitive control in older adults. *Nature* **2013**, *501*, 97–101. [CrossRef]
142. Antonenko, D.; Fromm, A.; Thams, F.; Grittner, U.; Meinzer, M.; Flöel, A. Microstructural and functional plasticity following repeated brain stimulation during cognitive training in older adults. *Nat. Commun.* **2023**, *14*, 3184. [CrossRef]
143. Assecondi, S.; Shapiro, K. The benefits of combined brain stimulation and cognitive training: A pilot study. *J. Vis.* **2018**, *18*, 119. [CrossRef]
144. Au, J.; Katz, B.; Buschkuehl, M.; Bunarjo, K.; Senger, T.; Zabel, C.; Jaeggi, S.M.; Jonides, J. Enhancing Working Memory Training with Transcranial Direct Current Stimulation. *J. Cogn. Neurosci.* **2016**, *28*, 1419–1432. [CrossRef]
145. Bentham, C.; Marco, M.D.; Venneri, A. The Modulatory Effect of Cerebrovascular Burden in Response to Cognitive Stimulation in Healthy Ageing and Mild Cognitive Impairment. *Neural Plast.* **2019**, *2019*, 2305318. [CrossRef]
146. Brehmer, Y.; Rieckmann, A.; Bellander, M.; Westerberg, H.; Fischer, H.; Bäckman, L. Neural correlates of training-related working-memory gains in old age. *NeuroImage* **2011**, *58*, 1110–1120. [CrossRef]
147. Bubbico, G.; Chiacchiaretta, P.; Parenti, M.; di Marco, M.; Panara, V.; Sepede, G.; Ferretti, A.; Perrucci, M.G. Effects of Second Language Learning on the Plastic Aging Brain: Functional Connectivity, Cognitive Decline, and Reorganization. *Front. Neurosci.* **2019**, *13*, 423. [CrossRef]

 https://doi.org/10.3390/mti10010005

148. Chen, Q.; Baran, T.; Turnbull, A.; Zhang, Z.; Rebok, G.; Lin, F. Increased segregation of structural brain networks underpins enhanced broad cognitive abilities of cognitive training. *Hum. Brain Mapp.* **2021**, *42*, 3202–3215. [CrossRef]
149. Cohen Kadosh, R. T007 Neural predictors of the effect of transcranial electrical stimulation on learning. *Clin. Neurophysiol.* **2017**, *128*, e3. [CrossRef]
150. Erickson, K.; Colcombe, S.; Wadhwa, R.; Bherer, L.; Peterson, M.; Scalf, P.E.; Kim, J.S.; Alvarado, M.; Kramer, A. Training-induced plasticity in older adults: Effects of training on hemispheric asymmetry. *Aging* **2007**, *28*, 272–283. [CrossRef] [PubMed]
151. Faber, T.; Dankbaar, M.; Van den Broek, W.W.; Bruinink, L.J.; Hogeveen, M.; van Merriënboer, J.J.G. Effects of adaptive scaffolding on performance, cognitive load and engagement in game-based learning: A randomized controlled trial. *BMC Med. Educ.* **2024**, *24*, 943. [CrossRef]
152. Falcone, B.; Wada, A.; Parasuraman, R.; Callan, D. Individual differences in learning correlate with modulation of brain activity induced by transcranial direct current stimulation. *PLoS ONE* **2018**, *13*, e0197192. [CrossRef] [PubMed]
153. Fang, P.; Gao, Y.; Li, Y.; Li, C.; Zhang, T.; Wu, L.; Zhu, Y.; Xie, Y. Effects of computerized working memory training on neuroplasticity in healthy individuals: A combined neuroimaging and neurotransmitter study. *NeuroImage* **2024**, *298*, 120785. [CrossRef] [PubMed]
154. Fatima, Z.; Kovacevic, N.; Mišić, B.; Mcintosh, A. Dynamic functional connectivity shapes individual differences in associative learning. *Hum. Brain Mapp.* **2016**, *37*, 3911–3928. [CrossRef]
155. Fehring, D.J.; Illipparampil, R.; Acevedo, N.; Jaberzadeh, S.; Fitzgerald, P.; Mansouri, F. Interaction of task-related learning and transcranial direct current stimulation of the prefrontal cortex in modulating executive functions. *Neuropsychologia* **2019**, *131*, 148–159. [CrossRef]
156. Filippi, M.; Riccitelli, G.; Mattioli, F.; Capra, R.; Stampatori, C.; Pagani, E.; Valsasina, P.; Copetti, M.; Falini, A.; Comi, G.; et al. Multiple Sclerosis: Effects of Cognitive Rehabilitation on Structural and Functional MR Imaging Measures—An Explorative Study. *Radiology* **2012**, *262*, 932–940. [CrossRef]
157. Frank, B.; Harty, S.; Kluge, A.; Cohen Kadosh, R. Learning while multitasking: Short and long-term benefits of brain stimulation. *Ergonomics* **2018**, *61*, 1454–1463. [CrossRef]
158. Fujino, J.; Tei, S.; Itahashi, T.; Aoki, Y.Y.; Ohta, H.; Izuno, T.; Nakamura, H.; Shimizu, M.; Hashimoto, R.-I.; Takahashi, H.; et al. A single session of navigation-guided repetitive transcranial magnetic stimulation over the right anterior temporoparietal junction in autism spectrum disorder. *Brain Stimul.* **2021**, *14*, 682–684. [CrossRef]
159. Gajewski, P.D.; Falkenstein, M. Training-Induced Improvement of Response Selection and Error Detection in Aging Assessed by Task Switching: Effects of Cognitive, Physical, and Relaxation Training. *Front. Hum. Neurosci.* **2012**, *6*, 130. [CrossRef]
160. Gallen, C.L.; Baniqued, P.L.; Chapman, S.B.; Aslan, S.; Keebler, M.; Didehbani, N.; D'Esposito, M.; Hayasaka, S. Modular Brain Network Organization Predicts Response to Cognitive Training in Older Adults. *PLoS ONE* **2016**, *11*, e0169015. [CrossRef]
161. Gangemi, A.; De Luca, R.; Fabio, R.A.; Lauria, P.; Rifici, C.; Pollicino, P.; Marra, A.; Olivo, A.; Quartarone, A.; Calabrò, R.S. Effects of Virtual Reality Cognitive Training on Neuroplasticity: A Quasi-Randomized Clinical Trial in Patients with Stroke. *Biomedicines* **2023**, *11*, 3225. [CrossRef] [PubMed]
162. Ha, J.; Fang, Y.; Cron, G.O.; Heo, J.; Jung, E.; Lee, D.; Kim, H.; Kim, E.; Park, J.Y.; Lee, J.H. In patients with late-life depression and cognitive decline, adding tDCS to cognitive training does not significantly affect depressive symptoms but shows potential benefits on cognition as measured by fMRI. *Brain Stimul.* **2024**, *17*, 202–204. [CrossRef] [PubMed]
163. Hadie, S.N.H.; Tan, V.P.S.; Omar, N.; Alwi, N.A.N.M.; Lim, H.L.; Marsilla, K.I.K. COVID-19 Disruptions in Health Professional Education: Use of Cognitive Load Theory on Students' Comprehension, Cognitive Load, Engagement, and Motivation. *Front. Med.* **2021**, *8*, 739238. [CrossRef] [PubMed]
164. Hauser, T.U.; Rütsche, B.; Wurmitzer, K.; Brem, S.; Ruff, C.C.; Grabner, R.H. Neurocognitive Effects of Transcranial Direct Current Stimulation in Arithmetic Learning and Performance: A Simultaneous tDCS-fMRI Study. *Brain Stimul.* **2016**, *9*, 850–858. [CrossRef]
165. Haut, K.M.; Lim, K.O.; MacDonald, A. Prefrontal Cortical Changes Following Cognitive Training in Patients with Chronic Schizophrenia: Effects of Practice, Generalization, and Specificity. *Neuropsychopharmacology* **2010**, *35*, 1850–1859. [CrossRef]
166. Henssen, D.J.; Heuvel, L.v.D.; De Jong, G.; Vorstenbosch, M.A.; Walsum, A.v.C.v.; Hurk, M.M.V.D.; Kooloos, J.G.; Bartels, R.H. Neuroanatomy Learning: Augmented Reality vs. Cross-Sections. *Anat. Sci. Educ.* **2019**, *13*, 353–365. [CrossRef] [PubMed]
167. Jaeggi, S. Maximizing Cognitive Training Outcomes with Simultaneous Brain Stimulation. *Innov. Aging* **2024**, *8*, 670. [CrossRef]
168. Jian, Y.; Abu Bakar, J.A. Comparing cognitive load in learning spatial ability: Immersive learning environment vs. digital learning media. *Discov. Sustain.* **2024**, *5*, 111. [CrossRef]
169. Jones, K.T.; Stephens, J.A.; Alam, M.; Bikson, M.; Berryhill, M.E.; Antal, A. Longitudinal Neurostimulation in Older Adults Improves Working Memory. *PLoS ONE* **2015**, *10*, e0121904. [CrossRef]
170. Kadir, M.S.; Yeung, A.S.; Caleon, I.S.; Diallo, T.M.O.; Forbes, A.; Koh, W.X. The effects of load reduction instruction on educational outcomes: An intervention study on hands-on inquiry-based learning in science. *Appl. Cogn. Psychol.* **2023**, *37*, 814–829. [CrossRef]

 https://doi.org/10.3390/mti10010005

171. Kelly, C.E.; Thompson, D.K.; Chen, J.; Josev, E.K.; Pascoe, L.; Spencer-Smith, M.M.; Adamson, C.; Nosarti, C.; Gathercole, S.; Roberts, G.; et al. Working memory training and brain structure and function in extremely preterm or extremely low birth weight children. *Hum. Brain Mapp.* **2019**, *41*, 684–696. [CrossRef]
172. Khalil, R.; Godde, B.; Karim, A. P093 Transcranial cortex stimulation, neuroplasticity and learning: An experimental and computational study. *Clin. Neurophysiol.* **2017**, *128*, e53–e54. [CrossRef]
173. Kober, S.E.; Witte, M.; Stangl, M.; Väljamäe, A.; Neuper, C.; Wood, G. Shutting down sensorimotor interference unblocks the networks for stimulus processing: An SMR neurofeedback training study. *Clin. Neurophysiol.* **2015**, *126*, 82–95. [CrossRef]
174. Küçük, S.; Kapakin, S.; Göktaş, Y. Learning anatomy via mobile augmented reality: Effects on achievement and cognitive load. *Anat. Sci. Educ.* **2016**, *9*, 411–421. [CrossRef]
175. Lampit, A.; Hallock, H.; Suo, C.; Naismith, S.L.; Valenzuela, M. Cognitive training-induced short-term functional and long-term structural plastic change is related to gains in global cognition in healthy older adults: A pilot study. *Front. Aging Neurosci.* **2015**, *7*, 14. [CrossRef]
176. Lee, D.R.; Kim, Y.H.; Kim, D.A.; Lee, J.A.; Hwang, P.W.; Lee, M.J.; You, S. Innovative strength training-induced neuroplasticity and increased muscle size and strength in children with spastic cerebral palsy: An experimenter-blind case study–three-month follow-up. *NeuroRehabilitation* **2014**, *35*, 131–136. [CrossRef] [PubMed]
177. Lee, H.; Voss, M.W.; Prakash, R.S.; Boot, W.R.; Vo, L.T.; Basak, C.; VanPatter, M.; Gratton, G.; Fabiani, M.; Kramer, A.F. Videogame training strategy-induced change in brain function during a complex visuomotor task. *Behav. Brain Res.* **2012**, *232*, 348–357. [CrossRef]
178. Leung, N.T.Y.; Tam, H.M.K.; Chu, L.W.; Kwok, T.C.Y.; Chan, F.; Lam, L.C.W.; Woo, J.; Lee, T.M.C. Neural Plastic Effects of Cognitive Training on Aging Brain. *Neural Plast.* **2015**, *2015*, 535618. [CrossRef]
179. Lin, C.-C.; Kao, S.-C.; Hung, C.-L.; Tsai, C.-L.; Huang, C.-J.; Chang, Y.-K.; Hung, T.-M. The Effects of Gymnastics Programs with Different Cognitive Loads on Working Memory and Prefrontal Cortex Oxygenation: A Randomized Controlled Trial. *Med. Sci. Sports Exerc.* **2025**, *57*, 1123–1136. [CrossRef] [PubMed]
180. Liu, X.L.; Reder, L.M. fMRI exploration of pedagogical benefits of repeated testing: When more is not always better. *Brain Behav.* **2016**, *6*, e00476. [CrossRef] [PubMed]
181. Looi, C.Y.; Duta, M.; Brem, A.-K.; Huber, S.; Nuerk, H.-C.; Kadosh, R.C. Combining brain stimulation and video game to promote long-term transfer of learning and cognitive enhancement. *Sci. Rep.* **2016**, *6*, 22003. [CrossRef]
182. Looi, C.Y.; Lim, J.; Sella, F.; Lolliot, S.; Duta, M.; Avramenko, A.A.; Cohen Kadosh, R. Transcranial random noise stimulation and cognitive training to improve learning and cognition of the atypically developing brain: A pilot study. *Sci. Rep.* **2017**, *7*, 4633. [CrossRef]
183. Novakova, L.; Gajdos, M.; Rektorova, I. Theta-burst transcranial magnetic stimulation induced cognitive task-related decrease in activity of default mode network: An exploratory study. *Brain Stimul.* **2020**, *13*, 597–599. [CrossRef]
184. Ludyga, S.; Gerber, M.; Schwarz, A.; Greco, A.; Müller, T.; Pühse, U.; Hanke, M. Effects of Cognitive and Physical Load of Acute Exercise on Inhibitory Control and Prefrontal Cortex Hemodynamics in Children. *Med. Sci. Sports Exerc.* **2024**, *56*, 1328–1336. [CrossRef]
185. MacInnes, J.J.; Dickerson, K.C.; Chen, N.-K.; Adcock, R.A. Cognitive Neurostimulation: Learning to Volitionally Sustain Ventral Tegmental Area Activation. *Neuron* **2016**, *89*, 1331–1342. [CrossRef]
186. Mahncke, H.W.; DeGutis, J.; Levin, H.; Newsome, M.R.; Bell, M.D.; Grills, C.; French, L.M.; Sullivan, K.W.; Kim, S.-J.; Rose, A.; et al. A randomized clinical trial of plasticity-based cognitive training in mild traumatic brain injury. *Brain* **2021**, *144*, 1994–2008. [CrossRef]
187. Mark, J.; Kraft, A.; Casebeer, W.D.; Ziegler, M.D.; Ayaz, H. Neuroimaging-guided Adaptive Training in Flight Simulators. *Front. Hum. Neurosci.* **2018**, *12*. [CrossRef]
188. Mattioli, F.; Bellomi, F.; Stampatori, C.; Capra, R.; Miniussi, C. Neuroenhancement through cognitive training and anodal tDCS in multiple sclerosis. *Mult. Scler. J.* **2015**, *22*, 222–230. [CrossRef]
189. McKendrick, R.; Ayaz, H.; Olmstead, R.; Parasuraman, R. Enhancing dual-task performance with verbal and spatial working memory training: Continuous monitoring of cerebral hemodynamics with NIRS. *NeuroImage* **2014**, *85*, 1014–1026. [CrossRef] [PubMed]
190. Nikolaidis, A.; Voss, M.W.; Elee, H.; Vo, L.T.K.; Kramer, A.F. Parietal plasticity after training with a complex video game is associated with individual differences in improvements in an untrained working memory task. *Front. Hum. Neurosci.* **2014**, *8*, 169. [CrossRef] [PubMed]
191. Nishiguchi, S.; Yamada, M.; Tanigawa, T.; Sekiyama, K.; Kawagoe, T.; Suzuki, M.; Yoshikawa, S.; Abe, N.; Otsuka, Y.; Nakai, R.; et al. A 12-Week Physical and Cognitive Exercise Program Can Improve Cognitive Function and Neural Efficiency in Community-Dwelling Older Adults: A Randomized Controlled Trial. *J. Am. Geriatr. Soc.* **2015**, *63*, 1355–1363. [CrossRef]

https://doi.org/10.3390/mti10010005

192. Nissim, N.R.; O'sHea, A.; Indahlastari, A.; Kraft, J.N.; von Mering, O.; Aksu, S.; Porges, E.; Cohen, R.; Woods, A.J. Effects of Transcranial Direct Current Stimulation Paired With Cognitive Training on Functional Connectivity of the Working Memory Network in Older Adults. *Front. Aging Neurosci.* **2019**, *11*, 340. [CrossRef]
193. Parmar, D.; Enticott, P.G.; Albein-Urios, N. Anodal HD-tDCS for cognitive inflexibility in autism spectrum disorder: A pilot study. *Brain Stimul.* **2021**, *14*, 1298–1300. [CrossRef] [PubMed]
194. Parsons, B.; Faubert, J. Enhancing learning in a perceptual-cognitive training paradigm using EEG neurofeedback. *Sci. Rep.* **2021**, *11*, 4061. [CrossRef]
195. Perlini, C. The Impact of cognitive remediation combined with mindfulness and social skills training on social functioning and neural plasticity in early psychosis: Preliminary results from a randomized clinical multicentric trial in Italy. *Eur. Psychiatry* **2024**, *67*, S33. [CrossRef]
196. Pietto, M.L.; Giovannetti, F.; Segretin, M.S.; Kamienkowski, J.E.; Lipina, S.J. Increased integration of functional connectivity after cognitive intervention in preschoolers from low socioeconomic status. *Dev. Psychol.* **2023**, *59*, 1823–1838. [CrossRef] [PubMed]
197. Pozuelos, J.P.; Combita, L.M.; Abundis, A.; Paz-Alonso, P.M.; Conejero, Á.; Guerra, S.; Rueda, M.R. Metacognitive scaffolding boosts cognitive and neural benefits following executive attention training in children. *Dev. Sci.* **2018**, *22*, e12756. [CrossRef] [PubMed]
198. Rebok, G.W.; Ball, K.; Guey, L.T.; ScD, R.N.J.; DrPH, H.K.; King, J.W.; Marsiske, M.; Morris, J.N.; Tennstedt, S.L.; Unverzagt, F.W.; et al. Ten-Year Effects of the Advanced Cognitive Training for Independent and Vital Elderly Cognitive Training Trial on Cognition and Everyday Functioning in Older Adults. *J. Am. Geriatr. Soc.* **2014**, *62*, 16–24. [CrossRef]
199. Richmond, L.L.; Wolk, D.; Chein, J.; Olson, I.R. Transcranial Direct Current Stimulation Enhances Verbal Working Memory Training Performance over Time and Near Transfer Outcomes. *J. Cogn. Neurosci.* **2014**, *26*, 2443–2454. [CrossRef]
200. Rischer, K.M.; Anton, F.; González-Roldán, A.M.; Montoya, P.; van der Meulen, M. Better Executive Functions Are Associated With More Efficient Cognitive Pain Modulation in Older Adults: An fMRI Study. *Front. Aging Neurosci.* **2022**, *14*, 828742. [CrossRef]
201. Roe, J.M.; Nesheim, M.; Mathiesen, N.C.; Moberget, T.; Alnæs, D.; Sneve, M.H. The effects of tDCS upon sustained visual attention are dependent on cognitive load. *Neuropsychologia* **2016**, *80*, 1–8. [CrossRef]
202. Román, F.J.; Iturria-Medina, Y.; Martínez, K.; Karama, S.; Burgaleta, M.; Evans, A.C.; Jaeggi, S.M.; Colom, R. Enhanced structural connectivity within a brain sub-network supporting working memory and engagement processes after cognitive training. *Neurobiol. Learn. Mem.* **2017**, *141*, 33–43. [CrossRef]
203. Romeo, R.R.; Leonard, J.A.; Grotzinger, H.M.; Robinson, S.T.; Takada, M.E.; Mackey, A.P.; Scherer, E.; Rowe, M.L.; West, M.R.; Gabrieli, J.D. Neuroplasticity associated with changes in conversational turn-taking following a family-based intervention. *Dev. Cogn. Neurosci.* **2021**, *49*, 100967. [CrossRef]
204. Rosa, V.d.O.; Franco, A.R.; Júnior, G.A.S.; Moreira-Maia, C.R.; Wagner, F.; Simioni, A.; Bassotto, C.d.F.; Moritz, G.R.; Aguzzoli, C.S.; Buchweitz, A.; et al. Effects of computerized cognitive training as add-on treatment to stimulants in ADHD: A pilot fMRI study. *Brain Imaging Behav.* **2019**, *14*, 1933–1944. [CrossRef] [PubMed]
205. Saiote, C.; Polanía, R.; Rosenberger, K.; Paulus, W.; Antal, A.; Avenanti, A. High-Frequency TRNS Reduces BOLD Activity during Visuomotor Learning. *PLoS ONE* **2013**, *8*, e59669. [CrossRef] [PubMed]
206. Sánchez-Pérez, N.; Inuggi, A.; Castillo, A.; Campoy, G.; García-Santos, J.M.; González-Salinas, C.; Fuentes, L.J. Computer-Based Cognitive Training Improves Brain Functional Connectivity in the Attentional Networks: A Study With Primary School-Aged Children. *Front. Behav. Neurosci.* **2019**, *13*, 247. [CrossRef]
207. Sankaranarayanan, G.; Odlozil, C.A.; Wells, K.O.; Leeds, S.G.; Chauhan, S.; Fleshman, J.W.; Jones, D.B.; De, S. Training with cognitive load improves performance under similar conditions in a real surgical task. *Am. J. Surg.* **2020**, *220*, 620–629. [CrossRef]
208. Schroder, H.S.; Moran, T.P.; Donnellan, M.B.; Moser, J.S. Mindset induction effects on cognitive control: A neurobehavioral investigation. *Biol. Psychol.* **2014**, *103*, 27–37. [CrossRef]
209. Sehatpour, P.; Dondé, C.; Adair, D.; Kreither, J.; Lopez-Calderon, J.; Avissar, M.; Bikson, M.; Javitt, D.C. Comparison of cortical network effects of high-definition and conventional tDCS during visuomotor processing. *Brain Stimul.* **2021**, *14*, 33–35. [CrossRef] [PubMed]
210. Smith, G.E.; Housen, P.; Yaffe, K.; Ruff, R.; Kennison, R.F.; Mahncke, H.W.; Zelinski, E.M. A Cognitive Training Program Based on Principles of Brain Plasticity: Results from the Improvement in Memory with Plasticity-based Adaptive Cognitive Training (IMPACT) Study. *J. Am. Geriatr. Soc.* **2009**, *57*, 594–603. [CrossRef]
211. Stephens, J.A.; Berryhill, M.E. Older Adults Improve on Everyday Tasks after Working Memory Training and Neurostimulation. *Brain Stimul.* **2016**, *9*, 553–559. [CrossRef]
212. Styliadis, C.; Kartsidis, P.; Paraskevopoulos, E.; Ioannides, A.A.; Bamidis, P.D. Neuroplastic Effects of Combined Computerized Physical and Cognitive Training in Elderly Individuals at Risk for Dementia: An eLORETA Controlled Study on Resting States. *Neural Plast.* **2015**, *2015*, 172192. [CrossRef]

 https://doi.org/10.3390/mti10010005

213. Sun, J.C.-Y.; Yu, S.-J.; Chao, C.-H. Effects of intelligent feedback on online learners' engagement and cognitive load: The case of research ethics education. *Educ. Psychol.* **2018**, *39*, 1293–1310. [CrossRef]
214. Tai, H.-C.; Chen, C.-M.; Tsai, Y.-H.; Lee, B.-O.; Dewi, Y.S. Is Instructional Scaffolding a Better Strategy for Teaching Writing to EFL Learners? A Functional MRI Study in Healthy Young Adults. *Brain Sci.* **2021**, *11*, 1378. [CrossRef]
215. Tatti, F.; Golemme, M.; Chrisostomou, L.; Panozzo, G.; Grande, G.; Di Bernardi, C.L.; Cappelletti, M. P255 Electrophysiological and behavioral monitoring of learning: An EEG and tRNS combined study. *Clin. Neurophysiol.* **2017**, *128*, e138. [CrossRef]
216. Trypke, M.; Stebner, F.; Wirth, J. The More, the Better? Exploring the Effects of Modal and Codal Redundancy on Learning and Cognitive Load: An Experimental Study. *Educ. Sci.* **2024**, *14*, 872. [CrossRef]
217. Tyagi, O.; Hopko, S.; Kang, J.; Shi, Y.; Du, J.; Mehta, R.K. Modeling Brain Dynamics During Virtual Reality-Based Emergency Response Learning Under Stress. *Hum. Factors J. Hum. Factors Ergon. Soc.* **2021**, *65*, 1804–1820. [CrossRef]
218. Valk, S.L.; Bernhardt, B.C.; Trautwein, F.-M.; Böckler, A.; Kanske, P.; Guizard, N.; Collins, D.L.; Singer, T. Structural plasticity of the social brain: Differential change after socio-affective and cognitive mental training. *Sci. Adv.* **2017**, *3*, e1700489. [CrossRef]
219. van Paasschen, J.; Clare, L.; Yuen, K.S.L.; Woods, R.T.; Evans, S.J.; Parkinson, C.H.; Rugg, M.D.; Linden, D.E.J. Cognitive Rehabilitation Changes Memory-Related Brain Activity in People With Alzheimer Disease. *Neurorehabilit. Neural Repair* **2013**, *27*, 448–459. [CrossRef] [PubMed]
220. Vieira, L.; Marques, D.; Melo, L.; Marques, R.C.; Monte-Silva, K.; Cantilino, A. Transcranial direct current stimulation effects on cognitive reappraisal: An unexpected result? *Brain Stimul.* **2020**, *13*, 650–652. [CrossRef]
221. Voss, M.W.; Prakash, R.S.; Erickson, K.I.; Boot, W.R.; Basak, C.; Neider, M.B.; Simons, D.J.; Fabiani, M.; Gratton, G.; Kramer, A.F. Effects of training strategies implemented in a complex videogame on functional connectivity of attentional networks. *NeuroImage* **2012**, *59*, 138–148. [CrossRef] [PubMed]
222. Wang, J.X.; Voss, J.L. Long-lasting enhancements of memory and hippocampal-cortical functional connectivity following multiple-day targeted noninvasive stimulation. *Hippocampus* **2015**, *25*, 877–883. [CrossRef] [PubMed]
223. Wang, J.; Antonenko, P.; Keil, A.; Dawson, K. Converging Subjective and Psychophysiological Measures of Cognitive Load to Study the Effects of Instructor-Present Video. *Mind Brain Educ.* **2020**, *14*, 279–291. [CrossRef]
224. Ward, N.; Paul, E.; Watson, P.; Cooke, G.E.; Hillman, C.H.; Cohen, N.J.; Kramer, A.F.; Barbey, A.K. Enhanced Learning through Multimodal Training: Evidence from a Comprehensive Cognitive, Physical Fitness, and Neuroscience Intervention. *Sci. Rep.* **2017**, *7*, 5808. [CrossRef]
225. Wards, Y.; Ehrhardt, S.E.; Filmer, H.L.; Mattingley, J.B.; Garner, K.G.; Dux, P.E. Neural substrates of individual differences in learning generalization via combined brain stimulation and multitasking training. *Cereb. Cortex* **2023**, *33*, 11679–11694. [CrossRef]
226. Weiss, M.; Lavidor, M. When Less Is More: Evidence for a Facilitative Cathodal tDCS Effect in Attentional Abilities. *J. Cogn. Neurosci.* **2012**, *24*, 1826–1833. [CrossRef]
227. Wild-Wall, N.; Falkenstein, M.; Gajewski, P.D. Neural Correlates of Changes in a Visual Search Task due to Cognitive Training in Seniors. *Neural Plast.* **2012**, *2012*, 529057. [CrossRef]
228. Woods, A.J.; Cohen, R.; Marsiske, M.; Alexander, G.E.; Czaja, S.J.; Wu, S. Augmenting cognitive training in older adults (The ACT Study): Design and Methods of a Phase III tDCS and cognitive training trial. *Contemp. Clin. Trials* **2018**, *65*, 19–32. [CrossRef]
229. Yang, H.-Y. Does multimedia support individual differences?–EFL learners' listening comprehension and cognitive load. *Australas. J. Educ. Technol.* **2014**, *30*. [CrossRef]
230. Yoon, M.; Zheng, H.; Jung, E.; Li, T. Effects of Segmentation and Self-Explanation Designs on Cognitive Load in Instructional Videos. *Contemp. Educ. Technol.* **2022**, *14*, ep347. [CrossRef] [PubMed]
231. Zondo, S.; Cockcroft, K.; Ferreira-Correia, A. Brain plasticity and adolescent HIV: A randomised controlled trial protocol investigating behavioural and hemodynamic responses in attention cognitive rehabilitation therapy. *MethodsX* **2024**, *13*, 102808. [CrossRef] [PubMed]
232. Zurita-Ortega, F.; González-Valero, G.; Ubago-Jiménez, J.L.; Melguizo-Ibáñez, E. Analysis of cognitively loaded physical tasks and active breaks for the improvement of executive functions in the school context. A systematic review and meta-analysis. In *Revista de Psicodidáctica*, English ed.; Elsevier: Amsterdam, The Netherlands, 2025. [CrossRef]
233. Kaur, V. The neurosocial alchemy of entrepreneurial transformation: A deep dive into extended mirror neuron system and neuroplasticity. *Entrep. Reg. Dev.* **2025**, 1–15. [CrossRef]
234. Swerdloff, M.M. *Measurement of Cognitive Load in Lower Limb Prosthesis Wearers: The P3 Event-Related Potential in Sitting, Standing, and Walking*; Northwestern University: Evanston, IL, USA, 2024.
235. Humble, G.; Geddes, H.; Baell, O.; Payne, J.E.; Hill, A.T.; Chung, S.W.; Emonson, M.; Osborn, M.; Caldwell, B.; Fitzgerald, P.B.; et al. TMS-EEG shows mindfulness meditation is associated with a different excitation/inhibition balance in the dorsolateral prefrontal cortex. *Mindfulness* **2025**, *16*, 347–365. [CrossRef]
236. Nguyen, Q.N.; Michon, K.J.; Vesia, M.; Lee, T.G. Dissociable Causal Roles of Dorsolateral Prefrontal Cortex and Primary Motor Cortex over the Course of Motor Skill Development. *J. Neurosci.* **2025**, *45*, e2015232025. [CrossRef]

 https://doi.org/10.3390/mti10010005

237. van Hell, J.G. The neurocognitive underpinnings of second language processing: Knowledge gains from the past and future outlook. *Lang. Learn.* **2023**, *73*, 172–181. [CrossRef]
238. Chmiel, J.; Stępień-Słodkowska, M.; Ramik-Mażewska, I. Efficacy of Transcranial Direct Current Stimulation (tDCS) on Neuropsychiatric Symptoms in Substance Use Disorder (SUD)—A review and insights into possible mechanisms of action. *J. Clin. Med.* **2025**, *14*, 1337. [CrossRef]
239. Haccou, G.L. Polarity Effects of HD-tDCS in a Gaming Setting: Investigating the Effect of Cathodal and Anodal Stimulation in a Visuospatial Working-Memory Task. Master's Thesis, University of Twente, Enschede, The Netherlands, 2024.
240. Contò, F.; Ellena, G.; Edwards, G.; Battelli, L. Modulation of learning-dependent plasticity in the attention network. *bioRxiv* **2024**. [CrossRef]
241. Meinzer, M.; Shahbabaie, A.; Antonenko, D.; Blankenburg, F.; Fischer, R.; Hartwigsen, G.; Nitsche, M.A.; Li, S.-C.; Thielscher, A.; Timmann, D.; et al. Investigating the neural mechanisms of transcranial direct current stimulation effects on human cognition: Current issues and potential solutions. *Front. Neurosci.* **2024**, *18*, 1389651. [CrossRef]
242. Bradley, C.; Nydam, A.S.; Dux, P.E.; Mattingley, J.B. State-dependent effects of neural stimulation on brain function and cognition. *Nat. Rev. Neurosci.* **2022**, *23*, 459–475. [CrossRef]
243. Tseng, P.-T.; Zeng, B.-S.; Hung, C.-M.; Liang, C.-S.; Stubbs, B.; Carvalho, A.F.; Brunoni, A.R.; Su, K.-P.; Tu, Y.-K.; Wu, Y.-C.; et al. Assessment of Noninvasive Brain Stimulation Interventions for Negative Symptoms of Schizophrenia. *JAMA Psychiatry* **2022**, *79*, 770. [CrossRef] [PubMed]
244. Vergallito, A.; Feroldi, S.; Pisoni, A.; Lauro, L.J.R. Inter-individual variability in tDCS effects: A narrative review on the contribution of stable, variable, and contextual factors. *Brain Sci.* **2022**, *12*, 522. [CrossRef]
245. Ojha, A.; Jones, N.P.; Henry, T.; Versace, A.; Gnagy, E.M.; Joseph, H.M.; Molina, B.S.G.; Ladouceur, C.D. Altered Lateral Prefrontal Cortex Functioning During Emotional Interference Resistance Is Associated With Affect Lability in Adults With Persisting Symptoms of Attention-Deficit/Hyperactivity Disorder From Childhood. *Biol. Psychiatry Cogn. Neurosci. Neuroimaging* **2024**, *9*, 588–596. [CrossRef] [PubMed]
246. Pengelley, J.; Whipp, P.R.; Malpique, A. A testing load: A review of cognitive load in computer and paper-based learning and assessment. *Technol. Pedagog. Educ.* **2025**, *34*, 1–17. [CrossRef]
247. Kakaria, S.; Saffari, F.; Ramsøy, T.Z.; Bigné, E. Cognitive load during planned and unplanned virtual shopping: Evidence from a neurophysiological perspective. *Int. J. Inf. Manag.* **2023**, *72*, 102667. [CrossRef]
248. Kalisch, R.; Russo, S.J.; Müller, M.B. Neurobiology and systems biology of stress resilience. *Physiol. Rev.* **2024**, *104*, 1205–1263. [CrossRef]
249. Wang, Z.; Donahue, E.K.; Guo, Y.; Renteln, M.; Petzinger, G.M.; Jakowec, M.W.; Holschneider, D.P. Exercise alters cortico-basal ganglia network metabolic connectivity: A mesoscopic level analysis informed by anatomic parcellation defined in the mouse brain connectome. *Brain Struct. Funct.* **2023**, *228*, 1865–1884. [CrossRef] [PubMed]
250. Roth, R.H.; Ding, J.B. Cortico-basal ganglia plasticity in motor learning. *Neuron* **2024**, *112*, 2486–2502. [CrossRef] [PubMed]
251. Gkintoni, E.; Antonopoulou, H.; Sortwell, A.; Halkiopoulos, C. Challenging Cognitive Load Theory: The Role of Educational Neuroscience and Artificial Intelligence in Redefining Learning Efficacy. *Brain Sci.* **2025**, *15*, 203. [CrossRef] [PubMed]
252. Zammouri, A.; Moussa, A.A.; Chevallier, S. Use of cognitive load measurements to design a new architecture of intelligent learning systems. *Expert Syst. Appl.* **2024**, *237*, 121253. [CrossRef]
253. Pradeep, K.; Sulur Anbalagan, R.; Thangavelu, A.P.; Aswathy, S.; Jisha, V.G.; Vaisakhi, V.S. Neuroeducation: Understanding neural dynamics in learning and teaching. *Front. Educ.* **2024**, *9*, 1437418. [CrossRef]
254. Khan, N.A.N.; Naheeda Tharannum, B.; Hassan, K.L.; Hussain, H. Proposed Framework to Map Virtual Reality with Ancient Indian Education System to Increase Neuroplasticity for Autistic Spectrum Disorder Children. In *Transforming Education with Virtual Reality*; Wiley-Scrivener: Beverly, MA, USA, 2024; pp. 351–378. [CrossRef]
255. Bassi, M.; Patti, L.; Silvestrini, I.; Strati, M.F.; Ponzano, M.; Minuto, N.; Maggi, D. One-year follow-up comparison of two hybrid closed-loop systems in Italian children and adults with type 1 diabetes. *Front. Endocrinol.* **2023**, *14*, 1099024. [CrossRef]
256. Grewlewicz, P.; Nowak, P.; Khuat, T.T.; Czeczot, J.; Klopot, T.; Gabrys, B. Practical implementation of computationally-efficient machine learning-based control performance assessment system for a class of closed loop systems. *Appl. Soft Comput.* **2023**, *146*, 110690. [CrossRef]
257. Gkintoni, E.; Vassilopoulos, S.P.; Nikolaou, G. Next-Generation Cognitive-Behavioral Therapy for Depression: Integrating Digital Tools, Teletherapy, and Personalization for Enhanced Mental Health Outcomes. *Medicina* **2025**, *61*, 431. [CrossRef]
258. Bruand, A.; Reatto, A.; Brossard, M.; Jouquet, P.; de Souza Martins, É. Long-term activity of social insects responsible for the physical fertility of soils in the tropics. *Sci. Rep.* **2023**, *13*, 12337. [CrossRef] [PubMed]
259. Forget, M.; Le Pertel, N. Enhancing neuroplasticity and promoting brain health at work: The role of learning and memory in workplace performance. In *Learning and Memory—From Molecules and Cells to Mind and Behavior*; IntechOpen: Rijeka, Croatia, 2024. [CrossRef]
260. Song, Y.-T.; Xiang, M.-Q.; Zhong, P. Differences in brain activation during working memory tasks between badminton athletes and non-athletes: An fNIRS study. *Brain Cogn.* **2024**, *175*, 106133. [CrossRef] [PubMed]

 https://doi.org/10.3390/mti10010005

261. Bomyea, J.; Caudle, M.M.; Dugas, N.; Moore, R.C.; Simmons, A.N.; Thomas, M.L. A randomized controlled trial of computerized cognitive training to improve working memory in individuals with elevated repetitive negative thinking: Behavioral and neural outcomes. *J. Mood Anxiety Disord.* **2025**, *9*, 100095. [CrossRef] [PubMed]
262. Krishnamurthy, R.; Schultz, D.H.; Wang, Y.; Natarajan, S.K.; Barlow, S.M.; Dietsch, A.M. Multimodal Adaptations to Expiratory Musculature-Targeted Resistance Training: A Preliminary Study in Healthy Young Adults. *J. Speech Lang. Hear. Res.* **2025**, *68*, 987–1005. [CrossRef]
263. Gkintoni, E.; Vassilopoulos, S.P.; Nikolaou, G.; Boutsinas, B. Digital and AI-Enhanced Cognitive Behavioral Therapy for Insomnia: Neurocognitive Mechanisms and Clinical Outcomes. *J. Clin. Med.* **2025**, *14*, 2265. [CrossRef]
264. Wagenblast, F.; Läubli, T.; Seibt, R.; Rieger, M.A.; Steinhilber, B. Wrist extensor muscle fatigue during a dual task with two muscular and cognitive load levels in younger and older adults. *Hum. Factors* **2024**, *66*, 2433–2450. [CrossRef]
265. Crivelli, D.; Angioletti, L.; Balconi, M. Neurocognitive empowerment, embodied practices, and peak performance in sports: Case studies and future challenges. *Neuropsychol. Trends* **2024**, *35*, 85–96. [CrossRef]
266. Saha, R. The exciting frontier of neuroplasticity: Innovations in brain health and recovery. *J. Behav. Brain Sci.* **2025**, *15*, 47–80. [CrossRef]
267. Gkintoni, E.; Vassilopoulos, S.P.; Nikolaou, G. Mindfulness-Based Cognitive Therapy in Clinical Practice: A Systematic Review of Neurocognitive Outcomes and Applications for Mental Health and Well-Being. *J. Clin. Med.* **2025**, *14*, 1703. [CrossRef]
268. Jurgina, L.Q.; Aquini, L.G.; de Aguiar, M.S.; da Rosa, L.S.; Lopes, J.P.; Mackedanz, T.D.; Klein, A.I.; Primo, T.T.; Iankowski, R.S. Neuroplasticity-Based Literacy Rescue: A Multisensory and Tangible Learning Methodology for Children at Risk. In Proceedings of the 2024 IEEE Global Engineering Education Conference (EDUCON), Kos Island, Greece, 8–11 May 2024; pp. 1–10. [CrossRef]
269. Olegário, R.L.; Goulart, C. Unravelling cognitive shifts: Neuroscience-based strategies in mathematics education. *Educ. Gerontol.* **2024**, 1–13. [CrossRef]
270. Vázquez-Guardado, A.; Yang, Y.; Bandodkar, A.J.; Rogers, J.A. Recent advances in neurotechnologies with broad potential for neuroscience research. *Nat. Neurosci.* **2020**, *23*, 1522–1536. [CrossRef] [PubMed]
271. Kourtesis, P.; MacPherson, S.E. An ecologically valid examination of event-based and time-based prospective memory using immersive virtual reality: The influence of attention, memory, and executive function processes on real-world prospective memory. *Neuropsychol. Rehabil.* **2021**, *33*, 255–280. [CrossRef] [PubMed]
272. Stangl, M.; Maoz, S.L.; Suthana, N. Mobile cognition: Imaging the human brain in the 'real world'. *Nat. Rev. Neurosci.* **2023**, *24*, 347–362. [CrossRef]
273. Chang, M.; Büchel, D.; Reinecke, K.; Lehmann, T.; Baumeister, J. Ecological validity in exercise neuroscience research: A systematic investigation. *Eur. J. Neurosci.* **2022**, *55*, 487–509. [CrossRef] [PubMed]
274. Prasad, S.M.; Khan, M.N.A.; Tariq, U.; Al-Nashash, H. Impact of electrical stimulation on mental stress, depression, and anxiety: A systematic review. *Sensors* **2025**, *25*, 2133. [CrossRef]
275. Soleimani, G.; Nitsche, M.A.; Bergmann, T.O.; Towhidkhah, F.; Violante, I.R.; Lorenz, R.; Kuplicki, R.; Tsuchiyagaito, A.; Mulyana, B.; Mayeli, A.; et al. Closing the loop between brain and electrical stimulation: Towards precision neuromodulation treatments. *Transl. Psychiatry* **2023**, *13*, 279. [CrossRef]
276. Bernabei, L.; Leone, B.; Hirsch, D.; Mentuccia, V.; Panzera, A.; Riggio, F.; Sangiovanni, L.; Piserchia, V.; Nicolò, G.; Pompili, E. Neuromodulation Strategies in Lifelong Bipolar Disorder: A Narrative Review. *Behav. Sci.* **2024**, *14*, 1176. [CrossRef]
277. Cheng, M.-Y.; Yu, C.-L.; An, X.; Wang, L.; Tsai, C.-L.; Qi, F.; Wang, K.-P. Evaluating EEG neurofeedback in sport psychology: A systematic review of RCT studies for insights into mechanisms and performance improvement. *Front. Psychol.* **2024**, *15*, 1331997. [CrossRef]
278. Roozbeh, M.; Pakdaman, H.; Naderi, N.; Roozbeh, M. Enhancing cognitive function and neuroplasticity assessed by diffusion tensor imaging in multiple sclerosis: The efficacy of combined transcranial direct current stimulation and application-assisted cognitive rehabilitation. *Mult. Scler. Relat. Disord.* **2024**, *92*, 105985. [CrossRef]
279. Qian, Y.; Schwartz, A.; Jung, A.; Zhang, Y.; Seitz, U.; Wilds, G.; Kim, M.; Kramer, A.F.; Chukoskie, L. The Influence of Separate and Combined Exercise and Foreign Language Acquisition on Learning and Cognition. *Brain Sci.* **2024**, *14*, 572. [CrossRef]
280. Gkintoni, E.; Dimakos, I.; Halkiopoulos, C.; Antonopoulou, H. Contributions of Neuroscience to Educational Praxis: A Systematic Review. *Emerg. Sci. J.* **2023**, *7*, 146–158. [CrossRef]
281. Yuan, X.; Li, H.; Feng, S.; Sun, M. Enhancing action recognition in educational settings through exercise-induced neuroplasticity. *Front. Neurosci.* **2025**, *19*, 1588570. [CrossRef]
282. Antonopoulou, H.; Halkiopoulos, C.; Gkintoni, E.; Katsimpelis, A. Application of Gamification Tools for Identification of Neurocognitive and Social Function in Distance Learning Education. *Int. J. Learn. Teach. Educ. Res.* **2022**, *21*, 367–400. [CrossRef]
283. Chang, C.; Chen, J.E. Multimodal EEG-fMRI: Advancing insight into large-scale human brain dynamics. *Curr. Opin. Biomed. Eng.* **2021**, *18*, 100279. [CrossRef]
284. Gkintoni, E.; Vassilopoulos, S.P.; Nikolaou, G. Brain-Inspired Multisensory Learning: A Systematic Review of Neuroplasticity and Cognitive Outcomes in Adult Multicultural and Second Language Acquisition. *Biomimetics* **2025**, *10*, 397. [CrossRef]

 https://doi.org/10.3390/mti10010005

285. Sortwell, A.; Trimble, K.; Ferraz, R.; Geelan, D.R.; Hine, G.; Ramirez-Campillo, R.; Carter-Thuiller, B.; Gkintoni, E.; Xuan, Q. A Systematic Review of Meta-Analyses on the Impact of Formative Assessment on K-12 Students' Learning: Toward Sustainable Quality Education. *Sustainability* **2024**, *16*, 7826. [CrossRef]
286. Niering, M.; Seifert, J. The effects of visual skills training on cognitive and executive functions in stroke patients: A systematic review with meta-analysis. *J. Neuroeng. Rehabil.* **2024**, *21*, 41. [CrossRef] [PubMed]

https://doi.org/10.3390/mti10010005

Multimodal Technologies and Interaction

MDPI

Article

Science Mapping of AI as an Educational Tool Exploring Digital Inequalities: A Sociological Perspective

Isotta Mac Fadden [1,*], Elena-María García-Alonso [1] and Eloy López Meneses [2]

[1] Department of Sociology and Communication, Faculty of Social Sciences, University of Salamanca, 37007 Salamanca, Spain; garelena@usal.es

[2] Department of Education and Social Psychology, Faculty of Social Sciences, University of Pablo de Olavide, 41013 Sevilla, Spain; elopmen@upo.es

* Correspondence: macfadden@usal.es

Abstract: This study aims to explore the evolution of the literature on the sociological implications of integrating artificial intelligence (AI) as an educational tool, particularly its influence on digital inequalities. While AI technologies, such as AI-based language models, have begun transforming educational practices by personalizing learning, fostering student autonomy, and supporting educators, concerns remain regarding access disparities, ethical implications, and the potential reinforcement of existing social inequalities. To address these issues, a bibliometric analysis employing science mapping was conducted on 1515 studies sourced from the Web of Science Core Collection. This analysis traces the thematic evolution of social science perspectives on AI's role in education and its relationship with digital inequalities. The results indicate a growing academic interest in AI in education, with a notable progression from understanding its basic impact to exploring complex themes such as vulnerability, disability, bias, and community. The studies show that AI's application has expanded from isolated research on specific populations to broader discussions on inclusivity, equity, and the impact of AI on governance, policy, and community. However, the findings also reveal a significant gap in sociological perspectives, particularly regarding issues like digital illiteracy and socio-economic access disparities. Although AI holds promise for promoting more inclusive education, further research is essential to address these sociological concerns and to guide the ethical, equitable implementation of AI as its influence on governance, policy, and community impact continues to grow.

Keywords: artificial intelligence; sociology; education; social exclusion; digital inequalities

1. Introduction

Artificial Intelligence (AI) represents a potential revolution in all spheres of society, the effects of which must be addressed scientifically: from computational science [1] to ethics [2], to medicine [3], to work [4], to economics and management [5], and even in the field of education [6]. A clear example of the wide range of risks and opportunities of introducing AI in a complex context of social and environmental sustainability is the management of water: from exploring better risk management for the sustainable use of water [7] or constructing smart cities [8] to the high risk represented by the enormous amount of water used for its production [9].

Digital innovations are a key pillar of our society's identity, particularly with the introduction of artificial intelligence (AI) into everyday life.

The risks and opportunities of AI in all fields of society need to be better understood, particularly in terms of equity and social sustainability. In this sense, social science—and particularly sociology—has the responsibility to explore and minimize the impact of AI on the reproduction of inequalities and disparities in our society [10]. From a sociological perspective, the role of new technologies is of crucial interest in the formation and development of both individual and community identity, focusing on the urban–rural dichotomy [11,12]. These technologies, by enabling new forms of social interaction, communication, and access to information, influence not only how individuals perceive themselves but also how communities are formed and evolve. In this context, digital platforms and AI-driven tools play a crucial role in mediating social relationships and shaping collective narratives, profoundly impacting the dynamics of belonging and social participation [13].

In the field of education, the impact of chatbots has been specifically evaluated [14–17]. It is important to consider that while applications like AI-based language models may offer significant benefits, it is also crucial to be aware of the differences in the type of social support provided through online chat services, as this can influence users' perceptions of service quality and well-being, in this case, students [18]. AI tools are transforming education by enabling the potential of personalized learning through machine learning algorithms (such as Carnegie Learning and Knewton). However, these systems can also inadvertently reinforce existing societal biases, such as gender biases in tutoring or reflecting historical inequalities in learning outcomes. Similarly, tools like speech-to-text software, smart glasses, and predictive text systems (for example, Google's Live Transcribe), improve accessibility for students with disabilities, enabling better engagement in learning. In lower-resource settings, services like Squirrel AI and Duolingo help bridge educational gaps, offering personalized learning experiences. Additionally, platforms cater to students from diverse family structures, including non-traditional environments, by providing flexible learning options. AI also plays a role in the college admissions process, where tools may assist minority and low-income students in gaining access to higher education, though concerns about bias remain. Specialized apps, such as Autism Expressed, are designed to support students with Autism Spectrum Disorder (ASD), helping them improve communication and social skills. Moreover, AI-driven grading tools aim to automate and streamline assessment, yet these systems require continuous refinement to ensure fairness and equity in educational evaluation.

Additionally, ethical and privacy concerns related to the use of chatbots in educational environments should be considered in this context [19]. Furthermore, technological limitations, novelty effects, and cognitive load have been pointed out as challenges in education [20]. Moreover, issues such as reliability [11,12] have also been discussed. All these elements can contribute to the deepening of social inequalities, whether due to the difficulties in accessing these technological tools or the quality of such tools, with certain groups relying on less precise or equitable solutions.

Sociology must increasingly prioritize the study of new technologies and their impact, especially as they reshape fundamental aspects of human interaction and identity. While education research has started to address how technology influences learning and access, sociology needs to investigate more deeply how these innovations transform social structures, shape personal identities, and alter community dynamics. Despite growing interest, this area remains largely unexplored, underscoring the need for comprehensive studies that examine the broader social implications of technology [21].

A sociological perspective enables an analysis not only of technologies themselves but also of how they interact with social structures, reinforcing or challenging existing power dynamics. Various theoretical frameworks—such as Critical Theory, Pierre Bourdieu's concept of cultural capital, digital divide theories, and Actor-Network Theory (ANT)—offer valuable tools for critically assessing the introduction of AI in education and its broader societal implications. These approaches allow for a nuanced understanding of how AI technologies may shape educational experiences, influence social hierarchies, and impact issues of equity and access. From Critical Theory, which invites ethical reflection on the implementation of AI [22–26], to Bourdieu's framework of cultural capital, which explains disparities in access to and use of technology [27,28], and Actor-Network Theory (ANT), which highlights the complex interactions between human and non-human actors, research in this area continues to evolve [27,28].

Critical Theory is particularly useful for analyzing how AI may reproduce existing power dynamics in education [22,24]. The commodification of education through AI, where learning becomes increasingly mechanized, risks alienating marginalized students by disconnecting them from the human aspects of the educational experience [23,25]. Similarly, Bourdieu's theory of cultural capital explains how students from different social backgrounds interact with AI-based educational tools, valuing certain knowledge and skills that could perpetuate generational inequalities [26,29]. Theories on the digital divide are also relevant in this context, as they address both disparities in access to digital technologies (first-level digital divide) and the unequal ability to effectively use these technologies (second-level digital divide) [26].

Meanwhile, Actor-Network Theory (ANT) offers a broader perspective by positioning AI not merely as a tool, but as an active participant within the network of educational actors, including students, teachers, administrators, and policymakers. ANT suggests that AI reshapes relationships, roles, and power dynamics within this network. By examining how different actors interact with AI systems, a deeper understanding can be gained of how educational practices and outcomes are reconfigured, and how inequalities are negotiated or reinforced [27,28].

The evolution of sociology in its approach to technology also reflects a significant shift. While sociological studies from the 1980s and 1990s primarily viewed AI as a field of scientific knowledge, more recent studies tend to focus on its practical applications and how they affect everyday life [25]. This shift implies an expansion in the way AI is understood, now seen not only as a matter of academic research but as a technology with a direct impact on social, cultural, and economic systems. For instance, the increasing commodification of AI in education raises concerns about its role in the reproduction of inequalities [10,30].

Moreover, recent sociological research examines how people interact with AI technologies and how these technologies shape social behaviors [14,31]. An analysis from the perspective of the sociology of technology allows for the observation not only of how scientists develop AI but also of how the applications of this technology can transform or reinforce power structures. AI can act as an agent of both transformation and perpetuation of inequalities, depending on how it is implemented and regulated within society [10,32].

It is undeniable that the literature in the context of social sciences and social studies reflects this dichotomy. The social impacts of these disparities show how, as these technologies become increasingly integrated into educational environments, new innovative ways to enhance learning outcomes coexist with the risk of exacerbating existing inequalities, particularly for vulnerable groups who face barriers such as lack of access to digital tools and low levels of digital literacy.

For this reason, this research aims to explore the sociological perspective on the introduction of AI as an educational tool and the risks associated with digital illiteracy, as well as its impact on vulnerable populations through a bibliometric analysis of various studies in the field that address this topic. The goal of this work is to go beyond and answer questions about the type of research that has been conducted in sociology regarding the impact of educational AIs on vulnerable populations, the widening of the digital divide, or the technological exclusion of certain social groups.

By analyzing these topics through the Web of Science Core Collection, extracting 1515 relevant studies, we can better understand how AI-driven educational practices contribute both to the mitigation and the amplification of issues related to social exclusion, fostering more equitable learning environments.

2. Methods

This study utilizes science mapping analysis to explore both the structural and dynamic aspects of scientific research, providing insights into the cognitive framework of the academic field [33]. The chosen approach offers a rationale for using SciMAT GPLv3 and other bibliometric tools due to their capacity to provide a comprehensive analysis of the scientific literature. SciMAT, in particular, offers unique features such as longitudinal mapping and thematic evolution analysis. SciMAT was selected precisely because it enables a detailed analysis aligned with the study's objectives. These functions enhance the understanding of trends and developments within a specific field over time, allowing for a richer, more nuanced view of how research evolves. By incorporating these features, we can identify and visualize conceptual subdomains within the field and monitor its thematic evolution over time [33,34].

The bibliometric analysis was conducted using the SciMAT software [33], which relies on the H-index [35] and co-word analysis [36]. The methodology follows a four-phase process:

1. "Detection of research topics": In this initial phase, a co-word network is created using keywords extracted from the articles. A clustering algorithm [36] is then applied. This phase helps identify and visualize the conceptual subdomains of a research field and track its thematic evolution.
2. "Visualization of research topics and thematic network": The second phase involves representing the identified topics through diagrams and thematic networks, with centrality (the relevance of a topic, calculated using c = 10 × Σekh) and density (internal cohesion of the network) as key dimensions.
3. "Identification of thematic areas": In the third phase, the analysis focuses on the frequency of occurrences and thematic significance by examining the overlaps in the clusters.
4. "Performance analysis": In the final phase, the association between keywords and thematic areas is examined using bibliometric indicators such as the number of publications, citations, and variations of the H-index [35]. The similarity between keywords is calculated using a word co-occurrence matrix and an equivalence index function [36].

The following outlines the key steps involved in the bibliometric analysis conducted in this study using the SciMAT tool. After selecting the relevant time periods, the next step is to choose the analysis units (such as periods, documents, references, authors, or terms). Data reduction techniques are applied to manage the massive and heterogeneous datasets by reducing millions of variables to a manageable scale [37]. Co-occurrence analysis follows, filtering the network using a minimum link weight threshold to highlight the most significant links [38]. The process also includes network analysis, reduction, normalization, grouping, document assignment, quality assessment, longitudinal analysis, visualization, and interpretation.

Following data export, the focus shifts to data preprocessing. This stage involves cleaning the data to remove duplicates and irrelevant entries, ensuring the dataset is focused and reliable. Normalization is also crucial, as it standardizes author names, journal titles, and keywords to eliminate inconsistencies that could affect the analysis. Researchers may apply filtering criteria to further refine the dataset, such as limiting the scope to publications within a specific date range or quality metrics.

After preprocessing, the cleaned and normalized dataset is imported into SciMAT, which facilitates various analytical processes. One key feature is longitudinal mapping, which allows researchers to create visual representations of the research landscape over time. This involves mapping publications across different years to illustrate trends, such as the growth of specific topics or research areas. Additionally, thematic evolution analysis is conducted to identify key themes within the literature, clustering similar publications and revealing dominant research themes while assessing how these themes have evolved over time.

The next phase involves the interpretation of results, where visual outputs generated by SciMAT are used to present findings clearly, including graphs and thematic maps. This analysis is followed by a thorough discussion of the implications of the findings in relation to the initial research questions, highlighting contributions to the existing body of knowledge and identifying gaps or opportunities for future research.

Finally, it is crucial to document the methodology comprehensively, detailing each step of the process from data collection to interpretation. This not only enhances the credibility of the research but also aids other scholars in replicating the study. In the conclusion, researchers summarize the key findings, emphasizing the significance of methodological rigor and the insights gained from the bibliometric analysis. Additionally, seeking peer reviews can provide valuable feedback, allowing for further refinement of the analysis and reporting to enhance clarity and impact. The methodology section should demonstrate the dynamic nature of the research landscape.

The bibliometric analysis process in SciMAT starts with data collection, focusing on the H-index [35] and co-word analysis [36]. A clear research topic is defined by specific questions and scope within the field. Appropriate bibliographic databases such as Scopus, Web of Science, or Google Scholar are selected to gather relevant publications. This involves executing search queries with carefully chosen keywords, authors, and publication years, utilizing Boolean operators to refine the results. Once the relevant literature is identified, data exportation follows, typically in a format such as CSV or RIS for easy import into SciMAT, including details like titles, abstracts, keywords, authors, publication years, and citation counts [33]. Only works published in the Web of Science Core Collection are selected in this study. This library offers a comprehensive and curated selection of academic articles that ensures high-quality, peer-reviewed content. This approach allows us to examine AI-related research trends, developments, and thematic evolution in a robust and reliable database.

This approach is based on a broad, non-systematic review of the relevant literature, which was subsequently validated by an expert panel in the field of AI, education, and social exclusion (ALM, RSC, RGO [14]). The selection of keywords is driven by the main objectives of the research project and is further supported by the literature, which underscores the issue of the introduction of AI as an educational tool in vulnerable settings. Engaging community members is vital for fostering genuine change in vulnerable environments, positively impacting health and well-being in urban areas, and enhancing social cohesion. Moreover, co-designing interventions with community members ensures that actions are tailored to local needs, boosting involvement and ownership of the solutions.

The study focuses on the following keywords and research strategy: "artificial intelligence" OR "educational innovation" OR "educational method" (Topic) AND exclusion OR "social exclusion" OR "digital illiteracy" OR "digital inequalities" OR vulnerability OR diversity OR "digital gap" (Topic) AND education (Topic) AND "social science" OR "social studies" (Topic) within the Web of Science Core Collection. This keyword selection, grounded in the main objectives of the project and supported by the existing literature, underscores the link between AI and inequalities [10,28,30].

Following data export, data preprocessing takes place. This involves cleaning the data to remove duplicates and irrelevant entries, ensuring the dataset is focused and reliable. Normalization is crucial, as it standardizes author names, journal titles, and keywords to eliminate inconsistencies that could affect the analysis. Researchers may apply additional filtering criteria, such as limiting the dataset to publications within a specific date range or by certain quality metrics, to further refine the dataset.

After preprocessing, the cleaned and normalized dataset is imported into SciMAT, which enables various analytical processes. The longitudinal mapping feature, for instance, allows researchers to create visual representations of the research landscape over time, illustrating trends in the growth of specific topics or research areas. Additionally, thematic evolution analysis identifies key themes in the literature, clustering similar publications to reveal dominant research themes and assessing how these themes have evolved over time.

To further enhance clarity and interpretation, SciMAT identifies "research topics" by creating a standardized co-word network from selected keywords and applying a clustering algorithm [37]. Topics are analyzed in terms of centrality (level of interaction between networks, calculated as $c = 10 \times \Sigma ekh$) and density (internal cohesion and strength of the network). The frequency of occurrences and thematic relevance are then analyzed within clusters, and bibliometric indicators (e.g., number of publications, citations, various h-index types) are used to examine relationships between keywords and thematic areas [35]. Additional detail regarding the steps within data processing (e.g., dimension reduction [38]) could help readers draw clearer conclusions about the analytical depth of this study.

Strategic diagrams are employed to examine the evolution of core themes, with centrality on the X-axis and density on the Y-axis (see Figure 1). The performance analysis assesses literature production by analyzing centrality and density, with relationships graphically represented in Cartesian coordinates. High centrality, for instance, may indicate a theme's strong relevance to various subfields, suggesting it is a point of convergence within the broader research network. Conversely, themes with high density but lower centrality may represent more specialized or isolated areas of inquiry that, while relevant, may have less connectivity with broader research trends.

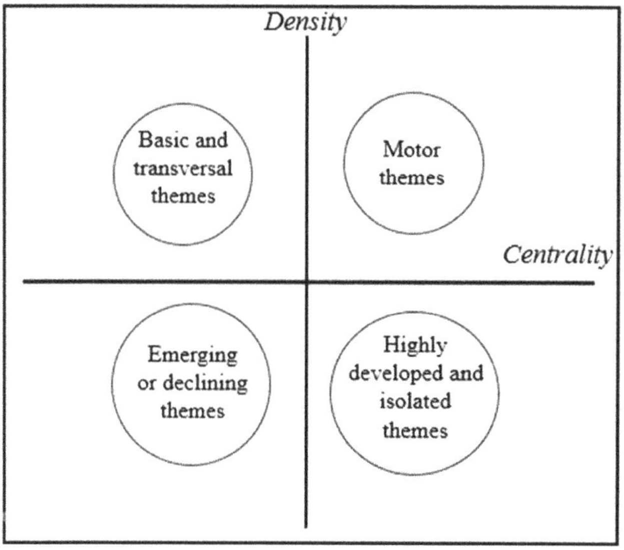

Figure 1. Adapted strategic diagram representing the cluster of a specific network, based on centrality (*X*-axis) and density (*Y*-axis) [33].

Thematic evolution highlights research themes that maintain conceptual continuity across different time periods. Solid lines between themes indicate the retention of the same name, while dashed lines represent thematic connections under different names. Thematic networks illustrate the clusters around specific networks. Although the Web of Science (WoS) indexes a substantial number of journals related to the topics of our analysis (2217), we have selected the top 10 journals with most papers in the research topic.

3. Results

The analysis of the data indicated a greater concentration of studies in "Education Research" (654). It highlighted the lack of a social studies research approach in this field. The most relevant journals publishing papers on this topic are the following (Figure 2): *Sustainability* (22); *BMC Public Health* (17); *Education Sciences* (16); *PLOS One* (14); *BMC Medical Education* (14); *Bordon-Revista de Pedagogía* (11); *Physical Education and Sport Pedagogy* (11); *International Journal of Inclusive Education* (11); *Teachers College Record* (10); *International Journal of Sustainability in Higher Education* (10).

The analysis was carried out across four defined periods (Figure 3): Period 1 (1996–2010), Period 2 (2011–2015), Period 3 (2016–2019), and Period 4 (2020–2024). The first period covers a longer time frame due to the lower volume of literature produced, whereas the following three periods are divided into five-year intervals.

Figure 2. Most relevant journals and number of papers published on the research topics using SciMAT.

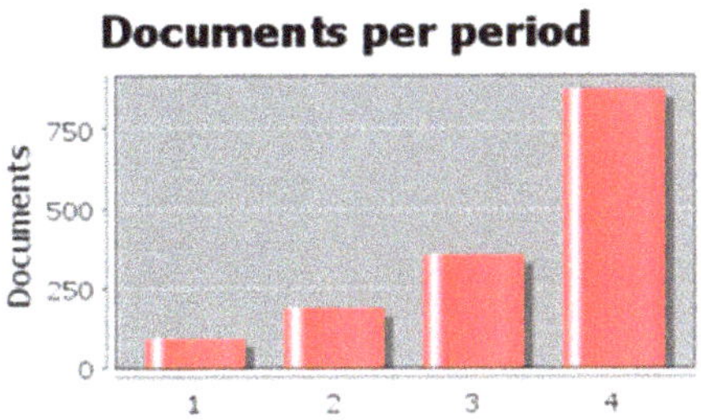

Figure 3. Documents per period.

A total of 96, 191, 356, and 872 documents were recorded for the four periods, respectively.

The results highlight the increasing interest among researchers in investigating the impact of artificial intelligence (AI) as an educational tool, particularly in relation to its effects on vulnerable populations and the digital divide. Recent years have seen a significant increase in technological innovation and the role of education in leveraging these tools to enhance learning outcomes [21]. However, there is a lack of studies from a sociological perspective that explore how these innovations could exacerbate existing inequalities.

Figure 4 illustrates the significant increase in the number of keywords and shared words, as indicated by the index values (0.33, 0.46, 0.66). In the first period, there are 61 words. In the second period, there are 119 words, with 16 disappearing, 45 in common, and 74 new words. The third period consists of 168 words, with 8 disappearing, 331 new words, and 330 words in common. The last period includes 897 words, with 610 shared from the previous period and 287 new words.

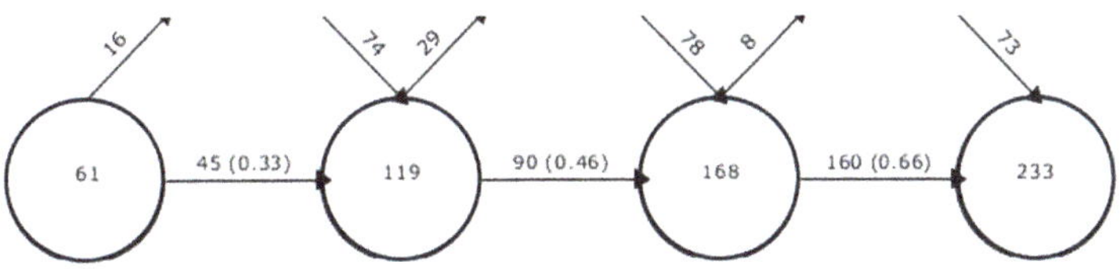

Figure 4. Incoming and outgoing keywords between sub-periods (1991–2023) using SciMAT.

As the graphs show, a clear evolution can be observed in both the complexity of the problems being addressed and the clustering of the network across the four periods.

The first ten words that appear most often are the following: Education (294); Diversity (133); Students (125); Higher Education (110); Children (82); Inclusion (74); Health (72); Gender (64); Impact (57).

Between positions 16 and 19 on the list of selected topics are those related to social exclusion (42), equity (42), and social justice (41). Other topics that have also been explored, highlighting the importance of artificial intelligence in community-related elements, include disability (34), mental health (35), exclusion (27), and vulnerability (25).

As shown in Figure 5, each of the four periods selected for analysis includes the primary keywords, showing an increasing diversity of topics over time. A detailed description of each analysis period follows.

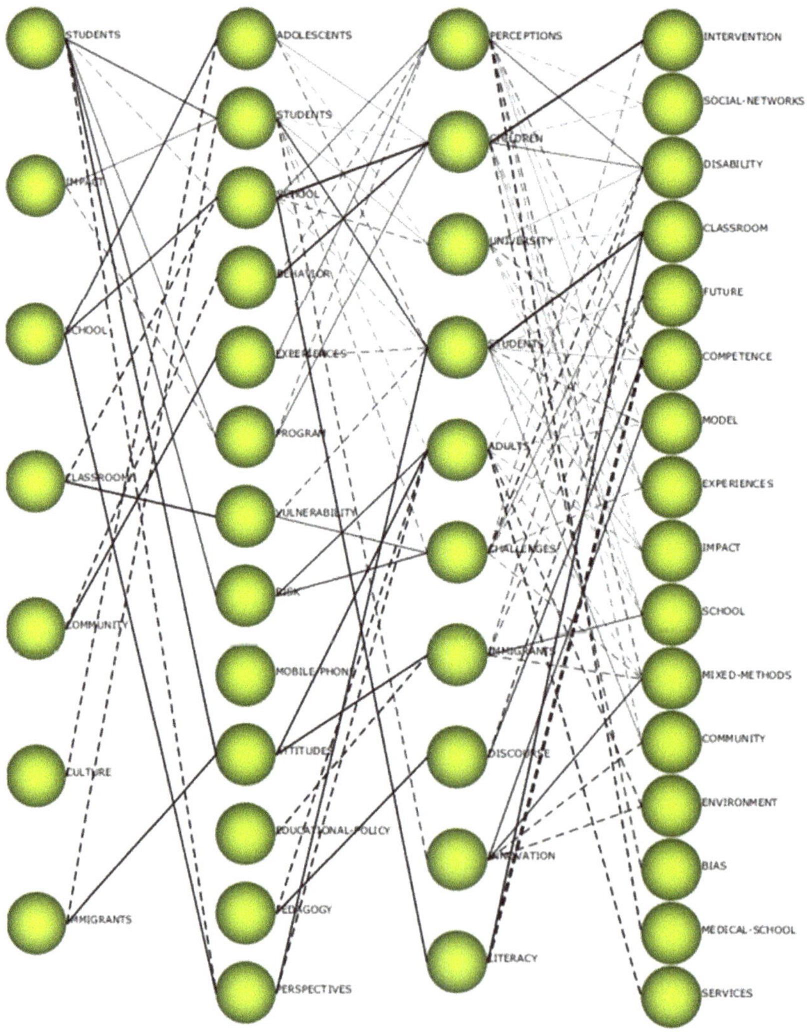

Figure 5. Thematic evolution in the field of AI as an educational tool across different periods using SciMAT (from the left: Period 1 to Period 4).

3.1. Period 1 (1996–2010)

The motor theme is "impact" while "immigrants", "school" and "students" are highly developed and isolated themes, and "impact" is a basic theme. "Classroom", "community", and "culture" are basic themes.

During the first period (1996–2010), the analysis of thematic distribution according to the clusters (Figure 6) reveals that the motor theme was "impact", suggesting that early research primarily focused on how AI influenced educational outcomes. Themes such as "immigrants", "school", and "students" appear as well-developed but isolated topics, indicating a focus on specific groups without broader contextual integration in other educational contexts. The centrality of "school" and "students" highlights their relevance during this period, reflecting the prominent role of AI in structured educational environments, such as schools and with students.

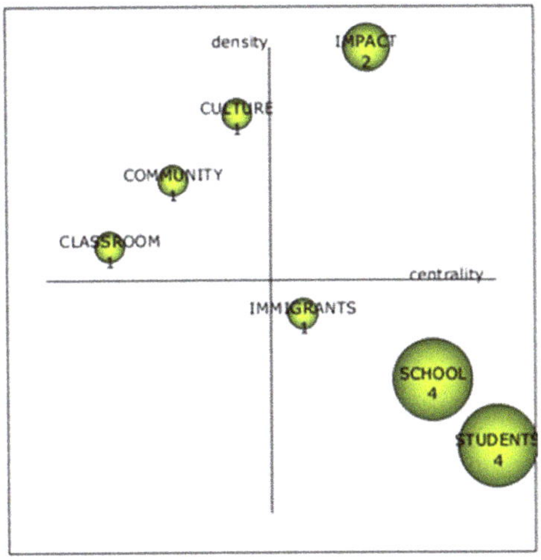

Cluster	Centrality
STUDENTS	28.81
IMPACT	2.67
SCHOOL	13.47
CLASSROOM	0
COMMUNITY	0
CULTURE	0
IMMIGRANTS	1

Figure 6. Strategic cluster diagram for Period 1 using SciMAT.

On the other hand, themes such as "classroom", "community", and "culture" are less central but appear as basic themes. These represent the initial discussions about AI's influence in traditional educational settings and its broader social implications, which could be expanded in future research.

The position of the theme "immigrants", near the center but with low density, suggests growing interest in this topic. However, it remains underexplored, highlighting its potential for further development as research in this area progresses.

This first period shows the initial concerns of researchers about AI's direct impact on educational outcomes, suggesting that research on AI was more focused on the structural aspects of formal education than on the broader social dynamics that can affect the overall educational experience.

3.2. Period 2 (2011–2015)

The motor themes are "adolescents", "students", "school", and "programs", while "experiences", "vulnerability" and "behavior" are highly developed and isolated themes, and "mobile phone", "pedagogy" and "risk" are basic themes. Emerging themes are "perspectives", "educational policy" and "attitudes".

During the second period, there was a shift in focus toward themes related to "adolescents", "students", "school", and "programs", which became motor themes (Figure 7). This indicates a broader integration of AI into educational environments, especially those involving younger populations. The emergence of themes like "vulnerability" and "behavior" as isolated but well-developed topics suggests that AI began to play a relevant role in addressing student challenges.

Cluster	Centrality
ADOLESCENTS	45.56
STUDENTS	48.19
SCHOOL	47.40
BEHAVIOR	35.92
EXPERIENCES	8.91
PROGRAM	30.31
VULNERABILITY	20.14
RISK	8.25
MOBILE-PHONE	0
ATTITUDES	2.21
EDUCATIONAL-...	3.83
PEDAGOGY	5
PERSPECTIVES	6.53

Figure 7. Strategic cluster diagram for Period 2 using SciMAT.

Meanwhile, "mobile phones", "pedagogy", and "risk" emerged as basic and transversal themes, highlighting a growing concern with integrating AI into educational practices through technology.

Finally, the emergence of new themes such as "perspectives", "educational policy", and "attitudes" suggests an increasingly broad conversation about how AI shapes and is shaped by policies and societal views. These emerging themes reflect growing interest in the social and regulatory impacts of AI in the field of education, which anticipates future debates on its implementation and the ethical and social consequences of its use.

The distribution of the clusters in Period 2 shows a diversification of research, shifting from a more structural and results-focused approach, as seen in the first period, toward a deeper integration of AI into students' daily lives. Additionally, it reveals growing interest in how technological tools can both mitigate and exacerbate inequalities, also addressing the ethical and political aspects of AI implementation in educational systems.

3.3. Period 3 (2016–2019)

The motor themes are "children", "adults", "university", and "perception", while "discourse" and "immigrants" are basic themes. Emerging themes are "literacy", "innovation" and "challenges". A highly developed and isolated theme is "students".

During Period 3, a notable shift in research focus is observed, especially with the emergence of new motor themes such as "children", "adults", "university", and "perception". This diversification reflects a growing interest in the role of artificial intelligence (AI) across all educational stages and age groups, spanning from primary education to higher education (Figure 8). As AI technology matured, discussions related to "literacy", "innovation", and the "challenges" posed by AI implementation in educational contexts emerged.

The inclusion of literacy as a central theme highlights the increasing awareness of the need to develop AI competencies among students and educators. This focus suggests that research began to recognize that, to leverage the benefits of AI, it is essential for users—both students and educators—to understand how this technology works and how it can be effectively utilized in educational environments.

Furthermore, the emergence of "innovation" as a prominent theme indicates that researchers were increasingly interested in how AI could transform educational practices, from personalized learning to the automation of administrative processes. However, the "challenges" associated with this transformation, which can range from ethical issues to technological barriers, became an integral part of the academic conversation.

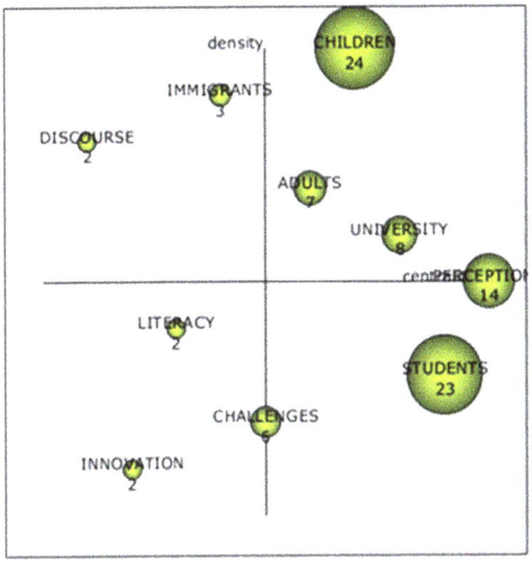

Cluster	Centrality
PERCEPTIONS	37.21
CHILDREN	26.63
UNIVERSITY	28.04
STUDENTS	33.41
ADULTS	20.54
CHALLENGES	18.75
IMMIGRANTS	14.27
DISCOURSE	2.57
INNOVATION	6.36
LITERACY	8.86

Figure 8. Strategic cluster diagram for Period 3 using SciMAT.

On the other hand, the themes of "discourse" and "immigrants" were classified as basic transversal themes. This finding implies that the discussion surrounding inclusion and equity in access to technology was still developing and could have been explored more thoroughly in future research.

Period 3 reveals an evolution towards a more holistic and nuanced approach to AI in education. There is a growing interest in how technology affects different demographic groups and educational levels, reflecting an increasing awareness of the diversity in educational experiences. Additionally, the focus on literacy and innovation suggests that research is beginning to address not only the impacts of AI but also how to prepare future generations for a world where artificial intelligence will be ubiquitous.

3.4. Period 4 (2020–2024)

The motor themes are "social networks", "classroom", "intervention", "future", "competence" and "disability", while "medical school", "services" and "model" are basic themes. Emerging themes are "environment", "school", "mixed methods", "bias" and "community" (returning themes). Highly developed and isolated themes are "impact" and "experiences".

During Period 4, a significant shift is observed in the motor themes of research, now including "social networks", "classroom", "intervention", "future", "competence", and "disability" (Figure 9). This evolution suggests that research began to explore the impact of artificial intelligence (AI) in more nuanced contexts, such as its role in fostering social networks, enhancing classroom interventions, and supporting students with disabilities.

The inclusion of "social networks" as a motor theme reflects a growing interest in how AI can facilitate communication and collaboration among students, as well as how these platforms can influence learning. On the other hand, the centrality of "classroom" and "intervention" indicates a renewed focus on specific pedagogical strategies that may benefit from AI, suggesting that researchers are considering not only the implementation of AI but also how it can be effectively utilized in learning environments.

The emergence of themes like "environment", "school", "mixed methods", "bias", and "community" introduces more complex issues, such as the AI-driven educational environment, interdisciplinary research methods, and concerns over bias in AI. This focus highlights the need for more critical and reflective research on AI tools, ensuring they are fair and equitable for all students.

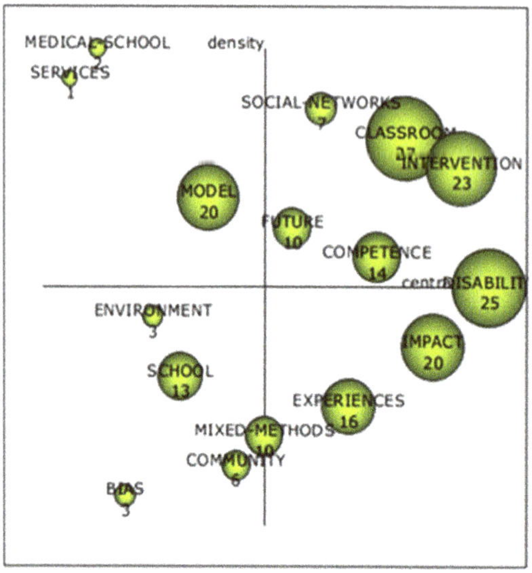

Figure 9. Strategic cluster diagram for Period 4 using SciMAT.

The presence of "impact" and "experiences" as highly developed but isolated themes suggests that, while these areas have been well studied, they still require further integration into broader discussions about AI's evolving role in education. This indicates that, although there is a solid knowledge base in these areas, it is crucial to continue investigating how the impact of AI can intertwine with the experiences of students and educators in a wider educational context.

In this final period, a more sophisticated and multifaceted approach to AI in education is presented. Researchers are exploring how AI can influence various dimensions of learning and teaching, reflecting a commitment to inclusion, equity, and innovation in education. This also suggests a transition toward a more holistic approach that considers not only the benefits of AI but also its ethical and social implications, which is crucial for developing an inclusive and sustainable educational future.

When analyzing the four periods, it becomes evident that the emergence of new topics and the increasing number of core themes represent a trend in the study of AI from a social sciences perspective. A fundamental element is the role of the community, which stands as one of the main subjects of sociological study (Figure 10). In this regard, there is a noticeable evolution: from being a marginal topic in the first period, associated with underdeveloped issues, to becoming an emerging theme connected to subtopics that directly address the lived experience of school dropout, communication in social interaction, digital inequalities, and, finally, the design and closure of unrelated subjects. Future studies should delve deeper into the development of this emerging theme, and greater efforts should be made to ensure that sociological issues surrounding inequality take on a more prominent role in studies on education and technology.

Although the term AI does not appear directly in the clusters or nodes, they have been carefully analyzed to better understand their underlying patterns and how they relate to the overall search, uncovering potential connections that may not be immediately visible. On the other hand, it is important to emphasize that all the findings are closely tied to a sociological perspective. This approach highlights the broader social implications of AI, particularly in terms of power dynamics, inequality, and the role of technology in shaping human interactions. The sociological lens allows for a deeper exploration of how AI systems influence educational practices, access to resources, and the reproduction of social inequalities, making it essential for understanding the full impact of AI on education and society at large. Findings in these areas underscore the importance of addressing the structural inequalities perpetuated through technology.

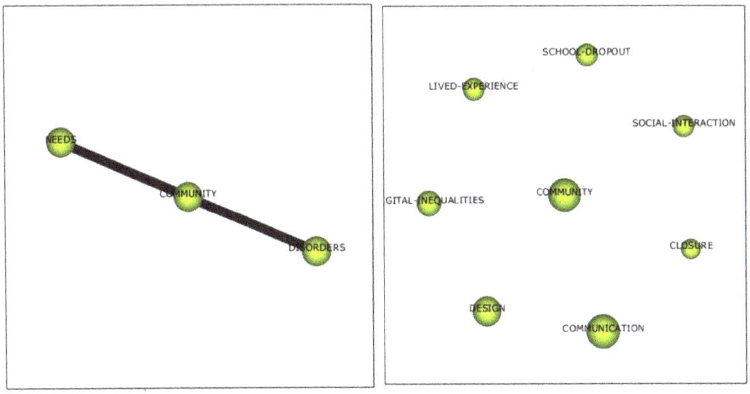

Figure 10. Evolution of the topic of community in Period 1 and Period 4.

4. Discussion

The growing integration of AI in the educational realm not only presents opportunities to enhance teaching and learning but also raises critical challenges that must be addressed. As research continues to develop, educators, researchers, and policymakers need to collaborate to ensure that AI is used equitably and accessibly for all students, especially those from disadvantaged socioeconomic backgrounds. This will require a multifaceted approach that considers both access to technology and the development of digital competencies necessary to navigate an increasingly AI-mediated world.

The integration of AI technologies in educational environments raises significant ethical and social concerns, particularly regarding how these systems can reinforce or exacerbate inequities. For instance, Madianou [24] emphasizes that AI systems, often designed with Eurocentric values, can perpetuate colonial power dynamics, suggesting that the role of AI in education is not neutral but rather reflects inherent biases in its design and implementation. This perspective aligns with Critical Theory's emphasis on understanding the sociopolitical contexts that shape the production and dissemination of knowledge.

The capacity of AI to transform educational practices is also examined in the context of personalized learning systems. Katiyar [39] discusses how AI-driven personalized learning can optimize educational outcomes by tailoring instruction to individual needs. However, this personalization can lead to a form of surveillance and control over students, raising questions about privacy and autonomy. The lens of Critical Theory allows for an examination of how these systems can inadvertently reinforce existing hierarchies by privileging certain learning styles or backgrounds over others. Additionally, the integration of AI in educational assessment, as explored by Du [25], reveals a gap between technological capabilities and practical implementation, particularly in terms of equity and bias.

The ethical challenges associated with AI in education, as discussed by Akgün and Greenhow [23], underscore the need for educators to critically engage with the technologies they employ. They argue that while AI can enhance learning experiences, it also presents ethical dilemmas that must be addressed to prevent reinforcing existing inequalities. This critical implication is essential for educators to navigate the complexities of AI integration and ensure that these technologies empower students rather than marginalize them.

The cultural capital posited by Bourdieu encompasses the knowledge, skills, and cultural competencies that individuals acquire through their education and upbringing, significantly influencing their educational trajectories and interactions with technology. Students from higher socioeconomic backgrounds often possess greater cultural capital, enabling them to navigate educational systems and technological tools more effectively. Educational tracking systems, which classify students based on their perceived ability, can exacerbate inequalities linked to cultural capital [40].

The evolution of the sociological perspective on artificial intelligence (AI) in education has revealed multiple dimensions and dynamics at play. A total of 37 documents were published with the Author keyword from 2012 to 2024, some of which are oriented to digital health and patient care. The narrative of artificial intelligence (AI) research in education has evolved significantly, reflecting growing integration across diverse educational contexts and societal needs. Early studies, like Khan [41], emphasized expanding access to learning for underserved populations using internet-based tools, laying the groundwork for future AI-driven educational technologies. The introduction of AI into augmentative communication for children with disabilities [42] further showcased the transformative potential of AI in enhancing learning for marginalized groups. This trend of integrating AI into education aligns with global goals, as highlighted by Galés and Gallon [43], who tied technological advancements to the Sustainable Development Goals (SDGs), promoting inclusive, equitable education worldwide.

As AI's role in governance and educational policy became more evident [44], attention turned to critical discussions on AI's ethical implications and its influence on educational practices [45]. Researchers like Kharbat et al. [46] identified gaps in AI's support for students with intellectual disabilities, urging a more inclusive design of AI technologies. Digital social innovations, particularly in Europe, started to reshape welfare systems, indicating a broader societal impact [47]. By 2022, concerns over social implications, including biases and ethical considerations in AI, were prominent in discussions [48], paralleled by the examination of AI's acceptance among younger learners [49].

In recent years, the intersection of AI and education has gained momentum with emerging technologies like the Metaverse [20] and AI-driven health applications [50], raising questions about the role of AI in personalized learning and social determinants of health. Chun and Elkins [51] responded to the "crisis" of AI by proposing a new digital humanities curriculum centered around human values, while Lai et al. [52] explored AI's impact on adolescent emotional perception in China. As AI technologies continue to develop, concerns about bias and equity remain central to discussions on best practices [53], along with growing interest in AI's role in higher education, particularly with the introduction of tools like ChatGPT [54].

The study reveals a significant gap in the thematic focus on the effects of AI in the field of education and the reproduction of inequality from a sociological perspective. This gap is evident in the limited number of publications addressing this topic and the analysis of clusters along their evolutionary lines. However, discussions on AI's impact appear transversally in studies from other fields, particularly within education. The results of this study call for sociology to take a leading role in investigating this area, using its essential tools to better understand the dynamics between new technologies, global society, and education.

The thematic network for "community" expands from two nodes in earlier periods to seven in later ones, indicating a broader engagement in integrating educational AI within community services. Studies associated with community are on services for children attending schools for the emotionally and behaviorally disturbed [55]. The research by Lai et al. [52] explores whether interaction with generative artificial intelligence can enhance learning autonomy, comparing the effects of virtual companionship and knowledge acquisition preferences over time.

The only study directly related to the research strategy is the study that explores the identity and cognition of English language teachers instructing students with visual impairments in Türkiye, examining how personal, social, cultural, and educational factors shape these teachers' experiences within the context of special education [56]. This aligns with the broader trend in AI research towards inclusive approaches that support diverse needs within educational settings, highlighting the importance of sociocultural factors in educational AI applications.

This work has explored various theoretical frameworks to tackle the issue of digital inequalities. From the perspective of Critical Theory, the importance of questioning and transforming power structures that limit human self-realization is emphasized, focusing on emancipation and resistance to social inequalities, which is essential for understanding how cultural capital influences access to and use of technologies like AI [22,24]. Bourdieu [57] defines cultural capital as the knowledge, skills, and competencies individuals possess, which are crucial for navigating educational and technological environments [58]. Students with high cultural capital tend to benefit more from AI platforms, as they possess the cognitive and social tools necessary to leverage these technologies effectively. In contrast, those with lower cultural capital face greater obstacles, creating a gap in access to and use of AI [25,26,58].

The Actor-Network Theory (ANT) broadens the perspective by presenting AI not only as a tool but also as an active participant in the educational ecosystem, reconfiguring relationships, roles, and power dynamics among students, teachers, and institutions. ANT considers both students and AI platforms as actors in a co-constructed network through their interactions [59]. This theory allows for analyzing how relationships among students, teachers, and AI technologies transform and evolve, highlighting the importance of connections and collaboration in learning [60]. AI platforms, far from being merely tools, influence relationships and knowledge construction between students and teachers [61], reflecting a dynamic and changing learning network in which cultural capital can either facilitate or hinder students' participation [62]. Thus, the theoretical framework provided by Critical Theory and ANT is invaluable for exploring how AI reconfigures educational practices, with profound implications for inequality and social justice [28,63].

A more detailed analysis of the challenges and benefits of AI, based on demographic subgroups, shows evidence of greater access barriers among students from rural areas due to limitations in technological infrastructure, while urban students can more readily benefit from these tools, thus exacerbating digital divides [64]. It would also be relevant to examine how AI could support students with disabilities or specific needs through adaptive platforms that respond to their particular requirements. This approach provides a more accurate picture of the various ways in which AI affects different populations, emphasizing the need for policies that consider the diversity and particularity of students.

Artificial intelligence (AI) is transforming education by addressing inequities through personalized learning experiences [30,65,66], early detection of learning difficulties [67], and automating administrative tasks [17,19]. By leveraging tools like natural language processing (NLP) and data analysis, AI enables educators to tailor resources to individual needs, improve accessibility, and identify gaps in knowledge. It helps bridge disparities across demographics and regions by optimizing teaching methods and making education more inclusive [28]. Ethical implementation ensures AI remains a powerful tool for fostering equity in education.

Simultaneously, AI has the potential to widen global inequality due to three main factors: economic divergence, where wealthier nations have better access to AI technology and its benefits; disparities in AI research resources, with leading countries dominating development; and the reinforcement of existing biases, as AI systems trained on biased data can perpetuate inequalities. Addressing these issues will require international cooperation and ethical frameworks to ensure AI advancements benefit lower-income countries and vulnerable populations [28,68].

The combination of Critical Theory and ANT enables a deeper understanding of inequalities in access to education and technology. Critical Theory invites questioning of the structures that perpetuate these inequalities, while ANT provides a framework for observing how these structures manifest in daily interactions [69]. For instance, students from disadvantaged socioeconomic backgrounds may have less access to technological and educational resources, limiting their ability to benefit from AI platforms [64]. ANT helps to make these dynamics visible by considering how relationships between different actors (students, teachers, technologies) are configured and affect learning [70].

Finally, the intersection between Bourdieu's theory of cultural capital and the concept of the digital divide offers a nuanced understanding of how generational inequalities are perpetuated in the context of AI-based educational tools. The digital divide is generally categorized into two levels: the first-level digital divide, which refers to disparities in access to digital technologies, and the second-level digital divide, which refers to the unequal ability to effectively use these technologies.

The first-level digital divide highlights disparities in access to technology, which can be influenced by socioeconomic status, geographical location, and educational resources. Students from lower socioeconomic backgrounds often lack access to essential digital tools, which can create significant educational disadvantages. According to van Dijk [63], access to technology is not just about physical availability, but also about the social and economic conditions that facilitate or hinder that access.

The second-level digital divide focuses on disparities in the ability to effectively use digital technologies. Even when students have access to technology, their capacity to use it effectively may vary significantly based on their cultural capital. Hargittai [71] emphasizes that digital literacy is a crucial component of the second-level digital divide. Students with higher levels of cultural capital tend to be more competent in using technology for educational purposes, as they are typically exposed to digital tools and resources from an early age.

The integration of AI in educational environments transforms the relationships among various actors. For example, educators may see their roles shift from knowledge providers to facilitators of AI-driven learning experiences. This change can create new power dynamics, where AI systems have significant influence over curriculum design and assessment methods. Selwyn [27] emphasizes that discussions about AI in education should be seen as inherently political, intertwined with issues of power, disadvantage, and marginalization.

To ensure that AI use in education benefits all students, especially those in vulnerable situations, various studies propose a set of practical recommendations for policymakers and educational institutions. First, it is necessary to establish clear privacy standards that regulate the use of AI in educational settings, protecting students' personal data and preventing misuse of information [23].

Different authors [12,13,64] highlight the importance of creating funding opportunities that allow under-resourced schools, particularly in rural or vulnerable areas, to access AI technologies. In addition to resources, it is crucial to implement training programs to ensure that teachers are equipped with the skills needed for appropriate and pedagogical use of AI tools, ensuring inclusive and responsible implementation.

Finally, a line of research has focused on promoting the availability of AI platforms that offer personalized learning, allowing students to progress at their own pace and meeting the needs of those requiring additional support [6,32]. These practical measures seek not only to improve access to AI but also to ensure that its implementation in the educational sector aligns with principles of equity and social justice. Furthermore, they call for educators, researchers, and policymakers to work together in developing an AI framework in education that is inclusive and accessible.

The evolution of sociology towards a more complex approach to technology, marked by the emergence of digital sociology, also reflects a significant shift. This branch seeks to understand how digital technologies influence human behavior, relationships, and social norms. The integration of AI across various sectors raises ethical considerations regarding accessibility and equity in education, highlighting the need for a sociological lens to navigate these challenges.

Policymakers have a crucial role in harnessing AI to foster equity in education, and several actionable strategies can guide their efforts. First, ensuring equitable access to technology is essential. This includes allocating funding to provide underserved schools with the necessary infrastructure to access AI tools, as well as implementing subsidized programs or partnerships with technology companies to offer AI-based educational tools at reduced costs for low-income families.

Promoting digital literacy and cultural capital is another important strategy. Policymakers should focus on developing curricula that integrate digital literacy and AI education from an early age, teaching students not only how to use AI tools but also how to critically evaluate and engage with these technologies. Additionally, community-based programs that educate families about AI can help build cultural capital and empower students to navigate AI-based platforms effectively.

Supporting teacher training and development is also vital. Policymakers should provide ongoing professional development for educators on effectively integrating AI tools into their teaching practices. This training should emphasize understanding diverse cultural backgrounds and fostering positive student–teacher relationships. Establishing mentorship programs that connect experienced educators with those new to AI technologies can further promote knowledge sharing and collaborative learning.

It is equally important to foster inclusive AI development. Policymakers should engage stakeholders, including educators, students, and community members, in the development and selection of AI tools to ensure these technologies are relevant and effective. Creating ethical guidelines for AI implementation in education that prioritize equity, transparency, and accountability will help address biases in algorithms that could impact student outcomes.

Implementing data-informed policies is crucial for driving meaningful change. Policymakers should fund research that evaluates the impact of AI on various student populations, focusing on how these tools affect equity in educational outcomes. Additionally, establishing feedback mechanisms for collecting insights from students and teachers about their experiences with AI tools can help inform policy decisions and improve the effectiveness of resources.

Encouraging collaboration across sectors will enhance the impact of AI in education. Policymakers should promote partnerships between educational institutions and technology companies to develop tailored AI solutions that meet the specific needs of diverse student populations. Fostering collaboration between schools and community organizations can also create support networks for students and families, leveraging AI tools to enhance learning opportunities beyond the classroom.

Finally, policymakers should address existing barriers through policy revisions and exploring new funding models that support equitable AI integration. By reviewing and revising education policies to remove obstacles to effective AI use and ensuring that financial resources are allocated based on need rather than uniform distribution, policymakers can create an educational landscape where AI tools enhance learning opportunities equitably. Through these strategies, all students can be empowered to thrive in a technology-driven world.

In summary, sociological theory allows for the identification of risks in the implementation of AIs, considering various mitigation strategies (Table 1), as has been outlined throughout the work.

This study has several limitations that should be acknowledged to contextualize the findings and guide future research. Firstly, the bibliometric analysis was confined to the Web of Science Core Collection, which, while comprehensive, may exclude relevant studies published in other databases or grey literature. This limitation could result in an incomplete representation of the existing research landscape on AI in education and digital inequalities. Additionally, the reliance on bibliometric methods inherently focuses on quantitative metrics, potentially overlooking the qualitative nuances and deeper sociological insights that qualitative analyses might capture. The so-called "grey literature", including reports

addressing or exacerbating social inequalities, emphasizing the need for thoughtful and inclusive strategies as AI becomes embedded in educational systems worldwide.

Author Contributions: Conceptualization, I.M.F., E.L.M. and E.-M.G.-A.; methodology, I.M.F.; software, I.M.F.; validation, I.M.F. and E.-M.G.-A.; formal analysis, I.M.F., E.L.M. and E.-M.G.-A.; investigation, I.M.F. and E.-M.G.-A.; writing—original draft preparation, I.M.F. and E.-M.G.-A.; writing—review and editing, I.M.F., E.L.M. and E.-M.G.-A.; visualization, I.M.F. and E.-M.G.-A.; supervision, I.M.F., E.L.M. and E.-M.G.-A. All authors have read and agreed to the published version of the manuscript.

Funding: This research received no external funding.

Institutional Review Board Statement: Not applicable.

Informed Consent Statement: Not applicable.

Data Availability Statement: The data presented in this study are available on request from the corresponding author.

Conflicts of Interest: The authors declare no conflicts of interest.

References

1. Rutkowski, L. *Computational Intelligence;* Springer: Berlin/Heidelberg, Germany, 2008. ISBN 978-3-540-76287-4/978-3-540-76288-1.
2. Bostrom, N.; Yudkowsky, E. The Ethics of Artificial Intelligence. In *Artificial Intelligence Safety and Security*, 1st ed.; Yampolskiy, R.V., Ed.; Chapman and Hall/CRC Artificial Intelligence and Robotics Series; CRC Press/Taylor & Francis Group: Boca Raton, FL, USA, 2018; pp. 57–69. ISBN 978-1-351-25138-9.
3. Holzinger, A.; Langs, G.; Denk, H.; Zatloukal, K.; Müller, H. Causability and Explainability of Artificial Intelligence in Medicine. *WIREs Data Min. Knowl. Discov.* **2019**, *9*, e1312. [CrossRef] [PubMed]
4. Howard, J. Artificial Intelligence: Implications for the Future of Work. *Am. J. Ind. Med.* **2019**, *62*, 917–926. [CrossRef] [PubMed]
5. Aghion, P.; Jones, B.F.; Jones, C. Artificial Intelligence and Economic Growth. In *The Economics of Artificial Intelligence;* National Bureau of Economic Research: Cambridge, MA, USA, 2019; Volume 23928. [CrossRef]
6. Chen, L.; Chen, P.; Lin, Z. Artificial Intelligence in Education: A Review. *IEEE Access* **2020**, *8*, 75264–75278. [CrossRef]
7. Xiang, X.; Li, Q.; Khan, S.; Khalaf, O.I. Urban Water Resource Management for Sustainable Environment Planning Using Artificial Intelligence Techniques. *Environ. Impact Assess. Rev.* **2021**, *86*, 106515. [CrossRef]
8. Szpilko, D.; Naharro, F.J.; Lăzăroiu, G.; Nica, E.; Gallegos, A.D.L.T. Artificial Intelligence in the Smart City—A Literature Review. *Eng. Manag. Prod. Serv.* **2023**, *15*, 53–75. [CrossRef]
9. Ren, S. How Much Water Does AI Consume? The Public Deserves to Know. OECD AI Policy Observatory. 2023. Available online: https://oecd.ai/en/wonk/how-much-water-does-ai-consume (accessed on 30 November 2023).
10. Lutz, C. Digital Inequalities in the Age of Artificial Intelligence and Big Data. *Hum. Behav. Emerg. Technol.* **2019**, *1*, 141–148. [CrossRef]
11. Dautenhahn, K. Socially Intelligent Robots: Dimensions of Human–Robot Interaction. *Philos. Trans. R. Soc. B Biol. Sci.* **2007**, *362*, 679–704. [CrossRef]
12. Salemink, K.; Strijker, D.; Bosworth, G. Rural Development in the Digital Age: A Systematic Literature Review on Unequal ICT Availability, Adoption, and Use in Rural Areas. *J. Rural Stud.* **2017**, *54*, 360–371. [CrossRef]
13. Fahmi, F.Z.; Arifianto, A. Digitalization and Social Innovation in Rural Areas: A Case Study from Indonesia. *Rural Sociol.* **2022**, *87*, 339–369. [CrossRef]
14. García-Alonso, E.M.; León-Mejía, A.C.; Sánchez-Cabrero, R.; Guzmán-Ordaz, R. Training and Technology Acceptance of ChatGPT in University Students of Social Sciences: A Netcoincidental Analysis. *Behav. Sci.* **2024**, *14*, 612. [CrossRef]
15. Firat, M. How Chat GPT Can Transform Autodidactic Experiences and Open Education? OSF Preprints. Available online: https://osf.io/preprints/osf/9ge8m (accessed on 12 January 2023).
16. Hakiki, M.; Fadli, R.; Samala, A.D.; Fricticarani, A.; Dayurni, P.; Rahmadani, K.; Astiti, A.D. Exploring the Impact of Using Chat-GPT on Student Learning Outcomes in Technology Learning: The Comprehensive Experiment. *Adv. Mob. Learn. Educ. Res.* **2023**, *3*, 859–872. [CrossRef]
17. Abdillah, H.Z.; Partino, P.; Madjid, A. Enhancing Student Well-Being through AI Chat GPT in the Smart Education University Learning Environment: A Preliminary Review of Research Literature. *E3S Web Conf.* **2023**, *440*, 05005. [CrossRef]
18. Van Dolen, W.; Weinberg, C.B. Child Helplines: How Social Support and Controllability Influence Service Quality and Well-Being. *J. Serv. Mark.* **2017**, *31*, 385–396. [CrossRef]
19. Cotton, D.R.E.; Cotton, P.A.; Shipway, J.R. Chatting and Cheating: Ensuring Academic Integrity in the Era of ChatGPT. *Innov. Educ. Teach. Int.* **2023**, *61*, 228–639. [CrossRef]

20. Tlili, A.; Huang, R.; Shehata, B.; Liu, D.; Zhao, J.; Metwally, A.H.S.; Wang, H.; Denden, M.; Bozkurt, A.; Lee, L.-H.; et al. Is Metaverse in Education a Blessing or a Curse: A Combined Content and Bibliometric Analysis. *Smart Learn. Environ.* **2022**, *9*, 24. [CrossRef]
21. Durak, G.; Çankaya, S.; Özdemir, D.; Can, S. Artificial Intelligence in Education: A Bibliometric Study on Its Role in Transforming Teaching and Learning. *Int. Rev. Res. Open Distrib. Learn.* **2024**, *25*, 219–244. [CrossRef]
22. Leander, K.M.; Burriss, S.K. Critical Literacy for a Posthuman World: When People Read, and Become, with Machines. *Br. J. Educ. Technol.* **2020**, *51*, 1262–1276. [CrossRef]
23. Akgun, S.; Greenhow, C. Artificial Intelligence in Education: Addressing Ethical Challenges in K-12 Settings. *AI Ethics* **2022**, *2*, 431–440. [CrossRef]
24. Madianou, M. Nonhuman Humanitarianism: When "AI for Good" Can Be Harmful. *Inf. Commun. Soc.* **2021**, *24*, 850–868. [CrossRef]
25. Du, K.; Geiger, J.; Killen, T.; Porta, A.E.; O'Brien, T. The Paradigm Shift in Education in Big Data Era: Exploring the Intersection of Historical Assessment Frameworks and AI-Powered Assessment Methods in Education. *J. Educ. Train. Stud.* **2024**, *12*, 22. [CrossRef]
26. Breinholt, A.; Jæger, M.M. How Does Cultural Capital Affect Educational Performance: Signals or Skills? *Br. J. Sociol.* **2020**, *71*, 28–46. [CrossRef] [PubMed]
27. Selwyn, N. The Future of AI and Education: Some Cautionary Notes. *Eur. J. Educ.* **2022**, *57*, 620–631. [CrossRef]
28. Li, H. AI in Education: Bridging the Divide or Widening the Gap? Exploring Equity, Opportunities, and Challenges in the Digital Age. *Adv. Educ. Humanit. Soc. Sci. Res.* **2023**, *8*, 355. [CrossRef]
29. Hart, C.S. Education, Inequality and Social Justice: A Critical Analysis Applying the Sen-Bourdieu Analytical Framework. *Policy Futures Educ.* **2019**, *17*, 582–598. [CrossRef]
30. Ansor, F.; Zulkifli, N.A.; Jannah, D.S.M.; Krisnaresanti, A. Adaptive Learning Based on Artificial Intelligence to Overcome Student Academic Inequalities. *J. Soc. Sci. Util. Technol.* **2023**, *1*, 202–213. [CrossRef]
31. Kuhail, M.A.; Thomas, J.; Alramlawi, S.; Shah, S.J.H.; Thornquist, E. Interacting with a Chatbot-Based Advising System: Understanding the Effect of Chatbot Personality and User Gender on Behavior. *Informatics* **2022**, *9*, 81. [CrossRef]
32. Roshanaei, M.; Olivares, H.; Lopez, R.R. Harnessing AI to Foster Equity in Education: Opportunities, Challenges, and Emerging Strategies. *J. Intell. Learn. Syst. Appl.* **2023**, *15*, 123–143. [CrossRef]
33. Cobo, M.J.; López-Herrera, A.G.; Herrera-Viedma, E.; Herrera, F. SciMAT: A New Science Mapping Analysis Software Tool. *J. Am. Soc. Inf. Sci. Technol.* **2012**, *63*, 1609–1630. [CrossRef]
34. Mac Fadden, I.; Santana, M.; Vázquez-Cano, E.; López-Meneses, E. A Science Mapping Analysis of 'Marginality, Stigmatization and Social Cohesion' in WoS (1963–2019). *Qual. Quant.* **2021**, *55*, 275–293. [CrossRef]
35. Hirsch, J.E. An Index to Quantify an Individual's Scientific Research Output. *Proc. Natl. Acad. Sci. USA* **2005**, *102*, 16569–16572. [CrossRef]
36. Callon, M.; Courtial, J.-P.; Turner, W.A.; Bauin, S. From Translations to Problematic Networks: An Introduction to Co-Word Analysis. *Soc. Sci. Inf.* **1983**, *22*, 191–235. [CrossRef]
37. Ward, R.M.; Schmieder, R.; Highnam, G.; Mittelman, D. Big Data Challenges and Opportunities in High-Throughput Sequencing. *Syst. Biomed.* **2013**, *1*, 29–34. [CrossRef]
38. Eck, N.J.v.; Waltman, L. How to Normalize Cooccurrence Data? An Analysis of Some Well-known Similarity Measures. *J. Am. Soc. Inf. Sci. Technol.* **2009**, *60*, 1635–1651. [CrossRef]
39. Katiyar, N.; Awasthi, M.V.; Pratap, R.; Mishra, M.K.; Shukla, M.N.; Tiwari, M. Ai-Driven Personalized Learning Systems: Enhancing Educational Effectiveness. *Educ. Adm. Theory Pract.* **2024**, *30*, 11514–11524. [CrossRef]
40. Zamfir, A.-M.; Aldea, A.B.; Molea, R.-M. Stratification and Inequality in the Secondary Education System in Romania. *Systems* **2024**, *12*, 15. [CrossRef]
41. Khan, E. Education for the Base of the Pyramid People (BOP) Using Voice Internet e-Learning. *Procedia Soc. Behav. Sci.* **2012**, *64*, 474–483. [CrossRef]
42. Neamtu, R.; Camara, A.; Pereira, C.; Ferreira, R. Using Artificial Intelligence for Augmentative Alternative Communication for Children with Disabilities. In *Human-Computer Interaction—INTERACT 2019*; Lamas, D., Loizides, F., Nacke, L., Petrie, H., Winckler, M., Zaphiris, P., Eds.; Springer International Publishing: Cham, Switzerland, 2019; Volume 11746, pp. 234–243. ISBN 978-3-030-29380-2/978-3-030-29381-9.
43. Universitat Autónoma de Barcelona Spain; Galés, N.L.; Gallon, R.; Universitat de Barcelona Spain. Integrating Education, Technology, and SDG's: A Three-Pronged Collaboration. In *Innovations, Technologies and Research in Education*; LU Akadēmiskais apgāds; University of Latvia Press: Riga, Latvia, 2019; pp. 10–22.
44. Sharma, G.D.; Yadav, A.; Chopra, R. Artificial Intelligence and Effective Governance: A Review, Critique and Research Agenda. *Sustain. Futures* **2020**, *2*, 100004. [CrossRef]
45. Ekström, S.; Fuentes, A. New critical imaginaries and reflections on robots and artificial intelligence: How teachers' programming knowledge could affect future educational technology. In Proceedings of the 14th International Technology, Education and Development Conference, Valencia, Spain, 2–4 March 2020; pp. 3475–3483.
46. Kharbat, F.F.; Alshawabkeh, A.; Woolsey, M.L. Identifying Gaps in Using Artificial Intelligence to Support Students with Intellectual Disabilities from Education and Health Perspectives. *Aslib J. Inf. Manag.* **2020**, *73*, 101–128. [CrossRef]
47. Davide, F.; Gaggioli, A.; Misuraca, G. (Eds.) *Perspectives for Digital Social Innovation to Reshape the European Welfare Systems*; IOS Press: Amsterdam, The Netherlands, 2021. ISBN 978-1-64368-157-3.

48. Tsvyk, V.A.; Tsvyk, I.V. Social Issues in the Development and Application of Artificial Intelligence. *RUDN J. Sociol.* **2022**, *22*, 58–69. [CrossRef]
49. Li, E.; Li, S.; Yuan, X. Adoption and Perception of Artificial Intelligence Technologies by Children and Teens in Education. In *Artificial Intelligence in HCI*; Degen, H., Ntoa, S., Eds.; Springer International Publishing: Cham, Switzerland, 2022; Volume 13336, pp. 69–79. ISBN 978-3-031-05642-0/978-3-031-05643-7.
50. Snowdon, J.L.; Scheufele, E.L.; Pritts, J.; Le, P.-T.; Mensah, G.A.; Zhang, X.; Dankwa-Mullan, I. Evaluating Social Determinants of Health Variables in Advanced Analytic and Artificial Intelligence Models for Cardiovascular Disease Risk and Outcomes: A Targeted Review. *Ethn. Dis.* **2023**, *33*, 33–43. [CrossRef]
51. Chun, J.; Elkins, K. The Crisis of Artificial Intelligence: A New Digital Humanities Curriculum for Human Centred AI. *Int. J. Humanit. Arts Comput.* **2023**, *17*, 147–167. [CrossRef]
52. Lai, T.; Zeng, X.; Xu, B.; Xie, C.; Liu, Y.; Wang, Z.; Lu, H.; Fu, S. The Application of Artificial Intelligence Technology in Education Influences Chinese Adolescent's Emotional Perception. *Curr. Psychol.* **2024**, *43*, 5309–5317. [CrossRef] [PubMed]
53. Roshanaei, M. Towards Best Practices for Mitigating Artificial Intelligence Implicit Bias in Shaping Diversity, Inclusion and Equity in Higher Education. *Educ. Inf. Technol.* **2024**, *29*, 18959–18984. [CrossRef]
54. Vartiainen, H.; Valtonen, T.; Kahila, J.; Tedre, M. ChatGPT and Imaginaries of the Future of Education: Insights of Finnish Teacher Educators. *Inf. Learn. Sci.* **2024**. *ahead-of-print*. [CrossRef]
55. Crawford, T.; Simonoff, E. Parental Views about Services for Children Attending Schools for the Emotionally and Behaviourally Disturbed (EBD): A Qualitative Analysis. *Child Care Health Dev.* **2003**, *29*, 481–491. [CrossRef]
56. Cinarbas, H.I.; Daloglu, A. Promoting Inclusivity: Exploring Turkish Language Teacher Identity and Cognition in Special Education for Students with Visual Impairments. *Qual. Assur. Educ.* **2024**, *32*, 611–627. [CrossRef]
57. Bourdieu, P.; Passeron, J.-C. *Reproduction in Education, Society and Culture*; Sage: Thousand Oaks, CA, USA, 1990; Volume 4. ISBN 0803983204.
58. Pecourt Gracia, J.; Martínez Morales, I.; Bernad i García, J.C. Hacia Una Concepción Crítica de La Sociología de La Educación: El Debate Entre Bourdieu y Boltanski. *Rev. Sociol. Educ.-RASE* **2022**, *15*, 184–200. [CrossRef]
59. Monterroza Ríos, Á. Una Revisión Crítica a La Teoría Del Actor-Red Para El Estudio de Los Artefactos. *Trilogía Cienc. Tecnol. Soc.* **2017**, *9*, 49–62. [CrossRef]
60. Hernández Gómez, C.A.; Vargas Aldana, C.M. Agua y Procesos de Educación Ambiental En Bogotá. *Rev. Educ. Ciudad* **2021**, *40*, 49–63. [CrossRef]
61. León, E.A. Latour, Deleuze y Harman Hacia Una Nueva Concepción de La Teoría Del Actor Red. *Isegoría* **2022**, *66*, e23. [CrossRef]
62. Pfeilstetter, R. Bourdieu y Luhmann. Diferencias, Similitudes, Sinergias. *Rev. Int. Sociol.* **2012**, *70*, 489–510. [CrossRef]
63. Van Dijk, J.A.G.M. *The Evolution of the Digital Divide-The Digital Divide Turns to Inequality of Skills and Usage*; IOS Press: Amsterdam, The Netherlands, 2012.
64. Flores Núñez, A.; Enríquez García, F. Educación Del México Rural y El Enfoque Autogestivo. *Rev. Biol. Agropecu. Tuxpan* **2023**, *11*, 29–44. [CrossRef]
65. Pawlik, S.; Rzeźnicka-Krupa, J.; Gierczyk, M.; Hornby, G. The Voices of Autistic Adolescents on Diversity, Education and School Learning in Poland. *Educ. Sci.* **2023**, *13*, 368. [CrossRef]
66. Ghergut, A. Education of Children with Special Needs in Romania; Attitudes and Experiences. *Procedia Soc. Behav. Sci.* **2011**, *12*, 595–599. [CrossRef]
67. Giménez, A.; Bordoy, S.; Sánchez, A.; López-Zamora, M.; Sopena, J.M.; Luque, J.L. A Supplemental computer-assisted Intervention Programme to Prevent Early Reading Difficulties in Spanish Learners: A Stratified Random Control Trial. *J. Comput. Assist. Learn.* **2021**, *37*, 510–520. [CrossRef]
68. Grashof, N.; Kopka, A. Artificial Intelligence and Radical Innovation: An Opportunity for All Companies? *Small Bus. Econ.* **2023**, *61*, 771–797. [CrossRef]
69. Carrasco-Aguilar, C.L.; Baltar-de Andrade, M.J. La Psicología y Las Metodologías Críticas de Investigación Educativa. *Memorias* **2015**, *12*, 21. [CrossRef]
70. Callén, B.; Domènech, M.; López, D.; Rodríguez Giralt, I.; Sánchez-Criado, T.; Tirado Serrano, F.J. Diasporas and Transitions in Actor-Network Theory. *Athenea Digital Rev. Pensam. Investig. Soc.* **2011**, *11*, 3. [CrossRef]
71. Hargittai, E. Second-Level Digital Divide: Differences in People's Online Skills. *First Monday* **2002**, *7*. [CrossRef]
72. Lea, M.R.; Goodfellow, R.; Jones, S. Digital Literacies Inhigher Education. In *Proceedings of the 3rd International Conference on e-Learning*; Remenyi, D., Ed.; Academic Publishing Limited: Reading, UK, 2008; pp. 255–260.
73. Kalambouka, A.; Farrell, P.; Dyson, A.; Kaplan, I. The Impact of Placing Pupils with Special Educational Needs in Mainstream Schools on the Achievement of Their Peers. *Educ. Res.* **2007**, *49*, 365–382. [CrossRef]
74. Wang, F.; Ni, X.; Zhang, M.; Zhang, J. Educational Digital Inequality: A Meta-Analysis of the Relationship between Digital Device Use and Academic Performance in Adolescents. *Comput. Educ.* **2024**, *213*, 105003. [CrossRef]

Multimodal Technologies and Interaction

MDPI

Review

A Comprehensive Review of Dropout Prediction Methods Based on Multivariate Analysed Features of MOOC Platforms

Saad Alghamdi [1], Ben Soh [1,*] and Alice Li [2]

[1] Department of Computer Science and Information Technology, School of Computing, Engineering and Mathematical Sciences, La Trobe University, Bundoora, VIC 3086, Australia; s.alghamdi@latrobe.edu.au

[2] La Trobe Business School, La Trobe University, Bundoora, VIC 3086, Australia; a.li@latrobe.edu.au

* Correspondence: b.soh@latrobe.edu.au

Abstract: Massive open online courses have revolutionised the learning environment, but their effectiveness is undermined by low completion rates. Traditional dropout prediction models in MOOCs often overlook complex factors like temporal dependencies and context-specific variables. These models are not adaptive enough to manage the dynamic nature of MOOC learning environments, resulting in inaccurate predictions and ineffective interventions. Accordingly, MOOCs dropout prediction models require more sophisticated artificial intelligence models that can address these limitations. Moreover, incorporating feature selection methods and explainable AI techniques can enhance the interpretability of these models, making them more actionable for educators and course designers. This paper provides a comprehensive review of various MOOCs dropout prediction methodologies, focusing on their strategies and research gaps. It highlights the growing MOOC environment and the potential for technology-driven gains in outcome accuracy. This review also discusses the use of advanced models based on machine learning, deep learning, and meta-heuristics approaches to improve course completion rates, optimise learning outcomes, and provide personalised educational experiences.

Keywords: MOOCs; dropout prediction; meta-heuristics; deep learning; accuracy optimisation; feature selection

1. Introduction

Massive open online courses (MOOCs) have brought about a new era of learning by providing easier access to high-quality educational materials worldwide [1]. This approach aims to address the challenges of accommodating large numbers of students, especially in developing countries, where traditional infrastructure is often inadequate. However, despite the initial high levels of engagement with MOOCs, many participants unfortunately drop out as the courses progress [2]. The dropout rate is a crucial metric for evaluating the effectiveness of cutting-edge approaches and frameworks designed to improve MOOC adoption and performance. A thorough understanding of the factors driving continuous MOOC acceptance and enhancing learning outcomes is essential for improving course completion rates. Continued use of MOOCs reflects a cognitive state involving a learner's personal attitude and willingness to adopt new technologies in education [3].

MOOC dropout prediction enhances the design of MOOCs and plays a crucial role in improving the user experience. The rise of machine learning (ML) and deep learning (DL) has introduced powerful methodologies for evaluating large datasets and extracting valuable insights [3]. These techniques can be applied to massive open online courses to build predictive models that not only forecast student behaviour but also increase the accuracy of learning outcome predictions. Given the complexity and diversity of learner interactions in MOOCs, the development of intelligent models to predict dropout rates is essential [4]. These models must capture complex patterns in learner data, adapt to varying learning contexts, and provide actionable insights for course designers and instructors to address the challenges associated with MOOC dropout prediction, as shown in Figure 1. In this regard, the selection of relevant MOOC features and feature selection methods are key factors that significantly impact the performance of dropout prediction models.

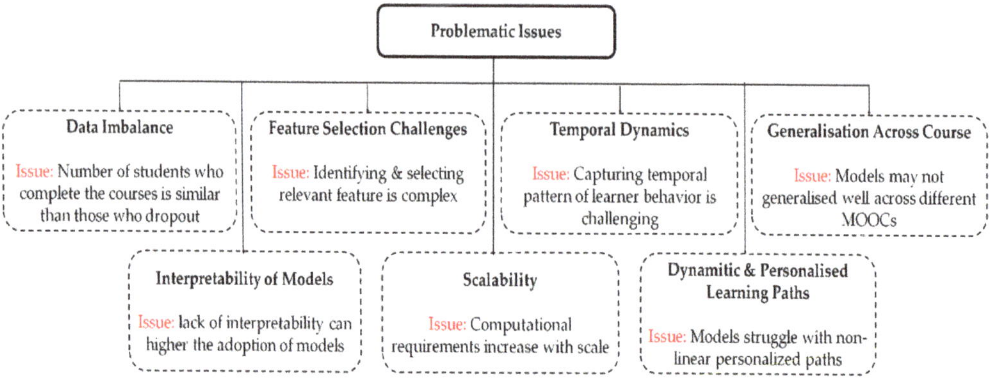

Figure 1. General problematic issues in MOOCs dropout prediction model.

MOOCs' feature types and selection methods are crucial components that significantly influence the performance of dropout prediction models [4]. The vast and diverse data generated by MOOC platforms include various features such as learner demographics, engagement metrics, interaction patterns, and course-specific variables. Identifying and selecting the most relevant features is essential for building accurate and robust predictive models. An effective feature selection process ensures that the model focuses on the most impactful variables, reducing noise and improving the ability of the model to generalise across different learning contexts [5]. Consequently, a well-considered approach to feature selection can lead to more precise dropout predictions and, ultimately, more effective interventions to enhance learner retention and success. There are specific features that must be carefully addressed in building MOOCs, which are reviewed according to the following objectives:

- Identify and select the most relevant learner attributes to ensure that the model accurately reflects diverse learning behaviours.
- Adapt to different learning contexts in MOOCs which may impact learner retention and dropout rates.
- Deal with the vast amount of data generated by MOOCs, which require robust attribute selection methods to filter out noise and focus on the most influential variables.
- Ensure that the model can generalise across different MOOC platforms and learner populations, improving its predictive accuracy and effectiveness.

1.1. Motivations

The purpose of this comprehensive review is to critically explore and evaluate the current literature on predicting dropout in MOOCs and to identify the key factors that contribute to learner dropout and the most effective AI-based approaches to address these challenges. By summarising findings from different studies, this review aims to provide a comprehensive understanding of the current state of research in this area and highlight the need for more sophisticated and intelligent models that can effectively mitigate dropout rates and improve learner outcomes in MOOCs. The motivations of this paper are listed as followings:

- Provide a compilation of MOOCs dropout prediction methods and their significance.
- Classify the potential MOOCs features, selection methods, and architecture.
- Identify and describe the key requirements to improve and optimise the MOOCs dropout prediction.
- Propose a thematic taxonomy of literature according to the most important dropout prediction features and provide a comprehensive review on recent advances MOOCs dropout models.
- Discuss the optimisation challenges related to MOOCs dropout prediction models, highlighting the most related methods and schemes.
- Illustrate the research gaps on MOOCs dropout prediction optimisation-based meta-heuristics and DL approaches, in addition to future works.

1.2. Contributions

This comprehensive review begins with a review of the methodologies used in many studies on MOOCs, with a particular focus on the interaction between their continued acceptance and the accuracy of predicting learning outcomes, through a review and critical analysis of current research on the dynamics of acceptance of MOOCs, with an emphasis on the role of the technology acceptance model. Moreover, this review will investigate the integration of predictive modelling, specifically ML, DL, and meta-heuristics, in improving the accuracy of outcome predictions in the MOOC environment. By deeply focusing into the complexities of these intersecting methods, this review aims to shed light on the mechanisms that underpin MOOC acceptance as well as the possibility for technology-driven advances in outcome accuracy.

This review offers readers a structured overview of the current body of research, providing a comprehensive synthesis of studies on MOOC acceptance and the application of predictive models. Furthermore, this study will review in depth and explore the challenges related to MOOCs optimisation, and will also provide insights into an integrated strategy that has the potential to shape the future of online learning approaches. In this study, numerous articles related to dropout prediction methods have been reviewed and analysed. The selected papers were evaluated based on criteria such as their titles, abstracts, contributions, resource quality, and journal impact factor. The review methodology is structured around the following paper selection and investigation criteria:

- Provide a taxonomical review for different MOOC dropout prediction methods by classifying the proposed studies according to methodologies, important impacts, contributions, and study directions.
- Review dropout prediction methodologies to efficiently increase the student completion rate and optimise the accuracy.
- Provide the main research direction questions related to dropout prediction optimisation methodologies.
- Highlight the weaknesses and expected improvements in the future with respect to the efficient optimisation in MOOCs' completion rate and accuracy.
- Present various approaches in tabular format and charts to help researchers clearly understand the key techniques and methodologies used in MOOC dropout prediction.

The rest of this paper is organised as follows: Section 2 provides an overview of the process and highlights the contributions of our comprehensive review. Section 3 reviews the existing literature on MOOC dropout prediction, highlighting important ideas like feature selection, architectural models, and the difficulties faced in MOOC optimisation. The many dropout prediction methods analysed are presented in detail in Section 4, along with comprehensive evaluations of their uses and limitations. We discuss the remaining issues and research gaps in MOOC dropout prediction and optimisation in Sections 5 and 6, respectively. In Section 7, future prospects in this field are reviewed and the limitations of existing research are reflected upon. This paper is finally concluded in Section 8, which provides a summary of our results and recommendations for further research.

2. The Review Methodology

MOOCs are regarded as a rapidly evolving educational technology that needs substantial attention and additional study on a number of topics, particularly dropout prediction across multiple application scenarios [5]. The integration of online learning platforms with advanced data analytics has led to significant technological advancements by combining various types of data from smaller and smarter sources, allowing for flexible interaction and operation across diverse educational environments. The MOOCs framework enables the use of cloud-based systems and ML techniques to provide real-time monitoring of student engagement and learning behaviours [6]. In addition, through these capabilities, MOOCs can effectively manage and operate various learning resources, and student retention can be significantly impacted by factors such as course design and learner motivation. According to this viewpoint, additional knowledge and approaches to enhance dropout prediction in MOOCs are needed. These approaches and insights may provide new technologies or techniques that guarantee stable and dependable MOOC deployments while enhancing learner results.

Throughout this article, readers will encounter many images, charts, and diagrams used as methodologies to analyse and evaluate past studies and techniques targeted at improving dropout prediction in MOOCs [6]. These review procedures serve to understand the benefits and drawbacks of the proposed prediction models and approaches provided in the field of MOOC dropout reduction. More precisely, this technique offers a thorough comprehension of the conditions pertaining to the existing MOOC dropout prediction systems, acting as a model for an all-encompassing methodology for examining and assessing different experimental outcomes in this field [7]. Future approaches and models to enhance learner retention and performance in MOOCs can be developed using the innovations and related difficulties in dropout prediction that have been presented as a roadmap.

A number of important questions were established to guide the research process and ease the discussion of material received from various investigations. The uniqueness of the models, the guidelines established for data gathering and analysis, and guaranteeing the caliber of the outcomes are the main topics of these inquiries [7]. The methodology of this study, which is shown in Figure 2, helped create an organised framework for evaluating pertinent studies on MOOC dropout prediction.

The sources of different publications were analysed as part of the study methodology that was chosen by looking for titles, abstracts, and keywords that were pertinent to enhancing dropout prediction in MOOCs. Many other studies were disregarded because they only addressed generic e-learning applications without addressing the unique difficulties associated with MOOCs. Consequently, the following methodological steps were followed in order to study and assess the chosen papers thoroughly.

2.1. Sources of Literature

The peer-reviewed research publications and conference proceedings were gathered from university libraries and internet research platforms including Research Gate and Google Scholar. Along with other sources like Tylor & Francis, ACM, Nature, Frontiers, and conferences, the majority of the articles gathered are from famous indexed journals like IEEE, MDPI, Springer, Elsevier, and Wiley. The papers that have been compiled have been published from September 2024 to the year 2018. The number of chosen articles assessed for dropout prediction in MOOCs is indicated in Figure 3, along with a summary of the publication sources.

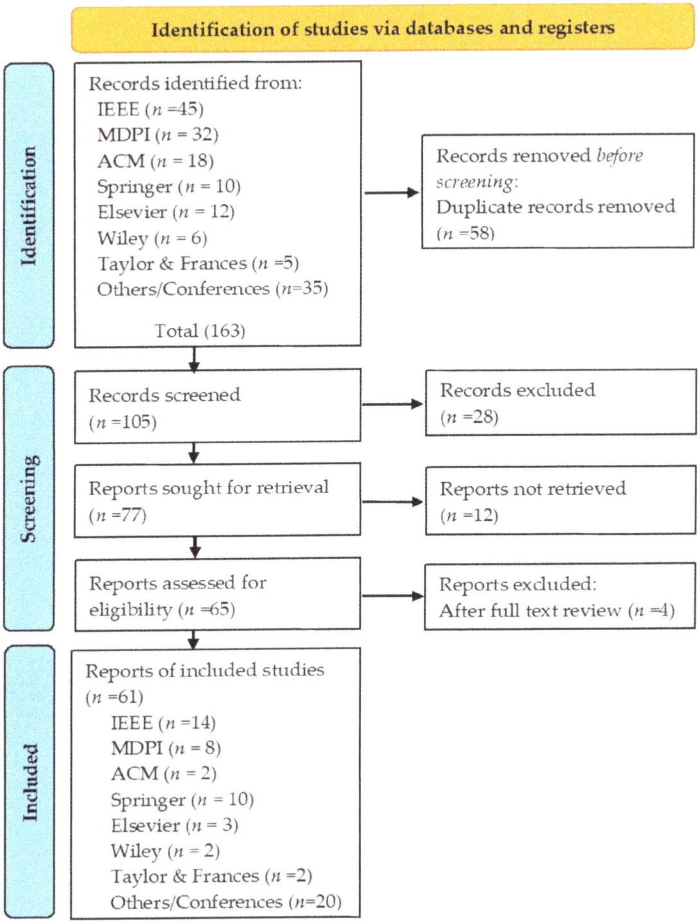

Figure 2. The methodology of studies selection criteria.

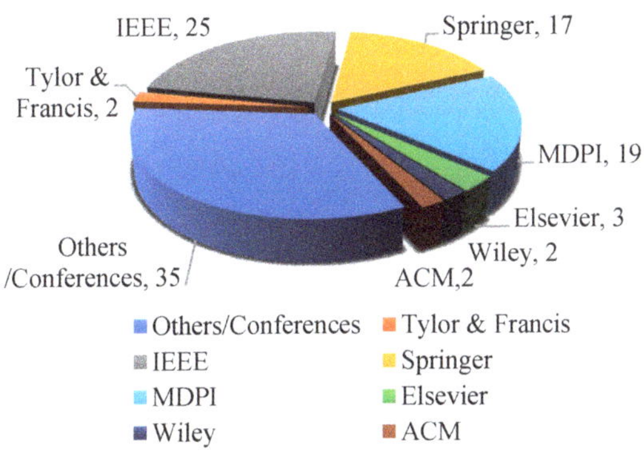

Figure 3. The number of total selected papers for review study (105 articles).

2.2. Key Questions and Inclusion Criteria

A set of guiding questions was formulated to review the papers related to this study, aiming to clarify various parameters used in different dropout prediction techniques for MOOCs. These questions are key to the presented study and were answered through the analysis of several discussed papers.

- Q1. What are the parameters that can impact MOOC dropout rates and learner engagement in general?
- Q2. What are the main factors that influence student retention in MOOCs?
- Q3. What technologies, methods, and algorithms can be used to improve dropout prediction in MOOCs?
- Q4. To what extent can recent methodologies achieve optimisation in dropout prediction accuracy?

Based on the guiding questions and the study selection process in Figure 2, a number of review and survey articles were selected following a specific strategy. First, search keywords or phrases were defined to find relevant articles, including MOOCs dropout prediction, MOOCs prediction optimisation, MOOCs feature selection, ML for dropout prediction, DL dropout prediction model, feature selection optimisation, meta-heuristic for feature selection, student retention in MOOCs, student engagement, MOOC completion rate analysis, predictive modeling for MOOCs, and intelligent dropout prediction models. Throughout the collection processed based on the keywords, Boolean operators such as AND and OR were used to combine the keywords during the search process. Next, duplicate articles were removed, along with irrelevant articles by checking the title, abstract, and full text. Finally, the articles most relevant to the proposed study were selected. This strategy allowed us to accurately present the literature related to this study and to identify other papers that provide methods and approaches for improving dropout prediction in MOOCs. The search of related articles collected from different resources yielded a total 163 records from IEEE (n = 45), MDPI (n = 32), ACM (n = 18), Springer (n = 10), Elsevier (n = 12), Wiley (n = 6), and Taylor & Francis (n = 5), as well as others from other databases and conferences (n = 35). The removed duplicated are (n = 32). A total of 105 articles screened as related to dropout prediction approaches in MOOCs were reviewed, as summarised in Figure 3. After reviewing the articles, we found that only 61 specifically addressed dropout prediction methods and solutions for MOOCs. These articles, summarised in Figure 4, were analysed, leading to the following outcomes:

- The concept of dropout prediction has been explored in the reviewed studies and analysed across various contexts, focusing on reducing dropout rates, enhancing student engagement, and optimising learning outcomes.
- Numerous studies have investigated the use of ML/DL as intelligent methods to improve dropout prediction in MOOCs. However, these studies often focus on select influencing factors and fail to encompass all the considerations required for a comprehensive approach to dropout prediction.
- Many papers were excluded as they focused on methods for improving student retention in general e-learning platforms, without specifically addressing dropout prediction in MOOCs.
- This study is expected to provide researchers with comprehensive coverage of the strengths and weaknesses of various relevant studies conducted between 2018 and 2022.

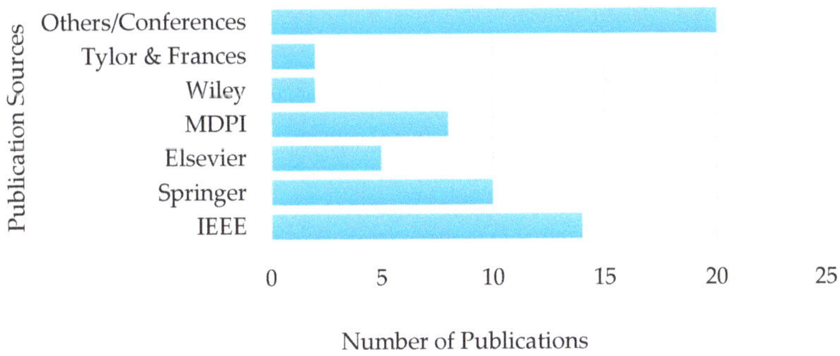

Figure 4. Summary of overall articles related to MOOCs dropout prediction corresponding to the publication sources (61 papers).

3. MOOCs Dropout Prediction Technical Background

MOOCs have received great attention in recent years from all educational levels, but they face major challenges related to a high dropout rate (reaching 92%), which reflects the extent of interaction with these platforms [8]. Various processes are employed to predict student activity on MOOC platforms and analyse their interactions across different courses. This helps in building new platforms or improving existing ones to enhance performance, leading to greater user acceptance and significantly reducing failure rates. Student interactions on a MOOC platform are influenced by the structure and functions of the platform, both of which can impact course completion rates and contribute to dropout levels [9]. The functions of a MOOC platform include managing large volumes of student data, handling independent course data, designing course videos to withstand high traffic, tracking online test scores and title settings, and managing course resources. Accordingly, MOOCs typically consist of four fundamental modules, namely, the user management module, the course outline module, the multimedia resource module, and the test management module, as shown in Figure 5.

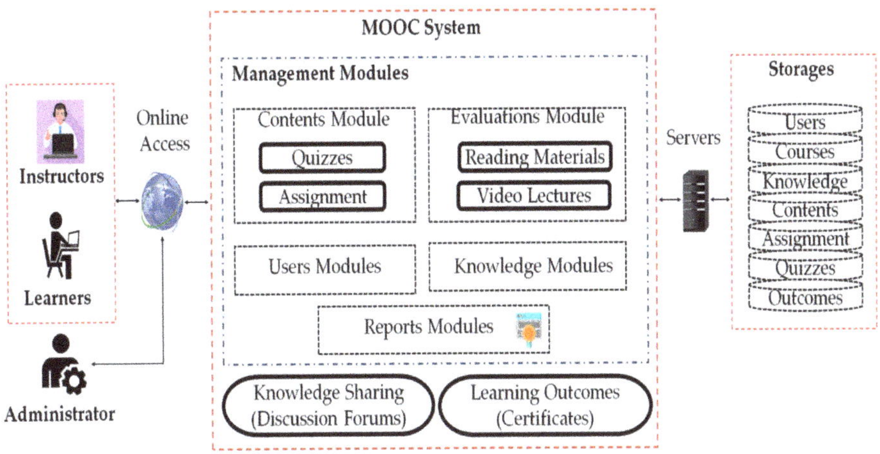

Figure 5. The MOOC structure.

One of the most prominent challenges of MOOCs, after design, is how to ensure acceptance by students and attract high retention rates. Low retention rates are often reflected in the course completion rates or dropout percentages [9]. According to the literature, MOOCs offered by elite universities, such as MIT, Stanford, and UC Berkeley, have reported dropout rates as high as 95%. These dropouts can be attributed to various factors related to both the students and the MOOC platforms themselves, as outlined in the following list.

A. Student factors

- Lack of student motivation, often cited as the most crucial factor contributing to high dropout rates, is influenced by personal and professional identity development, expectations of future economic benefits, the desire for challenge and achievement, and entertainment [9].
- Students may be reluctant to invest the considerable time required to watch videos, complete quizzes, and finish assignments.
- Students often lack the essential background knowledge and skills needed to comprehend the course content.
- Some researchers have noted that many enrolments in MOOCs are casual, i.e., from students who have no real intention to complete them.

B. MOOC factors

- Course design: A weak and non-interactive course design, including course content, structure, and information delivery technology, contributes significantly to high dropout rates.
- Hidden cost: The hidden cost could be another cause of a high dropout rate. Despite MOOCs' reputation as a free resource for online education, students need to pay for their certificates or sometimes buy costly textbooks recommended by lecturers [10].

According to the given factors, the most impactful factors are those related to the MOOCs' design. The way platforms are designed greatly affects the extent of user interaction, regardless of personal factors related to the user. These factors strongly influence the dropout rate, highlighting the need for a strategic approach to designing MOOCs and to assessing dropout predictions continuously for further improvement [10]. To reduce the dropout rate, the quality of instructional design in MOOCs is a crucial determinant and prerequisite for promoting active learning and enhancing learner experiences. Interaction among learners significantly contributes to lower dropout rates. In addition, integrating social tools in MOOCs can effectively assist peers in addressing challenges, encouraging discussions, and facilitating the sharing of new resources [11]. Further, the comfort level with technology for learners must be acceptable. Since MOOCs are online courses, they require technology to deliver content and communicate with students. Evaluation is important and is a crucial step in any educational process. The evaluation period after completing the course must not exceed a period of more than 48 h, and this is important to increasing the learners' connection to the platform [12]. The following subsections outline key details regarding the process of accurately predicting dropout rates in MOOCs, focusing on learning databases, feature selection, dropout prediction methodologies, and optimisation challenges.

3.1. MOOCs Database

The MOOC dataset, which collects extensive data on students' behaviour, engagement, and performance during the course, is essential to dropout prediction. These data contain a variety of information, including students demographics, learning interactions, such as video views and quiz completions, and the amount of time spent on various course activities [12]. In addition, the dataset shows patterns of involvement and disengagement that are important to know in order to identify children who might be at danger of not finishing school. Through the analysis of these patterns, educators and platform developers can acquire valuable insights into the causes that lead to dropout rates, which will facilitate the implementation of focused interventions [13].

The prediction models' performance is directly impacted by the quality of the dataset due to the complexity of dropout causes, which can be attributed to both MOOC-related issues like poorly designed courses and personal factors such a lack of enthusiasm or time [13]. A student's lack of motivation, for instance, could be reflected in the dataset by their decreased interest in the course materials, or their inconsistent participation in quizzes and assignments could suggest that they are pressed for time. It is also possible to deduce information about knowledge gaps from low exam results or little conversation participation. In order to create efficient algorithms that can anticipate dropouts early and give students appropriate support, a rich and well-labelled MOOC dataset is necessary.

The MOOC database structure is organised into three main content areas: course details, specialisation details, and student engagement. These domains are reinforced by crucial standalone blocks for educational institutions, instructors, and learners [14]. The structure of the platform is made up of these elements, which make it possible to handle courses, student data, and interaction effectively. A key component of the platform is the course details block, which arranges details on the materials, structure, and content of the course. Important details like course titles, descriptions, and the connections between courses and specialisations are captured by the model. Every course consists of several parts, each containing related assignments, tests, and videos as learning resources [15]. There is a clear hierarchy of content distribution thanks to the links between these assets and particular course sections.

In the specialisation details section, the model manages how courses are arranged into specialisations, each of which consists of several courses and culminating projects. In addition to facilitating the management of discounts and course bundles, this structure offers advanced learning pathways. In addition to enrolment information, session schedules, and performance goals, student participation tracks how students engage with courses and specialisations [15]. Tracking completions, keeping focus on student progress, and recognising dropout concerns all depend on this area. As essential data repositories, stand-alone blocks for educational institutions, instructors, and students offer the necessary cross-model references [16]. These tables ensure accurate associations between courses and their designers, as well as between students and their individual participation records. This database structure efficiently supports the fundamental features of a MOOC platform, allowing for the scalable and effective administration of large-scale virtual learning environments and opening up opportunities for future improvements to the capabilities and user experience of the platform.

3.2. MOOCs Feature Selection

As it entails determining which characteristics from the dataset are most pertinent to making accurate predictions, feature selection is a crucial step in the MOOC dropout prediction process. The effectiveness and efficiency of a prediction model can be enhanced by concentrating on its most noteworthy aspects as not all data points hold equal significance [17]. The model can better identify trends that signal the possibility of dropout by choosing the appropriate parameters, such as quiz scores, time spent on course materials, and student engagement indicators. With less complexity, the model can identify at-risk students more accurately and with less computational overhead due to this improved method.

In addition, feature selection improves the dropout prediction model's interpretability [17]. By focussing on the most important variables, instructors and platform developers can gain a deeper understanding of the reasons for student dropouts and the particular course components or student behaviours that are causing them. Certain aspects, like interaction with course videos or participation in discussion forums, may indicate a higher level of engagement, but low quiz scores may indicate a lack of expertise [18]. A more precise understanding of the reasons for dropouts and the ability to design retention-focused interventions are made possible by feature selection, which is effective in preventing the model from becoming overloaded with irrelevant data.

Figure 6 illustrates the many feature selection techniques that can be applied. The types of feature selection methods used in MOOCs have a direct impact on the effectiveness and performance of the dropout prediction models. Every selection technique, such as filtering, wrapping, and hybrid techniques, has unique properties with regard to optimising MOOC dropout prediction [18]. Statistical measures can be quickly and easily ranked and chosen with the help of filters. However, because they do not take into account the relationships between features, they may be less accurate. While embedded approaches incorporate feature selection into the learning process, wrappers allow for the evaluation of feature subsets depending on model performance and offer improved accuracy [19]. The strengths of the filter, wrapper, and embedded techniques can be used with the hybrid approach to balance prediction accuracy.

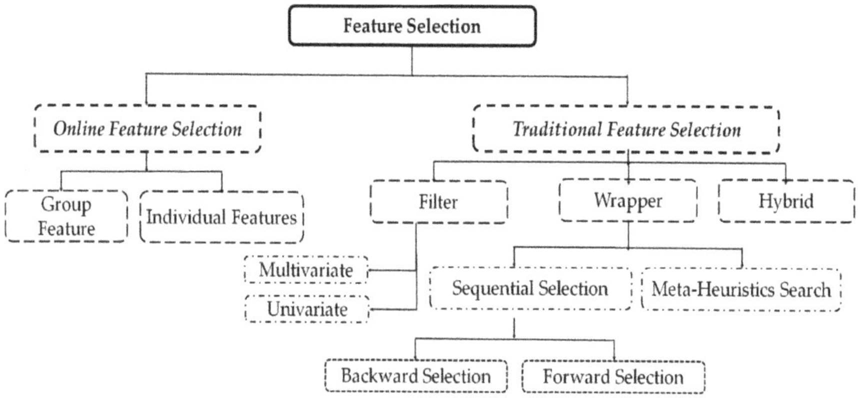

Figure 6. Feature selection approaches.

When the accuracy of wrapper techniques is combined with the filter strategy, the hybrid method proves very beneficial for dropout prediction in MOOCs. With the use of these combinations, it is possible to filter out features that are not important and then refine the features that remain, using strategies based on wrappers and model performance [19,20]. Optimising the dropout prediction process is possible with a hybrid strategy that uses a wrapper based on meta-heuristic algorithms. To identify the subset that optimises the prediction accuracy of the model, the meta-heuristic algorithms cleverly investigate various feature combinations. This can guarantee both efficiency and high accuracy, particularly for large-scale datasets. Dropout prediction is a critical issue that needs to be resolved in order to increase MOOCs' scalability, user engagement, personalisation, predictive accuracy, and high student retention rates [20]. Table 1 shows how these requirements relate to different feature selection factors based on MOOC applications.

Table 1 also shows that every component has an impact on every improvement need. Greater data quantities typically result in increased accuracy and engagement, but they are also needed for sufficient scalability and flexibility. Useful complexity encourages good scalability, prediction accuracy, and adaptability, but because it may make interpretation and use more challenging, it may have a mediocre effect on student engagement [20]. The flexibility of the algorithm offers low influence on student engagement, medium prediction accuracy, moderate scalability, and support for customisation and adaptability. This indicates that while adaptable algorithms may adapt to different data sources, engagement may not always be directly impacted by them. Though it has a small impact on adaptability, higher feature relevance across all criteria ensures that characteristics employed are essential for enhancing personalisation, scalability, accuracy, and engagement [21]. While real-time processing is necessary for fast modifications, it is not always suitable for handling extensive personalisation and adaptability. Finally, while varied data may not always immediately increase engagement, they have a significant impact on personalisation and scalability, which enhances model performance and adaptability.

Table 1. Feature selection factors and their impact on effectiveness and performance requirements.

Factors	Personalisation	Scalability	Predictive Accuracy	Learner Engagement	Adaptability
Data Volume	Moderate	High	High	High	Moderate
Model Complexity	High	High	High	Medium	High
Algorithm Flexibility	Moderate	Moderate	Medium	Low	High
Feature Relevance	High	High	High	High	Moderate
Real-Time Processing	Low	Medium	Medium	Medium	Low
Data Diversity	High	High	Medium	Medium	High

3.3. *MOOCs Dropout Prediction Methodology*

Many MOOC courses that facilitate the exchange of educational content over the internet are built on data-driven platforms and learning management systems. Along with other applications pertaining to personalised learning and evaluation, these programs are used to track and manage student progress, lower dropout rates, and improve learning outcomes [22]. Adaptive learning systems in educational settings use data-driven insights to modify support systems and course materials, enabling self-paced learning, better student retention through thoughtful feedback mechanisms, and a lower dropout rate.

Figure 7 illustrates the general structure for the dropout prediction approach, which consists of three key stages: dropout prediction model, feature selection and analysis, and dataset pre-processing. The output of the framework, which is dependent on the input, i.e., student learning behaviour data, is the number of dropouts [23]. The attributes of each form of learning record are derived based on the ranking approach after the students' learning records are grouped in the framework depending on the type of learning behaviour. Feature engineering and data pre-processing are essential components of a high-precision stall prediction model.

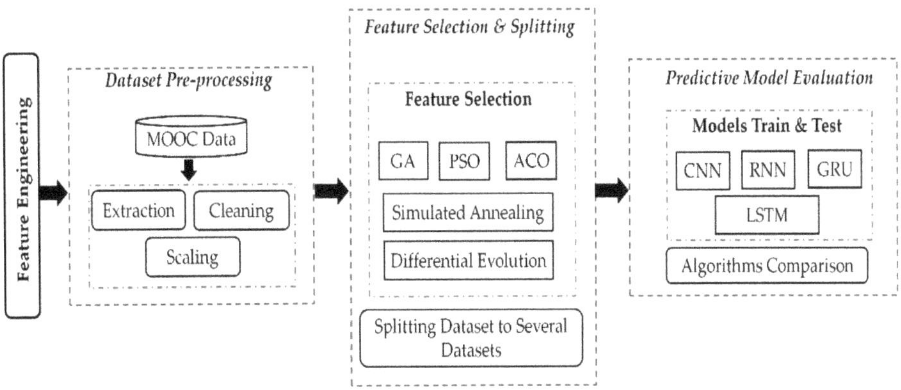

Figure 7. General model for MOOC dropout prediction.

A variety of techniques, including decision trees (DT), random forests (RF), support vector machines (SVM), and even deep learning (DL) models like recurrent neural networks (RNN), may be used in the dropout prediction stages [23,24]. Each student receives a categorisation or risk score from the dropout prediction framework, which indicates which students are most likely to discontinue their studies. For the purpose of assessing MOOC dropout risk, a carefully designed dropout prediction framework comprising feature selection, data pre-processing, and a reliable prediction model is essential. By increasing model correctness and efficiency, the process is further improved by the use of hybrid filtering and wrapper techniques. MOOC platforms are able to better assist students by anticipating dropouts with accuracy, which eventually increases student retention and course completion rates [24].

3.4. Dropout Prediction Optimisation Challenges and Solutions

Predicting dropout in MOOC is generally associated with a number of issues, as seen in Figure 8. The most notable of these is the insufficient sample size, which not only correlates with dropouts but also with graduates in order to produce findings for the classification process that are free of bias. The majority of machine learning algorithms rely on the abundance of positive and negative data [25]. However, a lot of people sign up for different MOOCs merely to try out online self-learning, sometimes even with the goal of obtaining a certificate, and they frequently discontinue the course before the end of the allotted time. Due to the difficulties of confirming the accuracy of the available data, missing data may also result from MOOC big data and unstructured data, which are the most significant prediction problems for ML [25,26]. Average values can occasionally be used to make up for missing data, but they are never a practical substitute for precise feature determination.

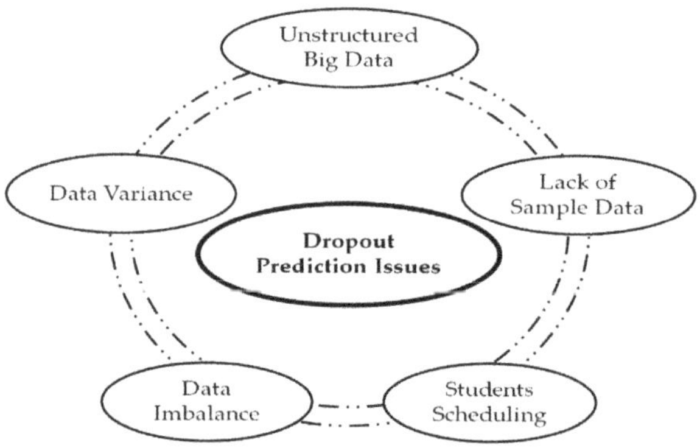

Figure 8. Main issues related to MOOCs dropout prediction.

Data variance and an imbalance in MOOCs are additional factors to take into account. Data variation can have a detrimental effect on the reliability of machine learning models because of self-paced learning. Unbalanced data negatively impact algorithms such as SVM. causing them to produce biased predictions that favour the majority class. This decreases the accuracy and dependability of the model, particularly when it comes to dropout prediction [26]. In addition, there is the problem of meeting the varied scheduling preferences of students. While some prefer to move through courses week by week, others prefer to study at their own speed or have access to all materials up front. While satisfying these diverse preferences is difficult, AI optimisation techniques can help. AI has a place in scheduling; it can aid with time constraints for students and enable more individualised learning.

3.4.1. Feature Availability

The quality and diversity of features have a direct impact on the efficacy and accuracy of machine learning models; hence, feature availability is crucial to the optimisation of dropout prediction models in MOOCs. An enormous quantity of data are produced by students' learning behaviours in MOOCs. Optimisation of dropout prediction models requires careful selection, engineering, and assurance of crucial feature availability [27]. Missing features can significantly impair model performance; therefore, having rich, comprehensive data is essential. Sparse or inconsistent datasets are produced when some characteristics of MOOCs are frequently inaccessible as a result of insufficient student activity data. Unreliable predictions can result from missing features, particularly in situations where behavioural patterns that are not recorded because data gaps cause dropouts [28]. Missing features also introduce noise.

The interpretability of the dropout prediction model is also impacted by feature availability. For educational institutions seeking to understand why specific students are in danger of dropping out, the model can yield clearer and interpretable findings when key attributes are regularly available [28]. The model may rely on less pertinent data if characteristics are absent or inadequately represented, which would reduce its interpretability and make it more difficult to extract useful insights from the forecasts. The efficacy of dropout prediction models in MOOCs is largely dependent on feature availability. Although a large feature set might improve the resilience and accuracy of the model, it can also present difficulties that affect optimisation [29,30]. Model performance can be negatively impacted by elements like noisy data, excessive dimensionality, irrelevant or duplicated features, and insufficient feature sets. It is imperative to comprehend these possible adverse effects in order to create efficient dropout prediction systems. Table 2 bellow lists some feature availability-related aspects and their potential detrimental effects on optimisation [30]. This table sheds light on how these problems may impair the general effectiveness and dependability of dropout prediction models.

Table 2. Feature selection factors and their negative effects.

Factors	Negative Impact Description
Missing Certain Features	Reduces model dependability by causing erroneous predictions based on missing data.
Variance	Accuracy may suffer from models' inability to generalise due to high variability.
Irrelevant Features	Low-impact or irrelevant elements can weaken the model's focus and cause it to perform lower.
Noisy Data	Features with noisy data might cause errors and lower prediction optimisation's dependability.
Feature Redundancy	Redundant features can make a model less efficient by increasing computational cost and causing overfitting.
Imbalance	Imbalanced data can still cause models to be biased towards the majority class, leading to poor performance on minority classes.
Overloaded Feature Set	A model that is overloaded with characteristics may find it difficult to determine which predictions are the most important and may require longer training times.

For dropout prediction models in MOOCs to be optimised, feature availability is essential. By giving a more accurate picture of student behaviour, comprehensive and pertinent features like temporal data and student engagement indicators greatly improve model accuracy. These features, which capture a wide variety of behaviours, alleviate data imbalance, facilitate effective feature engineering, and enhance model robustness [31]. They also help with the investigation of temporal engagement patterns, improve the interpretability of the model, and enable more precise feature selection. Having a wide range of high-quality characteristics makes it easier to handle missing data, make more accurate predictions, and ultimately improve learning outcomes and student retention.

3.4.2. Thematic Taxonomy of Optimisation Solutions

Numerous earlier studies that addressed how to improve dropout prediction in MOOCs have presented a range of techniques to increase predictability and lower dropout rates. These strategies include hybrid approaches, data-driven insights, adaptive learning techniques, and sophisticated algorithms [31]. As illustrated in Figure 9, which rates dropout prediction technologies and solutions, these techniques can be roughly divided into multiple groups.

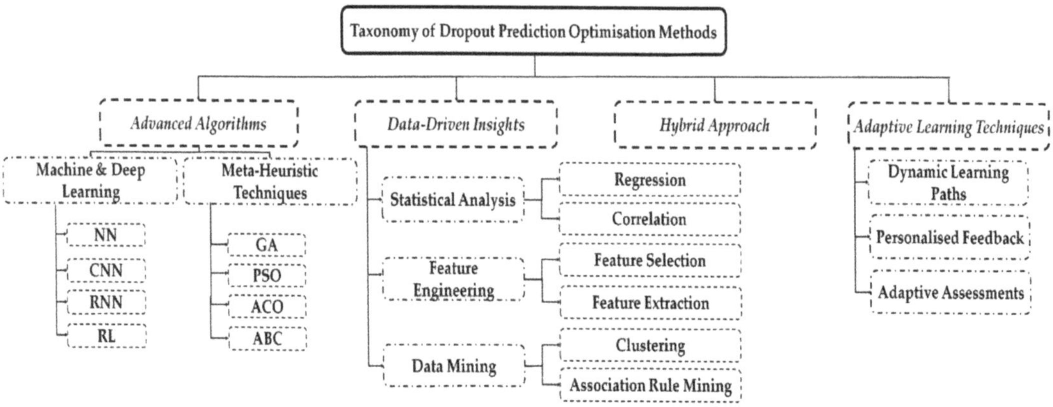

Figure 9. Thematic taxonomy of dropout prediction optimisation solutions.

Optimising dropout prediction in MOOCs can benefit greatly from the hybrid strategy that combines sophisticated algorithms with feature selection-based meta-heuristic methods. Meta-heuristic techniques, such particle swarm optimising (PSO), genetic algorithm (GA), and ant colony optimisation (ACO), are excellent at sifting through intricate feature spaces to find the most pertinent characteristics, improving model efficiency and predictive accuracy [32]. Feature selection is made easier, dimensionality is reduced, and model robustness is increased when these methods are combined with sophisticated ML algorithms like SVM, RF, NN, or deep learning techniques like CNN or RNN. By improving the feature set and better capturing dropout risks across several classes, this combination also solves data imbalance.

The hybrid approach also makes it easier to scale and adapt, which makes it appropriate for a variety of MOOC scenarios and expanding datasets. By concentrating on a pertinent subset of features, it improves interpretability and yields useful insights. In addition, it ensures effective model performance by optimising computational resources by lowering the number of features needed for training [32]. In general, meta-heuristic feature selection and sophisticated algorithms work in concert to maximise each other's advantages, producing dropout prediction models that are more precise, reliable, and scalable. With an emphasis on MOOC platforms, this review will examine numerous papers that have used hybrid methodologies along with ML/DL/Meta-heuristics applied to educational datasets. The discussion will focus on how these methods have been applied to forecast various student outcomes, such as learning performance, course completion rates, and dropout rates [33].

The focus will be on comparing methods, including feature selection techniques, model types used, and datasets used. The review will also address the current gaps in the literature, namely, the scant investigation of hybrid models that combine ML/DL and meta-heuristics in the framework of educational big data. The basis for comprehending how predictive models might be enhanced to enhance MOOC results and lower dropout rates will be provided by this analysis.

4. MOOCs Dropout Prediction Approaches

With the goal of increasing prediction accuracy and lowering dropout rates, a wide range of methods have been presented to improve MOOC dropout prediction. In order to retain high prediction performance while controlling computational resources, these techniques include tactics for modifying learning experiences, improving data analysis, and optimising algorithms [33]. In order to increase their efficacy and accuracy, dropout prediction models also need to make optimal use of data and computational resources. Therefore, preserving high prediction accuracy and enhancing overall MOOC efficacy require good resource utilisation. Enhancing retention rates and dropout prediction accuracy in MOOCs has been the subject of recent research. These studies, however, frequently ignore important elements unique to MOOC applications. A number of studies have recently examined and analysed dropout prediction techniques.

The current review papers on dropout prediction in MOOCs are summarised in Table 3. Although these surveys provide an overview of fundamental MOOC designs, models, and some treatments, they do not fully explore the particular needs for dropout prediction, current research directions, or technological developments.

Table 3. Comparison of proposed review papers with existing surveys on dropout prediction in MOOCs.

Contributions	Review Papers										Proposed Study
	[34]	[35]	[36]	[37]	[38]	[39]	[40]	[41]	[42]	[43]	
MOOC Architecture	✓	×	×	×	×	×	×	×	×	×	✓
Dropout Prediction	✓	✓	✓	✓	✓	✓	×	✓	✓	✓	✓
Feature Selection	✓	×	×	×	×	✓	✓	×	✓	✓	✓
Learning Models	✓	✓	✓	✓	✓	✓	×	×	×	×	✓
Predictive Analytics	✓	×	✓	×	✓	×	×	✓	✓	×	✓
Scalability Challenges	×	×	×	×	×	✓	×	✓	✓	×	✓
Open research Issues	✓	×	✓	✓	×	✓	×	✓	×	✓	✓
Prediction Optimisation	×	×	×	×	×	×	×	×	×	×	✓

While some studies have addressed dropout prediction in MOOCs, the comparison in Table 3 demonstrates that many have not sufficiently addressed important criteria associated with optimisation prediction accuracy and retention rates. The subsection that follows will cover a variety of approaches and strategies in the field of dropout prediction, offering a thorough analysis of prediction methodologies, cutting-edge research, and answers to major problems. A number of strategies are investigated to improve dropout prediction in MOOCs, including intelligent algorithms, feature selection techniques, and optimisation models. The following subsections will provide an in-depth analysis of the most recent approaches and strategies for boosting student retention and accuracy in MOOCs that have been researched for dropout prediction.

4.1. Data-Driven Approaches

Dropout prediction for MOOCs has always relied on statistical models and traditional methodologies because of their theoretical underpinnings, ease of interpretation, and simplicity. These methods work well for assessing the connections between different elements such as course parameters, student involvement levels, demographics, and the chance of student dropout because they are based on statistical principles [44]. One of the most popular methods for binary classification issues is logistic regression, which calculates the likelihood of a student dropping out of a course based on independent variables like time invested in the course or exam results. Considered transparent in determining crucial elements, this method continues to be a mainstay in dropout prediction models. Regression analysis is one of the most popular prediction methods used in assessing and forecasting student outcomes. Regression metrics like as mean square error (MSE), root mean square error (RMSE), R^2, and mean absolute error (MAE) are commonly employed in relevant studies. Each of the metrics are described in following equations [45]:

$$\text{RMSE} = \sum_{i=1}^{n} \sqrt{(x_i - \hat{x}_i)^2} \tag{1}$$

$$\text{MSE} = \sum_{i=1}^{n} (x_i - \hat{x}_i)^2 \tag{2}$$

$$R^2 = \frac{1}{n} \sum_{i=1}^{n} |x_i - \hat{x}_i| \tag{3}$$

$$\text{MAE} = 1 - \frac{\sum_{i=1}^{n} (x_i - \hat{x}_i)^2}{\sum_{i=1}^{n} (x_i - \overline{x})^2} \tag{4}$$

where n represents the total number of non-missing data points used in the analysis; x_i represents the actual observed value at data point I; and $\overline{x}$ and $\hat{x}_i$ represent the mean value of the observed data series and the predicted value corresponding to the observed value x_i, respectively.

Another statistical technique, the Naïve Bayes (NB) algorithm, is based on Bayes' theorem, which calculates the posterior probability of each class given a set of features. It assumes that features are conditionally independent of the target class. Despite this assumption, which may not always be true in actual scenarios, the technique is computationally efficient and generates fast, scalable predictions [45]. An alternative approach is survival analysis. It is a statistical method used to analyse and model time-to-event data. In the context of MOOCs, the event typically refers to student dropouts. The primary goal is to predict whether and when this event is likely to occur. This approach is particularly valuable because it can handle censored data, where dropout has not yet occurred by the end of the observation period. A key component of survival analysis is the survival function, which estimates the probability that a student will remain enrolled until a given time t. This methodology provides a powerful framework for studying patterns of student engagement and dropout over time [46]. For predicting student dropout, a variety of strategies have been created, ranging from sophisticated ML methods to statistical models. Because statistical approaches are transparent and easy to grasp, they are still frequently employed as basic tools for understanding the major determinants impacting student dropout [46]. In this framework, relevant research that has utilised both conventional and contemporary methods for dropout prediction in MOOCs is summarised in Table 4 and discussed in the section that follows.

A study by Anaíle et al. aims to forecast and reduce student dropout rates by using a model to enhance dropout prediction based on the characterisation of the dropout problem and the implementation of a knowledge discovery process [47]. The outcomes of three models used in the study—DT, NN, and LR (linear regression)—are combined in the ensemble model. The proposed model is able to effectively detect 98% of dropouts and correctly classify the student's enrolment and dropping. When the suggested model was compared to the RF ensemble approach, it showed positive traits that would help the management suggest measures to keep students in sessions. Neema focusses on how well different data balancing strategies work to increase machine learning models' predictive accuracy for student dropout rates [48]. The study highlights the difficulties caused by unbalanced datasets, which frequently contain an under-representation of dropout instances and hence skewed forecasts. The study shows notable gains in predicting accuracy by using techniques like SMOTE and assessing their effects on various ML algorithms. According to the findings, applying these balancing techniques can improve model accuracy, which makes them a useful addition to dropout prediction and educational data mining strategies.

Table 4. Summarised papers related to data-driven approaches for MOOC dropout prediction.

Citation	Contributions	Advantages	Shortcomings	Prediction Accuracy	Efficiency	Best Algorithm
[47]	Ensemble model integrates statistical approaches for dropout classification	High classification accuracy and enhancing reliability in predicting at-risk students	Does not capture all the factors that influence student dropout	89%	High	LR, DT, NN
[48]	Data balancing techniques	Use of SMOTE to enhance accuracy in predicting student dropouts	Weak selected features, and noise from the synthetic samples	83.2%	Moderate	LR, MLP and RF
[49]	Probabilistic technique for predicting university student dropout	Enhance prediction accuracy and handle binary outcomes effectively	Unable to capture complex relationships between variables	90%	High	LR
[50]	Predictive model for forecast dropout rates for ideological and political MOOC learners	Early identification of at risk students to improve retention rates	Potential biases in the data	Up to 83.7%,	Moderate	LR
[51]	DL-based temporal prediction	Accurate the personalised interventions for at-risk students	Heavy data dependency and complex implementation	Approx. 86 to 98%	High	DT, DL

Efficiency keys: high efficiency (>85%); moderate efficiency (70–85%); low efficiency (<70%).

B. Ujkani et al. investigate the probability of student dropout in higher education using LR as a predictive method [49]. Academic achievement, demographic characteristics, and socioeconomic position are among the important elements the authors identify as influencing dropout rates. To develop a model that can accurately identify students who are at risk of dropping out, the study analysed these factors using LR. According to the findings, educational institutions can improve student retention and success rates by using this prediction model to assist them in executing timely interventions and support measures. In tackling the issue of academic dropout, the study emphasises the value of data-driven strategies. Zhang, Y. et al. [50] use big data analytics to present a predictive model that predicts dropout rates among students in MOOC. Learner involvement, motivation, and demographics are the variables the authors examine when analysing dropout rates. The study creates a model that accurately predicts which students are at risk of dropping out by using the logistic regression method on massive datasets. This methodology can help MOOC providers execute timely interventions to improve student success and retention, according to the results.

A study by Wanli Xing et al. conducted research on how to improve dropout prediction models for MOOC by utilising DL algorithms [51]. The authors contended that high attrition rates result from traditional educational systems' frequent inability to promptly identify at-risk students. Their DL algorithm accurately forecasts the likelihood of individual dropouts by utilising a temporal prediction mechanism, which enables customised interventions based on the needs of the students. It enables customised interventions by predicting when students are most likely to drop out based on their engagement patterns over time. By analysing temporal data, such as student activity logs, participation frequency, and engagement levels throughout the course, this mechanism can identify students who may drop out at specific time points during the course. The research shows that this strategy not only outperforms baseline algorithms in prediction accuracy but also makes targeted support for learners who are at risk easier, with the ultimate goal of increasing student retention in MOOCs.

In MOOCs, feature engineering, which includes feature extraction and feature selection to improve model performance, is essential for dropout prediction. In order to identify pertinent patterns suggestive of dropout risk, feature extraction entails extracting useful measures from raw data, such as user engagement levels or interaction rates [52]. In order to increase the accuracy and efficiency of the model, feature selection then concentrates on finding the most important predictors from these measurements. Feature selection guarantees that the model employs only the most informative variables, minimising dimensionality and preventing over-fitting. This results in more accurate predictions and deeper insights into the causes impacting student attrition. Together, these processes transform raw data into actionable insights, enabling more effective dropout prediction [53]. The optimisation of feature selection is based on how to properly extract the feature subsets following the process of feature prediction.

DL techniques, like CNNs, make it possible to select the best input data and extract the most important features. Through the given CNN architecture, as shown in Figure 10, data simplification can be facilitated by the network and its automated feature extraction and selection [53,54]. CNNs are trained to selectively draw attention to important aspects while downplaying or disregarding less important or distracting ones. The CNN-based MOOC dropout prediction algorithm makes it possible to effectively capture local patterns and characteristics. Without further guidance, the model can use a filtering mechanism to gather information about the outside world once it has been educated [54]. One of the main benefits of such DL algorithms is their capacity for adaptive learning, feature extraction, and feature selection.

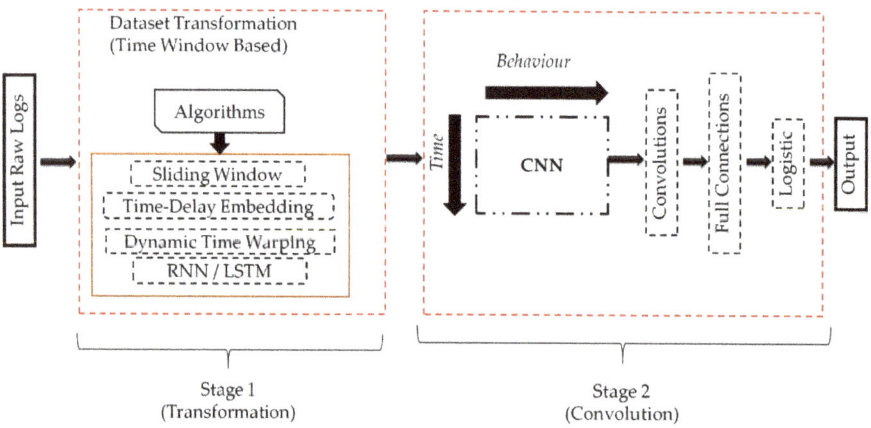

Figure 10. Overall architecture of CNN.

To handle the complexity of the data in MOOCs, DL's classification techniques, such as FNN, RNN, LSTM, and DRL, were applied in different related works. Depending on the type of data, the combination of these methods allows for improving generalisation by managing students' time series data and handling complex data patterns [54]. During data collection, the primary desirable qualities of the hybrid model that were taken into consideration were its capacity to comprehend multimodal input, its dependence on sequential and temporal data, and its reduction in overfitting.

For data with long-term dependencies, LSTM combined with other DL algorithms allows for greater performance. It uses a very complex network of memory cells to recall such small things over such long times. Input, forget, and output gates, as well as memory cells, make up an LSTM. It retains the most pertinent information and discards the remainder after going through these filters [55]. The forget gate is an essential operator that determines which data points can be safely deleted in the last step using a sigmoid function. Through backpropagation, the model adjusts the weights of the network during training by minimising the error in the predicted output. LSTM is trained, enabling it to draw conclusions from the past and modify its current state accordingly. Applying LSTM to time series data makes it a very useful tool. The following equations describe the operation of the LSTM model [56].

$$in\ (\mathrm{t}) = \sigma\ (w_{in} \times [h_s\ (\mathrm{t}-1),\ y(\mathrm{t})] + b_{in}) \tag{5}$$

$$f_g\ (\mathrm{t}) = \sigma\left(h_{fg} \times [h_s\ (\mathrm{t}-1),\ y(\mathrm{t})] + b_{fg}\right) \tag{6}$$

$$out\ (\mathrm{t}) = \sigma\ (h_{out} \times [h_s\ (\mathrm{t}-1),\ y(\mathrm{t})] + b_{out}) \tag{7}$$

$$c_s(t) = f_g(\mathrm{t})\ \times\ (h_{out} \times c_s(t) + in\ (\mathrm{t})\ \times\ tanh(w_{cs} \times [h_s\ (\mathrm{t}-1),\ y(\mathrm{t})] + b_{cs} \tag{8}$$

$$h_s(\mathrm{t}) = out\ (\mathrm{t})\ \times\ tanh(c_s(t)) \tag{9}$$

where σ denotes a sigmoid activation function; $y(\mathrm{t})$ denotes an input at time t; $h_s(\mathrm{t}-1)$ is for the hidden state; and b_{in}, b_{out}, b_{fg}, and b_{cs} represent the values of bias vectors; and *in* (t), *out* (t), and f_g(t) represent the gates for input, output, and forget, respectively. The weights of the matrices are represented by w_{in}, b_{in}, b_{out}, and b_{fg}.

In the above equations, the biases and weights are adjusted to pass the data through the neural layers to extract the expected outcome according to the pattern learned. These can help in adapting the LSTM model to accurately predict the dropout with effective feature selection. The model's performance can be strongly impacted by the calibre of the features that are retrieved and chosen [55,56]. Sophisticated methods like ML/DL models, which automatically choose and highlight key traits, improve this procedure even more. The relevant works that have investigated different feature engineering techniques to enhance dropout prediction in MOOCs are summarised in Table 5 and reviewed in the following paragraphs. The percentage of used algorithms and the methodologies' performances in the related papers discussed are shown in Figure 11.

A study by Alghamdi explores the different aspects of MOOCs that influence learner contentment [57]. The study uses ML approaches to discover important factors that influence the dropout, including peer interaction, instructor reputation, and the quality of the course material. Based on learner choices, the findings give educators and course designer's useful information to improve MOOC offerings. Although the study makes a substantial contribution to understanding of learner happiness, its reach is constrained by the dataset's narrow breadth, which might not fully capture the range of MOOC learner experiences. Lopa et al. emphasise providing relevant features to improve prediction results [58]. ML algorithms perform and analyse these predictions. The RFC achieved 86.14% accuracy, outperforming the LR, DT, GBC, and Xgb classifier used in the proposed study.

Blundo et al. present a novel method that uses a smaller collection of characteristics to train a set of dropout predictors [59]. The main concept is to utilise weekly data to identify students who are either likely to drop out or not with a good degree of accuracy. When there is uncertainty, the choice on classification is postponed until the following week, when fresh information becomes accessible. The results show that the method enables us to be cautious and mindful of the course schedule. Additionally, the study employs a rule-mining technique to enable the explicit characterisation of behaviour that leads to dropouts. A study by Psathas et al. uses self-regulated learning (SRL) behaviours to examine how early student dropout rates in MOOCs might be predicted [60]. The authors analyse dropout predictions using five well-known ML models: NB, LR, SVM, DT, and k-nearest neighbours. The study also improves forecast accuracy by combining traditional interaction measurements with SRL behaviours. The results show that adding SRL factors greatly enhances dropout predictions, emphasising certain aspects that are essential for determining students who are at risk.

Table 5. Summarised papers related to feature selection approaches for MOOC dropout prediction.

Citation	Contributions	Advantages	Shortcomings	Prediction Accuracy	Efficiency	Best Algorithm
[57]	Identify and evaluate key factors influencing learner satisfaction	Enhance the understanding of learner preferences and improves MOOC design	Limited scope in terms of the dataset because it does not fully capture the preferences of all MOOC learners	80.9%	Moderate	LDA, SVR
[58]	Proper feature selection for prediction outcomes	Improve prediction accuracy by selecting correct features	No production model is provided; weak performance measurements	86.14%	High	RFC
[59]	Novel process to train a set of dropouts predictors via reduced features	Improve a set of features extraction for efficient predict students' Dropout	Weak in enhancing the MOOC dropout performance	97%	High	RS, 3WD
[60]	Integrating self-regulated learning behaviours into ML	Improved accuracy of dropout predictions	Limited generalisability due to course variability static analysis; does not capture dynamic student behaviours	Approx. between 85 and 90%	High	LR, KNN
[61]	Novel approach to automatically select the optimal subset of features for dropout prediction	Efficient and accurate automatic feature selector	No dropout prediction method is reviewed after feature selection	NA	NA	DL, GA
[62]	Feature selection based on PCA and LDA approaches	Best prediction accuracy	Inherent error rate of 4.28% with a standard error of 0.82	>87.7%	High	SVM
[63]	Reliable prediction-based RF	Stable and accurate predictive methodology	Need for interpretable model to explain factors contributing to student dropout	87.5%	High	RF
[64]	Optimised SVR model	Efficient feature extraction	Focus on quantitative metrics and temporal dynamics	Up to 90%	High	SVR with quantum PSO
[65]	DFS method to predict MOOC students' performance	Better accuracy for generated features	Uninterpretable generated features; limited in understanding student factors	NA	NA	PCA, KNN
[66]	Integrated model for fine-grained feature generation and prediction	Improved prediction accuracy and model interpretability	Higher dropout	Approx. 85%	Moderate	LR

Efficiency keys: high efficiency (>85%); moderate efficiency (70–85%); low efficiency (<70%).

A unique method based on evolutionary algorithms is presented by Cheng, Y. et al. to automatically choose the best collection of features for dropout prediction [61]. The technique is tested using a dataset of about 248 k student records from a university in Brazil. The findings demonstrate that in comparison to earlier research in the literature, the suggested strategy considerably improves dropout prediction accuracy. A hybrid approach is provided by Poudyal et al. and is used to integrate several techniques such as feature extraction, regressions, and classifications [62]. They integrated principal component analysis and linear discriminant analysis. Two methods for extracting features are used: a linear and kernel SVM classifies attention patterns using extracted characteristics. The results show that the best outcomes in terms of recall, accuracy, precision, F1, and kappa were obtained via the hybrid approach. Given a collection of features designed from the daily learning progress of the students, a model to forecast student dropout from a MOOC course is presented by Dass et al. [63]. The study uses ML algorithms for prediction process to develop an RF model approach. The generated model has the ability to predict, with an accuracy of 87.5% and an F1-score of 87.5%, whether students will drop out or continue in the MOOC course on any given day.

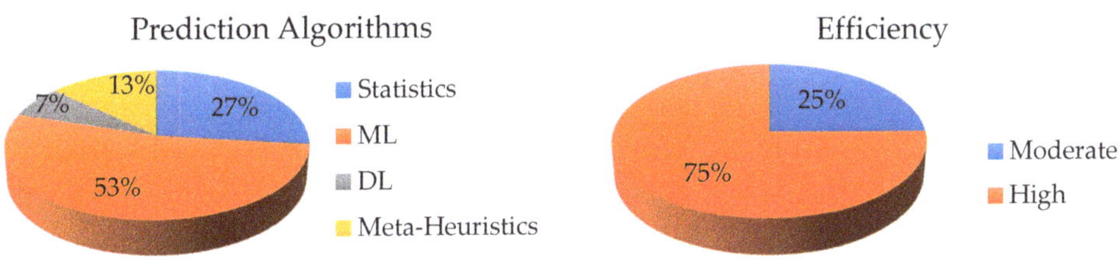

Figure 11. Related works featuring engineering algorithms and performance efficiency.

Cong Jin presented a learning behaviour data-driven student dropout prediction model for MOOCs. An enhanced quantum PSO (IQPSO) algorithm is used to calculate the parameters of an intelligently optimised SVR model, which is subsequently used in the study to reflect weekly student learning characteristics through a feature extraction method design [64]. Results from experiments using publicly available data show that the suggested model performs better in terms of prediction than a number of benchmark models, underscoring the significance of parameter optimisation and learning behaviour aspects for successful dropout prediction in MOOCs. Nadirah et al. describe the process of feature engineering for forecasting MOOC student success using the DFS method. The experiment creates features and the top features picked using PCA are the features generated by the procedure [65]. In terms of prediction, comparing both based and created features, the results demonstrate that generated features proposed using the k-nearest neighbours technique have higher accuracy, indicating that the method has the potential to be used for future prediction models.

The integrated framework with feature selection model proposed by LIN QIU et al., combines' dropout prediction, feature generation, and feature selection to predict the dropout rate in MOOCs [66]. The proposed model generates features using a fine-grained feature generation approach in days, selects valid features using an ensemble feature selection method, and then feeds the selected features into a LR model for prediction. The model obtained good results compared to existing dropout prediction algorithms according to extensive trials conducted on a public dataset. Ultimately, recommendations for building MOOCs are presented by means of an examination of the characteristics of the ultimate choice. The utilisation of data mining techniques is crucial for the analysis and comprehension of intricate datasets pertaining to MOOC dropout prediction. With the use of clustering, it is possible to find patterns and structures in data without the need for labels.

Clustering can be used to identify separate groups of students with similar behaviours or traits, such as engagement levels, performance patterns, or demographics, in the context of dropout prediction.

Researchers can gain a better understanding of the various learner types and their dropout risks by grouping students into clusters. This allows for more specialised interventions and individualised support plans. Clustering techniques, like K-means, hierarchical clustering, or DBSCAN, can identify at-risk groups and improve the efficacy of dropout prevention programs by offering insightful information about the underlying structure of the data. Classification metrics are particularly useful in data mining when attempting to uncover patterns and create models from the data [67]. Its applications include evaluating how effectively those models predict class labels for tasks such as classifying students as "enrolled" or "dropouts". Table 6 displays the categorisation metrics that have been applied in the relevant literature review research. Through the use of clustering techniques, researchers can improve the accuracy of dropout prevention efforts by gaining a greater understanding of at-risk populations [68]. A review of associated studies that have used classification metrics and clustering approaches to analyse and predicts MOOC dropout is summarised in Table 7 and discussed in the following paragraphs.

Table 6. Calcification metrics and corresponding formulae for production process.

Metric	Formulae	Terms Description
Recall (R)	$\frac{TP}{TP+FN}$	TP: True Positive; FN: False Negative
Accuracy	$\frac{TP+TN}{TP+TN+FN+FP}$	TN: True Negative; FP: False Positive
Precision (P)	$\frac{TP}{TP+FP}$	-
F-score	$2 \times \frac{R \times P}{R+P}$	R: Recall; P: Precision

A study by Xia, X et al. explored certain key aspects related to learning behaviour and achieved the fusion of sophisticated algorithms using data-driven approaches, incorporating lengthy short-term memory mechanisms to build dropout prediction methods and models [69]. Based on the experimental results, the study discussed the relevant problem of dropouts related to STEM learning behaviour, investigated the key dropout temporal sequences of the learning process, identified related factors that have a significant impact on learning behaviour, and proposed intervention measures and early warning suggestions. The study demonstrated effective approaches and decisions for researching MOOC STEM learning behaviour, as well as high research feasibility and urgency.

Xiaona et al. used the multi-temporal sequences of learning behaviours to study dropout prediction in MOOCs. Their study analyses the temporal dynamics of student engagement and creates a dropout prediction model using a multi-behaviour type association framework [70]. It highlights the significance of intervention tactics based on learning behaviour data and adaptive decision feedback. The results show how well the suggested model predicts dropouts, offering a dependable and workable method for selecting short-term learning methods and long-term monitoring. This makes a substantial theoretical and practical contribution to the field of educational technology. The study of C. Xu et al. takes into account the correlation data of students' learning behaviours across a number of days in a row. It is discovered via a thorough statistical analysis of learners' learning behaviour that the following day's learning behaviour is comparable to that of the days prior to it [71]. Drawing from this attribute, they suggest utilising a Lie group region covariance matrix to depict the local correlation data related to learning behaviour. Additionally, they build a convolutional neural network model featuring a multiple expansion assembly unit to extract the high-level local correlation characteristics of learning behaviour for dropout prediction.

Table 7. Summarised papers related to data mining approaches for MOOC dropout prediction.

Citation	Contributions	Advantages	Shortcomings	Prediction Accuracy	Efficiency	Best Algorithm
[69]	Novel behavioural data analysis integrating LSTM with DL	Improve the quality and effectiveness of dropout prediction	Not directly applicable to other online learning environments; complexity	NA	Moderate	LSTM, RNN, CNN
[70]	Multi-temporal learning behaviour for adaptive monitoring mechanism	Improve prediction accuracy and facilitate adaptive interventions	Complex models	Between 88% and 90%	High	DPM-MTS
[71]	Method of extracting the local correlation high-level features of learning behaviour for dropout prediction	Enhance the dropout prediction base on evaluating learning behaviour to improve the completion rate of MOOCs	Misses the consideration of external factors influencing dropout rates, in addition to low accuracy	Approx. 84.6%	Moderate	SVM, RF, GBDT
[72]	MOOC behaviour analysis performance prediction based on entropy	Best correlation between entropy and the corresponding behavioural features; efficient feature prediction	Focused only on feature prediction performance; does not consider MOOC dropout prediction	Up to 97%	Moderate	LR, DT, SVM, RF
[73]	Attention mechanisms via natural language processing	Improve prediction accuracy and enhance interpretability	Complex and contingent upon data quality	Between 85% and 90%	High	Attn-L
[74]	Synthetic minority over-sampling technique (SMOTE) for predictive performance	Improve the accuracy of predicting at-risk students and prediction performance	Limited scalability	97.50%	High	LR, RF, and KNN
[75]	Clustering techniques and tensor completion for predicting course drop-out rates	Promote the quality of education	Low precision and slightly higher dropout	NA	Low	Pigeon-inspired optimisation

Efficiency keys: high efficiency (>85%); moderate efficiency (70–85%); low efficiency (<70%).

A data mining technique is presented by Xiaoliang et al. to handle the substantial amount of learner log data that are available on the MOOCs platform and then analyse the association between learner behaviour and academic performance [72]. An entropy-based indicator is presented to quantify behaviour change trends based on the behaviour log data of learners taking part in 12 MOOC courses. The indicator investigates the connections between behaviour change trends and learners' academic achievement. The authors proceed to construct a collection of behavioural attributes in order to examine the connections between actions and academic achievement in more detail. The results show that the proposed method has a specific association that may be used to accurately depict behavioural change trends. Also, the results demonstrate that the suggested feature selection-based model can successfully pinpoint important characteristics and achieve strong prediction accuracy.

Shengjun et al. investigate the use of attention mechanisms to forecast dropout rates among students enrolled in MOOCs. Their paper presents a unique NN model that uses attention layers to focus on the most important aspects of student behaviour, improving prediction accuracy [73]. The results show that in terms of predictive performance, the attention-based model performs noticeably better than standard models, offering important new information about the aspects that most influence student dropout. A new method for improving student dropout prediction in MOOCs is proposed by Mulyani et al., which advances the field of educational data mining [74]. Using ensemble learning techniques to improve predictive accuracy, the study combines the application of the SMOTE to address class imbalance. Liao et al. propose a combined technique called MOOP which consists of a global tensor and local tensor. Their proposal is to utilise a global tensor structure to represent the data of online courses, and to capture the internal connections between courses, a local tensor structure is clustered [75]. In order to achieve drop-out prediction, a high-accuracy low-rank tensor completion method is utilised, together with a parameter-optimisation strategy inspired by pigeons. Using MOOC data, the suggested approach is empirically assessed and shown to provide a remarkably improved level of accuracy and efficiency compared to other options.

For all previously discussed studies, the fact that the difficulty of adapting models to different learning settings and user behaviours can affect prediction accuracy and effectiveness is one of the main problems with dropout prediction for MOOCs. Different algorithms has been used in these studies, and their percentage uses are illustrated in Figure 12. From the review, prediction improving, model adaption, and data gathering techniques that work well can greatly improve the accuracy of dropout prediction.

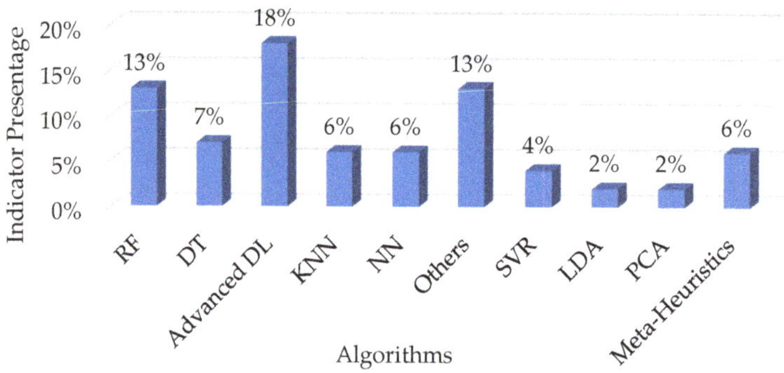

Figure 12. Distribution of data-driven insight models in the literature.

Moreover, dropout prediction faces a major difficulty due to the increasing complexity of MOOCs. Accurately identifying likely dropout learners becomes harder as the courses become larger and more diverse. This complexity is a common problem for traditional feature selection techniques used in dropout prediction algorithms, resulting in poor performance and high false-positive rates. An ensemble model that optimises complex problem spaces using meta-heuristic techniques could be suggested as a solution to this issue. The goal of this combination would be to increase the accuracy of dropout predictions, especially in complex learning contexts.

4.2. Advanced Approaches

ML algorithms are increasingly being used in MOOCs to provide new predictions and insights from data. With large datasets, DL has gained popularity as a predictive analytics technique and can make significant contributions to dropout prediction. When studying complex MOOC datasets, its ability to extract features from raw data automatically makes it very successful [76]. Models with multiple layers of nonlinear information processing and supervised or unsupervised learning techniques for feature representations at more abstract levels will help improve the accuracy of MOOC dropout predictions. The majority of ML-based classification approaches are frequent, where they function as fundamental instruments for classifying data into pre-established labels or classes. These methods use algorithms like LR, RF, DT, and SVM to create models that can forecast results based on input data. To increase the accuracy of the model, ML classification techniques in conventional contexts frequently call for manual feature engineering, in which particular features are chosen or altered from the data [76,77]. Despite their widespread effectiveness, these methods may have drawbacks when working with large, complicated datasets because they mostly rely on domain knowledge for feature extraction. When comparing DL models to traditional ML approaches, the former regularly yield superior predictive accuracy. This is primarily due to the fact that DL algorithms perform more accurately than ML as they can automatically recognise complex patterns and features from massive datasets.

DL models, such as the multi-layer artificial neural network process shown in Figure 13, can handle massive amounts of data and learn abstract representations that improve prediction accuracy, whereas traditional models rely on hand-picking features and simpler structures [77]. Moreover, when compared to ML, DL models regularly produce superior predicted accuracy, and they are able to automatically extract intricate patterns and characteristics from vast datasets. The reason behind DL outperforming ML is that it can handle enormous volumes of data and develop abstract representations that improve prediction accuracy. Prior to exploring the associated literature, it is critical to acknowledge the increasing significance of ML/DL models in attaining improved prediction accuracy in learning environments, especially on MOOC platforms. These sophisticated algorithms present fresh chances to improve the forecasting of student outcomes, such as course completion and dropout rates. The studies that have used ML/DL techniques are examined in the following paragraphs, which also highlight their methods and fill in some of the gaps, particularly with regard to hybrid model creation for large educational datasets. These studies are summarised in Table 8.

A study by Kowsar et al. provides early dropout prediction using ensemble models combining CNN and LSTM networks. The study provides at-risk students with timely treatments and highlights how crucial it is to anticipate dropout in the first week of classes [78]. The authors generate a thirty-day correlation matrix for learners and six novel ensemble classification models. The results show that these models greatly improve prediction accuracy; in addition, prediction errors can be successfully reduced when ensemble classifiers are used in conjunction with the NN approach. The learning behaviour feature-fused deep learning network model is suggested by Liu et al. for the prediction of MOOC dropout. The LBDL model separates the features of the data into two categories, namely, general information features and video learning behaviour characteristics, with time series information [79]. The model mines time series data for video learning behaviour features using Bi-LSTM and attention mechanisms, and it processes general information features using fully connected and embedding layers. To train the gradient boosting framework, LightGBM, the original feature information is integrated. The proposed model achieved greater AUC and F1-scores than other baseline models and performs better when it comes to dropout rate prediction.

Patel et al. investigate ML methods for forecasting MOOC dropout rates. They assess seven algorithms to forecast dropout rates and student outcomes. In order to improve student retention, the authors also suggest tailored treatments based on unique dropout probability [80]. The results highlight machine learning's potential to address MOOC dropout issues and provide guidance to educators on how best to support students who are at risk of dropping out. An innovative dropout prediction model for MOOC learning clickstream data analysis is presented by X. Zhang et al. It is named the Image Convolutional and Bidirectional Temporal Convolutional Network (IC-BTCN). The proposed study tackles the important problem of high dropout rates in MOOCs [81]. Utilising convolutional approaches, the technology extracts local features from a 3D learning behaviour matrix created by converting student learning data. Utilising dilated causal convolution to collect temporal learning features, these features are subsequently processed through a temporal convolutional network to further improve the input. According to the results, the proposed method's accuracy rate in forecasting student dropouts is 89.3%.

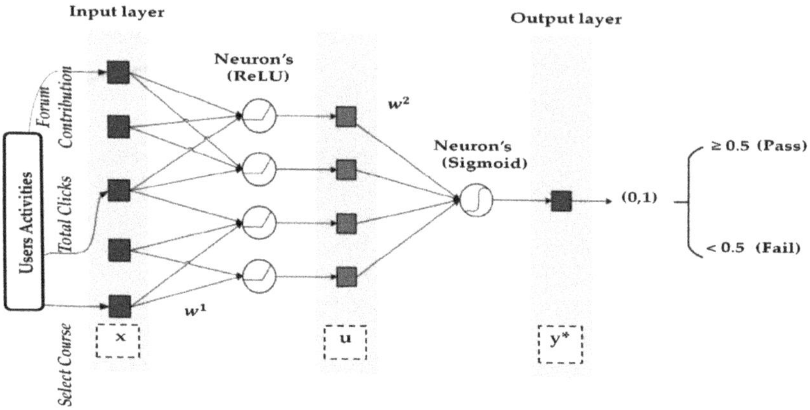

Figure 13. Artificial neural network model for student retention classification performance.

Pan F et al. address the difficulty of predicting student dropouts by providing a unique approach that uses multi-objective reinforcement learning (MORL) to maximise the trade-off between forecast accuracy and earliness [82]. The suggested method approaches dropout prediction as a partial sequence classification problem using a multiple-objective Markov decision process. The authors also describe an improved envelope Q-learning technique for thoroughly exploring the solution space, with the goal of identifying Pareto-optimal techniques that accommodate a variety of tastes. The model's usefulness is proven through rigorous testing on real-world MOOC datasets.

Amala et al. created an Arabic/English MOOC platform called the "Tadakul" system and assessed the impact of the learning analytics system. The authors also present a novel DL approach that is employed in the system to monitor learners' learning processes based on their interactions with registered courses. The input gained through the DL can be used to enhance the student learning experience [83]. They also study the learners' feedback and offer a new technique that combines a Bidirectional Long Short-Term Memory (BiLSTM) network with a CNN approach. Their results show that the proposed model outperformed traditional ML approaches in predicting learners' learning behaviour and enhanced the student experience by increasing teaching efficiency and effectiveness.

A study by Smaili et al. introduces a novel prediction model that offers at-risk learners the optimum learning path in order to address the problem of low retention rates in MOOCs [84]. The authors validated the efficacy of the proposed strategy with a case study that uses the ACO algorithm to optimise learners' routes and classification techniques for prediction. They suggest two complimentary strategies to lower MOOC dropout rates. The first is to use an adaptive boosting algorithm to forecast whether or not learners are at risk of quitting the MOOC program. The second approach entails developing profiles to assist in material selection and decision-making, thereby customising the educational experience for students identified as at risk. The proposed approach incorporates adaptive learning by dynamically modifying the course content to suit the needs of at-risk learners, drawing on the experiences of other learners with comparable profiles.

Table 8. Recent studies on dropout prediction based on ML/DL/meta-heuristic techniques.

Citations	Contributions	Baseline Algorithms	Proposed Models	Prediction Results	Efficiency	Datasets
[78]	Introduces six novel ensemble models that leverage CNN and LSTM for early dropout prediction in MOOCs	CNN, LSTM	Boosting CNN-LSTM	AC = 85.7% P = 87% R = 97.2% F = 91.8%	High	MOOCCube
[79]	Novel deep learning model integrates learning behaviour features to enhance the prediction of dropout rates	DL	Learning behaviour feature-fused DL network	AUC = 82.4% F = 74.9%	Low	NA
[80]	Build a prediction model for the early identification of at-risk students based on ML approaches	DT, RF, GNB, AdaBoost, ETC, XGBoost, and MLP	Multi-models-based approach	AC = 86% F = 92% R = 92% P = 99%	High	OULAD
[81]	Dropout prediction model based on image Convolutional and Bidirectional temporal Convolutional Network	CNN, MLP	IC-BTCN	AC = 89.3%	Moderate	KDD CUP 2015
[82]	Multi-objective reinforcement learning approach to optimise the trade-off between dropout prediction accuracy and earliness	RL	Multiple-objective Markov decision process	AC = 83.9%	Moderate	KDDCup2015 and XuetangX
[83]	Novel deep-learning approach monitors the learning process in a developing MOOC platform	CNN	Bidirectional LSTM	AC = 78% to 85%	Moderate	Kaggle platform
[84]	Adaptive boosting algorithm for predicting learners at risk of dropping out	DT, XGBost, AdaBoost, GBL	ACO with GBL	AUC = 86.63%	NA	OULAD
[85]	Dropout prediction model based on a fusion of behavioural data and ML	SVM, LR, NB, RT, LDA, RF, CNN	Multi-models	AC = 88.8% R = 96% P = 89% F = 93.1%	High	KDD CUP 2015
[86]	Learning model for dropout rate prediction based on high-dimensional vector features	CNN, SVM	Ensemble DL	AC = 97.4% R = 96% P = 97% F = 97.2%	High	KDD 2015
[87]	Efficient capture of nuanced learning patterns to accurately predict student dropout behaviour	CNN, LSTM, DNN	Federated learning pattern aware	AUC = 97.7% RMSE = 0.271 MAE = 0.2084	NA	XuetangX
[88]	A dropout prediction mode based on multiscale features of student behaviour time series data extraction	SVM, CNN, NB, LDA	MFCN-VIB	AC = 87% R = 96% P = 88% F = 92.2%	High	KDD CUP 2015
[89]	Develop an effective dropout prediction model to improve student retention rates	DNN	DNN-based model	AC = 98% R = 93% P = 82% F = 87% AUC = 99%	Moderate	MITx and HarvardX
[90]	Novel dropout prediction model utilises max neighbourhood and intelligent sample weighting to enhance ML predictive performance	DT, RF, SVM, LR	IQPSO-based model	AUC = 82.39% F = 79%	Moderate	KDD Cup 2015
[91]	Predicting student dropout in a MOOC for smart city professionals at an early stage	RF, LR, Ridge, Extra, GBC, CART, AdaBoost, SVM-SGD	GBDT	AC = 95.5% Kappa = 90.7% P = 97.7% F = 96.3%	High	NA

Table 8. *Cont.*

Citations	Contributions	Baseline Algorithms	Proposed Models	Prediction Results	Efficiency	Datasets
[92]	Hyper-model for MOOC feature extraction and dropout prediction	CNN	CNN- LSTM-based model	AC = 79% to 85% R = 88% to 87% P = 91% to 93% F = 89% to 90% (two datasets)	High	KDD Cup 2015 and XuetangX
[93]	Pipeline model based on CNN and long short-term memory to predict dropout rate	SVM, LSTM, CNN	CLSA	AC = 87.6% F = 86.9% P = 87% R = 86.5%	Moderate	KDD CUP 2015
[94]	Integration of feature weighting and behavioural time series to improve MOOC dropout prediction	LR, NB, RF, DT, SVM, CNN	FWTS-CNN	AC = 87.1% P = 86.3% R = 86.5% F = 86.4%	Moderate	KDD Cup 2015
[95]	Integrated feature extraction and classification for efficient end-to-end dropout prediction model	LR, GNB, DT, RF, GTB, AdaBoost, SVM	2D-CNN	P = 84.5% R = 84.9% F = 84.2% AUC = 87.8%	Moderate	KDD Cup 2015
[96]	Dropout rate prediction model to improve prediction accuracy	RF, GBDT	RNN-based model	$R^2 = 0.80$	NA	XuetangX

Metrics keys (P: precision; R: recall; F: F-score; AUC: area under the curve; AC: accuracy). Efficiency keys: high efficiency (≥90%); moderate efficiency (75–90%); low efficiency (<75%).

A dropout prediction model based on the combination of behavioural data and SVM is proposed by Yujiao et al. They use a creative model that integrates many behaviour traits with varying weights and uses them as input data. The proposed method is implemented on two trained datasets, which are used to train the SVM classifier [85]. Results show that the proposed model performs better and, according to experimental results on both datasets, gives the behaviour features the same weights. A dropout rate prediction based on an ensemble DL model and on learner behaviour data features was proposed by Gaurav et al. ResNet-50 is used in the proposed study to extract the local features, and a kernel method is then applied to construct feature relations. The high-dimensional vector characteristics are extracted; then, they are fed to a Faster RCNN to produce a vector representation that includes time series data [86]. The vector is then subjected to a static attention mechanism in order to acquire an attention weight for each dimension. The results demonstrated that the suggested model could perform on par with previous dropout prediction techniques.

Zhang et al. present a FLPADPM model as a bidirectional LSTM layer and a one-dimensional CNN integrated into a federated learning framework. The proposed approach is intended to capture complex learning processes and adjust to differences in a range of educational environments [87]. The author's conduct an empirical evaluation with the two datasets to assess the performance of FLPADPM. The results shows that FLPADPM is more effective than cutting-edge models at properly predicting the behaviour of dropout students. A dropout prediction model that combines a variation information bottleneck and a multiscale fully convolutional network is proposed by Shou et al. [88]. By building a multiscale full CNN, the model extracts multiscale features from student behaviour time series data. A variation information bottleneck approach is then used to reduce the impact of noise on the prediction outcomes. According to the results, the suggested method performed the best.

Anjali et al. present a study describing how DL techniques were used to create a dropout prediction system for at-risk MOOC participants. It draws attention to the rising acceptance of MOOCs and the alarming dropout rates that jeopardise their viability [89]. The study uses a DNN model to analyse learning patterns and predict student dropouts with two MOOCs datasets. The goal of this approach is to give teachers early warnings in order that they may step in and help at-risk pupils. According to the results, DL works better than other approaches, presenting a viable way to improve MOOC student retention. Ahmed et al. present a hyper-model of the LSTM and CNN models, known as CONV-LSTM, to automatically extract features from MOOC raw data and predict if each student will finish their courses or drop out [90]. The authors take into account the problem of class imbalance, which implies that models produce good results on most class cases and poor results on some class examples. In their study, the use of loss function employs a cost-sensitive method that takes into account the different misclassification costs for false positives and false negatives in order to reward improved prediction performance. In comparison to baseline approaches, the performance of the suggested model is better.

A pipeline model called CLSA is proposed by Qian et al. to forecast the dropout rate using information on student behaviour [91]. The CLSA model constructs feature relations using a kernel technique after first extracting local features using a convolutional neural network. After that, an LSTM network receives this high-dimensional vector produced by the CNN in order to produce a time series-integrated vector representation. To determine an attention weight for each dimension, authors apply a static attention mechanism to the vector. The proposed model outperforms baseline models by over 2.8%, with an accuracy of 87.6%. Cong Jin suggests a dropout prediction model based on ML to solve the high dropout rates in MOOCs. The study presents a novel idea known as max neighbourhood, which improves prediction accuracy by taking into account both the distance between student samples and their labels [92]. In addition, it creates an alternative to conventional random selection techniques for determining initial weights for every student sample by using this new neighbourhood definition. The study in question investigates the use of clever optimisation strategies to optimise these weights in more detail. The predictive ability of the dropout prediction model is greatly enhanced by the use of intelligent optimisation and sample weighting, as evidenced by the experimental results.

A study by Panagiotakopoulos et al. proposed that student dropout in MOOCs can be predicted using a variety of cutting-edge supervised machine learning methods [93]. Their study makes use of many predictive models that have their hypermeter learning parameters tuned for the best classification performance. Based on data gathered during the first week of the course, the experimental results demonstrate that accuracy surpasses 96%, enabling efficient intervention methods and support steps. Yafeng presents a CNN model that combines behavioural time series and feature weighting. The proposed study takes the learner's log of learning activities and extracts continuous behavioural features from it [94]. It then filters important features and uses a DT algorithm to rank them in order of importance. Finally, it weighs the continuous behavioural features according to their importance and uses behavioural time series and weighted features to create a convolutional neural network model. The suggested approach provides excellent accuracy with over 87% of the results.

Qiu et al. proposed an end-to-end dropout prediction model based on CNNs to predict the student dropout problem in MOOCs [95]. The model integrates feature extraction and classification into a single framework, automatically extracting features to improve feature representation and transforming the original timestamp data according to different time windows. Comprehensive tests on a publicly available dataset demonstrate that the proposed method can produce performance metrics scores that are on par with baseline dropout prediction techniques. Sun D et al. define the dropout prediction problem as forecasting how much content in the entire course syllabus can be finished by the student [96]. To address this issue, an RNN-based dropout rate prediction model is presented by the authors, together with a URL-embedding layer. The results reveal that the model's prediction accuracy outperforms that of the classic ML model.

Several ML and DL algorithms have been used in previous studies to improve dropout prediction and analyse students' learning behaviours in MOOCs. Figure 14 shows the percentage of algorithms used in these studies. In general, the majority of research has been focused on using DL algorithms to predict different student learning outcomes with different MOOCs platform, as illustrated in Figure 15. Though ML/DL is being used more frequently, not much research has integrated the two techniques to predict outcomes with huge data from education. The current study closes this research gap by offering a thorough evaluation of the predictive performance of various DL/ML models, with a particular emphasis on enhancing dropout prediction in MOOCs through the optimisation of feature selection and dropout prediction using meta-heuristic approaches.

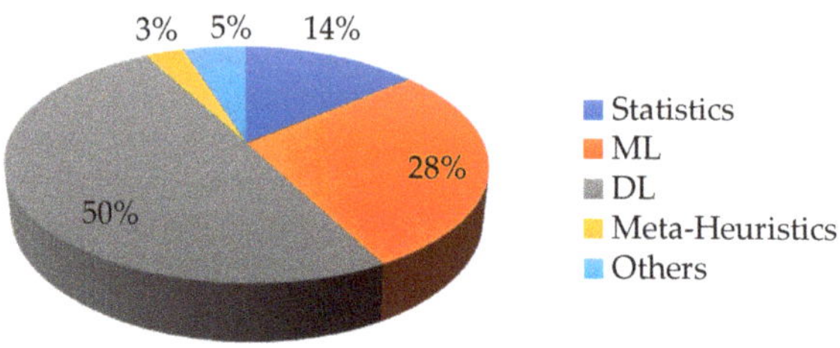

Figure 14. Distributions of algorithms used by related works (advanced approaches).

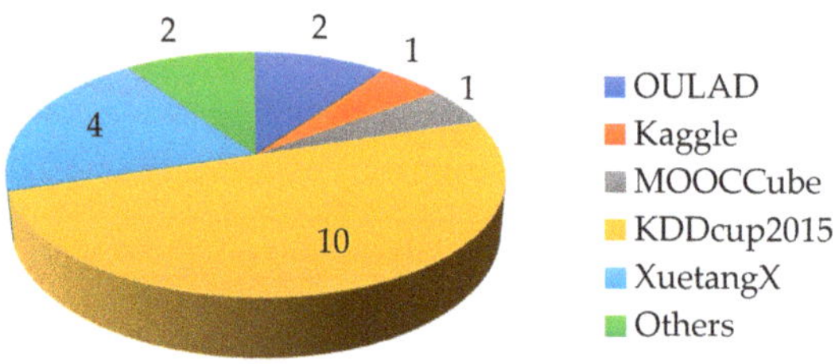

Figure 15. Distribution of MOOCs databases used by related works (advanced approaches).

Another issue with dropout prediction is the large amount of student data that needs to be analysed. Massive course enrolments and ongoing participation have led to a notable increase in the amount of learner interaction data generated every day. At this scale, manual dropout detection becomes impractical, and existing automated techniques often suffer from memory and precision issues. To address this, integrated meta-heuristic algorithms can be used to efficiently analyse large volumes of learner data and identify potential dropout patterns. This minimises the effect of data volume on prediction accuracy and makes the approach suitable for a range of learning scenarios.

4.3. Hybrid Approaches

It is important to emphasise that hybrid approaches that can combine ML, DL, meta-heuristic algorithms, and other techniques to maximise the accuracy of dropout prediction in MOOCs are increasingly being used. These hybrid models overcome the drawbacks of individual models and improve prediction accuracy by combining the advantages of several techniques. Researchers have obtained more robust predictions of student dropout and course completion by integrating multiple strategies, including intelligent learning techniques and improved feature selection. The following section discusses research that has used these hybrid approaches, compared their effectiveness, and examined potential avenues for further improvement of the dropout prediction model, as summarised in Table 9.

Table 9. Summary of most-relevant studies for dropout prediction hybrid approaches.

Citation	Year	Algorithms/ Approaches	Contributions	Dataset	Proposed Model	Prediction Results	Performance
[97]	2024	LightGBM, LMP	Utilises the learning process model to analyse learning behaviour and generate feature vectors to predict dropout	MOOCCube	LPM-LightGBM	AUC = 86.4%	NA
[98]	2024	DNN, LSTM, KNN, MLP, SVM, RF	Effectively identifies students at risk of dropping out early in their learning process, enabling timely interventions to improve retention rates	MOOCCube	DNN-LSTM	AUC = 82.4% F = 74.9%	Low
[99]	2024	NN, CNN, LSTM, SVM	Feature selection approach for prediction; opinion mining of learner comments	Coursera and MSIT datasets	Hybrid mutation-based earthworm	P = 90.9% R = 90.1% F = 91.2%	High
[100]	2023	CNN, LSTM	Hybrid NN for effective dropout prediction incorporating periodic learning behaviours and time distribution information	KDD Cup 2015	CGDC-LSTM	AC = 90.3% P = 91.2% R = 97.5% F = 94.25% AUC = 85.67	High
[101]	2023	DL, IQPSO	Hybrid novel dropout prediction model to enhance prediction accuracy effectively	MOOCCube video	IQPSO-PLSTM model	AUC = 88.45% F = 78.34%	Moderate
[102]	2022	GA, DL	Hybrid prediction model for early detection of students at high risk of drop-out in MOOC	KDD cup 2015	DL/GA-based models	AC = 94% AUC = 86%	High
[103]	2022	ANN, MLP, LR, DT, KNN	Highly accurate dropout prediction model to improve feature selection and learner retention	KDD Cup 2015	FIAR-ANN	AC = 92.42%	High
[104]	2022	CNN, TCN	Enhance and extract useful feature information from students' learning records for dropout prediction	KDD CUP 2015	CNN-TCN	NA	NA
[105]	2020	CNN, Squeesed/ excitation network (SE-Net)	Develop a DL-based model to predict learners' dropout behaviour	KDD Cup 2015	CNN-SE-gated recurrent unit (GRU)	AC = 94.5% P = 95.9% R = 97.2% F = 96.5%	High
[106]	2019	DT, ELM	Hybrid algorithm to improve dropout prediction process	KDD 2015	DT-ELM	AC = 89% AUC = 85% F = 91%	High

Metrics keys (P: precision; R: recall; F: F-score; AUC: area under the curve; AC: accuracy). Efficiency keys: high efficiency (≥90%); moderate efficiency (75–90%); low efficiency (<75%).

A MOOC dropout prediction approach utilising the LightGBM algorithm and learning process model is proposed by Nie, H. et al. To examine learning behaviour and produce feature vectors that will allow for a clear interpretation, the proposed method makes use of the learning process model [97]. To predict dropout, the LightGBM algorithm is used based on these feature vectors. The dropout prediction approach used in this study shows good performance when compared to baseline methods. El Aouifi et al. offer a hybrid deep learning model for predicting school dropout that is based on LSTM and DNN techniques [98]. The suggested model was contrasted with earlier research and a number of different ML techniques. According to the results, the accuracy and efficiency of the suggested DNN-LSTM model are superior to other evaluated models. A hybrid bio-inspired meta-heuristic feature selection strategy was presented by Jatain et al. for the analysis of learner comments on a course [99]. Experimental work is conducted over a real-world education dataset comprising of 110 K learner comments acquired from Coursera and learner data from academic institution MSIT. With respect to the gathered dataset, the experimental results show that the suggested model attains an accuracy of 92.24%.

A study by Y. Zhou introduces the notion of a periodic feature and discovers that varying the learning duration has distinct impacts on the prediction outcomes [100]. The authors provide a hybrid neural network model by using LSTM and CNN to simulate and forecast users' dropout behaviour in light of the new insights. CNNs enable the preservation of local correlations in student behaviour. The model combines dilated causal convolution and group convolution to capture students' periodic patterns. LSTM is integrated into the proposed model to extract learning time distribution information and assess the impact of different learning periods on outcomes. Experimental results show that the suggested model outperforms baseline techniques in prediction accuracy.

An improved quantum PSO technique and DL model are combined in a study by Xiao et al. The proposed methodology uses the derived behavioural feature importance as the initial weights of the features. It first pre-trains the data using random forests [101]. Then, weight finding is carried out using an improved quantum PSO technique to optimise the initial feature weights. Lastly, LSTM deep learning modelling is applied to the weighted data. The results show that the proposed model provides an acceptable performance compared to other baseline models. A hybrid feature selection and dimensionality reduction strategy were introduced by ALJ et al. to extract useful features and decrease model complexity and computation time [102]. Authors use supervised learning techniques to develop two models based on DL and GA. Their results show that both GA and DL outperform baseline algorithms employed in comparable investigations.

Nithya et al. focused on using video interaction analysis to describe important MOOC assignments such as forecasting student success and dropout rates [103]. To evaluate the dropout measure, the proposed method generates and selects the optimal characteristics depending on learner behaviour. The authors used frequent itemset-3 in the NN-based MLP for feature selection and calculated the evaluation metrics. Then, they contrasted their results with those of ANN for dropout prediction using the feature importance association rule. The proposed approach evaluated is compared to different ML and DL models, and the results show that it provides a high accuracy and improves the student retention and decreases dropout rates. In addition, the model outperformed other models by 18%. A hybrid model to predict learners' dropout behaviour is provided by H. Liu et al. [104]. This hybrid model uses an attention method to extract the crucial information from the learning records of students, rather than manually extracting features. It does this by designing a CNN model to automatically extract useful features. The authors also use TCN to capture the interactions between hidden features at various time scales. The proposed model was then evaluated, and the results show that it outperforms alternative dropout prediction techniques.

A hybrid DNN model for the prediction of learner dropout behaviour was proposed by Yan et al. The authors encrypt student recorded data, turn it into a 2D matrix, and then apply the CNN technique with squeesed and excitation networks to extract local features [105]. By obtaining the relationship between the learning behaviours, they are able to increase prediction performance. The results demonstrate that the suggested strategy outperforms the baseline in terms of performance. Chen, Jing et al. introduced an integrated DT algorithm with an extreme learning machines (ELM) hybrid model to eliminate the need for iterative training. Features that are well-suited for classification are chosen by the DT algorithm [106]. Moreover, the study establishes improved weights for the chosen characteristics to improve their capacity for classification. The authors translate the DT to ELM using entropy theory in order to improve ELM structure and obtain accurate prediction results. The results show that the proposed method outperforms baseline algorithms.

The related works discussed are the most relevant articles that focus on hybrid methodologies for MOOC dropout prediction. However, between 2018 and 2024, several other articles have proposed various hybrid solutions using ML/DL techniques, along with meta-heuristic approaches for addressing feature selection challenges and improving dropout prediction. Figure 16 shows the distributions of these publications. The primary focus on feature engineering represents the first stage as crucial to any ML/DL algorithm-based classification challenge since it involves extracting and choosing features from the initial data that are pertinent, meaningful, and information-rich. Data extraction based on the features selected in the first phase is the second most important stage. After that, these recovered data go through a scaling and cleaning processes to produce high-quality, standardised data that are prepared for the training phase.

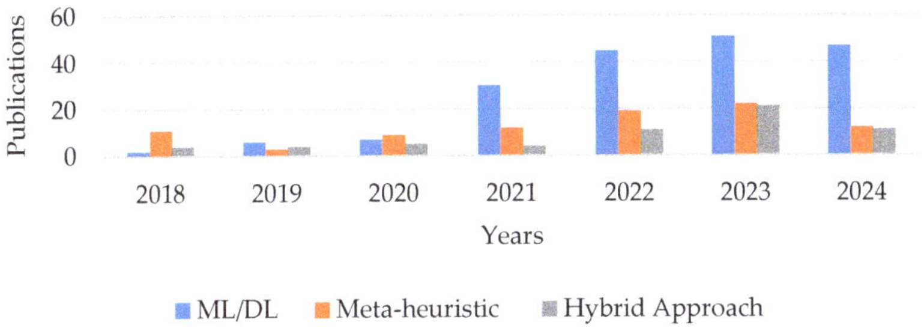

Figure 16. Distributions of hybrid ML, DL, and meta-heuristic approaches for MOOCs feature selection and dropout predictions (resource: Google Scholar).

To ensure an optimising prediction for MOOCs, the third phase involves creating data for every learner; then, the next stage looks for the best predictive traits based on wrapping techniques such as meta-heuristics algorithms. At this stage, many advanced algorithms can be used for optimisation, as shown in Figure 17. This methodology enables the classification of the original dataset into multiple subsets based on the features most relevant to each ML/DL method, which will then serve as input for the proposed prediction module. The final design stage of a hybrid model depends on the previous stages, after which the proposed model and other ML/DL algorithms are trained to compare the performance of each of them. This comparison will pit the presented predictive model against standard prediction models. Figure 17 shows the stages related to developing a hybrid dropout prediction model.

The framework illustrated in Figure 17 can be used for optimising MOOC dropout prediction models, combining a hybrid deep learning and meta-heuristic approach. This framework outlines the procedures necessary for achieving precise learning and improving dropout prediction. Initially, the collected dataset is pre-processed to eliminate errors and anomalies. Various imbalanced data learning techniques, such as SMOTE, boosting, ensemble methods, cluster-based approaches, and adaptive synthetic sampling, have been used in related works to resample the data during pre-processing [107]. The feature selection process for the next stage of the feature engineering procedure can be optimised according to meta-heuristics. To improve the prediction model, the prediction step depends on a DL-inspired hybrid learning mode. The efficacy of the model can be increased by using an optimisation function to minimise an ML/DL model's loss function. Many optimisers can be used, and some of them have been introduced in related works, such as the stochastic gradient descent optimiser, adaptive moment estimation, root mean square propagation, and the momentum optimiser. Q-learning functions as an optimiser and can be used to find the best action or series of actions to minimise or maximise a certain outcome.

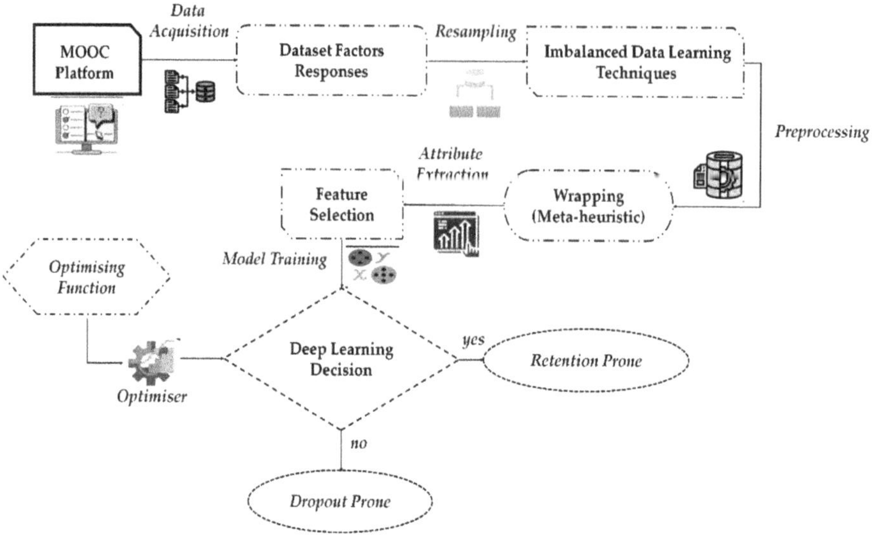

Figure 17. A hybrid framework of DL and meta-heuristic techniques for MOOC dropout prediction-based feature selection optimisation.

In summary, the various earlier studies pertaining to hybrid techniques for MOOC dropout prediction optimisation were covered in this section. We found a few papers linked to this topic since MOOCs have a specific criterion related to increasing the dropout prediction based on feature selection optimisation. More research is still needed on the MOOC performance and dropout prediction problems, which could lead to further advancements in this field. Nonetheless, numerous research projects based on ML/DL solutions are put out to improve dropout prediction. Prediction performance and accuracy can be raised by combining the optimisation of feature selection using meta-heuristic techniques with dropout prediction enhancement using ML/DL methods.

4.4. *Adaptive Learning Approach*

Three main components make up an adaptive learning model; these are the learner module, the learning environment module, and the decision-making module. The learning environment module offers specialised instructional materials designed to meet each learner's unique requirements. Enhancing learner motivation is mostly dependent on a carefully designed learning environment that encourages skill development and makes job completion easier [108]. Designing instructional materials and activities in a way that best supports and promotes learning objectives and learner development is therefore crucial. As shown in Figure 18, the learner module is responsible for learners' profiles, which are recognised based on data collected from their interactions with the system. Learner traits, including goals, preferences, knowledge level, learning styles, and academic motives, are often reflected in these profiles. The learner module delves into the imprints that students leave behind as they engage with the educational setting. After that, data pertaining to the learners' profiles are compiled, pre-processed, and kept in our database.

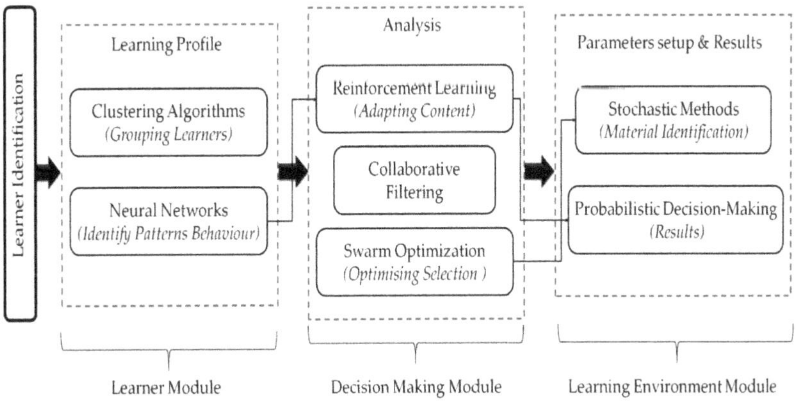

Figure 18. General adaptive learner architecture model.

The decision-making module is responsible for selecting the appropriate course materials that fit each learner's unique profile [108]. The module determines the sequence in which the learner will complete the tasks and assesses the student's readiness for the subsequent learning steps. The algorithm will automatically identify the suggested courses and the path that each learner should take based on their individual profiles. The profile, in this case, can play a crucial role by applying the meta-heuristics algorithm. In the research by Smaili et al., the authors tried to increase the effectiveness of online platforms and boost learners' academic performance by tailoring the MOOC materials to each individual learner [109]. The concept is intended to create a system that leverages learners' interactions with the learning environment to provide each learner with a personalised path that takes into consideration the diversity of their profiles. To achieve this, the authors propose building the best possible learning routes for the system using the PSO approach and perform a case study on online learning to demonstrate the efficacy of the suggested strategy.

4.5. Rationale and Review Objectives

This research aims to investigate recent developments in dropout prediction for MOOCs, as has been previously mentioned. The chosen papers show how predictive approaches have evolved and how they have been used in MOOCs. They were collected from prestigious journals and research databases between 2018 and 2024. Figure 19 shows the distribution of these studies based on the approaches used, highlighting a significant increase in the use of advanced algorithms, such as meta-heuristic methods and ML/DL techniques, for predicting student dropout.

The use of ML and DL has increased significantly over the years. While there were only a few studies on meta-heuristic methods between 2018 and 2020, research involving meta-heuristics has steadily grown in recent years. This indicates that MOOC dropout prediction studies are moving toward more advanced, data-driven models that integrate hybrid ML/DL/meta-heuristic approaches. This rise reflects growing awareness of the potential of these sophisticated techniques to improve prediction accuracy and adapt to diverse learning environments. These trends suggest that the field is rapidly evolving, with researchers employing more complex algorithms to enhance dropout prediction models. As a result, further advancements in dropout prediction methods are likely on the horizon, leading to more-effective strategies for retaining students in MOOCs and improving learning outcomes.

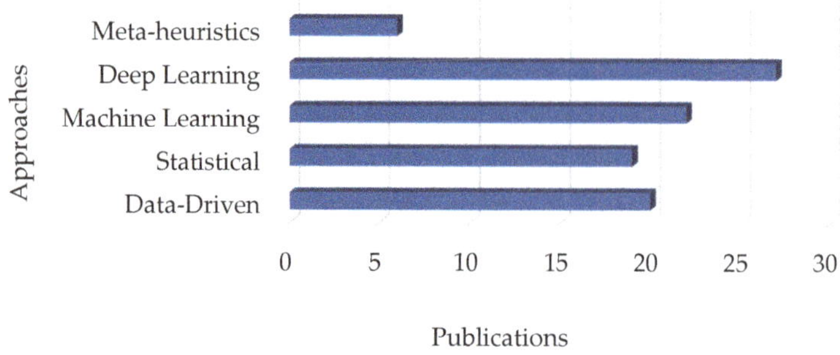

Figure 19. Distribution of related publications reviewed based on strategies used (statistical, data-driven, and intelligence approaches).

The percentage of articles gathered from various reliable and respectable sources for this study is highlighted by the distribution of publication sources. Several databases and publishers, including IEEE, MDPI, Elsevier, ACM, Springer, and Wiley, which were used as sources of collected papers. The distribution of various published sources as a proportion is shown in Figure 20. With 25% and 18% of the evaluated publications, respectively, IEEE and MDPI, according to the statistics, are the highest contributors to research on developing MOOCs dropout prediction models. Papers from these sources provide important new information on dropout prediction for MOOCs. ACM and IEEE digital libraries were the main sources of conference proceedings; other journals with respectable impact factors were also included such as Tylor & Francis, Nature, and Frontiers. Interestingly, IEEE and MDPI offer a good number of periodicals that are strongly recommended for scholars looking for MOOCs dropout prediction methods. This distribution highlights the important role that IEEE and MDPI have had in promoting this field of research.

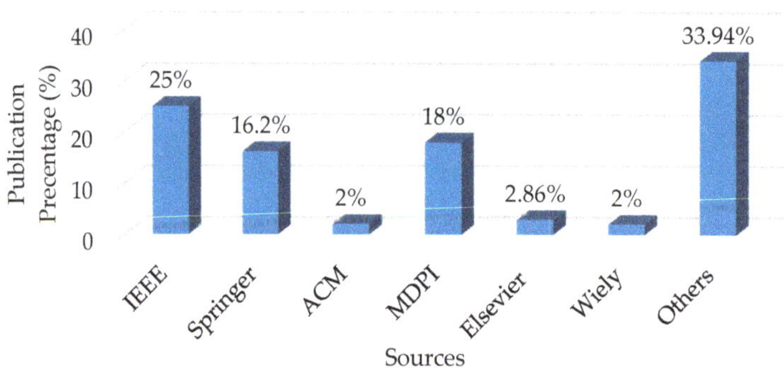

Figure 20. The percentage of all papers considered in this review based on publication venue.

5. Comprehensive Review Synthesis and Insights

Many techniques and methods have been utilised to predict dropout rates in MOOCs and increase student retention based on the earlier research, which is described in Section 4. A variety of dropout prediction strategies have been discussed in this review, with their efficacy and advantages and disadvantages noted. The review provides an informed analysis of existing prediction models and the viewpoints offered by scholars by examining the most recent research. In addition, it fills in the gaps in the literature that have not been thoroughly explored. This comprehensive analysis not only shows how far dropout prediction has come but also emphasises how much more work has yet to be done to close these gaps and improve prediction methods in order that they can be used more accurately and effectively in MOOCs.

It is evident from the discussed methodologies used in most MOOC dropout prediction studies that a range of predictive models and strategies can greatly enhance the accuracy of dropout forecasts. However, to maximise prediction performance, the right features and methods must be chosen. Numerous studies have concentrated on identifying pertinent features and optimising methods to increase model accuracy. Despite these developments, there are still a number of important variables that have a significant impact on prediction performance. These variables include learner engagement levels, the complexity of the course material, and user interaction patterns. Moreover, MOOCs dropout prediction is generally faced with a number of difficulties. These difficulties draw attention to important areas of research that could enhance learner memory and prediction accuracy. The evaluated research in this paper covers some of these problems, with many depending on advanced prediction models and ML/DL approaches [110]. To further improve forecast accuracy and efficacy in MOOCs, more thorough strategies that take into account a larger range of factors influencing dropout rates are still required.

Many of the reviewed studies often overlook the opportunity to optimise data exchange paths and select predictive models for dropout prediction based on key factors such as feature relevance, learner engagement, and model performance. Moreover, many of these studies also overlook the challenges of integrating diverse datasets and learner behaviours into predictive models, which can impact the accuracy and effectiveness of dropout predictions [110,111]. To address these limitations, future research could focus on implementing advanced algorithms and combining deep learning with meta-heuristic techniques. By refining feature selection, data integration, and model tuning, the accuracy of dropout predictions and the overall reliability of MOOCs can be improved. In addition, incorporating factors such as student engagement patterns and course interactions could further enhance prediction models and help reduce dropout rates.

Previous research has explored various techniques for feature selection and model training, but these methods often involve complex, resource-intensive processes that may not fully capture the nuances of learner behaviour. Future hybrid approaches could enable more efficient data processing and sophisticated routing mechanisms in predictive models, enhancing both energy efficiency and model performance [111].

6. Research Gaps in Dropout Prediction Optimisation Perspective

Reducing dropout rates in the MOOC space is still a major challenge. Due to the varied and dynamic nature of learner behaviour, one of the main problems found in recent studies is the difficulty faced in accurately predicting dropout rates. Conventional approaches frequently use static models that might not take into consideration changes in learner engagement and progress that occur in real time, resulting in forecasts and interventions that are not ideal. New developments in data analytics and ML present viable ways to improve dropout prediction models [112]. A variety of features, including student interaction patterns, engagement levels, and past performance data, are incorporated into these techniques. Many existing studies have not fully explored the potential of integrating real-time data with adaptive learning strategies. This gap indicates that additional study should be undertaken on creating models that can more accurately anticipate the future by dynamically adapting to the behaviour of learners. In addition, even while clustering techniques and other predictive models have demonstrated promise, they frequently run into issues like managing massive datasets and making sure the models hold up well across various course types and learner demographics [113]. For example, although clustering might be useful in identifying trends and putting comparable learners in one group, it might not always be able to convey the subtleties of each learner's experience. More advanced algorithms are required in order to handle a variety of datasets and offer insights into the reasons contributing to dropout.

Furthermore, the significance of combining intervention techniques with dropout prediction models is frequently disregarded in current research. It is not enough to just anticipate dropout; in order to improve student retention, customised interventions based on these predictions must be implemented. Future research should examine the efficient integration of prediction models with personalised learning tactics to support students who are considered to be at-risk and improve overall completion rates of courses [113,114]. Therefore, even if a lot has been accomplished in terms of comprehending and forecasting MOOC dropout, more sophisticated, real-time, and adaptable methods are still required. To tackle these obstacles, a blend of enhanced prediction models, enhanced integration with intervention tactics, and a more profound comprehension of student conduct and course dynamics will be necessary. To improve prediction accuracy and intervention tactics, recent developments in MOOC dropout prediction have increasingly used clever techniques. Algorithms such as DT and SVM are two popular ML algorithms that are used to detect at-risk students and forecast dropout rates based on different learning indicators and engagement patterns [114]. Predictive models, for example, can foresee dropout risks and recommend early interventions based on analysis of student interaction data, assignment completion rates, and forum participation. But even with these developments, there are still a number of important research gaps (RGs), as shown in the following sections.

A. RG1: Optimising Feature Selection to Enhance Prediction Model Accuracy

Dropout prediction models often take into account a wide range of factors, such as learning behaviour, engagement indicators, and demographic data. Model performance is greatly impacted by the choice of these features and the preparation of the data. Even though dimensionality reduction and feature selection are used to increase prediction accuracy, the efficacy of these strategies differs greatly throughout MOOC platforms and course types. Issues with data quality and feature relevance plague current models frequently, which negatively affects overall prediction performance. In order to increase the robustness and accuracy of dropout prediction models, future research should concentrate on enhancing feature selection procedures and data pre-processing techniques.

B. RG2: Developing Adaptive Prediction Models for Diverse MOOC Environments

To properly customise interventions, students with comparable traits and learning styles are grouped together using clustering and segmentation techniques. Many models now in use, however, fall short in addressing the context-specific elements and diversity of MOOC contexts, including learner background, course difficulty, and content type. Advanced models that can adapt to different contexts and learning environments, such as ensemble learning and deep learning approaches, show promise, but they often need significant computational resources and ongoing fine-tuning. In order to provide more precise forecasts and successful dropout prevention tactics, research should focus on the creation of adaptable and context-aware algorithms that can dynamically adapt to various MOOC venues and learner profiles.

Improving the accuracy and computing efficiency of prediction algorithms is necessary to optimise dropout prediction in MOOCs, given the dynamic and heterogeneous character of online learning environments. The capacity of dropout prediction algorithms to handle and evaluate large volumes of learner data in real-time, allowing for targeted and timely interventions, is a critical component of their efficacy. The development of sophisticated computational methods that can handle big datasets effectively and retain high prediction accuracy is necessary for this optimisation. The effectiveness of computational algorithms is critical for real-time applications because quick identification of at-risk pupils is essential for putting retention tactics into action. To increase dropout prediction systems' responsiveness, methods including dimensionality reduction, effective data processing, and algorithmic optimisation are crucial. Furthermore, the accuracy of predictions and intervention tactics will be improved by integrating adaptive learning algorithms that can dynamically adapt to changing learner behaviours and course circumstances.

7. Study Limitations and Future Directions

This comprehensive review provides valuable insights into MOOC dropout prediction models, but it has several limitations. The scope was confined to specific databases and MOOC-focused studies, potentially overlooking relevant research from other sources. The variability in methodologies, datasets, and models complicates consistent conclusions. While emphasising the importance of feature selection, this study identifies challenges such as integrating real-time data, managing diverse learner behaviours, and ensuring computational efficiency for large-scale MOOCs. In addition, it struggles to connect predictions to hybrid approaches and address scalability issues in advanced models, such as deep learning.

With MOOCs growing in complexity and size, it has become clear that the dropout prediction optimisation aspect is important and has a lot of potential to grow in the future. The issue comes in developing prediction algorithms to maximise accuracy and efficiency, ensuring early interventions that can improve learner retention and success. By offering flexible answers to the ever-changing problems MOOCs encounter, recent advances in ML have demonstrated promise in this field. Large-scale learner data can be analysed using ML/DL algorithms to find trends and more accurately forecast the likelihood of dropout [115]. These developments make it possible to create intelligent models that adjust to changing student behaviours and course dynamics, which enhances prediction accuracy and intervention techniques. A number of important considerations need to be made while creating dropout prediction models:

- Accuracy and efficiency: To manage massive amounts of data effectively, the model must be able to predict dropout risks with accuracy while consuming the least amount of computational resources.
- Adaptability: The model's adaptability is crucial as it needs to accommodate a range of learning contexts and student profiles. It must also account for differences in course content, learner engagement, and interaction patterns.
- Real-time capabilities: If dropouts need to be avoided before they happen, prompt prediction and action are essential.
- Effectiveness: Over time, the strategy should help maintain gains in student achievement and retention.

Even with this advancement, a lot of research has not adequately addressed all the factors, like varied student engagement levels, course complexity, and the effects of diverse teaching strategies, which influence the prediction of dropout rates. There is currently little research being conducted on advanced algorithms such as swarm intelligence and bioinspired techniques [116]. While these methods have the potential to yield more intelligent answers, more research is necessary to adapt them to a variety of MOOC scenarios.

Meta-heuristic techniques like swarm intelligence (SI) and bio-inspired (BI) techniques offer potential directions for future research, being intelligent means of improving dropout prediction in MOOCs. These approaches, which have their roots in collective behaviours and natural systems, have special benefits for dealing with the complexity and dynamic nature of online learning environments [116,117]. The effective contributions of several BI and SI approaches to dropout prediction optimisation are reviewed in the following paragraphs. As an example, Algorithm 1 describes the processes related to optimising the

MOOC dropout prediction based on optimised feature selection using hybrid ML/DL and meta-heuristic approaches.

Algorithm 1: MOOC dropout prediction optimisation using ML/DL and meta-heuristic approaches.

1. ***initialise processes***
2. ***data collection from dataset***
3. collect (user_interactions, course_progress, demographic_data, engagement_metrics, etc.)
4. ***data preprocessing***
5. clean_Data(), remove_noisy_values()
6. handle_class_imbalance() # use imbalanced data learning techniques
7. encode_categorical_variables(), normalise_or_scale_features()
8. ***feature extraction***
9. extract_key_features(), identify_temporal_patterns()
10. ***feature selection optimisation***
11. initialise_metaheuristic_algorithms()
12. select_algorithm (PSO, ACO, GA, FA, etc.)
13. optimise_dropout_features()
14. ensemble_metaheuristics(select_and combine_algorithms())
15. ***dropout prediction model using ML/DL approaches***
16. train_approaches() # e.g., RF, SVM, NN, etc.
17. fine_tune_Model_via_ensemble()
18. **repeat** step **15**
19. apply_metaheuristics())
20. apply_LSTM()
21. capture_temporal_dependencies()
22. predict_dropout_based_on_sequence()
23. ***model evaluation***
24. evaluate_model(accuracy, F1-score, precision, recall, ... etc.)
25. feedback_loop() # Incorporate feedback from dropout/persistent users
26. ***End***

Bio-inspired (BI) approaches, such as, ACO, GA, and PSO algorithms, offer effective solutions for dropout prediction. ACO-based models use ant foraging behaviour to efficiently analyse learner paths and inform intervention strategies for dropout risk. GA-based models optimise dropout prediction through evolutionary processes, while PSO models draw inspiration from the social behaviours of fish and birds to enhance prediction accuracy. Future research can explore how these algorithms can be modified to consider MOOC participant behaviours and changing course material [117].

The BI approaches with ML/DL models incorporate different prediction elements and parameters. By optimising parameters and more thoroughly examining the solution space, these hybrid methodology can be used to improve dropout prediction models' accuracy. Other SI techniques, like ABC and Firefly, can optimise feature selection for dropout prediction models. Future studies could explore how these algorithms can adapt to large-scale data in MOOCs and merge them with deep learning methodologies to tackle complex learner data correlations.

Hybrid approaches combining SI and BI methodologies with ML/DL techniques can enhance dropout prediction. These models are more resilient and flexible, allowing for real-time data management and adaptability to student behaviour. Future research should focus on creating BI and SI methodologies that can adapt to new information and expand to large student populations. Thus, more in-depth studies of these methods should be conducted in the future, with an emphasis on how they integrate with DL/ML, how flexible they are in real time, and how scalable they are [118]. By leveraging the natural principles underlying these approaches, researchers can develop innovative solutions to improve learner retention and success in MOOCs.

8. Conclusions

Predicting student dropout rates effectively is becoming more and more crucial as the area of education develops, especially in online learning contexts. To effectively customise interventions, educators and institutions use a range of variables, including academic achievement, engagement measures, and demographic data. Modern intelligence methods, especially data analytics and machine learning, have greatly improved dropout prediction models' accuracy and dependability. We can use these technologies to analyse large volumes of data and find trends and patterns that can point to a student's likelihood of disengaging. Furthermore, integrating both swarm intelligence and bio-inspired methodologies can lead to more-sophisticated predictive models. This combination not only enhances the accuracy of predictions but also allows for more targeted and timely interventions, ultimately supporting student success.

Despite the advancements in recent research, there are still difficulties in smoothly combining different predictors and modifying models to account for real-time variations in learner behaviour. Future research must concentrate on creating hybrid models that achieve a compromise between complexity, scalability, and adaptability because online education is dynamic and requires models that can change as student interactions do. Furthermore, continuous assessments and evaluations are essential to improve MOOC dropout prediction techniques. By enabling persistent methodological improvement, these assessments will guarantee that interventions are both successful and sensitive to the needs of a varied group of students. We can greatly improve student achievement and retention by utilising cutting-edge technologies and creative strategies, opening the door to a more effective and interesting online learning environment.

Author Contributions: Conceptualisation, S.A. and B.S.; methodology, S.A.; software, S.A. and B.S.; validation, S.A., B.S. and A.L.; formal analysis, S.A.; investigation, S.A. and B.S.; resources, S.A., B.S. and A.L.; data curation, S.A.; writing—original draft preparation, S.A.; writing—review and editing, B.S. and A.L.; visualisation, S.A., B.S. and A.L.; supervision, B.S. and A.L.; project administration, B.S. and A.L. All authors have read and agreed to the published version of the manuscript.

Funding: This research received no external funding.

Conflicts of Interest: The authors declare no conflicts of interest.

Abbreviations

The following abbreviations are used in this manuscript:

AdaBoost	Adaptive Boosting Learning
CART	Classification and Regression Tree Algorithm
CGDC	Combining Group Convolution and Dilated Causal Convolution
DFS	Deep Feature Synthesis
ETC	Extra Tree Classifier
Extra	Extremely Randomised Trees Algorithm
FIAR	Feature Importance Association Rule
FLPADPM	Federated Learning Pattern Aware Dropout Prediction Model
GBC	Gradient Boosting Classifier
GBL	Gradient Boosting Learning
GBDT	Gradient Boosting Decision Tree
GNB	Gaussian Naïve Bayes
GTB	Gradient Tree Boosting
IQPSO	Intelligent Quantum Particle Swarm Optimisation
KNN	k-nearest Neighbours Technique
LDA	Linear Discriminant Analysis

LightGBM	Light Gradient Boosting Decision Tree Implementation
LSTM	Long Short-Term Memory Network
MCC	Matthews Correlation Coefficient
MLP	Multilayer Perceptron
OULAD	Open University Learning Analytics Dataset
PCA	Principal Component Analysis
PLSTM	Pulsed Long Short-Term Memory
Ridge	Ridge Classification Method
RS	Rough Sets
SGD	Stochastic Gradient Descent Algorithm
SMOTE	Synthetic Minority Over-sampling Technique
SVR	Support Vector Regression
TCN	Temporal Convolutional Network
XGBoost	Extreme Gradient Boosting
3WD	Three-Way Decisions

References

1. Wang, W.; Zhao, Y.; Wu, Y.J.; Goh, M. Factors of dropout from MOOCs: A bibliometric review. *Libr. Hi Tech* **2023**, *41*, 432–453. [CrossRef]
2. Feng, W.; Tang, J.; Liu, T.X. Understanding Dropouts in MOOCs. In Proceedings of the AAAI Conference on Artificial Intelligence, Honolulu, HI, USA, 27 January–1 February 2019; Volume 33, pp. 517–524.
3. Goopio, J.; Cheung, C. The MOOC dropout phenomenon and retention strategies. *J. Teach. Travel Tour.* **2020**, *21*, 177–197. [CrossRef]
4. Borrella, I.; Caballero-Caballero, S.; Ponce-Cueto, E. Taking action to reduce dropout in MOOCs: Tested interventions. *Comput. Educ.* **2021**, *179*, 104412. [CrossRef]
5. Vitiello, M.; Walk, S.; Chang, V.; Hernandez, R.; Helic, D.; Guetl, C. MOOC Dropouts: A Multi-system Classifier. In *Data Driven Approaches in Digital Education. EC-TEL 2017*; Lavoué, É., Drachsler, H., Verbert, K., Broisin, J., Pérez-Sanagustín, M., Eds.; Lecture Notes in Computer Science; Springer: Cham, Switzerland, 2017; Volume 10474.
6. Li, J.; Li, S.; Zhao, Y.; Guo, L.; Hao, F.; Ren, M.; Li, K. Predicting Dropouts Before Enrollments in MOOCs: An Explainable and Self-Supervised Model. *IEEE Trans. Serv. Comput.* **2023**, *16*, 4154–4167. [CrossRef]
7. Mrhar, K.; Douimi, O.; Abik, M. A Dropout Predictor System in MOOCs Based on Neural Networks. *J. Autom. Mob. Robot. Intell. Syst.* **2021**, *14*, 72–80. [CrossRef]
8. Aldowah, H.; Al-Samarraie, H.; Alzahrani, A.I.; Alalwan, N. Factors affecting student dropout in MOOCs: A cause and effect decision-making model. *J. Comput. High. Educ.* **2020**, *32*, 429–454. [CrossRef]
9. Althibyani, H.A. Predicting student success in MOOCs: A comprehensive analysis using machine learning models. *PeerJ Comput. Sci.* **2024**, *10*, e2221. [CrossRef]
10. Li, Y. The factors influencing the continuance intention of MOOCs: The perspective of socio-technical approach. *Educ. Inf. Technol.* **2024**. [CrossRef]
11. Li, J. Construction of Modern Educational Technology MOOC Platform Based on Courseware Resource Storage System. *Int. J. Emerg. Technol. Learn. (iJET)* **2017**, *12*, 105. [CrossRef]
12. Goel, Y.; Goyal, R. On the Effectiveness of Self-Training in MOOC Dropout Prediction. *Open Comput. Sci.* **2020**, *10*, 246–258. [CrossRef]
13. Hafshejani, F.F.; Zeinalipour, H.; Ebner, M.; Fini, A.A.S.; Vajargah, K.F.; Jafari, E. Identifying the Essentials of Corporate MOOCs' Application to the Leading Organizations. *Int. J. Emerg. Technol. Learn. (iJET)* **2023**, *18*, 143–159. [CrossRef]
14. Loh, H.S.; Martins van Jaarsveld, G.; Mesutoglu, C.; Baars, M. Supporting social interactions to improve MOOC participants' learning outcomes: A literature review. *Front. Educ.* **2024**, *9*, 1345205. [CrossRef]
15. Dalipi, F.; Zdravkova, K.; Ahlgren, F. Sentiment Analysis of Students' Feedback in MOOCs: A Systematic Literature Review. *Front. Artif. Intell.* **2021**, *4*, 728708. [CrossRef]
16. Alexiou, A.T.; Sarup, P.; Kumar, A.; Gupta, G.K. MOOCs Theories, Trends, Critics, and Life Sciences Applications: Updates on MOOCs. In *Library and Information Science in the Age of MOOCs*; Kaushik, A., Ed.; IGI Global: Hershey, PA, USA, 2018; pp. 240–251.

17. Mehra, A.; Kant, P. A Comparative Evaluation of MOOCs and Classroom Learning in Engineering and Science in India: A MOOC Policy Assessment. In Proceedings of the European Conference on Education 2024: Official Conference Proceedings, Online, 11–15 July 2024; pp. 719–738.
18. Ardchir, S.; Rachik, A.; Ouassit, Y.; Moulouki, R.; Azzouazi, M. An Efficient Feature Selection Approach for MOOCs Dropout Prediction. In *Advanced Intelligent Systems for Sustainable Development (AI2SD'2020). AI2SD 2020*; Kacprzyk, J., Balas, V.E., Ezziyyani, M., Eds.; Advances in Intelligent Systems and Computing; Springer: Cham, Switzerland, 2022; Volume 1417.
19. Youssef, M.; Mohammed, S.; Hamada, E.K.; Wafaa, B.F. A predictive approach based on efficient feature selection and learning algorithms' competition: Case of learners' dropout in MOOCs. *Educ. Inf. Technol.* **2019**, *24*, 3591–3618. [CrossRef]
20. Mansouri, N.; Soui, M.; Abed, M. SFS feature selection with decision tree classifier for massive open online courses (MOOCs) recommendation. *J. Comput. Educ.* **2023**, *11*, 1089–1110. [CrossRef]
21. Bahi, H.A.A.; Boussaha, K.; Laboudi, Z. Meta-features Based Architecture for the Automatic Selection of Prediction Models for MOOCs. In *Novel & Intelligent Digital Systems: Proceedings of the 3rd International Conference (NiDS 2023). NiDS 2023*; Kabassi, K., Mylonas, P., Caro, J., Eds.; Lecture Notes in Networks and Systems; Springer: Cham, Switzerland, 2023; Volume 784.
22. Ige, O.P.; Gan, K.H. Ensemble filter-wrapper text feature selection methods for text classification. *Comput. Model. Eng. Sci.* **2024**, *141*, 1847–1865. [CrossRef]
23. Liu, L.; Wan, L. Innovative models for enhanced student adaptability and performance in educational environments. *PLoS ONE* **2024**, *19*, e0307221. [CrossRef]
24. Ardchir, S.; Ouassit, Y.; Ounacer, S.; Jihal, H.; Goumari, Y.E.L.; Azouazi, M. Improving Prediction of MOOCs Student Dropout Using a Feature Engineering Approach. In *Advanced Intelligent Systems for Sustainable Development (AI2SD'2019). AI2SD 2019*; Ezziyyani, M., Ed.; Advances in Intelligent Systems and Computing; Springer: Cham, Switzerland, 2020; Volume 1102.
25. Gligorea, I.; Cioca, M.; Oancea, R.; Gorski, A.-T.; Gorski, H.; Tudorache, P. Adaptive Learning Using Artificial Intelligence in e-Learning: A Literature Review. *Educ. Sci.* **2023**, *13*, 1216. [CrossRef]
26. Chi, Z.; Zhang, S.; Shi, L. Analysis and Prediction of MOOC Learners' Dropout Behaviour. *Appl. Sci.* **2023**, *13*, 1068. [CrossRef]
27. Márquez-Vera, C.; Cano, A.; Romero, C.; Noaman, A.Y.M.; Mousa Fardoun, H.; Ventura, S. Early dropout prediction using data mining: A case study with high school students. *Expert Syst.* **2016**, *33*, 107–124. [CrossRef]
28. Papadimitriou, A. Adaptive and Intelligent MOOCs: How They Contribute to the Improvement of the MOOCs' Effectiveness. *Int. J. Res. e-Learn.* **2023**, *9*, 1–21. [CrossRef]
29. Wu, F.; Zhang, J.; Shi, Y.; Yang, X.; Song, W.; Peng, Z. Predicting MOOCs Dropout with a Deep Model. In *Web Information Systems Engineering—WISE 2020*; Huang, Z., Beek, W., Wang, H., Zhou, R., Zhang, Y., Eds.; Lecture Notes in Computer Science; Springer: Cham, Switzerland, 2020; Volume 12343.
30. Deeva, G.; De Smedt, J.; De Weerdt, J. Educational Sequence Mining for Dropout Prediction in MOOCs: Model Building, Evaluation, and Benchmarking. *IEEE Trans. Learn. Technol.* **2022**, *15*, 720–735. [CrossRef]
31. Yang, F.; Xu, Z.; Wang, H.; Sun, L.; Zhai, M.; Zhang, J. A hybrid feature selection algorithm combining information gain and grouping particle swarm optimization for cancer diagnosis. *PLoS ONE* **2024**, *19*, e0290332. [CrossRef]
32. Asli, M.F.; Hamzah, M.; Ibrahim, A.A.A.; Ayub, E. Problem characterization for visual analytics in MOOC learner's support monitoring: A case of Malaysian MOOC. *Heliyon* **2020**, *6*, e05733. [CrossRef] [PubMed]
33. Khalid, A.; Lundqvist, K.; Yates, A.; Ghzanfar, M.A. Novel online Recommendation algorithm for Massive Open Online Courses (NoR-MOOCs). *PLoS ONE* **2021**, *16*, e0245485. [CrossRef]
34. Chen, J.; Fang, B.; Zhang, H.; Xue, X. A systematic review for MOOC dropout prediction from the perspective of machine learning. *Interact. Learn. Environ.* **2022**, *32*, 1642–1655. [CrossRef]
35. Dalipi, F.; Imran, A.S.; Kastrati, Z. MOOC dropout prediction using machine learning techniques: Review and research challenges. In Proceedings of the 2018 IEEE Global Engineering Education Conference (EDUCON), Santa Cruz de Tenerife, Spain, 17–20 April 2018; pp. 1007–1014.
36. Huang, H.; Jew, L.; Qi, D. Take a MOOC and then drop: A systematic review of MOOC engagement pattern and dropout factor. *Heliyon* **2023**, *9*, e15220. [CrossRef]
37. Moreno-Marcos, P.M.; Alario-Hoyos, C.; Munoz-Merino, P.J.; Kloos, C.D. Prediction in MOOCs: A Review and Future Research Directions. *IEEE Trans. Learn. Technol.* **2018**, *12*, 384–401. [CrossRef]
38. Liyanage, N.G.S.; Sandamali, K.A.D.; Fernando, W.M.A.P.S. Systematic review on high dropout rates in moocs—Reasons and solutions. In *Proceeding of the Open University Research Sessions (OURS 2023)*; The Open University of Sri Lanka: Colombo, Sri Lanka, 2023; ISSN 2012-9912.
39. Mduma, N.; Kalegele, K.; Machuve, D. A Survey of Machine Learning Approaches and Techniques for Student Dropout Prediction. *Data Sci. J.* **2019**, *18*, 14. [CrossRef]
40. Sharma, A. A Review on Various Developments in Moocs For Prediction of Dropouts To Form A Basis For Prescriptive Framework To Reduce Dropout Rate. *Think India J.* **2019**, *22*, 372–384.

41. Lin, Y.; Chen, H.; Xia, W.; Lin, F.; Wang, Z.; Liu, Y. A Comprehensive Survey on Deep Learning Techniques in Educational Data Mining. *arXiv* **2024**, arXiv:2309.04761v4.
42. Alhothali, A.; Albsisi, M.; Assalahi, H.; Aldosemani, T. Predicting Student Outcomes in Online Courses Using Machine Learning Techniques: A Review. *Sustainability* **2022**, *14*, 6199. [CrossRef]
43. Guo, T.; Bai, X.; Tian, X.; Firmin, S.; Xia, F. Educational Anomaly Analytics: Features, Methods, and Challenges. *Front. Big Data* **2022**, *4*, 811840. [CrossRef] [PubMed]
44. Khan, L.H.; Haque, M.A.; Ibrahim, E.A.; Mostakim, M.; Hossain, M.I. Interpretable MOOC Dropout Prediction using Different Ensemble Methods and XAI. In Proceedings of the 2023 2nd International Conference on Applied Artificial Intelligence and Computing (ICAAIC), Salem, India, 4–6 May 2023; pp. 636–643.
45. Syed Mustapha, S.M.F.D. Predictive Analysis of Students' Learning Performance Using Data Mining Techniques: A Comparative Study of Feature Selection Methods. *Appl. Syst. Innov.* **2023**, *6*, 86. [CrossRef]
46. Del Bonifro, F.; Gabbrielli, M.; Lisanti, G.; Zingaro, S.P. Student Dropout Prediction. In Proceedings of the Artificial Intelligence in Education: 21st International Conference, AIED 2020, Ifrane, Morocco, 6–10 July 2020; Proceedings, Part I; Volume 12163, pp. 129–140.
47. Rabelo, A.M.; Zárate, L.E. A Model for Predicting Dropout of Higher Education Students. *Data Sci. Manag.* **2024**, 1–33. [CrossRef]
48. Mduma, N. Data Balancing Techniques for Predicting Student Dropout Using Machine Learning. *Data* **2023**, *8*, 49. [CrossRef]
49. Ujkani, B.; Minkovska, D.; Stoyanova, L. Application of Logistic Regression Technique for Predicting Student Dropout. In Proceedings of the 2022 XXXI International Scientific Conference Electronics (ET), Sozopol, Bulgaria, 13–15 September 2022; pp. 1–4.
50. Zhang, Y.; Zhang, Q.; Liu, X. Dropout Predictions of Ideological and Political MOOC Learners Based on Big Data. In Proceedings of the WHICEB 2020 Proceedings, Wuhan, China, 5 July 2020.
51. Xing, W.; Du, D. Dropout Prediction in MOOCs: Using Deep Learning for Personalized Intervention. *J. Educ. Comput. Res.* **2019**, *57*, 547–570. [CrossRef]
52. Wang, W.; Yu, H.; Mia, C. Deep Model for Dropout Prediction in MOOCs. In Proceedings of the 2nd International Conference on Crowd Science and Engineering (ICCSE'17), Beijing China, 6–9 July 2017; Association for Computing Machinery: New York, NY, USA, 2017; pp. 26–32.
53. Kabathova, J.; Drlik, M. Towards Predicting Student's Dropout in University Courses Using Different Machine Learning Techniques. *Appl. Sci.* **2021**, *11*, 3130. [CrossRef]
54. El-Rashidy, M.A.; Farouk, A.; El-Fishawy, N.A.; Aslan, H.K.; Khodeir, N.A. New weighted BERT features and multi-CNN models to enhance the performance of MOOC posts classification. *Neural Comput. Appl.* **2023**, *35*, 18019–18033. [CrossRef]
55. Duru, I.; Sunar, A.S.; White, S.; Diri, B. Deep Learning for Discussion-Based Cross-Domain Performance Prediction of MOOC Learners Grouped by Language on FutureLearn. *Arab. J. Sci. Eng.* **2021**, *46*, 3613–3629. [CrossRef] [PubMed]
56. Altaf, S.; Asad, R.; Ahmad, S.; Ahmed, I.; Abdollahian, M.; Zaindin, M. A Hybrid Framework of Deep Learning Techniques to Predict Online Performance of Learners during COVID-19 Pandemic. *Sustainability* **2023**, *15*, 11731. [CrossRef]
57. Alghamdi, A. Evaluating Factors Influencing Learner Satisfaction in Massive Open Online Course Selection: A Data-Driven Approach Using Machine Learning. *Arab. J. Sci. Eng.* **2024**. [CrossRef]
58. Mandal, L.; Kar, A. Feature Engineering for Predicting Student Dropout in Massive Open Online Courses. *Tuijin Jishu/J. Propuls. Technol.* **2024**, *45*, 1–9.
59. Blundo, C.; Loia, V.; Orciuoli, F. A Time-Aware Approach for MOOC Dropout Prediction Based on Rule Induction and Sequential Three-Way Decisions. *IEEE Access* **2023**, *11*, 113189–113198. [CrossRef]
60. Psathas, G.; Chatzidaki, T.K.; Demetriadis, S.N. Predictive Modeling of Student Dropout in MOOCs and Self-Regulated Learning. *Computers* **2023**, *12*, 194. [CrossRef]
61. Cheng, Y.; Pereira Nunes, B.; Manrique, R. Not Another Hardcoded Solution to the Student Dropout Prediction Problem: A Novel Approach Using Genetic Algorithms for Feature Selection. In *Intelligent Tutoring Systems. ITS 2022*; Crossley, S., Popescu, E., Eds.; Lecture Notes in Computer Science; Springer: Cham, Switzerland, 2020; Volume 13284.
62. Poudyal, S.; Mohammadi-Aragh, M.J.; Ball, J.E. Hybrid Feature Extraction Model to Categorize Student Attention Pattern and Its Relationship with Learning. *Electronics* **2022**, *11*, 1476. [CrossRef]
63. Dass, S.; Gary, K.; Cunningham, J. Predicting Student Dropout in Self-Paced MOOC Course Using Random Forest Model. *Information* **2021**, *12*, 476. [CrossRef]
64. Jin, C. MOOC student dropout prediction model based on learning behaviour features and parameter optimization. *Interact. Learn. Environ.* **2020**, *31*, 714–732. [CrossRef]
65. Mohamad, N.; Ahmad, N.B.; Jawawi, D.N.A.; Hashim, S.Z.M. Feature Engineering for Predicting MOOC Performance. In *IOP Conference Series: Materials Science and Engineering*; IOP Publishing: Bristol, UK, 2020.
66. Qiu, L.; Liu, Y.; Liu, Y. An Integrated Framework with Feature Selection for Dropout Prediction in Massive Open Online Courses. *IEEE Access* **2018**, *6*, 71474–71484. [CrossRef]

67. Mohamed Nafuri, A.F.; Sani, N.S.; Zainudin, N.F.A.; Rahman, A.H.A.; Aliff, M. Clustering Analysis for Classifying Student Academic Performance in Higher Education. *Appl. Sci.* **2022**, *12*, 9467. [CrossRef]
68. Yağcı, M. Educational data mining: Prediction of students' academic performance using machine learning algorithms. *Smart Learn. Environ.* **2022**, *9*, 11. [CrossRef]
69. Xia, X.; Qi, W. Driving STEM learning effectiveness: Dropout prediction and intervention in MOOCs based on one novel behavioural data analysis approach. *Humanit. Soc. Sci. Commun.* **2024**, *11*, 430. [CrossRef]
70. Xia, X.; Qi, W. Dropout prediction and decision feedback supported by multi temporal sequences of learning behaviour in MOOCs. *Int. J. Educ. Technol. High. Educ.* **2023**, *20*, 32. [CrossRef]
71. Xu, C.; Zhu, G.; Ye, J.; Shu, J. Educational Data Mining: Dropout Prediction in XuetangX MOOCs. *Neural Process. Lett.* **2022**, *54*, 2885–2900. [CrossRef]
72. Zhu, X.; Ye, Y.; Zhao, L.; Shen, C. MOOC Behavior Analysis and Academic Performance Prediction Based on Entropy. *Sensors* **2021**, *21*, 6629. [CrossRef] [PubMed]
73. Yin, S.; Lei, L.; Wang, H.; Chen, W. Power of Attention in MOOC Dropout Prediction. *IEEE Access* **2020**, *8*, 202993–203002. [CrossRef]
74. Mulyani, E.; Hidayah, I.; Fauziati, S. Dropout Prediction Optimization through SMOTE and Ensemble Learning. In Proceedings of the 2019 International Seminar on Research of Information Technology and Intelligent Systems (ISRITI), Yogyakarta, Indonesia, 5–6 December 2019; IEEE: New York, NY, USA, 2019.
75. Liao, J.; Tang, J.; Zhao, X. Course Drop-out Prediction on MOOC Platform via Clustering and Tensor Completion. *Tsinghua Sci. Technol.* **2019**, *24*, 412–422. [CrossRef]
76. Basnet, R.B.; Johnson, C.; Doleck, T. Dropout prediction in Moocs using deep learning and machine learning. *Educ. Inf. Technol.* **2022**, *27*, 11499–11513. [CrossRef]
77. Sraidi, S.; Smaili, E.M.; Azzouzi, S.; Charaf, M.E.H. A Neural Network-Based System to Predict Early MOOC Dropout. *Int. J. Eng. Pedagog. (iJEP)* **2022**, *12*, 86–101. [CrossRef]
78. Talebi, K.; Torabi, Z.; Daneshpour, N. Ensemble models based on CNN and LSTM for dropout prediction in MOOC. *Expert Syst. Appl.* **2023**, *235*, 121187. [CrossRef]
79. Liu, H.; Chen, X.; Zhao, F. Learning behaviour feature fused deep learning network model for MOOC dropout prediction. *Educ. Inf. Technol.* **2024**, *29*, 3257–3278. [CrossRef]
80. Patel, K.K.; Amin, K. Predictive modeling of dropout in MOOCs using machine learning techniques. *Sci. Temper* **2024**, *15*, 2199–2206. [CrossRef]
81. Zhang, X.; Wang, X.; Zhao, J.; Zhang, B.; Zhang, F. IC-BTCN: A Deep Learning Model for Dropout Prediction of MOOCs Students. *IEEE Trans. Educ.* **2024**, *67*, 974–982. [CrossRef]
82. Pan, F.; Zhang, H.; Li, X.; Zhang, M.; Ji, Y. Achieving optimal trade-off for student dropout prediction with multi-objective reinforcement learning. *PeerJ Comput. Sci.* **2024**, *10*, e2034. [CrossRef] [PubMed]
83. Doss, A.N.; Krishnan, R.; Karuppasamy, A.D.; Sam, B. Learning Analytics Model for Predictive Analysis of Learners Behaviour for an Indigenous MOOC Platform (Tadakhul System) in Oman. *Int. J. Inf. Educ. Technol.* **2024**, *14*, 961–967.
84. Smaili, E.M.; Daoudi, M.; Oumaira, I.; Azzouzi, S.; Charaf, M.E.H. Towards an Adaptive Learning Model using Optimal Learning Paths to Prevent MOOC Dropout. *Int. J. Eng. Pedagog. (iJEP)* **2023**, *13*, 128–144. [CrossRef]
85. Yujiao, Z.; Ling Weay, A.; Shaomin, S.; Palaniappan, S. Dropout Prediction Model for College Students in MOOCs Based on Weighted Multi-feature and SVM. *J. Inform. Web Eng.* **2023**, *2*, 29–42. [CrossRef]
86. Kumar, G.; Singh, A.; Sharma, A. Ensemble Deep Learning Network Model for Dropout Prediction in MOOCs. *Int. J. Electr. Comput. Eng. Syst.* **2023**, *14*, 2. [CrossRef]
87. Zhang, T.; Liu, H.; Tao, J.; Wang, Y.; Yu, M.; Chen, H.; Yu, G. Enhancing Dropout Prediction in Distributed Educational Data Using Learning Pattern Awareness: A Federated Learning Approach. *Mathematics* **2023**, *11*, 4977. [CrossRef]
88. Shou, Z.; Chen, P.; Wen, H.; Liu, J.; Zhang, H. MOOC Dropout Prediction Based on Multidimensional Time-Series Data. *Math. Probl. Eng.* **2022**, *2022*, 2213292. [CrossRef]
89. Anjali, C.A.; Bai, V.R. An Early Prediction of Dropouts for At-risk Scholars in MOOCs using Deep Learning. In Proceedings of the 2022 International Conference on Computing, Communication, Security and Intelligent Systems (IC3SIS), Kochi, India, 23–25 June 2022; pp. 1–6.
90. Mubarak, A.A.; Cao, H.; Hezam, I.M. Deep analytic model for student dropout prediction in massive open online courses. *Comput. Electr. Eng.* **2021**, *93*, 107271. [CrossRef]
91. Fu, Q.; Gao, Z.; Zhou, J.; Zheng, Y. CLSA: A novel deep learning model for MOOC dropout prediction. *Comput. Electr. Eng.* **2021**, *94*, 107315. [CrossRef]
92. Jin, C. Dropout prediction model in MOOC based on clickstream data and student sample weight. *Soft Comput.* **2021**, *25*, 8971–8988. [CrossRef]

93. Panagiotakopoulos, T.; Kotsiantis, S.; Kostopoulos, G.; Iatrellis, O.; Kameas, A. Early Dropout Prediction in MOOCs through Supervised Learning and Hyperparameter Optimization. *Electronics* **2021**, *10*, 1701. [CrossRef]
94. Zheng, Y.; Gao, Z.; Wang, Y.; Fu, Q. MOOC Dropout Prediction Using FWTS-CNN Model Based on Fused Feature Weighting and Time Series. *IEEE Access* **2020**, *8*, 225324–225335. [CrossRef]
95. Qiu, L.; Liu, Y.; Hu, Q.; Liu, Y. Student dropout prediction in massive open online courses by convolutional neural networks. *Soft Comput.* **2019**, *23*, 10287–10301. [CrossRef]
96. Sun, D.; Mao, Y.; Du, J.; Xu, P.; Zheng, Q.; Sun, H. Deep Learning for Dropout Prediction in MOOCs. In Proceedings of the 2019 Eighth International Conference on Educational Innovation through Technology (EITT), Biloxi, MS, USA, 27–31 October 2019; pp. 87–90.
97. Nie, H.; Wen, Y.; Cao, D.; Liang, B. MOOC Dropout Prediction Using Learning Process Model and LightGBM Algorithm. In *Computer Supported Cooperative Work and Social Computing. Chinese CSCW 2023*; Sun, Y., Lu, T., Wang, T., Fan, H., Liu, D., Du, B., Eds.; Communications in Computer and Information Science; Springer: Singapore, 2024; Volume 2012.
98. El Aouifi, H.; El Hajji, M.; Es-Saady, Y. A hybrid approach for early-identification of at-risk dropout students using LSTM-DNN networks. *Educ. Inf. Technol.* **2024**, *29*, 18839–18857. [CrossRef]
99. Jatain, D.; Niranjanamurthy, M.; Dayananda, P. A Hybrid Bio-inspired Fuzzy Feature Selection Approach for Opinion Mining of Learner Comments. *SN Comput. Sci.* **2024**, *5*, 135. [CrossRef]
100. Zhou, Y.; Niu, K.; Lv, H.; Lu, G.; Pan, Y. CGDC-LSTM: A novel hybrid neural network model for MOOC dropout prediction. In Proceedings of the 2023 International Joint Conference on Neural Networks (IJCNN), Gold Coast, Australia, 18–23 June 2023; pp. 1–8.
101. Chen, X.; Liu, H.; Zhao, F. Prediction of MOOCs Dropout Based on IQPSO-PLSTM Model. In Proceedings of the 2023 8th International Conference on Mathematics and Artificial Intelligence (ICMAI '23), Chongqing, China, 7–9 April 2023; Association for Computing Machinery: New York, NY, USA, 2023; pp. 7–12.
102. Zakaria, A.L.J.; Anas, B.; Oucamah, C.M.M. Intelligent System for Personalised Interventions and Early Drop-out Prediction in MOOCs. *Int. J. Adv. Comput. Sci. Appl. (IJACSA)* **2022**, *13*, 700–710. [CrossRef]
103. Nithya, S.; Umarani, S. MOOC Dropout Prediction using FIAR-ANN Model based on Learner Behavioural Features. *Int. J. Adv. Comput. Sci. Appl. (IJACSA)* **2022**, *13*, 607–617.
104. Liu, H.; Zhang, W. A Hybrid Deep Learning Model for MOOCs Dropout Prediction. In Proceedings of the 2022 4th International Conference on Computer Science and Technologies in Education (CSTE), Xi'an, China, 6–8 May 2022; pp. 178–183.
105. Zhang, Y.; Chang, L.; Liu, T. MooCs dropout prediction based hybrid deep neural network. In Proceedings of the International Conference on Cyber-Enabled Distributed Computing and Knowledge Discovery (CyberC), Chongqing, China, 29–30 October 2020.
106. Chen, J.; Feng, J.; Sun, X.; Wu, N.; Yang, Z.; Chen, S. MOOC Dropout Prediction Using a Hybrid Algorithm Based on Decision Tree and Extreme Learning Machine. *Math. Probl. Eng.* **2019**, *2019*, 8404653. [CrossRef]
107. Al-Zawqari, A.; Peumans, D.; Vandersteen, G. A flexible feature selection approach for predicting students' academic performance in online courses. *Comput. Educ. Artif. Intell.* **2022**, *3*, 100103. [CrossRef]
108. El-Sabagh, H.A. Adaptive e-learning environment based on learning styles and its impact on development students' engagement. *Int. J. Educ. Technol. High. Educ.* **2021**, *18*, 53. [CrossRef]
109. Smaili, E.M.; Khoudda, C.; Sraidi, S.; Charaf, M.E.H. An Innovative Approach to Prevent Learners' Dropout from MOOCs using Optimal Personalized Learning Paths: An Online Learning Case Study. *Stat. Optim. Inf. Comput.* **2022**, *10*, 45–58. [CrossRef]
110. Findeisen, S.; Brodsky, A.; Michaelis, C.; Schimmelpenningh, B.; Seifried, J. Dropout intention: A valid predictor of actual dropout? *Empir. Res. Vocat. Educ. Train.* **2024**, *16*, 10. [CrossRef]
111. Imran, A.S.; Dalipi, F.; Kastrati, Z. Predicting Student Dropout in a MOOC: An Evaluation of a Deep Neural Network Model. In Proceedings of the 2019 5th International Conference on Computing and Artificial Intelligence (ICCAI '19), Bali, Indonesia, 19–22 April 2019; Association for Computing Machinery: New York, NY, USA, 2019; pp. 190–195.
112. Rahimi, A.R. A tri-phenomenon perspective to mitigate MOOCs' high dropout rates: The role of technical, pedagogical, and contextual factors on language learners' L2 motivational selves, and learning approaches to MOOC. *Smart Learn. Environ.* **2024**, *11*, 11. [CrossRef]
113. Matz, S.C.; Bukow, C.S.; Peters, H.; Deacons, C.; Dinu, A.; Stachl, C. Using machine learning to predict student retention from socio-demographic characteristics and app-based engagement metrics. *Sci. Rep.* **2023**, *13*, 5705.
114. Ahmed, E. Student Performance Prediction Using Machine Learning Algorithms. *Appl. Comput. Intell. Soft Comput.* **2024**, *2024*, 4067721. [CrossRef]
115. Mbunge, E.; Batani, J.; Mafumbate, R.; Gurajena, C.; Fashoto, S.; Rugube, T.; Akinnuwesi, B.; Metfula, A. Predicting Student Dropout in Massive Open Online Courses Using Deep Learning Models—A Systematic Review. In *Cybernetics Perspectives in Systems. CSOC 2022*; Silhavy, R., Ed.; Lecture Notes in Networks and Systems; Springer: Cham, Switzerland, 2022; Volume 503.
116. Li, J.; Xue, E. Dynamic Interaction between Student Learning Behaviour and Learning Environment: Meta-Analysis of Student Engagement and Its Influencing Factors. *Behav. Sci.* **2023**, *13*, 59. [CrossRef] [PubMed]

117. Potharlanka, J.L.; Nirupama Bhat, M. Feature importance feedback with Deep Q process in ensemble-based metaheuristic feature selection algorithms. *Sci. Rep.* **2024**, *14*, 2923. [CrossRef] [PubMed]
118. Goran, R.; Jovanovic, L.; Bacanin, N.; Stankovic, M.; Simic, V.; Antonijevic, M.; Zivkovic, M. Identifying and Understanding Student Dropouts Using Metaheuristic Optimised Classifiers and Explainable Artificial Intelligence Techniques. *IEEE Access* **2024**, *12*, 122377–122400. [CrossRef]

Multimodal Technologies and Interaction

Review

Innovative and Interactive Technologies in Creative Product Design Education: A Review

Ioanna Nazlidou, Nikolaos Efkolidis, Konstantinos Kakoulis and Panagiotis Kyratsis *

Department of Product and Systems Design Engineering, University of Western Macedonia, GR50100 Kila Kozani, Greece; dide00003@uowm.gr (I.N.); nefkolidis@uowm.gr (N.E.); kkakoulis@uowm.gr (K.K.)
* Correspondence: pkyratsis@uowm.gr

Abstract: When discussing the Education 4.0 concept and the role of technology-based learning systems along with creativity, it is interesting to explore how these are reflected as educational innovations in the case of design education. This study aims to provide an overview of interactive technologies used in product design education and examine their integration into the learning process. A literature search was conducted, analyzing scientific papers to review relevant articles. The findings highlight several categories of technologies utilized in design education, including virtual and augmented reality, robotics, interactive embedded systems, immersive technologies, and computational intelligence systems. These technologies are primarily integrated as supportive tools throughout different stages of the design process within learning environments. This study suggests that integrating such technologies alongside pedagogical methods positively impacts education, offering numerous opportunities for further research and innovation. In conclusion, this review contributes to ongoing research in technological advancements and innovations in design education, offering insights into the diverse applications of interactive technologies in enhancing learning environments.

Keywords: design education; interactive technologies; learning methods; product design; design process; Education 4.0

1. Introduction

In a continuously changing and challenging world, higher education institutions (HEIs) need to reimagine the current pedagogical approaches, in order to embrace the demands for new graduates with interdisciplinary skills. Today's education should adopt flexible learning methods that will allow students to experience education in new ways. At the same time, the ever-growing use of information and communication technologies on an educational scope has been modifying the traditional classroom scene. This brings up the need to rethink the paradigms of enhancing learning through technology-driven methodologies [1]. Emerging technologies in educational environments can improve the teaching and the learning process. It is a way to motivate learners and stimulate their interest to participate in the learning materials [2]. Specific digital technologies shape the way teaching and learning knowledge and skills activities are delivered and contribute to the transformation of the educational process i.e., immersive technologies, big data analytics, cloud computing, machine learning, Internet of Things (IoT), sensing and actuation technologies, and 3D printing [3].

Technology tools that promote innovative teaching, learning approaches and value-added student experiences are all part of the concept of Higher Education 4.0 [4]. The adaptation and implementation of current and emerging technologies combined with innovative pedagogical procedures and best practices are known as Education 4.0. Miranda et al. [5] defined Education 4.0 as "The current period in which higher education institutions apply new learning methods, innovative didactic and management tools, and intelligent and sustainable infrastructures complemented by emerging technologies that improve knowledge generation and information transfer processes".

In a more recent work, Miranda et al. [6] propose four components to shape the model of Education 4.0: (a) the developing of desirable competencies in students, (b) the incorporation of new learning methods, (c) the implementation of current and emerging Information and Communication Technologies (ICTs) and (d) the adaptation of innovative infrastructure. Their work suggests the redesign of traditional learning methods, with strategies, emerging technologies and activities that will allow access to all students in a variety of training programs. These programs are created based on student-centered or learner-centered models that require students to actively participate in the teaching learning processes. In this case, innovative learning methods are considered the use of emerging technologies along with pedagogical approaches, such as challenge-based learning, problem-based learning, learning-by-doing and gamification-based learning. In the same direction, according to Ramírez-Montoya et al., the Education 4.0 concept, seeks "best practices" of active learning, relying primarily on technological components for its implementation [7]. In addition, their proposed framework of five core components of Education 4.0 enables the designing of innovative pedagogical procedures to carry out best practices and dynamics, taking into account the appropriate technologies and infrastructure technologies. A main question that concerns the current paper is how this new way of thinking that reforms current pedagogies is reflected in the case of design education.

Design refers to the process of envisioning and creating ideas that form practical and attractive proposals; at the same time, design is the connection between creativity and innovation [8]. Design training requires the cultivation of a variety of thinking skills that promote creative thinking. According to Frascara [9] designers require to speak different disciplinary languages as they work on a multidimensional field that demands numerous skills. Recognizing the need for interdisciplinarity, design education builds on expanded knowledge, application in practice, and reflective learning [10]. Creativity is also a very essential component for design education [11]. Creativity must be cultivated from teachers to students as a guide in the design process [12].

Creativity in design education can be considered as a link point to the Education 4.0 concept. Creativity is the foundation of Education 4.0. It emphasizes the need to prepare students to take on challenges. On the other hand, [13] places design creativity and technology fluency at the forefront of Industry 4.0, due to the ever-growing complexity of the production lines. Therefore, technology is recognized as another key component of design education. Over the last decades, technological advancements such as Computer-Aided Design (CAD) software, pen computers and 3D printers, have changed the educational landscape in the design area. Today, the necessity for new competencies in graduates leads to the demand for skills in new design areas and the integration of new technological tools. As Norman [14] pointed out, speaking about industrial design, the design issues are far more complex and challenging and need more than just deep knowledge of forms, materials, sketching, drawing, and rendering skills. The designer requires a deep understanding of human cognition and emotion, sensory and motor systems, and sufficient knowledge of the scientific method, and experimental design. New design skills are linked with science, engineering, mathematics and are essential in design fields such as interaction and experience. Highlighting all the above characteristics as important aspects of design education, how can we rethink a new educational model that incorporates all the values of the design philosophy with the new perspective of innovative pedagogical procedures?

Design education has started to correspond to these new tech-challenges by promoting new pedagogies that embrace interactivity through technology-driven methodologies (T&L—teaching and learning). Interactivity is important in education, as it keep students actively involved in their learning process and increases their engagement to the material content. This study attempts to analyze whether the uses of innovative and interactive technologies in design education align with the expectations of Education 4.0.

For this reason, this paper presents a literature review-based discussion aimed at identifying innovative technology tools used in educational settings, specifically within the broad field of creative design education. More specifically, the research intends to examine how these tools are integrated into the educational process and the possible learning strategies or pedagogical approaches that may be employed for these purposes. The main research questions investigated are as follows:

- [Q1] What kind of innovative and interactive technology tools are being used in creative design education?
- [Q2] How are these technologies integrated into the educational process?
- [Q3] Is there any connection between technology tools and pedagogical methods?
- [Q4] How do these tools and methods affect the learning performance?

The types of technologies analyzed in this research are characterized by the element of interaction between the user and the technology—for example, technologies that support programming to perform specific tasks or technologies that contribute to the creation of interactive products, such as robotics, immersive technologies, and embedded systems.

The structure of this paper is organized as follows: Section 2 analyzes the structure of the methodology used for this review. Section 3 presents the research results, including the categorization of the identified technology types and a list of reviewed papers, followed by an analysis based on specific learning strategies. Section 4 summarizes this work and answers the defined research questions. Section 5 refers to the limitations of this study. Section 6 points out potential research gaps and suggests directions for future research.

2. Materials and Methods

The research method for performing the review was based on the examination of scientific papers indexed in Scopus and Google Scholar, including both academic journals and conferences papers, published in the last ten years. Scopus and Google Scholar databases were used during the current survey based on the University of Western Macedonia quality system procedures that calculate Key Performance Indicators from these databases. The purpose was to cover a wide range of topics regarding the identification of different technologies used in the learning process of product design-related courses. The PRISMA 2020 framework [15] guided the systematic process of literature identification and screening. An overview of the literature search strategy is shown in Figure 1.

2.1. Search Strategy and Data Collection

Because of the direct link of product design education with design-related courses, the intention of the research aimed to form a wider framework of cases concerning the utilization of technological tools in educational environments related to design, in order then to see how these are ultimately applied to product design. By choosing to restrict the search to only references from technological applications around product design education, it would create a very limited field of research, which would not respond to the objectives of the study that required a broader scope of research topics.

The relevant literature was acquired from Scopus and Google Scholar online databases and was performed over the months of February and March of 2024. The search concerned publications within the time span of 2013 to 2023, as the year 2024 was still ongoing. The search for papers was structured into two phases, using different sets of keywords. First, various keywords related to different technology terms were combined with "design education" and "design studies" (e.g., "innovative technologies in design education", "interactive technologies in design studies", "immersive technologies in design education"). This initial search identified the main types of technologies commonly reported in the literature and related to various types of technologies that involved in the creation of interactive applications. Specifically, "virtual reality", "augmented reality", "mixed reality", "extended reality", "spatial augmented reality", "holograms", robotics", "artificial intelligence", "machine learning", "Internet of things", "cloud computing", and "interactive interfaces". Then these terms were combined with "product design education", OR "industrial design education", OR "architectural design education", OR "engineering design education". Generally, the combination of keywords for the initial search aimed to identify publications covering a wide range of research papers related to design education and technologies involving interactive applications. During the second search, we combined terms of different technology types we identified at the previous stage with more specific design fields in education. The primary focus of the review was on product/industrial design-related education. Product design can be considered the subject of training in engineering design schools. Thus, we expanded the field of research to design fields covering cases from architectural and mechanical engineering education, when they explored design-related projects within the context of product/industrial design.

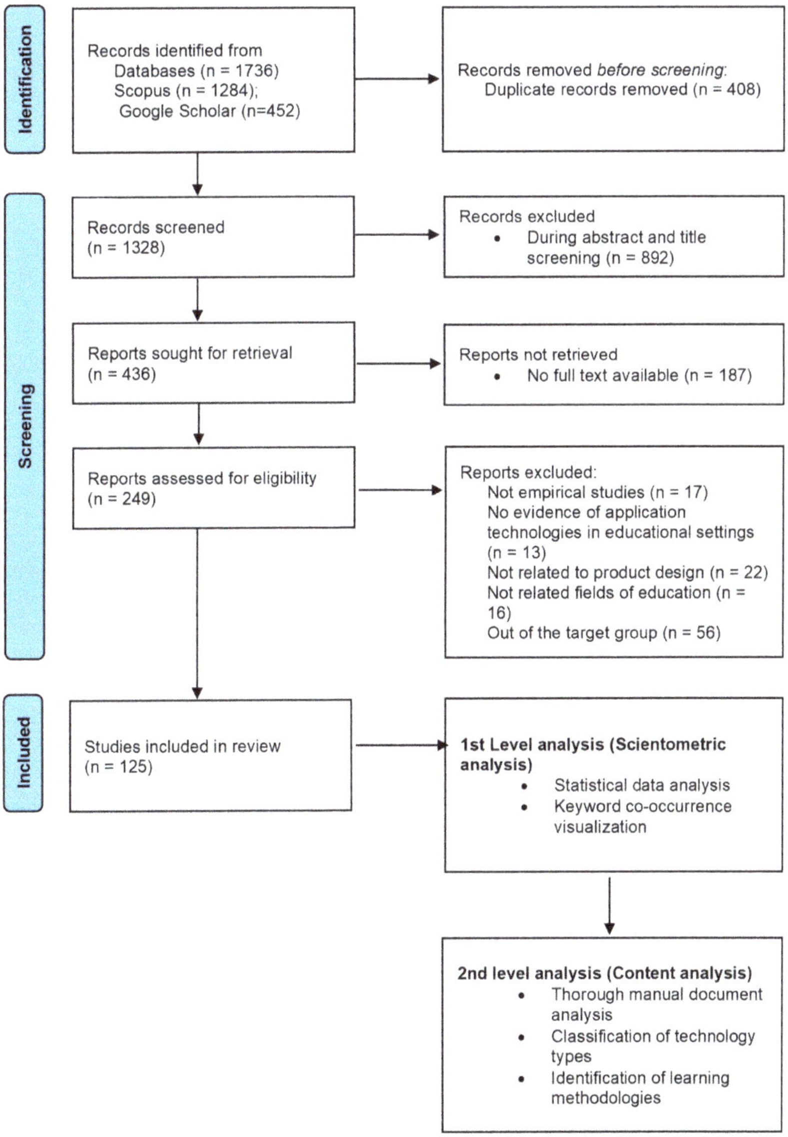

Figure 1. Overview of the research process guided by the PRISMA 2020 framework.

The initial database search returned 1736 articles, with 1284 sourced from Scopus and 452 from Google Scholar. When removing duplicates, 1328 documents were assessed for eligibility. The filtering process lasted five months from April 2024 to August 2024. First, the articles were screened based on the inclusion/exclusion criteria as presented in Table 1, by reading their titles and abstracts. Subsequently, three authors performed an in-depth analysis of the full text of each report against additional criteria, to uncover any discussions that were not reflected in the abstract. The presented review involves the application of design as an educational subject, whether taught in theoretical contexts or through studio-based practice. So, based on that, we selected only papers that involved the implementation of technologies in educational environments in three situations—when they concern their involvement in the development of educational applications, when technologies are used as part of a course design plan or when they concern research conducted in educational environments. The review also focused only on cases of adult education or student training in higher education institutions (HEIs). At this stage, a significant number of studies concerning applications in school educational environments at all grades were excluded. Finally, during the manual screening process, several more cases that did not meet the above criteria were excluded. In the end, we came up with 125 papers that were considered to cover more than the criteria set as the basis of our research.

Table 1. Inclusion and exclusion criteria for data selection.

Criteria	Inclusion	Exclusion
Time span of investigation	Between 2013–2023	Before 2013 and after 2023
Language	English	Not English
Access	Full text	Restricted access, limited availability, technical constrains
Type of documents	Journal article, conference paper	Poster, editorial, books
Research methodology	Empirical study	Extended abstract, review, theoretical study
General subject area	Engineering	Not related subject areas
Reference to specific technological applications (addressing RQ1)	Reported	Not reported
Field of design education	Product/Industrial, architecture, mechanical	Other not related fields
Research subject	Related to product design education	Unrelated subjects
Purpose of research	Educational application, course design plans or research regarding education	Applications that were not part of an educational context
Target group	Adults training and student education in higher education institutions (HEIs)	All other grades of education

2.2. 1st Level Analysis

Next, all references were organized firstly based on general information (year, title, authors, paper type) and secondly based on more specific categories of information (technology type, design field of application, objective, how the technology is used during the educational process, whether the paper uses pedagogical method to their case study, if it includes evaluation research at the end). Figure 2 presents some descriptive statistics of the total material review analysis, i.e., the distribution of references per year, the types of the selected articles, the research as per subject of studies and the design fields of application. To further analyze the extensive bibliometric data and gain deeper insights into potential connections between them, a scientometric analysis was conducted. Scientometric analysis involves creating virtual bibliometric networks to explore significant patterns and relationships among academic articles using scientometric indicators [16,17]. VOSviewer (v.1.6.20, Leiden University, Leiden, The Netherlands) was employed as a software tool to generate and visualize the co-occurrence of keywords extracted from the cited publications [18]. This stage constitutes a preliminary analysis aimed at identifying and visualizing the relative proximity of subject areas within the reviewed literature. The analysis conducted in VOSviewer resulted in a total of 998 keywords, with a minimum occurrence set to three to highlight more relevant keywords. Approximately 78 keywords were selected, and their co-occurrence network is depicted in Figure 3. The varying sizes of keywords indicate their frequency of occurrence, while different colors highlight distinct research themes. The findings suggest a concentration of research in areas such as "immersive technologies", "robotics", "artificial intelligence", "Internet of Things", and "interactivity terms" alongside their respective technologies. Keyword connections illustrate the interrelatedness of publications and their association with various aspects of design education.

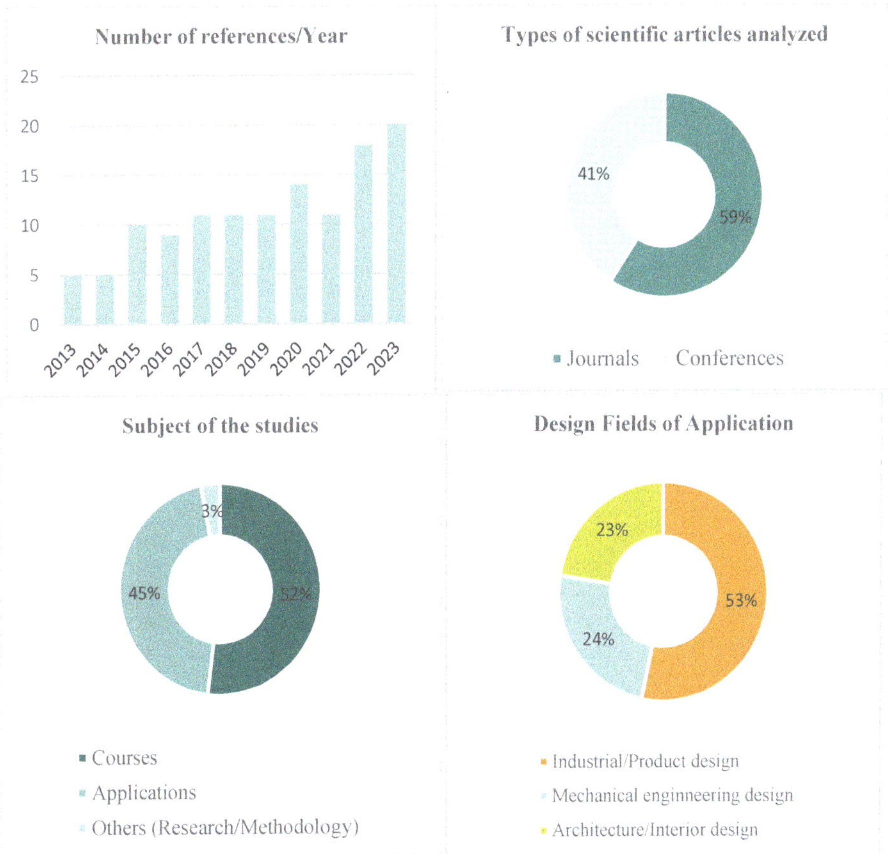

Figure 2. Descriptive analyses of the references used.

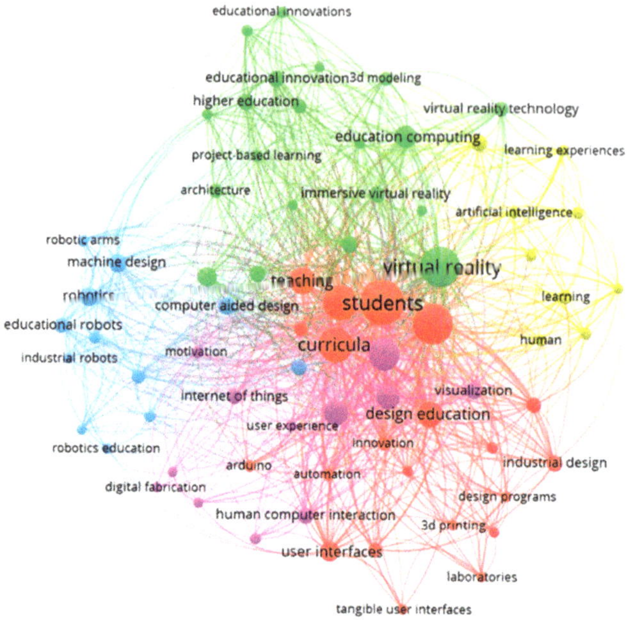

Figure 3. Network visualization of keyword co-occurrence.

2.3. 2nd Level Analysis

In the final stage of this methodology, content analysis is employed to thoroughly explore and categorize the reviewed literature. This analysis involves both quantitative and qualitative methods to process and categorize the data, providing deeper insights into the research findings [19]. The content analysis was conducted manually by rigorously reading each selected paper in order to create a more oriented research framework in accordance with the questions posed at the beginning of the paper. The first research question and the main goal of this review was to identify the technologies types used in product design-related educational environments that belong to the spectrum of interactive technologies. The technologies were categorized based on their common characteristics and their frequency of occurrence into five broader clusters. The first category includes the types of immersive technologies that appeared more often in the studies reviewed, virtual and augmented reality. The second category involved all technology types around robotics applications. Third category included all the supportive technology systems embedded in physical objects that are used in order to create interactive applications. Fourth category included all the other types of immersive technologies that are used more rarely in educational settings. And the final category involved computational systems based on several branches of artificial intelligence technologies.

Then for each cluster, a second categorization was made regarding the second research question and the way these technologies are used over the educational process. From this stage analysis emerged two general categorizations: the cases where technologies are used as support mechanisms in several aspects of educational activities and when they are involved in different stages of the design process, during studio-based practice. The review describes in detail all the ways related to the integration of technologies during education. In addition, it was considered appropriate to analyze further the second category, as there was a need to identify the exact stage of the design process that technologies were being used.

Finally, as the coexistence of pedagogical approaches along with technological tools in educational settings was another aspect of this review, regarding the third research question, all studies where analyzed from a pedagogical perspective to examine if and in how many cases the adoption of technology tools is being implemented in conjunction with specific learning methods.

3. Results

According to the review method described above, the identified technology tools were clustered into five categories: (a) virtual and augmented reality, (b) robotics, (c) interactive embedded systems, (d) other types of immersive technologies and (e) computational intelligence systems. These five categories cover a wide range of interactive technology types used in design educational settings that have been mostly addressed in literature and form the core structure of this research. As is depicted in Figure 4, immersive technologies, virtual and augmented reality are the technologies that concern the subject of study in most of the research works reviewed. However, robotics and interactive embedded systems follow with a significant percentage difference from the first category. Then there are other types of immersive technologies that are used more rarely according to the literature and on the last category, technologies based on computational intelligence systems can be found. The temporal distribution graphic stresses the distribution of references per year and per category. It shows that generally immersive technologies and robotics can be found in almost every year of the time span investigated, while papers referring to embedded technologies and computational intelligence systems mainly concern the last years.

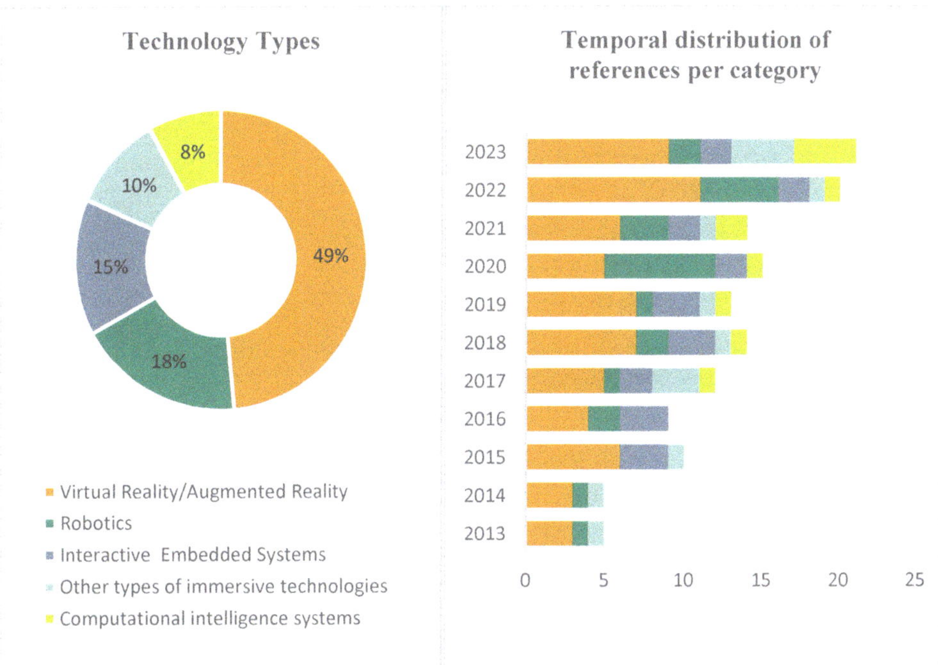

Figure 4. Classification of technology types and temporal distribution of references analyzed per year and category.

The following paragraphs present a description of the technologies and an analysis of the reviewed papers. Each technology category is followed by a graphic and a table that categorize the reviewed studies based on the way technologies are integrated into the educational process.

3.1. Technologies and Their Uses in Learning Environments

3.1.1. Virtual Reality (VR)/Augmented Reality (AR)

Virtual and augmented reality are the interactive technologies that appear most often in the studies reviewed. They belong to the kind of immersive technologies that become widely used in educational settings and work as supports tools in many learning environments [19]. Through virtual reality, a three-dimensional computer-generated environment is created, where the user can explore and interact with it, by manipulating objects or performing various actions [20]. On the other hand, augmented reality is an intermediate tool that integrates computer-generated data into real space, combining real and virtual objects together in real time [21,22]. In the field of design education, both VR and AR can enhance the teaching of design topics by enabling the students to visualize and interact with their designs in a more intuitive way.

A very large percentage of the studies uses VR/AR technologies as an integral part of the design process and during its various stages, when it is implemented in the context of studio-based educational practice. Neves and Duarte [23] examine the virtual reality technology and its potential as an innovative tool in Basic Design education. In the described course named "3D Design Lab", students have the opportunity to create a new, intangible design element, such as immersion in virtual realities. The study shows that VR can affect positively the creative process during the learning experience, enhancing the students' learning outcome. Another research [24] explores the use of virtual reality in the early stages of the design process, as an ideation and inspiration tool. In this study, they add a third dimension (i.e., depth) to the traditional 2D mood boards compositions and create a three-dimensional virtual mood board. This leads to a highly immersive and interactive experience for the designer, activating his interest and inspiration that helps to make style related decisions.

Continuing in the early design stages, Shih et al. [25] introduce VR as a 3D drawing tool during the sketching phase of the design process. Their case study focuses on industrial design education, where the designer uses hand-drawn forms to communicate his ideas with customers or for self-viewing. The research results show that the virtual reality drawing software Gravity Sketch™ can be an effective tool to increase students' creativity and completion. In line with this previous work, Joundi et al. [26] present research in a product design course that was carried out on Master level students, and investigates the effect of using VR as a sketch-based 3D modeling tool in the process of product styling. The results indicate that although the VR sketch tool (in this case Gravity Sketch™) was difficult to use as a form finding tool, students saw a lot of potential in the tool for visualizing their shape. VR can be a helpful tool in mediating from a shape idea towards the construction of that idea. In a more recent work, Rodríguez-Parada et al. [27] also use Gravity Sketch™ software for conceptual design in a studio-based course. In addition, they use it as a tool for functional evaluation tests of products within an immersive VR environment. This allows students to interact with their designs in 3D space and make early decisions that can enhance various aspects of their products.

On the design visualization stage, Moural et al. [28] explore the use of virtual immersive environments for visualization of architectural spaces. Their system provides the possibility of seeing and interacting with architectural models at real scale, giving students the chance to test and evaluate their projects. On the other hand, Ayer et al. [29] explore the pedagogical value of using augmented reality technology, combined with a simulation game, with an aim to enhance building engineering and design education. EcoCampus™ is the developed application that uses an augmented reality-based simulation game that allow users to visualize possible solutions for a given design problem. In this case, augmented reality helps students to visualize virtual information, in the context of its physical space, and simulation games can help present learning content during an applied scenario.

Salah et al. [30] introduce VR technology into product manufacturing in their study. Specifically, in alignment with the demands of Industry 4.0, students learn to design a product for a reconfigurable manufacturing system (RMS) using a virtual learning factory system. Their platform also supports a "learning by doing" strategy as a pedagogical tool. in their study, introduce VR technology in product manufacturing. More specifically, in line with the concept of Industry 4.0 demands, students learn to design a product of reconfigurable manufacturing system (RMS) using a virtual learning factory system. Their platform promotes also the learning by doing strategy as a pedagogical tool. From this point of view, Vo [31] gives student a luminaire design project and explores the influence of virtual reality technology combined with additive manufacturing (i.e., 3D printing) in design creativity. According to the findings, students show a very high level of interest and engagement in the use of these technologies with a very positive impact in their creativity. Roberts et al. [32] describe several case studies, highlighting the different applications of VR tools in a studio-based practice. First, they use VR at the beginning of the design process in order to initiate the design generation outcomes. In another case, they describe the application of VR for usability testing, as a mean to better understand user experiences and validate design outcomes. Finally, through training programs, they introduce digital modelling in virtual reality, giving students the opportunity to interact and feel the designed products at full size. Ibrahim and El Shakhs [33] introduce VR as a compelling design tool in education, where students can use to better communicate their proposed designs. Also, according to their research, VR is proved to be very effective in the case of visualizing abstract conceptual ideas of the 3D space. Banerjee et al. [34] study the impact of VR technology on industrial design students' cognitive skill as an instructional medium for 3D visualization. Specifically, their paper explores the learning experience of immersive technologies by comparing usability, engagement, enjoyment and acceptability between conventional 3D model-making software and VR-based 3D model-making software. The research indicate that VR is a very effective 3D concept visualization and presentation tool and has more engagement and enjoyment and acceptability comparing to conventional software.

Of great interest are the cases that utilize VR/AR technology as tools for understanding design. Serdar et al. [35] in their work examine the potential of an augmented reality system as an educational tool in an engineering course for solid modeling. By integrating AR into the Computer Aided Design system with SolidWorks™ software, students can better understand CAD drawings, geometric features and projection views. Alatta and Freewan [36] investigate the impact of immersive virtual environment on students' spatial perception within the design process. VR gives students the opportunity to explore and check their design's validity in greater depth, allowing them to better understand and comprehend complex morphologies. On the other hand, Horvat et al. [37], combines VR technology with a constructivism-based learning method in design education, with an aim to help students with lower expertise to better comprehend specific aspects of a design i.e., identification of rotation-based mechanisms.

Following the logic of using VR as a testing tool, Rentzos et al. [38] present a VR based methodology that is focused on the analysis of the human-product interaction. Through this technology, they use an immersive simulation session that enables the testing, experimentation and evaluation of the product in its full size. In their case, VR is proved to be a very effective tool in order to measure the complexity of the designed the product on the basis of human task. An interesting approach is the case study of Grajewski et al. [39] where they apply virtual reality for training and improving the skills of students in the field of eco-design. VR technologies are used for digital test evaluation of early prototypes of the product. Students have the opportunity to explore the product before it is constructed and make the right design decisions. Another approach that uses VR for testing and evaluating the product during the design phase is presented by Srihirun et al. [40]. In that case, they propose an integration of a virtual reality system with finite element analysis using e-learning and social media in the case of a plastic bottle package design. The results show that the VR system has significantly improved students' skills and learning performance. In the same direction, Jimeno-Morenilla et al. [20] introduce a methodological proposal, which integrates virtual reality into an industrial 3D design course. In this case, VR techniques are used as a product design support tool that helps students to understand complex concepts and make more efficient and better design decisions. It is also mentioned that the pedagogical method, followed in this course, is oriented to active learning, which is based on student participation, investigation, and autonomous learning. Halabi et al. [41] implement a project-based learning methodology combined with VR technology in an introductory engineering course, in order to teach engineering design process and skills. Students use the immersive environment of CAVE^{TM} display to visualize and interact with their design ideas, giving them the chance to inspect their projects in different stages and discover possible problems that need redesigning. In more recent work, Halabi [42] uses again VR as a form of 3D prototyping technique. In this paper, VR through immersive CAVE^{TM} display is used in conjunction with PBL (Project-based Learning) in self-directed approach to design and evaluate a product. On the other hand, Mourtzis et al. [43] present an approach of intuitive visualizing and evaluating product design, using augmented reality technology. The paper introduces the development of an augmented reality application that aims to enable engineering students to envision the product on 1:1 scale, interact with it, evaluate the current design, detect possible flaws and improve the design. Huang and Chen [44] propose the use of virtual reality technology so that students can check their preliminary three-dimensional models, in order to proceed with the required changes in shape and structure. This technique can reduce the cost of sample products and improve students' sense in creating more successful products. Jenek et al. [45] also investigate the use of virtual reality as a design-decision-making tool in the education process of architectural design. They present a case study, where students were asked to design a Media Architecture structure employing virtual-design-environment tools. Students approach the concept of Media Architecture as physical interactive structure with the virtual design environment. Agirachman et al. [46] in their paper introduce immersive virtual reality technology as an affordance-base design review tool in design process. The objective of the research was to determine if this technology, as a review method, effectively revise design concepts. The results show a very significant improvement of students' work, especially in their ability to perceive the qualitative characteristics in their original design work.

Following the logic of reducing costs of physical prototyping, Akundi [47] investigates the use of a virtual reality as a rapid prototyping (RP) simulator tool. Students through this immersive virtual experience, could learn and better understand the concept of additive manufacturing process at no significant cost. Yamada et al. [48] in their work, propose an educational method for creative design, based on synthetic design thinking that can enhance a person's ability to generate new concept of innovative products that are not merely extensions of existing ones. VR technology in this case is used at the final stage of their design procedure, as an immersive tool for creating an interactive virtual prototype. Häkkilä et al. [21] present different cases of various uses of VR technology in industrial design education. Students are introduced to this new technology and learn to use it in different phases of the design process. As an empathetic design tool to simulate visual disabilities, to create low-cost simulative prototypes and for exhibiting the final design proposal in an immersive display environment.

According to Topal and Sener [22] the main design activities that augmented technology could enhance, is in prototyping stages and in presentations. Especially in presentations, students can enrich their presentations and make them substantially more informative. In another research, Topal and Şener [49] present a case study that was carried out in an educational context with industrial design postgraduate students. The project was focused on using the mobile AR-App Metaio^{TM} in a bedside alarm clock, to enhance students' presentations of interactive and multimedia products. Saorín et al. [50] in their case study present an educational cloud-based collaborative 3D modeling platform, with an aim to train students in engineering graphics of product design. VR and AR technologies were used at the end of this experience as a presentation tool of their work. López Chao et al. [51] applied project-based methodology in a course, where students can learn several pieces of software for graphic simulations, including immersive tools, leading students to use these tools in their final project presentations.

Several studies investigate the use of virtual and augmented reality technologies as an interactive learning platform, without necessarily being part of a project's design process. Zhang [52] introduces virtual and augmented reality technology to the teaching course of cultural and creative product design. A flow field visualization method is used to create a virtual platform that simulates a 3D cultural scene, in order to help students deeply explore the technical aspects of the cultural environment. The immersive experience can enhance the student's perception ability and guide them to develop and evaluate cultural creative products. Bashabsheh et al. [53] developed a computer software using VR technology for building construction courses. The platform contains 4D model (3D model and time dimension) for certain building construction phases, using VR technology to introduce immersive and non-immersive virtual reality experience for the students during learning. Kassim and Md Zubir [54] presented their application called (AREEE), augmented reality (AR) on engineering equipment for education, which includes 3D images of engineering equipment and tools designed into an AR platform that uses as a valuable learning tool for students. On another approach, Urban et al. [55] presented an augmented reality (AR) platform called "AR-supported Teaching", applicable for both Architecture, Engineering and Construction (AEC) education and as a Construction 4.0 technology. The developed application enables students to access a variety of AEC AR content available for education. Following this, Onecha et al. [56] investigated also augmented reality metaverse environments in order to improve the learning process of construction and rehabilitation in architectural studies. Through this experiment work, students could visit and examine in detail various projects under construction without time or movement limitations.

On the other hand, González-Almaguer et al. [57] applied a gamification strategy with an aim to train industrial design students on a VEP (Virtual Enterprise Planning) simulator, which replicates the processes of a car assembly plant using ERP (Enterprise Resource Planning) with elements including quality, statistics, experiment design and problem solving. For this purpose, they use VR and AR technologies to enable the students experiencing the processes and products of the Meccano^{TM}'s manufacturing plant. The same authors in more recent research, González-Almaguer et al. [58] described the academic experience of redesigning a theoretical course by applying gamification and problem-solving methodologies, facilitated through virtual and augmented reality technologies. More specifically, they created a board game called Problem-Solving Race (PSR) that manage students to be more motivated and engaged to the learning process. From this point of view, Gill et al. [59] developed and evaluated a theoretical design course in an immersive virtual reality (iVR) environment, based on the theory of microlearning, embedded with gamification elements. The course material concerned a lesson about the Bauhaus design movement and the learning content was delivered through various interactive activities, including interactive videos and slideshows, 3D models, games and puzzles. Furthermore, on another research, Gill et al. [60] investigated the utilization of augmented-reality (AR) and gamification strategy in the teaching course of Design for Manufacturing and Assembly (DfMA). The developed application is an educational game which consists of a tangible puzzle with an AR interface that creates an enhanced learning experience for students, encouraging engaging and collaboration practices.

A different aspect of using VR/AR in an educational context concerns the development of technical skills that students are required to have. Gavish et al. [61] developed and evaluated VR/AR platforms for Industrial Maintenance and Assembly (IMA) tasks training. The IMA-VR platform concerns a controlled multimodal virtual environment, aimed at transferring the motor and cognitive skills involved in assembly and maintenance task. On the other hand, the IMA-AR training system allows the trainee to perform assembly operations on the real machines using real instruments for interaction. Jou and Wang [62] investigated the impact of virtual reality learning environments on technical skills, focusing more on knowledge, comprehension, simulation, application and creativity.

On another research, Chandramouli et al. [63] introduced a VR-based educational module for digital manufacturing that educate and train skilled technicians on advanced manufacturing processes. Their training module simulates various devices and equipment, allowing students to interact and test these devices without risking equipment damage. In addition, the VR modules are presented in the form of a game-like interface that makes the interaction more fun-based and reduces the cognitive load. Cordero-Guridi et al. [64] in their wok described the development of a virtual/augmented reality (VR/AR) laboratory to support learning, training, and collaborative ventures related to additive manufacturing for the automotive industry. In that direction, Mathur et al. [65] presented a framework that uses a VR immersive environment to train industrial design students on additive manufacturing (AM) process knowledge. Students through the VR application platform can interactively learn about AM systems and its components. The application's goal is not only to empower learners with the skills to design and evaluate digital artifacts for AM but also to foster them to solve emerging design problems with AM.

Focusing more on the pedagogical approach, Abbas et al. [66] investigated with the synergy between VR environments and adaptive-based learning as a method to develop a VR-based training system for educating train conductors on technical skills. The results of this approach show a higher learning preference and an increase in individual motivation of trainees. Acuña and Melón [67] created a multimodal and interactive virtual reality platform for the immersive teaching of high-risk equipment operation. They promote knowledge and active training in the use of the main wood and metal cutting machines in Industrial Design and Architecture workshops. Cassola et al. [68] also presented a virtual reality training platform in industrial training. But in their case study, they promote an autonomous interactive VR-based experiential training without the support of development experts. In this way, the learner plays an active role in the learning process. Yang et al. [69] presented an experiment with college students using an augmented reality (AR) system in an assembly task training. Their paper evaluates the results of the HoloLens-based AR training method based on natural human behaviors and knowledge retention. The findings indicate that AR system can improve the training effect and is more effective than ordinary training in increasing the knowledge retention. Maulana et al. [70] developed a furniture Augmented Reality Application (FunAR), which provide the basic information about existing equipment in Lab Furniture. The application is designed to contain digital content of information, images and 3D models that allow students to interact with the learning materials and help them to better understand lab workshop complex equipment.

Advanced virtual and augmented reality technologies are proved to be a valuable tool in developing students' spatial skills. Farzeeha et al. [71] in their study make use of augmented reality learning environments to ease undergraduates engineering students in understanding orthographic and isometric projection, especially in visualizing the 3D objects from the 2D projection images and vice versa. In addition, Omar et al. [72] introduce the use of mobile augmented reality in the teaching and learning of orthographic projection. They present the Augmented Reality Engineering Drawing Apps (AREDApps), as a new pedagogical approach to attract students' interest in engineering drawing courses and to enhance their visualization skills.

On the other hand, González [73] integrates virtual and augmented reality technologies during descriptive geometry for industrial design and architecture students. Through this course students learn to visualize any object by developing perception and spatial representation in understanding the spatial sense for the constructive visual representation. In that direction, Molina-Carmona et al. [74] in their work, conducted an experimental learning activity, based on a virtual reality application, in order to improve students' spatial ability, by applying various spatial visualization test. Gómez-Tone et al. [75] present the case study of a comparative analysis on first-year engineering students that were trained with an AR-based representational system, to improve their spatial skills. The results indicate significant gains in students' level of spatial perception and abilities. In the case of Akkus and Arslan [76], augmented reality (AR) is also used to investigate its effects on students' spatial skills and academic achievement. They presented three AR applications for a technical drawing course. The results of the research indicate an important contribution to the engineering education. A different approach is followed by Fonseca et al. [77]. Based on the use of virtual reality technology, the main aim of their work is to show how the implementation of gamified virtual strategies in architecture and urban design can increase students' spatial comprehension and citizens' interest in the collaborative/gamified/interactive design of spaces.

In most studies, virtual and augmented reality technologies are part of a course plan or integrated into the design process. Some studies, however, focus more on learning the specific type of technology. For example, Häfner et al. [78] presented the design of a teaching methodology for a practical course in virtual reality. The course focused on learning about virtual reality, by simulating interdisciplinary industrial projects with the purpose to develop skills for practical engineering problems, teamwork, working in interdisciplinary groups and time management.

Team work, on the other hand, has been the research subject of several studies. Many papers present their work on collaborative learning environments through the use of virtual reality technology. Gül et al. [79] presented three case studies on collaborative design teaching by integrating 3D virtual worlds into design education. Their platforms create virtual learning communities that include various collaboration tools, allowing students to develop, share, and document design ideas. An interesting aspect of these platforms is that they follow a constructivist learning approach by providing students opportunities for self-exploration and manipulation to actively build skills and knowledge that are close to their interest.

On another case study, Karmokar and Rive [80] also follow a constructivist approach and examine how teams of creative technologies learn design thinking, by creating and using collaborative tools, designed in a virtual world, while used in a virtual learning environment. By following this approach, Vogel et al. [81] present their science research project, which involves the development of a virtual reality application that allows design thinking teams to work on a collaborative environment. Their application serves as a virtual room that supports gestural interaction and hand tracking so that users can communicate during their collaboration. In addition, Huang et al. [82] present a 3D modeling learning experience, experiment based on virtual reality technology. Their learning model was designed to employ a learning community, where students could discuss design directions and freely come up with new ideas. The results indicate that students could effectively learn 3D modeling in this collaborative virtual environment.

Figure 5, summarizes the identified types regarding the ways virtual and augmented reality are integrated into learning environments of design educational subjects. According to the literature review, it shows that the most frequent use of VR and AR in education concerns its use as supporting tools during the design process. In other cases, they deal with the utilization of the tools in creating interactive learning environments and training platforms for various learning subjects, for collaboration or for developing specific skills that designers require to have. Table 2, depict every type of use, including the categorization of the references for each category. There are references that can be found in more than one category as the technology tools can be used with different ways for the same learning subject. In addition, the design stages are further analyzed to identify exactly where in the design process VR and AR technologies are used. Based on the number of references found in each category, VR and AR tools prove to be particularly useful in the stages, where there is a need to visualize the idea of a product, to evaluate its performance and make the right decisions for adjustments and improvements. Also, according to the review, prototyping in virtual environments is an effective way of significantly reducing design development time by creating low-cost prototypes. Another frequent use of VR and AR concerns the final stages of the design process and the creation of an immersive experience that enhances the final presentation style to attract the audience. Finally, the fewer case studies involving the integration of VR and AR are seen in the early stages of the design process.

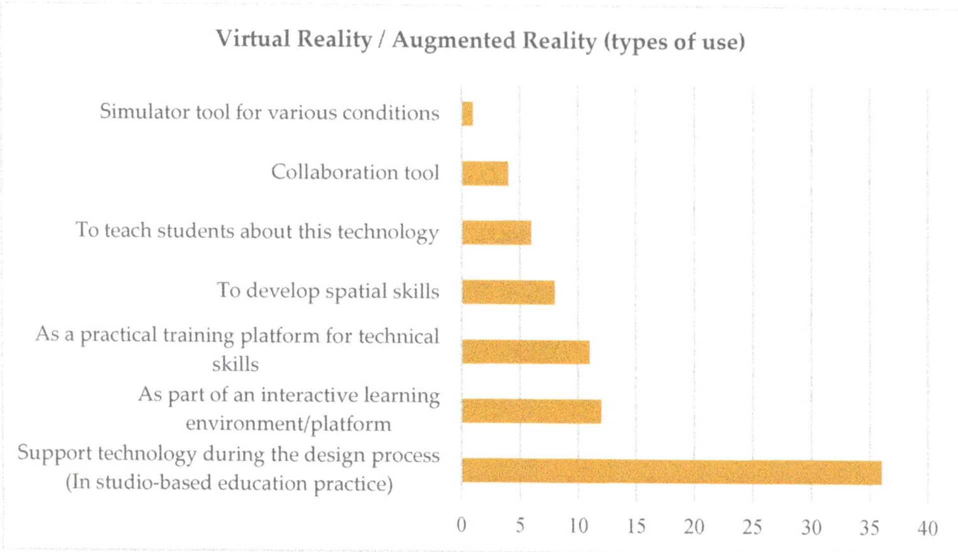

Figure 5. How virtual and augmented reality are used in educational environments.

Table 2. Studies related to the different types of virtual and augmented reality used in educational environments.

Types of Integration of Technology Tools into the Learning Process		Explanation	Authors
Support technology during the design process (In studio-based education practice)	Ideation and inspiration tool	At the very early stage of the design process as immersive tool for exploring potential abstract concepts.	Neves and Duarte, 2015 [23]; Rieuf et al., 2015 [24]
	Conceptual/Sketching tool	As a 3D drawing tool during the sketching phase of the design process to produce hand-drawn forms in the 3D space or to generate new concepts and communicate draft design ideas.	Shih et al., 2019 [25]; Joundi et al., 2020 [26]; Rodríguez-Parada et al., 2022 [27]; Roberts et al., 2020 [32];
	Visualization tool/Modeling tool	To visualize and model different aspects, possible functions and aesthetics of a specific design solution.	Moural et al., 2015 [28]; Ayer et al., 2016 [29]; Salah et al., 2019 [30]; Vo, 2022 [31]; Roberts et al., 2020 [32]; Ibrahim and El Shakhs, 2023 [33]; Banerjee et al., 2023 [34]; Serdar et al., 2013 [35]; Mourtzis et al., 2018 [43]; Huang et al., 2021 [82]; Camba et al., 2017 [83];
	Design comprehension tool	Helps students to better comprehend complex aspects of a design that would be difficult to understand in a conventional way. Improves students' visual perception.	Jimeno-Morenilla et al., 2016 [20]; Serdar et al., 2013 [35]; Alatta and Freewan, 2017 [36]; Horvat et al., 2022 [37]; Probst and Ebner, 2018 [84];

Table 2. *Cont.*

Types of Integration of Technology Tools into the Learning Process		Explanation	Authors
Support technology during the design process (In studio-based education practice)	Evaluation/Decision making tool	It evaluates a product's performance and other important characteristics. Identifies possible defects, in order to decide the appropriate design direction.	Jimeno-Morenilla et al., 2016 [20]; Rodríguez-Parada et al., 2022 [27]; Moural et al., 2015 [28]; Salah et al., 2019 [30]; Roberts et al., 2020 [32]; Serdar et al., 2013 [35]; Rentzos et al., 2014 [38]; Grajewski et al., 2015 [39]; Srihirun et al., 2015 [40]; Halabi et al., 2018 [41]; Halabi, 2020 [42]; Mourtzis et al., 2018 [43]; Huang and Chen, 2019 [44]; Jenek et al., 2020 [45]; Agirachman et al., 2022 [46];
	Prototyping tool	A tool that turns design solutions into product prototypes. It can be used as a way to create a low-cost physical version of real products and significantly reduce design development time.	Häkkilä et al., 2018 [21]; Rentzos et al., 2014 [38]; Halabi et al., 2018 [41]; Halabi, 2020 [42]; Huang and Chen, 2019 [44]; Akundi, 2017 [47]; Yamada et al., 2017 [48]; Topal and Şener, 2015 [49]; Probst and Ebner, 2018 [84]; Liu et al., 2021 [85]
	Presentation tool	As a tool to improve the presentation of projects, enriching the designs with more details and making them more informative, so that students can better communicate their design ideas to the audience.	Jimeno-Morenilla et al., 2016 [20]; Häkkilä et al., 2018 [21]; Topal and Sener, 2015 [22]; Ibrahim and El Shakhs, 2023 [33]; Banerjee et al., 2023 [34]; Yamada et al., 2017 [48]; Topal and Şener, 2015 [49], Saorín et al., 2019 [50]; López Chao et al., 2022 [51]; Camba et al., 2017 [83];
As part of an interactive learning environment/platform		When technology is used as part of a teaching system that creates an environment in which students are able to interact with the learning subject, contributing to an interactive learning experience.	Zhang, 2023 [52]; Bashabsheh et al., 2019 [53]; Kassim and Md Zubir, 2019 [54]; Urban et al., 2022 [55]; Onecha et al., 2023 [56]; González-Almaguer et al., 2022 [58]; Gill et al., 2022 [59]; Gill et al., 2023 [60]; Mathur et al., 2023 [65]; Maulana et al., 2023 [70]
As a practical training platform for technical skills		Referring to a training system that allows students to develop their technical skills by performing operations of various devices and equipment in a controlled environment without risking equipment damage.	González-Almaguer et al., 2022 [58]; Gavish et al., 2015 [61]; Jou and Wang, 2013 [62]; Chandramouli et al., 2018 [63]; Cordero-Guridi et al., 2022 [64]; Mathur et al., 2023 [65]; Abbas et al., 2023 [66]; Acuña and Melón, 2022 [67]; Cassola et al., 2022 [68]; Yang et al., 2023 [69]; Maulana et al., 2023 [70];
To develop spatial skills		A useful tool to improve students' understanding of three-dimensional (3D) morphologies, enhancing their spatial perception and their ability to visualize and understand the relationships between objects.	Alatta and Freewan, 2017 [36]; Farzeeha et al., 2017 [71]; Omar et al., 2019 [72]; González, 2018 [73]; Molina-Carmona et al., 2018 [74]; Gómez-Tone et al., 2020 [75]; Akkus and Arslan, 2022 [76]; Fonseca et al., 2021 [77]

Table 2. *Cont.*

Types of Integration of Technology Tools into the Learning Process	Explanation	Authors
To teach students about this technology	When the purpose of an educational activity is more focused on learning a specific type of technology.	Häkkilä et al., 2018 [21]; Roberts et al., 2020 [32]; Akundi, 2017 [47]; López Chao et al., 2022 [51]; Häfner et al., 2013 [78]; Camba et al., 2017 [83]
Collaboration tool	When the technology tool is used to create a learning community for the purpose of working in a collaborative environment.	Gül et al., 2014 [79], Karmokar and Rive, 2016 [80]; Vogel et al., 2021 [81]; Huang et al., 2021 [82];
Simulator tool for various conditions	When the tool is used to simulate specific environmental conditions or physical disabilities necessary for the design project that would be impossible to experience in any other way.	Häkkilä et al., 2018 [21]

3.1.2. Robotics

The second category includes robotics-related technologies. Robotics have a wide range of applications in the field of education, and can be found as: (a) learning objects, (b) learning tools and (c) learning aids. The aim of robotics is to improve the learning experience of students through the creation, implementation, improvement and validation of pedagogical activities. On the other hand, robotics enhances interdisciplinary thinking skills, such as problem solving, teamwork, logical reasoning and creative design, things that are also essential in the design studies. In design-related courses, robotics has several benefits in the process of solving various kinds of design problems and contribute in improving students' design skills i.e., problem definition, information gathering, solution generation, analysis of the solutions and test/implementation.

Robotics are integrated into the design process in various ways. An et al. [86] designed and implemented an online educational robotics course addressed to service teachers by applying instructional design factors as well as problem-solving and collaboration strategies. Telenko et al. [87] presented a multidisciplinary learning activity, based on the integration of problems from multiple educational subjects. Each described challenge combines problem clarification, concept generation and prototyping with subject content such as: circuits, biology, thermodynamics, differential equations or software with controls. Robotic systems are used as a support technology during these design processes. Tan et al. [88] presented a robot design competition as an effective tool for project-based education in undergraduate robotics. The designed problem that was posed to the students was to build and test mobile robots that can accomplish a task. The developed robotic systems were used as an education medium for a practical design experience on mechanical design, electronic circuits and programming. Almaguer et al. [89] described the use of Meccano^{TM}, a metal constructive game base, to help engineering and design students simulate the manufacturing process. The project is based on STEAM (Science Technology Engineering Art Mathematics) education and uses gamification learning techniques. Students used Meccano^{TM} parts to build their prototypes for the design challenges. Heyden et al. [90] presented their work on a Design Education Platform for a physical robotic system that was developed in the context of a problem-based interdisciplinary learning course. Students were asked to design and produce physical product variants of a robotic system and take part in a competition. The developed robotic systems are based on the design education course and technical specifications and divided into different modules, which are attached on the Design Education Platform.

Kuppuswamy and Mhakure [91] explored the project-based learning methodology in a mechanical engineering product design course. As part of the project, students were asked to design a Selective Compliance Assembly Robot Arm for a given application according to the industry demands. This case study focuses more on the learning methodology and uses robotics as the assigned project for the studio-based practice. Kleppe et al. [92] introduced an Industry 4.0 Idea Lab for bridging design and automatic manufacturing in Engineering Education 4.0. They designed a course based on activity-based learning methodology, which goal is to learn how to design products for Industry 4.0 manufacturing. Robots are used for the manufacturing and assembly process. Yazar et al. [93] presented an experiment on basic design studio students that investigates the utilization of a robotic arm as a design and production tool. Students were introduced to digital fabrication technologies and experiment with the integration in the design processes.

On other cases, robotics was used as the main learning subject. Phan and Ngo [94] proposed a novel framework for a multidisciplinary mechatronics program that introduces a community-based PBL learning approach. They investigated learning and teaching robotics systems from a collaborative perspective. As part of the designed course, students had to work together with other learners in the electronics, software, control automation, and mechanics fields, followed by the design of an open platform integrated multidisciplinary approach. Kilic-Bebek et al. [95] explored and presented the benefits of short online courses for the transdisciplinary competence development of graduate students for an Innovative Course on Wearable and Collaborative Robotics.

Deniz and Cakır [96] developed a novel interactive robot training platform that includes subjects related to robots in engineering education such as programming, kinematics, workspace, speed-acceleration and robot dynamic parameters. This platform recreates the conditions of an industrial environment, it is based on open-source libraries and is designed for the offline programming of industrial robots. Yu and Da Silva [97] presented their study on designing and implementing an online workshop for Robot Assembly. The assembly process through an automated system, like a robotic system, is crucial knowledge for students as it demonstrates that they understand the design rules and implement them in the actual product design. The objective of this research was to teach students, how to use and program a robot assembly that does not require access to lab facilities.

Other research approach the education of robotics not only as a subject to be learned but also as a teaching tool and support technology during the learning process. Grandi et al. [98] described a course, where students were required to mechanically design and program autonomous robots (to use in a competition among teams), in order to gain practical knowledge on mobile robotics. For this purpose, the Lego Mindstorms^{TM} Kit and Java-based firmware LeJOS had been selected as a tool to help in the learning process. Garcia et al. [99] described the methodology of designing a robotic hand, in order to facilitate and accelerate the teaching/learning process for mechatronics lecture-based courses. The study presents the design and implementation of a movement control system for recognition of hand gestures. The aim is to create a tool, based on mechatronics systems design that will help students gain a direct hands-on experience of the course topics. Montés et al. [100] explored the design of a challenge-based learning program, according to the STEAM product design education. The paper focuses on how STEAM learning can be integrated into the project, with an aim to improve students learning on topics concerning the engineering of product design.

Brell-Çokcan and Braumann [101] introduced robotic arm in architectural education, not just as a pure fabrication device, but as an open interface, allowing students to have an interactive and intuitive feeling for robotic fabrication. In their designed courses, robotic arms can act as a motivator that transfer valuable knowledge from many disciplines, such as geometry and programming. During courses, students went through the process of designing custom manufacturing workflows, according to their individual strengths, i.e., workflows that capture the movements of a dancer and transform it into robot toolpaths, adaptable structures used for form exploration. In the same design field, Shi et al. [102] introduced a new didactic pedagogical approach, based on the principles of robotic tectonics that provides interdisciplinary knowledge to architecture students and enables them to use advanced digital tools, such as robots for automated construction. Furthermore, Yi [103] describes an architectural robotic class that is structured to provide students with applied knowledge of kinematics and mechanisms. The courses are focused on design experimentation with kinetic (responsive) building prototyping and construction automation of a complex building form, using an industrial robot arm. Finally, Jiehan et al. [104] applied their work to engineering education, by designing a virtual remote lab, based on the title 'Robotic Automation Virtual Lab'. They built a system to remotely manipulate a robotic arm through a website.

Figure 6 illustrates the most common uses of robotics technology related to design education courses. Based on the literature review, robotic-based technology is used equally as both a learning object and an assistive technology, during the design process for various projects in the context of practical student training. Other uses involve the utilization of robotics as part of an interactive learning platform that help students in interacting with the learning subject, or works as supporting system that facilitates teachers in the teaching of specific topics. Finally, there are some cases that use of robotics as an aid to various manufacturing strategies, i.e., to test several manufacturing constraints and prototyping parameters. In Table 3, the reviewed studies are categorized in relation with the different types of robotics use that have been identified in educational settings. As far as it concerns the design process, it is observed that robotics is used exclusively in the prototyping stage. These cases involve the development of robotic prototypes as part of a problem-solving project, or the utilization of robotic technology as an auxiliary tool for building prototypes of specific projects.

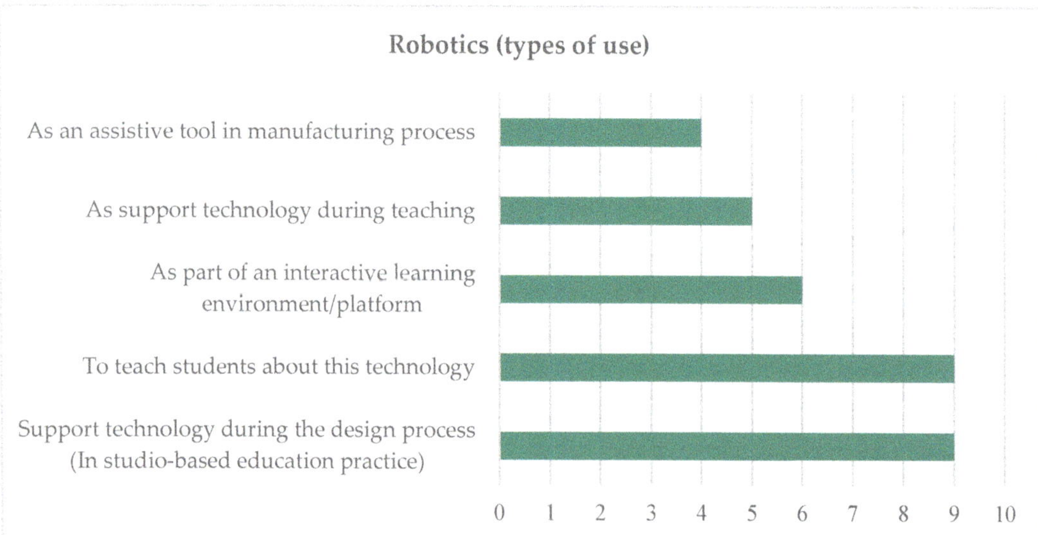

Figure 6. How robotics are used in educational environments.

Table 3. Studies related to the different types of robotics used in educational environments.

Types of Integration of Technology Tools into the Learning Process		Explanation	Authors
Support technology during the design process (In studio-based education practice)	Prototyping tool	When is used to create robotic prototypes or when robotic technology is used as an auxiliary tool in the process of developing the prototypes of specific projects.	Telenko et al., 2016 [87]; Almaguer et al., 2020 [89]; Heyden et al., 2020 [90]; Kuppuswamy and Mhakure, 2020 [91]; Kleppe et al., 2022 [92]; Yazar et al., 2023 [93]; Bedillion et al., 2018 [105]; Castelli and Giberti, 2019 [106]; Benitez et al., 2020 [107]
As part of an interactive learning environment/platform		When technology is used as part of a teaching system that creates an environment in which students are able to interact with the learning subject, contributing to an interactive learning experience.	Tan et al., 2016 [88]; Deniz and Cakır, 2017 [96]; Yu and Da Silva, 2021 [97]; Benitez et al., 2020 [107]; Carrasco-Navarro et al., 2022 [108]; Dewi et al., 2018 [109]
To teach students about this technology		When the purpose of an educational activity is more focused on learning a specific type of technology.	An et al., 2022 [86]; Kleppe et al., 2022 [92]; Phan and Ngo, 2020 [94]; Kilic-Bebek et al., 2023 [95]; Yi, 2021 [103]; Castelli and Giberti, 2019 [106]; Benitez et al., 2020 [107]; Dewi et al., 2018 [109]; Orsolits et al., 2022 [110];
As support technology during teaching		When technology supports the teaching of specific subjects and works as an auxiliary tool to facilitate the learning process.	Telenko et al., 2016 [87]; Grandi et al., 2014 [98]; Garcia et al., 2020 [99]; Montés et al., 2022 [100]; Carrasco-Navarro et al., 2022 [108]
As an assistive tool in manufacturing process		When the technology works as an aid to various manufacturing strategies, to test several manufacturing constraints and prototyping parameters.	Brell-Çokcan and Braumann, 2013 [91]; Shi et al., 2020 [102]; Yi, 2021 [103]; Jiehan et al., 2022 [104]

3.1.3. Interactive Embedded Systems

Interactive embedded systems (IES) describe the technology tools that are embedded on physical objects and communicate with other devices and systems over the internet by exchanging data. Refers to the Internet of Things (IoT), which is defined as a network of physical objects that collects environmental data through sensors and analyzes it, to make decisions for changing the environment through actuators [111]. It also includes control systems, where a person can interact with digital information through the physical environment, like Arduino^{TM}-based platforms and Tangible User Interfaces (TUI).

The majority of papers investigating the use of interactive embedded systems technologies in design learning environments, concern their integration into the design process and their contribution to the creation of interactive prototypes, during studio-based educational practice. Alsos [112] presents a project-based work for an industrial design course called "Prototyping Interactive Media". In this course, students were asked to design innovative interactive everyday products using Arduino^{TM}, an open-source electronics platform. The aim of the course was to teach students programming by introducing them into the processing language through project-based learning methodology. Narahara [113] also presents a project-based oriented course for beginning design students. The course concerned first the introduction of students in fundamental technical knowledge upon the new technological tools, i.e., sensors, actuators, and microcontrollers and secondly the designing and production of creative interactive prototypes. In similar research, Conradie et al. [114] combine Tangible User Interface and rapid prototyping technologies for a Mechatronic Product Design course. The course follows a project-based approach and starts with an introduction of mechatronics and the basics of Arduino^{TM}. Then students design and produce their own interactive products, based on real world problems in close collaboration with industry. 3D printing and laser-cut were used to materialize and finish the final prototypes.

Liu and Qu [115] structure an interactive prototyping course for students, concerning aged users. The objective of the course is to help students, learn and practice interactive prototyping skills, by developing interactive and experiential prototypes. On experiment research, Rodriguez-Sanchez et al. [116] present a case study, where they combine project-based learning (PBL) and Collaborative Learning (CL) integrated with information communication technologies for a Master's course in embedded systems. Open-source platform like Arduino^{TM}, as well as wireless communications, were also used for this course. According to the research results, this combination of pedagogical methods and technological tools, were proved to be beneficial for the students and the learning process itself. Velásquez-Montoya [111] on the other hand, describes a Human-Centered design course, which emphasize on the development of products with social impact, integrated with innovative and ubiquitous technologies i.e., IoT. In the context of the course, students were asked to design products or services that include technology components for user-product/service interaction.

Carulli and Bordegoni [117] present a problem-based multidisciplinary course, for designing and developing the prototypes of domestic products that allows tangible interaction with live-data streams. The innovation of the course lies on the instruction given to the students, not to use any kind of digital display to create their prototypes, but instead to use real effects, like moving some parts of the product or changing its shape or using lighting effects, sounds, and smells. Embedded systems, rapid prototyping and physical computing techniques and technologies were used in order to produce the final prototypes. Qu et al. [118] investigate the development of interaction design, considering the transmission of human emotions, through the human computer interaction process. The design of the interactive prototypes uses real material as the carrier, embedded in open-source hardware technology. The aim for the students is to learn designing products that interact with users through behavior and information exchange, resulting in a real 3D embodied interactive experience. Omar [119] presents a new approach in teaching automatic control by conducting Arduino^{TM}-based projects. More specifically, he has integrated Arduino^{TM} into carefully designed projects that supports all the course subjects that students need to learn. In that direction, Nam and Choh [120] experiment with the introduction of microcontroller interactive prototyping tools into design education. They developed a microcontroller board that allows quick prototyping of design ideas, without requiring any special coding training. The board can be easily used as a basic design prototype tool for industrial design students, with an aim to acquire relevant knowledge on design workshops.

Istanbullu and Taşçı [121] conducted a survey and evaluated the effect of using project-based learning (PBL) approach combined with open-source hardware, for a design course in engineering education. The course focused on the usefulness and ease of using Arduino^{TM} platform, in order to develop real-life projects for the learners. Kim [122] experiment with the implementation of technology in an interactive physical prototyping class. Students were provided with technical materials, such as sensors, actuators and display modules. This experience of matching a technology to an action helped students understand the relationship between electronic materials and actions. Allam and Alacame [123] use Arduino™ as a physical computation environment for a digital fabrication course. They designed a series of project-based exercises, combined with theoretical lectures, with the aim to develop diverse products or applications in the context of dynamic designs. Each course has tailored these methods to address Rhino3D™, Grasshopper™ and Arduino™ in a parametric–algorithmic–kinetic application within computational design and digital fabrication courses. Sun et al. [124] research refers to the contribution of IoT technology in the creation of a distance teaching system of interior design course. The course is designed based on an education platform and IoT, which is used to set the communication architecture of the software part.

Figure 7 presents the different ways of using interactive embedded systems in design education. Compared to previous types of technology, embedded systems present fewer ways of integration into the educational process. As before, most studies focus on the utilization of technology as supporting tool during the design process. Another way involves the use of embedded systems as a new learning object for students with an aim to introduce them to new technological tools, equipment and electronic materials. Finally, embedded technologies, usually combined with other types of technology, can contribute to the creation of interactive teaching systems and platforms. In Table 4, the reviewed studies are categorized based on the types of use identified earlier. With respect to the design process in the context of students' training practice, almost all cases involve the utilization of embedded systems in the final stages of developing interactive and experiential prototypes. There was one case though, where embedded technology combined with other technological systems contributed to the creation of a device that helped in the ideation phase of a design process, generating new concepts for future products.

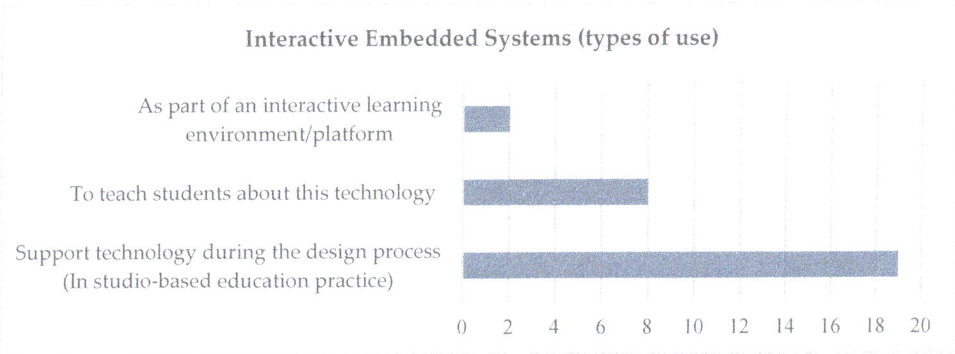

Figure 7. How interactive embedded systems are used in educational environments.

Table 4. Studies related to the different types of interactive embedded systems used in educational environments.

Types of Integration of Technology Tools into the Learning Process		**Explanation**	**Authors**
Support technology during the design process (In studio-based education practice)	Ideation and inspiration tool	When various applications and devices enhanced with embedded interactive technology helps in the ideation phase of the design process.	Jansen and Colombo, 2023 [125]

Table 4. *Cont.*

Types of Integration of Technology Tools into the Learning Process		**Explanation**	**Authors**
Support technology during the design process (In studio-based education practice)	Prototyping tool	A tool that turns design solutions into product prototypes. It can be used as a way to create a low-cost physical version of real products and significantly reduce design development time.	Velásquez-Montoya, 2016 [111]; Alsos, 2015 [112]; Narahara, 2015 [113]; Conradie et al., 2016 [114]; Liu and Qu, 2015 [115]; Rodriguez-Sanchez et al., 2016 [116]; Carulli and Bordegoni, 2017 [117]; Qu et al., 2017 [118]; Omar, 2018 [119]; Nam and Choh, 2019 [120]; Istanbullu and Taşçı, 2019 [121]; Kim, 2020 [122]; Allam and Alacame, 2023 [123]; Probst and Ebner, 2018 [84]; Bedillion, et al., 2018 [105]; Castelli and Giberti, 2019 [106]; Benitez et al., 2020 [107]; Carrasco-Navarro et al., 2022 [108]
To teach students about this technology		When the purpose of an educational activity is more focused on learning a specific type of technology.	Velásquez-Montoya, 2016 [111]; Alsos, 2015 [112]; Narahara, 2015 [113]; Conradie et al., 2016 [114]; Carulli and Bordegoni, 2017 [117]; Nam and Choh, 2019 [120]; Allam and Alacame, 2023 [123]; Castelli and Giberti, 2019 [106];
As part of an interactive learning environment/platform		When technology is used as part of a teaching system that creates an environment in which students are able to interact with the learning subject, contributing to an interactive learning experience.	Sun et al., 2022 [124]; Benitez et al., 2020 [107];

3.1.4. Other Types of Immersive Technologies

This category refers to the different types of immersive technologies that are more rarely found in the literature i.e., spatial augmented reality (SAR), mixed reality (MR), extended reality (XR) and holograms. These technologies are included on the spectrum between the real world and the complete virtual world. They introduce several ways of blending physical and digital information, allowing different degrees of sensing Reality-Virtuality, reshaping each time the way human-computer-environment interact [126]. In the field of design education, these technologies are integrated into the educational experience in various ways. As in the case of VR and AR, they are mostly found in the various stages of the design process in the context of design studios practice.

Tang et al. [127] developed an application based on mixed reality (MR) technologies, for teaching product design to university students. They used the application during design projects and tested its effectiveness in five main areas: (a) the ability of students to comprehend design, (b) understanding product functions, (c) visualizing 3D geometry, (d) understanding geometric relationship and (e) students' creativity. Ranscombe et al. [128] implement a mixed-reality visualization system in a prototyping process in order to support practice-based studio design projects. In the context of an industrial design studio project, students were asked to design a product for making food or hot drinks. The MR prototype system was used to contextualize students' preliminary concepts, as a basic test for product dimensions and proportions. Darwish et al. [126] test with the implementation of extended reality technology (XR) in the early design studio education and its impact on students' general spatial skills. Specifically, they examined students' cognitive levels, on their abilities to visualize and understand the relationships between objects. According to the results, XR technology significantly increased the scores of the students in the spatial ability test. Ricci et al. [129] on the other hand, use MR technologies within an industrial design program that develops novel interfaces for the Metaverse^{TM}. The research presents a multidisciplinary approach for a novel lab that aims to teach students, how to design innovative Graphical User Interfaces (GUIs) for home appliances, by exploiting MR technologies and promote a possible interaction in the Metaverse^{TM}. In addition, Mast et al. [130] present a workshop that concerned the design of an interactive system, beyond typical GUIs, based on spatial augmented reality (SAR). The prototyping methodology (Wizard of Oz) is a technique, for testing interface design ideas at an early stage in the design process. The interactive SAR technology was used to create the prototypes. Based on the results of the workshop, the students were very creative in the way, they chose to use SAR technology, such as choosing different sizes and different viewing angles and contexts for their interactions.

In the case of Park et al. [131] the use of spatial augmented reality (SAR) technology works as an evaluation tool for product appearance. The technique involves projecting a high-quality rendered image of the final product's appearance, onto a mock-up of the product, including a camera calibration to compensate the color distortion. This method allows a more intuitive evaluation of the product characteristics that define its appearance. Quintero et al. [132] used interactive video-mapping technology for a design project in a combined classroom from Digital Art, Architecture and Industrial Design programs. The project concerned the development of an architectural model and the video-mapping technology contributed to a different interpretation of the model, by creating the impression of a moving surface.

Experimenting with different technologies for creating interactive learning environments, Bringardner and Jean-Pierre [133] describe a case study of a flipped classroom pedagogy that was applied for the creation of instructional videos, for an introduction lab course to Engineering and Design. The video resources provide students with uniformity and expert guidance, through a visual representation of the topics. Holograms were one of the technologies used to contribute to the creation of an interactive learning environment. Specifically, the video editor was able to generate 3D hologram representations of the design, in order to promote visualization of potential solution. Hologram technology is also described in the study of Ramirez-Lopez et al. [134] but in this case for a distance synchronistic educational experience. Their research presents an educational technology ecosystem supported by hologram effect combined with an active learning pedagogy.

A different aspect of using spatial augmented reality (SAR) technology concerns, its support in cooperative learning environments. Rajeb and Leclercq [135] examine applications of SAR in collaborative design training. Their research focuses on four SAR configurations: (a) remote sharing of graphic documents and annotations in real time, (b) remote expert consultation, (c) collaborative design, (d) project review and group evaluation. In a more recent work, Rajeb and Leclercq [136] present the implementation of SAR technology on a project-based group, training in design education, aiming to develop the students' general and specific skills to devise complex projects in design. On another approach, Calixte and Leclercq [137] describe the implementation of an interactive projection mapping installation (referring to SAR), designed for a multidisciplinary collaboration in an architectural workshop. The created co-design environments were supported by the SAR technology during the design process. More specifically, all the required documents for the design work were projected on a surface for graphic work and were available for synchronous manipulation and annotation by all users. The technology also supported video-conference system and proved to be helpful tool for collective understanding of complex shapes.

Figure 8, presents and categorizes the most common uses of the above immersive types of technologies found in the reviewed studies. According to the literature, as proved in the cases of VR and AR, generally immersive technologies are mainly used as supporting tools for practice-based studio design projects. Other cases, involve the contribution of immersive technologies in developing interactive learning platforms or provide the equipment and conditions to create collaborative learning environments. Some case studies focus only on teaching of immersive technologies as a learning subject or use them as educational tools to improve students' spatial abilities and perception. Table 5, includes the categorization of the references found in each category. It shows from the further analysis of the studio-based design process, all the stages that other types of immersive technologies are used to facilitate the educational practice. Most cases use immersive types of technologies, in order to visualize and model the concept of a design project or use them as helpful tools for understanding complex aspects of design problems that would be difficult to understand in conventional ways. In addition, there are cases where immersive technologies are being used for evaluation of a products performance regarding various required specifications, or as prototyping tools to create low-cost prototypes or as tools to improve and enrich the designs in the final presentation stages. Generally, it could be concluded that immersive technologies of this category are found in all stages of the design process between visualizing the product to the final presentation style.

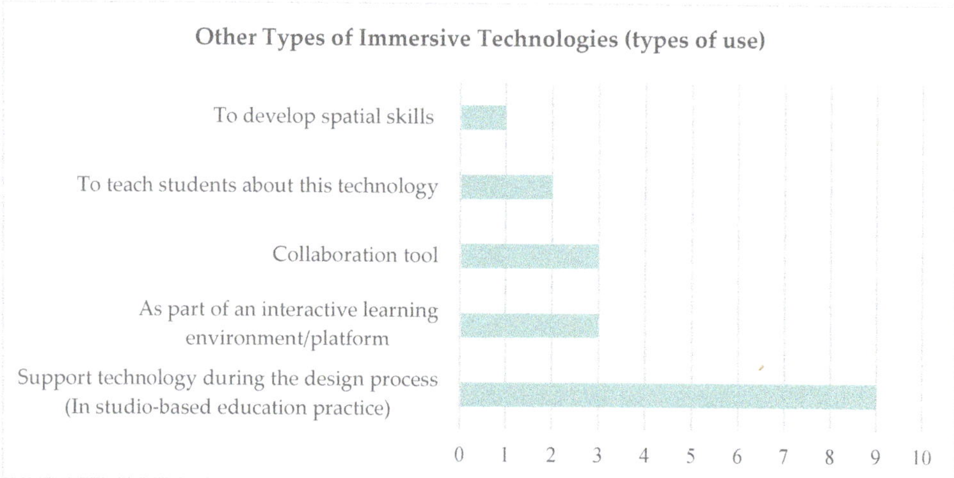

Figure 8. How other types of immersive technologies are used in educational environments.

Table 5. Studies related to the different types of other immersive technologies used in educational environments.

Types of Integration of Technology Tools into the Learning Process		**Explanation**	**Authors**
Support technology during the design process (In studio-based education practice)	Visualization tool/Modeling tool	To visualize and model different aspects, possible functions and aesthetics of a specific design solution.	Tang et al., 2018 [127]; Ricci et al., 2023 [129]; Camba et al., 2017 [83]
	Design comprehension tool	Helps students to better comprehend complex aspects of a design that would be difficult to understand in a conventional way. Improves students' visual perception.	Darwish et al., 2023 [126]; Tang et al., 2018 [127]; Calixte and Leclercq, 2017 [137];

Table 5. *Cont.*

Types of Integration of Technology Tools into the Learning Process		Explanation	Authors
Support technology during the design process (In studio-based education practice)	Evaluation/Decision making tool	It evaluates a product's performance and other important characteristics. Identifies possible defects, in order to decide the appropriate design direction.	Park et al., 2015 [131]
	Prototyping tool	A tool that turns design solutions into product prototypes. It can be used as a way to create a low-cost physical version of real products and significantly reduce design development time.	Ranscombe et al., 2023 [128]; Mast et al., 2023 [130];
	Presentation tool	As a tool to improve the presentation of projects, enriching the designs with more details and making them more informative, so that students can better communicate their design ideas to the audience.	Ricci et al., 2023 [129]; Quintero et al., 2019 [132]; Camba et al., 2017 [83]
As part of an interactive learning environment/platform		When technology is used as part of a teaching system that creates an environment in which students are able to interact with the learning subject, contributing to an interactive learning experience.	Bringardner and Jean-Pierre, 2017 [133]; Ramirez-Lopez et al., 2021 [134]; Orsolits et al., 2022 [110]
To develop spatial skills		A useful tool to improve students' understanding of three-dimensional (3D) morphologies, enhancing their spatial perception and their ability to visualize and understand the relationships between objects.	Darwish et al., 2023 [126]
To teach students about this technology		When the purpose of an educational activity is more focused on learning a specific type of technology.	Ricci et al., 2023 [129]; Camba et al., 2017 [83]
Collaboration tool		When the technology tool is used to create a learning community for the purpose of working in a collaborative environment.	Rajeb and Leclercq, 2013 [135]; Rajeb and Leclercq, 2014 [136]; Calixte and Leclercq, 2017 [137]

3.1.5. Computational Intelligence Systems

Computational intelligence systems refer to the type of computer technologies that have the ability to process vast amount of data in order to simulate the human intelligence and imitate the way that humans learn [138]. It refers to artificial intelligence and its several branches, combined with computer science (deep learning, machine learning, cloud computing, etc.) and focuses on the use of data and algorithms. These technologies work as recognition tools of several data patterns in order to generate ideas and prediction.

Technologies of computational intelligence systems in educational settings can mainly be found in different stages of the design projects. Chien and Yao [139] present a case study in product design education using artificial intelligence (AI) in the early stages of the design process. They propose an AI application that provides students with information regarding user behavior patterns and product preferences. Their AI userbot system constitutes an interaction platform with a dialog process mechanism that aims to be virtual representations of real product users, to help students carry out participatory design and develop their design skills. On another approach, Basarir [138] presents an experiment case study during the several design stages, by introducing AI tools and techniques to students of architecture. The research aimed at integrating AI in design workflow practice. AI tools and Machine Learning technology were used in the process of collecting data about user needs as well as analyzing various design parameters. More specifically, the course covered topics i.e., possible contributions of artificial intelligence implementations to problem-solving practices, training principles of artificial intelligence, role and significance of data towards solving design problems, collection of data on problems and their analysis using adequate techniques, evaluation of results by sensitivity analyses. Zhang et al. [140] developed a machine learning tool in product design education that uses an algorithm to analyze data from over 1000 concepts, thereby aiding the concept clustering process. The collection of data is based on natural language descriptions of concepts and the aim of the machine learning tool is to identify meaningful patterns in clustering, in order to enhance divergent concept generation processes. Tong et al. [141] explored the possibilities that AI technologies offer for design representation and visualization. Their case study investigates the integration of AI into first year design educational course. More specifically, they experiment with the combination of orthographic projections with AI-assisted generated images and evaluate the final outputs. According to the results, although there is an obvious need for careful implementation of AI tools in the design process, students benefit in expressing their ideas from AI tools during the development of their work. Wendrich [142] experimentally explored the integration of Creative AI (CAI) technology in conjunction with Hybrid Design Tools (HDTs), their environments (HDTEs), and cloud architecture. The aim is to develop a creative collaboration as the foundation for discovering new ideas in design engineering processes and education.

Exploring different aspects of AI technology, Meron and Tekmen Araci [143] investigated the potential of using an AI language model as a virtual colleague in the creation process of design-focused learning content. More specifically, they tested ChatGPT (Chat Generative Pretrained Transformer) during the collaboration with university educators in designing materials for higher education design students. The authors found that despite the weaknesses of this particular technology in creating content that was often generic, ChatGPT is proved to be a useful tool for brainstorming as well as structuring and editing language, which could significantly help save time from the process of designing masters-level course materials. Kuo and Xia [144] presented research on how AI-based technology can be used as a data processing and analysis tool with an aim to form the development of a more suitable design course. In their paper, design students were assigned to interact with smart home products with intelligent user interfaces, to evaluate their experience as users and submit a product experience report. ChatGPT was one of the different approaches that was used to collect and analyze the data from the course activity in order to provide feedback regarding evaluation aspects of smart home products from design students perspective.

Figure 9 summarizes the identified types of computational intelligence systems in design education. Computational intelligence systems are mainly used for the practical training of students and especially in the design phases, where research through data and parameter analysis is required. Other uses concern the teaching of this kind of technology as a new learning subject for students, who are not familiar with processing language before, or its contribution to the creation of teaching platforms as interactive learning systems. Finally, there are some cases that explore new aspects on the application of technology in design education as: (a) an auxiliary tool in developing content material for specific design courses, (b) a data processing and analysis tool for extracting valuable information for new products requirements that can be used for educational practice. In Table 6, the reviewed studies are categorized according to the types of use described earlier. Unlike the other types of technology, computational intelligence systems are used mainly in the initial stages of the design process. It can be used as a tool for identifying user needs or as a tool for collecting and analyzing data from specific design criteria that will help in choosing better design solutions. In the stages of ideation and concept generation, every technology based on intelligent systems through algorithmic mechanism, can act as a creative collaborator that supports increased creativity. At the same time, it can be used as visualization tool for students' ideas or can contribute with other technologies in developing product prototypes.

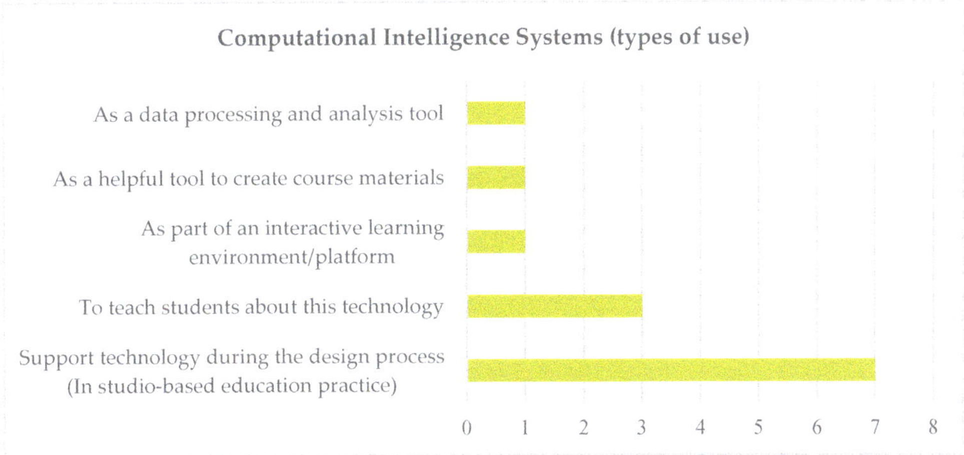

Figure 9. How computational intelligence systems are used in educational environments.

Table 6. Studies related to the different types of computational intelligence systems used in educational environments.

Types of Integration of Technology Tools into the Learning Process		**Explanation**	**Authors**
Support technology during the design process (In studio-based education practice)	Identification of user needs	To identify the user needs of a product or service, in terms of the required specifications it must have to fulfill user expectations.	Basarir, 2022 [138]; Chien and Yao, 2020 [139]
	Design parameter analysis tool	Collect and analyze data on the parameters of specific design problems and compare multiple solutions in order to optimize the best design solution.	Basarir, 2022 [138]
	Ideation and inspiration tool	When algorithmic mechanisms through an information-processing system can act as a creative collaborator in the early design stages of discovering new ideas and supporting the creative process.	Wendrich, 2021 [142]; Jansen and Colombo, 2023 [125]
	Conceptual tool	When the machine learning capabilities of intelligence technology can be used in the design process of multiple concept generation.	Zhang et al., 2017 [140]; Wendrich, 2021 [142]

Table 6. *Cont.*

Types of Integration of Technology Tools into the Learning Process		Explanation	Authors
Support technology during the design process (In studio-based education practice)	Visualization tool	When AI can act as an assisted-image visualization tool that helps in the process of representing and expressing students' ideas.	Tong et al., 2023 [141]
	Prototyping tool	When intelligent hardware combined with other technologies contributes in the creation of interactive prototypes.	Liu et al., 2021 [85]
As part of an interactive learning environment/platform		When technology is used as part of a teaching system that creates an environment in which students are able to interact with the learning subject, contributing to an interactive learning experience.	Dewi et al., 2018 [109]
To teach students about this technology		When the purpose of an educational activity is more focused on learning a specific type of technology.	Basarir, 2022 [138]; Jansen and Colombo, 2023 [125]; Dewi et al., 2018 [109]
As a helpful tool to create course materials		When technology is used in the process of creating and structuring content material for specific learning topics.	Meron and Tekmen Araci, 2023 [143]
As a data processing and analysis tool		When technology is used for collecting and analyzing data in order to extract valuable conclusions that can lead to defining specific requirements for the design of new products.	Kuo and Xia, 2023 [144]

3.1.6. Combinations of Different Technologies

An interesting approach is the research of Camba et al. [83] where they use Emerging Visualization Technologies" (virtual, augmented and holographic visualizations) in order to investigate, how these various types of interactive technologies can enrich presentations and simulations in a project-based course for undergraduate students in multidisciplinary Design Education. On another approach, Probst and Ebner [84] introduce an IoT platform with focus on augmented reality that aims to teach complex engineering design to students. The IoT application platform is a mobile App ThingWorx^{TM}, which uses a special code called ThingMark^{TM} to connect the app with data of the IoT server. The data concern a number of several 3D models of technical drawings that through the platform are embedded in an AR experience. In this way, students can navigate to the immersive environment, which makes it much easier for them to comprehend the functionality and other aspects of the 3D models. Liu et al. [85] present a case study, where the VR, AR and computational intelligence systems are combined in a transdisciplinary course for experiential concepts in user experience design (UX). The teaching method is focused on project-based practice and aims to cultivate practical abilities in students. Their research project entitled 'designing future life experience on smart home and wearables' involves the development of an application and a product prototype on virtual reality (VR), augmented reality (AR) and intelligent hardware systems that demonstrate human-computer interaction (HCI) and user experience (UX) design directions.

Bedillion et al. [105] present an Arduino^{TM}-based platform, developed for a design project in a Mechanical Engineering Sophomore Design Course. The projects are introducing students to mechatronic systems by developing a product concept and building a physical prototype of a small, remote-controlled, ground robot for USAR (Urban Search And Rescue). The students were provided with several laboratory activities, in order to familiarize themselves with the hardware, while a user manual created, specifically for the assigned tasks, include instructions for coding, driving actuators and handling sensors. Castelli and Giberti [106] describe a robotic system design course, enhanced by additive manufacturing and rapid electronic prototyping (Arduino^{TM}). Students are introduced to all aspects of a robotic system, from mechanical design to the final prototyping. Benitez et al. [107] combine robotics with IoT technology, for online teaching of robotic courses. Their research describes the design and construction of a robotic system. It is an open-source robot arm, empowered by IoT technology. IoT technology is used to demonstrate important robotic topics, regarding handling the robotic system and is embedded in a smartphone interface, deployed using wireless communication. The courses are based on project-based learning strategy and aim for students to understand the robotics design process, from the theoretical aspects to the actual coding and construction of a prototype.

In addition to the above, Carrasco-Navarro et al. [108] present their work on the development of a smart educational kit that takes advantage of the IoT technology, and creates an interactive remote simulation of a physical laboratory. The platform includes programmable features that allow it to be manipulated by the students in real time through remotely controlling and monitoring a mobile robot that works as an interactive actuator. In this case, robots are used as devices that can be programmed and optimized to conduct diverse tasks and desired movements with high accuracy. Jansen and Colombo [125] present the design and test of a Machine Leering toolkit (Mix and Match) that supports designers during the ideation process by providing Machine Leering (ML) knowledge and by enabling open exploration through a tangible approach. The toolkit consists of three elements: a set of tangible tokens, a sensing board, and a web interface. The tokens are placed on the sensing board and display detailed information in the web interface about data types and ML capabilities. Mix and Match ML toolkit could help in the ideation phase and could function as a purely educational tool for students to learn ML basic concepts and how to apply them to generate novel ideas. Dewi et al. [109] present an interactive application of an open-source and low-cost software simulation, designed for the purpose of introducing students to robotics and artificial intelligence. The paper discusses a project-based learning approach about the design and application of fuzzy logic controller in a mobile firefighter robot. Orsolits et al. [110] combine immersive technologies like mixed reality with robotics education. This novel approach aims to contribute to the use of a mixed reality, based on a digital twin platform for introducing students into robotic courses. Through this combined system of desktop robotics, students have the chance to explore robot behavior in class and experiment with the capabilities of mixed reality in industrial engineering without the need to access industrial robot systems.

3.2. Learning Methods

Education 4.0 seeks to improve the learning experience through innovative pedagogies supported by emerging technologies [145]. Another important parameter under investigation in the literature review are the cases where technologies and pedagogical methodologies coexist as complementary and supporting each other tools in learning environments. Most cases of those already presented in Section 2 focused exclusively on the use of technological tools. A significant number, however, referred also to learning methodologies depending on the desired objective of each study. Figure 10 depicts that 34% of the examined references, present case studies, where technology and specific learning methods are integrated together in the educational process. At the same time, their classification is included and presents the learning methodologies identified in the case studies, together with the number of references found in each category. It is evident that project-based methodology is being applied more often in design learning environments than any other learning method. Other methods like problem-based learning, methodologies that use game strategies, constructivism and active learning follow but with fewer cases of application.

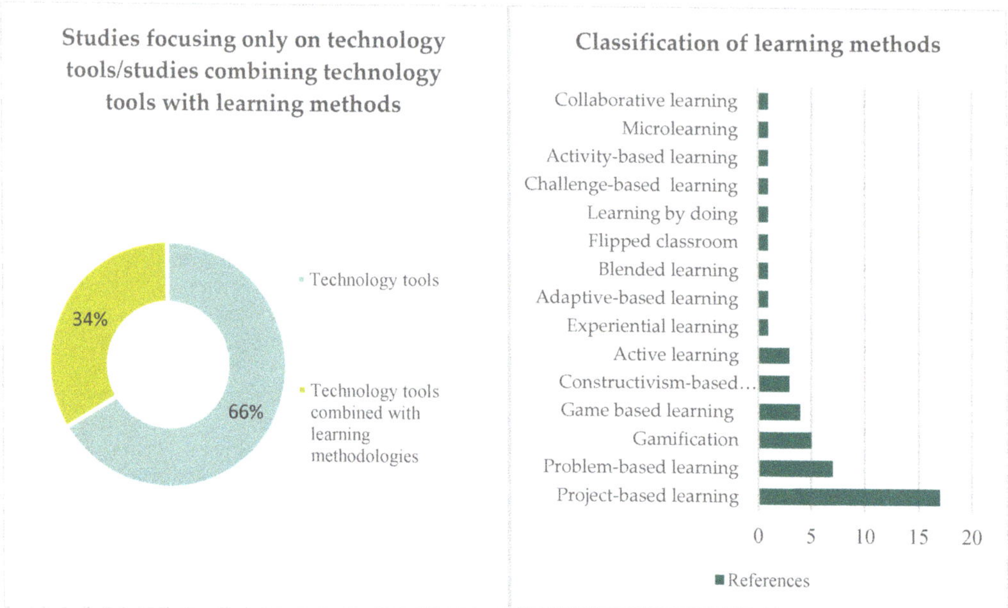

Figure 10. Technology tool focused studies and classification of learning methods found.

Figure 11 presents the categorization of the learning methods and the identified technological types, included in this review and shows the relations between those two pedagogical tools. Virtual and augmented reality appear in almost every category of the learning methods, while all the technology types are applied in a context of project-based learning approach. The following, Table 7, briefly describes the definitions of the methodologies and in which of the references they are used.

Summarizing about the above research results, it can be stressed that all the learning methods that have been identified promote a transition from the teacher-centered to the student-centered pedagogies and from passive to active learning. As opposed to traditional education and in accordance with Education 4.0 concept, the results indicate a tendency to centralize the student's role in the educational process. Students become the protagonists of their teaching, trying to face challenges and look for solutions that allow the construction of different areas of knowledge through multidisciplinary projects. Silva et al. [146] define active methodologies (such as project-based learning, collaborative-based learning, problem-based learning, blended learning, flipped classroom, game-based learning) as educational practices that allow students to relate reflection, questioning and searching for knowledge, based on its application in authentic contexts. These methodologies allow the development of practical knowledge and critical thinking through formal analysis and creative thinking.

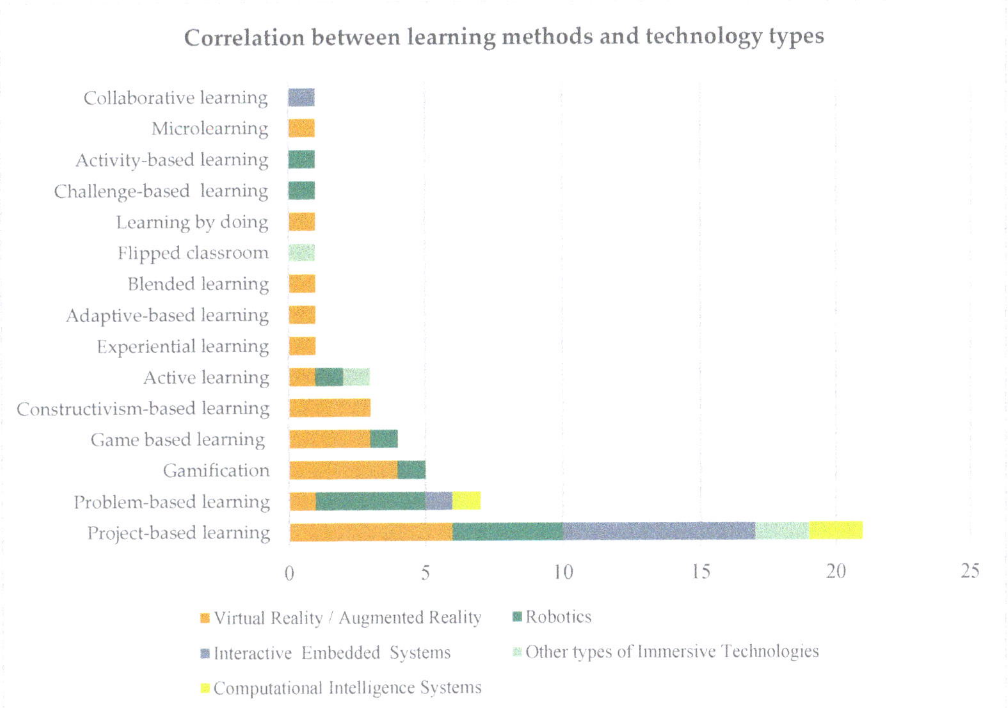

Figure 11. Learning methods in relation to the identified technology types.

Table 7. Learning methods found during the literature survey.

Learning Method	Description	Authors
Project-based learning	In Project-based learning students are introduced into the learning process by participating in real –world meaningful projects. Students are being involved in constructing hands-on multiple solutions to difficult or ill-structured problems. It also provides students the opportunity to apply their prior knowledge on new challenges while at the same time developing critical thinking skills through teamwork.	Halabi et al., 2018 [41]; Halabi, 2020 [42]; López Chao et al., 2022 [51]; Fonseca et al., 2021 [77]; Tan et al., 2016 [88]; Kuppuswamy and Mhakure, 2020 [91]; Alsos, 2015 [112]; Narahara, 2015 [113]; Conradie et al., 2016 [114]; Rodriguez-Sanchez et al., 2016 [116]; Istanbullu and Taşçı, 2019 [121]; Allam and Alacame, 2023 [123]; Rajeb and Leclercq, 2014 [136]; Camba et al., 2017 [83]; Liu et al., 2021 [85]; Benitez et al., 2020 [107]; Dewi et al., 2018 [109];
Problem-based learning	Problem-based learning is a student-centered pedagogy in which real-world problems are used as a mean in the effort for the students to learn about various subjects. Students' motivation to learn is indirectly enhanced by this need to solve the specific problem. It is based on the collaborative problem-solving process combined with individual initiative and creativity.	González-Almaguer et al., 2022 [58]; Telenko et al., 2016 [87]; Tan et al., 2016 [88]; Heyden et al., 2020 [90]; Phan and Ngo, 2020 [94]; Carulli and Bordegoni, 2017 [117]; Basarir, 2022 [138];

Table 7. *Cont.*

Learning Method	Description	Authors
Gamification	Gamification is referring to the pedagogical strategy of turning the learning environment itself into a game by entering game mechanics and game design elements in the learning process. It is considered as a very effective tool for engaging and motivating students in the educational content. Gamification also enhances enthusiasm and curiosity and leads learners to be active and take responsibility upon their own learning.	González-Almaguer et al., 2021 [57]; González-Almaguer et al., 2022 [58]; Gill et al., 2022 [59]; (Gill et al., 2023 [60]; Almaguer et al., 2020 [89]
Game based learning	Game-based learning can take use of a game as part of the learning process. It is a method that is designed to combine theoretical content and learning through the use of digital or non-digital games. It creates a playful environment by designing learning activities and gaming concepts that allow students to engage with educational material.	Ayer et al., 2016 [29]; Chandramouli et al., 2018 [63]; Fonseca et al., 2021 [77]; Almaguer et al., 2020 [89];
Constructivism-based learning	In constructivism learners construct their knowledge rather than just passively take in information. While experiencing the world and reflecting upon those experiences, they build their own representations and incorporate new information into pre-existing knowledge.	Horvat et al., 2022 [37]; Gül et al., 2014 [79]; Karmokar and Rive, 2016 [80]
Active learning	Active learning is based on student participation, investigation, and autonomous learning. Through active learning, students carry out various contextual activities to build their knowledge. They engage in learning through activities and discussions in class instead of passively listening to an expert. Active learning emphasizes higher-order thinking for analysis, synthesis, and evaluation. It often involves group work.	Jimeno-Morenilla et al., 2016 [20]; Yu and Da Silva, 2021 [97]; Ramirez-Lopez et al., 2021 [134]
Experiential learning	In experiential learning, which has its roots in the "learning by doing", the student plays an active role in the learning process. This learning model corresponds to a cyclical process of learning experiences, defined in four stages: (1) concrete experience; (2) abstract conceptualization; (3) reflective observation; and (4) active experimentation.	Cassola et al., 2022 [68]
Adaptive-based learning	Adaptive learning is a methodology for teaching and learning oriented to personalize lessons, readings, practice activities, and assessments for individual students based on their current skills progress, engagement and performance. It provides personalized learning experiences to all students regardless of individual differences and learning styles.	Abbas et al., 2023 [66]

Table 7. *Cont.*

Learning Method	Description	Authors
Blended learning	Blended learning is the integration of traditional face-to-face learning experiences with online distance learning, combining the best elements of each educational model. It is a learning approach that offers the opportunity to all students to advance the learning material at their own pace.	Roberts et al., 2020 [32]
Flipped classroom	Flipped classroom is a type of blended learning using instructional strategy through short video lectures on focused topics. It includes for learners to watch course videos or listen to course material online at any time they needed instead of being in a traditional classroom. In that case the teacher has more time to interact in class more effectively with each student individual.	Bringardner and Jean-Pierre, 2017 [133]
Learning by doing	Learning by doing is an educational approach that motivates students to learning experience through actions that are close to their needs and interests. The methodology allows learners a more meaningful learning experience through engaging activities. The role of the teacher is to drive students to learn by stimulating their curiosity.	Salah et al., 2019 [30]
Challenge-based learning	Challenge-based learning methodology engages students in real-world problems that exist in their environments that need a solution. It involves the use of technology, teamwork and self-directed learning as students apply the knowledge they acquired during their professional training. In this methodology, the teacher role is to accompany and guide the student through this challenge.	Montés et al., 2022 [100]
Activity-based learning	Activity-based learning is a learning methodology used in training process and based on various activities. This style of learning encourages students to actively engage in their training subject through practical exercises. It can be considered as a combination of problem-based learning and problem-oriented learning through an effective student-teacher interaction.	Kleppe et al., 2022 [92]
Microlearning	Microlearning is a way of teaching and delivering content to learners through small bursts of training materials that learners can comprehend in a short time, according to their preferred schedule and location. The theory of microlearning focuses on a single learning outcome, is multimodal, is typically delivered in short bursts, and is highly interactive. The learner is in control of what and when they are learning, and can complete their training at a time and place that suits their busy schedule.	Gill et al., 2022 [59]

Table 7. *Cont.*

Learning Method	Description	Authors
Collaborative learning	Collaborative learning is an educational approach to teaching and learning that involves groups of learners working together to understand an idea, complete a task, solve a problem or create a product. Is based on the idea that learning is a naturally social act in which participants talk among themselves. This learning style ensures learners remain engaged in content while thinking critically and sharing ideas with each other.	Rodriguez-Sanchez et al., 2016 [116]

It is evident that project-based learning is the method that is most frequently applied in design educational settings. Design education refers to the teaching of theory and application of design concepts that are applied in the context of tasks and projects. It is oriented around project work, preparing students for design practice. As Frascara [9] mentioned, "Design education has always been organized as problem-based learning, embedded in projects". This is another common point with Educational 4.0 philosophy, as it emphasizes on problem-solving training, where students are linked with real problems, by participating in real learning scenarios through projects and living laboratories [145,147] also points out that in design studios, which are consider the backbone for design education, students are mainly engaged in project-based learning.

The combination of technological tools with pedagogical methods is a field that is still under investigation. Most research usually focuses either on the use of technological tools or on specific learning methodologies. However, the way these two strategies can coexist and enhance each other in the educational process has not been sufficiently explored. The examined cases and the research results, whether they concern the development of educational applications or the creation of design courses, combine the technological tools with specific teaching-learning methods and thus increases significantly the added value offered.

4. Discussion

The present paper discusses innovative pedagogical procedures in learning environments of design education, based on the perspective of interactive technology tools. The main research questions concern the types of different technologies used today, the way these tools are incorporated into the educational process, the pedagogical learning methods used and how all these ultimately affect the learning outcome.

Answering the first research question [Q1] about the innovative and interactive technology tools that are being used in creative design education, it is evident that the research area of this review involved technologies that enable interactivity during the teaching and learning process. Interactivity was considered as part of the learning process, whether it was about its contribution to the creation of interactive products in educational environments or it was seen as a mean of interacting with other tools, in order to program them to perform specific tasks. Virtual and augmented reality, robotics, interactive embedded systems, other types of immersive technologies and computational intelligence systems are the technologies presented in this study. In summary, the identified types and their applications in design education show that virtual and augmented reality are most commonly used in learning environments. They present numerous ways of integrating into the learning process. Then there are the cases of robotics and interactive embedded technologies applications. Finally, more limited use in the cases examined concern the rarely types of immersive technologies and the computational intelligence systems as well, where they present the fewer references. In addition, it can be seen how significantly the number of reports regarding the use of technological tools in design educational environments, has increased in recent years. It is also evident that most types of technologies present cases of application in almost every year of the period under study and the papers referring to embedded technologies and computational intelligence systems mainly concern the latest period.

Regarding the second research question [Q2], about the way technology tools are used in design educational environments, there are essentially two main categories:

- When technology is used in different stages of the design process, during studio-based practice;
- When technology supports different aspects of the educational process and the learning material without necessarily being applied in specific projects.

According to the literature review, most of the learning environments that referring in the examined case studies concern the context of design studio courses, where technologies are used as supporting tools at various stages of the design process. Design studio courses are considered central pedagogical cells of design education and work as a simulation of the professional practice [148]. An interesting finding that emerged from the review, concerns this first category of application, where technology tools integrate into the design process. Figure 12, includes all case studies found to be applied in contexts of studio-based practice in relation with the design process. The studies are distributed based on their technology type, at all stages, from the identification of user needs to the final presentation. Based on this summary, there are some technologies that are used almost exclusively in specific stages and others that can be found in more than one stages even with different frequency. For example, robotics and interactive embedded technologies can be mainly involved with the creation of prototypes for products, as opposed to VR and AR technologies that are found in almost every stage of the design process, and other types of immersive technologies that are used from the middle of the design process to the end. On the other hand, computational intelligence systems proved more useful in the early design stages, as tools for identifying user needs and analyzing data from specific design parameters. Also observing the number of cases identified in each category and the upward trend of the diagram, it appears that in general the majority of technological applications in the case studies are incorporated in the final stages of the design process (towards project completion). There are significantly limited cases of technology application concerning the early stages of the design process. The lack of research topics around the use of interactive technologies in this area, can be seen as a research gap that creates many potentials for future investigation.

For the third research question [Q3], the term connection is used in order to examine three topics. First, as the study is focused in research of interactive technologies in design education, it is additionally examined if and in how many cases the adoption of technology tools is being implemented in a more delimited educational framework that is being strengthened from specific learning methods. Following, these methods were identified along with their appearance in research. Last, it was a matter of research to determine which of the learning methods are more often combined with specific technology tools.

As is mentioned in the results, approximately 34% of the analyzed studies refer to specific learning methods that are analytically presented in Figure 10 and Table 6. According to the findings, active methodologies (such as project-based learning, collaborative-based learning, problem-based learning, blended learning, flipped classroom, game-based learning) appear more frequently in the examined case studies. Generally, all the learning methods that were identified recognize the important role of the student in the educational process. Most of the methodologies encourage the student in taking initiatives and having the control of his own education. This can be achieved in many ways, for example by decisions needing to be taken for solving possible problems, or by combining new information with previous gained knowledge or by creating teams in order to solve issues that arise in a collaborative way. All these features are consistent with the design education philosophy of creating active and interactive learning environments through which students as protagonists can cultivate a variety of thinking skills. This study finds that there are connections of technologies and learning methodologies in design educational environments that are related to the implementation of interactive technologies. This is obviously considered relevant to the need of providing a more energetic educational setting where participants are invited to interact not only with technology tools but also with the general educational content.

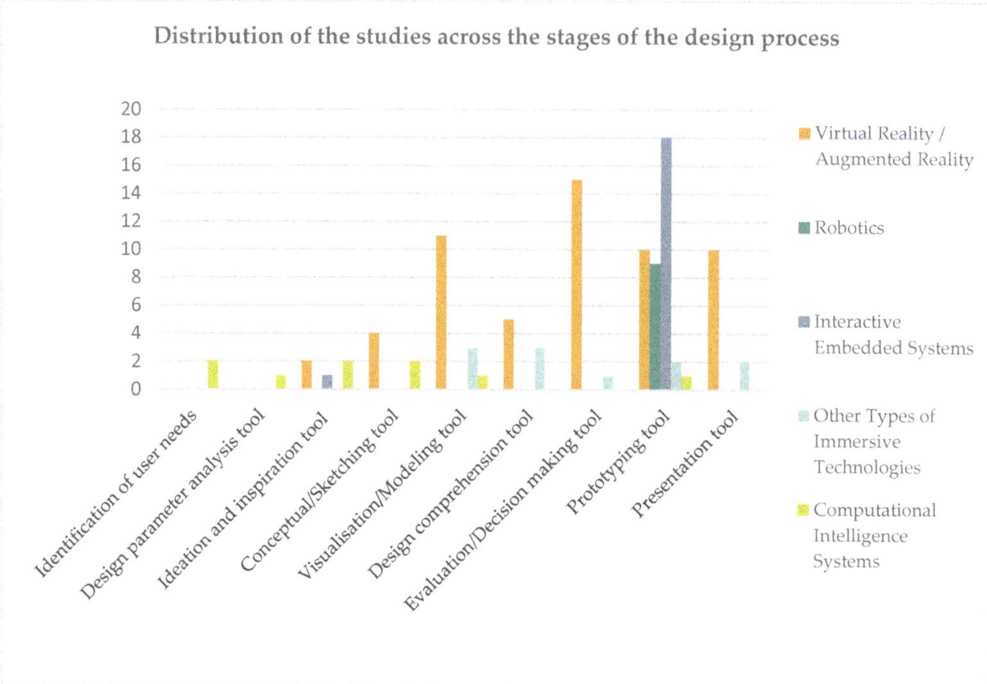

Figure 12. How the technology tools are used over the design process.

Moreover, according to the results, project-based learning represents by far the most common learning methodology used in education regarding design and is combined with all the identified technology types in this research. This is expected due to the nature of the specific learning subject, as design is mainly oriented around project work, taught in design studios, where students engage in project-based scenarios.

The final research question [Q4], is about the learning performance and whether technology tools and educational methods can ultimately be considered effective as innovative learning approaches. The technology tools identified in this review, have various uses in educational environments and affect students' academic performance in different ways. Using immersive environments for learning, improve students design skills in many areas i.e., in the process of generating, envisioning, testing, communicating ideas. Virtual and augmented reality technologies improve students' spatial abilities, imagination and creativity. Allow observation of design from multiple perspectives, which encourages diverse ways of thinking, affecting positively the creative process. All these results are contributing towards a very significant improvement of students' work. In their ability to perceive the qualitative characteristics in their original design and make design decisions in the revised design work. Other immersive technologies, such as spatial augmented reality, positively affects students' ability in comprehending design and geometric relationships, understanding product functions, or visualizing 3D geometry. Students also proved to be very creative in the way they chose to use SAR technology, enhancing the self-learning process, contributing to a more intuitive learning experience. Holograms, aim at increasing the creativity in student design solutions, resulting in positive learning outcomes. On the other hand, technology around robotics, act as motivator for transferring valuable knowledge from many disciplines and improve students learning on topics i.e., geometry, programming, kinematics, and mechanisms. They support the design process, mainly through gamified challenges, projects and problem-based learning activities that combine problem clarification, concept generation and interactive prototyping skills. Interactive embedded systems introduce students to new technical materials and equipment, like sensors, actuators, microcontrollers and display modules, in order to help them learn and practice interactive prototyping skills by creating experiential prototypes. Students have the opportunity to explore important aspects of interaction design by assessing parameters such as human behavior and emotions and how these are affected, when information is exchanged. Computational intelligence systems enhance the design process by providing students important information regarding user behavior patterns and product preferences, creating this way a valuable collaborator in discovering new ideas, helping students make design decisions and improving their design skills.

This study also showed that a significant percentage of 34%, which corresponds to 42 case studies of the examined papers refers to the involvement of specific pedagogical approaches in their proposed projects, along with the utilization of technological tools. Learning methodologies are applied as tools that facilitate the learning process at multiple levels. They can be used as a mean of creating an accessible and attractive learning environment that allows the development of critical thinking skills, encourages teamwork and self-directed learning. In some examples the use of VR in conjunction with project-based-learning method facilitated the attainment of desirable goals in engineering design projects, improved achievement of course learning outcomes and promoted effective communication. In many of the cases that involved the use of robotics technology, project-based-learning was used as an effective pedagogy that could offer students the opportunities to experience design the way it is practiced in real world-projects. There were cases that indicate that project-based learning has positive impact in students' performance regarding knowledge gained and skills. Other methodologies like problem-based learning from a perspective that reflects collaboration can help students be open to experimenting with innovative technologies. By collaborating with their peers in problem-based context, students become better equipped with specialized knowledge that helps them overcome their insecurities and increase their ability to solve multidisciplinary problems. Also, in collaborative environments, especially between nonheterogeneous teams, many case studies indicate positive results in learning performance. It is, for example, the benefit that students gain from exposure to a diversity of design backgrounds, coming from their colleagues, along with opportunities to share their areas of expertise within their groups. In studies concerning challenge-based learning approaches, results indicate that learning through knowledge discovery, when robotic technologies are involved, significantly improves students' understanding of basic concepts. Constructivism-based learning in relation to immersive technologies is providing opportunities for students to actively build skills and knowledge in relation to their interest. In addition, all the identified technologies that are found to be applied along with game-based learning methodologies, constitute examples of innovative pedagogies and emerging technologies working in harmony to positively influence motivation and learning performance. Pedagogies that use game strategies, can reduce the cognitive load, improve learning, develop students' competencies, and increase their motivation in material content.

Summarizing, from the above 42 case studies, which refer to the involvement of specific pedagogical methods, 93% refer exclusively to positive effects on the educational process and the impact they have on learning performance. The other percentage of 7%, along with the positive effects also mentioned some barriers that may arise during their implementation. These barriers, however, do not concern the combination of technological tools with educational methods but rather the supportive context around their implementation. For example, the proper training of teaching staff is considered a crucial factor for the successful development of a program that includes new technologies. Also, in cases where pedagogical methods include collaborative projects, although the majority of them showed positive results, generally, collaboration itself entails complications. Such as in cases where not all students start from the same cognitive level or they don't have the same attitude towards the projects, especially when one or more of them are not fully engaged in the project.

Concluding, the cases, where technologies and pedagogical methods coexist in learning design environments as complementary and mutually supporting tools, present very effective and encouraging educational results. Incorporating technology tools in the educational process, could attract students' interest, but when it is combined with specific pedagogical methodologies, it could engage them even more, leading to a very positive learning performance.

Another important issue regarding the implementation of new technologies in education concerns the social and psychological aspects that these innovations may have on students. Introducing new technologies to students especially for the first time, while it can create an interest and excitement in students, on the other hand, it can cause enough anxiety to undermine educational goals. In these cases, a more oriented educational context and a pedagogical method that can create a more friendly environment, can be very beneficial not only for the learning process and performance but also for these parameters. According to the above observations concerning some conclusions from the application of educational methods along with technology tools, some of the presented learning methods are directly linked with the social behavior of students and include educational aspects that are critical for the social status of students, and could indirectly affect their psychology.

5. Limitations

It is noted that this study follows the PRISMA 2020 statement guidelines for systematic reviews, and employs best practices in bibliometric analysis. Despite the measures taken to reduce bias in all of the critical steps of the review, this study still presents some limitations that must be acknowledged. Firstly, as already mentioned, the search strategy and data collection were restricted to two databases, Scopus and Google Scholar, based on the University of Western Macedonia quality system procedures. Although these databases cover a substantial proportion of the scientific literature, there might be relevant studies published in other databases that were not captured in this review. Future research could expand the search to additional databases and sources, to minimize the risk of missing relevant publications. Secondly, the study only focused on articles published in English, thus potentially missing relevant research published in other languages that could contribute to the research findings. Furthermore, the search strategy for data collection was based on the author's intention to initially create the broader research context regarding the utilization of interactive technologies in educational environments related to product design. However, due to the correlation of product design with design in general, there are potentially cases of technology applications that could not be identified. Future work could consider employing complementary inclusion criteria, to enhance the findings.

Moreover, the scope of this review focuses only on specific aspects of using technologies in educational environments, regarding mainly the identification of the different technology types, the ways these technologies are integrated into the educational process and how technologies can be applied in more structured educational contexts involving specific pedagogical methods. The practical implementation of technologies in education includes also aspects concerning several implications and effects like ethical considerations, or social and psychological aspects that need a more in-depth examination. This study indicates the importance of the contribution of specific pedagogical methods in introducing new technologies into learning environments. It is a wide area of research that could be explored further in the future, as is important to examine how such pedagogical tools can be effectively used to successfully support the educational process.

6. Conclusions

The Education 4.0 concept has started to reform the current pedagogical approaches in HEIs. Traditional learning methods are being upgraded including technologies, strategies and activities that place student at the center of the learning process. The literature discussed in this review attempts to clarify some aspects of this reformation in the field of design education. Focusing on the technological components that have emerged in recent years in the landscape of design education, 125 case studies have been examined based on the interactive technology tools that they use in their learning environments and the way these tools are integrate in the learning process. Subsequently, the case studies are analyzed from a pedagogical perspective, identifying the learning methodologies followed in each case.

According to the results, some research gaps are identified, which could be further investigated:

- Immersive technologies and robotics are presented in most of the examined papers. Significantly fewer studies focus on the use of more rare types of immersive technologies, interactive embedded systems or technologies based on computational intelligence systems. In addition, papers referring to embedded technologies and computational intelligence systems mainly have begun to appear in the recent years. So, there is a need to further investigate the application of these technologies in design education.
- Concerning the integration of technologies as supporting tools in the design process during studio-based practice, there are specific types of technologies like robotics and interactive embedded systems that are used exclusively on the prototyping stage. There are no cases studies, which to explore how these technologies could integrate to other design stages as well.
- Furthermore, the majority of technological applications in the case studies are incorporated in the final stages of the design process towards project completion. There are significantly limited cases of technology application concerning the early stages of the design process. There is a lack of research topics around the use of interactive technologies in this area, and that creates many potentials for future investigation.
- Regarding the learning methodologies, the results indicate that project-based learning present, by far, the most widely applied methodology in design educational settings. Other methodologies follow but with significantly fewer cases. So, it could be extremely useful to further investigate how other pedagogical approaches can be integrated into design education.
- There are few studies investigating different types of technologies combined with different learning methodologies. Only virtual and augmented reality appear in almost every category of the identified learning methods of this review. Generally, the cases where technologies and pedagogical methods coexistence in learning design environments is a field that is still under investigation and present many aspects that need to be explored in greater depth.

Finally, this review is expected to contribute towards the ongoing research in the field of technological advancements and applications in design education according to the Education 4.0 concept. Based on the research gap that have been discussed through the literature survey, more investigation is needed on further exploring the educational issues surrounding the utilization of interactive technological tools and learning methodologies. The coexistence and collaboration of these two educational tools could lead research work towards new directions. Future work will focus on developing methodological frameworks that will optimally combine adequate appropriate technology tools and learning methodologies in order to address innovative pedagogical strategies in design education. In relation to the gaps identified in this work, the areas to be investigated in the future concern the application of interactive technologies in the context of studio-based practice, focusing on the stages of the design process that present few research works. In addition, the contribution and integration of learning methodologies other than project-based learning could be further explored.

Author Contributions: Conceptualization, I.N., N.E., K.K. and P.K.; methodology, I.N. and P.K.; validation, I.N., N.E., K.K. and P.K.; formal analysis, I.N. and P.K.; investigation, I.N. and P.K.; resources, P.K.; data curation, I.N. and P.K.; writing—original draft preparation, I.N. and P.K.; writing—review and editing, I.N., N.E., K.K. and P.K.; visualization, I.N.; supervision, N.E., K.K. and P.K. All authors have read and agreed to the published version of the manuscript.

Funding: This research received no external funding.

Conflicts of Interest: The authors declare no conflicts of interest.

References

1. Herpich, F.; Guarese, R.L.M.; Tarouco, L.M.R. A Comparative Analysis of Augmented Reality Frameworks Aimed at the Development of Educational Applications. *Creat. Educ.* **2017**, *8*, 1433–1451. [CrossRef]
2. Halili, S.H. Technological Advancements in Education 4.0. *Online J. Distance Educ. E-Learn* **2019**, *7*, 63–69.
3. Chituc, C.-M. *A Framework for Education 4.0 in Digital Education Ecosystems*; IFIP Advances in Information and Communication Technology; Springer: Berlin/Heidelberg, Germany, 2021; Volume 629, pp. 702–709. [CrossRef]
4. Goh, P.S.C.; Abdul-Wahab, N. Paradigms to drive higher education 4.0. *Int. J. Learn. Teach. Educ. Res.* **2020**, *19*, 159–171. [CrossRef]
5. Miranda, J.; Lopez, C.S.; Navarro, S.; Bustamante, M.R.; Molina, J.M.; Molina, A. Open Innovation Laboratories as Enabling Resources to Reach the Vision of Education 4.0. In Proceedings of the 2019 IEEE International Conference on Engineering, Technology and Innovation (ICE/ITMC), Valbonne Sophia-Antipolis, France, 17–19 June 2019; pp. 1–7. [CrossRef]
6. Miranda, J.; Navarrete, C.; Noguez, J.; Molina-Espinosa, J.M.; Ramírez-Montoya, M.S.; Navarro-Tuch, S.A.; Bustamante-Bello, M.R.; Rosas-Fernández, J.B.; Molina, A. The core components of education 4.0 in higher education: Three case studies in engineering education. *Comput. Electr. Eng.* **2021**, *93*, 107278. [CrossRef]
7. Ramírez-Montoya, M.S.; Castillo-Martínez, I.M.; Sanabria-Z, J.; Miranda, J. Complex Thinking in the Framework of Education 4.0 and Open Innovation—A Systematic Literature Review. *J. Open Innov. Technol. Mark. Complex.* **2022**, *8*, 4. [CrossRef]
8. Design Council. Design for Innovation: Facts, Figures and Plans for Practical Growth. 2011. Available online: www.designcouncil.org.uk (accessed on 20 March 2024).
9. Frascara, J. Design, and design education: How can they get together? *Art Des. Commun. High. Educ.* **2017**, *16*, 125–131. [CrossRef]
10. Andreasen, M.M.; Hansen, C.T.; Cash, P. *Conceptual Design: Interpretations, Mindset and Models*; Springer International Publishing: Berlin/Heidelberg, Germany, 2015. [CrossRef]
11. McInerney, D. Insights into product design students' perception of, and engagement with, creativity in design education. *Int. J. Technol. Des. Educ.* **2023**, *33*, 1199–1219. [CrossRef]
12. Wong, Y.L.; Siu, K.W.M. A model of creative design process for fostering creativity of students in design education. *Int. J. Technol. Des. Educ.* **2012**, *22*, 437–450. [CrossRef]
13. Cropley, A. Creativity-focused Technology Education in the Age of Industry 4.0. *Create. Res. J.* **2020**, *32*, 184–191. [CrossRef]
14. Norman, D.A. Wir Brauchen Neue Designer! Why Design Education Must Change. 2011. Available online: http://www.jnd.org (accessed on 20 March 2024).
15. Page, M.J.; McKenzie, J.E.; Bossuyt, P.M.; Boutron, I.; Hoffmann, T.C.; Mulrow, C.D.; Shamseer, L.; Tetzlaff, J.M.; Akl, E.A.; Brennan, S.E.; et al. The PRISMA 2020 statement: An updated guideline for reporting systematic reviews. *Int. J. Surg.* **2021**, *88*, 105906. [CrossRef]
16. Martinez, P.; Al-Hussein, M.; Ahmad, R. A scientometric analysis and critical review of computer vision applications for construction. *Autom. Constr.* **2019**, *107*, 102947. [CrossRef]
17. Zhong, B.; Wu, H.; Li, H.; Sepasgozar, S.; Luo, H.; He, L. A scientometric analysis and critical review of construction related ontology research. *Autom. Constr.* **2019**, *101*, 17–31. [CrossRef]
18. Van Eck, N.J.; Waltman, L. Visualizing Bibliometric Networks. In *Measuring Scholarly Impact*; Springer: Berlin/Heidelberg, Germany, 2014; pp. 285–320. [CrossRef]
19. Kukah, A.S.K.; Owusu-Manu, D.G.; Edwards, D. Critical review of emotional intelligence research studies in the construction industry. *J. Eng. Des. Technol.* **2023**, *21*, 1925–1947. [CrossRef]
20. Jimeno-Morenilla, A.; Sánchez-Romero, J.L.; Mora-Mora, H.; Coll-Miralles, R. Using virtual reality for industrial design learning: A methodological proposal. *Behav. Inf. Technol.* **2016**, *351*, 897–906. [CrossRef]
21. Häkkilä, J.; Colley, A.; Väyrynen, J.; Yliharju, A.-J. Introducing Virtual Reality Technologies to Design Education. *Seminar.net* **2018**, *14*, 1–12. [CrossRef]
22. Topal, B.; Sener, B. Appraisal of augmented reality technologies for supporting industrial design practices. In *Virtual, Augmented and Mixed Reality*; Lecture Notes in Computer Science (including subseries Lecture Notes in Artificial Intelligence and Lecture Notes in Bioinformatics); Springer: Berlin/Heidelberg, Germany, 2015; Volume 9179, pp. 513–523. Available online: https://link.springer.com/chapter/10.1007/978-3-319-21067-4_52 (accessed on 17 March 2024). [CrossRef]

23. Neves, A.G.; Duarte, E. Using Virtual Environments in Basic Design Education. In Proceedings of the Senses and Sensibility'15: Design as a Trade Proceedings of the UNIDCOM/IADE 8th International Conference, Lisboa, Portugal, 5–7 October 2015; IADE—Creative University/Edições IADE: Lisbon, Portugal, 2015. Available online: https://www.academia.edu/38212750/Using_Virtual_Environments_in_Basic_Design_Education (accessed on 30 March 2024).
24. Rieuf, V.; Bouchard, C.; Aoussat, A. Immersive moodboards, a comparative study of industrial design inspiration material. *J. Des. Res.* **2015**, *13*, 78–106. [CrossRef]
25. Shih, S.L.; Ou, S.J.; Huang, Y.C.; Mu, Y.C. The Difficulties and Countermeasures of Applying Virtual Reality to Industrial Design Education. In Proceedings of the ACM International Conference Proceeding Series, Nagoya, Japan, 22–25 July 2019; Association for Computing Machinery: New York, NY, USA, 2019; pp. 269–272. [CrossRef]
26. Joundi, J.; Christiaens, Y.; Saldien, J.; Conradie, P.; De Marez, L. An Explorative Study Towards Using VR Sketching as a Tool for Ideation and Prototyping in Product Design. In *Proceedings of the Design Society: DESIGN Conference*; Cambridge University Press: Cambridge, UK, 2020; Volume 1, pp. 225–234. [CrossRef]
27. Rodríguez-Parada, L.; Pardo-Vicente, M.Á.; Sánchez-calle, A.; Pavón-Domínguez, P. Conceptual Design Using Virtual Reality: Case Study with Portable Light. In *Lecture Notes in Mechanical Engineering*; Springer Science and Business Media: Berlin/Heidelberg, Germany, 2022; pp. 81–90. [CrossRef]
28. Moural, A.; Eloy, S.; Dias, M.S.; Pedro, T. How Space Experimentation Can Inform Design: Immersive Virtual Reality as a Design Tool. In *Blucher Design Proceedings*; Blucher Proceedings: Sao Paulo, Brazil, 2015; Volume 1, pp. 182–185. [CrossRef]
29. Ayer, S.K.; Asce, A.M.; Messner, J.I.; Anumba, C.J.; Asce, F. Augmented Reality Gaming in Sustainable Design Education. *J. Archit. Eng.* **2016**, *22*, 4015012. [CrossRef]
30. Salah, B.; Abidi, M.H.; Mian, S.H.; Krid, M.; Alkhalefah, H.; Abdo, A. Virtual Reality-Based Engineering Education to Enhance Manufacturing Sustainability in Industry 4.0. *Sustainability* **2019**, *11*, 1477. [CrossRef]
31. Vo, H. Design creativity in Industry 4.0: Gravity Sketch and 3D printing in a Luminaire design project. *J. Eng. Des. Technol.* **2022**, *22*, 1413–1432. [CrossRef]
32. Roberts, S.; Page, R.; Richardson, M. Designing in Virtual Environments: The integration of Virtual Reality Tools into Industrial Design Research and Education. In Proceedings of the DRS Biennial Conference Series, Brisbane, Australia, 11–14 August 2020; Design Research Society: London, UK, 2020; pp. 11–14. [CrossRef]
33. Ibrahim, M.; El Shakhs, A. Virtual Reality as a Design Tool to Achieve Abstract Concepts of Spatial Experience: A Case Study of Design Studio Teaching. *Civ. Eng. Archit.* **2023**, *11*, 1010–1019. [CrossRef]
34. Banerjee, S.; Chowdhury, A.; Yein, N. User Experience Evaluation of a Virtual Reality Tool Used for 3D Modelling in Industrial Design Education: A Study in the Indian Context. *Designs* **2023**, *7*, 105. [CrossRef]
35. Serdar, T.; Aziz, E.S.S.; Esche, S.K.; Chassapis, C. Integration of Augmented Reality into the CAD Process. In Proceedings of the ASEE Annual Conference and Exposition, Conference Proceedings, Atlanta, Georgia, 23–26 June 2013. [CrossRef]
36. Alatta, A.R.; Freewan, A. Investigating the effect of employing immersive virtual environment on enhancing spatial perception within design process. *Archnet-IJAR Int. J. Archit. Res.* **2017**, *11*, 219–238. [CrossRef]
37. Horvat, N.; Martinec, T.; Lukačević, F.; Perišić, M.M.; Škec, S. The potential of immersive virtual reality for representations in design education. *Virtual Real.* **2022**, *26*, 1227–1244. [CrossRef]
38. Rentzos, L.; Vourtsis, C.; Mavrikios, D.; Chryssolouris, G. Using VR for complex product design. In *Virtual, Augmented and Mixed Reality. Applications of Virtual and Augmented Reality*; Lecture Notes in Computer Science (including subseries Lecture Notes in Artificial Intelligence and Lecture Notes in Bioinformatics); Springer: Berlin/Heidelberg, Germany, 2014; pp. 455–464. Available online: https://link.springer.com/chapter/10.1007/978-3-319-07464-1_42 (accessed on 17 March 2024). [CrossRef]
39. Grajewski, D.; Diakun, J.; Wichniarek, R.; Dostatni, E.; Buń, P.; Górski, F.; Karwasz, A. Improving the Skills and Knowledge of Future Designers in the Field of Ecodesign Using Virtual Reality Technologies. *Procedia Comput. Sci.* **2015**, *75*, 348–358. [CrossRef]
40. Srihirun, J.; Nimnual, R.; Netpradit, S. Plastic Bottle Structure Design Technique Using Virtual Reality Linked with Finite Element Analysis. *Comput. Educ. J.* **2015**, *6*, 87–107.
41. Halabi, O.; Abou El-Seoud, M.S.; Geroimenko, V. Teaching design project in introductory engineering course using 3D modeling and immersive virtual reality. In *Teaching and Learning in a Digital World*; Advances in Intelligent Systems and Computing; Springer: Berlin/Heidelberg, Germany, 2018; pp. 27–36.
42. Halabi, O. Immersive virtual reality to enforce teaching in engineering education. *Multimed. Tools Appl.* **2020**, *79*, 2987–3004. [CrossRef]
43. Mourtzis, D.; Zogopoulos, V.; Vlachou, E. Augmented Reality supported Product Design towards Industry 4.0: A Teaching Factory paradigm. *Procedia Manuf.* **2018**, *23*, 207–212. [CrossRef]
44. Huang, Y.C.; Chen, Y.R. The Study of Virtual Reality Product Design in Education Learning. In Proceedings of the ACM International Conference Proceeding Series, Yamanashi, Japan, 25–27 October 2019; Association for Computing Machinery: New York, NY, USA, 2019; pp. 9–11. [CrossRef]
45. Jenek, W.; Caldwell, G.; Donovan, J.; Garcia Hansen, V.; Adcock, M.; Xi, M. Exploring Media Architecture Design in Virtual Design Environments. *J. Des. Studio* **2020**, *2*, 159–163. [CrossRef]
46. Agirachman, F.A.; Shinozaki, M.; Koerniawan, M.D.; Indraprastha, A. Implementing Affordance-Based Design Review Method Using Virtual Reality in Architectural Design Studio. *Buildings* **2022**, *12*, 1296. [CrossRef]

47. Akundi, A. Enhancing Additive Manufacturing Education Using Virtual Rapid Prototyping Simulator Tool. In Proceedings of the ASEE Annual Conference and Exposition, Conference Proceedings, American Society for Engineering Education, Columbus, OH, USA, 25–28 June 2017. [CrossRef]
48. Yamada, K.; Tsumaya, A.; Taura, T.; Shimada, K.; Kaihara, T.; Yokokohji, Y.; Sato, R. An Educational Method for Enhancing the Ability to Design Innovative Products. In Proceedings of the 21st International Conference on Engineering Design (ICED 17), Vancouver, BC, Canada, 21–25 August 2017.
49. Topal, B.; Şener, B. Augmented Reality for Enhanced Student Industrial Design Presentations. In Proceedings of the 17th International Conference on Engineering and Product Design Education, E and PDE 2015, Loughborough Design School (LDS), University of Loughborough, Loughborough, UK, 3–4 September 2015; Code 117047. Available online: https://hdl.handle.net/11511/71474 (accessed on 20 March 2024).
50. Saorín, J.L.; de la Torre-Cantero, J.; Díaz, D.M.; López-Chao, V. Cloud-Based Collaborative 3D Modeling to Train Engineers for the Industry 4.0. *Appl. Sci.* **2019**, *91*, 4559. [CrossRef]
51. López Chao, V.; Luis Saorin, J.; Torre Cantero, J.L.; Melián Díaz, D. Collaborative Graphic Simulation Experience Through Project-Based Learning to Develop Spatial Abilities. *Int. J. Eng. Educ.* **2022**, *38*, 905–916.
52. Zhang, F. Teaching Reform of Cultural and Creative Product Design Based on Virtual Reality (VR) Technology. *Int. J. Web-Based Learn. Teach. Technol.* **2023**, *18*, 1–15. [CrossRef]
53. Bashabsheh, A.K.; Alzoubi, H.H.; Ali, M.Z. The application of virtual reality technology in architectural pedagogy for building constructions. *Alex. Eng. J.* **2019**, *58*, 713–723. [CrossRef]
54. Kassim, M.; Zubir, M.T.H.M. Design of augmented reality for engineering equipment in education. *Int. J. Adv. Trends Comput. Sci. Eng.* **2019**, *8*, 2773–2781. [CrossRef]
55. Urban, H.; Pelikan, G.; Schranz, C. Augmented Reality in AEC Education: A Case Study. *Buildings* **2022**, *12*, 391. [CrossRef]
56. Onecha, B.; Cornadó, C.; Morros, J.; Pons, O. New Approach to Design and Assess Metaverse Environments for Improving Learning Processes in Higher Education: The Case of Architectural Construction and Rehabilitation. *Buildings* **2023**, *13*, 1340. [CrossRef]
57. Gonzalez Almaguer, C.A.; Aguirre Acosta, A.C.; Perez Murueta, P.O. Gamification and Simulation: Distance Education for Industrial Engineering Students. In Proceedings of the Machine Learning-Driven Digital Technologies for Educational Innovation Workshop 2021, Monterrey, Mexico, 15–17 December 2021; Future of Educational Innovation Workshop Series. Institute of Electrical and Electronics Engineers Inc.: Piscataway, NJ, USA, 2021. [CrossRef]
58. Gonzalez-Almaguer, C.; Zubieta, C.; Rosas, E.; Rivas, C.; Aguirre, A.; Lule, M. Problem Solving Race: Gamification to Solve Industrial Engineering Problems in the Distance and Classroom Learning. In Proceedings of the DS 117: Proceedings of the 24th International Conference on Engineering and Product Design Education (E&PDE 2022), London South Bank University in London, London, UK, 8–9 September 2022; The Design Society: Glassgow, UK, 2022. [CrossRef]
59. Gill, A.S.; Irwin, D.S.; Mareta, S.; Towey, D.; Wang, A.; Zhang, Y. A Pilot Study Investigating Student Interaction Preferences in Immersive Virtual Reality Environments. In Proceedings of the 2022 IEEE International Conference on Teaching, Assessment and Learning for Engineering (TALE), Hong Kong, China, 4–7 December 2022; Institute of Electrical and Electronics Engineers Inc.: Piscataway, NJ, USA, 2022; pp. 133–140. [CrossRef]
60. Gill, A.; Irwin, D.; Towey, D.; Zhang, Y.; Li, B.; Sun, L.; Wang, Z.; Yu, W.; Zhang, R.; Zheng, Y. Effects of Augmented Reality Gamification on Students' Intrinsic Motivation and Performance. In Proceedings of the International Conference on Teaching, Assessment, and Learning for Engineering, Auckland, New Zealand, 28 November–1 December 2023. [CrossRef]
61. Gavish, N.; Gutiérrez, T.; Webel, S.; Rodríguez, J.; Peveri, M.; Bockholt, U.; Tecchia, F. Evaluating virtual reality and augmented reality training for industrial maintenance and assembly tasks. *Interact. Learn. Environ.* **2015**, *23*, 778–798. [CrossRef]
62. Jou, M.; Wang, J. Investigation of effects of virtual reality environments on learning performance of technical skills. *Comput Human Behav.* **2013**, *29*, 433–438. [CrossRef]
63. Chandramouli, M.; Jin, G.; Heffron, J.D.; Fidan, I.; Cossette, M.; Welsch, C.A.; Merrell, W. Virtual reality education modules for digital manufacturing instruction. In Proceedings of the ASEE Annual Conference and Exposition, Conference Proceedings, Salt Lake, UT, USA, 23 June–27 July 2018; American Society for Engineering Education: Washington, DC, USA, 2018. [CrossRef]
64. Cordero-Guridi, J.-d.-J.; Cuautle-Gutiérrez, L.; Alvarez-Tamayo, R.I.; Caballero-Morales, S.O. Design and Development of a I4.0 Engineering Education Laboratory with Virtual and Digital Technologies Based on ISO/IEC TR 23842-1 Standard Guidelines. *Appl. Sci.* **2022**, *122*, 5993. [CrossRef]
65. Mathur, J.; Miller, S.R.; Simpson, T.W.; Meisel, N.A. Designing immersive experiences in virtual reality for design for additive manufacturing training. *Addit. Manuf.* **2023**, *78*, 103875. [CrossRef]
66. Abbas, Y.; Martinetti, A.; Nizamis, K.; Spoolder, S.; van Dongen, L.A.M. Ready, trainer . . . one*! discovering the entanglement of adaptive learning with virtual reality in industrial training: A case study. *Interact. Learn. Environ.* **2023**, *31*, 3698–3727. [CrossRef]
67. Acuña, A.; Melón, M.E. Virtual Learning Environment for Immersive Teaching of the Operation of High-Risk Equipment in Architecture AND Industrial Design Workshops. In Proceedings of the DS 117: Proceedings of the 24th International Conference on Engineering and Product Design Education (E&PDE 2022), London South Bank University in London, London, UK, 8–9 September 2022; The Design Society: Glassgow, UK, 2022. [CrossRef]

68. Cassola, F.; Mendes, D.; Pinto, M.; Morgado, L.; Costa, S.; Anjos, L.; Marques, D.; Rosa, F.; Maia, A.; Tavares, H.; et al. Design and Evaluation of a Choreography-Based Virtual Reality Authoring Tool for Experiential Learning in Industrial Training. *IEEE Trans. Learn. Technol.* **2022**, *15*, 526–539. [CrossRef]
69. Yang, X.; Mao, W.; Hu, Y.; Wang, J.; Wan, X.; Fang, H. Does augmented reality help in industrial training? A comprehensive evaluation based on natural human behavior and knowledge retention. *Int. J. Ind. Ergon.* **2023**, *98*, 103516. [CrossRef]
70. Maulana, F.I.; Azis, B.; Primadani, T.I.W.; Hasibuan, P.R.A. FunAR-furniture augmented reality application to support practical laboratory experiments in interior design education. *Indones. J. Electr. Eng. Comput. Sci.* **2023**, *31*, 845–855. [CrossRef]
71. Farzeeha, D.; Omar, M.; Ibrahim, N.H.; Surif, J.; Ali, M.; Ismail, S. Overcoming the problems faced by student's in learning engineering drawing with the implementation of augmented reality learning environment. *Man India* **2017**, *97*, 147–159.
72. Omar, M.; Farzeeha, D.; Nasir, A.N. AREDApps: Integrating mobile augmented reality. in orthographic projection teaching and learning. *Int. J. Recent Technol. Eng.* **2019**, *8*, 821–825.
73. González, N.A.A. Development of spatial skills with virtual reality and augmented reality. *Int. J. Interact. Des. Manuf.* **2018**, *12*, 133–144. [CrossRef]
74. Molina-Carmona, R.; Pertegal-Felices, M.L.; Jimeno-Morenilla, A.; Mora-Mora, H. Virtual Reality Learning Activities for Multimedia Students to Enhance Spatial Ability. *Sustainability* **2018**, *10*, 1074. [CrossRef]
75. Gómez-Tone, H.C.; Martin-Gutierrez, J.; Anci, L.V.; Luis, C.E.M. International Comparative Pilot Study of Spatial Skill Development in Engineering Students through Autonomous Augmented Reality-Based Training. *Symmetry* **2020**, *12*, 1401. [CrossRef]
76. Akkus, İ.; Arslan, P.Y. The Effects of Augmented Reality in the Technical Drawing Course on Engineering Students' Spatial Ability and Academic Achievement. *J. Learn. Teach. Digit. Age* **2022**, *7*, 160–174. [CrossRef]
77. Fonseca, D.; Cavalcanti, J.; Peña, E.; Valls, V.; Sanchez-Sepúlveda, M.; Moreira, F.; Navarro, I.; Redondo, E. Mixed Assessment of Virtual Serious Games Applied in Architectural and Urban Design Education. *Sensors* **2021**, *21*, 3102. [CrossRef] [PubMed]
78. Häfner, P.; Häfner, V.; Ovtcharova, J. Teaching Methodology for Virtual Reality Practical Course in Engineering Education. *Procedia Comput. Sci.* **2013**, *25*, 251–260. [CrossRef]
79. Gül, L.F.; Kim, M.J.; Gu, N.; Wang, X. Methods for assessing 3D virtual worlds in design education. In *Cases on the Assessment of Scenario and Game-Based Virtual Worlds in Higher Education*; IGI Global: Hershey, PA, USA, 2014; pp. 152–174. [CrossRef]
80. Karmokar, S.; Rive, P. Design Thinking Methods and Creative Technologies in Virtual Worlds. In Proceedings of the European Conference on Innovation & Entrepreneurship, Jyvaskyla, Finland, 15–16 September 2016.
81. Vogel, J.; Schuir, J.; Koßmann, C.; Thomas, O.; Teuteberg, F.; Hamborg, K.-C. Let's Do Design Thinking Virtually: Design and Evaluation of A Virtual Reality Application For Collaborative Prototyping. In *ECIS 2021 Research Papers*; AIS eLibrary: Atlanta, GA, USA, 2021; Available online: https://aisel.aisnet.org/ecis2021_rp/112 (accessed on 20 March 2024).
82. Huang, H.; Lin, C.; Cai, D. Enhancing the learning effect of virtual reality 3D modeling: A new model of learner's design collaboration and a comparison of its field system usability. *Univers. Access Inf. Soc.* **2021**, *20*, 429–440. [CrossRef]
83. Camba, J.D.; Soler, J.L.; Contero, M. Immersive visualization technologies to facilitate multidisciplinary design education. In *Learning and Collaboration Technologies. Novel Learning Ecosystems*; Lecture Notes in Computer Science (Including subseries Lecture Notes in Artificial Intelligence and Lecture Notes in Bioinformatics); Springer: Berlin/Heidelberg, Germany, 2017; pp. 3–11. Available online: https://link.springer.com/chapter/10.1007/978-3-319-58509-3_1 (accessed on 28 February 2024). [CrossRef]
84. Probst, A.; Ebner, M. Introducing augmented reality at secondary colleges of engineering. In Proceedings of the 20th International Conference on Engineering and Product Design Education (EPDE2018), London, UK, 6–7 September 2018; I.C. Dyson School of Engineering, Ed.: London, UK; pp. 714–719.
85. Liu, W.; Lee, K.P.; Gray, C.M.; Toombs, A.L.; Chen, K.H.; Leifer, L. Transdisciplinary Teaching and Learning in UX Design: A Program Review and AR Case Studies. *Appl. Sci.* **2021**, *112*, 10648. [CrossRef]
86. An, H.; Sung, W.; Yoon, S.Y. Implementation of learning by design in a synchronized online environment to teach educational robotics to inservice teachers. *Educ. Technol. Res. Dev.* **2022**, *70*, 1473–1496. [CrossRef]
87. Telenko, C.; Wood, K.; Otto, K.; Elara, M.R.; Foong, S.; Pey, K.L.; Tan, U.X.; Camburn, B.; Moreno, D.; Frey, D. Designettes: An Approach to Multidisciplinary Engineering Design Education. *J. Mech. Des.* **2016**, *138*, 022001. [CrossRef]
88. Tan, N.; Mohan, R.E.; Foong, S.; Yamakita, M.; Iwase, M.; Hatakeyama, S.; Kamamichi, N.; Song, L.; Wang, Y.; Zhu, Q. IDC Robocon: A Transnational Teaming Competition for Project-Based Design Education in Undergraduate Robotics. *Robotics* **2016**, *5*, 12. [CrossRef]
89. Almaguer, C.G.; Maya, M.; Caballero, E.; Acuna, A.; Zubieta, C.; Yarto, C. Stem competency-based learning for engineering and design students of the educational model tec21. In Proceedings of the 22nd International Conference on Engineering and Product Design Education, E and PDE 2020, Herning, Denmark, 10–11 September 2020; The Design Society: Glassgow, UK, 2020. [CrossRef]
90. Heyden, E.; Küchenhof, J.; Greve, E.; Krause, D. Development of a Design Education Platform for an Interdisciplinary Teaching Concept. *Procedia CIRP* **2020**, *91*, 553–558. [CrossRef]
91. Kuppuswamy, R.; Mhakure, D. Project-based learning in an engineering-design course—Developing mechanical-engineering graduates for the world of work. *Procedia CIRP* **2020**, *91*, 565–570. [CrossRef]
92. Kleppe, P.S.; Bjelland, O.; Hansen, I.E.; Mork, O.J. Idea Lab: Bridging Product Design and Automatic Manufacturing in Engineering Education 4.0. In Proceedings of the IEEE Global Engineering Education Conference, EDUCON, Tunis, Tunisia, 28–31 March 2022; IEEE Computer Society: Washington, DC, USA, 2022; pp. 195–200. [CrossRef]

93. Yazar, T.; Oral-Karakoç, H.; Gündüz, G.; Yabanigül, M.N. Integrating Robotic Fabrication into the Basic Design Studio. *Nexus Netw. J.* **2023**, *25*, 999–1013. [CrossRef]
94. Phan, M.H.; Ngo, H.Q.T. A multidisciplinary mechatronics program: From project-based learning to a community-based approach on an open platform. *Electronics* **2020**, *9*, 954. [CrossRef]
95. Kilic-Bebek, E.; Nizamis, K.; Vlutters, M.; Bebek, O.; Karapars, Z.G.; Unal, R.; Yilmaz, D.; Ugurlu, B. Transdisciplinarity as a Learning Challenge: Student Experiences and Outcomes in an Innovative Course on Wearable and Collaborative Robotics. *IEEE Trans. Educ.* **2023**, *66*, 263–273. [CrossRef]
96. Deniz, C.; Cakır, M. A novel designed interactive training platform for industrial robot offline programming and robotics education. *Int. J. Robot. Autom.* **2017**, *32*, 665–672. [CrossRef]
97. Yu, F.; Da Silva, E.R. Design for robot assembly: Challenges of online education. *Procedia CIRP* **2021**, *100*, 482–487. [CrossRef]
98. Grandi, R.; Falconi, R.; Melchiorri, C. Robotic Competitions: Teaching Robotics and Real-Time Programming with LEGO Mindstorms. *IFAC Proc. Vol.* **2014**, *47*, 10598–10603. [CrossRef]
99. Garcia, I.; Guzmán-Ramírez, E.; Arias-Montiel, M.; Lugo-González, E. Introducing a robotic hand to support lecture-based courses on mechatronics systems design at the undergraduate level. *Comput. Appl. Eng. Educ.* **2020**, *28*, 1612–1627. [CrossRef]
100. Montés, N.; Aloy, P.; Ferrer, T.; Romero, P.D.; Barquero, S.; Carbonell, A.M. Exploria, Steam Education at University Level as a New Way to Teach Engineering Mechanics in an Integrated Learning Process. *Appl. Sci.* **2022**, *120*, 5105. [CrossRef]
101. Brell-Çokcan, S.; Braumann, J. Industrial robots for design education: Robots as open interfaces beyond fabrication. In *Global Design and Local Materialization*; Communications in Computer and Information Science; Springer: Berlin/Heidelberg, Germany, 2013; pp. 109–117. Available online: https://link.springer.com/chapter/10.1007/978-3-642-38974-0_10 (accessed on 28 February 2024). [CrossRef]
102. Shi, X.; Fang, X.; Chen, Z.; Phillips, T.K.; Fukuda, H. A Didactic Pedagogical Approach toward Sustainable Architectural Education through Robotic Tectonics. *Sustainability* **2020**, *12*, 1757. [CrossRef]
103. Yi, H. Robotics application for the advanced integration of design and technology in architecture. *Comput. Appl. Eng. Educ.* **2021**, *29*, 1146–1162. [CrossRef]
104. Jiehan, T.; Yee, T.C.; Zadhy, H.; Diallo, A.M.; Vickraman, M.; Royan, N.R.R. Integrating IR4.0 Technology in Engineering Education: Robotic Arm Remote Lab. *J. Eng. Educ. Transform.* **2022**, *36*, 83–94. [CrossRef]
105. Bedillion, M.; Muci-Kuchler, K.; Nikshi, W. An Arduino-Based Hardware Platform for a Mechanical Engineering Sophomore Design Course. In Proceedings of the ASEE Annual Conference & Exposition, Salt Lake City, UT, USA, 23 June–27 July 2018.
106. Castelli, K.; Giberti, H. Additive Manufacturing as an Essential Element in the Teaching of Robotics. *Robotics* **2019**, *8*, 73. [CrossRef]
107. Benitez, V.H.; Symonds, R.; Elguezabal, D.E. Design of an affordable IoT open-source robot arm for online teaching of robotics courses during the pandemic contingency. *HardwareX* **2020**, *8*, e00158. [CrossRef] [PubMed]
108. Carrasco-Navarro, R.; Luque-Vega, L.F.; Nava-Pintor, J.A.; Guerrero-Osuna, H.A.; Carlos-Mancilla, M.A.; Castañeda-Miranda, C.L. MEIoT 2D-CACSET: IoT Two-Dimensional Cartesian Coordinate System Educational Toolkit Align with Educational Mechatronics Framework. *Sensors* **2022**, *223*, 4802. [CrossRef] [PubMed]
109. Dewi, T.; Risma, P.; Oktarina, Y. Fuzzy logic simulation as a teaching-learning media for artificial intelligence class. *J. Autom. Mob. Robot. Intell. Syst.* **2018**, *12*, 3–9. [CrossRef]
110. Orsolits, H.; Rauh, S.F.; Estrada, J.G. Using Mixed Reality Based Digital Twins for Robotics Education. In Proceedings of the 2022 IEEE International Symposium on Mixed and Augmented Reality Adjunct, ISMAR-Adjunct 2022, Singapore, 17–21 October 2022; Institute of Electrical and Electronics Engineers Inc.: Piscataway, NJ, USA, 2022; pp. 56–59. [CrossRef]
111. Velásquez-Montoya, M. Social Innovation and Technology Implementation in Product Design Engineering. In Proceedings of the DS 83: Proceedings of the 18th International Conference on Engineering and Product Design Education (E&PDE16), Design Education: Collaboration and Cross-Disciplinarity, Aalborg, Denmark, 8–9 September 2016; pp. 15–20.
112. Alsos, O. Teaching Product Design Students How to Make Everyday Things Interactive with Arduino. In Proceedings of the Make2Learn@ICEC, Trondheim, Norway, 29 September 2015.
113. Narahara, T. Design exploration through interactive prototypes using sensors and microcontrollers. *Comput. Graph.* **2015**, *50*, 25–35. [CrossRef]
114. Conradie, P.D.; Vandevelde, C.; De Ville, J.; Saldien, J. Prototyping tangible user interfaces: Case study of the collaboration between academia and industry. *Int. J. Eng. Educ.* **2016**, *32*, 726–737.
115. Liu, W.; Qu, Y. Designing tangible interactions for aged users though interactive technology prototyping. In *Human Aspects of IT for the Aged Population. Design for Aging*; Lecture Notes in Computer Science (including subseries Lecture Notes in Artificial Intelligence and Lecture Notes in Bioinformatics); Springer: Berlin/Heidelberg, Germany, 2015; pp. 53–60. Available online: https://link.springer.com/chapter/10.1007/978-3-319-20892-3_6 (accessed on 20 March 2024). [CrossRef]
116. Rodriguez-Sanchez, M.C.; Torrado-Carvajal, A.; Vaquero, J.; Borromeo, S.; Hernandez-Tamames, J.A. An Embedded Systems Course for Engineering Students Using Open-Source Platforms in Wireless Scenarios. *IEEE Trans. Educ.* **2016**, *59*, 248–254. [CrossRef]
117. Carulli, M.; Bordegoni, M. Rapid prototyping products mapping live-data streams into tangible user interfaces. In Proceedings of the DS 87-9 Proceedings of the 21st International Conference on Engineering Design (ICED 17), Vancouver, BC, Canada, 21–25 August 2017.

118. Qu, Y.; Jia, Y.; Qu, T.; Chen, Z.; Li, H.; Li, W. Research on interactive prototype design and experience method based on open source. In *Design, User Experience, and Usability: Theory, Methodology, and Management*; Lecture Notes in Computer Science (including subseries Lecture Notes in Artificial Intelligence and Lecture Notes in Bioinformatics); Springer: Berlin/Heidelberg, Germany, 2017; pp. 633–651. [CrossRef]
119. Omar, H.M. Enhancing automatic control learning through Arduino-based projects. *Eur. J. Eng. Educ.* **2018**, *43*, 652–663. [CrossRef]
120. Nam, W.; Choh, I. Study on Microcontroller Board Design Planning for Design Education. In Proceedings of the 2nd IEEE International Conference on Knowledge Innovation and Invention 2019, ICKII 2019, Seoul, Republic of Korea, 12–15 July 2019; Institute of Electrical and Electronics Engineers Inc.: Piscataway, NJ, USA, 2019; pp. 557–560. [CrossRef]
121. İstanbullu, A.; Taşçı, M. Open source hardware-arduino: Case study on mechanical engineering students design project. *Int. J. Eng. Educ.* **2019**, *31*, 726–735.
122. Kim, H. Learning from two types of class projects in interactive physical prototyping: Comparison between technology-driven and experience-driven project results. *Arch. Des. Res.* **2020**, *33*, 75–86. [CrossRef]
123. Allam, S.; Alacame, S. Tailoring Arduino for Interactive Digital Fabrication: Mechanism, Algorithms, Cases. In Proceedings of the 20th International Learning and Technology Conference, L and T 2023, Jeddah, Saudi Arabia, 26 January 2023; Institute of Electrical and Electronics Engineers Inc.: Piscataway, NJ, USA, 2023; pp. 145–150. [CrossRef]
124. Sun, Z.; Zhang, X.; Peng, C.; Song, N.; Luo, C. Design of Distance Teaching System for Interior Design Course Based on Internet of Things and Education Platform. *Wirel. Commun. Mob. Comput.* **2022**, *2022*, 7440409. [CrossRef]
125. Jansen, A.; Colombo, S. Mix and Match Machine Learning: An Ideation Toolkit to Design Machine Learning-Enabled Solutions. In Proceedings of the Seventeenth International Conference on Tangible, Embedded, and Embodied Interaction, Warsaw, Poland, 26 February–1 March 2023; Association for Computing Machinery: New York, NY, USA, 2023. [CrossRef]
126. Darwish, M.; Kamel, S.; Assem, A. Extended reality for enhancing spatial ability in architecture design education. *Ain Shams Eng. J.* **2023**, *14*, 102104. [CrossRef]
127. Tang, Y.M.; Au, K.M.; Leung, Y. Comprehending products with mixed reality: Geometric relationships and creativity. *Int. J. Eng. Bus. Manag.* **2018**, *10*, 1847979018809599. [CrossRef]
128. Ranscombe, C.; Zhang, W.; Snider, C.; Hicks, B. A Critical Appraisal of Mixed Reality Prototyping to Support Studio Design Education. *Proc. Des. Soc.* **2023**, *3*, 81–90. [CrossRef]
129. Ricci, M.; Scarcelli, A.; Fiorentino, M. Designing for the Metaverse: A Multidisciplinary Laboratory in the Industrial Design Program. *Future Internet* **2023**, *15*, 69. [CrossRef]
130. Mast, D.; Roidl, A.; Jylha, A. Wizard of Oz Prototyping for Interactive Spatial Augmented Reality in HCI Education: Experiences with Rapid Prototyping for Interactive Spatial Augmented Reality. In Proceedings of the Conference on Human Factors in Computing Systems, Hamburg, Germany, 23–28 April 2023; Association for Computing Machinery: New York, NY, USA, 2023. [CrossRef]
131. Park, M.K.; Lim, K.J.; Seo, M.K.; Jung, S.J.; Lee, K.H. Spatial augmented reality for product appearance design evaluation. *J. Comput. Des. Eng.* **2015**, *2*, 38–46. [CrossRef]
132. Quintero, H.; Aguilera, N.; Ramirez, P.; Hosseini, S. Synergy of digital art, architecture and design using video-mapping in a combined classroom. In Proceedings of the 5th International Conference of the Virtual and Augmented Reality in Education, VARE 2019, Lisbon, Portugal, 18–20 September 2019; Dime University of Genoa: Genoa, Italy; pp. 1–6. [CrossRef]
133. Bringardner, J.; Jean-Pierre, Y. Evaluating a Flipped Lab Approach in a First-Year Engineering Design Course. In Proceedings of the 2017 ASEE Annual Conference & Exposition, Columbus, OH, USA, 25–28 June 2017.
134. Ramirez-Lopez, C.V.; Castano, L.; Aldape, P.; Tejeda, S. Telepresence with Hologram Effect: Technological Ecosystem for Distance Education. *Sustainability* **2021**, *13*, 14006. [CrossRef]
135. Rajeb, S.B.; Leclercq, P. Using spatial augmented reality in synchronous collaborative design applications in architectural design training. In *Cooperative Design, Visualization, and Engineering*; Lecture Notes in Computer Science (including subseries Lecture Notes in Artificial Intelligence and Lecture Notes in Bioinformatics); Springer: Berlin/Heidelberg, Germany, 2013; pp. 1–10. Available online: https://link.springer.com/chapter/10.1007/978-3-642-40840-3_1 (accessed on 20 March 2024). [CrossRef]
136. Rajeb, S.B.; Leclercq, P. Spatial augmented reality in collaborative design training: Articulation between I-space, we-space and space-between. In *Cooperative Design, Visualization, and Engineering*; Lecture Notes in Computer Science (including subseries Lecture Notes in Artificial Intelligence and Lecture Notes in Bioinformatics); Springer: Berlin/Heidelberg, Germany, 2014; pp. 343–353. Available online: https://link.springer.com/chapter/10.1007/978-3-319-07464-1_32 (accessed on 28 February 2024). [CrossRef]
137. Calixte, X.; Leclercq, P. The Interactive Projection Mapping as a Spatial Augmented Reality to Help Collaborative Design: Case Study in Architectural Design. In *Cooperative Design, Visualization, and Engineering*; Lecture Notes in Computer Science (including subseries Lecture Notes in Artificial Intelligence and Lecture Notes in Bioinformatics); Springer: Berlin/Heidelberg, Germany, 2017; pp. 143–152. Available online: https://www.researchgate.net/publication/319295601_The_Interactive_Projection_Mapping_as_a_Spatial_Augmented_Reality_to_Help_Collaborative_Design_Case_Study_in_Architectural_Design (accessed on 20 March 2024). [CrossRef]
138. Basarir, L. Modelling AI in Architectural Education. *Gazi Univ. J. Sci.* **2022**, *35*, 1260–1278. [CrossRef]

139. Chien, Y.H.; Yao, C.K. Development of an AI Userbot for Engineering Design Education Using an Intent and Flow Combined Framework. *Appl. Sci.* **2020**, *10*, 7970. [CrossRef]
140. Zhang, C.; Kwon, Y.P.; Kramer, J.; Kim, E.; Agogino, A.M. Concept Clustering in Design Teams: A Comparison of Human and Machine Clustering. *J. Mech. Des.* **2017**, *139*, 111414. [CrossRef]
141. Tong, H.; Türel, A.; Şenkal, H.; Ergun, S.F.Y.; Güzelci, O.Z.; Alaçam, S. Can AI Function as a New Mode of Sketching: A Teaching Experiment with Freshman. *Int. J. Emerg. Technol. Learn.* **2023**, *188*, 234–248. [CrossRef]
142. Wendrich, R.E. Computer aided creative thinking machines (Caxtus). *Comput. Aided Des. Appl.* **2021**, *18*, 1390–1409. [CrossRef]
143. Meron, Y.; Tekmen Araci, Y. Artificial intelligence in design education: Evaluating ChatGPT as a virtual colleague for post-graduate course development. *Des. Sci.* **2023**, *9*, e30. [CrossRef]
144. Kuo, J.Y.; Xia, Z. Exploring Intelligent User Interfaces from Design Students' Perspectives on Smart Home Products Through Peer Assessment, Focus Group and ChatGPT. *Adv. Transdiscipl. Eng.* **2023**, *41*, 161–170. [CrossRef]
145. López, H.A.; Ponce, P.; Molina, A.; Ramírez-Montoya, M.S.; Lopez-Caudana, E. Design Framework Based on TEC21 Educational Model and Education 4.0 Implemented in a Capstone Project: A Case Study of an Electric Vehicle Suspension System. *Sustainability* **2021**, *13*, 5768. [CrossRef]
146. Silva, D.E.; Lopes, T.; Sobrinho, M.C.; Valentim, N. Investigating Initiatives to Promote the Advancement of Education 4.0: A Systematic Mapping Study. In Proceedings of the International Conference on Computer Supported Education, CSEDU, Online, 23–25 April 2021; Science and Technology Publications: Lda Setúbal, Portugal, 2021; pp. 458–466. [CrossRef]
147. Emam, M.; Taha, D.; ElSayad, Z. Collaborative pedagogy in architectural design studio: A case study in applying collaborative design. *Alex. Eng. J.* **2019**, *58*, 163–170. [CrossRef]
148. Hamurcu, A.; Timur, Ş.; Rızvanoğlu, K. An overview of virtual reality within industrial design education. *J. Eng. Des. Technol.* **2020**, *18*, 1889–1905. [CrossRef]

Multimodal Technologies and Interaction

MDPI

Review

Combining Artificial Intelligence with Augmented Reality and Virtual Reality in Education: Current Trends and Future Perspectives

Georgios Lampropoulos [1,2,3]

[1] Department of Applied Informatics, School of Information Sciences, University of Macedonia, 54636 Thessaloniki, Greece; glampropoulos@uom.edu.gr
[2] Department of Education, School of Education, University of Nicosia, Nicosia 2417, Cyprus
[3] Department of Preschool Education, School of Education, University of Crete, 74100 Rethymno, Greece

Abstract: The combination of artificial intelligence with extended reality technologies can significantly impact the educational domain. This study aims to present an overview regarding the combination of artificial intelligence with augmented reality and virtual reality technologies and their integration in education through an analysis of the existing literature. Hence, this study examines 201 documents from Scopus and the Web of Science (WoS). This study focuses on examining the basic characteristics of the document collection, highlighting the most prevalent themes, areas, and topics, exploring the thematic evolution of the topic, revealing current challenges and limitations and on identifying emerging topics and future research directions. Based on the outcomes, a significant annual growth rate (60.58%) was observed indicating the increasing interest in the topic. Additionally, the potential of combining artificial intelligence with virtual reality and augmented reality technologies to provide personalized, affective, interactive, and immersive learning experiences across educational levels in both formal and informal settings supporting both teachers and students arose. Therefore, through this combination, intelligent tutoring systems (ITSs), which offer behavioral, cognitive, and social personalization, have a virtual presence, and can effectively be used as tutors or peer learners, can be created. Such ITSs can be characterized as affective and social entities that can increase students' learning performance, learning motivation, and engagement and promote both self-directed learning and collaborative learning. This study also highlights the need to examine how the physical presence that characterizes some new technologies compares to the virtual presence that extended reality technologies offer in terms of overall learning outcomes and students' development.

Keywords: artificial intelligence; AI; virtual reality; augmented reality; mixed reality; extended reality; metaverse; intelligent tutoring systems; review; bibliometric analysis; scientific mapping

1. Introduction

Digital technologies play a vital role in the educational process, as their integration into teaching and learning can yield several changes to the educational domain [1]. As students grow up with technological applications surrounding them, their educational interests and needs have drastically changed [2]. Specifically, students pursue to be actively involved in the educational process, they prefer learning based on hands-on experiences and real-world examples, and are in search of interactive, engaging, and personalized learning environments [3].

Personalized learning is an integral part of 21st-century education [4] as learning constitutes both a personal and a collaborative experience through which one can improve their knowledge and skills, expand their perspectives, and increase their understanding on subject matter [5]. Engaging students in technology-enhanced learning is vital to achieve personalized learning [6]. Since personalized learning can improve students' learning outcomes [7], emphasis has been put on the use of new technologies and how they affect personalized learning. For example, studies have focused on how intelligent tutoring systems [8], recommender systems [9], intelligent web-based learning systems [10], and artificial intelligence [11], among other technologies, can support and promote personalized learning. Additionally, studies have highlighted the role of motivation [12], interactivity [13], engagement [14], embodiment [15], and immersion [16] in education and in improving learning outcomes. Among the different technologies, the combination of artificial intelligence with extended reality technologies has shown great potential in transforming and enhancing the educational domain and in helping satisfy the new educational requirements [17].

The integration of artificial intelligence into various domains is increasing rapidly [18]. Among the different domains, the use of artificial intelligence in education has shown great potential to improve the educational process, by transforming and enriching traditional practices and approaches and by promoting the redesign of culture, cognition, and knowledge [19–22]. Artificial intelligence systems are inspired by the human nervous system and are characterized by their adaptability and their ability to learn from different sources as well as to reason and make decisions in an autonomous, sophisticated, and rational manner [23–25]. As a result, artificial intelligent systems mimic the way humans act, think, and communicate and, consequently, simulate human intelligence [26,27]. Recent studies have explored and highlighted the role, advantages, and disadvantages of adopting and integrating artificial intelligence in education and have revealed current challenges and issues [19,28–34]. As a result, and due to its potential, the field of artificial intelligence in education is rapidly advancing [35,36].

Extended reality technologies are increasingly being examined in educational settings. These technologies offer new reality formats and consist of virtual reality, augmented reality, and mixed reality [37]. In this context, the reality–virtuality continuum describes a continuum in which one end refers to the real environment and is closer to augmented reality while the other end refers to the virtual environments and is closer to virtual reality, and somewhere in between, a mixed reality exists in which both real and virtual objects and environments co-exist [38]. Specifically, virtual reality involves, either real or simulated, virtual environments that perceptually surround, immerse, and engage users by simulating their physical presence within them [39–42]. These fully virtual environments immerse users and separate them from the real environment while offering experiences that are characterized by high levels of immediacy, interactivity, immersion, and involvement [40,43,44]. Within virtual reality environments, emphasis is put on integrating social and psychological aspects so that the overall experiences and environments can be perceived as real [45]. As a result, virtual reality technology created an "all-inclusive, sensory illusion of being present in another environment" [46]. Furthermore, augmented reality enables users to interact with both the virtual and digital worlds in real time by enriching users' physical environment with virtual content, information, and objects that users can perceive through their senses and interact with using multiple sensory modalities [47–51]. Due to their potential to transform the educational domain, recent studies that have carried out literature reviews on the use of virtual reality [3,52–54], augmented reality [55–59], and mixed reality [60–62] technologies as well as the metaverse [63–65] have examined the use of extended reality technologies in educational settings and have revealed the related benefits, drawbacks, and implications that arise when using them in teaching and learning activities.

Based on the aforementioned, many recent studies have been carried out that explored the use of artificial intelligence, augmented reality, virtual reality, and the metaverse in education. Although these studies provide meaningful insights regarding their integration in education, as their use in educational settings and the research into these technologies are rapidly increasing, there is a clear need to map and analyze the existing literature to identify key topics and thematic areas regarding the current state of the art and future research directions. Consequently, this study aims to offer an overview of the existing literature regarding the combination of artificial intelligence with augmented reality and virtual reality in education and identify future research areas. This study adds to the existing body of knowledge by analyzing the basic characteristics of the documents (e.g., publication frequency, citation count, authors, sources, countries, affiliations, etc.), by identifying the most advanced research areas and those that are still in their early stages, by revealing the most prominent trends, themes, and topics, and by offering future research directions based on the limitations and challenges identified in the literature.

2. Materials and Methods

Due to the scope of this study, as it looks into the use of artificial intelligence within augmented reality and virtual reality environments and focuses on examining the topic from an interdisciplinary approach, a bibliometric analysis of the existing literature was carried out. This approach is regarded as appropriate to examine the current state of the art on specific topics, particularly, when they are looked at from a more general perspective [66]. As this study aims to present the current trends and future perspectives regarding the integration of artificial intelligence in extended reality environments across domains, to conduct a rigorous and valid analysis of the existing literature, the guidelines specified by Donthu et al. [67] and Gusenbauer and Haddaway [68] were followed. Additionally, the method presented by Aria and Cuccurullo [69] was followed to carry out the bibliometric analysis. Particularly, the open-source R package Bibliometrix [69] was adopted and used. Additionally, to further explore and analyze the document collection, VOSviewer [70] and topic modeling through Latent Dirichlet Allocation (LDA) [71] were also used. Both tools are validated and widely accepted as effective and suitable means to carry out reproducible and valid scientific mapping and bibliometric analysis studies.

A key component in any study that aims to examine and present the current state of the literature is the use of highly regarded databases to identify relevant documents. Following the outcomes of recent studies that revealed Scopus and Web of Science as the top databases based on the quality of indexed documents, their covering various topics and disciplines, and their being widely used to carry out similar studies [72,73], the specific two databases were selected. Another crucial part in opting to use these databases, besides their being widely used in similar studies, was the ability to use the related information extracted from them with the tools used in this study [69]. Data from other sources could also be used but it would require manual adjustments that could affect the reproducibility of this study. Hence, this study examined documents only from Scopus and Web of Science.

As this study aimed to provide an overview of the existing literature across domains, the only limitation set when searching for relevant documents was for them to be written in English. No other limitations or filters were utilized in the query. Given the scope and perspective of this study, keywords relevant to each topic were identified and focus was put on intelligent systems and how they are being integrated in education. In the case of artificial intelligence, the general term and its abbreviation was used, while chatbots, tutoring systems, and assistants were identified as key areas within the literature. The selection of keywords regarding extended reality technologies and the educational context was based on those of other related studies [3,59]. Additionally, after testing various combinations of keywords, the following set of keywords was selected and used: ("artificial intelligence" OR "ai" OR "chatbot*" OR "chat bot*" OR "automated tutor*" OR "personal tutor*" OR "intelligent tutor*" OR "intelligent agent*" OR "adaptive educational system*" OR "adaptive learning system*" OR "intelligent tutoring system*" OR "virtual assistant*" OR "personal assistant*" OR "intelligent assistant*" OR "ai assistant*") AND ("augmented reality" OR "AR" OR "virtual reality" OR "VR" OR "mixed reality" OR "MR" OR "extended reality" OR "XR" OR "metaverse") AND ("education" OR "teach*" OR "student*" OR "learner*" OR "universit*" OR "school*" OR "classroom*" OR "course*"). The reason for using the specific query was twofold. First, to identify all potentially relevant documents, acronyms related to the technologies that this study focused on were used despite their returning additional documents that were not relevant and were therefore eliminated. This decision resulted in an increased number of documents being identified as potentially relevant at the initial stage and their being removed afterwards. However, the tradeoff was that all related documents were identified. Second, as this study did not focus on a specific educational level nor on a specific type of artificial intelligence or extended reality technology to present the general state of this topic, no specialized keywords were used as they could provide explicit directions to specific domains, functions, or use cases. This decision resulted in a more general representation of the literature to be presented and for a larger number of documents to be examined to provide a more thorough and complete depiction of the state of the art.

The specific set of keywords was used to search for relevant documents on Scopus and Web of Science on a topic level. Hence, the set of keywords would have to match either the title, abstract, or keywords of a document for it to be identified as potentially relevant to the topic. Studies that provide a thorough analysis of the existing literature should also be reproducible, transparent, accurate, and valid. For this reason, the Preferred Reporting Items for Systematic reviews and Meta-Analyses (PRISMA) statement [74] was followed to ensure that all the required criteria in terms of quality and rigor were met. PRISMA is a widely used and validated method that is commonly used in systematic literature review studies and in bibliometric reviews [74].

Figure 1 showcases the complete PRISMA flowchart. Specifically, the aforementioned query was last used in December 2024 to search for suitable documents in Scopus and Web of Science. The query returned 4124 documents from Scopus and 1335 documents from Web of Science. As a result, the initial document collection consisted of 5459 documents. As both of these databases are used by most quality outlets, they do index some common documents. Hence, duplicates were identified and removed both automatically and manually. A total of 1061 duplicates were found and removed and 1919 documents were automatically removed using a keyword search as they were outside the scope of this study. Hence, 2479 documents remained in the document collection and were further examined for consideration manually. Specifically, 363 documents were removed because they were proceedings books, 118 were removed as they were books, 11 were removed since they were short communications, 14 were removed as they were editorials, 13 were removed due to their being erratum, and 18 were removed as they were retracted documents. Given the scope of this study, for a document to be regarded as relevant, it had to meet the inclusion criteria which were for it to focus on the use of artificial intelligence within either augmented reality, virtual reality, extended reality, mixed reality, the metaverse, or a combination of them in educational settings. Hence, documents that only referred to one of these technologies or that only mentioned the specific keywords but did not focus on them or their use in educational or training contexts were regarded as out of scope. Additionally, all documents that explored the combination of these technologies from a theoretical or experimental perspective in education were regarded as relevant. After processing the full text of the documents, 1741 documents were removed as they did not satisfy the inclusion criteria. As a result, the document collection examined and analyzed in this study consisted of 201 documents that were relevant to the topic. As previously mentioned, the use of abbreviations in the query resulted in a high number of documents being out of scope but simultaneously, ensured that all related documents would be identified. Moreover, it should be mentioned that although the vast majority of documents were duplicates between the two databases used, in total, most relevant documents were found in Web of Science while most of the irrelevant to the topic documents were reported from Scopus. This fact justified the difference in the number of articles initially retrieved.

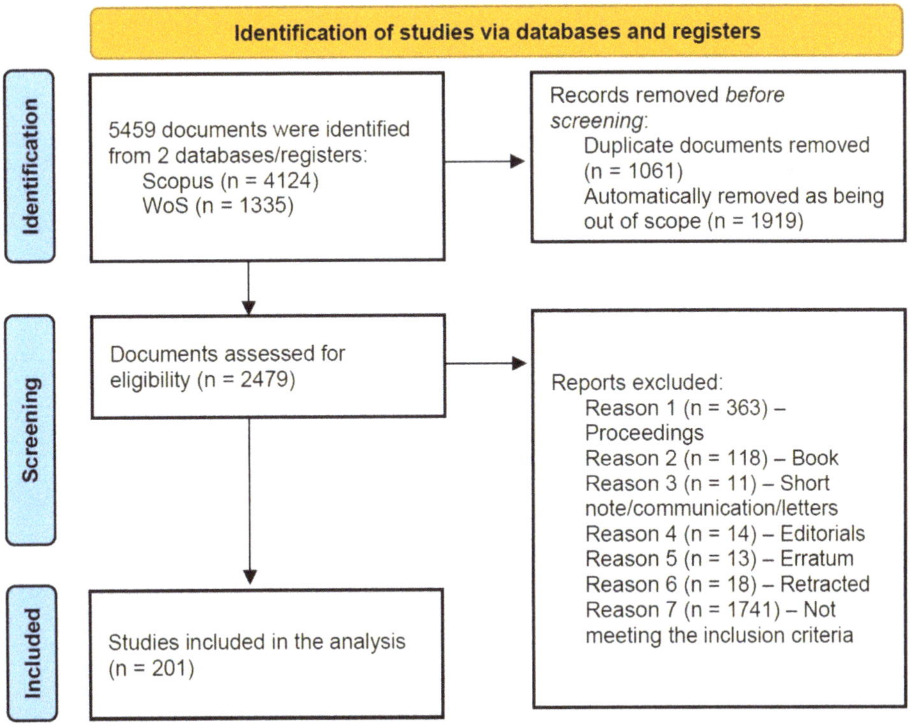

Figure 1. PRISMA flowchart.

3. Result Analysis

The document collection created was explored from various dimensions using different approaches to present the current state of the art regarding the combination of artificial intelligence with augmented reality and virtual reality technologies in education. Initially, the details of the document collection are presented. The publication frequency and the annual citation distribution are showcased. This study also looks into the authors' affiliation and countries and focuses on identifying the collaboration among the different countries. The relevant documents that have received the largest number of citations are also identified. Using keywords plus and author's keywords, the trends of the topic, its thematic map, and its thematic evolution are also examined. To identify more topics, the documents were clustered using both Bibliometrix and VOSviewer to carry out a keywords-based co-occurrence analysis. To further examine the topics, LDA [71] was used to carry out a topic modeling analysis of the document collection regarding the use of artificial intelligence and extended reality technologies in education.

3.1. Document Collection

The details of the complete document collection, which consists of 201 documents that were published during 2015–2024, are presented in Table 1. Most of the documents were published as conference/proceedings papers (42.8%), closely followed by journal articles (42.3%). To a lesser extent, the documents were published as book chapters (10.9%) or as review articles (4.0%) as indicated by the two databases. The documents were created and published by 642 authors. Each document had an average of 3.65 co-authors and the average citations per document was 13.82. In total, 32 authors contributed to the creation of 32 single-authored documents. It is worth highlighting that the average age of the documents is 1.63 and the annual growth rate demonstrates a significant positive rate of 60.58%. This fact highlights the importance and recency of the topic.

Table 1. Information regarding the document collection.

Description	Results	Description	Results
Main information about data		**Document types**	
Timespan	2015:2024	Article	85
Sources (journals, books, etc.)	142	Book chapter	22
Documents	201	Conference/Proceedings paper	86
Annual growth rate %	60.58	review	8
Document average age	1.63	**Authors**	
Average citations per document	13.82	Authors	642
		Authors of single-authored documents	32
Document contents		**Authors collaboration**	
Keywords plus (ID)	1293	Single-authored documents	32
Author's keywords (DE)	532	Co-authors per documents	3.65
		International co-authorships %	10.45

3.2. Publication Frequency and Citations

The significance of the topic and its high and positive annual growth rate (60.58%) become more evident when considering the distribution of the published documents from 2015 to 2024 (Figure 2). The majority of the documents were published in the last 3 years with the year 2024 having the most published documents (n = 71), followed by 2023 (n = 45) and 2022 (n = 34). Based on the specific period explored, three main time periods can be defined: (i) 2015–2020 (12.44% of the total documents published) was the period in which the initial interest in the combination of artificial intelligence with augmented reality and virtual reality in education sparked; (ii) 2021–2023 (52.24% of the total documents published) was the period in which the topic started to materialize; and (iii) 2024 (35.32% of the total documents published) was the breakthrough year. The outcomes are in line with the advancements in the respective fields in the recent years. When considering the applicability of these technologies and their potential to enrich and transform the educational process, the interest in the topic is expected to continue increasing. Moreover, the annual citations received were also explored as can be seen in Table 2. Specifically, Table 2 presents the year in which the documents were published (Year), the mean total citations that they have received (MeanTCperDoc), the number of published documents in that specific year (N), the mean annual total citations they have received (MeanTCperYear), as well as the total number of years that the documents of that year were citable (CitableYears). Certainly, besides the quality and impact of the studies, the citable years are a significant factor to the number of citations they have received. As a result, more recent studies have received fewer total citations on average when compared to older studies that helped establish this field of study. Hence, it becomes evident that documents published in 2019 (MeanTCperDoc = 46.5) and 2018 (MeanTCperDoc = 40.4), which were citable for 6 and 7 years respectively, had the highest mean total citations per document with the exception of the year 2015 in which a single document [75] was published that received 200 citations based on the data of the two databases. However, as this field of study is rapidly advancing and considering the average document age (1.63 years), it is expected that these outcomes will change in the future.

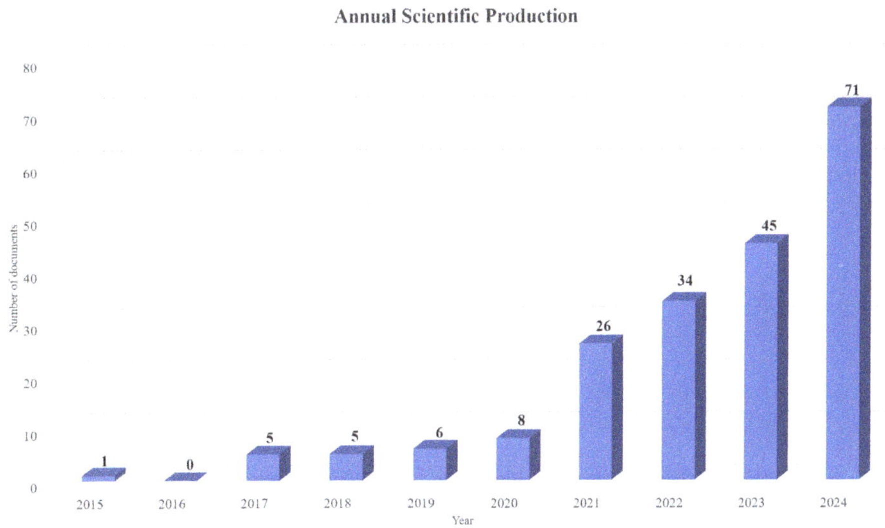

Figure 2. Number of documents published per year.

Table 2. Annual scientific production and citations.

Year	MeanTCperDoc	N	MeanTCperYear	CitableYears
2015	200	1	20	10
2017	8.2	5	1.02	8
2018	40.4	5	5.77	7
2019	46.5	6	7.75	6
2020	28.38	8	5.68	5
2021	22.12	26	5.53	4
2022	23.24	34	7.75	3
2023	8.27	45	4.14	2
2024	1.3	71	1.3	1

3.3. Sources

In total, the 201 documents that comprise the document collection examined in this study were published in 142 different sources, including journals, conference and proceedings, as well as edited book collections. Among the sources, the book series *Lecture Notes in Computer Science* (including subseries *Lecture Notes in Artificial Intelligence* and *Lecture Notes in Bioinformatics*) had the most published documents (n = 13) relevant to the topic. Moreover, three sources, namely, *Education and Information Technologies*, *Lecture Notes in Electrical Engineering*, and *Springer Series on Cultural Computing*, published four articles relevant to the topic. From the remaining sources, 13 sources published three relevant documents and 12 sources published two documents. A representation of the top four sources based on the number of relevant documents published that have published at least four documents is depicted in Table 3.

Table 3. Top sources based on the total number of relevant documents published.

Sources	Documents
Lecture Notes in Computer Science (including subseries *Lecture Notes in Artificial Intelligence* and *Lecture Notes in Bioinformatics*)	13
Education and Information Technologies	4
Lecture Notes in Electrical Engineering	4
Springer Series on Cultural Computing	4

Furthermore, the sources were also sorted based on their h-index and total citations received on the topic. The related outcomes are presented in Table 4 which depicts the h-index, g-index, m-index, total citations (TC), number of published documents (NP), and the publication start date (PY_start) of the sources. Based on the outcomes, *Computers and Education: Artificial Intelligence* (h-index = 3 and TC = 425), *Frontiers in Psychology* (h-index = 3 and TC = 62), and *Springer Series on Cultural Computing* (h-index = 3 and TC = 19) were the sources with the highest h-index (3). However, sources such as *International Journal of Artificial Intelligence in Education* (h-index = 2 and TC = 258) and *Lecture Notes in Computer Science* (including subseries *Lecture Notes in Artificial Intelligence* and *Lecture Notes in Bioinformatics*) (h-index = 2 and TC = 140) have also published impactful documents. The specific values that can be described as low, when compared to other bibliometric analysis studies that explore different topics, can be justified when we consider the average document age. Hence, given the fact that the topic is still in its infancy, the related outcomes are expected to change. However, the findings contribute by presenting the existing distribution of the documents among the various sources.

Table 4. Most impactful sources based on h-index.

Sources	h_Index	g_Index	m_Index	TC	NP	PY_Start
Computers and Education: Artificial Intelligence	3	3	0.75	425	3	2021
Frontiers in Psychology	3	3	0.75	62	3	2021
Springer Series on Cultural Computing	3	4	1.5	19	4	2023
International Journal of Artificial Intelligence in Education	2	3	0.2	258	3	2015
Lecture Notes in Computer Science (including subseries *Lecture Notes in Artificial Intelligence* and *Lecture Notes in Bioinformatics*)	2	11	0.25	140	13	2017
Computer Assisted Language Learning	2	2	0.667	91	2	2022
Nurse Education Today	2	2	0.5	68	2	2021
Education Sciences	2	3	0.5	58	3	2021
Applied Sciences (Switzerland)	2	3	0.5	48	3	2021
Mobile Information Systems	2	3	0.5	37	3	2021

Furthermore, Bradford's law was used to better comprehend the sources' impact and quality [76]. Specifically, three clusters were defined, namely, Cluster 1, Cluster 2, and Cluster 3, with Cluster 1 having the most impactful sources. Cluster 1 consists of 19 sources (13.4%) in which 68 documents (33.83%) were published, Cluster 2 comprises 57 sources (40.1%) in which 67 documents (33.33%) were published, and Cluster 3 has 66 sources (46.5%) in which 66 documents (32.84%) were published. Table 5 presents the top sources of Cluster 1 based on Bradford's law. Particularly, it presents the source name (Source), its rank (Rank), the number of documents published (Freq.), the cumulative frequency of published documents (CumFreq.), and the cluster (Cluster). Based on the outcomes, the top sources were *Lecture Notes in Computer Science* (including subseries *Lecture Notes in Artificial Intelligence* and *Lecture Notes in Bioinformatics*) (rank = 1 and freq. = 13), *Education and Information Technologies* (rank = 2 and freq. = 4), *Lecture Notes in Electrical Engineering* (rank = 3 and freq. = 4), *Springer Series on Cultural Computing* (rank = 4 and freq. = 4), *ACM International Conference Proceeding Series (ICPS)* (rank = 5 and freq. = 3), *Applied Sciences* (Switzerland) (rank = 6 and freq. = 3), *Cognitive Technologies* (rank = 7 and freq. = 3), *Computers and Education: Artificial Intelligence* (rank = 8 and freq. = 3), *Education Sciences* (rank = 9 and freq. = 3), and *Electronics* (Switzerland) (rank = 10 and freq. = 3).

Table 5. Most impactful sources based on Bradford's law.

Source	Rank	Freq.	CumFreq.	Cluster
Lecture Notes in Computer Science (including subseries *Lecture Notes in Artificial Intelligence* and *Lecture Notes in Bioinformatics*)	1	13	13	Cluster 1
Education and Information Technologies	2	4	17	Cluster 1
Lecture Notes in Electrical Engineering	3	4	21	Cluster 1
Springer Series on Cultural Computing	4	4	25	Cluster 1
ACM International Conference Proceeding Series (ICPS)	5	3	28	Cluster 1
Applied Sciences (Switzerland)	6	3	31	Cluster 1
Cognitive Technologies	7	3	34	Cluster 1
Computers and Education: Artificial Intelligence	8	3	37	Cluster 1
Education Sciences	9	3	40	Cluster 1
Electronics (Switzerland)	10	3	43	Cluster 1

3.4. Authors

Lotka's law was used to examine the number of authors that have contributed a set number of documents to the document collection included in this study. Based on the results presented in Table 6, it is evident that the vast majority of authors have contributed to a single study (89.7%). A total of 7.3% of authors have contributed to two documents and 13 authors (2.1%) have contributed to three studies. Finally, a total of six authors (0.9%) have contributed to four documents.

Table 6. Lotka's law analysis.

Documents Written	N. of Authors	Proportion of Authors
1	576	0.897
2	47	0.073
3	13	0.02
4	6	0.009

3.5. Affiliations

For a better understanding of the affiliations that have contributed the most in the creation and publication of documents relevant to the topic, the author affiliations were examined. Specifically, the affiliations of all authors involved in a document were taken into account. Hence, the total number of documents published by the authors of a specific country might be lower than the summation of the contribution from different affiliations of the same country. Hence, to examine the countries that have contributed the most, a separate analysis was carried out.

Among the different affiliations contained within the document collection, the top 10 affiliations, based on the number of contributions to documents, had contributed to at least four documents. Specifically, authors from McGill University, Canada (n = 11) and University of Essex, United Kingdom (n = 7) have contributed to the most documents.

Three affiliations, namely Texas A&M University, United States, University of Córdoba, Spain, and the University of Sydney, Australia, had authors who contributed to six documents. Two affiliations, namely AGH University of Science and Technology, Poland and Sungkyunkwan University, South Korea, had authors who contributed to five documents. Three affiliations, namely Delft University of Technology, Netherlands, National Chung Cheng University, Taiwan, and University of West Attica, Greece, had authors who contributed to four documents.

3.6. Countries

To examine the countries that have contributed the most to the creation of the document collection, the corresponding author's or the first author's country was taken into account. Specifically, the corresponding author's country was used and only if there was no corresponding author clearly defined, the first author's country was used. As a result, a total of 40 countries were identified.

In Table 7, the top 10 countries that have contributed the most documents on the topic are presented. Each of the remaining countries contributed three or fewer documents. Specifically, Table 7 presents the name of the country (Country), the number of documents (Documents), the intra-country collaboration (SCP), the inter-country collaboration (MCP), the frequency (Freq.), and the inter-country collaboration ratio (MCP_Ration). China (n = 61), the United States (n = 28), India (n = 13), and the United Kingdom (n = 8) were the countries that contributed the most documents. Additionally, China had the most intra-country (n = 57) and inter-country (n = 4) collaborations among all 40 countries.

Table 7. Country publication details.

Country	Documents	SCP	MCP	Freq.	MCP_Ratio
China	61	57	4	0.303	0.066
United States	28	26	2	0.139	0.071
India	13	12	1	0.065	0.077
United Kingdom	8	8	0	0.04	0
Canada	7	5	2	0.035	0.286
Italy	7	5	2	0.035	0.286
Australia	6	6	0	0.03	0
South Korea	6	6	0	0.03	0
Greece	5	5	0	0.025	0
Germany	4	4	0	0.02	0
Indonesia	4	4	0	0.02	0
Spain	4	2	2	0.02	0

Furthermore, Table 8 presents the countries that received the most citations based on the availability of the cited references information provided by the two databases used. China received the most citations (n = 954), followed by the United States (n = 527) and Canada (n = 453). Additionally, Canada has the highest number of average citations per document (64.7). Finally, the document contributed by authors in New Zealand [75] received a total of 200 references based on the information of the two databases which highlight its impact and significance.

Given that only 15.9% of the documents were single-authored, that the documents had on average 3.65 co-authors, and that the international co-authorship rate was 10.45%, it was deemed important to explore the collaboration among the different countries. As can be seen in Figure 3, in total, five clusters emerged. These clusters highlight the countries whose authors are actively involved in joint efforts to further advance this field of study and also present the countries that have been involved in more international collaborations. Of the countries presented, China, followed by the United States, had the most collaborations with other countries, having both direct and indirect connections.

Table 8. Countries that received the most citations.

Country	TC	Average Document Citations
China	954	15.6
United States	527	18.8
Canada	453	64.7
New Zealand	200	200
Australia	144	24
India	103	7.9
Italy	67	9.6
South Korea	62	10.3
Serbia	40	20
Spain	39	9.8

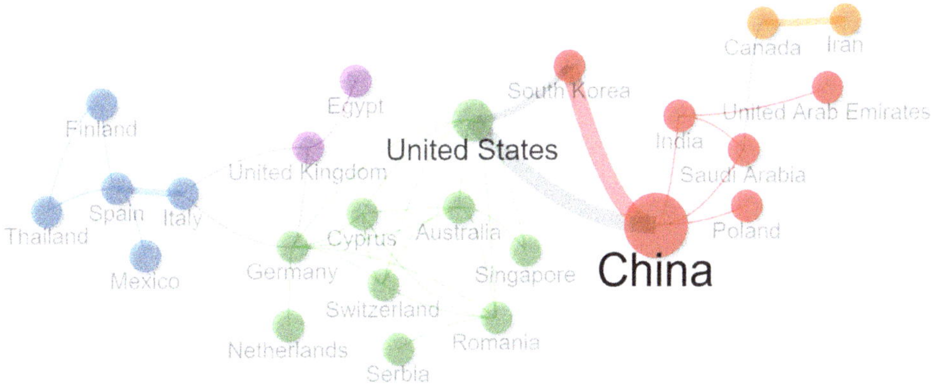

Figure 3. Country collaboration network.

3.7. Document Analysis

To further explore the related documents, the total number of citations they have received was considered. Additionally, using the keywords specified within the documents, the thematic evolution of the topic, the thematic map of the topic, and the main trends of the topic were explored. Specifically, Table 9 presents the documents that have received the most citations within the document collection.

Table 9. Documents with the highest number of citations.

Document	DOI	Total Citations	Total Citations Per Year	Normalized Total Citations
[77]	10.1016/j.caeai.2022.100082	372	124	16.01
[75]	10.1007/s40593-014-0032-x	200	20	1
[78]	10.1016/j.jsurg.2019.05.015	154	25.67	3.31
[79]	10.1371/journal.pone.0229596	150	30	5.29
[80]	10.1007/978-3-319-93843-1_12	135	19.29	3.34
[81]	10.1016/j.imr.2022.100917	89	44.5	10.77
[82]	10.2106/JBJS.18.01197	82	13.67	1.76
[83]	10.1080/09588221.2021.1879162	67	22.33	2.88
[84]	10.1001/jamanetworkopen.2021.49008	65	21.67	2.8
[85]	10.1155/2021/2637439	61	15.25	2.76

The keywords reported by the two databases are categorized into keywords plus and author's keywords. Specifically, keywords plus refer to the keywords used to classify the documents within the databases while author's keywords refer to the keywords specified by the authors within the documents. Both types of keywords can adequately represent the document knowledge structure [86]. Hence, both types of keywords are used in this study.

The top 10 most frequently used keywords plus were "artificial intelligence", "virtual reality", "augmented reality", "education", "metaverse", "extended reality", "deep learning", "human-computer interaction", "chatbots", "immersive learning", and "intelligent tutoring systems". The top 10 most common author's keywords were "artificial intelligence", "virtual reality", "students", "e-learning", "augmented reality", "engineering education", "learning systems", "teaching", "computer-aided instruction", and "education". The frequency of the related keywords is presented in Figures 4 and 5 for the keywords plus and author's keywords respectively. According to the keywords, the ability of these technologies to provide immersive learning environments that tend to students' needs is highlighted. Moreover, their ability to personalize the educational process through the provision of intelligent tutoring systems, chatbots, and agents as well as interactive learning systems is evident. The importance of focusing on human-computer interaction and on providing effective computer-aided instruction emerged. Finally, their potentials to support both teachers and students is also presented through the identification of relevant keywords.

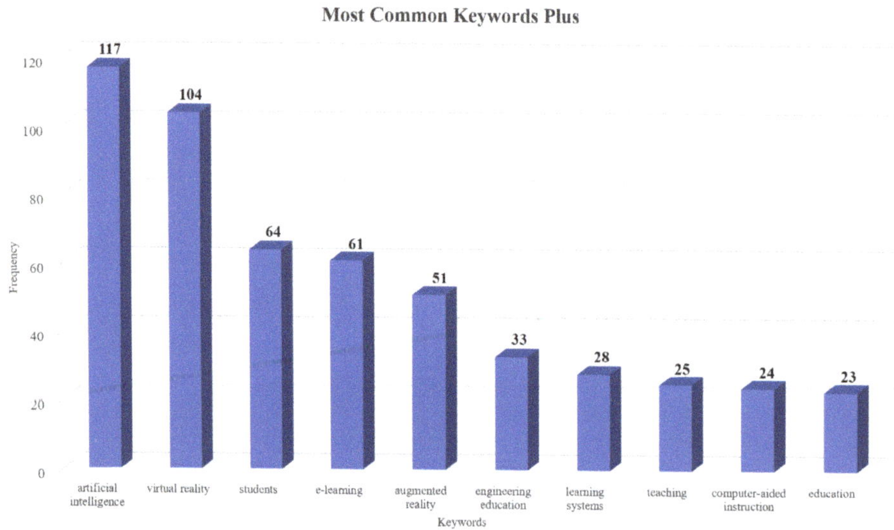

Figure 4. Most frequent keywords plus.

Besides the use of the Bibliometrix tool, VOSviewer was also used to explore the keyword co-occurrence network. The two networks are presented in Figures 6 and 7 respectively. For the networks generated via Bibliometrix (Figure 6), keywords plus were used, while for the network created via VOSviewer (Figure 7), author's keywords and keywords plus were used jointly. In the network created through Bibliometrix, a total of three clusters arose. The keywords of each cluster are as follows: (i) Green cluster: "virtual reality", "artificial intelligence", "students", "e-learning", "augmented reality", "engineering education", "learning systems", "teaching", "computer-aided instruction", "natural language processing", "education computing", "metaverse", "intelligent tutoring systems", "mixed reality", "learning", "deep learning", "extended reality", "curricula", "human-computer interaction", "learning experiences", "chatbots", "immersive learning", "immersive", "technology", "behavioral research", "speech recognition", "teachers", "artificial intelligence in education", "data handling", "language learning", "virtual assistants", "college students", "current", "learning environments"; (ii) Red cluster: "education", "machine learning", "medical education", "clinical competence", "medical", "simulation training", "nursing education", "procedures", "surgical training"; and (iii) Blue cluster: "virtual environments", "adversarial machine learning", "contrastive learning", "federated learning", "high education".

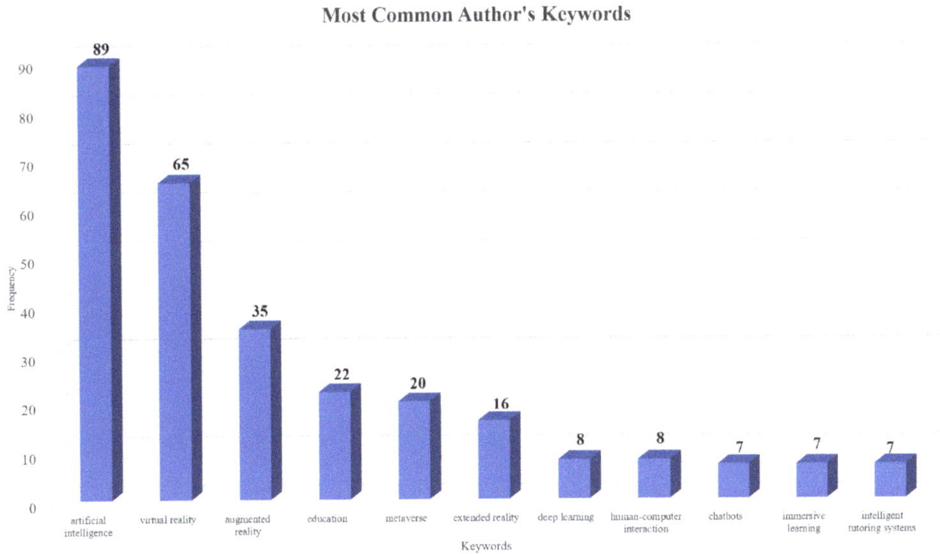

Figure 5. Most frequent author's keywords.

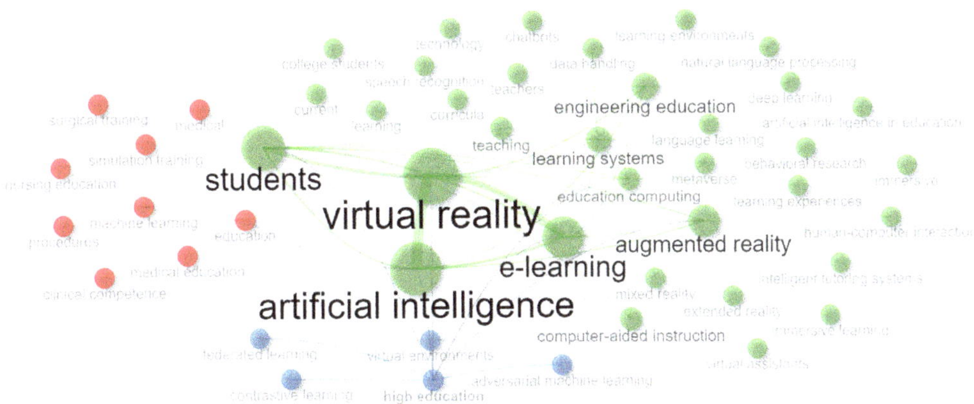

Figure 6. Keyword co-occurrence network—Bibliometrix.

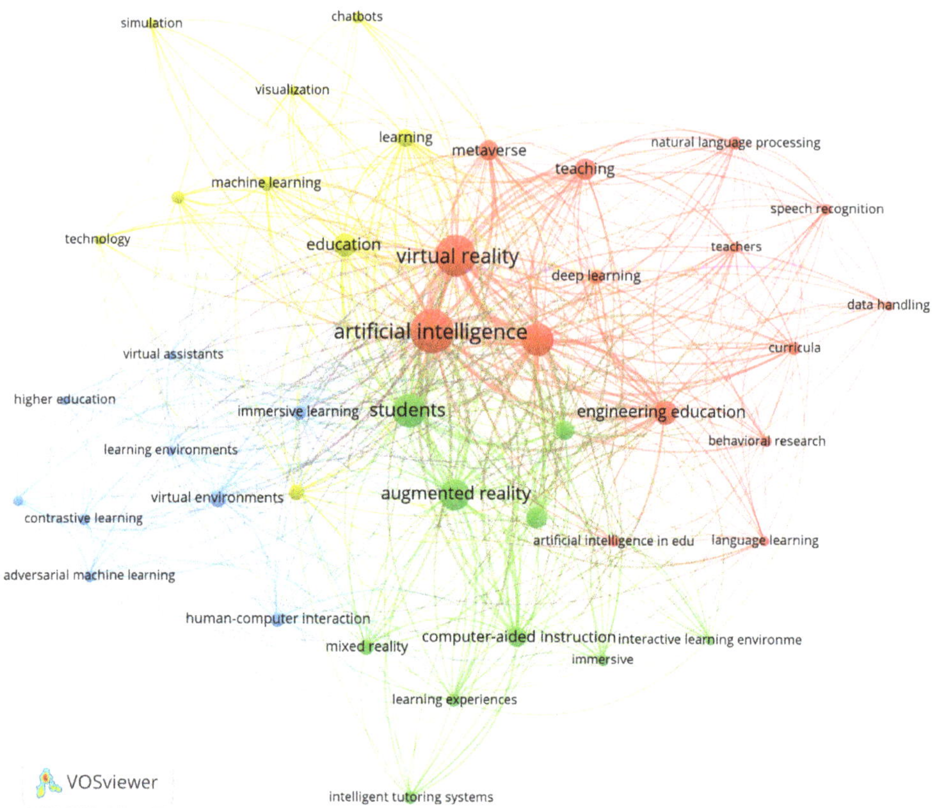

Figure 7. Keyword co-occurrence network—VOSviewer.

Moreover, the network generated through VOSviewer resulted in the creation of four clusters. The relevant to each cluster keywords are as follows: Cluster (1): "artificial intelligence", "artificial intelligence in education", "behavioral research", "curricula", "data handling", "deep learning", "e-learning", "engineering education", "language learning", "metaverse", "natural language processing", "speech recognition", "teachers", "teaching", "virtual reality"; Cluster (2): "augmented reality", "computer-aided instruction", "education computing", "immersive", "intelligent tutoring systems", "interactive learning environment", "learning experiences", "learning systems", "mixed reality", "students"; Cluster (3): "adversarial machine learning", "contrastive learning", "federated learning", "higher education", "human-computer interaction", "immersive learning", "learning environments", "virtual assistants", "virtual environments"; and Cluster (4): "chatbots", "education", "extended reality", "learning", "machine learning", "medical education", "simulation", "technology", "visualization". The applicability and multidimensional role of combining artificial intelligence with augmented reality and virtual reality technologies in educational settings is evident from the keywords and clusters.

Furthermore, through the use of VOSviewer, the total link strength among the keywords and their connections were explored. The related keywords were further processed and both keywords plus and author's keywords were used. Nonetheless, to avoid any bias, if a keyword existed in both keyword sets, it counted only once. Table 10 presents the top 10 keywords based on their total link strength. Artificial intelligence (occurrence = 111 and total link strength = 458), virtual reality (occurrence = 100 and total link strength = 444), and students (occurrence = 64 and total link strength = 361) were the keywords with the highest total link strength. Augmented reality also had a relatively high total link strength; however, it was less than that of the virtual reality keyword. This fact highlights the closer relation between artificial intelligence and virtual reality and that the research into the field of virtual reality has been more extensively examined.

Table 10. Total link strength of the keyword co-occurrence network—VOSviewer.

Keywords	Occurrences	Total Link Strength
artificial intelligence	111	458
virtual reality	100	444
students	64	361
e-learning	60	318
augmented reality	54	236
engineering education	33	178
learning systems	28	172
education	32	163
computer-aided instruction	24	150

Using Bibliometrix, the evolution of the topic throughout the years was also examined. Given the 10-year time period examined in this study (2015–2024), a total of three distinct time periods were set, as can be seen in (Figure 8). To examine the thematic evolution, the document keywords were used. Hence, each time period was associated with a set of keywords. Specifically, the following themes emerged over the years: (i) 2015–2018 period: virtual reality, computer-aided instruction; (ii) 2019–2021 period: artificial intelligence, extended reality, deep learning, education, learning efficiency, learning systems; and (iii) 2022–2024 period: artificial intelligence, metaverse, education, virtual environments, and tutoring systems. Based on the outcomes, the close relationship between extended reality technologies and artificial intelligence becomes evident. However, the field of virtual reality is more widely being examined in combination with artificial intelligence than with that of augmented reality. Additionally, the initial focus on general computer-aided instruction has shifted to exploring how the combination of artificial intelligence and extended reality technologies can constitute effective learning systems that can improve learning efficiency and support the educational process through the use of advanced technologies and approaches, such as deep learning techniques. In recent years, more emphasis has been placed on the metaverse and on creating effective virtual environments as well as personalized tutoring systems that can enrich the educational process.

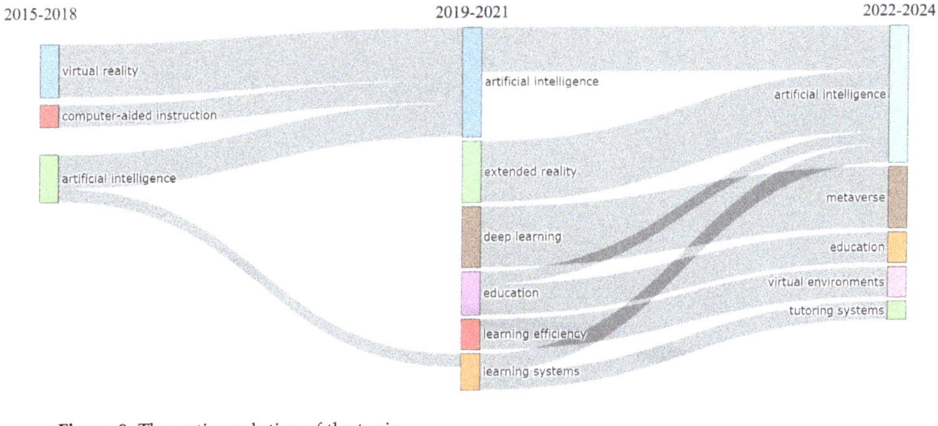

Figure 8. Thematic evolution of the topic.

The trend topics that emerged over the period of 2015–2024 were also explored. The related outcomes are presented in Figure 9 for the keywords plus and in Figure 10 for the author's keywords. Based on the author's keywords, the emphasis on intelligent tutoring systems is evident. Additionally, the focus on augmented reality and virtual reality started to appear more intensely in 2021 while on the metaverse in 2023. Creating immersive learning and personalized learning environments using extended reality and artificial intelligence technologies to support teaching and learning has been the main focus in the last years. According to the outcomes of the keywords plus analysis, the initial emphasis was placed in the field of medical and healthcare education. Gradually, the focus shifted to other fields and subjects as well. The interest in using new technologies and approaches to support teaching and learning by offering, intelligent tutoring systems, computer-aided instructions, and interactive learning systems was evident. Recently, emphasis has been put on different machine learning and deep learning techniques to provide personalized and immersive learning experiences in virtual environments while also capitalizing on virtual assistants and virtual avatars.

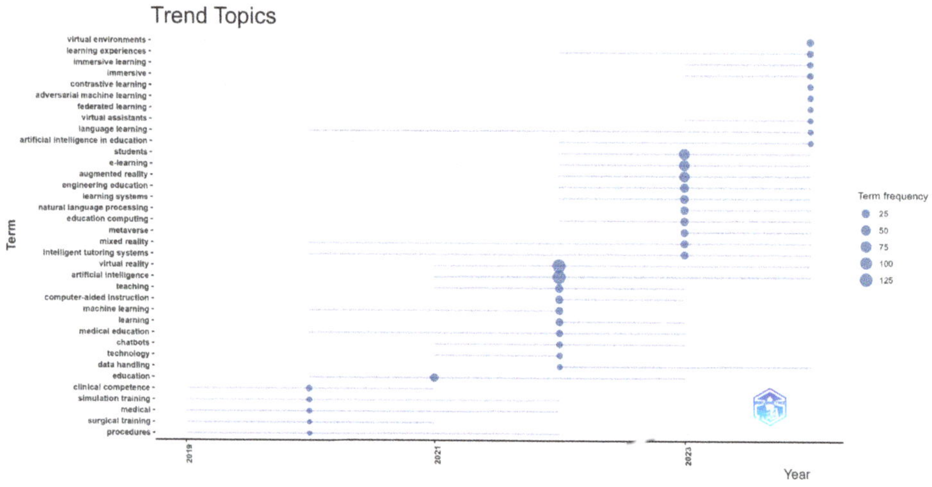

Figure 9. Trend topics based on keywords plus.

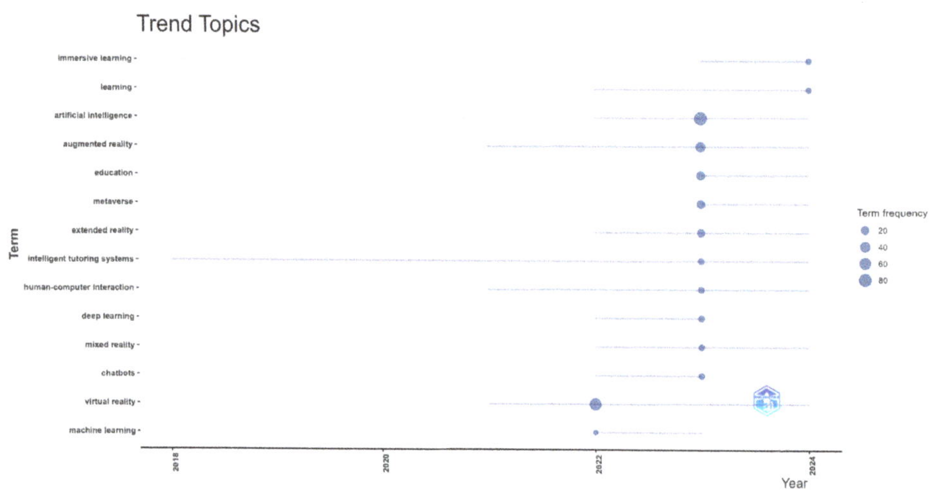

Figure 10. Trend topics based on author's keywords.

Keywords were also used to cluster the documents through the use of the clustering by coupling method using keywords plus as the coupling measurement and documents as the analysis unit. The related outcomes are presented in Figure 11, based on which six clusters arose. The first cluster (brown) was related to the keywords "artificial intelligence", "virtual reality", "education", "e-learning", and "clinical competence" while the second cluster (green) was related to the keywords "virtual reality", "artificial intelligence", "e-learning", "students", and "natural language processing". Both clusters highlight the close relation between artificial intelligence and virtual reality in educational settings. The third cluster (red) was associated with the keywords "artificial intelligence", "augmented reality", "mixed reality", "engineering education", and "learning systems", revealing the focus on combining augmented reality with artificial intelligence to create learning systems that promote learning in mixed reality environments, particularly in STEM-related fields. The fourth cluster (orange) was associated with the keywords "students", "augmented reality", "e-learning", "virtual reality", and "computer-aided instruction" while the fifth cluster (purple) was related to the keywords "adversarial machine learning", "contrastive learning", "federated learning", "students", and "virtual environments". These clusters present the use of new techniques and approaches to enrich learning in virtual environments and to provide students with personalized computer-aided instruction. The sixth cluster (blue) was related to the keywords "augmented reality", "intelligent tutoring systems", "students", "computer-aided instruction", and "education computing" which highlights the emphasis on using intelligent tutoring systems within augmented reality environments to provide students with personalized computer-aided instruction.

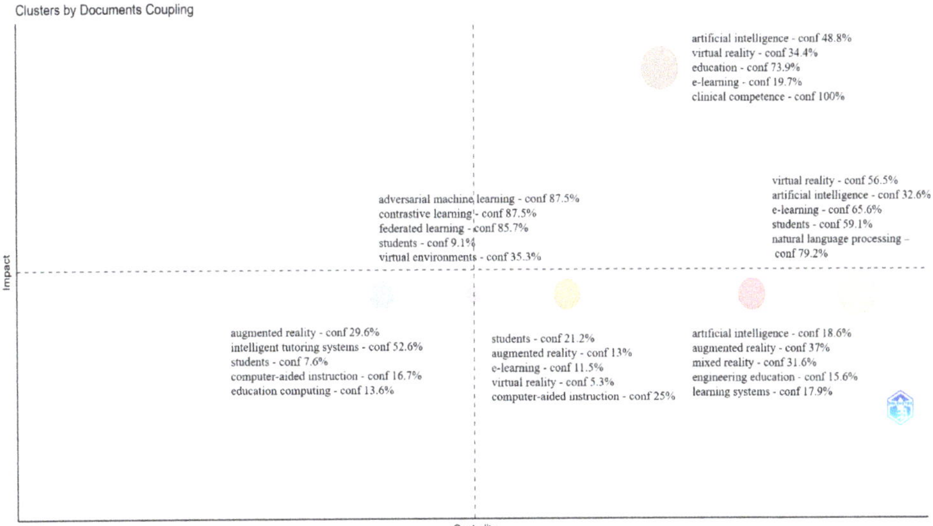

Figure 11. Document clusters.

Furthermore, using Bibliometrix, the thematic map of the topic, focusing on identifying the motor, basic, niche, and emerging or declining themes, was created. In total, 11 themes emerged. Motor themes (three clusters) were related to (i), "medical", "procedures", "surgical training", and "simulation"; (ii) "intelligent tutoring systems", "interactive learning environment", "user interfaces", and "virtual reality training"; and (iii) "nursing", "nursing education", and "nursing students". Basic themes (four clusters) were associated with (i) "teaching", "metaverse", "curricula", and "behavioral research"; (ii) "students", "e-learning", "augmented reality", and "engineering education"; (iii) "education", "machine learning", and "medical education"; and (iv) "virtual reality", "artificial intelligence", "learning", and "extended reality". Niche themes (two clusters) were related to (i) "instructional design", "intelligent robots", and "intelligent systems" and (ii) "artificial intelligence algorithms", "development prospects", and "efficiency". Emerging or declining themes (two clusters) were associated with (i) "adaptive learning", "design considerations", "innovation", and "learning technologies" and (ii) "college students", "motivation", and "sustainable development". Figure 12 depicts the related information.

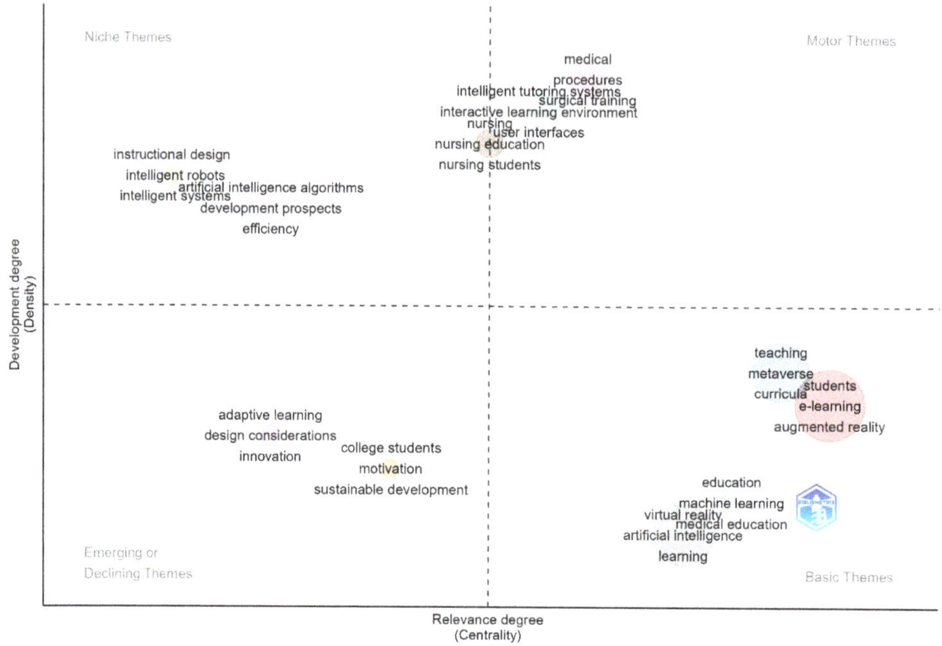

Figure 12. Thematic map of the topic.

In addition to the results of Bibliometrix and VOSviewer, which focused on keywords, topic modeling was also used through LDA. Specifically, LDA is used on discrete datasets to represent each item as a combination of topics from a finite set and constitutes a probabilistic Bayesian model with a three-level hierarchical structure [71]. The results of the topic modeling analysis are based on the bi-grams contained within the title and abstract of the documents and are presented in Table 11. The main keywords associated with the topic (e.g., artificial intelligence, augmented reality, virtual reality, extended reality, and mixed reality) are not reported to present more representative outcomes. In total, three topics arose from the topic modeling analysis. These topics were related to the wide applicability of artificial intelligence, augmented reality, and virtual reality in education. Specifically, the first topic is related to their role in higher education, to the focus on students' learning and improving their learning outcomes, as well as the design and adoption of appropriate teaching practices and methods. The second topic is related to the use of intelligent tutoring systems and virtual assistants and avatars within learning environments to promote and increase learning outcomes. The third topic is related to the wide range of educational subjects into which these technologies can be effectively integrated and to the emphasis on interactive and immersive learning experiences and environments. These outcomes are in line with those identified by the two tools used and provide additional details for each topic.

Table 11. LDA topic modeling.

No.	Topic	Bi-Grams
1	Higher education–Teaching practices and methods—Learning outcomes	higher education (8.856), application technology (6.281), learning outcomes (4.579), deep learning (4.143), machine learning (3.324), teaching method (3.054), teaching mode (3.042), student learning (2.999), learning technology (2.731).
2	Intelligent tutoring systems—Virtual assistants and avatars—Learning outcomes	intelligent tutoring (9.008), college students (4.921), educational environment (4.189), education research (3.814), virtual assistants (3.759), tutoring systems (3.743), students learning (3.512), improve learning (3.235), learning environments (3.005).
3	Interactive and immersive learning experiences—Educational subjects	learning experiences (6.909), language learning (6.818), nursing education (5.743), learning environment (5.729), real time (5.407), learning experience (5.299), interactive learning (4.817), engineering education (4.674), immersive learning (4.361), science education (4.329), computer science (3.339), medical education (3.240), emerging technologies (3.084).

4. Discussion

Both artificial intelligence and extended reality technologies can significantly impact teaching and learning activities; thus, transforming and enriching the educational domain. These outcomes can potentially be further amplified when these technologies are combined to yield intelligent, interactive, and immersive learning environments. However, despite the potential benefits that their use and the use of digital technologies in general can bring in education, it is important to consider the challenges associated with technology-enhanced learning in terms of the digital inclusion, digital exclusion, and the digital divide [87,88]. Specifically, the integration of more advanced technological applications into teaching and learning could create further inequalities between students who have access to them than those who do not [89,90].

To explore the advances of using extended reality technologies and artificial intelligence in education, the document collection focused on documents published in the last decade and their analysis looked into different dimensions and aspects of this collection. In total, 201 documents relevant to the integration of these technologies in educational settings comprised the document collection examined in this study. The PRISMA guidelines were adopted to ensure a valid, transparent, and reproducible study. The documents were retrieved from Scopus and Web of Science, which are highly regarded and widely used in systematic literature review and bibliometric analysis studies, and were utilized to search for documents relevant to the topic using a comprehensive query. The related documents were then processed and categorized. Using different tools and approaches, such as Bibliometrix, VOSviewer, and topic modeling through LDA, the documents contained within the specific document collection were analyzed.

The 201 documents contained in the document collection were published between 2015 and 2024. The documents had an average age of 1.63 years and a significantly high annual growth rate (60.58%). These outcomes highlight the importance and recency of the topic and indicate the use of artificial intelligence and extended reality in education as key technologies to shape up the future of the educational domain. The documents were published in 142 different sources with most documents having been published as conference/proceedings papers (42.8%), closely followed by journal articles (42.3%). The documents were written by 642 authors from 40 different countries and had an average of 3.65% co-authors. As the topic is still in its infancy, the international co-authorship rate (10.45%) reveals the multidisciplinary nature of the topic and it being widely examined by researchers of different expertise across countries and continents. Nonetheless, a relatively high number of single-authored studies (15.92%), in comparison to other topics, was also observed. Given the document publication period of 2015–2024, the time period was divided into three periods. Specifically, 2015–2020 was the period when interest in this topic sparked, 2021–2023 was the period when the topic began to materialize, and 2024 was the breakthrough year. Additionally, most documents were published in 2024 (35.32%), followed by those published in 2023 (22.39%) and 2022 (16.92%). Among the 201 documents, those that were published in 2019 and 2018 had the highest mean total citations per document. However, given the annual growth rate and the average age of the documents, it is expected that the outcomes regarding the publication year of the most impactful documents is subject to change. Moreover, using the number of published documents, the total citations, and the h-index on the topic, the sources in which the documents were published were also explored. Bradford's law was also used to cluster the sources based on their relevancy to the topic. Through the use of Lotka's law, it became evident that a significant majority of authors have contributed to a single study (89.7%); however, as the field advances, it is expected that these outcomes will change. Additionally, the countries and affiliations whose authors have contributed the most documents on the topic and received the most citations were also examined. Specifically, China, the United States, India, and the United Kingdom contributed the most documents while China, the United States, and Canada received the most citations. China also had the most intra-country and inter-country collaborations among all countries. Finally, five clusters of close collaborations among authors from different countries emerged when examining the international collaborations. These results highlight the interdisciplinary nature of the topic as well as the global interest in the integration and use of artificial intelligence, augmented reality, and virtual reality in education.

To identify topics and areas of interest, both author's keywords and keywords plus were used. When examining the frequency at which the keywords were used, the ability to offer immersive and interactive learning experiences through the convergence of artificial intelligence and extended reality technologies emerged. Additionally, the importance of human-computer interaction, machine learning and deep learning, computer vision, and natural language processing arose. The ability to support both teachers and students and offer computer-aided instruction was also evident. The potential to create intelligent tutoring systems and virtual assistants was highlighted as well. Although these technologies can be integrated into a plethora of learning subjects, most emphasis is being put on their use in engineering and STEM education. The multidimensional nature and wide applicability of these technologies were also revealed through the keyword co-occurrence network analysis in both Bibliometrix and VOSviewer. Specifically, using Bibliometrix, the documents were categorized into three clusters while using VOSviewer four clusters emerged. In both cases, the outcomes were similar and revealed their ability to be used as effective learning systems that can be integrated into the curricula, offer computer-aided instruction, provide interactive and immersive experiences, and support both teachers and students. Additionally, through intelligent agents, chatbots, intelligent tutoring systems, and virtual assistants, intelligent tutors that are characterized by high levels of realism, personalization, interactivity, as well as cognitive, emotional, and social skills can be created when combining artificial intelligence with augmented reality and virtual reality technologies. Among the clusters, the emphasis on higher education, engineering and medical education, as well as on hands-on learning experiences through immersive simulations is evident. The vital role of machine learning and deep learning methods for speech and motion recognition, computer vision, eye tracking, natural language processing, as well as content personalization and recommendation was highlighted. These outcomes were further highlighted and validated within the document clustering. When examining the link strength among the keywords, artificial intelligence, virtual reality, and students had the highest total link strength. This fact highlights the emphasis that is being put on students and student-centered learning environments as well as the focus on using artificial intelligence within virtual reality environments. Although augmented reality also had a relatively high total link strength, virtual reality being the prominent area of focus was evident throughout the analysis. This fact is in line with the keyword frequency analysis and further validates the outcomes of other related studies [91] which have indicated that the field of virtual reality has been more extensively examined than that of augmented reality on which more focus is being given in recent years. It should also be noted that of the different types of artificial intelligence, emphasis is being placed on the use of machine learning and deep learning approaches. Additionally, the topic modeling outcomes revealed the following three main topics: (i) the role of extended reality technologies and artificial intelligence in higher education and the focus on improving students' learning and outcomes as well as the design and adoption of appropriate teaching practices and methods; (ii) the use of intelligent tutoring systems and virtual assistants and avatars within learning environments to promote and increase learning outcomes; and (iii) their use in different educational subjects while emphasizing interactive and immersive learning.

Furthermore, the transition from virtual reality and augmented reality educational interventions to artificial intelligence-enabled extended reality systems and virtual environments was also highlighted in the thematic evolution of the topic in which three periods were defined. Based on the related keywords, emphasis is put on students' academic achievements, intelligent tutoring systems, personalized learning, immersive virtual environments, and learning efficiency. Besides augmented reality and virtual reality technologies, there has been increasing interest in the use of the metaverse in education. When examining the trend topics, the transition from the initial focus on medical and healthcare education to other fields and subjects was observed. Additionally, the gradual enrichment of extended reality experiences and environments with artificial intelligence and the emphasis on offering intelligent tutoring systems in the form of virtual avatars that provide personalized and immersive learning was highlighted. However, it should be noted that the advancements in this field are dependent on industrial productions and these changes are tightly coupled to other factors. For example, the wider use of generative artificial intelligence through tools such as Bard, ChatGPT, Gemini, etc., the hardware improvement in terms of processing capabilities, and the advancement of head-mounted devices (e.g., HoloLens, Meta Quest, etc.) may also influence the increased interest in the field and the increase in the number of published documents.

Moreover, the studies presented in Table 9, which identified the documents that have received the most citations within the document collection based on the data reported by the two databases, are discussed. In their study, Hwang and Chien [77] examined the research issues associated with the adoption of the metaverse in education from an artificial intelligence-based perspective. Their study also focused on presenting the potential applications of the metaverse in educational settings. Emphasis was also placed on the role of artificial intelligence in the metaverse. Ethical issues, the need for specialized hardware and software, and the lack of relevant technological support arose as the main challenges. Finally, the study highlights the need for future studies to focus on curriculum and learning design within the metaverse. Westerfield et al. [75] focused on combining augmented reality with intelligent tutoring system to aid in the learning and training of manual assembly tasks. Their study aimed at offering a more effective learning experience to assemble a motherboard. Based on their outcomes, students who learned through the intelligent augmented reality system completed the tasks faster and achieved better performance than those who learned through the basic augmented reality system. Hence, they highlighted the potential of intelligent augmented reality tutors as a means to improve learning.

Winkler-Schwartz et al. [78] put emphasis on improving and assessing surgical expertise in the context of medical education using machine learning and a virtual reality simulation. Aiming at effectively evaluating the performance on virtual reality simulators regarding surgical expertise, they created and presented the Machine Learning to Assess Surgical Expertise (MLASE) checklist. They examined published articles that used these technologies and found out that articles published in computer science journals had a more in-depth description of the study design and weaker discussion quality while articles that were published in medical journals were the exact opposite. Hence, this checklist aims to provide common ground for future studies to use to assess the effectiveness of their systems and applications. Mirchi et al. [79] explored the creation of a virtual operative assistant using virtual reality and explainable artificial intelligence tools. Specifically, they focused on simulation-based training in surgery and medicine in the context of medical education. Their virtual operative assistant was capable of effectively classifying the users into different categories based on their skills and performance and provided them with immediate visual feedback. Their study also highlighted the potential benefits that the use of artificial intelligence and virtual reality can have in education as well as the merits that can be yielded when combining instructor inputs, objective feedback, and expertise classification.

Focusing on artificial intelligence-enhanced classrooms, Holstein et al. [80] examined the influence of using a mixed-reality teacher awareness tool on students' learning in K-12 education. Their results revealed that through the use of intelligent tutoring systems and real-time analytics, it is possible to reduce the disparity in learning outcomes among students with different levels of prior ability. Finally, the study comments upon the potential benefits that can be yielded when integrating machine and human intelligence in classrooms to support students' learning. Divekar et al. [83] focused on the design and evaluation aspects of foreign language learning using extended reality technologies and artificial intelligence. Based on the outcomes, students had a positive learning experience and statistically significant differences were observed in knowledge acquisition and retention. Hence, the study highlighted that the combination of extended reality technologies with artificial intelligence can result in effective and naturalistic conversational interaction that can improve learning outcomes in the context of foreign language learning. Ma [84] also focused on exploring the combination of artificial intelligence, machine learning, and virtual reality as an immersive context teaching method for foreign language learning in higher education. The study revealed the immersive and interactive nature of virtual reality learning environments. Additionally, it highlighted the positive impact that this combination can have on students' learning outcomes as students who learned through this approach performed better than those of the control group who adopted common traditional teaching methods. Finally, the study pointed out the benefits of combining virtual reality with constructivism theory to improve students' learning.

Ahuja et al. [81] put emphasis on the potential applications of the metaverse in medical education, in integrative health, and in artificial intelligence. Their study went over the related concepts and highlighted the role and benefits of the metaverse in each domain. Additionally, the combination of the metaverse with artificial intelligence, virtual reality, and augmented reality technologies was highly regarded due to its potential applications in the field of healthcare in the context of medical education. The study quoted that this combination could revolutionize and shift the paradigm of traditional medical education.

Bissonnette et al. [82] also focused on the use of virtual reality and artificial intelligence within medical education focusing on surgical training. Their study put emphasis on different algorithms and their ability to effectively perform classification tasks within virtual reality training scenarios. Their approach showed a high level of accuracy across twelve metrics when retrieving and analyzing real-time data from the virtual reality environment. Finally, the study highlighted the potential of artificial intelligence to support and enrich current educational paradigms and better prepare future professionals. Focusing on examining the influence of artificial intelligence tutoring on medical students' surgical skills, Fazlollahi et al. [84] carried out a study involving a virtual operative assistant. According to their findings, when compared to instructor-based teaching and to the control group, the group of students, who learnt through the virtual operative assistant within the virtual reality environment, showcased significantly improved outcomes in practice expertise scores and realistic expertise scores. However, no significant differences were observed in terms of negative and positive emotions nor in cognitive learning among the three different groups.

5. Conclusions

The convergence of artificial intelligence with augmented reality and virtual reality technologies is being increasingly examined. Due to the benefits they can bring in the educational domain, emphasis is put on their role and integration into teaching and learning. This study aimed at examining the existing literature to present the state of the art regarding the combination of artificial intelligence with augmented reality and virtual reality technologies and its use in education and to reveal future research areas. As a result, using two databases, documents relevant to the topic were identified, processed, and analyzed using various tools and approaches. Specifically, this study explored the existing literature in terms of the main characteristics of the relevant documents, that is, publication frequency, citation, count, authors, countries, affiliations, and sources. Additionally, this study looked into the most prominent topics regarding the integration of artificial intelligence, augmented reality, and virtual reality in education, examined the trend topics and thematic evolution of the topic, and highlighted the most popular themes and areas through the use of Bibliometrix, VOSviewer, and topic modeling.

Although efforts were made to offer a broader look at the existing literature, there are a few limitations that should be considered. Firstly, due to the tools used (e.g., Bibliometrix and VOSviewer), this study did not involve an in-depth content-wise analysis of the documents but focused primarily on the bibliometric data. Secondly, the documents were retrieved from two databases based on the aforementioned reasons. Thirdly, only English documents were analyzed. Hence, future studies should focus on examining more specific areas of this field through systematic literature review studies to explore the impact that the combination of artificial intelligence with extended reality technologies can have in education and how it can affect teaching and learning practices. Finally, specifying and identifying the number of topics is a challenge when using LDA; hence, a perplexity metric was used to specify a number of topics that yielded distinct topics representative of the document collection.

According to the results and focusing on the keyword and topic analysis, the potential of combining artificial intelligence with virtual reality and augmented reality can contribute to creating personalized, interactive, and immersive learning experiences. Due to their nature, these technologies can be used in all educational levels in both formal and informal settings supporting both students and teachers. The ability to create intelligent tutoring systems that have a virtual presence and can effectively play the role of a tutor or peer learner was evident. Additionally, such immersive intelligent tutoring systems can be regarded as affective and social entities with cognitive, social, and emotional skills that can provide personalized and affective learning. Through the behavioral personalization that they offer and their ability to recommend appropriate content and modify learning resources, material, and activities based on each learner's skills, knowledge, needs, and preferences, such systems can improve students' engagement, learning motivation, and academic performance. Additionally, they enable students to be engaged in experiential-based learning and problem-based learning through their involvement in hands-on activities within immersive and safe virtual environments. Hence, by combining these technologies, students take part in self-directed learning and in collaborative learning experiences and settings within virtual environments without which they would not have the opportunity to experience them. Although the combination of artificial intelligence with extended reality technologies is mostly being examined in the fields of computer science, medical and healthcare education, and in engineering, studies have also revealed its potential to be integrated in other domains as well.

Although the specific topic is in its infancy, it is rapidly advancing as can be concluded based on the significantly high annual growth rate (60.58%). The interest in the topic and the wider adoption and integration of artificial intelligence, augmented reality, and virtual reality in educational settings is expected to further increase in the coming years. Nonetheless, there is a clear need for more empirical, experiential, and case study-based studies to be conducted following appropriate methodologies and involving students' prolonged exposure to learning through the use of artificial intelligence and extended reality technologies. Future studies should also focus on identifying the most effective approaches to design such tools and systems, to create related educational material, and to effectively introduce them to classrooms. Additionally, emphasis should be put on how to integrate them in teaching and learning activities and on creating common guidelines and standards for others to adopt and follow. Moreover, and as the field of artificial intelligence is rapidly progressing, future studies should explore how to design and create effective, interactive, immersive, and customizable intelligent tutoring systems that can be integrated into extended reality environments that offer personalized learning experiences. Additionally, there is a need to evaluate how these technologies affect students' soft skills and knowledge acquisition. Given the social traits of immersive intelligent tutoring systems and their virtual presence, future studies should also look into how the virtual presence influences students' cognitive and socio-emotional development. Therefore, it is important to examine how the physical presence that characterizes some new technologies (e.g., social robots) compares to the virtual presence that extended reality technologies offer in terms of overall learning outcomes and students' development. Given the scope of this study and the keywords used, future studies should focus on further examining different types of artificial intelligence. Finally, it is also vital to explore how these technologies can affect learning design, evaluation, and assessment, as well as the role of teachers in an ever-increasing digitally enriched classroom.

Funding: This research received no external funding.

Conflicts of Interest: The author declares no conflicts of interest.

References

1. Haleem, A.; Javaid, M.; Qadri, M.A.; Suman, R. Understanding the role of digital technologies in education: A review. *Sustain. Oper. Comput.* **2022**, *3*, 275–285. [CrossRef]
2. Admiraal, W.; Huizenga, J.; Akkerman, S.; Dam, G.t. The concept of flow in collaborative game-based learning. *Comput. Hum. Behav.* **2011**, *27*, 1185–1194. [CrossRef]
3. Lampropoulos, G.; Kinshuk. Virtual reality and gamification in education: A systematic review. *Educ. Technol. Res. Dev.* **2024**, *72*, 1691–1785. [CrossRef]

4. Bernacki, M.L.; Greene, M.J.; Lobczowski, N.G. A systematic review of research on personalized learning: Personalized by whom, to what, how, and for what purpose(s)? *Educ. Psychol. Rev.* **2021**, *33*, 1675–1715. [CrossRef]
5. Shemshack, A.; Spector, J.M. A systematic literature review of personalized learning terms. *Smart Learn. Environ.* **2020**, *7*, 33. [CrossRef]
6. Grant, P.; Basye, D. *Personalized Learning: A Guide for Engaging Students with Technology*; International Society for Technology in Education: Washington, DC, USA, 2014.
7. Pane, J.; Steiner, E.; Baird, M.; Hamilton, L. *Continued Progress: Promising Evidence on Personalized Learning 2015*; RAND Corporation: Santa Monica, CA, USA, 2015. [CrossRef]
8. Conati, C.; Barral, O.; Putnam, V.; Rieger, L. Toward personalized XAI: A case study in intelligent tutoring systems. *Artif. Intell.* **2021**, *298*, 103503. [CrossRef]
9. Raj, N.S.; Renumol, V.G. A systematic literature review on adaptive content recommenders in personalized learning environments from 2015 to 2020. *J. Comput. Educ.* **2022**, *9*, 113–148. [CrossRef]
10. Chen, C.-M. Intelligent web-based learning system with personalized learning path guidance. *Comput. Educ.* **2008**, *51*, 787–814. [CrossRef]
11. Pratama, M.P.; Sampelolo, R.; Lura, H. Revolutionizing education: Harnessing the power of artificial intelligence for personalized learning. *Klasikal J. Educ. Lang. Teach. Sci.* **2023**, *5*, 350–357. [CrossRef]
12. Deci, E.L.; Vallerand, R.J.; Pelletier, L.G.; Ryan, R.M. Motivation and education: The Self-Determination perspective. *Educ. Psychol.* **1991**, *26*, 325–346. [CrossRef]
13. Beauchamp, G.; Kennewell, S. Interactivity in the classroom and its impact on learning. *Comput. Educ.* **2010**, *54*, 759–766. [CrossRef]
14. Bond, M.; Buntins, K.; Bedenlier, S.; Zawacki-Richter, O.; Kerres, M. Mapping research in student engagement and educational technology in higher education: A systematic evidence map. *Int. J. Educ. Technol. High. Educ.* **2020**, *17*, 2. [CrossRef]
15. Shapiro, L.; Stolz, S.A. Embodied cognition and its significance for education. *Theory Res. Educ.* **2019**, *17*, 19–39. [CrossRef]
16. Dede, C. Immersive interfaces for engagement and learning. *Science* **2009**, *323*, 66–69. [CrossRef] [PubMed]
17. Lampropoulos, G. Augmented reality and artificial intelligence in education: Toward immersive intelligent tutoring systems. In *Augmented Reality and Artificial Intelligence*; Geroimenko, V., Ed.; Springer Nature: Hoboken, NJ, USA, 2023; pp. 137–146. [CrossRef]
18. Bughin, J.; Hazan, E.; Ramaswamy, S.; Chui, M.; Allas, T.; Dahlstrom, P.; Trench, M. *Artificial Intelligence: The Next Digital Frontier*; McKinsey Global Institute: Washington, DC, USA, 2017.
19. Chen, L.; Chen, P.; Lin, Z. Artificial intelligence in education: A review. *IEEE Access* **2020**, *8*, 75264–75278. [CrossRef]
20. Holmes, W.; Bialik, M.; Fadel, C. *Artificial Intelligence in Education: Promises and Implications for Teaching and Learning*; Center for Curriculum Redesign: Cambridge, MA, USA, 2020.
21. Hwang, G.-J.; Xie, H.; Wah, B.W.; Gašević, D. Vision, challenges, roles and research issues of artificial intelligence in education. *Comput. Educ. Artif. Intell.* **2020**, *1*, 100001. [CrossRef]
22. Pedro, F.; Subosa, M.; Rivas, A.; Valverde, P. *Artificial Intelligence in Education: Challenges and Opportunities for Sustainable Development*; United Nations Educational, Scientific and Cultural Organization: Paris, France, 2019.
23. Haenlein, M.; Kaplan, A. A brief history of artificial intelligence: On the past, present, and future of artificial intelligence. *Calif. Manag. Rev.* **2019**, *61*, 5–14. [CrossRef]
24. Duan, Y.; Edwards, J.S.; Dwivedi, Y.K. Artificial intelligence for decision making in the era of big data-evolution, challenges and research agenda. *Int. J. Inf. Manag.* **2019**, *48*, 63–71. [CrossRef]
25. Stone, P.; Brooks, R.; Brynjolfsson, E.; Calo, R.; Etzioni, O.; Hager, G.; Hirschberg, J.; Kalyanakrishnan, S.; Kamar, E.; Kraus, S.; et al. Artificial intelligence and life in 2030: The one hundred year study on artificial intelligence. *arXiv* **2016**, arXiv:2211.06318.
26. Brynjolfsson, E.; Mcafee, A. Artificial intelligence, for real. *Harv. Bus. Rev.* **2017**, *1*, 1–31.
27. Li, D.; Du, Y. *Artificial Intelligence with Uncertainty*; CRC Press: Boca Raton, FL, USA, 2017. [CrossRef]
28. Chen, X.; Zou, D.; Xie, H.; Cheng, G.; Liu, C. Two decades of artificial intelligence in education. *Educ. Technol. Soc.* **2022**, *25*, 28–47.
29. Baidoo-Anu, D.; Owusu Ansah, L. Education in the era of generative artificial intelligence (AI): Understanding the potential benefits of ChatGPT in promoting teaching and learning. *J. AI* **2023**, *7*, 52–62. [CrossRef]
30. Zhai, X.; Chu, X.; Chai, C.S.; Jong, M.S.Y.; Istenic, A.; Spector, M.; Liu, J.-B.; Yuan, J.; Li, Y. A review of artificial intelligence (AI) in education from 2010 to 2020. *Complexity* **2021**, *2021*, 8812542. [CrossRef]
31. Chiu, T.K.F.; Xia, Q.; Zhou, X.; Chai, C.S.; Cheng, M. Systematic literature review on opportunities, challenges, and future research recommendations of artificial intelligence in education. *Comput. Educ. Artif. Intell.* **2023**, *4*, 100118. [CrossRef]
32. Crompton, H.; Burke, D. Artificial intelligence in higher education: The state of the field. *Int. J. Educ. Technol. High. Educ.* **2023**, *20*, 22. [CrossRef]
33. Lin, C.-C.; Huang, A.Y.Q.; Lu, O.H.T. Artificial intelligence in intelligent tutoring systems toward sustainable education: A systematic review. *Smart Learn. Environ.* **2023**, *10*, 41. [CrossRef]

34. Ouyang, F.; Zheng, L.; Jiao, P. Artificial intelligence in online higher education: A systematic review of empirical research from 2011 to 2020. *Educ. Inf. Technol.* **2022**, *27*, 7893–7925. [CrossRef]
35. Song, P.; Wang, X. A bibliometric analysis of worldwide educational artificial intelligence research development in recent twenty years. *Asia Pac. Educ. Rev.* **2020**, *21*, 473–486. [CrossRef]
36. Hinojo-Lucena, F.-J.; Aznar-Díaz, I.; Cáceres-Reche, M.-P.; Romero-Rodríguez, J.-M. Artificial intelligence in higher education: A bibliometric study on its impact in the scientific literature. *Educ. Sci.* **2019**, *9*, 51. [CrossRef]
37. Rauschnabel, P.A.; Felix, R.; Hinsch, C.; Shahab, H.; Alt, F. What is XR? Towards a framework for augmented and virtual reality. *Comput. Hum. Behav.* **2022**, *133*, 107289. [CrossRef]
38. Milgram, P.; Kishino, F. A taxonomy of mixed reality visual displays. *IEICE Trans. Inf. Syst.* **1994**, *77*, 1321–1329.
39. Sherman, W.R.; Craig, A.B. *Understanding Virtual Reality: Interface, Application, and Design*; Morgan Kaufmann: San Mateo, CA, USA, 2018.
40. Sherman, W.R.; Craig, A.B. Understanding virtual reality—Interface, application, and design. *Presence Teleoperators Virtual Environ.* **2003**, *12*, 441–442. [CrossRef]
41. Anthes, C.; Garcia-Hernandez, R.J.; Wiedemann, M.; Kranzlmuller, D. State of the art of virtual reality technology. In Proceedings of the 2016 IEEE Aerospace Conference, Big Sky, MT, USA, 5–12 March 2016; IEEE: New York, NY, USA, 2016. [CrossRef]
42. Burdea, G.C.; Coiffet, P. *Virtual Reality Technology*; John Wiley & Sons: Hoboken, NJ, USA, 2003.
43. Ryan, M.-L. *Narrative as Virtual Reality 2: Revisiting Immersion and Interactivity in Literature and Electronic Media*; JHU Press: Baltimore, MD, USA, 2015.
44. Psotka, J. Immersive training systems: Virtual reality and education and training. *Instr. Sci.* **1995**, *23*, 405–431. [CrossRef]
45. Blascovich, J.; Bailenson, J. *Infinite Reality: Avatars, Eternal Life, New Worlds, and the Dawn of the Virtual Revolution*; William Morrow & Co: New York, NY, USA, 2011.
46. Biocca, F.; Delaney, B. Immersive virtual reality technology. *Commun. Age Virtual Real.* **1995**, *15*, 127–157. [CrossRef]
47. Azuma, R.T. A survey of augmented reality. *Presence Teleoperators Virtual Environ.* **1997**, *6*, 355–385. [CrossRef]
48. Lee, K. Augmented reality in education and training. *TechTrends* **2012**, *56*, 13–21. [CrossRef]
49. Cipresso, P.; Giglioli, I.A.C.; Raya, M.A.; Riva, G. The past, present, and future of virtual and augmented reality research: A network and cluster analysis of the literature. *Front. Psychol.* **2018**, *9*, 2086. [CrossRef]
50. Carmigniani, J.; Furht, B. Augmented reality: An overview. In *Handbook of Augmented Reality*; Borko Furht Springer: Berlin/Heidelberg, Germany, 2011; pp. 3–46. [CrossRef]
51. Carmigniani, J.; Furht, B.; Anisetti, M.; Ceravolo, P.; Damiani, E.; Ivkovic, M. Augmented reality technologies, systems and applications. *Multimed. Tools Appl.* **2011**, *51*, 341–377. [CrossRef]
52. Radianti, J.; Majchrzak, T.A.; Fromm, J.; Wohlgenannt, I. A systematic review of immersive virtual reality applications for higher education: Design elements, lessons learned, and research agenda. *Comput. Educ.* **2020**, *147*, 103778. [CrossRef]
53. Freina, L.; Ott, M. A literature review on immersive virtual reality in education: State of the art and perspectives. In Proceedings of the International Scientific Conference Elearning and Software for Education, Bucharest, Romania, 25–26 April 2015; pp. 1–8.
54. Kavanagh, S.; Luxton-Reilly, A.; Wuensche, B.; Plimmer, B. A systematic review of virtual reality in education. *Themes Sci. Technol. Educ.* **2017**, *10*, 85–119.
55. Akçayır, M.; Akçayır, C. Advantages and challenges associated with augmented reality for education: A systematic review of the literature. *Educ. Res. Rev.* **2017**, *20*, 1–11. [CrossRef]
56. Chen, P.; Liu, X.; Cheng, W.; Huang, R. A review of using augmented reality in education from 2011 to 2016. In *Innovations in Smart Learning*; Springer: Singapore, 2017; pp. 13–18. [CrossRef]
57. Avila-Garzon, C.; Bacca-Acosta, J.; Kinshuk; Duarte, J.; Betancourt, J. Augmented reality in education: An overview of Twenty-Five years of research. *Contemp. Educ. Technol.* **2021**, *13*, ep302. [CrossRef]
58. Garzón, J. An overview of Twenty-Five years of augmented reality in education. *Multimodal Technol. Interact.* **2021**, *5*, 37. [CrossRef]
59. Lampropoulos, G.; Keramopoulos, E.; Diamantaras, K.; Evangelidis, G. Augmented reality and gamification in education: A systematic literature review of research, applications, and empirical studies. *Appl. Sci.* **2022**, *12*, 6809. [CrossRef]
60. Maas, M.J.; Hughes, J.M. Virtual, augmented and mixed reality in k-12 education: A review of the literature. *Technol. Pedagog. Educ.* **2020**, *29*, 231–249. [CrossRef]
61. Sala, N. Virtual reality, augmented reality, and mixed reality in education. In *Advances in Higher Education and Professional Development*; IGI Global: NewYork, PA, USA, 2020; pp. 48–73. [CrossRef]
62. Banjar, A.; Xu, X.; Iqbal, M.Z.; Campbell, A. A systematic review of the experimental studies on the effectiveness of mixed reality in higher education between 2017 and 2021. *Comput. Educ. X Real.* **2023**, *3*, 100034. [CrossRef]
63. López-Belmonte, J.; Pozo-Sánchez, S.; Moreno-Guerrero, A.-J.; Lampropoulos, G. Metaverse in education: A systematic review. *Rev. De Educ. A Distancia* **2023**, *23*, 1–25. [CrossRef]

64. Lin, H.; Wan, S.; Gan, W.; Chen, J.; Chao, H.-C. Metaverse in education: Vision, opportunities, and challenges. In Proceedings of the 2022 IEEE International Conference on Big Data (Big Data), Osaka, Japan, 17–20 December 2022. [CrossRef]
65. Zhang, X.; Chen, Y.; Hu, L.; Wang, Y. The metaverse in education: Definition, framework, features, potential applications, challenges, and future research topics. *Front. Psychol.* **2022**, *13*, 1016300. [CrossRef]
66. Ellegaard, O.; Wallin, J.A. The bibliometric analysis of scholarly production: How great is the impact? *Scientometrics* **2015**, *105*, 1809–1831. [CrossRef] [PubMed]
67. Donthu, N.; Kumar, S.; Mukherjee, D.; Pandey, N.; Lim, W.M. How to conduct a bibliometric analysis: An overview and guidelines. *J. Bus. Res.* **2021**, *133*, 285–296. [CrossRef]
68. Gusenbauer, M.; Haddaway, N.R. Which academic search systems are suitable for systematic reviews or meta-analyses? Evaluating retrieval qualities of google scholar, PubMed, and 26 other resources. *Res. Synth. Methods* **2020**, *11*, 181–217. [CrossRef] [PubMed]
69. Aria, M.; Cuccurullo, C. Bibliometrix: An r-tool for comprehensive science mapping analysis. *J. Informetr.* **2017**, *11*, 959–975. [CrossRef]
70. van Eck, N.J.; Waltman, L. Software survey: VOSviewer, a computer program for bibliometric mapping. *Scientometrics* **2010**, *84*, 523–538. [CrossRef] [PubMed]
71. Blei, D.M.; Ng, A.Y.; Jordan, M.I. Latent dirichlet allocation. *J. Mach. Learn. Res.* **2003**, *3*, 993–1022. [CrossRef]
72. Mongeon, P.; Paul-Hus, A. The journal coverage of web of science and scopus: A comparative analysis. *Scientometrics* **2015**, *106*, 213–228. [CrossRef]
73. Zhu, J.; Liu, W. A tale of two databases: The use of web of science and scopus in academic papers. *Scientometrics* **2020**, *123*, 321–335. [CrossRef]
74. Page, M.J.; McKenzie, J.E.; Bossuyt, P.M.; Boutron, I.; Hoffmann, T.C.; Mulrow, C.D.; Shamseer, L.; Tetzlaff, J.M.; Akl, E.A.; Brennan, S.E.; et al. The PRISMA 2020 statement: An updated guideline for reporting systematic reviews. *Int. J. Surg.* **2021**, *88*, 105906. [CrossRef] [PubMed]
75. Westerfield, G.; Mitrovic, A.; Billinghurst, M. Intelligent augmented reality training for motherboard assembly. *Int. J. Artif. Intell. Educ.* **2015**, *25*, 157–172. [CrossRef]
76. Bradford, S.C. Sources of information on specific subjects. *Engineering* **1936**, *137*, 85–86.
77. Hwang, G.-J.; Chien, S.-Y. Definition, roles, and potential research issues of the metaverse in education: An artificial intelligence perspective. *Comput. Educ. Artif. Intell.* **2022**, *3*, 100082. [CrossRef]
78. Winkler-Schwartz, A.; Bissonnette, V.; Mirchi, N.; Ponnudurai, N.; Yilmaz, R.; Ledwos, N.; Siyar, S.; Azarnoush, H.; Karlik, B.; Del Maestro, R.F. Artificial intelligence in medical education: Best practices using machine learning to assess surgical expertise in virtual reality simulation. *J. Surg. Educ.* **2019**, *76*, 1681–1690. [CrossRef]
79. Mirchi, N.; Bissonnette, V.; Yilmaz, R.; Ledwos, N.; Winkler-Schwartz, A.; Del Maestro, R.F. The virtual operative assistant: An explainable artificial intelligence tool for simulation-based training in surgery and medicine. *PLoS ONE* **2020**, *15*, e0229596. [CrossRef]
80. Holstein, K.; McLaren, B.M.; Aleven, V. Student learning benefits of a Mixed-Reality teacher awareness tool in AI-Enhanced classrooms. In *Lecture Notes in Computer Science*; Springer Nature: Berlin/Heidelberg, Germany, 2018; pp. 154–168. [CrossRef]
81. Ahuja, A.S.; Polascik, B.W.; Doddapaneni, D.; Byrnes, E.S.; Sridhar, J. The digital metaverse: Applications in artificial intelligence, medical education, and integrative health. *Integr. Med. Res.* **2023**, *12*, 100917. [CrossRef]
82. Bissonnette, V.; Mirchi, N.; Ledwos, N.; Alsidieri, G.; Winkler-Schwartz, A.; Del Maestro, R.F. Artificial intelligence distinguishes surgical training levels in a virtual reality spinal task. *J. Bone Jt. Surg.* **2019**, *101*, e127. [CrossRef] [PubMed]
83. Divekar, R.R.; Drozdal, J.; Chabot, S.; Zhou, Y.; Su, H.; Chen, Y.; Zhu, H.; Hendler, J.A.; Braasch, J. Foreign language acquisition via artificial intelligence and extended reality: Design and evaluation. *Comput. Assist. Lang. Learn.* **2022**, *35*, 2332–2360. [CrossRef]
84. Fazlollahi, A.M.; Bakhaidar, M.; Alsayegh, A.; Yilmaz, R.; Winkler-Schwartz, A.; Mirchi, N.; Langleben, I.; Ledwos, N.; Sabbagh, A.J.; Bajunaid, K.; et al. Effect of artificial intelligence tutoring vs expert instruction on learning simulated surgical skills among medical students. *JAMA Netw. Open* **2022**, *5*, e2149008. [CrossRef]
85. Ma, L. An immersive context teaching method for college english based on artificial intelligence and machine learning in virtual reality technology. *Mob. Inf. Syst.* **2021**, *2021*, 2637439. [CrossRef]
86. Zhang, J.; Yu, Q.; Zheng, F.; Long, C.; Lu, Z.; Duan, Z. Comparing keywords plus of WOS and author keywords: A case study of patient adherence research. *J. Assoc. Inf. Sci. Technol.* **2016**, *67*, 967–972. [CrossRef]
87. Afzal, A.; Khan, S.; Daud, S.; Ahmad, Z.; Butt, A. Addressing the Digital Divide: Access and Use of Technology in Education. *J. Soc. Sci. Rev.* **2023**, *3*, 883–895. [CrossRef]
88. Khalid, M.S.; Pedersen, M.J.L. Digital Exclusion in Higher Education Contexts: A Systematic Literature Review. *Procedia-Soc. Behav. Sci.* **2016**, *228*, 614–621. [CrossRef]
89. Lythreatis, S.; Singh, S.K.; El-Kassar, A.N. The Digital Divide: A Review and Future Research Agenda. *Technol. Forecast. Soc. Change* **2022**, *175*, 121359. [CrossRef]

90. Livingstone, S.; Helsper, E. Gradations in Digital Inclusion: Children, Young People and the Digital Divide. *New Media Soc.* **2007**, *9*, 671–696. [CrossRef]
91. Lampropoulos, G.; Fernández-Arias, P.; Antón-Sancho, Á.; Vergara, D. Affective computing in augmented reality, virtual reality, and immersive learning environments. *Electronics* **2024**, *13*, 2917. [CrossRef]

MDPI AG
Grosspeteranlage 5
4052 Basel
Switzerland
Tel.: +41 61 683 77 34

Multimodal Technologies and Interaction Editorial Office
E-mail: mti@mdpi.com
www.mdpi.com/journal/mti

www.ingramcontent.com/pod-product-compliance
Lightning Source LLC
Chambersburg PA
CBHW061455220926
51850CB00004B/100
* 9 7 8 3 7 2 5 8 7 8 2 3 9 *